Mammals of Indiana

DATE DUE

Mammals

RUSSELL E. MUMFORD
and
JOHN O. WHITAKER, JR.

of Indiana

BLOOMINGTON

INDIANA UNIVERSITY PRESS

Manufactured in the United States of America

Library of Congress Cataloging in Publication Data
Mumford, Russell E.
    Mammals of Indiana.

    Bibliography: p.
    Includes index.
    1. Mammals—Indiana. I. Whitaker, John O. II. Title.
QL719.I6M86   599.09772   79-2175
ISBN 0-253-30387-7   AACR2
1 2 3 4 5 86 85 84 83 82

To our wives, Vivian and Royce

Contents

Preface

This book is intended as a tribute to all the people who have conducted research on or written about the mammals of Indiana. Although neither of us is a native Hoosier—Mumford was born in Illinois and Whitaker in New York—we have lived and worked in Indiana, and have come to think of these mammals in an Indiana setting. Mumford began collecting mammals as a student at Purdue University in 1946 and has conducted fieldwork in each of Indiana's ninety-two counties. Whitaker arrived at Indiana State University in 1962 and was trapping mammals before his bags were completely unpacked. We have since learned much about these Indiana species while conducting research and teaching mammalogy in the state.

It became apparent to us after some years of research on the mammals of Indiana that we had obtained much new information. When we decided to write this book several years ago, we wanted to present an up-to-date review of the data available on Indiana mammals. In doing this, we hoped to establish some sort of base from which future changes in mammal populations, habitats, and distributions might be assessed more accurately. No one knows more surely than we that much remains to be learned concerning the mammals of the state. We hope this review of Indiana mammals may stimulate further work in this area, and we have attempted to point out where additional data are required to produce a more complete picture of the state's mammals.

We feel that the information we have com-piled will be useful to diverse groups of readers—biologists, veterinarians, students, teachers, naturalists—anyone who has an interest in Indiana mammals. Perhaps those responsible for conducting impact studies in the state will draw on the data presented regarding habitats and distributions of the various species. The people who identify and endeavor to preserve endangered or threatened species may find something of interest here with which to work. And finally, we hope through this book to share with the people of Indiana even a small amount of the many pleasures we have experienced during our work and travels throughout the state.

When we think of the plains pocket gopher, we think of the sand ridges vegetated with black oaks, interspersed with marshes and cultivated fields that were formerly prairie grasslands, in Jasper and Newton counties. We recall the booming of the now-extirpated greater prairie chickens on cold, windy spring mornings and the huge, wheeling flocks of golden plover that appear in April in that region. But we also have watched as, one by one, the larger prairie remnants were divided, drained, plowed, and planted to corn, wheat, or soybeans. The prairie chickens are gone, along with their native grassland habitats that were really never adequately studied by any mammalogist. But in summer, six-lined racerunners still scurry over the loose soil of some of the blow sand regions. We have watched as the western harvest mouse has invaded the area in recent years.

Swamp rabbits remind us of the sloughs choked with buttonbush, lying between low ridges vegetated with floodplain trees and shrubs, where cane, greenbrier, and other herbaceous plants render it difficult to walk or to observe clearly. In such habitats in Gibson and Posey counties, we have walked about among the few remaining bald cypress trees, listening to the pileated woodpecker by day (and the barred owl by night), while searching for the telltale signs of swamp rabbits. In summer, these haunts are hot, humid, calm, and infested with mosquitoes. The prothonotary warbler flashes its bright colors as it flies along the slough borders, where dead snags providing nest sites abound. As the shallow sloughs and overflows dry up in late summer, yellow-crowned night herons wade in them catching crayfish and small fishes that have been stranded. And at night raccoons prowl these same haunts.

Star-nosed moles bring back memories of mucky lake shores and marshes, scattered tamarack swamps, and meandering streams with scarcely any banks. Here, in the northeastern corner of Indiana, is the unique habitat of the lake district, where spotted turtles and Blanding's turtles (though becoming more rare) can be found. In early fall, the poison sumac's leaves turn a brilliant color and gentians bloom about the marsh borders. The wooded areas are full of red squirrels and eastern chipmunks, and numerous woodcocks settle into the swamps during fall migration. This region is evidently one of the best Indiana habitats for the badger, which finds the gravelly ridges and moraines easy digging and the abundant thirteen-lined ground squirrels tasty food.

The cave region of the south-central hills we associate with bats, eastern woodrats, gray squirrels, and gray foxes. We remember tending a bat net from sundown to sunrise one night in late August, when bats flew throughout the night at the mouth of Big Wyandotte Cave. The night was warm and katydids and screech owls serenaded us. We thrilled at the sight, just before dawn, of a gray bat in our net, one of the few ever seen in Indiana. We have spent uncomfortable hours crawling, wading, and slipping through the caves in search of bats and woodrats. But we have also been fortunate enough to watch the cave blindfish, white crayfish, cave salamanders, and other interesting inhabitants of these natural caverns. In summer, eastern phoebes and Carolina wrens build their nests near cave entrances. And the large, pendant egg sacs of the cave spiders glisten like cut glass in the beam of a flashlight. Hoosiers in this region (Brown County) know that when the oak leaves are the size of squirrels' ears it is time for spring corn planting.

The large central section of the state is characterized by cornfields, soybean fields, wheat fields, small woodlots, borrow pits, riparian strips of timber, and houses. It is nearly impossible to find a spot from which one cannot see at least one house. When we trap in this region, we expect our traps to hold many house, deer, and white-footed mice. The woodlots, mostly grazed and located in the center of the farms, harbor fox squirrels and eastern chipmunks. The open fields are the domain of the red fox and, in recent years, the coyote, a comparative newcomer to much of the section. The barred owl is largely absent, except in certain low-lying woods, but the great horned owl is common.

We have known the Virginia pine / chestnut oak knobs of Clark County, the numerous limestone caves and sinkholes of the karst region, the extensive cornfields of the Tipton Till Plain, the fascinating life of the marshy potholes of Lagrange and Steuben counties, the shifting sand dunes along Lake Michigan, the old fields of broom grass and red cedar in Perry County, the swamps, sloughs, and canebrakes of Gibson County. And there have been discomforts: the mosquito-infested summer days in the Jasper-Pulaski Fish and Wildlife Area; the prairie wind and the late spring ice storms; the muggy, hot, wilting atmosphere of Hovey Lake in midsummer; the Lake Michigan storms and ice packs; the dry, hot, rugged forest lands of Jackson and Monroe counties in August; the flooded cypress swamps and sloughs of Posey County in winter; the floodplain haunts of the swamp rabbit in Warrick County, where waist-high poison ivy grows so dense one has to push through it.

We have arrived at some chosen trapping site late on a winter evening and placed our hundreds of traps in dewberry-infested fields until darkness stopped us, noticing later the numerous broken-off briers embedded in our hands, which had by then thawed. And who can forget setting long lines of mousetraps in the snow, when cold, aching fingers seemed to make the task twice as difficult—indeed, each time a trap accidentally snapped on a cold finger, we questioned our sanity. Then, after the traps were set, we repaired to a motel room, usually with inadequate lighting, and skinned mammals half the night.

We have noted with amazement the amount of peanut butter required to bait 3,000 mousetraps—which we set in one afternoon in late November. And we have known the agonizing realization that a short, driving rain in late afternoon was going to spring many of the traps we had just set. Somehow, resetting those long strings, after dark with the aid of a flashlight, was far from satisfying.

We have experienced many disappointments in not being able to capture a certain species at a particular site where we suspected it might occur. But, in compensation, we have sometimes taken a species in a site where it was totally unexpected. We have made long drives back home over icy roads after several days in the field far from our base of operations. We have had crickets and other insects strip the peanut butter from our traps between the time they were set and when darkness came. And we have had traplines swept away in flash floods, covered with several inches of sudden snow, burned by highway crews, and plowed under by farmers. Sometimes part of our traps have been stolen; at other times, persons unknown, although probably meaning well, have spoiled our sampling by picking up several hundred traps and neatly arranging them in piles.

Meeting people around the state has been an enjoyable part of our work. Many were amazed at the variety of small mammals we were able to capture in their hayfields, woodlots, fencerows, or waste areas. Most people have been quite helpful. But we have been suspected of shooting squirrels at dusk about some woodlot, when we were actually shooting bats. And we have spent long periods explaining our work (sometimes not very effectively) to curious landowners. We have been treated to many interesting stories about mammals and other animals, although some of these tales could most kindly be described as folklore. We have attempted to convince people that bats do not intentionally get into one's hair, red squirrels do not castrate other squirrels, opossums do not breed through the nose, and gray wolves do not occur in Indiana. Mumford was once investigated by two state troopers as he sat at a roadside rest area skinning a flying squirrel on the picnic table.

Many people have assisted our efforts by collecting specimens, stuffing road-killed mammals into their freezers, informing us of interesting specimens, answering our inquiries, allowing us to hunt or trap on their properties, ignoring our curious activities, and in many other ways. Some have even sheltered us overnight, allowed us to skin mice in their warm living room on the family card table, fed us hot coffee and cookies and other foods, let us prowl about in their attics catching bats, taken us through their basements in search of some unknown animal, permitted us to set traps in their homes for flying squirrels, and watched with interest as we performed a multitude of other tasks associated with our work.

We have been helped immensely by our students, many of whom have assisted in fieldwork or in the preparation of specimens. We realize some thought that their professors were insane, for no one in his right mind outruns and captures Franklin's ground squirrels by hand, swims through deep pools of cold water in caves in search of bats, or walks through the woods with a stick, tapping on dead snags, looking for flying squirrels. They might also question the intelligence of someone who sits up most of the night in a motel room sorting through yards and yards of intestines from vole specimens in search of parasites. It must also have been difficult for them to understand why that trapline had to be set through those thickets of black locust / greenbrier / blackberry. And why risk life and limb chasing agile fleas jumping about a smashed mammal carcass on a busy highway? Moreover, who would attempt to prepare a decent museum skin from a mangled, beginning-to-turn-green carcass salvaged from the road on a hot July day—standing along the roadside, using the hood of his car for a workbench, and stitching up the numerous holes in the skin as curious drivers passed by?

But we have enjoyed our work—with its pleasures, its discomforts, its apparent insanities—and it is our hope that the reader will enjoy the results of our efforts.

Acknowledgments

We have received a great deal of help during the preparation of this book. Our families, friends, colleagues, students, and others have assisted us in the collection and preparation of specimens, in cataloguing data from collections, in obtaining literature references, and by calling our attention to various reports and records. We have benefited from our conversations with landowners, hunters, naturalists, and other interested persons throughout the state. Many of those who have helped are mentioned below, but we have, no doubt, failed to list many others who have also contributed in important ways.

Many of our students have assisted us, by helping in the field or laboratory, by contributing specimens or data, or by discussing various phases of the work or analysis. We express our thanks to all. Some are partially acknowledged by being authors or coauthors on various papers in the literature cited. Several former students now hold important positions with the Indiana Division of Fish and Wildlife and other organizations. Some are our colleagues at our respective universities. Many have continued their aid to our research efforts.

Among the Indiana State University graduate students who made significant contributions to our work are Cheryl Bauer, Ronald S. Caldwell, Dennis E. Clark, Paul G. Fish, Steven D. Ford, Thomas W. French, Rebecca J. Goff, Wayne C. Houtcooper, Gwilym S. Jones, D. David Pascal, Jr., David Rubin, Larry Schmeltz, George R. Sly, Edwin J. Spicka, and Mary Beth Wassel. Undergraduates Donna Gehring and Martha Smith have done outstanding work in preparing slides and in summarizing data.

We are also grateful to the following former students at Purdue University who have assisted us in collecting and preparing mammal specimens or in supplying photographs and performing other services: Larry L. Allsop, Glenn A. Baker, David W. Berrey, Larry W. Bledsoe, Anthony D. Burnside, James Cook, Robert L. Cooksey, Jr., Charles R. Danner, Jr., Robert L. DeLong, David A. Easterla, Dennis R. Eger, Louis H. Ehinger, Jim M. Eloff,

Robert D. Feldt, Mark Fitzsimmons, Billie E. Gahl, J. Scott Grundy, Randy J. Haney, Jon F. Heisterberg, Don R. Helms, Donovan E. Hendricks, David L. Herbst, Thomas W. Hoekstra, Roger S. Hoffman, Marion T. Jackson, Dean E. Jessup, Arthur Johanningsmeier, William W. Knauer II, Michael N. Kochert, Herbert C. Krauch, Jr., David A. Manuwal, L. David Mech, Glenn R. McCormick, Dennis L. McGroarty, Fredrick H. Montague, Jr., Kenneth C. Nettles, Thomas A. Parker, Richard E. Phillips, Charles L. Rippy, Larry J. Roop, Larry L. Schmeltz, Philip C. Shelton, Phillip R. Smith, Donald T. Sporre, Robert C. Stones, Ted L. Terrel, Alan T. Theriak, Richard C. Tuszynski, John D. Wade, Dale G. Waldbieser, Harmon P. Weeks, Jr., Ann J. Wheatley, Nixon A. Wilson, Larry J. Workman, Richard A. Zackman, M. Dean Zimmerman. In addition, Steven D. Ford and Gwilym S. Jones were graduate students at both Purdue University and Indiana State University.

The Indiana Department of Natural Resources granted permission to trap and study mammals on areas under the supervision of the Division of Fish and Wildlife, the Division of Forestry, the Division of State Parks, and the Division of Nature Preserves. Since 1951, the Division of Parks has granted permission to band bats in certain parks. The United States Forest Service and the United States Fish and Wildlife Service allowed us to work on their properties in Indiana. We have also been granted the opportunity to conduct limited research within the Indiana Dunes National Lakeshore, where we were particularly pleased to be able to trap small mammals in the bogs. The Nature Conservancy gave us permission to trap some areas under its care. Although we conducted much of our study on public lands, numerous private landowners gave us access to their properties.

We are indebted to the following for data regarding specimens of Indiana mammals in collections: Rollin H. Baker, Laurence C. Binford, Elmer C. Birney, William H. Burt, James B. Cope, Carol Davidson, John L. Diedrich, J. Kenneth Doutt,

William R. Eberly, William H. Elder, James S. Findley, Hugh H. Genoways, Eugene E. Good, Robert Goslin, Jack L. Gottschang, Robert R. Grant, Jr., Raymond Grow, Harvey L. Gunderson, E. Raymond Hall, William J. Hamilton, Jr., Charles O. Handley, Jr., Don R. Helms, Donald F. Hoffmeister, J. Knox Jones, Jr., Ralph D. Kirkpatrick, Mike Kowalski, Barbara Lawrence, William Z. Lidicker, Jr., Dwight M. Lindsay, James C. List, Robert L. Livezey, Charles A. Long, T. J. McNitt, Joseph C. Moore, Robert T. Orr, Charles L. Rippy, Robert K. Rose, William Royalty, Colin C. Sanborn, Damian Schmelz, Frederick H. Test, Richard G. VanGelder, J. Dan Webster, Nixon A. Wilson, Samuel W. Witmer, Earl G. Zimmerman.

We have had a great deal of cooperation for many years from various workers who have helped in identification and verification of parasites. Among these are: K. C. Emerson, Arlington, Virginia (lice); Alex Fain, Institut de Medecine Tropicale Prince Leopold, Antwerpen, Belgium (mites); S. D. Herrin, Center for Environmental Studies, Brigham Young University, Provo, Utah (mites of the genus *Hirstionyssus*); E. W. Jameson, Department of Zoology, University of California, Davis (myobiid mites); G. W. Krantz, Department of Entomology, Oregon State University, Corvallis (macrochelid mites); E. E. Lindquist, Research Branch, Biosystematics Research Institute, Agriculture Canada, Ottawa, Ontario (cyrtolaelapid and other mites); Richard R. Loomis, Department of Biology, California State University, Long Beach (chiggers); B. McDaniel, Entomology–Zoology Department, South Dakota State University, Brookings (mites); F. J. Radovsky and J. A. Tenorio, Bernice P. Bishop Museum, Honolulu, Hawaii (macronyssid mites); Nixon A. Wilson, Department of Biology, University of Northern Iowa, Cedar Falls (fleas, ticks, mites); William Wrenn, Department of Biology, University of North Dakota, Grand Forks (chiggers).

We have learned much from talks with our colleagues and friends throughout the state. Many people are good wildlife observers, yet never get their records into print unless by chance they relate some interesting event to someone engaged in writing about the subject. It is regrettable that good data are lost because of lack of personal contacts, but it would be impossible for us to know who these people are and then to find the time to visit with them. Bird watchers are organized and have ample chance to report and record their sightings in a variety of publications, but "mammal watchers" are fewer in number and have no societies or clubs. Just as they have been invaluable in gathering significant information on birds, amateurs could add a tremendous amount of information on our native mammals.

For their help in many ways, we would like to recognize and thank the following: Durward L. Allen, Wilson W. Baker, William B. Barnes, Walter F. Beineke, David M. Brooks, Robert Brown, Mr. & Mrs. John P. Buck, Larry L. Calvert, Ted Chandik, Leland Chandler, Herdis Conder, James B. Cope, Kenneth R. Cougill, John F. Datena, Herald A. Demaree, Jr., William R. Eberly, William E. Ginn, John Goold, Raymond Grow, Robert W. Guth, Max Hamilton, Rex Hamilton, Harold Hawkins, Bruce J. Hayward, William Hendrickson, Dave Howell, Richard Hudson, James A. Hughes, Emery Jenkins, James H. Keith, Robert Kern, Charles M. Kirkpatrick, Ralph D. Kirkpatrick, Richard K. LaVal, Larry E. Lehman, Dwight M. Lindsay, Frank R. Lockard, Eugene Ludlow, Wayne Machan, James D. McCall, Will E. Madden, Dale N. Martin, Karl Maslowski, Peter E. Meyer, Robert W. Meyer, Harold H. Michaud, Nancy Ann Miller, Wendell Nickolson, Phillip N. Ohmit, John Olson, George R. Parker, Richard L. Powell, Maurice C. Reeves, Warren S. Rowe, Rodney D. Royce, Charles E. Scheffe, Damian Schmelz, Donald L. Schuder, Duane Shroufe, Eric W. Stark, Donald E. Stullken, Terry P. Tichenor, Merlin D. Tuttle, Thomas M. Uzzell, Jr., Victor Walter, Gertrude L. Ward, William J. Wayne, Arthur H. Westing, J. R. Whitehouse, Samuel W. Witmer.

We have been given permission to use data from materials previously published by many individuals named above. Their works have been cited in the text, and full citations are given in the list of references. We also wish to acknowledge the following sources for granting permission for the use of such previously published materials: the *American Midland Naturalist;* the C. C. Adams Center for Ecological Studies, Western Michigan University; the National Research Council of Canada, for materials in the *Canadian Journal of Zoology;* the Ecological Society of America, for materials in *Ecology* and in *Ecological Monographs; Entomological News;* the Indiana Academy of Science, for materials in the various *Proceedings* of the Academy; the State of Indiana, Department of Natural Resources, Division of Fish and Wildlife, for materials contained in various research reports; the Kentucky Academy of Science, for materials in the *Transactions* of the Academy; the American Society of Mammalogists, for materials in the *Journal of Mammalogy;* the *Journal of Medical Entomology;* the *Journal of Parasitology;* the *Journal Review,* Crawfordsville, Indiana; and the U.S. Fish and Wildlife Service, United States Department of the Interior.

Laura Bakken typed several drafts of most of the manuscript for Whitaker, and went beyond the call of duty in eliminating inconsistencies, ambiguities, and a host of other problems. Mumford acknowledges the excellent typing of Diana Keller and Jeannie Navarre, especially the latter, who prepared at least two complete drafts of the entire manuscript.

Our wives, Vivian and Royce, and our children, Jim, Lynne, and Russell Mumford, and John, Lynne, and Bill Whitaker, have had to sacrifice much time normally spent with husbands and fathers when we were afield, in the laboratory, or incommunicado while "in the den"—writing. We apologize to them and we thank them for their indulgence. In addition, Jim Mumford and John and Bill Whitaker contributed materially to this study by their aid in the field.

Mammals of Indiana

Introduction

The term *animal* is often used incorrectly to mean *mammal*. But birds, frogs, snakes, fishes, insects, and spiders are also animals. Mammals (technically, the class Mammalia) constitute but one group of vertebrate (backboned) animals. Man is a mammal, as are all other animal species which have hair and in which the females feed milk to their young by means of mammary glands. Mammals, like birds, are warm-blooded (homoiothermic; that is, they maintain a relatively constant body temperature (except during hibernation), regardless of the environmental temperature, by utilizing energy from their food. The normal body temperature of man is about 98.6 degrees Fahrenheit. Body temperatures of smaller mammals are generally slightly higher, but are relatively constant for any particular species. Lower vertebrates—fishes, amphibians, reptiles— are cold-blooded (heterothermic, or poikilothermic); their body temperatures vary with environmental temperatures. Most mammals have two types of teeth (milk, deciduous, or "baby" teeth, and permanent teeth) set in sockets. Platypuses, some whales, and a few other species of mammals have no teeth, having lost them secondarily, through evolution. The mammal skull articulates with the vertebral column by means of two principal, lateral structures, the occipital condyles; birds and reptiles have one occipital condyle. Mammals breathe by lungs and have a muscular diaphragm separating the body cavity into two sections. The heart and lungs are in the upper (thoracic) part; the stomach and intestines are in the lower (abdominal) part.

The two major groups or subclasses of living mammals are the egg-laying species (Prototheria) and those which produce living young (Theria). Prototherians include a single mammalian order, the Monotremata, containing the duckbill platypus and the echidnas (spiny anteaters) of the Australia–New Guinea region. These animals lay round, leathery-shelled eggs. Platypus eggs are laid in a nest in a burrow in the ground; echidnas lay their eggs and incubate them in an abdominal pouch (or marsupium). The mammary glands of these unique animals lack nipples; young echidnas suck milk from two lobule areas in the pouch, while young platypuses lap milk from the abdominal fur of their mother. These primitive mammals have a cloaca, a common receptacle for materials from the urogenital and digestive systems. The ordinal name, Monotremata, means single opening, in reference to the presence of a cloaca.

All other mammals produce living young and are in the subclass Theria, which contains the infraclasses Metatheria (pouched mammals) and Eutheria (placental mammals). Metatheria contains only the order Marsupialia (mammals with a marsupium or pouch), although a few marsupials have secondarily lost their pouches. Marsupials have mammary glands supplied with nipples and located inside the pouch. The young are born in a very immature state, then climb into the pouch and remain there for an extended period. Marsupials lack the type of "true" placental attachment found in the Eutheria. The unique epipubic bones of the pelvic girdle in the marsupials (and in the Monotremata) help support the pouch. Pouched mammals are most characteristic of the Australian region, where there are eight families of marsupials. In the absence of some mammalian types which have evolved on other

1

continents, Australian marsupials have developed in such a way as to fill many of the ecological niches (living situations) occupied by various types of mammals in other parts of the world. For example, Australia has marsupial "mice," "cats," a "mole," and a "wolf." On other continents, mammals occupying similar ecological niches are represented not by marsupials, but by different orders, such as Insectivora (moles), Rodentia (mice), and Carnivora (cats, wolves). In addition, some Australian bandicoots are roughly similar to rabbits (order Lagomorpha) and wombats to woodchucks (order Rodentia) in their lifestyles. The process by which one group of organisms diverges and evolves diverse forms to fill various niches is called *adaptive radiation*. And the process whereby unrelated forms develop to look superficially alike and to live in similar ecological niches is called *convergent evolution*, or convergence. There are also two families of marsupials in the New World, and one family (Didelphidae) has a representative, the Virginia opossum, in Indiana.

All other living mammals are called eutherians and have a similar type of placental attachment between mother and developing young for the exchange of nutrients and oxygen. There are sixteen extant orders of placental mammals, and members of six of these orders occur in Indiana.

In teaching mammalogy courses at our respective universities, we have been aware that the average student knows relatively little about our native mammals. This is not too surprising, for most Indiana mammals are small, secretive, and nocturnal. Mammal watching is much more difficult than bird watching and is not as popular in this country (except where larger, more easily observed species are found). When taking a class into the field, we can be reasonably sure of seeing some variety of birds. In contrast, planning field trips to observe mammals is quite difficult and much is left to chance. Mammals are generally encountered at unexpected times and may involve such incidents as a fleeting glimpse of a fox dashing across the road at night, a raccoon at a garbage can in a campground, a chipmunk running across the road or a woodland trail, a ground squirrel sitting along the grassy shoulder of a road, a muskrat swimming, or a bat flitting across the

sky at dusk. These short encounters usually do not give one a satisfactory view or time to savor the observation.

Most field observations regarding mammals do not involve seeing the animals themselves, but consist of seeing "signs" left by them as they go about their normal activities. Such signs include burrows in the ground, nests, houses, tracks, droppings, mounds of soil, gnawed objects, scratches on trees, rubbing posts, slides in the mud, prey refuse, debris left from feeding, and the like. From time to time, the carcass or partial carcass of a mammal is also found, mostly along roads.

Several species of mammals are well known for their vocalizations—the barking of a squirrel or a fox, the howl of a coyote, the chitter of a ground squirrel, flying squirrel, or chipmunk, the whistle of a woodchuck, the snort of a deer, the tail slap of a beaver, the squeaking of a bat, the squeal of a rabbit in distress. Other sounds made by mammals (many of them at night) are less well known and consist of screams, yelps, howls, and other calls. These are sometimes attributed to "panthers," "wildcats," or other imagined animals.

And one can hardly ignore the odor of a skunk. Other mammalian odors may be recognized by the initiated. These include the musky odor of a fox or deer, the scent of mink or badger at their dens, and the distinctive odor of some bats and the short-tailed shrew.

The mammals included in this book are the species currently living within the state. Most are native, but two (the house mouse and the Norway rat) were introduced from the Old World. Two species, the white-tailed deer and the beaver, were once extinct in Indiana but were successfully reintroduced. We have not included domesticated, captive, or escaped species, or species that have for a time been released (or escaped) or introduced without becoming established as part of the mammalian fauna of the state. This group includes the elk, the nutria, and the San Juan rabbit. Additional information on extirpated mammals has been published by Hahn (1909), Lyon (1936), and Mumford (1969c). From Table 1 it can be noted that numerous larger mammals have been extirpated from Indiana since 1800. Some of the latest dates of occurrence for these species are no more than estimates.

Table 1

Mammals reported in Indiana within the past 150 years
but now apparently absent

Order and Species	Approximate year of last report
Order Rodentia	
Black Rat / *Rattus rattus*	1845
*Woodland Jumping Mouse / *Napaeozapus insignis*	1930
Porcupine / *Erethizon dorsatum*	1918
Order Carnivora	
Gray (Timber) Wolf / *Canis lupus*	1908?
Red Wolf / *Canis rufus*	1832
Black Bear / *Ursus americanus*	1850
Fisher / *Martes pennanti*	1859
Wolverine / *Gulo gulo*	1852
Eastern Spotted Skunk / *Spilogale putorius*	1920?
River Otter / *Lutra canadensis*	1942
Mountain Lion / *Felis concolor*	1851
Lynx / *Felis lynx*	1832?
Order Artiodactyla	
Elk (Wapiti) / *Cervus elaphus*	1830
Bison / *Bison bison*	1830

*See page 5 for further comments concerning this species.

Fifty-four species of mammals are now found in Indiana.* These are divided among seven orders. The order Rodentia (mice, rats, squirrels, beaver) is represented by twenty-two species. By far the greatest number of mammals of the world are rodents—a group that has successfully invaded practically all portions of the land surface of the earth. Rodents as a group are quite variable, and our native forms include the flying squirrel, pocket gopher, jumping mouse, woodchuck, beaver, and many others. All show interesting adaptations and special characteristics that enable them to survive.

*Just as this book was going to press, a very nice use of the experimental method by Ronald Caldwell has resulted in the finding of two additional species of mammals in Indiana. Caldwell (unpublished) had been trapping *Microsorex hoyi* and *Sorex fumeus* in the oak-maple sandstone areas of the western coal fields of Kentucky. He noted that this same outcropping and vegetative type protruded northward into Indiana and hypothesized that *Microsorex* might occur there. He subsequently introduced 24 sunken cans on the Harrison-Crawford State Forest in Crawford County, Indiana, in May 1981. These cans were checked a few days later and yielded nine smoky shrews, *Sorex fumeus*, and one Pygmy shrew, *Microsorex hoyi*.
Additional data now being collected on the distribution and biology of these species in the state.

The next most important group (twelve species) is the order Chiroptera, containing the only mammals that truly fly—the bats. Several Indiana species are little known. We still are unable to state where the evening bat spends the winter. And we would like to know more about the winter range of the tree-inhabiting red bat, hoary bat, and silver-haired bat, which migrate in the fall to as yet largely undisclosed sites. One of our most common bats, the big brown bat, is present in hundreds of buildings throughout the state during the summer. When winter comes, the summer quarters are deserted, to be reoccupied the following spring. Where these thousands and thousands of big brown bats spend the winter is still a mystery. The species is not considered to be highly migratory, yet we know the animals move. So far, our searching in caves in southern Indiana has not revealed any large numbers—certainly only a very small percentage of the huge numbers present in the state in summer. Our banding studies, begun in 1951, have shed no light on the problem. And we do not know whether the gray bat, southeastern myotis, or big-eared bat breed in the state. A fourth species, the silver-haired bat, may be present in small numbers during the summer in extreme northern Indiana.

Only one member of the order Mar-supialia—the Virginia opossum—occurs in the state. Most of the species in this group live in the Australian region or in tropical or semitropical portions of Mexico, Central America, and South America. North of Mexico, only the common Virginia opossum that Hoosiers know so well has been able to survive away from warmer environments. Even here, it frequently suffers frostbite, which causes the tips of the tails and ears to freeze and slough off.

Indiana is home to four species of shrews* and two species of moles, all in the order Insectivora. Shrews are small mammals that live in damp places where there is sufficient humidity to prevent the desiccation of their small bodies. They must feed almost constantly to stay alive, for such small warm-blooded animals need much energy to maintain a constant, warm body temperature. This is especially true in cold winters, for none of the shrews hibernate. Both native moles are burrowers (and hence fossorial) and spend much of their time belowground in tunnels which they construct with their powerful digging feet. The star-nosed mole is semi-aquatic and has special structures which enable it to dive and swim underwater. Both moles appear to feed mainly on earthworms.

Two species of rabbits, order Lagomorpha, inhabit Indiana, but the larger swamp rabbit is severely restricted in range to extreme southwestern Indiana and is not known to most people in the state. These animals are found in wooded floodplain remnants, where the habitat will still support them. The swamp rabbit may be the mammal species most vulnerable to extirpation from Indiana in future years; its habitat is still decreasing and its numbers are not large. The common eastern cottontail is the "rabbit" that everyone knows. Although its numbers have also decreased considerably because of loss of habitat, it is still common.

The order Carnivora has ten Indiana representatives. These include the weasels, the mink, the striped skunk, and the badger in the family Mustelidae. Another family, the Canidae, includes the coyote, the gray fox, and the red fox. The bobcat and the raccoon

*See the preceding note on two additional species of shrews recently found in Indiana.

each belong to still different families (Felidae and Procyonidae). In the recent past, several species of carnivores have disappeared from the state. These include the gray wolf, red wolf, black bear, fisher, wolverine, eastern spotted skunk, river otter, lynx, and mountain lion. It is a shame that some, or all, of these fine mammals could not survive in Indiana, but they were simply not compatible with the current number of humans and the lack of available habitats (mostly wilderness areas). There is reasonable doubt that the wolverine and lynx actually occupied the state in early times, but there are some references to them (none backed by preserved specimens, however).

The order Artiodactyla is now represented in Indiana only by the white-tailed deer. Elk (wapiti), once present, have been reintroduced without success and the bison has long been extinct.

The mammals of Indiana are quite similar to those of Illinois, which has a few more species (59). There are about 60 species in Michigan and 63 each in Ohio and Kentucky. In contrast, New Mexico has 139 species and California 163. Thus, the mammalian fauna of our state is not nearly as rich and varied as that of many other states. Indiana's geographical position is interesting, however, in that some southern, northern, and western species occur here. Indiana species that occupy geographic ranges mostly to the west of the state are the Franklin's ground squirrel, the thirteen-lined ground squirrel, the plains pocket gopher, the badger, the coyote, and the western harvest mouse. (Before 1969, the western harvest mouse was not known to occur in Indiana, but it invaded from Illinois and is probably still extending its range eastward.) Northern species include the masked shrew, least weasel, red squirrel, star-nosed mole, and meadow vole. Those with ranges more to the south are the southeastern shrew, southeastern myotis, gray myotis, Rafinesque's big-eared bat, swamp rabbit, and eastern woodrat. The remainder of the species found in Indiana are more widespread throughout the United States and are difficult to categorize as southern, northern, eastern, or western.

Other mammals may be added to the state list in the future. It seems possible that the small-footed myotis (*Myotis leibii*) and the eastern harvest mouse *(Reithrodontomys humulis)* may occur. Both have been found in close proximity to Indiana. A specimen of the woodland jumping mouse *(Napaeozapus insignis)* in the University of Michigan Museum of Zoology was reportedly taken in Parke County, Indiana (possibly in Turkey Run State Park), on 26 July 1930. We have trapped extensively for this species at Turkey Run, where there appears to be suitable habitat for this mouse, but have taken no specimens. Nor has it been collected elsewhere in the state. Possibly the species no longer occurs in Indiana. Another possibility is that the specimen may have been incorrectly labeled as to locality. For these reasons, we have not included the woodland jumping mouse on our current list. There are several earlier records (none substantiated by collected specimens) of the black rat *(Rattus rattus)* in Indiana. This Old World species evidently was carried to our state via boats coming up the Ohio River and Wabash River. The *R. rattus* specimen mentioned by Hahn (1909) from New Albany, Indiana, was submitted by us to the National Museum of Natural History for verification. It proved to be a melanistic specimen of the Norway rat, according to David H. Johnson.

That the mammalian fauna of Indiana is constantly changing to some degree is also evidenced by the number of species that have become extinct over the past 150 years (see Table 1). No doubt other species will be extirpated in the future. For this reason, most states have now compiled lists of endangered and threatened species. The Indiana list currently carries the Indiana myotis, the gray myotis, Rafinesque's big-eared bat, and the bobcat as endangered (in danger of extirpation). On the list of threatened species (those which are likely to become endangered within the foreseeable future) are the southeastern myotis, southeastern shrew, star-nosed mole, swamp rabbit, eastern woodrat, badger, plains pocket gopher, Franklin's ground squirrel, and western harvest mouse. We feel that some of these are not truly threatened and should be removed from the list. Several species in this category have geographic ranges that barely reach into Indiana, and thus are considered peripheral species. Over the major part of their ranges these species are in no danger of extirpation.

No doubt the current Indiana list of threatened and endangered species will be modified to reflect more accurately the true status of these species. (Mammals we feel should be on the threatened list for Indiana include the southeastern myotis, the eastern woodrat, the swamp rabbit, and the badger.)

There are several earlier publications on the mammals of Indiana. Evermann and Butler published a "Preliminary List of Indiana Mammals" (1894b), which was amended by Butler in 1895. These authors included 43 of the 54 species presently known to exist in the state. Species not included (some were on their hypothetical list) were the southeastern shrew *(Sorex longirostris)*, southeastern myotis *(Myotis austroriparius)*, gray myotis *(Myotis grisescens)*, Keen's myotis *(Myotis keenii)*, Indiana myotis *(Myotis sodalis)*, evening bat *(Nycticeius humeralis)*, swamp rabbit *(Sylvilagus aquaticus)*, eastern woodrat *(Neotoma floridana)*, deer mouse *(Peromyscus maniculatus)*, western harvest mouse *(Reithrodontomys megalotis)*, and least weasel *(Mustela nivalis)*.

Hahn published the first book on the mammals of Indiana (1909). This excellent work evidently received relatively little of the credit due it. Hahn's unfortunate death at an early age cut short a promising career as a mammalogist, and surely he would have maintained his interest in Indiana, his home state. Species that Hahn added to the state list were *Sorex longirostris, Myotis grisescens, Myotis keenii, Peromyscus maniculatus,* and *Sylvilagus aquaticus.*

The comprehensive book *Mammals of Indiana* (1936) by Lyon was a classic for its day, although it contained little original information on mammals gathered in Indiana since Hahn's work. Lyon was not a mammalogist by profession and his work with mammals represented a side interest. He did relatively little fieldwork in the state. Species added to the state fauna by Lyon were *Mustela nivalis, Myotis austroriparius, Myotis sodalis,* and *Neotoma floridana.*

Mumford (1969c) summarized information on the history, habitat, distribution, and taxonomy of Indiana mammals, and with the addition of *Nycticeius humeralis* (Kirkpatrick, 1943) brought the number of known living mammal species in the state to 53. About two weeks after Mumford's book appeared in

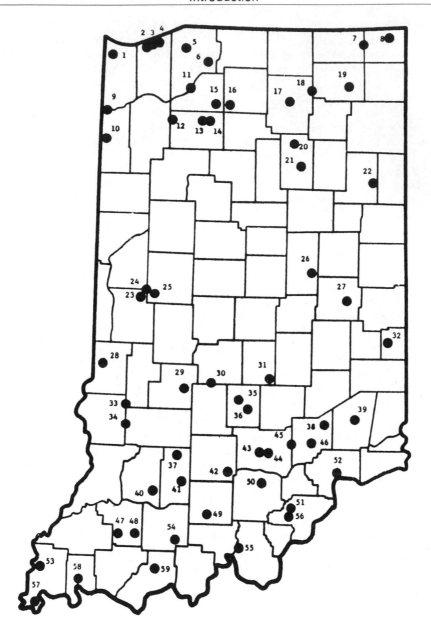

Some natural areas of Indiana

1 Hoosier Prairie
2 Cowles Bog
3 Indiana Dunes State Park
4 Indiana Dunes National Lakeshore
5 Pinhook Bog
6 Kingsbury Fish & Wildlife Area
7 Pigeon River Fish & Wildlife Area
8 Pokagon State Park
9 LaSalle Fish & Wildlife Area

10 Willow Slough Fish & Wildlife Area
11 Kankakee Fish & Wildlife Area
12 Jasper-Pulaski Fish & Wildlife Area
13 Winamac Fish & Wildlife Area
14 Tippecanoe River State Park
15 Bass Lake State Park
16 Lake Maxinkuckee
17 Winona Lake
18 Tri-County Fish & Wildlife Area

19 Chain O'Lakes State Park
20 Laketon Bog
21 Salamonie River State Forest
22 Ouabache State Park
23 Turkey Run State Park
24 Shades State Park
25 Pine Hills Nature Preserve
26 Mounds State Park
27 Wilbur Wright Fish & Wildlife Area
28 Little Bluestem Prairie
29 McCormick's Creek State Park
30 Morgan-Monroe State Forest
31 Atterbury Fish & Wildlife Area
32 Whitewater State Park
33 Shakamak State Park
34 Greene-Sullivan State Forest
35 Yellowwood State Forest
36 Brown County State Park
37 Crane Naval Weapons Support Center
38 Brush Creek Fish & Wildlife Area
39 Versailles State Park
40 Glendale Fish & Wildlife Area
41 Martin State Forest
42 Spring Mill State Park
43 Jackson-Washington State Forest
44 Starve Hollow State Forest
45 Muscatatuck National Wildlife Refuge
46 Crosley Fish & Wildlife Area
47 Patoka Fish & Wildlife Area
48 Pike State Forest
49 Springs Valley Fish & Wildlife Area
50 Jackson-Washington State Forest
51 Clark State Forest
52 Clifty Falls State Park
53 Harmonie State Park
54 Ferdinand State Forest
55 Harrison-Crawford State Forest
56 Dean Lake State Forest
57 Hovey Lake Fish & Wildlife Area
58 Angel Mounds State Memorial
59 Lincoln State Park

State Parks and Recreation Areas

15 Bass Lake
36 Brown County
19 Chain O'Lakes
52 Clifty Falls
53 Harmonie
3 Indiana Dunes
59 Lincoln
29 McCormick's Creek
26 Mounds
22 Ouabache
8 Pokagon
24 Shades
33 Shakamak
42 Spring Mill
14 Tippecanoe River
23 Turkey Run
39 Versailles
32 Whitewater

Fish and Wildlife Areas

31 Atterbury
38 Brush Creek
46 Crosley
40 Glendale
57 Hovey Lake
12 Jasper-Pulaski
11 Kankakee
6 Kingsbury
9 LaSalle
47 Patoka
7 Pigeon River
49 Springs Valley
18 Tri-County
27 Wilbur Wright
10 Willow Slough
13 Winamac

State Forests

51 Clark
56 Dean Lake
54 Ferdinand
34 Greene-Sullivan
55 Harrison-Crawford
43
50 Jackson-Washington
41 Martin
30 Morgan-Monroe
48 Pike
21 Salamonie River
44 Starve Hollow
35 Yellowwood

Other Areas Frequently Mentioned in the Text

58 Angel Mounds State Memorial
2 Cowles Bog
37 Crane Naval Weapons Support Center
1 Hoosier Prairie
4 Indiana Dunes National Lakeshore
16 Lake Maxinkuckee
20 Laketon Bog
28 Little Bluestem Prairie
45 Muscatatuck National Wildlife Refuge
25 Pine Hills Nature Preserve
5 Pinhook Bog
17 Winona Lake

print, the western harvest mouse *(Reithro-dontomys megalotis)* was collected in Indiana for the first time (Whitaker and Sly, 1970).

Throughout this book, we have attempted to use primarily information obtained in and pertaining specifically to Indiana. We wanted the book to have a "Hoosier flavor." We have drawn heavily from the publications, reports, and field notes of researchers and early settlers in the state. And, during the past fifteen years especially, we ourselves have accumulated much information, a considerable amount of which has been published elsewhere.

Latin names, vernacular names, and sequence of species follow Jones *et al.* (1979). Other common names included are those either currently in use in Indiana or definitely known to have been applied to Indiana mammals. Vernacular names for a particular species may vary from place to place in the state or in other sections of the country. For example, "gopher," as used in much of northern Indiana, refers not to the pocket gopher but to the Franklin's ground squirrel and the thirteen-lined ground squirrel. These squirrels are further separated into "gray gophers" and "striped gophers," respectively. In southern Indiana, the eastern chipmunk is called a "ground squirrel." The red squirrel *(Tamiasciurus hudsonicus)* is usually called "piney squirrel" or simply "piney" throughout its northern range. But in southern Indiana, where the red squirrel is quite rare, the fox squirrel *(Sciurus niger)* is often called "red squirrel" to differentiate it from the gray squirrel *(Sciurus carolinensis)*.

Weights and measurements are from specimens taken in Indiana, when such information is available; there are a few exceptions, as noted in the species accounts. These data are from specimens we collected and from the labels of preserved specimens examined by us in other collections. Some of the weight and measurement information is broken down by sex or by different sections of the state. Many species of mammals do not exhibit significantly different weights and measurements between sexes, but there are exceptions—some mustelids and a few bats. Populations of the same species from various sections of the state exhibit minor differences

in weights and measurements (and color), as our data show.

Distribution maps have been provided in the species accounts to show localities from which we have examined preserved specimens or have reliable published observations. When the exact location from which a preserved specimen was taken is known, a solid circle is plotted as precisely as possible on that site. If the specimen has a label showing only the county from which it came, the solid circle is plotted in the middle of the county. Other records (open circles) plotted on the distribution maps consist of reliable observations of live or dead (but not preserved) specimens, photographs, or references in the literature.

Distribution maps cannot be taken too literally. It will be noted that for some common species we have no records from numerous counties. This does not imply that the species in question does not occur in those counties. It simply points up the fact that no one has placed on record (by specimen or by published information) its occurrence. We know that some species occur in every Indiana county, but we may not have been able to find records for certain counties and so we plotted no observations for those counties. On the other hand, some species (especially some of the small shrews) may occur at various places throughout Indiana but may not be found in every county. The species may be present only where there are suitable, but often isolated, habitats. For such species, apparent gaps in the ranges may be actual.

In addition to the references in the text, a list of references is given at the end of each species account, to help the reader locate some additional pertinent data for that species. All references refer to the bibliography, which contains essentially all papers known to us dealing with Indiana mammals.

We have included what we think are useful innovations for a state mammal book. One of these is the material dealing with parasites, which should be useful to parasitologists, veterinarians, wildlife biologists, students in mammalogy, and (perhaps to a lesser extent) laymen. Relatively little is known about the relationships of ectoparasites to most Indiana mammals. Even less is known about endoparasites, but unfortunately most of those we report are not identified to species. This field of study is quite challenging and possibly important to farmers, wildlife managers, and other groups. The same can be said regarding diseases. Except for a few diseases (rabies, tularemia) that have been known in wild mammals for many years, there is little information regarding diseases that afflict wild mammals and regarding the implications of such diseases to man or to domestic animals.

Another departure from many state mammal books is our inclusion of a discussion of mammal food habits. In recent years, mammalogists have conducted more extensive research on mammal (especially non-game) food habits. In earlier years, most of this type of work involved predatory or important game species. Now, it is becoming more and more apparent that before we can have a well-rounded understanding of how a mammal utilizes its ecological niche we must have more data on food habits. New and better techniques are being described for this type of analysis, which in the past was either considered unimportant or too difficult.

One function of a book of this kind is to stimulate others to become more actively engaged in the study of our native mammals. We feel that much pleasure can be derived from such studies. Sometimes what begins as a cursory observation may end up as a published paper of some significance. Indeed, mammals can be enjoyed in many ways, but we feel that those who enjoy them most are those who know most about them. We hope we have added to such knowledge and enjoyment for the people of the Hoosier state.

Indiana
The State as an Environment

Mumford (1969c) characterized Indiana as follows·

Indiana lies in the middle-eastern part of the United States, near the eastern border of the great interior plains, between 41°49′ and 37°40′ north latitude and 84°49′ and 88°2′ longitude. The total area is 36,555 square miles, of which Lake Michigan occupies 230 and interior lakes and rivers 280. The greatest dimensions are about 155 by 275 miles. The average elevation is about 715 feet; the highest point (1285 feet) is in Randolph County and the lowest (313 feet) is at the mouth of the Wabash River. Approximately five-sixths of the State are covered with glacial drift, while about 6,000 square miles in the south-central portion are unglaciated. Almost nine-tenths of the State drain southwestward and westward into the Mississippi Basin, the remainder into the St. Lawrence Basin. [Map 1]

The state is divided into 92 counties (Map 2); we have found it useful to use the counties as points of reference in reporting distribution data and other aspects of our research.

Physiographic Features

Wayne (1966) has related the geologic events that shaped the physiography of the state, from the late Paleozoic Era, when what is now Indiana first rose above sea level, to the present. He wrote, "After the land that was to become Indiana rose above sea level late in the Paleozoic Era, it probably underwent almost continuous weathering and erosion until the first of the Ice Age glaciers spread across it." The Paleozoic Era began about 620 million years ago and ended about 195 million years ago. From the time the land rose and throughout the Mesozoic Era (from

some 195 million to 60 million years ago) and the Tertiary Period of the Cenozoic Era (from 60 million to 1 million years ago) weathering and erosion played a major role in shaping the landscape. Early in the Tertiary, part of what is now Indiana was inundated by a sea.

The geologic events that took place from the Paleozoic Era through the Tertiary Period of the Cenozoic Era were important in determining the physiography of the state, but the more recent geological history is primarily responsible for what we see today. The last million years of the Cenozoic Era have been called the Quaternary (or Pleistocene Epoch), and Wayne had this to say regarding that period:

During the Pleistocene Epoch, glacial ice extended into Indiana at least three times. Each of the cold periods was followed by a warmer interglacial episode, during which the glaciers melted. The total effect of these several glaciations on the landscape and resources of northern Indiana as well as all of northeastern North America was vast. Shale lowlands, trenched limestone plains, and sandstone-capped escarpments, which made up the preglacial surface features of the State, were buried beneath a great volume of rock debris carried and dumped by the glacier. The present relief in much of central and northern Indiana is slight, if compared to that of the buried rock surface.

The first of the Pleistocene glaciers (the Nebraskan stage), which occurred from half a million to one and a half million years ago (estimates vary), apparently did not reach Indiana. Some 350,000 to 400,000 years ago, the Kansan stage ice reached central and southern Indiana from the northeast. The warm Yarmouth interglacial period that fol-

11

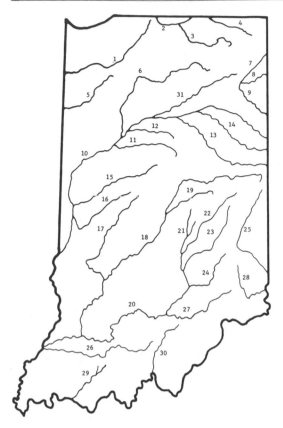

Map 1.   Major drainage systems of Indiana

Map 2.   The counties of Indiana

1 Kankakee River	17 Eel River
2 St. Joseph River	18 White River W. Fork
3 Elkhart River	19 Fall Creek
4 Pigeon River	20 White River E. Fork
5 Iroquois River	21 Sugar Creek
6 Tippecanoe River	22 Big Blue River
7 St. Joseph River	23 Flat Rock River
8 Maumee River	24 Sand River
9 St. Mary's River	25 Whitewater River
10 Wabash River	26 Patoka River
11 Wildcat Creek	27 Muscatatuck River
12 Deer Creek	28 Laughery Creek
13 Mississinewa River	29 Little Pigeon Creek
14 Salamonie River	30 Big Blue River
15 Sugar Creek	31 Eel River
16 Raccoon Creek	

lowed evidently persisted for at least 200,000 years. The Illinoian ice age followed, possibly as little as 125,000 years ago (estimates vary to 400,000 years). The Illinoian glaciers, which extended into the lowlands along the Wabash River, reached further south than did any other ice sheet during the Pleistocene.

The Illinoian ice disappeared, perhaps

105,000 years ago. Records of fossil pollen show that the next warmer (Sangamon) period was characterized by hardwood forests, rather than the previous coniferous vegetation. But toward the end of the Sangamon, conifers reappeared.

The last glacial ice sheet (Wisconsin) began about 70,000 years ago, and covered nearly two-thirds of Indiana (Map 3). It reached its maximum penetration some 21,000 years ago, receded, and re-advanced short of the initial margin 1,000 years later. At that time central Indiana was covered with tundra-like vegetation and scattered spruce trees. The Pleistocene epoch ended and glaciers melted about 8,500 years ago. Wayne wrote:

The record from peat bogs shows that a cool climate conifer forest was followed, about 8,000 years ago, by a change to a deciduous forest. . . . Pleistocene vertebrates were many, but only a few — mostly the big ones — are known from Indiana. Someone remarked once that every bog that is big-

Map 3. Selected glacial boundaries in Indiana

Map 4.   Physiographic regions of Indiana
(from Wayne, 1956)

ger than an acre probably contains the bones of at least one mastodon. This may be true; certainly Indiana has been an exporter of mastodon and mammoth skeletons. . . . In addition to these behemoths, giant beavers, elk, muskox, and ground sloths roamed the area. Mice and other small vertebrates surely were abundant, too, but they are so tiny and unspectacular they have been overlooked almost completely so far.

Malott (1922) described the physiographic regions of the state, basing his nine divisions ("natural units") on elevation, relief, and related types of topographic forms present. Wayne (1956) modified and refined some of the boundaries established by Malott, but retained Malott's names for these areas (Map 4). Schneider (1966) closely followed Wayne, pointing out that data accumulated since 1956 warranted only "relatively minor" modifications. Our brief descriptions of the physiographic units that follow are adapted from these papers, which should be consulted for more details.

1 Northern Lake
  and Moraine Region
2 Tipton Till Plain
3 Wabash Lowland
4 Crawford Upland
5 Mitchell Plain

6 Norman Upland
7 Scottsburg Lowland
8 Muscatatuck Regional
  Slope
9 Dearborn Upland

Schneider, in commenting upon the general physiographic aspects of Indiana, noted that the state "can be divided into three broad physiographic zones that trend in a general east-west direction across the State." The central of these zones is the Tipton Till Plain, 12,000 square miles of deposition plain with low relief and slightly modified by postglacial stream erosion. The northern zone, the Northern Moraine and Lake Region, covers about 8,500 square miles and contains landforms that are mostly of glacial origin. These include end moraines, outwash plains, kames, lake plains, valley trains, kettles (potholes), lakes, sand dunes, and peat bogs. The southern zone has seven subdivi-

NORTHERN MORAINE AND LAKE REGION. Pothole lake near Albion in Noble County. Meadow voles, meadow jumping mice, short-tailed shrews, and masked shrews live here. Photo by Mumford

sions, and the central portion of it was not glaciated during the Pleistocene. Landforms throughout this 15,000-square-mile zone are mostly the result of normal weathering, stream erosion, and mass movement.

Northern Moraine and Lake Region. Although this region has been divided into five minor portions (see Schneider, 1966), our discussion will treat it as a unit. The region covers roughly the northern one-fourth of the state and is of variable relief. Most of Indiana's natural lakes are within its borders, although a few small lakes (some nearly gone) occur south of the region in Blackford, Grant, Warren, and Wells counties. Deep peat deposits in Hamilton, Madison, and perhaps other counties are indicative of such lakes. Most of the lakes are small and more or less restricted to terminal moraines. The numerous outwash and lacustrine plains are often indicated by wide marshes (or marshes now drained) broken by low sand ridges or knolls. Massive, rugged moraines are numerous and many were named by Malott. Tamarack (*Larix laricina*) bogs occur across the north-

ern end of Indiana; most are small and many have been drained. The best developed remaining bogs are Cowles Bog and Pinhook Bog, both in the northwestern part of the state.

Tipton Till Plain. This region covers approximately the central one-third of the state. The land surface is a relatively flat, glacial plain, but marked by many terminal moraines, resulting in gently rolling topography in some portions. Some wide areas are monotonously flat. This till plain has not undergone excessive modification or dissection by streams, but the Wabash River traverses it and provides some relief (see Map 1). Some tributaries (especially Sugar Creek, Indian Creek, and Clifty Creek) of the Wabash River in west-central Indiana have cut through glacial drift to form narrow, rocky valleys with steep sandstone cliffs as much as 150 feet high. Examples may be seen at the Pine Hills Nature Preserve and in Shades and Turkey Run state parks. The highest elevations in the state are in Jay and Randolph counties, where huge terminal moraines have

TIPTON TILL PLAIN. A railroad right-of-way often provides good trapping areas of relatively natural habitat. Prairie voles, short-tailed shrews, and deer mice would be expected in this Benton County area. Photo by David W. Berrey

been formed. The best agricultural land in Indiana is found in the Tipton Till Plain and this region (once heavily forested) has lost almost all of its woodlands within the past one hundred years. Most remaining forested areas are present as small woodlots or riparian growth.

Wabash Lowland. This region, as described by Malott, contains about 4,900 square miles in the southwestern quarter of the state. The northern two-thirds of this lowland were glaciated. In general, the region is characterized by wide expanses of alluvial land, some of which is lacustrine in origin, along the Ohio, Wabash, and White rivers. The average elevation is about 500 feet above sea level. Upland areas are undulating to rolling plains, with some divides and isolated hills rising from 100 to 150 feet above the valley floors. The maximum local relief is at Merom (Sullivan County), where a massive sandstone bluff rises 170 feet above the Wabash River. Much of the Wabash Lowland

is (or was) inundated annually. Sand dunes are present, and deposits of windblown sand or silt (loess) cover much of the uplands. One sand area forms the terrace of the Wabash River from Vigo County southward to Posey County. In parts of Knox County, this terrace is more than a mile wide. Peculiarly isolated bedrock hills commonly occur as islandlike areas in the broad stream valleys. Such hills vary in size and shape from low conical knolls a few feet high to uplands 100 feet or more in height and covering from one to several square miles.

Crawford Upland. This region of approximately 2,900 square miles contains the maximum diversity of relief and topographic variability in the state. Local relief of 300 to 350 feet is common, and elevations range from 350 to 980 feet. The Crawford Upland is an exceedingly rugged highland embracing low and high hills, sharp and rounded ridges, trenchlike valleys, flat-bottomed valleys, rock benches, rolling peneplain remnants, sink-

WABASH LOWLAND. Flooding causes problems for species living in this area along the Wabash River at Terre Haute. Photo by Whitaker

CRAWFORD UPLAND. Rather rugged topography such as this area at McCormick's Creek State Park marks much of the Crawford Upland. Photo by Whitaker

holes, escarpments, canyonlike gorges, and caves. It is the least accessible area in Indiana. Nonresistant shales alternating with resistant sandstones and limestone in this largely unglaciated area, combined with a long period of weathering and erosion, have resulted in a scenic maze of landforms. Perry County, bordering the Ohio River, is the most rugged county in Indiana, but Crawford County has nearly the same terrain.

Mitchell Plain. This westward-sloping limestone plain of about 1,125 square miles exhibits some of the best karst topography in the world (Schneider, 1966). Sinkholes of various sizes are abundant and reach a density of 100 per square mile in some sections. Surface water drains into subterranean passages through open sinks. Many sinks have become plugged to form small ponds. Most of Indiana's caves are located in the Mitchell Plain, although caves are present throughout much of the unglaciated portion of the state (Map 5). The entire plain varies in elevation from about 600 to more than 900 feet, although much of it has low relief. The western part is marked by numerous outlying hills from the Crawford Upland, and in some places the

MITCHELL PLAIN. Donnehue's Cave is only one of many caves in the
Mitchell Plain area. This cave is heavily used by several species of bats.
Photo by Whitaker

deeply entrenched streams provide local relief of some magnitude.

Norman Upland. This region is an upland of some 2,075 square miles, containing great local relief due to uniform dissection by stream action over a long period. Long, sharp ridges and V-shaped valleys have resulted and form rugged, picturesque hills. Such features reach their maximum in Brown County, and result in one of the most famous scenic panoramas in Indiana. The elevation reaches its maximum of 1,050 feet on Weedpatch Hill, near Nashville. The Knobstone Escarpment, which bounds the Norman Upland and Scottsburg Lowland, is the most prominent regional topographic feature in Indiana. Throughout much of its 150-mile length (from southern Jackson County to Harrison County), it rises about 300 feet above the Scottsburg Lowland. The escarpment is most prominent north of the Ohio River near New Albany (Floyd County), where its crest is 400 to 600 feet above the lowland valleys to the east. In Harrison County, a descent of 610 feet occurs in a horizontal distance of barely

one-half mile. Escarpment crests in Clark, Floyd, Scott, and Washington counties reach elevations above 1,000 feet. Outliers of the escarpment appear as conical hills and are referred to as "the Knobs."

Scottsburg Lowland. This lowland is broad, shallow and with slight relief, and characterized by wide expanses of flat valley land along streams and a notable lack of bluffs or steep slopes. This region's 950 square miles all range in elevation below 700 feet, much below 600 feet. A deeply dissected upland area of 25 to 30 square miles in Jackson County is known as the "Brownstown Hills" and represents an upland mass isolated from the Norman Upland by stream erosion. The upper portions of these hills stood above the continental ice sheet during the Illinoian glacial stage and today rise 300 feet above the surrounding lowland.

Muscatatuck Regional Slope. This gently sloping plain encompasses an area of about 1,875 square miles. At its northern end, the plain slopes from 1,100 feet above sea level

NORMAN UPLAND. Brown County State Park provides an excellent view of original Norman Upland terrain. White-footed mice, short-tailed shrews, woodland voles, raccoons, fox squirrels, gray foxes and opossums are a few of the common mammals here. Photo by Whitaker

SCOTTSBURG LOWLAND. Wide flat valleys are characteristic of the Scottsburg Lowland. The Norman escarpment is in the background. Deer mice and prairie voles would be expected here, in corn stubble and grassy fields respectively. Photo by Whitaker

MUSCATATUCK REGIONAL SLOPE. Streams form canyons to the south in this area, smaller ravines to the north. Areas between streams are generally flat. Photo by Whitaker

DEARBORN UPLAND. Varied terrain in southeastern Indiana provides a variety of habitats and ground cover. Photo by Whitaker

CATTAIL MARSH. Extensive cattail marshes mark many areas of northern
Indiana, but are much less common to the south. The muskrat is the most
characteristic mammal of the Indiana marshes. Meadow voles, jumping mice,
short-tailed and masked shrews, and many other species occur about the
peripheries of cattail marshes. This marsh is at Willow Slough Fish and
Wildlife area in Newton County. Photo by Whitaker

at its eastern border to about 725 feet on the
west. Elevations near the Ohio River are
about 225 feet lower. Descent to the south
occurs at about 15 feet to the mile. Only the
northern portion of the region was glaciated
during the Wisconsin age, but the entire region was covered with ice earlier in the
Pleistocene. Stream valleys of the southern
half of the region are canyonlike in character,
but are never entrenched deeper than 175
feet below the gently inclined plain. Areas
between streams are typically quite flat. The
border along the Ohio River has steep bluffs
400 to 450 feet high. In Clark, Jefferson,
Jennings, and Ripley counties are level,
poorly drained areas with an acid soil; these
areas are known locally as "the Flats." Deam
(1940) made a distinction between "high
flats" and "low flats" on the basis of their
vegetative cover. Upland areas are generally
broad and nearly flat to undulating.

Dearborn Upland. This interesting unit,
which contains about 1,925 square miles in
the southeastern corner of the state, consists
of the drainage basin of the Whitewater River

and a number of smaller basins. Elevations
range from about 425 feet, at the Ohio River,
to maxima of 850 to 1,100 feet. The streams
are short, have a relatively great fall, and
have deeply trenched the upland plain from
200 to 500 feet below its general surface.
Local relief is often measured in hundreds of
feet; slopes are steep, as a rule, but bluffs are
rare. Long, evenly elevated upland tongues
of land lie between the deeply dissected valleys. In western Dearborn and eastern Ripley
counties, a rather extensive and markedly flat
upland occurs. It rises slightly above the
1,100-foot contour and has not been so severely dissected by streams.

Vegetation

The plants that grow on an area determine
in great part what animals will be found
there. There is a basic, natural relationship
between plants and mammals. In many cases
the absence of certain plants will result in the
absence of certain mammals. In the following
species accounts of Indiana mammals, we
have cited many specific examples of plant-

Map 5.
Locations of caves mentioned in the text

1 Porter's	17 Hamer's
2 Boone's	18 Upper Twin
3 Mayfield's	19 Endless
4 Grotto	20 River
5 Coon's	21 Beck's Mill
6 Saltpeter	22 Dillon
7 Eller's	23 Bentz
8 Buckner's	24 Wildcat
9 May's	25 Wyandotte
10 Leonard's Spring	26 Salt Petre
11 Clyfty	27 Bear
12 Ray's	28 Sheep
13 Sullivan's	29 King's
14 Donnehue's	30 Wilson's
15 Bronson's	31 Tunnel
16 Donaldson's	
(= Shawnee)	

mammal relationships with regard to food, shelter, escape sites, and nesting locations.

The voles are most likely to occur where green grass is available most of the year. Grasses constitute much of their food, and their nests are constructed of dried grasses.

The surface runways of voles are mostly hidden by grassy and weedy vegetation, which also serves to hide the voles from the eyes of potential predators. Muskrats eat a wide variety of emergent plants in their marshy habitat, and construct their houses of the same materials. Tree squirrels all feed heavily on nuts, acorns, seeds, and fruits of trees; they use leaves and twigs in making their nests, they hide these nests in tree cavities or place them in the open canopy, they use trees to escape from dogs and other terrestrial predators, they sun themselves on tree branches, and they store food in trees. These are a few examples of the dependence of mammals on vegetation.

Plants, in turn, may benefit from mammals, in the scattering of their seeds or the fertilization of their flowers. Some tropical and semitropical plants are partially pollinated by bats. Seeds, nuts, and acorns stored in the ground by various mammals may give rise to new plants. Some seeds may germinate better after they have passed through the digestive tract of a mammal. The tiny spores of the fungus *Endogone* are probably widely distributed by the small mammals that eat them.

Thus, to study the mammals of an area, one should learn something about plant distribution and the vegetational zones which form the major types of habitats. Throughout the glacial history of Indiana, vegetation varied from tundra to coniferous to deciduous over the portion of the state that was covered by various glaciers. With time, climatic changes triggered vegetation changes, which in turn dictated what mammals were present. Most of our knowledge of mammals present during these periods is from the fossil record and involves large species. Small species do not persist as easily in fossil form. Much of Indiana is covered with deep layers of glacial drift, so many fossils are deeply buried. The chance of a dead mammal being preserved well as a fossil depends upon several things. The animal, once dead, must come to rest in a site where it is free from depredation by scavengers and has an opportunity to be preserved. This may mean in a deposit of silt, which through the years is converted to limestone, sandstone, or other sedimentary rock. Dead mammals must be relatively undisturbed after deposition to lessen chances of breakage and scattering of the skeletal re-

mains by scavengers or water currents. Once
fossilized, the remains must again be unearthed for study. Fossil deposits are often
exposed by erosion or by man's excavating
activities.

The early vegetation of Indiana is not particularly well known. About 160 years ago, 87
percent of Indiana was covered by deciduous
forests, the remainder, in the northwestern
portion of the state, with tall grass prairie.
Lindsey *et al.* (1965) analyzed the presettlement vegetation of Indiana by using original
land survey records and modern soil surveys.
Their resulting map depicts the vegetation as
it existed about 1820, four years after Indiana
became a state. Gordon (1936) prepared a
vegetation map of Indiana based on recon-
naissance by automobile in 1928 (Map 6). His
map, though out of date, appears best suited
to present-day conditions for determining
mammal distributions. Deam (1940) included
a map of the floral areas of Indiana in his
monumental work on Indiana flora. More recently, Petty and Jackson (1966) have discussed the plant communities of the state.
Our discussion is based on data from these
authors.

Prairie. The three general types of prairie
once found in Indiana were wetland prairie,
upland dry prairie, and areas where grasslands and forest occurred together. Prairie in
Indiana was an extension of the "Grand
Prairie" of Illinois and possibly reached its
best development in Indiana in Benton
County. Small, isolated patches of prairie also
occurred along stream terraces and within the
forest proper. They varied in size from a few
acres to a few hundred acres. Elmore Barce
(1925) described the Benton County prairie
as "mile upon mile . . . covered in most
places with giant blue-stem" and wrote that
"A party of land hunters riding through Benton County in the fall of 1824 and following
the line of an old Indian trail, found bluestem so high that a horseman could tie the
ends over the top of his head." One notable
feature of the early grasslands was that about
half of the northern one-fourth of Indiana was
ponded in winter and spring; wetlands and
wet prairie were widespread there. The acreage that was originally dry prairie was relatively small.

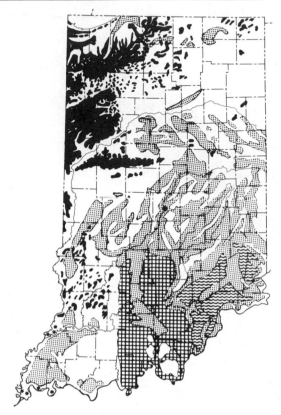

Map 6.   Vegetation types in Indiana
(after Gordon, 1936)

Black = Prairie grasslands
White = Upland oak forests
Stipple = Beech forests
Wavy lines = Beech / sweet gum forests
Crosshatch = Mixed mesophytic
Asterisks = Bald cypress

According to Gordon (1936), wet prairies
and sloughs were covered with water in early
spring and supported such plants as cordgrass, tuberous Indian-plantain, swamp
milkweed, blazing-star, and rattlesnake-
master. The natural "marsh hay" meadows of
reed bent-grass and other species were included as wet prairies. Much of the Kankakee
River valley and parts of Benton, Clinton,
Jasper, Newton, Tippecanoe, and Warren
counties were formerly covered with this
type of vegetation. Mesophytic prairies supported such plants as bluestem, Indian grass,
hard-leaved goldenrod, prairie dock, tall
sunflower, and tick-clover. Dominant plants
of dry prairies were little bluestem, dense

WET PRAIRIE. Hoosier Prairie in Lake County is an outstanding example of wet prairie. It harbors good populations of meadow voles, jumping mice, and short-tailed shrews. In spring, meadow voles here were feeding extensively on willow catkins. Photo by Whitaker

blazing-star, round-headed bush clover, flowering spurge, compass-plant, and tall coreopsis.*

Conditions of the vegetation in Jasper and Newton counties were mentioned by Hamilton and Darroch (1916), who wrote:

On the high lands the grass did not reach its normal height, while on the lower lands its growth was of astonishing proportions, frequently reaching a height which would hide a man on horseback, and thus would tend to create the illusion of a perfectly level plain. . . . Then the timber, save along the rivers, was marked only by scattered oaks and hickories, which favoring localities preserved from the annual fires which swept the prairies.

*An appendix giving the scientific names for the various plants and animals referred to in the text is provided at the end of the book.

Where prairie and oak forests merged, a mosaic of grassland and oak stands was present, forming what were often referred to as "oak openings." The oaks most frequently found in these situations were white oak, black oak, bur oak, and jack oak, in that order of abundance (Petty and Jackson, 1966). These island forest stands were generally situated on sandy knolls, especially on the higher parts of terminal moraines, and were frequently surrounded by wetland prairies. Forest invasion of the prairie progressed most rapidly along ravines where erosion had broken the prairie sod.

Bliss and Cox (1964) described five prairie community types in northern Indiana. These are big bluestem, little bluestem, prairie dropseed, poverty grass / bluegrass, and slough grass. (For information regarding the principal plant species occurring in these types, one should consult their paper.) Of the communities recognized, big bluestem and little bluestem were most important and extensive. Big bluestem communities dominated lower moist slopes and the better aerated portions of lowlands. Although forbs were noticeably more abundant in this prairie type than in any other, they rarely constituted more than 5 percent of the total ground cover. Indian grass often became an important component of the community after fires or floods, and heavy grazing encouraged bluegrass.

Little bluestem occurred in all community types except those excessively wet. It was dominant on well-drained upper slopes or ridges. The prairie dropseed community was usually restricted to mid and lower slopes. Poverty grass / bluegrass communities were restricted to eroded sites on steeper slopes on soils low in organic matter and moisture. This type, found throughout Indiana, is not considered to have been important in the original prairie vegetation, but has been enhanced by disturbance of both original prairie and previously wooded soils. Slough grass (or cordgrass) communities are typical of poorly drained soils and bottomlands.

The prairie has not always been distributed as settlers first observed it. It required several thousand years to become established. It invaded deglaciated regions, covering knolls and lowlands and areas previously vegetated with forests; and it followed fire. It has con-

DRY PRAIRIE. This dry prairie is on the Beaver Lake Prairie Chicken Refuge in Newton County. Prairie voles and deer mice were the dominant small mammals here. Photo by David W. Berrey

tinuously advanced and retreated, as it continues to do today.

Remnants of prairie vegetation can still be found in old cemeteries, on bluffs, along roads or railroads, and on lands reclaimed for fish and wildlife areas. Lindsey (1966) knew of no place in Indiana where prairie currently existed as a landscape type except near Schererville (Lake County). Part of this tract has now been set aside as the Hoosier Prairie Nature Preserve. The Grand Marsh of the Kankakee River valley once covered 1,000 square miles in Indiana, but drainage, initiated as early as 1873, had effectively drained the region by 1917. And ditching and tiling is still taking place.

Deciduous Forests. Lindsey *et al.* (1965) prepared a map depicting the presettlement vegetation of Indiana and showing the boundaries of the major forest community types then present. These types included western mesophytic, constituting about 8 percent of the original vegetation; beech / maple, which made up 50 percent; and oak / hickory, making up 29 percent. Gordon

(1936) divided the forests of Indiana into upland oak (four subdivisions); northern swamp (three subdivisions); beech (three divisions); mixed mesophytic; beech / sweet gum; southern swamp; bald cypress; and relic (relict) associations. We have drawn on data from these authors, but in the following discussion of forest lands we have relied most heavily on the paper by Petty and Jackson (1966). They, in turn, used the vegetation map of Lindsey *et al.*

Western Mesophytic

This mixed forest type occupies mainly the limestone-derived soils on the Mitchell Plain and the steeper slopes of the Ohio River and Laughery Creek drainages of the Dearborn Upland. Small outliers also occur in the southwestern quarter of the state. "Although this mixed forest is not extensive in Indiana, it is one of the most interesting plant communities of the state because of the great number of species sharing dominance. Frequently 10 to 20 species share in the crown cover and exert their controlling influence on the forest community" (Petty and Jackson, 1966).

SAND PRAIRIE. Little Bluestem Prairie just north of Terre Haute in Vigo County is one of the very few remaining sand prairies in southern Indiana. This particular one was studied by W. S. Blatchley in the 1890s. Principal small mammals here are prairie voles, deer mice, cottontail rabbits, and, in the patches of black oak, fox squirrels. Photo by Whitaker

In dissected areas in southeastern Indiana (Jefferson County), yellow buckeye and white basswood are important components. These species are considered to be most typical of the true mixed mesophytic forests of the Cumberland Mountains, showing the affinity of this type in Indiana to the parent type to the south. The principal tree species in sample plots (Dearborn, Jefferson, and Lawrence counties), based on relative density, were beech, sugar maple, white oak, red oak, white ash, white basswood, tulip poplar, pignut hickory, yellow buckeye, red maple, black gum, and shagbark hickory, in descending order. Beech is the dominant species in most mixed forests in southeastern Indiana, where sugar maple, tulip poplar, white ash,

basswood, black walnut, white oak, red oak, red elm, and black gum also occur.

In the unglaciated hills of south-central Indiana, mixed forests usually are found in ravines and on the cooler slopes; oak or oak / hickory forests occupy the drier slopes and ridges. Mixed forests in this region generally have a greater abundance of beech and maple (instead of buckeye and basswood) than do the southeastern mixed forests. Probably the best remaining virgin stand of mixed forest in south-central Indiana is Donaldson's Woods in Spring Mill State Park (Lawrence County). This forest is dominated by white oak, sugar maple, and beech. Since this woods is changing toward an increase of beech and maple, it probably is not a climax forest.

VIRGIN TIMBER. Donaldson's Woods at Spring Mill State Park is an example of southern Indiana virgin timber. Few mammals were taken in the extensive rather bare areas, but white-footed mice, woodland voles, and short-tailed shrews were taken in patches of vegetation in the moist spots. Also a southeastern shrew was caught by hand here. Photo by Whitaker

Originally, American chestnut was present in mixed forests of southern Indiana, but the Asian chestnut blight totally destroyed this species as a mature tree. Chestnut oak and tulip poplar appear to have invaded to replace the chestnut.

The understory tree layer in mixed forests often contains flowering dogwood, redbud, and blue beech, and shrubs such as pawpaw, spicebush, greenbrier, and leatherwood are common. The pronounced herb layer includes wake-robin (trillium), slender toothwort, rock larkspur, twinleaf, and other species.

The rugged topography of the area has discouraged extensive clearing of this forest land for agriculture. This forest association covers a significant portion of the Hoosier National Forest.

Beech / Maple

Forests of this type usually have beech as the most abundant canopy tree, but sugar maple is co-dominant in the canopy and frequently most abundant in the understory. Beech / maple communities are most common within the area once covered by the Wisconsin glacier, but are also present in the Illinoian age till in both southeastern and southwestern Indiana. The prairie border marks the northwestern extension of this type in the state.

Since beech has never been a valuable tree for timber, it has been favored by the removal of more "desirable" species such as black walnut, tulip poplar, white oak, and ash through selective logging practices. Most remaining woodlots now are dominated by beech, especially among the larger trees. Usually the dominant beech and maple are distributed widely and evenly throughout the stand, while trees such as sassafras, black cherry, tulip poplar, and black walnut are most often encountered in groups.

In six beech / maple stands analyzed for species composition in Franklin, Kosciusko, Montgomery, Orange, Owen, and Wayne counties, the principal species (based on relative basal area)* were beech, sugar maple, tulip poplar, American elm, white ash, cork elm, red elm, black gum, black walnut, black

*Basal area is the cross-sectional area, in square feet, of all plant stems four inches and more diameter at breast height (4.5 feet above the ground).

BEECH/MAPLE FOREST. Beech/maple is often the climax forest in cooler portions of northern Indiana, especially in ravines. Photo by Whitaker

cherry, red oak, basswood, white oak, mockernut hickory, and bur oak, in descending order (Petty and Jackson, 1966). Thus, beech and maple commonly constitute 50 percent or more of the Indiana stands of this association. In the lowland beech / maple communities, elm often makes up 25 percent of the crown cover. Since Dutch elm disease has virtually eliminated American elm as a canopy tree in many remnant stands, it will be interesting to determine which species will take its place.

The small-tree understory of beech / maple communities is usually either redbud / dogwood / blue beech or dogwood / hop hornbeam. The shrub layer usually contains one or a combination of the following: pawpaw, greenbrier, spicebush, elderberry, leatherwood, wahoo, mapleleaf viburnum. In undisturbed beech / maple forests, the display of spring flowers includes rue anemone, jack-in-the-pulpit, spring beauty, cutleaf toothwort, pretty bedstraw, mayapple, false Solomon's seal, and wild ginger.

Most of the beech / maple association that once covered a large portion of Indiana is farmland today, for the soils that supported such stands were among the better agricultural soils. Also, when drainage lowered the water table, many lowland communities were cleared and put under cultivation. The following statement of Petty and Jackson (1966) is certainly true: "As one drives across the gently rolling Tipton Till Plain of central Indiana, only a few scattered, well cut-over beech-maple forests break the horizon of the best crop lands."

Oak / Hickory

This type occurs throughout much of Indiana (except the large central section) in a mosaic pattern with prairie, western mesophytic, and beech / maple communities. The distributions of oak / hickory and beech / maple forests are closely correlated with physiography. In areas of pronounced slopes, beech / maple communities are best developed on north-facing and east-facing slopes, oak / hickory on south-facing and west-facing slopes. Soil moisture is generally lower in the oak / hickory type. White oak was much more important in the original Indiana forests, but has been selectively logged because of its value as a timber tree. Beech and maple are frequently important species in oak / hickory associations, because the former are invading in natural successional stages.

The most important trees (based on relative basal area) of four oak / hickory associations studied in Clinton, Dubois, Owen, and Parke counties were white oak, red oak, black oak, sugar maple, pignut hickory, shagbark hickory, swamp white oak, American elm, beech, white ash, chinquapin oak, mockernut hickory, red elm, black gum, and bur oak (listed in descending order). In the lowland phases of the oak / hickory association, bur oak, pin oak, swamp white oak, Shumard's oak, shellbark hickory, and bitternut hickory increase in importance. In the lower Wabash River valley, pecan, swamp chestnut oak, and overcup oak are important locally. And on dry ridges of the unglaciated region, chestnut oak, scarlet oak, post oak, and mockernut hickory are more frequent.

Oak / hickory forests frequently have a less well-developed understory stratum than that found in other Indiana forest types. One or two species such as hop hornbeam, blue beech, serviceberry, or dogwood may dominate the understory along with young maples. In the forests on dry sandy ridges of northern Indiana, common shrubs are blueberry, huckleberry, snowberry, nannyberry, New Jersey-tea, ninebark, witch-hazel, wild gooseberry, and Virginia creeper. While the most prominent herbaceous plants in the beech / maple forests are evident in spring, herbaceous flowers of the oak / hickory associations are more noticeable in late summer and in autumn. Oak / hickory forests contain from 45 to 50 percent more herbaceous species than do beech / maple; the following are most prominent: pussy-toes, common cinquefoil, wild licorice, tick-clover, blue phlox, waterleaf, bloodroot, Joe-Pye weed, woodland asters, goldenrods, wild geranium, and bellwort.

OAK/HICKORY FOREST. This is the dominant forest climax in much of Indiana. This area is in Clay County, near Brazil, and harbors many white-footed mice, short-tailed shrews, woodland voles, fox squirrels, opossums, and raccoons. Photo by Whitaker

Hollow tree in oak/hickory forest in Clay County woodland gives refuge to fox squirrels, opossums, and raccoons. Photo by Whitaker

The oak / hickory association grades into the prairie in northwestern Indiana, where forests are generally limited to slopes, ravines, or morainic ridges. Over most of the area where oak / hickory and prairie were mixed, heavily grazed oak / hickory woods are most likely to be found on the rougher topography, which is not cultivated.

Climate

Climate has been described by Newman (1966) as "the aggregate of all weather changes over a period of time for a given place." We have extracted much of the following from his discussion of the bioclimate of Indiana. Indiana has a humid, continental climate. There are no definite dry seasons or periods with an average humidity of less than 50 percent—as any Hoosier knows, it is humid throughout the year. The continental

influence is expressed in the seasonal changes from extreme cold in winter to extreme hot in summer. The climate of Indiana is transitional from north to south. The southern half has a warm temperate climate, more like that to the south and east. Northern Indiana has a cool temperate climate, similar to that found to the north and east.

The "normal" frost-free growing season varies from 150 days in northeastern Indiana to more than 200 days in parts of the extreme southwestern section of the state (Posey County). Newman wrote:

Perhaps the most dramatic transition in the state is found in the areas bordering Lake Michigan. Here the normal frost-free growing season varies from approximately 190 days near the shoreline to less than 160 days in the Kankakee River basin 15 to 20 miles to the south. The dramatic change in the local climate for the lakeshore area of northwestern Indiana is further evident in summer temperatures, cloudiness and winter snowfall.

Landforms in Indiana that influence local climatic conditions include the major stream valleys, the shores of larger lakes, and the highest plateau areas. In addition, cities and large artificial bodies of water exert their influence. On a smaller scale, climatic conditions may be modified by slope, woodlands, large buildings, large areas of concrete, and other major wind obstructions. Although these "local climates" may influence relatively small areas, they can be of importance to certain small mammals (shrews, bats). The major control for local climate is slope, for the amount of solar energy received at the earth's surface depends upon the angle of incidence of sunlight. Certain plant associations grow best on slopes facing specific directions, and deep slopes may support different vegetation than nearby level terrain.

Temperature. Visher (1944) presented a detailed study of the climate of Indiana and his book should be consulted for additional information. Some data from his study are included in our discussion below. The average annual temperature of Indiana is about 52° Fahrenheit; July, the hottest month averages slightly more than 75° and January, the coldest month, about 30°. Nocturnal summer temperatures normally average 60° to 64° for June, July, and August. Even in the coolest part of the state, July nocturnal temperature does not normally fall below 60°. Based on day and night temperatures averaged together, Indiana has about 100 days with temperatures 68°F or higher, about 100 days with 50° to 68°, and about 100 days with temperatures from 32° to 50°. The remaining 65 days are below freezing. In July 1936, the temperature reached 116°F at Rensselaer (Jasper County), and on 2 January 1887 the temperature at Lafayette (Tippecanoe County) was −33°F.

Precipitation. Annual precipitation averages about 45 inches for southern Indiana, 40 inches for central Indiana, and 35 inches for northern Indiana. Precipitation is distributed rather evenly throughout the year and the wettest months are in late spring. Prevailing winds across the state are from the southwest, and nearly all rainfall is associated with cyclonic disturbances. Most moisture is drawn from the Gulf of Mexico, with little coming from the west, north, or east. Northern Indiana receives an average of 30 inches to more than 50 inches of snowfall annually; most of central Indiana gets about 20 inches, and part of southwestern Indiana receives less than 15 inches. The area of heaviest snowfall is just east of the southern tip of Lake Michigan, where more than 50 inches is normal. Occasionally more than 100 inches is recorded in that region, and in the winter of 1977-78 nearly 200 inches was recorded at South Bend (St. Joseph County).

Habitats

Simply stated, the habitat of an animal is the place where that animal lives. But to be more specific, it may be best to say it is the environment in which the animal lives. Habitats may be small or large—a small pond, or an ocean. Examples of mammal habitats in Indiana are woodlands, fields, marshes, fencerows, and caves. Major habitats may be subdivided; for example, woodlands may be deciduous, coniferous, or mixed. And fields may be cultivated or uncultivated, while those under cultivation can be classed as cornfields, hayfields, wheat fields, soybean stubble, and so on. A particular type of field may contain various smaller units of habitat. A fallow field may be inhab-

ited by masked shrews, but since the shrews are likely to be present only where there is sufficient moisture for them, the actual area occupied by the shrews may be quite small. Such areas are sometimes called microhabitats. Thus, a particular animal is not usually distributed evenly over its geographic range, but occurs only in those sites where living conditions are favorable. There may be a single site within a township, or a county, that is suitable to some species. The next suitable site may be in an adjoining township or county, or several counties away. Even though the particular mammal may be found "throughout" Indiana, it may in fact occur in relatively few localities and be absent from most of the area of the state. Published range maps are misleading in this respect, and a better method of showing mammal distributions may be to plot only precise locations where the species is known to live. Unfortunately, we seldom have such detailed information concerning even our common species, so we tend to map the range of a species by showing an area formed by connecting the outside points of its known distribution.

Habitats are constantly changing. Even noncultivated habitats pass through various stages of plant succession and are altered by floods, winds, fires, disturbance by man or other animals, and other agencies. Day to day and year by year the changes may not be evident to inexperienced persons. On the other hand, cultivated fields undergo drastic changes overnight. A corn stubble may be plowed in one day's time, making the area immediately unsuitable for some mammals. There are also changes in habitats from one season to another. Snow and cold of winter give way to warmer days, green, succulent vegetation, and the abundant insects of spring; the hot, sometimes dry summer passes into a cool, wet fall that in turn completes the cycle back to winter. Insect food and various seeds are abundant in summer and early fall but are very difficult to find in winter. Green vegetation, so abundant in spring, summer, and early fall, mostly dries and withers by winter. And the shelter from the sun and wind offered by plant growth in summer may largely be absent in winter. Thus, the numbers of a particular species of mammal in a given habitat may fluctuate greatly through the various seasons. There is much movement by larger species, hibernation by some species, and even migration by others (bats).

Now that state and federal agencies are involved in determining which species are endangered and how we may be able to save them from extinction, our knowledge of habitat must be more detailed. We must ascertain which habitats are necessary for the survival of various mammal species. The critical habitat for a species may differ from summer to winter, or even from season to season. We need to protect critical habitats whenever they occur. For example, summer habitats may be plentiful for a species, but if it lacks sufficient winter habitats it will not survive. All too often we have discovered that our knowledge of critical habitats is woefully inadequate.

Indiana contains relatively few large-scale, major habitats for mammals. Originally, about nine-tenths of the state was covered with deciduous forests and the remainder was primarily prairie grasslands. Throughout the past century, the prairie has all but disappeared and most of the forests have been logged off. The result has been a trend toward uniformity of habitat characterized by more and more cultivated land (17,100,000 acres are in farmland) and the division and subdivision of large land holdings into smaller tracts. In 1977, there were 12,832,000 acres of cultivated land planted in major crops—corn, soybeans, wheat, oats, rye, barley, hay, sorghum. This figure does not include orchards, vegetable gardens, or pastures (data provided by Earl L. Park). Since there are about 23,000,000 acres of land in the state, one can easily see how important cultivated fields have become for wildlife.

We have spent considerable effort sampling small mammal populations in various Indiana habitats. In the beginning, we were curious to know just what was there. But it is now apparent that such information may hold the key to the preservation of some of our threatened or endangered mammals. Habitat information is being sought by various agencies who must comply with the Endangered Species Act by conducting impact studies on proposed sites where bridges, roads, airports, reservoirs, or other projects are to be constructed. We probably shall not be able to

stop the loss of some species, but with the accumulation of more knowledge of habitats, and with the intelligent use of such data, we might be able to slow the process for some species and to save others.

We feel that our habitat data will be most useful to workers concerned with these problems. We have attempted to sample most habitat types, but a few relict areas have not been trapped intensively. For example, we have few data for bogs, a habitat that has nearly been eliminated in the state. Our habitat data represent the species composition of small mammals only—those species most likely to be captured in ordinary snapback mousetraps. We made no attempts to census larger mammals.

Although Indiana is mostly a rather flat agricultural state, it has its share of interesting and diverse habitats. Besides the cultivated fields of corn, wheat, soybeans, sorghum, the plowed fields between plantings, and the grassy or clover fields planted for livestock feed, Indiana also has considerable fallow land, ranging from large dry fields of broom grass on the poor-soil areas of southern Indiana to the grassy, weedy, and brushy fields of the north. Indiana also has much woodland, varying from the cypress swamps of the southwestern part to the widespread hickory and oak forests throughout the state and the beech / maple forests of many areas, particularly in the northern portions. Along Lake Michigan are series of dunes varying in vegetation from early seral stages of dunes grass or cottonwood, through pine or basswood to black oak, and finally to beech / maple climax forests on those dunes farthest from Lake Michigan.

Indiana also has marshes, swamps, and a few bogs. Marshes contain primarily herbaceous plants; swamps have woody vegetation. True bogs are lakes or ponds that have been overgrown by floating mats of vegetation on which one often can walk. Unfortunately, many former wetlands have been drained for cultivation, but there are still swamplands throughout the state. Marshland is not as common, but numerous areas still have at least remnants of cattail marshes. True bogs contain a very specialized community of plants, characterized by such species as pitcher plants, sundew, chain fern, cottongrass, and cranberries. Tamaracks also often grow in bogs, along with poison sumac (especially around the edges). The few remaining bogs are in the northern part of our state.

Just north of the Ohio River along the southern edge of the state are high bluffs, giving still more diversity to the habitat types in Indiana. Also, there are many scattered pine plantations, which contribute to habitat diversity. Both the Ohio and Wabash rivers have cut great swaths through or along Indiana, providing relief and a floodplain habitat. Also present is a large number of lake, pothole, and muckland areas in the northeastern part of the state.

Thus, although Indiana cannot boast the wide range of habitats found in some other states, it does have variety and habitat diversity, which quite naturally lead to diversity of mammal species present. Intermixing of habitat types in contiguous areas creates conditions favorable to many types of wildlife. In homogeneous habitats, there may be abundant food and cover for animals at one time but these items may be almost totally lacking at another time; thus many species will not prosper there. When habitat diversity exists, it is much more likely that the needs of a species can be met throughout the year, a fact which is worth the consideration of the farmer or rural resident as well as the professional wildlife manager wishing to contribute to the well-being of our various wildlife species.

Cultivated Habitats

There is relatively little published information from Indiana or elsewhere on the mammals living in cultivated fields. We have accumulated many data of this sort in Indiana, especially in Vigo County (Table 2), and some of the cultivated habitats are discussed below.

Corn, sorghum, and soybeans. Normally only one or two species of mammals occurred in number in these major cultivated fields in west-central Indiana. If ground cover was scant or nearly lacking, the deer mouse (*Peromyscus maniculatus*) was the only species regularly found, but with increased amounts of ground cover, the house mouse (*Mus musculus*) occurred in larger numbers. In areas of good cover, the deer mouse was

less numerous and the house mouse was abundant.

Winter wheat, clover, rye, and other grain or grassy fields. The major small mammals in cultivated grassy type fields or hay meadows were generally the prairie vole (*Microtus ochrogaster*) and the house mouse, or, in fairly wet situations, the meadow vole (*Microtus pennsylvanicus*). All were more abundant in areas with increased amounts of herbaceous ground cover. In areas with little ground cover, the deer mouse dominated.

Plowed fields. We were very surprised to learn that even perfectly bare plowed fields contained small mammals. The 48 study plots trapped in plowed fields of Vigo County contained essentially no ground cover. Only one species of small mammal (the deer mouse) was present, but it occurred in numbers (2.39 per 100 trap-nights; one mousetrap set for one night is one trap-night). This species apparently used the soil as its cover, while all other species moved out when fields were plowed. On winter mornings when light snow was present, the tracks of deer mice leading between burrows were abundant in plowed fields.

Soybean fields. The house mouse and the deer mouse were the two major species present in soybean fields. Only four white-footed mice (*Peromyscus leucopus*) were taken in the 16 sample plots. It is interesting that in soybeans deer mice were taken in the greatest numbers, while in cornfields the house mouse was most frequently taken.

Cornfields. The house mouse was by far the most abundant species of small mammal taken in Vigo County cornfields; 139 were taken in the 38 sample plots. Deer mice and white-footed mice were next in abundance, but most of the white-footed mice taken in cornfields were near hedgerows or dumps, from which they probably moved into the corn.

Soybean stubble. After soybean fields were harvested, only soybean stubble remained. Like plowed fields, this habitat contained very small amounts of herbaceous cover, and thus contained the single species of small

Table 2

Small mammals trapped in cultivated fields, Vigo County

Random plots in . . .	plowed fields	soybean fields	corn-fields	soybean stubble	corn stubble	wheat fields	wheat stubble	other*
Number of plots	48	16	38	22	50	9	37	22
Number of trap-nights	3,600	1,200	2,850	1,650	3,750	675	2,775	1,650
Number of mammals taken (and number per 100 trap-nights)								
Deer mouse	86 (2.39)	34 (2.83)	35 (1.23)	39 (2.36)	44 (1.17)	40 (5.93)	73 (2.63)	71 (4.30)
White-footed mouse	5 (0.14)	4 (0.33)	31 (1.09)		2 (0.05)	8 (1.19)	7 (0.25)	6 (0.36)
House mouse	1 (0.03)	25 (2.08)	139 (4.88)		78 (2.08)	42 (6.22)	82 (2.95)	33 (2.00)
Prairie vole			3 (0.11)		2 (0.05)	2 (0.30)	6 (0.22)	10 (0.61)
Masked shrew			1 (0.04)					
Least shrew			1 (0.04)					2 (0.12)
Short-tailed shrew			1 (0.04)					
Meadow vole					2 (0.05)		2 (0.07)	
Totals:								
Mammals trapped (and number per 100 trap-nights)	92 (2.56)	63 (5.25)	211 (7.40)	39 (2.36)	128 (3.41)	92 (13.63)	170 (6.13)	122 (7.39)

*Consists of other types of mixed cropfields, sorghum, oats, garden crops, etc.

Indiana mammal that tolerates removal of ground cover—the deer mouse.

Corn stubble. Corn stubble, unlike soybean stubble often had greater amounts of cover, and here the house mouse was, as in cornfields, the most abundant species, although it was not as abundant as in corn. Also, as in corn, the deer mouse was the second most abundant species but it did not decrease at harvesting time.

Thus, there were two major species in corn and soybean fields, *Mus musculus* and *Peromyscus maniculatus.* The house mouse occurred in better cover, while the deer mouse occurred when cover was lacking and did not change much in abundance throughout the full cycle of crop cultivation, harvested field, plowed field, back to crop.

Noncultivated Habitats

It is well known that a plowed field, if allowed to remain idle and undisturbed, will go through a regular progression of vegetation changes from early stage, or weedy field, through grassy field, to brushy field, to woods. These "stages" are really parts of a continuum. The progression is referred to as *succession,* and is one of the important ecological processes. Various successional stages were obvious during our Indiana mammal study, and the mammals taken during random trapping of noncultivated study plots in Vigo County are indicated in Table 3.

Grassy field. The vegetation of early stage grassy fields often consisted of the grasses foxtail and / or wild rye, while later stage grasses were bluegrass, orchard grass, purpletop, fescue, and others. The most abundant mammal taken in grassy fields during

WINTER WHEAT FIELDS AND STUBBLE. Winter wheat fields harbor only deer mice during the fall and winter when the green sprouts are only about 1 to 5 inches high and form little cover. The deer mice are joined by house mice, which form large populations as the wheat grows rapidly in spring until harvesting, usually in June. If much stubble remains, such as in this field in Vigo County, house mice will remain. Otherwise, they will move out to some other area where ground cover is adequate. Photo by Whitaker

PLOWED FIELD. Only the deer mouse regularly inhabits plowed fields such as this one at Willow Slough Fish and Wildlife Area in Newton County. It feeds on seeds found in the soil and blown into the furrows. Photo by David W. Berrey

SOYBEAN FIELD. Soybeans are now grown extensively in Indiana. House mice and deer mice are the only regular small mammal inhabitants of such areas. This field is in Vigo County. Photo by Whitaker

CORNFIELD. Two species of small mammals inhabit fields with row crops: deer mice and, when ground cover is adequate, house mice. Photo by Whitaker

the random trapping was the house mouse. It was particularly abundant in the early stage fields of foxtail, which often invaded when fields were left idle for any length of time. The house mouse is very successful in the midwest because it is highly nomadic, utilizing rapidly appearing and disappearing habitats associated with the harvest and plowing of cultivated areas. Besides moving between cultivated fields, it will move into areas of good grassy cover when crops are harvested, and it will winter there. This species reproduces rapidly, and thus supplies new individuals which quickly repopulate new cultivated fields as cover becomes adequate.

The second most abundant small mammal was the white-footed mouse. Though primarily a woodland form, it often enters areas with relatively large amounts of ground cover. Many white-footed mice trapped were immatures, however, and were possibly simply moving through the sample plots to establish themselves in other areas. Some were probably foraging there from nearby woodlands and brush areas where they made their homes. Deer mice were also found in grassy fields, but most often in areas of sparse cover, such as in field openings, especially on sandy areas. In addition, prairie voles and meadow voles were important members of the small mammal community in mature, dense, relatively homogeneous grassy fields; meadow voles occur most abundantly in the more moist and pure grassy areas, whereas prairie voles occur most often in the drier, more well-drained, sparser vegetation where the flora is more diverse.

Information in Table 3 is from random trapping plots in Vigo County, but to illus-

Table 3

Small mammals trapped in various noncultivated habitats, Vigo County

Random plots in . . .	grassy field	weedy field	brushy field	brush	upland woods	bottomland woods	pasture
Number of plots	33	29	23	16	54	15	17
Number of trap-nights	2,475	2,175	1,725	1,200	4,050	1,125	1,275
Number of mammals taken (and number per 100 trap-nights)							
House mouse	74 (2.99)	63 (2.90)	2 (0.12)			2 (0.18)	
White-footed mouse	30 (1.21)	37 (1.70)	48 (2.78)	17 (1.42)	65 (1.60)	54 (4.80)	2 (0.16)
Deer mouse	26 (1.05)	38 (1.75)	7 (0.41)	1 (0.08)			1 (0.08)
Prairie vole	25 (1.01)	20 (0.92)	2 (0.12)				1 (0.08)
Meadow vole	16 (0.65)	4 (0.18)	1 (0.06)			1 (0.09)	
Woodland vole	3 (0.12)				8 (0.20)	1 (0.09)	
Least shrew	3 (0.12)						1 (0.08)
Masked shrew			1 (0.06)			2 (0.18)	
Short-tailed shrew	2 (0.08)		4 (0.23)		17 (0.42)	2 (0.18)	
Meadow jumping mouse		1 (0.05)	2 (0.12)			1 (0.09)	
Totals: Mammals trapped (and number per 100 trap-nights)	179 (7.23)	163 (7.49)	67 (3.88)	18 (1.50)	90 (2.22)	63 (5.60)	5 (0.39)

trate the diversity of small mammals that may sometimes be found in grassy fields, we have also summarized data from 17,862 additional trap-nights in grassy fields in Vigo, Newton, and Dearborn counties (see Table 4). The numbers of mammals taken varied, of course, depending on the part of the state trapped; much of the trapping represented in these data occurred in northern Indiana (Newton County), in most habitats of the kind in which meadow voles, short-tailed shrews (*Blarina brevicauda*), and masked shrews (*Sorex cinereus*) thrive.

Results of further trapping by Steven Ford in five categories of grassy, grassy / weedy, and weedy field habitats of northwestern Indiana are shown in Table 5. The short-tailed shrew was the most abundant species in these habitats, followed by the deer mouse,

the meadow vole, the meadow jumping mouse (*Zapus hudsonius*), the prairie vole, and the house mouse. If more trapping in southern Indiana had been included, the more abundant of these species would undoubtedly have occurred in lower numbers and the prairie vole in higher numbers. And if earlier stages rather than mature stages were included, the house mouse would have been more abundant.

Weedy field. The house mouse was the most abundant small mammal in weedy fields of Vigo County (see Table 3), followed by the deer mouse, the white-footed mouse, and the prairie vole. This is another of the habitats to which the house mouse moves, especially when crops are harvested. The prairie vole is much more successful in dry mixed and

GRASSY FIELD. Road right-of-ways, like railroads, often provide good habitat for small mammals. This roadside habitat and ditch at Willow Slough Fish and Wildlife Area in Newton County harbored prairie voles, deer mice, house mice, long-tailed shrews, and western harvest mice. Photo by David W. Berrey

Table 4

Small mammals trapped in grassy fields in Vigo, Newton, and Dearborn Counties (17,862 trap-nights)

Species	Number trapped	Number per 100 trap-nights
Meadow vole	124	0.69
White-footed mouse	105	0.59
Deer mouse	64	0.36
Prairie vole	58	0.32
Masked shrew	28	0.16
Short-tailed shrew	27	0.15
House mouse	18	0.10
Western harvest mouse	16	0.09
Meadow jumping mouse	10	0.06
Southern bog lemming	8	0.04
Southeastern shrew	6	0.03
Least shrew	2	0.01
	466	2.61

Table 5

Mammals trapped in northwestern Indiana during the summers of 1973 and 1974 (from Ford, 1975)

Species	Number trapped	Percentage of total
Short-tailed shrew	910	25.1
Deer mouse	824	22.7
Meadow vole	537	14.8
Meadow jumping mouse	305	8.4
Prairie vole	275	7.6
House mouse	225	6.2
White-footed mouse	195	5.4
Masked shrew	178	4.9
Western harvest mouse	129	3.6
Thirteen-lined ground squirrel	31	0.9
Norway rat	6	0.2
Eastern chipmunk	6	0.2
Franklin's ground squirrel	2	0.1
Southern bog lemming	2	0.1
	3,625	100.2

WEEDY FIELD. This weedy field at Willow Slough contains the cactus
Opuntia, sensitive fern, bracken fern, and prairie clover, among many other
plant species. It yielded the first Indiana individual ever taken of the
western harvest mouse. Photo by David W. Berrey

weedy fields than is the meadow vole, which usually reaches its greatest abundance in moist, dense, more uniformly grassy fields.

An additional 20,163 trap-nights in mature "weedy fields" in Newton, Posey, and Vigo counties provided slightly different results (Table 6). Here, the white-footed mouse was most numerous, followed by the deer mouse. The house mouse was not taken at all, supporting the conclusion that it is found in early plant successional stages. The prairie vole was much more abundant than the meadow vole, since the former is most frequently associated with a diverse, rather than a more uniformly grassy, flora. The western harvest mouse *(Reithrodontomys megalotis)* occurs only in northern Indiana.

Brushy field. This stage, in which enough time has elapsed for woody vegetation to become established, follows a grassy or weedy field. In this habitat, as shown by the Vigo County randomized trapping, the white-footed mouse was by far the most abundant. Next was the deer mouse, represented by

Table 6

Small mammals trapped in mature weedy fields in Newton, Posey, and Vigo counties (20,163 trap-nights)

Species	Number trapped	Number per 100 trap-nights
White-footed mouse	75	0.37
Deer mouse	60	0.30
Prairie vole	42	0.21
Western harvest mouse	41	0.20
Short-tailed shrew	39	0.19
Meadow jumping mouse	37	0.18
Meadow vole	21	0.10
Masked shrew	11	0.05
Southern bog lemming	2	0.01
	328	1.63

only seven individuals. The decrease in the number of house mice in later seral stages is evident, for only two were taken.

Relatively little trapping was done in other "brushy field" habitats around the state. Extensive trapping was conducted only in Vigo and Newton counties (7,964 trap-nights), and

BRUSH. This brushy roadside at Willow Slough Fish and Wildlife Area
harbors white-footed mice, short-tailed shrews, and meadow jumping mice.
Photo by David W. Berrey

this trapping was generally in areas with
much less woody vegetation than was present
in the randomly selected plots (Vigo County).
The results are presented in Table 7.

The influence of the dense grassy vegetation of moist areas of northern Indiana is
shown strongly in these data, with the
meadow vole the most abundant species, followed by the meadow jumping mouse. The
relatively small amount of woody vegetation
present probably has led to the smaller
number of white-footed mice than one might
otherwise expect.

Brush. Brush is the next later major successional stage. It was represented by only 16
plots in the Vigo County randomized trapping, and the white-footed mouse was the
only species regularly taken there.

Woods. During the randomized trapping,
woods habitat was divided into upland woods
and bottomland woods (see Table 3). The
white-footed mouse was the dominant small
mammal in both. In bottomland woods it was
the only important species, while in upland

Table 7

Small mammals trapped in brushy field
habitats in Vigo and Newton counties
(7,964 trap-nights)

Species	Number trapped	Number per 100 trap-nights
Meadow vole	29	0.36
Meadow jumping mouse	27	0.34
White-footed mouse	17	0.21
Short-tailed shrew	9	0.11
Masked shrew	8	0.10
House mouse	4	0.05
Prairie vole	2	0.03
Deer mouse	2	0.03
	98	1.23

woods it was followed in abundance by the
short-tailed shrew and the woodland vole
(*Microtus pinetorum*). These latter two species are burrowers in the forest floor and
probably were absent from the bottomland
woods because of the periodic flooding there.

Table 8 indicates the small mammals taken
in 27,688 additional trap-nights in wooded

NORTHERN INDIANA WOODLAND. Red squirrels, fox squirrels, southern flying squirrels, and eastern chipmunks were all common in this woodlot at Willow Slough Fish and Wildlife Area in Newton County. Photo by David W. Berrey

areas, mostly at Turkey Run State Park, but also including some trapping in Ripley and Posey counties.

Both sets of data (Tables 3 and 8) indicate that the white-footed mouse was the dominant small mammal in Indiana woodlands, followed by the short-tailed shrew and the

Table 8
Small mammals trapped in wooded areas in Parke, Ripley, and Posey counties
(27,688 trap-nights)

Species	Number trapped	Number per 100 trap-nights
White-footed mouse	309	1.12
Short-tailed shrew	104	0.38
Meadow jumping mouse	51	0.18
Woodland vole	10	0.04
House mouse	6	0.02
Masked shrew	4	0.01
Eastern chipmunk	3	0.01
Prairie vole	2	0.01
Meadow vole	1	0.004
Southern bog lemming	1	0.004
Southeastern shrew	1	0.004
	492	1.78

RAVINE AT TURKEY RUN. This heavily vegetated moist ravine bank at Turkey Run State Park in Parke County harbors white-footed mice, meadow jumping mice, and short-tailed shrews. Photo by Whitaker

woodland vole, which occur in lower numbers. The occurrence of the meadow jumping mouse in such abundance, and the occurrence of the house mouse, the prairie vole, and the meadow vole might not be expected. However, much of the trapping was done in Turkey Run State Park in an area where ground vegetation was luxuriant. Also, some trapping occurred at the edge of the woods in

in 4,600 trap-nights (28 to 30 November 1969), 69 white-footed mice, 3 masked shrews, 6 short-tailed shrews, and 3 woodland voles were taken

Pasture. One of the poorest habitats for small mammals in Indiana is pasture inhabited by livestock or pasture which has been so recently occupied that the soil is severely

CYPRESS SWAMP. Few cypress swamps remain in southwestern Indiana. This area at Hovey Lake in Posey County harbored white-footed mice and masked shrews. Photo by Mumford

thick grassy vegetation where the house mouse and the prairie vole occurred. The meadow jumping mouse occurred in greatest abundance in thick stands of touch-me-not (*Impatiens*) along the small streams at Turkey Run. A total of 1,172 trap-nights in one such stand yielded 26 jumping mice, 13 white-footed mice, 6 short-tailed shrews, and 1 meadow vole.

Also of particular interest are the cypress swamps of southwestern Indiana. We trapped along the edges of the cypress swamps at Hovey Lake (Posey County). There, black willow, silver maple, and pecan trees occurred in addition to the numerous cypress trees. Ground cover was relatively poor, but

trodden and compacted. During the Vigo County random trapping, 17 pasture plots were trapped, both in woodland and in open areas, but only 5 mammals were taken. These included 2 white-footed mice and a single deer mouse, 1 prairie vole, and 1 least shrew (*Cryptotis parva*).

Habitat Relationships of Major Species of Small Mammals

Habitat relationships of four of the major species of small mammals of Vigo County were studied by Whitaker (1967a), using random plot data (Tables 2, 3). The four species were the white-footed mouse, the deer

WOODED PASTURE. We have watched southern flying squirrels frolic at dusk in these black oaks near Willow Slough Fish and Wildlife Area. Photo by David W. Berry

mouse, the house mouse, and the prairie vole.

The white-footed mouse was the only important species in upland woods, river bottomland woods, brush, and brushy fields, and the deer mouse was the only species regularly found in plowed fields and soybean stubble. Two habitats, grassy fields and weedy fields, had relatively large populations of all four species. Winter wheat and corn yielded relatively large numbers of house mice, deer mice, and white-footed mice, but not meadow voles. The remaining four habitats, soybeans, wheat stubble, corn stubble, and other cultivated fields (containing mainly clover, lespedeza, or sorghum), had major populations of house mice and deer mice.

The four species inhabit four generally separate sets of ecological conditions. Competition is thus kept to a minimum. The prairie vole and the white-footed mouse occupy the two permanent types of habitats, open field and woodland areas, respectively. Apparently neither has been able to adapt to the abrupt changes required to exist in cultivated areas. The house mouse and the deer mouse occupy the two major cultivated habitats, areas with adequate ground cover and areas with little ground cover. Both are able to adapt to abrupt major habitat changes, the house mouse by moving about within cultivated areas as adequate cover becomes available, the deer mouse by being able to exist in areas with no herbaceous ground cover.

Since, if given enough time, the plowed land can progress through seral stages of cultivated field, weedy field, grassy field, to woodland, and since the changes are continual and gradual unless interrupted, there are numerous intermediate situations allowing for species overlap, at least for a time.

Other Noncultivated Habitats

Strip-mined land. Strip-mining for coal has occurred for many years in Indiana. Strip-mined land is a familiar sight to Hoosiers, and usually consists of series of small hills and valleys. Succession proceeds on the stripped land at various rates, depending primarily on the quality of the overturned soil at the particular sites. Early stage vege-

STRIP-MINED LAND. Much strip mining for coal has occurred in southwestern Indiana. Presently land after stripping is restored, but earlier "spoils" are common. Strip mines are inhabited by deer mice where cover is sparse and by house mice where it is more dense, and by white-footed mice when brush or trees have taken hold. Photo by Whitaker

tation often consists of grasses, whereas later stages often have shrubby species, particularly blackberry. Still later, trees of various species become dominant, although quite often plantings of pines or other species are present.

Sly (1976) studied three strip-mined areas in Vigo County about 5, 12, and 28 years after stripping. The two species found to be dominant on stripped areas were the deer mouse (in the 5- and 12-year-old stands) and the white-footed mouse (in the 12- and 28-year-old areas).

We have studied some stripped areas and are in agreement with Sly, except that in early stages when adequate ground cover is present, the house mouse, rather than the deer mouse, may be the dominant species.

Broom-sedge fields of southern Indiana. The broom-sedge (broomgrass) field is an important habitat of southern Indiana, where it covers extensive acreage on the poor soils of the hill country. We have twice trapped in this habitat, once with 300 and once with about 400 traps. Dominant vegetation was broom-sedge, which formed clumps over the ground. Other major species present were blackberry, purpletop, bluegrass, clover, and other grasses and herbs. Cover was fair to good, and the soil was dry. Trapping dates were 20 March and 3 April 1973, in the vicinity of Leavenworth (Crawford County). The complete catch consisted of 6 prairie voles and 3 bog lemmings (*Synaptomys cooperi*).

Indiana Dunes. Another prominent Indiana habitat is the extensive dunes area of the southern end of Lake Michigan. These dunes have been built up over many years, and the older dunes (those farther from the lake), being the first formed, are now covered with woodland. This is one of the classic cases of succession, as many seral stages are present within a relatively short distance, from newly formed dunes at lakeshore to the oldest dunes 3 to 5 miles or so away. Both plant and

BROOMGRASS. Large fields of broomgrass (*Andropogon*) are found on the dry slopes of southern Indiana. Southern bog lemmings, prairie voles, and deer mice are commonly found here. This field is in Harrison County. Photo by Whitaker

SAND DUNES. This scene is along the Dunes National Lakeshore in Lake County. Deer mice and white-footed mice inhabit this area. Photo by Whitaker

animal life have been rather intensively studied there, although little information is available on the mammals of these stages.

We trapped twice in the Indiana Dunes National Lakeshore area. The first trapping occurred on 11-13 May, 1974, when 1,300 traps were used in beachgrass (*Ammophila*), other grasses and herbs, and in shrubby vegetation. The traps were set in lines along the first row of dunes, at the eastern edge of Dunes State Park. This trapping was relatively unsuccessful, both because of weather conditions (a rain snapped many of the traps the first night) and because someone, apparently displeased with our trapping efforts, snapped many of our traps the second night. The four mammals taken during this effort were 3 deer mice and 1 meadow vole.

On our second trapping effort (16 to 18 October 1974) we set four lines of traps, one in each of the major seral stages close to Lake Michigan. This trapping was conducted in Porter County, at the Bailley Generating Station, 4 miles northwest of Chesterton. The vegetation along the traplines is described and the results are summarized below.

In line one, 288 traps were set in pure beachgrass in full fruit. The cover was fair to good, with 80 to 90 percent of the ground covered. The soil was pure, dry white sand. Piles of beachgrass cuttings and seed heads were abundant. The catch consisted of 8 white-footed mice, 2 meadow voles, 1 short-tailed shrew, and 1 masked shrew.

Line two contained 288 traps set in pure beachgrass (most plants lacking fruit) in a grassy depression behind the fore dune. Beachgrass cuttings and seed heads were present. This site is periodically inundated. The cover was nearly 100 percent in most places. The soil was moist humus. Ten meadow voles, 7 white-footed mice, 1 meadow jumping mouse, and 1 short-tailed shrew were caught.

Line three consisted of 288 traps set in a mixture of brushy, weedy, grassy vegetation along the first line of older dunes. Dominant plants were little bluestem, purpletop, goldenrod, aster, and bittersweet. Cover was poor (10 to 30 percent) and was mostly of clumps of the two major grasses. The soil was sand. The catch included 9 white-footed mice, 3 meadow voles, and 1 masked shrew.

In line four, 288 traps were set in the black oak woods along the front of the first dunes. Black oak, grape, and goldenrod were the dominant plants, but several others were present. In depressions, some moss and some leaf litter had accumulated. The soil was mostly dry. Cover was poor (5 to 15 percent). The catch consisted of 3 white-footed mice and 1 masked shrew.

Thus the most abundant mammal in three of the four habitats was the white-footed mouse. In the moist depression, the meadow vole was the most abundant.

Tamarack Swamp. Two traplines were set in swamps along the Pigeon River about 2.5 miles southeast of Mongo (Lagrange County). Principal woody plants were tamarack, poison sumac, poison ivy, alder, and red maple. Herbaceous cover was dense and consisted of mosses, sensitive fern, skunk cabbage, cowslip, and other vegetation. Standing water was present throughout the area. The 326 traps (set three nights, 14 to 17 May 1973) were placed on the many hummocks and fallen logs present. Mammals taken were 12 white-footed mice, 12 short-tailed shrews, 7 masked shrews, 2 meadow jumping mice, 1 meadow vole, 1 bog lemming, and 1 star-nosed mole (*Condylura cristata*).

Bogs. Bogs are interesting habitats and in some states contain relict communities of northern mammals not found elsewhere. There are very few bogs remaining in Indiana and all are small. We trapped the two best known (Cowles Bog, Porter County; Pinhook Bog, LaPorte County) from 21 September to 11 October 1978.

At Cowles Bog, one trapline was located in the edge of the bog and another in the adjacent swamp. The former site was quite wet and numerous trap locations were on hummocks elevated above standing water. The vegetation consisted mainly of willow, poison sumac, elm, alder, Indiana holly, mountain holly, cattail, and sensitive fern. This trapping site produced 32 masked shrews, 4 meadow voles, 1 short-tailed shrew, and 1 meadow jumping mouse. In the nearby swamp, standing water 3 to 5 inches deep was present along much of the trapline, but there were numerous drier hummocks, fallen logs, branches, and old tree stumps along the

TAMARACK SWAMP. Floor of tamarack swamp at Pigeon River. Burrow shown was that of a star-nosed mole. Photo by Mumford

TAMARACK SWAMP. These skunk cabbages were along the edge of the tamarack swamp at Pigeon River Fish and Wildlife Area in Steuben and Lagrange counties. Here masked shrews, white-footed mice, and star-nosed moles were common. Photo by Whitaker

SWAMP. This swamp is at the edge of Cowles Bog in Lake County. Masked shrews, short-tailed shrews, and white-footed mice were abundant here. Photo by Whitaker

BOG. Pinhook Bog in LaPorte County is home for masked shrews, short-tailed shrews, and white-footed mice. We were surprised to take two house mice here. Photo by Whitaker

ground. The vegetation was mostly yellow birch, red maple, spicebush, cinnamon fern, royal fern, touch-me-not, sensitive fern, mayflower, nettles, skunk cabbage, partridge berry, and sedge. In this trapline we captured 33 masked shrews, 10 white-footed mice, and 2 short-tailed shrews.

At Pinhook Bog, trapping occurred in a plant community made up mainly of blue-berries, cranberries, spirea, sphagnum, tama-rack, leatherleaf, bog rosemary, pitcher plant, sundew, and cottongrass. A short trapline was set around the border of a small pond. Mam-mals taken here were 14 masked shrews, 1 short-tailed shrew, and 1 meadow vole. The second trapline was far from open water and on a drier site. The catch here consisted of 33 masked shrews, 8 short-tailed shrews, 5 white-footed mice, 5 meadow jumping mice, 2 meadow voles, and 2 house mice. The most

surprising results of sampling the bogs were the unexpected abundance of masked shrews and the relatively small numbers of other species.

The Nature Conservancy recently acquired Laketon Bog (at Laketon, Wabash County), which we trapped on one occasion. The site appears to be a late stage bog and we saw no pitcher plants, sundew, heath plants, cotton-grass, and no floating mat of vegetation (re-portedly such a mat occurs). The area might be better called a tamarack swamp, although tamaracks are dominant in only a portion of it. Various brushy plants are dominant over most of it.

We visited Laketon Bog on 5 October 1977 and set about 900 traps. We began the trap-line at the bog entrance and crossed the cat-tail marshy section to the tamaracks, then went around the edge of the wetter portion to the maple woods on the side opposite the en-trance. Lee Brubaker had previously found two star-nosed moles in the bog. Although we searched diligently for signs of this mole, we found few burrows that could have been made by it. Many crayfish tunnels and bur-rows were present. We captured no moles in our traps, which were set the nights of 5 and 6 October. The results of our trapping in each of the several described habitats follow.

Woods—35 traps at entrance to bog. Soil: moist sandy black humus. Numerous bur-rows, fair cover, hackberry trees, walnut, blackberry. Ground cover: mint, goldenrod, aster, other herbs. The catch was 4 short-tailed shrews, 1 masked shrew, and 1 white-footed mouse.

Cattails—93 traps. Cover: very good. Soil: muck, wet, but no standing water at time of trapping. Cattails, vervain, goldenrod, sedges, and some poison sumac. The catch was 4 white-footed mice, 2 masked shrews, 2 short-tailed shrews, and 1 meadow vole.

Brushy area—191 traps. Cover: very good. Ninebark, poplar, sedges, aster, goldenrod, cattail, willow, other shrubs, marsh shield fern. The catch was 9 masked shrews, 5 short-tailed shrews, 4 white-footed mice, and 1 meadow vole.

Tamarack woods—380 traps. Cover: poor to fair. Soil: moist. Tamarack, poison sumac, much moss, marginal shield fern, woodbine, dogwood, highbush cranberry, honeysuckle, elm, bedstraw, skunk cabbage. The catch was

7 white-footed mice, 5 short-tailed shrews, 3 masked shrews, and 1 meadow vole.

Wet weedy area—60 traps. Cover: good. Soil: black muck, very wet. Touch-me-not, bedstraw, mint, much stinging nettle. The catch was 3 short-tailed shrews.

Maple woods—160 traps. Cover: fair. Soil: black muck. Red maple, stinging nettle, grass, goldenrod, sensitive fern. The catch was 7 white-footed mice, 4 short-tailed shrews, and 1 masked shrew.

In addition we set 30 traps along the edge of the woods at the bog entrance. In these were taken 5 eastern chipmunks *(Tamias striatus)*, 3 white-footed mice, and 1 red squirrel *(Tamiasciurus hudsonicus)*.

Prairie. A large section of northwestern Indiana was previously climax grass or grass / herb prairie, but little of that habitat is left. We have trapped three areas of relatively undisturbed dry sandy prairie, and one in wet prairie (see Table 9). The dry prairie trapping sites were the Beaver Lake Prairie Chicken Refuge (Newton County); a small strip of prairie at the Willow Slough Fish and Wildlife Area (Newton County); and Little Bluestem Prairie just north of Terre Haute (Vigo County). The single wet prairie sampled was the so-called Hoosier Prairie recently obtained by the Indiana Division of Nature Preserves between Griffith and Schererville (Lake County).

The major species caught in all three dry prairie habitats were the white-footed mouse and the deer mouse. The masked shrew and the meadow vole were also common at Beaver Lake, whereas the western harvest mouse and the house mouse were common at Willow Slough.

The meadow vole was the most abundant mammal trapped on the Hoosier Prairie, followed by the masked shrew, the white-footed mouse, and the short-tailed shrew.

Table 9

Small mammals trapped on Indiana prairies

	Beaver Lake Prairie Chicken Refuge	Willow Slough Prairie	Little Bluestem Prairie	Hoosier Prairie
Dates of trapping	16-19 April 1970	19-23 Oct. 1969	18-24 Jan. 1973	27-28 April 1977
Number of trap-nights	1,812	7,500	4,336	3,016
Number of mammals taken (and number per 100 trap-nights)				
White-footed mouse	19 (1.05)	32 (0.43)	42 (0.97)	16 (0.53)
Masked shrew	17 (0.94)	11 (0.15)		17 (0.56)
Deer mouse	13 (0.72)	39 (0.52)	8 (0.18)	
Meadow vole	12 (0.66)	1 (0.01)		60 (1.99)
Prairie vole	2 (0.11)	23 (0.31)	2 (0.05)	
Southern bog lemming	1 (0.06)	1 (0.01)		
Western harvest mouse	1 (0.06)	33 (0.44)		
Short-tailed shrew	1 (0.06)	12 (0.16)		10 (0.33)
House mouse		31 (0.41)	4 (0.09)	

The Mammals of Indiana

Distribution

In presettlement Indiana, the prevailing vegetation was probably the most important single factor in determining geographic ranges of mammals. Under primitive conditions (as shown by Lindsey *et al.*, 1965), the mammals of the state had three major habitat types available to them—prairie grasslands, deciduous forests, and aquatic areas (including wet prairies, swamps, and marshes). Based on available information, some of which may not be authentic, we believe that 62 species of mammals were present within Indiana as of 1820. It is impossible to be precise, because several species attributed to the state by various authors may have been erroneously listed.

Grassland-inhabiting species—the plains pocket gopher is a good example—were confined to a relatively small area in northwestern Indiana, and some were even more restricted locally by the large percentage of unsuitable aquatic and semiaquatic habitat predominating within the prairie grassland vegetation type. The forest-inhabiting species had most of the state open to them as potential habitat. Mammals occurring in aquatic habitats were probably rather evenly distributed throughout the state, especially along streams and rivers. As a whole, the mammalian fauna during this period was characterized by a number of forest species spread over an extensive area and another group of species restricted to the grasslands. Where the prairie and woodlands met, there was a wide ecotone of interdigitated habitats. Elsewhere in predominantly wooded areas, edaphic conditions and fires probably influenced the formation of grassland-type habitats of various sizes.

Logging, drainage, and farming have drastically altered all early Indiana habitats. Only the unglaciated hills of south-central Indiana have retained a significant vestige of their former identity; even these hills show the effects of intensive logging operations near the turn of the last century and of subsequent cultivation (especially in stream valleys and flat-topped ridges). In general, man's activities have caused a trend toward a rather uniform habitat in the state. Cultivation enables this trend to continue. With the shift toward a sameness of habitat, species distribution began to change, some to a great degree. In many cases, prairie grassland species invaded previously forested regions. And as trees and brush encroached upon the original grasslands, mammals of the deciduous forests moved in also. Some species greatly expanded their ranges, some had their ranges restricted, and others were extirpated.

Most grassland-inhabiting species benefited from man's activities, and many that were formerly quite restricted by habitat now occur over extensive areas that were once forested (thus unsuitable). Of this group of mammals, only the bison *(Bison bison)* was eliminated. This "prairie element" portion of the current mammalian fauna of Indiana is quite important and includes several species, some of which have now extended their ranges to include the entire state. Forest inhabitants suffered drastic reductions in species, ranges, and numbers after Indiana was settled. Much of the forested area was cleared by logging before 1900 (Butler, 1898). Among the species eliminated were the porcupine *(Erethizon dorsatum)*, the mountain lion *(Felis concolor)*, the lynx *(Felis lynx)*, the fisher *(Martes pennanti)*, the gray wolf *(Canis lupus)*, the red wolf *(Canis rufus)*, the black bear *(Ursus americanus)*, and the wolverine *(Gulo gulo)*.

Drainage, especially in the northern two-thirds of Indiana, had considerable effect on ranges and numbers of aquatic mammals. The beaver *(Castor canadensis)* population was probably nearly depleted by 1830 and the species apparently disappeared from Indiana by 1900. Since 1930, it has been successfully reintroduced. The river otter *(Lutra canadensis)*, possibly never abundant, persisted longer than the beaver along some of the larger rivers, but also was extirpated. The elimination of large marshes, especially along the Kankakee River, destroyed thousands and thousands of acres of habitat utilized by the muskrat *(Ondatra zibethicus)*, the mink *(Mustela vison)*, the river otter, the beaver, and the raccoon *(Procyon lotor)*. The Grand Marsh of the Kankakee originally covered more than 500,000 acres. Beaver Lake (northern Newton County) occupied 28,500 acres in 1834. Through drainage, it was reduced to 10,000 acres by 1917 and has since disappeared.

Both the elk *(Cervus elaphus)* and the white-tailed deer *(Odocoileus virginianus)* were gone from Indiana by 1900, but the latter has been reestablished. The elk was probably not abundant, but deer populations were locally large, according to historical accounts. Another species which early occurred in small numbers in southern Indiana (as evidenced by cave deposits) was the spotted skunk *(Spilogale putorius)*.

The data at hand are insufficient for proper evaluation of the effect of man on many native mammals. The mammals eliminated were mostly species of considerable size and many were in direct conflict with man's interests. Some were mammals which in other parts of their present-day ranges seem most successful where human populations are sparse. Historical information on small mammals of the state is notably nonexistent and one can only infer past status and distribution from prevailing habitats.

The present mammalian fauna of Indiana comprises 54 species, to which a few may eventually be added. The physical features of the state and its mammal habitats are relatively uniform, with no obvious, important barriers to mammal distribution (a possible exception may be that the pocket gopher appears to be limited by rivers). This uniformity

is reflected in the fact that 36 of Indiana's 54 mammal species probably occur, in suitable habitat, throughout the state (see Table 10); of these, the beaver and the white-tailed deer were reintroduced after they became extinct.

Three additional species—the masked shrew, the meadow vole, and the prairie vole—may eventually be found to occur throughout Indiana in suitable habitat. To

Table 10
Mammals found in suitable
habitat throughout Indiana

Order Marsupialia
  Virginia Opossum / *Didelphis virginiana*
Order Insectivora
  Short-tailed Shrew / *Blarina brevicauda*
  Least Shrew / *Cryptotis parva*
  Eastern Mole / *Scalopus aquaticus*
Order Chiroptera
  Little Brown Myotis / *Myotis lucifugus*
  Keen's Myotis / *Myotis keenii*
  Indiana Myotis / *Myotis sodalis*
  Silver-haired Bat / *Lasionycteris noctivagans*
  Big Brown Bat / *Eptesicus fuscus*
  Evening Bat / *Nycticeius humeralis*
  Red Bat / *Lasiurus borealis*
  Hoary Bat / *Lasiurus cinereus*
Order Lagomorpha
  Eastern Cottontail / *Sylvilagus floridanus*
Order Rodentia
  Eastern Chipmunk / *Tamias striatus*
  Woodchuck / *Marmota monax*
  Gray Squirrel / *Sciurus carolinensis*
  Fox Squirrel / *Sciurus niger*
  Southern Flying Squirrel / *Glaucomys volans*
  Beaver / *Castor canadensis*
  Deer Mouse / *Peromyscus maniculatus*
  White-footed Mouse / *Peromyscus leucopus*
  Woodland Vole / *Microtus pinetorum*
  Muskrat / *Ondatra zibethicus*
  Southern Bog Lemming / *Synaptomys cooperi*
  Norway Rat / *Rattus norvegicus*
  House Mouse / *Mus musculus*
  Meadow Jumping Mouse / *Zapus hudsonius*
Order Carnivora
  Coyote / *Canis latrans*
  Red Fox / *Vulpes vulpes*
  Gray Fox / *Urocyon cinereoargenteus*
  Raccoon / *Procyon lotor*
  Long-tailed Weasel / *Mustela frenata*
  Mink / *Mustela vison*
  Striped Skunk / *Mephitis mephitis*
  Bobcat / *Felis rufus*
Order Artiodactyla
  White-tailed Deer / *Odocoileus virginianus*

date, we have few records of the masked shrew *(Sorex cinereus)* from much of southern Indiana. This shrew appears to be rare south of the border of Wisconsin glaciation, and is known from a single station (Hovey Lake, Posey County) within the unglaciated portion of Indiana. It probably entered Indiana from the north and may be retreating northward following modification of the post-Pleistocene climate. It reaches one southern extension of its total geographic distribution in Illinois and Indiana.

The prairie vole *(Microtus ochrogaster),* a grassland species, has apparently not yet invaded the northeastern corner of Indiana, a region that was originally oak / hickory and beech / maple forest. This is most curious, for this vole currently occupies all of the remainder of the state which was formerly deciduous forest. Perhaps adequate trapping in suitable habitats in northeastern Indiana will reveal its presence, but it also appears to be absent from south-central Michigan and northwestern Ohio.

The meadow vole *(Microtus pennsylvanicus)* seems to be absent from much of southwestern Indiana. Possibly it occurs there in suitable scattered habitats that have not been trapped, but it is at the southern limit of its distribution in this region. Many of the former wetlands of this section of Indiana have been drained for agricultural purposes.

Fifteen other species now have restricted Indiana ranges, and some from the south, north, west, and southeast reach the limits of their total distributions in Indiana.

If the early records of Butler (1895) and True (1896) are correct, the star-nosed mole *(Condylura cristata)* once occurred over a considerable portion of Indiana. The Bartholomew County specimen recorded by Butler was not examined by a mammalogist and was not preserved. There is no definite locality cited for the specimen mentioned by True. Today, the star-nosed mole appears to be restricted mainly to northeastern Indiana, with some animals occurring as far west as LaPorte County. We feel that the continual drainage of bogs, lakes, and marshes has probably caused the original range to shrink.

The southeastern shrew *(Sorex longirostris)* probably invaded Indiana via the Mississippi River valley and appears to reach its northernmost continental distribution in northwestern Indiana. Its range may still be expanding, but there are two few records at the northern border of its range to make such a determination. Specimens have been taken in both the glaciated and unglaciated regions of Indiana, but we have much to learn about the absence or presence of the species within the known boundaries of its range in the state.

Three bats, the southeastern myotis *(Myotis austroriparius),* the gray myotis *(Myotis grisescens),* and Rafinesque's big-eared bat *(Plecotus rafinesquii),* all reach northern limits of their ranges here. The presence of all three is probably closely correlated with their cave habitats in south-central Indiana. Relatively little is known of these species and they possibly have wider distribution in the state than currently known.

The apparent absence of another bat, the eastern pipistrelle *(Pipistrellus subflavus),* from much of northern Indiana is interesting. To the east and west, this species occurs far to the north of the state. There seems to be no barrier to prevent it from occurring in northern Indiana. Possibly more collecting in this section will reveal its presence.

The swamp rabbit *(Sylvilagus aquaticus)* is evidently confined to the southern swamp (floodplain) forests of the Wabash Lowland, for all specimens have been taken there. The species reaches the northern limit of its range in extreme southwestern Indiana but was possibly at one time found farther northward along the Wabash River. No doubt its range in the state has been drastically reduced by logging, by drainage, by the construction of levees to control floodwaters of the Wabash River, and by cultivation. Within the past few years, one of the best-known localities for swamp rabbits was greatly disturbed by the construction of a large power plant (Gibson County).

Available evidence indicates that the red squirrel *(Tamiasciurus hudsonicus)* has at various times occurred throughout Indiana. A specimen was taken near Evansville (Vanderburgh County) in 1902 and another near Madison (Jefferson County) in 1933. Only a few additional records from the next 35 years have come to our attention for the southern end of the state. But in 1969 a specimen was shot in Switzerland County. Perhaps more fieldwork should be conducted throughout the southern one-third of the state in search of this species. The red squirrel is another northern species whose range has probably become more restricted in comparatively recent years.

The distribution of the thirteen-lined ground squirrel (*Spermophilus tridecemlineatus*) was summarized by Mumford and Kirkpatrick (1961), who concluded that since about 1900 this animal had extended its range southeastward across Indiana from its original prairie habitat. Evidently its range is still expanding, but the southern boundary of its known range is approximately that of the Wisconsin glacial boundary. It will be most interesting to observe whether range extension continues, but we suspect that it will.

Franklin's ground squirrel (*Spermophilus franklinii*) still exists in northwestern Indiana within approximately the same area it occupied 70 years ago. Ecological factors preventing its range extension are unknown, although within the past 15 years a few animals have been observed or collected somewhat east of the previously known range. Perhaps the species has already reached the eastern limits of suitable environment; it does not occur east of Indiana. The apparent sedentary nature of Franklin's ground squirrel is in sharp contrast to the dynamic expansion of the thirteen-lined ground squirrel. Both species formerly occupied Indiana ranges that were no doubt quite similar in extent.

Available records indicate that the plains pocket gopher (*Geomys bursarius*) also occupies much the same area today as it did in earlier times. The present population occurs in a region bounded by the Kankakee, Tippecanoe, and Wabash rivers, which apparently are sufficient barriers to deter range extension. There have probably been considerable local range extensions within the total range boundary, for the pocket gopher now is present in regions that were formerly lakes, marshes, or swamps. Soil texture and moisture no doubt play some role in the distribution of this species, which is also inhibited from occupying forested areas where roots interfere with burrowing. Perhaps both the pocket gopher and the Franklin's ground squirrel have been unable to increase to the level where population pressures affect range

expansions. The pocket gopher reaches its easternmost limit of distribution in Indiana.

The eastern woodrat (*Neotoma floridana*) occupies a small portion of south-central Indiana along the Ohio River. Here, at the northern limit of its range, it is closely associated with caves and limestone escarpments. Bader and Hall (1960) and Richards (1972) have reported on the finding of woodrat remains in a dozen caves in Harrison, Jennings, Lawrence, Monroe, Orange, and Owen counties. With the exception of Harrison County, all of these sites are outside the current known distribution and attest to the fact that in earlier times this woodrat had a much wider range in Indiana. We suspect it is found today in localities other than those we know about. Conceivably, the entire karst and cave region of the state is potentially open to occupancy by this species.

The least weasel (*Mustela nivalis*) is a northern species that has its southern range limits in Indiana. There are relatively few early records of this small carnivore and we assume that its Indiana range today may be much the same as that of 150 years ago. The southern limit of its range in the state has not been adequately determined.

The badger (*Taxidea taxus*) appears to have extended its range southward along the western side of Indiana and southeastward from the prairie across central Indiana. It has not yet penetrated (to our knowledge) the unglaciated portion of the state, but may well do so if the dynamic pattern of range expansion continues.

The western harvest mouse (*Reithrodontomys megalotis*), a relative newcomer to the state, was first detected in Indiana in 1969 (Newton County). This is another western species that reaches its eastern distributional limits here. Since its discovery in the Hoosier state, some attention has been paid to its Indiana range. Surprisingly, this mouse has already been collected 40 miles east of the Illinois-Indiana border and no doubt will continue to take up new range.

We can expect that mammal ranges will continue to shift, as land use, climate, and other ecological factors exert their influence on various species. Sometimes over the short term one fails to recognize that such alterations are occurring, and in most cases limits of distribution are difficult to ascertain and may be invisible to casual inspection. Some species—the western harvest mouse is a good example—are capable of rapid range expansion across a fairly broad front. But other species—the plains pocket gopher and Franklin's ground squirrel are examples— exhibit little or no movement for decades. To more fully understand these differences between species, we need detailed data on population dynamics, habitat and food requirements, and other phases of the total ecology of the animals. The answers to biological problems of this type are rarely simple; indeed, they are more likely to be exceedingly complex.

Reproduction

The reproductive system differs from other organ systems in one very important way. All other systems are of direct importance to the individual. The digestive system is involved with food intake and breakdown, and thus supplies energy. The respiratory system is involved with oxygen intake and expulsion of carbon dioxide. The circulatory system provides a means of transport, whereas the excretory system provides a means of waste elimination. Muscles provide a means of getting things accomplished; the skeleton provides support; the skin provides protection and a means of communication with the environment.

The reproductive system provides *no* substantial service to the individual. Rather, the whole process of reproduction represents a major energy drain to individuals, both during precopulatory proceedings and in the actual production of and caring for the young. Individuals may also be more vulnerable to predation or accidents during reproductive activities. Anyone who has observed the carefree, rambling chases of squirrels over the ground and up and down trees or the meanderings of eastern cottontails during the courtship period can appreciate both the energy drain and the increased exposure. The vulnerability of a female deer mouse frightened from the nest with young attached to her nipples, or of a red bat stranded on the ground with four attached young is also obvious.

Although the reproductive system is of lit-tle or no direct use to the individual, it is of great significance to the species. Production of young allows continuation of the species, maintenance or increase of populations in inhabited areas, and the invasion of unoccupied areas. At the same time, reproduction produces variations among individuals by bringing together new genetic material in various combinations. Variation is the raw material of the evolutionary process. Through natural selection, those variants that best enable the individual to cope with its environment are retained in greater number, and those less well suited are eventually eliminated. This rather orderly progression of events leads to populations of individuals better able to withstand the rigors of the environment. Thus the reproductive system is of long-term or indirect benefit to the individual.

The mammalogist can obtain much information from the examination of male and female reproductive systems throughout the year. One can determine when young are produced, how many are born per litter, how many litters are produced each year, sex ratios of young, and what age group of the population bears young. Additional data of various types can also be gathered from both males and females.

For males, testis size (length and width) or seminal vesicle length can be measured. Both structures increase in size with the onset of the breeding period in animals old enough to breed. The seminal vesicles are measured as they lie in their natural position in the body cavity, from their point of connection to the urethra (the main tube which becomes the penis) to the outermost point of their bend. These organs provide much of the liquid part of the seminal fluid and seem more sensitive to changes in reproductive activity than the testes. Sperm is produced in the testes, then enters the epididymis for maturation and storage. One can often see living sperm by examining the fluid from the epididymis under a microscope.

The female reproductive system can be examined for embryos, placental scars, corpora lutea, unimplanted blastocysts, or sperm. Ovulation is the erupting or expelling of a mature ovum (egg), which then enters the uterus via the Fallopian tube. Fertilization, if it occurs, is usually in the Fallopian tube.

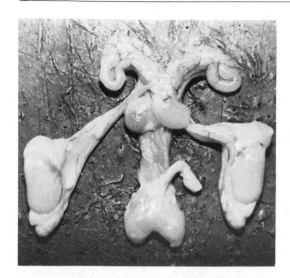

MALE REPRODUCTIVE SYSTEM. Shown here is the male reproductive system from *Rattus norvegicus*. The testis length and width are often used as an indicator of reproductive capacity; seminal vesicle (at top) is a more sensitive indicator. Photo by Whitaker

The occurrence of fertilization stimulates the ovarian follicles to become full-fledged endocrine glands called corpora lutea (yellow bodies), which produce hormones that help maintain the female tract during pregnancy and help prepare it for giving birth. The corpora lutea can be observed as bulges on the ovaries. After birth of the young, the corpora lutea rapidly disappear, but are called corpora albicantia while still observable.

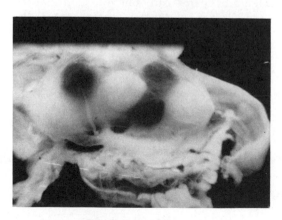

CORPORA LUTEA. Corpora lutea (yellow bodies) in the ovary of a mammal secrete hormones which help prepare the female for maintenance of pregancy. This view is of a white-footed mouse. Photo by Whitaker

The uterus can be examined directly for embryos or placental scars. Embryos may show simply as bulges or swellings in the early stage, or as well-formed embryos later. If only bulges are present, one usually measures their diameters. If the outline of the embryo can be discerned, one usually measures the greatest distance from crown to rump (C-R). Data may be recorded as follows: 18 mm C-R, 2L, 3R (= embryos average 18 mm in crown-rump measurement as they lie in the tract; there are 2 in the left, 3 in the right horn of the uterus). Also, notations should be made if one or more embryos are radically smaller than the others; such embryos probably are being resorbed and would not have been born.

The uterine attachment sites (placental scars) of the young are readily seen for some time after birth and show up as reddish, brown, or black spots along the uterine horns (Fig. 38). Their presence usually indicates that birth has occurred rather recently. It takes about 42 to 44 days for placental scars to disappear in some voles, for example (although scar tissue persists much longer, as evidenced by histological examination).

In weasels or other mammals with delayed implantation, one can attempt to find unimplanted blastocysts by cutting off the ends of the uterine horns and flushing out the tubes with a syringe. In the case of bats with de-

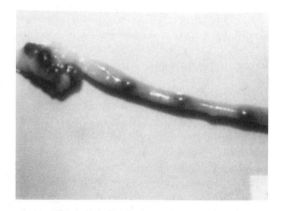

PLACENTAL SCARS. Placental scars in *Rattus norvegicus* twenty days after giving birth to litter. Corpora lutea are evident in ovary also. The dark spots mark the points where embryos were attached during pregnancy, although their number is not a very accurate indication of the number of young produced. Photo by Whitaker

layed fertilization, one can make a uterine smear to determine if sperm is present. In voles, the presence of a whitish or yellowish "copulation plug" in the vagina indicates recent mating.

Most of the specimens taken during our studies of Indiana mammals have been examined for reproductive information. Some of these data are summarized in this section. Many species of mammals have only one litter per year. This is often indicative of low predatory pressure or high survival of young in the species. Also, large animals require a longer period for breeding activities, gestation, and rearing of the young; time may not allow more than one litter per year in these species. Other species may produce two, or even several, litters per year. The number of offspring per litter correlates closely with the number of litters per year as an index to reproductive potential of the various species. A low number of offspring per litter is also probably primarily a reflection of low predation rates or is indicative that most of the young are reaching maturity and entering the breeding population.

One Litter per Year

Indiana mammals with only one breeding season and one litter per year are listed in Table 11. The moles, pocket gopher, ground squirrels, and woodchuck are burrowers or spend much time in burrows, and thus are probably much less subject to predation than many other species. Larger species—beaver, coyote, foxes, raccoon, bobcat—are also less subject to predation; in addition, these larger mammals require so much time to raise a litter that second litters cannot be reared. Single litters per year are the rule for these species.

Another large group of mammals with a single litter per year is the bats, which probably are preyed upon but little because of their rapid flight, the time of their activity, and the protected places in which they spend their inactive periods. In addition to producing one litter per year, they have low numbers of young per litter. Most species of *Myotis* have one young per litter, while the eastern pipistrelle (*Pipistrellus subflavus*), the silver-haired bat (*Lasionycteris noctivagans*), the evening bat (*Nycticeius humeralis*), the big brown bat (*Eptesicus fus-*

cus), and the hoary bat (*Lasiurus cinereus*) usually have two. The red bat (*Lasiurus borealis*) normally has three, frequently four, and varies from one to five per litter. It would appear that the red bat is the bat most subject to predatory pressure, presumably because of its habit of roosting in less protected places (among foliage) during the day.

It should be mentioned that bats of the genera *Myotis*, *Pipistrellus*, and *Eptesicus* display delayed fertilization. The sperm may remain in a pouch off the uterus of the female for extended periods of time between mating, which occurs in the fall, and fertilization, which occurs in early spring. This is generally thought to be an energy conservation measure. Since mating takes energy, and since these bats are hibernators and cannot replenish their energy supplies by feeding during the winter, mating occurs during the fall while ample food is still available. Delayed fertilization allows the young embryo to develop in the spring and the young to be born later at the optimum time. (However, bats of some species—the big brown bat, for example—tend to move about and even to copulate during the winter. If energy conservation is so important, we wonder why these movements and matings occur. We have speculated that perhaps a major function of delayed fertilization is to help ensure mating of all females by allowing copulation to occur whenever males and females come together during fall or winter. Mating of all females would be particularly important in species producing one litter per year and small litters.)

Delayed implantation also occurs in some of the weasels (genus *Mustela*). Copulation is soon followed by fertilization and the zygote develops to the blastula stage. Implantation does not take place immediately, however, and the blastula remains free in the uterus. In *Mustela*, copulation occurs in midsummer, but implantation, followed by normal development, occurs in the very early spring. This process is also probably one of energy conservation.

Two Peaks of Breeding, or Two Litters per Year

In some species two litters per year are produced, by the same or (more often) by different individuals of the population. For

Table 11

Indiana mammals producing only one litter per year

Species	Young per litter		Time of birth	Gestation period (days)
	Average	Range		
Virginia opossum	6.73[a]	1-13	early spring	12-13
Eastern mole	3	2-4	Feb.–May	45
Star-nosed mole	4	4	April–May	45?
Little brown myotis	1	1-2	June–early July	
Southeastern myotis	2[b]	—	May	
Gray myotis	1[c]	—	—	
Keen's myotis	1	1	June	
Indiana myotis	1	1	June–July	
Silver-haired bat	2[c]	2	—	
Eastern pipistrelle	2	1-4	late June–early July	
Big brown bat	2	1-2	late May–June	
Evening bat	2	1-2	June	
Red bat	3.2	1-5	June	
Hoary bat	2	2	late May–early June	
Rafinesque's big-eared bat	2[d]	2	—	
Woodchuck	4.9	3-8	March–April	28
Thirteen-lined ground squirrel	8	4-12	May	27-28
Franklin's ground squirrel	8?	4-12?	June	28?
Plains pocket gopher	4	1-7	April–May	about 30?
Beaver	3.5	3-4(9)	May–July	128+
Eastern woodrat[e]	3?	1-4	March	33-42?
Coyote	?	4-8	April	60-63
Red fox	6.8	4-13	early spring	about 53
Gray fox	4	2-6	early spring	51
Raccoon	4.5	1-9	April–May	63
Bobcat	2	1-4	April?	62
Least weasel[f]	4.7	1-6	April–Sept.?	34-36
Long-tailed weasel	?	4-6?	April–May?	about 280
Mink	?	3-6	April–May	40-75?
Badger	2.5	1-5	April–May	about 240
Striped skunk	4.5	2-10	May–early June	63
White-tailed deer	1 and 2[g]	1-3	May or June	201

[a]pouch young
[b]no young observed in Indiana
[c]young probably not produced in Indiana
[d]possibly does not breed in Indiana
[e]probably more than one litter
[f]likely one litter
[g]one young the first year, then two young

example, in the eastern chipmunk (*Tamias striatus*) the older adults breed in early spring, while the animals about a year old produce a litter in July. An individual female chipmunk usually produces only one litter per year, but there are two peaks of litter production. Species in this category are listed in Table 12.

Several Litters per Year

Other species produce several litters throughout much of the year, and some are thus able to invade and quickly populate an area as it becomes available. Species of this type are listed in Table 13.

Much more information on reproduction is needed for many Indiana mammals. For some relatively rare and secretive species, we have little or no data. We would like to know more about nesting sites and structures, precise numbers of litters produced per year by various species, and the age at which breeding commences. Additional information regarding annual reproductive cycles would

Table 12

Indiana mammals with two peaks of breeding, or two litters per year

Species	Young per litter		Time of birth	Gestation period (days)
	Average	Range		
Eastern chipmunk	4.1	2-5	Spring	31
			Aug.–Oct.	
Southern flying squirrel	4.7	3-8?	Mar.–Apr.	40
			Aug.–Oct.	
Gray squirrel	3	1-5	Feb.–Mar.	45
			June–Aug.	
Fox squirrel	3	1-5	Feb.–Mar.	45
			June–Aug.	
Red squirrel	—	—	—	38
Muskrat	6.9	3-10	Apr.–June	28-30
Meadow jumping mouse[a]	5.5	2-9	June–Sept.	18

[a]possibly three peaks of breeding

be useful to biologists, wildlife managers, and others concerned with the welfare of our Indiana mammals.

Populations

It is difficult to get accurate absolute population estimates (number of individuals per unit area) for most mammals, and there is little such information for most Indiana species. To get such data for many terrestrial mammals, it is necessary to establish study plots, to trap, mark and release, and recapture individuals to estimate home range size, and to add a strip half the width of the home range diameter to the outside of the study plot (to compensate for the animals' movements), and finally to calculate the number of animals for the corrected unit of area. There are numerous pitfalls in employing this (or any other) method.

Mammal populations fluctuate with the season. They are largest in late summer or early fall when the young of the year have been added. Thus the researcher's trapping season affects estimates of population numbers. There is also an unknown number of mammals that are not captured. This number cannot be determined and may be a source of considerable error in population estimates.

Table 13

Indiana mammals producing several litters per year

Species	Young per litter		Time of birth	Gestation period (days)
	Average	Range		
Masked shrew	6.5	4-10	Spring, fall	about 18?
Southeastern shrew	4.5	3-9	March–Oct.	about 18?
Short-tailed shrew	5.9	3-8	March–Oct.	21-22
Least shrew	5.8	3-7	June–Sept.	21-23
Eastern cottontail	4.8	3-7	Jan.–Oct.	26-30
Swamp rabbit	3.5	3-7	Feb.–Sept.	39-40
Deer mouse	4.5	2-8	Jan.–Dec.	25
White-footed mouse	4.5	2-8	mostly Feb.–Nov.	21
Meadow vole	4.81	2-8	Mar.–Dec.	21
Prairie vole	3.48	1-7	Jan.–Dec.	21
Woodland vole	2.5	2-4	Feb.–March	20-21
Southern bog lemming	3	2-5	Feb.–Dec.	23
Western harvest mouse	3.8	2-6	Mar.–Nov.	19?
Norway rat	7.4	4-12	Feb.–Nov.	21-26
House mouse	6.02	3-10	Feb.–Nov.	21

Climatic conditions during the trapping period can play an important role in determining the catch of various species. Some species are quite cyclic and, depending upon which part of the cycle the trapping occurs in, estimates can vary greatly. We are also aware that some mammals are less easily trapped than others, and a few are extremely difficult to capture at all. All these factors should be taken into account when working with population data. We have had to assume that our data, though subject to these and possibly other factors, can be used to make comparisons between species and between habitats.

Our best absolute population estimates are the result of Whitaker's work in Vigo County (1967c). Whitaker snap-trapped 429 study plots randomly selected from among 1,640,331 available plots in Vigo County (excluding the city of Terre Haute). Since he did not determine home range sizes, we used one-half acre as a general home range for our calculations. For any individual species or habitat, home range size might actually be smaller or larger. Each plot was 25 by 25 meters, which is rather small for this type of population estimation. By assuming a home range of one-half acre (a 45-meter square), the "effective plot size" was figured by adding half the home range diameter (22.5 meters) around the actual plot size; thus, the effective plot size was a 70-meter square, or 4900 square meters (1.2114 acres). There were 209,226 plots of this size in the study area, so we multiplied that number by the average number of animals in the original plots to obtain our estimate of the total number of each species in Vigo County (Table 14). Since the "effective plot size" was 4900 square meters (1.2114 acres), we divided the number of animals per plot by the number of acres per effective plot to get the average number of animals per acre (Tables 15, 16). These data should be interpreted, then, in light of the methods of calculation and keeping in mind the various factors affecting data collection.

For example, house mice *(Mus musculus)* were estimated overall at 3.85 per acre in winter wheat fields. However, they would not occur at that rate at all times. They would be absent or very sparse (and with larger home ranges) in early stage wheat fields, and much more abundant (and with smaller home ranges) in mature wheat fields. Thus, for population estimates, the investigator needs to develop data for the specific time and place of interest.

In cases where one is unable to get absolute estimates, (those in numbers per unit area), it is often possible to get relative values; that is, one can determine which species are most abundant and then indicate relative degrees of abundance. Snap-trapping data are widely used to show relative abundance and species composition of mammals per habitat type. Such data are highly biased toward species that are more likely to be trapped. In Indiana, for example, these include the deer mouse, the white-footed mouse, the harvest mouse, the house mouse, some voles, and the short-tailed shrew. Snap-trapping works less well for other shrews, bog lemmings, and other small-mammal species. Thus, data on

Table 14

Estimated numbers of various small mammals in
Vigo County in 1962-63

Species	Number trapped	Average trapped per plot	Estimated total number
House Mouse	541	1.26	263,625
Deer Mouse	495	1.15	240,610
White-footed Mouse	316	0.74	154,827
Prairie Vole	71	0.17	35,568
Meadow Vole	26	0.06	12,554
Short-tailed Shrew	26	0.06	12,554
Woodland Vole	12	0.03	6,277

Table 15

Estimated numbers per acre of various small mammals in cultivated habitats in
Vigo County (calculated from random plot trapping data, using home range size
of one-half acre)

Effective Acres	19.38	10.90	46.03	26.65	44.82	60.57	58.15
Habitats	Soybeans	Winter Wheat	Corn	Soybean Stubble	Wheat Stubble	Corn Stubble	Plowed Fields
Number of Plots	16	9	38	22	37	50	48
Species							
House Mouse	1.30	3.85	3.02	—	1.83	1.29	0.02
Deer Mouse	1.75	3.67	0.76	1.46	1.63	0.73	1.48
White-footed Mouse	0.21	0.73	0.67	—	0.16	0.03	0.09
Prairie Vole	—	0.18	0.07	—	0.13	0.03	—
Meadow Vole	—	—	—	—	0.04	0.03	—
Woodland Vole	—	—	—	—	—	—	—
Short-tailed Shrew	—	—	0.02	—	—	—	—

Table 16

Estimated numbers per acre of various small mammals in
noncultivated habitats in Vigo County (calculated from random
plot trapping data, using home range size of one-half acre)

Effective Acres	65.42	18.17	27.86	35.13	39.98
Habitats	Upland Woods	River Bottom- land Woods	Brushy Fields	Weedy Fields	Grassy Fields
Number of Plots	54	15	23	29	33
Species					
House Mouse	—	0.11	0.07	1.79	1.85
Deer Mouse	—	—	0.25	1.08	0.65
White-footed Mouse	0.99	2.97	1.72	1.05	0.75
Prairie Vole	—	—	0.07	0.57	0.62
Meadow Vole	—	0.06	0.04	0.11	0.40
Woodland Vole	0.12	0.06	—	—	0.05
Short-tailed Shrew	0.26	0.11	0.14	—	0.08

relative abundance are quite useful in comparing species composition and numbers per
habitat type for the easily trapped species,
but are less useful, because of small sample
size, for determining the same information
regarding the species more difficult to take in
snap-traps. Despite this, we have sometimes
had to rely on such data for inclusion in the
species accounts and in the section on
habitats.

One cannot say that the white-footed
mouse is ten times more abundant than the
masked shrew because ten times more of the
mice than of the shrews were taken in traps.
But one can usefully compare trapping results from one time and place to those of another time or place. For example, if the
white-footed mouse is taken at the rate of 4
per 100 trap-nights and the masked shrew at
a rate of 1 per 100 trap-nights in the fall, but
both occur at rates of 2 per 100 trap-nights in
the spring, there are strong indications that
the mouse has decreased from fall to spring
by about half, whereas the shrew has approximately doubled in numbers. (We might
further caution readers here that perhaps one
or both species was more easily caught in
spring than in fall, perhaps because of reduced food supply or for some other reason.)

Other types of data may be used for relative population estimates. Among these are
data on bats submitted for rabies testing during different seasons and years; additional
information on bats can be obtained by

mist-netting or by shooting them at dusk. Systematic observations of mammals killed on roads might be compared on a seasonal or an annual basis, or with similar studies from other states. Comparisons of such data between various places and for various seasons reflect the behavior, distribution, numbers, movements, and other aspects of the biology of the species being studied and may be useful for several types of investigations.

Bats Submitted for Rabies Examination. Residents of Indiana submit large numbers of bats to the Indiana Board of Health for rabies examination, and these animals are then submitted to us for identification (Whitaker *et al.*, 1969, 1974). It is not clear how the numbers of bats submitted for examination relate to the proportions of the various species of bats occurring in the state. We suspect at least two major sources of bias in these data. We believe that those bats most closely associated with human habitations appear more often in this sample than in the population at large, and that sick animals are more apt to be captured than healthy ones.

In all, 1,315 bats were submitted for rabies tests from 1965 through 1972 (Table 17). The most abundant bat in the sample was the big brown bat *(Eptesicus fuscus),* followed in numbers by the red bat *(Lasiurus borealis).* We believe these are the two most abundant species of bats in Indiana, except in winter, but we doubt that the big brown bat is twice as abundant as the red bat as the data seem to

indicate. The big brown bat is closely associated with humans because of its habit of roosting and establishing maternity colonies in houses, barns, churches, and other structures where man is apt to come in contact with the species. Although red bats are quite common in residential sections of cities and towns, this species is a tree-roosting bat and seldom enters houses; it is likely to be found, however, in spring, summer, and fall in parks, cemeteries, wooded residential areas, orchards, and other suitable roosting sites. The hoary bat *(Lasiurus cinereus)* is represented in these data by disproportionately high numbers, in our opinion. This is a relatively uncommon bat that is not taken in large numbers by shooting or by mist-netting. In view of the relatively large number (51) submitted to the rabies laboratory and the number (10) proven to be rabid, it may be that the species is taken so often because it has a high risk of becoming sick. It has much the same roosting habits as the red bat and thus occurs near humans where suitable tree habitats are available. It is also possible that the hoary bat is much more abundant in the state than our other records indicate, for we know of only 65 preserved specimens from Indiana in museum collections. It is doubtful, however, that the species listed in Table 17 can be ranked for relative abundance according to the numbers examined in the rabies laboratory.

Bats Mist-netted at Cave Entrances. Another means of estimating bat populations is by capturing bats at night with Japanese mist nets at cave entrances. This technique is most effective in late summer. Some species of bats circle into and out of caves (a behavior called swarming), and thus a net across the cave entrance will often capture them in fairly large numbers. We used this method to sample bats at the entrance to Donnehue's Cave (Lawrence County) on twenty occasions from August 1970 through August 1971, and again in February 1973 (Mumford and Whitaker, 1975). Data from this effort are summarized in Table 18. Overall, the little brown myotis *(Myotis lucifugus)* and the eastern pipistrelle *(Pipistrellus subflavus)* were the most numerous of the bats netted, followed by the big brown bat. These were also probably the most abundant bats — with the addi-

Table 17

Species composition and numbers of bats submitted by Indiana citizens for rabies tests, 1965 through 1972

Species	Number Examined	Number Rabid	Percent Rabid
Big Brown Bat	776	29	3.7
Red Bat	338	24	7.1
Little Brown Myotis	80	1	1.3
Hoary Bat	51	10	19.6
Eastern Pipistrelle	24	3	12.5
Indiana Myotis	23	0	0
Evening Bat	10	0	0
Silver-haired Bat	7	0	0
Keen's Myotis	6	0	0
Totals	1,315	67	5.1

Table 18

Bats captured by mist-netting the entrance to Donnehue's Cave (Lawrence County), from approximately dusk to midnight (netting ceased earlier in colder months)

	Southeastern Myotis	Little Brown Myotis	Indiana Myotis	Keen's Myotis	Big Brown Bat	Red Bat	Eastern Pipistrelle	Totals
February	1	—	—	—	2	—	—	3
March	—	6	—	—	2	—	—	8
April	—	3	—	1	—	—	—	4
May	1	7	—	2	7	—	10	27
June	—	5	—	3	2	—	2	12
July	—	7	—	2	4	1	16	30
August	10	89	1	4	29	4	91	228
September	9	61	—	3	2	2	23	100
October	3	12	—	—	6	—	1	22
November	1	—	—	—	2	—	—	3
December	—	1	—	—	2	—	—	3
Totals	25	191	1	15	58	7	143	440

tion of the red bat—in that vicinity during the study period. The red bat is much more abundant (except in winter) than these data indicate, but is less subject to capture by mist-netting at caves. Relatively few red bats join the other bats swarming about the cave entrances, presumably because the red bat is not a cave dweller.

Mist-netting of the entrance of Big Wyandotte Cave (Crawford County) was carried out throughout the night of 22-23 August 1974 (Table 19). We suspect that the relative abundance of the top five species of bats netted correlates quite accurately with the bats present in the area. However, the red bat (represented by two netted individuals) certainly ranks near the top of the abundance list in the vicinity of the cave at that time of year. The gray myotis (*Myotis grisescens*) is a rare bat in Indiana at all seasons. The time of entrance of each bat into the net was recorded at this cave, as were the species and sex of each bat. The four most abundant species were active all night. At around 5:20 to 5:35 A.M., when the sky was getting light, many bats were in the air outside the net; by 5:35 to 5:40 it had become light and the bats were milling closer to the cave entrance. By 5:57 most of these bats had found their way around the net and had entered the cave or else had gotten caught. At 5:58 an additional four bats were milling about the entrance, and at 6:00, six more. All activity had stopped by 6:02 and the net was removed at 6:08 A.M.

Bats taken by mist-netting cave entrances during the swarming (or any other) season provide data not necessarily indicative of the relative numbers of the various species in the area, however. Only certain species take part in swarming and some of these may be present in disproportionately large numbers, especially at the peak of the swarming period. Numbers captured and species composition also vary greatly from week to week and from cave to cave. Species taken in the largest numbers—the little brown myotis, the Indiana myotis (*Myotis sodalis*), and the pipistrelle—are those that use caves during hibernation. In addition, the big brown bat and Keen's myotis (*Myotis keenii*) may be relatively common and may occur at some seasons in much larger numbers than one finds during hibernation. The red bat is frequently netted at cave entrances but seldom occurs in caves. Thus, data gathered by mist-netting must be interpreted in light of our knowledge of the biology of the various species.

Bat Shooting. Some idea of relative abundance of bats can be obtained by shooting at dusk near suitable feeding or drinking areas, although the animals collected are more likely to reflect evening activity patterns than true relative abundance. For example, the little brown bat is common, but it is shot in extremely small numbers, because it emerges at dusk too late to be seen and shot. Even the

Table 19
Bats captured by mist-netting the entrance to Big Wyandotte Cave (Crawford County),
night of 22-23 August 1974
(m / f / u = male / female / sex undetermined)

	Little brown myotis			Big brown bat			Indiana myotis			Eastern pipistrelle			Keen's myotis			Red bat			Gray myotis		
	m	f	–	m	f	u	m	f	–	m	f	u	m	f	–	m	f	–	m	–	–
7:20-7:30		2			–		1	–		2	–										
7:30-8:00	14	5			–		9	–		2	–										
8:00-8:30	6	4				1	12	5		6	–										
8:30-9:00	8	1		3	–		1	–		1	–										
9:00-9:30	8	–		2	3		–	–		1	–										
9:30-10:00	6	–		5	–		1	–		–	–	1	–	–		1	–				
10:00-10:30	7	4		4	–		1	–		1	–	1	2	–							
10:30-11:00	3	–		5	–		5	1		3	–	2	1	–							
11:00-11:30	1	1		6	2		1	–		2	–	2	1	–							
11:30-12:00	–	–		8	2	1	6	1		6	1										
12:00-12:30	4	1		3	5	1	3	–		3	–										
12:30-1:00	3	1		6	3	1	1	–		4	1		–	–		–	–		1	–	
1:00-1:30	2	–		5	2	2	2	1		2	3										
1:30-2:00	2	3		3	–	1	2	2		1	2										
2:00-2:30	3	1		6	3	1	5	–		2	–										
2:30-3:00	6	1		2	1	1	4	–		3	–		1	–							
3:00-3:30	4	3		3	2	–	2	–		2	1										
3:30-4:00	4	1		1	1	1	3	1		4	–	1									
4:00-4:30	1	2		1	–	1	–	1		3	–	–	–	–		–	1				
4:30-5:00	7	–		1	–	–	1	1		2	1	–									
5:00-5:30	5	4		1	–	–	2	1													
5:30-6:00	5	–		–	–	–	15	–					–	1							
6:00-6:08																					
totals	99	34		65	25	10	77	14		50	9	7	5	1		1	1		1		

big brown bat, probably one of the two most abundant bats in the state in summer, is taken in much smaller numbers than would be expected, for the same reason. On the other hand, the red bat and the eastern pipistrelle are early fliers. Both can frequently be observed when there is sufficient light to see their colors, and shooting is easier. Species that feed in more protected sites (low, over streams; in wooded areas) are less vulnerable to shooting. Three species of bats occurring in Indiana have not been taken by shooting. These are the southeastern myotis (*Myotis austroriparius*), the gray myotis, and Rafinesque's big-eared bat (*Plecotus rafinesquii*).

Bats vary in their vulnerability to shooting, depending on such factors as their size and foraging habits. For example, the pipistrelle is a low, relatively slow flyer that feeds close to the ground, and thus is easily shot. Other slow-flying species include the big brown bat, the silver-haired bat (*Lasionycteris noc-*

tivagans), and the evening bat (*Nycticeius humeralis*). Lasiurine bats (the red bat and hoary bat) are capable of extremely swift flight (especially on windy evenings) and frequently feed very high, often out of effective shotgun range. Female red bats near term appear quite vulnerable to shooting, however, probably because they cannot maneuver as easily or fly as fast or as erratically while carrying large embryos. Pregnant females may also tend to feed in more open locations (away from trees and brush that might further impede their maneuverability), where they are shot and retrieved more easily. The unhampered males are not as vulnerable to shooting.

Bats of several species may congregate over favorite feeding or watering sites, where shooting may be quite productive. However, on certain evenings one species may predominate in an area and on another evening another species may predominate; we know little about what causes this (an indication of how little we know about bat biology). Climatic conditions or availability of insects may affect various species differently. The activity patterns of the bats' insect prey may affect foraging height, since some insect species remain near the ground and others fly about high in the air. Some prey may be active near trees and shrubs and other prey may move about in the open. Insect activity, in turn, may be influenced by barometric pressure, wind, temperature, relative humidity, and other environmental factors, and may at times be related to mating, swarming, migration, or other biological processes.

Species composition of the bats may also differ depending upon the habitat hunted. Some factors involved include proximity of a daytime roost (or maternity colony), presence or absence of water, number and spacing of large trees, predominant ground cover (which also affects the ease of finding the downed bats), and abundance and species composition of insect prey. Thus the number and species of bats shot and collected in a given evening in a given area depend upon a variety of factors—not the least of which may be the shooter's skill.

We have spent considerable time bat-hunting in Indiana. We frequently shoot along small streams with wooded banks, over small ponds in wooded or unwooded areas, along woodlot borders, or along cleared powerline right-of-ways and roads through forested tracts. A greater variety of bats may frequent ponds, where the animals come to drink. In Indiana, there are few areas where water is not readily available near bat roosts. Our data on bat hunting should not be interpreted as representing relative species abundance. Basically the data reveal what species bat shooters can expect to collect, and indicate the relative numbers of the early-emerging species of bats shot at different localities at different times. Hence, our data do reflect the success one is likely to have and the species composition of the kill for areas we have sampled in Indiana.

The results of bat hunting by Mumford in 34 counties throughout the state have been compiled for analysis. Only hunts during which at least one bat was collected were included, and these totaled 121 hours of effort. (There were many additional hunts that

OTTER CREEK IN VIGO COUNTY. Feeding site for many bats, particularly big brown, red, little brown, Keen's, Indiana, pipistrelle, and, during migration, silver-haired. Photo by Whitaker

resulted in no bats being taken.) Of 318 bats shot and retrieved, 192 were red bats, 59 were eastern pipistrelles, 23 were big brown bats, 18 were silver-haired bats, and 17 were evening bats. Smaller numbers of Indiana myotis, little brown myotis, and hoary bats were also taken. Red bats were shot at the rate of 1.6 per hour and eastern pipistrelles at 0.5 per hour. Species taken at the lowest rate were little brown myotis and hoary bats, each at 0.02 per hour.

Whitaker's data for bat hunting in Vigo County were somewhat different. Of 90 bats he shot over several years at one site near Terre Haute, 48 were red bats, 17 were big brown bats, and 7 were pipistrelles; also taken were 6 little brown myotis, 5 Indiana myotis, 3 silver-haired bats, 2 hoary bats, 1 Keen's myotis, and 1 evening bat. This is an interesting and diversified sample, but again points to the preponderance of red bats taken by this method.

In Indiana, wherever one samples summer bat populations by shooting at dusk, the red bat constitutes a large part of the total bag. It may frequently be the only species taken. Where red bats and eastern pipistrelles occur together in south-central Indiana, the two species tend to be collected in about equal numbers. In Mumford's analysis, where these species were both collected at the same time and place, 24 eastern pipistrelles and 16 red bats were shot. (Mumford's data are biased by the fact that he often passed up shots at pipistrelles and red bats in watching for other species; these bats would have consituted even larger percentages of the kill had they been taken at every opportunity.) Where pipistrelles are absent (the northern half of the state), the red bat constitutes a large percentage of all bats killed.

The best data have been collected in Clay, Jackson, and Tippecanoe counties. In Clay County, in 13.5 hours of bat hunting, the following were shot: 23 red bats, 2 eastern pipistrelles, 5 big brown bats, 3 evening bats, and 1 silver-haired bat. During 20.75 hours of hunting in Jackson County, 22 red bats, 8 pipistrelles, 2 little brown myotis, and 1 hoary bat were collected. The Tippecanoe County data cover 26.5 hours of shooting. The species composition was 63 red bats, 2 pipistrelles, 6 big brown bats, 4 evening bats,

9 silver-haired bats, 1 Indiana myotis, and 1 little brown myotis. It will be seen that of the 153 bats taken in these three counties, 108 were red bats. The eastern pipistrelle is not common in Tippecanoe County, which appears to be about the northward limit of its geographic range in Indiana.

Mammals Killed on Roads by Vehicles. We have accumulated some data concerning mammal mortality on Indiana highways. Much of the information was gathered by Philip Clem in south and west-central Indiana (Table 20). Some of Indiana's most common larger mammals — opossums, cottontails, woodchucks, raccoons, striped skunks, and fox squirrels — are those most often noted dead along roads. The opossum was recorded in the greatest numbers, but we suspect that it may be disproportionately represented because of its tendency to feed on other dead animals on roads. A surprisingly small number of chipmunks was recorded; this species is relatively uncommon in southern Indiana where Clem accumulated much of his data. In some other portions of the state, it is often observed dead along roads. The species composition of such sampling would probably vary somewhat from one section of the state to another, especially varying with habitat. One might expect differences in the

Table 20

Mammals seen dead on Indiana roads, 1972 to 1974,
by Philip Clem, Gwilym S. Jones, and J. O. Whitaker, Jr.

	Jan.	Feb.	March	April	May	June	July	Aug.	Sept.	Oct.	Nov.	Dec.	Totals
Virginia opossum	6	11	13	28	34	29	32	34	39	10	6	2	244
Eastern cottontail	13	17	33	14	15	5	9	3	29	5	4	4	151
Raccoon	2	3	8	8	6	5	14	6	1	24	1	1	79
Striped skunk	—	12	6	6	7	12	8	11	4	5	2	—	73
Fox squirrel	4	10	—	12	8	4	—	2	17	6	2	1	66
Woodchuck	—	1	6	3	7	15	9	10	—	—	1	—	52
Norway rat	—	—	1	—	2	—	—	—	—	2	—	—	5
Red fox	—	—	—	—	2	1	—	2	—	—	—	—	5
Gray fox	—	2	—	1	—	—	—	—	—	1	—	—	4
Muskrat	—	—	1	1	1	—	—	—	—	—	—	—	3
Eastern mole	—	—	—	—	—	—	—	—	—	2	—	—	2
Eastern chipmunk	—	—	—	—	1	1	—	—	—	—	—	—	2
Red squirrel	—	—	—	—	1	—	—	—	—	—	1	—	2
Mink	—	—	—	—	1	—	1	—	—	—	—	—	2
White-tailed deer	—	1	—	—	—	—	—	—	—	—	—	—	1
Badger	—	—	—	—	1	—	—	—	—	—	—	—	1
	25	57	68	73	86	72	73	68	90	55	17	8	692

numbers of mammals killed with regard to types of roads, amount of traffic, abundance of scavenging animals that remove carcasses, season of the year, and time of day of census. Small mammals are few in numbers in these data because of the greater probability of pickup by scavengers, and quicker breakdown and decay, as well as the greater likelihood of being overlooked by the observer. Information from systematic observations of animals killed on roads has been and can be used by biologists and various game agencies, primarily to determine relative populations of some of the more common larger mammals between areas, between habitats, and between seasons. In addition, changes in populations, and relative amount of movement over the year, can be estimated for some species.

Annual Fur Harvest. Some states are able to use data from the annual catch of fur animals to obtain population trends. Data concerning the marketing of mammals for furs in Indiana are of interest, but for several reasons are not very useful in drawing conclusions regarding population fluctuations or relative abundance. Not all fur dealers submit annual reports of their activities, and the percentage that do varies from year to year. Prices paid for raw pelts fluctuate tremendously over a span of years. When prices are high, more effort is expended to hunt and trap mammals and the numbers sold increase. High fur prices also encourage more new trappers and hunters to participate, thus adding another variable. In the 1950s, fox pelts were valued at less than a dollar, but in the 1970s they brought thirty dollars (or more) each. Raccoon pelts have also increased greatly in value over the past 10 to 20 years.

D. M. Brooks (1959) collected data on fur-bearing animals in Indiana for many years. He found that some animals killed for fur were never sold; this figure fluctuated depending upon the prices paid for pelts. Some Indiana-taken animals are sold out of the state. In earlier years, undetermined numbers of pelts were shipped to Sears, Roebuck and Company and to other fur buyers who operated by mail. Also, an unknown quantity of pelts are taken outside of but sold in Indiana.

Table 21 lists data for average annual Indiana fur harvests for various periods since 1933. Available figures for 1933 to 1937 were obtained by Brooks from the United States Fish and Wildlife Service; for 1943 to 1947, he used data from the Sportsman's Questionnaire; fur buyer reports were used for compiling data for 1953 to 1957. In the 1970s the fur catch was assessed by the Indiana Department of Natural Resources.

It is clear from these data that the muskrat is the longtime favorite animal of Indiana trappers, with average harvests running at about 400,000 per year, followed by the raccoon, varying between 20,000 and 225,000

Table 21

Fur harvest data, Indiana, for selected periods and years

Species	Average Annual 1933-1937[a]	Average Annual 1943-1947[a]	Average Annual 1953-1957[a]	1970-71[b]	1971-72[b]	1972-73[b]	1973-74[b]	1974-75[b]
Beaver	No season	No season	101	157	238	507	608	596
Muskrat	464,288	453,084	226,082	126,296	182,795	366,804	468,760	403,425
Mink	19,802	28,106	12,784	4,257	8,464	8,962	12,253	11,993
Raccoon	25,824	126,792	112,213	42,367	89,434	166,892	225,421	22,175
Opossum	220,689	183,895	30,801	3,777	8,788	24,962	47,339	45,039
Striped skunk	63,437	23,835	2,456	47	194	455	1,032	831
Weasels	4,663	7,479	684	4,259	194	180	350	328
Badger	No data	201	4	0	0	0	0	0
Red fox	No data	44,064	1,816	2,936	2,920	5,843	12,421	10,276
Gray fox	No data	10,249	775	1,284	2,816	7,639	9,654	10,411

[a]from Brooks (1959)
[b]from Indiana Department of Natural Resources

pelts annually. Many opossums are still recorded, but not as many as in the 1930s and 1940s, and minks have ranged from about 5,000 to about 30,000 per year. Reported catch of skunks and weasels has declined, whereas that of foxes was large earlier, then declined, but has again increased.

Food Habits

Getting enough food of the right kind is a prime requisite for sustaining life, and finding food occupies a good many of the waking hours of wild species. Green plants make their own food by capturing the sun's energy and combining it with carbon dioxide and water to form simple sugars, a process known as photosynthesis. Green plants (and a few other primitive forms) are the only organisms that can produce their own food, and are referred to by ecologists as producers (or autotrophic forms = self-feeding). All other organisms depend on this initial source, directly or indirectly, as a food supply, and are referred to as consumers. Primary consumers feed directly on producers, secondary consumers feed on primary consumers, and tertiary consumers feed on secondary consumers. As one considers the various mammals, however, it becomes obvious that most species function in more than one category, and the relationships rapidly become confused and complex.

Meadow voles, muskrats, and white-tailed deer feed almost entirely on green vegetation and thus are primary consumers. However, meadow voles sometimes eat insects (crickets, at least) and may also be considered, albeit marginally, as secondary consumers. One might think the mammals of the order Carnivora would fit neatly into the secondary and tertiary consumer levels. Such is not the case. The name Carnivora is a misnomer, for many or most of these species are strongly omnivorous. For example, foxes feed on corn and berries (and hence are considered primary consumers), on meadow voles (and thus are secondary consumers), and on short-tailed shrews (and are therefore tertiary consumers).

Among the most important factors influencing the food habits of any particular species of mammal are evolutionary adaptation, availability of food sources, and predilection. The various mammal species have carved out and adapted to ecological niches where they have managed to survive. Those that were unable to fit themselves into such niches have, of course, perished. In order to survive, a species must find a continuous means of obtaining food despite competition with other species for the available energy sources. If a species or group of organisms can make use of a group of foods not widely eaten by potential competitors, that species will have a considerable advantage. Such "specialization" may in turn lead that species to evolve in ways that enable it to make even more use of that group of foods. Voles, for example, are nearly strict herbivores and have evolved in such a manner as to better feed on cellulose, a principal component of green vegetation, which is, however, difficult to eat and to digest. Voles have developed rather complicated, greatly folded occlusal surfaces (for grinding) on ever-growing molariform teeth, and the caecum (corresponds to our appendix) has also undergone specialized development. The caecum in voles contains a microflora and secretions which aid in plant digestion. In weedy or grassy situations, these adaptations enable the voles to reign supreme, but their capabilities are severely limited in other habitats.

Other species have maintained themselves with less specialization and can eat more varied foods. Thus they maintain a different type of advantage. It is more likely that there will be something for them to eat at all times and in a greater variety of ecological situations.

Animals must select their foods from what is available to them. Hence, availability of potential food sources is another important factor influencing the food habits of mammal species. Potential foods are organisms—dead or alive; as a whole or in part—that are present, digestible, and of a size that can be handled (small enough to be subdued, if necessary) and consumed (large enough to make it worthwhile to eat in terms of energy gained). An item too high in a tree to be reached, or buried too deep in the ground to be dug out, is not available. Neither is a living organism that is too alert and watchful to be captured or too strong to be subdued.

Beyond this, if more than one type of food is available, predilection (likes and dislikes) and relative ease of obtaining the various foods may come into play. Many species (voles, the meadow jumping mouse, foxes) shift from their more standard foods and eat certain delectable items such as strawberries, blueberries, or blackberries when they become ripe.

Thus the foods eaten by various species differ, based primarily on adaptation, availability, and predilection. A major interest during our studies has been food habits research, since the food habits of Indiana mammals had not been well studied. The latter part of this section lists the various species by major food groups. Details for the various species will be found in the individual species accounts. Since the methods we have used in food habits research may be of interest to other researchers, we will outline them here.

Food Habits Research

The most direct and usually the most satisfactory approach to food habits research is simply to collect the animals and identify and estimate the amounts of various foods found in their stomachs. It is usually less satisfactory to examine fecal materials or contents of the intestines since digestion rates of various foods differ. Soft items tend to digest faster than hard ones and hence may occur in the animals' intestines in relatively lower proportions than they occur in the diet. This problem is less severe in bats, which feed almost entirely on flying insects. Essentially all flying insects contain the relatively indigestible substance chitin. However, we have examined stomachs rather than fecal material in our food habit studies of bats.

Another means of obtaining food habits information is by direct observation of the feeding animals. Yet another is by examining cuttings or other remains after a species has been feeding; an obvious problem with this method, however, is to identify the mammals involved. Also, one is much less well able to assess the relative importance of various foods in the diet by either of these methods.

Still another approach is to examine the food materials in cheek pouches (chipmunks, pocket gophers) or in caches of stored foods (chipmunks, red squirrels, deer mice, white-footed mice). It should be cautioned, however, that the foods in cheek pouches or in storage caches may not be the same as those being consumed at that time. The animals may be storing some foods for later use and eating perishable foods on a daily basis.

The mechanics of food habits analysis are intricate and time-consuming. The stomach contents of an animal being examined are emptied into a petri dish and mixed thoroughly with water. If the water becomes too cloudy, it may be necessary to wash the material one or more times by pouring off changes of water, being careful not to lose anything but suspended materials. The excess water should then be poured off, leaving only enough to barely cover the remaining materials. The materials are examined with a dissecting microscope, preferably a zoom type, of perhaps 10 to 70 power. A standard microscope may be used for more detailed examination of cellular structure. Identifications are made by comparing materials in the stomachs to materials found in the field. It is best to examine the stomachs soon after the animals are collected, so that the researcher can return to find materials in the field that he is unable to identify in stomachs. If one cannot examine the stomachs immediately, it is beneficial to make rather extensive collections of potential food items in the field and preserve them for future reference.

Collections of materials from the field at the time and place of collection of the mammals to be examined is probably the most beneficial and important part of food habits analysis and cannot be overemphasized. In food habits work, good keys and good reference collections of plants or animals are very important, and we constantly attempt to develop and improve them. However, when it comes to identifying an unknown material in the stomach there is no substitute for fresh materials from the specific place from which the animal was taken. There are many items included in keys and collections which are not found at the locality in question; these "extra" items can be quickly eliminated when fresh field materials are available for comparison and identification. Also, materials in stomachs are not always (or even any great percentage of the time) complete enough to be "keyed." Rather, one must compare them with "knowns," using whatever identifying characters one has. Often items have to be listed as "unidentified insect," or as "Coleoptera," or simply as "unidentified" when foods cannot be determined more precisely.

Once identifications have been determined, visual estimates of the percentage of each item in each stomach are made. The estimate will, of course, be 100 percent when only one item is present, but making the estimates becomes more complicated with increased numbers of kinds of foods. We usually begin by estimating the percentages for those items which occur in very large or very small amounts, and we proceed in this way until all food items have been estimated. We have tested this method with classes in mammalogy and then compared class results to volumes as measured by water displacement. We found that, even without previous experience, the students made reasonable estimates.

A standard form is used for recording data. Information concerning the collection of mammals is written at the top and numbers of individuals are listed down the left side. Food items are listed on slanted lines at the top. The values across the lines for each numbered individual should total 100 percent. The criticism can be made that since all stomachs do not have exactly the same amount of food in them the data are not strictly comparable. This is true; but if a stomach is less than half filled we do not record it. Otherwise, we treat the stomach as being full, assuming that minor differences will cancel out.

Once the data are tabulated, both the columns and the rows should give a grand total equalling 100 (100 percent of each stomach) times the number of stomachs examined. Data are summarized as percent volume and percent frequency. Percent volume provides an estimate of the amount of each food in the stomachs at the time and place of collection. Percent frequency is an estimate of the percentage of animals eating a particular food at that time and place. These data are then tabulated for each mammal (see tables in the various species accounts).

Food Consumer Types

Indiana mammals can be divided into several categories with respect to food habits.

Insectivorous Feeders. The most completely insectivorous species are the bats, and all feed almost entirely on flying insects. The kinds of insects most heavily consumed vary among species. The bats found in Indiana are little brown myotis, southeastern myotis, gray myotis, Keen's myotis, Indiana myotis, silver-haired bat, pipistrelle, big brown bat, evening bat, red bat, hoary bat, and big-eared bat.

The species of *Myotis* tend to feed on smaller insects, particularly Diptera, while *Pipistrellus* feeds heavily on homopterans (leafhoppers and froghoppers, particularly). *Eptesicus* eats many larger beetles, while the species of *Lasiurus* tend to feed heavily on adult moths, although *Lasiurus borealis* consumes a number of homopterans and beetles also. Thus, there is considerable food partitioning among bats.

Herbivorous (plant) Feeders. Another group with relatively homogeneous feeding habits includes the mammals which feed only on vegetative parts of plants, such as roots, stems, leaves, and (sometimes) seeds. Indiana mammals which are entirely or almost entirely herbivorous are the eastern cottontail, the swamp rabbit, the woodchuck, the pocket gopher, the beaver, the meadow vole, the prairie vole, the woodland vole, the muskrat, the bog lemming, and the white-tailed deer.

Many of these mammals have evolved morphological adaptations, such as highly modified grinding surfaces and rootless (evergrowing) teeth, to handle the cellulose of plant material. The kinds of plants consumed vary with mammal species, plant availability, and season. Many of these mammals feed on green vegetation when it is available, and on twigs, bark, or roots when it is not.

Invertebrate Feeders. Six species feed primarily on invertebrates other than insects, although all are in the order Insectivora. These are the masked shrew, the southeastern shrew, the least shrew, the short-tailed shrew, the eastern mole and the star-nosed mole. Of these, the largest shrew (*Blarina brevicauda*) and the two moles feed mostly on earthworms, and all may occasionally feed on vegetation. The short-tailed shrew often feeds on the fungus *Endogone*, while the eastern mole sometimes eats seeds (especially those of grasses).

Vertebrate Feeders. Only five Indiana mammals are primarily vertebrate feeders ("carnivorous"), despite the fact that ten species are in the order Carnivora. The five vertebrate feeders are the least weasel, the long-tailed weasel, the mink, the badger, and the bobcat.

Omnivorous Feeders. Some species tend to be more or less omnivorous, and most of these animals can be divided into three groups according to the types of foods they eat in greatest quantity.

The first group, the nut eaters, are all tree squirrels—the eastern chipmunk, the gray squirrel, the fox squirrel, the red squirrel, and the southern flying squirrel. All, especially the flying squirrel, also feed upon other foods, including generous amounts of insects. And all evidently consume some flesh and reportedly prey on birds.

The second group, the seed eaters, eat seeds and a great variety of other items, but especially various invertebrates. Members of this category are the thirteen-lined ground squirrel, Franklin's ground squirrel, the deer mouse, the white-footed mouse, the harvest mouse, the eastern woodrat (possibly more properly a herbivorous feeder), the meadow jumping mouse (also eats the fungus *Endogone*), and the house mouse. At least part of this group also eats some flesh.

The third group, the carnivorous feeders, all eat a great amount of plant material along with the animal foods. This category includes the coyote, the foxes, the raccoon, and the striped skunk.

Two Indiana mammals are not categorized above. Both feed on many types of food, including garbage, but because of their foraging habits neither can be classified beyond being "omnivorous." They are the Norway rat and the opossum.

Parasites and Other Associates

Most mammals host several species of parasites, and thus the study of parasites is an important part of ecological studies of mammals. Parasites are technically organisms living on or in a host and causing some degree of harm. It is easy to see how some parasites harm their hosts. For example, lice, ticks, fleas, and some mites insert their mouthparts into the host's body tissue and withdraw blood and other body fluids. They perhaps also cause the host discomfort. However, it is difficult to discern any degree of harm that other parasites cause to their hosts, and many of those species studied as "external parasites" are not really parasitic at all. In fact, since the host's body is the habitat of the parasite, there is a natural evolutionary tendency toward parasitic lifestyles that harm the host as little as possible. Parasites which kill their host or weaken it to the point that it does not reproduce are harming their own habitat—hence, their own existence. Natural selection operates against such conditions, and we see evidence for this trend away from parasitism and toward symbiosis when we study the natural parasites of mammals. Indeed, most naturally occurring parasites appear to do little harm to their hosts.

In many cases we do not know the type of host / "parasite" association. Some species (ticks, sucking lice, myobiid mites) are clearly parasitic. Many others are not. It would be difficult to show harm being caused to the host by many of the hair-clasping hypopi, which remain firmly attached to the host's pelage by means of a posterior ventral clasping organ. Hypopi are simply larval transport stages; they have no mouthparts, hence cannot feed. We know even less about the lifestyles of *Pygmephorus*, *Bakerdania*, *Macrocheles*, listrophorids, atopomelids, and labidocarpids. These mites may feed on dead skin or on other parasites in the pelage. It would be interesting to understand more fully the relationship between these forms and their "hosts."

The first step in understanding various host / parasite associations is to determine the presence and abundance of internal and external "parasites." During our work on Indiana mammals, we have routinely examined the digestive tracts and pelage of collected specimens for parasites and associated forms. We have attempted to identify only external forms. Unidentified endoparasites have here simply been listed as numbers of cestodes, trematodes, nematodes, acanthocephalans, and the like. We have included rather detailed parasite data in the species accounts and hope such information may be a welcome addition to the ecological study of Indiana mammals. We hope that these data and notes on processing parasites will introduce others to the very interesting and somewhat isolated ecological communities existing in and on mammals. Perhaps our efforts will also provide a basis for future work on parasite / host associations.

Other state mammal books contain little (if any) information on parasites. *Mammals of Wisconsin* (Jackson, 1961) and *Mammals of Louisiana* (Lowery, 1974) are notable exceptions, although even in these works parasite data are not original for those states. Probably one reason most authors do not gather such information is that it takes a great deal of effort and expertise to find, process, and identify parasites. In most cases, if the authors do not conduct this type of work themselves, it simply is not done.

Before our studies began, there was relatively little published information on the ectoparasites of Indiana mammals. The best single piece of research appeared in 1961 and was an excellent doctoral dissertation by Nixon A. Wilson. He summarized the known data on fleas, sucking lice, and ticks. We found few species in these groups not listed by Wilson, although we have collected additional information. We concentrated primarily on other ectoparasites, especially mites. A work on the external parasites of Indiana mammals, with figures and keys for parasite identification, is in progress.

Methods of Parasite Collection

During our fieldwork, mammal specimens, when collected, were immediately placed in individual plastic bags to keep parasites separate by host and to prevent their escape. We then used one or more of three methods for collecting ectoparasites: (1) direct examination of the hair and skin of the mammal specimen with a dissecting microscope; (2) washing the skin of the mammal in detergent; (3) dissolving the fur of the mammal in potassium hydroxide and centrifuging the fur / KOH mixture. Actual counts of parasites were made at this time when possible, but when counts could not be made, numbers were estimated. The parasites were then preserved in a solution of 75 percent ethanol and 5 percent glycerol.

The standard method employed in our data collection was that of direct examination of mammal specimens for parasites and other associates. The hair and skin of specimens were examined under a 10- to 70-power binocular dissecting microscope; dissecting

needles were used to manipulate the hair. This method, rather than simply brushing the hair of the specimen over white paper as is often done, allowed us to find many species—including several described as new—that we otherwise likely would not have found. This is true especially for many of the smaller mites which cling to individual hairs or embed their mouthparts in the skin. Once we located parasites or other associates, they were removed from the host with a dissecting needle dipped in alcohol, or with tiny forceps. Often the hair with attached parasite was removed.

The second method for collecting parasites was that of washing the skin of the animal in detergent. This technique is useful for mammals too large for direct examination with a dissecting microscope. The equipment needed for this method consists of a Buchner funnel and some filter papers, a filtering flask and a rubber stopper, a length of noncollapsible hose, an aspirator attached to a source of running water, some Alconox (or other detergent), and a container with lid. We placed the mammal specimen in a container of appropriate size (such as a pint container for a mouse or shrew, a quart for a chipmunk, a gallon for a squirrel) and filled the container three-fourths full with water. A small amount of detergent was then added to the container. (A pinch, about 0.1 gram per pint, is usually sufficient. Too much produced excess suds which clogged the filter paper. This was corrected by dilution with more water, transferring the solution to a larger container if necessary.) We capped the container and shook it vigorously for 30 seconds to a minute. The faucet was turned on and part or all of the liquid from the specimen was poured into the funnel. The vacuum draws the water through, leaving the parasites on the filter paper. The parasites were then examined under a dissecting microscope and were removed from the filter paper with a dissecting needle. Washing was repeated until parasites no longer appeared on the paper.

The third method of collecting ectoparasites was by dissolving the fur of the mammal in potassium hydroxide (see Hilton, 1970, for more details). The complete skin of each animal was placed in an individual container with about 500 ml of 5 percent KOH. After the skin soaked for 24 hours, all remaining

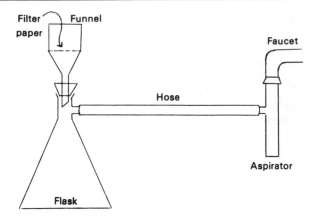

Apparatus used for washing technique for collecting of parasites. Equipment consists of Buchner funnel, filter paper, filtering flask, rubber stopper, length of noncollapsible hose, aspirator attached to a source of running water, Alconox (or other detergent), and a container with lid.

hair was scraped away with a metal spatula. The KOH and dissolved hair were heated 1 to 4 hours on a hot plate at about 95°C under a hood. The mixture was allowed to settle overnight. Excess KOH was decanted and the remaining mixture was centrifuged for 5 minutes at about 1,200 rpm. Again, excess KOH was decanted and enough zinc sulfate solution was added to almost fill the centrifuge tubes. The tubes were agitated until the pellet at the bottom was completely broken up and the sample was again centrifuged. The solution and parasites were decanted into petri dishes and examined with the dissecting microscope. Although we employed this method sparingly, we no longer recommend it. The parasites were too macerated to be of much value beyond counting. We found at least one form which appeared to be new, but the specimens were in too poor shape to be described.

Slides were made of the smaller parasites for microscopic study. Specimens were transferred from the alcohol preservative to Nesbitt's solution for clearing (five days to two weeks), then were mounted, ventral side up, on slides in Hoyer's solution and ringed with Euparal to prevent the Hoyer's from drying during permanent storage. (Nesbitt's solution is made with 80 gms chloral hydrate, 50 ml water, and 5 ml hydrochloric acid. Dissolve the ingredients and add a tiny amount of acid fuchsin to color the solution red. Hoyer's so-

lution is prepared with 50 gms distilled water, 30 gms gum arabic, 200 gms chloral hydrate, and 20 gms glycerine. Mix and dissolve the ingredients *in the above sequence* at room temperature; if incorrect sequence is used, the materials will not dissolve.)

Parasites and Their Hosts

The four major types of larger endoparasites are tapeworms (cestodes), flukes (trematodes), roundworms (nematodes), and spiny-headed worms (acanthocephalans). Most live as adults in the digestive tract, primarily in the small intestines of their hosts. Eggs generally pass out with the feces and must then be picked up by another mammalian host (in the case of nematodes and cestodes) or by a secondary host. Acanthocephalans are not common in Indiana mammals, and the only record we have is from one small area in Vigo County where infestations were common in meadow voles. Crickets are apparently major secondary hosts for this species of acanthocephalan, and traces of crickets were found in meadow voles at this locality. Flukes require a snail as an intermediate host; thus, as one would expect, the short-tailed shrew often harbors these parasites. Much more intriguing is the question of why bats are so commonly infested with flukes. They do not eat snails. Do they eat insects which have fed on snails? Are the larval flukes that emerge from snails in the water picked up by the bats when drinking?

A total of 206 species of ectoparasites has now been recorded from Indiana mammals. Detailed information on these ectoparasites is presented in the mammalian species accounts, and figures of and keys to the forms are being included in a separate publication on ectoparasites of Indiana mammals (Whitaker, in press). A summary of the numbers of species of ectoparasites known from Indiana mammals is given in Table 22. Sixty-seven of the species had been recorded previously, whereas 139 were taken for the first time from Indiana during these studies. A complete listing of the ectoparasites known from Indiana mammals is given in Appendix A.

Both sucking and biting lice live their entire lives on mammals. Their eggs (nits) are attached to hairs. Fleas and batbugs come onto the body of the mammal to feed on blood, but their eggs and larvae are found in the nests or habitat of the host. Ticks lie in wait for mammal hosts on vegetation; at the stimulation of warmth (body heat), they drop and presumably land on the host. They then take a prolonged blood meal and fall off. Several blood meals are taken during the lifetime of a tick. Ticks feed on hosts either as larvae (three pairs of legs) or as adults.

Chiggers are very familiar to Hoosiers, especially to those who pick wild blackberries. Chiggers are larval trombiculid mites, the adults of which are nonparasitic. Adults are the "large" (for mites) orange spider mites that we find crawling about on the ground. *Eutrombicula alfreddugesi* is the main chigger that attacks man, but we have found 20 species on wild mammals (see individual species accounts).

Last, among the mites proper, a number of

Table 22

Ectoparasites from Indiana Mammals

	Species taken during these studies	Species known from Indiana mammals	New state records	New species
Insects				
Fleas (Siphonaptera)	25	31	1	
Sucking lice (Anoplura)	15	17	3	
Biting lice (Mallophaga)	10	10	8	
Beetles (Coleoptera)	2	2	2	
Batbugs (Hemiptera)	1	1	1	
Ticks and Mites (Acarina)				
Ticks (Ixodoidea)	11	11	—	
Chigger mites (Trombiculidae)	20	20	19	
Other mites				
Ascidae	1	1	1	
Atopomelidae	1	1	1	
Cheyletidae	4	4	4	
Chirodiscidae	2	2	2	1
Chortoglyphidae	2	2	2	1
Glycyphagidae	12	12	12	4
Laelapidae	23	23	19	—
Listrophoridae	12	12	12	2
Macrochelidae	3	3	3	1
Macronyssidae	9	9	7	—
Myobiidae	18	18	18	4
Myocoptidae	4	4	4	—
Pygmephoridae	19	19	18	16
Spinturnicidae	3	3	1	—
Uropodidae	1	1	1	—
	198	206	139	29

families and genera of widely different behavior are represented. Only a few are discussed here. The largest, most easily found, and best studied are the laelapid and macronyssid mites, many of which have piercing sucking mouthparts and suck blood or other body juices. Listrophoroid mites are generally cigar-shaped and cling to individual hairs by modified legs or mouthparts. Glycyphagid mites (*Dermacarus* and allies) are very abundant but, in common with the listrophorids, are seldom collected because of their small size and their habit of clinging to hairs. They occur on mammals as immature forms (hypopi). Adult glycyphagids are generally found in the nest of the host.

The new species that have been or are being described based on material collected during the present studies are listed in Appendix B.

Taxonomy

In our treatment of Indiana mammals, we have chosen to ignore subspecies. Whitaker (1970a) has written his views on the current subspecies concept, which stresses morphology. We feel that until a more purely biological concept is adopted for the determination and naming of subspecies their inclusion here would add little to our work.

There are two native species with type localities in Indiana, the Indiana myotis *(Myotis sodalis)* and the prairie vole *(Microtus ochrogaster)*. The former was described by Miller and Allen (1928), who designated Big Wyandotte Cave (Crawford County) as the type locality. There was long doubt as to where the specimens from which the prairie vole was described originated, but Bole and Moulthrop (1942) fixed the type locality at New Harmony (Posey County).

In the synonymy of each species, we have listed all scientific names known by us to have been applied by authors writing about those species in Indiana. It is readily apparent that some names have changed many times. And changes are still being made by taxonomists. We hope our synonymies will be useful to persons who study and write about Indiana mammals in the future.

The keys that follow should help one to identify the species of Indiana mammals discussed in this book, although determinations of some may be quite difficult (the separation of certain species of bats, shrews, or voles). The task is easier if one has both the skin and the skull for reference. We have prepared a key to be used in the identification of entire animals and another for determining skulls only.

KEY TO WHOLE ANIMALS OR
STUDY SKINS

1   Front limbs modified as wings; thin interfemoral membrane (uropatagium) connecting hind limbs and tail (Fig. 1) . . . Order CHIROPTERA 2

    No wings; uropatagium absent or not as described above . 13

2   Interfemoral membrane with hairs above, either completely or on basal half... 3

    Interfemoral membrane without hairs above 5

3   Interfemoral membrane with hairs on basal half; body color dark chocolate or blackish, with few silvery tipped hairs dorsally . . . Silver-haired Bat *(Lasionycteris noctivagans)*

    Interfemoral membrane with hairs above; body coloration much paler, reddish or rich brown and grayish mixed 4

4   Forearm more than 45 mm; dorsal hairs rich brown with tips obviously "frosted" with white . . . Hoary Bat *(Lasiurus cinereus)*

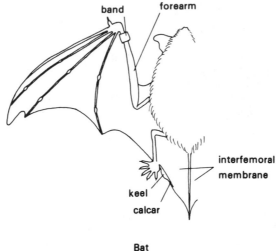

Bat

Fig. 1

Forearm less than 45 mm; body color usually brick red or yellowish red; dorsal hairs lightly frosted or unfrosted . . . Red Bat *(Lasiurus borealis)*

5   Small, reddish bat (forearm 35 mm or less), with tricolored dorsal hairs (dark at base, pale in intermediate portion, dark tips); *or* brownish bat with very large ears (more than 30 mm long)   6

Brownish or grayish bat; dorsal hairs not tricolor (or indistinctly so), ears much less than 30 mm long   7

6   Small, reddish, with tricolor hair on back . . . Eastern Pipistrelle *(Pipistrellus subflavus)*

Brownish, ears more than 30 mm long . . . Rafinesque's Big-eared Bat *(Plecotus rafinesquii)*

7   Forearm more than 41 mm long   8

Forearm not more than 41 mm long, usually shorter   9

8   Dorsal hairs uniform gray (sometimes brownish) from base to tips . . . Gray Myotis *(Myotis grisescens)*

Dorsal hairs dark at base, brown at tips . . . Big Brown Bat *(Eptesicus fuscus)*

9   Tragus about 9 mm long, pointed, somewhat sickle-shaped (Fig. 2) . . . Keen's Myotis *(Myotis keenii)*

Tragus 4 to 7 mm long, rounded at tip (Figs. 3, 4)   10

10   Tragus about 4 to 5 mm long, blunt and curved (Fig. 3); membranes, ears, and nose black (only one upper incisor on each side) . . . Evening Bat *(Nycticeius humeralis)*

Tragus about 6 to 7 mm long, not curved (Fig. 4); membranes, ears and nose not black   11

11   Calcar well keeled (Fig. 1), not easily seen in dried specimens; dorsal hair dull, dark pinkish gray or (rarely) brownish, some dorsal hairs may be faintly tricolor . . . Indiana Myotis *(Myotis sodalis)*

Calcar not keeled, or indistinctly so; dorsal hairs not tricolor, body some shade of brown, or grayish   12

tragus quite long,
pointed tip

Keen's Myotis
Fig. 2

short
blunt
tragus

Evening Bat
Fig. 3

tragus relatively long,
rounded tip

Little Brown Myotis
Fig. 4

12   Ventral hairs white-tipped; dorsal hairs appear woolly . . .
      Southeastern Myotis (*Myotis austroriparius*)
          Ventral hairs not white-tipped, but color varies consid-
      erably in this species; dorsal fur not woolly . . . Little Brown
      Myotis (*Myotis lucifugus*)

13   Toes terminating in hooves . . . Order ARTIODACTYLA . . .
      White-tailed Deer (*Odocoileus virginianus*)
          Toes terminating in claws   14

14   Innermost toe of hind foot thumblike and without claw;
      female with abdominal pouch; ears thin and naked; tail
      round, naked, black at base, whitish on terminal half or more;
      fur grayish . . . Order MARSUPIALIA . . . Virginia Opossum
      (*Didelphis virginiana*)
          Not as above   15

15   Always five clawed toes on front foot (first toe sometimes re-
      duced, high on inside of foot, and not touching ground when
      animal walks)   16
          Usually only four well-clawed toes on front foot (thumb
      may be present as small knob with nail); if five, then tail
      either naked and much flattened (laterally or dorsoventrally)
      or a short cottony tuft   31

16   Length of head and body less than 115 mm, or if more than
      115 (in some moles) no ears visible and belly not white . . .
      Order INSECTIVORA   17
          Length of head and body more than 115 mm, ears visible . .
      Order CARNIVORA   22

17   Forefeet greatly developed for burrowing, more than twice as
      wide as hind feet and turned outward; eyes not visible . . .
      Moles   18
          Forefeet less than twice as wide as hind feet and not turned
      outward; eyes small but visible . . . Shrews   19

18   Tail more than 60 mm; 22 fleshy tentacles on snout . . . Star-
      nosed Mole (*Condylura cristata*)
          Tail short, generally not more than 45 mm; snout lacking
      tentacles . . . Eastern Mole (*Scalopus aquaticus*)

19   Tail generally less than 28 mm and about 20 percent or less of
      the total length   20
          Tail generally 27 mm or more and about 30 to 40 percent of
      the total length . . . *Sorex*   21

20   Color gray; total length 95 mm or more . . . Short-tailed Shrew
      (*Blarina brevicauda*)

Color brownish; total length less than 95 mm . . . Least Shrew (*Cryptotis parva*)

21   Tail shorter, about 32 to 38 percent of total length; longest hairs at end of tail when unworn about 2 to 3 mm . . . Southeastern Shrew (*Sorex longirostris*)

Tail longer, about 35 to 46 percent of total length; longest hairs at end of tail when unworn about 4.5 to 6 mm . . . Masked Shrew (*Sorex cinereus*)

22   Tail bushy and ringed, or else animal catlike with very short tail (shorter than hind foot)   23

Not as above   24

23   Tail bushy and ringed; face with black mask . . . Raccoon (*Procyon lotor*)

Animal catlike with very short tail (less than length of hind foot); cheek and throat hair tuft present . . . Bobcat (*Felis rufus*)

24   Animal doglike . . . Canidae   25

Animal not doglike   27

25   Size large, adult weight more than 20 pounds . . . Coyote (*Canis latrans*)

Size smaller, weight less than 20 pounds   26

26   General color reddish; tail tip white . . . Red Fox (*Vulpes vulpes*)

General color grayish; tail tip black . . . Gray Fox (*Urocyon cinereoargenteus*)

27   Color black and white, or else grayish brown with a white longitudinal stripe on forehead   28

Color brown, often with a black tail tip, or color sometimes white in winter   29

28   Color black and white, or occasionally solid black or nearly so . . . Striped Skunk (*Mephitis mephitis*)

Color grayish brown with a white longitudinal stripe on forehead . . . Badger (*Taxidea taxus*)

29   Tail black tipped . . . Long-tailed Weasel (*Mustela frenata*)

Tail not black tipped   30

30   Size small, less than 300 mm total length; tail about 1 inch long . . . Least Weasel (*Mustela nivalis*)

Size large, more than 300 mm total length; tail much more than 1 inch long . . . Mink (*Mustela vison*)

31   Ear longer than tail; hind foot with four claws covered with fur; soles of feet completely covered with dense fur; tail forming a cottony tuft . . . Order LAGOMORPHA   32

Ear shorter than tail; hind foot with five well clawed toes; soles of feet not completely covered with dense fur; tail not a cottony tuft . . . Order RODENTIA   33

32   Nape rich cinnamon; hind foot about 90 mm; dorsum of hind foot white . . . Eastern Cottontail (*Sylvilagus floridanus*)

Nape not rich cinnamon; hind foot about 105 mm; dorsum of hind foot brown . . . Swamp Rabbit (*Sylvilagus aquaticus*)

33   Tail horizontally flattened, well furred or scaly   34

Tail not flattened   42

34   Tail flat, broad, and scaly; hind feet well webbed . . . Beaver (*Castor canadensis*)

Tail densely furred; hind feet not webbed   35

35 Tail short, less than one-fourth of total length; animals large, averaging 6 to 8 pounds . . . Woodchuck *(Marmota monax)*
  Tail more than half total length; animals smaller, weighing less than 4 pounds 36

36 Furred patagium present between front and hind legs, or else obvious stripes on dorsum 37
  No patagium, no dorsal stripes 39

37 Furred patagium between front and hind legs . . . Southern Flying Squirrel *(Glaucomys volans)*
  No patagium 38

38 One pair of pale dorsolateral stripes . . . Eastern Chipmunk *(Tamias striatus)*
  Several pale dorsal stripes . . . Thirteen-lined Ground Squirrel *(Spermophilus tridecemlineatus)*

39 Tail with relatively small amount of hair; ears relatively small; dorsal pattern of obscure spotting . . . Franklin's Ground Squirrel *(Spermophilus franklinii)*
  Not as above; tail very bushy 40

40 Total length less than 400 mm . . . Red Squirrel *(Tamiasciurus hudsonicus)*
  Total length more than 400 mm 41

41 Tail hairs yellow tipped . . . Fox Squirrel *(Sciurus niger)*
  Tail hairs silvery tipped . . . Gray Squirrel *(Sciurus carolinensis)*

42 Hind legs very long and tail at least one and one-third times as long as head and body . . . Meadow Jumping Mouse *(Zapus hudsonius)*
  Tail shorter... 43

43 Prominent fur-lined external cheek pouches . . . Plains Pocket Gopher *(Geomys bursarius)*
  No external cheek pouches 44

44 Tail short, less than one-third the length of head and body; ears small 45
  Tail longer than one-third the length of the head and body 48

45 Tail very short, about the length of the hind foot 46
  Tail longer 47

46 Hairs very fine . . . Woodland Vole *(Microtus pinetorum)*
  Hairs grizzled . . . Southern Bog Lemming *(Synaptomys cooperi)*

47 Belly hairs silvery; tail usually more than twice the length of the hind foot . . . Meadow Vole *(Microtus pennsylvanicus)*
  Belly hairs usually buff colored; tail usually about twice the length of the hind foot . . . Prairie Vole *(Microtus ochrogaster)*

48 Animal at least 285 mm in total length; tail naked and laterally compressed . . . Muskrat *(Ondatra zibethicus)*
  Animal smaller; tail not flattened dorsoventrally.......... 49

49 Belly gray or brown; tail scaly and sparsely furred 50
  Belly usually white (sometimes buffy in *Reithrodontomys*); tail furred 51

50 Total length less than 250 mm; tail less than 110 mm . . . House Mouse *(Mus musculus)*
  Total length more than 250 mm; tail more than 110 mm . . . Norway Rat *(Rattus norvegicus)*

51   Size large, more than 250 mm total length . . . Eastern Wood-rat *(Neotoma floridana)*

        Size smaller, less than 220 mm total length   52

52   Eyes small; hind feet usually less than 17 mm; incisors grooved . . . Western Harvest Mouse *(Reithrodontomys megalotis)*

        Eyes prominent; hind feet usually 17 mm or more; incisors not grooved   53

53   Hind foot usually 17 or 18 mm; tail usually much less than one-half total length . . . Deer Mouse *(Peromyscus maniculatus)*

        Hind foot usually 19 mm or more; tail usually just under one-half of the total length . . . White-footed Mouse *(Peromyscus leucopus)*

KEY TO THE SKULLS

1   Prominent, sharp-pointed canine teeth present in upper and lower jaws (Fig. 5)   2

        Canines absent, or if present, not noticeably differing from adjacent teeth (in *Condylura* the third upper incisor looks like a canine, but canines are in the maxillary bones, incisors are in the premaxilla)   25

2   Five incisors above and four below on each side . . . Virginia Opossum *(Didelphis virginiana)*

        Incisors never more than three per side, above or below . .   3

3   Premaxillary bones and their corresponding upper incisors separated in front by a distinct gap (Fig. 6); one or two incisors per side   4

        Premaxillary bones confluent, thus upper incisors forming a continuous row between the canines   15

4   One incisor on each side of upper jaw   5

        Two incisors on each side of upper jaw   7

5   Five upper molariform teeth, the first reduced in size and behind the canine in lateral view (Fig. 7); skull short and squarish   6

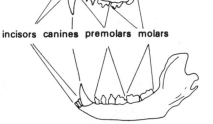

incisors canines premolars molars

Raccoon

Fig. 5

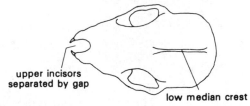

upper incisors separated by gap

low median crest

Bat

Fig. 6

Four upper molariform teeth, none reduced . . . Evening Bat *(Nycticeius humeralis)*

6   Skull short, less than 15 mm total length . . . Red Bat *(Lasiurus borealis)*

Skull longer, more than 15 mm total length . . . Hoary Bat *(Lasiurus cinereus)*

7   Four upper molariform teeth on each side, all about the same size (Fig. 8) . . . Big Brown Bat *(Eptesicus fuscus)*

Five or six upper molariform teeth on each side, the first one or two reduced in size (Figs. 9, 10) thus appearing as a gap in the toothrow, between the canines and the larger posterior molariform teeth   8

8   Five upper molariform teeth, the first one reduced in size (Fig. 9)   9

Six upper molariform teeth, the first two reduced (Fig. 10) . . . *Myotis* (it is very difficult to separate skulls of this genus)   11

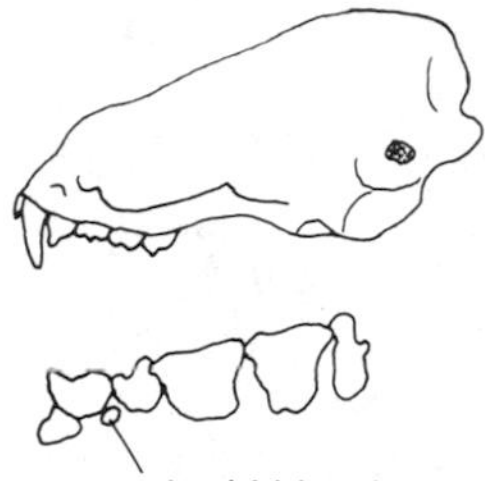

premolar hidden from
lateral view

Red Bat
Fig. 7

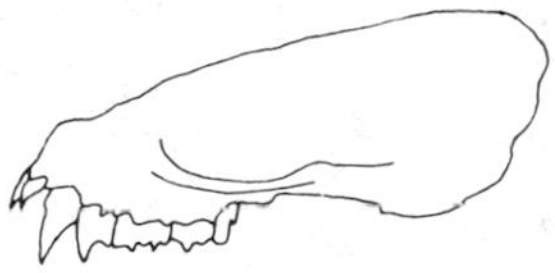

no small premolar immediately
behind canine

Big Brown Bat
Fig. 8

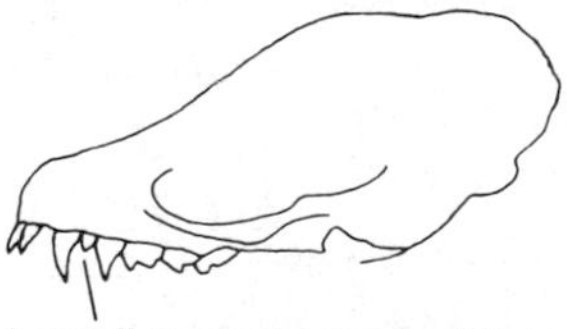

1 small premolar immediately
behind canine

Eastern Pipistrelle
Fig. 9

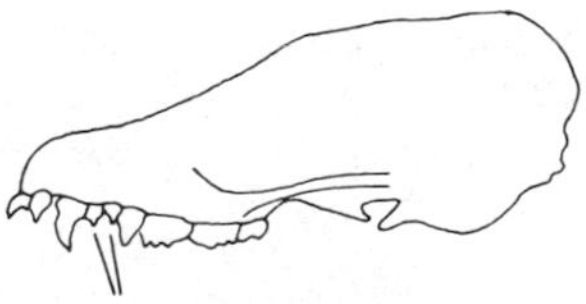

2 small premolars immediately
behind canine

Little Brown Myotis
Fig. 10

9   Skull about 15 mm in length; dorsal aspect of skull very convex or "humped"; auditory bullae very large; an accessory cusp on first molar . . . Rafinesque's Big-eared Bat *(Plecotus rafinesquii)*

Skull not humped, or else less than 14 mm long; no accessory cusp   10

10   Skull very flat or concave dorsally as viewed from side . . . Silver-haired Bat *(Lasionycteris noctivagans)*

Skull very small, less than 14 mm in length and convex in lateral view . . . Eastern Pipistrelle *(Pipistrellus subflavus)*

11   Least width of interorbital constriction 4 mm or more   12

Least width of interorbital constriction less than 4 mm ...   14

12   Total length of skull usually 15.7 mm or more . . . Gray Myotis
      (*Myotis grisescens*)
          Total length of skull less than 15.7 mm   13
13   Skull with low median crest (Fig. 6) . . . Southeastern Myotis
      (*Myotis austroriparius*)
          Skull lacking median crest . . . Little Brown Myotis (*Myotis
      lucifugus*)
14   Skull lacking median crest; length from front of canine to
      back of last molar greater than width across molars in upper
      jaw . . . Keen's Myotis (*Myotis keenii*)
          Skull with median crest; length from front of canine to back
      of last molar less than width across molars . . . Indiana myotis
      (*Myotis sodalis*)
15   Six upper and six or seven lower molariform teeth   16
          Usually four upper (three in bobcat) and less than six lower
      molariform teeth   19
16   Posterior end of hard palate ending far beyond posterior
      molariform teeth; six lower molariform teeth (Fig. 5) . . . Rac-
      coon (*Procyon lotor*)
          Posterior end of hard palate ending at about level of
      posterior molariform teeth; seven lower molariform teeth . . .   17
17   Postorbital processes thickened, convex dorsally; basal length
      of skull more than 147 mm . . . Coyote (*Canis latrans*) . . . (the
      skull may be smaller, but the domestic dog also keys out
      here; it has a relatively shorter, broader rostrum. Measure the
      inside distance between the two anterior premolars, and di-
      vide this into the length of the molariform toothrow. In a
      coyote this ratio will generally be more than 3.66, in a dog it
      will generally be less than 3.00, and in a coyote-dog hybrid it
      will generally be 3.0 to 3.5)
          Postorbital process thin, concave dorsally; skull smaller . .   18
18   Sagittal ridges U-shaped (Fig. 11); posterior end of lower jaw
      with distinct notch . . . Gray Fox (*Urocyon cinereoargenteus*)
          Sagittal ridges V-shaped (Fig. 12); posterior end of lower
      jaw without notch . . . Red Fox (*Vulpes vulpes*)

notch

no notch

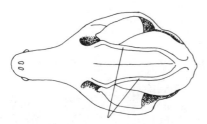

U-shaped ridges

Gray Fox
Fig. 11

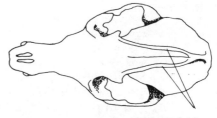

V-shaped ridges

Red Fox
Fig.12

19   Skull short with smoothly rounded braincase; no sagittal
      crest; three or four upper molariform teeth   20
          Skull elongate, differently shaped and with a sagittal crest
      in adults; four or five upper molariform teeth   21
20   Three upper molariform teeth . . . Bobcat *(Felis rufus)*
          Four upper molariform teeth . . . Domestic Cat *(Felis catus)*
21   Palate not extending appreciably beyond last upper
      molariform teeth (Fig. 13); top of skull as viewed from side
      forming an angle of about 60° . . . Striped Skunk *(Mephitis*
      mephitis)
          Palate extends appreciably beyond posterior edge of last
      molariform teeth (Fig. 14)   22

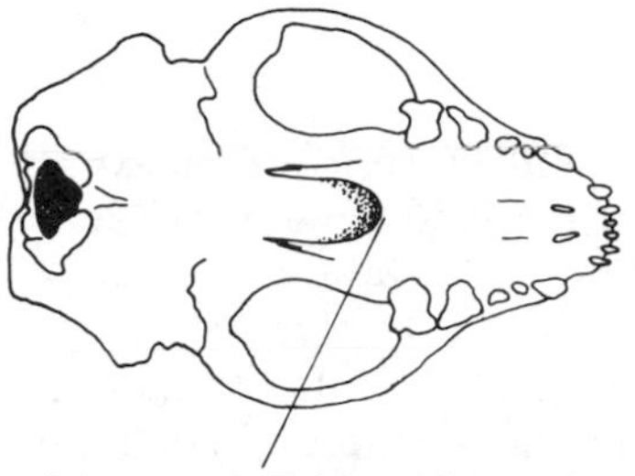

palate extends little past last molar

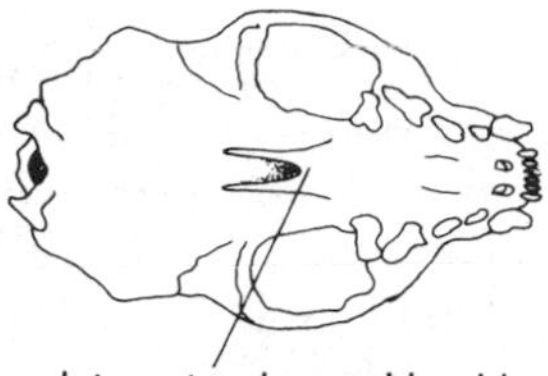

palate extends considerably
past last molar

Striped Skunk   Mink
Fig. 13   Fig. 14

22   Braincase triangular (Fig. 15); skull more than 90 mm long;
      last molar with triangular grinding surface . . . Badger
      (Taxidea taxus)
          Braincase elongate (Fig. 14); skull less than 90 mm long;
      last molar with dumbbell-shaped grinding surface   23
23   Total length of skull more than 55 mm . . . Mink *(Mustela*
      vison)
          Total length of skull less than 55 mm   24
24   Total length of skull less than 33 mm . . . Least Weasel
      (Mustela nivalis)
          Total length of skull more than 33 mm . . . Long-tailed
      Weasel *(Mustela frenata)*
25   Upper incisors absent; orbits forming a bony ring; antlers
      present in males . . . White-tailed Deer *(Odocoileus vir-*
      ginianus)
          Upper incisors present; orbits not forming a bony ring ...   26
26   Large prominent chisel-shaped upper incisors separated from
      molariform teeth by wide diastema (Fig. 16); never more than
      eight teeth on each side of upper jaw   32
          Incisors not as above; no diastema; nine to eleven teeth on
      each side of upper jaw...................................   27
27   Teeth white; zygomatic arch (Fig. 15) complete (but often
      broken)   28
          Teeth with chestnut-colored tips; zygomatic arches absent   29
28   Third upper tooth resembling a canine; premaxillaries ex-
      tending well forward of the narial aperture (Fig. 17); eleven
      teeth above on each side . . . Star-nosed Mole *(Condylura*
      cristata)

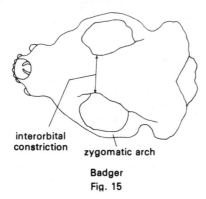

interorbital
constriction   zygomatic arch

Badger
Fig. 15

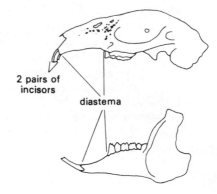

2 pairs of
incisors

diastema

Eastern Cottontail
Fig. 16

Third upper tooth not resembling a canine; premaxillaries not extending well forward of the narial aperture (Fig. 18); ten teeth above on each side . . . Eastern Mole *(Scalopus aquaticus)*

29   Either four unicuspids present (Fig. 19), or the lateral edge of the braincase ending in a sharp angle (Fig. 20)   30
      Five unicuspids present; no such angle, braincase rounded   31

30   Five unicuspids present, the fifth hidden behind a projection of the fourth (Fig. 20); braincase edge ending in a sharp angle . . . Short-tailed Shrew *(Blarina brevicauda)*

      Four unicuspids (Fig. 19); braincase edge rounded . . . Least Shrew *(Cryptotis parva)*

31   Rostrum long and narrow (Fig. 21); third unicuspid not smaller than fourth; inner ridge of upper unicuspids with pigment . . . Masked Shrew *(Sorex cinereus)*

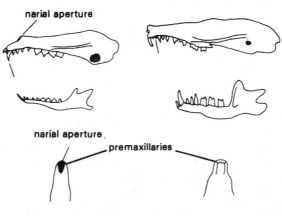

narial aperture

narial aperture   premaxillaries

3rd tooth like canine;   3rd tooth not like canine;
2nd upper tooth minute   2nd and 3rd upper teeth
and often lost in cleaned   small and equal in size
skull

Star-nosed Mole   **Eastern Mole**

Fig. 17   **Fig. 18**

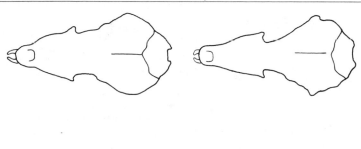

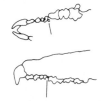

3 unicuspids visible in lateral
view

5th unicuspid often hidden in
lateral view

Least Shrew
Fig. 19

Short-tailed Shrew
Fig. 20

Rostrum short, wider; third unicuspid often smaller than fourth (Fig. 22); inner ridge of upper unicuspids lacking pigment . . . Southeastern Shrew *(Sorex longirostris)*

32   Two pairs of upper incisors, a small pair directly behind the larger pair (Fig. 16); lateral rostral area with perforations ..   33
        One pair of upper incisors; lateral portions of rostrum solid bone   34

33   Posterior extension of postorbital process connected to braincase for most of its length (Fig. 23), leaving no opening (or if opening present, tiny and not much more than 1 mm in length); anterior palatine foramina extending posteriorly not quite to the level of the first pair of molariform teeth . . . Swamp Rabbit *(Sylvilagus aquaticus)*

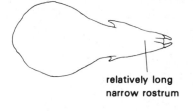

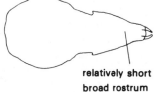

relatively long
narrow rostrum

relatively short
broad rostrum

3rd and 4th unicuspids about
equal size

3rd unicuspid usually smaller
than 4th

Masked Shrew
Fig. 21

Southeastern Shrew
Fig. 22

postorbital process fused to braincase

postorbital process not fused to braincase

Swamp Rabbit
Fig. 23

Eastern Cottontail
Fig. 24

Posterior extension of postorbital process not connected to braincase (Fig. 24), or separated by a larger fenestra; anterior palatine foramina extending posteriorly to just beyond the level of the anterior edge of the first molariform teeth . . . Eastern Cottontail *(Sylvilagus floridanus)*

34   More than three upper molariform teeth per side   35
     Three upper molariform teeth per side   45
35   Skull with prominent postorbital processes (Fig. 25)   36
     Skull lacking prominent postorbital processes   43
36   Incisors white; top of skull flat; postorbital processes at right angles to skull . . . Woodchuck *(Marmota monax)*
     Incisors orange or yellow; top of skull rounded; postorbital process not at right angle to skull   37
37   Infraorbital opening a foramen (opening through a thin plate) rather than a canal; four upper molariform teeth . . . Eastern Chipmunk *(Tamias striatus)*
     Infraorbital opening (Fig. 26) a canal (opening through a thick plate)   38
38   Skull large, about 60 mm   39
     Skull smaller, no larger than about 54 mm   40
39   Four upper molariform teeth, none minute . . . Fox Squirrel *(Sciurus niger)*
     Five upper molariform teeth, the first minute (less than one-half width of second) . . . Gray Squirrel *(Sciurus carolinensis)*
40   Five upper molariform teeth, three posterior ones largest, the first small (but not minute, more than half the width of second); anterior portion of zygomatic arch bent out and downward, forming a relatively flat plate; distance from tip of rostrum to posterior edge of this plate is about 48 to 52 percent of total length of the skull   41

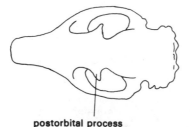

postorbital process
Woodchuck
Fig. 25

infraorbital opening

Deer Mouse
Fig. 26

Four or five upper molariform teeth, if five, the first small to minute; anterior portion of zygomatic arch more vertically positioned; distance from tip of snout to posterior edge of zygomatic plate is less than one-half total length of skull, usually less than 45 percent 42

41   Length of skull about 50 to 60 mm . . . Franklin's Ground Squirrel (*Spermophilus franklinii*)

       Length of skull about 40 to 45 mm . . . Thirteen-lined Ground Squirrel (*Spermophilus tridecemlineatus*)

42   Total length of skull about 43 to 49 mm; four large molariform teeth, but a tiny premolar is sometimes present anterior to these; notch over orbit absent or not well developed . . . Red Squirrel (*Tamiasciurus hudsonicus*)

       Total length of skull less than 38 mm; four large molariform teeth preceded by a small premolar; smoothly rounded notch over orbit . . . Southern Flying Squirrel (*Glaucomys volans*)

43   Skull very large, more than 70 mm long; incisors not grooved . . . Beaver (*Castor canadensis*)

       Skull smaller, less than 70 mm; incisors grooved 44

44   Infraorbital opening large; skull less than 35 mm long . . . Meadow Jumping Mouse (*Zapus hudsonius*) (Fig. 33)

       Infraorbital opening tiny; skull more than 35 mm long . . . Plains Pocket Gopher (*Geomys bursarius*) (Fig. 34)

45   Molariform teeth with three longitudinal rows of cusps (Fig. 27).. 46

       Molariform teeth with two rows of cusps (Fig. 28), or with loops and triangles (Figs. 29, 30) rather than cusps 47

46   Skull rounded and less than 25 mm long . . . House Mouse (*Mus musculus*)

       Skull flat above and more than 25 mm long . . . Norway Rat (*Rattus norvegicus*)

47   Cheek teeth usually with cusps, teeth rooted 48

       Cheek teeth with loops and triangles, teeth usually rootless 49

48   Upper incisors grooved (Fig. 31) . . . Western Harvest Mouse (*Reithrodontomys megalotis*)

       Upper incisors not grooved 49

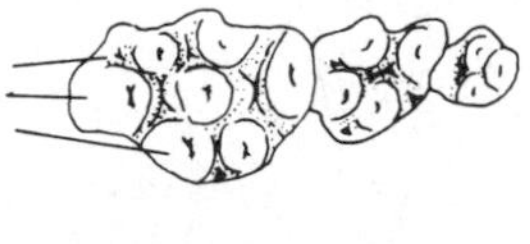

3 longitudinal rows of cusps
House Mouse
Fig. 27

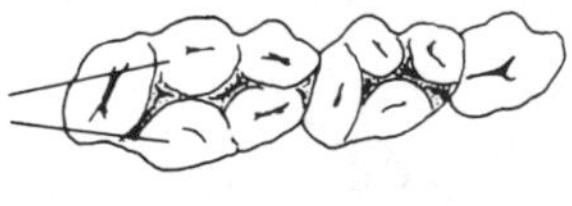

2 longitudinal rows of cusps
Deer Mouse
Fig. 28

at least 3 triangles between anterior and posterior loops of last molar
Meadow Vole
Fig. 29

1 or 2 triangles between anterior and posterior loops of last molar
Prairie Vole
Fig. 30

49   Skull large, more than 35 mm; molars with prismatic pattern
      resembling rootless teeth . . . Eastern Woodrat *(Neotoma
      floridana)*
            Skull smaller, less than 35 mm; molars with cusps   50
50   Skulls of these two species are very similar; we have found
      no good characters that work for Indiana material . . . White-
      footed Mouse *(Peromyscus leucopus)* and Deer Mouse
      (Peromyscus maniculatus)
51   Basal length of skull more than 50 mm . . . Muskrat *(Ondatra
      zibethicus)*
            Basal length of skull less than 40 mm   52
52   Incisors with faint longitudinal groove (Fig. 32), outer and
      inner angles of molariform teeth acute . . . Southern Bog
      Lemming *(Synaptomys cooperi)*
            Incisors lacking grooves, angles of molariform teeth
      rounded   53
53   Third upper molariform teeth with four triangles between the
      anterior and posterior loops (Fig. 29) . . . Meadow Vole *(Mic-
      rotus pennsylvanicus)*
            Third upper molariform teeth with two (sometimes one in
      Microtus ochrogaster) triangles between the anterior and
      posterior loops (Fig. 30)   54
54   Squamosal width (Fig. 35) divided by total length usually less
      than 0.49; foramen above ear opening more than 3 mm long
      . . . Prairie Vole *(Microtus ochrogaster)*
            Squamosal width divided by total length usually more than
      0.49; foramen above ear opening less than 3 mm long . . .
      Woodland Vole *(Microtus pinetorum)*

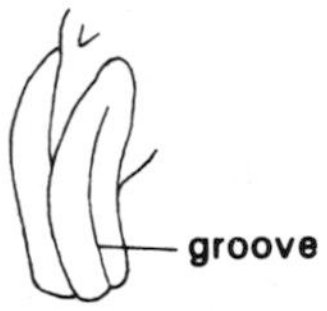

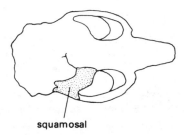

Western Harvest Mouse
Fig. 31

Southern Bog Lemming
Fig. 32

Meadow Jumping Mouse
Fig. 33

Plains Pocket Gopher
Fig. 34

squamosal
Fig. 35

Order MARSUPIALIA

Family Didelphidae

Virginia Opossum
Didelphis virginiana Kerr

Common Opossum, Opossum, 'Possum

Didelphys virginiana: Wied, 1839
Didelphis marsupialis: Mumford and Handley, 1956
Didelphis virginiana: Plummer, 1844

DESCRIPTION. The opossum is pale colored (usually gray), medium sized (about the size of a domestic cat), and has a long, nearly naked, scaly, prehensile tail. The large, dark eyes are conspicuous in the white to pale grayish face. The prominent, naked, leathery looking ears are black with pale tips (the tips sometimes are missing due to frostbite). The snout is long and pointed. The five toes on the front feet bear claws; the hind feet have four claw-bearing toes and an opposable toe without a claw. Females have a fur-lined pouch for carrying the young. Inside the pouch are usually 13 teats (in a circle or a U), but the number varies from 9 to 17.

An opossum skull can be immediately distinguished from that of all other Indiana mammals by its greater number of incisors (five on each side above and four below), its small braincase, and its high, thin sagittal crest. The dental formula is

$$\text{I } \frac{5}{4} \text{ C } \frac{1}{1} \text{ P } \frac{3}{3} \text{ M } \frac{4}{4} = 50.$$

The coloration of the opossum ranges from nearly white, through various shades of gray, to nearly black. We have noted specimens from Indiana that exhibited all shades of color in that range. A specimen in the Joseph Moore Museum (Earlham College) is an albino that had pink eyes.

We have tabulated measurements and weights of Indiana opossums more than 555 mm in total length (Table 23). Lindsay (1960) reported the capture of a large male weighing 5.4 kg. This animal had a large skull measuring 141 mm in total length. We examined a skull that measured 142 mm in total length, recovered from a carcass in Clay County. These may be near maximum size for the species, for Hall and Kelson (1959) gave 139 mm as the greatest length of skull of North American opossum specimens.

STATUS AND DISTRIBUTION. Of 4,640 mammals identified from skeletal remains found at the Angel Mounds archaeological site (Vanderburgh County), 67 were opossums, which appear "to have been relatively important at this site" (Adams, 1950). The earliest recorded observation of the opossum in Indiana seems to be that of Father Hennepin (1683), who accompanied La Salle across northern Indiana in December 1679. Hennepin described La Salle's return to camp at the St. Joseph–Kankakee river portage after a night's absence: "He had two animals of the size of muskrats, hanging from

Table 23

Weights and measurements of
Didelphis virginiana from Indiana

	Males	Females
Total length(mm)		
n	75	51
x̄	739.6	691.61
range	559-964	562-797
SD	93.3	58.9
SE	10.8	8.4
Tail length (mm)		
n	76	50
x̄	284.5	264.5
range	206-394	234-320
SD	46.4	35.6
SE	5.3	5.0
Hind foot (mm)		
n	76	51
x̄	66.8	60.75
range	52-79	54-69
SD	7.8	4.6
SE	0.9	0.6
Weight (grams)		
n	58	32
x̄	2839.13	1990.0
range	418-5556	576-3515
SD	1475	809.7
SE	193.7	143.1

his belt . . . which he had killed with blows of a stick, without these little animals taking flight, and which often let themselves hang by the tail from branches of trees, and . . . they were very fat." *La Salle at the Portage,* a widely acclaimed mural in the St. Joseph County Courthouse (South Bend), depicts the famous explorer with two opossums hanging at his waist (Engels, 1933).

Wied (1839-41) reported the presence of the opossum at New Harmony (Posey County) in the winter of 1832–33. Plummer (1844) considered the species "rare" in Wayne County. It was plentiful in Noble County and abundant in Miami County until the severe winter of 1854–55, which decimated populations in these and other Indiana counties. The following winter, opossums were greatly decreased in Howard County, where they had formerly been abundant. W. B. Van Gorder saw none in Noble County from that winter until 1900 (Hahn, 1909). Opossums were reportedly rare in some counties (Jasper, Newton) of northwestern

Indiana from 1869 to 1880 but their numbers increased later (Butler, 1895). Dinwiddie (1884) noted: "Some few opossums have been killed in Lake County, but they were probably stragglers from counties farther south." For some reason, there was a noticeable increase of opossums in several places during the winter of 1892–93. Numbers were reported in St. Joseph County, the species was "unusually abundant" in Hendricks County, one killed in Huntington County was noteworthy for that northern locality, and opossums were more abundant in Franklin County. The general trend before about 1900 appears to be one of periodic fluctuation, especially in northern Indiana. Perhaps the opossum invaded the northern portion of the state several times, being decimated between invasions by extremely cold winters.

The trend in southern Indiana is more difficult to evaluate, because the species was no doubt common (and fluctuated much less) throughout that region. About 1859, the species must have been abundant in Knox County, for one evening after butchering hogs the Chansler family killed eight opossums in the dooryard before bedtime (E. J. Chansler). In the fall of 1890, seven were captured in one night near Rockville (Parke County). B. W. Evermann noted that many were brought to market at Terre Haute (Vigo County) each winter. Locally, there appear to have been some declines, however, possibly due to the extensive logging that took place shortly before 1900. For example, Cox (1893) reported the opossum as "Formerly common, but now very rare" in Randolph County, further noting that "a few are killed each year." In Knox County the species was "becoming rare" in 1894, according to E. J. Chansler. And Hahn (1909) made the comment that opossums were not so abundant in southern Indiana as formerly.

Lyon (1936) listed reports of the opossum from almost every Indiana county, but made no comment on abundance.

Today, the opossum is evidently common throughout Indiana, but more abundant in the southern half. Charles M. Kirkpatrick trapped seven opossums at his residence in the city of West Lafayette (Tippecanoe County) in the fall of 1952. In 1957, 79 percent of the opossums bought in the state by fur dealers were from southern Indiana

(Brooks, 1959). It is difficult to draw conclusions from the numbers of animals bought by fur dealers for various years, for fur prices have fluctuated greatly. For instance, dealers bought 378,968 opossum skins in the state in 1934 and only 3,430 in 1957. We have examined specimens from 63 counties (Map 7).

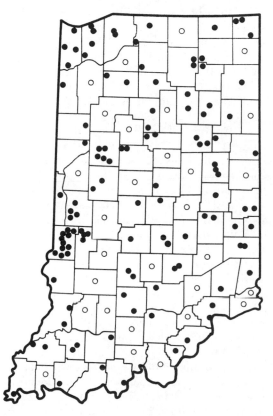

Map 7.   The Virginia Opossum, *Didelphis virginiana*, in Indiana

HABITAT.   Although wooded areas are favored, the opossum occupies a variety of habitats in wooded, brushy, and semiopen country, especially along fencerows, ditches, streams, and roads. Tracks in the soft mud reveal that it spends considerable time along watercourses. It lives in burrows constructed by woodchucks and other mammals or in drainage tiles along ditch banks. Individuals take up residence in and beneath buildings. Opossums often are found in cities, where they appear to prosper.

ASSOCIATED SPECIES.   Many other species of Indiana mammals occupy the same habitats with opossums. Schmeltz and Whit-

aker (1977) gathered information on the use of woodchuck burrows by other mammals (Vigo County) and captured twenty opossums at the entrances of these burrows. Raccoons, gray and red foxes, striped skunks, eastern cottontails, white-footed mice, and deer mice were also taken, in addition to woodchucks. Hahn (1908b), in writing about the opossum in Lawrence County, stated that "Most often it seems to use a woodchuck hole for its home."

HABITS.   Although it is mostly nocturnal, the opossum is often abroad by day. It does not hibernate, but in the fall becomes quite fat, which allows it to remain inactive for varying periods during inclement weather. Tracks in the snow and observations of individuals out of their dens at temperatures of 0°F reveal that the species may emerge even on inclement days. We have examined several Indiana specimens that lacked the tips of their ears or tails; the tips had apparently been lost to frostbite.

Opossums den or nest under brush piles or other debris, in burrows, hollow logs, trees and stumps, or drainage tiles. They also take shelter in buildings, caves, and even in garbage cans. They may not be regular visitors to caverns, for Hahn, who intensively studied the caves in what is now Spring Mill State Park, wrote, "I never saw tracks or other signs of the opossum in the caves" (Hahn, 1908b). There are records of opossum remains from several Indiana caves; however, these could have been carried there by other animals. Nests are constructed of dry leaves, grasses, corn husks, or similar materials. Nesting material is carried in a loop of the prehensile tail, after being gathered by mouth and passed to the tail.

The opossum is well adapted to an arboreal life and evidently does considerable climbing to obtain food or to reach dens. It can hang by its tail, and the tail also provides a useful "fifth hand." The usual walking gait is a slow waddle, but when sufficiently frightened the opossum can cover the ground in leaping bounds (Dellinger, 1951). Animals found on the ground can often be captured by hand, but a frightened individual may expose the teeth, hiss, and exude saliva. Feigning death (playing possum) is a rather common behavior of *Didelphis virginiana*. Sometimes, when cornered, it will "play dead" by lying

Virginia opossum, juvenile. Photo by J. Hill Hamon

immobile on its side and letting its tongue hang out. Even when handled, the animal may retain this posture. After the disturbance has passed, the opossum resumes its normal activities. Such passive display in the face of danger would appear ineffective, but it evidently serves the purpose for this species. Dellinger (1951) reported that large opossums, when cornered on the ground by dogs, will fight. Other raccoon hunters have told us that opossums confronted by dogs may open the mouth and hiss, but the opossums are quickly dispatched. Francq (1969) described feigned death as a brief nervous shock accompanied by a slowed heartbeat. Dellinger found an opossum, caught only by the tail, dead in a steel trap; since the animal appeared otherwise uninjured, perhaps shock was a factor contributing to death.

The swimming ability of the opossum has been reported upon by several authors, who have noted that it can even swim considerable distances under water. Gwilym S. Jones made the following observations on an Indiana opossum he released from a live trap. The animal entered a lake without hesitation and swam across (an estimated 310 feet). On the surface, it used a "dog-paddle" stroke, but a good portion (not measured) of the swim was under water. The opossum did not stop to rest, and upon emerging shook itself in the manner of a dog.

FOOD. The omnivorous diet of the opossum is characterized by its indiscriminate feeding upon fruits, such as persimmon and apples, animal matter of all kinds, including carrion (Hahn, 1909), and garbage, and its attraction to live traps baited with corn, apples, hickory nuts, and sunflower seeds. One specimen examined by Nixon A. Wilson had only grasshoppers in the stomach. The legendary fondness of the opossum for persimmons has been referred to at least twice in the literature on Indiana mammals. Plummer (1844), noting that the opossum was rare in Wayne County, wrote that "his favorite food, the persimmon, is not found in the county." Butler (1895), in discussing early Knox County, wrote: "In those days, in that land of the persimmon, the edges of the prairies were the places where, in the fall and winter, the two were found together— the persimmon and the opossum." Evermann and Clark (1911) noted that opossums "are also fond of pawpaws" and eat mussels.

Whitaker, Jones, and Goff (1977) reported upon foods in the stomachs of 83 Indiana opossums (Table 24). As in previous studies, a great variety of food items (71) were found. Mammal remains totaled 22.2 percent, birds 21.3, amphibians (mostly Fowler's toad) 2.2, reptiles (turtle) 0.1, and unidentified flesh 1.8 percent of total food volume. Carrion constituted 4.9 percent of the volume, and it is likely that much of the vertebrate remains listed as bird and mammal was carrion. Insects amounted to 11.7 percent of the food volume, and other invertebrates totaled 13.6 percent. The only important individual item in the latter category was earthworms (10.9 percent of the volume), which were eaten by 34.9 percent of the opossums examined. This was the third most abundant food, after birds and unidentified vegetation. A total of 19 percent of the overall volume was plants, 2 percent of which were cultivated (corn, wheat, sorghum). A food was considered garbage when obvious items used by humans (wrapping paper, etc.) were present with it in the stomachs, but many items in other categories could also have been scavenged from dumps, garbage pails, and the like.

REPRODUCTION. The gestation period of the opossum is only about 12 to 13 days and the young are poorly developed at birth. The young find their way into the female's pouch, where they remain for several weeks. Ten females carrying pouch young which we were able to count completely had from 1 to 13 (average 6.7) young each. These, and three other females with young not completely counted in the pouch, were all examined from March through July (Table 25). Evermann and Clark (1911) reported capturing a female with young still in the pouch on 3 September in Marshall County. Mumford captured and confined a female with 8 pouch young on 1 March, at which time the largest young was 15 mm long (in its natural, suckling position). On 6 March it was noted that this young was 18 mm and that 4 of the litter were larger than the others. The largest young was 21 mm long on 11 March and 30 mm in length on 18 March. By this latter date, the young were moving about more than formerly as they were examined. Joseph

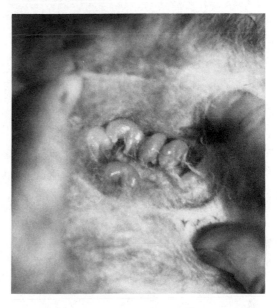

Virginia opossum, pouch young. Photo by Larry Roop

Table 24

Foods eaten by *Didelphis virginiana* (n = 83) from Indiana
(from Whitaker, Jones, and Goff, 1977)

Food Item	Percent Volume	Percent Frequency
Mammal (total 22.2% volume)		
Mammal (unidentified)	4.2	8.4
Blarina brevicauda (short-tailed shrew)	3.8	4.8
Microtus ochrogaster (prairie vole)	2.7	3.6
Didelphis virginiana (opossum)	2.5	3.6
Tamias striatus (eastern chipmunk)	2.2	2.4
Sylvilagus floridanus (eastern cottontail)	2.1	2.4
Microtus pennsylvanicus (meadow vole)	1.5	2.4
Sciurus niger (fox squirrel)	1.2	1.2
Peromyscus sp.	0.9	1.2
Peromyscus maniculatus (deer mouse)	0.7	1.2
Mus musculus (house mouse)	0.2	1.2
Cryptotis parva (least shrew)	0.2	3.6
Bird (total 21.3% volume)		
Bird (unidentified)	15.4	22.9
Colinus virginianus (bobwhite)	2.4	2.4
Turdus migratorius (American robin)	1.9	2.4
Domestic chicken	1.3	2.4
Colaptes auritus (common flicker)	0.3	2.4
Other Vertebrates (total 9.0% volume)		
Carrion	4.9	8.4
Bufo woodhousei (Fowler's toad)	2.1	6.0
Flesh (unidentified)	1.8	6.0
Turtle	0.1	1.2
Salamander	0.1	1.2

Table 24 continued

Food Item	Percent Volume	Percent Frequency
Insects (total 11.7% volume)		
Carabidae (ground beetle)	2.8	10.8
Acrididae (grasshopper)	2.7	8.4
Gryllidae (cricket)	1.9	14.5
Lepidopterous larvae (caterpillar)	1.2	13.3
Pentatomidae (stinkbug)	0.5	4.8
Gryllacrididae (mole cricket)	0.4	1.2
Tettigoniidae (long-horned grasshopper)	0.4	2.4
Scarabaeidae (scarab beetle)	0.2	3.6
Muscoid fly	0.2	2.4
Tipulid larvae (crane fly)	0.2	3.6
Scarabaeid larvae (scarab beetle)	0.2	1.2
Lampyrid larvae (firefly)	0.1	2.4
Lygaeidae (chinch bug)	0.1	1.2
Coleoptera	0.1	1.2
Diptera	0.1	1.2
Coleopterous larvae	0.1	3.6
Hemiptera	0.1	1.2
Acalypterate Diptera	0.1	1.2
Tabanid larvae	0.1	1.2
Tenebrionidae (darkling beetle)	0.1	1.2
Alleculidae (comb-clawed bark beetle)	trace	1.2
Chauliognathus larva	trace	1.2
Nitidulidae (nitidulid beetle)	trace	1.2
Formicidae (ant)	trace	1.2
Staphylinidae (rove beetle)	trace	1.2
Other Invertebrates (total 13.6% volume)		
Annelida (earthworms)	10.9	34.9
Gastropoda (snails & slugs)	0.8	
Decapoda (crayfish)	0.7	2.4
Invertebrates	0.6	6.0
Isopoda (sowbug)	0.5	3.6
Araneae (spider)	0.1	2.4
Vegetation (total 19.0% volume)		
Vegetation (unidentified)	13.4	47.0
Wheat seeds	1.2	2.4
Dead leaves	1.1	1.2
Apple	1.1	3.6
Physalis sp. (fruit)	0.8	6.0
Corn	0.4	2.4
Sorghum	0.4	1.2
Grass seeds	0.2	3.6
Phytolacca americana (pokeweed)	0.2	1.2
Seeds (unidentified)	0.2	1.2
Chenopodium (pigweed) seeds	0.1	1.2
Prunus serotina (black cherry) seeds	trace	1.2
Ambrosia trifida (ragweed) seeds	trace	1.2
Moss	trace	1.2
Garbage	3.1	6.0
Unidentified material	trace	1.2
	99.9	

Table 25

Reproductive information from *Didelphis virginiana* from Indiana

Month	Number examined	Number females with pouch young	Number of young in those counted	Adult Males		
				Number examined	Testis Size (mm) Average Length	Width
Jan.	1	0	—	6	22.8	13.3
Feb.	5	0	—	10	19.9	12.4
March	3	2	5, 8	7	20.3	13.0
April	4	3	10, 13	2	25.0	13.0
May	4	4	7, 4, 4	3	22.7	13.6
June	2	2	10, 1	0	—	—
July	4	2	8, 4	1	14.0	10.0
Aug.	1	0	—	1	14.0	12.0
Sept.	4	0	—	6	18.8	13.0
Oct.	1	0	—	4	16.8	12.0
Nov.	1	0	—	4	19.9	12.4
Dec.	1	0	—	3	24.3	17.3

(1975) reported a female carrying 9 pouch young, of which 2 were estimated to be about 66 days old and the rest about 42 days old. He wondered whether the young represented two litters or delayed implantation.

We have examined immatures from twenty litters; these specimens were taken from 4 April to 18 October. At least 5 young, found with a female killed on 4 April, ranged from 40 to 45 mm in total length. But the smallest young (23 mm total length and weighing 1 gram) were from the pouch of a female killed 28 May. The largest (total length 480 mm) was taken 22 July, while the specimen taken latest in the year (18 October) was only 366 mm long. It is obvious that litters are not produced at any particular time, but are born over a relatively long period from early spring into summer.

We have no records of females with litters in their nests. Most of our information has accumulated through the examination of females with young killed on roads. Nine young were flushed from a burning brush pile in early May. After the young leave the female's pouch, they accompany her for another period of several weeks. Females and their litters evidently remain together for about three months. Females probably produce two litters per year. Evermann and Clark (1911) reported the capture on about 1 October of an adult with 12 young. The young were "about two-thirds as large as rats." During the first night in captivity the adult killed 9 of them. These authors wrote, "Devouring its young in captivity seems to be a common habit of the Opossum, and almost everyone who has tried to keep them together has had the young destroyed by the mother."

Testis sizes for 47 males collected in each month of the year except June were analyzed (see Table 25). Throughout most of the year, testis length averaged between 18 and 23 mm. Only a single specimen each was collected in July and August and each had testes 14 mm long; it is possible that both were immature animals. We need additional data on adult males collected from June through August to complete the picture of testis size throughout the year.

PARASITES. Wilson (1961) examined 21 opossums and 4 additional collections of opossum parasites from Indiana for sucking lice, fleas, and ticks. He found no lice, but among the fleas were 1 *Cediopsylla simplex*, 7 *Ctenocephalides felis*, and 1 *Orchopeas howardii*. Ticks consisted of 11 *Dermacentor variabilis* and 2 *Ixodes cookei*. Whitaker and Corthum (1967) took a specimen of the flea *Orchopeas leucopus* from 1 of 13 Indiana opossums, and the hypopial mite *Marsupialichus brasiliensis* was recorded by Fain and Whitaker (1973).

Whitaker, Jones, and Goff (1977) reported on ectoparasites from 66 Indiana opossums (Table 26). The major forms found were 4

Table 26

Ectoparasites and other associates of *Didelphis virginiana* (n = 66) from Indiana
(from Whitaker, Jones, and Goff, 1977)

	Parasites		Hosts Parasitized	
Parasites	Total	Average	Total	Percent
Fleas (Siphonaptera)				
Ctenocephalides felis	147	2.23	17	25.8
Orchopeas leucopus	6	.09	6	9.1
Ctenocephalides canis	3	.05	2	3.0
Orchopeas howardii	2	.03	1	1.5
Ctenophthalmus pseudagyrtes	1	.02	1	1.5
Chaetopsylla lotoris	1	.02	1	1.5
Biting Lice (Mallophaga)				
Trichodectes octomaculatus	1	.02	1	1.5
Mites (Acarina) other than chiggers				
Marsupialichus brasiliensis	16,920	256.36	17	25.8
Archemyobia inexpectatus	4,436	67.21	19	28.8
Ornithonyssus wernecki	1,138	17.24	26	39.4
Didelphilichus serrifer	903	13.68	21	31.8
Zibethacarus ondatrae	259	3.92	3	4.5
Androlaelaps fahrenholzi	9	.14	6	9.1
Listrophorus dozieri	5	.08	2	3.0
Anoetidae	3	.05	1	1.5
Laelaps multispinosa	2	.03	1	1.5
Macrocheles sp.	2	.03	1	1.5
Haemogamasus reidi	1	.02	1	1.5
Androlaelaps casalis	1	.02	1	1.5
Lophuromyopus sp.	1	.02	1	1.5
Ornithonyssus sylviarum	1	.02	1	1.5
Ornithonyssus bacoti	1	.02	1	1.5
Chigger Mites (Trombiculidae)				
Neotrombicula whartoni	137	2.08	14	21.2
Eutrombicula alfreddugesi	2	.03	1	1.5
Ticks (Ixodides)				
Ixodes cookei	4	.06	2	3.0
Dermacentor variabilis	1	.02	1	1.5

mites (*Marsupialichus brasiliensis, Archemyobia inexpectatus, Ornithonyssus wernecki, Didelphilichus serrifer*), a chigger (*Neotrombicula whartoni*), and the cat flea (*Ctenocephalides felis*). Of these, *Archemyobia inexpectatus* (Myobiidae) and *Ornithonyssus wernecki* (Macronyssidae), common parasites on North American *Didelphis*, occurred in large numbers. As noted above, *Marsupialichus brasiliensis* had previously been reported from Indiana opossums. However, there is some question as to whether it is specifically distinct from *Marsupialichus marsupialis*, described by Fain,

DeCock, and Lukoschus (1972) from Surinam (South America). Pence (1973) identified hypopi from Louisiana opossums as *M. marsupialis*. The hypopi of *M. marsupialis* and *M. brasiliensis* differ only in minor characteristics, and preserved material from Indiana and Louisiana may represent a single species rather than two. A third species (*Marsupialis andretti*) from the opossum also is involved. The life stages of these three forms require further study before final conclusions can be drawn regarding their identity at the species level.

The only previous description and record

of *Didelphilichus serrifer* (Listrophoridae) was from *Didelphis azarae* from Brazil (Fain, 1970); thus the report of Whitaker, Jones, and Goff (1977) constitutes a new mite record for North America and a new host record for *D. virginiana*.

Although a variety of fleas was found, the cat flea *(Ctenocephalides felis)* was the only one of regular occurrence. Seven of nine fleas found by Wilson (1961) on Indiana opossums were this species, which occurs primarily on domestic cats and dogs. The few dated records in the literature indicate that this flea may be present on opossums mostly in winter, for most records are for September to March. Our data support this hypothesis. The 13 opossums collected from April to August had a total of 7 fleas of this species (0.53 per opossum), while 140 fleas were found on 53 opossums taken from September through March (2.64 per opossum) (Chi-square = 20.74, 1 df). The fact that *C. felis* is the only flea of regular occurrence on the opossum probably reflects the close affinity of the opossum with man and his domesticated animals.

Few ticks were found and they represented the two species previously reported on opossums from Indiana.

The rather large number of species of parasites taken, including a few normally considered to be host-specific on other mammals, probably reflects the food habits of the opossum. It eats a great variety of foods, and much as carrion. We suspect that parasites are more likely to move from a dead, cold carcass than from a warm, fresh one to a predator feeding on the original host. Thus, a carrion feeder might be expected to carry a higher number of parasites. During our laboratory studies of dead mammals, we have often observed that host parasites have moved to the tips of the hairs when the host has become cold. We believe this tendency helps explain the occurrence on *Didelphis* of some of the more host-specific forms such as *Zibethacarus ondatrae*, *Listrophorus dozieri*, and *Laelaps multispinosus* (normally on muskrats), *Ornithonyssus sylviarum* (normally on chickens), *Trichodectes octomaculatus* (normally on raccoons), and *Androlaelaps casalis*, *Orchopeas howardii*, and *Haemogamasus reidi* (normally on squirrels).

The presence of these species probably indicates that the opossum had recently fed on the respective hosts. That two of the three opossums that harbored *Zibethacarus ondatrae* were also the only ones found to host *Listrophorus dozieri* further supports this idea. Only one opossum harbored *Orchopeas howardii*, but the same animal was the only one that hosted *Haemogamasus reidi*.

The most comprehensive study of *Didelphis virginiana* ectoparasites is that of Morlan (1952), who examined 349 opossums from Georgia. He found major parasites to be the fleas *Echidnophaga gallinacea* (322 individuals), *Ctenocephalides felis* (615), *Orchopeas howardii* (80), and *Polygenis gwyni* (501), the mites *Androlaelaps fahrenholzi* (222), *Ornithonyssus bacoti* (206), and *O. wernecki* (195), the tick *Dermacentor variabilis* (411), and the chigger *Eutrombicula splendens* (196). Smaller numbers of other parasites were also reported.

Internal parasites that we collected from the digestive tracts of 60 Indiana opossums included more than 4,500 nematodes, 1 trematode, and 17 cestodes, none of which has been identified to species. Of the 60 specimens examined, 56 (93.3 percent) carried nematodes in their stomachs and intestines. Joseph (1974b) described a new protozoan, *Eimeria indianensis*, from 2 of 15 Indiana opossums he examined. He also reported a few oocysts of *Isospora* sp. from one.

DECIMATING FACTORS. Motor vehicles and domestic dogs probably are the most important causes of mortality in Indiana opossums. Kase (1946a) and Mangus (1950) found opossum remains in 3 of 211 and 1 of 80 red fox stomachs, respectively. We have identified opossum remains in 1 of 14 red fox, 1 of 8 coyote, 1 of 41 raccoon, and 3 of 83 opossum stomachs examined. The latter is probably a case of cannibalism through feeding on carrion. As noted earlier, severe winters are evidently a factor in determining opossum populations in northern Indiana; after the extremely cold winter of 1976-77, persons in that part of the state remarked on the decrease in opossums. On 13 April 1978, after an extremely severe winter, Steven D. Ford live-trapped an opossum that exhibited considerable damage attributed to frostbite. The toes of all four feet were represented only by bone; all softer portions were missing. And part of the tail tip was gone.

TAXONOMY. The subspecies in Indiana is *Didelphis virginiana virginiana* Kerr.

SELECTED REFERENCES. Fitch and Sandidge, 1953; Francq, 1969; W. Hamilton, 1958a, 1958b; Hartman 1920, 1923, 1928; Joseph, 1974a, 1974b; Lay, 1942; Reynolds, 1945, 1952; Sandidge, 1953; Stuewer, 1943b; Taube, 1947; Whitaker, Jones, and Goff, 1977; Wiseman and Hendrickson, 1950.

Order **INSECTIVORA**

Family **Soricidae**

Masked Shrew
Sorex cinereus Kerr

Common Shrew, Long-tailed Shrew,
Ohio Shrew, Cinereous Shrew

Amphisorex lesueurii: Duvernoy, 1842
Blarina platyrhinus: Butler, 1892b
Sorex personatus: Merriam, 1895a
Sorex longirostris: Hollister, 1911b
Sorex cinereus: Jackson, 1928

DESCRIPTION. The masked shrew and the southeastern shrew *(Sorex longirostris)* are the smallest Indiana mammals. Both are long-tailed, with long pointed snouts and tiny beady eyes. The ears are small and nearly concealed in the fur, which is fine, soft, and dense. Coloration and measurements of the masked shrew and the southeastern shrew are similar. The southeastern shrew, however, is usually reddish brown above, while the masked shrew is grayer (and less reddish) above and tends toward blackish in some populations in winter. Both have pale, silvery colored undersides. The masked shrew tends to have a longer, more haired tail. The two species are best separated by skull characteristics. Both have five unicuspids, the posteriormost (fifth) being much reduced in size. In the southeastern shrew, the third unicuspid is usually smaller than the fourth. The rostrum of the southeastern shrew is shorter and broader than that of the masked shrew (see Figs. 21, 22). In all shrews, the

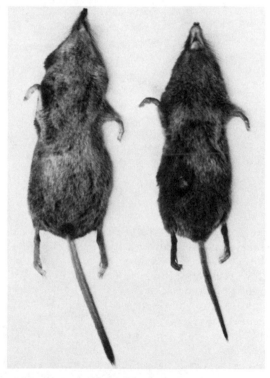

Masked shrew and southeastern shrew. Note the longer and more hairy tail of the masked shrew (left). Photo by Anthony Brentlinger, ISU AV Center

zygomatic arches are incomplete and auditory bullae are absent.

Table 27

Weights and measurements of
Sorex cinereus from Indiana

	Males	Females
Total length (mm)		
n	36	43
x̄	88.3	87.6
range	74-109	70-103
SD	7.5	7.3
SE	1.3	1.1
Tail length (mm)		
n	36	43
x̄	33	34
range	25-38	28-39
SD	2.8	2.43
SE	0.5	0.4
Hind foot (mm)		
n	36	42
x̄	11.2	11.4
range	9-13	10-12
SD	0.7	0.7
SE	0.1	0.1
Weight (grams)		
n	34	39
x̄	3.8	3.5
range	2.4-7.8	2.6-5.3
SD	1.01	1.00
SE	0.2	0.1

Weights and measurements are shown in Table 27. The dental formula is

$$I \frac{3}{1} \ C \frac{1}{1} \ P \frac{3}{1} \ M \frac{3}{3} \ = \ 32.$$

STATUS AND DISTRIBUTION. *Amphisorex lesueurii*, described by Duvernoy (1842) from the Wabash River Valley, Indiana (probably New Harmony, Posey County), is evidently the first record of the masked shrew from the state. Although the type of Duvernoy's *A. lesueurii* is lost, his colored plate of the specimen appears to represent *Sorex cinereus*. Butler (1892b) next mentioned the species (from Wabash County) and Hahn (1909) added a record from Cass County. But the masked shrew remained little known and was represented from Indiana by only a few specimens until Engels (1931) reported the taking of 11 specimens in St. Joseph County. Engels wrote:

While trapping about fifteen miles south of Notre Dame during the first week of March, 1931, I caught 11 specimens of *Sorex cinereus cinereus*. During this period the same line yielded but five other small mammals, two *Microtus pennsylvanicus pennsylvanicus* and three *Peromyscus leucopus noveboracensis*. The total absence of *Blarina* was especially noticed, since in trapping elsewhere about the county last year I found the short-tailed shrews so numerous as to be pests, as far as collecting was concerned. But the catch of the long-tailed shrew is interesting in itself, in view of the apparent scarcity of this mammal in Indiana. Hahn (Mammals of Indiana, 1909) noted that through several years collecting in the state he had never taken a single long-tailed shrew. I trapped rather extensively in the vicinity of Notre Dame from March to November in 1930 without success as far as this species was concerned. There are but five published records of *Sorex cinereus cinereus* from Indiana, four from Porter County, taken by Dr. Marcus Ward Lyon, Jr., and one from New Harmony.

Lyon (1936) wrote that it was "apparently a rare animal in Indiana" and knew of specimens from only six counties. With increased and more extensive collecting in the late 1940s and during the 1950s, additional masked shrews were taken from various parts of the state. During this period, for example, Lindsay (1958) collected a dozen in Ripley County.

We consider the masked shrew in Indiana to be common in good habitat, especially in the northern part of the state, although its distribution is spotty, reflecting the distribution of suitable habitat. In good habitats we have often trapped from 6 to 15 in a few days. In twenty days' trapping (using a combination of cans and snap-traps) in and around Cowles and Pinhook bogs, we easily took 112 masked shrews, and Ford (1975) took 178 in two summers' trapping in northwestern Indiana. More extensive (and intensive) trapping with pitfall traps is greatly altering our present notion of abundance and distribution of this species. Pitfall trapping by Thomas W. French (in press) for *Sorex* in Vigo County from 1976 through 1979 has resulted in the capture of 161 additional individuals. At present this species seems to be fairly rare over the southern half of the state. We have examined specimens from 39 counties (Map 8).

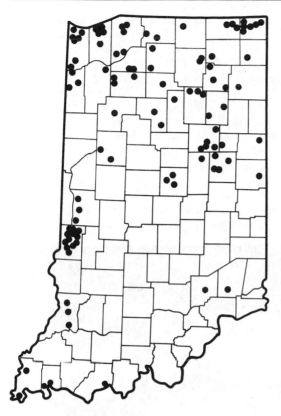

Map 8. The Masked Shrew, *Sorex cinereus,*
in Indiana

Compared to the number of house mice, white-footed mice, deer mice, prairie voles, and meadow voles taken per 100 trap-nights, the catch of masked shrews is very low. The size of this shrew may render it less vulnerable to regular snap-traps. We have noticed that if the trapline is left in place for several days (during which few or no masked shrews may be taken), the catch of this species frequently increases over the next few days. We cannot explain this phenomenon.

HABITAT. Masked shrews seem to favor moist habitats with fairly dense ground cover. Lyon (1924) published the following habitat notes:

Two specimens from Porter County caught in mouse traps baited with bacon placed in the quaking bog at the south end of the tamarack swamp opposite Mineral Springs station of the Chicago, Lake Shore and South Bend Railway. They were taken in the last week of October, 1923. The vegetation where the traps were placed consisted of tall rushes, sphagnum, cranberries, pitcher plants, etc.

The bog is very wet and when standing in it one's feet are always in an inch or more of water. Traps placed in the drier adjacent wooded swamp yielded only northern white-footed mice. Several specimens of this mouse were also taken in the line of traps which caught the shrews.

The shrews trapped by Engels "were collected in two weeks in a little used pasture bordering a creek, and in rank, damp grass along the foot of a low ridge on the opposite side." Engels also noted, "In three weeks of collecting in a drained tamarack swamp west of Sousley Lake, near the LaPorte County line, one shrew was taken. Mr. Phil Trexler collected one close to the bank of a small creek near State line."

Lindsay (1958) described the habitat where he captured 12 *S. cinereus ohionensis* in Ripley County:

Nine of these shrews were caught in runways along the edge of a well-rotted white oak log (*Quercus alba*) in a hydromesophytic forest in which the larger trees have been cut in logging operations. . . . Woody vegetation consists chiefly of red oak (*Q. rubra*), pin oak (*Q. palustris*), red maple (*Acer rubrum*), sweet gum (*Liquidambar styraciflua*), black gum (*Nyssa sylvatica*), white oak (*Q. alba*) and poison ivy (*Rhus radicans*). The leaf mold of the forest floor is irregularly distributed in depth. In the lowest areas it has been so completely decomposed that very little, if any, is present, while in slightly elevated regions, especially near logs and brush, a considerable quantity has accumulated. The runways of the shrews may be found in this leaf mold. The remaining specimens were taken in traps set in grassy surface runways along the edge of this forest.

We have trapped masked shrews in swampy deciduous woods; marshy areas covered with grasses and brush; tamarack bogs; weedy and grassy fencerows bordering bluegrass pastures; rank weedy growths along the floodplain of small creek and ditch banks; young pine plantations in old field; fairly dense grasses on sandy prairies; and around the border of a bald cypress pond.

ASSOCIATED SPECIES. Since the masked shrew is found in such diverse habitats, many other mammals associate with it. But in northern Indiana, in moist habitats where this shrew is most common, the meadow vole, the short-tailed shrew, the white-footed mouse, and the meadow jumping mouse are the usual small species that share the habitat.

HABITS. The masked shrew is active mostly at night, but has been trapped and observed in the daytime. There appears to be an active period just after dark; traps, empty at sunset, often hold animals an hour later. The species is active all year and its tracks have been seen in the snow in extremely cold (−10°F) weather. Its movements are quick, as it darts back and forth, constantly starting, stopping, and shifting about.

Individuals may sometimes be found hiding under rotten logs, stumps, boards, fallen fence posts, or other debris on the ground. When uncovered these shrews usually manage to dash away before they can be grabbed.

swamp hardwood trees), we trapped 15 masked shrews in three nights (November 1969). Most of them entered traps set beneath fallen limbs or logs or along the edge of fallen logs lying on the ground. A few were captured away from such objects, among the leaves. David M. Brooks once captured a masked shrew that was living in a muskrat house, and one was reported in a beehive. Mabel Thorne trapped several masked shrews in the basement of an abandoned house.

It is difficult to obtain live *Sorex* for study. Many are found dead in live traps or die shortly after being found therein. Evidently

Masked shrew. Photo by Roger W. Barbour

Richard E. Phillips observed several masked shrews at midday running about on the ground in a thicket of quaking aspen. Lindsay (1958) captured one by hand as it ran along the side of a log during the daytime; he also trapped eight others along this same log. Evidently the animals maintained a barely visible runway there. Lindsay also mentioned runs in the leaf mold. In grassy areas, runs utilized by this shrew are not evident, and the animals are frequently trapped in runways made by voles or other species. Nests are constructed of grasses under logs, stumps, and other objects.

About the border of Hovey Lake (an oxbow lake surrounded by cypress, pecan, and other

they succumb to some type of "shock disease." This has made it difficult to study either masked shrews or southeastern shrews in captivity.

FOOD. Whitaker and Mumford (1972a) analyzed the stomach contents of 50 masked shrews from Indiana (Table 28). Lepidopterous larvae, coleopterous larvae, and slugs and snails were the three most frequent groups of foods, followed by spiders, crickets, and unidentified Hemiptera. Earthworms, important to larger shrews, were seldom eaten by this species, and the fungal food *Endogone* constituted only 1.2 percent of the diet. Orthopteran internal organs made up 2.0 percent, while a variety of other invertebrates, especially insects, was also eaten. Vegetation, other than *Endogone*, made up only 0.2 percent of the volume of food in the sample.

As in other small shrews, the metabolic rate is high and the animals have to eat throughout the day to stay alive.

REPRODUCTION. We have relatively little information on reproduction from Indiana masked shrews. Two females taken 5 April (Ripley County) were lactating. A female taken 22 April contained 6 embryos 8 mm in crown-rump length. On 15 May a female had 7 placental scars. Four other females taken in

the same area from 15 to 17 May were gravid, two each with 7 and two each with 8 embryos. These embryos ranged from 6 to 7.5 mm in crown-rump length. In addition, Thomas W. French (1980) examined 9 pregnant masked shrews from Vigo County. Embryos ranged from 4 to 7, averaging 6.1. It appears that masked shrews produce large litters, but we have no record of litters found in the field in Indiana. The gestation period is thought to be about 18 days.

From the examination of 43 male masked shrews, taken in each month but August, we have made the following observations. The

Table 28

Foods eaten by *Sorex cinereus* from Indiana
(including data from Whitaker and Mumford, 1972a)

Food Item	50 stomachs previously reported upon (Whitaker & Mumford, 1972a)		17 additional stomachs	
	Percent Volume	Percent Frequency	Percent Volume	Percent Frequency
Lepidopterous larvae	17.2	28.0	23.8	41.2
Coleopterous larvae	11.9	18.0	11.5	17.6
Gastropoda (slugs & snails)	10.9	14.0	—	—
Araneae (spiders)	9.1	14.0	20.9	29.4
Gryllidae (crickets)	8.1	10.0	5.9	5.9
Hemiptera	6.0	8.0	4.4	11.8
Coleoptera, miscellaneous	4.8	10.0	7.9	23.5
Insect (unidentified)	4.7	18.0	2.9	5.9
Cicadellidae (leafhoppers)	4.6	8.0	—	—
Annelida (earthworms)	3.3	6.0	0.6	5.9
Isopoda (sowbugs)	2.1	4.0	0.6	5.9
Pentatomidae (stinkbug)	2.1	4.0	—	—
Orthopteran internal organs	2.0	2.0	—	—
Formicidae (ant)	2.0	2.0	—	—
Diptera	2.0	2.0	8.5	11.8
Chironomidae (midge)	2.0	2.0	—	—
Nabidae (nabid bugs)	1.6	2.0	—	—
Chilopoda (centipedes)	1.2	4.0	—	—
Endogone	1.2	2.0	—	—
Hymenoptera	1.2	2.0	—	—
Carabid larvae (ground beetles)	1.0	2.0	—	—
Tingidae (lace-bugs)	0.4	2.0	—	—
Diplopoda (millipedes)	0.2	2.0	—	—
Vegetation	0.2	2.0	0.9	5.9
Enchytraeidae (enchytraeid worms)	0.2	2.0	—	—
Lonchopteridae (spear-winged flies)	0.1	2.0	—	—
Chrysomelidae (leaf beetles)	—	—	5.6	11.8
Adult Lepidoptera	—	—	4.7	5.9
Chauliognathus larvae	—	—	0.9	5.9
Dipterous larvae	—	—	0.9	5.9
	100.0		102.0	

testes are small, probably reproductively quiescent, from November through January, but are larger in February. It would appear that much copulation occurs from March through July, perhaps later. One male with testes 2.5 by 4 mm was trapped in October. Those with small testes in June and September were probably immatures.

PARASITES. Whitaker and Wilson (1968) recorded a single specimen of the mite *Androlaelaps fahrenholzi* from Indiana *Sorex cinereus*. Whitaker and Mumford (1972a) reported the following mites (percent of hosts infested, followed by mites per shrew, in parentheses after each): *Orycteroxenus soricis* (37.5; 7.25); *Androlaelaps fahrenholzi* (15.0; 0.18); *Protomyobia claparedei* (5.0; 0.18). They also found the mite *Protomyobia claparedei* (5.0; 0.18) and 2 specimens each of the mites *Blarinobia cryptotis* and *Amorphacarus hengererorum*. We have since taken 11 specimens of the chigger *Euschoengastia ohioensis* and 1 of the phoretic mite *Pygmephorus equitrichosus* from this host. We have found no ticks, fleas, or lice on Indiana masked shrews.

Of 110 shrews examined for internal parasites, only 27 were infected. Cestodes, mostly a tiny species, presently unidentified, were the most abundant (491 in 19 shrews). A few nematodes (38 in 10 animals) were found, including some in the bladder, under the skin, and in the intestines. In contrast to the situation in the short-tailed shrew, no trematodes were found in masked shrews.

DECIMATING FACTORS. An occasional masked shrew is found dead. Hawks and owls undoubtedly take these shrews. We have a record of 5 masked shrews from long-eared owl pellets. What work has been conducted on food habits of mammalian carnivores in Indiana has not revealed masked shrews among the food items. Some are caught by domestic cats.

TAXONOMY. Bole and Moulthrop (1942) assigned the name *Sorex cinereus lesueurii* to *Amphisorex lesueurii* of Duvernoy (1842), who designated the Wabash River Valley, Indiana, as the type locality. Although some controversy has ensued regarding the specific identity of Duvernoy's lost type of *Amphisorex lesueurii*, his colored plate appears to represent *Sorex cinereus*. On the basis of available specimens, the name *Sorex cinereus lesueurii* can probably be retained for the dark (in winter pelage) Indiana populations. Illinois specimens examined from Carroll (1), Cook (5), DuPage (1), and Lake (9) counties are paler than the Indiana series; however, the Illinois animals are browner (less gray) than either *S. c. cinereus* or *S. c. haydeni* and thus tend toward *lesueurii*. We are aware that some Iowa and Wisconsin animals have been referred to *lesueurii*. Seven Washtenaw County, Michigan, specimens are somewhat paler than Indiana *lesueurii*, but nearer that race than the Illinois specimens seen. A series of 20 specimens from Mercer County, Ohio, are likewise dark and nearer Indiana *lesueurii* in color. Typical *lesueurii* may have a rather restricted geographic range.

Twelve specimens from Ripley County, Indiana, are referable to *Sorex cinereus ohionensis* Bole and Moulthrop (Lindsay, 1960). The few winter Indiana specimens from localities between *ohionensis* and *lesueurii* populations tend to approach *S. c. ohionensis* in size and color, although *S. c. ohionensis* is less grayish and more reddish than the intergrades examined.

SELECTED REFERENCES: Blossom, 1932; French, 1980; Hamilton, 1930; Hollister, 1911b; Jackson, 1928; Moore, 1949; Pruitt, 1954; Whitaker and Mumford, 1972a.

Southeastern Shrew
Sorex longirostris Bachman

Bachman's Shrew, Southern Shrew, Carolina Shrew

Sorex longirostris: Hahn, 1909

DESCRIPTION. The southeastern shrew is a small brown or reddish brown long-tailed shrew similar in appearance to the masked shrew. One gray colored *S. longirostris* specimen from Vermillion County stands out among the other skins examined by us. We have discussed the characteristics of the southeastern shrew and the masked shrew in the *S. cinereus* species account.

Weights and measurements data for *S. longirostris* are shown in Table 29. The dental formula is

$$I \frac{3}{1} \ C \frac{1}{1} \ P \frac{3}{1} \ M \frac{3}{3} = 32.$$

Table 29

Weights and measurements of *Sorex longirostris* from Indiana
(data courtesy of Thomas French)

	Males	Females
Total length (mm)		
n	40	21
x̄	80.8	80.6
range	77-84	73-87
SD	2.6	3.9
SE	0.4	0.8
Tail length (mm)		
n	40	21
x̄	29.6	29.3
range	26-32	26-33
SD	1.6	2.1
SE	0.3	0.5
Hind foot (mm)		
n	40	21
x̄	10.1	10.1
range	9.5-11.0	9.5-11.0
SD	0.4	0.4
SE	0.06	0.1
Weight (grams)		
n	32	16
x̄	3.1	3.1
range	2.0-3.7	2.3-4.0
SD	0.4	0.5
SE	0.06	0.1

STATUS AND DISTRIBUTION. In the early years, there was much confusion regarding the correct identification of small shrews of the genus *Sorex* from southwestern Indiana. Hahn (1909) and Howell (1909b) recorded the first specimen of *S. longirostris* from the state. It was taken at Bicknell (Knox County) in 1895, preserved in alcohol, and sent to the United States Biological Survey, Washington, D.C. C. H. Merriam identified this specimen

as *Sorex personatus* (=*S. cinereus*), but when Hahn suggested that it might be another species, the skull was removed and the specimen was found to be *S. longirostris*. Two other specimens of the southeastern shrew, taken at Bicknell in 1910, are also in the National Museum of Natural History. Together, these are probably the three specimens listed by Jackson (1928).

The next specimen of southeastern shrew from Indiana was taken by J. Dan Webster in 1955 (Lindsay, 1958). Mumford and Rippy (1963) recorded specimens from additional counties, including 14 specimens from near Lafayette. Through our collecting and the work of others, there were specimen records from 12 counties by 1969 (Mumford, 1969c). We still have much to learn about the distribution of this shrew in Indiana, but it appears likely that it occurs over much of the southern two-thirds of the state, at localities that provide suitable habitat. For example, in recent years 128 specimens have been collected in Vigo County, the great majority of them in sunken cans by Thomas W. French from 1976 to 1979 (1980), indicating that this method of trapping will greatly add to our knowledge of this species. French's information, when published, will increase our knowledge of both species of *Sorex* in Indiana. Persons working in the state should be aware of the lack of detailed information on *Sorex longirostris* (and *S. cinereus)* and that these two species are easily confused with each other. Specimens of *Sorex* from throughout Indiana, particularly the southern half of the state, should be preserved and the identification carefully checked. We currently have records from 17 counties (Map 9).

POPULATIONS. We formerly assumed that the southeastern shrew was rare in Indiana, but recent data indicate that locally it is considerably more abundant than available records lead us to believe. Local abundance in Tippecanoe and Vigo counties may be real, or may reflect the increased effort expended in trapping small mammals at these locations. We have received recent information from the late Jack McCormick and his associates, who took 28 southeastern shrews near Rockport (Spencer County).

HABITAT. The collector recorded nothing concerning the habitat of the Knox County

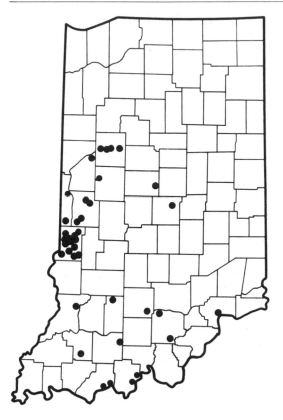

Map 9.   The Southeastern Shrew, *Sorex longirostris*, in Indiana

specimens. Most of the 19 southeastern shrews taken in Tippecanoe County were trapped in dense grasses and sedges at the border of a marsh, not far from the water's edge. Another was taken in a wet area along a small creek in a woods. One was captured in dense grass at the base of a wooded, deciduous slope bordering a small stream. The Marion County specimen came from a small, seasonally damp patch of grasses, weeds, and scattered sprouts not far from a creek. The ground cover was fairly dense bluegrass, with scattered *Andropogon, Aster,* Canada thistle, milkweed, sedges, goldenrod, and mullein. Sprouts of ash and other trees from 2 to 8 feet tall grew sparsely in the area. The area appeared to have been an overgrown field or old homesite.

One southeastern shrew was trapped on a fairly dry site along a fencerow between an upland pastured slope and the roadside (Fountain County). The only vegetation in the pasture was badly overgrazed, sparse

bluegrass. A fringe of weeds, including lesser ragweed, red clover, goldenrod, ground cherry, aster, and foxtail, grew in the fencerow, which was only 3 feet wide. Rather dense bluegrass formed the ground cover.

T. M. Uzzell, Jr., captured three southeastern shrews in sunken can traps, which he placed near temporary ponds in deciduous woods to capture salamanders (Boone and Tippecanoe counties). Larry L. Roop saw a southeastern shrew at the edge of a woods bordering a field (Washington County) and caught it by hand after it crawled beneath the loose bark of a tree. On land formerly strip-mined for coal and grown up to briers and weeds (Pike County), G. S. Jones trapped three of these small shrews.

Most of the Vigo County specimens were taken in moist to dry grassy fields with a mixture of grasses and other herbaceous plants and rather dense ground cover. Two others were taken in sunken bottles set for catching salamanders at the edge of a pond. Vegetation about the pond was less dense than in the grassy fields, and the soil was sandy. Most of those taken by French in Vigo County were in upland woods. One specimen was taken alive by hand by Whitaker in climax forest at Donaldsons Woods (Spring Mill State Park) as it darted in and out among leaves.

ASSOCIATED SPECIES. Most of the small mammals that occupy habitats suitable for the

Southeastern shrew. Photo by Tom French

southeastern shrew have been collected in the same traplines with it. In one field near Terre Haute, the southeastern shrew, the masked shrew, the meadow vole, and the prairie vole were all taken. In other areas in the same county, masked shrews, short-tailed shrews, least shrews, meadow voles, woodland voles, meadow jumping mice, and white-footed mice were trapped in the same habitats with the southeastern shrew. In the marsh near Lafayette, where numerous southeastern shrews have been trapped, a single masked shrew has been caught, but prairie voles, meadow voles, short-tailed shrews, least shrews, meadow jumping mice, white-footed mice, and deer mice have been captured in the same area.

HABITS. Little information has been obtained regarding the habits of this shrew in Indiana, but it is assumed that they are similar to those of the masked shrew. The southeastern shrew is partially diurnal. Roop observed one during the day and Charles L. Rippy captured one in a sunken can trap between 10 A.M. and 1 P.M. When he checked the trap at 10 A.M., it held two short-tailed shrews. Eight of the specimens taken near Lafayette were found dead (usually beneath the treadle) in wire Havahart live traps set for voles. Evidently the shrews attempted to hide beneath the treadle after being captured. One specimen was discovered in the daytime beneath a large wooden platform lying on the ground.

FOOD. Whitaker and Mumford (1972a) examined the stomachs of 7 Indiana southeastern shrews, which contained the following foods (percent volume and percent frequency, respectively, for each in parentheses): spiders (20.0, 42.9); lepidopterous larvae (19.3, 42.9); slugs and snails (14.3, 14.2); vegetation (14.3, 14.3); centipedes (11.4, 14.3); harvestmen (10.0, 14.3); roaches (5.0, 14.3); earthworms (1.4, 14.3); unidentified insects (1.4, 14.3); unidentified Hemiptera (1.4, 14.3); miscellaneous Coleoptera (0.7, 14.3); ants (0.7, 14.3). An additional stomach examined later contained 100 percent Hemiptera. From this small sample, we were unable to determine whether southeastern shrews and masked shrews differ greatly in food habits.

REPRODUCTION. Thomas W. French (1980) collected 13 pregnant southeastern shrews during his studies of *Sorex* in Vigo County. At least one was taken in every month from April through September. Embryos ranged in number from 4 to 6 (average 4.55).

From our relatively small sample, it appears that testes are largest in southeastern shrews from late February to October. Three males with large testes (4 by 6 mm) were taken on 14, 19, and 20 April.

PARASITES. External parasites were recovered from only 2 of 12 southeastern shrews examined by Whitaker and Mumford (1972a). A single specimen of the labidophorine hypopial mite *Orycteroxenus soricis* was found on one, and 8 mites (subsequently lost) were on the other. Since that report, another specimen has been found to host an estimated 400 individuals of *O. soricis* and 2 individuals of the laelapid mite *Hirstionyssus talpae*, both commonly found on shrews.

One shrew was host to 5 cestodes of an unidentified species.

DECIMATING FACTORS. Three animals were found dead (two along roads), presumably having been killed and left by predators. One found dead on the Hanover College campus may have been dropped there by a domestic cat (Lindsay, 1958).

TAXONOMY. *Sorex longirostris longirostris* (Bachman) probably occurs in Indiana. The cranial measurements of 9 specimens from Georgia, North Carolina, Tennessee, and Virginia averaged larger than those of 12 Indiana specimens. This variation may be clinal, but specimens are too few to be certain (see also Jackson, 1928).

SELECTED REFERENCES. Hollister, 1911b; Jackson, 1928; Mumford and Rippy, 1963; Whitaker and Mumford, 1972a.

Short-tailed Shrew
Blarina brevicauda (Say)

Large Blarina, Carolina Shrew, Carolina Short-tailed Shrew, Mole Mouse, Large Shrew, Common Short-tailed Shrew, Northern Short-tailed Shrew, Lake States Blarina, Mole-shrew

Brachysorex brevicaudatus: Duvernoy, 1842
Sorex brevicaudatus: Plummer, 1844
Sorex brevicaudis: Plummer, 1844
Sorex Blarina (brevicaudatus): Kennicott, 1858
Blarina brevicauda: Butler, 1892b

DESCRIPTION. *Blarina brevicauda*, the largest of the Indiana shrews, is silvery gray to black, with a tail that is much shorter than the body. The underparts are paler than the dorsal areas. As in other shrews, the snout is long and pointed and projects beyond the mouth. The eyes are tiny and black, and the external ear opening is large but concealed in the fur. There are five clawed toes on each foot, and the hind feet are somewhat larger than the front. The fur is velvety, with no differentiation into guard hairs and underfur; the hairs have whiplike tips.

We are aware of at least 10 specimens of short-tailed shrews from Indiana that are white or whitish spotted. Murray (1939) reported a *Blarina* specimen (now lost) which was "pure unblemished white throughout." No record was made of the eye color. A specimen from Vigo County is almost completely a soiled whitish color. We have examined 6 other specimens (all from different counties) that exhibit white spots, mostly on a leg or on the back. An interesting specimen from Wayne County has the anterior half of the body normal color (silver gray), but the posterior half is white, except for two small, irregular patches along the middorsal line.

As in all North American shrews, *Blarina* has teeth with chestnut colored enamel. There are five unicuspids, but the fifth is hidden, in lateral view, behind a lobe of the fourth. The third and fourth unicuspids are much smaller than the first and second, and the fifth is still smaller. The anteriormost incisors are enlarged, protrude forward, and have a posterior lobe. The skull is flattened

with posterolateral ridges. As in other North American shrews, there is no zygomatic arch.

Measurements and weights are shown in Table 30. The dental formula is

$$I \frac{3}{1} C \frac{1}{1} P \frac{3}{1} M \frac{3}{3} = 32.$$

Table 30
Weights and measurements of
Blarina brevicauda from Indiana

	Males	Females
Total length(mm)		
n	60	69
x	115	111.5
range	100-126	95-125
SD	6.5	6.1
SE	0.8	0.7
Tail length (mm)		
n	60	69
x	23	22.3
range	19-28	17-26
SD	2.2	2.7
SE	0.3	0.3
Hind foot (mm)		
n	60	70
x	14.3	14.2
range	9-16	9-20
SD	1.4	1.6
SE	0.2	0.2
Weight (grams)		
n	53	67
x	17.5	16.3
range	11.0-26.3	11.4-24.8
SD	3.4	2.9
SE	0.5	0.4

STATUS AND DISTRIBUTION. The short-tailed shrew is common or even locally abundant over much of the state. As Hahn (1909) noted, it is more common in northern than in southern Indiana and appears to be scarce in some parts of south-central Indiana. It shares with the white-footed mouse (*Peromyscus leucopus*) the distinction of being one of the most common native Indiana mammals. Its range includes the entire state and we have specimen records from most of the 92 counties (Map 10).

Plummer (1844), possibly the first to men-

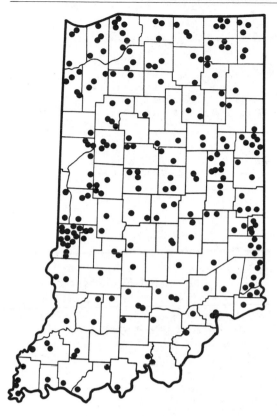

Map 10.   The Short-tailed Shrew, *Blarina brevicauda*, in Indiana

tion the short-tailed shrew from Indiana, gave no indication of its abundance. Butler (1892b) called it the most abundant shrew in the state. A single specimen was mentioned from Randolph County by Cox (1893). McAtee (1907) recorded it as abundant in Monroe County. In August 1905, when Walter Hahn collected mammals in the Kankakee River valley of northwestern Indiana, he found the species "common everywhere except in the lower marshes." It was especially abundant at Bluegrass Landing (Newton County), both in the woods and in the fields. Hahn studied mammals on the Indiana University Farm (now part of Spring Mill State Park, Lawrence County) from September 1906 to September 1907. He wrote about *Blarina* there as follows: "This shrew is common, yet not nearly so abundant as at some other places I have collected" (Hahn, 1908b). Hahn (1909) thought it probably occurred in every township of Indiana.

At Lake Maxinkuckee (Marshall County) 10

records of *Blarina* were accumulated from 1899 to 1907 by Evermann and Clark (1911). They thought that in the vicinity it was "probably not uncommon." In the sand dune country of Porter County, Lyon (1923) collected only 5 specimens in the fall of 1922 and wrote that "This shrew did not appear to be common." These specimens may be the 5 in the National Museum of Natural History which were collected from 4 to 13 October 1922. In the same museum, however, are 12 short-tailed shrews taken in October and November 1923 and 5 taken in October and November 1924, all by Lyon, in Porter County. Engels (1933) noted that *Blarina* was "the most common small mammal" in St. Joseph County. He wrote, "It is not an uncommon experience to take nothing but these shrews in trap-lines with five percent yield." Lyon (1936) had specimen records from 18 Indiana counties and other records from 13 more.

Kirkpatrick and Conaway (1948) captured 25 short-tailed shrews in more than 400 trap-nights at the Jasper-Pulaski Fish and Wildlife Area (Jasper and Pulaski counties) in 1946. It was "the most frequently caught mammal." These animals were taken in various habitats. Lindsay (1960) collected some 600 small mammals in Jefferson and Ripley counties; from November 1952 to July 1955, he took 28 short-tailed shrews but did not break down his catch for trap-nights or habitats.

We have summarized some trapping records from our work in the state in order to show numbers of *Blarina* taken per 100 trap-nights in varied habitats. Our best data resulted from Whitaker's work in Vigo County (Table 31).

The local abundance of small mammals may sometimes be indicated by other records, such as small mammal remains identified from owl pellet material. Frequently, a comparison of species composition by trapping and from owl pellets from the same area shows large differences in relative abundance of certain species, especially shrews. The following data should be interpreted with this caution in mind. Analyses of more than 100 pellets each of the barn owl, the long-eared owl, the short-eared owl, and the great horned owl in Tippecanoe County, collected during the winter of 1946–47, re-

Table 31

Blarina brevicauda taken in random trapping program in Vigo
County
(from Whitaker, 1967)

Habitat	Number of trap-nights	Number of *Blarina* taken	Number taken per 100 trap-nights
Plowed fields	4,800	0	0
Field crops or stubble	14,550	1	0.01
Pasture	1,275	0	0
Grassy field	2,475	2	0.08
Weedy field	2,175	0	0
Brushy field	1,725	4	0.23
Brush	1,200	0	0
Woods	5,175	19	0.37

vealed that *Blarina* ranked between third and sixth in abundance of prey species taken by these birds (Kirkpatrick and Conaway, 1947). Of 270 mammals identified from owl pellets collected in Jackson County from 1952 to 1955, only 2 short-tailed shrews were represented (Mumford and Handley, 1956).

Relative abundance of prey items also may differ between species of owl. In the Tippecanoe County study, 145 barn owl pellets contained 391 mammals, of which 58 were short-tailed shrews. In 83 long-eared owl pellets, only 1 of 153 mammals identified was a *Blarina*. A single *Blarina* was found among 165 mammals in 100 short-eared owl pellets. And of 205 mammals in 102 great horned owl pellets only 3 were short-tailed shrews (Kirkpatrick and Conaway, 1947). In another study, conducted by Bowles (1962), 3 of 103 mammals in 50 long-eared owl pellets (Fayette County) were short-tailed shrews; 25 short-tailed shrews were represented among 179 mammals from 47 barn owl pellets (Marion County); a single *Blarina* was among 22 mammals identified from 18 saw-whet owl pellets (Fayette County).

HABITAT. The short-tailed shrew occurs in most Indiana habitats. The species has been taken in moist bog and marsh borders where the soil was saturated and small pools of water were present. It is locally abundant in woodlands, open fields, marsh borders, and shrubby areas. Fencerows grown up to weeds, grass, or brush and bordering almost any type of habitat are good locations in which to trap this shrew. It enters buildings and possibly caves (Hahn, 1907b). Relatively

mature woodlands with a thick ground litter and partially rotted logs and stumps on the forest floor frequently harbor large populations. In some sections of the state, *Blarina* is more abundant in nonwooded areas than in wooded ones, although in most of these situations a reasonably heavy ground cover appears to be essential to support large numbers. We have the best systematic trapping data from Vigo County, where *Blarina* was absent in plowed fields, pastures, weedy fields, and brush areas. It would be interesting to compare the preferred habitats of the species in various sections of the state to determine whether differences might be traced to historical vegetation patterns. Of the 29 short-tailed shrews taken in southeastern Indiana by Lindsay (1958), 14 were trapped in wooded areas.

ASSOCIATED SPECIES. The species most commonly associated with *Blarina* in wooded areas is the white-footed mouse. In mature forested tracts, both may be quite abundant and may constitute most of the small mammal population present. In moist woods with soft soil, *Blarina* and the woodland vole (*Microtus pinetorum*) sometimes occur together, even using the same underground burrows. Burrows of the short-tailed shrew can often be identified from those of the woodland vole because the latter tend to be round in cross-section instead of somewhat flattened on two sides. Since the short-tailed shrew is found in a wide variety of habitats, most species of mammals found in Indiana are at some place associated with it.

Short-tailed shrew. Photo by John Tester

HABITS.   The short-tailed shrew appears to spend considerable time running (and sniffing) from place to place, apparently quite oblivious of its surroundings. Much of its time is evidently spent searching for food. It can run along slanting tree trunks with ease, but is probably not an exceptionally good climber, and rarely jumps. One was found on the second floor of a building. In confinement, this shrew will usually run around the perimeter of its cage or room, but will seldom attempt to run across it. This may explain why in snap-trapping for this species many animals are caught along the edges of logs lying on the ground. Other good trap sites are the bases of stumps (especially rotted) or trees, and in the numerous underground burrows constructed by *Blarina* just below the leaf litter. Along the burrows, openings to the surface show as clear, round holes with no soil about them. Traps placed at these tunnel openings frequently take short-tailed shrews.

This shrew swims when necessary, and we have trapped numerous specimens in marshy or swampy habitats. Engels (1933) mentioned one that took to the water without hesitation when disturbed. Vision appears to be quite poor, and some authors have suggested that the sense of smell is not effective at great distances. Hearing is quite acute and must certainly play in important role in the life of this

species. Plummer mentioned that a captive he observed would come out its hiding place in response to the buzzing of a fly.

The short-tailed shrew is active both day and night, but appears to be primarily nocturnal at most seasons. It remains active throughout the year. The extent of nocturnal activity is reflected in the numbers of short-tailed shrews one finds in the pellets of several species of owls. McAtee (1907) wrote that "many of this species forage in the evenings under the street arc lights" at Bloomington. We have trapped numerous specimens during daylight hours. On 14 April 1961, we took 7 short-tailed shrews between 1:30 and 4:30 P.M. in 40 mousetraps in a fallow field (Boone County).

Little information is available on observed behavior of short-tailed shrews in their natural habitats. Captive animals adjust well to confinement when provided with ample cover, but spend much time out of sight. Plummer noted that his captives were tidy and clean, but he did not report observing any pelage maintenance behavior. When a captive kept by Mumford was first placed on the bare floor of a small aquarium, it defecated and urinated, then it appeared to drink (?) some of the urine. Water was immediately provided and the shrew drank. It did not visibly use the tongue in drinking, but immersed the tip of the snout in the water then raised its head. The snout was sometimes moved from side to side when drinking.

Captive short-tailed shrews observed by Plummer and by Mumford became conditioned to come for food, in one case in response to the human voice and in the other to a tapping on the side of the aquarium. In the case of the latter, which was confined for 48 days, we failed to record at what point it became so conditioned. Both animals would appear to feed when called, by day or by night. And both would readily take food (although quickly) from the hand. Plummer observed, however, that on very hot days his captive tended to respond more slowly to his call. This could indicate that the short-tailed shrew moves about less on hot, summer days, as one might expect.

Vocalizations of *Blarina* include squeaks, chipping or clicking sounds, and chattering. Plummer noted a "shrill chirp" from an individual being closely pursued by another, and a rapidly uttered chip-chip-chip call, "almost precisely" like that of the eastern chipmunk *(Tamias striatus)*. Mumford observed that when some cotton was dropped into a can containing a newly live-trapped *Blarina*, the shrew lifted its snout straight up and gave a sharp, rachetlike call, similar to that given by a disturbed hoary bat *(Lasiurus cinereus)*. Other sounds produced by this shrew are ultrasonic (thus out of the range of human hearing) and are used in echolocation.

One captive did a considerable amount of gnawing and constructed itself a bed from paper and rags it had cut into small bits. Captives readily formed burrow systems in the substrate within their cages. In one case, these burrows were constructed in the 4-inch layer of sod and soil provided for the shrew. The animals must possess considerable strength, for one of Plummer's animals escaped from a glass container 5 inches tall, with vertical sides, by pushing aside a covering weighing a pound.

In confinement, short-tailed shrews usually fight (sometimes quite furiously) when confronted by individuals of the same species. Vocal sounds often accompany these encounters. After Plummer had studied one of his captives for some time, a second individual was placed in the same cage. It spent much time out of sight in the tunnel system of the cage, but was frequently chased, although seldom overtaken, by the original captive, which was larger. Sometimes the two shrews met on the surface of their living area. This resulted in "vigorous combat" and eventually resulted in the death of the smaller (nonresident) shrew. At one point in the pursuit, the smaller animal, detecting the presence of the larger close behind, gave a "shrill chirp," wheeled about, and faced its pursuer.

The short-tailed shrew has small flank glands which produce a strong, musky secretion. This odor is evidently produced in males all year and in females during the nonbreeding season. Secretions from the glands scent the shrews' tunnels and individuals seem to avoid tunnels scented by another individual, although males enter unscented (female) tunnels during the breeding season. There is also a single, large gland on the abdomen of the short-tailed shrew, but its function is unknown. The submaxillary glands of *Blarina* release a mixture of saliva and a strong poison, which apparently functions to immobilize prey. These glands open into the mouth between the large lower incisors.

Few short-tailed shrew nests have been discovered in natural habitats of Indiana. Plummer captured a *Blarina* by hand under a rotten log, which the shrew had "converted into a perfect labyrinth" of tunnels. In the largest excavation was a nest of dry leaves. Nixon A. Wilson also found a family of short-tailed shrews in a nest in a rotten log. The nest was composed of loosely packed leaves, the inner ones being somewhat shredded. A nest located below the surface of the ground in an anthill was reported by Caldwell and Jones (1973). This nest was of unshredded leaves and measured about 6 inches in diameter. Edgren (1948) reported the capture of a short-tailed shrew "from what appeared to be an abandoned mouse nest under a log."

FOOD. Food habits of Indiana *Blarina brevicauda* have been studied by Whitaker and Mumford (1972a). The most important foods (listed in order of decreasing percent volume) were earthworms, slugs and snails, lepidopterous larvae, crickets, and centipedes; these foods formed 63.1 percent of the food volume (Table 32). The short-tailed shrew occasionally appears to split open the outer covering of some larger insects and eat the internal organs; this food formed 0.7 percent of the total. The fungus *Endogone* was found in 11.2 percent of the stomachs, but made up only 3.6 percent of the volume of food in the stomachs. It appears that shrews dig out spore masses of the fungus in top layers of the soil, probably detecting the fungus by olfaction. We found 3.6 percent of the

food in the stomachs of short-tailed shrews to be vegetable, including a few seeds. Mouse flesh has often been reported as food of *Blarina*, but we examined only a single shrew with mouse flesh in its stomach. This could have resulted from the shrew's feeding

Table 32

Foods eaten by *Blarina brevicauda* (n = 125) from Indiana

(from Whitaker and Mumford, 1972a)

Food Item	Percent volume	Percent frequency
Annelida (earthworms)	35.7	48.1
Gastropoda (slugs and snails)	8.5	14.4
Lepidopterous larvae	8.2	16.8
Gryllidae (crickets)	6.2	8.8
Chilopoda (centipedes)	4.5	8.0
Coleoptera, unidentified	4.2	7.2
Coleopterous larvae	4.0	7.2
Insect (unidentified)	3.8	14.4
Endogone	3.6	11.2
Carabidae (ground beetle)	2.7	4.0
Dipterous larvae	1.8	5.6
Isopoda (sowbug)	1.6	1.6
Pentatomidae (stinkbug)	1.4	3.2
Vegetation	1.2	8.8
Scarabaeidae (scarab beetle)	1.1	3.2
Hemiptera	1.0	2.4
Elymus seeds	0.8	0.8
Coleopterous pupae	0.8	0.8
Muscoid fly	0.8	0.8
Acrididae (grasshopper)	0.8	0.8
Scarabaeid larvae (scarab beetle)	0.8	0.8
Orthopteran internal organs	0.7	0.8
Plecoptera (stonefly)	0.6	0.8
Curculionidae (snout beetle)	0.6	1.6
Mast	0.6	1.6
Araneae (spider)	0.5	2.4
Formicidae (ant)	0.5	4.5
Seeds (unidentified)	0.5	0.8
Fraxinus (ash) seeds	0.5	0.8
Gryllacrididae (mole cricket)	0.4	0.8
Larvae	0.3	1.6
Diptera	0.3	1.6
Mouse flesh	0.3	0.8
Enchytraeidae (enchytraeid worm)	0.2	0.8
Syrphidae (hover fly)	0.2	0.8
Adult Lepidoptera	0.1	0.8
Cicadellidae (leafhopper)	0.1	0.8
Staphylinidae (rove beetle)	0.1	0.8
Rubus (blackberry) seeds	trace	0.8
Reduviidae (assassin bug)	trace	0.8
Hymenopterous larvae	trace	0.8
Aphididae (aphid)	trace	0.8
	100.0	

Corn storage by short-tailed shrew. Photo by Whitaker

on a dead mouse in our mousetraps, rather than from its taking live mice as prey. Captives will devour mice put into their cages.

Blarina often stores food in small caches. In the fall of 1979, a short-tailed shrew lived for several weeks under a large piece of plywood in a hedgerow along a cornfield. The shrew made a labyrinthine series of tunnels with several caches of corn in blind passages. The corn remained for several days before being completely consumed.

Some data are available on the food habits of captive short-tailed shrews. Plummer (1844) published his observations, which have been quoted by Hahn (1909) and Lyon (1936). Since these works are not readily available, we have extracted parts of Plummer's account and included them here. Foods eaten were slugs, worms, flesh, insects, millipedes, oats, corn, and other grains. Excess food was stored, but when cached food spoiled, the shrew brought it to the surface, evidently to discard it. Living food was preferred. When feeding on large earthworms, the shrew partially restrained the struggling worms with its forefeet. The shrew waded about in a container of water to take worms placed there. A full-grown mouse (species not specified) placed in the cage with the shrew was relentlessly pursued and killed by

the latter. This shrew was "very adroit in catching flies" placed in its cage.

A captive observed by us ate a dead creek chub 4 inches long, earthworms, dead mice (*Peromyscus*), red-backed salamanders, and the carcasses of voles, jumping mice, various birds, and even the carcass of another *Blarina*. Large earthworms were usually grasped by the mouth at one end, then the worm was chewed and swallowed like a strand of spaghetti. Legs of various small mammals such as meadow voles (*Microtus pennsylvanicus*) were avidly consumed, leaving only the well-picked bones.

Kenneth M. Brown regularly trapped white-footed mice and short-tailed shrews in his country home. But he told us that when he caught shrews he captured no mice in the house. One winter George R. Parker captured three live shrews which climbed a stick to get into a bucket of moist dog food stored in a garage. The shrews were unable to escape from the bucket once they dropped in.

Hahn (1908b) once saw a wild short-tailed shrew carrying a dead woodland vole, and later (1909) Hahn stated that *Blarina* sometimes ate "large quantities of snails." McAtee (1907) observed that a female he captured "ate blue bottle flies as fast as they could be given to her." Butler (1892b) wrote that *Blarina* was fond of beechnuts. We took a specimen in early October that had a soybean in its mouth.

Edgren (1948) determined that a captive consumed an average of 25.6 grams of food (crayfish and minnows) per day, over a ten-day period. On the first day of the experiment, the shrew weighed 14.8 grams. The mean daily water consumption for five days was 9.1 cc.

REPRODUCTION. We have relatively little information on reproduction in short-tailed shrews but have examined adult females in every month but January. Numbers examined, followed by numbers pregnant or with placental scars, are: February–7, 0; March–5, 2; April–7, 6; May–4, 3; June–5, 1; July–2, 1; August–3, 1; September–7, 3; October–18, 3; November–10, 2; December–5, 1. We conclude that there is some breeding activity among females during much of the year, but the scant information available would appear to indicate breeding peaks from March through May, and perhaps a less pronounced one in the fall. No females with embryos were taken between October and February. The gestation period is about 17 to 21 days. Placental scars in 9 females ranged from 3 to 6 each, with a mean of 4.3. Embryo counts on 11 females ranged from 4 to 8 (1 with 4 embryos; 3 with 5; 4 with 6; 1 with 7; 2 with 8) with a mean of 6.0.

Testis measurements of 100 males (representing every month but June) also indicate a major peak of breeding in spring. Some individuals are likely capable of breeding from January through October. Testis length measurements are given in Table 33.

An adult and 5 half-grown young (eyes still closed) were found in a nest on 12 April (Posey County) by Nixon Wilson. McAtee collected a female with 4 young on 15 June. Young evidently remain in the nest until nearly full-grown, for we have very rarely trapped specimens smaller in body size than adults.

Table 33

Testis measurements from *Blarina brevicauda* (n = 100) from Indiana (every month but June)

Month	Number examined	Testis length (mm) Average	Range
January	6	5.7	2-9
February	11	6.7	2-9
March	7	8.0	7-10
April	7	8.1	7-9
May	7	8.0	4-10
July	2	5.5	3-8
August	4	4.5	2-9
September	26	3.7	2-9.5
October	21	3.5	2-9.5
November	6	2.7	1-3
December	3	2.7	2-3

PARASITES. Whitaker and Mumford (1972a) reported on the ectoparasites of Indiana short-tailed shrews (Table 34). Since then, other species of ectoparasites have been reported. The most notable is *Asiochirus blarina*, which has proved to be the most abundant form to date, being present on 15.2 percent of shrews examined. This listrophorid mite was in the process of being described (Fain and Hyland, 1972) when our paper went to press. The same species was also being described by McDaniel and Whitaker (1972) as *Olistrophorus blarinae*. However, since the description of Fain and Hyland appeared earlier, it takes precedence. The generic name *Olistrophorus* McDaniel and Whitaker 1972 therefore becomes a synonym of *Asiochirus* Fain and Hyland 1972, and *Olistrophorus blarinae* McDaniel and Whitaker 1972 becomes a synonym of *Asiochirus blarina* Fain and Hyland 1972.

The second most abundant mite is the nonfeeding hypopus of *Orycteroxenus soricis*, a tiny form that clings to individual hairs by means of its posterior clasping organ. The other mites most common on *Blarina* in Indiana are, in order of decreasing abundance, *Androlaelaps fahrenholzi*, *Myonyssus jamesoni*, *Haemogamasus liponyssoides*, and *Protomyobia americana*. *Hirstionyssus blarinae*, another mite, has been added since our 1972 paper.

The more common fleas of *Blarina* are *Ctenopthalmus pseudagyrtes* and *Doratopsylla blarinae*. Wilson (1961) had previously reported all the species of fleas listed in Table 34 except *Orchopeas howardii*, while Whitaker and Corthum (1967) reported *C. pseudagyrtes*, *D. blarinae*, and *Stenoponia americana*. *C. pseudagyrtes* is found on many species of small mammals, but *D. blarinae* appears to be a true parasite of *Blarina*. In addition, Wilson (1961) recorded the following fleas: *Atyphloceras bishopi*, *Corrodopsylla curvata*, *Peromyscopsylla hamifer*, *Megabothris asio*. *Megabothris asio* was represented by two specimens, the others by single specimens.

Although we recovered no ticks from *Blarina*, Wilson (1961) found single specimens of *Dermacentor variabilis* and *Ixodes muris*, from Posey County and Steuben County respectively.

Five beetles, *Leptinus americanus*, were taken. Wilson had previously reported this species from the eastern mole *(Scalopus aquaticus)*, while Blatchley (1910) listed it as "frequent" in mouse and shrew nests in Indiana, with specific reports from Lake, Marion, Perry, and Putnam counties.

Mites of the genus *Pygmephorus* (Pygmephoridae) often occur (sometimes in large numbers) on *Blarina*; they have large claw-like first appendages, apparently for clinging

Table 34

Ectoparasites and other associates of *Blarina brevicauda* (n = 92) from Indiana
(from Whitaker and Mumford, 1972a)

Parasites	Parasites		Hosts Parasitized	
	Total	Average	Total	Percent
Fleas (Siphonaptera)				
Ctenophthalmus pseudagyrtes	29	0.32	14	15.2
Doratopsylla blarinae	17	0.18	7	7.6
Epitedia wenmanni	4	0.04	3	3.3
Stenoponia americana	2	0.02	1	1.1
Corrodopsylla hamiltoni	1	0.01	1	1.1
Orchopeas howardii	1	0.01	1	1.1
Beetles (Coleoptera)				
Leptinus americanus	5	0.05	4	4.3
Mites (Acarina) other than chiggers				
Asiochirus blarina	2,610	28.37	14	15.2
Orycteroxenus soricis	1,245	13.53	14	15.2
Androlaelaps fahrenholzi	68	0.74	22	23.9
Myonyssus jamesoni	27	0.29	2	2.2
Haemogamasus liponyssoides	25	0.27	10	10.9
Protomyobia americana	13	0.14	3	3.3
Eulaelaps stabularis	7	0.08	7	7.6
Haemogamasus longitarsus	5	0.05	1	1.1
Blarinobia simplex	3	0.03	3	3.3
Haemogamasus ambulans	1	0.01	1	1.1
Hirstionyssus blarinae	1	0.01	1	1.1
Dermacarus hypudaei	1	0.01	1	1.1
Laelaps kochi	1	0.01	1	1.1
Pygmephorus (taken in large numbers; numbers identified are listed below)				
P. hamiltoni	27			
P. rackae	16			
P. horridus	6			
P. scalopi	5			
P. whitakeri	4			
P. designatus	3			
P. johnstoni	3			
P. equitrichosus	2			
P. faini	2			
P. spinosus	1			
P. brevicauda	1			
P. hastatus	1			

to hairs. Mites of this genus are apparently phoretic. We sent a number of these mites from *Blarina* to Dr. S. Mahunka (Hungarian Natural History Museum, Budapest), who described from the material six new species of *Pygmephorus* which occur on short-tailed shrews in Indiana: *P. designatus, P. equitrichosus, P. hastatus, P. moreohorridus, P. scalopi,* and *P. whitakeri,* as well as *P. spinosus* Kramer (Mahunka, 1973, 1975). More recently Smiley and Whitaker (1979) have described an additional five species

occurring on Indiana *Blarina: P. brevicauda, P. faini, P. hamiltoni, P. johnstoni,* and *P. rackae.* This brings to 12 the number of species in this genus that have been found on short-tailed shrews from Indiana.

All 92 short-tailed shrews we examined from Indiana harbored external parasites. We also examined 181 animals for internal parasites and 118 yielded some form, as indicated in Table 35.

Nixon A. Wilson (letter to Mumford) reported finding larval cysts of the nematode

Table 35

Endoparasites of *Blarina brevicauda* (n = 181) from Indiana

Parasites	Parasites		Hosts Parasitized	
	Total	Average	Total	Percent
Nematodes	84	0.46	17	9.4
Trematodes	287	1.59	54	29.8
Cestodes	796	4.40	79	43.6

Porrocaecum encapsulatum in *Blarina* from Indiana.

DECIMATING FACTORS. Remains of short-tailed shrews have been identified in the regurgitated pellets of six species of owls (barn, long-eared, short-eared, screech, saw-whet, great horned), and these shrews have been eaten by two species of hawks (marsh, rough-legged) in Indiana. Mumford saw an American kestrel with a freshly killed *Blarina*. Cats and dogs often kill this shrew, but usually discard kills rather than eat them. Engels (1933) mentioned that a short-tailed shrew had been found in the stomach of a gar pike (probably a gar, *Lepisosteus*). Red foxes evidently kill *Blarina*, but seldom eat it (F. H. Montague, Jr., personal communication). Numerous dead short-tailed shrews are found along paths, roads, and trails where they are probably discarded by foxes and possibly by other predatory mammals.

TAXONOMY. Judging from current information, it appears that *Blarina brevicauda kirtlandi* Bole and Moulthrop occurs throughout Indiana. Mumford (1969c) has corrected the literature reference to *B. c. carolinensis* from Indiana. The specimen in question was actually taken in Illinois. Considerable research is now being conducted regarding the status of *Blarina brevicauda* and its subspecies. Perhaps more intensive collecting should be done in southwestern Indiana to complete the picture, especially since *Blarina carolinensis* is no doubt a good species. If this smaller form occurs in the state, it would most likely inhabit this region.

SELECTED REFERENCES. Blair, 1940a; Hamilton, 1929, 1930, 1931a; Merriam, 1895b; Pearson, 1944; Shull, 1907; Whitaker and Mumford, 1972a.

Least Shrew
Cryptotis parva (Say)

Bee Shrew, Bee Mole, Mole Mouse, Cinereus Shrew, Gray Cryptotis, Little Shrew, Small Blarina, Small Shrew, Small Short-tailed Shrew

Brachysorex Harlani: Duvernoy, 1842
Blarina exilipes: Butler, 1892b
Blarina parva: Butler, 1892b
Blarina cinerea: Butler, 1892b
Cryptotis parva: Lyon, 1925

DESCRIPTION. *Cryptotis parva*, the smaller of the two species of short-tailed shrews in Indiana, is tiny, and has a very short tail (see measurements). Least shrews are usually brown or grayish brown (rarely grayish),

slightly paler below than above, including the tail. The snout is long, extending well beyond the mouth. The eyes are black, and the external ears are small. The ear openings are large, but are hidden in the fur. The legs and feet are small, with five toes and claws on both front and hind feet. The fur is soft, with no differentiation into underhair and guard hairs, and, as in other shrews (and moles), the tips of the hairs are whiplike.

There are usually thirty teeth in *Cryptotis*, but two are sometimes missing. As in all Indiana shrews, the anterior upper incisor is enlarged, with a forward projection and a posterior cusp. The teeth have chestnut colored tips. The skull of this species can be

Least shrew. Photo by Roger W. Barbour

immediately separated from that of other Indiana shrews since it has only four unicuspids, the fourth hidden behind the third in lateral view (see Fig. 19). Other species of Indiana shrews have five unicuspids. As in other North American shrews, the zygomatic arch is absent.

Weights and measurements are shown in Table 36. The dental formula is

$$I \frac{3}{1} C \frac{1}{1} P \frac{2}{1} M \frac{3}{3} = 30.$$

STATUS AND DISTRIBUTION. *Cryptotis parva* is probably relatively common throughout much of the state, but is not usually taken in numbers. The apparent scarcity of this species is probably due more to our trapping methods than to a lack of shrews. Kirkpatrick and Conaway (1948) took 22 least shrews in 92 trap-nights in Tippecanoe County, and Lindsay (1960) took 26 among 600 mammals trapped in southeastern Indiana. Mumford (1969c) took only 11 in six years of extensive trapping over the state, but Whitaker and Mumford (1972a) reported on the food and external parasites of 142, taken mostly in Vigo County. Cope (1949) found 27 least shrews in the digestive tract of a rough-legged hawk from Wayne County. Other people have reported large numbers taken by hawks and owls (especially barn owls) in

Table 36
Weights and measurements
Cryptotis parva from Indiana

	Males	Females
Total length (mm)		
n	66	72
x̄	74	76.5
range	61-86	63-88
SD	5.71	6.2
SE	0.7	0.7
Tail length (mm)		
n	65	72
x̄	15.2	15.6
range	9-21	11-20
SD	2.65	1.9
SE	0.3	0.2
Hind foot (mm)		
n	66	71
x̄	10.2	10.2
range	9-12	9-12
SD	0.62	0.9
SE	0.1	0.1
Weight (grams)		
n	62	61
x̄	4.4	4.6
range	2.9-6.3	2.0-10.5
SD	0.7	1.1
SE	0.1	0.1

other states, often at places where these shrews were not being taken readily in traps.

Butler (1892b) appears to have been among the first to record the least shrew from Indiana. He wrote that it "seems to be comparatively common in Vigo County" and "rather common in the Whitewater valley." Cox (1893) knew of a single specimen from Randolph County. Evermann and Butler (1894b), who knew of specimens from Franklin, Jefferson, Marion, Randolph, and Vigo counties, reported that a man's domestic cat captured "four or five" least shrews every year in Terre Haute. McAtee (1907) noted its presence in Monroe County, and in 1908 Walter L. Hahn recorded it from Lawrence County. A year later, Hahn (1909) listed records from nine Indiana counties. Specimens from nine counties were known to be in museums and there were records from seven additional counties by 1936 (Lyon). Kirkpatrick and Conaway (1948) recorded *Cryptotis* specimens from Carroll, Ripley, and Tippecanoe counties, and the presence of least shrew skulls in owl pellets gathered in Dearborn County. The species was evidently rather common in Ripley County in the 1950s; during the same period several were trapped in Jefferson County (Lindsay, 1960). By 1961, more specimens had been accumulated and this shrew was definitely known from 21 counties (Mumford, 1961). To date, we have examined specimens from 45 Indiana counties (Map 11).

Most people who have written about *Cryptotis* in Indiana have considered it relatively rare to uncommon. There are some records, however, which indicate local (and possibly seasonal) abundance. The 22 least shrews taken in 92 trap-nights in Tippecanoe County were trapped on 22 and 23 October 1946 (Kirkpatrick and Conaway, 1948). The rough-legged hawk with 27 least shrews in its digestive tract was killed in Wayne County on Christmas Day (Cope, 1949). Lindsay (1960) found this shrew relatively common in Ripley County, where he trapped 10 from 22 to

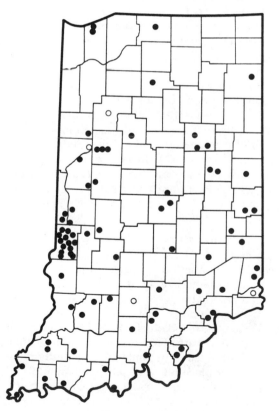

Map 11.   The Least Shrew, *Cryptotis parva,*
in Indiana

26 December 1952 and 10 from 3 to 11 October 1953.

Kirkpatrick and Conaway (1947) reported on the small mammals in the pellets of four species of owls (Tippecanoe County). The remains of 47 least shrews were identified from 145 barn owl pellets. In 83 complete and 139 whole or fragmentary pellets of the long-eared owl, 22 least shrews were represented. Only 1 least shrew was identified in 100 pellets of the short-eared owl. And at least 4 least shrews were represented in 102 pellets of the great horned owl.

Bowles (1962) reported on the small mammal remains found in owl pellets. Five least shrews were found in 47 barn owl pellets from Marion County and 3 in 50 long-eared owl pellets from Fayette County. A single barred owl pellet contained the remains of a *Cryptotis.*

HABITAT.   The least shrew in Indiana is primarily a mammal of old fields, particularly drier ones. Lindsay (1960) trapped most of his specimens in Ripley County in fields that had lain fallow for two to three years. Other field habitats from which the species has been collected include the following: old field with dense bluegrass and weeds; overgrown field; hilltop weed field; dry, open field; field of fescue three years old; along fencerows between cultivated fields; a harvested lespedeza field; marsh border. Hahn (1909) collected specimens "in grassy places, usually where briars and shrubs were mingled with the grass." He took none in woods. Those that he took in Lawrence County were mostly in the vicinity of small sinkholes. A few specimens were taken in a "permanent, heavily grazed pasture" in Carroll County (Kirkpatrick and Conaway, 1948). Lyon (1924) trapped one "on the surface of a damp woods, not far from a damp meadow" in Porter County. Mumford found one dead in a mature deciduous woods mixed with hemlock and yew (Turkey Run State Park), but the animal may have been dropped there by a predator. John C. Kase found several dead least shrews lying along roadsides in wooded areas (Ripley County), but thought they were probably left by foxes. At least two specimens have been found in buildings. One was captured in a hole at the base of a small tree, along the edge of a woods.

ASSOCIATED SPECIES. The species most often associated with the least shrew in Indiana are the house mouse *(Mus musculus)* and the prairie vole *(Microtus ochrogaster)*, but numerous other species share old field habitats.

HABITS. There appears to be little published material on the habits of the least shrew under natural conditions. It is evidently quite secretive and mostly nocturnal. There is evidence, however, that some activity takes place in the daytime. McAtee (1907) apparently observed both *Cryptotis* and *Blarina* foraging beneath the street lights in Bloomington (Monroe County), but he did not record the time of day when they were noted. Hahn (1908b) thought that the least shrew was largely diurnal. We assume he based his judgment on trapped specimens, for he wrote (Hahn, 1909) that he had "never seen it alive." It is active throughout the year.

The least shrew evidently forms runways, which are small and not readily apparent. Hahn and Lindsay both mentioned such runways in Indiana, and other authors have noted their presence elsewhere. No doubt the runways of other small mammals are also used by *Cryptotis*. We have noted no burrows, but they are undoubtedly small and easily overlooked, as others have suggested. Individuals have been captured in the daytime under a log, under a board, and beneath a burlap bag on the ground. Another was captured on 15 February inside the partial, mummified carcass of a snapping turtle on which it was feeding. Cox (1893) captured one by hand that was running on top of the snow at night.

Nests are usually constructed in hidden sites. Evermann and Butler (1894b) mentioned that the least shrew sometimes built its nest inside a beehive. Lindsay (1960) found two least shrews in a nest beneath a board at the edge of a pond on 17 August. The nest, constructed of dry grasses in a cup-shaped depression in the soil, was approximately 4 inches in diameter and 2.5 inches deep. The nest had two entrances, one at the top and one at the bottom, which led to the ground surface through a short tunnel.

Studies conducted outside Indiana indicate that *Cryptotis* is a social animal and that numerous individuals will occupy the same nest (Jackson, 1961; Davis and Joeris, 1945; McCarley, 1959). Conaway (1958) described the behavior of four adults (one with a litter) confined in the same cage. The nest and litter were intentionally scattered about the cage. All adults immediately began moving the young, finally depositing them at the original site of the nest, which they then reassembled. Davis and Joeris described how two least shrews cooperated in digging a burrow. One dug while the other removed the loose soil and packed it along the burrow walls.

The least shrew often utters chirping sounds.

FOOD. Whitaker and Mumford (1972a) have reported on the food habits of 109 least shrews from Indiana (Table 37). The five most abundant foods by volume were lepidopterous larvae, earthworms, spiders, internal organs of orthopterans, and coleopterous larvae (unidentified insects ranked fifth but were not considered one type of food). Nearly 10 percent of the food appeared to be internal organs of larger insects, especially Orthoptera and Coleoptera, indicating that the shrews sometimes discarded the outer hard parts of these insects. Vegetation constituted 5.6 percent of all foods; one stomach was almost completely full of seeds and flowers of a composite.

The least shrew often roots into the soil with its snout, apparently searching for food. In the laboratory, this shrew fed on large grasshoppers and frogs, which were immobilized by repeated biting on the hind legs. Crickets and beetles, however, were immobilized by biting about the head (Moore, 1943).

REPRODUCTION. Although we have taken a number of least shrews, we have relatively little information on their reproduction in Indiana. Totals of 11, 1, 4, 1, 1, and 11, 28, and 6 females were taken in the months of January through May and October through December respectively; none had embryos or placental scars. Three females taken in June and three taken in September had either embryos or placental scars. One contained 6 and one 3 placental scars, while two each had 6 and 7 embryos. We examined no females taken in July or August. This meager information indicates that least shrews in Indiana produce young at least in June and Septem-

Table 37

Foods eaten by *Cryptotis parva* (n = 109) from Indiana
(from Whitaker and Mumford, 1972a)

Food Item	Percent Volume	Percent Frequency
Lepidopterous larvae	17.9	29.4
Annelida (earthworms)	11.2	15.6
Araneae (spider)	6.8	11.0
Orthopteran internal organs	6.6	7.3
Insect (unidentified)	5.8	11.9
Coleopterous larvae	4.7	7.3
Aphididae (aphid)	3.8	6.4
Chilopoda (centipede)	3.6	7.3
Mast	3.5	4.6
Gastropoda (slugs and snails)	3.3	3.7
Gryllidae (cricket)	3.2	4.6
Coleoptera	3.0	6.4
Coleopterous larvae; internal organs	2.8	2.8
Dipterous larvae	2.4	3.7
Hemiptera	2.2	6.4
Miridae (leaf bugs)	2.2	3.7
Isopoda (sowbug)	1.9	2.8
Hymenoptera	1.8	1.8
Carabidae (ground beetle)	1.7	4.6
Diptera	1.6	4.6
Scarabaeidae (scarab beetle)	1.2	1.8
Seeds (unidentified)	1.2	2.8
Acrididae (grasshopper)	1.1	1.8
Cicadellidae (leafhopper)	1.0	2.8
Endogone	0.9	0.9
Membracidae (treehopper)	0.9	0.9
Formicidae (ant)	0.8	0.9
Fungal spores	0.8	0.9
Vegetation	0.5	1.8
Setaria (foxtail grass) seeds	0.4	0.9
Cantharidae (soldier beetles)	0.4	0.9
Vespidae (vespid wasp)	0.3	0.9
Scarabaeid larvae	0.2	0.9
Muscoid fly	0.1	0.9
Mites	0.1	0.9
Enchytraeidae (enchytraeid worm)	trace	0.9
	99.9	

ber, but likely all through the summer. A summary of published records plus our information indicate embryo counts range from 2 to 7, with a mean of 4.9. The mean number of young in 16 litters was 4.5 (range, 3 to 7). The gestation period is about 21 to 23 days.

PARASITES. Few internal parasites were found in the digestive tracts of 139 Indiana least shrews. None of the 14 trematodes, 4 cestodes, or 3 nematodes (from 3, 2, and 2 shrews respectively) has been identified. Eight species of mites and four species of fleas were identified from 108 specimens (Table 38). Only the mites *Orycteroxenus soricis, Androlaelaps fahrenholzi,* and *Protomyobia americana* are considered regular associates of *Cryptotis*. The fleas *Corrodopsylla hamiltoni* and *Ctenophthalmus pseudagyrtes* are considered "normal" parasites on this shrew.

Two mites (*O. soricis* and *Dermacarus hypudaei*, Labidophoridae) are tiny hypopial (transport, nonfeeding) forms that cling to individual hairs. *Protomyobia americana* and

Table 38

Ectoparasites and other associates of *Cryptotis parva* (n = 108) from Indiana

| | Parasites | | Hosts Parasitized | |
Parasites	Total	Average	Total	Percent
Fleas (Siphonaptera)				
Corrodopsylla hamiltoni	137	1.27	18	16.7
Ctenophthalmus pseudagyrtes	25	0.23	8	7.4
Peromyscopsylla scotti	1	0.01	1	0.9
Epitedia wenmanni	1	0.01	1	0.9
Mites (Acarina) other than chiggers				
Orycteroxenus soricis	1,934	17.91	46	42.6
Androlaelaps fahrenholzi	71	0.66	25	23.1
Protomyobia americana	34	0.31	13	12.0
Hirstionyssus talpae	32	0.30	6	5.6
Blarinobia cryptotis	11	0.10	7	6.5
Dermacarus hypudaei	6	0.06	2	1.9
Myonyssus jamesoni	1	0.01	1	0.9
Haemogamasus liponyssoides	1	0.01	1	0.9
Pygmephorus designatus	6			

Blarinobia cryptotis are small, white mites most often found on or near the surface of the skin. They have a piercing-sucking proboscis and apparently feed on body juices. The remainder of the mites are larger and are normally found crawling about in the fur.

Wilson (1961) examined only one least shrew during his studies of the lice, ticks, and fleas of Indiana; it harbored one specimen of *Ctenophthalmus pseudagyrtes*. Whitaker and Corthum (1967) reported one specimen of *Epitedia wenmanni*, and other fleas on *Cryptotis*. One shrew examined during this study harbored 73 individuals of *Corrodopsylla hamiltoni*.

No chiggers, ticks, or lice have been found on least shrews in Indiana.

DECIMATING FACTORS. Cats regularly kill least shrews, and there is circumstantial evidence that foxes also kill (and discard) this species. As indicated earlier, various birds of prey feed on least shrews. Raymond J. Fleetwood noted that "several" least shrews were found trapped in freshly dug postholes, a type of unintentional pitfall trap.

TAXONOMY. Hall and Kelson (1959) indicated that *Cryptotis parva parva* (Say), *C. p. harlani* (Duvernoy), and *C. p. elasson* Bole and Moulthrop all occurred in Indiana. Until a more detailed study is made, it is our opinion that all Indiana specimens should be referred to *C. p. parva*.

SELECTED REFERENCES. Choate, 1970; Davis, 1941; Davis and Joeris, 1945; Hamilton, 1944; Whitaker and Mumford, 1972a.

Family **Talpidae**

Eastern Mole
Scalopus aquaticus (Linnaeus)

Mole, Common Mole, Prairie Mole, Shrew Mole

Scalops canadensis: Wied, 1839
Scalops argentatus: Kennicott, 1858
Scalops aquaticus: Wied, 1862
Scalopus aquaticus: McAtee, 1907

DESCRIPTION. The eastern mole is grayish in color, and has greatly enlarged front feet, short legs, a short and nearly naked tail, and small eyes concealed in the fur. Color varies (in part, seasonally) and some individuals appear silvery, others blackish, some gray, and some brownish. The hairs from their bases to near the tips are usually grayish, but the tips are paler in color. Lyon (1936) noted that the winter coat was dark brown above and more grayish below, while in summer the pelage was usually paler and more grayish. The fur is dense, soft, and not differentiated into guard hairs and underfur. Moles molt twice a year, once in spring and once in fall.

The front feet are broader than long, naked below and lightly furred above, and equipped with large flattened claws on the toes. The elongate hind feet are considerably smaller than the forefeet and have smaller claws. The palms of all feet are surrounded by a fringe of hairs, which aid in digging. The front feet are rotated outward so that the palmar surfaces are more or less vertical.

The separation between head and body is not distinct, and the anterior portion of the snout is small, conical, naked, flexible, and projects beyond the mouth. No external ears or eyes are visible.

There are 36 teeth in the skull; none of the teeth has a typical canine form. The zygomatic arches are complete (but thin), and are often broken in cleaned skulls.

The sexing of moles by external examination may be difficult. Males have one urogenital opening (in the penis) anterior to the anus; females have an anterior urinary papil-

Eastern mole. Photo by Gary Tieben

lar opening, the vaginal opening, and the anus. Females have 6 teats.

We have noted a considerable amount of abnormal coloring among mole specimens from Indiana (Fig. 36). Of 297 examined, 47 have white, whitish, yellowish, or orangish patches of color in the pelage. These specimens are from widely scattered localities, but 24 are from the Richmond-Centerville area (Wayne County) and 9 are from near Lafayette (Tippecanoe County). Spotting is confined to the venter on 40, to the dorsum on 3, and is present on both the dorsum and venter on 4 of the specimens. A mole taken in Putnam County is completely cream colored, and two others we have examined are totally

white or whitish. Some animals have orangish to rusty colored spots on various parts of the body; once thought to have taxonomic importance, these spots are now thought to be the result of glandular secretions. Whitish spotting of Indiana eastern moles was reported by Evermann and Butler (1894b), and Jackson (1915) described an unusually colored animal from Madison (Jefferson County). A specimen (Clay County) in the Indiana State University collection is primarily cream colored with three dark spots about 3–4 cm diameter, one around the right eye, one around the tail, and one on the posterior dorsum.

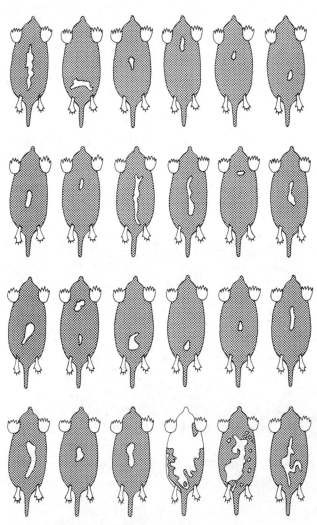

Figure 36.   Extent and variation of white or cream-colored spotting on venter of Indiana *Scalopus.*

Weights and measurements are listed in Table 39. The dental formula is

$$\text{I}\ \frac{3}{2}\ \text{C}\ \frac{1}{0}\ \text{P}\ \frac{3}{3}\ \text{M}\ \frac{3}{3}\ =\ 36.$$

Table 39
Weights and measurements of *Scalopus aquaticus* from Indiana

	Males	Females
Total length (mm)		
n	52	46
x̄	193.9	183.7
range	167-223	164-209
SD	9.62	9.0
SE	˙ 1.3	1.3
Tail length (mm)		
n	52	46
x̄	29.9	27
range	24-35	22-33
SD	3.0	3.5
SE	0.4	0.5
Hind foot (mm)		
n	52	46
x̄	23.3	22.4
range	20-29	19-28
SD	1.6	1.1
SE	0.2	0.2
Weight (grams)		
n	49	46
x̄	119.7	94.4
range	82.5-139.8	80-123
SD	16	17.5
SE	2.3	2.5

STATUS AND DISTRIBUTION. David Thomas (1819; in Lindley, 1916) seems to have been the first to record *Scalopus aquaticus* from the state. Wied (1839) mentioned its occurrence at New Harmony (Posey County), and Plummer (1844) and Haymond (1870) both regarded it as "very numerous," in Wayne and Franklin counties respectively. Cox (1893) recorded it as "common but not abundant" in Randolph County. It was listed from 7 counties by Evermann and Butler (1894b), who remarked about the moles in Franklin County that "many moles taken here are more or less marked with white on throat and lower parts." Hahn (1909) wrote that this mole "apparently occurs throughout the State" but included "reliable" records from only 14 counties.

About Lake Maxinkuckee (Marshall County) the eastern mole was reported to be "very common" by Evermann and Clark (1911). Lyon (1923), writing about the dune region of Porter County, noted that "Residents state that moles are not uncommon in the region, but they have escaped my personal observation." His comments were based mainly on work done there in 1922. Engels (1933) called the eastern mole "very common" in St. Joseph County. Lyon (1936) listed specimens from 13 counties and "records" from about 70 more. Dwight M. Lindsay studied mammals in Jefferson and Ripley counties in the early 1950s, but of 600 small mammals he collected, only 3 were eastern moles. He reported that "nowhere are they common" (Lindsay, 1960). He thought the scarcity he noticed might be correlated to soil types present in the counties studied. He further commented that "Not a single molehill was seen in the course of this investigation, although they had been observed previously in this area by the author."

It is obvious that the eastern mole is found throughout the state and that it is common in most sections. An intensive study of distribution and populations as they may relate to vegetation and soil types has not been made. We have examined specimens from 66 counties (Map 12).

We have no numerical information concerning the size of mole populations in Indiana, although moles certainly occur commonly and in large numbers. It is true, however, that the number of moles in an area is probably less than one might think from the number of burrows, for a single mole constructs many feet of burrows. The home range of an eastern mole is probably less than one acre, but determining species density for a given area is quite difficult. Engels (1933) reported that "from two to three moles per day" were captured in the same trap in a runway "for several days." Whether this instance involved a single mole family or indicated that several adults used the same runway is unknown.

HABITAT. The eastern mole is found in most Indiana habitats, even in some areas that are periodically inundated by flood waters. Open fields, especially with sandy or other loose soils, lawns, roadsides, open woods, gardens, and cultivated fields are all habitats likely to be invaded by moles.

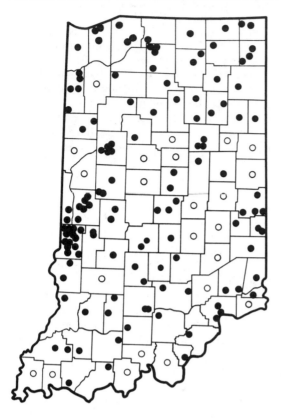

Map 12.   The Eastern Mole, *Scalopus*
          aquaticus, in Indiana

Loose, fairly moist soil would appear to be a
factor necessary for this species to thrive,
while excessive soil moisture would seem to
inhibit it. Dellinger (1951) described how
tunneling moles were "frequently forced to
turn aside to by-pass small puddles" when
burrowing in marshy places. The strength of
the eastern mole is surprising. We once found
one extending its forage tunnel through very
dry, clay soil in a woods. It seemed impossible that the mole could tunnel through this
type of substrate.

ASSOCIATED SPECIES.   Other small mammals often travel runways constructed by
moles. Lyon (1923) trapped in runs evidently
made by moles in sand dunes in Porter
County and captured the white-footed
mouse, the woodland vole, and the prairie
vole. In northwestern Indiana, where pocket
gophers occur, moles and gophers often have
burrows and mounds side by side, and moles
have been trapped in gopher burrows.

HABITS.   Since the eastern mole is almost
completely fossorial (only occasionally coming above the ground) it is seldom seen. One
captured crossing a road in January may have
been forced from its burrow by rain and melting snow. The presence of moles in an area,
however, is easily detected by the characteristic mounds of soil (molehills) pushed
up on the surface of the ground and by the
elevated ridges across the ground that mark
the location of shallow forage tunnels beneath. One easily breaks through these ridges
when walking in habitats supporting moles.
Burrowing is such an important aspect of the
life of the mole that most of its characteristics
are adaptations for the fossorial life. These
include large front feet for digging, a mova-
ble snout, a naked tail that serves as a sensory
organ (especially when the mole moves
backward), and eyes and ears that are
covered with fur. The eyes are fused shut and
serve only to distinguish between light and
dark.

Burrow of eastern mole taken at Willow Slough,
Newton County. Photo by Whitaker

Mound of soil pushed up by eastern mole, in Spencer County. Photo by Whitaker

When digging, *Scalopus* uses the front feet to loosen the soil and braces itself with the hind feet. Soil is pushed backward beneath the animal until a pile has accumulated, then the mole turns around and pushes the soil farther to the rear with its front feet. A narrow pelvic girdle and relatively small hindquarters allow the mole to turn around more easily (by a partial somersault) inside the tunnel. Excess soil excavated in tunneling may be pushed into an unused burrow or to the ground surface, where it forms somewhat conical molehills. Forage tunnels are near the surface of the ground, and when a mole is actively extending a forage tunnel, an observer can see the soil being pushed up to form the characteristic ridges. During this time, the mole can often be captured by hand by inserting the blade of a shovel or spade behind it so that it cannot retreat back into the completed burrow. Burrowing speed varies with the texture of the soil, but may occur at the rate of 4.5 meters in an hour. Walker *et al.* (1964) reported that a mole constructed 31 meters of forage tunnel in a day.

Moles are active day and night and throughout the year. When the ground surface becomes frozen, they use deeper burrows. Walter F. Beineke captured two eastern moles in late December that were burrowing on his lawn when the upper half inch of soil was frozen. Mounds may be pushed up through the snow when soil conditions permit. Numerous new mounds may be observed after a heavy rain, particularly when

the rain follows a dry period. When the spring thaw occurs, a flurry of mole activity takes place and many forage tunnels and mounds are constructed. Mounds pushed up by moles are sometimes confused with those made by pocket gophers (in northwestern Indiana), although the molehills are usually smaller and are shaped differently.

A live mole placed on the ground does not usually attempt to escape by running, but immediately begins to dig into the soil.

A musky secretion from a gland on the belly of *Scalopus aquaticus* marks the burrow as the mole passes. It appears that such markings serve in communication between moles, primarily during the breeding season. The sounds made by moles include squeals, squeaks, snorts, and grating of the teeth, but it is not clear how these sounds function in the daily life of the species.

Eastern moles can swim, but, unlike the star-nosed mole, probably do so only under emergency conditions.

FOOD. Whitaker and Schmeltz (1974) reported on the food habits of 90 eastern moles from Indiana. The most important food item was earthworms (26.8 percent of the total), followed by scarabaeid larvae, vegetation, ants (Formicidae), and ground beetles (Carabidae). Numerous other foods were present in lesser amounts (Table 40, and see below). Animal material constituted 80.8 percent of the total volume of food eaten, insect larvae (especially scarabaeid) alone accounting for 23.3 percent. It appears that moles often encounter ant nests and feed upon adults, larvae, and especially pupae, for 10.5 percent was this food. A mole taken on 31 July contained 98 percent ants and had 3 ants firmly attached to one leg. Adult beetles constituted 9.6 percent of the food.

Of the 18.2 percent of vegetation in the stomachs, seeds (especially of the grass *Digitaria*) occurred fairly often and all seeds made up 7.3 percent of total food volume. Miscellaneous vegetation (bits of roots, stems, etc.) may have been ingested along with other foods. Foods representing less than 1 percent of the total volume do not appear in Table 40, but, in decreasing abundance, were as follows: unidentified Coleoptera, *Elymus* seeds, cantharid larvae (*Chauliognathus*=soldier beetles), Lepidoptera, corn, unidentified insect larvae, elaterid

Table 40

Foods eaten by *Scalopus aquaticus* (n = 90) from
Indiana

Food Item	Percent Volume	Percent Frequency
Annelida (earthworm)	26.8	87.8
Scarabaeid larvae (scarab beetle)	13.9	32.2
Miscellaneous plant foods	9.0	40.0
Formicidae (ant)	7.2	48.9
Carabidae (ground beetle)	5.6	28.9
Ant pupae	3.3	17.8
Insect (unidentified)	3.1	16.7
Chilopoda (centipede)	3.1	21.1
Coleopterous larvae	3.0	18.9
Scarabaeidae, adults (scarab beetle)	2.6	7.8
Lepidopterous pupae	1.9	8.9
Digitaria (crab grass) seeds	1.9	2.2
Lepidopterous larvae	1.9	7.8
Oats or wheat seeds	1.5	2.2
Unidentified material	1.4	6.7
Carabid larvae (ground beetle)	1.2	6.7
Sorghum seeds	1.1	1.1
Endogone	1.1	2.2
Araneae (spider)	1.0	5.6

Foods constituting less than 1 percent of the total volume are
listed in the text.

larvae, grass stems, tiger beetles (*Cicindela repanda*), *Prunus* seeds, *Physalis* fruit, unidentified fungi, insect eggs (*Orthoptera?*), unidentified Hymenoptera, flesh, Lygaeidae, grass seeds, slug (*Deroceras*), sowbug, tipulid larvae, unidentified dipterous pupae, unidentified seeds, snout beetles (Curculionidae), *Cerastium* seeds, Cyclorrhapha pupae, crickets, dipterous larvae, moss, hymenopterous larvae, adult Staphylinidae (rove beetles), gall wasps (Cynipoidea), stratiomyid (soldier fly) larvae.

REPRODUCTION. We have accumulated little information concerning reproduction in Indiana *Scalopus*. Conaway (1959) studied the reproductive tracts of 6 females from Dearborn County and concluded that the height of the breeding season for eastern moles in southern Indiana was probably about mid-February. Of the females he examined (all trapped in February), 3 were in estrus, 1 was implanting, and 2 were in late pregnancy; he provided no further details. We have records of gravid females, as follows: 6 March (Floyd County), 3 embryos 10 mm long; 30 March (Vigo County), 4 em-

bryos; 5 April (Tippecanoe County), 3 embryos 23 mm crown-rump length; 8 April (Cass County), 2 embryos 2 mm crown-rump length; 15 April (Clay County), 2 embryos 33 mm crown-rump length; 7 May (Tippecanoe County), 3 well developed embryos.

We observed 15 females with placental scars; 2 had 5, 9 had 4, 1 had 3, and 3 had 2 each. Females with placental scars were collected in April, May, June, July, and September (Table 41). We do not know how long such scars persist following parturition, but the September record appears quite late to us. McAtee (1907) collected a subadult *Scalopus* on 2 May that was 156 mm in total length and about three-fourths grown. We have examined 3 immatures from Wayne County, taken on 14 and 18 April, that measured from 120 to 132 mm in total length.

The eastern mole supposedly produces a single litter per year, in early spring, after a gestation period of about 30 to 42 days. Clearly we need additional data on reproduction in this species. Data on testis size in males are shown in Table 41. Moles lack a scrotum and the testes are retained permanently in the abdominal cavity. We found testes were smallest in the summer (June to August), enlarged in September and October, reached a maximum size in February, March, and April, and retrogressed through May. These data are consistent with the view that eastern moles produce a single litter per year and suggest that copulation may reach a peak in March. There may be some variation in the breeding season from southern to northern Indiana.

Harmon P. Weeks, Jr., found a *Scalopus* nest in the edge of his lawn and provided the following description. The nest was a ball of leaves constructed of fragments less than an inch square. It was 12 inches below the surface of the ground and in a nongrassy area. When found on 28 April, it contained 4 young about 3 inches long. The nest, which was excavated by a dog, was re-covered, but the adult mole evidently moved the young. Since practically all mole specimens seen by us are adult or near-adult size, it appears that young may remain in the nest until nearly full grown before venturing into forage burrows.

PARASITES. Of 104 eastern moles examined for external parasites (Whitaker and Schmeltz, 1974), 80 (76.9 percent) were infested with at least one individual. Four species of fleas, one biting louse, and thirteen species of mites were recovered (Table 42). In addition, 78 miscellaneous mites (apparently free-living forms) were noted but not included in Table 42.

The only common flea on Indiana *Scalopus* was *Ctenopthalmus pseudagyrtes*, represented by 134 specimens. Two specimens of *Nearctopsylla genalis* (St. Joseph County) constituted the first record of this flea from Indiana. There are relatively few records of this flea, which Hubbard (1947) considered a parasite of shrews and moles. The flea *Stenoponia americana* has also been reported from shrews and other Indiana mammals (Whitaker and Mumford, 1972a; Whitaker and Wilson, 1968; Wilson, 1961). One specimen of *Cediopsylla simplex*, a flea found primarily on rabbits *(Sylvilagus)*, can be considered accidental on moles.

A few beetles *(Leptinus americana)* found on *Scalopus* were previously reported from Indiana by Whitaker and Mumford (1972a) and by Wilson (1957). The sucking louse *Haematoponoides squamosus*, from only two moles, had not previously been recorded from Indiana.

The most abundant mite was listed as *Pygmephorus* sp., but several species of this genus are included (see Table 42) and have been described as new by Dr. S. Mahunka of the Hungarian Natural History Museum in Budapest (Mahunka, 1973, 1975) and by Smiley and Whitaker (1979). These tiny mites were sometimes in large numbers and have also been found on several other species, especially *Blarina*. These mites are apparently phoretic. One specimen of *Macrocheles* was also taken.

The two labidophorids taken proved to be

Table 41

Reproductive information from *Scalopus aquaticus* from Indiana

Month	Adult Females			Adult Males		
			No. with		Testis size (mm) Average	
	Number examined	Number pregnant	placental scars	Number examined	Length	Width
Jan.	3	—	—	1	10.0	6.0
Feb.	0	—	—	1	13.0	8.0
March	4	1	—	4	16.3	9.0
April	10	1	8	3	15.0	9.7
May	4	—	2	5	11.8	7.4
June	12	—	1	4	5.5	3.5
July	10	—	3	10	6.0	3.8
Aug.	6	—	—	5	7.4	4.8
Sept.	3	—	1	5	8.4	4.4
Oct.	6	—	—	8	9.9	6.3
Nov.	0	—	—	3	9.0	5.3
Dec.	2	—	—	1	11.0	6.0

Table 42

Ectoparasites and other associates of *Scalopus aquaticus* (n = 104) from Indiana
(from Whitaker and Schmeltz, 1974)

Parasites	Parasites		Hosts Parasitized	
	Total	Average	Total	Percent
Fleas (Siphonaptera)				
Ctenophthalmus pseudagyrtes	139	1.34	46	44.2
Nearctopsylla genalis	2	0.02	1	1.0
Stenoponia americana	1	0.01	1	1.0
Cediopsylla simplex	1	0.01	1	1.0
Sucking Lice (Anoplura)				
Haematopinoides squamosus	32	0.31	4	3.8
Coleoptera (Beetles)				
Leptinus americanus	9	0.09	4	3.8
Mites (Acarina) other than chiggers				
Pygmephorus sp.*	925±	8.89	42	40.4
*Pygmephorus identified:				
P. scalopi	64			
P. whitakeri	15			
P. hastatus	2			
P. designatus	1			
P. horridus	1			
P. mahunkai	1			
P. whartoni	1			
Scalopacarus obesus	823±	7.91	12	11.5
Haemogamasus harperi	282	2.71	13	12.5
Androlaelaps fahrenholzi	146	1.40	21	20.2
Haemogamasus liponyssoides	97	0.93	30	28.8
Eulaelaps stabularis	13	0.13	6	5.8
Xenoryctes latiporus	7	0.07	2	1.9
Bakerdania plurisetosa	5	0.05	—	—
Ornithonyssus bacoti	2	0.02	1	1.0
Ornithonyssus sylviarum	1	0.01	1	1.0
Haemogamasus ambulans	1	0.01	1	1.0
Hirstionyssus blarinae	1	0.01	1	1.0
Macrocheles sp.	1	0.01	1	1.0
Chigger mites (Trombiculidae)				
Euschoengastia trigenuala	3	0.03	1	1.0

new species (one was a new genus, *Scalopacarus*) and were described by Fain and Whitaker (1973) as *Scalopacarus obesus* and *Xenoryctes latiporus*. Both are hypopi or transport forms, adults of which are unknown. The remainder of the mites are normally thought of as parasitic forms. *Haemogamasus harperi, H. liponyssoides,* and *Androlaelaps fahrenholzi* occur regularly on eastern moles in Indiana, but *Eulaelaps stabularis* is infrequent. Whitaker and Schmeltz (1974) reported the first records for the mites *Haemogamasus harperi* and

Hirstionyssus blarinae from Indiana and the following species for the first time from eastern moles: *Euschoengastia trigenuala, Ornithonyssus bacoti, Hirstionyssus blarinae.*

Of 107 eastern moles examined for internal parasites, 12 (11.2 percent) were infected. Five each had from 1 to 9 intestinal cestodes; 7 each had from 1 to 16 nematodes, all in the stomach.

DECIMATING FACTORS. Owls and domestic dogs and cats are known to prey on eastern moles. Dogs and cats usually dig the moles from their forage burrows. Cats sometimes watch the tunnels being formed and then pounce and dig the moles out; they often abandon the moles then, apparently because of their bad odor. How owls catch moles is unknown; perhaps they take some as carrion or find the moles aboveground. Minton (1944) found a "mole" (probably *Scalopus*) in the stomach of a black rat snake. One August day, Mumford and David L. Herbst found a prairie king snake with half of its body in the forage tunnel of an eastern mole; the snake was captured and found to have a dead adult *Scalopus* in its mouth. We have found the remains of *Scalopus* in 1 of 5 mink stomachs and 1 of 34 gray fox stomachs examined. Thomas W. Hoekstra found a late June food cache (thought to be that of a red fox) that contained two eastern moles, an eastern chipmunk, and a vole (*Microtus* sp.). The remains of three eastern moles have been identified in the pellets of unidentified owls, and two were found in long-eared owl pellets. Numerous moles are found dead (frequently on roads); some have probably been captured and discarded by mammals which found the strong odor of moles offensive. It is suspected that foxes kill and abandon moles, and dogs probably behave similarly.

TAXONOMY. The subspecies in Indiana is *Scalopus aquaticus machrinus* (Rafinesque).

SELECTED REFERENCES. Arlton, 1936; Christian, 1950; Conaway, 1959; Henning, 1952; Hisaw, 1923a, 1923b; Jackson, 1915; West, 1910; Whitaker and Schmeltz, 1974.

Star-nosed Mole
Condylura cristata (Linnaeus)

Condylura cristata: Evermann, 1888

DESCRIPTION. The star-nosed mole is blackish above and below, with dense fur that is soft and shiny but coarser than that of the eastern mole. The eyes and ears are small, and the long pointed snout has 22 fleshy tentacles (the star) around its tip. The tail is long, scaly, black, covered with coarse blackish hairs, and constricted at the base; it becomes much enlarged with deposits of stored fat in the winter. The feet are large and sparsely scaled above. The hind feet are elongate, the front feet shorter and broad with the plantar surfaces turned somewhat outward. The skull is narrow, with incomplete auditory bullae, and the third incisor is caniform in shape.

Weights and measurements are shown in Table 43. The dental formula is

$$\text{I } \frac{3}{3} \text{ C } \frac{1}{1} \text{ P } \frac{4}{4} \text{ M } \frac{3}{3} = 44.$$

STATUS AND DISTRIBUTION. The first published record of this species from Indiana should be credited to either Butler (1888) or Evermann (1888), both of whom recorded a specimen taken 5 July 1887 near Denver (Miami County). This specimen was later destroyed by a fire that burned the museum at Indiana State Normal School (now Indiana State University) on 8 April 1888. Professor W. B. Van Gorder had seen a specimen (not preserved) from Noble County in 1886 (Hahn, 1909). Evermann and Butler (1894b) reported a star-nosed mole captured near Deedsville (Miami County) on 19 March 1894, and Hahn (1909) mentioned that two were taken near Denver on 3 June 1890 and 30 March 1894.

A record from Bartholomew County may not be reliable. Butler (1895), who did not see the specimen, wrote as follows: "A specimen described by Miss Elizabeth Wright appears to be this species. It was taken in their garden near Grammar." Even more surprising, since it was reported from so far south in Indiana, was the record by True (1896), who quoted from a letter he received from Charles Dury, secretary of the Cuvier Club of Cincinnati, as follows: "There is a specimen of *Condylura cristata* in the Cuvier Club collection that was sent to us from Indiana, near the Ohio State line, a few miles north of due west from Cincinnati. This is the only specimen I have seen from the vicinity of this city. In twenty-five years collecting in

Star-nosed mole. Photo by Clarence Owens

this vicinity, I have never run across it my-self."

Lyon (1936) listed records (but no speci-mens) from four counties. He did not com-ment on the report by True, but listed True's record. Perhaps the specimen had been lost in the meantime; we have been unable to verify its existence. The oldest extant speci-men may be that in the Field Museum of Natural History and was collected on 19 June 1941 (Steuben County). In March 1959, M. Dale Harbaugh sent Mumford a mounted specimen of the star-nosed mole, taken near South Bend, and made these comments in the accompanying letter. "The one I'm send-ing to you is in terrible condition but still can be identified. I must have got this at least 15 to 18 yrs. ago. My apologies for not having the date on the specimen. I sort of remember that I mounted it myself."

Through the following years, specimens and reports of *Condylura cristata* in Indiana have been accumulated from various locali-ties. Mumford (1969c) knew of 8 extant specimens, from Allen, Kosciusko, Lagrange, Steuben, and St. Joseph counties, and con-sidered the species as "probably rare and confined to northern Indiana." Since 1969, we have obtained or examined an additional 23 specimens of this mole from Indiana. Based on new evidence, we feel that the cur-rent status of this species in the state must be modified from earlier thinking. It seems to be

common in some parts of its northeastern Indiana range and has a wider distribution than previously known to us. There are re-

Table 43

Weights and measurements of *Condylura cristata* from Indiana

	Males	Females
Total length (mm)		
n	15	9
$\bar{x}$	178.2	171.9
range	167-190	152-198
SD	7.70	12.55
SE	1.98	4.18
Tail length (mm)		
n	15	9
$\bar{x}$	66.8	66.7
range	58-70	57-71
SD	5.60	5.21
SE	1.43	1.73
Hind foot (mm)		
n	15	9
$\bar{x}$	26	25.6
range	21-29	22-27
SD	2.42	1.58
SE	0.6	0.52
Weight (grams)		
n	13	8
$\bar{x}$	42	41
range	31.2-57.3	30.0-58.6
SD	7.49	9.30
SE	2.1	3.3

cently collected specimens from nine counties, but its range is still imperfectly known and requires further study (Map 13).

Previous authors considered the star-nosed mole rare in Indiana, and the records from scattered localities are insufficient to draw conclusions regarding population size. Our best data on numbers were gathered on the Pigeon River Fish and Wildlife Area (Lagrange and Steuben counties) in mid-May 1973. During a three-night session of trapping with snap-back mousetraps, we captured 14 star-nosed moles from three different sites. The species is obviously common there, in the correct habitat, and we believe we could take large numbers of specimens on that property. Dean L. Zimmerman has obtained 5 specimens for us from a small area in Noble County, indicating a sizable population at that site.

It appears that relatively few specimens of the star-nosed mole were previously collected because no one really trapped for them. Many of the earlier specimens were obtained by accident ("caught by cat," "found dead," etc.). Several persons who trap muskrats along the Pigeon River have captured star-nosed moles in their traps (*fide* Dale N. Martin and others), but these specimens never reached a museum and were not made known to us in time to preserve them. A population study of this interesting mammal would add much to our knowledge and make a worthwhile research project.

HABITAT. Marshes, bogs, ditch and stream banks, and swampy areas are the favored habitats of the star-nosed mole. Such areas usually have an abundance of food and loose soil that allows the mole to burrow easily. *Condylura* is semiaquatic and probably spends considerable time in the water. It is unable to burrow in more compact soils in which the larger and stronger *Scalopus aquaticus* can work. In Steuben County, specimens of star-nosed moles were trapped in surface runways in a damp depression that floods in the spring and is surrounded by pasture. A rank growth of weeds nearly three feet tall at the site included goldenrod, vervain, mint, thistle, boneset, and milkweed. Plants from previous seasons had fallen so that the ground was in most places well covered by a thick layer of decaying plant material. Runs in which star-nosed moles were taken were at the surface of the ground, but depressed somewhat into the soft soil and covered by fallen stems. The protecting cover was pulled aside and traps were placed across the runs.

Don R. Helms captured a star-nosed mole in a marshy area bordering a lake. One was taken in a muskrat trap along the bank of the Pigeon River, just upstream from where it flows along the border of a rather extensive tamarack swamp. Along the shore at this site the soil was saturated and plants growing there were alder, dogwood, poison sumac, and other typical swamp species. On the Pigeon River Fish and Wildlife Area, we captured star-nosed moles in burrows in a grass-covered bank along a pond, a brushy willow thicket along a lake, a tamarack swamp, brush and brushy river bank, and a shallow, leaf-filled gulley draining into a lake. Some of the trap sites were saturated, others were rela-

Map 13.   The Star-nosed Mole, *Condylura cristata*, in Indiana

Star-nosed mole habitats at Pigeon River Fish and Wildlife Area. Photos by Whitaker

tively dry, but the soil in most cases was mucky.

ASSOCIATED SPECIES. The most abundant small mammals sharing the habitat with the star-nosed mole are the meadow vole, the masked shrew, the short-tailed shrew, and the meadow jumping mouse. Star-nosed moles have been trapped at underwater burrow entrances to muskrat dens.

HABITS. Star-nosed moles construct forage tunnels, ridges, and mounds (molehills), but evidently do not push up as many ridges as eastern moles. We also noted rather extensive areas where the muck had been disturbed by *Condylura*, on the Pigeon River Fish and Wildlife Area. We have observed burrows in banks along lakes and ponds, in saturated soil along lake shores, and under a thick layer of leaves in partially dried-up swamps. This species also enters wet portions of lawns, where it may push up characteristic mounds. It is said to be semicolonial.

The star-nosed mole is active day and night and throughout the year. Jackson (1961) reported that in Wisconsin it often makes burrows in and under the snow and sometimes appears on top of snow. In the manner of other moles, it digs through soil or mud with the forefeet, pushing the loosened soil ahead of it as the tunnels are extended. It is an excellent swimmer and diver, well-adapted for its semiaquatic habitats. Entrances to its burrows often are below water. In winter it is said to be active beneath the ice. Jackson (1961) observed that its swimming movements resemble those of a frog, except that the front feet, moved alternately, provided the momentum. The hind feet also move alternately and the tail is not used in swimming.

Don R. Helms was sitting at a lake shore (Lagrange County) about 5:00 on an early September evening, when a star-nosed mole walked out of a marshy area about two feet from the water's edge and onto a bare sand beach, where Helms captured it by hand. Two Indiana specimens were found in the basements of buildings and one was observed under a house that was being moved. Another fell into the cellar window well of a house. Lee Brubaker found one in an upright drainage tile in a bog. We captured one in a mousetrap set at the mouth of a burrow completely filled with water in a swampy area.

FOOD. We have examined 18 star-nosed moles with food in their stomachs. The only major dietary item was earthworms, comprising 100 percent of the food in nine stomachs and 10, 66, and 90 percent in three others. The remainder of the food items identified were insects, slugs, vegetation, and aquatic foods (three stomachs). Two individuals caught in muskrat traps contained 8 and 100 percent aquatic insect larvae and annelids. Another specimen, taken in March, contained chironomid and tipulid larvae. We have one report from northern Indiana of a star-nosed mole captured in a plot where earthworms were being raised for fish bait.

Hamilton (1931b) examined the stomachs of 107 moles of this species from New York and found 49 percent of the food to be annelids (80 percent of the aquatic food was leeches and aquatic oligochaetes), 33 percent insects (mostly aquatic), 8 percent extraneous matter, 6.5 percent Crustacea, 2.2 percent mollusks, and 2.2 percent vertebrates.

REPRODUCTION. Star-nosed moles produce one litter a year, in the spring. The gestation period is believed to be about 45 days (Jackson, 1961). The single gravid female we have examined from Indiana was trapped on 15 May and contained four embryos measuring 24 mm in crown-rump length and 34 mm in total length. The nose tentacles of these young were well formed. Jackson stated that newborn young were about 70 to 75 mm in total length. We were surprised that only one of seven females taken by us from 15 to 17 May was gravid. All were about the same size, ranging from 30.8 to 58.6 grams in weight and from 161 to 177 mm in total length. Perhaps most, or all, were in their first year and were mostly nonbreeders. The sole pregnant female weighed 58.6 grams and measured 170 mm in total length.

Hamilton (1931b) recorded the reproductive season of this species in central New York as extending from mid-April to mid-June, most young being born in early May. Litter size for seven pregnant females ranged from 6 to 7.

Jackson (1961) stated that the nest of the

Table 44

Ectoparasites and other associates of *Condylura cristata* (n = 21) from Indiana

Parasites	Parasites		Hosts parasitized	
	Total	Average	Total	Percent
Fleas (Siphonaptera)				
Ctenophthalmus pseudagyrtes	13	0.62	6	28.6
Mites (Acarina) other than chiggers				
Orycteroxenus canadensis	5,586	266.00	14	66.7
Haemogamasus ambulans	20	0.95	8	38.1
Eadiea condylurae	10	0.48	4	19.0
Androlaelaps fahrenholzi	9	0.43	5	23.8
Pygmephorus sp.	6(+)	0.29	6	28.6
Pygmephorus identified				
P. moreohorridus	1	—	—	—
Haemogamasus liponyssoides	4	0.19	3	14.3
Eulaelaps stabularis	1	0.05	1	4.8
Hirstionyssus talpae	1	0.05	1	4.8
Cyrtolaelaps sp.	1	0.05	1	4.8
Macrocheles sp.	1	0.05	1	4.8
Euryparasitus sp.	1	0.05	1	4.8
Anoetidae	1	0.05	1	4.8

star-nosed mole is of grasses or leaves, about 5 to 7 inches in diameter, and a flattened sphere placed above high water, usually in a little hillock or knoll, often beneath a stump or log.

We recorded testis size for twelve Indiana star-nosed moles. From this small sample, the four males with the largest testes (12 to 19 mm in length) were collected on 15 February, 22 March, and 28 April. All of seven taken in mid-May, one in June, one in September, and two in November had testes ranging from 3 to 6 mm in length. It would appear from these meager data that copulation takes place mainly in March and April.

PARASITES. Wilson (1961) examined one Indiana *Condylura* from Steuben County for external parasites and found two specimens of the flea *Ctenopthalmus pseudagyrtes*. We have examined 21 star-nosed moles from Indiana for external and internal parasites; all but one had ectoparasites (Table 44). By far the most abundant form (as many as 1,000 per host) was the host-specific hypopial gly-

cyphagid mite *Orycteroxenus canadensis*. The next most common species, in descending order, were the laelapid mite *Haemogamasus ambulans*, the flea *Ctenopthalmus pseudagyrtes*, and the laelapid mite *Androlaelaps fahrenholzi*. Small numbers of the host-specific myobiid mite *Eadiea condylurae* and other species of mites were also found, including species of *Pygmephorus: P. faini, P. horridus, P. moreohorridus, P. spinosus,* and *P. whitakeri*.

None of 18 moles examined harbored endoparasites.

DECIMATING FACTORS. Two Indiana specimens were captured by cats and one by a dog. Several others, found dead, were probably dropped by predators. Mumford once found a saw-whet owl perched with a decapitated star-nosed mole in its talons, in southern Michigan.

TAXONOMY. The subspecies in Indiana is *Condylura cristata cristata* (Linnaeus).

SELECTED REFERENCES. Hamilton, 1931b; Jackson, 1915.

Order CHIROPTERA

Family Vespertilionidae

Little Brown Myotis
Myotis lucifugus (LeConte)

Little Brown Bat, Cave Bat

Vespertilio gryphus: Allen, 1894
Vespertilio subulatus: Blatchley, 1897
Myotis subulatus: Elliott, 1907
Myestis lucifugus: Van Gorder, 1916
Myotis lucifugus: Hahn, 1909

DESCRIPTION. The little brown myotis is a small, brownish bat with relatively short ears. It is easily confused with several other species of *Myotis*, or with the evening bat *(Nycticeius humeralis)*, the eastern pipistrelle *(Pipistrellus subflavus)*, and even the big brown bat *(Eptesicus fuscus)*. In the hand, an examination of the teeth will enable one to determine if he is dealing with a species of *Myotis*, for in this genus there is a space containing two tiny molariform teeth between the canine and the four large, posterior molariform teeth (see Fig. 10). *Myotis lucifugus* can be separated from *M. sodalis* (the Indiana myotis), with which it is most often confused, by the fact that *sodalis* has dark grayish pink, duller fur, smaller feet, and a distinct keel on the calcar (see Fig. 1; keel can be seen in fresh specimens, not in study skins); also in *sodalis* the hairs on the toes are shorter and do not extend to the tips of the claws. Keen's myotis *(M. keenii)* is dis-

tinguished from other Indiana *Myotis* by its longer ears and by the tragi, which are frequently curved and pointed (see Fig. 2). The gray myotis *(M. grisescens)*, a rare bat in Indiana, has dorsal fur that is the same color from base to tip; the gray myotis is usually grayish, but females may be brownish in summer. The forearm of *grisescens* averages about 44 mm in length; and that of other *Myotis* in Indiana ranges from 35 to 40 mm. The southeastern myotis *(M. austroriparius)* has a more dense, woollier fur than other species in Indiana; the color above is usually gray, with some individuals in late summer exhibiting a brownish cast; the belly fur is usually white-tipped, but may have a tan to pale brownish tinge on certain individuals. The foot is relatively large in *austroriparius* and live animals have a pinkish nose (other than *M. sodalis* and *M. austroriparius*, other *Myotis* in Indiana have dark noses).

Myotis lucifugus in Indiana ranges in color from tan to chocolate brown; adults have shiny fur, but immatures have duller, darker pelage than adults. Several color variations may occur in a single maternity or hibernating aggregation. We have examined a little brown myotis specimen that has white wing tips and a white venter. White-blotched individuals may occur from time to time, as they do in other species of mammals.

135

Little brown myotis. Photo by Merlin Tuttle

Weights and measurements are shown in Table 45. The dental formula is

$$I \ \frac{2}{3} \ C \ \frac{1}{1} \ P \ \frac{3}{3} \ M \ \frac{3}{3} \ = \ 38.$$

STATUS AND DISTRIBUTION. The little brown myotis is common and is found throughout Indiana (Map 14). It is the second most abundant bat (after the Indiana myotis) in hibernating quarters, but possibly less abundant than the big brown bat and the red bat *(Lasiurus borealis)* in the summer. Numerous breeding colonies have been found, ranging from Martin, Lawrence, Jackson, and Franklin counties northward (Cope *et al.*, 1961; Humphrey and Cope, 1976). Animals occupying the noncave regions of Indiana withdraw from those areas in the fall, and many little brown bats hibernate in the caves of southern Indiana (see Map 5). The northernmost wintering record is from an old coal mine in Turkey Run State Park (Parke County), where a single male was found 12 February 1962. The largest known winter populations of *Myotis lucifugus* have been recorded in Coon's Cave and Grotto

Table 45
Weights and measurements of *Myotis lucifugus* from Indiana

	Males	Females
Total length (mm)		
n	39	41
x̄	83.7	84.3
range	72-94	66-91
SD	6.4	6.2
SE	1	1
Tail length (mm)		
n	40	41
x̄	33	33
range	26-43	24-48
SD	4.5	4.6
SE	0.7	0.7
Hind foot (mm)		
n	39	40
x̄	8.7	8.5
range	7-11	5-11
SD	1.5	1.4
SE	0.2	0.2
Weight (grams)		
n	37	36
x̄	6.15	6.15
range	3.1-10.0	3.2-14.4
SD	1.7	2.5
SE	0.3	0.4

Cave (Monroe County), Big Wyandotte Cave (Crawford County), and Ray's Cave (Greene County), but numerous other caves in south-central Indiana have occasional winter concentrations of up to 100 or more little brown bats. There is evidently considerable movement of *M. lucifugus* out of Indiana in the fall, for the numbers known from the breeding colonies are greater than the numbers known to hibernate. As with most species of bats in Indiana, population decreases are evident over the past twenty years.

Humphrey and Cope (1976) published winter population estimates for four Indiana caves (Table 46).

HABITAT. During spring and fall migration and in the summer, the little brown myotis has been encountered by day in buildings, picnic pavilions, on the sides of buildings, beneath shutters, in caves or mines, beneath concrete bridges, and in a wooden covered bridge. At dusk we have shot individuals flying about the borders of

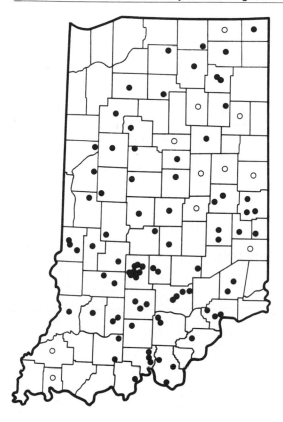

Map 14.   The Little Brown Myotis, *Myotis lucifugus*, in Indiana

Table 46

Winter population estimates of *Myotis lucifugus* in four Indiana caves (from Humphrey and Cope, 1976)

Year	Ray's Cave	Grotto Cave	Wyandotte Cave	Coon's Cave
1960-61	—	2,000	—	900
1961-62	2,680	1,525	350	—
1962-63	—	—	175	—
1963-64	1,800	—	150	225
1964-65	5,600	1,377	900	—
1965-66	1,300	—	500	350
1966-67	1,800	1,180	550	—
1967-68	70	—	140	—
1968-69	350	190	24	—
1969-70	575	266	4	—

wooded areas and along streams lined with trees, in Jackson, Tippecanoe, and Vigo counties. Except for one record from a mine, all wintering bats of this species have been found in caves. Of 36 Indiana caves surveyed

for wintering *M. lucifugus*, 27 harbored this bat. Hibernation sites in the caves "were relatively uniform and stable in microclimate, being cool and humid with almost no air flow" (Humphrey and Cope, 1976). All known breeding colonies have been in buildings; the bats are most often found in attics, but also roost behind shutters, behind the large, wooden, sliding doors of barns, and in other protected places. A group of 15 little brown myotis found beneath the loose bark of an American elm on 22 May could have been a nursery colony (Humphrey and Cope, 1976).

ASSOCIATED SPECIES. The most common bats that hibernate in caves with the little brown myotis are the Indiana myotis, the big brown bat, and the eastern pipistrelle. Other bats that utilize caves along with the little brown bat are Keen's myotis and the southeastern myotis. Of these species, we have found the little brown bat clustered only with the Indiana myotis and the southeastern myotis. In summer maternity colonies, we have noted the big brown bat and (once) the southeastern myotis with the little brown myotis. *Myotis lucifugus* has been shot at dusk while foraging with Keen's myotis, the Indiana myotis, the red bat, the big brown bat, and the eastern pipistrelle. A few little brown bats, Keen's myotis, and Indiana myotis roosted in the daytime beneath a large concrete bridge in Turkey Run State Park; a maternity colony of big brown bats also used this bridge.

HABITS. The little brown myotis is colonial; large congregations are found in hibernation, and assemblages of females (plus some males) form maternity (nursery) colonies. In summer, relatively few adult males are found, although a few roost in caves and some occupy nursery colonies. It would be most interesting to know where adult males roost in the summer and whether they form groups or become more solitary.

From about November to April, the little brown myotis is found almost exclusively in caves. The females leave the caves earlier in the spring than do the males, and begin to congregate in buildings to bear their young; most bats of both sexes have left the caves by 1 June. A very small number of little brown bats (nearly all males) inhabit certain caves during June and July; for example, only four males were found on eighteen June and July visits to twelve caves known to be used for hibernation by *M. lucifugus*. Evidently, when one finds this species in caves during these months, most of the animals are males. Adult male little brown bats were caught in nets set across the entrance to Donnehue's Cave (Lawrence County) on the following nights: 30 June, 5 bats; 14 July, 1 bat; 26 July, 6 bats. We do not know why *M. lucifugus*, and other species of bats, can be netted at cave entrances during these months, even when they do not inhabit the caves during the daytime.

In August, individuals begin returning to the caves, building up to their winter peak in December. As a rule, hibernating little brown bats do not form huge, compact clusters. A common pattern of roosting groups is to form irregular, more or less horizontal rows on the side walls of the caves. This species, however, does hang from cave ceilings and squeezes into both vertical and horizontal crevices. Wintering groups are composed of both sexes, and other species of *Myotis* may be present in the groups. Many little brown bats also hang singly in the caves; lone individuals may wedge themselves into tiny holes in the cave ceiling just large enough to house a single bat. There appears to be little activity by *M. lucifugus* in the hibernating quarters from November to March; one male was netted on 2 December at a cave entrance.

Emergence from day roosts during the nonhibernating season occurs relatively late in the evening. On 18 June, practically none of the members of a nursery colony left the attic until the light outside was so dim that shooting the bats was impossible. This may explain why so few little brown myotis have been obtained by bat hunting at dusk in Indiana. As with other species of bats, time of emergence is closely correlated with time of sunset and with light intensity. In a study of bat activity at the entrance of Donnehue's Cave, we caught no little brown bats in our nets until after sunset, although both Keen's myotis and pipistrelles entered the nets before sunset. Only 16 of 178 little brown myotis netted were caught within the first hour after sunset.

The extensive use of buildings and other man-made structures for roosting and maternity sites by *M. lucifugus* and other bats certainly reveals how these species have adapted since man came on the scene. One wonders whether little brown bats gathered to produce young in trees (perhaps they still do) or made more use of caves in earlier days. It seems evident that buildings provide excellent conditions for the formation of nursery colonies and the rearing of young. One factor may be the warm temperatures that prevail in the attics of houses during the summer. (Caves are relatively cool in summer.) Also, houses afford more protection from natural predators. It is of interest that none of the twelve species of bats that occur in Indiana are known to breed in caves in the state.

On 18 May, a cage of little brown myotis was removed from a cave for banding. Some of the bats were banded near the cave and released before a rain shower began. As the cage with the rest of the squeaking bats was carried one-fourth mile to an automobile, several bats flew about the investigator's head. When he reached the car and paused for a few minutes, four bats circled about and two even lit momentarily on his jacket. All four of these bats were banded and must have been attracted by the noisy animals in the cage.

MIGRATION. Since 1946, many thousand little brown myotis have been banded in Indiana to help researchers learn something about movements, longevity, and other aspects of this bat's natural history. Data from the recapture of banded individuals have not been spectacular, but some information has resulted from this work. Humphrey and Cope (1964) reported the movements of 47 little brown myotis from a maternity colony at Thorntown (Boone County) over a six-year period. Banded bats were recaptured in eight caves in Indiana and two caves in Kentucky, at distances up to 200 miles from the banding site. The general direction of movement was mostly due south-north. Half of the recoveries were made in four caves in Monroe County, Indiana, about 70 miles south of the breeding colony. Band recoveries from studies by Mumford reveal roughly the same type of movement—a general southward movement in fall and a general northward movement in the spring. In both of these banding studies, a few bats were retaken to the east and west of the usual line of movement, indicating a certain amount of sporadic movement in all directions. Humphrey and Cope summarized the recapture of 845 little brown bats away from the banding site. They found that the net distance of autumn migration ranged from 10 to 455 kilometers and averaged 100 kilometers.

Few data are available regarding the speed of migration, but Humphrey and Cope (1964) provided some information. Three bats from Thorntown (Boone County) were captured in Big Wyandotte Cave (Crawford County) 20, 32, and 36 days after being banded; the distance traveled was 132 miles. Two others moved 88 miles to Donnehue's Cave (Lawrence County) in 12 and 13 days. All these periods are maxima, so that the bats may actually have covered these distances much faster. Later, Humphrey and Cope reported movements of 60 kilometers in one night.

Fall migration from the breeding colonies appears to take place from late July to mid-October. At a Boone County colony, 450 bats were present 14 August, 32 on 29 September, and 3 on 10 October (Humphrey and Cope, 1964). Spring migration data are less abundant, but it seems that bats leave the hibernating sites in the caves the last half of April and may be migrating throughout most of May, or even during the first week of June. Some intensive studies of the spring buildup of maternity colony populations would shed more light on spring movements.

In late summer and early fall, relatively large numbers of little brown bats, and other bats, gather about certain cave entrances between dark and midnight. (There is similar spring behavior involving smaller numbers of bats.) Such gatherings of bats can be netted at the cave entrances for banding programs, and offer to the investigator the opportunity to handle fairly large samples of several species. Most of the bats that make up such gatherings are transients, evidently on migration, and on days following this "swarming" activity at the cave entrances only a few bats will be found inside the caves.

Swarming is known to occur at Big Wyandotte, Donnehue's, and Ray's caves in Indiana; it probably also takes place at other, as yet undiscovered, sites. A good example of the pattern of swarming in *Myotis lucifugus* was obtained by Wilson Baker at Big Wyandotte Cave. On the nights of 3, 4, 5, 6, and 7 September 1962, he captured, respectively, 63, 231, 229, 306, and 117 little brown bats. Of these, 627 were males and 319 were females. Three isolated nights of netting at Ray's Cave resulted in the following catches of *Myotis lucifugus:* 301 on 2 September 1962; 246 on 3 September 1964; 205 on 8 September 1971. Smaller numbers were taken at Donnehue's Cave, the largest catches being 61 on 26 August 1970 and 41 on 16 September 1970.

Other species of bats netted with *Myotis lucifugus* at these sites included *M. sodalis*, *M. keenii*, *M. austroriparius*, *M. grisescens*, *Eptesicus fuscus*, *Pipistrellus subflavus*, and *Lasiurus borealis*. The Indiana myotis was most abundant at Big Wyandotte and at Ray's Cave; Keen's myotis was most numerous at Ray's Cave.

HOMING. Cope *et al.* (1961) carried out homing experiments with a summer colony of little brown myotis at Brookville (Franklin County) using radioactive bands. Forty females were banded and released 20 air miles due west of Brookville between 9:00 and 9:34 P.M. From 75 to 80 percent of these bats returned to the original roost within 4 hours 55 minutes and 6 hours. Unfortunately, the ages of the bats used in the experiment were not stated; one might expect adults to home more successfully and at a greater speed than immatures. Four bats that did not return to the original roost were located in another roost just across the street, within 7 hours 45 minutes.

Cope *et al.* (1958) reported on homing of little brown myotis at a nursery colony at Tunnelton (Lawrence County). Groups of a total of 364 bats (67 subadults of both sexes and 297 adult males and females) were released at air mile distances of 120 miles (north-northwest), 93 miles (north-northwest), 66 miles (north-northwest), and 4 miles (west) from Tunnelton. The colony was next visited 34 days later. From 120 miles, 20 percent of the females and 25 percent of the males were back; the release from 120 miles was composed of 110 adult females and 8 adult males. The highest proportion (31 percent) of bats returning had homed from 66 miles north-northwest; the release was made up of 51 adult females, 8 adult males. Only 1 bat homed from 4 miles west, where the release consisted of 32 subadult females and 22 subadult males. Homing from the fourth release (93 miles) involved 18 percent of 120 adult females and 13 subadult males. Although there is an imperfect correlation between the number of adults in the samples, the mileage traveled, and success of homing, it may be significant that adults homed more successfully than subadults.

In another homing experiment at this same colony, none of 15 subadults released 82 miles south or 40 subadults released 107 miles northeast had homed three, twelve, or thirteen months later.

LONGEVITY.   From banding between 1952 and 1959, and recaptures analyzed in 1974, there were 100 little brown myotis that had attained a minimum age of 5 years. Of these animals 69 were females and 31 were males; it should be mentioned however, that many more females than males were banded. The complete breakdown of these recaptures (in minimum years of age) is as follows: 4 males and 8 females at least 5 years of age; 4 males and 20 females recaptured 6 years after banding; 10 males and 11 females at least 7 years old; 3 males and 16 females at least 8 years old; 7 males and 12 females recaptured at 9 years; 1 male and 2 females at least 10 years of age; 1 male recaptured 11 years after banding; 1 male at least 12 years of age.

It is quite probable that some bats banded during the latter part of this longevity study are still alive; thus the percentage of recaptures will ultimately increase and additional data will be forthcoming. Also, we are reporting minimum ages; many bats could have been several to many years old when banded. There is a suggestion that males may live longer than females, as Hitchcock (1965) has pointed out for this species in Canada.

HUMAN USES OF BATS.   Lyon (1931) uncovered the interesting possibility that people in southern Indiana used bat oil for rheumatism; he thought that *Myotis lucifugus* was probably the species involved. Hibernating bats do attain great deposits of subcutaneous fat in early fall and this fat has a low melting point.

Over the past twenty years, many thousands of bats have been removed from Indiana caves for physiological research. This has resulted in conflicts between bat banders and physiologists, and has, more importantly, been an additional decimating factor on hibernating bat populations. Bats have been much used as research animals by various scientists conducting life history, food habits, parasite, homing, longevity, and other studies. Bats from Indiana were also used in various radiation experiments. (It was at one time thought that bats might be immune to radiation!)

Bat guano has been used in other parts of the country (and the world) for fertilizer. We have found no indication that Indiana residents have made use of this commodity. Mumford once removed 49 gallons of bat guano from the attic of a house where a maternity colony of little brown bats was present; this represented only about one-third of the droppings present in the attic. In most Indiana caves, large deposits of bat guano are not present. Many caves housing large numbers of bats have streams of water flowing through them; these streams apparently carry the droppings away and they do not accumulate. Also, much more guano is deposited by summer colonies of bats than by wintering colonies, and no large summer colonies are known in Indiana caves.

MOLT.   We have little data regarding molt in little brown myotis. Three adult females collected on 10 July were molting heavily (two were undergoing a complete body molt and one of these two was still lactating). An immature female taken with the adults was also undergoing a complete body molt. Two of four males (age unknown) taken 30 June had complete body molts in progress. Another unaged male taken 22 June was molting heavily. An immature male and 7 males and 3 females of undetermined age taken 30 August showed no evidence of molt.

FAT STORAGE.   Adults evidently build up fat deposits earlier in the fall than do young of the year. An adult female taken 7 August 1957 was so fat she appeared to be pregnant when captured and examined. Two immature females taken with her had no body fat, and an adult male had moderate fat; an unaged male taken the same day had no fat. An immature male taken 20 August had no fat; 3

unaged males the same day had moderate fat, and 2 unaged females had heavy fat. Nine unaged males and 2 unaged females taken 31 August had no fat. Three females and 1 male taken 3 to 26 September were very fat; another male was medium fat on 10 September. More data are needed to determine the timing of the deposition of body fat during the prehibernating period. The sample collected 31 August may have been composed of migrants, for it was netted at the mouth of a cave. Perhaps migrants have not yet accumulated their winter fat when they pass through Indiana. On the other hand, nonmigrants that may move short distances to winter quarters may take on large amounts of fat rather early in the fall. Migration would deplete stored fat, and excess fat might be extra weight for bats to transport on migration.

Adult females may accumulate body fat earlier than any other sex and age class. Males may be slower (and more active) because copulation occurs in the fall (and winter). Immatures probably gain fat reservoirs more slowly because of the energy expended in growing and perhaps there is thus less physiological potential to add fat rapidly during the first fall of their lives.

FOOD. Sixteen stomachs of little brown bats from Indiana were examined by Whitaker (1972b) for food analyses (Table 47). The food of this species from May through September was more similar to that of the red bat than to that of the big brown bat, with Lepidoptera and Trichoptera the foods most often eaten. Cicadellidae and Delphacidae (Homoptera) were also important, but Coleoptera formed only 12.4 percent of the total volume. A single coleopterous larva formed the entire contents of one stomach, and it and crickets were the only nonflying items eaten. The Lepidoptera eaten were small forms as compared to those eaten by the red bat.

REPRODUCTION. The events leading up to copulation are unknown for most species of bats; further study may reveal whether or not there is courtship or other precopulatory

Table 47

Foods eaten by *Myotis lucifugus* (n = 16) from Indiana
(from Whitaker, 1972b)

Food Item	Percent Volume	Percent Frequency
Lepidoptera (moths)	21.6	31.3
Trichoptera (caddis flies)	13.1	25.0
Diptera (flies)	11.9	31.3
Cicadellidae (leafhoppers)	11.6	43.8
Delphacidae (planthoppers)	8.8	25.0
Coleopterous (beetle) larvae	6.3	6.3
Ichneumonidae (Ichneumon flies)	3.8	12.5
Carabidae (Ground beetles)	3.4	18.8
Reduviidae (Assassin bugs)	2.8	12.5
Scarabaeidae (June beetles)	2.5	6.3
Coleoptera (Unidentified beetles)	2.2	18.8
Tipulidae (Craneflies)	1.9	12.5
Hemerobiidae (Hemerobiids)	1.9	6.3
Chironomidae (Midges)	1.6	12.5
Cerambycidae (Long-horned beetles)	1.6	6.3
Formicidae (Ants)	1.3	12.5
Chrysomelidae (Leaf beetles)	0.9	6.3
Chrysomelidae, *Diabrotica undecimpunctata*	0.9	6.3
Nitidulidae (Nitidulid beetles)	0.9	6.3
Miridae (Leaf bugs)	0.6	6.3
Gryllidae (Crickets)	0.3	6.3
Insects (Unidentified)	0.3	6.3
	100.2	

behavior. Little brown bats in Indiana have been observed copulating on 20 August (one pair, in a maternity colony), on 30 August (at least ten pairs, in a maternity colony), on 16 November (a pair in a cave), and on 11 January (a pair hanging from a cave ceiling; the male of this pair hanging from the cave ceiling grasped the fur on the back of the female's head with his teeth and pulled her head back slightly while copulating with her). Sperm are stored in the uterus of the female until spring, when fertilization occurs.

In April, females begin gathering in maternity (nursery) colonies, where the young are born and reared. Most nursery colonies have been located in the attics of houses, but some are also known in barns, churches, and other buildings. Some nursery sites are dark and poorly ventilated; others (in barns) are well ventilated and well lighted. Daytime temperatures in some of the attics used as nurseries are well in excess of 100 degrees Fahrenheit. This heat evidently has no adverse effect on the bats and it is possible that they choose such sites to promote rapid growth of the young. On the hottest days, the bats tend to hang more in the open places in the attic (exposed rafters, faces of chimneys); they utilize crevices more when temperatures are cooler. In colonies used by the bats for many years, we have seen "stalactites" of crystallized urine hanging from the rafters. In other colonies, deposits of bat droppings at least a foot deep have been noted. In some cases, the weight of accumulated droppings has caused the ceiling of the room below to sag or break through.

As many as 1,000 or more females may occupy a single maternity colony. The 50 nursery colonies examined by Humphrey and Cope ranged in size from about 20 to about 3,000 bats (females and young), but most colonies contained from 300 to 1,200 bats. Humphrey and Cope also noted that the larger nursery colonies were nearer the caves, and in northern Indiana (where there are no hibernacula) the colonies were smaller. Maternity colonies of *Myotis lucifugus* usually averaged considerably larger than maternity colonies of other species of bats that breed in Indiana. Most nurseries of little brown myotis were within a few hundred meters of a pond or stream, to which the bats flew when leaving the colony at dusk.

In the maternity colonies, bats may hang from the rafters, on the sides of brick chimneys, inside the walls or between the roofing and the attic ceiling. It is not usually easy to catch or observe all individuals in a colony at any one time. Young bats are frequently found dead on the attic floor; some may become separated from adult females and succumb without being retrieved, and some probably are born dead or die and fall to the floor. From time to time a dead bat is found hanging from a wire or cord in which it has become entangled in flight.

Maternity colonies usually contain a single species of bat, but we have found big brown bats sharing a building with little brown myotis on seven occasions, and we found a single southeastern myotis (a transient?) in a little brown myotis colony on 1 October. Once selected, breeding sites are evidently used for years; one such colony in Jackson County was in continuous use for at least sixty-five years, and Cope *et al.* (1961) suggests a colony in use for a hundred years.

Small numbers of adult males may inhabit the maternity colonies. One colony contained 2 percent males on 20 April, and another contained 3 percent males on 30 April. At a third colony, 7 males and 121 females were present on 29 May. As the season progresses, a higher percentage of males sometimes occupies the colony. One colony contained 32 percent males in late August, 84 percent the first of October, and 96 percent the second week of October (Cope *et al.*, 1958). Whether the colonies are staging areas for males in preparation for fall migration, or whether the gathering of males in the nurseries facilitates mating is unknown, but copulation has been observed there as early as August. More intensive studies are needed to determine what percentage of these males are animals reared there during the summer and how many are transients.

Many animals from a maternity colony tend to return each year to that colony, but banding studies have also revealed that individuals may occupy different maternity colonies in different years. In general, it is felt that many adult females return to the same maternity colonies year after year throughout their lives. Some males also may be found in a particular maternity colony more than one year. One male was banded at Tunnelton (Lawrence County) in a breeding colony on

30 August 1954 and released at Terre Haute (Vigo County) that night. He was again in the Tunnelton colony on 4 July 1957 and on 25 July 1962. He was also captured twice during the fall at Big Wyandotte Cave (Crawford County), on 7 September 1961 and 13 September 1963. Another male banded 7 August 1957 at Tunnelton was not caught again there but was found 9 August 1958 and 14 August 1963 in a maternity colony at Thorntown (Boone County), 95 miles north-northwest. A male banded 18 June 1953 in a nursery colony near Cortland (Jackson County) and released at Freetown (8 miles west) was back at Cortland 2 July 1953. On 14 June 1954, he was taken again from Cortland and released near Kossuth (Washington County), and was found at Cortland on 31 August 1954; this time he was released at Bedford (Lawrence County), but was found again at Cortland on 18 August 1961.

The return of adult female little brown myotis to a particular maternity colony has been determined from banding studies. From 18 June 1953 to 17 August 1962, there have been ten visits made to a maternity colony near Cortland. One female *M. lucifugus* has been present in this colony over a span of seven years, six females over a span of eight years, and nine females over a span of nine years. Since the colony has not been visited since 1962, we do not know whether some females actually used the colony for longer periods. Two males were found here over periods of seven and eight years, but seven males are known to have been present in a single year and three for two years. Only four

little brown bats banded as young of the year in this colony have been recaptured there in later years; these were found one, two, two, and nine years later.

Cope and Hendricks (1970) reported on the fate of twelve "well-established" little brown bat nursery colonies in Indiana; some of these had been active for at least ten years. Of these colonies, checked from June to August 1969, three were no longer present, four showed declines of 48 to 96 percent, and five retained their former levels.

A single young is generally produced each year by the adult female; occasionally twins may be born. Parturition usually occurs in late May, in June, or in early July. The young are capable of flight about four weeks after birth. One newborn little brown myotis weighed 1.4 grams, had a total length of 48 mm, a forearm length of 12.5 mm, and a wingspan of 94 mm. The young in a nursery colony are not all born at the same time; twelve young from Fountain County (21 June) ranged from newborn to well-furred individuals and seemed to represent three rather distinct developmental stages on the basis of their morphological characteristics. Ten of them had forearm lengths from 12 to 30.5 mm (average 21 mm). Two adult females collected from this colony on the same date each contained a single fetus, measuring 20 and 21 mm respectively in crown-rump length. At a maternity colony in Pulaski County (2 July) sixteen young had forearm lengths of 15 to 34 mm (average 26 mm). On 21 June, eleven young from a colony in Clay County had forearms ranging from 13.5 to 21

Table 48

Ectoparasites of *Myotis lucifugus* (n = 84) from Indiana

Parasites	Parasites		Hosts Parasitized	
	Total	Average	Total	Percent
Fleas (Siphonaptera)				
Myodopsylla insignis	1	0.01	1	1.2
Mites (Acarina) other than chiggers				
Macronyssus crosbyi	8	0.10	5	6.0
Acanthophthirius lucifugus	1	0.01	1	1.2
Chigger Mites (Trombiculidae)				
Euschoengastia pipistrelli	109	1.30	20	23.8
Ticks (Ixodides)				
Ornithodoros kelleyi	7	0.08	2	2.4

mm (average 18.2 mm). And nine young from Kosciusko County (1 July) had forearms from 12 to 28 mm (average 17.9 mm).

Growth of young bats is relatively rapid; some reach adult proportions and weights and are capable of flight by early July. For example, one immature male weighed 6.4 grams and had a 36-mm forearm by 1 July.

PARASITES AND DISEASES. Only 1 little brown myotis of 80 examined for rabies tested positive (Whitaker and Miller, 1974).

We found external parasites on 25 of 84 little brown bats examined, and internal parasites in 14 of 92 specimens. Two mites, a chigger, a tick, and a flea were the external parasites (Table 48). Internal parasites found were nematodes and trematodes (as yet unidentified). Wilson (1961) reported additional data on parasites, including a flea, *Nycteriodopsylla chapini*, not found in our sample.

The little brown bat harbors relatively few external parasites. Of the six species found on this bat to date, only the chigger is very common. The flea *Nycteriodopsylla chapini* is normally found on the big brown bat; Wilson's (1961) specimen from the little brown bat probably represents a case of straggling. *Myodopsylla insignis* is often found on *Myotis lucifugus* in summer colonies, and Wilson collected 207 fleas of this species in 22 Indiana counties. *Ornithodorus kelleyi* is primarily found on the big brown bat, but Wilson reported 49 ticks of this species on little brown bats from 7 counties. Whitaker (1973) recovered 8 specimens of the mite *Macronyssus crosbyi*, 1 of *Acanthophthirius sp.*, 109 of the chigger *Euschoengastia pipistrelli*, 7 ticks, *Ornithodoros kelleyi*, and 1 flea, *Myodopsylla insignis*, from 84 little brown bats. The *Acanthophthirius* has since been described as new, *A. lucifugus* Fain and Whitaker, 1976.

DECIMATING FACTORS. Little is known about the natural predators of *Myotis lucifugus* but some bats of this species are undoubtedly taken by hawks, owls, and snakes. Martin (1961) reported on the probable predation on bats in Ray's Cave by the prairie vole, but the bat remains noted were not identified to species. One day when Mumford was releasing banded little brown myotis outside a cave, a blue jay actively pursued one of the released bats for some distance but evidently was unable to catch it in flight. Some years ago, the floor of a low passage in Big Wyandotte Cave was littered with bat wings, said to have been the remains of bats (a species of *Myotis*) captured and eaten by a domestic cat.

The worst known enemy of bats is man, who uses various methods in attempting to drive nursery colonies from buildings. We know of the use of tear gas, sulphur candles, moth balls, automobile exhaust fumes, and heavy grease. DDT and cyanide gas have been used in some roosts to eliminate the bats. The most successful way to prevent bats from entering attics is to close all entrance holes that the animals can use; this is sometimes difficult, if not impossible, but it is the most satisfactory and permanent method. The remodeling of houses, churches, and other buildings has eliminated many summer colonies.

Vandalism has resulted in the loss of bats at various seasons. Fire, sticks, stones, and BB guns have all been used to kill and mutilate bats in their roosts. During hibernation, the mere disturbance of bats can be harmful to them; if they are awakened and fly about, they use up some of their stored fat reserves. Repeated disturbances may cause them to deplete so much fat that they cannot live through the winter.

Researchers have probably caused considerable damage to bats. We know, for example, that large numbers of bats have been removed from some Indiana caves and other roosts for physiological studies. Others have been collected for scientific specimens or to be examined for food habits, parasites, or other data. Moderate collecting of specimens by scientists who know the species and keep abreast of the status of various bats in Indiana does relatively little harm. But in 1949, a cluster of several dozen of the relatively rare southeastern myotis was removed from a cave for specimens. This cave has housed only a few of that species each winter since then. Now that the Indiana myotis is on the national endangered species list and is rather common as a hibernator in some Indiana caves, it becomes more important that those people working with bats are able to identify the various species readily. The unjustified removal of excessive numbers of this species (either accidentally or intentionally) could deal a damaging blow to its future in Indiana.

We also feel that bat banding could have been a factor in the decline of some bat populations in the state. Banding was begun in Indiana, at Big Wyandotte Cave, in 1946. Numerous workers have banded bats since 1946, and the disturbance caused by catching, confining, banding, and otherwise causing the animals to waken during hibernation may have produced casualties, although we have no proof of this. Also, it is well known that bands applied to the wings of bats can cause irritation, inflammation, the formation of scar tissue, and possibly infection. We cannot evaluate the effect of banding on the well-being of bats, but it is possible that deaths have occurred as a result of banding activities.

In more recent years, we have been concerned about man's increased use of insecticides and the possible detrimental effect on bats. All bats that occur in Indiana feed exclusively on insects and thus are subject to high levels of insecticides that may be present in their food. We do know that the decline in the numbers of some bats in the state has been dramatic since 1951, but we still cannot pinpoint the reasons for these decreased populations.

TAXONOMY. The subspecies in Indiana is *Myotis lucifugus lucifugus* (LeConte).

SELECTED REFERENCES. Anthony and Kunz, 1977; Barbour and Davis, 1969; Belwood and Fenton, 1976; Benton and Scharoun, 1958; Cagle and Cockrum, 1943; Cope, Baker, and Confer, 1961; Cope and Hendricks, 1970; Cope, Koontz, and Churchwell, 1961; Cope, Mumford, and Wilson, 1958; Davis and Hitchcock, 1965; Fenton, 1970, 1977; Humphrey, 1964; Humphrey and Cope, 1964, 1976; Kunz, Anthony, and Rumage, 1977; Walley, 1970.

Southeastern Myotis
Myotis austroriparius (Rhoads)

Rhoads' Bat

Myotis subulatus: Hahn, 1908b (in part)
Myotis austroriparius: Miller and Allen, 1928

DESCRIPTION. Most Indiana specimens of the southeastern myotis have a gray dorsum and a whitish venter. These animals closely resemble gray-pelaged gray myotis in color, but the gray myotis has a longer forearm, dorsal fur the same color from base to tip, and less white (more grayish) on the venter. The hairs on the dorsum of the southeastern myotis are more woolly and have dark bases and paler tips. Brown-pelaged individuals are best separated from other *Myotis* in Indiana by forearm length and (in life) by pink noses.

Color in Indiana *Myotis austroriparius* appears to be best correlated with season; animals tend to be grayish in winter and spring and brownish in summer. Most of our brownish-pelaged specimens were collected in August. For example, seven captured on 4 August were quite variable in color; three were brown above and tan below, and four were grayish above (some with brownish

Southeastern myotis. Photo by Bruce J. Hayward

patches). All were in heavy molt. Four older specimens, taken by Hahn from 2 August to 9 August 1907, show the same variations. In addition, three taken 20 August 1969 were all molting; two were undergoing nearly complete molts.

We suspect that the brownish color is related to the reproductive cycle, as it seems to be in the gray myotis we have examined from Kentucky, with females becoming quite brownish during the summer. Most of our brownish southeastern myotis taken in August are females.

Weights and measurements are shown in Table 49. The dental formula is

$$I \frac{2}{3} C \frac{1}{1} P \frac{3}{3} M \frac{3}{3} = 38.$$

STATUS AND DISTRIBUTION. The first Indiana specimens of *Myotis austroriparius* were taken by Walter Hahn near Mitchell (in what is now Spring Mill State Park) in 1906. We have examined 13 extant specimens taken by Hahn, who had identified 12 as *Myotis subulatus* (= *Myotis keenii*) and 1 as *Myotis lucifugus*. Miller and Allen (1928) first realized the true identity of 4 of Hahn's specimens after they almost described them as a new species. Lyon (1936) reported no new records.

The southeastern myotis is rare and evidently occurs most commonly in south-central Indiana, where it is known from Crawford, Greene, Lawrence, and Washington counties (Map 15); for all but Lawrence County, these are single records. There has been a decided decrease in Indiana wintering populations since 1949. The species is present throughout the year, but there is no record of breeding in the state.

HABITAT. Except for a female found in a breeding colony of little brown bats in a building, all Indiana records of the southeastern myotis are from caves.

ASSOCIATED SPECIES. The only other bat we have found clustered with *Myotis austroriparius* was *M. lucifugus*. On 28 December 1955 there were 27 southeastern myotis and 2 little brown myotis in a compact group in Donnehue's Cave; not far away a single southeastern myotis was in a clump of 10 little brown myotis. In this same cave, on 30 December 1959, a southeastern myotis was clustered with 6 little brown myotis. One southeastern and 2 little brown myotis occupied a small hole in the ceiling of Don-

Table 49
Weights and measurements of *Myotis austroriparius* from Indiana

	Males	Females
Total length (mm)		
n	43	13
x̄	83.3	87.2
range	70-91	80-95
SD	5.5	4.6
SE	0.8	1.3
Tail length (mm)		
n	42	13
x̄	34.4	35.8
range	27-40	30-41
SD	4.1	3.0
SE	0.6	0.8
Hind foot (mm)		
n	41	13
x̄	8.8	9.6
range	7-10	9-11
SD	1.1	0.8
SE	0.2	0.2
Tragus (mm)		
n	32	7
x̄	7.0	7.0
range	5.5-9.0	5.2-8.0
SD	0.8	0.9
SE	0.1	0.3
Forearm (mm)		
n	35	10
x̄	38.1	38.1
range	32-41	35.5-40.0
SD	1.9	1.5
SE	0.3	0.5
Weight (grams)		
n	27	16
x̄	6.5	7.2
range	4.1-9.2	5.1-9.1
SD	1.1	1.3
SE	0.2	0.3

aldson's Cave, 30 December 1959. During the year, Indiana myotis, gray myotis, Keen's myotis, big brown bats, eastern pipistrelles, and silver-haired bats have been found in caves with southeastern myotis. The caves that harbor the largest numbers of southeastern myotis contain practically no Indiana myotis, perhaps suggesting a subtle habitat preference between the species.

POPULATIONS. We have no record of southeastern myotis for Indiana between 17

Map 15. The Southeastern Myotis, *Myotis austroriparius*, in Indiana

December 1907 (Hahn specimen) and 8 November 1947 (R. G. Prasil specimen). Before 1953, all records were from the caves at Spring Mill State Park, mostly from Bronson's Cave or Donaldson's Cave.

A few southeastern myotis can still be found in the caves at Spring Mill. We have not adequately checked the several "wet" caves there often enough to determine the status of this bat in the park. There were about 50 individuals observed in Bronson's Cave on 7 February 1949; the following day, 40 of these were collected. The largest number recorded since in Bronson's Cave was 8 on 30 March 1966. A cluster of about 25 was located in Donaldson's Cave on 23 November 1951 and about two-thirds of them were caught and banded; 6 were observed in the same spot the next day. Since then, the maximum number seen in this cave was 3, on 6 March 1954.

On 8 January 1954, at least 9 southeastern myotis were found in Donnehue's Cave at Bedford. This cave has been visited by us more than a hundred times over the past twenty years. Small numbers of the southeastern myotis still use the cave and the species has been found there every month of the year except July. The maximum number found on a visit was 28, on 28 December 1955; the second largest number was 19, on 12 February 1955.

This bat has been reported once in each of four other caves: Ray's Cave (Greene County), a female, 7 December 1953; Salt Petre Cave (Crawford County), about 15 on 23 February 1953; Endless Cave (Washington County), 1 male, on 28 January 1961; Big Wyandotte Cave (Crawford County), 2 females, 12 February 1966.

HABITS. During the hibernation period, *Myotis austroriparius* has been found in compact clusters of up to 50 individuals, hanging from the ceilings or on the side walls of caves. Most clusters were on side walls, but the largest was on a ceiling. Singles and small groups are usually found, especially today, since the population decline. Solitary individuals, usually males, often wedge themselves into tiny holes in the cave ceiling. Some of these holes are just large enough for a single bat. We collected at least three southeastern myotis from one such hole, and observed others; more than once we have also found a single southeastern myotis in another tiny, favored roosting hole. Holes and crevices too large for a single bat to fill have been found occupied by a southeastern myotis and 1 to 4 little brown myotis, or by up to 3 southeastern myotis. On one occasion, we found a single southeastern myotis roosting inside a hollow stalactite.

Of the four largest clusters of southeastern myotis found, two were in dry portions of the cave where no water was present below them, one was in a completely dry cave (Salt Petre Cave), and one was over a gravel bar at the edge of the cave stream. Singles and small groups have been observed both in dry passages and hanging directly over water.

During the winter these bats are readily awakened and are more active than are other *Myotis*. On 23 November 1951, we found an active cluster of southeastern myotis because of their squeaking and probably would have missed them otherwise. Individuals dislodged from the ceiling or a crevice may escape by taking flight. Our attempts to catch two on 13 April were unsuccessful. One of the bats, in a crevice in the ceiling, immediately squeezed itself into a tiny hole when it was touched with a stick. Repeated careful prodding caused it to drop from the crevice and fly away. The second was inside the hollow core of a broken stalactite, but also dropped out and flew when touched with a stick. On 11 January 1949, a cluster of about 35 to 40 southeastern myotis was observed on the ceiling of a cave. One, dislodged from the edge of the group with a stick, fell to the floor, but the rest immediately flew farther back into the cave.

On the night of 23 November 1951, 16 southeastern myotis were banded in Donaldson's Cave. About 15 minutes later one of these was recaptured in Bronson's Cave, which is one-half mile from Donaldson's Cave, with which it has, however, an underground connection. One or two individuals have quickly taken flight when the beam of a flashlight was shined on them.

These experiences and others suggest that *Myotis austroriparius* does not tolerate disturbances and is likely to change its roosting site quite readily, even in hibernation quarters. On 23 February 1953, there were clusters of 7 and 8 on the side wall of Salt Petre Cave; a single bat was carefully taken from one cluster for a specimen, but none of the bats flew. On 7 March 1953, not a bat of this species could be found in the cave (which is easy to census for bats), nor have we seen *M. austroriparius* there again. After we captured and banded 16 of a cluster of about 25 one night, we returned the next day and found only 6 hanging at the same spot. However, in two instances we have found groups in two successive winters hanging at identical spots; such roosting spots may be particularly favorable to the species for hibernation.

Seasonal Activity. We obtained some information on this aspect of behavior from our work at Donnehue's Cave. Periodic netting of the entrance to the cave throughout a year resulted in our capturing a single southeastern myotis on 18 November and one on 4 February. These captures indicate that this bat may move about during the winter, especially when the temperature is above freezing. That the bats mentioned above left Salt Petre Cave

between 23 February and 7 March also points up this possibility.

Daily Activity. *Myotis austroriparius* emerges from its daytime roosts in caves relatively late in the evening. Our Donnehue's Cave data with regard to this behavior were interesting. We summarized the comparative times of netting the first southeastern myotis, the first little brown myotis, and the first bat on seven evenings, recording only animals that struck the inside face of the nets (and thus were presumably leaving the cave). On the six occasions when we captured both *M. lucifugus* and *M. austroriparius*, the latter was caught consistently later than the former by 24 to 186 minutes. *Myotis lucifugus* was not always the first species netted each evening, and the time between the netting of the first bat of any species and the first *M. austroriparius* ranged from 34 to 186 minutes, for seven dates.

A southeastern myotis was netted as late as 12:16 A.M. (26 August) and we captured 11 others between 10:00 P.M. and 12:05 A.M. (26 August to 14 October). One was captured on 4 February at 7:17 P.M., one on 11 May at 9:44 P.M., two on 30 October at 8:45 P.M. and 9:10 P.M., 1 on 18 November at 8:42 P.M. and 2 on 20 August at 9:12 and 9:37 P.M.

MIGRATION. Although numerous southeastern myotis have been banded in Indiana, band recoveries have shed no light on movements of the species. We have no proof that migration occurs; no individuals have been collected or observed north of the known wintering distribution in the state. The bats obviously move into and out of the hibernating caverns periodically and the female found in a little brown bat nursery colony probably did not hibernate there. Perhaps this species is more sedentary than other *Myotis*.

LONGEVITY. The relatively small number of southeastern myotis recaptured after banding revealed little regarding the life-span of the species. Of 21 animals recaptured, 16 were at least 1.5 years old, 2 were at least 2.5 years of age, 1 was at least 3, and 2 were at least 4 years old.

SEX RATIOS. Of 62 southeastern myotis collected in caves during nine months of the year, 48 were males and 14 were females (77.4 percent males); no specimens were taken in May, September, or October. Of 25 collected in February, only 5 were females (20 percent), but of 15 taken in August, 6 were females (40 percent). Of 104 southeastern myotis banded in caves (every month except May, June, July) 61 were males and 43 were females (58.6 percent males). For Donnehue's Cave, where 80 of the 104 were banded, 45 (56.3 percent) were males; also, 11 males and 5 females were collected there, giving a total of 58.3 percent males for this cave.

FOOD. We have examined no bats of this species which had food in the stomachs.

REPRODUCTION. We have no direct evidence that the southeastern myotis breeds in Indiana, although adults have been captured in each month of the year. Elsewhere, females each produce two young in May. We netted a female on 4 August that evidently had been nursing young; she had areas devoid of hair around each nipple. A group of about 25 southeastern myotis observed on 23 November was quite active and noisy; one female had moisture, which could have been semen, about the vulva. J. B. Cope saw a pair that "seemed to be copulating" on 7 March. Males with scrotal testes have been collected or examined in March, April, and August; those with the largest testes were taken in August. In this species, each testis descends to a conspicuous position on either side of the base of the tail.

PARASITES. We examined 6 southeastern myotis for parasites and found the mite *Olabidocarpus whitakeri*, the chigger *Euschongastia pipistrelli*, and some unidentified intestinal trematodes (Whitaker and Mumford, 1971a; Whitaker, 1973). *Olabidocarpus whitakeri* was described by McDaniel and Coffman (1970) from material collected from three southeastern myotis taken from Donnehue's Cave, 20 August 1969.

DECIMATING FACTORS. Man is probably the major enemy of the species. One southeastern myotis was found dead in a cave on 30 December, hanging by one foot from the ceiling. On the night of 18 November, during netting of Donnehue's Cave, a screech owl struck the mist net immediately after a southeastern myotis was caught; it appeared that the owl was pursuing the bat, or possibly attempting to take it from the net.

A southeastern myotis found in a cave on 7 April had the tips of both ears somewhat shortened and devoid of pigment, a condition suggesting frostbite.

TAXONOMY. *Myotis austroriparius mumfordi* Rice (1955) was described from Indiana specimens taken at Spring Mill State Park, but LaVal (1970) has since concluded that the species is monotypic. Thus, the current name for the species is *Myotis austroriparius* (Rhoads).

SELECTED REFERENCES. Barbour and Davis, 1969; Foster, Humphrey, and Humphrey, 1978; LaVal, 1970; Rice, 1955, 1957; Sherman, 1930.

Gray Myotis
Myotis grisescens Howell

Large-winged Bat, Howell's Bat

Myotis velifer: Hahn, 1908b
Myotis grisescens: Howell, 1909a

DESCRIPTION. This relatively large, gray myotis can be separated from other species of the same genus in Indiana by its forearm length (42-45 mm), dorsal hair the same color from base to tip, and the attachment of the wing membrane to the tarsus instead of to the side of the foot. In Indiana, only *Myotis au-* stroriparius has the grayish dorsal color of *M. grisescens;* we suspect that the two species exhibit roughly the same seasonal color variations. For example, an adult female *M. grisescens* taken on 9 August and examined by Howell was described by him as being "sepia above, with a russet tinge" and "hair-brown" below. This specimen (now lost) was evidently similar in color to about a dozen female gray myotis we have seen taken from a maternity colony in Adair County, Kentucky, on 2 June 1958. Indiana specimens taken in April, August, and September are gray above and grayish white below. We need specimens taken at other times of the year to more completely evaluate color variations.

Weights and measurements are shown in Table 50. The dental formula is

$$I \frac{2}{3} C \frac{1}{1} P \frac{3}{3} M \frac{3}{3} = 38.$$

STATUS AND DISTRIBUTION. The gray myotis is evidently rare in Indiana (Map 16), and has been collected only in Crawford and Lawrence counties. Ralph D. Kirkpatrick banded and released an individual in a cave in Jennings County. James B. Cope and a field party netted 8 gray myotis in Clark County. Anthony F. DeBlase captured 4 in a mist net at the mouth of Big Wyandotte Cave (Crawford County) on the night of 31 August 1963. This bat probably occurs elsewhere in the southern part of the state, where it appears to be closely associated with caves. Most of the records for this species in Indiana have been for August (9 records) and Sep-

Gray myotis. Photo by Anthony Brentlinger, ISU AV Center

Table 50
Weights and measurements of *Myotis grisescens* from Indiana

	Males	Females
Total length (mm)		
n	5	3
x̄	98.8	94.5
range	94-107	92.5-96.0
SD	5.2	1.8
SE	2.3	1.0
Tail length (mm)		
n	5	3
x̄	41.0	39.3
range	38-46	35-43
SD	3.3	4.0
SE	1.5	2.3
Hind foot (mm)		
n	5	2
x̄	10.8	10.5
range	9-12	10-11
SD	1.1	0.7
SE	0.5	0.5
Tragus (mm)		
n	5	3
x̄	8.8	7.2
range	8-10	7.0-7.5
SD	0.8	0.3
SE	0.4	0.2
Forearm (mm)		
n	5	3
x̄	43.5	43.3
range	42-45	43-44
SD	1.4	0.6
SE	0.6	0.3
Weight (grams)		
n	2	1
x̄	11.4	11.0
range	10.7-12.0	–
SD	0.9	–
SE	0.7	–

tember (2 records), suggesting that perhaps there is a postbreeding wandering of individuals northward in late summer from Kentucky or other states where the species is known to breed. Single individuals of gray myotis have been found in Indiana in February, in March, in April, and in October.

The first specimen of this bat was taken by Walter L. Hahn on 9 August 1907, in Lawrence County in what is now Spring Mill State Park; this specimen is now lost. The

Map 16. The Gray Myotis, *Myotis grisescens,* in Indiana

second Indiana specimen was netted at Donaldson's Cave (Spring Mill State Park) on 14 August 1958 by J. B. Cope and J. H. Schnell. There are only 9 extant *M. grisescens* specimens from the state known to be in museums.

HABITAT. Most gray myotis found in Indiana were in caves, but in other states this species also utilizes buildings. Those captured in Clark County were netted over a stream during the summer.

ASSOCIATED SPECIES. The other species of bats normally found in Indiana caves have been found in association with the gray myotis (see under *Myotis lucifugus*). On 14 April, a gray myotis was clustered with 3 little brown myotis about 7 feet up on the ceiling of a passage in Donnehue's Cave, about 275 feet from the cave entrance.

HABITS. Most of the gray myotis captured in Indiana were netted at night at cave entrances, during the fall swarming period. One has been found roosting in a cave in February, one in March, one in April, and one in October. The one taken 25 March was not far inside the entrance of Big Wyandotte Cave and was torpid (A. F. DeBlase). We know little about the duration of nocturnal activity, but we netted one at 12:34 A.M. on 23 August at a cave entrance.

FOOD. There appears to be nothing published on the food of this bat. The bat collected by mist netting on 23 August 1974 contained 10 percent Chironomidae, 15 percent Trichoptera, 60 percent Lepidoptera, and 15 percent unidentified insect.

REPRODUCTION. Hahn (1908b) stated that the female he collected on 9 August "apparently had nursed during the present season, as there was a new growth of short, whitish hairs about the mammae," and in 1909 he again mentioned this specimen by writing that "The condition of the mammae showed that the animal had nursed during that summer." The species possibly breeds in Indiana. Of the five females examined from Indiana, four were captured in August and one in February. Single males taken 14 and 22 August had testes measuring 4.5 by 6.5 and 5 by 8 mm, respectively. Another male collected on 14 April had 1.5 by 4-mm testes.

PARASITES. Two anal mites (probably *Spinturnix globosus*) were taken from a specimen collected at Big Wyandotte Cave. The one individual examined by us harbored 3 fleas *(Myodopsylla insignis)*, 3 mites *(Macronyssus jonesi)*, and no internal parasites. Ubelaker (1966) has reported on the parasites of *Myotis grisescens* in Kansas.

DECIMATING FACTORS. No information is available on predation of this species in Indiana. As in other bats, man is probably the major destructive agent.

TAXONOMY. No subspecies of the gray myotis is recognized, thus the Indiana population is composed of *Myotis grisescens* Howell.

SELECTED REFERENCES. Barbour and Davis, 1969; Elder and Gunier, 1978; Gunier and Elder, 1971; Guthrie, 1933; Hall and Wilson, 1966; Hays and Bingman, 1964; Smith and Parmalee, 1954; Tuttle, 1975, 1976a, 1976b, 1979; Tuttle and Stevenson, 1977; Ubelaker, 1966.

Keen's Myotis
Myotis keenii (Merriam)

Keen's Bat, Say's Bat, Trouessart's Bat

Vespertilio subulatus: Allen, 1864 (probably)
Vespertilio gryphus: Allen, 1894 (probably)
Myotis subulatus: Miller, 1897
Myotis keenii: Miller and Allen, 1928

DESCRIPTION. Among Indiana species, *Myotis keenii* is most similar in appearance to *Myotis lucifugus.* The upper parts are brownish, but in life may have a "brassy" color not always evident in dried skins. The underparts are tan to yellowish, especially on the tips of the hairs. Immatures are darker and duller in color than adults. The best distinguishing characters of Keen's myotis are the long ears (average 17 mm) and long tragi (average 9 mm); the tragi are often sickle-shaped (see Fig. 2).

Keen's myotis. Photo by Merlin Tuttle

Weights and measurements are shown in Table 51. The dental formula is

$$I \frac{2}{3} \ C \ \frac{1}{1} \ P \ \frac{3}{3} \ M \ \frac{3}{3} \ = \ 38.$$

STATUS AND DISTRIBUTION. Miller (1897) was evidently the first author to record *M. keenii* from Indiana; reports of Allen (1864, 1894) and Evermann and Butler (1894b) are subject to doubt since part of the specimens mentioned are now lost. Evermann and But-

ler's record of one taken in 1889 at Terre Haute possibly represents the earliest extant Indiana specimen. Lyon (1936) reported specimens from four counties.

Keen's myotis probably occurs throughout the state, but specimens have been taken from only 27 counties (Map 17). It is an uncommon bat at any season and is evidently most abundant at certain caves in southern Indiana during August and September.

Although we have found Keen's myotis hibernating in at least twenty Indiana caves, the greatest number of these bats observed was 11 in a cave near Kent (Jefferson County) on 3 January 1959. We usually find from 1 to 3 or, more infrequently, 4 to 6 per cave. During the swarming period of late August and early September, as many as 40 Keen's myotis have been netted at the entrance to Ray's Cave (Greene County) and more than

Table 51
Weights and measurements of *Myotis keenii* from Indiana

	Males	Females
Total length (mm)		
n	26	10
x̄	86.5	86.1
range	75-95	74-89
SD	4.8	4.6
SE	0.9	1.4
Tail length (mm)		
n	26	10
x̄	35.5	34.8
range	27-42	28-40
SD	3.6	4.4
SE	0.7	1.4
Hind foot (mm)		
n	26	10
x̄	8.3	7.6
range	5-11	7-8
SD	1.1	0.8
SE	0.2	0.1
Weight (grams)		
n	25	9
x̄	6.4	5.4
range	4.7-9.2	3.7-8.5
SD	1.2	1.5
SE	0.2	0.5

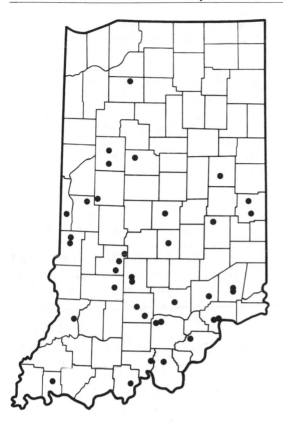

Map 17. Keen's Myotis, *Myotis keenii,*
in Indiana

20 were taken in one night by net at the mouth of Boone's Cave (Owen County). We have found no more than 3 Keen's bats at either of these caves at any one visit during the winter; we do not know where those go that can be netted in the fall, but they presumably migrate.

HABITAT. Keen's myotis is usually found in caves, which it frequents throughout the year; all winter records are from caves. During the nonhibernating season, individuals have been found roosting by day in, on, and about buildings, in a mine, and under concrete bridges. A few have been netted at night over small streams in farmland or ponds in woodlots; others have been shot at dusk along tree-lined streams. Keen's myotis seems to prefer wooded areas and it probably uses tree roosts in summer. It hangs on the sides or under the eaves of buildings, behind window shutters, in attics, or in rather well-lighted rooms of abandoned houses. It seems to show a high tolerance for sunlight.

ASSOCIATED SPECIES. *Myotis keenii* shares its hibernating caves with all other species of bats that hibernate in or otherwise use caves. In Turkey Run State Park, Keen's myotis, big brown bats, little brown myotis, and Indiana myotis all roosted by day beneath a large concrete bridge. Two Keen's myotis have been shot at dusk along streams while foraging with red bats, big brown bats, little brown myotis, and pipistrelles.

J. B. Cope reported *Myotis keenii* and *Pipistrellus subflavus* maternity colonies in the same barn (Jackson County). Nixon A. Wilson caught a Keen's myotis and a little brown myotis in September in the rafters of a small, open-sided shelter house.

HABITS. *Myotis keenii* is generally a solitary species, except during the breeding season, when aggregations of females (and females with young) form. In caves, most individuals are found in small crevices in the ceilings. A favored roosting site is the hollow core of a broken stalactite, often just large enough for a single bat. On 16 November 1968, we found 3 bats of this species in a small cave in Jennings County; each was inside a stalactite. Some also hang on the side walls or ceilings of cave passages. We have never found Keen's myotis hibernating in clusters, and our records fail to show that we found even two or more hanging together.

For several years (1948 to 1954) Mumford found lone males roosting by day beneath three small signs on the staff cabins at Turkey Run State Park. The signs (about 8 by 12 inches) were fastened to the cabins in such a way that a space roughly an inch wide was formed between the sign and a 4-inch post supporting the cabin porch. A single male was removed from behind one of these signs on 30 July 1948, in July 1949, on 1 July 1952, and on 24 July 1954.

Keen's myotis for some reason enters caves in southern Indiana at night during the summer, but is not present there through the day. Robert Goslin first recorded this behavior (letter to Mumford) at Ray's Cave on 16 June 1932. He found no *M. keenii* in the cave at dusk, but 8 males were there at 10:30 P.M. We netted a male entering Big Wyandotte Cave at 10:37 P.M. on 18 May.

We have little data regarding when *M. keenii* enters or leaves its hibernation quarters. The fact that males may be present throughout the summer in caves makes it difficult to determine these movements. And there were so few females present during the winter that it was impossible to gather adequate data. However, on four visits in May to as many caves where *M. keenii* was present, only males were observed. We have recorded females in one cave on 10 August, but we do not know the age of these animals.

Banding studies have shed very little light on the movements of this species in Indiana. A male banded at Boone's Cave (Owen County) on 24 August was killed in a barn at Wingate (Montgomery County) in September or October the same season. The barn is about 65 miles north-northwest of the point of banding and in a direction one would not expect a migrant bat to take in the fall. A male banded on 8 June at Donnehue's Cave (Lawrence County) appeared to be rather sedentary; he was recaptured there 14 July and 23 October the same season.

Swarming behavior of Keen's myotis has been evident at the mouth of Ray's Cave in the early fall, where we netted the species as follows: 19 between 5:45 and 9:30 P.M., 2 September 1962; 38 between 6:30 and 9:00 P.M. on 3 September 1964; 18 on 8 September 1971 between 7:15 and 11:30 P.M. In addition, 22 were netted at the entrance of Boone's Cave from 6:15 to 10:35 P.M., on 24 August 1962. At noon on 3 September 1962 (following the netting of Ray's Cave the night before), 19 Keen's myotis, all unbanded, were caught inside the cave; we had banded those captured the night before, so they obviously had not remained in the cave.

The seasonal activity of *M. keenii* requires more study. During a year of netting the entrance to Donnehue's Cave, we caught the species from 16 April to 30 September; 15 males and a single female were netted throughout this period and not more than 3 were caught in a single night. A male was netted just inside the mouth of Porter's Cave (Owen County) on 1 October. A female was collected in Rush County on 17 November, but we do not have details of this capture. Adult females were taken at Lafayette on 26 April and on 2 May, which may be some indication of when females migrate in the spring. One was in a building and the other on the side of a building, but it is unknown whether they hibernated in the area. A very active male *M. keenii* was observed in Donnehue's Cave on the night of 7 April.

Keen's myotis appears to be a relatively early flyer, some emerging from their daytime roosts before sunset. Four of the 11 we netted at the mouth of a cave were captured from 31 to 60 minutes after sunset. A few have also been shot at dusk, suggesting that some are on the wing before dark.

Whether males and females have different roosting and foraging habits or actually occur in Indiana in a strongly unbalanced sex ratio, as our data indicate, we do not know. Males greatly outnumber females. Of collected specimens, 71 are males and 24 are females. Of the 117 Keen's bats banded by Mumford in Indiana, 95 were males. Many of those banded were caught at caves during the swarming period. It is of interest that all 22 netted 24 August at Boone's Cave were males. At Ray's Cave, 24 males and 18 females were caught 2-3 September 1962, 28 males and 10 females on 3 September 1964, and 14 males and 4 females on 8 September 1971. Since our data were collected throughout the year, and much of it during the hibernation season, they probably reflect the true sparsity of females.

FOOD. Whitaker (1972b) reported on the stomach contents of 3 Keen's myotis. One contained 60 percent Reduviidae (assassin bugs), 10 percent Cicadellidae (leafhoppers), and 30 percent Ichneumon wasps. Another held 70 percent unidentified Lepidoptera and 30 percent unidentified Diptera. The third contained 100 percent unidentified insects.

REPRODUCTION. Three breeding colonies of *Myotis keenii* have been reported in Indiana. On 8 July 1954, Mark Wright found about 50 bats beneath the loose bark of a dead tree in Wayne County; several were collected and some were unable to fly. About 30 females with young were routed from a cabin in the Clark County State Forest, in June 1953; the animals had been found beneath the window shutters and in the cabin. A maternity colony in a barn in Jackson County contained 24 adult females, 10 adults of undetermined sex, and 30 immatures on 22 June 1966 (J. B. Cope; S. R. Humphrey).

Parturition evidently occurs during June,

but over a span of perhaps two to three weeks. Litter size is one. A female taken on 15 June contained an embryo 15 mm in crown-rump length, and 1 of 24 adult females examined on 22 June was pregnant; the others were lactating.

We have little data on growth of the young, but one immature taken 8 July had a total length of 68 mm. Immature males captured on 22 June had forearm lengths ranging from 18 to 32 mm and weighed from 2.0 to 4.2 grams. Young still unable to fly have been observed on 8 July.

Males have large, scrotal testes in August and September. All of 14 (unaged) males collected on 8 September had scrotal testes, ranging in length from 3.5 to 6 mm (average 4.6 mm). Two males taken 5 and 7 April had testes 2 and 3 mm long; two males collected 11 and 18 May had testes 3.5 and 3 mm long. The male taken 7 April had live sperm in its reproductive tract.

PARASITES AND DISEASES. Of 35 Keen's myotis examined for external parasites (Whitaker, 1973), 19 were parasitized with mites *(Macronyssus crosbyi, Acanthopthirius* sp., *Olabidocarpus whitakeri, Spinturnix americanus),* a chigger *(Euschoengastia pipistrelli),* and a batbug *(Cimex adjunctus)* (Table 52). The *Acanthopthirius* was described as a new species (Fain and Whitaker, 1976), *A. gracilis.*

Unidentified trematodes, cestodes, and nematodes were recovered from 7 of 34 Keen's myotis examined for internal parasites.

None of 6 Keen's myotis checked for rabies proved positive (Whitaker and Miller, 1974).

TAXONOMY. The subspecies in Indiana is *Myotis keenii septentrionalis* (Trouessart).

SELECTED REFERENCES. Barbour and Davis, 1969; Miller, 1897; Miller and Allen, 1928.

Table 52

Ectoparasites of *Myotis keenii* (n = 33) from Indiana

Parasites	Parasites		Hosts Parasitized	
	Total	Average	Total	Percent
Batbugs (Cimicidae)				
Cimex adjunctus	1	0.03	1	3.0
Mites (Acarina) other than chiggers				
Olabidocarpus whitakeri	47	1.42	4	12.1
Acanthopthirius gracilis	9	0.27	5	15.2
Macronyssus crosbyi	4	0.12	2	6.1
Spinturnix americanus	1	0.03	1	3.0
Chiggers (Trombiculidae)				
Euschoengastia pipistrelli	48	1.45	9	27.3

Indiana Myotis
Myotis sodalis Miller and G. M. Allen

Indiana Bat, Social Bat

Vespertilio gryphus: Evermann and Butler, 1894b (in part)
Vespertilio subulatus: Blatchley, 1897 (in part)
Myotis subulatus: Elliott, 1907 (in part)

Myotis lucifugus: Hahn 1909 (in part)
Myotis sodalis: Miller and Allen, 1928

DESCRIPTION. The Indiana myotis is usually dull, dark pinkish gray (some nearly blackish) above and paler (more pinkish) below. A few individuals have a brownish cast to the dorsal fur. We have examined three Indiana specimens (all from Big Wyandotte Cave) which had areas of white in the pelage. In good light, color alone will enable one to separate the Indiana myotis from all other Indiana species of *Myotis* about 90 percent of the time. The little brown myotis is the most difficult to distinguish from the Indiana myotis. Although the little brown myotis is normally brown above, it is quite variable in color and darkish specimens occur. Most little brown myotis have a glossy sheen to the dorsal fur. The Indiana myotis has smaller feet than does the little brown myotis, and the hairs on the toes are fewer and shorter (not extending beyond the claws). Most Indiana myotis also have a more or less distinct keel on the calcar. The keel is usually easy to see under a dissecting microscope in whole specimens but may be impossible to see in dry skins. Although we have included all species of Indiana bats in the key, the skulls of Myotis are very similar to one another.

Measurements and weights are shown in Table 53. The dental formula is

$$I \frac{2}{3} C \frac{1}{1} P \frac{3}{3} M \frac{3}{3} = 38.$$

STATUS AND DISTRIBUTION. Miller and Allen (1928) described *Myotis sodalis* as a new species with the type locality as Wyandotte Cave, Crawford County, Indiana. The type specimen (Museum of Comparative Zoology, No. 10980) is a female collected 7 March 1904 by J. O. Sibert. This is one of the two species of extant mammals whose type locality is in Indiana (the other is the prairie vole, *Microtus ochrogaster*). That *Myotis sodalis* is very similar to *Myotis lucifugus* is indicated by the fact that it was not described as a separate species until 1928. Many earlier specimens undoubtedly were collected, but such records are hopelessly confused with *M. lucifugus*, *M. keenii*, and *M. austroriparius*. A specimen in the National Museum of Natural History taken 30 June 1896 from Bicknell (Knox County) by E. J. Chansler seems to be the earliest authentic record from Indiana. Elliott (1907) and Hahn (1909) were probably discussing *M. sodalis* along with other species. Lyon (1936) recorded specimens from Crawford, Greene, and Knox counties.

Myotis sodalis evidently occurs throughout the state. In the nonhibernating season, it

Table 53
Weights and measurements of *Myotis sodalis* from Indiana

	Males	Females
Total length (mm)		
n	26	19
x̄	87.23	86.52
range	73-100	77-97
SD	6.2	4.32
SE	1.21	1.0
Tail length (mm)		
n	28	19
x̄	35	33.6
range	26-40	26-39
SD	3.14	3.4
SE	0.6	0.8
Hind foot (mm)		
n	28	19
x̄	7.9	8.15
range	6.5-10.0	6-10
SD	1.2	1.3
SE	0.22	0.3
Forearm (mm)		
n	21	15
x̄	38.1	37.8
range	34-41	36-39
SD	1.53	1.0
SE	0.33	0.3
Tragus (mm)		
n	12	13
x̄	5.8	6
range	4-7	4-8
SD	1.0	1.3
SE	0.3	0.4
Weight (grams)		
n	27	19
x̄	5.7	6.62
range	3.3-9.0	4.1-10.5
SD	1.4	1.8
SE	0.26	0.42

may be present in relatively small numbers, but there are few data for this time of the year. Hundreds can be netted in August and September at some cave entrances in south-central Indiana, and many of these are probably migrants. During the winter, more than 150,000 hibernate in a few caves, but some winter populations have been declining in recent years, especially in Big Wyandotte Cave. It was believed that about 4,000 Indiana myotis were left in Indiana in 1974. This bat undoubtedly breeds in most of Indiana, but only two maternity colonies have been located, in Henry County and in Wayne County. Gravid or lactating females and weakly flying young have been found during the summer, however, in Lagrange, Parke, and Steuben counties. Mumford and Cope (1958) have published other summer records.

Our best winter population data are from Buckner's Cave (Monroe County), Ray's Cave (Greene County), and Big Wyandotte Cave (Crawford County), which we and others have visited periodically for more than twenty years (Table 54). During this period, the Indiana myotis has drastically declined in Big Wyandotte Cave. It will be noted that winter populations have fluctuated considerably in Ray's Cave, while the numbers in Buckner's Cave remained fairly constant. We do not know how to account for winter fluctuations in populations; perhaps such cycles are natural. Some persons have suggested that human disturbance may be an important factor; we agree that this may be, although it is difficult to prove. Others have been concerned with the effects of insecticides on bat populations; again, we need positive evi-

dence. There are few data on the normal, long-term fluctuations or population cycles of bats. This subject needs a great deal of study. In the meantime, we can deal practically with only one possible agent of decline— human disturbance. Closing caves to humans when the bats are hibernating would be a step in the right direction; this procedure is already in effect at some caves in the United States and will certainly be instituted at others.

In an earlier draft of this species account, we had written that there may be wintering *Myotis sodalis* populations not known to biologists, for spelunkers had reported large congregations in southern Indiana caves. Such has since proved to be the case. On 26 March 1976, James B. Cope and others, checking a report of large numbers of bats in a cave, discovered an estimated 100,000 Indiana myotis. On 5 February 1977, Cope and his crew located another population estimated at 50,000 in a second cave not far from the first. The 100,000± population mentioned above is the largest extant wintering colony

Table 54

Winter population estimates of *Myotis sodalis* in selected Indiana caves

Winter	Ray's Cave	Buckner's Cave	Big Wyandotte Cave
1951-52	2,700	500±	—
1952-53	—	—	10,000*
1953-54	—	400	1,000
1954-55	1,000	270	550
1955-56	—	295	—
1956-57	1,000±	—	700
1957-58	2,700	—	—
1960-61	—	—	980
1961-62	500	—	1,700
1962-63	500	—	2,500
1963-64	960	—	2,500
1964-65	3,200	—	3,200
1965-66	3,000	—	—
1966-67	1,700	—	—
1967-68	2,800	—	1,330
1968-69	600	—	1,400
1969-70	1,300	—	1,000
1970-71	—	—	1,200
1971-72	2,700	—	1,700
1972-73	1,500	—	1,100
1973-74	2,500	300	1,900
1974-75	2,000	—	—

*probably overestimated

Indiana myotis. Photo by Mumford

of *M. sodalis* now known (Richter *et al.*, 1978). There are hundreds of caves in the state and many have not been investigated for bats during the hibernating season. In addition to the caves already mentioned, there are records of smaller numbers of Indiana myotis from at least 16 other caves: Bear, Bentz, Salt Petre, and Sheep caves (Crawford County); Clyfty Cave (Greene County); Bronson, Donaldson's, Donnehue's, Hamer, and Sullivan caves (Lawrence County); Coon's, Grotto, and Saltpeter caves (Monroe County); Boone's Cave (Owen County); Endless and River caves (Washington County). More research is clearly warranted in order to accurately evaluate the population status of *M. sodalis* in winter in Indiana.

Some indication of abundance during the nonhibernating season can be gained by examination of data on relative numbers shot by us over streams, and by the relative numbers submitted to the state health department for rabies examination (see Table 17). Mumford and Cope (1958) had previously summarized the summer occurrence of *M. sodalis* in Indiana, but additional records are now at hand and will be discussed in the section on reproduction. This bat has now been collected in 21 counties (Map 18).

HABITAT. Caves are used extensively during the hibernation season and to a lesser extent in late summer. Most observations on this species have been made in caves during the hibernating season. During the nonhibernating period, individuals have been found in buildings, beneath the loose bark of trees, and under a concrete bridge. A dead, mummified specimen was found hanging 12 feet from the ground on the face of a sandstone escarpment, on 18 April. Three observations of Indiana myotis were made in mature, deciduous forests (Turkey Run and Shades state parks) containing some hemlock and yew. A few Indiana myotis have been shot along small streams with wooded banks; others have been shot in open, grazed woodlots composed of scattered, deciduous trees. One was collected over a small lake. A specimen collected on 30 June was foraging over a road bisecting a low, damp woods composed mainly of pin oak, sweet gum, and other swamp species.

The two known maternity colonies (Henry

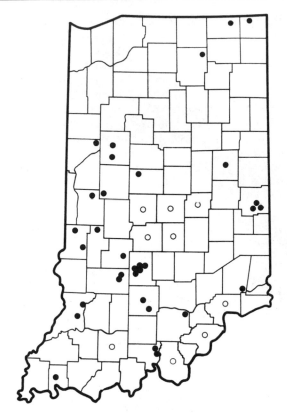

Map 18.   The Indiana Myotis, *Myotis sodalis*, in Indiana

and Wayne counties) were found in wooded, riparian areas along small streams (Humphrey, *et al.*, 1977). Humphrey and others studied the foraging habitat of a nursery colony of *Myotis sodalis* for two summers. They found that the foraging habitat "was confined to air space from 2 to 30 m high near the foliage of riparian and floodplain trees." It was also reported that the "total foraging range of the population was a linear strip along 0.82 km of creek." In early summer the foraging area included 1.47 hectares, but by midsummer the bats foraged over 4.54 hectares. Foraging in early summer was restricted to riparian habitat and later was extended "to other solitary trees and forest edge on the floodplain." No foraging was detected in forest, open pasture, cornfield, upland hedgerow, or along creeks from which riparian trees had been removed. "Dominant trees about which the bats fed were *Platanus occidentalis* [sycamore], *Populus deltoides* [cottonwood], *Juglans nigra* [black walnut],

Salix nigra [black willow], and *Quercus* sp. [oak]." Additional information on summer habitat of this species may be vital to its survival. *Myotis sodalis* is currently on the federal list of endangered species, and the United States Fish and Wildlife Service Recovery Team is most interested in the determination of critical summer habitat.

ASSOCIATED SPECIES. Hibernating Indiana myotis share their cave quarters with all other species of bats found in Indiana caves, but are most closely associated with the little brown myotis. Mixed groups of the two species are frequently seen hanging together. A concrete bridge at Turkey Run State Park was used as a daytime roost by Indiana myotis, Keen's myotis, and big brown bats in the summer of 1948. Other bats shot while foraging with Indiana myotis are eastern pipistrelles, red bats, hoary bats, big brown bats, evening bats, little brown myotis, and silver-haired bats.

HABITS. The period from about mid-November to mid-April is spent in hibernation in caves. A few animals, primarily males, may inhabit caves periodically during the summer. Two immature male Indiana myotis were taken in Ray's Cave on 5 August 1957; about 65 unidentified bats *(Myotis)* were seen in the cave that day. No Indiana myotis could be found in Ray's Cave on 4 July 1956, 5 August 1969, or 10 August 1954. Likewise, none were present in Buckner's Cave on 11 July 1953, 7 June 1954, or 4 July 1956; two unidentified bats *(Myotis)* were there on 18 August 1954. Relatively little research has been done in Indiana caves during the summer, so there are few data on this aspect of bat biology in the state. Females tend to leave the caves before the males in the spring, and the large winter congregations disperse each year by early May, with little evidence of their whereabouts until they enter the caves again in the fall. However, it does appear that they spread out from their hibernating caves; they can be shot in many portions of the state, and specimens from various portions of Indiana have been submitted to the Health Department for testing for rabies. The same behavior is characteristic of this species throughout its range, and the young are raised in areas yet largely unknown to us.

Hibernating groups containing both sexes usually form dense, roughly circular clusters on cave ceilings, but singles and small groups of all sizes are commonly found. At times, *M. sodalis* is also seen in vertical or horizontal crevices in cave walls or in cracks in cave ceilings. Although numerous hibernating clusters are composed solely of Indiana myotis, other clusters may be mixed little brown myotis and Indiana myotis. These dense gatherings may contain about 300 bats per square foot. Blatchley's (1897) report that he removed 401 "*Vespertilio subulatus*" (*M. keenii*) from an area 0.7 feet wide and 1 foot long almost certainly refers to *M. sodalis*.

In Ray's Cave, most of the wintering Indiana myotis hang fairly close to the cave entrance. At one point where many are found annually there is a crevice about 50 yards long that runs along the ceiling. The bats pack themselves tightly into this cleft and on the ceiling bordering it. In addition, dense clusters also form on the ceiling elsewhere in the cave, and some of the population can be found in crevices in the cave walls. In several different years, the first Indiana myotis noted in this cave in the fall (usually in August or September) formed a cluster some distance back in the cave, at a point where some breakdown from the ceiling formed a domelike structure about twice the average height of the rest of the ceiling in the cave.

In Buckner's Cave, we usually found most of the Indiana myotis present in one to three tightly packed clusters. One such clump on 16 January 1954 contained by actual count 400 Indiana myotis and 1 little brown myotis. For several years in succession a large cluster was present at the identical spot on the cave ceiling, a behavioral tendency we have noticed for Indiana myotis in other caves where they hibernate. In Buckner's Cave we recorded *M. sodalis* as follows: 15 November 1953, at least 300 in one dense cluster; 6 December 1953, practically all in three clusters, of 200, 100, and 50; 16 January 1954, 400 in one cluster; 15 November 1954, clusters of 60, 40, and 30, and 10 to 15 others in a crevice in the cave wall; 9 January 1955, several clusters containing about 200; 28 December 1955, clusters of 188, 57, and 87.

On the evening of 2 August 1961, several small bats were feeding beneath, around, and sometimes within the crowns of some large oak and hickory trees in a woodlot in Boone County. The trees were spaced closely enough that when one looked up there were only a few small openings against the sky between the crowns. The bats appeared to be flying into spaces between the branches and within the overall span of the crowns. Three bats were shot; two were not retrieved and the other was a *Myotis sodalis*. On 7 August 1959, in a similar woodlot in Warren County, a *M. sodalis* exhibiting the same type of behavior was shot. The bats spent most of their time foraging near the tops of the crowns (about 40 feet high), but from time to time descended and flew about the head of the observer.

About twenty small, dark bats came from the edge of a woodlot, flew across the adjacent road, then disappeared into (or over) a second woodlot at dusk on the evening of 27 July 1957 in Steuben County. The bats flew rather slowly, but made sudden swerves, turns, and circles as though feeding; they flew from 15 to 50 feet above the ground. As they approached the road, they flew lower, then lower still as they passed along a wooded fencerow. They all came from the same direction and took about 15 minutes to pass; they were undoubtedly coming from a daytime roost, probably in the woodlot. We never saw more than two bats at any one time, and usually singles flew the route described above. L. C. Binford shot three of these bats between 8:30 and 9:00 P.M.; all were immature Indiana myotis. On the evening of 31 August 1957, seven *Myotis*-sized bats were seen at this same site, but the only one shot was lost in the weeds.

MIGRATION.   We have little relatively solid evidence to indicate where Indiana myotis go when they leave their Indiana hibernacula in the spring. Based on some bats shot, and some submitted to the rabies laboratory, we suspect that the large wintering populations disperse widely and in all directions. To date, our banding returns have shed little light on this aspect of behavior. We do have spring, summer, and fall records of the species north of any known wintering quarters; thus at least some spring movement is generally northward. Recoveries from hibernating Indiana myotis banded in Kentucky also reveal this pattern. A female banded in winter in Bat Cave, northeastern Kentucky, was recovered in southeastern Indiana. Four males and seven females banded during hibernation at Mammoth Cave, central Kentucky, were recaptured in the southern half of Indiana, mostly in the southeast quarter (Barbour and Davis, 1969).

Also, a few Indiana myotis banded at Big Wyandotte Cave, Indiana, have been retaken in Kentucky. A female banded 12 March 1955 at Big Wyandotte Cave was found in Coach Cave (Edmonson County, Kentucky) on 7 March 1959. A female banded in Buckner's Cave (Monroe County, Indiana) on 16 January 1954 was recaptured in Mammoth Cave National Park, Kentucky, on 2 March 1958. James B. Cope has records of banded Indiana myotis moving 300 miles from Indiana to Kentucky.

Most of our band recoveries for wintering Indiana myotis in Indiana have been from caves where the bats were originally banded, but a few have been found in different caves. Two females banded 13 December 1952 in Ray's Cave were recaptured in Buckner's Cave on 16 January 1954. A male banded in Salt Petre Cave on 7 March 1953 was caught in Ray's Cave on 17 March 1956. Two other males and two females banded in Salt Petre Cave were found later in Big Wyandotte Cave, a short distance away. A female banded in Buckner's Cave, 16 January 1954, was captured in Leonard Springs Cave on 23 January 1955.

SWARMING.   Netting at the entrances to Big Wyandotte Cave and Ray's Cave in August and September has enabled us and others to learn something about the swarming behavior of *Myotis sodalis* in Indiana. Wilson Baker caught 157, 226, 38, 10, and 2 Indiana myotis nightly from 3 to 7 September 1962, at the entrance of Big Wyandotte Cave. We netted this cave from dusk to dawn on the night of 22-23 August 1974 and captured 92 Indiana myotis. We caught the first one at 7:25 P.M. and the last at 6:00 A.M. Indiana myotis entered our net throughout the intervening period, with the longest time span between captures being 58 minutes (8:48 to 9:46 P.M.). The breakdown of our catch, based on hourly periods from the time of netting the first Indiana myotis, is shown in Table 55. This same night, we also netted 133 little brown myotis, 6 Keen's myotis, 1 gray myotis, 66 pipistrelles, 100 big brown bats, and 2 red bats.

Table 55

Myotis sodalis taken in mist-netting the entrance to Big Wyandotte Cave from 7:25 P.M. August 22 to 6:00 A.M. August 23, 1974

7:25 to 8:25	21 males, 4 females
8:25 to 9:25	2 males, 1 female
9:25 to 10:25	2 males, no females
10:25 to 11:25	5 males, 1 female
11:25 to 12:25	9 males, 1 female
12:25 to 1:25	4 males, 1 female
1:25 to 2:25	6 males, 2 females
2:25 to 3:25	7 males, 1 female
3:25 to 4:25	4 males, 1 female
4:25 to 5:25	2 males, 2 females
5:25 to 6:00	16 males, no females

Ray's Cave has been netted by us during the swarming period on four occasions. On 2 September 1962, from 5:45 P.M. to 9:30 P.M., 306 little brown myotis, 6 Indiana myotis, 42 Keen's myotis, and 9 pipistrelles were caught. Between 6:30 and 9:00 P.M. on 3 September 1964, we captured 244 little brown myotis, 23 Indiana myotis, 38 Keen's myotis, 39 pipistrelles, and 2 big brown bats. On 8 September 1971, between 7:20 and 11:30 P.M., we netted about 210 little brown myotis, 50 Indiana myotis, 18 Keen's myotis, 20 pipistrelles, 2 big brown bats, and 2 red bats. We caught 200 little brown myotis, 1 Indiana myotis, 12 Keen's myotis, 15 pipistrelles, and 7 big brown bats between 6:30 and 10:00 P.M. on 5 September 1974.

Our netting during the swarming season has shed no light on the pattern of buildup of wintering congregations of Indiana myotis, and it appears that swarming and fall buildup may not be closely correlated. It is obvious that we need more study on the subject. Visits to the cave at more frequent intervals are required to determine just how the wintering populations are formed in the fall and how they break up in the spring. We have some data from Ray's Cave, but not nearly enough to draw any conclusions at this time. We are indebted to James Cope for supplying his notes on *Myotis sodalis* in this cave.

LONGEVITY. From banding by Mumford between 1952 and 1959 and recaptures analyzed in 1974, data were obtained on longevity in *Myotis sodalis*. There were 36 Indiana myotis that had attained a minimum age of 5 years. Of these 36 bats, 12 were at least 5 years old, 3 were a minimum of 6 years of age, 9 were at least 7 years of age, 10 were at least 8 years old, 1 was at least 9, and 1 was at least 12 years old. Humphrey and Cope (1977), who studied survival rates of *M. sodalis* banded in Indiana and Kentucky, came to the following conclusions: "Survival rates are high for 10 years after marking in females and 6 years in males. Females can live as long as 14.8 years and males as long as 13.5 years."

FOOD. Whitaker (1972b) reported on the stomach contents of 4 Indiana myotis; percent volumes of insects were as follows: Hymenoptera (Ichneumonidae) 42.5 percent; Homoptera (Cicadellidae) 18.8 percent; unidentified Coleoptera 17.5 percent; unidentified Hymenoptera 7.5 percent; Coleoptera (Scarabaeidae 5.0 and Curculionidae 1.3) 6.3 percent.

REPRODUCTION. A gravid female, shot in Lagrange County on 18 June 1959 by Larry L. Calvert, was the first breeding *Myotis sodalis* examined (Mumford and Calvert, 1960). She contained a single embryo 39 mm in total length. Nixon Wilson banded two juvenile Indiana myotis on 27 July 1957 (Hall, 1962). They were hanging under a bridge in Turkey Run State Park (Parke County). They were still quite young and must have been born near where they were taken. Several subadults have been shot in flight in late July; 3 shot on 27 July were of adult body and skull proportions. The smallest *M. sodalis* examined was taken 24 July and measured only 71 mm in total length; it seems unlikely that this animal was capable of flight. A lactating female was shot in Kosciusko County, on 20 July.

The discovery of the first known maternity colony of Indiana myotis was detailed by Cope *et al.* (1974):

On 3 August 1971, Mark Wright bulldozed a dead elm (*Ulmus americana*) tree in a hedgerow near the Nolands Fork River, north of Webster, Wayne County, Indiana. He captured 8 of an estimated 50 bats which flew from under the loose bark of this tree as it was pushed over. These bats, two adult females, two immature males and four immature females, were taken to the Joseph Moore Museum on the Earlham College campus where they were identified as *Myotis sodalis* and entered in the Museum collection. . . . These bats represent the first reported maternity colony of *Myotis sodalis*.

During the summers of 1972 and 1973, Cope and his co-workers captured 31 Indiana myotis along Nolands Fork River, but no maternity colony was located. In the summer of 1974, the investigators were successful in finding the colony (Humphrey *et al.*, 1977):

The nursery roost was located under the loose bark of a dead bitternut hickory (*Carya cordiformes* . . .), that was alive in 1969. The bats used spaces behind several different patches of bark, some interconnected and others evidently isolated. The two places most consistently occupied by the largest numbers of animals had ESE and SSW exposures and consequently received much solar heat on their outer surfaces. During the winter of 1974–1975 much of the bark used for roosting the previous summer fell off the tree, while new slabs curled away from the trunk to form new potential roosting spots.

It was found that part of this population also used an alternate roost under the loose bark of a living shagbark hickory about 30 meters away. Another alternate roosting site was suspected, but not found.

The resident population in 1974 consisted of 25 females and 23 young that were reared to the volant stage. In 1975, there were at least 23 young weaned by 28 females. The first bats arrived at the nursery site in 1975 on 4 May, and substantial numbers appeared beginning 18 May. Available data suggest that each female bore a single young. Parturition in 1974 took place from 25 June to 4 July. Young were volant at 25 to 37 days of age. In 1975, young reached the volant stage 16 days earlier than they did in 1974. Indiana myotis were present at the roost until 10 October 1974 and until 19 September 1975.

Some observations were made on parental care, although the colony was in a difficult site to observe. One evening, about half the adults of the colony each carried their single young to new locations, from one patch of bark to another. The young were easily visible and clung to a teat while being carried. These young appeared to be from 7 to 10 days old and were about one-quarter to one-third the size of their mothers. From 21 July to 19 August 1974, when young were begin-

ning to fly and forage, the observers noted "pairs of *M. sodalis* flying in tandem." Such flights were characterized by the following bat staying within 1 meter of the leader, and it was thought that such pairs were composed of an adult and young. Such pairs occasionally returned to the nursery tree and landed together. One pair flew 290 meters from the roost to a foraging site.

The male embryo removed from a gravid *Myotis sodalis* shot on 18 June 1959 in Lagrange County measured 39 mm in total length. The teeth were not completely through the gums, but the tips were quite evident. There were few hairs present on the head, but some hairs were located posterior to the nostrils, on the chin and muzzle. No hairs were present between the nostrils. There were fringes of hair along the upper and lower lips. The chin region was heavily haired over an extensive area. One hair was present at the angle of the jaw on either side of the head. There appeared to be a chin gland present. On the dorsum, short hairs were over the rump area down to below the level of the knees and along the legs to the base of the feet. Sparse hairs were present on the toes. The only hair on the venter was as described above and was confined to the head.

Five immature males taken in late July and early August had testes ranging from 1.5 by 2.5 mm to 2.5 by 4 mm. Males with the largest testes (9 mm long) were collected in mid-August; specimens taken in September had testes that averaged smaller in size than August specimens, but our sample (19 animals) is rather small.

PARASITES AND DISEASES.   None of 34 Indiana myotis tested for rabies by Whitaker and Miller (1974) was infected with this disease.

Whitaker (1973) examined 43 Indiana myotis for external parasites and found 15 (44.1 percent) to be infested. The mite *Macronyssus crosbyi*, a normal parasite of this species, was the only parasite regularly found (70 taken). *Spinturnix globosus* is a peculiar large spinturnicid mite found in the anus of *M. sodalis*. It was originally described from *M. sodalis* from Ray's Cave, in Greene County, Indiana (Rudnick, 1960). Six individuals of this species were found. Also two myobiid mites were taken. They were listed by Whitaker (1973) as *Acanthopthirius* sp., but have since been described as *A. lucifugus* (Fain and Whitaker, 1976). Wilson (1961) reported two fleas, *Myodopsylla insignis*, on this species. A nonvolant young *M. sodalis* examined by Humphrey *et al.* (1977) was host to 7 bat bedbugs (*Cimex* sp.) and about 125 unidentified mites.

DECIMATING FACTORS. DeBlase and Cope (1967) reported the discovery of a dead *M. sodalis* impaled on a barbed-wire fence. The remains of numerous individuals have been found in various caves, but cause of death is generally unknown for these specimens. Cope reported about 1,000 Indiana myotis destroyed by vandals in one cave. Some years ago, the floor of a low passage in Big Wyandotte Cave was littered with bat wings. The tour guide told us that a domestic cat had been capturing and eating the bats (discard-

ing the wings). Although we could make no positive identification from only the wings, the bats were all *Myotis* and undoubtedly some were *sodalis*. Others have reported that cats have fed on *M. sodalis* in this cave. Humphrey *et al.* (1977) reported the unsuccessful attempt of a screech owl to catch a foraging *M. sodalis* near the nursery colony.

TAXONOMY. *Myotis sodalis* Miller and Allen was described in 1928 from specimens taken in Big Wyandotte Cave, Crawford County, Indiana. No subspecies are recognized.

SELECTED REFERENCES. Cope and Humphrey, 1977; Cope, Richter, and Mills, 1974; Easterla and Watkins, 1969; Hall, 1962; Humphrey, 1978; Humphrey and Cope, 1977; Humphrey, Richter, and Cope, 1977; Mumford and Calvert, 1960; Mumford and Cope, 1958; Richter, Seerley, Cope, and Keith, 1978.

Silver-haired Bat
Lasionycteris noctivagans (LeConte)

Lasionycteris noctivagans: Evermann and Butler, 1894b

DESCRIPTION. The silver-haired bat is a medium sized, blackish bat with whitish hair tips (frosting) both above and below. The amount of silver tipping on the dorsum varies considerably among individuals. Three Indiana specimens seen by us exhibit a "chocolate" color phase, in which the blackish color is replaced with brown. One of these specimens has about the same amount of frosting that black-pelaged animals have, but gives the overall appearance of a cocoa-colored individual (Kirkpatrick and Conaway, 1948); the membranes of this specimen are also paler than those of the usual, blackish animals. The brown phase, then, may represent some type of genetic variation (dilution) from the normal color. *Lasionycteris* is not likely to be confused with any other species of bat occurring in Indiana.

Weights and measurements are shown in Table 56. The dental formula is

$$I \frac{2}{3} C \frac{1}{1} P \frac{2}{3} M \frac{3}{3} = 36.$$

Silver-haired bat. Photo by Anthony Brentlinger, ISU AV Center

Table 56

Weights and measurements of
Lasionycteris noctivagans from Indiana

	Males	Females
Total length (mm)		
n	17	38
x̄	98.2	100.4
range	87-112	84-113
SD	7.0	7.2
SE	1.7	1.2
Tail length (mm)		
n	17	38
x̄	37.9	39.2
range	31-41	27-47
SD	4.0	4.3
SE	1.0	0.7
Hind foot (mm)		
n	15	34
x̄	7.6	8.5
range	7-10	7.5-11.0
SD	0.9	1.0
SE	0.2	0.2
Tragus (mm)		
n	16	26
x̄	5.6	6.0
range	4-7	5-8
SD	1.0	1.0
SE	0.2	0.2
Forearm (mm)		
n	16	29
x̄	41.4	41.5
range	39-44	39-43
SD	1.5	1.3
SE	0.4	0.2
Weight (grams)		
n	11	28
x̄	10.6	10.4
range	7.4-16.4	7.0-15.7
SD	2.5	2.0
SE	0.7	0.4

STATUS AND DISTRIBUTION. The silver-haired bat is evidently an uncommon spring and fall migrant and a rare winter resident; its exact status is poorly known. It evidently occurs throughout Indiana (Map 19). Spring specimens were taken from 18 April to 28 May and fall specimens from 29 August to 6 November. Hibernating individuals have been found on occasion in caves and buildings. Most of the winter records and specimens are from Tunnel Cave, Clifty Falls State Park (Jefferson County). In the collection of the Joseph Moore Museum are three specimens from Tunnel Cave, a male dated 10 December 1960, and two females dated 16 February 1964. An unsexed specimen taken from a building on the Earlham College campus, Richmond, on 16 January 1956 is also in this collection. It is possible that March and November records of the silver-haired bat from Indiana represent migrants, rather than wintering individuals.

In spring and fall, one may occasionally observe four or five silver-haired bats foraging about the edges of a woodlot at dusk, but more often singles or two or three bats are present. On the evening of 23 April 1954, four silver-haired bats were shot by James B. Cope as they foraged at one site on the Clark State Forest (Clark County) near Henryville. We have practically no data concerning the numbers of this bat in Indiana during various seasons of the year. There is no indication

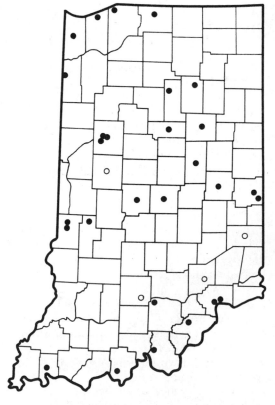

Map 19.   The Silver-haired Bat,
Lasionycteris noctivagans, in Indiana

that it is at all common in winter; in fact, it is quite rare and has only been seen in three caves. We have no reports of large numbers during migration.

HABITAT. Most Indiana specimens of *Lasionycteris* were shot flying about the borders of woodlots, over ponds, or along streams. One was shot on 3 May as it foraged about the edge of a wooded slope, bordering a clover field. Two, shot on 18 April, were feeding over a road and along a mowed power line, both through a mature, deciduous woods. Most of those taken in Tippecanoe County have been shot about the borders of two mature, deciduous woodlots surrounded by pasture or cultivated fields.

One silver-haired bat was observed (date not recorded) beneath the loose bark of a tree (Porter County) by Raymond Grow; A. H. Westing and W. C. Bramble caught two beneath the loose bark of a dead tree (Perry County) on 6 November. Dan Bloodgood caught one beneath the loose bark of a shagbark hickory on 14 September. One was shot over a small pond surrounded by pasture, but near a wooded area. In Newton County, one was shot at dusk as it foraged around large, scattered oak trees on a sand ridge.

Several silver-haired bats have been found in caves, and a few have been captured in or on the sides of houses. One was hanging on the side of a house on 6 September, at 11:30 A.M. At 6:45 on the morning of 3 September 1959, a silver-haired bat was noted flying about a small concrete lighthouse 100 yards from shore at the end of a breakwater extending out into Lake Michigan, at Michigan City. The bat lit on the side of the structure, then crawled into a narrow crevice between the building and the end of a steel catwalk, where it was easily captured by hand. A second *Lasionycteris* was then noted flying weakly about and it was easily knocked down by hand and caught. The morning was clear and cool (55 to 58°F) and there was a 7- to 8-mile-an-hour wind; the bats flew mostly on the lee side of the structure and gave the appearance of being quite tired.

R. D. Kirkpatrick found a female hanging 8 feet above the ground on a cliff face, just outside a cave entrance (Jennings County) on 3 January.

ASSOCIATED SPECIES. While shooting bats at dusk, we have collected the following species along with *Lasionycteris noctivagans: Lasiurus borealis, Nycticeius humeralis, Eptesicus fuscus, Myotis sodalis, Myotis lucifugus,* and *Pipistrellus subflavus.* The red bat has been the most common associate at these times, but this may be because it, too, emerges early in the evening and is more easily shot than species that may emerge to forage later. Two silver-haired bats found in Donaldson's Cave on 6 March shared the room in which they roosted that day with little brown myotis, southeastern myotis, big brown bats, and eastern pipistrelles. Silver-haired bats share Tunnel Cave with little brown myotis, Keen's myotis, big brown bats, and pipistrelles.

HABITS. Silver-haired bats are usually observed foraging rather early in the evening—about the same time that red bats, pipistrelles, and evening bats are flying about. At some collecting sites, the silver-haired bat was the first species noted at dusk. We should point out, however, that most of the silver-haired bats collected by shooting in Indiana have been taken where pipistrelles (a noted early flyer) are absent or very rare. Where *Pipistrellus subflavus* is common, as in southern Indiana, it is normally the first species to become active at dusk.

Lasionycteris usually flies fairly low, hawking insects from 15 to 30 feet above the ground, along woods borders. On 15 May, however, several were feeding above the crowns of trees in a woodlot at Lafayette; these bats were feeding 50 to 75 feet from the ground when over the canopy. They occasionally made forays away from the trees out over the adjacent pasture, where they tended to fly nearer the ground. Two silver-haired bats shot on 18 April were feeding along a mowed strip beneath a power line, parallel to an adjacent woods; the bats flew rather slowly back and forth along this open strip, feeding not more than 20 feet from the ground.

Most silver-haired bats seen in Indiana are migrants, but we have no idea where these spring and fall flights originate or terminate. Only a few bats of this species have been banded in Indiana (most of these were captured in caves), and band recoveries have shed no light on migratory movements. J. B. Cope recaptured one a year after banding in a cave. It is possible that in winter this bat is more abundant in Indiana than is now known; it may hibernate in the crevices of rock outcrops, in caves, buildings, or in tree cavities. Spring migration seems to occur in a relatively short period from about mid-April to the end of May, but fall migration is more prolonged, extending at least from late August to early November. Six of eight silver-haired bats shot in April and fifteen of seventeen shot in May were females. Eight of fourteen shot from August to October were females. Adult males are evidently not common in Indiana or have habits that reduce their vulnerability to being shot.

Relatively few silver-haired bats have been observed in their roosts in Indiana. On 6 March, a male and a female were extracted from a narrow fissure in Donaldson's Cave. The bats were wedged together at the back of this crevice, about 18 inches from its opening; the crack had been formed when a piece of limestone had pulled away from the cave wall at the point where the wall met the ceiling, about 10 feet from the cave floor. Both bats were very torpid. Their roosting site was at least 120 feet from the cave entrance, in a rather large, dry room. The male and female found 6 November in Perry County were beneath the bark of a 14-inch dead black oak tree; the bats were 7 feet from the ground. In the fall of 1952, Raymond Grow captured and released a silver-haired bat he found beneath the loose bark of a tree in Lake County.

In September 1954, Raymond Grow saw one clinging to the outside of a screen door at the Northern Indiana Public Service Plant, Michigan City; this plant is located on the shore of Lake Michigan. The two silver-haired bats captured at the lighthouse were near this plant. When we caught these bats (3 September) we noted that they appeared weak; they were easily captured, although a few moments before they had been flying about. We believe the bats had just reached land after migrating from over Lake Michigan. Perhaps bats that fly over a portion of this lake are exhausted when they reach land and take the first opportunity to hang on some available structure, such as the screen door mentioned above. (We will have more to say on this subject under the discussion of *Lasiurus borealis*, another migratory species.)

Most silver-haired bats collected in Indiana in the fall were quite fat.

FOOD. Whitaker examined two Indiana silver-haired bats with food in their stomachs. One contained only Trichoptera and the other 90 percent Trichoptera and 10 percent Scarabaeidae. Gould (1955) reported a stable fly *(Stomoxys calcitrans)* in the mouth of a silver-haired bat from Massachusetts. Novakowski (1956) recorded the feeding of this bat on dipterous larvae, presumably obtained from a tree hole in which the bats were living.

REPRODUCTION. Single females collected 26 April and 12 May contained no visible embryos. A female collected 9 May contained 2 embryos weighing 0.2 grams each. Another female taken 12 May had at least one 5-mm embryo; part of her reproductive tract was destroyed by shot. The label notation on a specimen shot on 14 May mentions that embryos were present, but gives no other details. One of two females taken on 20 May (Vigo County) contained two embryos measuring 2.4 mm, but the other showed no visible embryos or placental scars.

We have relatively little information on testis size in *Lasionycteris noctivagans*. A male shot on 4 May had testes only 3 mm long and represents the only spring-taken specimen for which we have data. Two males taken on 3 September each had testes 7 mm long. Single males had testis lengths of 5, 3, 5, 5, and 3 mm on 6 September, 20 September, 7 October, 8 October, and 24 October respectively.

PARASITES AND DISEASES. One batbug *(Cimex adjunctus)* and one myobiid mite *(Acanthopthirius* sp.) were found on 8 silver-haired bats examined by Whitaker (1973). Of 11 bats of this species examined for internal parasites, 4 harbored a total of 6 cestodes and 8 harbored 63 trematodes. These parasites have not been identified to species.

A male silver-haired bat captured in a house in Montgomery County on 12 September 1960 tested positive for rabies. The bat had bitten a woman on the finger during the night as she was sleeping. Mumford identified the bat for the Public Health Service. None of 7 Indiana silver-haired bats examined by Whitaker and Miller (1974) were rabid.

DECIMATING FACTORS. We have no records of predation or of enemies of this species.

TAXONOMY. No subspecies of *L. noctivagans* is recognized.

SELECTED REFERENCES. Barbour and Davis, 1969; Miller, 1897.

Eastern Pipistrelle
Pipistrellus subflavus (F. Cuvier)

Georgian Bat, Northern Pipistrelle

Vespertilio georgrenus: Quick and Langdon, 1882
Vesperugo carolinensis: Evermann and Butler, 1894b
Pipistrellus subflavus: McAtee, 1907

DESCRIPTION. The eastern pipistrelle is the smallest species of bat found in Indiana. The upper parts range from pale yellowish brown or grayish brown to dark reddish brown. Immatures tend to be the most grayish. There is considerable variation in the pelage color of this bat. Most of the hairs on the dorsum are tricolored, having a broad, blackish basal band, then a narrower, yellowish band, and dusky tips. The venter is much the same color as the dorsum, but usually has less of a grayish cast because the belly hairs are not dark-tipped. The forearm is usually reddish and contrasts sharply with the blackish wing membranes, especially in live animals. Four specimens showing varying amounts of white in the pelage have been taken; in one, whitish blotches are present on the wing membranes, as well.

Weights and measurements are shown in Table 57. The dental formula is

$$I \frac{2}{3} C \frac{1}{1} P \frac{2}{2} M \frac{3}{3} = 34.$$

STATUS AND DISTRIBUTION. This little bat is a common permanent resident in southern Indiana, and an uncommon summer resident in northern Indiana (Map 20). There are few records for the northern half of the state. The northern extent of its known range is Tippecanoe County and Wells County, in western and eastern Indiana respectively. It win-

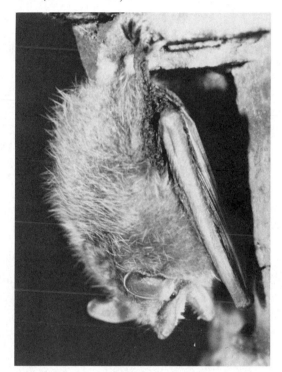

Eastern pipistrelle. Photo by Richard LaVal

ters as far north as Parke County (in Turkey Run State Park). *Pipistrellus subflavus* is one of the most abundant bats in summer throughout the southern one-third of Indiana. Winter populations there are quite small in comparison, indicating that most pipistrelles leave the state in the fall. The largest wintering population found in one cave was 112, in Wilson's Cave (Jefferson County). Only one breeding area has been discovered (Cope, Baker, and Confer, 1961), in Jackson County, where maternity colonies have been found for several years.

Almost every cave examined during the

Table 57
Weights and measurements of
Pipistrellus subflavus from Indiana

	Males	Females
Total length (mm)		
n	28	24
x̄	83.5	82.5
range	74-91	76-90
SD	5.0	4.46
SE	0.94	0.91
Tail length (mm)		
n	28	24
x̄	34.3	36.4
range	31-39	31-42
SD	2.75	3.14
SE	0.52	0.64
Hind foot (mm)		
n	28	24
x̄	8.6	7.9
range	7-11	6-9
SD	1.49	0.97
SE	0.28	0.19
Forearm (mm)		
n	19	9
x̄	34.3	34.2
range	32-41	33-36
SD	2.06	1.3
SE	0.47	0.43
Tragus (mm)		
n	15	3
x̄	5.4	5.0
range	3.5-6.5	4-6
SD	0.90	1
SE	0.23	0.57
Weight (grams)		
n	26	23
x̄	6.0	5.6
range	2.8-9.2	2.6-7.5
SD	1.58	1.35
SE	0.31	0.28

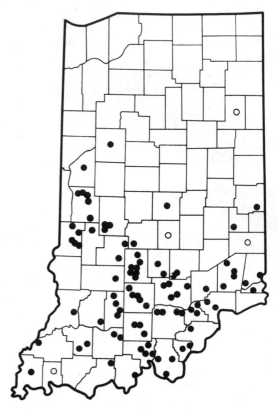

Map 20.   The Eastern Pipistrelle,
Pipistrellus subflavus, in Indiana

winter has contained at least one pipistrelle; some of these caves are quite small and no other species of bat hibernates in them. The number of pipistrelles seen per visit to 72 Indiana caves ranged from 1 to 112. In 49 of these caverns, 1 to 10 were present; 11 to 24 were found in 10 caves; 25 to 50 were in 10 caves. In only 3 caves did we find more than 50 pipistrelles: in Dillon Cave (Orange County), Coon's Cave (Monroe County) and Wilson's Cave (Jefferson County).

There are few data for making comparisons of pipistrelle populations for different years. Walter L. Hahn observed "not more than 50" eastern pipistrelles in Coon's Cave on 29 March 1908. We have records of 31, 80, and 40 there on 23 February 1952, 13 December 1952, and 22 February 1954 respectively. Hahn saw "about 10" pipistrelles in Eller's Cave (Monroe County) on 29 March 1908. Our records show 18 there on 26 March 1952 and 25 on 3 January 1953. Banta (1907) worked in Mayfield's Cave (also Monroe County) from 1903 to 1905 and noted that *P. subflavus* was "fairly abundant," but gave no figures. Hahn observed 17 pipistrelles there on 11 January 1907; only 4 were found on 26 January 1952. We can conclude little concerning population trends from these comparisons until we learn more about normal, annual fluctuations in winter populations.

We also know little about summer populations of *Pipistrellus subflavus*, and very few breeding colonies have been located. But judging from the number of pipistrelles observed and shot throughout southern Indiana during the summer and early fall, the summering population must be many times greater than the wintering population. For example, on the evening of 8 August 1957, Mumford observed at least 75 pipistrelles along a 3-mile stretch of road in Martin County. At one spot there were 30 to 40 feeding over a small area; at another site at least 25 were foraging over an area 100 yards square. Smaller congregations of pipistrelles have been noted in several parts of southern Indiana during the summer.

HABITAT. *Pipistrellus subflavus* appears to be most abundant in well-wooded regions which contain streams and ponds. It probably roosts by day in trees (there are no observations to confirm this), for at dusk it emerges about woodland borders. Observed day roosts are caves, mines, and (rarely) buildings. On 6 May 1961, there were 5 pipistrelles hanging beneath the roof of a small, open-sided picnic shelter. Two females were hanging from the ceiling of a room in an abandoned house on 5 May 1954. On 27 April 1952, a male was captured while hanging under a small porch of a building. All of these roosting sites were well lighted. Maternity colonies discovered in Indiana have been associated with buildings. Eight pregnant pipistrelles were taken from one maternity colony in a barn 3 miles south of Riley (Vigo County) 1 June 1964.

ASSOCIATED SPECIES. In southern Indiana, red bats and pipistrelles are most frequently seen foraging together in spring, summer, and fall. Both species emerge early in the evening and perhaps our data are biased somewhat by this fact. For example, the little brown myotis has seldom been shot while feeding with pipistrelles at dusk, but *Myotis lucifugus* appears to emerge from its daytime roost considerably later than *Pipistrellus subflavus*. In fact, relatively few little brown myotis have been collected in Indiana by shooting in the evening, and observations at their maternity colonies suggest that they do not emerge to feed until deep dusk, often too late for the bat hunter to collect them. Other bats collected with eastern pipistrelles by shooting were big brown bats, evening bats, hoary bats, red bats, silver-haired bats, and Indiana myotis.

During the winter, eastern pipistrelles hibernate in caves with all other species of bats that use caves at this season. It is not unusual, however, to find only *P. subflavus* hibernating in small caves. Pipistrelles do not hang in clusters with other species of bats during the winter.

HABITS. When hibernating, *Pipistrellus subflavus* is normally solitary; individuals are found hanging singly throughout the caves. We have only once found even two hanging together: on 3 September 1963, two pipistrelles hanging on the wall in Ray's Cave appeared to be copulating; the bats were captured and both were males, but one had an erect penis.

Most pipistrelles hang on the walls of the caves during hibernation; relatively few roost on the ceiling, but some enter dome-like depressions in the ceiling or hang inside hollow stalactites. Where there are breakdowns, consisting of large chunks of limestone which have fallen from the walls or ceilings, pipistrelles frequently hibernate on the underside of these chunks, sometimes not more than two feet from the cave floor. They also hang on the underside of ledges along the cave wall, again frequently near the cave floor or the surface of the cave stream. On rare occasions, a single bat of this species may be found in a small crevice in the cave ceiling.

Once the wintering site is selected, an individual bat may hang there for long periods. Two pipistrelles occupied the same spots from at least 1 March to 5 May in a small cave in Washington County. Hahn (1908) found that the eastern pipistrelle moved about inside the cave during the winter less than other species he studied in what is now Spring Mill State Park. He reported that an individual remained in the same spot an average of two weeks, and one hung at the identical spot for 44 days. We have the general impression that others may actually use the roosting site for even longer periods, when not unduly disturbed. In fact, Banta (1907) recorded one that hung at the same spot from 20 November to 5 April; he implied that others spent long periods at other sites. The fur of many hibernating eastern pipistrelles is covered with fine droplets of condensed moisture, possibly indicating that these bats have spent long inactive periods at one spot.

We have little information on the buildup

of hibernating populations in the fall. A few pipistrelles (principally males) may be found in caves throughout the summer. There are evidently some interesting movements involving numbers of pipistrelles into certain caves at times. For example, there were no more than 8 pipistrelles in Ray's Cave at 5:00 P.M. on 2 September 1963; the next morning, 63 (including both sexes) were found in the cave. The new arrivals had obviously entered the cave during the night. We were unable to study these animals to determine how many, if any, remained in the cave during the winter. But our periodic censuses of wintering pipistrelles in Ray's Cave have revealed that more than half a dozen present on a single winter visit is unusual; the more than 25 seen on 7 February 1953 is an exception.

Banta's work in Mayfield's Cave also furnished some data on the pattern of seasonal activity of pipistrelles. He found one in the cave on 24 September; the number of pipistrelles had increased considerably by 30 October. By 20 November, he felt all had entered the cave that were to hibernate there. There was very little movement noted after 1 December; the bats became more easily aroused in late winter and early spring. During April there appeared to be some fluctuation in numbers present on Banta's weekly visits. Pipistrelles were "very seldom" seen in the cave later in the spring and during the summer. We have noticed that at least from May to July pipistrelles hang near the cave entrance; in winter, they are normally found farther inside the cave.

We have records for *Pipistrellus subflavus* in Indiana caves for each month of the year, but relatively few are present from mid-May to mid-August. From our meager information, we cannot determine whether most of the pipistrelles found in caves in summer are males; both sexes have been taken in June and July. Further research may shed some light on this problem. That females are found in caves during the season of the year when young are being reared suggests that all females do not bear young each year; perhaps some are not bred or some immatures do not breed. We have no evidence that this species forms maternity colonies in caves.

We know practically nothing about the daytime roosting habits of *P. subflavus* during the nonhibernating season. At dusk this bat appears about the borders of wooded areas, along streams lined with trees, and about ponds or lakes near forested areas. We assume that the normal daytime roost is among the foliage of or in hollow trees, but we have never actually seen one in such a site.

The pipistrelle emerges early in the evening, and the earliest individuals to appear often forage quite high, about the treetops or above them. As dusk deepens, the bats usually feed closer to the ground, coming down to hawk insects and to drink. On 3 August 1948, about 20 pipistrelles were feeding over and along Sugar Creek, in Turkey Run State Park. The first bat appeared at 7:05 P.M., then the group centered its activity over a gravel bar and swift riffle in the stream; perhaps some type of insect was emerging from the water or most of this activity was concerned with drinking. The bats fed actively for about 30 minutes then dispersed. The following evening, at the same site, a pipistrelle appeared at 6:57, it fed, drank, and flew about for at least 10 minutes before other pipistrelles were seen. During this period, it drank only in the quiet water of an eddy beneath an overhanging rock or just downstream from a large rock in the water. Its foraging area was 30 to 40 yards long and 10 yards wide. Within the next 45 minutes, 25 to 30 pipistrelles were present. As it became darker, these bats left the creek and began feeding among the treetops along it; in this case, it appeared that the early part of the evening activity was centered around drinking. On 14 August 1948, at a small farm pond about 2 miles from the Sugar Creek site, at least 20 pipistrelles were feeding and drinking at 7:15 P.M. By 7:30 only 2 or 3 were present; the bats had dispersed rather quickly, evidently after drinking. On 27 July 1961, along Coal Creek (Fountain County), the first pipistrelles seen at dusk were foraging about 75 feet in the air about the crowns of tall trees bordering the stream. The same behavior was observed along a small stream in Jackson County, on 8 July 1952.

On 11 August 1959, in Monroe County, Mumford was watching for bats at dusk near a small pond adjacent to a low, flat woods composed mostly of pin oak. A few red bats were foraging at 8:05; at 8:10, about 20 pipistrelles suddenly appeared in the air and fed over the woods, the pond, a soybean field, and a nearby weed field. There were no buildings or caves in the vicinity and the bats had evidently emerged from the trees.

From 15 to 20 pipistrelles were feeding at dusk in Vigo County on 5 June 1958 over a fallow field bordering a woods. The bats foraged in small circles low over the field and along the woods border at elevations below the treetops. On 25 July 1954, in Bartholomew County, at least 15 pipistrelles and 2 red bats were feeding over a wheat stubble near the edge of a woods, and 15 red bats and 30 pipistrelles were observed along the road within a few miles. In Martin County, on 8 August 1957, approximately 40 pipistrelles were foraging over a weed field along a small creek near the edge of a forested area.

Pipistrelles are among the first bats to emerge from their daytime roosts at dusk. In southern Indiana, they can frequently be seen feeding with red bats and chimney swifts while there is still considerable light. As has been noted several times with red bats, a pipistrelle occasionally flies toward a swift. Whether the bat and the bird are after the same insect we do not know, but this is a possibility. Sometimes pipistrelles appear at dusk before red bats are on the wing; on other occasions, red bats are seen earlier than pipistrelles. Both of these species have also been seen at dawn, flying about after the sky is quite light. On 28 July 1954, at 5:32 A.M., at least three pipistrelles were watched with binoculars as they flew about just above the treetops. They appeared to fly into the foliage of a large oak and disappeared from sight at 5:40. The morning was clear and calm and the temperature was about 64°F. One pipistrelle was shot at 2:00 on a bright, sunny afternoon in either October or November in Posey County.

In our study of the emergence of bats from Donnehue's Cave (Lawrence County) we found that pipistrelles were the first bats to leave the cave on eight of eleven nights (May to October) that we netted this species (Mumford and Whitaker, 1975). We captured 4 before sunset in a net set across the mouth of the cave. Although *P. subflavus* left Donnehue's Cave relatively early in the evening, the species remained active over a considerable period of time on certain nights. Some were netted five hours after sunset, and this species was probably active throughout the night on occasion (we did not tend the nets all night to determine this). Since we caught the greatest number (114 of 143) of pipistrelles during August and September, most of them were undoubtedly in migration. The activity patterns of migrants may differ from that of more sedentary animals; this requires further study. The pattern of bats, especially transients, emerging from a cave may differ from that of bats emerging from noncave roosts at other, or the same, seasons. Other bats using the cave during the period of our study were the little brown myotis, Keen's myotis, the southeastern myotis, the Indiana myotis, and the big brown bat.

We have been interested in determining how long individual bats are active at night and whether they return periodically to their daytime roost after dark. Since practically all summer daytime roosts of *P. subflavus* are probably in trees, this type of information is lacking. Bats are efficient feeders, and they can fill their stomachs with food in a period of minutes at dusk when insects are abundant. But what does a bat do the rest of the night after it has fed at dusk? And how often does a bat feed during the night? While netting the cave entrances, we have usually banded and released each bat shortly after it was netted. A pipistrelle banded and released at 8:30 P.M. on 18 May at Big Wyandotte Cave was again netted as it entered the cave at 10:25 P.M. Some clue as to nightly activity was obtained the night of 22-23 August, when we netted Big Wyandotte Cave throughout the night. We captured pipistrelles from 7:20 P.M., to 5:00 A.M., netting 1 to 6 (average 3.3) in each half-hour interval of the period.

In attempting to capture pipistrelles by the use of fine wires stretched just above the water of pools where bats drink, Mumford noted that bats knocked into the water by striking the wires would frequently fly directly from the water's surface. Others would swim to the edge of the pool and could be easily captured by hand. Perhaps those that got their pelage excessively wet when they struck the water were then unable to fly as easily as those that did not; also, some may have been stunned by striking the wires.

SEX RATIOS. We have obtained some sex ratio data from netting cave entrances and some from banding or observations in caves. During the winters of 1951–52 and 1952–53, a total of 137 eastern pipistrelles were banded in Coon's Cave (Monroe County); of these, 105 were males. Males outnumbered females in smaller samples from thirteen other caves. In Beck's Mill Cave (Washington County) females outnumbered males 9 to 2 on 22 December 1952, and in Upper Twin Cave (Lawrence County) 5 males and 7 females were present on 23 November 1951. The overall percentage of males banded in fourteen caves during the winter was 75.4.

Sex ratio data from the netting of eastern pipistrelles at cave entrances during the fall swarming period are available from four caves. At Donnehue's Cave on three nights in August and one in September, we captured 98 males, 12 females, and 4 for which sex was unrecorded. On the night of 22-23 August 1974, we netted Big Wyandotte Cave from dusk to dawn, catching 50 males, 9 females, and 7 for which sex was unrecorded. A net set across the mouth of Ray's Cave from 6:30 to 9:00 P.M. on 3 September 1964 captured 30 male and 9 female pipistrelles. At Boone's Cave (Owen County), 15 males and no females were netted on 24 August 1962.

Most of the relatively few pipistrelles seen in caves in June and July were males. Representative observations follow: Salt Petre Cave (Crawford County), 10 June 1954, a single male; Bronson's Cave (Lawrence County), 11 July 1949, 1 male; May's Cave (Monroe County), 7 June 1954, 5 males; Buckner's Cave (Monroe County), 7 June 1954, 7 males. On three nights in June and July 1971, at Donnehue's Cave, 16 males and 2 females were netted at the cave entrance.

LONGEVITY. The relatively few banding returns of hibernating pipistrelles have shed little light on longevity. Of 314 males and 104 females banded, 19 males and 8 females have been recaptured. Only 3 of these animals had been banded more than two years previously; these were recaptured after 26, 36, and 57 months. The average length of time between banding and the last recapture of these 27 pipistrelles was about 18 months.

MIGRATION. We know practically nothing about the migration of *P. subflavus* in Indiana, where the bat lives near the northern borders of its geographic range. A male shot 26 May in Tippecanoe County, north of any

known wintering sites, was undoubtedly a migrant. Circumstantial evidence for the movements of large numbers of animals is the fact that summer populations in southern Indiana are high, but hibernating numbers are quite low.

HOMING. A male pipistrelle taken from Sullivan's Cave on 1 March 1955 was banded and then released the next day in Donnehue's Cave. On 1 February 1958, the bat was again captured in Sullivan's Cave. The caves are about 8 miles apart. We have carried out no homing experiments with this bat in Indiana, since so few maternity colonies have been found and they were all small.

FOOD. Whitaker (1972b) examined the stomachs of 23 pipistrelles from Indiana (Table 58). Homopterans of the family Cicadellidae (leafhoppers) were the most commonly eaten food, followed by ground beetles (Carabidae). Other foods represented at higher volumes were Diptera, Coleoptera, Lepidoptera, and delphacids (Homoptera). Ross (1967) found the stomach of one pipistrelle from Indiana to contain 80 percent Cicadellidae and 20 percent Formicidae. Since the pipistrelle is the smallest Indiana bat, most of the foods eaten were small.

We were surprised that seven eastern pipistrelles netted at the entrance of Donnehue's Cave on the evening of 20 August between 8:31 and 10:00 had empty stomachs. Five of these were captured between 9:01 and 10:00 and seemingly had had ample time to feed, for it was dark shortly after 8:30 that evening.

REPRODUCTION. The usual number of young at birth is probably two. We have records of twelve gravid females with twin embryos and two females each with a single embryo. In addition, each of sixteen gravid females examined (but not collected) appeared to contain two embryos (Cope and Humphrey). Walter L. Hahn (1908) took a female on 6 June that contained three small (2-mm) embryos, and Lindsay (1958) examined a female taken on 21 May that had four embryos measuring 3 mm. Perhaps some embryos are resorbed before parturition in this species. Parturition in pipistrelles in Indiana evidently occurs in late June and early July. We have no actual dates, although two females confined to cages gave birth (perhaps prematurely) to young on 21 June and 30 June. Another caged female, injured by shot

Table 58
Foods eaten by *Pipistrellus subflavus* (n = 23) from
Indiana
(from Whitaker, 1972b)

Food Item	Percent Volume	Percent Frequency
Cicadellidae (leafhoppers)	21.7	52.2
Carabidae (ground beetles)	18.1	34.8
Diptera	10.7	26.1
Coleoptera	7.8	34.8
Lepidoptera	7.3	21.7
Cercopidae (froghoppers)	7.2	13.0
Muscoid flies	4.6	8.7
Formicidae (ants)	4.6	8.7
Reduviidae (assassin bugs)	3.7	13.0
Chrysomelidae (leaf beetles)	3.7	13.0
Chrysopidae (lacewings)	2.8	4.3
Tipulidae (craneflies)	2.2	4.3
Hemiptera (true bugs)	2.2	4.3
Ichneumonidae (ichneumon-flies)	1.1	8.7
Grass stems	0.9	4.3
Insects (unidentified)	0.7	8.7
Culicidae (mosquitos)	0.7	4.3
Chironomidae (midges)	0.2	4.3
	100.2	

on 7 July, gave birth to twins on 9 July. Mumford and Handley (1956) published an account of the behavior of one of these families just after birth. The combined weight of two embryos removed from a female on 22 June was 2.3 grams.

Males with the largest testes have been collected from July to September. Four males taken in July had testes averaging 4.8 mm in length; 35 males taken in August had testes averaging 4.8 mm in length; 3 males collected in September had testes ranging from 3.5 to 6 mm (averaging 4 mm) in length. From our data, testis size is smallest in mid-winter (one male with 1-mm testes on 24 February), then increases to a maximum in summer, with a rather abrupt decrease in fall (3 males with 2-mm testes on 1 October). We suspect that a considerable amount of copulation takes place in August.

PARASITES AND DISEASES. The single internal parasite found in 55 individuals of this bat was one nematode in one bat. Only the chigger *Euschoengastia pipistrelli* (54 individuals) was found on 13 pipistrelles examined for external parasites. The only previous parasite records for this species are those of Wilson (1961), who found two specimens of the bat flea (*Nycteridopsylla*

chapini), normally found on *Eptesicus fuscus*.

Of twenty-four pipistrelles from Indiana examined for rabies, 3 (12.5 percent) were rabid (Whitaker and Miller, 1974).

DECIMATING FACTORS. We occasionally find a dead pipistrelle hanging in a cave, but we have no idea of the cause of death of these individuals. Some must meet with accidents, for we have examined several with part of the wing membrane or uropatagium missing. A maternity colony in Jackson County was discouraged from using its roost of the previous year when heavy grease was smeared on the rafters where the bats hung. A pipistrelle shot while flying about on a sunny day had part of its body covered with what appeared to be red paint. No doubt a few of these bats are killed by vandalism in caves.

TAXONOMY. The subspecies in Indiana is *Pipistrellus subflavus subflavus* (F. Cuvier). There is considerable color variation in Indiana specimens.

SELECTED REFERENCES. Barbour and Davis, 1969; Cope, Baker, and Confer, 1961; Davis and Mumford, 1962; Jones and Suttkus, 1973; Lindsay, 1956b; Mumford and Cope, 1964; Walle·· and Jarvis, 1971.

Big Brown Bat
Eptesicus fuscus (Beauvois)

Brown Bat, Large Brown Bat

Eptesicus melanops: Rafinesque, 1820
Vespertilio fuscus: Quick and Langdon, 1882;
  Banta, 1907
Adelonycteris fuscus: Evermann and Butler,
  1894b
Eptesicus fuscus: Hahn, 1909

DESCRIPTION. *Eptesicus fuscus* is a rather large (the second largest species of bat in Indiana), brownish bat with blackish membranes and ears. The wings are brown. The body pelage varies in color from tan to chocolate brown and may be reddish brown in some individuals. It is difficult to describe a "typical" specimen other than to say that it is some shade of brown. We have seen several Indiana specimens with white spots and a few scattered, whitish guard hairs. The tragus is broad and blunt-tipped, and the ears are relatively short for so large a bat. The wingspan is about 310 to 355 mm, and the forearm varies from about 42 to 54 mm (average 46 mm). The tail protrudes a few mm beyond the end of the interfemoral membrane. The calcar has a distinct keel. There are prominent odoriferous glands on the upper lips.

The only other brownish colored bat in Indiana with a forearm reaching 42 mm is the rare gray myotis, which has a forearm ranging from 42 to 45 mm and a relatively long, narrow, pointed tragus. *Myotis grisescens* is usually gray, but females may develop a brown pelage during the reproductive season.

Big brown bat. Photo by Whitaker

Weights and measurements are shown in Table 59. The dental formula is

$$I \frac{2}{3} C \frac{1}{1} P \frac{1}{2} M \frac{3}{3} = 32.$$

STATUS AND DISTRIBUTION. The big brown bat is a common resident throughout the state (Map 21), especially in spring, summer, and fall. It is probably the most or second most abundant bat in the state. In winter it is much less conspicuous and either hibernates in protected sites or possibly migrates. During the hibernation season, big brown bats are observed most often in the various limestone caves of south-central Indiana; these bats hibernate also in heated buildings in other parts of the state, but we have relatively few winter records from the northern one-third of Indiana. There is some evidence from banding that the big brown bat is somewhat migratory. Numbers present in Indiana in the summer are far greater than the relatively few found in Indiana caves during the winter.

HABITAT. Summer roost sites of *Eptesicus fuscus* include buildings, bridges, rocky escarpments, and caves, but the species is most common in old buildings. We have seen barns or other buildings that harbor 200 to 400 or more individuals in the summer. Trees and mines are also undoubtedly used, but definite records are lacking. We have one report of a maternity colony in a tree cavity. In the nonhibernating season, *E. fuscus* has been taken by shooting over ponds, around deciduous woodlots, along streams, and in residential areas.

Many big brown bats winter in caves, and others winter in heated buildings; the percentage that uses buildings is unknown, but may be considerably greater than records now indicate. Little is known about the species in hibernation, but 26 big brown bats were found in apparent hibernation on March 26 in a barn north of Terre Haute. It is possible that they came there from some other area after initial arousal from hibernation, although this did not seem likely since the bats were wedged very tightly into tiny crevices,

Table 59

Weights and measurements of *Eptesicus fuscus* from several counties of Indiana

	Vigo		Jefferson		Vanderburgh		Northern Indiana	
	Males	Females	Males	Females	Males	Females	Males	Females
Total length (mm)								
n	26	61	23	21	13	6	19	11
x̄	108.4	113.4	113.0	111.9	112.2	108.0	112.9	112.9
range	99-124	106-129	106-121	101-126	105-123	94-113	100-129	102-119
SD	20.85	13.61	4.95	8.14	5.16	7.42	5.65	4.61
SE	4.08	1.74	1.03	1.77	1.43	3.03	1.29	1.39
Tail length (mm)								
n	30	64	22	21	13	6	19	11
x̄	39.0	42.3	40.5	42.4	41.2	39.8	42.4	41.3
range	29-47	37-50	33-47	36-50	35-48	35-43	34-46	35-47
SD	4.64	3.81	3.14	4.91	4.59	2.71	3.46	4.00
SE	0.84	0.47	0.65	1.07	1.28	1.10	0.79	1.20
Hind foot (mm)								
n	30	62	22	19	13	6	18	10
x̄	10.0	10.0	10.5	10.5	10.2	10.3	10.3	10.5
range	8-12	8-13	9-12	8-13	7-13	8-13	8-12	8-13
SD	1.07	1.07	1.02	1.42	1.87	1.63	1.57	1.50
SE	0.19	0.13	0.21	0.32	0.52	0.66	0.37	0.47
Forearm (mm)								
n	24	46	23	20	10	6	17	13
x̄	45.8	46.5	45.8	46.9	46.2	46.5	46.1	47.3
range	42-48	42-50	41-54	42-50	43-49	44-51	44-50	44-50
SD	1.48	1.89	2.90	2.05	1.81	2.88	1.49	2.05
SE	0.30	0.27	0.61	0.46	0.57	1.17	0.36	0.57
Tragus (mm)								
n	11	29	6	6	2	3	3	6
x̄	6.5	6.9	6.8	6.2	5.8	6	6.2	6.9
range	6-7	5-8	5-7	6-8	5.5-6.0	6	6.0-6.5	4.5-6.0
SD	0.52	0.91	0.75	0.75	0.35	0	0.28	3.52
SE	0.15	0.16	0.30	0.30	0.25	0	0.16	1.44
Weight (grams)								
n	29	63	22	19	9	4	19	12
x̄	15.2	16.7	15.7	16.7	14.5	15.8	14.2	15.2
range	12.2-19.5	12.1-26.1	13.0-19.5	12.8-26.5	12.0-20.6	12.6-17.1	12.0-16.5	12.4-18.6
SD	2.59	2.82	1.85	3.9	2.48	2.12	1.42	1.68
SE	0.48	0.35	0.39	0.89	0.82	1.06	0.32	0.48

both as individuals and in groups. The bats were wedged so tightly that many were torn as they were removed with large forceps, and many myobiid mites attached to their abdomens were squashed. This same barn was visited in midwinter the next year, but no bats were found in these crevices. We suspect that some of the bats found in large numbers in buildings in summer squeeze into narrow crevices in the same buildings for hiberna-

tion, while some migrate to caves (in southern Indiana?). However, we have no idea where the majority of big brown bats summering in Indiana spend the winter. Much more work is needed on this.

Our winter population data (gathered from 1951 to 1975) for 67 Indiana caves show that 23 caves contained no big brown bats; 33 caves had from 1 to 10; in 7 caves 11 to 24 were present; 1 contained 25 to 50; and 3

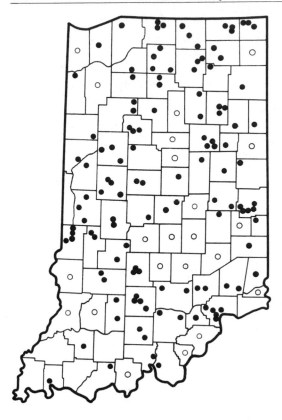

Map 21.   The Big Brown Bat, *Eptesicus fuscus*, in Indiana

caves contained more than 50. The largest numbers of big brown bats were found in Donaldson's Cave and Donnehue's Cave (both in Lawrence County) and in Tunnel Cave (Jefferson County), where maxima of 74, 58, and 93 were found, respectively. Kirkpatrick and Conaway (1948) reported "about 200" big brown bats in Donaldson's Cave on 29 December 1946. To our knowledge, this is the largest number recorded in an Indiana cave. It is surprising that relatively few big brown bats hibernate in Indiana caves, since the species is so plentiful in summer in the state. It is also interesting that certain caves appear to attract a particular species of bat and other caves do not. This is true for *Eptesicus fuscus* as it is for most (or all) native species that hibernate in caverns. The three Indiana caves that contain the largest winter populations of *E. fuscus* may have been favored traditionally by this bat, although data from Donaldson's Cave, gathered in the early 1900s by Hahn, indicate

that very few big brown bats used this cave during that period. Donaldson's and Donnehue's caves have streams running throughout their entire length; Tunnel Cave is dry.

In 1906 and 1907, Hahn found small numbers of big brown bats in the caves where we have worked. He stated (1908b) that six was the largest number of big brown bats he found in one cave; this was in Mayfield's Cave (Monroe County) on 21 December 1906. Banta (1907) recorded this species only in Mayfield's Cave on four occasions between January 1903 and August 1905. We found none in this cave on 26 January 1952. Hahn studied the caves on the University Farm (now within Spring Mill State Park) from September 1906 to September 1907. He reported *E. fuscus* as "comparatively rare" and collected only three specimens (Hahn, 1908b). He does not list the species in his paper on the mammalian remains of Donaldson's Cave (Hahn, 1907b). Further evidence of the rarity of big brown bats in caves in Spring Mill State Park and in other southern Indiana caves is Hahn's statement that he found "only ten of this species" in Indiana and Kentucky caves he visited. Certainly, the status of *Eptesicus fuscus* had drastically changed in Donaldson's Cave by 1946, when Kirkpatrick and Conaway found 200 present on a single visit. We have records of 74 in this cave on 12 February 1955, only 12 on 22 January 1962, and 3 on 13 February 1975. Again, we do not know how much these figures actually reflect population changes. A single visit to a cave per winter does not provide a reliable estimate of the hibernating population of big brown bats (or any other species).

We have practically no records of *Eptesicus fuscus* in caves during June or July, but our visits to caves during this season have not been numerous or systematic. Ten June and July trips to seven caves known to harbor big brown bats in winter resulted in a single observation—two big brown bats in Donnehue's Cave on 22 July. No doubt some caves are used periodically for night roosting by this species in summer, but we need more study of this phenomenon. In August, a few big brown bats begin to roost by day in some caves, and this number gradually increases until the winter population is more or less stable, from about mid-December to mid-

February, when, weather permitting, the bats may begin leaving the caves.

ASSOCIATED SPECIES. *Eptesicus fuscus* hibernates in caves used by all other species of bats that utilize caves in this season. In a concrete culvert at Lafayette, studied for 20 years, a single *Plecotus rafinesquii* was the only other bat found in winter with *E. fuscus*. Possibly this hibernaculum is too cold for less hardy species to winter there successfully. Big brown bats do not mix with other species in the caves. Many hang singly; others are found in small groups; the largest aggregations are invariably found in crevices, and large clusters are not formed on the walls or ceilings. Also, big brown bats tend to hang nearer the cave entrance than do other bats; this is especially true in winter.

When feeding, big brown bats have been shot along with red bats, hoary bats, evening bats, pipistrelles, silver-haired bats, Indiana myotis, and little brown myotis.

On 3 September, 3 big brown bats and 12 little brown myotis were found behind the window shutters on an occupied house. Our notes do not indicate whether separate shutters were used by each species; there were twelve shutters, all on one side of the house. In the summer of 1948, big brown bats, Indiana myotis, Keen's myotis, and little brown myotis all roosted by day beneath a large concrete bridge in Turkey Run State Park. The species were separated from one another, however.

An evening bat was shot at dusk on 8 May as it emerged from the roof of a house; the following evening, a big brown bat was shot as it flew from the same exit hole.

HABITS. *Eptesicus fuscus* appears to be quite hardy and able to withstand more cold than most other species of bats found in Indiana. For example, on 5 March 1954, there were 4 big brown bats in a crevice just outside the mouth of King's Cave (Harrison County). Four feet directly below the bats was a pool of water covered with one-fourth inch of ice. In a somewhat similar situation, 11 females were found in a crevice outside the mouth of May's Cave (Monroe County) on 20 February 1954. Many big brown bats that hibernate in caves choose sites near the cave mouth, where considerable air movement and freezing temperatures may occur.

Most other bats of this species are found in winter in the front sections of the caves. In an intensive study of Donnehue's Cave, only 2 big brown bats were observed more than 364 feet from the cave entrance (Mumford, 1958). Since this is a hardy species, it would not be surprising to learn that it also winters in holes in trees. One is drawn to this conclusion by several facts: there is a dramatic decrease in numbers of big brown bats from summer to winter in Indiana; banding has failed to establish that there are extensive migrations out of Indiana in the fall; the known number hibernating in buildings does not account for the summer population; *Eptesicus fuscus* moves in and out of at least some of its hibernacula throughout the winter. Clearly, caves are not required for successful hibernation; thus, until we obtain more data on the use of buildings by big brown bats during the winter, we feel that trees may be housing a large part of the wintering bats. It seems that *E. fuscus* is really less of a cave-dweller than are the various native species of *Myotis* or *Pipistrellus subflavus* (Hahn, 1909), but perhaps it is in the process of changing its habits in this regard. We have some evidence that big brown bats more readily seek caves in colder weather. There were 12 in Ray's Cave (Greene County) on 30 January 1975, but 18 to 20 there on 13 February 1975; during this period the outside temperature dropped to 10 to 15 degrees below zero Fahrenheit.

In the caves, most big brown bats hang singly on the side walls. They often use small crevices formed by flakes of limestone that have become partially separated from the walls. Both vertical and horizontal crevices are used; some bats in a horizontal crack will be lying on their backs. Bats often wedge themselves into narrow places from which they cannot be removed without injury to the bats. Choice crevices normally are occupied annually. There were 40 big brown bats in such a site (Tunnel Cave) on 6 January 1954; the 18 that could be extracted for examination were all males.

SEX RATIOS. The sex ratios of wintering *Eptesicus fuscus* evidently differ from place to place. In the culvert studied in Tippecanoe County from 1951 to 1971, the total known population for the period consisted of

29 males, 86 females, and 2 for which sex was unrecorded. Males outnumbered females here in only two seasons of those studied. This culvert was used by only 3 to 12 big brown bats per winter, so our sample is rather small. Sex ratios of big brown bats banded during hibernation in caves in southern Indiana generally favor males, with some exceptions. In Donnehue's Cave, 40 males, 34 females, and 2 unsexed individuals were banded during one winter season. For three different winters combined, there were 86 males, 40 females, and 15 unsexed big brown bats in Donaldson's Cave, about ten miles away. In May's Cave, on 20 February 1954, we found 1 male, 18 females, and a bat that could not be captured for examination.

We have no data on the survival of bats that choose to hibernate in heated buildings. On the Purdue University campus, 29 big brown bats have been captured between 26 November and 14 March during the past 17 years. Some of these animals were found on the ground (some alive, some dead), but most were found flying about in buildings. Of these, 17 were males, 8 were females, and the sex was not recorded for 4. Most of those examined had very little or no fat, even during the middle of the hibernation season. This may indicate that temperatures in the buildings are too high for successful hibernation. We need data on banded individuals to clarify this point.

On 10 March, a big brown bat was found on the ground (alive) in the snow at Ft. Wayne (Allen County); its pelage was covered with what appeared to be soot. Perhaps the bat had entered a chimney shortly before being found. A male banded in Kosciusko County on 23 July 1959 was found in that county on 24 December 1960.

Nonhibernating big brown bats have been found in and on buildings, in caves, on rock escarpments, beneath concrete bridges, and in covered wooden bridges. About buildings they have been found in attics, hanging on the side of a brick structure, in vines on the side of a building, beneath loose tarpaper on the sides of a house, behind window shutters, in the rafters of small, open-sided structures, and between the stone side of a building and the gutter downspout.

MIGRATION. Banding has revealed little about the movements of *Eptesicus fuscus*.

Perhaps the species migrates little, or perhaps the lack of recoveries of banded animals is because most of the population winters in unknown sites. A female banded in Donnehue's Cave on 9 January 1954 was killed near Sullivan, 52 miles westnorthwest, on 16 April 1955. A male banded at the same cave on 9 January 1954 was found alive near Elkton, Kentucky (142 miles south-southwest, on 31 December 1954. A female banded at May's Cave on 20 April 1954 was killed near Hidalgo, Illinois (85 miles west), in April 1962. And a female banded in Donaldson's Cave on 12 February 1955 was captured and released in a cave near Georgia, Indiana (7 miles west), on 29 November 1958.

Each year in August we receive telephone calls and letters from homeowners about bats in houses, garages, or breezeways. Most of these animals that we have examined were big brown bats. There is undoubtedly considerable movement in August, when bats probably wander from summer to winter habitats; transients evidently enter houses and other buildings temporarily at this season. Frequently an individual is seen only for a day.

Many of the known maternity colonies in Indiana are in unheated barns, from which the bats depart in winter. Although a considerable number of big brown bats has been banded in these summer colonies, few animals have been recaptured at sites other than where banded. Thus, we know the species moves from summer to winter localities but we do not know the distances involved in these movements.

Banding has revealed little seasonal or annual changes of cave roosts by *E. fuscus*. Most marked individuals have been recaptured in the same caves where they were banded.

HOMING. Cope *et al.* (1961) conducted several homing experiments with *Eptesicus fuscus* in southeastern Indiana. From 70 to 90 percent of 20 big brown bats released 20 miles west of the capture site homed within 4.5 to 9 hours. About 32 to 40 percent of 47 released 40 miles south of another site returned, but none came back before two nights had elapsed. An estimated 8 of 11 returned after three nights after being released 100 miles north of their colony. From four to six nights after release, 31 of 36 homed from 250 miles south. Only 1 of 18 released 250 miles north returned to the colony, after an absence of four nights. The experimental animals were all adults (males and females) and the work was carried out in July and August. We can offer no explanation for the difference in homing performance in these animals. The variation in the percentage that successfully homed from 250 miles south and 250 miles north is interesting.

On 30 August 1954, a sample of 41 males and 48 females was taken from a maternity colony in Bedford, banded, and released later that night at Terre Haute (80 miles northwest). The colony was next visited in April 1955, when at least 5 banded males and 9 banded females were present. Since this group was banded with regular aluminum bands only, it is possible that some individuals were not located visually in the colony. Cope and his co-workers had used radioactive bands on their animals and were able to detect unseen bats in the roosts.

LONGEVITY. Of 12 males and 11 females banded during hibernation and recovered three or more years later, 1 male and 1 female were at least seven years old, 4 females and 2 males were at least six years old, 2 males and 2 females were at least five years old, 2 males and 1 female were at least four years old and 5 males and 3 females were at least 3 years old. The age of none of these animals was known at the time of banding.

Another sample of unknown age, banded during hibernation, contained 1 male and 2 females at least three years old, 1 male and 2 females at least four years old, 1 female at least five years old, 1 female at least six years old, and a female at least nine years old.

HABITS. Evidently *Eptesicus fuscus* wakens and becomes active periodically during the winter. On unusually warm evenings (temperature around 60°F) in January and February, big brown bats may be seen in flight on the Purdue University campus, where they hibernate in buildings. Gwilym S. Jones saw a big brown bat flying slowly over Farmersburg (Sullivan County) in the pre-dusk on 21 February 1976; the day was clear, but a storm was moving in. Winter observations in caves also reveal that a particular bat does not remain long in one spot, but

moves about throughout the hibernating period. Some individuals enter and leave the caves all winter long and evidently have alternate (unknown) roosts which they occupy when absent from the caves. We suspect that the prevailing winter temperatures outside the hibernacula are correlated with these movements. The extent of winter movement in and out of Donnehue's Cave was reported by Mumford (1958). Although 109 big brown bats used this cave from August to April, the maximum number observed on any one of 76 visits to the cave was 39 (36.1 percent). More than 30 bats per visit were seen on 3 and 29 December, 7, 12, and 16 January, and 17 February—the three coldest months of the year. Temperature minima for five of these dates ranged from 19°F to 28°F; the minimum for the other date was 33°F. From August 1970 to August 1971 and in February 1973 we netted the entrance to Donnehue's Cave on twenty nights, including each month but January. We captured big brown bats each month but April, again demonstrating winter activity of this species (Mumford and Whitaker, 1975).

The big brown bat is a fairly early flyer at dusk, but does not emerge from its daytime roost as early as do red bats or pipistrelles. We have often shot big brown bats in the early evening while the sky was fairly bright. In netting Donnehue's Cave, we caught only one big brown bat within the first half hour and six within the first hour after sunset. In the second, third, fourth, and fifth hours after sunset we netted 16, 14, 13, and 6 big brown bats respectively. Since we did not tend the nets later than 12:20 A.M., we do not know whether this species was active all night. A net at the mouth of Big Wyandotte Cave (Crawford County), tended from 7:20 P.M. to 6:30 A.M. the night of 22-23 August, took *E. fuscus* during each half-hour period from 8:15 P.M. to 5:10 A.M. Of the 100 captured 66 were taken between 10:30 P.M. and 2:30 A.M.; during this four-hour period, we netted 13, 20, 19, and 14 respectively per hour.

The time of emergence from a maternity colony in a building was correlated with the time of sunset and, presumably, therefore with light intensity. As the days became shorter, the bats began emerging earlier in the evening (Table 60).

Hahn (1908a) estimated that *E. fuscus* flew

faster than 10 to 12 mph, but his figures were largely guesswork.

FOOD. Hahn (1909) reported that in captivity *Eptesicus fuscus* ate "any kind of meat." A female shot at dusk on 24 July had a chafer *(Cyclocephala borealis)* in her mouth.

The stomachs of 184 big brown bats were examined for food (Table 61). Ground beetles (Carabidae) formed the greatest volume of food. These were probably taken on the wing. The food second in abundance was Scarabaeidae, and third was the spotted cucumber beetle, *Diabrotica undecimpunctata* (Chrysomelidae), common in stomachs in late summer. (It is not clear why this particular species was so common in stomachs, but this agricultural pest was seen in numbers at lights.) Thus the three most heavily consumed foods were beetles—indeed, beetles formed 49.1 percent of the entire volume of food in the sample. The fourth most prevalent food taken was stinkbugs, which occurred in nearly a third of the stomachs and constituted nearly 10 percent of the volume of food. Most were a bright green species, possibly *Acrosternum hilare* (Say). It was not clear why stinkbugs were so often taken. Most of the forms mentioned above (48.0 percent of the total volume) were large, being at least a centimeter in total length. Flying ants were fifth in abundance, sometimes occurring in numbers of 10 to 50 per stomach. Crickets (Gryllidae), although including a few flying forms, constituted a part of the nonflying food, which also included vegetation, Curculionidae, insect larvae, Diplopoda, and mites. The total volume of food considered to be of nonflying forms was 4.3 percent. Four bats had eaten internal organs of larger insects, possibly Scarabaeidae, presumably by splitting the insect open and removing the abdominal contents. The cockroach eaten was apparently *Parcoblatta*, a flying form. No cellular structure was apparent in the unidentified amorphous material. It had the appearance of milk seen in the stomachs of juveniles, and was found in female bats with young. Vegetation consisted of grass stems in one stomach (about ¼ full), and 95 percent wheat seeds in another. Other items taken from stomachs of big brown bats in trace amounts and not included in the table were click beetles (Elateridae), insect larvae, rhysodid beetles, syrphid flies, mites, millipedes, and various other flies (Otitidae, Chironomidae, and Mycetophilidae).

Data were available from several sources to determine whether big brown bats feed in winter. The stomachs of 178 bats taken from

Table 60

Emergence of *Eptesicus fuscus*, at 5-minute intervals, from a maternity colony, Bedford, Indiana, 1954
(from Mumford and Whitaker, 1975)

Time Periods P.M.	Date and Number Leaving Roost				
	9 Aug.	18 Aug.	29 Aug.	31 Aug.	8 Sept.
7:20 to 7:25	—	—	—	—	4
7:25 to 7:30	—	—	—	—	30
7:30 to 7:35	—	—	1	1	82
7:35 to 7:40	—	—	9	1	70
7:40 to 7:45	—	—	20	7	44
7:45 to 7:50	—	2	65	28	21
7:50 to 7:55	—	17	38	48	12
7:55 to 8:00	4	62	31	44	
8:00 to 8:05	11	54	36	34	
8:05 to 8:10	47	75	7	3	
8:10 to 8:15	60	45	13		
8:15 to 8:20	72	23			
8:20 to 8:25	83	19			
8:25 to 8:30	49	10			
8:30 to 8:35	16				
8:35 to 8:40	7				

Table 61

Foods eaten by *Eptesicus fuscus* (n = 184) from Indiana
(from Whitaker, 1972b)

Food Item	Percent volume	Percent frequency
Carabidae (ground beetles)	14.6	29.8
Scarabaeidae (scarab beetles)	12.4	25.0
Chrysomelidae, *Diabrotica undecimpunctata*	11.5	21.7
Pentatomidae (stinkbugs)	9.5	29.3
Formicidae (ants)	8.5	16.8
Coleoptera	6.6	15.2
Ichneumonidae (ichneumon flies)	5.0	14.1
Lepidoptera	4.5	7.6
Cicadellidae (leafhoppers)	4.4	20.7
Insects (unidentified)	3.1	11.4
Chrysomelidae (leaf beetles)	3.0	9.8
Gryllidae (crickets)	3.0	9.2
Diptera	1.8	7.1
Reduviidae (assassin bugs)	1.8	7.6
Insects (internal organs)	1.5	2.2
Trichoptera (caddis flies)	1.4	3.3
Vegetation	1.1	1.6
Amorphous material (unidentified)	0.9	1.6
Alleculidae (comb-clawed bark beetles)	0.8	2.2
Delphacidae (planthoppers)	0.7	3.3
Hymenoptera	0.5	1.6
Muscoid flies	0.5	0.5
Chrysopidae (lacewings)	0.5	2.7
Curculionidae (snout beetles)	0.4	2.7
Blattidae (roaches)	0.3	0.5
Coccinelidae (ladybird beetles)	0.2	0.5
Miridae (leaf bugs)	0.2	2.2
Coreidae (squash bugs)	0.2	0.5
Tipulidae (crane flies)	0.2	1.1
Mydaidae (mydas flies)	0.1	0.5
Calliphoridae (blow flies)	0.1	0.5
Rhagionidae (snipe flies)	0.1	0.5
Nabidae (nabid bugs)	0.1	0.5
Anthicidae (anthicid beetles)	0.1	0.5
Chironomidae (midges)	0.1	0.5
Total	99.7	

A few foods found in trace amounts are listed in the text.

November through March (not included in Table 61) were examined. All were empty except for one from December, which contained gray amorphous material, apparently not food. Many of these bats were active and apparently had been flying around, since they appeared in and on the outside of buildings. Four bats were caught as they entered Donnehue's Cave in the late fall (one on October 30, two on November 18, and one on December 2) in 1970. The stomachs and intestines of all were completely empty. The digestive tracts of 17 torpid big brown bats taken from a barn in Vigo County on 26 March 1970 were empty, except for small masses of insect material in the posterior end of the intestines of some. This apparently had been present for a long time, judging by the discoloring of the material and by the amount of digestion which had taken place, even of the hard parts. Another group of 11 bats was taken in the third week of October 1965, also at Terre Haute. The intestines of all and the stomachs of 10 were empty. One specimen, however, had a full stomach. It contained 60 percent *Diabrotica undecimpunctata* (a leaf beetle), 10 percent unidentified Coleoptera, and 30 percent Ichneumonid flies. It would appear that big brown bats do not feed during the winter. These data give some indication that feeding in the species probably ceases for the year in late October. This supports Beer and Richards (1956), who concluded that it was not necessary for *Eptesicus* to feed in the winter. For comparison, 184 of 505 bats (36.4 percent) of this species taken from April through October had food in their stomachs.

Two series of juvenile bats were examined to determine when feeding on solid foods by the young occurred, and how the foods eaten by the juveniles compared with that eaten by adults. A group of 12 was taken 22 June 1965, from a breeding colony in a barn at Terre Haute, Vigo County. In these the forearm ranged from 32 to 43 mm, and the weights of two were 9.1 and 4.7 grams. They had only milk in their stomachs. A series of 18 juveniles, taken from a barn 1 July 1968 in Johnson County, contained, by percentage volume, milk, 52.0; Carabidae, 15.0; Pentatomidae, 9.7; Formicidae, 8.1; Scarabaeidae, 7.5; Ichneumonidae, Cicadellidae, Reduviidae, and the chrysomelid beetle *Diabrotica undecimpunctata*, each 0.8; and unidentified insects and mites each 0.1 percent. Of the 18 juveniles, 5 had 100 percent milk, 5 more had part milk and part solid food, while 8 had apparently been completely weaned and were eating food similar to that of the adults. It would appear that weaning was taking place about July 1 in these bats.

REPRODUCTION. Copulation has been observed in *Eptesicus fuscus* in Indiana caves on 23 November, 27 December, 5, 6, and 8 January, 7 February, and 12 March. In most cases, the bats were hanging from the cave ceiling while copulating; one pair was on the cave wall. On 7 February, three active big brown bats were observed in a crevice in the ceiling in Donnehue's Cave. One of the bats flew before it could be captured, but the remaining two were copulating at 7:34, 7:39, and 7:43 P.M.; they had ceased by 8:17, the final observation. On 8 January, a pair hang-

ing about five feet above the cave floor on the wall were copulating; both were captured, examined, then replaced in the spot. The male flew, but the female remained; ten minutes later, when the observer returned to this spot, a pair (presumably the same) was again copulating. This time, the male flew when the beam of a flashlight was played on him. On 5 January, just inside the entrance to Big Wyandotte Cave, two pairs of big brown bats hanging fifteen feet apart on the cave ceiling were copulating.

We have previously summarized data on testis size of 366 big brown bats collected throughout the year (Whitaker and Mumford, 1972c). In August and September the highest percentage of males had testes more than 5 mm long and testis size averaged greatest in these months. This probably indicates that copulation occurs mostly in August and September. However, if testis size alone is a criterion of ability to copulate successfully, male big brown bats may be capable of fertilizing females much of the year.

Most known maternity colonies of *Eptesicus fuscus* in Indiana are in buildings. At least three colonies have been found beneath concrete bridges; these bridges are of similar construction and are the only bridges of this type examined by us. Donna J. Howell found a nursery colony in a tree cavity (Tippecanoe County). Barns seem to be favorite sites for the establishment of maternity colonies, but many colonies are also found in churches, schools, houses, and other buildings. Landrum (1971) studied fifteen nursery colonies in Delaware, Grant, Hamilton, and Madison counties. Twelve of the colonies were in barns. Some colonies may persist for a long time. The owner of a building containing a colony in Bedford told us that the bats had been there for at least 25 years. Cope, Baker, and Confer (1961) reported on 142 *Eptesicus fuscus* colonies in 51 counties throughout Indiana. The number of bats per colony ranged from "about a dozen" to 216. Most contained 25 to 50 adults. In seven cases, big brown bats and little brown myotis each had maternity colonies in the same building. The attic of a house in Clay County supported colonies of big brown bats and evening bats simultaneously.

Some of 18 adult female big brown bats we

have examined the first half of April showed signs of pregnancy; 7 of 14 females taken from a maternity colony in Putnam County on 14 April contained "tiny" embryos and the rest either appeared nongravid or had enlarged uteri. All 26 females examined from this same colony on 14 May were pregnant; 3 contained single embryos and 23 had twins. Embryo size in this sample ranged from 8.8 to 21 mm in crown-rump length and averaged 15.0 mm. The 15 females collected here on 24 May had embryos ranging from 13 to 20 mm (average 17.3 mm) in crown-rump length; 2 females had single embryos, 13 had twins. The owner of the house reported the first young of the year on 12 June. A sample of 16 females from the colony on 14 July revealed that although all had nursed young recently only 3 still retained visible placental scars (2 scars each). Evidently placental scars do not persist for an extended period after parturition in *E. fuscus*.

On 8 June, 3 small young were found (alive) below a maternity colony situated high under the eaves of a building in Montgomery County. One was on the ground, but the other two had climbed a short distance up the side of the concrete foundation of the building. In another colony beneath a bridge (Montgomery County), we found most females carrying young on 3 July; some young were unable to fly. Most (or all) of the females in a maternity colony in a barn (Hamilton County) were carrying small young on 11 June. We have examined lactating females as late as 20 July.

Parturition probably occurs mainly in June, with some young being born in May. We have examined few adult female big brown bats or maternity colonies of this species in June; more precise dates on parturition in Indiana are unavailable. Gravid females have been collected as late as 1 June (Ripley County), 5 June (Adams County), 6 June (Franklin County), 8 June (Montgomery County), 9 June (Parke County), 10 June (Wayne County), 11 June (Hamilton County), 12 June (Putnam County), and 14 June (Lagrange County).

Parturition dates evidently vary from colony to colony. Perhaps they vary geographically, but we can not confirm this pattern at present because of insufficient data. That some young are born in May is evidenced by the fact that a flying young of the year was shot on 12 June (Tippecanoe County). In a particular nursery colony, young are evidently born over a relatively short span of time. On 14 June, we examined 10 young from a colony in Lagrange County. Forearm lengths of these animals ranged from 17 to 27 mm and averaged 21.4 mm. Eleven young killed by a long-tailed weasel on 11 June in a colony in Hamilton County had forearms from 12.5 to 26 mm (average 20.2 mm).

We have no data on the forearm length of *E. fuscus* at birth. The smallest attached young we have examined and the dates they were taken are summarized below. The 24 immatures we examined that had forearm lengths less than 30 mm were all found between 1 and 14 June; their forearms ranged from 12.5 to 27 mm (average 20.7 mm). The 16 collected between 5 and 30 July had forearms measuring from 33 to 49.5 (average 43.3) mm. Adult big brown bats have an average forearm length of 46-47 mm; thus young have full-sized wings by August. Our small sample of known young of the year taken in August totals 6 animals, with forearms from 42 to 50 mm (average 46 mm).

PARASITES AND DISEASES. Data on external parasites taken by us from *Eptesicus fuscus* are summarized in Table 62. The most common forms are the macronyssid mite *Steatonyssus occidentalis* and the tick *Ornithodorus kelleyi*. *Steatonyssus occidentalis* is common on the big brown bat throughout its range. Young individuals were commonly crawling on the wing membranes, with the adult mites often being about the bases of the wings and tail. *Ornithodorus kelleyi* is a normal parasite of *Eptesicus* and was found commonly on big brown bats in their summer colonies by Wilson (1961). He found 649 specimens, constituting 14 records. Wilson found *Ornithodorus kelleyi* on *Eptesicus fuscus*, on *Myotis lucifugus*, and in roosts, from 16 February to 30 December, but mostly in July and August. Summer colonies are found in buildings. This tick has also been found on *Pipistrellus subflavus*, but not in Indiana. This species was reported from 16 counties by Wilson, and is presumed to be statewide. Ticks of this species are most often attached

Table 62

Ectoparasites of *Eptesicus fuscus* (n = 491) from Indiana

Parasites	Parasites		Hosts parasitized	
	Total	Average	Total	Percent
Batbugs (Cimicidae)				
Cimex adjunctus	30	0.06	20	4.1
Mites (Acarina) other than chiggers				
Steatonyssus occidentalis	1,470	2.99	143	29.1
Alabidocarpus sp.	71	0.14	2	0.4
Acanthopthirius caudatus	61	0.12	24	4.9
Spinturnix bakeri	10	0.02	7	1.4
Cheletonella vespertilionis	1	0.002	1	0.2
Chiggers (Trombiculidae)				
Euschoengastia hamiltoni	34	0.07	5	1.0
Leptotrombidium myotis	7	0.01	4	0.8
Euschoengastia pipistrelli	3	0.01	2	0.4
Neotrombicula microti	1	0.002	1	0.2
Ticks (Ixodides)				
Ornithodorus kelleyi	126	0.26	71	14.5

to the venter of the bats, apparently because this area is more available to the ticks. Some maximum numbers of *O. kelleyi* per bat were 91, 65, and 62 from *Eptesicus* (Wilson, 1961).

The batbug *Cimex adjunctus* is sometimes found on the big brown bat. We have taken a total of 20 specimens from it.

One cheyletid, probably *Cheletonella vespertilionis* Womersley (1941), was taken from a big brown bat from Donnehue's Cave. The specimen was identified by Robert Smiley, and when taken was only the second known specimen of the species ever taken, the other being from Glen Osmon, South Australia. Additional specimens have since been taken from soil in California.

We have taken one specimen of *Alabidocarpus* sp. from *Eptesicus fuscus* hibernating in a barn in Vigo County, 26 March 1970. It is similar to *A. minor* from *Rhinolophus* sp. (the horseshoe bat) from France.

Whitaker (1973) took a total of 24 individuals of *Acanthopthirius caudata* from the big brown bat from Indiana, and also 7 spinturnicid mites, *Spinturnix bakeri*. Also he took chiggers as follows: *Euschongastia hamiltoni*, 5; *E. pipistrelli*, 2; and *Leptotrombidium myotis*, 4.

Wilson (1961) found a total of 126 individuals of the flea *Nycteridopsylla chapini*, 123

of them on *Eptesicus* (only 27 specimens of this flea were previously known). This species of flea was found only during the winter in caves, and mostly on the hibernating bats. Colonies of big brown bats other than in caves did not harbor this species; eggs, larvae, and cocoons were found in the cracks of the caves with the infested *Eptesicus* colonies.

Whitaker and Miller (1974) examined 776 big brown bats from Indiana for rabies and found 29 (3.7 percent) to be positive. An especially large number and proportion from Madison (Jefferson County) were found to have the disease in the summer in 1967, with 10 positive for rabies of 69 examined (14.5 percent).

DECIMATING FACTORS. Accidents probably take a toll of this species, as well as of other bats. One big brown bat found dead in a stone structure in a cemetery had caught its wing in a crack and died there. Another, found dead in the attic of a house, had become entangled in some wire hanging from a rafter. One hibernating group in a cave had been the object of vandals, who had killed many of the bats with a BB gun. Colonies in buildings are frequently exterminated by a variety of methods.

Predation on *E. fuscus* by a long-tailed weasel has been reported by Mumford

(1969a). W. B. Buskirk (1963) found 2 skulls of *E. fuscus* in pellets thought to have been those of a screech owl.

Mumford once struck an *E. fuscus* at night with his automobile, and has also examined a mounted specimen in a taxidermy shop that had been removed from the radiator of a car.

TAXONOMY. The subspecies in Indiana is *Eptesicus fuscus fuscus* (Beauvois).

SELECTED REFERENCES. Beer, 1955; Beer and Richards, 1956; Christian, 1956; Hamilton, 1933a; Rysgaard, 1942.

Evening Bat
Nycticeius humeralis (Rafinesque)

Nycticejus humeralis: Evermann and Butler, 1894b
Nycticeius humeralis: Hahn, 1909

DESCRIPTION. The evening bat is a small, brown bat with relatively short ears and tragi (see Fig. 3). It resembles certain species of *Myotis*, or a small *Eptesicus fuscus*. The membranes and ears are black. Adults are usually bronze-brown, and the pelage has a "greasy" appearance. Immatures are blackish and have duller pelage than adults. The evening bat can be separated from the little brown myotis and the Indiana myotis by its short, rounded tragi. These two *Myotis* have longer, more pointed tragi, as well as longer ears.

Weights and measurements are shown in Table 63. The dental formula is

$$I \frac{1}{3} \ C \frac{1}{1} \ P \frac{1}{2} \ M \frac{3}{3} \ = \ 30.$$

STATUS AND DISTRIBUTION. The evening bat is an uncommon summer resident

Evening bat. Photo by Richard LaVal

Table 63
Weights and measurements of *Nycticeius humeralis* from Indiana

	Males	Females
Total length (mm)		
n	25	77
x̄	84.6	91.8
range	70-94	67-106
SD	5.9	8.1
SE	1.2	0.9
Tail length (mm)		
n	24	77
x̄	33.6	35.6
range	26-38	23-42
SD	2.8	3.9
SE	0.5	0.4
Hind foot (mm)		
n	25	73
x̄	7.2	7.6
range	5.5-9.5	6.0-10.5
SD	0.9	1.0
SE	0.18	0.1
Tragus (mm)		
n	18	55
x̄	5.2	5.8
range	3.0-6.5	3.0-8.5
SD	0.9	1.3
SE	0.2	0.2
Forearm (mm)		
n	23	82
x̄	34.9	36.8
range	28-38	28-40
SD	2.3	2.0
SE	0.5	0.2
Weight (grams)		
n	15	72
x̄	7.2	10.1
range	4.2-10.5	5.8-14.8
SD	1.7	2.1
SE	0.5	0.2

throughout Indiana, and is most abundant in the southern half of the state (Map 22). It is evidently absent in winter. All specimens were taken between 8 April and 15 November. The species was first recorded from Indiana in 1942 (Kirkpatrick, 1943). Much remains to be learned concerning its distribution and movements.

Four maternity colonies of evening bats, in Clark, Clay, Orange, and Washington counties, were reported on by Cope *et al.* (1961); these colonies contained an estimated total of 460 animals. Humphrey and Cope (1970) provided more data on nursery colony size and on sex and age ratios for three of the four colonies, plus data from another (Montgomery County). Single visits to the nurseries in Orange and Clark counties in August 1958 and August 1961 resulted in sample counts of 26 and 4 adult females and 90 and 11 immatures. Estimated total population sizes were not given for these colonies. The Washington County colony was visited once each year in

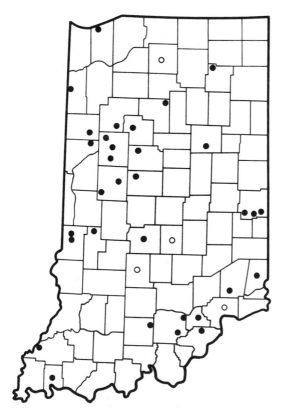

Map 22.   The Evening Bat, *Nycticeius humeralis,* in Indiana

August in 1958, 1960, and 1961 and once in July in 1962. For these years, 108, 67, 58, and 4 adult females were recorded; immatures were not counted for 1958, but there were 62, 88, and 103 immatures recorded for the other years respectively. More extensive data were provided for the Montgomery County colony, visited fourteen times between 15 August 1964 and 29 July 1965. On two August visits, 86 and 39 adult females and 64 and 40 immatures were captured. On one September visit, 68 adult females were captured but no count was obtained for immatures. On 28 May, 15 July, and 29 July 1965, the numbers of adult females and immatures captured were 140 and none, 8 and 107, and 5 and 25.

The largest number of evening bats captured in the Washington County colony on a single visit was 155 (of an estimated 165 present), on 9 August 1960. The largest number of bats captured on a single visit to the Montgomery County colony was 151 (of an estimated 275), on 15 August 1964; an estimated 250 were present at this colony on 15 July 1965. These are the two largest known maternity colonies of evening bats in Indiana. A colony in Carroll County consisted of 50 to 60 animals on 15 July. Evidently maternity colonies of evening bats are not as large as some for other house-inhabiting bats, such as the little brown myotis.

Population data for other times of the year are not available. We have found no evening bats in winter, and numbers passing through the state during spring and fall migration are unknown.

HABITAT.   All of the known breeding colonies in Indiana were in buildings. This is the only species of bat in the state that we have not found in a cave. Some probably live in summer in trees, either in cavities or beneath loose bark, for they have been found in such situations in other parts of their range. We have collected them at dusk by shooting in and about the borders of woodlots and over small ponds. Several have been netted over small streams flowing through pastured areas. We have taken this species over a pasture next to a woods; along a stand of oaks bordering a marsh; over a pond in a small, pastured woodlot; in an open stand of tall oaks and hickory trees, formerly pastured; in an open, pastured woodlot of oak / hickory;

along a road crossing a low, flat, pin oak / sweet gum swampy woods.

ASSOCIATED SPECIES. A nursery colony of evening bats in Clay County was shared with big brown bats. The bats were in the attic of a house to which we did not have access, so we could not determine how the two species utilized this site. At dusk, we have collected several species of bats along with evening bats; these include red bats, silver-haired bats, pipistrelles, and big brown bats.

HABITS. Evening bats emerge relatively early in the evening, but a bit later than red bats or pipistrelles. The flight of *Nycticeius* is rather slow and steady; foraging bats of this species frequently fly at and below treetop height. They sometimes feed among the crowns of scattered trees in pastured wood-lots, even darting into the edges of the crowns and sometimes brushing the leaves. Like some other species, the evening bat appears to forage higher in the air in the early part of the evening, coming lower as dusk advances.

One mid-May evening Mumford shot and injured a flying silver-haired bat, which fell to the ground. Almost immediately a small bat began circling Mumford's head and hovering over the fallen bat. Attempts were made to knock this bat down with the gun barrel. For about two minutes it fed near the observer and the fallen bat, cruising over an area about 15 by 35 yards. It was finally shot and found to be an evening bat. Mumford could hear no sounds being made by either bat. In hovering, the evening bat held the tip of the interfemoral membrane cupped forward, forming a deep pocket. This bat definitely appeared to be attracted to the fallen *Lasionycteris*.

HOMING. Cope and Humphrey (1967) performed homing experiments with evening bats from a nursery colony in Montgomery County in 1964. On 15 August, they removed 83 adult females and 62 immatures from the colony, transported them 96 air miles to Wayne County, and banded and released them there the same night. Ten days later, they recaptured 12 adult females and 2 immatures from this sample back at the nursery colony; 12 additional adult females were back at the colony 27 days after their release. On 25 August, 38 new immatures were banded and released 38 air miles away, in Hamilton County, and 27 new adult females were banded and released at the previous release site in Wayne County. An additional group (number not stated) of bats that had homed once were released 56 air miles away, in Hancock County. When the colony was checked 18 days later, 7 adult females and 3 immatures had returned to it. It was thus demonstrated that *Nycticeius humeralis* has a strong homing ability, and that immatures homed without being released with adults.

MIGRATION. Although *Nycticeius* has not been found during the winter (from 15 November to 8 April) in Indiana, little is known of its movements within or outside the state. Humphrey and Cope (1968) provided the first definite migration data. A female banded 10 July in Clark County was found 110 miles southwest, at Onton, Kentucky, on 17 August the same year. Although there was some discussion about the legibility of this band, it appears to be a valid record. An immature male banded 25 July in Washington County was recovered 120 miles southeast in early August of the same year, at Cooperville, Kentucky. Finally, another immature male released in Fulton County on 1 August was recaptured 187 miles south-southeast, near Eminence, Kentucky, eight days later. That these animals migrated from Indiana during the first half of August is of interest. As Humphrey and Cope mentioned, it sheds new light on their data for August and September from a nursery colony at Darlington (Montgomery County), Indiana. The evident decrease there in numbers of evening bats was possibly the result of normal prewinter dispersal and not a population decline.

There are no data substantiated by the recovery of banded individuals on the spring migration of evening bats. The species has been found on 8 April in Tippecanoe County, so the appearance of the species might be expected earlier in counties further south. At the Darlington nursery colony, no evening bats were observed on 10 or 23 April. Two were seen on 1 May, 42 on 7 May, 106 on 14 May, and 159 on 21 May. On 28 May, what was thought to be the entire population (140) was captured, since all of the bats were torpid.

FOOD. The stomachs of two evening bats from Indiana were examined by Ross (1967). One contained beetles and flies, including Scarabaeidae and Drosophilidae; the other was nearly empty but contained one flying ant and a cercopid. Whitaker (1972b) examined two additional stomachs. One contained Homoptera (Delphacidae, 35 percent), Hemiptera (Coreidae, 20 percent), Coleoptera (Scarabaeidae, 35 percent; unidentified, 10 percent), and the second held Lepidoptera (50 percent), Coleoptera (Carabidae, 30 percent), and Hemiptera (20 percent).

REPRODUCTION. Two young per litter are usually produced by this species. In 11 of 12 gravid evening bats we examined, 2 embryos were present in each; the other contained a single embryo. Embryos ranged in size from 4 mm (12 May, Newton County) to 22 mm (1 June, Ripley County) in crown-rump length. A female taken on 20 June (Clay County) had embryos 20 mm in crown-rump length. Parturition probably occurs in early June in extreme southeastern Indiana and in late June in the northern half of the state. Our latest dates for gravid females are 27 June (Marshall County) and 29 June (Clay County). We have examined lactating females as late as 24 July. The female with 4-mm embryos was not lactating.

We have records of maternity colonies from Carroll, Cass, Clark, Clay, Clinton, Montgomery, Orange, Tippecanoe, Washington, and White counties, all in attics of houses.

On 30 July, 5 immature males and 5 immature females were examined from a nursery colony in Clinton County. The females ranged from 84 to 90 mm (average 87.6) in total length and had forearms from 36 to 38 mm (average 36.9) long. The males had total lengths ranging from 78 to 88 mm (average 83) and forearms 34 to 37 mm (average 35.7) long. The females averaged 7.7 grams (7.0 to 8.2) and the males 6.7 grams (6.4 to 8.0). From another colony, in Tippecanoe County, 13 immature males and 14 immature females were taken on 24 July. Males had forearms from 28 to 36 mm (average 33.4) and weighed from 5.3 to 8.7 grams (average 6.8). Females had forearms from 28 to 37 mm (average 34.1) and weighed from 5.6 to 8.3 grams (average

7.1). We tested 23 of these young to determine whether they could fly. Of these, 8 males and 10 females flew; 3 males and 2 females did not fly. The 18 flying young had forearms ranging from 31.5 mm (this bat flew weakly) to 37 mm; nonflying young had forearms ranging from 28 to 31.5 mm. Thus, it appeared that flight was attained when the forearm was from 31 to 32 mm in length. Volant young weighed from 6 to 8.3 grams; nonflying young weighed from 5.3 to 6.2 grams.

We recorded testis size for 10 immature evening bats. One individual (unable to fly) examined on 24 July had testes 1 by 2 mm. Testis size increased throughout July and into early August. The 3 young with the largest testes were taken on 2, 4, and 7 August and had testes measuring 3 by 5, 4 by 6, and 4 by 7 mm respectively. Three unaged specimens, examined 5 September, 16 August, and 19 August, had testes measuring 2 by 4, 3 by 6, and 3 by 6.5 mm respectively.

PARASITES AND DISEASES. Five of twelve evening bats from Indiana examined by Whitaker (1973) for ectoparasites were found to be parasitized. All were hosts only to the macronyssid mite *Steatonyssus ceratognathus* (average = 2.4 per bat), a mite normally associated with *Nycticeius* (Radovsky, 1967).

Cestodes have been found in four specimens, and trematodes, nematodes, and tapeworms in one specimen each.

Ten Indiana evening bats examined for rabies tested negative (Whitaker and Miller, 1974).

DECIMATING FACTORS. Other than the attempted eradication of maternity colonies from buildings by man, we have detected no enemies of *N. humeralis.*

TAXONOMY. *Nycticeius humeralis humeralis* (Rafinesque) is the subspecies in Indiana.

SELECTED REFERENCES. Cope, Baker, and Confer, 1961; Cope and Humphrey, 1967; Easterla and Watkins, 1970; Humphrey and Cope, 1968, 1970; Jones, 1967; Kirkpatrick, 1943; Lindsay, 1956a; Mumford, 1953c; Ubelaker and Kunz, 1971; Watkins, 1970, 1972a, 1972b.

Red Bat
Lasiurus borealis (Müller)

New York Bat, Northern Rat Bat

Vespertilio Noveboracensis: Plummer, 1844
Atalapha noveboracensis: Evermann and Butler, 1894b
Nycteris borealis: Lyon, 1923
Lasiurus borealis: McAtee, 1907

DESCRIPTION. The red bat can be distinguished from all other bats of Indiana by its reddish coloration. Males are a clear, brick red and females are a duller and more dusky, sometimes yellowish red, a unique example of sexual dimorphism in color among mammals. Dorsal hairs are blackish at the base, then have a broad band of yellow, a narrow band of red, and whitish tips. White-tipped hairs are also present on other parts of the body. There is a small whitish yellow patch in front of each shoulder. Red bats have short, rounded ears and tragi. The dorsal and ventral surfaces of the wing are furred close to the body and along the forearm. The interfemoral membrane is densely furred above over its entire surface, but sparsely furred (near the base) below. Although *Lasiurus borealis* shows variation in color, much of the variation appears to be related to sex and age.

Skulls of *Lasiurus* can be separated from those of other species of bats in Indiana by their short, squarish shape, and *L. borealis* can be separated from *L. cinereus* by size. The skulls of red bats are about 13 to 14 mm in total length, while those of hoary bats are about 17 to 20 mm.

Weights and measurements are shown in Table 64. The dental formula is:

$$I \frac{1}{3} C \frac{1}{1} P \frac{2}{2} M \frac{3}{3} = 32.$$

The minute, anterior upper premolar, which is inside the toothrow, behind the canine (see Fig. 7), is occasionally lacking.

STATUS AND DISTRIBUTION. The red bat occurs throughout Indiana. Specimens have been collected in 73 counties, and there are reliable sight records for several additional counties (Map 23). It is an abundant summer

Table 64
Weights and measurements of *Lasiurus borealis* from Indiana

	Males	Females
Total length (mm)		
n	18	96
x̄	100.9	107.7
range	90-109	91-123
SD	5.68	6.75
SE	1.33	0.68
Tail length (mm)		
n	20	103
x̄	40.7	44.3
range	32-48	28-59
SD	4.93	4.73
SE	1.10	0.46
Hind foot (mm)		
n	20	101
x̄	8.7	7.8
range	7-10	6-11
SD	1.31	0.94
SE	0.29	0.094
Forearm (mm)		
n	17	88
x̄	39.4	40.6
range	38-42	36-47
SD	1.22	1.71
SE	0.29	0.18
Tragus (mm)		
n	12	61
x̄	5.2	5.5
range	4-6	3.0-7.5
SD	0.83	0.94
SE	0.24	0.12
Weight (grams)		
n	19	102
x̄	10.4	12.3
range	9.0-11.7	8.8-22.0
SD	1.74	2.44
SE	0.40	0.24

resident in many sections of the state; it is probably least numerous in the relatively treeless prairie region of northwestern Indiana, but even there the species occurs about small woodlots and in riparian areas. An undetermined percentage evidently winters. We have specimen records for each month of the year except January and February, but we have sight observations for those months; the species appears to be a rare winter resident. There is thought to be an extensive migration of red bats in spring and fall. Actual breeding records (females with young or nonflying young) are available from 9 counties. In summer, the red bat is probably one of the most abundant bats in Indiana, and ranks second in number to the big brown bat among bats submitted to the rabies laboratory and bats shot by us.

Lasiurus borealis is extremely difficult to census because of its habit of roosting almost exclusively in tree foliage. We have made some attempts to estimate numbers by counting individuals seen in flight as we drove slowly along roads at dusk. Two such July counts resulted in estimates of 0.35 and 0.37 bats per acre for the habitats censused. One October count showed 0.45 bats per acre. These counts were for driving distances of 2.3 and 3 miles (Mumford, 1973). The Octo-

ber count may include some migrant or transient bats.

Red bats may be locally common at some seasons. As many as 10 have been seen foraging together for insects above street lights in a city. On at least three occasions (one in June; two in August), from 15 to 20 red bats have been observed foraging at one site; on another August evening, there were 25 red bats feeding over a small area. Between 27 May and 17 June, 4 adult male and 7 adult female red bats were shot from an area measuring 25 by 25 yards. Additional red bats were seen here, but not collected, on nearly all of seven visits to this site during this period. The females shot here were probably on their summer breeding grounds. During migration, red bats may suddenly appear in numbers at favored sites. For example, 13 were captured by hand on a single day in early September 1968 at their roost inside ring-necked pheasant pens on the Jasper-Pulaski Fish and Wildlife Area.

HABITAT. Red bats seem to favor areas of scattered deciduous trees, and thus are often seen about orchards, parks, cemeteries, grazed woodlots, and residential areas. We have little data from regions covered by extensive forests, although we have observed red bats to be fairly common at dusk along roads through such forests. Where large forested areas are absent (as in most of Indiana), *L. borealis* forages in and about small woodlots and along wooded stream banks. It is seldom found in caves, but can be captured in mist nets set at cave entrances at night, especially in late summer and early fall. Most records of red bats from caves in Indiana involve dead bats or skeletal materials (Hahn, 1907b; Mumford, 1953b). Red bats occasionally enter buildings, and we have 10 to 12 records of this habit. Red bats are sometimes found in daytime roosts, mostly hanging in trees, bushes or tall weeds. This bat is occasionally found in large trees in residential districts. Val Nolan, Jr., has observed 20 to 25 red bats over the past ten years hanging by day in bushes and small trees in an overgrown field in Monroe County (Mumford, 1969c).

ASSOCIATED SPECIES. The red bat, a solitary tree-roosting species, does not generally have roosting associates. However, we have

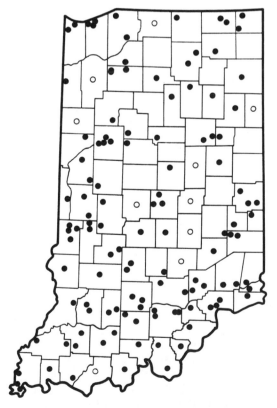

Map 23. The Red Bat, *Lasiurus borealis*, in Indiana

observed pipistrelles, hoary bats, big brown bats, evening bats, silver-haired bats, Indiana myotis, and little brown myotis foraging with red bats at dusk. The most frequently observed feeding associate of the red bat is the pipistrelle; this may be because both species emerge early at dusk to feed when the sky is relatively bright. In the southern one-third of Indiana, where pipistrelles are common in summer, these two species are nearly always found together.

HABITS.   It appears that *Lasiurus borealis* spends the day hanging among vegetation, flying out to feed at night. This early flyer is usually on the wing before dark. Its flight can be exceptionally rapid, especially on windy evenings, and the maneuvers performed by a red bat at such times are marvelous to watch. The bat may make sudden side forays to pursue an insect, or it may dive at high speed to chase prey close to the ground. At times red bats flying at altitudes of more than 100 feet have been seen to dive suddenly, almost vertically, to the surface of a pool, level off, and gracefully drink by skimming the surface.

Foraging height varies, but we have watched many red bats at dusk flying at heights from 20 to 50 feet. Most of them fed at a height of about 35 to 45 feet. Others have been observed feeding at 200 feet in the air; some even appeared to be higher than this. In contrast, most of the 25 red bats foraging on 3 August over a mowed clover field were flying from 2 to 15 feet off the ground. No doubt several factors determine the foraging height of bats: the height at which insects are flying; wind conditions; the habits of the particular insects being captured. Red bats normally seem to forage from 20 to 50 feet above the ground, flying back and forth along the edges of wooded areas, along roads through a forest, along small streams, or among the crowns of scattered trees in residential areas. It appears that red bats often chase individual prey items, rather than forage indiscriminately by flying through large numbers of small insects. An individual bat often appears to fly the same irregular route over and over for several minutes. Later, it may depart, possibly to drink or to hang up while digesting its food.

An individual bat may forage over a given area each evening, but until such animals are marked in such a way that they can be positively identified, we cannot be certain of this behavior. It has been noted that on several successive evenings a red bat will appear at about the same time and place, forage for a while, then depart. Other authors have observed this same behavior (Barbour and Davis, 1969). One is tempted to say that the same bat was observed each night on such occasions. However, our experience with collecting bats by shooting at dusk has shown that a dozen or more red bats may use the same foraging site during a three-week period. There seems little doubt that foraging areas overlap greatly.

One individual fed over an area 50 by 60 yards for about 4 minutes; throughout this time, it fed within 75 feet of the ground. Another red bat foraged along a roadside over an area 15 feet by 100 yards. It is sometimes possible to keep such a bat in view for up to ten minutes, but usually a bat appears and then leaves in a shorter period. One was seen feeding for two minutes after first appearing, then drinking, and continued feeding for ten minutes before leaving.

Based on the amount of food found in the stomachs of red bats shot soon after they emerge in the evening, it appears that this animal can undoubtedly fill its stomach with food in a matter of minutes. Several factors may influence feeding behavior: the type and abundance of insect prey, prevailing weather conditions, sex of the bat, and the stage of the reproductive cycle. For example, adult males would not be restricted to feeding in an area near where the young were roosting, whereas the adult female who was rearing these young might not venture far away or stay over extended periods of time without returning.

On cold afternoons and evenings from November to February, red bats emerge earlier to forage. These bats are evidently taking advantage of the warmest part of the day to be active, when their insect prey is also most likely to be available. Thus, the bats may be seen before the sun sets and the ambient temperature takes a sudden drop. H. P. Weeks, Jr., observed a red bat flying at 5:50 P.M. on 4 February (Montgomery County). The temperature was an estimated 45°F and the sun was shining on the bat. A male shot at 5:00 P.M. on 16 December by H. A. Demaree,

Jr., in Hamilton County was foraging along the edge of a woodlot. On 12 January (Decatur County) one was flying about in the late afternoon and was easily identified by C. M. Kirkpatrick and R. E. Mumford. D. L. McGroarty saw a red bat flying at 2:00 in the afternoon in a forest (Martin County) on 21 January; that evening, 5 or 6 were seen there. There are several observations for late November, with the bats flying about relatively early in the evening.

The red bat can evidently tolerate a temperature well below freezing, since some individuals have been shot during times of the year just after below-freezing temperatures prevailed. For example, a male shot on 9 March (Orange County) would have had to withstand a temperature of 9°F on 6 March (if it had remained in the area during this time). One can argue that this bat had flown to the site between 6 and 9 March, for the maximum temperature on 8 March was 59°F (the minimum for that date was 24°F). It has been noted in several years that when temperatures exceed 60 to 65°F in midwinter red bats may be seen foraging in the evenings. Surely, these bats do not suddenly migrate into the region; they are probably present throughout the winter in unknown roosts, from which they emerge when the temperature allows such activity.

Red bats do not require large bodies of water for drinking. They can maneuver about relatively small intermittent pools along creeks and brush-bordered ponds of small size in wooded areas. Red bats continued to drink from a pool along an intermittent stream after the pool was only 4 by 6 feet. Four were netted over a temporary pool 12 by 23 feet and scarcely more than an inch deep (the pool was originally four times this size). Red bats knocked into the water by wires stretched across the surface of their drinking pools frequently fly from the water's surface. At other times, apparently when their pelage becomes too wet, the bats swim strongly to shore, climb up on some object and reach sufficient height to launch themselves into flight.

Except for females and their young, which hang in a cluster, red bats roost singly. The height at which a roosting bat hangs is seemingly somewhat correlated with the total height of the roost tree; bats tend to roost

Litter of young red bats. Photo by Grady Franklin, Crawfordsville *Journal Review*

nearer the ground in shorter trees or shrubs. We have data on 39 daytime roost sites, which ranged from 2 to 40 feet (average 8.5) above the ground. Val Nolan located 14 of these roosts in old overgrown fields near Bloomington (Monroe County) while conducting studies on the prairie warbler. The fields, which contained weeds, briars, bushes, saplings, and scattered trees, were censused daily from early April to late September each year between 1953 and 1961. These bat roosts varied from 4 to 25 feet (and averaged 7.8 feet) from the ground. Nolan located 2 roosts in April, 5 in July, and 7 in August. It is interesting (and possibly significant) that he found no roosting bats there in May or June. The bats should have been easier to detect in those months than later, when leaves had reached their full development. Perhaps for some reason most of the bats sought this habitat only after their young were capable of flight. Unfortunately, we do not know the sex of any of the bats, although some were surely females with large young.

Trees in which the 14 roosts were found were as follows: sugar maple, 3; maple (sp.), 2; American elm, 3; flowering dogwood, 2; Virginia pine, 1; black cherry, 1; redbud, 1; tulip poplar, 1. The bats were found in various parts of these trees, but most were fairly easily seen from below. Several were hanging at or near the tips of branches, but one hung next to the trunk, only 58 inches above the ground, and below the tops of surrounding, weedy cover. Most were shaded by leaves above them, but the bats were not well hidden.

SEX RATIOS. Of the 424 *Lasiurus borealis* specimens from Indiana that we examined in collections, 180 were males and 244 were females. Females with young are probably much more vulnerable to being found than males. Also, gravid females are no doubt more easily shot than males. Thus, one might expect a larger number of females in collections. It is difficult to obtain an unbiased sample for these reasons.

Nevertheless, it appears that female red bats generally outnumber males in Indiana. This appears to be strikingly true for adult red bats.

LONGEVITY. Of 11 males and 22 females banded by Mumford, only one has been recovered (one month after banding). Thus, we have been unable to obtain longevity data on this species. Other banders have had much the same results.

MIGRATION. It has been long accepted that the red bat migrates, but band recoveries have not demonstrated the distances or numbers of bats involved. Also, there is no southern locality where the species is absent or is in relatively low numbers in the summer and then appears or increases in the winter, nor is there any evidence of migratory movements based on banding records. There are winter records for the species in Indiana, as mentioned before, and from other nearby states (Davis and Lidicker, 1956). It appears possible that some individuals hibernate in Indiana, perhaps in such isolated sites as hollow trees. More information is needed regarding the migration of the red bat.

Certain observations made in Indiana suggest migratory animals were involved. The 15 that suddenly appeared flying about at Jasper-Pulaski Fish and Wildlife Area at 1:45 P.M. on 24 August evidently constituted a migratory flock. Robert Buskirk saw 5 red bats flying south, high overhead, at Lafayette on 22 September, at 4:30 P.M. These records may indicate that some fall migration takes place in the daytime. Raymond Grow has observed red bats flying south, coming from over Lake Michigan, at the south end of the lake, during daylight hours. Further evidence of the movement of *Lasiurus borealis* over Lake Michigan is provided by the fact that after a severe thunderstorm (with hail) on the night of 16-17 April 1960, at least 4 dead red bats were washed ashore, with hundreds of dead birds, along the south end of the lake. These animals were most likely in migration over the water when they encountered the storm. Raymond Grow has occasionally found red bats roosting by day in trees and bushes along the Lake Michigan shore. On 1 September 1969, he found 4.

FOOD. Whitaker (1972b) examined the stomachs of 128 red bats from Indiana (Table 65). The most abundant food item was adult Lepidoptera (26.2 percent of total volume), which had been eaten by 32 percent of the bats. The second most abundant food was Scarabaeidae, followed by Cercopidae, Formicidae, and Cicadellidae. The total amount of Coleoptera was 28.1 percent. The red bat and big brown bat were the most abundant bats flying at dusk along streams at Terre Haute, where many of the bats used for Whitaker's food habits analysis were collected. The foods of the two species were very different: Lepidoptera was the most important food of red bats but was seldom eaten by big brown bats; beetles were the dominant food of big brown bats.

Ross (1961) examined 10 fecal pellets of red bats from California and found remains of 60 moths, 29 unidentified orthopterans, 10 acridids, and one ptilodactylid. In 27 red bats from Indiana and Illinois, Ross (1967) found 10 cicadellids, 620 cercopids (primarily *Philaenus pumaria*), another homopteran, an anthicid, 8 scarabaeids, 2 chrysomelids, 9 other coleopterans, 12 lepidopterans, 4 drosophilids, 7 other dipterans, and 35 formicids. Of six additional digestive tracts examined by Ross from Mexico and New Mexico, five contained only moths, and one contained moths and 6 small scarabaeid beetles. Lewis (1940) found red bats (and one pipistrelle) congregating over corn cribs to feed on grain moths (*Angomous*). Our data are similar to those of other workers in that Lepidoptera formed a major portion of the food of the species and homopterans were

Table 65

Foods eaten by *Lasiurus borealis* (n = 128) from Indiana
(from Whitaker, 1972b)

Food item	Percent volume	Percent frequency
Lepidoptera	26.2	32.0
Scarabaeidae (scarab beetles)	12.1	21.9
Delphacidae (planthoppers)	11.8	25.8
Formicidae (ants)	6.3	11.7
Cicadellidae (leafhoppers)	5.9	20.3
Coleoptera (unidentified beetles)	5.6	21.9
Carabidae (ground beetles)	5.6	10.9
Reduviidae (assassin bugs)	4.1	14.1
Muscoid flies	2.5	6.3
Hydrophilidae (water scavenger beetles)	1.8	3.9
Diptera	1.8	7.0
Insects (unidentified)	1.6	4.7
Gryllidae (crickets)	1.6	4.7
Miridae (leaf bugs)	1.2	3.1
Chrysomelidae (leaf beetles)	1.1	3.1
Curculionidae (snout beetles)	1.0	3.9
Soft material	0.8	0.8
Dirt	0.8	0.8
Alleculidae (comb-clawed bark beetles)	0.8	0.8
Tipulidae (craneflies)	0.8	3.1
Nabidae (nabid bugs)	0.8	0.8
Fulgoridae (lanternflies)	0.8	0.8
Pentatomidae (stinkbugs)	0.7	2.3
Lygaeidae (chinch bugs)	0.7	0.8
Blattidae, *Parcoblatta* (roaches)	0.6	0.8
Ichneumonidae (ichneumon flies)	0.6	4.7
Chrysopidae (lacewings)	0.5	1.6
Chironomidae (midges)	0.5	0.8
Trichoptera (caddisflies)	0.4	1.6
Vegetation	0.4	2.3
Anthomyidae (anthomyid flies)	0.2	0.8
Hymenoptera	0.2	1.6
Syrphidae (hover flies)	0.2	0.8
Flesh (baby bat or placenta?)	0.2	0.8
Chrysomelidae, *Diabrotica undecimpunctata*	0.1	0.8
Araneae (spider)	trace	0.8
Ephemeridae (mayflies)	trace	0.8
Drosophilidae (pomaceflies)	trace	0.8
	100.3	

prominent. Jackson (1961) thought that red bats might feed from foliage, or even near the ground, since crickets *(Gryllus)* were found in their stomachs.

REPRODUCTION. We have been unable to obtain definite data regarding copulation in Indiana *Lasiurus borealis.* While hunting or observing red bats at dusk, we have frequently seen one bat pursue another; several of these "chases" have resulted in the two

bats making actual contact in the air. In one case (9 April), the bats came into contact while flying 30 feet above the ground, fell together until about 5 feet from the ground, then separated. We have no way of knowing the sexes of the bats involved or if they were actually copulating. We have recorded chases in April (two), June (two), July (eight), August (nine), September (four), and October (one). On 24 July and 4 September, one of the two participating in a chase was shot; in each case it was a male. Two others, shot as they made contact on 15 August, were both males. Thus, one wonders whether observed chases have anything to do with copulation. Thomas W. Hoekstra watched a red bat chase another on 12 April; the bats came together, then fell to the surface of a road, where Hoekstra captured them. One was a male, the other a female. He was of the opinion that they were copulating. On 5 September, Peter Phendler caught two red bats that were lying on the ground (evidently fighting); both were males, one of which tested positive for rabies.

We have found that testis size in red bats is largest in July, August, and September (Whitaker and Mumford, 1972c). If testis size can be taken as an indicator of the mating season, we assume that most copulation takes place during these months. Hamilton (1943) collected female red bats with sperm in their uteri the first week of August.

Most young of red bats are evidently born around mid-June in Indiana, but actual dates of parturition are quite difficult to obtain from noncaptive individuals. Females near term may abort their young prematurely in confinement, so one should be cautious in accepting parturition dates for captive (frequently injured) gravid females. We found small (1.8 mm diameter) embryos in a female collected 30 April, and embryos as late as 19 June (10 mm crown-rump length). Since we have seen embryos as large as 22 mm crown-rump length, the female taken 19 June was not at term.

The 32 gravid red bats examined each contained from 2 to 5 embryos. The average number of young per female was 3.2 and the mode was 3. A summary of the number of embryos per female follows: 2 young (1 female); 3 young (24 females); 4 young (6 females); 5 young (1 female).

We have records of 33 adult female red bats (6 June–26 July) with attached young; many of these were found on the ground. Of these females, 14 had 4 young, 12 had 3, 6 had 2, and 1 had 1. It was surprising to note that such a large percentage had 4 young per litter, because from embryo counts 3 young per litter was the most common. Perhaps the fact that a female is carrying 4 young makes her more vulnerable to storms or other disturbances that may dislodge her from her roost and cause her to fall to the ground.

Placental scars were observed in 19 females. Seven of these animals exhibited scars in June and 10 in July; none was found in females taken in August. One individual said to have been taken on 3 May had placental scars, as did another female supposedly taken on 18 September. Both of these dates seem unusual, in light of the other data; perhaps there were errors in the dates; both females were among bats found and sent to the Indiana State Board of Health. Five other adult females collected in September had no visible placental scars, nor did six taken in August. It appears that placental scars do not persist for long periods after parturition. A female found with four attached young averaging 74 mm in total length (1 July) contained four faint scars. Another female taken with three attached young averaging 75 mm in total length on 20 June had at least two very faint scars. In the collection of Manchester College is an adult female red bat and five small young of equal size preserved in alcohol. No label accompanies the specimens, but it is possible that they represent a female and her litter.

We have examined females in lactation from 14 June to 3 August, but no doubt these dates could both be extended with more data.

GROWTH OF YOUNG. There are evidently few weight and size data for newborn red bats. Barbour and Davis (1969) lacked information on this point, and Jackson (1961) must have erred in stating that they weighed only 0.5 grams each at birth. We have not examined known, full-term, newborn red bats, but from a few observations we have made some interpolations. On 17 June a female with two young, still carrying umbilical cords, were found on the ground. Forearm measurements for these young were 12 and 13 mm. The largest embryos we have examined in a gravid red bat measured 22 mm in crown-rump length and had total lengths of 44, 44, and 41 mm. Three embryos measuring 20 mm each in crown-rump length had forearms of 10 mm each. We feel that these must have been near term. Another female was found on the ground with 3 attached young on 20 June. These young had forearms measuring 24, 21, and 20 mm and weighed 3.1, 2.9, and 2.5 grams respectively. This family represents the smallest attached young that we have data for and may be an indication of the size of young at, or shortly after, parturition.

The largest young we have found with their mother was on 26 July. When disturbed, two of the young flew away and the other glided to the ground and was captured. It weighed 8.4 grams, was 85 mm in total length, and had a forearm length of 38 mm. Three young found with a female on 14 July measured 79, 79, and 81 mm in total length and weighed 6.4, 7.4, and 7.6 grams respectively. An immature male shot in flight on 4 July weighed 6.6 grams, was 81.5 mm in total length, and had a forearm of 36 mm. More information is needed to determine at what size *Lasiurus borealis* young become independent, but the animals mentioned here may have been near this stage.

Stomach analyses of immatures provided some interesting information (Whitaker and Mumford, 1972c). One young weighing only 4.4 grams and having a total length of 64 mm had 60 percent chironomid and 40 percent coleoptera remains in the stomach, but no milk. All of the 29 other immatures found without accompanying females and with total lengths of less than 80 mm and having food in their stomachs contained milk. But 2 of them (forearms 27 and 31 mm) also contained parts of ants and other insects. Two lone immatures, collected 28 July and 11 August, contained only insect remains and thus were evidently independent. They had total lengths of 85 and 86 mm and forearms of 36 and 39 mm respectively. One young, measuring 91 mm in total length and with a 38-mm forearm, had milk in its stomach and intestines. This indicates that some young, though able to feed on insects, continue to nurse, and some become quite large before they are off milk.

PARASITES AND DISEASES. There is relatively little information on external parasites. Tipton and Boese (1958) described *Steatonyssus furmani* from a red bat taken in Jefferson County. A report of *Steatonyssus occidentalis* on *L. borealis* by Whitaker and Wilson (1968) was in error; the two individuals found were juvenile *S. furmani*. Two

larval specimens of the tick *Dermacentor variabilis* were taken from a red bat in Tippecanoe County (Wilson, 1961). Whitaker (1973) reported on the ectoparasites of 234 Indiana red bats. Of the two species of parasites found, 59 were macronyssid mites *(Steatonyssus furmani)* and 13 were a new species of myobiid mite *(Acanthopthirius lasiurus)* recently described by Fain and Whitaker (1976).

Particularly large numbers of trematodes and a few cestodes were found in the intestines of Indiana red bats. None of these internal parasites has been identified.

Rabies was diagnosed in a red bat from Tippecanoe County in September 1960, and 24 of 338 Indiana red bats examined for rabies by Whitaker and Miller (1974) tested positive. In this study the red bat ranked third in incidence of rabies, following the hoary bat and the pipistrelle, both of which were represented by small numbers.

DECIMATING FACTORS. Several authors have reported the attacks of blue jays on red bats (Strecker, 1924; McClure, 1942; Allan, 1947; Elwell, 1962; Hoffmeister and Downes, 1964; Mumford, 1973). This type of predation might be of significant importance in the extensive area where the summer ranges of the red bat and the blue jay overlap. Evidently the jay discovers roosting red bats while it is foraging among tree foliage. Other avian enemies of red bats are known, including hawks and owls. Mumford found the skull of a *L. borealis* in the pellet of an unidentified owl from Jackson County. Workers at the Jasper-Pulaski Fish and Wildlife Area watched captive ring-necked pheasants pursue and kill a red bat that got inside the pheasant pen.

Automobiles kill some foraging animals; we have eight records of red bats found either dead on roads or on the radiators or front ends of cars. Various accidents have befallen other individuals. One was found alive in a swimming pool, the sides of which were evidently too high and too smooth for the bat to climb out. Another was found caught on a fence. Several have been found in insect light traps (Wilson, 1965), to which they may have been attracted by the insects or by the sound produced by certain types of traps ("black" lights). One was found, dead, impaled on the ripe seed head of a burdock plant *(Arctium minus)*. At least nine red bats have been found dead along the beach at the south end of Lake Michigan; four of these were found by Raymond Grow in mid-September. The implication is that these were migrants caught over the lake by adverse weather conditions and forced into the water.

TAXONOMY. *Lasiurus borealis borealis* (Müller) is the subspecies in Indiana.

SELECTED REFERENCES. Barbour and Davis, 1969; Constantine, 1966; Davis and Lidicker, 1956; Kunz, 1968; McClure, 1942; Mumford, 1973; Whitaker, 1972b, 1973.

Hoary Bat
Lasiurus cinereus (Palisot de Beauvois)

Vespertilio pruinosis: Plummer, 1844
Atalpha cinereus: Langdon, 1881b
Atalapha cinerea: Evermann and Butler, 1894b
Lasiturus cinerus: Engels, 1933
Lasiurus cinereus: McAtee, 1907

Hoary bat. Photo by Bruce J. Hayward

DESCRIPTION. *Lasiurus cinereus* is a large, grayish bat with short, broad, rounded ears bearing black borders. It is the largest species of bat in Indiana. The whitish tips of the body hairs give the bat the appearance of being covered with hoarfrost, hence its common (vernacular) name. The dorsal surface of the interfemoral membrane is completely furred. The throat is yellowish, and there is a small, irregular yellowish spot at the base of each thumb. Immatures are somewhat paler in color than adults. Individual hairs on the back often have four bands of color—a blackish base, then yellowish, followed by blackish or brown near the whitish tip. Males and females are colored alike, in contrast to the sexually dimorphic coloration of *Lasiurus borealis*. The skull of *L. cinereus* is squarish and similar to that of *L. borealis*, but larger.

Weights and measurements are shown in Table 66. An immature male taken 20 July weighed 18.4 grams and had light fat. An adult female taken on 9 August and an unaged male collected 28 August were both very fat, weighing 33.6 and 21.0 grams respectively. The dental formula is

$$\text{I } \frac{1}{3} \text{ C } \frac{1}{1} \text{ P } \frac{2}{2} \text{ M } \frac{3}{3} = 32.$$

STATUS AND DISTRIBUTION. The hoary bat no doubt occurs throughout Indiana, but is probably uncommon. Specimens are now in museums from 27 counties (Map 24). Reliable sight records or reports of lost and discarded specimens are at hand from additional counties. Findley and Jones (1964) summarized the seasonal distribution of the hoary bat throughout its contiguous range, and Mumford (1969b) supplemented their data for Indiana. Of 83 records of occurrence in the state for which the month is known, 52 are for the months of June (29) and July (23). Most dates fall between 12 April and 5 October; the majority of these are for May to August, evidently the period when hoary bats are most abundant in Indiana. There are

Table 66

Weights and measurements of
Lasiurus cinereus from Indiana

	Males	Females
Total length (mm)		
n	20	41
x̄	124.0	134.8
range	110-138	102-152
SD	8.7	9.6
SE	1.9	1.5
Tail length (mm)		
n	19	39
x̄	52.8	56.5
range	44-64	49-65
SD	5.4	5.0
SE	1.2	0.8
Hind foot (mm)		
n	19	41
x̄	10.2	10.6
range	8-14	6.0-13.5
SD	1.5	1.9
SE	0.3	0.3
Forearm (mm)		
n	16	35
x̄	52.2	54.9
range	47-57	42-59
SD	2.4	3.4
SE	0.6	0.6
Tragus (mm)		
n	14	37
x̄	7.8	7.9
range	5-10	5-11
SD	1.5	1.7
SE	0.4	0.3
Weight (grams)		
n	10	27
x̄	18.1	28.5
range	14.0-28.2	18.0-38.3
SD	4.1	6.1
SE	1.3	1.2

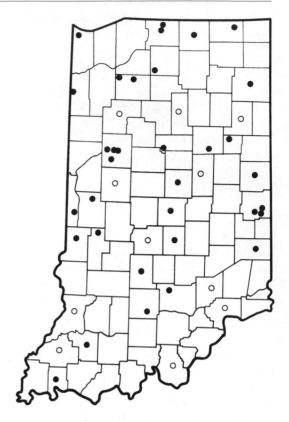

Map 24.   The Hoary Bat, *Lasiurus cinereus*,
in Indiana

Since *Lasiurus cinereus* is a tree-inhabiting bat, accurate censusing is virtually impossible. At times, several may be seen foraging together or coming to watering areas. On the evening of 29 May 1948, at least three were feeding together along the border of a wood-lot (Tippecanoe County); two of them were shot and both were females. Thomas W. Hoekstra and J. Scott Grundy shot five hoary bats at dusk on 27 June 1962, as the bats flew over a small pond near Munster (Lake County); four were females and one a male. Bats were numerous there that evening, but all appeared to be the same species, according to Hoekstra. James B. Cope and his students netted three hoary bats the night of 12 July 1962, near Richmond (Wayne County).

HABITAT.   The hoary bat is considered to be essentially a tree-inhabiting bat, roosting by day among the foliage. It appears to show a definite tendency to roost in areas where trees are scattered and have openings below their crowns. Such known roosting sites in Indiana include a pasture, residential areas, a

single records for 20-29 October (Allen County), 21 November and 18 December (both Tippecanoe County), and 31 January (Vigo County). There is a good possibility that some individuals are present in winter. Since the species is presumed to be highly migratory, considerable movements must take place across the state in spring and fall, but we have little indication of the numbers of animals involved. Breeding occurs throughout Indiana, although we have relatively few actual records of females with attached young.

wooded lake shore, a wooded campus, and an open stand of mixed woodland, brush, and old fields. Two individuals were taken in buildings; another was found clinging to the side of a building. There are a few records of skulls and other remains of hoary bats in Indiana caves (Hahn, 1907b; Mumford, 1953b), but neither a live nor an intact animal has been discovered in caverns in this state. It would be interesting to know at what seasons and under what conditions hoary bats enter caves.

Most Indiana specimens of *L. cinereus* have been shot or netted about woodlot borders, along small streams through pasture or cropland, or over ponds (mostly in unwooded areas). Eight females were shot at Lafayette around the borders of a pastured, deciduous woodlot surrounded on three sides by pasture and on the fourth by a cultivated field. Judging by the frequency with which hoary bats are submitted to the Indiana State Board of Health, residential areas may be used by this species to a considerable extent.

ASSOCIATED SPECIES. Other bats shot along with hoary bats at dusk include big brown bats, Indiana myotis, pipistrelles, silver-haired bats, red bats, and evening bats. Red bats are a common associate in Indiana, possibly indicating that both species of *Lasiurus* find certain habitats to their liking. A man tearing down a small building on his residential lawn (Lafayette) on 21 November found a hoary bat and three smaller bats in the building. He destroyed the smaller bats before giving the *L. cinereus* to Mumford.

HABITS. The hoary bat is primarily a solitary species, except at favored feeding and drinking areas, where three or more may be seen together. Family groups consisting of a female and her two young are also encountered. It appears to us that the hoary bat emerges to forage a bit later on the average than does the red bat, although some hoary bats have been observed in the evening when it was still relatively bright. Many of the individuals that have been noted early in the evening were flying quite high (often out of shotgun range). Some of these passed overhead in rather straight flight and may have been animals moving from their daytime roosts to feeding or drinking areas some distance away. As dusk deepens, the bats seem to forage nearer the ground. This may

partially explain why fewer hoary bats have been collected by shooting.

The flight of the hoary bat is usually strong, fast, and direct. The wingbeats seem regular, rather deliberate, and somewhat birdlike. Amazingly erratic flight may be exhibited by foraging individuals, especially on windy evenings. On calm evenings, hoary bats have been watched lazily circling about 200 feet in the air for periods of up to twelve minutes. One watched (and later shot) on a windy evening seemed to feed mostly into the wind, then it climbed slightly and "hung" motionless for a few moments, before going into a downward glide on set wings. We think that *L. cinereus* glides more than do other Indiana species of bats when feeding.

The size of the foraging area has not been precisely determined, but our impression is that an individual bat ranges rather widely. On one occasion, however, a single hoary bat was kept under observation for ten minutes, as it fed near the ground and over an area probably not more than 50 feet in diameter. As many as three hoary bats have been noticed feeding together (two of them were collected) about the border of a woodlot; the bats fed mostly from 12 to 25 feet from the ground and roughly 15 yards from the edge of the woods, over the edge of a pasture.

On six evenings from 14 June to 12 July, a hoary bat (presumably the same each night) left its daytime roost (not discovered) in a large tree in a residential area between 8:16 and 8:35. Its behavior was about the same each evening; it appeared to emerge from an area about 40 feet above the ground, circle briefly, then fly directly away until out of sight. The bat appeared each evening at about the same time after sundown.

Only a few hoary bats have been found in their day roosts; four roost sites were in trees. On 15 June an adult female with two attached young was hanging 25 feet from the ground in a thornless honey locust. A male was captured in a honey locust at an unspecified height above the ground on 29 August. On 26 September, Fred Miller found one hanging 6 feet from the ground on a green fruit of a black walnut tree in a pasture. The bat hung in full sunlight. A female was caught in an unidentified tree on 6 May and a female with two young was roosting in a box elder tree on 14 June. A male was captured in a small building on 21 November; it hung with three smaller bats (which we were unable to obtain for examination). Another male was found clinging to the side of a brick building on 31 January (Whitaker, 1967b). An adult female was captured while clinging to the roof inside a ring-necked pheasant pen constructed of poultry netting supported by poles. When the bat Miller found was stroked with a finger, it snapped its jaws and gave the usual chittering noise characteristic of agitated hoary bats.

Most observations and collections of hoary bats have been made at dusk. The activity patterns of the species are largely unknown. An adult female was netted at 12:20 A.M. on 29 July.

Adult male hoary bats are evidently quite rare in Indiana. One was taken 31 May in Jennings County. Males collected 21 November (Tippecanoe County) and 31 January (Vigo County) could not be definitely aged as young of the year or fully adult. In contrast, we have some 40 records of adult females from the state. We have about 40 additional records of hoary bats collected in Indiana from July to November, but accurate age data are not available for most of them.

Little is known about the winter habits of this species, but most authors indicate that hoary bats migrate south to spend the winter. The evidence for this is somewhat scanty and not based on recoveries of marked animals.

FOOD. We have accumulated relatively little information regarding the food of *Lasiurus cinereus* in Indiana. Three specimens had insects in their stomachs. Two contained 100 percent Lepidoptera and the third contained 65 percent Lepidoptera, 25 percent Chrysomelidae, and 10 percent muscoid flies. One individual taken in July had only vegetation in its stomach. Details of collection were not available, but vegetation is probably not a normal food. Possibly the bat had been hurt and confined to the ground, where it consumed plant material as an emergency food. A hoary bat taken 31 January (Vigo County) after a warm period of four to five days, had a "plug" of well digested grass stems in the posterior end of the intestine. This material appeared to have been there for a considerable period. Fresh grass stems and some shed snake skin were in the stomach (Whitaker, 1967b).

Ross (1967) examined the digestive tracts

of 139 hoary bats from New Mexico. Of these, 136 contained Lepidoptera (Phalaenidae, Geometridae, Gelechiidae) in numbers up to 25 per bat. Other insects present were Formicidae (78 individuals), Acrididae (1), Isoptera (7), Chrysopidae (1), Coleoptera (9), Scarabaeidae (4), Chrysomelidae (2), and Cerambycidae (1). Poole (1932) found a pentatomid and a culicid in a stomach of *L. cinereus* from Pennsylvania. Bishop (1947) found a hoary bat feeding on *Pipistrellus subflavus* in New York, and Orr (1950) observed one pursuing a small bat in California. Low numbers of coleopterans have been found in stomachs of this species, and Brisbin (1966) reported *L. cinereus* as reluctant to take beetles. Overall, this species is primarily a moth feeder.

REPRODUCTION. Each of eleven gravid hoary bats collected in Indiana from 5 May to 8 June contained two embryos. Parturition evidently occurs mostly in late May and early June. A female captured on 28 May (Vigo County) gave birth (perhaps prematurely) to two young the same day. Three adult females with attached young have been recorded on 14 June (Wayne County), 15 June (Tippecanoe County), and 19 June (Vigo County). Two partially grown young were obtained (without a female) on 12 June (Clay County) and a small young was collected on 30 June (Wayne County). Four lactating females were collected between 28 May and 14 July.

A female taken 5 May contained embryos only 6 mm in crown-rump length. The largest embryos examined by us (1 June) had forearm lengths of 16.5 mm each and were probably near term. These two young weighed 3.9 and 4.0 grams. Two young born to a captive female on 28 May had forearm lengths of 15 and 17 mm and total lengths of 55 and 57 mm respectively. Two embryos, each with 16-mm forearms, examined 29 May, weighed 3.3 and 3.5 grams, while two others on 3 June had 15-mm forearms and weighed 3.1 grams each. From these data, it appears that newborn hoary bats have forearms of about 16 mm, total lengths of from 55 to 57 mm, and weights of about 3.5 to 4.0 grams. Our measurements are nearly identical with those of Bogan (1972), although he presented no weights for newborn young. Barbour and Davis (1969) stated that

Table 67
External parasites of several species of bats from Indiana,
listed by host, in order of decreasing abundance

Species	No. examined	Parasites		Hosts parasitized	
		Total	Average	Total	Percent
Southeastern Myotis	5				
Mites (Acarina) other than chiggers					
Olabidocarpus whitakeri		52	10.40	3	60.0
Chigger mites (Trombiculidae)					
Euschoengastia pipistrelli		1	0.20	1	20.0
Indiana Myotis	43				
Mites (Acarina) other than chiggers					
Macronyssus crosbyi		70	1.63	14	32.6
Paraspinturnix globosus		6	0.14	4	9.3
Acanthophthirius lucifugus		2	0.05	1	2.3
Silver-haired Bat	8				
Batbugs (Cimicidae)					
Cimex adjunctus		1	0.13	1	12.5
Mites (Acarina) other than chiggers					
Macronyssus macrodactylus		19	2.38	5	62.5
Acanthophthirius sp.		1	0.13	1	12.5
Eastern Pipistrelle	56				
Chigger Mites (Trombiculidae)					
Euschoengastia pipistrelli		54	0.96	13	23.2
Evening Bat	12				
Mites (Acarina) other than chiggers					
Steatonyssus ceratognathus		12	1.00	5	41.7
Red Bat	234				
Mites (Acarina) other than chiggers					
Steatonyssus furmani		59	0.25	26	11.1
Acanthophthirius lasiurus		13	0.06	7	3.0
Hoary Bat	25				
Mites (Acarina) other than chiggers					
Pteracarus completus		2	0.08	2	8.0
Acanthophthirius lasiurus?		13	0.52	1	4.0

newborn young have forearm lengths of 18 to 19 mm.

We have few data on growth rates of young hoary bats from Indiana. Relatively few young have been examined and all kept in confinement died within seven or eight days, thus weight and measurement data for them are probably not meaningful. An immature female was shot in flight on 18 July; it had a forearm length of 53 mm and a total length of 114 mm. It was flying slowly and steadily in a straight line, with rather deliberate wingbeats. It exhibited none of the driving, erratic flight characteristics of adults and probably had not been independent very long. A young male, shot in flight on 19 July, had a 53-mm forearm and was 135 mm in total length. An immature male collected 6 July weighed 17 grams, had a forearm of 51 mm and a total length of 124 mm; the specimen label does not indicate whether this animal was capable of flight.

Data for adult males are lacking. Testis size was not recorded for the only adult male we examined. A male taken 31 January had testes 2.4 mm long. Testis lengths for nine subadults varied from 3 to 6 mm and averaged 4.1 mm.

PARASITES AND DISEASES. Whitaker (1973) examined 25 Indiana hoary bat specimens, but the only external parasites found were 13 unidentified individuals of *Acanthophthirius* and 2 other myobiid mites originally listed as *Pteracarus chalinobus* but now reidentified as *Pteracarus completus*. Table 67 summarizes data on external parasites from several species of bats in Indiana.

Nixon A. Wilson found the cestode *Cyclo-skrjabinia taborensis* in a hoary bat from Indiana (Stunkard, 1962).

Whitaker and Miller (1974) found 10 of 51 Indiana hoary bats positive for rabies.

DECIMATING FACTORS. One hoary bat specimen obtained had flown into a guy wire. Boys with a BB gun shot a female carrying two young from her daytime roost in a tree. Another family was found on the ground after the wind blew its roost tree down. McAtee recorded a female and two large young that were chased from their daytime roost in a tree by a robin. On 18 December 1976, the wings and most of the skin of a hoary bat were found beneath some pines being used as a roosting site by long-eared owls (Tippecanoe County). The bat remains were quite fresh, and circumstantial evidence suggests the owls captured the bat.

TAXONOMY. The subspecies in Indiana is *Lasiurus cinereus cinereus* (Beauvois).

SELECTED REFERENCES. Barbour and Davis, 1969; Poole, 1932; Provost and Kirkpatrick, 1952; Mumford, 1969b; Whitaker, 1967b.

Rafinesque's Big-eared Bat
Plecotus rafinesquii Lesson

Big-eared Bat

Corynorhinus macrotis: Butler, 1895
Corynorhinus megalotis: Allen, 1916
Corynorhinus rafinesquii: Miller, 1924
Corynorhinus townsendii: Hall and Kelson, 1959 (probably)
Plecotus rafinesquii: Handley, 1959

DESCRIPTION. This medium sized bat is brownish above, whitish below, and has extremely long ears (more than one inch long) unlike those of any other species of bat in Indiana. The hairs on the dorsum are dark brown or blackish on the basal two-thirds, then pale reddish or yellowish brown on the distal one-third. The ventral hairs are black or blackish at their bases, with white or whitish tips. The throat and chin may be about the color of the back in some individuals. As the pelage becomes worn, the overall color of the dorsum becomes darker.

Weights and measurements are shown in Table 68. The dental formula is

$$I \frac{2}{3} C \frac{1}{1} P \frac{2}{3} M \frac{3}{3} = 36.$$

STATUS AND DISTRIBUTION. *Plecotus rafinesquii* is rare in Indiana and seemingly restricted to the south-central portion of the state. Most of our records are from Lawrence and Washington counties (Map 25); three are from two small caves about 2 miles northeast of Saltillo and eight are from the caves on Spring Mill State Park, east of Mitchell. The last observation known to us from Spring Mill was made in November 1907. Two individuals of *Plecotus* (presumably this species) were seen and one collected near Greencastle (Putnam County) on 26 December 1894. A big-eared bat was collected (Ohio State Museum1741) from a small cave near Kossuth (Washington County) on 25 October 1955; another was captured in a cave near Smedley (Washington County) on 21 December 1962. The presence of a *Plecotus rafinesquii* at West Lafayette (Tippecanoe County) on 13 December 1959 was a surprise; this specimen represents the northern-most known record of this species in the United States (Wilson, 1960).

HABITAT. All records except one of *Plecotus rafinesquii* for Indiana are from caves; a single specimen was taken from a long, concrete culvert. The caves where the big-eared bat has been found in Lawrence and Washington counties are located in areas of deciduous woodlands. The Spring Mill State Park caves where Walter L. Hahn made his observations of this species are located in a solid, near-virgin tract of large trees. The Washington County sites are not so extensively wooded, but have cultivated and wooded areas intermixed. We do not know what the appearance of the Putnam County site was in 1894, when *Plecotus* was found

Rafinesque's big-eared bat. Photo by Philip C. Shelton

there, but today it is sparsely wooded and mostly cultivated land. The culvert mentioned above is located beneath a well-timbered slope near the Wabash River; this forested area has probably been relatively undisturbed for many years. It would appear, then, that *P. rafinesquii* is a forest-inhabiting bat. In other parts of its range it has frequently been found in buildings.

Some of the caves housing big-eared bats in Indiana have a stream flowing throughout their length, but some are without streams. The culvert where a big-eared bat was collected frequently has the floor covered with water, as it was the day the specimen was taken there.

ASSOCIATED SPECIES. The caves at Spring Mill were also used by little brown myotis, Keen's myotis, Indiana myotis, southeastern myotis, gray myotis, pipistrelles, and big brown bats when Hahn made his observations there on the big-eared bat. The *Plecotus rafinesquii* found near Kossuth on 25 October 1953 was the only bat noted in the cave. Two big-eared bats captured on 28 December 1954 shared the cave with six pipistrelles and one little brown myotis. Big brown bats also used the culvert where a *Plecotus* was taken at West Lafayette; this big-eared bat represents the only other species of bat observed in this culvert during periodic checks between December 1946 and the winter of 1972–73.

Table 68

Weights and measurements of *Plecotus rafinesquii* from Indiana

Character	n	$\bar{x}$	Range	SD	SE
Total length (mm)	6	96.5	84-104	8.0	3.3
Tail length (mm)	6	45.8	43-50	2.8	1.1
Hind foot (mm)	5	10.0	9-11	0.7	0.3
Ear (mm)	6	32.1	27-35	1.1	2.7
Tragus (mm)	5	13.6	13-15	0.9	0.4
Forearm (mm)	6	43.8	43-45	0.4	1.0
Wing expanse (mm)	3	276.3	225-305	25.7	44.6
Weight (grams)	3	10.6	10.2-11.2	0.5	0.3

Map 25. Rafinesque's Big-eared Bat,
Plecotus rafinesquii, in Indiana

HABITS. Most of the 17 big-eared bats observed in Indiana were single animals, but two were found in a cave on three occasions. Two found on 28 December were hanging about 2 inches apart on a cave wall, according to R. D. Kirkpatrick, who first observed them. Hahn observed six big-eared bats in the Spring Mill caves during the winter of 1906–07 and another during May 1907. He was making almost daily visits to these caves over that time period.

The big-eared bat appears to prefer to roost, even in winter, in the twilight zone near cave entrances. Here, the temperature is often quite cool and air movement is sometimes considerable. The only other bat occurring in Indiana that chooses similar winter roosting sites is the big brown bat. Evidently both species are equally hardy. The *Plecotus rafinesquii* that Wilson captured in Tippecanoe County had entered the culvert between 6 and 13 December. Minimum daily temperatures at a nearby

weather station during this period ranged from 22 to 37°F, and maximum temperatures ranged from 30 to 49°F. At the site where the bat hung the temperature was 48°F. Hahn (1909) reported two big-eared bats that "flew out into the cold air" from a cave on 22 February, but he did not indicate the air temperature at the time. Hahn (1908b) found that big-eared bats at Spring Mill in 1906–07 were all "not far within the cave." Other observers have found big-eared bats 25 feet within a small cave, two others about 60 feet from the cave entrance, and one 137 feet from a culvert entrance. Most were hanging from the cave wall, but the one in the culvert was suspended from the ceiling. Two individuals were hanging separately about 6 feet from the cave floor, and two were hanging near each other 12 feet from the floor of a cavern.

Evidently this bat is easily aroused from hibernation or is more alert than most other bats during the winter. Hahn was able to capture only two of the seven he observed. A few minutes after Kirkpatrick found two hanging near each other, one had moved to a new location in the cave. When the bats are sleeping, their long ears are usually curled along either side of the neck, and the end of the forearm of the bat overlaps the ear. As the bats awaken, the ears are uncurled slowly until they are straight. A male found in deep torpor on 28 December had the ears laid along the neck and shoulders, but the ears were uncurled.

Despite Hahn's intensive work in the Spring Mill caves and the fact that he observed more big-eared bats than any other person in Indiana, he did not see the species flying about at dusk and decided that it was a late flyer, probably not emerging until the light was too dim for observation. Bats of this species that Hahn kept in captivity were swift and steady flyers. Like Hahn, we have never seen a *Plecotus* in flight outside a cave, and none have been collected by shooting bats at dusk in Indiana.

FOOD. We have no data on the food habits of this species in Indiana, but we assume that it feeds heavily on moths. Captive animals kept by Hahn refused to eat and soon died.

REPRODUCTION. No *Plecotus* has been recorded from Indiana during the breeding season. A male taken 13 December had testes measuring 2 by 4 mm, but single males collected 28 December and 12 January had scrotal testes measuring 4 by 7 mm.

PARASITES AND DISEASES. We have no data from Indiana specimens.

DECIMATING FACTORS. No data are available from Indiana.

TAXONOMY. The subspecies in Indiana is currently known as *Plecotus rafinesquii rafinesquii* Lesson. Other names that have been applied to Indiana big-eared bats appear in the synonymy at the beginning of this account. On the assumption that the two *Plecotus* mentioned by Butler (1895) from Putnam County were *P. townsendii*, some authors have indicated that *P. townsendii* occurs in Indiana. The specimen that Butler examined (now lost) was never seen by these authors, but Hall and Kelson (1959) mapped the range of *P. townsendii* across Indiana. Since all extant specimens of *Plecotus* from the state are *rafinesquii*, we think *P. townsendii* should be eliminated from the Indiana list. We are aware that both *P. townsendii* and *P. rafinesquii* breed in Kentucky. Clearly, further research on this genus is needed in our region.

SELECTED REFERENCES. Barbour and Davis, 1969; Hall, 1963; Handley, 1959; Hoffmeister and Goodpaster, 1963; Jones and Suttkus, 1975; Wilson, 1960.

Order LAGOMORPHA

Family Leporidae

Eastern Cottontail
Sylvilagus floridanus (J. A. Allen)

Cottontail Rabbit, Rabbit, Common Rabbit, Gray Rabbit, Cottontail, Prairie Cottontail, Middle Western Cottontail, Northeastern Cottontail, Mearn's Cottontail, Hare

Lepus americanus: Wied, 1839
Lepus sylvaticus: Haymond, 1870
Lepus floridanus: Elliott, 1907
Sylvilagus floridanus: Hahn, 1907b

DESCRIPTION. This is the only rabbit common throughout Indiana, and among native mammals can be confused only with the larger swamp rabbit, found in a few localities in the extreme southwestern part of the state. Released or escaped domestic (or "San Juan") rabbits (*Oryctolagus cuniculus*) may be encountered occasionally. The eastern cottontail is grayish to brownish above, sprinkled with black. The upper surfaces of the hind feet are whitish; the upper surface of the tail is grayish. The swamp rabbit is more reddish-brown and has more blackish on the back; the upper surface of its tail is brownish and the upper surfaces of the hind feet are tan or pale brown. Both species have a reddish nape patch, which is somewhat variable in color. Young and subadult cottontails have a white spot on the forehead, absent in the swamp rabbit. We have observed only minor color variations in Indiana cottontails, mainly in the color of the dorsum, which is more brownish in some individuals. The skull of the cottontail is smaller and differs in other ways from that of the swamp rabbit (see Figs. 23 and 24 and the species account for the swamp rabbit). *Sylvilagus* is the only genus of Indiana mammal in which the two pairs of upper incisors are situated one pair directly posterior to the other (see Fig. 16).

Weights and measurements are shown in Table 69. The dental formula is

$$I \frac{2}{1} C \frac{0}{0} P \frac{3}{2} M \frac{3}{3} = 28.$$

STATUS AND DISTRIBUTION. Although drainage and clearing of brushlands and cultivation have depleted much habitat, the cottontail still is the most common and most sought after game mammal in Indiana. It occurs throughout the state where suitable habitat is present, and may be locally abundant. For many years, about two million cottontails have been harvested annually by hunters in the state.

Miscellaneous reports indicate that cottontails were not common throughout Indiana at the time of settlement. No doubt the forested areas harbored relatively few, but the species must have occurred in some numbers on and

Table 69

Weights and measurements of
Sylvilagus floridanus from Indiana

	Males	Females
Total length (mm)		
n	52	39
x̄	420.1	408.6
range	355-537	312-476
SD	34.4	36.6
SE	4.8	5.9
Tail length (mm)		
n	50	38
x̄	47.4	47.9
range	30-64	30-67
SD	8.2	9.4
SE	1.2	1.5
Hind foot (mm)		
n	52	39
x̄	96.2	95.1
range	88-105	80-104
SD	4.2	4.7
SE	0.6	0.8
Weight (grams)		
n	21	28
x̄	1176.5	1252.2
range	907-1392	798-1570
SD	141.9	250.2
SE	31.0	47.3

near the prairies. John Johnston, a fur trader at Fort Wayne (Allen County) handled few rabbit skins between 1804 and 1811. He shipped only 39 skins, all in 1908 (Griswold, 1927). David Thomas found cottontails "very numerous" in southern Indiana in 1816 (Lindley, 1916). There were reportedly "no rabbits" at Deer Creek (Carroll County) in 1827 (Stewart, 1872). Wied (1839) recorded the cottontail as common at New Harmony (Posey County) in 1832. In writing about this rabbit in Wayne County, Plummer (1844) noted that "The hare is common, and does considerable mischief to our nurseries and young orchards, by gnawing the bark off the trees during winter." Cox (1893) listed the species as "very abundant" in Randolph County. The cottontail was said to be "very numerous" in places in Lake County in 1884 (Ball, 1884). Evermann and Butler (1894b) simply stated that it was "abundant all over the state." Evermann and Clark (1920) wrote the following about the status of this rabbit about Lake Maxinkuckee (Marshall County):

During the fall of 1899 up to January 21, one man who hunted only occasionally and only in the immediate vicinity of the lake, killed 76 rabbits. In the fall of 1900 one hunter had killed 56 by December 31. In 1901 they were said to be plentiful in February and on December 10, one hunter shot 19. On January 2, 1903, hunters obtained 21 in the vicinity of Mud Lake near the head of Aubeenaubee Creek; December 14, four hunters got 20 and on December 30, one got 8.

These authors also commented on rabbit hunting in the region and its effect on rabbit populations:

In this region the Rabbit is hunted rather persistently every fall and winter from October to February and the total number killed is great; nevertheless the animals are so prolific that the supply usually keeps up pretty well. During some years it is less abundant. The season of 1908–9 was a period of scarcity. Generally these periods last only for a single season, and the next season is one of usual abundance. They are in best condition in November to January and these are the principal months when they are hunted. Unfortunately a few local pothunters have been using ferrets, a method which affords no sport, is entirely unsportsmanlike, gives the Rabbit no chance, and which cannot be too severely condemned. . . . The Rabbit as an article of food is becoming more highly appreciated in recent years and there is also an increasing market for its fur. With proper laws providing adequate protection a large and valuable catch can be made every year.

Ralph W. Stark, in a letter to Mumford, related that two men killed 54 cottontails in a

Eastern cottontail. Photo by Larry E. Lehman

single day in 1902 within 640 acres in Boone County. Cockrum (1907), speaking of cottontails in Indiana as a whole, remarked that "There are 20 here now where there was only one in 1840." McAtee (1907) reported the cottontail as "abundant" in the Bloomington area. Near Mitchell (Lawrence County) Hahn (1908b) found the species "very abundant" in 1906 and 1907. Hahn (1909) failed to write anything regarding the status of the cottontail on a statewide basis, but did record the following comments:

I think it is safe to say that where sinkholes, stony hillsides or thickets and uncultivated land have been left for retreats, the rabbits have not been reduced in numbers since the country was first settled. Although shotguns play havoc with their numbers, these agencies of destruction have been counterbalanced by the extermination of wolves, coyotes, wildcats and other enemies. But where intensive cultivation removes harboring places the rabbits are rapidly thinned out, although they do not completely disappear, even in the suburbs of the largest cities.

Evermann and Clark (1920) wrote, "The Rabbit or Cottontail is an abundant and well known animal of the Maxinkuckee region" of Marshall County. Lyon (1923) found the species "fairly common" in the dunes region of Porter County. Engels (1933) considered rabbits "common" in St. Joseph County and noted that "while not numerous enough to excite attention, [they] seem to be holding their own with the hunters." Lyon (1936) summarized the status of the cottontail in Indiana by saying, "It is found everywhere throughout the state except in the centers of large cities."

Mumford and Handley (1956) noted that this rabbit was scarce in most parts of Jackson County during the 1952–53 and 1953–54 hunting seasons, and relatively few were observed dead along roads in the county. Lindsay (1960) found it "very common throughout the area" in Jefferson and Ripley counties in the early 1950s. Data tabulated concerning mammals found dead along Indiana roads (see Table 20) may indicate the current abundance of the cottontail, which ranked second (the opossum ranked first).

Data gathered from hunter questionnaires by Barnes (1946a) indicated that more than two million cottontails were killed annually in the state, nearly three million in 1941. There was a decrease in the annual kill between 1945 and 1952, then a gradual increase to 1956. But the average kill for the ten-year period 1950 to 1959 was still more than two million. In 1960, the kill dropped and remained below that figure through 1966. We have no data for the period 1967 to 1977. Although the questionnaire does not give precise data, mostly due to the type of sample taken each year, the trend indicates that cottontail populations have declined considerably.

Specimens have been preserved from the majority of Indiana counties (Map 26).

Population data for the cottontail in Indiana are largely lacking, for no one has yet intensively studied this species in the state. Rabbits may have high populations locally, as evidenced by the numbers killed by hunters in certain areas. On 7 January 1943, six hunters allegedly shot 35 cottontails in a 1.5-acre field dominated by sweet clover and giant

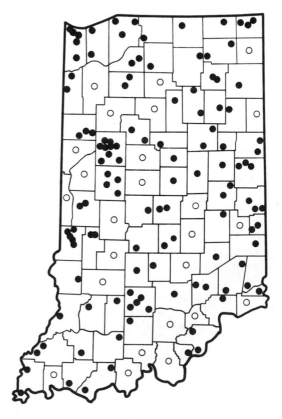

Map 26.   The Eastern Cottontail, *Sylvilagus floridanus*, in Indiana

ragweed. Three inches of snow had fallen the previous night. During the same season, 239 rabbits were shot on a 710-acre farm in Hancock County. During the 1965–66 hunting season, 1,148 were shot on the Pigeon River Fish and Wildlife Area. In the 1954 and 1955 hunting seasons, hunters killed one rabbit for every 16 and 12 acres respectively, on the Willow Slough Fish and Wildlife Area (Newton County). In 1955 and in 1956, there was a rabbit killed for every 3.5 and 2.9 acres respectively, on the Tri-County Fish and Wildlife Area (Kosciusko County). About 900 acres were hunted at Tri-County and 3,000 acres at Willow Slough.

Through the years, many attempts have been made to increase the cottontail population in Indiana by introducing animals from other states. In the May 1934 issue of *Outdoor Indiana*, the caption of a photograph of one such release reads: "Steps to relieve the scarcity of rabbits in some parts of the state were taken recently by the Department of Conservation when 1,800 rabbits trapped in Kansas, were distributed through game wardens." Such ventures are generally a waste of money, but appeal to various clubs and other agencies who do not understand ecological principles. Restocking depleted habitats that have a potential for supporting cottontails may be warranted, depending upon the situation, but usually, if the habitat requirements of the rabbits are fulfilled, the animals will most likely populate the area on their own. If habitat conditions are not suitable, the animals simply cannot live there, regardless of how many are introduced.

HABITAT. Cottontails are encountered in most types of habitats but are most numerous in overgrown fields of weeds, briers, and brush near croplands. They occur in extensive woodlands sparingly, usually near openings, but may be found in ungrazed woodlots, smaller wooded tracts, and in young pine tree plantations. Many thrive in cities where they can find vacant lots, gardens, shrub plantings, golf courses, parks, and other areas which afford enough shelter and food. Heavy ground cover is one prerequisite for optimum cottontail habitat. It is especially favorable when interspersed with thickets of blackberries and roses of various species. Old fields with a mixture of weeds, bluegrass, some shrubs, and the low, sprawling briers of dewberry

may support high populations. The burrows of woodchucks are used extensively by rabbits, especially in inclement weather.

In Lawrence County, Hahn (1908b) found that "sink holes and rocks afford homes and hiding places" for rabbits. And he noted that "Now and then rabbits wander into the caves and usually perish if they get away from the sinkholes through which they enter the larger chambers." Later (Hahn, 1909) he again stressed the importance of sinkholes, stony hillsides, thickets, and uncultivated land in providing good habitat for cottontails. In the Lake Maxinkuckee region, Evermann and Clark (1920) made observations on habitats:

The large areas of uncultivated swamp-land, abounding in tall grasses, sedges and small brushy shrubs, the tamarack and other swamps, and the considerable tracts of timber, often with heavy undergrowth, give a wide choice of location and refuge. In all these, Rabbits are usually quite abundant. Although apt to be found almost anywhere, there are choice places where they are particularly common. Among these are the thickets, fields, and Farrar's woods at the south end of the lake; the shores of Lost Lake and the woods and fields from Green's to Walley's and beyond; the fields, swamps and prairie westward to Manitou and Houghton lakes, including the tamarack swamp; and the low ground along Aubeenaubee Creek on the east side.

In the dunes region of Porter County, Lyon (1924) observed rabbits "in nearly every locality except the fore dunes." Engels (1933) noted that "In South Bend, they live and breed in small empty lots with scant cover, within a mile and a half of the center of the city." In writing about Indiana habitats, Lyon (1936) stated, "I have seen them in the alleys of South Bend within ten blocks of the business district. I have flushed them in all sorts of situations from open fields to dense woods and swamp land. They are probably more frequently found in thickets, brushy places and open woods." In the early 1950s, when cottontails were relatively scarce in Jackson County, some hunters reported the best success where there was abundant cover along small stream valleys, rather than in upland areas (Mumford and Handley, 1956).

Haller (1949) reported on the utilization of habitat by cottontails in the fall during farming operations. During harvesting, one cottontail was flushed for every 4.4 acres of wheat and one for every 13 acres of oats. "After the harvest of small grain, cottontails were primarily concentrated in soybean fields, although corn fields were used to a lesser degree. The harvest of the soybeans results in concentrations in corn fields. Corn picking caused another movement to the small grain stubble; however, after completion of this operation, use of the corn fields was again noted." On Haller's study area in Tippecanoe County, live-trapping was conducted for 32 nights between 17 January and 1 March 1947 in cultivated fields. The best results were obtained in unpastured corn stubble and fallow fields. The number of trap-nights required to capture one cottontail in each habitat was as follows: permanent pasture, 224; pastured corn stubble, 224; wheat stubble, 112; soybean stubble, 74.6; unpastured corn stubble, 56; fallow field, 56. None was trapped in hayfields.

At dusk on the evening of 14 July 1976, Fredrick H. Montague, Jr., counted 25 cottontails within one mile while driving along a country road bordered by a railroad grade and a cornfield (Tippecanoe County).

ASSOCIATED SPECIES. The eastern cottontail shares its habitat with both the red and gray fox, the opossum, the striped skunk, the long-tailed weasel, the mink, the badger, the woodchuck, and the white-tailed deer. There is a close association with the woodchuck, whose burrows are commonly used by cottontails in winter (Schmeltz and Whitaker, 1977). Smaller associates are the prairie vole, meadow vole, deer mouse, white-footed mouse, meadow jumping mouse, thirteen-lined ground squirrel, house mouse, shrews, and other small mammals, depending upon the area. Both species of foxes prey on rabbits rather extensively, but the habitat of the red fox is more similar to that of the cottontail than is the habitat of the gray fox; the gray fox is more inclined to inhabit wooded terrain.

HABITS. Cottontails spend most of the daylight hours in a form, "bed," or "nest" on the ground. Forms are usually in good cover, so that the animal is sheltered from sight from all directions except the one it faces and escapes to when disturbed. Forms may be in quite heavy cover in cold weather or in sparse cover in warmer weather. Sometimes old rolls of fence wire, old car or farm machinery discards, stacks of lumber, brush piles, piles of stumps, steel pipes, or other objects serve as resting sites. Drainage pipes, tiles, and small culverts are also used; in these cases no vegetation is present. A form may be used by an individual more than once, but a new form may also be used each day. A cottontail occupied a form in a small clump of grass on Whitaker's closely mowed lawn for several days. If one looked closely, the rabbit could easily be seen from several feet away. In pine plantations, shrubby areas, and woodlots, cottontails frequently construct a form at the base of a stump or tree, so that they are more protected from the rear. Ground burrows made by other, larger mammals also serve as daytime resting places for cottontails. On a cold day in late November, George R. Parker and Mumford were hunting cottontails in Fulton County. Two nights before, from 6 to 8 inches of snow had fallen, but rabbit tracks were almost nonexistent. The few tracks noted were all within 20 yards of burrows. One rabbit was seen near the entrance to a burrow about noon; it may have emerged to sun itself.

Most cottontail activity is in early morning, late evening, or at night. It is not unusual in early spring to see rabbits out in the daytime, but many of these are possibly females with nests or young. There is sometimes marked activity just before dark, especially in late summer when young are out and about. At other seasons, dawn and shortly after are good times to observe cottontails. Herald A. Demaree, Jr., had some data on animals killed by cars and by shooting that suggest females emerge earlier in the evening than males. One can most easily observe rabbits where roads parallel good rabbit cover, for during their active periods they spend much time along or actually on the road. They are also attracted to other open areas at night and appear on lawns, mowed areas, in cemeteries, on golf courses, in pastures, and in other places where vegetation is low.

An individual probably spends most of its life within a fairly small area. When a cottontail is chased by dogs, it will soon circle back near the site where it was originally flushed. Rabbit hunters take advantage of this behavior.

Cottontails swim well, although Dellinger (1951) noted that they swam with convulsive kicks of the hind feet.

This is not normally a gregarious species,

and even where rabbits are plentiful they are not usually seen in large groups. Two or more may be seen together during the courtship and mating season, but one most often sees a single animal. Nancy Miller has seen as many as eight at a time, however, chasing and playing on her farm lawn. She has also observed five lying on their bellies, legs stretched out behind, as they nibbled white clover heads.

Although swamp rabbits often get on top of logs and stumps, cottontails are not thought to do so regularly. Sean Kelly captured a cottontail in a mirror trap set for ruffed grouse on top of a drumming log being used by the grouse in April.

Cottontails sometimes squeal loudly, almost a scream, when handled by humans or captured by predators.

Adult cottontails (presumably females) have been observed several times trying to protect their nests or young from the depredations of crows (Kirkpatrick, 1950). In these cases, the rabbits excitedly hopped about near the crows, and in one instance seemed to rush at the birds.

FOOD. We have done no stomach analyses on cottontails from Indiana. The vegetable food it consumes no doubt includes many species of plants. Specific food plants mentioned by other writers include hydrangea, hepatica, "red" locust, "ironwood," shellbark hickory, black walnut, clover, Christmas fern, wahoo, sugar maple, dogwood, sassafras, alfalfa, corn, cabbage, peas, beets, and apples. Both Hahn and Evermann and Clark (1920) mentioned damage (sometimes extensive) done to fruit trees in winter, when the rabbits may completely girdle the trees in obtaining their bark. Such damage usually occurs when snow cover hides more desirable food items. It has also been noted that during heavy snows cottontails will strip the bark from sumac, black cherry, and *Ailanthus*. We have observations of their feeding on multiflora rose, cultivated beans in a garden, red osier dogwood, sycamore, persimmon, and briers. Blackberry briers as large as 3/8 inch in diameter have been seen that were clipped off by cottontails during periods of deep snow. At the same time, sprouts were noticed that had their bark removed to a height of 2.5 feet above the ground. H. P. Weeks, Jr., has observed that cottontails completely consume dried lamb's-quarters plants during winter;

they seem to seek out this plant. Dellinger noted that rabbits ate fallen apples in orchards.

The cottontail has the ability to eat a great amount of food in a relatively short time, thus reducing its period of exposure to predators while it is feeding in the open. The food is partially chewed and gulped down, but not immediately digested. It moves into the small intestine, where it forms soft, green fecal pellets. When the rabbit reaches a protected spot, it defecates these green pellets and reingests them, a process called coprophagy. This time, the pellets are digested more fully as they pass again through the digestive tract. The green pellets are about the same size and shape as completely digested pellets, but are merely masses of green vegetation. Kirkpatrick (1956) reported on this behavior in Indiana cottontails.

Hahn (1909) described the behavior of cottontails eating soil:

During the summer evenings rabbits will lie at full length on bare patches of compact clay and gnaw at the earth. This may be for the purpose of obtaining salt or other mineral matter, but I have watched them doing it along paths and in fields where there was no reason to believe that there was a considerable quantity of salt in the soil. At Mitchell I used to see them repeatedly in the same place in the open woods near the cabin on University Farm. The tooth marks were plainly visible as long as there was no rain, and in this way it was possible to form an idea of how much they ate. During one period of ten days they gnawed away the earth to a depth of from one-fourth to one-half an inch, or even more, on an area of approximately a square yard.

There is the possibility that the animals seen by Hahn were frequenting natural salt licks, which occur in other parts of southern Indiana. During his studies on various species of mammals and their need for salt (at the Crane Naval Ammunition Depot, Martin County), H. P. Weeks, Jr., noticed that at certain seasons of the year cottontails tended to sit on the roads in early morning and late evening. Some of these animals were actually licking the roads (which were constructed of asphalt), and were assumed to be obtaining salt from the road surface. Others sitting on the roads were assumed to be seeking salt. Regular roadside counts made by Weeks throughout the year revealed that cottontails were noted only from April through August. More were seen in July than in any other month. Of 104 cottontails counted on 606 miles of road in July, 22 were along the road (grassy shoulders) and 82 were on the road surface. Of the 82 on the road surface, 6 were actually licking the road. In June, 9 of 39 seen on the road were licking the surface; all 3 seen in May were licking the surface; 1 of 14 noted on the road in August was licking; none of 3 observed in April was licking the surface of the road. Mileages for the various months were about equal. It is interesting that for the months September through March not a single rabbit was seen either along the roadside or on the road during 4,566 miles of censusing.

Hahn (1908b) made a point of observing winter food habits of rabbits on his study area in Lawrence County during the winter of 1906–07.

During the winter I was at the University Farm the State Forester complained vigorously of the damage done by rabbits to the young trees on the forest reservation about 50 miles farther south. Accordingly I paid close attention to their winter food in my locality. Comparatively little damage was done to the young hard-wood trees. The vegetation most often eaten was as follows: Wahoo, hydrangea, Christmas fern, sassafras, hepatica, red locust, and ironwood. The shellbark hickory, walnut, and sugar maple shoots were eaten infrequently. I did not observe an oak, ash, or tulip-tree which had been injured by the rabbits, the abundance of the more tender vegetation serving as an effective protection to the more valuable species.

He also remarked on the general feeding habits of this rabbit. "Occasionally they damage gardens, eating cabbage, beets and other vegetables. I have seen a small plot of peas in an unfenced garden cropped so closely by the rabbits that they never reached the height of an inch. Clover, alfalfa, corn in the shock or the growing ears in the milk are also eaten." They also eat green bean and broccoli plants in gardens.

REPRODUCTION. In late winter and early spring, courtship activities commence. Pairs or small groups may be seen actively chasing each other about. Courting is quite intensive and physical; at times one or more individuals may jump straight up into the air for a considerable height. After this strenuous pre-

copulatory activity, the females are bred, and the members of the pairs then go separate ways. The gestation period is about 28 to 32 days.

The breeding season is long. Young cottontails were found at Brookville (Franklin County) on 8 January (Evermann and Butler, 1894b). A gravid female with "acorn size" embryos was examined by H. A. Demaree, Jr., on 19 October. Several litters are probably produced each year. Of 26 females collected by Demaree between 13 March and 9 April, 17 were in their first pregnancy and 9 were in the early stages of a second pregnancy. Haller (1949) examined 3 females (Tippecanoe County) trapped between 11 and 20 February that contained "pea-sized" embryos; lactating females were first trapped during the first week of April. He also obtained information regarding testis size in males, by examination of live animals. The 40 males captured in January had an average testis length of 29.6 mm; 9 taken in February had an average testis length of 43.2 mm; 2 March-taken specimens each had 47 mm testes; 8 males in April averaged 50.1 mm in testis length.

The young are born in a nest constructed of grasses and other soft plant materials, to which is added considerable hair from the female's body. Nests are usually constructed in rather open sites, with sparse vegetation, and are shallow, cuplike depressions in the ground. They are so well hidden and covered that even on a well-kept lawn they may be difficult to detect. Recorded nest sites include lawns, flower beds, close-cropped pastures, weed fields, roadside ditches, the center of an old road, weed stubble, and other treeless areas. Haller (1948) recorded the location of 13 nests plowed up in one season; 9 were in hay fields, 2 in wheat stubble, 1 in corn stubble, and 1 in a pine plantation. The excavated nest depressions are usually 3 to 6 inches wide. Kirkpatrick (1960) reported on a nest made mainly of alfalfa stems, which the female must have transported from the nearest source 50 yards away. The nest had been constructed in the side of a pile of topsoil about 2 feet tall.

The behavior of an adult female at her nest containing young was witnessed by Mumford on 5 April. At 6:30 P.M. (sunset was at 7:15), the female came slowly hopping and walking across a lawn to the nest near the foundation of a house. She stopped at the nest site and scratched briefly with her feet (undoubtedly uncovering the young in the hidden nest). She then sat perfectly motionless for 10 minutes nursing the young. The next 4 minutes she sat in the same position, but preened her feet and chest. The last minute she was at the nest she scratched at the leaves and grass briefly, turned 90 degrees and scratched again, then turned another 90 degrees and repeated the process before hopping away. Thus, she spent 15 minutes at the nest. Although the nest site was watched each evening through 13 April, when the young left it, the adult was not seen there again.

D. L. Allen observed a cottontail's nesting cycle on his lawn. The freshly dug nesting hole was found 18 May and the 6 young were observed 6 feet from the nest on 1 July. On the afternoon of 2 July, all of the young were back in the nest; the young were without covering. The nest was empty on 3 July.

The number of embryos in 26 gravid females ranged from 3 to 7 and averaged 4.8. In 5 nests for which we have complete counts of the young, 4, 4, 5, 6, and 6 were found. Haller (1949) reported that 30 litters contained from 3 to 7 young and averaged 4.8. He also recorded 58 young in 13 nests destroyed by plowing operations in one year and 101 young in 21 nests plowed under another year. Kirkpatrick (1960) recorded a nest with 12 young.

At birth, young cottontails are blind and without hair. A warm nest is, obviously, important to their survival. When they leave the nest, they are still relatively small (about 4 to 5 inches long). Their size and the fact that they are mainly on their own after leaving the nest make them vulnerable to many predators and accidents. On two occasions young were released from the sunken entrance to a crawl space beneath a house. Others are sometimes trapped by falling into window wells from which they cannot escape.

PARASITES AND DISEASES. Wilson (1961) recorded the ticks *Ixodes dentatus*, *Dermacentor variabilis*, and *Haemophysalis leporis-palustris* on cottontails from Indiana. He found the fleas *Cediopsylla simplex*, *Odontopsyllus multispinosus*, and *Epitedia wenmanni*. About half the cottontails exam-

ined by Wilson were parasitized by the flea *Cediopsylla simplex*. In turn, this flea was found to have the mite *Cheyletiella parasitivorex* attached to it. A cottontail from Gibson County was host to a single specimen of a tick tentatively identified as *Amblyomma americanum*. This tick was previously known in Indiana from a dog, from man, and from a wood thrush. *Dermacentor variabilis* and *Epitedia wenmanni* are most often found on rodents, although both have been recorded from a wide variety of hosts. The tick *H. leporis-palustris* has been recorded from an Indiana cottontail as late as 5 December (Lopp, 1943). Demaree (1978) recorded the fleas *Cediopsylla simplex*, *Odontopsyllus multispinosus*, and one specimen of *Atyphloceras bishopi*, ticks *Haemaphysalis leporis-palustris* and one specimen of *Ixodes dentatus*, and *Cuterebra* sp. from Indiana cottontails. He also recorded fibroma tumors on 29 rabbits from Indiana.

We have examined 131 Indiana cottontails for ectoparasites (Table 70). Major parasites were the flea *Cediopsylla simplex*, the ticks *Ixodes dentatus* and *Haemophysalis leporis-palustris*, the mite *Cheyletiella parasitivorax*, and the chiggers *Neotrombicula whartoni* and *Eutrombicula alfreddugesi*.

Lopp reported that 36 of 40 cottontails examined in the fall of 1942 had tapeworm cysts; the species of tapeworm was not determined.

Tularemia is perhaps the most important known disease of Indiana rabbits, because man is susceptible to it. The first report from Indiana of tularemia in man was in 1928, and from 1928 to 1941 there were 528 cases recorded by the Indiana State Board of Health. The highest incidence (32 cases) was in Vanderburgh County and the next (29 cases) was in Marion County. In 66 case histories studied, 58 of the afflicted persons had been in direct contact with rabbits, 3 with cats, 1 each with a squirrel, a dog, or a tick (Lopp, 1942).

DECIMATING FACTORS. The cottontail has a number of enemies. It makes up a large percentage of the diets of both red and gray foxes. Many fall prey to domestic cats and dogs, and no doubt other carnivores prey on them. Domestic cats are capable of killing full-grown adult cottontails. Rabbit remains have been identified in the pellets of barn

Table 70

Ectoparasites and other associates of *Sylvilagus floridanus* (n = 131) from Indiana
(from Wassel, Whitaker, and Spicka, 1980)

Parasites	Parasites		Hosts Parasitized	
	Total	Average	Total	Percent
Fleas (Siphonaptera)				
Cediopsylla simplex	249	1.90	53	40.5
Odontopsyllus multispinosus	15	0.11	9	6.9
Ctenocephalides felis	3	0.02	2	1.5
Orchopeas leucopus	1	0.01	1	0.8
Flies (Diptera)				
Cuterebra sp.	5	0.04	4	3.1
Mites (Acarina) other than chiggers				
Cheyletiella parasitivorax	1313±	10.02	19	14.5
Marsupialichus brasiliensis	150±	1.15	1	0.8
Psorobia sp.	100±	0.76	1	0.8
Androlaelaps fahrenholzi	12	0.09	9	6.9
Dermanyssus sp.	2	0.02	2	1.5
Glycyphagidae	2	0.02	2	1.5
Ornithonyssus bacoti	1	0.01	1	0.8
Pygmephorus designatus	1	0.01	1	0.8
Chigger mites (Trombiculidae)				
Eutrombicula alfreddugesi	531±	4.05	6	4.6
Neotrombicula whartoni	200	1.53	17	13.0
Euschoengastia setosa	6	0.05	2	1.5
Neotrombicula lipovskyi	3	0.02	2	1.5
Ticks (Ixodides)				
Ixodes dentatus	353	2.69	38	29.0
Haemaphysalis leporis-palustris	277	2.11	45	34.4
Dermacentor variabilis	49	0.37	10	7.6

owls, long-eared owls, and great horned owls (Kirkpatrick and Conaway, 1947). The larger hawks take a toll; Frank D. Haller observed a rough-legged hawk capture a cottontail in a stubble field during a period of heavy snow. Mumford and Danner (1974) found cottontail remains in marsh hawk pellets. Merle E. Jacobs saw adult marsh hawks bring partial rabbit carcasses to their nest to feed the young. Kirkpatrick (1950) reported several observations of crows killing and eating nestling cottontails.

Mumford captured a large black rat snake that contained a young cottontail; Minton (1944) recorded a similar incident. Large numbers of rabbits are killed on roads and highways each year, and hunting now accounts for about 1.5 million annually in Indiana. Evermann and Clark (1920) suggested that spring flooding drowned many young in

nests, and Haller noted that spring plowing destroyed nests and young. Hahn (1907b) and Bader and Hall (1960) found remains of cottontails in Indiana caves. Herald A. Demaree, Jr., told us that in the fall of 1976 some cottontails found dead had become impacted by eating agricultural lime.

TAXONOMY. The subspecies in Indiana is *Sylvilagus floridanus mearnsii* (J. A. Allen). For at least forty years, cottontails have been imported from various states for release in Indiana (*Outdoor Indiana*, 1934). Among the states supplying these animals are Kansas, Missouri, and Wyoming. The fate of the imported animals is unknown, but certainly other subspecies were introduced by these importations.

SELECTED REFERENCES. Haugen, 1942, 1943; Nelson, 1909.

Swamp Rabbit
Sylvilagus aquaticus (Bachman)

Water Hare

Lepus aquaticus: Evermann and Butler, 1894b

Sylvilagus aquaticus: Harrison and Hickie, 1931

DESCRIPTION. The swamp rabbit resembles a large cottontail and under most field conditions is extremely difficult to distinguish from the cottontail. In general the swamp rabbit is darker brown and has a more liberal sprinkling of blackish on the back. The rump tends to be brownish, rather than grayish as in the cottontail. The tail is narrower and browner above than that of *S. floridanus*. In addition, the dorsal surface of the hind feet are tan in the swamp rabbit, whitish in the eastern cottontail. There is a distinct reddish or rusty colored nape patch in both species, but that of the swamp rabbit is duller.

The skulls of the two species are similar, but that of the swamp rabbit is larger (greatest length about 90 mm, compared to about 70 mm in the eastern cottontail). In adult swamp rabbits, the supraorbital process is completely fused to the skull; in the eastern cottontail there is incomplete fusion of these bones (see Figs. 23, 24). C. M. Kirkpatrick noted an odor given off by the swamp rabbit's anal glands.

Weights and measurements are summarized in Table 71. The dental formula is

$$I \frac{2}{1} C \frac{0}{0} P \frac{3}{2} M \frac{3}{3} = 28.$$

STATUS AND DISTRIBUTION. Evermann and Butler (1894b) included the swamp rabbit on their list of mammals to be searched for in Indiana. The next year, Butler (1895) wrote the following: "Knox Co., Mr. Chansler says a brown rabbit has been seen there by different persons. It is said to be much larger than the common gray rabbit. It seems probable that two forms of swamp hares will be found in the lower Wabash valley, the one above noted, . . . and the smaller, *Lepus palustris*. . . ." The large, brown rabbits

mentioned by E. J. Chansler were undoubtedly swamp rabbits, but *Lepus (Sylvilagus) palustris* probably never reached Indiana. Hahn (1909) evidently contacted E. J. Chansler about the presence of the swamp rabbit in Knox County, for he wrote, "I have no additional records excepting Chansler's statement to me which is as follows: 'A very few of these are found here (Knox County). They are larger than the common rabbit and of a brownish color. One of these rabbits was seen by my brother Will, September 17, 1898; also another by Will Staley. It was also seen in 1894; no recent records; seems to be rare; usually found about water and swampy places.'" Hahn went on to say, "I consider these reliable enough to give the species a place in the fauna of the State, although no specimens are extant." But later he added, "The water hare is doubtless extinct within our limits at the present time, but it has always been too rare to have been of much importance in the fauna of the State."

The first specimens of the swamp rabbit to be preserved from Indiana were four collected in Posey County, on 24 June, 1 July, and 27 August 1930 by Harrison and Hickie (1931). Although no specimens had been collected in the locality, Lyon (1936) added the following information: "A youth near Yankeetown, Warrick County, described rather accurately very large, dark colored rabbits which he had shot in a cane brake in the vicinity." Charles M. Kirkpatrick and Mumford shot a swamp rabbit near Halfmoon Pond (Posey County) on 22 March 1949. On 9 January 1959, Ralph D. Kirkpatrick and others collected the first specimen for Spencer County (Kirkpatrick, 1961). According to David Howell, a swamp rabbit was killed in Spencer County in the fall of 1976 (newspaper clipping). Don R. Helms told Mumford that he thought swamp rabbits occurred near Yankeetown; on 29 October 1960 they shot one there. We do not know how long hunters had been shooting swamp rabbits in Gibson County (and other counties), but Terry Tichenor gave Mumford the skull of one he shot in the Broad Pond area on 20 October 1966. (We are indebted to Carol Davidson,

Swamp rabbit. Photo by Karl H. Maslowski

formerly in the Biology Department, Oakland City College, for making us aware of this specimen; Tichenor was one of her students.)

Ted L. Terrel studied the swamp rabbit in southwestern Indiana (mostly in Gibson County) from September 1967 to June 1969. Most of the following discussion on the species is from Terrel's thesis (1969) and from a subsequent paper (Terrel, 1972). The area studied was a narrow ridge about a mile long and one-fourth mile wide (approximately 120 acres) in the Broad Pond Swamp. The swamp was an old oxbow abandoned by the Wabash River, located about 9 miles west-northwest of Princeton. The site was known locally as Cane Ridge. The study area has since been logged and mostly flooded in the creation of a cooling lake for Northern Indiana Public Service Company.

Conservation Officer Phillip N. Ohmit wrote to Mumford (16 April 1959) that he had seen swamp rabbits killed by hunters in the southern tip of Vanderburgh County, just up-river from Dam No. 48. We have received other, unverified reports of swamp rabbits from Vanderburgh County, but have not seen a specimen from this county. Adams (1950), who studied the mammal remains at the

Angel Mounds archaeological site (Vanderburgh County) mentioned a large rabbit from that material that "may well represent this species." Terrel also found S. *aquaticus* in southwestern Knox County, where rabbit hunters have shot numerous animals over the years. Terrel and Mumford tried to obtain specimens there during the winter of 1968–69, but although they saw one swamp rabbit, it escaped.

Terrel (1969) knew of 27 localities in six counties where S. *aquaticus* was thought to occur in Indiana. He calculated that there was 1 swamp rabbit per 6 acres on his Cane Ridge study area of 150 acres. He trapped and tagged 16 animals, but it required 197 trap-nights to catch each. In all, he handled 22 specimens from Cane Ridge (6 of them were untagged and shot by hunters). On the basis of about 10,000 acres of occupied swamp rabbit habitat known to exist in Indiana, and adjusting density to the quality of the various habitats, Terrel estimated that perhaps 1,000 swamp rabbits were present in the state. It seems probable that the species was never abundant in Indiana because of the limited amount of suitable habitat. The number of swamp rabbits observed per hec-

Table 71

Weights and measurements of
Sylvilagus aquaticus from Indiana

	Males	Females
Total length (mm)		
n	9	9
x̄	510.3	518.3
range	476-530	462-545
SD	16.8	25.4
SE	5.6	8.5
Tail length (mm)		
n	9	9
x̄	52.0	50.8
range	44-60	40-57
SD	5.2	5.8
SE	1.7	1.9
Hind foot (mm)		
n	9	9
x̄	106.9	105.1
range	101-113	100-110
SD	4.0	3.7
SE	1.3	1.2
Weight (grams)		
n	10	10
x̄	2184.4	2185.6
range	1814.4-2721.6	1786.0-2494.4
SD	268.0	226.1
SE	84.8	71.5

tare in selectively logged forest, mature forest, and old field growth was 3.5, 1.0, and 0.6 respectively. Compared to studies conducted in Georgia and Missouri, the Indiana population on Cane Ridge indicates that this was good habitat. No one has made a survey since Terrel's work. We have examined specimens from four counties (Map 27).

HABITAT. The vegetation of the drier portions of the Cane Ridge study area included at least 47 species of trees, 9 erect shrubs, 13 woody vines, and 49 herbaceous plants. Because of the presence of 21 species of plants generally associated with the southern swamp forest type (Shantz and Zon, 1936), the study area was classified in this category. Among the trees commonly found in more southern latitudes were swamp cottonwood, sugarberry, sweet gum, pecan, water locust, pondbrush, pumpkin ash, southern red oak, and overcup oak. Herbaceous or shrubby species more common in southern plant associations were possumhaw, sweet winter

grape, cane, crossvine, yam, wild senna, Carolina moonseed, yellow passionflower, and Missouri violet.

The major components of the plant communities inhabited by swamp rabbits at 13 Indiana sites were summarized by Terrel. Major tree species, in order of decreasing abundance, were shellbark hickory, sugarberry, sugar maple, bitternut hickory, pecan, elm, sweet gum, ash, pin oak, cottonwood, sycamore, Shumard's oak, box elder, and black walnut. For the forest floor vegetation the most important species were heath aster, poison ivy, stinging nettle, grasses, sedges, trumpetvine, cane, lizard's-tail, greenbrier, and spotted touch-me-not. Vegetation in the sloughs on the study areas was dominated by such trees as black willow, sugar maple, and pumpkin ash. Other important trees were swamp cottonwood, cottonwood, green ash, sycamore, river birch, and pecan. Buttonbush dominated large areas of the sloughs where the water was too deep for tree survival. Pondbrush often occurred in dense stands,

Map 27.   The Swamp Rabbit, *Sylvilagus aquaticus*, in Indiana

The specimen collected in Posey County by Kirkpatrick and Mumford was on a small island along the Wabash River; the island was wooded mostly with cottonwood, willow, and silver maple trees and the dominant shrubs and vine vegetation consisted of poison ivy and grape. There was no ground cover at the time, but the island had recently been inundated and was covered with soft mud.

The Yankeetown swamp rabbit site was a wooded floodplain on which the canopy trees were pin oak, red elm, black gum, pecan, silver maple, shagbark hickory, sycamore, sassafras, mulberry, honey locust and swamp white oak. The understory consisted mainly of young hackberry trees. Most of the ground cover was poison ivy, nettles, trumpetvine, aster, greenbrier, and the sprouts of red elm, pin oak, and hackberry. Poison ivy was extremely abundant and luxuriant. A narrow border of cane was located along the edge of a then-dry slough (in which buttonbush was the predominant plant) about one-eighth of a mile from where the rabbits were flushed.

The collecting site of the Spencer County specimen was a forested floodplain.

ASSOCIATED SPECIES.   On his Cane Ridge study area and the immediate vicinity, Terrel found swamp rabbits and eastern cottontails in equal numbers. Trapping, hunting, and collecting accounted for 25 of each species. Other larger mammals most abundant on the area were the raccoon, woodchuck, fox squirrel, and opossum. Additional species recorded on the study area were white-tailed deer, red fox, gray fox, striped skunk, long-tailed weasel, mink, muskrat, southern flying squirrel, eastern mole, white-footed mouse, meadow vole, meadow jumping mouse, and Norway rat. Red bats, eastern pipistrelles, and evening bats were collected by shooting at dusk.

HABITS.   Terrel calculated the home ranges of swamp rabbits by several methods and obtained maxima and minima for each. By following the tracks of rabbits in the snow, he found that home ranges for three animals varied from 10.3 to 15 acres. Fourteen rabbits chased by beagles ranged over areas from 10.5 to 20.6 acres. Four rabbits with collars equipped with radio transmitters utilized areas of 11.3 to 15.8 acres. The fourth method (trap-retrap) involved four animals

but was mixed with other tree species. Common herbaceous plants on the better drained portions of the sloughs were false nettles, grasses, sedges, and trumpetvine. In wetter sites, not inundated for long periods of time, arrowhead, lizard's tail, and smartweed grew. Swamp dock was found in the deeper water.

Harrison and Hickie (1931) obtained their specimens in the summer of 1930 near stands of cane in Posey County. They stated that rabbits "appeared to be closely confined to the canebrakes." They also wrote,

The cane where this rabbit is found in Indiana forms a dense, almost impenetrable undergrowth in thick woods, composed in part of hickory, walnut, pecan, sweet gum, swamp cottonwood, and various oaks. The ground is low and portions are covered with water during the wet season. The cane which apparently cannot grow in water is confined to long, narrow, knoll-like ridges. During the summer of 1930 these places were completely dry due to an almost rainless summer.

each trapped a minimum of three times. Calculated home ranges were quite small (4.0 to 8.8 acres) and may reflect the low number of recaptures. Terrel concluded that in his Indiana study, where there was determined to be one swamp rabbit per 6 acres, the average home range size was 11 acres. He also obtained figures on the movements of individual rabbits by calculating linear travel distance (the longest distance between observations) for each animal. This distance varied from 160 to 440 yards and averaged about 329 yards. However, one immature swamp rabbit was shot by a hunter 750 yards from the spot where it had been tagged two months earlier. Swamp rabbits being chased by beagles will usually move in a circular fashion, finally returning near the site where first flushed, like the eastern cottontail.

During the day, swamp rabbits were found resting in a variety of places. When each rabbit was flushed, its resting site was examined and the cover type noted. Usually, the rabbit was using a form (again, similar to that used by cottontails). The sites most utilized (in order of decreasing usage) were brushpiles; treetops or grape vine tangles; cane thickets; grassy open areas; standing hollow tree; in form at base of tree; buttonbush slough; blackberry thicket; on the ice in a slough. Terrel also tracked rabbits in the snow, with similar results. C. M. Kirkpatrick and Mumford flushed a swamp rabbit from its daytime retreat beneath a pile of driftwood in an area which had been inundated a few days previously. Don R. Helms and Mumford flushed two swamp rabbits along the floodplain of the Little Pigeon River (Warrick County) on 29 October. The first was in a form in a mass of tree branches and limbs lying on the ground. The second was resting in a form at the edge of a dense stand of aster about 40 yards from the first.

Swamp rabbits frequently deposit fecal pellets on top of stumps and logs. This habit appears to be quite rare in eastern cottontails. Terrel studied the types of logs used by swamp rabbits for the deposition of pellets and the seasonal pattern of such behavior. He marked 225 logs which he considered potential sites for pellet deposition. The typical log most often used by swamp rabbits averaged 12 inches wide by 14 feet long and was rotted on the upper side. It was felt that the rotting surface of the log was an important factor, for 91 percent of the logs used were of this type.

Habitat of swamp rabbit, Gibson County. Photo by Don Helms

Fecal pellets of swamp rabbit, deposited on log, Gibson County. Photo by Don Helms

Of the logs used five or more times, 90 percent were found on the ridges; 60 percent of logs not used were in the sloughs. The higher utilization of logs on ridges no doubt was correlated with the percentage of time rabbits spent on ridges and the percentage of time logs in the sloughs were inundated. Log usage was virtually nonexistent from early June to mid-September, and usage stabilized between mid-October and early November.

The specific daytime cover sought by swamp rabbits probably varies with weather conditions and other environmental factors. For example, most of the swamp rabbits flushed from grassy areas were observed there on rather sunny, warm days; none was found there when tracked in the snow. No swamp rabbits were found in hollow trees except when snow was on the ground, but without snow cover perhaps these animals would simply have been overlooked. One can wonder, however, whether or not the rabbits seek such retreats to be less noticeable against the snow. In all, Terrel recorded seven instances of the rabbits using hollow, standing trees.

Terrel made numerous observations of the behavior of swamp rabbits being found and chased by beagles. In 80 percent of such chases, the rabbits entered sloughs almost immediately after being flushed by the dogs.

The dogs pursued the rabbits for varying lengths of time, but often lost the scent when the rabbits swam across water-filled sloughs or evaded the dogs in several inches of water. In one case, the rabbit crossed a slough on thin ice which did not support the weight of the pursuing dogs. The rabbits also walk along logs or climb about in the tops of fallen trees. Frequently they will walk the length of a log, backtrack, jump from the log and run off at a right angle. Terrel observed this behavior when he was tracking rabbits in the snow. These tactics frequently confuse the pursuing dogs. Hunters reported that occasionally a swamp rabbit entered a standing hollow tree to escape dogs, and in one instance a rabbit entered a burrow in the ground when being chased by beagles. It was seldom possible to dislodge rabbits from hollow trees; the animals would climb up inside the tree as far as 6 feet, and the cavities were small enough that the investigator could not remove the rabbit without serious injury to it. Beagle chases of swamp rabbits were usually quite prolonged and covered considerable distances. Half-mile chases were not uncommon. The dogs seldom drove the rabbits at a fast pace for very long before temporarily losing the trail and slowing the chase. Terrel observed a small (1 pound 6 ounces) swamp rabbit hopping quite leisurely about within a blackberry thicket with a beagle in full cry on its trail only 50 feet away.

In Terrel's search for rabbits, he found that they flushed 2 to 50 feet from him (average, 23 feet). Most flushed at a distance of about 30 feet. Some individuals flushed only after he came past them a second time, so undoubtedly some failed to flush when he passed near them. One, sitting in a cane thicket, allowed Terrel to approach to within 2 feet and flushed only after the observer had backed away. On three occasions, rabbits flushed, ran short distances, and stopped to groom themselves when they detected no pursuit by the observer. Swamp rabbits were more docile in traps than were eastern cottontails, and seldom damaged themselves by leaping against the sides of the trap (a common behavior pattern of cottontails).

Swamp rabbits readily enter the water when not being pursued and swimming and wading about in water is part of their normal daily behavior. On two days when Terrel had sufficient tracking snow and slush covered the sloughs, he observed six instances where swamp rabbits fed, hopped leisurely to the water's edge, walked into the water and swam out into the sloughs. On some occasions the rabbit swam to a log, walked along its length, returned to the water and swam back to shore; then it followed the shoreline and repeated the performance. One individual was found resting a short distance from shore on a floating brushpile. Other investigators have remarked on the willingness of swamp rabbits to enter the water and this type of behavior separates them ecologically from eastern cottontails, which will seldom swim unless forced to do so.

When flushed by a human, a swamp rabbit will frequently run off rather slowly. It may even walk or otherwise move slowly about, evidently watching the observer. This rabbit can also move quite rapidly by long leaps or jumps. Terrel measured one leap which was 12.5 feet and others up to 9 feet in length. One swamp rabbit evaded pursuing beagles for several minutes by climbing on top of a snow-crusted mass of lodged aster plants and allowing the dogs to pass directly beneath it. The dogs relocated the rabbit after several minutes and flushed it. Because of the difficulty of flushing and observing swamp rabbits in their best habitats, most successful hunters use dogs.

FOOD. Terrel obtained data on the food habits of swamp rabbits by tracking rabbits in the snow, by making observations of plant cuttings at sites where swamp rabbit pellets were present, and by an intensive study of the utilization of fifty food study plots by the rabbits. Practically all of this information was collected during the winter. Fieldwork revealed, however, that swamp rabbits were feeding on cane and spotted touch-me-not during the first week of August. The major winter foods eaten by swamp rabbits, as revealed by tracking the rabbits in the snow, were as follows: crossvine leaves (eaten nine times); poison ivy and sedge (eaten six times); greenbrier (eaten five times); willow bark and shoots (eaten three times); blackberry and silver maple seedlings (eaten twice); trumpetvine, cane, box elder, aster, and ragweed (eaten once each).

On fifty study plots on the Cane Ridge study area in January 1969, Terrel (1972) obtained considerable information regarding the species of plants being cut and eaten by the rabbits (Table 72). Crossvine was by far the most important food item. It is a member of the trumpetvine family, but (unlike trumpetvine) retains green leaves at least through February. Swamp rabbits often stripped the leaves from crossvine entwined with greenbrier, leaving the greenbrier leaves untouched. Succulent leaves of primrose-leaved violet and bedstraw were quite abundant throughout the Cane Ridge study area but were rarely eaten by swamp rabbits. The rabbits did appear to have a preference for honey locust, blackberry, shellbark hickory, and wahoo, all species that appeared in low numbers in the vegetation sample. Wahoo stems up to the size of a lead pencil were consumed by rabbits.

REPRODUCTION. The gestation period in the swamp rabbit is about 38 days. Young are produced in a nest much like that of the eastern cottontail but larger. Terrel flushed an adult swamp rabbit from what appeared to be the beginning of a nest on 4 April. The site was in a dense growth of blackberry and grass in an old field. A depression 2 inches deep and 8 inches long had been scooped out in the ground, within a large hollow formed by blackberry stems. No further nest construction occurred after the initial observation. Nests of both species of rabbits in Indiana are difficult to locate, for they are well hidden and are covered throughout the time when the female is away.

Terrel estimated the birth dates for 15 juvenile swamp rabbits he handled. Earliest and latest dates were 23 February and 5 September, respectively. Peaks in the production of young were indicated in April and July. Females collected on 11 January were near ovulation and would probably have had young in late February. Five adult females averaged 6.7 developing follicles each (both ovaries combined), but no gravid females were examined and litter size was not determined. An adult female taken on 17 February had 4 very faint placental scars.

A low concentration of sperm was found in the epididymis of an adult male taken on 12 September. Another adult male taken in December contained sperm, but much greater concentrations were present in animals taken

Table 72

Food consumption by *Sylvilagus aquaticus* in January 1969
on fifty plots, Cane Ridge, Gibson County
(from Terrel, 1972)

Species	Total stems available	Stems fed upon	% fed upon	Frequency % where found	Frequency % where eaten
Bignonia capreolata	707	151	21.4	72	44
*Carex grayii**	302	95	31.5	66	62
Rhus radicans	974	45	4.6	86	36
*Elymus virginicus**	89	25	28.1	20	12
Smilax spp.	100	19	19.0	54	18
Celtis spp.	59	10	17.0	38	14
Galium obtusum	393	10	2.5	50	4
*Carex muskingumensis**	69	7	10.1	28	10
Evonymus atropurpureus	22	7	31.8	14	4
Menispermum canadense	55	4	7.3	40	8
Aster pilosus	809	4	0.5	68	6
Arundinaria gigantea	690	4	0.6	90	8
Rubus argutus	7	3	42.9	4	4
Gleditsia spp.	2	2	100.0	2	2
Campsis radicans	71	2	2.8	30	2
Fraxinus spp.	15	1	6.7	14	2
Carya laciniosa	2	1	50.0	2	2
Laportea canadensis	38	1	2.6	4	2

*Indicates the number of "clumps" or bunches of this species

in January and February. An immature male taken on 6 January was sexually active with sperm in low concentrations in the epididymis. Testis weights of adult and immature males taken in midwinter showed some overlap; adult testes averaged 1,203 mg and immature testes averaged 728 mg.

PARASITES. Ted Terrel examined 16 swamp rabbits from Gibson County for larger ectoparasites. He found 80 specimens of the flea *Cediopsylla simplex* and 15 specimens of the tick *Haemaphysalis leporis-palustris*. Both are normal ectoparasites on *Sylvilagus aquaticus*. Wilson (1961) recorded 9 larval forms of *H. leporis-palustris* on a swamp rabbit from Warrick County.

Among the endoparasites Terrel recovered from swamp rabbits were 2 nematodes (*Dirofilaria scapiceps, Longistriata novibariae*). A single rabbit was host to 2 specimens of the former and 91 of the animals were infected with the latter. *Obeliscoides cuniculi* was present in 96 percent of the swamp rabbit stomachs. *Taenia pisiformis* occurred in 26 percent of this species. Additional endoparasites collected were not identified to species.

DECIMATING FACTORS. Hunting was the single most important mortality factor discovered by Terrel in the Gibson County study area, where a known 52 percent of the estimated swamp rabbit population was shot during the fall and winter of 1968–69. The kill may have been even higher, for all hunters were not checked. Some southwestern Indiana hunters go afield specifically to hunt swamp rabbits, which they consider unique trophy animals. These hunters use dogs and the average hunting party chased 3.1 swamp rabbits and killed 0.94 in four hours of hunting. For each animal shot, 3.3 were involved in chases by dogs. High water and ice later in the season altered the success of hunters, and nearly 50 percent of the kill occurred when these conditions prevailed. Swamp rabbits are good eating and taste much like the eastern cottontail. We have found no direct evidence of predation on swamp rabbits in Indiana. An occasional animal is killed by an automobile.

TAXONOMY. The subspecies in Indiana is *Sylvilagus aquaticus aquaticus* (Bachman).

SELECTED REFERENCES. Hunt, 1959; Lowe, 1958; Nelson, 1909; Smith, 1940; Svihla, 1929; Terrel, 1969, 1972.

Order **RODENTIA**

Family **Sciuridae**

Eastern Chipmunk
Tamias striatus (Linnaeus)

Ground Squirrel, Fisher's Chipmunk, Northeastern Chipmunk, Ohio Brown Chipmunk, Carolinian Chipmunk

Sciurus striatus: Plummer, 1844
Tamias Lysteri: Wied, 1862
Tamias striatus: Wied, 1839

DESCRIPTION. The chipmunk is a small, brownish squirrel with two pale and five blackish longitudinal stripes on the back, and two pale and two brownish stripes on each side of the face. The underparts are white and the rump is rusty colored (variable among populations). The tail is dorsoventrally flattened, and has long, reddish hairs, tipped with black. For some reason many chipmunks have broken tails. We have seen one completely white specimen (but with dark eyes), and another specimen that is all white except for a tiny blackish spot on the forehead, another at the dorsal base of the tail, and an irregular blackish patch more than an inch long in the middorsal region at the shoulders.

Chipmunks have well-developed internal cheek pouches. The female has four pairs of teats. Musk glands are present on either side of the anus. The skull is about 45 to 50 mm in length and has 4 molariform teeth; among Indiana mammals, it is most likely to be confused with the skull of the thirteen-lined

Albino eastern chipmunk. Photo by Don Hendricks

ground squirrel, which has 5 molariform teeth. Also, the infraorbital foramen goes through a thin plate in the chipmunk, but forms a canal through a thick plate in the ground squirrel.

Weight and measurement data are shown in Table 73. The dental formula is

$$\text{I } \frac{1}{1} \text{ C } \frac{0}{0} \text{ P } \frac{1}{1} \text{ M } \frac{3}{3} = 20.$$

223

Table 73

Weights and measurements of
Tamias striatus from Indiana

	Males	Females
Total length (mm)		
n	183	184
x̄	242.3	240.5
range	205-275	183-260
SD	14.5	14.2
SE	1.1	1.0
Tail length (mm)		
n	172	179
x̄	86.5	85.4
range	68-106	70-111
SD	10.8	7.0
SE	0.8	0.5
Hind foot (mm)		
n	193	185
x̄	35.5	35
range	32-44	28-39
SD	2.2	1.8
SE	0.2	0.1
Weight (grams)		
n	106	94
x̄	113.2	109.4
range	94-149	90-139
SD	13.4	13.0
SE	1.3	1.3

STATUS AND DISTRIBUTION. Early authors noted the chipmunk in Indiana but usually made few comments regarding its status. Wied (1839) found it scarce at New Harmony (Posey County) when he was there in 1833–34. In Wayne County, Plummer (1844) noted that it "often greets the eye, as it skims along the prostrate tree." Haymond (1870) recorded it as "very numerous all over the woods and fields" in Franklin County, and he thought "it is probably more numerous than in the early settlement of the country." The chipmunk was "very common" in Randolph County, according to Cox (1893). Evermann and Butler (1894b) noted that it was abundant in Carroll, Monroe, and Vigo counties. In Lake and Porter counties, Blatchley (1898) regarded it as "common among the upland wooded ridges." Walter L. Hahn (1907a) wrote that it apparently "does not occur" at Bluegrass Landing but was "abundant" at Mountayr (both in Newton County). He also mentioned that it occurred "in fewer numbers" at Aylesworth (Porter County). In this region along the Kankakee River, where much land was then subject to periodic flooding, the species may have been locally present or absent, depending upon the elevation of the land above flood stage. It seems surprising that Hahn (1908b) found the chipmunk "not very abundant in the woods" on the Donaldson tract near Mitchell (Lawrence County). This mature forest should have provided excellent habitat for chipmunks. Hahn (1909) thought that the chipmunk was found all over Indiana in suitable habitat. He further wrote, "It is most abundant at the present time in the fields that are partially overgrown with bushes and covered with stones."

The species was reported as "still rather common" about Lake Maxinkuckee (Marshall County) by Evermann and Clark (1911). They made the following comments about chipmunks in the state: "Though still abundant in most parts of Indiana they are less so than formerly. At one time they were so numerous as to be regarded as a serious pest and bounties were paid for their scalps." We have been unable to elaborate on the payment of bounties. Lyon (1923) wrote that chipmunks "do not appear to be very common in the dunes" where he worked in Porter County. They were considered "fairly common" in St. Joseph County by Engels (1933). Lyon (1936) mapped records from throughout the state, but knew of specimens from only 14 counties. Allen (1952a) found chipmunks rare on his two squirrel study areas in Orange County, from May 1946 to January 1949. Mumford and Handley (1956) reported the chipmunk as "fairly common" in Jackson

Eastern chipmunk. Photo by Whitaker

County in the early 1950s. Lindsay (1960) collected few specimens in Jefferson and Ripley counties, but thought that the species was then more widely distributed in this region than it was 20 years ago. It appears to us that *Tamias striatus* is uncommon along the Ohio River. It may be present in each Indiana county; we have specimen records from 72 counties (Map 28). Chipmunks are locally abundant in northeastern and west-central Indiana, in particular, and possibly in other localities. We have noted large numbers on the Pigeon River and the Jasper-Pulaski fish and wildlife areas and in Turkey Run State Park. W. E. Madden reported that in 1977 he saw the first chipmunks on the Willow Slough Fish and Wildlife Area (Newton County) in 25 years.

HABITAT. The eastern chipmunk is essentially a woodland-dwelling animal which also inhabits woodland border habitats such

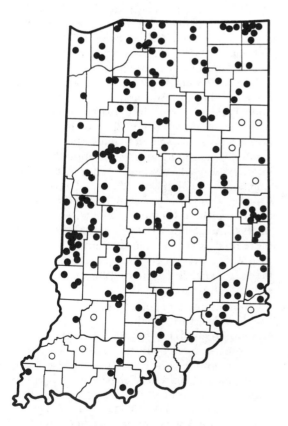

Map 28.   The Eastern Chipmunk, *Tamias striatus*, in Indiana

as cemeteries, parks, residential tracts, roadsides, lake borders, and brushy localities. McAtee (1907) described it as an "inhabitant of roadsides and fields as well as woods" about Bloomington (Monroe County), and Hahn (1908b) found it "in the fields and open woods" near Mitchell. Later (1909) Hahn wrote, "The chipmunk is found all over Indiana where there are moderately open woods or dry pastures, overgrown with bushes or filled with stumps and rocks." Evermann and Clark (1920) also commented on the habitat of Indiana chipmunks, as follows: "Wherever there are open woods or pastures and old decaying trees, rocky ledges overgrown with vines, fallen timber and brush piles, and Virginia rail fences that have not been well kept, there the Chipmunk is quite sure to be found." In St. Joseph County, Engels (1933) noted its preference for "dry bushy areas." Animals observed in Jackson County were usually in "wooded areas and along brushy fencerows" (Mumford and Handley, 1956). Lindsay (1960) reported that chipmunks were found both in the flats and in dissected areas of Jefferson and Ripley counties, but that 20 years ago they were restricted to the latter.

At both Turkey Run and Shades state parks, chipmunks are plentiful in the deeply dissected, mature deciduous / evergreen woods abounding with deep canyons and sandstone outcrops. At the Jasper-Pulaski Fish and Wildlife Area they are at times abundant in flat oak / hickory woods with a rather dense understory, where numerous fallen logs and stumps are present. Much the same type of habitat supports large numbers of chipmunks on the Pigeon River Fish and Wildlife Area (Lagrange and Steuben counties). We have also noted that numerous chipmunks can sometimes be found in brushy fencerows and in old, eroded brushy fields that are reverting to forest. Individual animals are sometimes noted along roads some distance from woodlots, and about bridges, piles of rocks, or erosion gullies. In the hill country of south-central Indiana, chipmunks occur about cave entrances and other rocky places. Habitat notes on specimen labels include the following trapping sites: at burrow in pine plantation; low, swamp woods, with tall ferns; brushy fencerow bordering cornfield; board pile in tall weeds along railroad track; brush and weeds along levee through marsh; about stone walls and buildings; in abandoned buildings.

ASSOCIATED SPECIES. All of the tree squirrels (fox, gray, red, flying) occur with the chipmunk somewhere in the state. In more open situations, the woodchuck is an associate. Woodland species of mammals usually found in good chipmunk habitats are the white-footed mouse, short-tailed shrew, eastern mole, raccoon, opossum, gray fox, and white-tailed deer.

HABITS. Chipmunks are diurnal, largely terrestrial mammals that spend much of the winter in hibernation. In late fall or early winter, they prepare to enter hibernation by storing large amounts of food, but they put on little fat. Although some individuals remain inactive for much of the winter, others may be sometimes active during this period. Even relatively inactive animals probably wake occasionally to feed. The hibernation period ends about late February or early March, but there are records of chipmunks aboveground during every month of the year and specimens have been collected in each month.

At Lake Maxinkuckee a chipmunk was watched daily about its burrow. It was last seen above the ground on 27 November and emerged on 20 March (Evermann and Clark, 1920). We have no other precise data regarding when chipmunks become inactive, but there are numerous observations of the animals aboveground in November and December. No doubt dates of entrance into and emergence from hibernation vary from year to year, depending upon the prevailing temperatures and other environmental factors in various sections of the state. F. H. Test (1932) observed a chipmunk chasing another on 1 February 1932 (Parke County) on a "cold and wet" day. George Dellinger trapped 2 chipmunks in the snow at a den entrance on 12 February 1950 (Montgomery County). On 20 February 1977, during one of the coldest winters on record in Indiana, a chipmunk was observed in a woodlot (Clay County). The temperature reached about 30°F that day.

We have examined 30 specimens of the eastern chipmunk taken in Indiana from 11 November to 9 March and have observations of 25 individuals during the same period.

The two sets of data combined reveal that we have 12 reports for November, 9 for December, 8 for January, 17 for February, and 9 for March. The sex ratios for specimens collected between 11 November and 9 March are: November, 8 males, 1 female; December, 3 males, 2 females; January, 1 female; February, 5 males, 3 females; March, 4 males, 1 female. These data suggest that males are more apt to be aboveground during the "winter" than are females. Schooley (1934) thought that males emerged earlier in the spring than did females. In general, few chipmunks are seen in Indiana from mid-November to mid-March. Many observations of chipmunks during the winter season were made on sunny days or during periods of above-normal temperatures, but some have been made during inclement weather. For example, Mumford noted two or three chipmunks running about on 23 February 1972 (Tippecanoe County) during a sleet storm; the temperature was 20 to 25°F at the time. On an overcast, windy day (temperature about 25°F), one chipmunk was seen in Spencer County (30 December 1970). On 12 February 1954, a clear, sunny day (temperature 18°F), one was seen in Clay County. Others were noted on more pleasant days, such as four running about in Spring Mill State Park on 4 February 1973, a sunny day with the temperature at 50°F. One gets the impression that on such days the animals come aboveground mostly to enjoy the sun, but they also actively feed. Walter F. Beineke watched a chipmunk daily (Tippecanoe County) at noon from 12 to 15 January 1969; the animal took birdseed mix and sunflower seeds from a feeder and stored them. Another individual was watched at South Bend (St. Joseph County) on 26 February 1966 "out in the sun." On 12 February 1961, John Tritch saw ten chipmunks in Greene County.

Chipmunks are good climbers, but are usually observed on the ground. They are most apt to climb trees to feed, to gather food, or to escape some disturbance. We have seen them several times collecting acorns from white oaks. A frightened chipmunk will often scamper away and climb a few feet up the trunk of a tree, where it may then watch or scold the intruder. Chipmunks hold the tail straight up when running.

Hahn (1909) commented on some of the habits of *Tamias striatus:*

. . . they may be seen, ever watchful and alert, about almost any heap of stones, logs, or the old-fashioned rail fences that have not yet disappeared. If they are approached too closely they dart away for a short distance, taking care not to expose themselves in the open and probably uttering a shrill protest as they go. If pursued they are apt to dart into some burrow or other hiding place at a point where there seems the least probability of escape. If a burrow is not within reach they can run up a tree without difficulty, but their claws are not as sharp as those of a tree squirrel and they can be easily shaken down.

Evermann and Clark (1920) noted that chipmunks were often observed near their burrows, "into which they would scamper, on the slightest alarm, with a rapid succession of sharp chipping noises." Alarmed individuals will often sit quietly near a safe retreat and repeat a short chipping or chirping note for extended periods. Evermann and Clark remarked that this note might be given for "hours at a time."

The vocal sounds of *T. striatus* are variable and evidently play an important role in the daily life of the species. Hahn (1909) remarked on the vocabulary of the eastern chipmunk:

For a rodent, the chipmunk has a remarkable vocal ability. His name chipmunk or chipping-squirrel was given to him because of the chipping song he sings as he sits in the bright autumn sunshine. I have heard this chipping at intervals of two or three seconds for fifteen or twenty minutes, with scarcely a note missed. What its purpose may be, I cannot conceive. A second noise is the rapid chatter he makes in defiance as he dashes away from danger along a fence or wall. But the most startling sound that I have ever known to proceed from any rodent's throat, is the shrill whistle of this little animal. Its exact nature is indescribable, but it resembles the whistle of a bird more than any mammal note that I know of. I have been fooled by it myself, and I once knew two very good ornithologists to search all over a hillside for some unknown bird, only to discover that the call that had lured them was not that of some feathered creature, but the ventriloquistic whistle of one of these little squirrels.

Hahn (1908b) had also written, "During the autumn they were often heard giving their chipping call . . ., but I have never heard them chipping" in the spring. In speaking of the calls of the chipmunk in the fall, Evermann and Clark (1920) wrote, "At this time of the year they have a call or note quite different from the sharp chipping noise usually heard in the summer, it being a succession of hollow clucking sounds, most interesting when heard at some distance through the autumn woods."

We have never heard the whistle that Hahn refers to and perhaps it is infrequently given by chipmunks. In our experience, most of the chirping calls are given in spring and fall; in July we have noted much less calling. We have heard calling in all months but January, but we have few observations for that month. The low, clucking sounds so often heard somewhat resemble some calls of the yellow-billed cuckoo, and many persons think that this bird is uttering the calls. When calling, chipmunks often twitch their tails.

Schooley (1934) thought that the apparent cessation of chipmunk activity in July, noted by some authors and based primarily on vocalizations, was probably due to the summer breeding season. He thought males did more calling than did females at this time. He also noted that during this July period chipmunks escaping into their burrows would utter no sounds (unlike the chattering earlier in the season); suckling females exhibited this same quiet behavior. Males became relatively inactive during July.

Burrows are usually excavated under rocks, tree stumps, logs, buildings, bridges, walls, standing trees, or other objects, but some are also located in the open. There is usually no soil piled before the burrow entrance, which is sometimes rather inconspicuous. Hahn (1909) mentioned that "a colony has lived for years in the foundation of Owen Hall" on the Indiana University campus. We occasionally receive reports of chipmunks which have found their way into the basements of newly constructed houses. The entrance burrow to the underground tunnel system usually slants downward steeply or may even be vertical for nearly a foot or more. Burrows may be 20 to 30 feet long, and enlarged chambers up to 12 inches long and 8 inches high may be constructed along them. Portions of the burrow are used for nesting and food storage. Hahn

(1909) stated that the nest "is nearly always placed underground." We have not examined an active chipmunk nest.

On bright, sunny days chipmunks may spend considerable time sunning or preening while perched on rocks, logs, stumps, about buildings, or even (more rarely) in trees. They appear to be less active above the ground on dark, cool, windy, or overcast days, but we have observed them under these conditions, also. At 1:30 P.M. on a humid, cloudy day on 19 May, Mumford watched a chipmunk stretched out at full length on the ground in the sun along the side of a gravel road; the animal appeared to be sunning. There had been a thunderstorm and heavy rain the night before. On two occasions in late February, we have noted that several animals out at the same time were frequently chasing one another. Perhaps this behavior is part of the courtship and mating cycle, but it appears to be play. Evermann and Clark witnessed such chasing from May or June until late October.

As one walks about through good chipmunk habitat in late summer or early fall, he may not hear many animals. But if he watches closely he will see chipmunks sitting on some lookout perch, unmoving, totally silent, and aware of the observer. On occasion an animal will stand straight up on its hind legs to obtain a better view of some disturbance. As many as ten to twelve individuals may be in view at one time.

FOOD. The chipmunk spends a considerable amount of its active period foraging for, gathering, transporting, and storing food. Evidently much foraging takes place near the burrow, but when pursued individual animals have been observed to run up to at least 75 feet to enter their burrows. One can find small piles of food refuse dropped by the animals on top of stumps, logs, rocks, or other objects where they have fed. Food is carried in the large, internal cheek pouches, which will accommodate items up to the size of a red oak acorn. Hahn (1909) had this to say regarding the cheek pouches:

The capacity of the cheek pouches is surprisingly large. They open between the lips and the molars and extend along the cheeks and neck beneath the outer skin. They are simply folds of skin that have grown back from the lining of the lips and are not furred inside. They can be stretched to hold a considerable quantity of grain or seeds, . . .

The storing of food for winter use is a noticeable activity that requires much time in the fall, when nuts, berries, seeds, and other foods are gleaned and cached in underground burrow systems. The chipmunk pushes the food into its cheek pouches with the front feet. To remove the food from the pouches, the chipmunk pushes its front feet forward along the cheeks, squeezing items from the pouches.

Chipmunks eat a wide variety of vegetable matter (mostly seeds, nuts, and fruits), but also consume some amounts of animal material. There are few early published accounts of the food habits of Indiana chipmunks. Banta (1907) watched one "picking up seeds" inside the mouth of a cave. McAtee (1907) reported that on the Indiana University campus (Bloomington) chipmunks fed in the fall on beechnuts and "berries of the Virginia creeper *(Parthenocissus quinquefolia)."* Hahn (1909) wrote:

The food of the chipmunks is quite varied. In the oak woods they store up quantities of acorns in the autumn, and these form the staple article of food for several months. All kinds of nuts are eaten when they can be secured, and one of the favorite dwelling places of the animals is in an old pasture where clumps of hazel bushes are interspersed with stone piles or stumps. In the spring they sometimes do considerable damage by digging up sprouting corn from the furrows. In the autumn some corn is taken from the shocks. They also levy tribute on the wheatfields, separating the chaff from the grains and filling their cheek pouches with the latter to be carried to the den and stored for time of need. I have taken 145 grains of wheat from the pouches of an animal killed beside a shock of wheat. Many kinds of wild seeds and fruits are no doubt eaten.

Hahn went on to say that in Maryland he observed chipmunks storing the seeds of sweet gum. Hahn commented further on the feeding behavior of the chipmunk:

As a rule, the chipmunk does not eat much food at the place where he finds it growing, for he knows his enemies are legion, and therefore gathers it hastily and carries it to his burrow and stores it there to be eaten at leisure. A quantity is stored up for winter use, for these animals, unlike the woodchuck, do not sleep soundly all through the cold season.

Hahn made reference to the fact that chipmunks "have also been known to rob the nests of birds" and that they "eat some insects."

Evermann and Clark (1920) noted that chipmunks ate beechnuts, hickory nuts ("particularly the thinner shelled species"), hazelnuts, acorns, and corn. They observed a chipmunk on 4 October "going from one ragweed to another, stripping off the seeds and cramming his pouches with them." Henderson (1932) reported the removal of a large nestling cardinal from its nest by a chipmunk. H. P. Weeks, Jr., has observed chipmunks eating land snails. Howard H. Michaud told us they eat petunia blossoms and dig up bulbs of crocuses and tulips.

We examined foods in the stomachs of 59 chipmunks collected in Indiana (Table 74).

Of the total food volume, 61 percent was classified as "mast," probably consisting mainly of chewed nuts and acorns. One identifiable food was fruits of blackberry, which made up 8.3 percent. Most of the food volume was composed of vegetation, although numerous animal items (15.5 percent) were present in the stomachs. We also recorded the food found in the cheek pouches of 19 chipmunks collected in various months (Table 75).

A specimen shot in October had a large acorn in each cheek pouch. The combined weight of the acorns was 4.6 grams. At bird feeders, chipmunks consume various seeds, including sunflower, and several specimens have been taken in bird traps baited with grain. Mumford saw a chipmunk on 22 May sitting 6 feet above the ground in a mulberry

Table 74

Food eaten by *Tamias striatus* (n = 59) from Indiana

Food item	Percent Volume	Percent Frequency
Mast	61.0	69.0
Rubus (blackberry)	8.3	10.0
Vegetation	4.0	14.8
Lepidopterous larvae	3.7	15.3
Vertebrate flesh	3.7	5.1
Seeds	2.0	5.1
Scarabaeidae (scarab beetle)	1.9	5.1
Adult Lepidoptera	1.9	3.4
Grass seeds	1.8	3.4
Prunus serotina (black cherry) seeds	1.7	3.4
Roots	1.7	3.4
Coleoptera	1.0	8.5
Dipterous larvae	0.9	3.4
Endogone	0.8	6.8
Hymenoptera	0.8	3.4
Cerastium (chickweed) seeds	0.8	1.7
Pseudacris triseriata (striped chorus frog)	0.6	6.8
Reduviidae (assassin bug)	0.5	1.7
Acrididae (grasshopper)	0.5	1.7
Chilopoda (centipede)	0.5	5.1
Insect	0.4	6.8
Curculionidae (snout beetle)	0.3	1.7
Araneae (spider)	0.3	3.4
Annelida (earthworm)	0.3	1.7
Adult Diptera	0.3	6.8
Chrysomelidae (leaf beetle)	0.2	1.7
Polygonum sp. (knotweed)	0.1	1.7
Gryllidae (cricket)	0.1	1.7
Formicidae (ant)	trace	1.7
	100.1	

Table 75

Items from cheek pouches of
Tamias striatus from Indiana

18 April	3 snails, 1 slug, 1 earthworm, 1 seed
9 May	acorn parts
10 May	corn and maple seeds
5 June	seeds
25 June	mulberries
26 August	acorns
8 September	black cherry fruits
15 September	black cherry fruits
15 September	red oak acorn
18 September	black cherry fruits
18 September	black cherry fruits
28 September	black cherry fruits
3 October	37 seeds, 1 Coleoptera larva
8 October	red oak acorn
16 October	red oak acorn
17 October	46 grains of corn
4 November	1 pin oak acorn, 1 black oak acorn
27 November	11 grains of corn
3 December	38 soybeans

tree, eating green mulberries about 6 to 8 mm in diameter. We have trapped chipmunks with peanut butter or apple as bait.

REPRODUCTION. The gestation period of *Tamias striatus* is about 31 days. Schooley (1934) established that there were two breeding seasons for chipmunks in Indiana, and had this to say:

The factors producing a breeding season are not simple. There is evidence from embryological studies by the author to indicate that even though the chipmunks emerge and are active early in the spring, even ovulating and being inseminated, a period of unfavorable weather will cause cessation of mating activities and even the resorbtion of embryos already present. However, there is no doubt that there is a definite breeding season beginning as early in the spring as activity above ground can be undertaken. Mating activities began during the first week of April in Monroe County, Indiana, in 1932, a year of about average temperatures, but ovulations were not found until the last week of April. In addition to the spring breeding season, the chipmunks of northern Indiana have a definite cycle running through the latter half of July and the earlier part of August. Breeding is not continuous during the summer among these animals in that locality.

Schooley's data were gathered from 1929 to 1932 at Winona Lake (Kosciusko County) and near Bloomington. His studies also revealed that older females bred in the spring and younger females ("even those born the preceding spring and summer") bred during the July cycle. Old females that did not become pregnant in the spring also bred during the summer. Schooley further stated, "The presence of old females pregnant at the spring mating season explains the large number of non-pregnant females taken during the peak of the summer breeding season. They represent about one-fourth of the non-pregnant animals taken at that time. They can usually be recognized by the presence of placental spots in the uteri."

Of the hundreds of eastern chipmunks we have examined from Indiana, only six gravid females were represented. One each of these was collected on 14 March, 13 April, 29 July, 6 and 11 August, and 3 October. Two females contained 3, two contained 4, and two contained 5 embryos (average 4.0). Schooley did not include embryo counts or litter size information in his paper, and there appears to be practically nothing known regarding these aspects of the reproductive biology of Indiana chipmunks. We examined ten females which had from 2 to 6 (average 4.4) placental scars each. Placental scars were observed in females collected from 29 March to 10 October. Our records include the examination of lactating females from 29 March to 11 August, but our sample is not large. We observed what appeared to be a copulation plug in one female taken on 27 July.

Males that we collected from March through July had enlarged testes, but the testes of males collected from August through November were smaller. The maximum testis size recorded was 9 by 20 mm (one animal in April and one in June). Six immature males taken in May, June, and July had testes averaging only 2 by 5 mm. Schooley was of the opinion that "most of the insemination of a given year is accomplished by males more than a year old, since not many year-old males were found to have scrotal testes during the breeding season."

It appears that young chipmunks do not emerge from their nesting burrows until they have attained considerable size. Young estimated to be halfgrown were observed aboveground in Brown County on 2 May. The smallest specimen we have examined from

Table 76
Ectoparasites and other associates of *Tamias striatus* (n = 81) from Indiana
(from Whitaker, Pascal, and Mumford, 1979)

Parasites	Parasites		Hosts Parasitized	
	Total	Average	Total	Percent
Fleas (Siphonaptera)				
Ctenophthalmus pseudagyrtes	13	0.16	6	7.4
Tamiophila grandis	2	0.02	2	2.5
Orchopeas leucopus	1	0.01	1	1.2
Sucking Lice (Anoplura)				
Hoplopleura erratica	313	3.86	26	32.1
Mites (Acarina) other than chiggers				
Dermacarus hylandi	1877	23.17	31	38.3
Aplodontopus sciuricola	504	6.22	3	3.7
Eucheyletia bishoppi	20	0.25	5	6.2
Pygmephorus sp.	13	0.16	5	6.2
Androlaelaps fahrenholzi	6	0.07	3	3.7
Bakerdania sp.	6	0.07	4	4.9
Xenoryctes latiporus	3	0.04	3	3.7
Euryparasitus sp.	3	0.04	2	2.5
Haemogamasus ambulans	2	0.02	1	1.2
Cyrtolaelaps sp.	2	0.02	2	2.5
Androlaelaps casalis	1	0.01	1	1.2
Pygmephorus hastatus	1	0.01	1	1.2
Pygmephorus tamiasi	1	0.01	1	1.2
Chigger Mites (Trombiculidae)				
Neotrombicula whartoni	151	1.86	10	12.3
Eutrombicula alfreddugesi	3	0.04	3	3.7
Walchia americana	3	0.04	3	3.7
Euschoengastia peromysci	2	0.02	1	1.2
Neotrombicula fitchii	1	0.01	1	1.2
Ticks (Ixodides)				
Dermacentor variabilis	3	0.04	3	3.7

Indiana measured 129 mm in total length; we do not know how the specimen was obtained. We have only examined 6 others that were less than 200 mm in total length. An immature taken on 24 May and weighing 43 grams is the lightest we have recorded. Another taken on 13 May weighed 48.6 grams. By late August, many animals reared during the season are approaching adult size and weight. But 14 known young of the year taken in October ranged from 52.8 to 81.3 grams and averaged 66.6. A specimen taken on 1 November weighed only 70.6 grams and measured 215 mm in total length.

PARASITES AND DISEASES. Several species of parasites have been reported from Indiana chipmunks. Wilson (1961) mentioned a specimen of the tick *Dermacentor variabilis*,

5 specimens of the flea *Ctenopthalmus pseudagyrtes*, and 2 specimens of the flea *Orchopeas howardii*. Whitaker and Corthum (1967) found a specimen of *C. pseudagyrtes*. None of these species is host-specific or a principal parasite on the chipmunk. The host-specific louse *Hoplopleura erratica* was first recorded on Indiana chipmunks by Ferris (1921). Wilson (1961) took 4 specimens of the host-specific flea *Tamiophila grandis*. Whitaker and Corthum added one more record and this flea is now known from Carroll, Steuben, and Vigo counties. It does not appear that either of the host-specific parasites restricted to *T. striatus* is very abundant in Indiana.

Larvae of the botfly (*Cuterebra* sp.) have been collected from four Indiana chipmunks.

On 3 September 1958, Wilson and Mumford found two larvae in one specimen and another larva in a second specimen collected in Shades State Park (Montgomery County); the latter was in the scrotum. A chipmunk taken in Turkey Run State Park (Parke County) on 7 September 1958 had a botfly larva in the inguinal region. Another infected animal was taken on 30 July 1969 in Vermillion County.

During the present studies, 81 chipmunks were examined for external parasites, of which 58 (71.6 percent) were infected (Table 76). The most abundant forms were the hypopial mites *Dermacarus hylandi* and *Aplodontopus sciuricola*, the louse *Hoplopleura erratica*, and the chigger *Neotrombicula whartoni*. *Aplodontopus sciuricola* was found by E. J. Spicka late in the study, and was probably on many more individuals. It occurs in the hair follicles of the tail and thus is not found without special searching.

Sixty chipmunks were examined for internal parasites. Three of these harbored a total of three cestodes, one harbored 13 trematodes, and seventeen harbored a total of 42 nematodes. None of the internal parasites has been identified.

Not one of the 505 chipmunks examined from Indiana for rabies from 1970 through 1976 was positive.

DECIMATING FACTORS. According to label notations, three of the *T. striatus* specimens we examined were brought in by domestic cats. Others were taken in bird-banding traps and one in a snake trap. Many chipmunks are killed by automobiles and other vehicles. A long-tailed weasel was observed chasing chipmunks. One chipmunk, two eastern moles, and an unidentified vole were found on 25 June in a food cache left by an unidentified fox. Remains of *T. striatus* were found in the stomach of the least weasel and in 2 of 83 stomachs of the opossums we examined. At dusk on the evening of 2 December, a chipmunk became entangled and was captured in a mist net placed at the entrance to a cave. H. P. Weeks, Jr., saw a Cooper's hawk carrying a chipmunk.

TAXONOMY. Mumford (1969c) stated that the taxonomy of chipmunks in Indiana was an unsolved problem, and discussed the situation. *Tamias striatus ohionensis* Bole and Moulthrop appears to be the relatively dull, dark chipmunk occurring over most of Indiana. In the northern portion of the state are small, pale individuals which could be assigned to *T. s. rufescens* Bole and Moulthrop. Chipmunks from Parke and Vermillion counties (west-central Indiana) are paler and larger, and could be included in the race *T. s. griseus*. A single specimen from New Harmony tends to approximate *T. s. striatus* in color and was assigned to that race by Bole and Moulthrop.

SELECTED REFERENCES. Allen, 1938; Condrin, 1936; Howell, 1929; Klugh, 1923; Yerger, 1953.

Woodchuck
Marmota monax (Linnaeus)

Wood-chuk, Groundhog, Southern Woodchuck, Whistle-pig

Arctomyx pruinosus: Wied, 1839
Arctomyx monax: Plummer, 1844
Marmota monax: McAtee, 1907

DESCRIPTION. The woodchuck is the largest member of the squirrel family in Indiana. It is grizzled, grayish brown above, sometimes with decided blackish or reddish tones. The underparts are pale reddish brown, often slightly grizzled. The hair is coarse, and that of the belly is so sparse that the skin shows through it. The ears and eyes are small, and the tail is relatively short and slightly bushy. There are four claws on the toes of each front foot and five on the hind foot. The enamel of the incisors, unlike other Indiana sciurids, is white. The skull is flat above, with prominent transverse postorbital processes projecting outward from the upper rim of the orbit (see Fig. 25).

A woodchuck killed in Adams County was

Woodchuck, molting. Photo by Roger W. Barbour

all white except for some dark hairs on the tail, shoulders, and face (*fide* D. Bickel and Dale N. Martin). One taken in Vigo County was completely white, with pink eyes; another from the same county was completely tan and probably represented an imperfect albino. A white woodchuck was observed by several persons near Rochester (Fulton County) during 1976 and 1977 (*fide* Robert Kern). Black individuals have also been reported from time to time.

Abnormal growth of the ever-growing incisors has been reported. When the tips of the lower and upper incisors fail to meet cor-

Table 77

Weights and measurements of
Marmota monax from Indiana

	Males	Females
Total length (mm)		
n	64	73
x̄	599	594.9
range	475-673	440-700
SD	34.8	42
SE	4.3	4.9
Tail length (mm)		
n	62	71
x̄	138.5	133.8
range	117-172	107-182
SD	15.9	17.9
SE	2	2.1
Hind foot (mm)		
n	64	74
x̄	90.3	82.2
range	77-100	75-95
SD	4.4	9
SE	0.6	1
Weight (grams)		
n	62	74
x̄	3511.7	3462
range	2175.0-5273.1	2000.0-5783.4
SD	642	769.3
SE	81.6	89

rectly, wear does not maintain their normal length and individual incisors may form a complete circle, grow unduly long, or grow at abnormal angles from the jaw. Such anomalies have been reported by Newlin (1897) and Hess (1926) for Indiana woodchucks, and we have examined an additional skull of this type.

Weights and measurements are presented in Table 77. The dental formula is

$$ I \ \frac{1}{1} \ C \ \frac{0}{0} \ P \ \frac{2}{1} \ M \ \frac{3}{3} \ = \ 22. $$

STATUS AND DISTRIBUTION. The woodchuck is common throughout the state, although it may be locally rare to abundant. Certain areas hunted intensively by "vermin" shooters may contain low populations. Specimens are in collections from 53 counties (Map 29).

Wied (1839) recorded the woodchuck at New Harmony in the winter of 1832–33, but

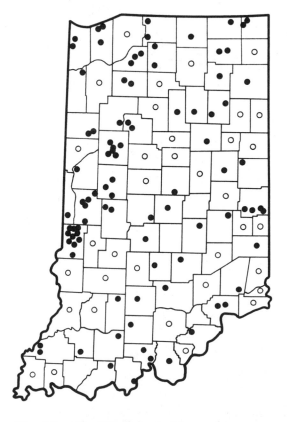

Map 29.   The Woodchuck, *Marmota monax*, in Indiana

mentioned nothing concerning its abundance. Plummer (1844) stated that it was "seldom met with" in Wayne County, but Haymond (1870) reported it as "very numerous" in the Whitewater River valley. Although "formerly quite common," it was only "occasionally found" in Randolph County by 1893 (Cox). Evermann and Butler (1894b) listed it from 7 counties, noting that it was "generally very abundant." Around 1890 it was evidently rare in parts of southeastern Indiana, but increased there later. Hahn (1909), whose home was in Ohio County, described the situation, as follows: "The writer can remember when, somewhat more than twenty years ago, an older brother killed a woodchuck and all the boys and some of the men in the neighborhood were ignorant as to the identity of the animal. At the present time the same farm in southeastern Indiana harbors from 25 to 50 'ground pigs,' as they are popularly called. . . ." The woodchuck was considered "common" around Bloomington (Monroe County) by McAtee (1907) and "very abundant" in what is now Spring Mill State Park (Lawrence County) by Hahn (1908b). In August 1905, Hahn found the species "very abundant" in the sections of the Kankakee River valley he studied in northwestern Indiana. In 1909, he stated that it was found in every county in the state.

Evermann and Clark (1911) stated that the woodchuck was "not rare" about Lake Maxinkuckee (Marshall County). In the wooded portions of the sand dunes of Porter County, Lyon (1923) found the woodchuck "very common" and Engels (1933) assigned the same status to it for St. Joseph County. Lyon (1936) did not give any details regarding the status of the woodchuck in Indiana other than to state that it was one of the commonest large mammals. Dwight M. Lindsay (1960) recalled that approximately 25 years ago the woodchuck was "rare" in the flats of Ripley County but very common in the hilly portions. At the time of his writing, it was found throughout the county, but still most frequently in the dissected areas. Charles M. Kirkpatrick found woodchucks plentiful in Decatur County from 1928 to 1938.

We have little information concerning the numbers of woodchucks in specific areas or habitats in Indiana. Relatively few are killed on roads in comparison to the numbers of rabbits or opossums (see Table 20). Schmeltz and Whitaker found at least 35 woodchucks living along a 3,500-meter stretch of dike along the Wabash River (Vigo County). Assuming them all to be present at the same time, this is about one every 100 meters (Table 78).

An interesting possible indication of woodchuck numbers locally is found in entries in the daybook of Samuel S. Strong (who ran a store and tannery), between 1845 and 1851, at Lebanon (Boone County), Indiana. "Strong bought hundreds of woodchuck hides for 8¢ each, with the price occasionally going up to 15¢, and paid 62¢ per gallon for the oil rendered from the carcasses." " . . . one supplier . . . brought in from eight to ten woodchuck hides at a time, with an accompanying half-gallon of oil, receiving 8¢ a hide, and 31¢ for the oil" (Stark, 1964).

Hahn (1907a) supplied some information on the numbers of woodchucks in one part of the Kankakee River valley, northwestern Indiana. He wrote, "Porter County pays a bounty of 10 cents for each animal killed and a statement furnished me by the county treasurer shows that an average of about 1,400 woodchucks a year have been killed for the five years ending with 1905, at a total cost to the county of $700. Apparently the bounty has not caused any appreciable diminution in numbers." Blatchley (1898) remarked that the woodchuck was "common among the upland wooded ridges" in Lake and Porter counties. Hahn (1907a) observed that it seemed "to inhabit every sand hill and elevated point throughout the region" where he worked along the Kankakee River in August 1905.

HABITAT. Lyon (1936) considered the woodchuck to be primarily a forest animal that was able to adapt successfully as the land was cleared and settled. Earlier (Lyon, 1923) he had noted that in the Indiana dunes it was found "in the wooded portions." Near Mitchell (Lawrence County) Hahn (1908b) observed that the woodchuck was "very abundant in the woods and fields." Today, woodland is certainly not necessary for this common mammal and, in fact, it appears to be more abundant in nonwooded habitats. Large numbers of woodchucks occur along railroad grades and ditch banks far from forested areas. McAtee (1907) noted that railroad embankments were favorite locations for their burrows in Monroe County, where they also lived in sinkholes. In Franklin County, where woodchucks were abundant, Haymond (1870) remarked that "the gravelly terraces, wherever covered with brushwood, they seem to prefer to all other situations." Evermann and Clark (1911) wrote that the woodchuck "most delights in the more hilly districts covered with open forests or grassy meadows, particularly those near fields of red clover." Whatever the optimum habitat originally in Indiana, the woodchuck has now adapted to more open areas. We have observed its burrows under buildings, in cultivated and fallow fields, in abandoned gravel pits, in a drainage culvert, on a mowed lawn, along railroads, in fencerows and drainage ditches, along levees, about stonepiles in a field, beneath a pile of old stumps in a pasture, under a brushpile, in woodlots and more heavily wooded areas, about culverts and bridges, in sinkholes, and in berry patches. Brushy, uneven land interspersed

Table 78

Use of woodchuck burrows by large mammals on a flood control levee along the Wabash River at Terre Haute, Vigo County, Indiana (from Schmeltz and Whitaker, 1977)

	Animals Taken		Captures and Recaptures	
	Number	Percent	Number	Percent
Woodchuck	35	42.2	74	57.4
Virginia opossum	20	24.1	21	16.3
Eastern cottontail	18	21.7	24	18.6
Raccoon	8	9.6	8	6.2
Gray fox	1	1.2	1	0.8
Red fox	1	1.2	1	0.8
	83	100.0	129	100.1

with cultivated fields appears to be chosen when available.

ASSOCIATED SPECIES. Woodchucks share their habitats with many other species, but the best assessment of closely associated mammals is the work of Schmeltz and Whitaker (1977), who studied the use of burrows by woodchucks and other mammals in Vigo County (Tables 78, 79). A series of 94 woodchuck burrow openings which appeared to have been in use recently (as indicated by presence of cuttings, fresh soil, odor, tracks) was studied along a section of dike built many years ago as a flood deterrent for farmland along the west side of the Wabash River, north of Terre Haute. Live-traps were used to sample the medium-sized mammals (gray squirrel to fox) using these burrows. Traps

were placed in the mouth of each burrow in such a way that they would be likely to capture an animal which was inside the burrow at the time the trap was set. Traps were used at two- to three-month intervals from October 1970 through April 1972. Use of the burrows by small mammals was determined with snap-back mousetraps set inside the burrow entrances for five two-day periods during the study.

Six species and 83 individuals of large mammals were taken among a total of 129 captures and recaptures. Mammals were caught at 62 of the 98 burrow entrances. The woodchuck was captured most frequently, as expected, constituting 42.2 percent of the larger mammals taken. Eastern cottontails constituted 21.7 percent of the mammals taken and were captured primarily during the

Table 79

Use of woodchuck burrows by small mammals on a flood control levee
along the Wabash River at Terre Haute, Vigo County, Indiana
(from Schmeltz and Whitaker, 1977)

	Number of burrows		White-footed Mouse	Deer Mouse	House Mouse	Short-tailed Shrew	Meadow Jumping Mouse	Meadow Vole	Masked Shrew	Totals
Nov. 22-24, 1970	78	Number	47	1	17	2	—	—	—	67
		Avg. per burrow	0.60	0.01	0.22	0.03	—	—	—	0.86
March 28-30, 1971	75	Number	1	4	3	1	—	—	2	11
		Avg. per burrow	0.01	0.05	0.04	0.01	—	—	0.03	0.15
May 30-June 1, 1971	94	Number	1	17	3	—	2	—	—	23
		Avg. per burrow	0.01	0.18	0.03	—	0.02	—	—	0.24
Nov. 22-24, 1971	75	Number	46	—	8	7	—	1	—	62
		Avg. per burrow	0.61	—	0.11	0.09	—	0.01	—	0.83
April 18-20, 1972	48	Number	9	7	1	—	—	1	—	18
		Avg. per burrow	0.19	0.15	0.02	—	—	0.02	—	0.38
		Number	104	29	32	10	2	2	2	181
		Avg. per burrow	0.28	0.08	0.09	0.03	0.005	0.005	0.005	0.49

colder months: October, six captures; November, ten; December, two; February, four. Twenty opossums were taken, involving twenty initial captures and one recapture. These data indicate that opossums were not living in the burrows but were simply visiting them. Of eight raccoons taken, none were recaptured; thus, raccoons appeared to investigate the openings then move on.

The most common small mammals in the general vicinity of the burrows were white-footed mice, meadow voles, house mice, and deer mice. About burrows in grassy areas, the meadow vole was particularly abundant, but seldom used the burrows. The most common small mammal trapped in the burrows was the white-footed mouse (104 individuals). The deer mouse and the house mouse used burrows less, probably because their habitats were less closely associated with the burrows studied. The white-footed mouse lived in the brushy areas along the dike itself, while the other two species lived primarily in cultivated fields a few feet away. The overall capture rate of small mammals in the burrows was 0.49 per burrow; however, the greatest utilization was in the fall, when 0.86 small mammals per burrow were taken in November 1970 and 0.83 in November 1972. Respective values for March 1971 and April 1972 were 0.15 and 0.38.

Helen Hendricks (1970) observed a gray fox burrow beneath a brushpile that was used by the foxes and by a woodchuck with four young.

Dellinger (1951) knew of several instances where bobwhites took refuge in woodchuck burrows during snowy, cold weather. And we have heard of at least one case where a ring-necked pheasant, shot and wounded by a hunter, ran into a woodchuck burrow to escape.

HABITS. The woodchuck is primarily diurnal and terrestrial, and most individuals are observed along railroads, roadsides, and the borders of open areas during the day. Evermann and Clark (1920) wrote about the nighttime activities of woodchucks (but without further elaboration) as follows: "They are, however, to some extent nocturnal and may remain abroad well into the night." McAtee (1907) had previously reported observing a nocturnal woodchuck at Washington, D.C. James L. Mumford saw one that appeared to be feeding along the roadside about an hour after midnight.

Although the woodchuck spends most of its time on or in the ground, we have observed several animals in trees and have gathered reports of several other climbing individuals. Tree climbing appears to be relatively common and is often associated with feeding. In most cases, the animals were within 10 feet of the ground. Some of the trees had branches that came near the ground or were leaning, but at least two had vertical trunks with no branches near the ground. In general, trees climbed by woodchucks are relatively small in diameter. A woodchuck with a burrow beneath a large pile of tree stumps that had been bulldozed into a pile in a pasture frequently climbed to the topmost stump (more than 6 feet above the ground) and sat there in the sun. Another, that lived beneath a large pile of bulldozed trees, was observed at the distal end of a long tree trunk that jutted at an angle from the pile; the perch was at least 6 feet from the ground. Again, it appeared the animal was simply sunning or using the site as an observation post. Considerable time seems to be spent sunning, and an animal will often lie flat on the mound of soil at the burrow entrance to sun.

The most obvious evidence of the presence of woodchucks are the burrow entrances that lead into an extensive underground system. The animals excavate the tunnel system so that it usually has one major entrance and two or three subsidiary ones. The main entrance usually has a pile of soil (removed from the burrow) at its mouth; the others often lack such mounds and may be more hidden by vegetation. Such mounds of soil are often large enough to interfere with mowing, harvesting, or the operation of other farm machinery. Burrow systems along railroad embankments may be so extensive that the roadbed is damaged. Underground burrows may extend from 15 to 50 feet horizontally, may have several side passages leading to the nest, may contain a latrine area or a hibernating chamber, and may reach depths of 3 to 4 feet. Nests of leaves are built in the underground burrows. F. H. Montague, Jr., observed an adult woodchuck carrying leaves, a mouthful at a time, into its den.

Burrows are most likely to be constructed

on a hillside or the side of a bank, embankment, or levee, but some are dug into level ground. Evermann and Clark (1920) observed burrows in the middle of a level field; the holes led downward vertically for several feet. We, also, have noted burrows in open, level areas. Several were in use in 1959 on a large, closely mowed bluegrass lawn at Turkey Run State Park. It is not unusual to see burrow openings beneath a stump, at the base of a tree, or beneath other objects. Burrows that have been in use for some time have well-worn trails leading from their entrances to feeding sites. Such trails are often worn down to bare soil and are about 5 inches wide. Woodchucks are slow, clumsy runners, but the presence of well-used trails probably enables them to return to the safety of their underground dens more easily.

The woodchuck feeds mostly in the morning and evening, but, depending upon the season, weather conditions, and perhaps other factors, it may be seen aboveground nearly any time of day. There appears to be a minor feeding period around noontime. Feeding forays may take the animals 75 feet or more from their dens, to which the woodchucks return quickly if disturbed sufficiently. Rarely does a woodchuck stray more than a few hundred feet from its den. Individuals emerge from their burrows with much caution, often rising on their haunches at the burrow entrance to look about for some time before venturing away. While foraging or feeding, they stand up about every 30 seconds or so and scan their surroundings. They can detect moving objects at a considerable distance, but frequently an observer who stands perfectly still can watch them at close range. When alarmed, the animals scurry back to the burrow, usually by the shortest and most direct route. If a potential enemy (even man) is standing in its path, a woodchuck is likely to run directly past it, sometimes giving the impression that the intruder is being charged. It is apparent that woodchucks spend a great deal of time in their burrows, presumably sleeping.

Hahn (1909) wrote the following concerning woodchuck activity aboveground:

In the spring, while lean and hungry, he may stay out for an indefinite length of time. Later in the summer he usually returns in an hour or two, and perhaps does not come out again till late afternoon. At this time he sometimes goes for a visit to his neighbor across the field, but most often he stays near home, although he may prolong his supper till after nightfall. Sometimes he comes out for a midday lunch also.

The behavior of woodchucks in early spring has been described by Evermann and Clark (1920):

In the early spring, soon after the first warm days have come and the only remaining reminders of the passing winter are a few snow banks in protected places or occasional little flurries of snow, and when the first green blades of grass are just peeping through the matted dead grass of the previous year on warm hillsides and along fence-rows, the first Groundhog of the season is apt to be seen. He will most likely be found out in the open in some old meadow, preferably a clover-field, and near his den. Here he appears early in the afternoon when the sun shines warm on the hillside. He comes out not only to feed upon the young and tender stems and leaves of the clover and other early spring plants, but he also delights to lie in the warm sunshine or to sit upright near his burrow looking about over the fields and renewing his acquaintance with the scenes which have remained only as a memory since he went into winterquarters the previous fall. Later in the spring and in summer and fall, if you should be abroad in the early morning when the sun is just showing and the dew still hangs heavy and sparkling on the tender new grass, you will almost certainly be rewarded by seeing one or more Woodchucks in any cloverfield you chance to pass. Then they come out for their morning repast of red clover stems and leaves, and the tender shoots of windflower and cinnamon fern. At this time they will be quite busy. When done feeding they will return to their burrows where they probably sleep until one or two o'clock when they reappear, not so much for feeding as to bask in the warm sun or to look about over the country. Again late in the evening, between sundown and dusk, they come out again to feed. Then they usually remain out until nearly dark when they are apt to retire to their burrows. They are, however, to some extent nocturnal and may remain abroad well into the night.

The woodchuck becomes very fat in the late summer and early fall in preparation for hibernation. The date that hibernation begins (or that woodchucks are no longer observed out of their burrows) varies, evidently with prevailing weather conditions. As a general rule, woodchucks in northern Indiana probably enter hibernation earlier than those in southern Indiana. We have few precise data on this subject, but have gathered information from various observers and other sources. In Lawrence County, Hahn (1908b) observed woodchucks "running about late in October" but thought they "probably were not active later than the end of that month." Later he wrote, "In southern Indiana the animals usually retire about the middle of October. I have seen them on the 14th of that month after the severe early frost of 1906, but I have never seen them as late as November, although it is possible that a few may venture out in the sunshine of that month" (Hahn, 1909). A summary of our own observations and those of others reveals that an occasional woodchuck may be seen at any time of the year. There are numerous sightings for October and November, a few records for December, and at least one for January, the month when the animals are least likely to be seen. Schmeltz and Whitaker (1977) reported an individual that appeared to remain active all winter (Vigo County). Before woodchucks hibernate, they plug the entrances to their dens with soil. The earthen plugs no doubt modify the temperature, relative humidity, and air movement within the dens and furnish additional protection to the sleeping animals.

Emergence from hibernation, contrary to popular belief and folklore, does not occur on Groundhog Day (2 February). We do not know whether the single January observation (date not available) indicated an animal late to enter hibernation, one early to emerge, or one that simply came aboveground for some reason. The observer (Gary Witmer) noted that this animal had a severe case of what appeared to be mange. A woodchuck was seen dead on the highway (Boone County) on 1 February, and there are numerous other February dates for counties as far north in the state as Lafayette. James Cook saw a woodchuck with its head out of its burrow on 9 February and another digging out its burrow on 15 February (both in Tippecanoe County). Hahn (1909) wrote, "I do not know that they ever appear as early as February 2," but added that "before the end of February, however, they usually begin to clean out and enlarge their burrows or dig new ones." Schmeltz and Whitaker recorded the earliest

emergence on 5 February 1971 and 8 February 1972 during their study, but in 1978, a year of record cold temperature, Whitaker observed a freshly opened burrow on 2 February, with the excavated soil deposited directly on the snow. Hahn (1909) was of the opinion that once the woodchuck left its burrow in the spring, inclement weather later did not cause it to again enter hibernation. He observed numerous woodchuck tracks in the snow early on the morning of 6 March, after a "heavy snow storm late in the evening" of 5 March. Such activity caused Hahn to wonder why the species hibernated at all, pointing out that its food was quite similar to that of the eastern cottontail, which did not find it necessary to hibernate.

Although woodchucks are so alert and have such good vision that they are difficult to surprise away from their burrows, when cornered they will fight furiously. Evermann and Clark (1920) reported that when a half-grown young was pursued and overtaken by humans, it turned and showed fight. Woodchucks are more than a match for some dogs, and their strong incisors are formidable weapons. They are good swimmers; Mumford once saw one swimming across the White River. Woodchucks have been abundant from time to time along a narrow levee (on top of which is a one-way road) between the Kankakee River and flooded marsh or forest on the Kankakee Fish and Wildlife Area. Perhaps in this area the animals are sometimes forced to swim to obtain food or for other reasons.

The usual vocal sound made by the woodchuck is a shrill, somewhat quavering whistle (giving rise to the name "whistle-pig"). One animal under observation repeated this call several times after it had been frightened into its burrow at dusk by Mumford. C. M. Kirkpatrick observed that startled individuals gave sharp, explosive whistles; we have often heard such sounds coming from a burrow into which a woodchuck had just fled.

We have little information concerning the movements of woodchucks. For the most part, they seem to remain in a relatively small area. However, that many are killed each year by vehicles along roads perhaps indicates that some movement takes place. McAtee (1907) wrote that "they appear to wander to some extent in late May and early

June." Evermann and Clark (1920) were of the opinion that some woodchucks living in fields during the summer moved into the woods to hibernate in other burrows. Six animals marked and released by Schmeltz and Whitaker (1977) were recaptured at an average distance of 1,456 meters from the original capture sites.

Several persons have kept captive woodchucks. Evidently if woodchucks are captured when they are quite small, many will become very tame. Years ago, a pet woodchuck at the museum in McCormick's Creek State Park was a star attraction to visitors.

FOOD. The woodchuck evidently eats practically 100 percent vegetable matter. Detailed food habits analyses have not been conducted, but Whitaker grossly examined 95 stomachs. The animals involved were collected as follows: March, 16; April, 43; May, 22; June, 3; July, 7; October, 2; November, 2. Of these, 85 contained essentially 100 percent unidentified vegetation composed primarily of the green parts of herbaceous plants and some root material. The remaining stomachs each contained from 10 to 95 percent unidentified vegetation. Few plants were identified to species. One stomach contained much wild onion. In 8 stomachs, corn composed 5, 10, 45, 50, 50, 90, 90, and 100 percent of food volumes. Apples and dandelion blossoms made up 40 and 5 percent of the volumes of 2 stomachs. In addition to vegetation, 5 woodchucks had ingested (no doubt incidentally) much gravel. A trace of mouse remains, present in 1 stomach, also may have been consumed by accident. Haymond (1870), the only other author writing about Indiana mammals who referred to the possibility that woodchucks eat animal matter, wrote, "They have been accused of preying upon domestic fowls, but I apprehend unjustly."

Woodchucks have been reported to eat a wide variety of plant foods. Hahn (1907a) secured a specimen that dogs had "treed" in a sassafras bush; its "stomach was gorged with sassafras leaves." Hahn remarked that to his knowledge it was unusual for woodchucks to obtain food from trees. Harmon P. Weeks, Jr., has frequently observed woodchucks feeding on the leaves of small red elm trees; in most cases the trees climbed were less than 6 inches in diameter. He also observed that woodchucks ate persimmon pulp but not the seeds of that fruit. Howard H. Michaud watched a woodchuck in his yard feeding on the blossoms of petunias and marigolds; it ate nothing but the flowers of these plants. Mumford once saw a woodchuck eating blooming spring beauties. Evermann and Clark (1920) recorded windflower and cinnamon fern as foods of the woodchuck.

Several persons have told us that woodchucks do extensive damage to their gardens by feeding on beans and other crops. They are also said to eat pumpkin, squash, cabbage, and celery. Considerable amounts of soybeans are sometimes consumed, and the animals also eat large quantities of young corn on occasion. Dellinger (1951) noted that where dens were located in crop fields, woodchucks might clip off all corn or soybean plants within "several rods" of the entrance. Red clover, wheat, sorghum, and alfalfa are locally important food plants. Hahn reported that woodchucks eat ferns, shrubs, grasses, the tender shoots of young trees, and ripe apples. Schmeltz and Whitaker observed that a woodchuck that appeared to remain active all winter (Vigo County) fed on standing corn near its burrow. Not only are the cropland feeding habits of woodchucks a problem for landowners, but the mounds the animals build at their burrow entrances, and the burrows themselves, interfere with farming; also, in making their numerous trails, woodchucks trample crops.

REPRODUCTION. The woodchuck presumably mates soon after emerging from hibernation in February and March. Our data suggest that copulation takes place mainly from mid-February to mid-March. Although we have no testis measurement data for December or January, males with the largest testes were collected from February to May (Table 80). The gestation period is about 28 days (Hamilton, 1934). Most females probably produce litters from late March to late April, with the majority of young being born the first three weeks of April. We examined a single female taken in February and she was gravid; 9 of 14 taken in March were pregnant and 2 had placental scars; 15 of 40 taken in April were gravid and 21 had placental scars. None of 23 females taken in May were pregnant, but 18 had placental scars. Few specimens were available from June and July, and no females were examined that had been collected in August, September, and October. More data are needed to determine whether litters are produced after April 18, the latest date we obtained a gravid female. Evidently a female bears a single litter per year. Evermann and Clark (1920) observed a young woodchuck, said to be one-third grown, on 10 September (Marshall County) and they considered this as evidence that the species might produce two litters per season.

Relatively few specimens of immature woodchucks have been collected, and our data on growth rates of the young are based on a few observations and museum skins. On 19 May, an adult with 3 young, each about 10 inches in total length, was observed in Harrison County. An immature, taken in Wayne County in April (no date), weighed 430 grams and measured 320 mm in total length. Another young taken 6 May (Martin County) weighed 755 grams and measured 379 mm in total length. On 17 June, a young animal estimated to be only half-grown was seen in Warren County.

We have few records of complete litter counts for Indiana woodchucks. We examined 21 gravid females, which contained from 3 to 8 embryos each (average 4.9) (SD = 1.51; SE = 0.32). To determine whether larger (presumably older) females produced more young per litter than did smaller females, we grouped the data for gravid females into weight classes (by grams) as follows: 2,000-2,499, 2,500-2,999, 3,000-3,499, 3,500-3,999, 4,000 +. For these groupings 4, 5, 3, 7, and 3

Table 80

Testis measurements from
Marmota monax from Indiana

Month	Number examined	Testis size (mm)	
		Average Length	Width
February	2	22.5	17
March	15	24.3	13.6
April	31	23.1	13.3
May	16	23.4	12.8
June	2	19.0	9.5
July	5	16.2	9.6
August	1	11	5
September	0		
October	2	13.5	7
November	1	15	8

females averaged 3.5, 4.2, 5.0, 5.4, and 6.7 embryos respectively. Since our sample size was not large, it would be interesting to gather additional information on this aspect of reproduction. In particular, it would be good to know if the relative ages of female woodchucks can be correlated with numbers of embryos.

PARASITES. Two papers (Wilson, 1961; Whitaker and Schmeltz, 1973) contain rather extensive information on the external parasites of Indiana woodchucks. Wilson examined 16 animals for ticks, lice, and fleas only, but Whitaker and Schmeltz reported on all ectoparasites on 91 specimens (Table 81). The most abundant parasite (28.9 per animal) was the mite *Androlaelaps fahrenholzi* (=*Haemolaelaps glasgowi* and probably also = *Androlaelaps sternalis*). The second most abundant parasite (131 specimens) was the chigger *Euschoengastia marmotae*, and 12 specimens of another chigger (*Eutrombicula alfreddugesi*) were also taken. Two other mites (*Eulaelaps stabularis* and *Macrocheles* sp.) were recorded. *Macrocheles*, a nonparasitic form that probably has a phoretic relationship with the woodchuck, represents a new species being described by G. W. Krantz.

Two ticks (*Dermacentor variabilis; Ixodes cookei*) were reported by both Wilson and Whitaker and Schmeltz. In both studies *I. cookei* was slightly more numerous. A single species of louse (*Enderleinellus marmotae*), typical of woodchucks, was found. Wilson reported 127 and Whitaker and Schmeltz 437 specimens.

Only 2 specimens of the flea *Oropsylla arctomys*, a normal parasite of *Marmota monax*, were recorded by Wilson from an Indiana woodchuck (Noble County). Whitaker and Schmeltz found no fleas on 39 woodchucks collected in southern Indiana, and 3 of 51 woodchucks taken in northern Indiana (Marshall, St. Joseph, and Tippecanoe counties) harbored 12, 1, and 1 *O. arctomys*. Wilson took one specimen of the flea *Orchopeas howardii*, but this is normally found on tree squirrels and is considered a straggler on the woodchuck.

DECIMATING FACTORS. Automobiles (and to a lesser extent, trains) take a considerable toll of woodchucks each year. The animals

Table 81

Ectoparasites and other associates of *Marmota monax* (n = 91) from Indiana
(from Whitaker and Schmeltz, 1973)

Parasites	Parasites		Hosts parasitized	
	Total	Average	Total	Percent
Fleas (Siphonaptera)				
Oropsylla arctomys	14	0.15	5	5.5
Sucking Lice (Anoplura)				
Enderleinellus marmotae	437	4.80	26	28.6
Mites (Acarina) other than chiggers				
Androlaelaps fahrenholzi	2628	28.88	71	78.0
Macrocheles sp.	17	0.19	6	6.6
Eulaelaps stabularis	1	0.01	1	1.1
Chigger mites (Trombiculidae)				
Euschoengastia marmotae	131	1.44	5	5.5
Eutrombicula alfreddugesi	12	0.13	1	1.1
Euschoengastia peromysci	2	0.02	1	1.1
Ticks (Ixodides)				
Ixodes cookei	34	0.37	21	23.1
Dermacentor variabilis	31	0.34	7	7.7

feed along the roadsides and often construct their burrows along roadside ditches and in railroad embankments. Woodchuck hunting has always been a popular sport and has led to local decimation of populations. Some hunters eat woodchucks (*Outdoor Indiana*, July 1938, p. 30). Hahn wrote, "The flesh of these animals is said to be tender and well flavored. . . . There is, however, a strong antipathy among many people to eating most kinds of animals with whose flesh they are unfamiliar. If a taste for the meat of these animals could be cultivated, it would help to solve the problem of getting rid of a serious pest." And Evermann and Clark (1920) stated, "The flesh is abundant in quantity, sweet, palatable and very nutritious; it ought to be more extensively utilized as an article of food." We are acquainted with a recent graduate student and his family who used woodchuck as a meat staple and liked it as well as they did beef. Early settlers in eastern Illinois tanned woodchuck hides (usually with a solution consisting mainly of wood ashes) and made leather shoe laces and thongs for other uses. The tough hide is well suited to these purposes.

Farmers generally look upon the animal as a troublesome pest and wage campaigns to eradicate it from their cultivated fields. Poisoning of woodchucks has been conducted on an extensive basis for many years, and even today large numbers of cyanide cartridges are dispensed annually to kill woodchucks throughout the state. Hahn (1909) reported that "An ounce of bisulphide of carbon soaked into cotton or an old rag and thrown as far as possible down the hole of a woodchuck will usually asphyxiate the inhabitants." He mentioned another method which consisted of placing poison in ripe apples and leaving them along woodchuck trails or near their dens. Bounties for woodchucks have been paid in several Indiana counties.

Red foxes, gray foxes, domestic dogs, and badgers are known to kill woodchucks, but some dogs are not a match for a large specimen. Abnormal incisor growth is evidently sufficiently common to lead to the death of some animals because they cannot feed normally.

TAXONOMY. The subspecies in Indiana is *Marmota monax monax* (Linnaeus).

SELECTED REFERENCES. Grizzell, 1955; Hamilton, 1934; Schmeltz and Whitaker, 1977; Whitaker and Schmeltz, 1973.

Thirteen-lined Ground Squirrel
Spermophilus tridecemlineatus (Mitchill)

Striped Ground Squirrel, Eastern Striped Ground Squirrel, Striped Gopher, Thirteen-lined Gopher, Striped Spermophile, Thirteen-striped Spermophile, Spotted Prairie Squirrel

Citellus tridecemlineatus: Hahn, 1907a
Spermophilus tridecemlineatus: Bailey, 1893

DESCRIPTION. This is a chipmunk-sized, short-legged ground squirrel with a tail of medium length. Its unique dorsal color pattern consists of alternating brownish and buffy longitudinal bands from the ears to the tail. Inside the dark bands are rows of pale spots. The sides are buffy and the underparts are buffy to yellowish white. The hair is relatively sparse and individual hairs are rather stiff. The ears are short and protrude little beyond the hair of the head. The skull is most similar to that of the eastern chipmunk, from which it can be separated by the presence of five upper molariform teeth (the chipmunk has four). The skull of the thirteen-lined ground squirrel is considerably smaller than that of the Franklin's ground squirrel, except in immature specimens of the latter species.

There is moderate variation in the dorsal color of *S. tridecemlineatus* from Indiana, mostly in the color of the dark stripes, which may vary from chocolate brown to tan or dark buff. Some variation is due to age, for immatures tend to be darker than adults, and some appears to reflect seasonal changes, wear, and fading. In addition, partial albinos are occasionally captured. We have seen two pink-eyed, immature specimens that at a distance appeared white. Upon close examination, both retained faint dorsal markings. Hoffmeister and Hensley (1949) have provided an excellent description of a similar specimen from Illinois. The Indiana specimens, taken 10 July (Wabash County) and 30 June (Kosciusko County), had total lengths of 155 and 168 mm respectively.

Weights and measurements are shown in Table 82. The dental formula is

$$I \frac{1}{1} C \frac{0}{0} P \frac{2}{1} M \frac{3}{3} = 22.$$

STATUS AND DISTRIBUTION. *Spermophilus tridecemlineatus* was not mentioned from Wayne County (Plummer, 1844), Franklin County (Haymond, 1870) or Randolph County (Cox, 1893), although it is now known from all of these. Kennicott (1857) possibly first recorded the species from Indiana. Evermann and Butler (1894b) knew of its existence in seven counties (Benton, Carroll, Lagrange, Newton, Tippecanoe, Vigo, White) and mentioned that it was "rather common" in Vigo County and "pretty common" in Newton County. Butler (1895) was told that the species was "abundant along hedges and banks" in Newton County (*fide* W. W. Pfrimmer). This ground squirrel was considered to be "common on the prairies and among the sand ridges" of Lake and Porter counties (Blatchley, 1898). During the summer of 1905, Hahn (1907a) noted burrows of this species along railroad embankments along the Kankakee River and stated, "it is probable that it has extended its range, locally, at least, by following these embankments through the marshes." In 1909 he wrote, "In Indiana it is found only in the prairie portion, not extending much south or east of the Wabash River." He added records from Kosciusko, LaPorte, Steuben, and St. Joseph counties.

Adult thirteen-lined ground squirrel. Photo by Whitaker

Table 82

Weights and measurements of *Spermophilus*
tridecemlineatus from Indiana
(squirrels under 95 grams were not included)

	Males	Females
Total length (mm)		
n	53	56
x̄	252.6	247.9
range	232-276	235-291
SD	15.78	19.15
SE	2.16	2.55
Tail length (mm)		
n	53	56
x̄	83.35	81.37
range	71-79	41-97
SD	7.37	10.36
SE	1.01	1.38
Hind foot (mm)		
n	53	58
x̄	35.6	35.1
range	32-40	33-39
SD	1.68	1.5
SE	0.23	0.19
Weight (grams)		
n	51	56
x̄	139.49	137.97
range	95.5-223.4	96.3-234.0
SD	32.5	35.48
SE	4.55	4.74

Evermann and Clark (1911) elaborated on the status and distribution of this ground squirrel about Lake Maxinkuckee (Marshall County) and elsewhere:

This gopher is an intrusion from the prairie fauna to the westward of Maxinkuckee. It appears to be gradually extending its range eastward. Thirty years ago it was very rare or entirely unknown in Indiana except in the prairie counties along the western border of the State. During 1883–1885 the senior writer of this report had exceptional opportunities to become quite familiar with all parts of Carroll County, which lies some 50 to 80 miles south and a few miles west of Maxinkuckee, and in those years he saw a total of only three or four pairs of Striped Gophers within its borders and they were all in the extreme western part of the county where the land is largely prairie. During many years of almost continuous residence in that county (1858 to 1885) the species was never seen east of the Wabash River, but recently it is said to have appeared there. In Vigo County it was common from 1886 to 1891 and has so increased in abundance since then as to have become a serious pest.

In 1899 when our field work began at Lake Maxinkuckee the Striped Gopher was rare in that region; in fact, only one or two pairs were seen during that season. They had their home at the Gravelpit and were observed most frequently in August. In 1900 they were more numerous. Besides the colony at the Gravelpit, one or more were seen occasionally further south along the railroad, several about the sandy hills southeast of the lake, and now and then one was noted on Long Point. In 1904 they had still further increased. On July 3 one was found dead on the railroad near Murray's where it had evidently been killed by a passing train, and several others were seen at the Gravelpit. One or more were seen on Long Point, and in the autumn of 1906 several were observed there. In 1907, soon after corn-planting, these little rodents were found to have increased greatly in numbers about the Gravelpit. They became very destructive to the young corn in a field nearby. . . . The owner of the field shot 20 of them in May and early June. . . . The colonies on the sandy farms south and southeast of the lake had also increased considerably in numbers, as had also that on Long Point. . . . In 1910 it was learned that they were becoming more and more abundant every year. . . . Observations made in the fall of 1913 indicate that they are still increasing. . . . On the farms south, southwest and southeast of the lake they are getting to be a pest. They are probably now found west, north and east of the lake in suitable situations, but we have not observed them there, as our field work has not recently extended into those regions.

During the fall of 1922, Lyon (1923) conducted fieldwork in part of the sand dunes area of Porter County. He wrote:

This species is not uncommon along the Chicago, Lake Shore and South Bend Railway just south of the dunes. In the dunes proper just north of Oak Hill station and a few feet above the subdunal swamp my wife saw one of these spermophiles. It is not improbable that these animals have entered the region by following the railway and that the one seen opposite Oak Hill had followed the road leading from the station to the dunes.

In St. Joseph County, Engels (1933) considered this ground squirrel "one of the most numerous rodents" and noted that "Dozens live on the main campus at Notre Dame." Lyon (1936) reported *S. tridecemlineatus* from roughly the northern one-third of Indiana, within an area northwest of a line connecting Vigo and Blackford counties. He stated, "Undoubtedly in primitive times it was confined to the native prairie region of Indiana, but with the opening up of the country it has extended its distribution to take in the upper third of the state." At that time, there were preserved specimens from only six counties.

Mumford and Kirkpatrick (1961) summarized the distribution of this ground squirrel in Indiana, noting its progressive movement southeastward across the state from 1909 to 1936 and from 1936 to 1960. By 1960, its range extended over the northern two-thirds of the state north of a line connecting Vigo, Johnson and Franklin counties. Some of the first recorded dates of the species in these marginal counties are of interest. A specimen in the Joseph Moore Museum, Earlham College, taken in 1948 is the earliest for Wayne County. Aaron Nigh, who had lived in Shelby County since 1920, saw his first ground squirrel in that county in 1948, when a farmer brought him one for identification. Conservation Officer Dale Hood observed the first one in Franklin County in 1956 and one in Union County between 1957 and 1959. Ralph D. Kirkpatrick collected a specimen in a cemetery in Johnson County in 1959. On this date, the caretaker who had worked there since 1947 told Kirkpatrick that he saw the first ground squirrel in 1954.

Since 1961, we have obtained additional information regarding the continued movement of *S. tridecemlineatus* southward in the state. Conservation Officer Adolphus Schosker told Mumford he saw one at the north edge of Decatur County in 1965. In May 1965, Charles L. Rippy saw one along U.S. Route 31 a mile north of Edinburg (Johnson County). Rippy observed one in June 1966 (along U.S. 31) 2.5 miles north of Taylorsville (Bartholomew County). Richard Bartholomew told Mumford in February 1970 that the species was now on Camp Atterbury, in the northwest corner of Bartholomew County. And in July 1970, Charles M. Kirkpatrick saw one 4 miles northeast of Columbus, in the same county. James R. Gammon observed this squirrel in the fall of 1970 about a mile north of Greencastle (Putnam County). And on 27 June 1976, Mumford and his wife saw one along Route 59 about 2.5 miles north of Brazil (Clay County). The Mumfords have driven this road constantly for the past thirty years and this is the first

ground squirrel they have seen in this area. Since *S. tridecemlineatus* appears to use roadsides and railroad right-of-ways in dispersing, we can probably expect records from more southern localities, especially along U.S. 31 and along Interstate 65, which parallels it from Indianapolis to Louisville. We think it will be very interesting to determine just how far south this species will expand its range. Currently, the southern edge of its distribution in Indiana (Map 30) coincides fairly well with the southern boundary of Wisconsin glaciation.

Since this ground squirrel is colonial, it is often locally abundant. In three consecutive days of trapping with a dozen rattraps, 21 animals were captured on a lawn approximately 60 by 100 feet (Terre Haute, Vigo County). Several times we have trapped 8 to 10 animals in a couple of hours in an acre area on a golf course. In the early 1950s, this

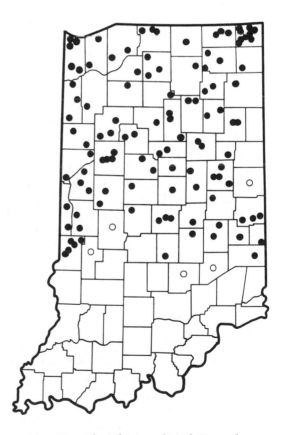

Map 30.   The Thirteen-lined Ground Squirrel, *Spermophilus tridecemlineatus,* in Indiana

species was so abundant in pastures at the edge of the Purdue University campus (Tippecanoe County) that Mumford sometimes snared as many as 8 animals per hour by hand. In August 1977, Whitaker's family collected 147 ground squirrels in a ten-day period from a cemetery north of Terre Haute. The capture area was about 28 acres of mowed lawn with scattered trees. It was felt that three or four times the number of squirrels taken were occupying this area. Thus, the 5.25 animals per acre actually caught could likely have been expanded to 15 to 20 per acre had all squirrels been removed.

HABITAT. Large populations have been observed in cemeteries and pastures, on airports and golf courses, and in other open habitats of similar nature, such as grassy roadsides or school campuses. Sometimes colonies are established in abandoned gravel pits, on lawns, or in taller vegetation (usually weeds) with some brush. The latter type of habitat is frequently present along railroad embankments and ditch banks. Weedy or cultivated fields, sand dunes, and fencerows are also inhabited, but the species shuns the woods.

The northwestern portion of Indiana, where S. *tridecemlineatus* formerly had a restricted range on the prairie grasslands, was quite wet much of the year. Little of this region was dry prairie, and large marshes and swamps were common. Ground squirrels no doubt had a spotty distribution, living only on the drier sites. Thus, in the late 1890s and early 1900s it was noted that these animals inhabited fencerows, banks, railroad embankments, sand ridges, and upland pastures. As the Kankakee River was dredged and most of northwestern Indiana was drained for cultivation, the species was able to take up new habitat. About this same time, much of the forest was removed from the state, further opening up the land to invasion by grassland species that had not yet penetrated the heavily forested areas. Dispersal routes were furnished by ditch banks, railroads, and roadsides.

Dellinger (1951) made observations on habitat utilization of the thirteen-lined ground squirrel in Montgomery County, noting its tendency to be colonial. He wrote:

[It] is commonly found grouped within a restricted area of a grassland with many individuals occupy-

ing only a small part of a large field and leaving the rest of the field uninhabited. For example, you may find four groups occupying only one-eighth to one-half an acre per group scattered about in a ten to forty acre pasture. In most cases, there does not appear to be any difference between the sites which each group occupies and the remainder of the field. This would indicate that they prefer to group together rather than to scatter out over the entire area. Year after year the groups occupy the same general area and seldom does a new group establish in another part of the field.

In one pasture, a colony occupied only an area of thirty by one hundred and fifty feet within a twenty acre pasture. This spot localization is partly attributable to the poor internal drainage of the pasture because of which most of the pasture is quite damp. The colony is occupying a small ridge; thirty feet wide, two hundred feet long, and rounded up to a height of three feet which was thrown up by men some years before. However, there are other high rolls naturally formed within the pasture which are also well drained. Yet it is claimed that these ground squirrels have never occupied any other part of the pasture but the forementioned man made ridge.

Hahn (1909) found them living "in a field of ripened oats."

ASSOCIATED SPECIES. Because of the lack of ground cover where this species exists there are few mammals that occur in close association with it. Possibly the deer mouse is most closely associated with it. The eastern mole and the woodchuck live underground in the same areas. In northwestern Indiana, Franklin's ground squirrel may live along the same roadsides where the thirteen-lined ground squirrel is found. However, S. *franklinii* appears to require much more ground cover, and the two species seldom occur together.

HABITS. This is a diurnal species and thus is easily observed in the open habitats it occupies. It spends the winter in deep hibernation. Ground squirrels are burrowers and excavate numerous and sometimes complicated tunnel systems beneath the ground. Because of their burrowing habit and the fact that they prefer cemeteries, golf courses, lawns, pastures, and other open locations, they frequently are in conflict with man. The animals seldom venture far from their burrows to feed, sun themselves, or play, and are always alert for danger. When disturbed, they may stand straight up on their hind feet, thus resembling a short wooden stake driven into the ground. Standing enables them to obtain a better view of the disturbance. If sufficiently frightened, they return to the burrow, sometimes again standing at the entrance to look about before entering. The animals usually then go just inside the burrow and may partially or completely emerge in a few minutes (or sooner). This behavior pattern enables one to snare them quite easily. Imminent danger causes the squirrels to retreat further into the burrow system. They run with the body near the ground and the tail straight out behind.

Burrows are usually from 1 to 2 feet beneath the surface of the ground and have one or two openings to the surface. Burrows may be 15 to 20 feet long and often have side passages branching off at various intervals. Burrow openings may have a mound or scattered loose soil at their entrances, or they may lack soil. Sometimes they are partially obscured by vegetation and are thus quite inconspicuous. Burrows are generally less than 2 inches in diameter. Evidently many burrows used for escape by the ground squirrels are shallow and short, for a few gallons of water poured into them will usually force the squirrels to emerge. Whitaker's family captured more than a hundred animals by this method in the summer of 1977, and again in 1978, for use in hibernation studies.

On 6 August an occupied burrow system was excavated by Whitaker and E. G. Zimmerman in the yard (mentioned earlier) where 21 squirrels had been trapped in three days. This system was exceedingly long and complicated and we do not know how many animals may have been using it, or portions of it. There were numerous openings to the surface and many side branches, most of them short, blind passages. Whitaker and Zimmerman could not completely map the system, because one tunnel extended into an adjacent lawn they were unable to dig up. The total length of the main passage was more than 16 meters, and there were more than 10 meters of side passages.

Hendricks (1967) excavated eight ground squirrel burrows in June and July. These varied in length from 28 to 186 inches and averaged 73 inches. Three had single entrances, the rest two each. The maximum depth of the burrows ranged from 8 to 24 inches and averaged 12 inches. Five burrows each contained single nests and one held two nests. The burrow enlargements where nests were located measured 5, 6, 6, 7, 7, 7, and 7 inches in diameter. Exclusive of the nest cavities, tunnels varied in diameter from 1.75 to 3 inches. Hendricks noted that "burrow systems generally were at least 4 feet from any isolated projecting object, such as a tree or utility pole; however, fencerows seemed favored excavation sites. Most burrow holes were obscured by tufts of grass, making them difficult to see, since mounds of soil did not mark the openings. Runways in the grass formed irregular patterns and often could be followed to a burrow system." Four of the burrow systems excavated were oriented north-south, three east-west; the other was L-shaped, with one opening each to the north and east.

Spermophilus tridecemlineatus is active mostly during the warmest part of the daylight hours. On warm summer days the animals emerged on a golf course (Terre Haute) about the time the dew had dried up (roughly between 8:30 and 9:30 A.M). In other locations we have noticed that the species does not emerge early in the morning. Much of the time aboveground is spent foraging for food or engaging in chases, some of which are apparently associated with reproductive activity. Dellinger noted that "On sunny warm days they are out in numbers scampering about usually in close proximity to a hole." They are wary animals, constantly watching for possible danger and difficult to approach closely or to catch unaware at any distance from an escape burrow. They give a birdlike chattering call, which probably serves as a warning between members of the colony. The call is often heard as one approaches a burrow into which a squirrel has just disappeared. This rapid chatter or chirping call is similar to the prolonged chirping of the common house cricket (*Acheta domesticus*). Groups of immature ground squirrels foraging about the burrow entrance will scamper into the burrow when disturbed, and then, one by one, poke their heads and forequarters out of the burrow to look about. Mumford photographed seven such animals (evidently a litter), with their heads and forequarters out, their hindquarters and bodies entwined in the burrow entrance. A sudden move on Mumford's part sent them scrambling into the burrow, from which they again emerged to repeat the performance.

Juvenile thirteen-lined ground squirrels. Photo by Mumford

In some habitats well-used runways radiate from the burrow openings into foraging sites. Such runways are not always readily visible. H. P. Weeks, Jr., noted in August that the ground squirrels were using runways located beneath tall, lodged bluegrass in old fields on the Purdue Wildlife Area (Tippecanoe County). Voles were also using the runways. We do not know if the use of such runs by ground squirrels is unusual, but this is the first time it has been called to our attention.

Hibernation probably begins in October or November and lasts until March or April. It is difficult to obtain precise dates when animals enter into and emerge from hibernation in the wild. From specimens collected and observations made throughout Indiana we have compiled information regarding the appearance of *S. tridecemlineatus* aboveground from late fall to early spring. Many of our observations during the last thirty years have been made near Lafayette (Tippecanoe County), where this ground squirrel is common. Ground squirrels were noted aboveground there on 23 and 26 November 1960 and on 29 November and 2 December 1961. We have November sightings of the species from Benton, Fayette, Union, and Vigo counties. On 22 December 1957, a fresh, dead thirteen-lined ground squirrel was found on a road near Crown Point (Lake County).

Individuals were seen on 2 January 1971 (Tippecanoe County), 4 January 1966 (La Porte County), and 5 January 1965 (Benton County). One was recorded in Tippecanoe County on 3 February 1962, a day when the temperature was around 50°F. The earliest March dates are the 13th (Delaware and Newton counties), 16th, 23rd, 25th, 26th (all Tippecanoe County), 27th (Johnson County), 28th (Benton County), and 30th (Lake County). We have seven dates of observations (for five different years) from 2 to 10 April (Benton, Grant, Tippecanoe, and White counties).

At Terre Haute, where many specimens of this ground squirrel have been collected, the latest date of collection is 18 October; 14 animals (10 males, 4 females) were taken during that month. Whitaker gathered additional information during the fall of 1977. Until about 1 October, numerous squirrels were out nearly every day. One to three ground squirrels were aboveground on 5, 10, 20, 22, 23, 29, and 30 October. One was seen on 4 and 5 November. No doubt animals were actually aboveground later than this date, but systematic visits were not made later in the fall. On the dates mentioned above, the daily temperature ranged from 59 to 72°F. One ground squirrel was found in hibernation on 17 March 1964. Dates of the earliest animals trapped aboveground were for two females taken on 26 April 1964. No concentrated effort was made to determine dates of spring emergence or fall disappearance, so the dates we do have are probably subject to change with more intensive fieldwork. In Wisconsin, Jackson (1961) did not see a ground squirrel aboveground later than 1 November, but W.L. Engels saw one on a golf course at Green Bay on Christmas Day, 1931.

During hibernation, the animals curl into a ball in a nest of leaves or grasses. The nests are usually placed below the frost line, for obvious reasons. It is unknown what percentage fail to hibernate successfully, for flooding, low temperature, predators, and disturbance of the hibernacula all probably take a toll. In preparation for hibernation, the animals accumulate large quantities of fat during the fall. Even in late September and October some individuals were found to have as much as 11 grams of fat under the skin. The one hibernating ground squirrel we examined was an adult female, found on 17 March in a nest 6 feet below the surface of the ground. The respiration and heartbeat rates slow dramatically during hibernation, so animals in deep hibernation feel cool to the touch and appear dead. Johnson (1928) recorded respiration rates of 187 to 213, 13 to 27, and 7 to 9 per minute respectively for *S. tridecemlineatus* awake, sleeping but not hibernating, and hibernating. Heart rates ranged from 350 beats per minute in excited animals, 100 to 113 in sleeping individuals, and 5 to 7 in hibernation. He also found that laboratory animals lost up to 39 percent of their body weight during hibernation.

Captives kept by Hendricks (1967) were studied under simulated hibernation conditions.

When refrigerated at 1 to 5°C., the squirrels assumed an upright prenatal position in the nests within 48 hours. They hibernated in this position but could be dislodged mechanically while nest material was sampled. As the temperature rose, the squirrels became more active and generally entered the upper cage at temperatures above 10°C. They took food and water during 48-hour periods of elevated temperatures and quickly returned to a torpid state as the temperature decreased to 1 to 5°C.

This ground squirrel can be kept in captivity with relative ease. J. O. Dunn told Ever-

mann and Butler (1894b) that he had "kept two striped gophers in a cage for nearly a year." Physiologists at Purdue University have conducted much research on the hibernation of the species and maintained caged animals for extended periods. A few animals exposed to direct solar radiation in traps when the air temperature was in excess of 95°F died in the traps.

FOOD. Hahn (1909) examined a specimen of *S. tridecemlineatus* that had its cheek pouches full of Canada thistle seeds, and remarked that the species also ate insects, especially crickets and grasshoppers. Certainly on the prairie remnants of northwestern Indiana at certain seasons crickets and grasshoppers are abundant. We once set a trapline on the Beaver Lake Prairie Chicken Refuge in summer and these insects rendered it almost useless by feeding on the bait and snapping the traps. Evermann and Clark (1920) noted that ground squirrels fed on corn at Lake Maxinkuckee in 1907: "They became very destructive to the young corn in a field nearby. They would pull up and eat the young plants. One individual was seen to pull up 20 stalks." They also mentioned its feeding on wheat, oats, grass and other tender plants, and upon grains and seeds of various kinds. We collected a male on 2 April that had its mouth full of corn. Nixon A. Wilson found one dead on the road on 9 July that had 328 grains of wheat in its cheek pouches. Since this ground squirrel does consume animal material, it probably eats eggs and young of ground nesting birds. Mumford observed an adult killdeer chase a ground squirrel that ventured near the killdeer's nest containing eggs. On 22 April 1970, when Mumford was censusing birds on a sandy prairie area in Newton County, a very weak thirteen-lined ground squirrel, which had apparently been injured, was observed feeding on the partially mummified carcass of an eastern cottontail. The squirrel was dragging its hindquarters and was easily captured by hand. It was badly emaciated and evidently starving.

Whitaker (1972c) examined the stomachs of 135 Indiana ground squirrels, *S. tridecemlineatus* (Table 83). Lepidopterous larvae was the single most important food item (14.9 percent by volume) and had been eaten by about half the individuals. The various parts of clover plants (leaves, seeds, flowers, and fruits) combined, however, constituted the most important food (18.5 percent). Some of the material listed as "green vegetation" was probably also clover. Heads of clover and chickweed were eaten whole. Other foods eaten often were the seeds of finger grass,

Table 83

Foods eaten by *Spermophilus tridecemlineatus* (n = 135)
from Vigo County, Indiana
(from Whitaker, 1972c)

Food Item	Percent Volume	Percent Frequency
Lepidopterous larvae	14.9	48.9
Trifolium (clover) leaves	12.0	28.1
Digitaria (crab grass) seeds	11.4	21.5
Cerastium (chickweed) seeds & fruit	9.0	16.3
Green vegetation	7.6	32.6
Acrididae (grasshopper)	7.3	29.6
Oxalis (wood sorrel) seeds	4.3	14.8
Carabidae (ground beetle)	3.7	25.9
Trifolium (clover) seeds, flowers & fruits	3.6	7.4
Mast	3.0	5.9
Scarabaeidae (scarab beetle)	2.3	12.6
Grass seeds	1.5	8.9
Scarabaeid larvae (scarab beetle)	1.4	4.4
Bird flesh	1.4	3.0
Elymus canadensis (wild wheat)	1.2	3.0
Seeds	1.2	3.7
Coleoptera	1.2	11.9
Annelida (earthworm)	1.1	9.6
Polygonum (knotweed) seeds	1.1	2.2
Taraxacum officinale (dandelion) heads	0.9	2.2
Chrysomelidae (leaf beetle)	0.8	8.1
Triodea flava (tall redtop) seeds	0.8	1.5
Oxalis (wood sorrel) leaves	0.7	0.7
Curculionidae (snout beetle)	0.7	8.9
Lepidopterous pupae (caterpillar)	0.7	4.4
Brassicaceae (mustard family)	0.6	2.2
Arthropod	0.6	8.1
Apple	0.5	0.7
Gryllidae (cricket)	0.4	3.0
Araneae (spider)	0.4	4.4
Unidentified material	0.4	3.0
Blarina brevicauda (Short-tailed Shrew)	0.4	0.7
Formicidae (ant)	0.3	11.1
Adult Lepidoptera	0.3	3.0
Lespedeza seeds	0.3	1.5
Hemiptera	0.3	5.2
Setaria (foxtail grass) seeds	0.2	0.7
Cicindella sexguttata (cicindellidae)	0.2	2.2
Lepidium (peppergrass) seeds	0.1	0.7
Coleopterous larvae	0.1	4.4
Carex (sedge) seeds	0.1	0.7
Coccinellidae (ladybird beetle)	0.1	1.5
Plecoptera (stonefly)	0.1	1.5
Blattidae (roach)	0.1	0.7
Amaranthus (amaranth pigweed) seeds	0.1	0.7
Endogone	0.1	3.0
	99.5	

and grasshoppers and beetles of the families Carabidae and Scarabaeidae (adults and larvae). Three kinds of vertebrates were found in the stomachs. Four stomachs contained birds, one a short-tailed shrew, and one a young prairie king snake. There are other literature references to ground squirrels feeding on vertebrates, including mice, chickens, young birds, cottontail rabbits, and a six-lined racerunner.

The most important foods (more than 3 percent by volume) were summarized on a seasonal basis (Table 84). From April to June, the two most important foods were seeds and fruiting bodies of chickweed; this food was not used later, presumably because it was not available. The second most important April–June food was lepidopterous larvae, followed by clover leaves and other green vegetation. In July and August, clover leaves were the most heavily used food, followed by lepidopterous larvae, wood-sorrel seeds, green vegetation, and clover. In September and October, the seeds of finger grass *(Digitaria)* became the most important food, followed by grasshoppers. Lepidopterous larvae were used at their lowest rate at this time (9.7 percent by volume).

REPRODUCTION. According to literature references, the thirteen-lined ground squirrel in other states copulates two to four weeks after emerging from hibernation, usually in April, and the period of copulation continues for two or three weeks (Wade, 1927). McCar-

ley (1966) reported that the breeding season extended from April to late June in northern Texas. The gestation period is about 27 to 28 days. Young are born later in the more northern parts of the species' range. There is usually one litter per female per year, but some females produce two litters.

A female dug out of hibernation on 17 March (Vigo County) exhibited no visible reproductive activity. We have examined a gravid female taken 18 April (Tippecanoe County) that contained embryos 11 mm in crown-rump length. Kirkpatrick and Conaway (1948) collected a female on 25 April (Tippecanoe County) that "had enlarged ovaries with young follicles." And on 31 May they captured two lactating females. Two females taken on 29 April (Vigo County) had no placental scars or visible embryos, but fertilization could have occurred by that date. We have examined nine gravid females taken on 7, 8, 11, 12, 14, 17, 18, and 25 May and 17 June. One of eight embryos in the female taken 11 May and four of seven in the female collected on 17 June were being resorbed.

In nine gravid Indiana thirteen-lined ground squirrels, the average number of embryos per female was 8.6, which corresponds with an 8.1 average (n = 269) reported by Criddle (1939) from Manitoba, Canada, and an 8.7 average reported by Rongstad (1965) from 27 southern Wisconsin ground squirrels. In our Indiana sample, the number of embryos per female ranged from 4 to 12. We have no information regarding litter size after

Table 84

Seasonal variations in food habits of *Spermophilus tridecemlineatus* from Vigo County, Indiana (percent volumes)
(from Whitaker, 1972c)

	April-June	July-August	Sept.-October
Number of stomachs	48	47	40
Lepidopterous larvae	16.4	17.8	9.7
Trifolium (clover) leaves	9.0*	19.5	6.3
Digitaria (crab grass) seeds	0.0	5.3	32.3
Cerastium (chickweed) seeds & fruit	25.4	0.0	0.0
Green vegetation	7.5	6.9	8.9
Acrididae (grasshopper)	2.6*	4.6	16.2
Oxalis (wood-sorrel) seeds	3.7*	8.6	0.1
Carabidae (ground beetle)	3.2*	5.7	1.9
Trifolium (clover) seeds, flowers & fruits	3.8*	6.5	0.0
Totals	71.6	74.9	75.4

*All in June.

parturition in Indiana ground squirrels. McCarley (1966) found that old females produced more young per litter than did younger females in Texas, and that the number of young that emerged from the burrows was less than the number of young born. According to various authors, young appear aboveground when they are from 4.5 to 7 weeks old. In Vigo County, the first young were trapped aboveground on 22 June, and ten were captured from 22 to 30 June. These young weighed from 11.9 to 41.7 grams each (average 31.4). Johnson (1931) reported the average weights for various aged ground squirrels as follows: 40 days, 27 grams; 50 days, 40 grams; 60 days, 59 grams; 70 days, 66 grams. From these data, some of the young trapped in Vigo County must have been considerably less than 4.5 weeks old.

Placental scars were present in many females taken from May through August, but none was found in females taken in September or October. These data probably indicate that none of the females examined had produced two litters during the season. It appears that most Indiana litters are born in May. The average litter size for 26 females with placental scars was 7.2, but it is possible that some scars had disappeared from some animals before the counts were made. At the Vigo County study area, all adult females taken in June had placental scars, but only 5 of 14 taken in August had visible scars (on 3 and 7 August). We have estimated that placental scars persist for about 50 days, using 20 May as the average latest date of parturition.

We have summarized testis sizes in males taken monthly from April to October (Table 85). Testis size was significantly larger in April than in any other month for which we have samples, then size declined rapidly in May and June and remained small until October. Testis size correlates well with the period of breeding indicated by gravid females. It appears that most copulation takes place in April, and our data do not indicate a second litter during the reproductive season.

Young are born in a nest of dry grasses and similar materials in the burrow system. Hendricks found that nests he examined were "constructed of tightly interwoven strands of grass from 2 to 7 inches long" and that "Nests were hollow and spheroid and completely

Table 85

Testis measurements from *Spermophilus tridecemlineatus* from Indiana

Month	Number examined	Testis size (mm) Average Length	Width
April	8	23.0	10.3
May	9	14.0	7.3
June	7	9.2	4.2
July	5	6.8	3.0
August	13	7.3	3.7
September	15	6.6	3.4
October	9	8.6	4.5

lined the enlarged burrow cavities which were above the floor of subterranean tunnels that lead to and from the atria." Five burrows each contained one nest atrium; another contained two. Two captive squirrels, held in the laboratory from November to March, constructed nests in simulated hibernacula within 5 days after grass nesting material was supplied. Evidently some nests are constructed in blind, side passages off the main burrow and others are along the main burrow. Young are said to be weaned at about 30 days of age, but others have observed young nursing after they emerged from the burrow system. We have obtained little data regarding young ground squirrels in Indiana. Mumford once observed an adult carrying a young in its mouth across a gravel road on 15 June. Mumford's car apparently frightened the adult and it dropped the young, which weighed 35.3 grams, measured 167 mm in total length, was well furred, and had its eyes open. It could crawl, but was easily captured by hand, and in captivity gave the typical "chitter" call of the species.

We have no growth information based on marked animals repeatedly weighed, but we have examined young animals taken aboveground (Table 86). By applying the age versus weight data from Johnson (1931), one can estimate approximate birth dates for these animals.

PARASITES. Wilson (1961) recorded 70 specimens of the louse *Enderleinellus suturalis*, 70 ticks (*Ixodes sculptus*), and 72 fleas (*Opisocrostis bruneri*) as the common ectoparasites on Indiana S. *tridecemlineatus*.

Hendricks (1967) studied the ectoparasites

Table 86

Weights and measurements of young
thirteen-lined ground squirrels from Indiana

Date	County	Weight (grams)	Total Length (mm)
10 July	Wabash	23.4	155
2 July	Vigo	28.2	133
30 June	Kosciusko	32.3	168
2 July	Vigo	33.0	139
26 June	DeKalb	36.1	154
5 July	Vigo	38.3	155
11 July	Whitley	58.4	198
14 July	Rush	71.1	209
10 July	Lagrange	73.5	204
2 July	White	98.9	221

on 117 specimens (73 males, 44 females) of this squirrel in Tippecanoe County. He found the three most abundant parasites were the same three listed by Wilson. Hendricks collected 141 individuals of *E. suturalis*; of these, 105 lice were on males and 36 on females. The lowest percentage of parasitism was in mid-May (none); the two periods of highest parasitism were in mid-March (about 35 percent) and mid-June (about 83 percent). He took 436 specimens of *O. bruneri*. Of these, 346 fleas were from males and 90 from females. The highest incidence of parasitism by these fleas was about mid-October (about 75 percent), with a much smaller peak in mid-June (about 27 percent). The lowest percentage of parasitized squirrels was examined in May and from July through September. Hendricks took 537 specimens of the tick *Ixodes sculptus*, 440 from males and 97 from females. Peaks of percentage of parasitized hosts occurred in mid-October (55 percent) and mid-August (about 90 percent). The lowest incidence of parasitism was mid-May (none). Other arthropod associates collected from ground squirrels by Hendricks were lepidopterous larvae and flies (11 identified as *Pegomyia finitima*). In addition, 5 adult diplura *(Parajapyx isabelle)* were found in a ground squirrel's nest and unidentified mites were found on several of the *O. bruneri* fleas. (Five of these mites were also found on 2 squirrels from Vigo County). The 54 specimens of the flea *Ctenophthalmus pseudagytes* were taken mostly (52) from nests. A single flea *(Nosopsyllus fasciatus)* found on one squirrel was thought to be a straggler. One specimen of the flea *Oropsylla arctomys* was found in a squirrel's nest, where it too may have been a straggler.

Whitaker (1972c) obtained detailed data on these and other parasites on 123 Indiana specimens (Table 87). He found 60 fleas *(O. bruneri)* on 31 specimens (0.49 per squirrel, overall), 453 lice *(E. suturalis)* on 31 animals (3.7 per squirrel), and 278 individuals of the

Table 87

Ectoparasites and other associates of *Spermophilus tridecemlineatus* (n = 123) from Indiana
(from Whitaker, 1972c)

Parasites	Parasites Total	Parasites Average	Hosts parasitized Total	Hosts parasitized Percent
Fleas (Siphonaptera)				
Opisocrostis bruneri	60	0.49	31	25.2
Beetles (Coleoptera; Staphylinidae)				
Atheta sp.	40	0.33	11	8.9
Sucking Lice (Anoplura)				
Enderleinellus suturalis	453	3.68	31	25.2
Mites (Acarina) other than chiggers				
Xenoryctes latiporus	500±	4.07	1	0.8
Androlaelaps fahrenholzi	278	2.26	56	45.5
Macrocheles sp.	56	0.46	11	8.9
Aplodontopus micronyx	15	7.50	2	100.00
Kleemania sp.	13	0.11	11	8.9
Dermacarus reticulosus	10+	—	1+	0.8

mite *Androlaelaps fahrenholzi* on 56 animals (2.26 per squirrel). Other ectoparasites found on Indiana *S. tridecemlineatus* included a species of *Macrocheles* (being described as new), of which 56 specimens were obtained from 11 hosts. This mite apparently has a phoretic relationship with the squirrel. Several hundred hypopial mites *(Xenoryctes nudus)* were found on one animal. And two additional species of hypopial mites *(Dermacarus reticulosus* Spicka and Gerrits, 1977; *Aplodontopus micronyx* Fain and Spicka, 1977) have been described from this species in Indiana. The former was found in the fur and the latter in hair follicles on the tail. Eleven specimens of *S. tridecemlineatus* from Vigo County were hosts to 40 staphylinid beetles. These insects were identified by N. D. Downie as *Atheta (fide* Leland Chandler). Their relationship to the squirrel is not clear, but they were found in the fur of animals dead but a few minutes.

The 137 Indiana thirteen-lined ground squirrels examined for internal parasites yielded 1 nematode, 90 cestodes in 11 animals, and 86 trematodes in 6 animals. None of the endoparasites have been identified.

DECIMATING FACTORS. Evermann and Clark (1920) mentioned a ground squirrel caught by a domestic cat and another struck by a train. Many are killed along roads by vehicles, and no doubt various predators take their toll of this diurnal species. We have one observation of a marsh hawk carrying a thirteen-lined ground squirrel (Newton County), and Mumford observed a carcass of this squirrel in the nest of a marsh hawk in southern Michigan. Ralph D. Kirkpatrick caught a ground squirrel that had severe malocclusion of the incisors.

TAXONOMY. The subspecies in Indiana is *Spermophilus tridecemlineatus tridecemlineatus* (Mitchill).

SELECTED REFERENCES. Evans, 1951; Fain and Spicka, 1977; Fitzpatrick, 1925, 1927; Hendricks, 1967; Howell, 1938; Johnson, 1928, 1931; Spicka and Gerrits, 1977; Wade, 1927, 1930, 1950; Whitaker, 1972c.

Franklin's Ground Squirrel
Spermophilus franklinii (Sabine)

Franklin's Spermophile, Gray Spermophile, Prairie Squirrel, Franklin's Gopher, Gray Gopher, Gray Ground Squirrel

Citellus franklini: Hahn, 1907a
Spermophilus franklinii: Bailey, 1893

DESCRIPTION. *Spermophilus franklinii* is a relatively large ground squirrel, exceeded in size among the ground-inhabiting squirrel tribe in Indiana only by the woodchuck. *Spermophilus franklinii* is near the size of the gray squirrel, for which it is sometimes mistaken. The upperparts are a grizzled, brownish gray and may appear spotted. The underparts are dull yellowish white. The tail is relatively long and bushy for a ground squirrel and is flattened dorsoventrally. The ears are rounded and short, and the legs are relatively short. There are only minor varia-

Franklin's ground squirrel. Photo by Roger W. Barbour

tions in color among the specimens we have examined from Indiana. Immatures are darker than adults.

Weights and measurements are shown in Table 88. The dental formula is

$$I \frac{1}{1} C \frac{0}{0} P \frac{2}{1} M \frac{3}{3} = 22.$$

STATUS AND DISTRIBUTION. The first published observation of this species in Indiana may have been by David Thomas (1819), who wrote about the "prairie squirrel." An 1880 list of the mammals of St. Joseph County includes "the large gray prairie squirrel." Dinwiddie (1884) reported its presence, under the name gray ground squirrel, in Lake County. It was recorded by Bailey (1893) from Benton and Newton counties. The following year, Evermann and Butler (1894b) remarked on its occurrence in Jasper and White counties. Blatchley (1898) recorded it from Porter County. Hahn (1909) collected specimens in Newton County, and listed it from Porter County as well. Lyon (1924) found the species in St. Joseph County

Table 88

Weights and measurements of *Spermophilus franklinii* from Indiana

	Males	Females
Total length (mm)		
n	30	14
x̄	350.2	352.8
range	265-390	295-378
SD	34.3	25.4
SE	6.2	6.8
Tail length (mm)		
n	30	14
x̄	119.2	124.6
range	73-152	101-138
SD	17.4	13.0
SE	3.2	3.5
Hind foot (mm)		
n	28	13
x̄	53.0	51.9
range	49-66	45-55
SD	4.9	2.9
SE	0.9	0.8
Weight (grams)		
n	24	12
x̄	378.9	347.3
range	229-520	182.2-509.0
SD	125.1	89.2
SE	25.5	25.7

and wrote that it "appears to be extending its range eastward." He summarized the available Indiana records in 1932. Lyon (1936) knew of specimens from only four counties and the known range of Franklin's ground squirrel was then bounded by Warren, Cass, and St. Joseph counties. Engels (1933) mentioned a farm in southwestern St. Joseph County where *S. franklinii* first appeared "only within recent years."

By 1958 there were specimens from Benton, Jasper, Lake, LaPorte, Newton, Porter, Pulaski, St. Joseph, Tippecanoe, and White counties. Glenn Baker observed Franklin's ground squirrels just southeast of Tyner (Marshall County) on 30–31 July 1961. On 14 August 1961, Mumford picked up a specimen killed on the road at the east edge of Tyner. On 13 June 1961, Ralph D. Kirkpatrick saw one 3.2 miles east of Pine Village (Warren County). Robert D. Feldt later observed one a mile west of Tab (Warren County) on 30 August 1962 and Mumford and R. Tuszynski saw another 2 miles south-southeast of Stewart (Warren County) on 7 July 1969. In May 1964, Robert Kern, who had lived in the vicinity for 45 years, saw his first Franklin's ground squirrel near Rochester (Fulton County); he trapped specimens the following year. In the summer of 1966, J. Masteller wrote a letter to the Indiana Department of Natural Resources describing *S. franklinii*, which he stated had been observed near Kewanna (Fulton County) "for some years." Carroll County was added to the range of the species in the spring of 1965, when Bill Willsey saw one enter a burrow along the roadside near the junction of routes 18 and 421. Dean Zimmerman obtained a specimen from Carroll County in 1976. It may occur in northern Montgomery County, for an individual was found dead on the road just 0.6 miles north of the Montgomery-Tippecanoe county line on 30 August 1958 by Nixon A. Wilson.

Spermophilus franklinii is currently known to occur in 16 contiguous counties in the northwestern quarter of Indiana (Map 31). We have seen specimens from 13 of these counties. Except for Carroll and Fulton counties, this is approximately its geographic range of 40 years ago. Unlike the smaller thirteen-lined ground squirrel, which has expanded its former range greatly and seems to still be doing so, Franklin's ground squirrel has exhibited little tendency to occupy new areas, even though the available habitat appears suitable to it. Persons should be aware, however, of the possibility of finding this species in new areas near the borders of its present range. We have had much the same experience as Lyon, who wrote: "Franklin's Ground Squirrels are comparatively rare in Indiana. In making inquiries about them in counties where they are known to occur it is often difficult to find persons who are familiar with them" (Lyon, 1932a).

Nothing is known regarding Indiana population size for this species. It is evidently colonial, for landowners speak of colonies or groups of the animals on their properties. However, we have no evidence that *S. franklinii* forms as large colonies as *S. tridecemlineatus*.

HABITAT. Most observations of *S. franklinii* in Indiana have been made along road-

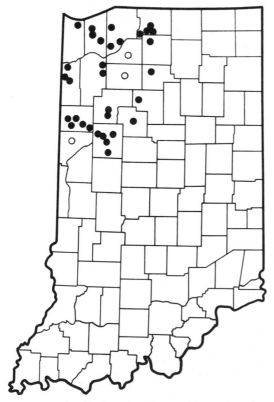

Map 31. Franklin's Ground Squirrel, *Spermophilus franklinii*, in Indiana

sides and railroad embankments, where mixed grasses and tall weeds were dominant. In some sites, scattered shrubs or small trees were also present. Other animals have been noted in weedy pastures, weedy / brushy old fields, along ditch banks, in a cemetery, and in waste areas in shrub and mixed weeds. Blatchley (1898) reported it "along hedge rows on the borders of prairie" in northwestern Indiana. Hahn found a colony in an oat field about a stone pile. One found dead on the road in Tippecanoe County was evidently living in an abandoned gravel pit. We have seen them along the sand dunes bordering Lake Michigan and in overgrown marsh borders with scattered trees around Wolf Lake (Lake County). Under present-day patterns of land use in Indiana, the best remaining habitat seems to be provided by railroad embankments, where dense grass / weed communities often form good cover and the embankments provide abundant sites for burrow locations. Kirkpatrick and Conaway (1948) also noted this preference. This ground squirrel does not occur in woodlands, and appears to prefer much more dense, tall cover than does *S. tridecemlineatus*.

ASSOCIATED SPECIES. The major associates of the Franklin's ground squirrel are the woodchuck, the plains pocket gopher, the thirteen-lined ground squirrel, the eastern mole, the prairie and meadow voles, the white-footed mouse, deer mouse, western harvest mouse, and meadow jumping mouse, the short-tailed shrew, and the masked shrew. In some habitats, the eastern chipmunk is also present.

HABITS. This diurnal species has been observed out of its burrow between 8:45 A.M. and 6:30 P.M. No doubt earlier and later daily observations could be made if someone studied *S. franklinii* intensively. Most sight records have been incidental and no research has been conducted on this animal in Indiana. It hibernates for several months, but details are lacking on dates of entering and leaving hibernation. The species has been seen aboveground from 20 April to 21 October. Blatchley (1898) mentions one that was dug out of the ground on 6 October (Porter County) that "had already entered a state of hibernation." Two were reported by a farmer to be hibernating under a haystack (no date was given). A specimen (no details) was collected 5 February 1890 in Benton County.

The habits of *S. franklinii* and those of *S. tridecemlineatus* are similar. Both live in burrows and forage out in all directions from the burrow entrances. Well-defined trails may be present from the burrows into favored feeding areas. Although *S. tridecemlineatus* often has a mound of excavated soil piled at the burrow entrance, *S. franklinii* most frequently does not construct such a mound. Soil excavated by the latter is normally scattered about, so the mouth of the burrow is more difficult to see. Burrows of *S. franklinii* are a little more than 3 inches in diameter. This is considerably larger than the burrows of *S. tridecemlineatus*. Nixon A. Wilson has trapped both species of *Spermophilus* in Indiana at the same burrow entrance. Evidently *S. tridecemlineatus* at times enters the larger burrows of *S. franklinii*. There appears to be some tendency for burrows to be constructed near some object. David A. Manuwal took two specimens "in a grassy area near a bridge." Lyon (1932a) trapped a specimen "in a rockpile near a culvert." Hahn (1909) found them living near and about a stone pile. A burrow being used by one in Carroll County was at the base of a telephone pole. Another lived under a cottage.

Lyon (1936) stated that *S. franklinii* was a good swimmer. He also mentioned the ease with which animals could be trapped in small steel traps placed at their burrow entrances. They can also be snared by hand quite easily as they emerge from their burrows.

They are often seen near the edge of highways, where they feed on vegetation, and possibly insects. We have wondered whether they might salvage insects killed by passing cars, since they feed so close to the edge of the road. When startled, they quickly retreat toward their burrows, which may be some distance away and so well hidden that they cannot be easily found by attempting to follow the animal. A chattering call somewhat like that (but louder) of the thirteen-lined ground squirrel is often given by startled individuals. Captives frequently gave this call. Captive animals also seemed to give off a musky odor, similar to that of a long-tailed weasel. Franklin's ground squirrels appear to take well to captivity, and Jon Heisterberg kept one through the winter (at Lafayette)

that successfully hibernated in a burrow Heisterberg provided in its outside cage.

Robert Kern found that if he stopped his car near the burrows of *S. franklinii* then sat in the car and made squeaking noises, the squirrels would approach him through the grass, then stand upright and look around. Even though some landowners are aware that the animals live on their properties, they tell us that the squirrels are seldom observed. It appears, then, that there is a tendency for *S. franklinii* to be more secretive than *S. tridecemlineatus*. This, and the fact that the former prefers heavier cover, probably are the reasons Franklin's ground squirrel is so poorly known.

Stullken (1950) found that some individuals of both species of ground squirrels that he captured by pouring water into their burrows and chasing them out died later from a respiratory infection.

FOOD. Vegetable matter evidently makes up the bulk of the diet. Hahn collected one with oats and another with several crickets in its cheek pouches. One killed on the road on 11 October had its cheek pouches filled with corn. Most animals observed along roads appeared to be eating grass or other vegetation. We have examined the stomachs of ten individuals from Indiana (Table 89). Green vegetation (including clover leaves) was the most important food, making up 43 percent of the volume, and all forms of vegetation, collectively, made up 85 percent of the total volume. Lepidopterous larvae were the most prominent animal food (8.5 percent of the volume), followed by ants (Formicidae, 3.5 percent). Flower heads of clover and dandelion were sometimes eaten.

REPRODUCTION. Females taken 9-11 May (Tippecanoe County) were in estrus, and captives were observed copulating 17 and 23 May (Kirkpatrick and Conaway, 1948). A female taken on 10 June (Fulton County) contained 11 embryos; 6 in the right horn of the uterus measured 25 mm each in crown-rump length, while 4 in the left horn were of similar size and 1 was only 9 mm in crown-rump length and was evidently being resorbed. A nonlactating female taken on 27 July had suckled young. Another female collected on 18 August appeared to be nursing young, and one taken on 14 September had

Table 89

Foods eaten by *Spermophilus franklinii* (n = 10)
from Indiana

Food item	Percent Volume	Percent Frequency
Green Vegetation	40.5	70.0
Corn	17.0	20.0
Trifolium (clover) heads	10.0	10.0
Lepidopterous larvae	8.5	20.0
Unidentified vegetation	8.5	10.0
Wheat seeds	4.0	10.0
Formicidae (ant)	3.5	10.0
Trifolium (clover) leaves	2.5	10.0
Taraxacum (dandelion) flowers	2.0	10.0
Acrididae (grasshopper)	1.7	30.0
Ant pupae	0.5	10.0
Carabidae (ground beetle)	0.5	10.0
Unidentified seeds	0.3	10.0
Gryllidae (cricket)	0.3	10.0
Unidentified fruit	0.2	10.0
	100.0	

suckled young earlier. A female taken 19 July had 10 placental scars.

We have little data on parturition or growth of the young. A 7 July specimen was 310 mm in total length and weighed 182 grams. Two immatures taken on 24 July measured 295 and 318 mm in total length. Two others captured 25 July were 265 and 280 mm in total length and weighed 146 and 149 grams. Three taken 31 July ranged from 304 to 336 mm in total length and from 229 to 264 grams in weight. On 1 August, two others were 310

and 321 mm long and had weights of 240 and 254 grams. A young female with very little fat, taken 4 August, was 325 mm in length and weighed 260 grams, while a 6 August specimen was 305 mm long and weighed 200 grams. On 18 August an adult and two immatures were seen foraging among clumps of grass on the foredunes (Indiana Dunes State Park).

A male taken on 26 April had scrotal testes (not measured). Males trapped on 9 May, 11 June, and 23 June had testes 21, 18, and 19

Table 90

Ectoparasites and other associates of *Spermophilus franklinii* (n = 9) from Indiana

Parasites	Parasites		Hosts Parasitized	
	Total	Average	Total	Percent
Fleas (Siphonaptera)				
Opisocrostis bruneri	14	1.56	5	55.6
Sucking Lice (Anoplura)				
Enderleinellus suturalis	516	57.33	4	44.4
Mites (Acarina) other than chiggers				
Androlaelaps fahrenholzi	184	20.44	6	66.7
Laelaps alaskensis	1	0.11	1	11.1
Macrocheles sp.	1	0.11	1	11.1
Ticks (Ixodides)				
Ixodes sculptus	115	12.78	3	33.3
Dermacentor variabilis	12	1.33	3	33.3

mm in length respectively. An immature male captured on 24 July had testes 6 mm long.

PARASITES. Few individuals of *S. franklinii* from Indiana have been examined for parasites. Wilson (1961) recorded a tick (*Ixodes sculptus*), a flea (*Opisocrostis bruneri*), and a louse (*Enderleinellus suturalis*) on specimens from Tippecanoe County. He also found another tick (*Dermacentor variabilis*) on this species, but considered it a straggler.

Of 9 Franklin's ground squirrels from Indiana examined by us, 7 were found to harbor parasites (Table 90). The major forms were the louse *Enderleinellus suturalis*, the laelapid mite *Androlaelaps fahrenholzi*, the ticks *Ixodes sculptus* and *Dermacentor variabilis*, and the flea *Opisocrostis bruneri*. The only other parasites found were one macrochelid mite (*Macrocheles* sp.) and a single specimen of another laelapid mite (*Laelaps alaskensis*).

Two of ten individuals examined for endoparasites harbored 11 unidentified cestodes.

DECIMATING FACTORS. Automobiles are responsible for the death of many Franklin's ground squirrels. The habit of feeding and living near roadsides makes the animals vulnerable to this type of mortality. We know of one instance where a domestic cat captured an immature Franklin's ground squirrel. Some years ago, personnel at the Purdue University Agronomy Farm, near Lafayette, killed several animals with poison.

TAXONOMY. No subspecies of *Spermophilus franklinii* is recognized.

SELECTED REFERENCES. Howell, 1938; Lyon, 1932a; Sowls, 1948.

Gray Squirrel
Sciurus carolinensis Gmelin

Southern Gray Squirrel, Northern Gray Squirrel, Black Squirrel

Sciurus cinereus: Wied, 1839
Sciurus leucotis: Plummer, 1844
Sciurus niger: Plummer, 1844
Sciurus Migratorius: Audubon and Bachman, 1846
Sciurus Carolinensis: Plummer, 1844

DESCRIPTION. The gray squirrel is slightly smaller than the other large (and more familiar) tree squirrel of Indiana, the fox squirrel. The underside and lateral portions of the tail are silvery in the gray squirrel, yellowish in the fox squirrel. The tail is long, bushy, and dorsoventrally flattened. The upperparts of the gray squirrel are usually grizzled gray, with scattered buffy tones. Many color variations occur. Allen (1952a) examined Indiana specimens "varying from a maroon through shades of rust, tan and white." The underparts are white or whitish, sometimes with buffy color or areas of deep chocolate. Albinos were reported by Plummer (1844), but no specimen is in collections. In the early 1950s, several albinos (probably introduced) lived in the city park at Linton (Greene County). Mumford saw a gray squirrel with a completely white tail on the Morgan-Monroe State Forest. Melanistic animals are now unusual, but formerly a considerable number of this color phase occurred in northern Indiana. In the summer of 1905, along the Kankakee River in Jasper and Porter counties, Hahn (1907a) found that "black or partially black squirrels were nearly as numerous as the gray." Blatchley (1898) mentioned that "jet black" specimens were occasionally seen in Lake and Porter counties. The flourishing colony of black gray squirrels now found in Goshen (Elkhart County) was introduced from Michigan (*fide* Samuel W. Witmer). B. W. Evermann recalled that the black phase was "not rare" in Carroll County when he was a boy (Evermann and Butler, 1894b). Rufus Haymond (1870) stated that some 30 to 40 years ago, about one-sixth of the gray squirrel population in Franklin County consisted of black animals. Plummer (1844) listed the black squirrel as occurring in Wayne County. At New Harmony (Posey County) LeSueur reputedly saw but a single black phase gray squirrel in many years. As will be noted later, the black animals evidently disappeared from Indiana after the early 1900s.

Walter L. Hahn examined specimens in northwestern Indiana that varied from "light grizzled back and white belly" to "grizzled back and dark belly." Kirkpatrick and Conaway (1948) trapped a female on 6 August that had a "reddish-fawn coat." "The usual grizzled gray color appears in only a few irregular spots about the head and fore legs." Numerous animals we have seen had dark, brownish black areas on the chin, face, feet, or belly. One is first inclined to think that this color is imparted by the stain from black walnuts, but the dark areas are usually too symmetrical to have been caused by staining. From time to time, individual gray squirrels have been observed that were the normal gray pelage except for the tails, which were pale chestnut. In the Lafayette area, many gray squirrels in winter show conspicuous white, furred surfaces on the backs of the ears.

The skull of the gray squirrel is about 59–64 mm long and is rounded above, with orange fronted, rootless incisors. The infraorbital foramen forms a canal through the zygomatic arch. The gray squirrel has a small premolar anterior to the molariform tooth row. This small tooth is lacking in the fox squirrel.

Weights and measurements are shown in Table 91. The dental formula is

$$I \frac{1}{1} C \frac{0}{0} P \frac{2}{1} M \frac{3}{3} = 22.$$

Gray squirrel. Photo by Mumford

Table 91
Weights and measurements of *Sciurus carolinensis* from Indiana

	Males	Females
Total length (mm)		
n	119	60
x̄	469.4	467.8
range	404-530	422-530
SD	21.9	24.1
SE	2.0	3.1
Tail length (mm)		
n	120	59
x̄	208.6	211.5
range	177-285	185-247
SD	25.8	33.0
SE	2.3	4.3
Hind foot (mm)		
n	118	52
x̄	64.9	64.2
range	50-76	60-71
SD	6.93	8.8
SE	0.63	1.23
Weight (grams)		
n	99	48
x̄	503.89	521.9
range	403-610	430-598
SD	44.5	73.5
SE	4.4	10.6

STATUS AND DISTRIBUTION. The gray squirrel occurs in suitable habitat throughout Indiana (Map 32), but is decreasing (or absent) over much of the northern one-third of the state. It is most abundant and maintaining its numbers in the more heavily wooded, unglaciated south-central region, and is more or less common in most other portions of the southern half of the state. In certain parts of northern Indiana, the species has been introduced in parks, cities, and other areas. For example, in the city of Wabash (Wabash County) gray squirrels occur that were brought there for release from southern Indiana (*fide* Raymond E. Wilson). The black squirrels in Goshen have already been mentioned. On the Jasper-Pulaski Fish and Wildlife Area gray squirrels were reestablished by releases begun about 1966. These animals were mainly from Lafayette and were released about the headquarters of the Fish and Wildlife Area after being on exhibition at the Indiana State Fair. By 1975, they had spread at least 2 miles from the release

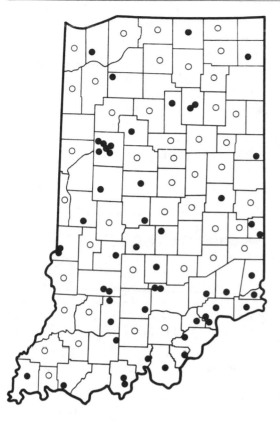

Map 32.   The Gray Squirrel, *Sciurus carolinensis*, in Indiana

site, according to personnel who checked squirrel hunters on the area. Other northern populations may also be the result of reintroductions.

Prior to the settlement of Indiana, *Sciurus carolinensis* was undoubtedly abundant in the entire forested portion. If it was present in the prairie region, it was probably largely confined to stream valleys and swamps. In these types of native habitats (such as along the Kankakee River) it has held out the longest.

There is comparatively little information regarding the current status of the gray squirrel in the northern half of Indiana. E. M. Chamberlain mentioned the gray and the black phases in Elkhart County in 1834. Evermann and Butler (1894b) noted that the gray squirrel was "common in places" in Randolph County and "formerly abundant" in Carroll County. Blatchley (1898) listed it as "common" in Lake and Porter counties, but Williamson (1900) considered it "rare" in

the vicinity of Round Lake and Shriner Lake (Whitley County). Hahn reported a spotty distribution in the portion of the Kankakee River valley where he worked during August 1905. He found none at Mountayr (Newton County), and at Bluegrass Landing (Newton County) it was "rare"; but in the swamps south of Aylesworth it was "very abundant" on both sides of the river (Jasper and Porter counties). The species was thought to be extinct in Noble County by 1909 (*fide* W. B. Van Gorder). It was reportedly "nearly extinct" in Lagrange County by 1909, and no black squirrels had been reported there since 1879 (Hahn, 1909). A single gray squirrel seen at Furnessville (Porter County) in 1918 was considered unusual (Brennan, 1923). At Lake Maxinkuckee (Marshall County) it was "very rare" in 1911, and only a few were known to have been killed near the lake the previous six or seven years (Evermann and Clark). Although a historian had mentioned the presence of gray squirrels in St. Joseph County in 1880, Engels (1933) knew of no definite record for the county. Of interest, then, is the observation of one at South Bend in 1972 (possibly introduced?). Lyon (1936) considered the gray squirrel "rare" in extreme northern Indiana.

We have seen specimens from Auburn (DeKalb County) taken in 1962, in Carroll County (1964), Wabash County (1970), and in Hammond in Lake County (1976). At one site at Crown Point (Lake County), where the gray squirrel was previously unknown by older residents, it is now common (*fide* J. F. Heisterberg). Over the past few years, several gray squirrels have been shot by hunters on the La Salle Fish and Wildlife Area (*fide* A. Burnside), and the species is said to occur at Hebron (Porter County). Mumford saw gray squirrels within the city limits of Hobart (Lake County) in the fall of 1979 and was told by residents there that the animals first appeared in 1977. We have no way of knowing whether these records are the results of introductions or represent remnant populations.

There is still a good number of gray squirrels in Turkey Run State Park, and in other areas in Parke County; these animals are considered to be natural populations. The species is also present in Shades State Park (Montgomery County). At West Lafayette

(Tippecanoe County) the gray squirrel is abundant in the city, and occurs in lesser numbers in suitable habitats in the vicinity. Gray squirrels live on the Ball State University campus (Delaware County). Robert H. Cooper and others told R. D. Kirkpatrick that this species had been there since at least 1923. This, then, appears to be a remnant, native population. Additional data are much desired from other parts of northern Indiana.

In 1947 and 1948, conservation officers from throughout the state were asked to report on the relative abundance of gray squirrels and fox squirrels in their counties. The average percentages of gray squirrels were summarized for the six districts set up for the administration of the Pittman-Robertson program: northwestern (12 counties), 2.5 percent; northeastern (17 counties), 0.3 percent; central (17 counties), 3.0 percent; southwestern (15 counties), 17.4 percent; south-central (14 counties), 50.3 percent; southeastern (17 counties), 21.8 percent. In the northern half of Indiana, gray squirrels appeared to be mostly along the Kankakee, Wabash, and White rivers and their tributaries (Allen, 1952a). In the southern half of Indiana, gray squirrels were more abundant, constituting an estimated 30 percent of the two species within the three southernmost districts. In the south-central district (the unglaciated portion of Indiana) the gray squirrel and fox squirrel were found in about equal numbers. The gray squirrel is almost absent in Vigo County (one taken in fifteen years that we are aware of), but is common in Clay County to the east and Parke County to the north. At Crane Naval Weapons Support Center (Martin County) about 73 percent of the squirrels killed are gray and 27 percent are fox squirrels (H. P. Weeks, Jr., personal communication).

Few detailed population studies have been conducted in the state, but Allen (1952a) has provided some data as a result of his work in Orange County. On a 70-acre study area of good gray squirrel habitat (where no fox squirrels were present and hunting was not permitted) he trapped 66 and 67 gray squirrels in two consecutive years. The number of animals that might have been present and not captured is unknown. Clearly, more such studies are needed in various gray squirrel habitats. On another Orange County area, consisting of 59 acres of lightly grazed de-

ciduous woods isolated from other woodlots, Eugene E. Good trapped 21 gray squirrels and 23 fox squirrels.

It seems probable that one gray squirrel per acre is a good population, but it would be interesting to determine numbers present in Turkey Run State Park, Spring Mill State Park, and other seemingly good habitats. Within the city limits of West Lafayette, where gray squirrels are abundant, a woman live-trapped 25 in a month on her lawn in the early spring of 1964 in a residential portion of the city. At another residence, C. M. Kirkpatrick trapped 18 animals in a yard in four days (1–4 August, 1971).

Based on data obtained from a questionnaire sent to 4 percent of Indiana hunters for many years, the annual gray squirrel kill has been estimated (Barnes, 1946a). For the six years 1943 through 1948, the average annual estimated kill was 350,600. And for the years 1963 through 1966, an average of 378,700 was harvested annually.

HABITAT. The best gray squirrel habitat in Indiana is probably extensive, mature, mixed deciduous woodlands with a well-developed understory on hilly terrain. In some of the most productive areas today these woodlands are interspersed with brushy fields. Mature and overmature trees usually provide more den sites, which are evidently essential for high populations. A good habitat also offers a wide variety of natural foods, some of which are available throughout the year. Young or second-growth forests do not contain these essentials in the same numbers and are likely to be inferior for gray squirrels. Heavily grazed woodlands or woodlots are also less desirable and usually are inhabited more by fox squirrels than by gray squirrels; the grays are often totally absent. Some hilly portions of south-central Indiana that support many gray squirrels are extremely dry in late summer, and little or no surface water is available over large areas. Gray squirrels have been introduced successfully into several towns, where they often do quite well. No doubt part of their success is due to the presence of old trees with natural cavities and protection from hunting. In such situations, they tend to replace the fox squirrel.

ASSOCIATED SPECIES. The closest single associate of the gray squirrel in most habitats is the fox squirrel. Where these two species do not occur together, the flying squirrel is probably the closest associate. In some areas fox squirrels and gray squirrels may occur in about equal numbers, but usually one far outnumbers the other. No one has studied closely the relationship of these species in Indiana. Allen trapped both species in the same traps during his study and found a nesting box that was used by one species one year and by the other species the next year. There seems to be a somewhat general belief that gray squirrels will drive fox squirrels out of an area, but proof is lacking. To our knowledge, few observations have been made of direct conflict between them. Both have been seen foraging near each other on the same lawn. We have observed one instance where a gray squirrel chased a fox squirrel. There were three gray squirrels, two fox squirrels, and a red squirrel foraging in the same small area. Suddenly a fox squirrel came down a tree trunk and a gray squirrel followed close behind. Both reached the ground and the chase continued for about 30 feet, until the fox squirrel ran through a woven-wire fence. The gray squirrel did not cross the fence and ceased its pursuit. We do not know in what context this brief encounter occurred, but certainly the gray squirrel put the larger fox squirrel to flight.

Red squirrels are closely associated with gray squirrels in relatively few areas, some being in cities. No doubt all other tree squirrels compete with the gray squirrel to some extent for dens and food. It appears to us that this subject would make an excellent study, for there are some areas where all four species occur in the same woods.

Other important associates of *S. carolinensis* in its woodland habitats are the eastern chipmunk, woodchuck, raccoon, opossum, white-tailed deer, gray fox, long-tailed weasel, white-footed mouse, woodland vole, eastern mole, and a few others. Of these, opossums, raccoons, and weasels may compete for dens. Chipmunks, mice, and deer consume many of the same foods. The weasel, gray fox, and raccoon are potential predators on the gray squirrel.

HABITS. Under natural conditions, the gray squirrel is more elusive than the fox squirrel. For this reason squirrel hunters are able to kill a higher percentage of the fox squirrels sighted than they do gray squirrels.

Data gathered in Indiana over four hunting seasons show that an average 40.7 percent of the gray squirrels seen and 50.6 percent of the fox squirrels seen were shot by hunters. Gray squirrels are not only more adept at hiding in trees, they frequently leave the tree quickly when disturbed and do not stop running until safely in their dens.

Gray squirrels also tend to be more active earlier in the morning than fox squirrels. On the Morgan-Monroe State Forest, where both species occur, 70.1 percent of 150 gray squirrels shot by hunters in one season were killed before 9 A.M. Only 56.5 percent of 92 fox squirrels were shot before this hour. The peak of the gray squirrel kill was between 7 and 8 A.M. Many gray squirrels were shot as soon as there was sufficient light at dawn for hunters to see. Few animals were reportedly seen between noon and 4 P.M. On the other hand, fox squirrels were fairly active throughout the day. Gray squirrels do have a second activity period in the evening, continuing until dark. But the best hours for hunting this species were determined to be between 6 and 9 A.M. Midday activity occurs in cool weather, seldom in warm weather.

Prevailing weather conditions vary daily activity somewhat. Allen found that on cloudy days with light rain, the morning activity was prolonged. If the rain was insufficient to wet the trunks and major branches of large trees, some squirrels remained out throughout the day. Heavy rain usually kept them in their dens. Wind reduced daily activity. The evening period of foraging and other activity may continue into deep dusk, even to darkness. An individual may occasionally be active at night, but more data are required on this phase of behavior.

The gray squirrel normally spends more time in trees than does the fox squirrel. However, both forage, feed, store food, gather nesting material, and travel on the ground. During the early part of the hunting season (15 August to 15 September) most squirrels are shot from trees, where they are feeding on ripening fruits of oaks, black cherry, black gum, tulip, and other trees; slightly later, they also feed on hickories. Shortly after mid-September (in central Indiana) many squirrels are observed on the ground, where they forage for and bury acorns and nuts, including walnuts. Both species of squirrels are more difficult to shoot at this season, for tree foliage is still dense and the animals are often able to escape on the ground rather than by climbing trees.

Gray squirrels may sunbathe on occasion, but little seems to be recorded regarding this behavior. J. M. Allen mentioned that individuals would stretch out on platforms of leaves and twigs in trees; this may possibly be sunbathing. We have seen one animal lying stretched out at full length along the peak of a roof on a warm April day (in town). Although this animal appeared to be sunning, there is a possibility that it was hiding there.

The usual vocal sounds given by *S. carolinensis* are a short "bark," a rather drawn out nasal call, a squeal, and, occasionally, a chattering call. The first two appear to be scolding or alarm notes. They are often heard when man, a dog, or some other intruder has been detected. Allen noted that a tame, pen-reared individual responded with the typical barking notes when it was roughly handled by him. Tail-jerking usually accompanies the barking call. Animals squeal when being handled in live-trapping operations or when unduly frightened. The captive above gave this type of call when it became entangled in some wire in its cage. Part of the vocabulary of the gray squirrel resembles some of the notes given by a domestic cat, hence in some southern states the name cat squirrel is given to the gray squirrel.

The gray squirrel normally lives in tree cavities or in leaf and twig nests which it constructs among the tree crowns and in buildings. It readily takes to nesting boxes, also. The leaf nests are temporary shelters, occupied mainly in warmer weather. The coldest weather is spent in tree holes and cavities where it is warmer and there is more protection from wind and other climatic features. Leaf nests are of three major types and have somewhat different uses. One seems to be a rather shallow, cup-shaped platform of leafy twigs. The animals lie on top of it. Such structures are sometimes called "cooling beds" and may be used primarily in hot weather, possibly to sunbathe. A more substantial, roughly globular nest of leaves and twigs is most commonly constructed. The squirrels cut twigs with leaves attached, usually in spring or summer (thus the cut twigs retain their leaves for some time). Nests are usually placed in a limb or tree fork

where they can be anchored more easily. Some nests are built in the treetops, where the small branches supporting them are incorporated into the nest materials. We have noticed that frequently a nest is placed in a tree where it can be partially supported by a grapevine or a poison ivy vine. The average nest is about 12 inches high and 14 inches wide, but size varies from smaller masses to nests as large as a bushel basket. Some nests have a definite entrance hole, but others do not. The squirrels simply push their way into the nest through the loose leaves. Some nests are lined with shredded bark (usually of grape or tulip poplar). Nests are built at various heights, ranging from perhaps 20 to 70 (or more) feet.

The third type of nest contains more twigs than the others and is more compact. Twig nests are usually built after leaf fall and are sometimes so well constructed that they are used during the winter. Such nests are usually somewhat basket-shaped structures made mostly of twigs and filled inside with leaves, to which is added shredded bark for more warmth. This type of nest is relatively uncommon in Indiana, possibly because it is usually too cold to permit the squirrels to live in such shelters throughout the winter.

Evidently leaf nests are seldom built in den trees. Allen found very few, and they were usually temporary structures that disappeared after leaf fall. A single squirrel appears to build each nest, sometimes completing the job in a day. Normally only one leaf nest per tree is noted, but two per tree may occur and we saw a tree at Lafayette that contained four nests. Damaged nests are frequently rebuilt. Allen found that only 7 percent of the leaf nests first found in July 1946 were still in good condition in December 1948. In 21 months, 74 percent of the nests were gone and 13 percent were no longer serviceable. Only 37 percent of the nests built in 1947 were serviceable and 37 percent were completely gone 11 months later. On the other hand, some nests were evidently maintained in good condition by the squirrels for at least three years.

On his Orange County study area of 70 acres, Allen noted that leaf-nest construction was initiated on 23 May and reached a peak about 15 July. From 15 to 18 July, he located 95 nests (1.36 per acre). For the entire year of

1946, squirrels constructed 141 leaf nests on this area. The known minimum population of gray squirrels (based on trapped and tagged animals) was about 65 to 70. No fox squirrels occupied the area. In February and March 1947, Allen found 91 leaf nests and from January to May 1947 he trapped 66 gray squirrels. It is evident that caution is required if one attempts to correlate the number of leaf nests with the number of gray squirrels present on a given area.

Den trees are of major importance to squirrels, for they are required for escape, shelter in inclement weather, and sites to rear the young. Most dens cannot be examined adequately without some degree of destruction, and thus few data are available from them. The squirrels carry leaves and other nesting materials into suitable cavities and holes in trees and construct warm retreats. Since the animals are usually not able to survive outside the dens throughout the winter, the number of den trees on an area may be a determining factor in regulating the winter population. On Allen's study area, a tree-by-tree census conducted in 1947 revealed 158 tree cavities that were "possible" denning sites. How many of these were actually used by the squirrels is unknown. The 158 possible dens were located in 119 trees, 60.5 percent of which were beech. There was a known minimum gray squirrel population of 66 on this study area in 1947. Without knowing more about competitive pressures from other wildlife species, it would appear that adequate den trees were present. Individual squirrels released from traps and then tracked with a dog did not seek a particular tree, but made use of many. Thus, an animal is no doubt familiar with a number of dens into which it can escape, and is not dependent on a single tree. It is unknown whether more than one squirrel used a tree containing multiple dens.

Cavities at the ground level (usually at the bases of trees) and within 3 to 4 feet of the ground were normally not used as dens by healthy animals. Crippled individuals or those released from traps would sometimes seek shelter in such sites. Numerous tree holes harboring gray squirrels on the study area had been constructed by pileated woodpeckers. Since some of these were excavated in living trees, squirrels often gnawed at the edges of openings which were growing shut, in attempts to keep them open. The number of adult gray squirrels per den was not ascertained. It would be good to know more about the seasonal usage of dens by squirrels.

All tree squirrels readily inhabit nesting boxes erected in their habitats. Nesting boxes are probably treated pretty much like tree holes, although they are probably not as warm in winter as most natural cavities in trees. Squirrels carry leaves and other vegetable materials to the boxes and construct warm nests. Gray squirrels in Orange County were found to use such boxes mostly from January through April. By May, few boxes were in use. In a year when litters were produced later than usual, the boxes were used all summer. Normally, the animals again seek the shelter of boxes in late October. In early winter, the boxes were completely filled with leaves, and animals entered through a small hole and went down a tunnel to reach the center of the nest, which was usually composed of shredded bark. In April or May, the squirrels often cleaned out the boxes and added fresh, green leaves. Two adult gray squirrels were often found in a single box during the winter months. Droppings did not accumulate in the boxes, indicating that the squirrels defecated outside their nests.

The gray squirrel does not hibernate, but may remain relatively inactive for some period of time during extremely cold weather. More research is needed on this. Squirrels store food for winter and also enter winter (in normal years) at their greatest weight. During the winter they progressively lose weight until spring foods are available. In April, the animals consume developing tree buds and quickly regain the lost weight. Food stored in the ground during the fall is located and excavated in winter. The animals locate this food by an excellent sense of smell, which operates through several inches of snow and soil. Edible nuts and acorns can also be distinguished from non-edible ones by olfaction. During a severe winter, George R. Parker observed gray squirrels burrowing under deep snow beneath his bird feeder. The squirrels would retreat into tunnels in the snow to escape dogs, and one hid in a brushpile until a pursuing dog departed.

The home range of a gray squirrel in good habitat may be relatively small. Allen's work with marked animals revealed that daily movements were generally within 100 yards of the den. As one would expect, home range was influenced by the abundance and location of available food. Also, it appeared that adults and immatures ranged over areas of different size in their daily activity. Winter home ranges of individual squirrels varied from 2.3 (adult female) to 18.3 acres (immature male). During a winter of scarce food, immatures had an average maximum range (farthest distance between traps where caught) of 200 yards, while adults averaged only 160 yards. The known maximum distance traveled by an adult (male) was 368 yards, for an immature (male), 425 yards. An immature male trapped 9 times one winter ranged over 6 acres; the same animal (caught 13 times) the next winter covered 18.3 acres. An adult male trapped within 8 acres one winter ranged over only 5 acres the next winter. Similar results for an immature female revealed that she ranged over 8.3 and 6 acres in consecutive winters, while an adult female was trapped within 2.3 and 5 acres during the same periods. Marked animals did not move long distances even when miles of continuous forest, broken only by dirt roads, were available to them. Gray squirrels are easy to trap and J. M. Allen found that several became "trap-happy" and were recaptured time and time again. An adult female was captured 19 times from January to May; two males were trapped 22 and 23 times each over two years.

There is a general fall dispersal of gray squirrels that occurs from about the first week of August through October. The peak of this "fall shuffle" is usually about the first half of September and coincides with the ripening of much of the mast. Southern Indiana squirrel hunters sometimes attribute poor early season hunting success to the fact that the squirrels have not yet arrived. We have no detailed data on the extent of the fall dispersal in Indiana.

Long-distance movements of gray squirrels (mostly in earlier years) are well known. Such irregular occurrences have been generally called migrations or immigrations. John J. Audubon witnessed a mass movement of gray squirrels across the Ohio River between Indiana and Kentucky in 1819 (Audubon and Bachman, 1849). No mention was

made regarding the direction the animals were moving. There was reportedly a great migration of gray squirrels in Wabash County in 1834. And large numbers of this species moved through Knox County in 1834, 1836, and 1837. Haymond (1870) mentioned an eastward migration in Franklin County in 1865. There was another movement of *S. carolinensis* across the Ohio River about 1933 or 1934; the animals entered Indiana in Spencer County, where local residents shot, clubbed, and otherwise killed the squirrels and carried them away by the sackful.

Gray squirrels routinely cross busy city streets by walking or running along horizontal cables strung between utility poles. These cables are about one-half inch in diameter and from 15 to 20 feet from the ground. John Miller told Mumford that he watched a gray squirrel run the length of a clothesline constructed of a single strand of No. 9 wire. Anyone who has fed birds in areas frequented by gray squirrels has been amazed at the success these animals enjoy in reaching bird feeders seemingly constructed and positioned so as to make it impossible for squirrels to reach the food. Feeders suspended from tree branches by a single strand of wire are not immune to pirating by the squirrels. Temple Pearson hung a feeder in such a fashion, but greased the supporting wire with lard. Several squirrels slid down the wire, struck the feeder, and fell to the ground, but one individual managed to hang on and get to the food.

FOOD. The gray squirrel consumes a wide variety of vegetable foods, but few data on food habits are available from stomach analyses. General accounts describe how the squirrels destroy corn, and it is well known that acorns, nuts, berries, seeds, fruits, buds, bark, and other foods are eaten from season to season. Garbage and trash containers are raided in parks and cities. Considerable information has been obtained from interviews with squirrel hunters, who recorded what foods the animals they hunted were feeding on during the hunting season. In many cases it is easy to determine by direct observation which foods are being taken. In mid-February we have seen *S. carolinensis* feeding on the bark of small basswood twigs, in the treetop. Red maple buds are taken in

March. Some observed April foods include elm and maple seeds; oak, maple, cottonwood, and Chinese elm buds; flowers of shagbark hickory and green ash. Other spring foods included tulip poplar flowers, maple leaves and stems, and mushrooms. Red elm seeds were being eaten in May. We have seen gray squirrels feeding on buckeye fruits. H. P. Weeks, Jr., has seen them eating oak galls.

There appears to be little recorded on summer feeding habits. Allen noted that mockernut hickory nuts were first being "cut" on 20 July. By August, green hickory nuts, tulip poplar seed heads, acorns, black walnuts, butternuts, and the seeds and / or fruits of black cherry, black gum, hackberry, dogwood, sassafras, blackberry, huckleberry, corn, beech, honey locust, and the like are being consumed. On Allen's study area, black oak and white oak acorns, shagbark and mockernut hickory nuts, and black walnut, black cherry, and tulip poplar fruits were part of the diet by 10 August. By 14 August, most feeding was confined to black oak and white oak acorns, hickory nuts, and flowering dogwood fruits. He found that acorns of the black oak group appeared to be less palatable than those of the white oak group. One summer John C. Callahan watched gray squirrels eating green tomatoes from his garden.

Food caching was observed to begin about 1 September on the Morgan-Monroe State Forest, and about ten days later much of the activity of the squirrels was confined to the ground, where food was being buried. The animals dig holes about 1.5 to 2 inches deep with their front feet, place one or two acorns or nuts in each hole, pushing and tamping them with the head, jaws, and shoulders, then scrape soil and leaves over the site with the front feet. The animals usually tamp down the covering with their feet. Cached food may be unearthed and consumed until a new crop is available the next fall.

Insects probably are readily eaten by gray squirrels when they are obtainable. Persimmons and mulberries are also included in the diet. H. P. Weeks, Jr., has observed that the pulp and not the seeds of persimmon is taken by gray squirrels. Birds are no doubt taken, also. Mrs. J. C. Callahan saw a gray squirrel retrieve a stunned American goldfinch that had flown into a windowglass and dropped to the ground. The squirrel carried the bird into a tree, but when the observer shouted at the squirrel it dropped the bird.

Feeding aggregations of gray squirrels are not unusual. Allen observed eleven individuals eating buds simultaneously in a single red maple tree. We have noted at least six feeding together in a beech tree.

REPRODUCTION. Pairing begins rather early; in January and February one can see precopulatory chases involving males and females. A female collected 14 January had a copulation plug. The gestation period is about 45 days. Females evidently produce one or two litters per year, depending upon the age of the females and on food conditions the previous season. Litters are produced from February through October, although two major peaks of litter production occur, the earliest probably in February and March and the second from June to August. Allen noted that after a good mast year most adult females had first litters in February and March, then produced second litters about June. Following a season of poor mast, most first litters were not born until July or August and few second litters were noted. The next season, due to the lateness of their birth the previous summer, most first-year females did not bear young. Thus, there may be considerable variation in parturition dates from various portions of the state. Food abundance appears to play an important role in determining the breeding season.

C. M. Kirkpatrick, R. A. Hoffman, and E. H. Barnett have provided much information pertaining to reproduction in Indiana gray squirrels. Their work concerned males primarily, but some data were obtained through the examination of females taken along with the males. Kirkpatrick and Hoffman (1960) found "that spring and summer born males attain sexual maturity at about 10-11 months of age. Spring males remain sexually active for 6-8 months while summer males are sexually potent for approximately 3 months." No sexually functional male was found in September. Both groups show sexual degeneration in late summer. Males born in summer breed for the first time the following May; those born in spring breed during the following January to March. Though Kirkpatrick and Hoffman presented the most recent analysis of the reproductive cycle in male gray squirrels, other details may be found in Hoffman (1952), Barnett (1955), Mossman, Hoffman, and Kirkpatrick (1955), Hoffman and Kirkpatrick (1956), and Kirkpatrick and Barnett (1957).

Since the reproductive period is long, it overlaps the hunting season. Allen estimated that 14 percent of the adult females shot in 1946 and 67 percent of those shot in 1947 were lactating. The 1947 season, however, followed a winter when mast was scarce; squirrels were in poor condition and the breeding period was evidently much prolonged or retarded.

At Lafayette, the number of embryos in 13 females averaged 3; 5 females contained 4 while a single female contained 1. We have relatively few embryo counts for gray squirrels, but a sample of 7 gravid females contained from 2 to 5 each and averaged 3.3.

Allen reported an average of 2.1 young per litter in 19 litters he examined in nesting boxes (Orange County).

Young squirrels apparently spend much of the first several weeks of their lives in the den. Their eyes are open at about 5 weeks of age. Allen reported that young are about 90 days old when they leave the den.

PARASITES. Plummer (1844) removed a *Cuterebra* or botfly larva "from the back" of a gray squirrel (Wayne County). J. M. Allen examined 5 gray squirrels in Morgan-Monroe State Forest carrying these larvae from 1946 to 1948. The parasites were embedded in the shoulder region. In the fall of 1976, squirrel hunters in southern Indiana (especially in Dubois County) began finding *Cuterebra* larvae in the neck region and front feet of both gray squirrels and fox squirrels. Some of the hunters had not seen such parasites in twenty years of squirrel hunting in the area. It is interesting that in one year this phenomenon would become so obvious. Whitaker, Spicka, and Schmeltz (1976b) found a single *Cuterebra* on the back of the neck of a gray squirrel.

Allen also recorded ticks, fleas, and mange mites from gray squirrels. Flea infestations of large numbers were observed in nesting boxes and dens. The first major work on ectoparasites of gray squirrels in Indiana was done by Wilson (1961), who reported a tick (*Ixodes marxi*), two lice (*Enderleinellus longiceps, Neohaematopinus sciuri*), and three fleas (*Ctenocephalides felis, Conorhinopsylla stanfordi, Orchopeas howardii*). The single specimen of *Ctenocephalides felis* was considered to be a straggler and not a normal parasite on *S. carolinensis*. Wilson considered *Conorhinopsylla stanfordi* a normal parasite of the gray squirrel in view of this association elsewhere, but he found only one specimen of this flea on 192 gray squirrels he examined from Tippecanoe County, Indiana. Some researchers think that this flea is primarily a nest-inhabiting species, thus few are found on the hosts themselves. Whitaker and Corthum (1967) took a total of eight specimens from ten southern flying squirrels collected in Indiana. It seems possible that the flying squirrel is a more important host of this flea than is the gray squirrel in the state.

Whitaker, Spicka, and Schmeltz (1976b) reported on the ectoparasites of 47 gray squirrels from several Indiana counties. Their results considerably enlarged the list of known parasites, and included three lice, one flea, three ticks, six chiggers, five other mites, and one dipteran (Table 92). Sucking lice were the most abundant, mainly *Enderleinellus longiceps* and *Neohaematopinus sciuri*. The common flea on the gray squirrel was *Orchopeas howardii*, but single specimens of *Ctenocephalides felis* and *Conorhinopsylla stanfordi* were recorded by Wilson. Of the three species of ticks, a single species (*Ixodes marxi*) had been reported by Wilson. It should be noted, however, that the rather large numbers of *Amblyomma americanum* were all taken from gray squirrels collected in Perry County. This tick probably occurs only in the southern part of Indiana (Wilson, 1961). Gray squirrels are host to at least six species of chiggers, the most regularly occurring species being *Neotrombicula fitchi* and *Walchia americana*. There are five other species of mites recorded from Indiana gray squirrels, the most abundant form being *Echimyopus orphanus*. This mite was described by Fain and Phillips (1977) from the nest of an unidentified bird of prey. Two other mites (*Haemogamasus reidi* and *Androlaelaps casalis*) have been commonly found on squirrels of the genus *Sciurus*. The presence of *Androlaelaps fahrenholzi* is not surprising, for it appears to be one of the least host-specific of North American mites (Whitaker and Wilson, 1974). An unidentified

Table 92

Ectoparasites and other associates of *Sciurus carolinensis* (n = 47) from Indiana
(from Whitaker, Spicka, and Schmeltz, 1976b)

Parasites	Parasites		Hosts Parasitized	
	Total	Average	Total	Percent
Fleas (Siphonaptera)				
Orchopeas howardii	52	1.11	25	53.2
Sucking Lice (Anoplura)				
Enderleinellus longiceps	1,018	21.66	31	66.0
Hoplopleura sciuricola	37	0.79	4	8.5
Neohaematopinus sciuri	968	20.60	29	61.7
Flies (Diptera)				
Cuterebra sp.	1	0.02	1	2.1
Mites (Acarina) other than chiggers				
Haemogamasus reidi	34	0.72	8	17.0
Androlaelaps casalis	60	1.28	6	12.8
Androlaelaps fahrenholzi	2	0.04	2	4.3
Echimyopus orphanus	51	1.09	5	10.6
Macrocheles sp.	1	0.02	1	2.1
Chigger Mites (Trombiculidae)				
Neotrombicula fitchi	13	0.28	8	17.0
Walchia americana	13	0.28	6	12.8
Neotrombicula whartoni	10	0.21	3	6.4
Eutrombicula alfreddugesi	4	0.09	4	8.5
Leptotrombidium peromysci	14	0.30	3	6.4
Microtrombicula trisetica	—	0.02	—	2.1
Ticks (Ixodides)				
Amblyomma americanum	57	1.21	3	6.4
Dermacentor variabilis	9	0.19	5	10.6
Ixodes marxi	7	0.15	5	10.6

mite of the genus *Macrocheles* rounds out the list of mites known from Indiana gray squirrels.

Endoparasites known from Indiana specimens are *Bohmiella wilsoni* and *Citellinema bifurcatum*. During the present studies, 32 gray squirrels were examined for internal parasites. One of these yielded 57 nematodes, but no cestodes or trematodes were found.

DECIMATING FACTORS. There are relatively few records of predation on Indiana gray squirrels. Floyd Moffatt described to J. M. Allen (1952a) an observation of a long-tailed weasel chasing an adult gray squirrel. The pursuit took place up and down trees and on the ground, "with both the squirrel and weasel squealing at every bound." Glenn A. Baker saw a great horned owl carrying an adult gray squirrel. Temple Pearson saw a

red-tailed hawk attempt to catch one of three gray squirrels on her bird feeder. Cats and dogs undoubtedly prey on this squirrel, especially in cities and in residential areas near good gray squirrel woods. Allen remarked that dead gray squirrels were seldom noticed on highways in southern Indiana. In the city of West Lafayette, however, many are killed annually on the streets by cars. Haller (1951a) found remains of gray squirrels in 1 of 92 red fox stomachs and 1 of 29 gray fox stomachs he examined.

Hunters harvest a large number of *Sciurus carolinensis* each year. Whether parasites or diseases have adverse effects has not been ascertained. Animals with severe cases of mange have been observed, but their fate is unknown.

TAXONOMY. *Sciurus carolinensis carolinensis* Gmelin presumably occupies the southern half and *S. c. pennsylvanicus* Ord the northern half of the state. Good series of specimens are not available except from Tippecanoe County, where *pennsylvanicus* is present. The taxonomy of gray squirrels may be further complicated by the transportation

of animals from southern to northern Indiana for restocking purposes.

SELECTED REFERENCES. Brown and Yeager, 1945; Fitzwater and Frank, 1944; Schorger, 1947; Uhlig, 1956; Whitaker, Spicka, and Schmeltz, 1976b.

Fox Squirrel
Sciurus niger Linnaeus

Middle Western Fox Squirrel, Red Squirrel

Sciurus rufiventris: Wied, 1839
Sciurus magnicaudatus: Kennicott, 1857
Sciurus rufiventer: Wied, 1862
Sciurus vulpinus: Haymond, 1870
Sciurus ludovicianus: Bangs, 1896b
Sciurus niger: Cox, 1893

DESCRIPTION. The fox squirrel is the largest tree squirrel in Indiana. Its upperparts are a tawny brown grizzled with gray, the underparts are yellowish brown or rufous. The dorsoventrally flattened tail is mixed rufous and black, and underneath it appears yellow, in contrast to the gray squirrel, in which the tail looks silvery. The ears are medium-sized, rounded, and yellowish in the fox squirrel.

Fox squirrels with entirely black underparts have been taken. Evermann and Butler (1894b) refer to black-bellied animals from Randolph and Wabash counties. In the fall of 1958 Mumford saw such a specimen that was killed along the Kankakee River (Newton County). Fox squirrels with black underparts have also been observed or collected in Daviess, Fulton, Hendricks, and Marion counties. Evermann and Butler refer to a nest that contained two red, two white, and two black young, but we have no further records of black-phased fox squirrels from Indiana. Albinos have been reported from Brown, Miami, Ohio, Porter, and Vigo counties. There are also several records of partial albinos.

Two fox squirrels with white tails were seen on the lawn at the New Harmony (Posey County) Library in August 1964. At the

Riverside Fish Hatchery (Indianapolis), on 2 June 1961, Mumford observed two fox squirrels of normal color except that each had a yellowish white tail. A specimen from near Liberty (Union County) has a partially white tail. An animal of unusual color was shot near Stockwell (Tippecanoe County) in October 1972. Its dorsum was all white, the belly was normal color, but there was a thin stripe of grayish on each side, separating the color of the belly and that of the dorsum. The remainder of the animal appeared to be normal.

The skull of the fox squirrel is about 62–70 mm long, is rounded above, and has rela-

Fox squirrel. Photo by Jack Smith

tively small postorbital processes. The infraorbital opening forms a canal. The incisor enamel is orange. The skull is similar in size and appearance to that of the gray squirrel, but has only four upper molariform teeth; the small anterior premolar is absent in *Sciurus niger*.

Weights and measurements are shown in Table 93. The dental formula is

$$I \frac{1}{1} C \frac{0}{0} P \frac{1}{1} M \frac{3}{3} = 20.$$

STATUS AND DISTRIBUTION. It seems evident that most historical accounts of squirrel numbers and their damage to settlers' crops in Indiana involved the gray squirrel. When Indiana was being settled, the fox squirrel undoubtedly had a much more restricted range and occurred in lesser numbers than it does today. Wied (1862) reported fox squir-

rels as common at New Harmony (Posey County) during the winter of 1832–33. Plummer (1844) listed *Sciurus niger* from Wayne County, but called it the black squirrel. He probably was discussing the black phase of the gray squirrel, not the fox squirrel. Haymond (1870) stated that "about 30 years ago the fox squirrel made its first appearance in the neighborhood of Brookville" (Franklin County, not far from Wayne County). *Sciurus niger* was included on a list of mammals occurring in St. Joseph County in 1880. Cox (1893) considered this species "quite common" in Randolph County. Evermann and Butler (1894b) had records of the fox squirrel from only 7 Indiana counties, calling it common in Carroll, Monroe, and Vigo counties. Surprisingly, Blatchley (1898) considered the fox squirrel "very scarce" in Lake and Porter counties, where one would expect the habitat to favor this species. Both

Table 93

Weights and measurements of
Sciurus niger from Indiana

	Males	Females
Total length (mm)		
n	113	103
x̄	529.3	539.1
range	418-620	445-627
SD	30	27.4
SE	2.8	2.7
Tail length (mm)		
n	110	103
x̄	242.1	246
range	200-342	190-330
SD	20.5	19.6
SE	1.9	1.9
Hind foot (mm)		
n	105	98
x̄	70.9	70.7
range	61-79	60-82
SD	3.9	4.0
SE	0.38	0.41
Weight (grams)		
n	75	83
x̄	768.6	803.21
range	504.0-1061.5	540.0-1207.2
SD	121.0	123.2
SE	13.9	13.5

of these counties lie within the region that was formerly mixed prairie and oak woodland, in which fox squirrels must have occurred. This squirrel was not noted at Lake Maxinkuckee in 1899, but one was observed the following year and others through 1907 (Evermann and Clark, 1911). In August 1905, when Walter Hahn collected and studied mammals in part of the Kankakee River valley, he found the fox squirrel common at each site he visited. It was considered "very common" in Monroe County in 1907 (McAtee). In 1906–07 *Sciurus niger* was common in small, more open woods in the Mitchell (Lawrence County) area, but in a mature forest studied by Hahn (1908b) a single individual was noted. Lyon (1923) reported that this squirrel was "frequently seen" in the dunes area of Porter County. Engels (1933) listed the fox squirrel as "fairly common" in St. Joseph County. For the state as a whole, Lyon (1936) did not consider the species common, but it was much more abundant than the gray squirrel in northern Indiana. Lyon had records from throughout the state and we have specimen records from 78 counties (Map 33). We are unable to determine whether or not the fox squirrel has always had such a wide distribution, but it seems likely that it may have been absent from some heavily forested portions of Indiana before settlement. This is speculative, and there is the possibility that enough openings, stream valleys, and other habitats existed to allow the species to enjoy a wide distribution. But it certainly did not occur in such numbers as the gray squirrel.

An estimated 1,425,000 fox squirrels were harvested annually by hunting in Indiana from 1943 to 1948 (Allen, 1952a). The estimated average kill for the years 1963 to 1965 was 1,136,000.

We have relatively little information on fox squirrel populations in Indiana. There has been no study conducted on areas where gray squirrels did not also occur. Between December 1942 and March 1943, E. E. Good trapped 23 fox squirrels and 21 gray squirrels on a 58-acre study area in Orange County. The tract was a lightly pastured deciduous woods separated from other woodlots by 200 yards. About 2 percent of the area was open fields.

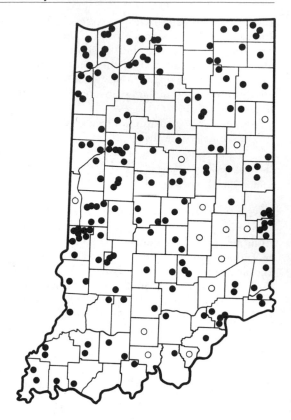

Map 33.   The Fox Squirrel, *Sciurus niger*, in Indiana

HABITAT.   In general, fox squirrels occupy less dense woodlands with less understory than do gray squirrels. Fox squirrels do not require extensive wooded tracts and readily adapt to pastured woodlots, windbreaks, residential areas, city parks, cemeteries, wooded fencerows, and even isolated clumps of non-mast-bearing trees in intensively farmed regions. Hahn (1909) knew of only a single fox squirrel in a 180-acre mature, undisturbed forest in Lawrence County during the winter of 1906–07. However, this same tract abounded with gray squirrels.

ASSOCIATED SPECIES.   What has been said about the gray squirrel holds in a general way for the fox squirrel. The major difference is that the red squirrel is more closely associated with the fox squirrel because of their overlapping ranges in the northern two-thirds of the state.

HABITS.   Some aspects of habits have been discussed for this species in the account of the gray squirrel. Fox squirrels spend more daylight hours out of their dens than do gray squirrels. *Sciurus niger* is also evidently somewhat nocturnal. George Dellinger (1951) reported that while hunting raccoons along cornfields on moonlit nights his dogs treed fox squirrels. Homer Martin and George R. Parker both told Mumford that their dogs also had treed fox squirrels on moonlit nights. On 14 March, Parker's dogs treed two fox squirrels at about 10:00 P.M.; the night was relatively warm and there was a full moon. Although the areas hunted by Parker contain many gray squirrels, he noted none at night.

Both gray squirrels and fox squirrels are excellent swimmers (gray squirrels swim the Ohio River), and fox squirrels have been found living in nest boxes attached to trees standing in 2 feet of water. In such habitats it may also be possible for the animals to reach the nest boxes by moving through the tree crowns. Adults flushed from such boxes jumped into the water and swam strongly to the nearest shore.

A fox squirrel running along the ground was clocked at 10 miles per hour for 50 yards by William E. Ginn, who was following it in a vehicle. In general, squirrels depend upon short bursts of speed to elude predators, then seek the shelter of a tree. When caught at a distance from a suitable retreat, they are often captured by dogs. After reaching a safe perch in or on a tree, some animals will pause, watch the intruder and scold with barking notes and jerking tails. The speed and agility with which both gray squirrels and fox squirrels can move from tree crown to tree crown are remarkable. They can leap gaps of several feet in moving from one tree to another. Occasionally an animal misses its footing and falls to the ground; but, seemingly unhurt, these individuals run rapidly away.

Where cornfields border wooded areas occupied by fox squirrels, there is much evidence of the squirrels' feeding on corn. The animals forage into the fields and carry ears (or partial ears) of corn back to the trees. They usually climb a tree and feed from an elevated perch, dropping the corncobs to the ground. If the ear of corn is too heavy, they feed on the ground, usually at the base of a tree, into which they can climb if danger threatens. Dozens of corncobs may be scattered about trees used frequently as feeding sites by these squirrels. If corncribs are in the vicinity of such wooded tracts, the squirrels will also take corn from them, sometimes traveling some distance to do so.

Dens and nests of fox squirrels are similar to those of gray squirrels. Stoddard (1920b) observed and described nests of fox squirrels in the dunes region of the state. He found that in early spring young were brought forth in open nests, which he described as follows:

These nests are round or oval in shape, tightly woven of freshly cut oak or other tough twigs. Inside of this twig shell comes a thick compact wall of large leaves, evidently pressed into shape while damp, making a smooth, tough lining capable of resisting wind, cold and rain. The nest proper is then made of soft inner bark, shredded leaves and other material. The entrance hole is on one end. . . . These nests are entirely different from the loosely constructed summer nests and are so compactly built that they frequently remain in place many years, the squirrels using them a great deal even in coldest weather.

Many nests found by Stoddard were in jack pines and were placed 20 to 40 feet or more above the ground. C. M. Kirkpatrick found *S. niger* nests not over 15 feet high in small pin oaks on the Jasper-Pulaski Fish and Wildlife Area. We have seen fox squirrel nests on the Beaver Lake Prairie Chicken Refuge (Newton County) that were constructed only 8 feet above the ground in trees. Trees are relatively scarce on this area and we feel that low nests have a much better chance of surviving the almost constant winds. Higher, more exposed nests would be difficult to construct and to maintain.

The relative wariness of fox squirrels and gray squirrels (with respect to man) has been discussed under the latter species. Fox squirrels are more likely to stay in the tree where first observed. They hide in clumps of leaves, by flattening themselves out on top of horizontal branches, and by keeping the tree trunk or large branches between them and the observer. This behavior allows hunters to harvest them more easily than gray squirrels, which are more active in movements and more likely to run to a den when first detected. Sometimes fox squirrels will climb a tree and enter a leaf nest to escape man. Unfortunately, some hunters will then shoot through the nest to obtain the squirrel; this is an illegal practice. Some of the animals thus shot do not fall, but remain in the nest and are not retrieved. A few individuals have been seen to enter burrows in the ground to escape danger. Squirrels seem less wary when approached quietly in a boat, a favorite way of hunting them along Indiana streams.

At least some individual fox squirrels wander in the fall. This is evident as one drives about the countryside from August to October. Robert D. Feldt and Marion Jackson observed two such animals on 29 August (Newton County). One was at least one-fourth mile from a single, large cottonwood tree; the other was the same distance from trees about farm buildings. At times an animal will be encountered along the road at least half a mile from any suitable habitat; others undoubtedly wander farther. Animals killed on the highways in nonwooded areas are also indications of these movements. Most of the early accounts of large squirrel migrations in Indiana concerned gray squirrels, but a few fox squirrels sometimes accompanied them (Hahn, 1909).

The calls of fox squirrels consist mostly of barking sounds. This species evidently does not give the catlike notes one hears from the gray squirrel. Trapped animals of both species may squeal when handled. Tail-twitching accompanies the barking of both species.

In hot weather, fox squirrels may come out of their nests and dens and lie in more exposed sites. Feeding and sunning during midday are not unusual for the fox squirrel. We have seen one photograph taken in July of an individual sprawled on top of a horizontal branch, with all four legs hanging down, among the foliage of a tree.

All tree squirrels found in Indiana appear to be subject to "shock disease" when trapped. Live-trapping programs usually result in some casualties. A number of animals are found dead in the traps or in a comatose state, from which they may not recover when removed from the trap.

FOOD.   Food habits of the fox squirrel and gray squirrel are very similar, though the fox squirrel probably eats more corn. In fact, corn may have been one food that greatly facilitated the range extension of this species in Indiana. Hickory nuts are a major food of the species from late summer through fall, although acorns and beechnuts are also important, and walnuts are occasionally used. In spring and early summer a variety of buds, flowers, and seeds are eaten, along with nuts from the previous year. Maple seeds are often eaten when ripening, and the young fruit of the tulip tree is a staple food in July and early August. Some bark is eaten; in one instance at Rochester (Fulton County), maples were girdled by fox squirrels which stripped off and chewed the bark. This occurred in June and may have had some nutritional significance to these city-dwelling animals (Allen, 1952a). Lindsay (1958) observed both fox and gray squirrels licking at something (perhaps salt) on highways in southeastern Indiana, and a fox squirrel habitually licked a brick walk. H. P. Weeks, Jr., has also seen S. *niger* licking asphalt roads. Bones, turtle shells, and even boards are gnawed by squirrels, perhaps for minerals. Fox squirrels extract the seeds from the large globular fruits of Osage orange, and Hahn recorded their feeding on blackberries. Evermann and Clark (1911) described how cockleburs were harvested by squirrels. Elinor Vesey (*in* Meek, 1960) watched a fox squirrel "reaching inside a hornet's nest . . . and feeding on the larvae" at South Bend, the winter of 1959–60. F. H. Montague, Jr., has seen fox squirrels eating soybeans.

Fox squirrels and gray squirrels both readily come to bird feeders to eat grain, sunflower seeds, and other food items placed there for birds. Occasionally, birds are captured by the squirrels at such feeders. Harold Bruner reported that a fox squirrel caught a sparrow-sized bird at his bird feeder and carried its prey into a nearby nesting box in a tree. H. P. Weeks, Jr., observed fox squirrels digging through 12 inches of snow to find food they evidently located by olfaction. Wood duck nests in nesting boxes have been destroyed by fox squirrels on some of the fish and wildlife areas.

REPRODUCTION.   Kirkpatrick (1955) has summarized information on the reproductive cycle in male fox squirrels. He found that males capable of breeding were present in the population each month of the year except August; undoubtedly, a larger sample would reveal their presence in this month also. Males usually become sexually mature at about 11 months of age.

Courtship begins at least by January. What appeared to be a courtship chase was observed by Mumford on 27 December (Martin County). His attention was first attracted by a series of sharp, birdlike chirps given at intervals. The site was an old planting of white pines in which the trees were about 75 feet tall. Two fox squirrels were running, one behind the other, among the tree tops. The sexes of the animals could not be determined, but it is assumed they were a male and a female. The animals moved from tree to tree and probably occupied about twenty trees in all during the period they were under observation (4:15 to 4:30 P.M.). Wherever the first animal went, the pursuer followed. It was not possible to determine which animal was giving the occasional chirping note. The animals were usually from 2 to 4 feet apart, but twice the "male" appeared to attempt copulation with the "female." The maximum temperature for the day was 14°F, and it was windy and partly cloudy. Neither the beginning nor the end of the chase was observed.

The gestation period is about 45 days. Gravid females have been examined from February to December. F. H. Montague, Jr., observed an obviously gravid female constructing a nest in a nesting box on 13 February (White County). She was gathering leaves from a shingle oak near a black walnut tree containing the nesting box. She did not climb the oak, but climbed the walnut tree and crossed from it into the oak.

As in *S. carolinensis*, most young are born from February to March and from June to August. The average number of embryos contained by 12 gravid females was 3.0; individuals had from 1 to 5 embryos each, but 8 females contained 3 each. Four newborn young of one litter averaged 15.5 grams and had total lengths of 112, 114, 115, and 120 mm. Two naked young, found 10 March in Jasper County, measured 98 and 99 mm in total length and weighed 17.4 and 16.8 grams respectively. Two young estimated to be 7 and 8 weeks old averaged 240 grams.

The opening of the squirrel-hunting season in Indiana (usually about 15 August) overlaps the reproductive period of the fox squirrel. During the season of 1948 on the Morgan-Monroe State Forest, Allen found that 28 percent of the females shot by hunters and examined by him were lactating. In 1946, he had found no lactating females during the hunter bag check. At the Willow Slough Fish and Wildlife Area (Newton County), only 4 of 30 adult females examined between 13 August and 10 September were lactating. It appears that the abundance of food available during the fall preceding the breeding season determines to some extent the timing of litter production (as it does in *S. carolinensis*). But Allen thought that possibly *S. niger* exhibited less variation in annual breeding seasons because it fed on more agricultural crops.

PARASITES AND DISEASES. Wilson (1961) recorded a tick (*Dermacentor variabilis*), three lice (*Enderleinellus longiceps*, *Hoplopleura sciuricola*, *Neohaematopinus sciurinus*), and two fleas (*Orchopeas howardii*, *Orchopeas leucopus*) from Indiana fox squirrels. He recorded a single specimen of *O. leucopus*, which is usually found on the genus *Peromyscus*. Wilson examined 47 animals for ectoparasites.

Whitaker, Spicka, and Schmeltz (1976b) summarized information on the ectoparasites they found on 137 fox squirrels from several Indiana counties (Table 94). In addition to the six species reported by Wilson, one tick (*Amblyomma americanum*), four chiggers (*Neotrombicula fitchii*, *Walchia americana*, *Neotrombicula sylvilagi*, *Miyatrombicula cynos*), five other mites (*Haemogamasus reidi*, *Androlaelaps casalis*, *A. fahrenholzi*, *Echimyopus orphanus*, *Dermacarus* spp.) and one *Cuterebra* were added. Sucking lice were the most abundant parasites recorded, and the three species found by Whitaker *et al.* were also found by Wilson, and in the same order of abundance.

Three species of ticks were found on both *S. niger* and *S. carolinensis*. Of interest is the fact that *Amblyomma americanum* occurred only on fox squirrels collected in Martin County. Likewise, all of this tick found on gray squirrels were from Perry County. That tick is evidently a southern Indiana species. One fox squirrel had two *Cuterebra* larvae

Table 94

Ectoparasites and other associates of *Sciurus niger* (n = 137) from Indiana
(from Whitaker, Spicka, and Schmeltz, 1976b)

Parasites	Parasites		Hosts Parasitized	
	Total	Average	Total	Percent
Fleas (Siphonaptera)				
Orchopeas howardii	198	1.45	47	34.3
Orchopeas leucopus	1	0.01	1	0.7
Sucking Lice (Anoplura)				
Enderleinellus longiceps	2,578	18.81	66	48.2
Neohaematopinus sciurinus	1,212	8.85	50	36.5
Hoplopleura sciuricola	502	3.66	25	18.2
Flies (Diptera)				
Cuterebra sp.	2	0.01	1	0.7
Mites (Acarina) other than chiggers				
Echimyopus orphanus	342	2.50	11	8.0
Androlaelaps casalis	56	0.41	8	5.8
Haemogamasus reidi	19	0.14	7	5.1
Androlaelaps fahrenholzi	7	0.05	4	2.9
Dermacarus sp.	2	0.01	1	0.7
Chigger Mites (Trombiculidae)				
Neotrombicula whartoni	68	0.50	9	6.6
Walchia americana	65	0.47	8	5.8
Neotrombicula fitchi	47	0.34	15	10.9
Neotrombicula sylvilagi	5	0.04	1	0.7
Eutrombicula alfreddugesi	4	0.03	3	2.2
Leptotrombidium peromysci	4	0.03	2	1.5
Miyatrombicula cynos	2	0.01	2	1.5
Ticks (Ixodides)				
Amblyomma americana	46	0.34	7	5.1
Dermacentor variabilis	15	0.11	9	6.6
Ixodes marxi	15	0.11	5	3.6

embedded in the abdominal area; this seems to be the first published record of this parasite from *S. niger* in Indiana.

Merle L. Kuns (unpublished) listed the following endoparasites from Indiana fox squirrels: *Bohmiella wilsoni, Citellinema bifurcatum, Strongyloides* sp., *Eimeria sciurorum, Ascaris* sp., *Physaloptera* sp. He also recorded coccidiosis in a male taken in January 1947.

Mange appears to be a common affliction of fox squirrels. Charles M. Kirkpatrick examined a male taken in June that had the "body practically bare except for tail and feet." A weakened adult female, observed on 20 May at Lafayette, hopped (did not run) from an observer in pursuit, climbed a short distance up a tree trunk, fell, and died. There were approximately 225 ticks attached to this animal and it was suffering from a moderate infection of coccidiosis. Allen examined a healthy appearing animal with 63 attached ticks.

DECIMATING FACTORS. Kase (1946a) found the remains of fox squirrels in 3 of 27 gray fox stomachs and 5 of 221 red fox stomachs he examined. In other states, great horned owls have been determined to take fox squirrels. Allen (1952a) found two 45-day old fox squirrels (one dead, with puncture wounds) in a nesting box with a screech owl, which may have killed the squirrel. Large numbers of fox squirrels are killed on the roads by cars and other vehicles. The fox squirrel appears to be much more vulnerable to this type of mortality than the gray squirrel. Grant Henderson saw a red-tailed hawk with a fox squirrel.

TAXONOMY. The subspecies in Indiana is *Sciurus niger rufiventer* E. Geoffroy St.-Hilaire.

SELECTED REFERENCES. Allen, 1943; Baumgartner, 1939, 1943; Brown and Yeager, 1945; Hicks, 1949; Packard, 1956; Whitaker, Spicka, and Schmeltz, 1976b.

Red Squirrel
Tamiasciurus hudsonicus (Erxleben)

Piney, Piney Squirrel, Chickaree, Boomer, Mountain Squirrel, Eastern Red Squirrel, Middle Western Red Squirrel

Sciurus hudsonius: Kennicott, 1857
Sciurus hudsonicus: Cox, 1893
Tamiasciurus hudsonicus: Rand and Rand, 1951

DESCRIPTION. The red squirrel is the smallest diurnal tree squirrel in Indiana. It is rusty reddish above and whitish below. The dorsum exhibits a distinct summer and winter pelage. In summer, the upperparts are uniformly reddish to reddish brown, the belly is white or whitish, and a short black stripe separates the underparts from the upperparts. In winter the middorsal region is reddish, bordered by grayish olive, the upper surface of the tail is mostly reddish (about the same color as the stripe down the back), the belly is whitish to grayish white, and the black stripe on either side becomes much faded and nearly disappears. The ears usually bear tufts of relatively long hairs in winter, but these tufts are absent in summer. Albinistic specimens have been reported from at least five counties. Bangs (1896b) mentioned albino red squirrels from Denver (Miami County). We have specimens or photographs of albinos from LaPorte and Tippecanoe counties. Another specimen has whitish areas in the tail. Engels (1933) wrote, "Mr. Al Tansey of South Bend says that about 1915 there were a pair of albino pineys living on the campus" at the University of Notre Dame. An albino was seen in the park at Delphi (Carroll County) in December 1961 (William Myers, conversation with Mumford). The skull size of this species is intermediate for Indiana sciurids. It is about 45

Red squirrel. Photo by Roger W. Barbour

mm in total length in adults—larger than the chipmunk, flying squirrel, or thirteen-lined ground squirrel, and smaller than the fox squirrel, gray squirrel, Franklin's ground squirrel, or woodchuck. The red squirrel skull has a short rostrum. The anterior upper premolar is usually absent, and when present is small and poorly formed.

Weights and measurements are shown in Table 95. The dental formula is

$$I \frac{1}{1} C \frac{0}{0} P \frac{2}{1} (or \frac{1}{1}) M \frac{3}{3} = 22 (or \ 20).$$

STATUS AND DISTRIBUTION. There is no information regarding the occurrence of the

Table 95

Weights and measurements of
Tamiasciurus hudsonicus from Indiana

	Males	Females
Total length (mm)		
n	77	67
x̄	310.0	316.7
range	262-390	280-385
SD	44.1	17.8
SE	5	2.18
Tail length (mm)		
n	69	66
x̄	127.5	128.10
range	100-190	100-172
SD	14	13.79
SE	1.69	1.69
Hind foot (mm)		
n	73	67
x̄	47.8	47.1
range	40-51	42-52
SD	2.79	2.98
SE	0.32	0.36
Weight (grams)		
n	57	54
x̄	204.4	199.1
range	150.0-252.3	151.0-241.4
SD	36.4	23.5
SE	4.8	3.20

red squirrel in Indiana for many years after the state was settled. The earliest published reference appears to be that of Haymond (1870), who stated that he knew of only one red squirrel ever having been observed in Franklin County. Plummer (1844) did not list it for Wayne County, where it is now locally common. Cox (1893) considered the red squirrel "very rare" in Randolph County. Records from Blackford, Franklin, Fulton, Huntington, Lagrange, Miami, Randolph, and Wabash counties were cited by Evermann and Butler (1894b). The Fulton County record was of an individual shot near Kewanna in December 1889. According to Cox, the red squirrel was abundant in Blackford County. It was listed as "the most common squirrel" in Huntington County. W. W. Pfrimmer informed Butler (1895) that he (Pfrimmer) had "heard of" the red squirrel in Newton County but had "not seen" it there. Blatchley (1898) reported that *Tamiasciurus* was "common in the timbered areas" of Lake and Porter counties. Hahn (1907a) thought the

red squirrel was present "only in restricted portions" of the Kankakee River valley. He found none at Roselawn or Mountayr, but collected a specimen near Aylesworth (Porter County) in 1905. He was told that the species was present "in large numbers" about the village of Boone Grove (Porter County) and he knew of records from LaPorte. Later Hahn (1909) noted its presence in the following additional localities: South Bend (St. Joseph County), Ray (county not known), Winona Lake (Kosciusko County), and Delaware, Fulton, Huntington, Lagrange, Marion, Miami, Randolph, and Wabash counties. He wrote: "In Indiana its range includes the northern part of the State only, and there are localities within its range where it is wholly unknown. I was unable to hear of it near Roselawn in northern Newton County. In southern Porter County, 30 miles east of Roselawn, it was abundant in a country that does not differ in the character of the soil, drainage or timber." In the autumn of 1922, Lyon (1923) found the red squirrel "fairly common in the wooded portions" of the dunes region of Porter County. Engels (1933) commented that this was the only species of squirrel living on the University of Notre Dame campus (St. Joseph County) and mentioned records as early as about 1915. When Evermann and Clark (1920) began their studies at Lake Maxinkuckee in 1899, red squirrels were not common. By 1904 "they were quite numerous." Evidently they continued to increase there until 1920. These authors also commented on the general range of this squirrel in Indiana:

The Red Squirrel, Pine Squirrel, Chickaree or Boomer, as it is variously called, is a northern species which is gradually extending its range southward in Indiana. Until within the last decade it was rare or wholly unknown in most parts of the state south of Logansport, though it is not uncommon in the more northern counties. On December 24, 1889, one was shot near Kewanna which is about 12 miles south of Maxinkuckee. It was regarded as a rarity in that region. About 1900 one was seen near Frankfort, about 70 miles south of Maxinkuckee, the first ever noted in that county. We have learned from Mr. Sidney T. Sterling of Camden, Carroll County, that it has recently appeared in that county.

Lyon (1934a, 1936) summarized the records known to him. In his 1936 work, he listed records (many unsubstantiated by specimens) from 55 counties (most of the northern two-thirds of the state). Some persons had expressed belief that the red squirrel was extending its range locally. This is possible, judging from what we have observed in Newton County over the past decade. The range extension mentioned by Walker (1923) was over a distance of about 8 miles.

Since the publication of Lyon's book on Indiana mammals (1936), there have been reports of *Tamiasciurus* in new areas. However, part of these may represent small, relict populations not previously detected. The early specimen records of red squirrels from Vanderburgh County (1902) and Jefferson County (1933) are interesting. Both counties border the Ohio River, considerably south of most present-day records. From Vanderburgh County north, along the western edge of the state, we know of no other specimen records closer than 115 miles (Warren County). Along the eastern border, red squirrels have been recorded as far south as Franklin County for some years. The collecting of a specimen in Switzerland County in November 1969 was unexpected. There are two reports for Owen County, the most recent being for 1961, when Harold Hasse shot one northeast of Gosport (conversation with Mumford). C. M. Kirkpatrick heard a red squirrel on the Purdue Southern Indiana Forage Farm, near Cuzco (Dubois County) in 1967. And there are unverified reports of red squirrels in Gibson County around 1957 or 1958. We have accumulated records for 14 counties not included by the range of *Tamiasciurus* indicated by Lyon (1936). The most interesting of these are probably reports from Clark, Decatur, Dubois, Gibson, Jackson, Jennings, Owen, and Switzerland counties, all in the southern one-third of Indiana. We wonder if the widespread planting of pines has been a factor in some apparent range extensions. Although red squirrels do not require evergreen trees, practically all pine stands within the range of the species are occupied by this squirrel. White pine stands are an exception.

One of the difficulties of determining red squirrel populations by live-trapping and tagging is that trap mortality appears to be quite high. For example, from September to March, Mark Fitzsimmons trapped 35 red squirrels on his study area in Tippecanoe County; of these, 14 were found dead in the traps. An additional individual that was re-trapped and released in what appeared to be good condition was found dead the following day in a hole at the base of a tree. Mr. O. L. Chance of Connersville (Fayette County) wrote Mumford in May 1960 that a man in that town had trapped 17 red squirrels "in his buildings." We do not know the time period involved or if more than one set of buildings harbored the animals. Near the headquarters of the Jasper-Pulaski Fish and Wildlife Area (Pulaski County) there has been a local abundance of red squirrels for many years. We trapped 5 each on 26 October and 30 November 1972 in a few hours. There was a large number of red squirrels at Garrett (DeKalb County) in 1922, when Victor Walter reported "100" in a single beech tree; even allowing for considerable over-estimation, this must have been an unusual aggregation. Walter related this incident to Mumford in conversation.

One area for which we have fairly good data regarding the arrival and distribution of the red squirrel is the Willow Slough Fish and Wildlife Area (Newton County) and surrounding territory. Willow Slough was established in the early 1950s and many biologists, naturalists, and others have worked on or visited the area continually since that time. Elmer Rix, who lived on the south edge of the property, first observed red squirrels at his home in 1971; the same year, others noted signs of this squirrel at a different location on Willow Slough. By 1977, red squirrels were present throughout the area and at numerous sites (mostly pine plantations). We do not know how the squirrel invaded this region, which is mostly prairie. There were reports of red squirrels 5 miles east of Enos and 5 miles northwest of Kentland (near the Iroquois River) in 1967. In March 1968, Mumford found red squirrels in a jack pine planting just off the southeast corner of the Beaver Lake Prairie Chicken Refuge. This is an isolated stand of pines, but near a large drainage ditch, along the banks of which at that time were scattered large trees (mostly cottonwoods). The squirrels may have moved along this ditch. Not far south of the Beaver Lake site, in another pine plantation one-half mile north of North Newton High School, Mumford also found signs of red squirrels in March 1969. He revisited this site in December 1971 and was unable to find indications that the animals were then present. We suspect that movements of this species into new areas in country like Newton County are via waterways (ditches, streams, rivers), for contiguous stands of timber do not exist and even most fencerows have been kept free of trees and brush for many years.

It will be interesting to follow future changes in the distribution of the red squirrel in Indiana. We have plotted the current range as accurately as possible (Map 34).

HABITAT. Hahn (1909) noted the red squirrel's preference for open groves near buildings in northern Indiana, and earlier (Hahn, 1907a) wrote that it "appears to avoid the swamps" along the Kankakee River. However, it is common now in hardwoods along the Kankakee River in the La Salle Fish and Game Area. Whitaker shot five there in less than an hour and observed several more on 19 February 1974. Near Lafayette,

Red squirrel habitat along Kankakee River in Lake County. Photo by Whitaker

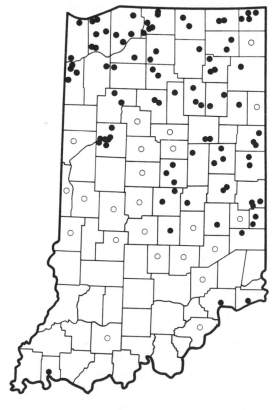

Map 34.   The Red Squirrel, *Tamiasciurus hudsonicus*, in Indiana

Kirkpatrick and Conaway (1948) thought it was apparently restricted to ungrazed wooded areas with good undergrowth. Evermann and Clark (1920), regarding habitats of the red squirrel at Lake Maxinkuckee, said, "Their favorite haunts about Lake Maxinkuckee are the heavier woodlands at the south end of the lake, Walley's woods, the timbered areas on the east side and the groves north and east of the Academy grounds." Wooded stream borders and adjoining swamps are also favored habitats. The red squirrel occurs in isolated woodlands and woodlots surrounded by cultivated fields in east-central Indiana. Other populations are present in residential areas, parks, cemeteries, and on campuses, especially where some conifer trees are present. It is common in conifers and deciduous woods along the anterior row of dunes in Dunes State Park (Porter County). Hahn (1909) noted that red squirrels had taken up residence in a row of catalpa trees bordering a street within the city limits of South Bend. In the extensive forests of south-central Indiana, the species is evidently quite rare and occurs in widely scattered localities.

ASSOCIATED SPECIES. All four native Indiana tree squirrels live in similar habitats. We have previously discussed the fox squirrel and the gray squirrel. Little can be added here to the comments for the gray squirrel. In some relatively small woods, the four tree squirrels, the eastern chipmunk, and the woodchuck all occur together. An example is McCormick's Woods (Tippecanoe County), on the edge of the Purdue University campus. Time and time again, we have read and been told that red squirrels drive out gray squirrels and fox squirrels. We know of no Indiana studies indicating that this has happened. Possibly changes in some areas favor the red squirrel more than other tree squirrels, so that red squirrels become dominant. Harold Hasse saw a gray squirrel and a red squirrel in the same tree.

HABITS. *Tamiasciurus* is essentially diurnal, but George R. Parker's dogs treed one at night (11 P.M.) while raccoon hunting on 27 January. Parker shined his flashlight on the animal and noted that it was quite active in the tree. Nancy Miller also reported nocturnal activity in an attic. The red squirrel spends much more time on the ground than do the other Indiana tree squirrels. It also makes extensive use of burrows in the ground and it burrows in the snow. Such burrows are mostly in evidence in pine plantations, where the squirrels store piles of cones for the winter. Burrows frequently are made in the cone (and their refuse) piles. Tracks in the snow attest to the use of these burrows in winter. The red squirrel is active all year, but may stay in its den for two or three days at a time in severe weather.

Red squirrels are ever-active, nervous, and alert. Most of their movements are fast. They move about in trees and from tree to tree with astonishing speed and can run swiftly on the ground. They appear to be good swimmers, also. They seem inquisitive and can be called within view, sometimes quite near, by squeaking noises. The squirrel peers intently at the disturbance, apparently poised for instant movement, and may call. The usual call is a distinctive chatter, often heard before one sees its source. At times, red squirrels are quite noisy. As with other tree squirrels, the tail is an expressive appendage. It can be twitched, curled over the back, hung loosely downward, or held in other positions, depending upon the occasion and the behavior of the individual animal.

Nests are constructed in tree holes and cavities or among the crowns of trees. Many tree-top nests we have seen in Indiana were built in the crowns of conifers. Such nests are globular and are smaller and more compactly built than those of the fox squirrel or gray squirrel. Red squirrel nests also contain more soft materials, including shredded bark, burlap, grasses, or other soft vegetation, and less leaves and twigs than those of the larger tree squirrels. A nest found in a nesting box in mid-April was composed mostly of fine grasses and other soft materials. The box was nearly full of the loosely packed material, but there was a hole in the top of this mass about 2 inches in diameter. This hole was the entrance to a short tunnel leading to the interior of the nest, which contained young (H. P. Weeks, Jr.). Nesting boxes are evidently used at all times of the year.

On 6 March, Weeks and Mumford examined a red squirrel nest from a tree. It was constructed mainly of grasses (99 percent), a few small bits of green mosses, about 15 feathers of a bobwhite quail and a cardinal feather, and a few shreds of a thin plastic bag. They also noted several other nests the same day in pine trees; most nests were in branches some distance from the tree trunks, but nests in conifers are often at the trunk near the top of the trees. Nests were generally globular and about 10 inches in diameter.

Red squirrels readily enter houses (both occupied and unoccupied) and other buildings, building nests in convenient sites. Sometimes this creates quite a nuisance, for the animals carry in nesting material and food in some quantity. Food refuse is scattered about. Gnawing is also a problem; the squirrels may gnaw through house siding to gain access to an attic and may gnaw at insulation or electric wires. Mothballs have been used successfully to drive red squirrels from an attic, according to Nancy Miller.

In a hardwood forest with several large hollow beech and other large trees on the

Willow Slough Fish and Wildlife Area, Whitaker watched red squirrel behavior patterns several hours one day in April. Several squirrels were present and much chasing was evident. At one point the observer approached too closely to two squirrels involved in a chase. They retreated to separate trees about 80 yards apart, and one squirrel entered, and stayed just inside, a tree hole. After about ten minutes the squirrel emerged and soon started calling. The call was immediately answered by the other squirrel; they called back and forth for about 4 minutes, then returned to a fallen tree between them which had been used during the previous chase, and continued the chase. At dusk, other squirrels were still chasing and calling, and one squirrel, calling from inside a hollow beech tree, continued calling until 12 to 15 minutes after dark. The presence of a red squirrel is often first detected by hearing the characteristic chattering call. Some individuals are quite vocal and will call persistently when disturbed.

One winter on the University of Notre Dame campus, a red squirrel used the burrow of a thirteen-lined ground squirrel and another an underground drain pipe (Engels, 1933).

Evermann and Clark (1920) obtained a small young red squirrel, which they kept as a pet. It reportedly became quite tame and would sit on one's shoulder and gently nip an ear to get attention. Evermann and Butler (1894b) quoted W. E. Bardsley as saying "Some neighbor boys raised fourteen young in 1892" (Huntington County).

FOOD. We have relatively little data on the food habits of *Tamiasciurus* in Indiana, although it consumes a great variety of seeds, fruits, nuts, and other plant materials (Table 96). Several persons have complained about the red squirrel robbing birds' nests of young or eggs. Lyon (1936) reported how one individual harvested blackberries by hanging upside down in the briers, suspended by its hind feet and picking the berries with its front feet. We have seen red squirrels eating ripe mulberries in late June. In mid-September they have been noted eating black oak acorns. The cones of several conifers are eaten and stored for winter. Among these are jack pine and Scotch pine. The squirrels do not appear to eat white pine; we have noted several times, even where white pines were adjacent to Scotch pine or jack pine stands heavily used by the squirrels, that white pine cones were untouched. We observed in late November that red squirrels had been feeding on the large fibrous fruits of Osage orange at the Jasper-Pulaski Fish and Wildlife Area. And in the camping area at the Indiana Dunes State Park some animals were

Table 96

Foods eaten by *Tamiasciurus hudsonicus* (n = 51) from Indiana

Food item	Percent volume	Percent frequency
Mast	79.5	82.4
Seeds	8.9	9.8
Green vegetation	2.2	3.9
Tubers	1.8	3.9
Grass seed	1.8	3.9
Lepidopterous larvae	1.8	2.0
Prunus serotina (black cherry)	1.7	2.0
White material, unidentified	1.7	2.0
Hemiptera	0.3	2.0
Lepidoptera	0.3	2.0
Curculionidae (snout beetle)	0.1	2.0
Formicidae (ant)	trace	2.0
Coleopterous larvae	trace	2.0
Cercopidae (froghopper)	trace	2.0
	100.1	

noted gleaning food scraps from the picnic tables.

Several red squirrels have been captured in bird-banding traps, which they may have entered either for the bait or to obtain birds. Baits used successfully for trapping this squirrel include apple, peanut butter, and corn. Various types of grains are taken from bird-feeding stations. Red squirrels store much food in the ground (nuts and pine cones mainly) for the winter (and early spring?). They also store food such as mushrooms by placing them on top of horizontal branches or branch forks in trees. Pine cones are gathered in large stores, often called middens. This behavior pattern is sometimes made use of by foresters who search out the middens to obtain pine seed rather than cutting cones from the trees. In a small planting of jack pines (Newton County) where red squirrels have lived for ten years we made some observations on stored jack pine cones on 14 October 1977. We located at least ten caches of cones, some at the base of trees and others under the large branches or trunks of fallen trees. The largest cache contained 187 cones and the second largest 84. Three other caches held an estimated 35, 50, and 75 each.

Red squirrels have a characteristic method of extracting the meat from black walnuts and butternuts. The animals gnaw an irregular hole on either side of the shell and remove the meat through these holes, each of which measures about one-half by three-quarters of an inch. The entire shell is not gnawed into frgaments (a habit of gray squirrels and fox squirrels), but remains mostly intact.

Fredrick H. Montague, Jr., told us that a tree stump on which he had placed a salt block (now gone) near his house is frequently visited by red squirrels, which gnaw away the wood of the stump. Fox squirrels in the same vicinity do not visit the stump.

REPRODUCTION. We have obtained meager information regarding reproduction in red squirrels. The gestation period is about 38 days. Gravid females have been examined from 19 February to 1 September. Lactating females have been examined as early as the week of 4–10 April. Six gravid females contained young as follows: 19 February, 5 embryos (5 mm); 16 March, 3 embryos (27 mm); 18 July, 3 embryos; 31 July, 3 embryos (15 mm); 15 August, 5 embryos; 1 September, 2 embryos (9 mm). Placental scars were observed in females taken 13 March (3 scars), 15 May (5 scars), and 17 December (7 scars).

Complete litters observed on 12 April, 15 April, and 1 May each contained 5 young. Those examined on both April dates were

Pine cones cached by red squirrel, Beaver Lake Prairie Chicken Refuge. Photo by David W. Berrey

Black walnuts and butternuts opened by a red squirrel. Photo by David W. Berrey

estimated to be only two to three days old. One collected from the 1 May litter weighed 26.9 grams. The litter found on 15 April was in a wood duck nesting box from which a red squirrel nest had been removed on 5 April. There are two peaks of litter production, one in spring and another in late summer. Additional data regarding this aspect of reproduction are desirable.

Males with enlarged testes have been collected in most months of the year, as follows: January, 22 × 10 mm; February, 17.9 × 9.6 mm; March, 20.3 × 12 mm; May, 18 × 9.5 mm; June, 17 × 10 mm; August, 11 × 4 mm; October, 8 × 5 mm; November, 10.5 × 5.5 mm; December, 18 × 9 mm. For these months, 1, 7, 3, 4, 1, 1, 2, 2, and 1 animals were examined (respectively). These data are too few to be more than indicative, but they suggest that males are capable of breeding

from about December through midsummer, so copulation may occur over an extended period.

Newborn red squirrels weigh about 6.7 grams and measure about 70 mm in total length (tail, 20 mm; hind foot, 10.5 mm) (Layne, 1954). We have examined relatively small specimens through the first half of November. For example, one killed on 14 November weighed only 42 grams and had a total length of 191 mm.

PARASITES. Wilson (1957) recorded a flea *(Orchopeas howardii)* from Indiana *Tamiasciurus*. Some animals appeared to have mange, but no mange mites were discovered. Wilson (1961) reported *Ixodes marxi* (8 individuals) and *Orchopeas howardii* (4 individuals) from Indiana specimens of this species.

Whitaker, Pascal, and Mumford (1979) ex-

Table 97

Ectoparasites and other associates of *Tamiasciurus hudsonicus* (n = 93) from Indiana. (from Whitaker, Pascal, and Mumford, 1979)

Parasites	Parasites		Hosts Parasitized	
	Total	Average	Total	Percent
Fleas (Siphonaptera)				
Orchopeas howardii	39	0.42	14	15.1
Ctenophthalmus pseudagyrtes	8	0.09	1	1.1
Epitedia wenmanni	2	0.02	2	2.2
Sucking Lice (Anoplura)				
Enderleinellus tamiasciuri	107	1.15	18	19.4
Neohaematopinus semifasciatus	105	1.13	13	14.0
Hoplopleura erratica	1	0.01	1	1.1
Mites (Acarina) other than chiggers				
Dermacarus tamiasciuri	449	4.83	20	21.5
Androlaelaps fahrenholzi	128	1.38	17	18.3
Haemogamasus reidi	108	1.16	15	16.1
Euryparasitus sp.	3	0.03	3	3.2
Haemogamasus ambulans	1	0.01	1	1.1
Androlaelaps casalis	1	0.01	1	1.1
Orycteroxenus soricis	1	0.01	1	1.1
Chigger mites (Trombiculidae)				
Neotrombicula whartoni	60	0.65	6	6.5
Euschoengastia setosa	38	0.41	12	12.9
Neotrombicula fitchi	35	0.38	4	4.3
Walchia americana	21	0.23	3	3.2
Miyatrombicula cynos	8	0.09	5	5.4
Leptotrombidium peromysci	2	0.02	1	1.1
Ticks (Ixodides)				
Ixodes marxi	32	0.34	9	9.7

amined 93 red squirrels for external parasites (Table 97). Although several other forms were found, major parasites were two species of sucking lice (*Enderleinellus tamiasciuri* and *Neohaematopinus semifasciatus*), one flea (*Orchopeas howardii*), one hypopial mite (*Dermacarus tamiasciuri*), two laelapid mites (*Androlaelaps fahrenholzi* and *Haemogamasus reidi*), and four species of chiggers (*Neotrombicula whartoni*, *Euschoengastia setosa*, *N. fitchii*, and *Walchia americana*).

Eighty-six squirrels were examined for internal parasites. Only three had internal parasites—one, one, and two nematodes respectively.

DECIMATING FACTORS. We have examined at least four specimens that were captured by domestic cats, evidently a major enemy of this squirrel in Indiana. Some animals are shot by hunters, although most of those killed are not used for food. For example, on some of the fish and wildlife areas where public hunting is allowed, squirrel hunters bring red squirrels to the checking station but discard them there. In some cases, these animals are not well known to the hunters and are shot out of curiosity. Perhaps more hunters should consider the red squirrel as a food animal, for Evermann and Clark (1920) wrote that "it makes a delicious stew."

TAXONOMY. The subspecies in Indiana is *Tamiasciurus hudsonicus loquax* (Bangs).

SELECTED REFERENCES. Allen, 1898; Hatt, 1929; Klugh, 1927; Layne, 1954; Whitaker, Pascal, and Mumford, 1979.

Southern Flying Squirrel
Glaucomys volans (Linnaeus)

Flying Squirrel

Pteromys volucella: Wied, 1839
Sciuropterus volans: Cox, 1893
Glaucomys volans: Howell, 1918

DESCRIPTION. This small brownish-gray squirrel is the only Indiana rodent with a well-developed gliding membrane (patagium) extending from the wrist to the ankle on either side of the body. The tail is greatly flattened dorsoventrally. The upperparts of *Glaucomys volans* are pale brownish or pinkish gray, with brownish tones (more common in summer). The underparts are white. The fur is dense and soft. The eyes are relatively large and black. About 1963, James A. Hughes reported a captive pink-eyed albino.

The skull is most similar to that of the thirteen-lined ground squirrel and the eastern chipmunk, among Indiana mammals. It is about 33 to 36 mm long, and has five upper molariform teeth; the infraorbital foramen is formed as a canal through a thick plate. (The eastern chipmunk has only four molariform teeth; the infraorbital foramen opens through a thin plate). In contrast to the thirteen-lined ground squirrel, the flying squirrel skull has the zygoma turned outward in such a way that their anterior portions are more horizon-

Southern flying squirrel. Photo by Philip C. Shelton

tal. Also, *Glaucomys* has a shorter rostrum, set off at a more abrupt angle than that of the ground squirrel.

Weights and measurements are shown in Table 98. The dental formula is

$$I \frac{1}{1} C \frac{0}{0} P \frac{2}{1} M \frac{3}{3} = 22.$$

STATUS AND DISTRIBUTION. The flying squirrel is found in suitable habitat throughout Indiana. It may be locally common, but, statewide, should probably be considered

Table 98

Weights and measurements of
Glaucomys volans from Indiana

	Males	Females
Total length (mm)		
n	27	34
x̄	223.4	231.7
range	196-248	204-256
SD	14.5	14.1
SE	2.8	2.4
Tail length (mm)		
n	27	34
x̄	99.6	100.6
range	82-133	75-118
SD	11.7	10.1
SE	2.3	1.7
Hind foot (mm)		
n	27	34
x̄	29.8	30.2
range	25-34	25-32
SD	2.30	1.9
SE	0.4	0.3
Weight (grams)		
n	16	26
x̄	60.2	66.5
range	45.0-87.0	42.2-113.6
SD	15.0	17.7
SE	3.7	3.5

uncommon. It has been collected in 39 counties and observed in 6 more (Map 35).

Wied (1862) first recorded the flying squirrel from Indiana (Posey County). Plummer (1844) recorded it from Wayne County, and Haymond (1870) stated that it was "very numerous" in Franklin County. It was thought to be common in Randolph County (Cox, 1893). Although Evermann and Butler (1894b) listed the species from only 7 counties, they mentioned no specimens. McAtee (1907) recorded it as common at Bloomington. Hahn (1909) wrote that it "doubtless occurs in every county." This statement was probably true, but Lyon (1936) recorded specimens from only 7 counties and observations or reports from 13 additional counties. Flying squirrels are not easily observed, and their presence in an area may go undetected. No doubt the removal of the native forest from most of Indiana reduced the numbers of this interesting animal in our state.

No one has conducted a population study of the flying squirrel in Indiana. We believe it is considerably more abundant than available data indicate. Plummer (1844) remarked that five or six were found together in trees that were being cut, and Cox (1893) wrote that "In November a few years ago I found fifteen in one old stump." The flying squirrel was evidently plentiful in Franklin County (in early spring) according to Evermann and Butler (1894b), who stated, "It is remarkable what a number of these animals can be found by going from snag to snag and pounding upon it at that time of year." Hahn (1909) wrote that flying squirrels were almost as numerous as gray squirrels in some localities, but gave no details. In Jefferson County, Lindsay (1958) was told that flying squirrels sometimes were so numerous that untrained dogs, used to hunt raccoons at night, treed the squirrels so often that raccoon hunting was unsatisfactory. Mr. and Mrs. Jack E. Young, who feed birds at their country home near Brazil, see eight to ten flying squirrels at one time coming to their bird feeders. The

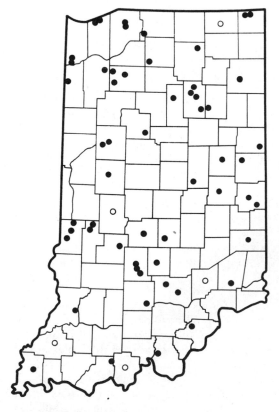

Map 35.   The Southern Flying Squirrel,
Glaucomys volans, in Indiana

animals come from various directions and from distances of at least several hundred feet.

Larry L. Allsop put out nesting structures for flying squirrels on the Crosley Fish and Wildlife Area, near North Vernon (Jennings County). Most of the boxes, placed in a deciduous hardwood forest, were constructed of folded sections of discarded automobile tires (a few boxes were made of wood) and were hung in trees at heights ranging from 6 to 30 feet. On 28 June 1973, the 8 occupied boxes contained 22 flying squirrels; numbers per box were 1, 1, 2, 2, 3, 3, 4, and 6. At two other areas, on 16 January 1974, he found 7 of 34 boxes occupied by a total of 41 flying squirrels; numbers per box were 1, 1, 2, 3, 7, 11, and 16. The use of these artificial shelters indicates that a rather high population of flying squirrels occupied the area.

HABITAT. Most wooded areas that provide den sites may support populations of flying squirrels, but the species is most abundant in mature woods, particularly if numerous dead snags are present. The squirrels readily take over holes made by woodpeckers, and will occupy such holes and natural cavities ranging from 5 feet above the ground upward. In some of the black oak stands along the sand ridges on the Willow Slough Fish and Wildlife Area, this squirrel appears to be common. Individuals are present in towns and cities and often take up residence in buildings.

ASSOCIATED SPECIES. The southern flying squirrel is probably closely associated with the red squirrel (particularly in northern Indiana), the gray squirrel, fox squirrel, white-footed mouse, eastern chipmunk, and raccoon. All occur together in certain localities in the same woods. The extent of competition among them for food and nest or den sites is unknown.

HABITS. *Glaucomys volans* is largely nocturnal and arboreal. Some time is spent on the ground, and individuals are occasionally trapped there. Some activity also takes place after daybreak and before dusk, for squirrel hunters shoot a few flying squirrels. The day is normally spent in a dark place, usually a tree hole. We observed one on a tree trunk at 9 A.M., but perhaps it had been flushed from its daytime roost. One that took up residence in a nesting box erected for purple martins was seen at 2:30 P.M. on a hot (90°F), late June day, sitting for several minutes with its head out of one of the holes leading to a nesting chamber. One can imagine that the temperature inside the nesting box must have been quite high.

Old woodpecker nesting and roosting holes are excellent flying squirrel retreats and nesting sites. The squirrels also use natural cavities in both dead and living trees, sometimes choosing a site that is not more than 5 feet from the ground in a tree scarcely 6 inches in diameter. We have observed flying squirrels most often in fairly small dead snags containing woodpecker holes. It is obvious, however, that the chance of finding a flying squirrel in such a site is greater than that of locating the animal in larger trees. George Dellinger (1951) found several singles, a group of 2, and a congregation of 13 in one day (Montgomery County). The singles were in woodpecker holes in dead snags and limbs from 10 to 30 feet from the ground. Two animals were flushed from their roost 25 feet from the ground in the top of a broken-off tree. The cavity was 3 feet deep and 10 inches in diameter and well filled with leaves. Dellinger thought it had been previously used by a fox squirrel. It contained fresh acorns and hickory nuts. The group of 13 occupied the dead top of a sassafras tree and the roosting hole was 30 feet from the ground. Two animals glided from the tree and traveled 100 feet down a slope. Some of the group refused to leave the tree even when prodded with a stick. Dellinger described the roosting site:

The top of the main trunk had been killed and broken off at thirty feet. A three foot section below the break off was dead and had been hollowed out into single compartments, one at each of five levels, with a main shaft running up the inside edge from top to bottom and connecting all levels. It could be compared to a five story building with one room per floor and an elevator shaft connecting all floors. The stresses of weather had cracked open the vertical shaft and left a quarter inch crack through which I could survey the whole interior. There were three outside entrances, one at the top compartment, one at the bottom and a third about midway on the shaft and on the opposite side from the other two holes. It was a notch enlarged in the vertical crack. I do not maintain that they constructed this hotel but it did appear unique. I am of the opinion that the woodpeckers hollowed the cavities and abandoned it when the top cracked the full length.

Nests are usually built in the den site. Nesting materials of the two nests we have examined closely consisted of grasses and shredded bark. Evermann and Clark (1911) found some small flying squirrels on the ground. An adult came and transported all of the young to a large globular nest of fibrous material in the crotch of a small oak tree. Presumably the young had fallen from this nest earlier. We have one record of *Glaucomys* using a nest in the crown of a tree. In this case, a hunter shot a fox squirrel in a leaf nest, at the same time killing four flying squirrels in the nest. The date was early October. This nest was probably originally constructed by a fox squirrel.

Flying squirrels are most easily found by searching wooded areas for dead snags or small trees with holes in them. By tapping on the tree with a stick or by kicking the tree, one can induce the squirrels to poke their heads out of the holes. If the disturbance is stopped, the animals will retreat back into their roosts. But if one persists in tapping or kicking, the animals will climb out of the holes, usually remaining nearby on the trunk of the tree. Additional disturbance will then usually cause the animals to climb to the top of the tree and glide to another. When the squirrel first emerges from its dark retreat (especially on a bright day), it seems rather dazed or blinded. Frequently such individuals can be captured by pinning them against the trunk with the hand. We have watched *Glaucomys* glide from the top of one tree to another tree 90 feet away. We recorded another glide between trees 75 feet apart. Most glides are shorter, for the squirrels are usually found in wooded areas where trees are more densely situated. The animal may initiate the glide at a considerable angle; just before alighting at the end of the glide, the squirrel can pull up to a nearly vertical position and strike the tree with all four feet. The tail is held straight out behind and is moved, probably as a rudder.

Flying squirrels often call attention to themselves with their chittering, high-pitched squeaking, or birdlike calls, most frequently heard at dusk. Calling is most likely to be heard in spring. Merle E. Jacobs, who made almost daily nature observations on the Jasper-Pulaski Fish and Wildlife Area in the spring of 1943, wrote in his notes on 6 April that "the flying squirrel began to chip today." Mumford wrote to Jacobs in 1976 and asked him about this entry. Jacobs replied that he had observed that there usually was a spring date when the squirrels were first heard. Hahn (1909) refers to their "shrill, bird-like calls" heard on warm nights in late February, March, and April. We have frequently heard and seen flying squirrels at dusk as we were watching for bats, but we failed to record the date they were heard. It has also been noticed that at such times if one gives an imitation of the barred owl's call, flying squirrels in the immediate vicinity will chatter in response.

Adults readily move their young when they have been disturbed sufficiently. Evermann and Clark (1911) described how an adult flying squirrel moved four naked young from the ground to a nest in a tree. The observers stood a few feet away as the adult carried the young, one by one, in her mouth. They related another observation of an adult carrying young that had been taken from a nest and placed on the ground. The adult had left the nest area when disturbed, but came back shortly, discovered the young, then took them one at a time to the top of the nest tree, glided to another tree 30 feet away, and deposited the young in a hole in the second tree 50 feet from the ground.

Aggregations of flying squirrels too large to represent family groups have repeatedly been observed together in tree holes or nesting structures. The largest groups have been discovered from late November to February. Nine such observations involved 6, 7, 8, 8, 11, 11, 13, 15, and 16 animals per roost. Four collected from a group of 8 (13 February) consisted of 3 males and a female. We have no sex ratio data for the remainder, but assume that the sexes are mixed in these winter aggregations. Other Indiana tree squirrels do not exhibit this gregarious habit. We do not know whether winter groups assemble in buildings, but Warren S. Rowe once observed 8 flying squirrels in the attic of a house at one time. These animals became a nuisance through their noise, by gnawing away insulation around furnace ducts and using it in their nests, and by drowning themselves in an open toilet bowl, where they attempted to drink at night.

Dellinger (1951) described the behavior of a group of 13 flying squirrels he found in a single tree at one time; the roost was about 30 feet from the ground and he climbed to it.

Before I had climbed ten feet, two leaped out and sailed off down the slope and curved up into a large white oak a hundred feet away. I had paused to watch when they sailed out, but now started up again. Before I had climbed another five feet, three more sailed out after the first two. With five squirrels gone, I did not expect to find any more but continued up to look over the den. When but a few feet below it, I heard scratching from the snag but nothing was visible on the outside. Finally, when I had reached the level of the snag top, I saw two squirrels peaking [sic] out of the holes at me. I then slapped the snag with my hand and was amazed to see five more come out. None of these sailed off; but just climbed to the top of the snag and in a group hung to the outside just above reach of my hand. With a small branch, I prodded each in turn. Three sailed off after the first five but the other two ran down and re-entered the hole. Further slapping of the snag produced only inquisitive noses at the holes. Finally I noted the long crack and began to prod them through this. There were five still in the snag, giving a total of thirteen. These were very reluctant to leave and would run from one level to another when prodded. Finally, two more leaped forth and sailed away. Only one more could be chased out and it refused to jump. After constant pestering it ran down the trunk between my feet and entered a hole in the base of the tree. The remaining four refused to leave the chambers and I finally gave up for fear of injuring them.

Young flying squirrels are easily tamed and are considered good pets, except for their largely nocturnal habits.

FOOD. Of seven flying squirrel stomachs that we examined, five contained 100 percent nuts, one held 90 percent nuts, 5 percent Hemiptera, and 5 percent Gryllidae, and the third contained only wheat seeds. Acorns and hickory nuts evidently make up much of the diet, for remains of such foods are present in dens and roosts. Flying squirrels are said to eat young birds and eggs, and Evermann and Clark mentioned a captive that ate a prepared bird skin. Stoddard (1920a) reported that a captive *Glaucomys* ate a healthy yellow-bellied sapsucker with which it was confined overnight. Captives kept by Mumford ate a house sparrow and part of a whole dead mouse *(Peromyscus)* placed in the cage. They also ate seeds of bittersweet, English ivy, and butternut, red oak acorns, bread, doughnuts, cookies, potato chips, apple cores, dry and cooked rolled oats, shredded wheat cereal, prunes, peanuts, crickets, and grasshoppers.

People who maintain bird-feeding stations sometimes find that flying squirrels come to the stations at night to feed on the various seeds (such as sunflower or grains) and other foods placed there for the birds. Food is often carried away and stored, in tree holes.

REPRODUCTION. The breeding season extends over a long period. Seven litters were found in Indiana from 29 March to 26 October; three were observed in April, one in May, and one in August. Litter size ranged from 2 to 5 and averaged 3.1. Three gravid females contained 3, 5, and 6 embryos (average 4.7). The five young found on 26 October weighed from 23 to 26 grams each two days later, and their average total length was 151 (145 to 165) mm. Larry Schmeltz found two young about 2 inches in total length on 26 September (Parke County). The young were in a nest in a tree that was cut down. One young was killed. The adult (presumably the female) came near the observer and seemed concerned before carrying the second young away.

The gestation period of *Glaucomys* is about 40 days. The earliest copulations probably occur in February and March, but obviously there are later copulations to account for fall litters. It appears that two peaks of copulatory activity occur—one in early spring and another in summer. An individual female probably produces a single litter per year. Young are born naked and blind, and the eyes open in about 28 days.

We have examined relatively few adult males, which are poorly represented in collections from Indiana. Males with the largest testes were collected from mid-February to mid-May. A male with scrotal testes (size not stated on museum label) was taken on 2 October.

Table 99

Ectoparasites and other associates of *Glaucomys volans* (n = 10) from Indiana
(11 examined for chiggers)

Parasites	Parasites		Hosts parasitized	
	Total	Average	Total	Percent
Fleas (Siphonaptera)				
Orchopeas howardii	22	2.20	6	60.0
Conorhinopsylla stanfordi	8	0.80	1	10.0
Ctenocephalides felis	1	0.10	1	10.0
Sucking Lice (Anoplura)				
Neohaematopinus sciuropteri	88	8.80	5	50.0
Hoplopleura trispinosa	9	0.90	2	20.0
Mites (Acarina) other than chiggers				
Haemogamasus reidi	1	0.10	1	10.0
Dermacarus sp.	19	1.90	1	10.0
Chigger mites (Trombiculidae)				
Neotrombicula fitchi	40	3.64	1	9.1

PARASITES. Wilson (1961) reported the host-specific lice *Hoplopleura trispinosa* (9 specimens) and *Neohaematopinus sciuropteri* (20 specimens) and the flea *Orchopeas howardii* from Indiana *Glaucomys volans.*

We examined 10 flying squirrels for ectoparasites (Table 99). The flea *O. howardii,* the two host-specific lice, a mite (*Dermacarus* sp.), and a chigger (*Neotrombicula fitchii*) appeared to be the main ectoparasites.

Seven individuals were examined for internal parasites. Four (57.1 percent) yielded 48 nematodes (6.6 per squirrel) and one (14.3 percent) yielded 7 trematodes.

DECIMATING FACTORS. We have very little information regarding predators of flying squirrels. Mumford and Handley (1956) reported *Glaucomys* remains in the pellets of an unidentified owl. Domestic cats are known to capture this squirrel. Timber cutting probably accounts for some casualties, and the modern practice of removing dead snags and unsound trees from the woods decreases available nest and den sites. Evermann and Clark (1911) reported flying squirrels killed by fire that burned their den tree. A few are evidently killed by vehicles on the roads. John M. Allen (1952a) found several dead flying squirrels in box traps set for other squirrels. Ann Wheatley and Anne Zimmerman encountered the same problem when live-trapping flying squirrels. The squirrels apparently succumbed to some type of shock disease, brought on by the confinement. Hunters take relatively few flying squirrels and probably most of those are shot by accident. Accidental deaths that have come to our attention are the drownings already mentioned and the taking of at least two animals in mist nets set for bats.

TAXONOMY. *Glaucomys volans volans* (Linnaeus) is the form in Indiana.

SELECTED REFERENCES. Hatt, 1931; Howell, 1918; Jordan, 1948; Sollberger, 1940, 1943.

Family Geomyidae

Plains Pocket Gopher
Geomys bursarius (Shaw)

Eastern Pocket Gopher, Illinois Pocket Gopher

Pseudostoma bursarius: Kennicott, 1858
Geomys pinctis (probably misprint for *pinetis*): Ball, 1900
Geomys illinoensis: Lyon, 1936
Geomys bursarius: Evermann and Butler, 1894b

DESCRIPTION. This gopher is nearly the size of a gray squirrel and has a relatively short, hairless, tapered tail. Males average larger than females. The eyes are small, and the ears are small, naked, and flattened against the head. The front feet are larger than the hind feet and are equipped with large, elongated claws for burrowing. *Geomys* has external, fur-lined cheek pouches that extend back to the shoulder region. Color varies geographically, usually in correlation with the prevailing soil color. The animals in Indiana, however, are uniformly slate gray above and below, the undersides often having a wash of beige or whitish. The feet and distal half of the tail are white or whitish, and white spotting is often present on the chin. Specimens in fresh pelage are dark and glossy, while those in worn pelage are paler and dull. A small percentage of the population exhibits a purplish gloss on the fur. D. F. Hoffmeister noted this coloration on Indiana specimens, but told us that the color disappears from prepared skins after a period of time. Tuszynski (1971) reported that 12 of the 128 pocket gophers he examined from Indiana had "a slight purple coloration on the ventral surface." He further stated that this color occurred only on animals taken in sand. In many specimens, scattered whitish guard hairs are mixed through the fur. There are no white-spotted or albino individuals among about 220 Indiana specimens we have seen.

The skull of *Geomys* is relatively broad and flattened; at first glance it is similar in size and shape to that of the muskrat, with which it has often been confused. Each upper incisor of the gopher has two distinct grooves on the anterior face (see Fig. 34). The muskrat has no such grooves.

Plains pocket gopher. Photo by Anthony Brentlinger, ISU AV Center

Weights and measurements are shown in Table 100. The dental formula is

$$I \frac{1}{1} C \frac{0}{0} P \frac{1}{1} M \frac{3}{3} = 20.$$

STATUS AND DISTRIBUTION. Few early writers mentioned the presence of *Geomys bursarius* in Indiana. Even today, many persons are unaware that the species is found in the state. Evermann and Butler (1894b) stated that it occurred in Newton County. Ball (1900) mentioned it from Jasper and Newton counties. Hahn (1909) collected none during his fieldwork along the Kankakee River, and knew of no specimens in collections. He did write, "There is no doubt of its occurrence in Lake and Newton counties. The only definite records I have are Shelby, Lake County, and Lake Village, Newton County." We assume that Hahn had observed gopher mounds or had other evidence of its existence at these localities. Komarek and Spencer (1931) were evidently

the first to actually collect this species in Indiana, in 1930 (we have been unable to locate their specimens). They described a new subspecies from their Illinois and Indiana material. Galen C. Oderkirk noted the presence of *Geomys* in Tippecanoe County around 1930 (Lyon, 1932b), and a specimen was collected there in 1932.

The plains pocket gopher has a limited distribution (Map 36), and is known from six counties between the Kankakee and Wabash rivers and east to Pulaski County, all in northwestern Indiana. The mounted specimen that represents the sole record for Pulaski County was said to have been taken "near Winamac" (we have no date), but we (and others) have been unable to find *Geomys* there. Perhaps it represents a population now extirpated. Within the range of the species it is locally quite common to completely absent. There are small, isolated colonies in Benton, Tippecanoe, and Warren

Table 100

Weights and measurements of
Geomys bursarius from Indiana

	Males	Females
Total length (mm)		
n	48	90
x̄	294.3	258.5
range	252-324	212-296
SD	21.4	17.9
SE	3.1	1.9
Tail length (mm)		
n	48	89
x̄	85.4	73.6
range	67-105	51-100
SD	11.1	10.9
SE	1.6	1.2
Hind foot (mm)		
n	47	90
x̄	34.6	31.8
range	35-38	28-37
SD	1.6	1.8
SE	0.2	0.2
Weight (grams)		
n	41	84
x̄	333.0	231.2
range	230-451	128-380
SD	54.7	41.1
SE	8.5	4.5

Map 36.   The Plains Pocket Gopher,
Geomys bursarius, in Indiana

counties, but most of the population occurs in Jasper and Newton counties. Lyon (1932b) corrected an erroneous record from St. Joseph County. The Kankakee, Wabash, and Tippecanoe rivers appear to form barriers to the distribution of the pocket gopher in Indiana, but Conaway (1947) noted that a captive he placed in the water could swim well.

We have made no attempt to determine statewide populations of the pocket gopher, although the range is quite restricted. Within the geographic area where it is found, colonies are scattered and there are no large, contiguous aggregations that would allow one to make reasonable estimates of numbers per area. Conaway (1947) trapped all of the pocket gophers he could from an 11-acre study plot near Battle Ground (Tippecanoe County) and took 7 animals. We have no way of determining whether this density of 0.64 gophers per acre represents a high, a low, or an intermediate population. In the fall of 1970, Tuszynski removed 15 pocket gophers from an isolated grassy area of 1.2 acres (Benton County). It was thought that all animals were captured, for no indications of gopher activity could be observed on the site a month after the removal trapping. The resulting population estimate of 12.5 animals per acre may indicate a high density.

HABITAT. The major habitat requirements of the species appear to be open areas and a well-drained soil that permits easy burrowing. Pocket gophers occur in fine sand, sandy loam and gravel, silt loam, and silty clay loam. A colony near Battle Ground lived along a railroad grade that was composed mostly of cinders. *Geomys* lives mostly in grasslands, in grassy and weedy ditch banks, along roadsides and railroad grades, and in fallow fields. It also may be found in cultivated fields. Some colonies have been observed in open savanna-like stands of trees. Where trees are too dense, burrowing is hampered and gophers do not persist.

Tuszynski (1971) studied the distribution of *Geomys* in Indiana with regard to soil type, drainage, vegetation, and land use. He concluded that soil type alone was of minimal importance, for the animals were found in a wide variety of soils. Drainage was of major importance; many colonies of gophers were located on moraines which were slightly higher and better drained than surrounding

areas. Tuszynski found that current gopher distribution was correlated fairly well with original dry prairies and oak/hickory associations, as described by Lindsey (1966). Artificial drainage by man has rendered some habitats suitable on lands that were originally wet prairies or lowlands subject to flooding, and the gophers have invaded some of these low-lying areas. Man's activities can be either beneficial (drainage) or harmful (intensive cultivation) to the pocket gopher. Perhaps the reason *Geomys* is found in greatest abundance in northern Jasper and Newton counties today is because much of this region was relatively dry and sandy, thus less attractive to the farmer for growing crops. Plowing destroys the shallow forage burrows of the gopher and (at least temporarily) eliminates the vegetation.

ASSOCIATED SPECIES. The same general habitats occupied by the pocket gopher are shared by the eastern mole, the deer mouse, prairie and meadow voles, the eastern cottontail, thirteen-lined and Franklin's ground squirrels, the red fox, and others. Of these, the eastern mole is probably the most closely associated, for it sometimes uses gopher burrows, and probably the forage burrows of the two species at times intersect. Most other mammals probably have little opportunity to come into contact with *Geomys*, since it spends so much of its time belowground. Mice, voles, and ground squirrels may occasionally dig into gopher burrows and perhaps make use of them (especially those that are abandoned). We have no evidence that mammalian predators capture pocket gophers.

HABITS. The pocket gopher is largely subterranean, rarely venturing aboveground (mostly to feed). One will occasionally be observed in the daytime at the mouth of an open burrow as it works on its extensive tunnel system. The species is active day and night and throughout the year, but the details of daily activity patterns are unknown. Individuals are evidently solitary most of the year, male and female coming together in spring to copulate. Later, an adult female and her offspring may occupy a burrow system until the young are weaned.

Geomys is apparently an aggressive animal. Most of the time when two are confined together (regardless of sex), fighting ensues. The long incisors are formidable weapons and occasionally inflict deep cuts on an opponent. Conaway observed lacerations on the rostrum of one wild-trapped animal that were similar to cuts noted on individuals that had fought in captivity. In fighting, a gopher elevates the head and makes short, somewhat aimless rushes and retreats, at the same time clicking the teeth together and hissing. Since vision is poor, any object (animate or inanimate) contacted on these rushes is bitten, and the combatants do not necessarily direct their attacks toward one another each time. Fighting animals may push loose soil forward with the front feet, probably in an effort to plug the burrow against the intruder. In the wild, the plugging of the burrow system no doubt decreases clashes between individuals.

The most obvious behavior of *Geomys* is its burrowing. Underground tunnel systems constructed by this species are extensive and on several levels. Foraging tunnels are usually 6 to 8 inches below the surface. Vertical or near vertical short burrows connect the foraging burrows to another series of deeper ones, which may connect with even deeper tunnels. Soil excavated in digging is pushed above the ground surface in the form of mounds. After a mound has been constructed, the opening used in its construction is plugged with soil. Mounds vary in size from several inches to 2 feet (or more) in diameter and may be nearly a foot high. In open areas, dozens of mounds may be visible from any one spot. Their locations indicate to the observer the extent of digging and direction taken by foraging burrows. Foraging tunnels make up the major portion of a single burrow system. Conaway (1947) examined 386 feet of burrows in excavating what he estimated was two-thirds of the complete system. He noted that forage tunnels were slightly less than 4 inches in diameter and were about 9 inches below the ground surface. Forage tunnels were ordinarily free from debris, but unused portions were often plugged with soil. Food storage pockets and nesting chambers were situated in the deeper burrows. The deep tunnel system examined by Conaway varied from 24 to 36 inches below the surface. More intricate and deeper burrow systems have been reported from other states.

Pocket gopher mounds are fan-shaped or crescent-shaped and are composed of finely

Mound of plains pocket gopher at Willow Slough Fish and Wildlife Area, Newton County. Photo by David W. Berrey

divided soil, in contrast to the smaller, more rounded mounds made of chunks of soil and constructed by the eastern mole.

The pocket gopher digs mostly with the claws on its front feet, but may use the incisors to cut through roots encountered along the tunnels. Conaway's captive *Geomys* frequently paused when digging to clean accumulated soil from the foreclaws by working each claw in turn between the incisors. After a quantity of soil had been loosened with the foreclaws, and pushed beneath the body with the hind legs, the gopher turned around and pushed it toward the tunnel opening with its front feet and chest. To hold loose soil in place on a sloping tunnel wall, the gopher tamped the soil by holding the forefeet with palmar surfaces down at the level of the nose and rapidly vibrating the body "with considerable force." We have observed the burrowing activity of captive gophers placed on top of the ground. One such individual tunneled out of sight in damp soil within five minutes.

The incisors of *Geomys* grow at a rapid rate. Conaway trapped one animal that had broken off both lower incisors when captured. The teeth extended only 4 mm above the gums; these teeth were 15 mm long seven days later. It was thought that the rate of growth was about 2 mm per day, for this animal was actively feeding while in captivity during this time. Pocket gophers are such persistent gnawers that they sometimes damage underground telephone cables and other buried structures. We have seen mounds pushed up by gophers in the center of a much-used gravel-surfaced road.

Gophers kept by Conaway were observed to have poorly developed vision, as one might expect. Captives gave no indication of perceiving movement, even very close to their eyes, but responded when a light was flashed in their eyes. For a subterranean animal, vision beyond the ability to detect light and dark is of little use, especially if the sense of smell is highly developed. Conaway found that food placed in the cage was detected rapidly. "One individual repeatedly awoke from a sound sleep within a minute after a bit of tangerine had been dropped into its cage three feet from the sleeping animal." The tactile sense of this gopher is also highly developed. Lightly touching a captive on any part of its body caused the individual to immediately whirl to face that direction. Blowing lightly on individuals aroused them, and vibrations of their cage elicited an immediate response. Wild gophers "ceased activity and plugged their holes in response to vibrations of the ground caused by walking."

When sleeping lightly, a gopher remained "upright on its haunches with tail tucked around one hind leg and then under the body." The head was brought down between the foreclaws until the latter were at the level of the cheek pouch openings. On occasions the foreclaws were actually within the openings of the cheek pouches. At other times, the animals assumed much the same position described above except that they lay on their sides. In deep sleep, the animals were "observed lying on their side [*sic*] in a completely relaxed position." Such animals were difficult to arouse and could be handled rather roughly before awakening.

Fresh *Geomys* droppings examined by Conaway were dark brown, averaged 4 by 11 mm, and resembled the droppings of the Norway Rat. Dehydrated scats were darker in color, shrunken, and averaged about 3.5 by 8 mm. No scats were observed in the forage burrows, but a few were in mounds. In one deep burrow numerous scats and old nesting material were noted sealed off from the main tunnel system in a small pocket.

Seasonal activity as indicated by the construction of mounds was studied by Conaway near Battle Ground, in 1946–47. He found

"activity was greatest during the late summer and fall months. This was in part the result of young of the year constructing new burrows and in part due to increased foraging on the part of adult animals." By mid-November the number of new mounds decreased markedly and continued to decrease through December. Only a few new mounds were observed in January, and none was seen in February or the first two weeks of March. With the thawing of the soil in mid-March, mound-building activity resumed.

The number of mounds constructed per day varied. A single gopher sometimes constructed two or three mounds a day, but this rate was the exception. One gopher, actively extending its burrow into a field of winter wheat in early April, made six mounds in seven days. These mounds were in a relatively straight line, and between the first and sixth mound the surface distance was 53 feet. Conaway thought that the actual length of the burrow excavated below the ground was nearly 70 feet.

Tuszynski live-trapped 56 pocket gophers, of which he recaptured 9. The greatest distance moved by an individual was 230 feet.

Much has been made of the fact that a burrow system is normally used by a single animal for most of the year. Tuszynski gathered data on "multiple use" (more than one animal per burrow system). He did no trapping in December, January, and early February because the ground was frozen. Of 143 captures and recaptures, 23 were "multiple" as defined above. Ten of them were for June to August and probably represented family units of an adult and young. Seven were for March to May, probably the mating season when male and female may be found together. Six were for September to November; these may have represented immatures extending their ranges. More data would be valuable in evaluating the incidence of solitary versus multiple use of burrow systems. Burrow occupants other than gophers observed by Tuszynski were three eastern moles, two tiger salamanders, and an unidentified snake that laid its eggs in a burrow.

FOOD. Conaway recorded the following foods of free-living pocket gophers on his study area: alfalfa, red clover, wheat, oats, rye, soybeans, bluegrass, roots of ragweed, sunflower, and black-eyed susan. In unc-ultivated sites, "almost all of the plants growing were used as foods." The two food caches discovered in the burrows consisted almost entirely of heavy rootstocks of alfalfa. Captive animals ate a wide variety of foods, including oranges, tomatoes, and watermelon. One trapped by us had wheat plants in its cheek pouches.

Roots and tubers are discovered and collected by the gopher during the construction of forage tunnels. Sometimes the roots are eaten away and the dead plant will still be standing in place aboveground. Succulent vegetation is gathered mostly at night; the animals probably come to the surface, remain near their burrow openings, and graze about the opening. Food is transported in the cheek pouches. Conaway observed a captive individual that carried 54 grains of corn without difficulty. Plant stems 3 inches long were also carried in the pouch. Material too large for the pouch was grasped by the incisors and dragged along the burrow, the gopher moving backward to do so. Food is routinely stored in the burrows.

A fondness for bluegrass is indicated by the fact that *Geomys* often occurs in lawns, where its mounds interfere with mowing and kill some of the grass. We have trapped one gopher a considerable distance out in a wheat field.

REPRODUCTION. The gestation period of *Geomys bursarius* is estimated to be about a month. One litter is produced per year. The breeding season of the pocket gopher in Indiana appears to extend from late February through early June. Conaway collected 2 females on 21 March; both had enlarged reproductive tracts and large ovarian follicles; one contained sperm in the vagina. A female trapped 4 April had "pea sized" embryos, and another taken on 10 April contained embryos 6 mm in crown-rump length. Tuszynski collected 2 gravid pocket gophers in March, 9 in April, and 2 in May. A female taken on 29 June appeared to have suckled young, but had no placental scars and was not lactating. The status of placental scars in *Geomys bursarius* requires more study.

The number of embryos in 15 gravid pocket gophers ranged from 1 to 7 each, and averaged 4.1. Two of the 7 found in one female were being resorbed. Of the 18 embryos that could be sexed, 55.5 percent were males. Most authors have noted the preponderance of females in *Geomys* populations. Tuszynski captured 128 animals, of which 66.4 percent were females. Of the 37 specimens that Conaway collected, 23 were females (62 percent). Perhaps there are fundamental differences in the activity of males and females, or perhaps one sex is more vulnerable to trapping than the other. Indications are, however, that males are subject to a higher mortality than females, from birth to adulthood.

Tuszynski found that males with the largest testes were taken from March to May, with one exception (June). The maximum testis size recorded was 14 by 18 mm (20 March). Conaway recorded the combined weight of both testes for 9 adult males. The 4 animals with the largest testes were taken 28 March and 4 April. Various authors have noted that not all adult females taken in spring have been bred. Tuszynski examined 44 adult females between March and June and found that only 16 (36.3 percent) showed signs (lactating, gravid, placental scars) of pregnancy. The imbalance in the sex ratio of adults could be an important factor with regard to reproductive success in this species.

PARASITES. Conaway (1947) examined 37 Indiana pocket gophers for parasites. He found 55 percent to be infested with the mite *Atricholaelaps* (= *Androlaelaps*) *glasgowi* and all with the louse *Geomydoecus geomydis*. Unidentified cestodes were found in 41 percent of the animals. Malecki (1949) reported the mites *Androlaelaps fahrenholzi* (= *Atricholaelaps glasgowi*) and *Listrophorus* sp., the biting louse *Geomydoecus geomydis*, and the cestodes *Andrya macrocephala* and *Paranoplocephala infrequens* from Indiana pocket gophers. Wilson (1961) reported an average of 15.3 fleas (*Dactylopsylla ignota*) on 3 pocket gophers he examined from Newton County. Tuszynski and Whitaker (1972), who examined 85 Indiana pocket gophers, found one species of biting louse, one flea, and four species of mites to be regularly associated with this species (Table 101). The form they listed as *Listrophorus* sp. has now been identified as *Geomylichus floridanus*. *Macrocheles* sp. is not a true parasite, but presumably uses its host for transportation.

Table 101

Ectoparasites and other associates of *Geomys bursarius* (n = 85) from Indiana
(from Tuszynski and Whitaker, 1972)

Parasites	Parasites		Hosts Parasitized	
	Total	Average	Total	Percent
Fleas (Siphonaptera)				
Dactylopsylla ignota	155	1.82	26	30.6
Biting Lice (Mallophaga)				
Geomydoecus illinoensis	1,817	21.38	85	100.0
Mites (Acarina) other than chiggers				
Geomylichus floridanus	810	9.53	40	47.1
Androlaelaps geomys	309	3.64	40	47.1
Hirstionyssus longichelae	44	0.52	19	22.4
Hirstionyssus geomydis	33	0.39	12	14.1
Macrocheles sp. (free living form)	1	0.01	1	1.2
Pygmephorus whitakeri	1	0.01	1	1.2

DECIMATING FACTORS. We have no direct evidence of predation on Indiana pocket gophers, and assume that the living habits of the species lessens the possibility of predation. The skin and skull of one *Geomys*, found in a field, were cleaned of most flesh, but we do not know what killed the animal. Conaway found the remains of an adult male at the base of a telephone pole. The animal was fresh and part of the head and shoulder had been eaten. Laceration about the back and the manner of eating suggested that a hawk may have taken it. Dogs and foxes frequently dig into gopher burrow systems, but there is no evidence that they have captured gophers. Where gophers invade lawns and other places where they are not wanted, control campaigns are usually waged to eliminate them. Plowing may kill a few animals, but most are probably able to escape to deeper burrows.

TAXONOMY. The form in Indiana is *Geomys bursarius illinoensis* Komarek and Spencer.

SELECTED REFERENCES. Conaway, 1947; English, 1932; Malecki, 1949; Komarek and Spencer, 1931; Mohr and Mohr, 1936; Scheffer, 1931; Tuszynski, 1971; Tuszynski and Whitaker, 1972.

Family Castoridae

Beaver
Castor canadensis Kuhl

Carolina Beaver

Castor fiber: Plummer, 1844
Castor canadensis: Hahn, 1909

DESCRIPTION. The beaver is a large, dark reddish brown rodent with a broad, dorsoventrally flattened, scaly tail. The pelage consists of a soft, dense underfur and long, coarse guard hairs. The upperparts usually appear to be chestnut brown (the color of the guard hairs), but the underparts are paler brown and lack any reddish tinge. The hind feet are webbed, and the two inner claws on each foot are split and are used in grooming the pelage. Each foot has five toes. The ears are small and round. The large, rugose skull contains large incisors with orange enamel on their anterior surfaces. The dental formula is

$$I \frac{1}{1} C \frac{0}{0} P \frac{1}{1} M \frac{3}{3} = 20.$$

WEIGHTS AND MEASUREMENTS. There are relatively few data for Indiana specimens, and all of those are for reintroduced animals. No information appears to be available on weights or measurements of the beavers that originally occupied the state. Six adult females weighed from 22 to 56.5 pounds each and averaged 35.6 pounds. Two adult males weighed 25.2 and 26.8 pounds. The largest female measured 1,145 mm in total length, had a tail 305 mm long and 137 mm wide, and a hind foot of 192 mm. The male weighing 26.8 pounds had the following measurements: total length, 880 mm; tail, 260 mm; hind foot, 147 mm; ear, 30 mm. Jackson (1961) listed beaver weights as ranging from 45 to 60 pounds and total length measurements from 900 to 1170 mm.

STATUS AND DISTRIBUTION. The beaver was once found throughout Indiana (Lyon, 1936), but evidently disappeared from nearly all of the state by 1840, perhaps even earlier. Evidence from fur-trader records indicates that in northern Indiana the beaver was present in extremely low numbers by 1800. William Burnett, who traded for furs on the St. Joseph River (St. Joseph County) received only 9 beaver skins for the period 1800 to 1801 (Engels, 1933). At a trading post near Fort Wayne (Allen County), John Johnston shipped the following beaver pelts from 1804 to 1811: 14 April 1804, 13 pounds; 23 April 1805, 6 pelts; 13 May 1806, 46.5 pounds; March, April, May 1808, 26 pounds; 31 May 1809, 37.5 pounds; May, June 1810, 2 pounds; April, June 1811, 3.75 pounds (Griswold, 1927).

Wied (1862) reported that beavers were formerly abundant along the lower Wabash River. Plummer (1844), in writing about Wayne County, said, "Beaver dams are still found in a dilapidated condition along our streams, but the animal has not been seen by any of the white settlers." Haymond (1870) had no recent report of it from Franklin County. About Randolph County, Cox (1893) wrote that the beaver was "not found at pres-

Beaver. Photo by Larry E. Lehman

ent, but a few old beaver dams can be located." Evermann and Butler (1894b) mentioned that, according to S. D. Steininger,
"there are traces of the beaver still to be seen
in La Grange county." They wrote about
Franklin County, as follows:

Beavers were formerly found in some numbers in
Franklin county. In Bath and Springfield town-
ships were extensive colonies, and the remains of
their dams are still to be seen. They were also
found along the rivers. In the spring of 1883 Mr.
Edward Hughes obtained the skull of a beaver
from the alluvial deposit at the mouth of Yellow
Bank creek four miles from Brookville. The specimen is in the collection of the Brookville Society of
Natural History.

It is impossible to determine just when the
beaver became extinct in Indiana. One was
supposedly seen in the Wabash River above
Lafayette in the summer of 1889. B. W.
Evermann (Evermann and Butler, 1894b) saw
a beaver skull said to have been found near
New Harmony "not many years ago." Beaver
Lake (Newton County) was undoubtedly
named for the abundance of beaver that once
occurred there; W. W. Pfrimmer reported to
Butler (1895) that the "remains of their work
is yet seen." There was formerly a place
called Beaver Pond in Bartholomew County
where beavers "built their houses." On the
Official Highway Map of Indiana for 1975–
76, are the towns Beaver City (Newton
County) and Beaver Dam (Kosciusko
County). A beaver skull was found on Goose
Island, in the Wabash River (Tippecanoe
County) in 1894, according to Stanley Coul-
ter. Butler (1895) reported that a beaver was
trapped in Knox County in 1840, and that
beaver dams were still visible in that county.
E. J. Chansler told Butler that some persons
claimed that Monteur's Pond (now drained)
was formed when beavers dammed Pond
Creek (Knox County). Hahn (1909) doubted
some of the later records listed above. Dinwiddie (1884) thought that the beaver was
gone from Lake County "before the advent of
the white man." Lindsay (1960) mentioned a
skull which may have been from a beaver
trapped in Jefferson County between 1879
and 1926.

Evermann and Clark (1911), commenting
about the beaver in the Lake Maxinkuckee
(Marshall County) area, wrote, "The Beaver

was at one time pretty common in the northern part of Indiana. There still exist vestiges
of one or more beaver dams in the Outlet between Lost Lake and the Tippecanoe River."
The mammals of historic St. Joseph County
were studied by Engels (1933), who wrote:

Bartlett and Lyon (1899) says that La Hontan, who
viewed this region during La Salle's time, represents the Kankakee as arising in a lake (Chain
Lakes?) surrounded by a great beaver town, (p. 62).
The same authors mention an enthusiastic letter to
the French crown by D'Iberville declaring that this
western land had great wealth, and that the region
of the Kankakee and the St. Joseph was the place
where "beavers are plenty" (p. 63). Almost every
farmer in the county claims to know of old beaver
dams which are still visible in the drained Kankakee district. One such that may be authentic is
located near the north end of Sousley Lake, about
eight miles southwest of South Bend.

Lyon (1936) discussed "a so-called beaver
dam at Sousley Lake," possibly the one mentioned by Engels, and described it from his
personal observation as being "wide and
solid enough to drive a car across," also noting that "it appears as a solid earth affair at
the present time."

Although we do not know when the beaver
became extinct in Indiana, there was a long
period during which it was not a part of the
fauna of the state. Beaver cuttings were photographed in Wells County in 1932 (Lyon,
1936); the origin of these animals is unknown. The Indiana Department of Conservation (now the Department of Natural Resources) obtained beavers from Wisconsin
and Michigan in 1935 and released them on
the Jasper-Pulaski Fish and Wildlife Area
(Jasper and Pulaski counties) and on the
Kankakee Fish and Wildlife Area (Starke
County). Some of these animals came from
Loana, Wisconsin, according to Willard H.
Kaehler, who helped transport them (letter to
Mumford, 21 March 1960). After the introduction of small numbers of beavers at these
two sites, the animals rapidly moved into adjacent areas (*Outdoor Indiana*, November
1939). By 1938, beavers were present in
Jasper, LaPorte, Marshall, Noble, Porter,
Pulaski, and Starke counties. Other introductions and transplantings were made (some in
southern Indiana) and by 1947 an estimated
5,000 beavers were thought to be living in

the state (Denney, 1952). David M. Brooks interviewed all conservation officers in the state in 1955 to obtain his data on the distribution and number of beavers (Brooks, 1959). He concluded that 1,695 animals were present in the 326 known Indiana beaver colonies in 43 counties in 1955. However, he felt that perhaps 20 percent of the colonies were unknown or unreported; by including these, he arrived at an estimated statewide population of about 2,100 in 1955. His calculations were based on the assumption that 5.2 was the average number of beavers per colony. Brooks wrote, "The heaviest concentrations of beaver are in the drainages of the Kankakee and upper half of the Tippecanoe rivers. Over 73 percent of the known beaver colonies of Indiana are in Lake, Newton, Porter, Jasper, Laporte, Starke, Marshall, and Kosciusko Counties." Colonies were present at localities throughout the state.

Beavers have done well in Indiana and today have a wide distribution. Reports have been received in recent years from all corners of the state and beavers are continually moving and establishing new colonies. Colonies may be abandoned or destroyed after a short period. Such has been the case near Terre Haute and in other parts of Vigo County and near Lafayette (Tippecanoe County). No recent survey has been made to determine the current distribution and population of the beaver in Indiana. We have specimen records from few counties but reports from many counties (Map 37).

The historical accounts of beavers in Indiana frequently refer to the abundance of this species, but we have been unable to find a reference that includes definite numbers per area. Cockrum (1907) wrote that the Black River (Patoka River?) was formerly one of the best streams for trapping beaver in Indiana. As mentioned earlier, the few Indiana fur trading post records we have examined indicate that the beaver was not common from 1800 to 1811. Denney (1952) estimated that there were about 5,000 beavers in Indiana, but we do not know how he derived this figure.

HABITAT. Beavers are most abundant in lakes, marshes, streams, and drainage ditches in northern Indiana. They live in burrows in the ground along rivers too large and swift for

Map 37.   The Beaver, *Castor canadensis*, in Indiana

them to dam up. This is especially noticeable along the Kankakee River, where beavers have been reestablished for more than 40 years. In southern Indiana, beavers have been introduced into some of the strip-mined land, where they have numerous ponds available for den and lodge sites.

ASSOCIATED SPECIES. The closest associate of the beaver in Indiana is probably the muskrat. Both species construct their houses in close proximity in marshes and use burrows along the banks of rivers and ditches. Other mammals frequenting these areas include the raccoon and mink.

HABITS. The beaver is seldom encountered out of water, but goes on land to feed and to travel. Most activity takes place at night, although in areas where the animals are not unduly disturbed by man, they may be seen by day. Beavers are excellent swimmers and can spend considerable time beneath the water. Entrances to their lodges and dens are usually under water. Where beavers enter and leave the water over extended periods of time, well-marked paths and slides devoid of most vegetation are formed. One slide we observed was 15 inches wide and was depressed into the sandy soil to a depth of 6 inches.

Burrows used as dens are usually situated at the edge of the water. Burrowing into levees upon which roads have been constructed frequently results in the collapse of portions of the road surface, the formation of deep holes, and increased water erosion of the levee. Where possible, beavers construct lodges of sticks, mud, and other items. Brooks reported that a typical beaver lodge in Indiana is usually a modified bank burrow and has one or two tunnels leading from below water level into a nesting chamber above water level. Nesting chambers are about 2 feet high and 4 to 6 feet in diameter. Above the nest chamber, on top of the bank in which it is constructed, there is often a pile of interlacing sticks and branches plastered with mud. This covering structure is quite variable in size, ranging from a few sticks to a mound 5 to 6 feet tall and 10 to 20 feet in diameter. The size of the house depends

upon its age, the size and strength of the bank, and the number of beavers inhabiting it. Nests of shredded bark or grasses are built in the nesting chamber. Mumford observed a beaver lodge on the Jasper-Pulaski Fish and Wildlife Area (3 April 1960) that rose 8 feet above the water. It had been constructed around and over a wooden observation blind standing in water about 4 feet deep.

The most important and obvious activity of the beaver is the building of dams, which are constructed of sticks, mud, rocks, old fence posts, boards, discarded rolls of wire, and other items. Most of the dam, however, is made of sticks and mud. Brooks reported that one dam contained a discarded door from an automobile. Much dam material consists of sticks cut from brush and small trees. Many beavers in this region inhabit drainage ditches and small creeks, whose banks are frequently kept cleared of large trees by landowners. Large trees are cut by the beavers, however, when available. We have seen a cottonwood tree more than 2 feet in diameter that beavers had gnawed extensively (but did not fell) along the Kankakee River. A photograph published in *Outdoor Indiana*

Beaver dam at Willow Slough Fish and Wildlife Area, Newton County.
Photo by David W. Berrey

(November 1939) shows a 24-inch diameter cottonwood tree that beavers felled. Although cottonwood, willow, and aspen are frequently cut, both for food and for the construction of dams, trees of harder wood are also used. We have noted oaks, maples, birches, and pines gnawed down by beavers. As long as the dams are useful to them, beavers kept them in good repair. This involves keeping leaking spots sealed and replacing materials carried away by water erosion (or by man). Evidently the adult male does much of the repair work. A surprising amount of dam can be constructed or repaired in a single night. Where sufficient water is available for storing winter food and for other activities, the animals do not construct dams.

Startled beavers will often slap their broad tail on the water with a loud smacking sound, then submerge noisily, causing a sound "like a huge boulder being dropped into the water." This alarm signal is heeded by other beavers in the area. At other times, a swimming beaver or one at the water's edge will silently slip beneath the water with scarcely a ripple. An individual can remain submerged for up to 6 minutes. Swimming speed has been estimated at about 2 to 2.5 miles per hour, according to Brooks. The tail may be used as a rudder or as an aid in propelling the beaver through the water. When a tree is being cut, the beaver's tail is used as additional support for the upright body.

Transplanted beavers travel extensively up ditches, small streams, and rivers. Although they may be introduced into an area where man would like them to remain, they are quite likely to move until they find a spot to their own liking.

FOOD. Beavers are primarily vegetarians, and bark and twigs form the bulk of their diet. Aspen, cottonwood, and willow are apparently favorite food trees; they are easily gnawed because of their relatively soft wood and their widespread occurrence near water. Many aquatic plants are also consumed, such as cattail, arrowhead or duck-potato, water lily, sedges, and grasses. Young blackberry canes and corn are also eaten. Bark and twigs are consumed mostly in cold weather, and many tree branches (and larger sections of trees) are stored under water for the winter season. These materials are cut and depos-

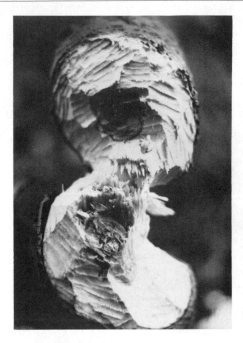

A beaver cut. A small poplar tree felled by beaver. Note the tooth marks. Photo by Rita Veal

ited on the bottom as a large brushpile; the newly cut material is rather heavy when green and most of it sinks to the bottom quite readily when waterlogged. Food piles are stored near the lodge or den and can be reached by the animals after the water areas have frozen over. Food may be carried back inside the lodge, where the bark is eaten off, then the peeled stick or tree branch is carried outside and dropped. Almost any herbaceous plant growing in beaver habitats is eaten during spring and summer.

REPRODUCTION. The gestation period of the beaver is about 128 days. Brooks stated that in Indiana beavers, the period for copulation occurred from January through March. Breeding first occurs in animals about 2.5 years old. One litter is produced per year, usually between May and July, and litter size varies from 1 to 8 (probably averaging 3 to 4). A large female taken on the Willow Slough Fish and Wildlife Area contained 9 embryos on 12 April. Newborn beavers weigh about a pound each, and the young are kept in the nest until about a month old. Brooks found that young about 6 months old averaged 14 pounds 6 ounces. The smallest beaver he handled during the legal trapping season weighed 8 pounds 13 ounces and was probably born in late summer.

A beaver colony usually consists of two adults with their young from the two previous breeding seasons. When young reach an age of almost two years they are driven away by the parents and seek homes of their own. It is thought that an average colony consists of from five to six beavers. The members of a colony evidently are intolerant of individuals from another colony and family groups tend to be rather isolated. Once a colony is established and water and food conditions remain sufficient to sustain it, it may persist for years. Studies in other states have revealed that some beavers leave the colonies when only yearlings and that tagged animals moved distances up to 31 air miles.

PARASITES. Four beavers from Indiana have been examined to date for external parasites, three of them from the Jasper-Pulaski Fish and Wildlife Area and one from the Wabash River south of Lafayette. The common parasites were chirodiscid mites of the genus *Schizocarpus*. Previously these mites had been listed as *S. mingaudi* but Dubinina recently (1964) studied parasites of beavers in Asia and found that this genus was represented by a complex of species. Additional study is thus needed on *Schizocarpus* from beavers from North America to determine the situation here. Large numbers (500±) of *Schizocarpus* sp. were found on all four beavers from Indiana, and three individuals of the beetle *Platypsylla castoris* (Platypsyllidae), found only as a parasite of

beavers, were found on two beavers. Also, one macronyssid mite, *Ornithonyssus bacoti*, was found on one beaver.

DECIMATING FACTORS. Indiana beavers have few enemies other than man. We have no record of predation, but assume that dogs might be able to kill young beavers found out of the water. Just two years after beavers were reintroduced into Indiana, there were complaints from landowners of damage (usually flooding) they had caused. In 1951 alone, 319 complaints were registered with the Division of Fish and Game. Personnel hired to handle the complaints were unable to do so, and an open season on beavers was initiated in November 1951. Before this time, the destruction of dams by dynamiting had been common. Whether lodges were also destroyed, we do not know. A beaver is occasionally killed when the tree it is felling drops on it.

TAXONOMY. *Castor canadensis carolinensis* Rhoads may formerly have occupied most of Indiana (Hall and Kelson, 1959). Michigan beavers have been assigned to *C. c. michiganensis* V. Bailey, and Wisconsin beavers to *C. c. canadensis* Kuhl by the same authors. Beavers from both of these states were transplanted to Indiana, but no one has made subspecific determinations of the current Indiana animals. To our knowledge, only two skulls from beavers originally native to Indiana exist in collections (Lyon, 1936; Lindsay, 1960).

SELECTED REFERENCES. Bradt, 1938, 1939; Grasse and Putnam, 1950; Tevis, 1950.

Family Cricetidae

Western Harvest Mouse
Reithrodontomys megalotis (Baird)

Reithrodontomys megalotis: Whitaker and Sly, 1970

DESCRIPTION. This is a small, rather long-tailed, short-eared mouse. It is brownish gray (somewhat grizzled) above and white or

whitish below. The sides of the head and body have a fulvous wash, which is brighter in adults. Subadults are grayer above and below than are adults. The tail is distinctly bicolored, dark above and whitish below. In Indiana, the harvest mouse is most likely to be confused with the house mouse, the white-footed mouse, or the deer mouse. From all three the harvest mouse can be immediately distinguished by the grooves on the front of the upper incisors (see Fig. 31). Although adult harvest mice, white-footed mice, and deer mice may have similar color patterns, young white-footed mice and deer mice of comparable size to adult harvest mice are uniformly slate gray above and white below. Adult white-footed mice and deer mice are considerably larger than harvest mice. House mice are quite variable in color, and some individuals may resemble harvest mice; however, house mice do not have a bicolored tail and normally do not have a whitish venter. Indiana specimens of *Reithrodontomys megalotis* collected thus far exhibit relatively little color variation.

Weights and measurements are shown in Table 102. The dental formula is

$$I \ \frac{1}{1} \ C \ \frac{0}{0} \ P \ \frac{0}{0} \ M \ \frac{3}{3} \ = \ 16.$$

STATUS AND DISTRIBUTION. The first harvest mice found in Indiana were trapped on the Willow Slough Fish and Wildlife Area (Newton County) in 1969 (Whitaker and Sly, 1970). By 1972, we had collected 182 specimens on or near Willow Slough. Many of these were trapped in or near a large, unharvested rye field, which appears to have served as a population and dispersal center. In 1973, we took a single specimen in Jasper County, about 20 miles east of Willow Slough. Mumford and others captured a single harvest mouse near Lafayette (Tippecanoe County) in 1974 and 4 others there

Western harvest mouse. Photo by Whitaker

in 1975. In the summers of 1973 and 1974, Steven D. Ford undertook to determine the distribution of this mouse in Indiana. With Willow Slough as a starting point, he trapped at approximately 5-mile intervals south, east, and west in 13 northwestern Indiana counties (Ford, 1977). He trapped 129 harvest mice from 35 of 154 sites sampled, adding specimens from Benton, Carroll, Vermillion, and Warren counties. Ford was unable to capture any harvest mice north of the Kankakee River, although he trapped at 15 locations (18,000 trap-nights). The easternmost site yielding harvest mice was a half mile west of the Tippecanoe River in Carroll County,

Table 102

Weights and measurements of *Reithrodontomys megalotis* from Indiana

Character	n	x̄	Range	SD	SE
Total length	84	126.81	114-146	7.48	0.82
Tail length	83	58.29	50-69	8.33	0.91
Hind foot	85	16.28	15-18	0.78	0.09
Weight	85	10.76	9.1-21.9	0.70	0.08
Skull length	55	20.37	19.0-21.4	0.61	0.08
Braincase breadth	61	10.04	9.6-10.7	0.26	0.03
Length of palate	64	3.58	3.2-4.0	0.20	0.03
Maxillary toothrow length	65	3.11	2.8-3.5	0.24	0.03
Interorbital breadth	65	3.18	2.7-3.8	0.17	0.02
Basilar length	53	14.63	13.6-15.7	0.46	0.06

where 12 specimens were taken. Five trapping sites on the east side of the river and within 6 miles of the above site yielded no harvest mice. Ford did not obtain specimens east or south of the Wabash River, even though he trapped 16 locations (19,200 trap-nights) in 1974. Two mice taken just east of the Illinois-Indiana state line (1 mile north of Rileysburg, in Vermillion County) represent the southernmost station for the species in Indiana. It is interesting that in October 1976 Ford trapped a western harvest mouse south of the Wabash River (9 miles southwest of Lafayette). No doubt, the species also occurs in additional counties and we hope to sample new areas outside the known range.

Some indication of population density may be derived from trapping data. In the prairie association of *Andropogon / Sorghastrum* (bluestem / Indian grass), 1 harvest mouse was taken in 1,800 trap-nights. Along a grassy dike at Willow Slough, 2 were taken in 1,600 trap-nights, while a ditch bank near a rye field and a nearby *Monarda / Opuntia* (horsemint / prickly-pear) field produced 15 and 14 specimens in 4,000 and 3,650 trap-nights respectively. In the rye field, however, 150 harvest mice were taken in 11,452 trap-nights. Pearson (1964) reported that populations of *R. megalotis* on a study area in California fluctuated between less than 1 to more than 50 per acre.

We believe the western harvest mouse is a relatively recent immigrant to Indiana, probably arriving not much before 1969, although it has penetrated at least 40 miles into the state. Jones and Mursaloglu (1961) stated that it was extending its range eastward in Illinois, and Birkenholz (1967) felt that it had moved into Illinois during the present century. Their absence in trapping in earlier years at Urbana and Normal, Illinios, and at Willow Slough and Lafayette, Indiana, substantiate the theory of recent immigration. Before 1969, a number of localities had been trapped at Willow Slough. Since the first harvest mice were taken there, that species has been trapped by us, except for one time (April 1979), on each subsequent visit and in numerous locations. Similarly, at least one site near Lafayette had been trapped at intervals for more than 15 years before the first *R. megalotis* was obtained. In view of the fact that this mouse apparently has the ability to invade new areas and to undergo rapid population increases, it seems unlikely that it remained undetected in low numbers for long at Willow Slough or Lafayette.

The western harvest mouse is now known from at least 38 localities in 7 counties (Map 38). It appears to be common only on the Willow Slough Fish and Wildlife Area. We expect the western harvest mouse to become part of the mammalian fauna in additional counties and to extend its range eastward along Interstate 74, which provides a ready avenue of dispersion and good habitat.

It is interesting that Evermann and Butler (1894b), Hahn (1909), and Lyon (1936) all more or less predicted that the eastern harvest mouse (*Reithrodontomys humulis*) might eventually be discovered in Indiana; this possibility is not ruled out, although we have been unable to trap *R. humulis*.

HABITAT. Birkenholz (1967) felt that the harvest mouse was moving eastward in Il-

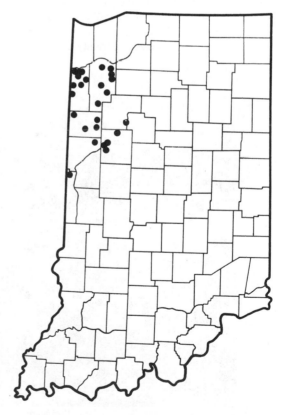

Map 38.   The Western Harvest Mouse,
Reithrodontomys megalotis, in Indiana

linois in response to clearing of woodlands, as de Vos (1964) had reported for the ground squirrels *(Spermophilus tridecemlineatus* and *S. franklinii)* and the white-tailed jack-rabbit *(Lepus townsendii).* Mumford and Kirkpatrick (1961) have shown how the thirteen-lined ground squirrel has extended its range in Indiana. Birkenholz found the largest Illinois harvest mouse populations associated with stands of foxtail in recently cultivated habitats; such stands existed for a short time and the mice decreased or disappeared as the areas progressed through plant succession to old fields. Verts (1960) found that *R. megalotis* in Illinois occurred most often in "grassy areas with scattered clumps of tall stemmed herbs and small shrubs," where common grasses were bluegrass, little bluestem, fescue, oats, panic-grass, and foxtail.

The first Indiana harvest mice were taken at two localities about one mile apart. One site was a grassy dike bordering a cornfield; the vegetation on the dike was mostly bluegrass, fescue, and clover, growing on a dark, sandy loam soil. The second trapping station was an old field containing many species of plants, the most conspicuous being horsemint, bracken, prickly-pear, flowering spurge, and round-headed bush clover. Other plants present were panic-grass, alfalfa, Joe-Pye weed, yarrow, ragweed, Russian thistle, blunt-leaved milkweed, ground-cherry, partridge pea, purpletop, knotgrass, wild lettuce, goat's-beard, self-heal, and rye. This plant association was on a light, sandy soil.

A third collecting site was a sparsely vegetated sandy field, where the predominant plants were horsemint and an unidentified grass; much of the ground here was bare. Subsequent trapping revealed that harvest mice were also present adjacent to the horsemint / prickly-pear field in fairly large numbers along a ditch bank, and in even larger numbers in a rye field. When initially trapped in 1969, the 25- to 30-acre field contained nearly pure rye. This field was left undisturbed until 1971, during which time the composition of the plant cover was altered by the presence of less and less rye and the appearance of more herbs. A fifth collecting site was on the Beaver Lake Prairie Chicken Refuge, where a single harvest mouse was trapped in an association of

Habitat of western harvest mouse at Willow Slough Fish and Wildlife Area, Newton County. Photo by Mumford

prairie grasses composed mainly of bluestem and Indian grass. This site approaches a natural prairie grassland condition.

Ford summarized his trapping data (179,500 trap-nights) in five vegetation types, which he categorized as grassy, grassy/weedy, weedy, tall weeds, and marsh. Grassy sites had an estimated 70 percent or more vegetative cover of grass, of which bluegrass was the most common. Other important grasses were fescue, quack grass, timothy, redtop, cheat, foxtail, bottlebrush grass, Indian grass, and panic-grass. Most grassy habitats were along highways and other roadsides.

Grass constituted 40 to 70 percent of the vegetation of grassy/weedy sites. All herbs and small shrubs (except wet site species) were considered weeds. This type of habitat was found along roadsides, fencerows, and railroad right-of-ways.

Weedy sites had less than 40 percent grassy vegetation and included hayfields (red clover, alfalfa, timothy, goldenrod, ragweed, etc.), many railroad right-of-ways, and some roadsides.

The tall weedy class consisted of many species found in the weedy category, but most of the vegetation was at least 3.5 feet tall. Plants commonly growing in this type of habitat were giant ragweed, wild parsnip, prickly lettuce, horseweed, ironweed, sunflower, wild carrot, rose, and blackberry. Willows were sometimes present. Grasses (usually timothy) were often present, but were considered an unimportant part of the vegetative cover. Tall weedy habitat was restricted mostly to railroad right-of-ways, except for a few fields on fish and wildlife areas.

Five of the six marsh habitats sampled were well within the range of the harvest mouse. Common plants in marshes were cattail, bog rush, sedge, willow, slough-grass, and boneset, which generally reached heights of more than 3.5 feet.

Ford trapped significantly more harvest mice in the grassy/weedy vegetation type than in the other four types sampled. The highest rate of catch (3.9 per 1,000 trap-nights) was in plots with 90 to 99 percent cover, the next highest (2.1 per 1,000 trap-nights) in 70 to 79 percent cover. Sample plots with 0 to 69, 80 to 89, and 100 percent cover yielded respectively 1.4, 1.4, and 1.1

mice per 1,000 trap-nights. Ford captured no western harvest mice in six "miscellaneous" plots, which included a cornfield (with no undergrowth), a wheat field (no undergrowth), a white oak woodlot, and three barnlots (with corncribs, haylofts, and other outbuildings).

ASSOCIATED SPECIES. Small mammals taken in the same traplines (only regular mousetraps were used) with harvest mice in Indiana were recorded, by collecting sites. In the rye field, where we trapped most, deer mice, white-footed mice, prairie voles, and harvest mice were taken in roughly the same numbers in October 1969 (Table 103). The deer mouse, the prairie vole, and the harvest mouse continued to be the three most commonly trapped species through December 1970. But in February 1971, the meadow vole became the third most abundant and the prairie vole dropped to fifth, after the white-footed mouse. The remainder of small mammals taken consisted of the shrews *Sorex cinereus*, *Blarina brevicauda*, and *Cryptotis parva*, and the house mouse, *Mus musculus*.

In the field near the rye, deer mice, white-footed mice, house mice, and prairie voles were most commonly taken with the western harvest mouse. On the Beaver Lake area, associates of the harvest mouse were masked shrews, deer mice, white-footed mice, and meadow voles. The plains pocket gopher was common in many of the same fields with harvest mice.

Ford (1975) found the deer mouse to be the major species taken with harvest mice, and the short-tailed shrew, the prairie and meadow voles, the white-footed mouse, the masked shrew, the house mouse, and the meadow jumping mouse were also found with it.

Catlett and Shellhammer (1962) found that the harvest mouse and the house mouse were compatible in captivity, and in salt marshes studied by these workers the house mouse was about 5.6 times as abundant as the harvest mouse. In the rye field we studied, the house mouse was present at the beginning, but essentially disappeared later, even though the field should have provided good habitat for this mouse.

HABITS. There is little specific information on the habits and behavior of the harvest

Table 103

Trapping results from rye field, grassy field, and sandy field in Newton County, Indiana, where *Reithrodontomys megalotis* has been taken

	Trapping In Rye Field							
Dates	18-23 Oct. 1969		7-12 Mar. 1969		29 Oct. 1970		5 Dec. 1970	
Trap-nights (TN)	750		4,200		590		572	
Animals trapped	Total	(per 100TN)	Total	(per 100TN)	Total	(per 100TN)	Total	(per 100TN)
Western harvest mouse	13	1.73	85	2.02	11	1.86	21	3.67
Deer mouse	17	2.27	16	0.38	8	1.36	19	3.32
Prairie vole	11	1.47	11	0.26	11	1.86	10	1.75
White-footed mouse	14	1.87	1	0.02	6	1.02	6	1.05
Masked shrew	—	—	2	0.05	2	0.34	1	0.17
Short-tailed shrew	—	—	1	0.02	2	0.34	—	—
Meadow vole	—	—	—	—	2	0.34	1	0.17
House mouse	6	0.80	—	—	1	0.17	—	—
Least shrew	—	—	—	—	—	—	1	0.17

	Trapping in Old Fields Near Rye		Trapping in Beaver Lake Prairie Chicken Refuge	
Dates	18-23 Oct. 1969		16-19 Apr. 1970	
Trap-nights (TN)	7,842		1,812	
Animals trapped	Total	(per 100TN)	Total	(per 100TN)
Western harvest mouse	20	0.26	1	0.06
House mouse	25	0.32	—	—
White-footed mouse	18	0.23	19	1.05
Deer mouse	22	0.28	13	0.72
Prairie vole	17	0.22	2	0.11
Meadow vole	1	0.01	12	0.66
Southern bog lemming	1	0.01	1	0.06
Masked shrew	11	0.14	17	0.94
Short-tailed shrew	12	0.15	1	0.06

mouse in Indiana. It would appear from the stomach contents and from debris in the rye field that the mice gather rye by getting seeds from the ground or from the stalks, peeling away the glumes and taking the enclosed seeds. Nests have not been found, although we have watched for them in our activities in the field on numerous occasions. Numerous pocket gopher mounds and burrows are present in this field and may provide some shelter for harvest mice.

The harvest mouse builds a globular nest in grass or weeds, under bushes, and sometimes above the ground in a bush. The nest is of shredded grass or other vegetation, and the opening on one side leads into a cavity lined with thistledown, milkweed, fine grass, or other soft material.

Harvest mice may be active day or night,

but are primarily nocturnal. They are good climbers and will climb up grass and other plant stems in search of food. They do not make runways, but often use those of other species. Harvest mice are particularly active in the late summer and fall, when they store seeds for winter use. The species does not hibernate, but during cold periods may remain in the nest. Harvest mice make a series of birdlike squeaks.

FOOD. Whitaker and Mumford (1972b) summarized the food habits of 155 Indiana harvest mice; of these, 127 were trapped in the rye field and 28 in other habitats. In the rye field sample, rye seeds and lepidopterous larvae were by far the most important foods. Most of the rye was mature seeds, but sprouts of germinated seeds were also taken. In non-rye habitats, lepidopterous larvae, foxtail grass seeds, and unidentified grass seeds were the most important food items. The volume of animal food in the 106 mice taken from the rye field from March to October was 36.1 percent (Table 104); a winter sample of 21 mice from this same field contained 7.6 percent animal food. The volume of animal food in the 28 mice taken in other habitats was 49.9 percent. Harvest mice, unlike many other species of small mammals, consumed little of the subterranean fungus *Endogone*. The stomach of one mouse taken in December contained 50 percent *Endogone*; December is late in the season for this food to appear in stomachs (Whitaker, 1962). Harvest mice occasionally contained only the internal organs of larger insects.

Table 104

Foods eaten by *Reithrodontomys megalotis* (n = 134) from Newton County, Indiana, including 106 individuals from a rye field, and 28 individuals from other habitats, taken from March through October
(from Whitaker and Mumford, 1972b)

Food items	Mice from rye field		Mice from other habitats	
	Percent volume	Percent frequency	Percent volume	Percent frequency
Rye seeds	55.7	93.4	3.4	3.6
Lepidopterous larvae	21.9	61.3	31.1	42.9
Vegetation	4.4	18.9	0.9	3.6
Coleopterous larvae	2.4	9.4	0.5	3.6
Dipterous larvae	1.9	26.4	0.5	7.1
Gryllidae (cricket)	1.8	4.7	2.7	7.1
Coreidae (squash bugs)	1.2	4.7	—	—
Araneae (spider)	1.2	5.7	3.9	7.1
Cicadellidae (leafhoppers)	1.2	12.3	6.1	10.7
Hemiptera	0.9	8.5	0.5	3.6
Asclepias (milkweed) seeds	0.9	2.8	3.6	3.6
Coleoptera	0.8	5.7	—	—
Setaria (foxtail grass) seeds	0.8	2.8	19.5	25.0
Endogone	0.8	2.8	2.5	7.1
Insect (unidentified)	0.7	5.7	0.5	7.1
Seeds (unidentified)	0.6	1.9	0.4	3.6
Lepidopterous pupae	0.6	1.9	—	—
Miridae (leaf bugs)	0.4	1.9	0.7	3.6
Internal organs of Orthopterans	0.3	1.9	0.5	3.6
Rumex (dock) seeds	0.2	0.9	—	—
Chrysomelidae (leaf beetles)	0.2	0.9	—	—
Psychodidae (moth flies)	0.2	1.9	—	—
Green vegetation	0.2	1.9	—	—
Carabidae (ground beetles)	0.1	1.9	0.7	3.6
Panicum (witchgrass) seeds	0.1	0.9	—	—
Feather	0.1	1.9	—	—
Chilopoda (centipede)	0.1	1.9	—	—
Moss	0.1	0.9	—	—
Annelida (earthworm)	0.1	0.9	—	—
Collembola (springtails)	trace	0.9	—	—
Unidentified grass seeds	—	—	14.1	25.0
Triodia flava (tall redtop) seeds	—	—	4.3	7.1
Curculionidae (snout beetles)	—	—	1.8	3.6
Festuca (fescue) seeds	—	—	1.3	7.1
Diptera	—	—	0.4	3.6
Hymenogaster	—	—	0.2	3.6
	99.9		100.1	

REPRODUCTION. Breeding activity begins in March; 23 of 33 adult females taken in that month had embryos and 1 had placental scars. Whether breeding continues through the spring and summer we cannot say, but of 3 adult females taken in August, 2 had embryos and 1 had placental scars. All adults taken in October showed evidence of reproductive activity; 5 of 13 contained embryos and 10 had placental scars (2 had both). None of 4 adults taken in December was pregnant, but 3 had placental scars. Late litters were probably produced in November. In a sample of 20 animals collected in February, all but 2 were "adults" in terms of total length and all but 5 were "adults" in terms of weight. We arbitrarily set a total length of 114 mm and a weight of 9.1 grams as the lower limits of "adult" criteria, for these were the smallest weights and / or total lengths of females showing evidence of reproduction (embryos or placental scars). None of 7 females (5 of them "adults") taken in February was pregnant or had placental scars. Verts (1960) reported breeding activity in Illinois harvest mice from March through June; he lacked data from 19 June to December. Jackson (1961) and Hooper (1952) stated that *R. megalotis* breeds throughout the year, but mostly from April to October. Other authors reported a more restricted breeding season and some mentioned a reduced breeding period in midsummer.

In our sample, 30 gravid females averaged 3.8 embryos (range from 2 to 6); 10 had 3 and 12 had 4 embryos.

Ford found that 88.6 percent of the females he took weighing 9.1 grams or more had embryos or placental scars. The number of embryos in Ford's sample of 33 ranged from 2 to 6, with an overall mean of 4.4.

PARASITES. Of 177 harvest mice examined for internal parasites, only 11 were infested. From one mouse 14 unidentified cestodes were recovered. Unidentified nematodes ranged from 1 to 4 per mouse; of 19 nematodes collected, 12 were in the stomach and 7 were in the intestines.

External parasites were found on 65 of 180 harvest mice examined. The only parasite found regularly was a myobiid mite (*Radfordia subuliger*), of which 234 were found on 49 animals (1.30 per mouse on 27.2 percent of the animals); there were 1 to more than 50 per host. The next most common mite was *Androlaelaps fahrenholzi* (23 on 17 animals). Another mite found was the labidophorid *Dermacarus hypudaei* (4 individuals). Two species of fleas (*Epitedia wenmanni*, 6 individuals; *Orchopeas leucopus*, 4 individuals) were also taken, along with one individual of the pygmephorid mite *Bakerdania equisetosa*.

DECIMATING FACTORS. The skulls of 4 harvest mice were recovered from pellets of long-eared owls; the pellets were picked up in a pine plantation at least a mile from the nearest harvest mouse trapping station.

TAXONOMY. Mensural variation among 41 male and 51 female harvest mice from Indiana was greater than that in a sample from Nebraska reported on by Jones and Mursaloglu (1961). The Indiana sample was composed of animals meeting our "adult" criteria. The Indiana population is considered to represent the subspecies *Reithrodontomys megalotis dychei* J. A. Allen.

SELECTED REFERENCES. Birkenholz, 1967; Ford, 1977; Hooper, 1952; Smith, 1936; Svihla, 1931; Verts 1960; Whitaker and Sly, 1970; Whitaker and Mumford, 1972b.

Deer Mouse
Peromyscus maniculatus (Wagner)

Prairie Deer Mouse, Prairie White-footed Mouse, Michigan Field Mouse, Baird Deer Mouse

Peromyscus michiganensis: Elliott, 1907
Calomys michiganensis: Evermann and Butler, 1894b
Peromyscus maniculatus: Osgood, 1909

DESCRIPTION. The species of *Peromyscus* in Indiana are *P. maniculatus* and *P. leucopus*. For many years, the species were evidently confused and some earlier authors listed a single species. Both have been commonly called deer mice or white-footed mice. Certain individuals of either species are sometimes quite difficult to identify to species; both may be brownish above, white below, and have white feet. The deer mouse is usually grayer above than the white-footed mouse, but color varies considerably. Some deer mice are uniformly tan above, while some are nearly blackish gray. Immatures of both species are slate gray above and white below. Deer mice are smaller and have shorter ears, shorter hind feet, and shorter tails than do white-footed mice. *Peromyscus maniculatus* usually has a tail length much less than half its total length and averaging about 50 to 55 mm; tail length almost never exceeds 65 mm. *Peromyscus leucopus* has a tail length slightly less than half its total length and averaging about 75 mm. The hind foot measurement of *P. maniculatus* is normally 19 mm or less, but *P. leucopus* usually has a hind foot 19 mm or longer (even in obvious gray-pelaged juveniles). The deer mouse has shorter ears (about 13 mm) than does the white-footed mouse (16 mm). In life, the deer mouse appears to have a blunter facial area than does the white-footed mouse. Tails of adult deer mice are distinctly bicolored (dark above and white below, with a sharp demarcation) and are often more heavily furred than the tails of white-footed mice. Unfortunately, the latter also has a bicolored tail (more evident in subadults) at times. But the combination of size, coloration, and measurements will usually allow one to separate the species in the flesh. Prepared museum specimens may be more difficult to identify.

The dorsal coloration of the deer mouse

Deer mouse and litter. Photo by Anthony Brentlinger, ISU AV Center

may be nearly a uniform tan, a grayish brown, or darkish gray with little brown. Often there is a dark central stripe down the back. In the darker populations, this stripe is nearly black. The white-footed mouse also has a central back stripe that is darker than the rest of the dorsum, but usually this stripe is not so distinct as it is in *P. maniculatus*, and *P. leucopus* never has a pelage as dark as the darkest deer mouse.

The skull characteristics of these species in Indiana are quite similar and we have not found good characters to distinguish between them with any degree of certainty.

Weights and measurements for the deer mouse are shown in Table 105. The dental formula is

$$\text{I } \frac{1}{1} \text{ C } \frac{0}{0} \text{ P } \frac{0}{0} \text{ M } \frac{3}{3} = 16.$$

STATUS AND DISTRIBUTION. Evermann and Butler (1894b) included the deer mouse

Table 105

Weights and measurements of
Peromyscus maniculatus from Indiana
(data from random trapping in Vigo County;
deer mice under 12 grams were not included)

	Males	Females
Total length (mm)		
n	221	167
x̄	135.42	136.55
range	106-162	107-155
SD	45.40	37.82
SE	3.05	2.92
Tail length (mm)		
n	222	167
x̄	52.36	51.64
range	28-68	42-68
SD	2.92	5.08
SE	0.19	0.39
Hind foot (mm)		
n	223	167
x̄	16.8	16.64
range	15-19	15-19
SD	1.09	3.92
SE	0.07	0.30
Weight (grams)		
n	218	161
x̄	15.87	16.59
range	12.2-20.3	12.1-25.6
SD	2.05	4.72
SE	0.13	0.37

on the list of mammals suspected to occur in Indiana. At that time, the two species of *Peromyscus* in the state may have been confused with each other, or the deer mouse may have actually been quite rare except in the prairie section of northwestern Indiana. But there are specimens of *P. maniculatus* collected by C. F. Fite near Denver (Miami County) in 1894. Waldo L. McAtee (1907) took specimens near Bloomington (Monroe County) in 1903, and he wrote, "I do not recall having seen this species recorded from Indiana." Hahn (1907a) and Elliott (1907) also reported on specimens of the deer mouse taken in Indiana, and Hahn (1909) knew of records from five counties. The species was known from as far south as Knox, Monroe, and Ohio counties by Lyon (1936). However, up to that time, little mammal collecting had been conducted in the Ohio River valley. More extensive collecting has shown that the deer mouse now occurs in suitable habitats (mostly cultivated fields) throughout Indiana (Map 39).

The numbers of deer mice taken per 100 trap-nights in randomly selected plots in different Vigo County habitats and in different seasons are shown in Table 106. Populations appeared to remain relatively constant throughout the year in cultivated fields, the highest number per 100 trap-nights being 2.45 in the March–April period, and the lowest being 1.37 in the July–August period. Since herbaceous cover was not necessary for deer mice, but was necessary for all other species studied, one habitat—plowed field —which furnished little or no vegetative cover was available to deer mice and unsuitable for other species. The deer mouse populations were highest in plowed fields from November through April. Essentially no hiding places were available except under the soil, although many of the fields in this category had been planted and contained some vegetation. Fifteen plots had winter wheat 2 to 3 inches tall; ten plots had winter wheat about 1 inch high; ten plots had corn or soybeans 2 to 3 inches tall; thirteen plots included only bare ground. Numbers of deer mice per 100 trap-nights in these various plots were 3.02, 2.53, 2.13, and 1.74 respectively. The observed differences were not significant ($X^2 = 3.84$, 3 df). Even the plots with no ground cover at all yielded relatively large numbers of mice.

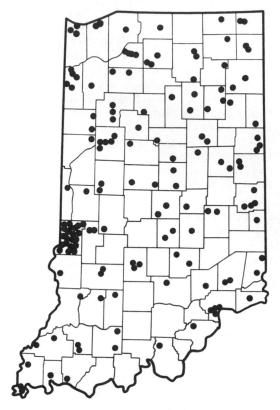

Map 39.   The Deer Mouse, *Peromyscus maniculatus*, in Indiana

Little additional work has been conducted on population size of deer mice in Indiana. Kirkpatrick and Conaway (1948) mentioned that they captured 10 specimens in 18 traps set overnight in an "open weed field" on 10 November 1946 in Tippecanoe County. This indicates a high population level. Barrett and Darnell (1967) gathered comparative population data on deer mice, house mice, and prairie voles on 7.9 acres of a 22.5-acre red clover field in Gibson County. They reported that 90 house mice, 25 deer mice, and 18 prairie voles occupied the sampled area.

HABITAT. The deer mouse was probably originally most common in the relatively dry, open fields of the prairie areas of northwestern Indiana and in the isolated, smaller prairies in the western part of the state. It undoubtedly occurred also on the front line of sand dunes along Lake Michigan where vegetation is sparse. Since it is not an inhabitant of wooded areas, it was probably absent (or occurred in isolated openings) in the nine-tenths of Indiana originally covered by forests until the late 1800s. With the removal of most of the forest vegetation by logging around the turn of the last century, and with the steady increase of cultivation, suitable habitat became available and enabled the species to enjoy a much wider geographic distribution. There are no data to determine how rapidly the deer mouse might have immigrated into this newly created area. (Mammalogists very seldom study cultivated field habitats.) Lyon (1936) stated that the deer mouse was "an inhabitant of cleared

land, fields, natural meadows, prairies, and the sand beaches of Lake Michigan." Today, it occurs in what is left of prairie grasslands, pastures, fallow fields, hay and grain fields, and other open areas. We have taken it along grassy roadsides, railroad grades, ditch banks, and in cemeteries and old gardens. Other collecting sites include fencerows between or bordering cultivated fields, the edge of a pond in a pasture, on a spit of land between two ponds in a marl marsh, in gravel pits, and along the edge of woods.

Around Terre Haute (Vigo County), Whit-

Table 106

Numbers of *Peromyscus maniculatus* taken in randomly trapped plots in Vigo County, by habitat and season
(from Whitaker, 1967a)

	Jan. Feb.	March April	May June	July August	Sept. Oct.	Nov. Dec.
Grassy field						
Trap-nights	900	900	825	450	600	975
P. maniculatus	7	13	8	3	21	77
No./100 TN	0.78	1.44	0.97	0.67	3.50	7.90
Plowed field						
Trap-nights	690	825	1,050	—	300	750
P. maniculatus	26	25	16	—	1	18
No./100 TN	3.77	3.03	1.52	—	0.33	2.40
Soybeans						
Trap-nights	150	225	—	375	300	150
P. maniculatus	5	8	—	11	4	6
No./100 TN	3.33	3.56	—	2.93	1.33	4.00
Winter wheat						
Trap-nights	—	375	300	—	—	—
P. maniculatus	—	35	5	—	—	—
No./100 TN	—	9.33	1.67	—	—	—
Corn						
Trap-nights	225	150	—	975	1,050	450
P. maniculatus	1	11	—	16	6	1
No./100 TN	0.44	7.30	—	1.64	0.57	0.22
Misc. cultivated fields						
Trap-nights	75	300	225	150	525	375
P. maniculatus	9	14	5	6	15	22
No./100 TN	12.0	4.67	2.22	4.00	2.86	5.87
Wheat stubble						
Trap-nights	450	525	75	525	675	525
P. maniculatus	19	10	4	2	23	19
No./100 TN	4.22	1.90	5.33	0.38	3.41	3.62
Corn stubble						
Trap-nights	1,275	1,725	75	—	150	525
P. maniculatus	21	19	0	—	1	3
No./100 TN	1.65	1.10	—	—	0.67	0.57

aker (1967a) found *P. maniculatus* to be most common in cultivated fields, but gathered data on its occurrence in 15 habitats (Table 107; see also Tables 2 and 3). In 85 study plots established in river bottom woods, upland woods, and brush, a single deer mouse was trapped (in brush). Other investigators have reported similar habitat preferences in this region. In brushy fields, only 7 deer mice (0.41 per 100 trap-nights) were taken. Low capture rates were also obtained from pastures, where continual soil compaction by livestock inhibits burrowing and affects vegetation types. Whitaker's study showed that the deer mouse was most abundant in cultivated fields; the seven best habitats were all agricultural fields. *Peromyscus maniculatus* was very common in fields plowed in the fall and left barren all winter. One such habitat on a floodplain had been inundated by spring flooding and, when the area was trapped after the water receded, the soil was sunbaked and cracked. The 5 mice taken in three nights with 25 traps each night were deer mice, which were evidently living in the cracks and feeding on seeds accumulated there. Mumford has also trapped this mouse in similar sites, on the dry, cracked mud of small depressions in old fields. Houtcooper (1972) found more deer mice in floodplains (6.04 per 100 trap-nights) than on an old glacial terrace of the Wabash River (2.38 per 100 trap-nights) or on an upland (1.95 per 100 trap-nights) in Vigo County.

Whitaker's Vigo County data were summarized to test the effects of vegetative ground cover on the distribution of deer mice in the 11 best habitats sampled. There were 52 mice (1.24 per 100 trap-nights) taken in 60 plots with good cover, and 233 mice (2.49 per 100 trap-nights) in 125 plots with poor cover. This difference was significant ($X^2 = 26.95$). On these same plots, there was also a significant difference ($X^2 = 16.96$, 1 df) between the numbers of deer mice trapped on dry soil (2.13 per 100 trap-nights; 296 plots) and on moist soil (0.86 per 100 trap-nights; 31 plots).

Since there is considerable interest in the effects of strip-mining for coal on wildlife populations, the seven study plots situated on strip-mining lands were analyzed. One plot was classified as upland woods, three as brush, two as brushy fields, and one as weedy field. One of the brushy field plots had poor woody vegetation and the dominant plant was the grass *Setaria faberi;* 4 deer mice were taken in this plot. The other brushy

Table 107

Numbers of *Peromyscus maniculatus* taken in random plots
in various habitats in Vigo County, Indiana
(from Whitaker, 1967a)

	Number of plots	Trap-nights	Number of deer mice taken	Number per 100 trap-nights
Winter Wheat	9	675	40	5.93
Miscellaneous Cultivated Fields	22	1,650	71	4.30
Soybean	16	1,200	34	2.83
Wheat Stubble	37	2,775	73	2.63
Plowed Fields	48	3,600	86	2.39
Soybean Stubble	22	1,650	39	2.36
Weedy Field	29	2,175	38	1.75
Corn	38	2,850	35	1.23
Corn Stubble	50	3,750	44	1.17
Grassy Field	33	2,475	26	1.05
Brushy Field	23	1,725	7	0.41
Brush	16	1,200	1	0.08
Pasture	17	1,275	1	0.08
Upland Woods	54	4,050	0	—
River Bottom Woods	15	1,125	0	—

field plot had a fair cover of woody vegetation and practically no grass; 2 white-footed mice were trapped on it. On the single weedy field plot, 6 deer mice were captured. The four plots in upland woods and brush yielded 8 white-footed mice. The results indicate that the deer mouse invades the early stages of stripped land and is replaced by the white-footed mouse when woody plant species become dominant over herbaceous plants.

ASSOCIATED SPECIES. The species most closely associated with the deer mouse in Indiana are the house mouse, which occupies cultivated fields with moderate to heavy ground cover, and the prairie vole, in dry old fields. The white-footed mouse also occurs with the deer mouse, sometimes in dry fields, especially those with greater amounts of ground cover, and sometimes in cornfields, especially along woods. In early seral stage fields of northwestern Indiana where the western harvest mouse has invaded, it, too, is a common associate.

HABITS. The deer mouse is nocturnal and evidently spends the day in underground burrows, in holes or cavities in fence posts and trees (rarely), or in piles of hay or other vegetation in fields. Houtcooper (1972) studied the burrowing habits of deer mice in cultivated fields near Terre Haute. Diagrams of two burrows excavated by him in February and March are shown in Figure 37. Twelve burrows studied in detail by Houtcooper averaged 16 feet in length and varied from 5 to 35 feet; they ranged from 1 to 12 inches below the ground surface and averaged 4.1 inches in depth. The deepest point of the burrow was often near the entrance. Usually a single opening (0.75 to 1.5 inches in diameter) led to the underground system of tunnels, which was rather complex, with up to 12 branches off the main burrow. The average number of side passages was 6. Three of the burrows contained caches of stored seeds and eight of the burrows each terminated in a large chamber, three of which contained

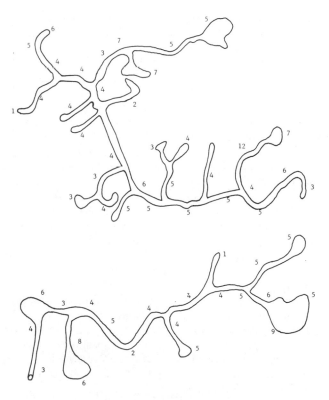

Figure 37. Two *Peromyscus maniculatus* burrows, Vigo County, Indiana. Numbers indicate burrow depth, in inches. From Houtcooper, 1971.
Linear scale: 0.25 inch = 1 foot.

nesting materials of grasses, straw, leaves, or paper. Lyon (1923) trapped two deer mice near burrows thought to have been constructed by crayfish.

The deer mouse climbs well, and nests have been observed in hollow fence posts or bushes some distance from the ground. Perhaps some food is obtained by climbing, also. But the deer mouse is undoubtedly much less arboreal than the white-footed mouse. The deer mouse is so well adapted for living in habitats devoid of woody vegetation that climbing is probably not very important to its livelihood and survival.

When moving about over the surface of the ground, deer mice evidently do not leave well-defined runways. Lyon (1923) noted, however, that in the soft sand along Lake Michigan, tracks of deer mice merged and sometimes seemed to form "almost a runway." The foraging technique used by the deer mouse evidently precludes well-formed runs (such as those used by voles). Deer mice are often trapped, however, in runways of voles. Lyon noted that *P. maniculatus* moved about over the sand usually by short jumps on all four feet at once. He also noticed that at times it walked, sometimes dragging its tail in the sand. When jumping, the tail was evidently held high, for it failed to leave such a mark.

The home range of a deer mouse is probably confined to 0.5 to 1.5 acres, the larger home ranges tending to be in poorer habitats. Males have larger home ranges than do females. Whitaker's studies in Vigo County indicate that individuals do not move about much, remaining in cultivated fields even after the fields have been plowed. *Peromyscus maniculatus* is unique in this respect among Indiana mice.

FOOD. The food habits, as determined by the contents of the stomachs of 444 deer mice from Vigo County (Whitaker, 1966), are summarized in Table 108. Lepidopterous larvae were the most important food, constituting 15.4 percent of the volume. Seeds of wild plants made up 14.6 percent, and nearly a third of the diet consisted of cultivated crops. Soybeans and wheat each constituted about 10 percent and corn made up 5.6 percent. About half of the 32.9 percent animal food was lepidopterous larvae. Nearly 20 percent of the material in the stomachs consisted of miscellaneous or green vegetation. One can readily see from Table 108 that deer mice consume a wide variety of food items.

Food habits data were summarized for the principal food items in major habitats (Table 109). In soybeans and wheat stubble, soybeans and wheat seeds were the major foods. In wheat fields, weedy fields, and corn fields, lepidopterous larvae were eaten in the greatest abundance. In corn stubble or grassy fields, miscellaneous vegetation was consumed in greatest abundance. Considering its abundance, corn was largely avoided as a food by *P. maniculatus*, except in corn stubble or otherwise when it was about the only food readily available.

Food data were also summarized by season (Table 110). Certain foods greatly restricted by season are not included in the table. Seeds of lespedeza were eaten only in winter and spring, forming 4.5 and 1.8 percent of the food volume at those times. Cultivated sorghum seeds were eaten only in fall, when they constituted 10.8 percent of the diet. Seeds of Johnson grass and panic-grass each made up only 0.4 percent of the diet, but in winter and summer respectively. Many of these data undoubtedly reflect different availabilities of various foods at different times (or in different habitats). Corn in Vigo County was available to some degree throughout the year, but it was particularly abundant in winter after it had matured and been harvested. At that time there were numerous kernels and even whole ears of corn on the ground. During this period there were relatively few other foods available in the cornfields, except *Setaria* seeds, which also were important in winter. Lepidopterous larvae were very important dietary items in all seasons except winter. Presumably they would have been eaten more extensively in winter if they had been more abundant or available. The most important winter foods of *P. maniculatus* were wheat seeds and soybeans, which littered the ground after harvest in their respective areas. These two foods were still available and were major foods in the fields even after plowing destroyed all vegetative cover. As spring progressed, soybeans remained important for a time, but in areas where there was herbaceous vegetation, lepidopterous larvae became a major food and was the single most important item of diet throughout summer and fall.

Table 108

Foods eaten by *Peromyscus maniculatus* (n = 444)
from Vigo County, Indiana
(from Whitaker, 1966)

Food Item	Percent Volume	Percent Frequency
Lepidopterous larvae	15.4	30.0
Miscellaneous vegetation	14.7	28.4
Wheat seeds	11.8	16.0
Soybeans	10.5	12.8
Unidentified seeds	7.2	11.9
Corn	5.6	8.3
Green vegetation	5.1	11.0
Coleoptera	3.6	12.2
Lespedeza seeds	2.3	3.8
Flesh (mouse, salamander)	1.8	4.1
Hemiptera	1.7	5.9
Annelida (earthworms)	1.7	5.0
Animal material	1.7	8.6
Setaria (foxtail grass) seeds	1.6	2.7
Coleopterous larvae	1.6	3.8
Chilopoda (centipedes)	1.2	3.2
Chenopodium (pigweed) seeds	1.2	2.9
Echinochloa (barnyard grass) seeds	1.2	2.7
Diptera	1.2	3.4
Lepidopterous pupae	1.1	2.0
Dipterous larvae	1.0	4.5
Cultivated sorghum seeds	0.9	1.1
Ambrosia trifida (giant ragweed) seeds	0.6	0.7
Digitaria (crabgrass) seeds	0.5	0.9
Araneae (spider)	0.5	1.4
Elymus seeds	0.5	0.7
Xanthium (cocklebur) seeds	0.4	0.5
Rye, Oat seeds	0.4	0.7
Portulaca oleaceae (common purslane) seeds	0.4	0.7
Prunus serotina (black cherry) seeds	0.3	0.7
Phytolacca (pokeweed) fruit	0.2	0.2
Panicum (witch grass) seeds	0.2	0.2
Corn; anthers, pollen	0.2	0.2
Gastropoda (slugs)	0.2	0.5
Phleum (timothy) seeds	0.1	0.5
Miridae (leaf bugs)	0.1	0.2
Leerzia (rice cutgrass) seeds	0.1	0.2
Gryllidae (cricket)	0.1	0.5
Endogone	0.1	0.7
Amaranthus (amaranth pigweed) seeds	0.1	0.2
Fungus	0.1	0.9
Acrididae (grasshoppers)	0.1	0.5
Polygonum (knotweed) seeds	0.1	0.2
Oxalis (wood sorrel) seeds	0.1	0.5
Formicidae (ant)	0.1	0.9
Enchytraeidae (enchytraeid worms)	trace	0.2
Sorghum halepense (Johnson grass) seeds	trace	0.2
Piesmidae (ash-gray leaf bugs)	trace	0.2
Juncus (rush) seeds	trace	0.2
Nematode (roundworm)	trace	0.2
Collembola (springtails)	trace	0.2
	99.5+	

Table 109

Major foods eaten by *Peromyscus maniculatus*
in major habitats of Vigo County, Indiana
(sample sizes ranged from 24 to 67 animals; food data given as percent volumes)

	Soybeans	Wheat	Wheat Stubble	Corn Stubble	Weedy Field	Grassy Field	Corn
Soybeans	24.5	—	1.7	2.3	—	—	—
Lepidopterous larvae	15.6	26.8	14.2	12.4	24.3	9.8	22.7
Miscellaneous vegetation	8.3	22.2	14.2	13.5	11.4	22.2	6.6
Wheat seeds	8.2	9.3	35.5	2.7	—	—	—
Annelida (earth-worms)	5.8	4.3	—	0.5	—	—	—
Flesh	3.9	0.4	1.5	6.7	—	1.7	1.8
Unidentified seeds	3.0	5.7	5.8	5.7	15.6	9.4	5.2
Coleoptera	2.7	5.0	1.8	1.5	6.9	5.6	7.7
Hemiptera	1.8	0.4	1.5	1.4	1.9	1.3	4.0
Coleopterous larvae	0.4	6.3	—	2.8	2.4	0.4	—
Green vegetation	—	3.4	4.4	0.7	13.6	8.3	4.2
Endogone	—	0.1	0.9	—	—	—	—
Setaria (foxtail grass) seeds	0.0	0.4	1.0	4.9	0.0	0.0	9.3
Corn	0.0	0.0	1.1	37.4	5.3	0.0	8.2

Table 110

Seasonal variation in food habits of
Peromyscus maniculatus from Vigo County, Indiana
(sample size listed below season;
food data given as percent volumes)

Food item	Winter n = 162	Spring n = 172	Summer n = 37	Fall n = 73
Setaria seeds	1.4	2.1	2.7	0.6
Lepidopterous larvae	4.8	20.6	34.5	16.7
Corn	8.7	4.1	4.2	3.2
Misc. vegetation	13.4	15.8	3.1	8.0
Wheat seeds	23.7	6.5	1.6	3.2
Digitaria seeds	0.6	0.0	2.6	0.7
Ambrosia seeds	0.6	0.0	0.0	2.2
Coleopterous larvae	1.0	1.8	0.7	1.6
Unidentified seeds	8.3	5.4	5.0	8.8
Endogone	0.0	trace	0.0	0.8
Green vegetation	3.7	7.6	0.0	4.3
Echinochloa	0.0	0.0	1.2	6.4
Coleoptera	1.4	3.9	5.3	5.1
Soybeans	10.7	13.4	3.1	6.9
Hemiptera	0.9	1.3	2.7	4.2
Earthworms	1.7	2.9	0.0	0.0
Prunus	0.0	0.2	1.2	0.7
Elymus seeds	0.0	0.3	0.0	0.0
Chilopoda	0.3	2.1	0.0	2.0
Spider	0.0	0.7	1.8	0.3

Foods eaten by juveniles were tabulated (Table 111) and can be compared with foods eaten by all deer mice (Table 108). Lepidopterous larvae were the most important food in both cases, followed by wheat seeds, soybeans, miscellaneous vegetation, and unidentified seeds. The order of abundance was different, but there was little difference between foods eaten by juveniles and adults.

REPRODUCTION. The gestation period in the deer mouse is about 25 days. At least some females produce more than a single litter per year. In Indiana, pregnant females have been trapped in each month of the year. Thus, it is potentially possible for the deer mouse population to increase quite rapidly.

Most females appear to bear young in spring and early summer; the smallest percentage of gravid females was taken in midwinter.

In a sample of 62 gravid deer mice examined from Vigo County, Whitaker (1967a) found the number of embryos per female to average 4.73 and range from 2 to 8. The most common number of embryos per female was 4 (in 22 females), and 19 females each contained 5 embryos. Four of 9 females trapped in January and 3 of 9 caught in February were pregnant. Additional data concerning this sample are presented in Table 112. Overall, 62 of the 132 adult females examined were gravid and 59 had placental scars; 3 individuals contained both embryos and placental scars. The average number of pla-

Table 111

Foods eaten by juvenile *Peromyscus maniculatus* (n = 69) from Indiana

Food Item	Percent Volume	Percent Frequency
Lepidopterous Larvae	18.1	28.9
Wheat Seeds	17.9	24.7
Soybeans	14.7	17.3
Miscellaneous Vegetation	6.9	14.5
Seeds	4.6	8.7
Green Vegetation	4.4	8.7
Lespedeza seeds	3.1	4.3
Hemiptera	2.9	4.3
Diptera	2.8	4.3
Setaria (foxtail grass) seeds	2.2	4.3
Unidentified Grass seeds	2.2	4.3
Chenopodium (pigweed) seeds	2.0	2.8
Unidentified seeds	1.6	10.1
Annelida (earthworm)	1.5	1.4
Green clover seeds	1.5	1.4
Sorghum	1.4	1.4
Phytolacca americana (pokeweed) fruit	1.4	1.4
Panicum (witch grass) seeds	1.4	1.4
Corn	1.4	2.8
Vegetation	1.3	4.3
Coleoptera	1.1	5.8
Echinochloa (barnyard grass) seeds	1.1	2.8
Flesh	0.7	1.4
Digitaria (crabgrass) seeds	0.7	1.4
Amaranthus (amaranth pigweed) seeds	0.7	1.4
Curculionidae (snout beetle)	0.7	1.4
Coleopterous larvae	0.5	1.4
Insect larvae	0.2	1.4
Piesmidae (ash-gray leaf bugs)	0.2	1.4
Lepidopterous pupae	0.2	1.4
Dipterous larvae	0.1	2.8
Araneae (spider)	0.1	2.8
	99.6	

Table 112

Reproductive data from adult female deer mice from Vigo County random trapping program (from Whitaker, 1967a)

Months	Number adult females examined	Number pregnant	Average number embryos per pregnant female	Number with placental scars	Average number placental scars
Jan.-Feb.	26	9	4.50	10	5.70
March-April	60	33	4.82	26	5.72
May-June	6	4	4.50	2	7.00
July-August	9	4	4.00	5	3.80
Sept.-Oct.	17	7	5.29	10	7.18
Nov.-Dec.	14	5	4.50	6	5.40

cental scars per female was 5.82. Since this figure is higher than the average number of embryos per female (4.73), some animals evidently exhibited two sets of scars when examined. One female had 9, four had 10, and one had 13 placental scars. Disregarding these six females, the average number of scars per female was 5.29, more nearly equal the number of embryos per female. The average number of embryos contained by 20 additional females collected throughout the state was 5.0 (range from 2 to 7). A female trapped on 19 October was lactating (and appeared to be suckling) and contained 7 small embryos. Seven of the 20 females in this sample had 5 embryos each.

Young are born in nests constructed of various plant materials and placed in sheltered sites. Lindsay (1960) found nests in hollow fence posts and under piles of soybean hay lying in the field. McAtee (1907) discovered a nest under a log. Deer mice appropriate old birds' nests and dome them over for winter living quarters. The nest forms the foundation and the mice transport soft materials (such as milkweed fluff or thistledown) and form a warm globular structure nearly 6 inches in diameter, with an entrance low on one side. Mumford found such a nest on 14 December (Tippecanoe County) situated 7 feet from the ground in a hazelnut bush along a brushy fencerow between a picked cornfield and a fallow field. The foundation appeared to be an old cardinal's nest and was domed over completely with feathers from a ring-necked pheasant. As the observer jarred the nest in attempting to pull it down for examination, two deer mice left it. One went to the ground and escaped; the other climbed

out to the tip of a small branch and was captured by hand.

PARASITES. Evermann and Clark (1920) reported deer mice heavily infested with fleas at Lake Maxinkuckee and wrote, "On one occasion when trapping these mice for specimens it was observed that they were quite seriously infested by fleas. The examples thus afflicted could usually be recognized at once by their having the hair gnawed or scratched out from about the root of the tail." One of 11 deer mice collected in the sand dunes of Porter County between 26 September and 14 October was infected with a *Cuterebra* larva (Lyon, 1923). Nixon A. Wilson (1961) reported the tick *Dermacentor variabilis* and the louse *Hoplopleura hesperomydis* from Indiana deer mice. *H. hesperomydis* is found on both *P. maniculatus* and *P. leucopus* in Indiana.

Wilson (1961) recorded 3 fleas (*Orchopeas*

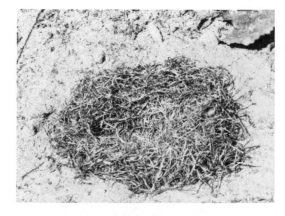

Deer mouse nest, found under litter at Beaver Lake Prairie Chicken Refuge, Newton County. Photo by David W. Berrey

leucopus) on 25 deer mice from Grant County and 2 fleas from a *P. maniculatus* nest in White County. Other fleas he collected were 3 *Epitedia wenmanni* and 1 *Megabothris asio*. Whitaker and Corthum (1967) collected 40 fleas (four species) from deer mice in Vigo County (Table 113). Of the mice examined, 25 (5.14 percent) yielded fleas. It appears that fleas are not commonly found on *P. maniculatus* in Indiana and that of the fleas that are found, *Orchopeas leucopus* is the most abundant.

Data on parasites of Indiana deer mice are summarized in Table 113. The more important mites found on this species were *Androlaelaps fahrenholzi, Hirstionyssus utahensis, Dermacarus hypudaei, Ornithonyssus bacoti,* and *Radfordia subuliger,* although none occurred in great abundance.

Whitaker examined 457 deer mice from Vigo County for internal parasites and found a total of 230 cestodes (average 0.50; 23 mice infested), 45 nematodes (average 0.10; 17 infested), and 15 trematodes (average 0.03; 1 infested).

DECIMATING FACTORS. The deer mouse is undoubtedly one of the major prey species of nocturnal, predatory mammals and owls. We have no definite data regarding the remains of deer mice in the stomachs or pellets of mammals or birds because most investigators did not distinguish between deer mice and white-footed mice in their analyses.

TAXONOMY. The subspecies in Indiana is *Peromyscus maniculatus bairdii* (Hoy and Kennicott). Deer mice from northwestern Indiana are much darker dorsally than those from elsewhere in the state, but most populations show considerable color variation. The darkest specimens we have seen were trapped on black muck soils in Lake County. Some deer mice with extremely worn teeth are a pale, rather uniform golden color dorsally; we think at least part of this coloration is correlated with age, for we have seen similar individuals of *P. leucopus*.

SELECTED REFERENCES. Blair, 1940b; Houtcooper, 1972; Howard, 1949; Osgood, 1909; Svihla, 1932; Whitaker, 1966.

Table 113

Ectoparasites and other associates of *Peromyscus maniculatus* from Indiana
(data summarized from Whitaker and Corthum, 1967, and Whitaker and Wilson, 1968)

Parasites	Parasites		Hosts Parasitized	
	Total	Average	Total	Percent
Fleas (Siphonaptera) (486 mice examined)				
Orchopeas leucopus	31	0.06	31	6.4
Ctenopthalmus pseudagyrtes	6	0.01	6	1.2
Epitedia wenmanni	2	0.004	2	0.4
Stenoponia americana	1	0.002	1	0.2
Sucking Lice (Anoplura) (472 mice examined)				
Hoplopleura hesperomydis	72	0.15	31	6.6
Mites (Acarina) other than chiggers (454 mice examined)				
Androlaelaps fahrenholzi	199	0.44	43	9.5
*Hirstionyssus utahensis	94	0.21	12	2.6
Dermacarus hypudaei	42	0.09	7	1.5
Ornithonyssus bacoti	30	0.07	6	1.3
Radfordia subuliger	8	0.02	7	1.5
Radfordia affinis	2	0.004	2	0.4
Eulaelaps stabularis	1	0.002	1	0.2
Laelaps kochi	1	0.002	1	0.2
Macrocheles sp.	1	0.002	1	0.2
Chigger mites (Trombiculidae)				
Euschoengastia peromysci	1	0.002	1	0.2
Ticks (Ixodides)				
Dermacentor variabilis	2	0.004	2	0.4

*Originally reported as *H. talpae*

White-footed Mouse
Peromyscus leucopus (Rafinesque)

Deer Mouse, Woodland White-footed Mouse, Dormouse, Rustic Mouse, Common Deer Mouse, Common White-footed Mouse, Northern Deer Mouse, Wood Mouse

Mus leucopus: Wied, 1839
Mus agrarius: Plummer, 1844 (*agrarias* of Lyon, 1936)
Hesperomys leucopus: Wied, 1862
Calomys americanus: Butler, 1892a
Peromyscus leucopus: Elliott, 1907

DESCRIPTION. The white-footed mouse is reddish brown to fawn above and white below, with large ears and large black eyes. The pelage is grayer in summer than in winter. The tail is slightly shorter than the combined head and body length and is brownish above and whitish below. Juvenile white-footed mice are uniform gray above and white below. We have seen at least two specimens that each had a white patch on the forehead. Another specimen was all white except for a tan middorsal stripe and tan nape and top of head; its eyes were dark. It was one of three "white" animals trapped in a house. Quick (1881) reported the taking of an "albino" white-footed mouse at Brookville (Franklin County). Animals with extremely worn teeth and pale, faded, rather unicolored dorsal pelage have been examined. Lindsay (1958) described one of these specimens as follows:

"The pelage is quite distinct from the others in being uniformly lighter in color and having a 'bleached' appearance. Upon examination of the skull it is evident that this mouse was quite senile when captured. All cusps of the molar teeth are worn away, causing the cutting surface to be flat." Mumford also trapped a specimen that fit this description.

In Indiana, this species is most likely to be confused with the deer mouse, which has a shorter tail, smaller ears, and shorter hind feet. In general, adult Indiana white-footed mice seldom have a hind foot length less than 19 mm; the hind foot of the deer mouse is usually 16 to 18 mm long. We have been unable to distinguish adequately between the skulls of the two species, although that of the deer mouse averages smaller. Both species of *Peromyscus* can be separated from other Indiana mice by having two rows of cusps on the grinding surfaces of the cheek teeth (see Fig. 28) and no grooves on the anterior faces of the incisors. Jackson (1961) mentioned characters that distinguish the skulls of *P. maniculatus* from those of *P. leucopus* in Wisconsin.

Weights and measurements for the white-footed mouse are tabulated for three sections of Indiana, in Table 114. The dental formula is

$$I \frac{1}{1} C \frac{0}{0} P \frac{0}{0} M \frac{3}{3} = 16.$$

STATUS AND DISTRIBUTION. Although the white-footed mouse has probably always been one of the most common Indiana mammals, there is relatively little written about it by earlier authors. Haymond (1870) noted that "This mouse is very common in the woods" of Franklin County. In Randolph County, it was said to be common in the woods and along fences (Cox, 1893). Evermann and Butler (1894b) reported the species from 6 counties. McAtee (1907) termed it abundant in the Bloomington (Monroe County) area. In August 1905, Walter Hahn (1907a) found *P. leucopus* "abundant everywhere" in the Kankakee River valley where he worked. Hahn (1908b) considered it to be "the most abundant mammal" on the

White-footed mouse. Photo by Dennis E. Clark

Table 114

Weights and measurements of *Peromyscus leucopus* from Indiana
(showing regional variations)

	Northwestern (Porter Co.)	West Central (mostly Vigo Co.)		Southwestern (Posey Co.)
		Males	Females	
Total length (mm)				
n	58	112	97	34
x̄	171.6	165.1	167.2	171.9
range	155-190	147-184	148-199	153-187
SD	9.10	18.2	11.82	9.96
SE	1.19	1.7	1.2	1.70
Tail length (mm)				
n	58	111	98	34
x̄	77.8	73.3	73.7	78.9
range	65-90	62-90	63-88	65-86
SD	5.66	9.77	7.96	5.32
SE	0.74	0.92	0.80	0.91
Hind foot (mm)				
n	58	112	101	34
x̄	20.8	19.91	19.7	20.3
range	20-23	18-21	17-22	18-22
SD	0.74	0.91	1.91	0.92
SE	0.09	0.1	0.2	0.15
Weight (grams)				
n	—	110	96	—
x̄	—	20.5	21.7	—
range	—	17-25	17.2-33.0	—
SD	—	1.1	3.47	—
SE	—	0.10	0.4	—

Donaldson Farm (now within Spring Mill State Park) from September 1906 to September 1907, and in 1909 he wrote that it occurred in every Indiana county. Evermann and Clark (1911) reported the white-footed mouse as abundant at Lake Maxinkuckee. Lyon (1923) considered *P. leucopus* the "commonest mammal in the region" among the sand dunes of Porter County. In St. Joseph County, Engels (1933) thought that it was "certainly the most common rodent" and stated that "it rivals *Blarina brevicauda* in numbers." Lyon (1936) wrote, "The Woodland White-footed Mouse is probably the most abundant mammal in Indiana and is found in suitable localities everywhere throughout the state." His range map, however, listed specimen records from only 20 counties and other records from 5 additional counties.

We now have specimen records from each of the 92 Indiana counties and consider the species common to abundant in suitable habitats throughout Indiana (Map 40). The continual destruction of woodland habitat has undoubtedly greatly decreased the numbers of white-footed mice in Indiana over the years.

HABITAT. *Peromyscus leucopus* is primarily a woodland species that occurs occasionally, but generally in low numbers, in fields. Getz (1961b) and Bendell (1961) thought it might avoid wooded areas with grassy ground cover, and Getz concluded that soil moisture was not a major factor in habitat selection by *P. leucopus* in his Michigan study area.

Several early authors in writing about the white-footed mouse in Indiana refer to its living in the woods, but other habitats are mentioned. Cox and McAtee noted its occurrence along fencerows. McAtee also found it "even in the open meadows and fields." Hahn (1909) wrote that *P. leucopus* was equally at

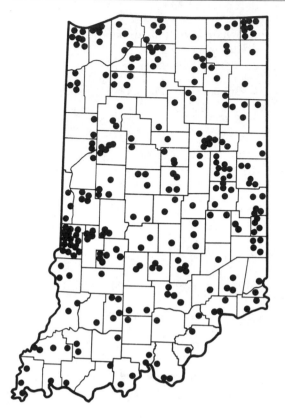

Map 40.   The White-footed Mouse,
Peromyscus leucopus, in Indiana

home in woods and fields. About Lake
Maxinkuckee, it was reportedly "abundant
not only in the fields and woods but also
about the cottages around the lake." Along
the Kankakee River in northwestern Indiana,
Hahn (1908a) found white-footed mice in
small numbers at places in the swamps
where all land within a one-mile radius was
submerged for weeks at a time. *Peromyscus
leucopus* also inhabits such habitats in Vigo
County (and doubtless other counties) today.
During flood season, the mice evidently live
in trees. The species was found on the
brush-covered and wooded sand dunes in
Porter County, but not on the sparsely vegetated dunes along the lake shore, according to
Lyon (1923). Several authors have reported
the occurrence of the white-footed mouse in
caves, and we have several records of them in
such habitats. A "colony" of white-footed
mice inside the entrance of Marengo Cave
(Crawford County) had existed there since
1883 (Hahn, 1909). Sometimes the mice

occur a considerable distance from the entrance. D. M. Lindsay found a *P. leucopus*
nest 100 yards inside a cave. Banta (1907)
found this species at least 1,500 feet inside
Mayfield's Cave (Monroe County).

During a random trapping program conducted by Whitaker in Vigo County, 316
white-footed mice were taken. They were
relatively common in eight habitats—river-
bottom woods, brushy field, weedy field, upland woods, brush, grassy field, winter wheat,
and corn (Table 115). Only four of the
habitats contained woody vegetation. The
species was most abundant (4.8 per 100 trap
nights) in river-bottom woods. It was relatively common in winter wheat and corn, but
most of the white-footed mice trapped in corn
were actually captured along the edges of the
fields. They were apparently living in adjacent fencerows, for black cherry seeds constituted the majority of their diet and black
cherry trees were a major component of the
fencerow vegetation.

The effect of cover on the distribution of
white-footed mice in Vigo County was rather
difficult to assess. The following discussion is
based on an analysis of the data only from
habitats where the species was common. In
the best habitats, 51 plots with good herbaceous ground cover, 105 plots in fair cover,
and 61 plots in poor cover yielded, respectively, 2.77, 1.54, and 1.31 mice per 100
trap-nights. There were significantly more
mice in areas with better herbaceous ground
cover ($X^2 = 28.03$, 2 df). In 38 plots in dense
woody vegetation, 1.40 mice per 100 trap-
nights were taken, while in 87 plots with
moderate or sparse woody vegetation, 2.45
per 100 trap-nights were captured. And in the
92 plots with no woody vegetation, 3.75 per
100 trap-nights were caught. These data
would indicate that among the habitats in
Vigo County supporting major populations of
P. leucopus dense woody vegetation was the
poorest and areas with no woody vegetation
were the best habitats for the species ($X^2 =
22.57$, 2 df). The complete picture of the
situation is somewhat different. It should be
emphasized that mature wheat and corn
habitats, where the white-footed mouse was
common, were present only during summer
and fall, when mouse populations were large
and young animals were moving into new
areas. Moderate or sparse woody vegetation

Table 115

Numbers of *Peromyscus leucopus* taken in random plots
in various habitats in Vigo County, Indiana
(from Whitaker, 1967a)

	Number of plots	Trap-nights	Number of mice taken	Number per 100 trap-nights
River bottom woods	15	1,125	54	4.80
Brushy field	23	1,725	48	2.78
Weedy field	29	2,175	37	1.70
Upland woods	54	4,050	65	1.60
Brush	16	1,200	17	1.42
Grassy field	33	2,475	30	1.21
Winter wheat	9	675	8	1.19
Corn	38	2,850	31	1.09
Cultivated field	22	1,650	6	0.36
Soybean	16	1,200	4	0.33
Wheat stubble	37	2,775	7	0.25
Pasture	17	1,275	2	0.16
Plowed field	48	3,600	5	0.14
Corn stubble	50	3,750	2	0.05

yielded significantly more individuals than dense woody vegetation (X^2 = 10.32, 2 df). This was probably because the sparser woody vegetation favored the development of herbaceous ground cover favorable to white-footed mice. Numbers of immature mice were often taken in grassy and weedy fields, especially in late summer and fall, probably as a result of dispersal into these areas. Few adults were taken in such habitats.

Peromyscus leucopus is often abundant in Indiana woodlands. Whitaker once attempted to catch every white-footed mouse in a 2.8-acre wooded plot surrounded by open fields (Vigo County). In ten days, 84 were taken, an average of 30 per acre and only 0.82 per 100 trap-nights. The habitat sampled was considered ideal for the species, for there was a small stream through the woodlot, and numerous brushpiles and fallen logs were present on the ground. Numbers of white-footed mice captured per 100 trap-nights in other habitats in Vigo County are in Table 115. Data on seasonal populations of *P. leucopus* in major habitats are presented in Table 116. It will be seen that numbers were fairly high through the winter, decreased in early spring, and increased again by late summer.

ASSOCIATED SPECIES. The white-footed mouse occurs in such a variety of habitats

that it has many other Indiana mammals as associates. In wooded areas, the short-tailed shrew is often a co-dominant associate, and the woodland vole is sometimes present. In cornfields, the white-footed mouse occurs with the house mouse and the deer mouse, and in brushy fields it often occurs with the meadow vole, the meadow jumping mouse, and the masked shrew.

HABITS. The white-footed mouse is primarily a nocturnal, woodland-inhabiting species that spends a considerable amount of time on the ground and some time climbing about in bushes and trees. It is not confined, however, to wooded areas. At times, *P. leucopus* is somewhat diurnal. From our observations, one is most likely to observe these mice moving about in the daytime when nighttime temperatures are near 0°F or colder. Under such conditions, the mice evidently forage to some extent during the day, when temperatures are normally higher than at night. McAtee (1907) wrote, "They are at least occasionally seen abroad by day." He saw a white-footed mouse in the afternoon at some distance from its burrow, others running about in barnyards near woods in the early morning, and one feeding at high noon. Hahn (1907a), in writing about this mouse in the Kankakee River valley, said that "in these wooded swamps the white-footed mouse is not as exclusively nocturnal as it is supposed

Table 116

Numbers of *Peromyscus leucopus* taken in randomly trapped plots in Vigo County,
by habitat and season
(from Whitaker, 1967a)

	Jan. Feb.	March April	May June	July Aug.	Sept. Oct.	Nov. Dec.
Upland and river bottom woods						
Trap-nights	750	1,275	225	600	825	1,500
P. leucopus	36	20	5	19	5	35
No. /100 TN	4.80	1.57	2.22	3.17	0.61	2.33
Brush & brushy field						
Trap-nights	525	1,200	225	450	—	525
P. leucopus	17	22	2	12	—	12
No. /100 TN	3.24	1.83	0.89	2.67	—	2.29
Weedy and grassy field						
Trap-nights	900	900	825	450	600	975
P. leucopus	8	9	5	2	7	36
No. /100 TN	0.89	1.00	0.61	0.44	1.17	3.69
Winter wheat						
Trap-nights	—	375	300	—	—	—
P. leucopus	—	4	4	—	—	—
No. /100 TN	—	1.07	1.33	—	—	—

to be elsewhere." On 2 February, Mumford saw a white-footed mouse which appeared to be sunning itself along a brushy fencerow about noon. The same day, one was captured at 1:00 P.M. in a trap set only 10 minutes earlier. The previous night's low temperature had been −4°F. and the ground was covered with crusted snow and ice.

P. leucopus is a good climber. Engels (1933) reported a white-footed mouse nest 20 feet above the ground in a tree cavity. D. M. Lindsay trapped two on the trunks of beech trees in traps 6 feet from the ground. There are other records of this mouse in trees, as well as in the upper stories of buildings. Bird nesting boxes fastened on the tops of fence posts and wood duck nesting boxes 15 to 20 feet high on tree trunks are easily reached and used (especially during the winter) by *P. leucopus*.

Nests are constructed in almost any site that affords enough protection. We have seen nests in holes in trees, in rotten stumps or tree snags with cavities or woodpecker holes, in buildings, caves, bird boxes, idle farm machinery, fence posts, discarded tires, metal structures or other objects, beneath bridges, in rock crevices, and other places. Other nests have been recorded beneath boards, logs, stones, or rubbish on the ground. The white-footed mouse readily invades houses (both abandoned and occupied) and other buildings, particularly during the colder months, and nests may be observed in almost any nook or cranny in such buildings. F. H. Montague, Jr., told us that white-footed mice sometimes built their nests overnight among the burners in the top of his stove. It is not unusual to find bird nests which the mice have capped over with soft materials for winter use. Such nests appear rather globular and have an entrance hole on one side. We have noticed that multiflora rose fencerows are excellent places to find this type of winter nest. Hahn (1909) had previously noticed that bird nests were used by this mouse.

Nesting materials include grasses, bits of paper or other soft materials, feathers, hair, milkweed, thistle or cattail down, pieces of leaves, or other items. Nests constructed in open areas, such as on a ledge in a cave or on the horizontal supports of a bridge, are spherical (about 6 inches in diameter) with thick walls and have an opening on one side. Nests built in other sites are, of course, in various shapes to fit the available space. W. L. Hahn noted that nests were sometimes underground. He also noticed that often the mice constructed nests "in a woodpile" and that nests were made of "bark, small twigs, dry grass or leaves and lined with some kind of soft material." Winter nests in trees and bird boxes sometimes harbor single animals, but may be used simultaneously by several individuals. The mice also use bird nesting boxes at least in May and June. In twelve bird boxes for which he maintained records, four held a single mouse, seven contained 2 each and the other harbored 13 (in winter, *fide* James M. Dietz). On 3 January 1978, H. P. Weeks, Jr., examined five nesting boxes originally provided for bluebirds and found 4, 6, 6, 8, and 9 white-footed mice in the five boxes. Both sexes were represented and more than one male was found per box. In renovated bird nests we have found the following: 27 January, 1 adult; 2 November, 1 adult; 10 November, 1 adult and 5 large young; 24 November, 1 adult; 24 November, 2 adults; date unknown, 2 adults; October, 4 young.

White-footed mice also live in small burrows in the ground. Such tunnels may open to the surface about the base of a tree or stump. The mice also use the burrows of larger mammals (such as the woodchuck), and probably travel along tunnels constructed by the eastern mole or the plains pocket gopher. In some areas, they also appear to enter the burrows made by crayfishes. Lyon (1923) trapped numerous white-footed mice in subterranean burrows where he had placed traps for woodland voles (Porter County).

When *P. leucopus* is discovered during the daytime in a remodeled bird nest, a slight disturbance (such as shaking the nest gently) usually causes the mouse to peer out of the entrance. Additional disturbance may cause it to climb from the nest to the ground; once it reaches the ground, it runs rapidly away or hesitates and hides momentarily. Mice often escape from low nests by jumping directly from the nest or from branches to the ground. The nest containing an adult and 5 young was shaken rather gently to determine whether any mice were inside. One by one the mice left the nest, climbed down the same small branches supporting the nest and ran off along the ground. One bird nest that the mice had domed over was that of either a yellow warbler or an American goldfinch. Both birds construct small, compact nests with thick walls of soft downy materials similar to the nesting materials used by the mice. This type of nest no doubt provides a warmer retreat than would bird nests constructed of grasses. But it appears that other types of bird nests are also used, thus the bird nest may be chosen more for a supporting structure on which to place the additional nesting materials. Bird nests are also used as feeding platforms by white-footed mice, as will be discussed later.

Hahn (1908b) recorded some of his observations on a captive white-footed mouse:

A male taken when half grown became so tame that it would eat from my hand. It remained under cover of its box during the day, but toward sunset would leave its retreat and begin to run about the cage looking for food and clambering about, often hanging downward from the roof of the cage. It would not allow me to pick it up, but would voluntarily come to my hand and nibble it or take food from it.

H. P. Weeks, Jr., noted that some captives vibrated their tails rapidly when an observer was near.

The usual method of locomotion on the ground appears to be a series of jumps, on all four feet at once, about the length of the mouse's body; some jumps are longer (10 to 12 inches). The tracks in such cases appear in groups of four, similar to miniature rabbit tracks, and no tail marks are present with the tracks. Sometimes tracks suggest that the animals have walked, and occasionally tail-drag marks are present (Lyon, 1923). *Peromyscus leucopus* travels along the surface runways made by voles.

FOOD. The white-footed mouse is primarily a seed eater, but also eats other vegetation and some animal material. No doubt a complete list of the plant species consumed would be quite long, for the mouse has a tremendously varied diet.

Haymond (1870) mentioned that *P. leucopus* ate large quantities of cockleburs, which it stored in song sparrow nests and in the nests of other small songbirds. Evermann and Clark (1920) thought beechnuts were an important food and noted that large numbers were stored by the mice for winter food. The same authors included three genera of snails

(*Physa, Limnaea, Sphaerium*) among the diet of white-footed mice. In Mayfield's Cave, *P. leucopus* ate seeds, myriopods, insects, and even part of a label from a bottle. Beef and cheese placed in the cave as bait for insects were also consumed by the mice. The mice dug into the soil to retrieve seeds buried there. Food mentioned by other authors includes acorns, hickory nuts, seeds of redbud, wahoo, bittersweet, sunflower, wild plum, tulip poplar, and giant ragweed, berries of coralberry, and corn. We have also observed that multiflora rose hips are readily eaten, and some mice have been trapped with pokeberry seeds in their cheek pouches. Pits from the fruits of black cherry are eaten in considerable quantities; a quart of the opened pits can sometimes be found about the base of a black cherry tree.

Captive white-footed mice have eaten a pasteboard box, dry rolled oats, cheese, and raw meat. A caged female ate her three offspring, and two cages in which three white-footed mice were confined together overnight each contained a single live mouse and two partially eaten mice the next morning (Hahn, 1908b). Two other white-footed mice, confined with a live screech owl overnight, "ate a considerable portion of the bird" (McAtee, 1907). Mumford once put a dead *P. leucopus* and a second mouse of the same species (thought to be dead) in a paper bag when running a trapline. Five hours later, when the bag was opened, the second mouse had consumed the dead mouse.

Jones (1970) studied the food habits of white-footed mice in Pike County by analyzing the contents of 489 stomachs (Table 117). The most frequent foods were unidentified starchy material and insects. Insect larvae and unidentified seeds were the next two most important food items. Small amounts of food (less than 0.1 percent volume) not included in the table were listed and consisted of "composite" seeds and the seeds of crowfoot, touch-me-not, pokeberry, tick treefoil, trumpet creeper, redbud, oxeye daisy, avens, sedge, daisy fleabane, lettuce, bluets, St. John's-wort, and plantain. Also listed were Annelida, insect pupal cases, metal, Coleoptera larvae, flower petals, and bones.

The food habits of 272 white-footed mice collected in Vigo County were studied by Whitaker (1966). Various kinds of wild seeds

and nuts made up 42.7 percent of the food volume, and cultivated plants were of minor importance, constituting only 3.4 percent of the foods (Table 118). Animal material accounted for more than 30 percent of the contents of the stomachs. Lepidopterous larvae were an important item. Unidentified seeds and miscellaneous vegetation constituted about 25 percent of the food; mast (probably acorns and nuts mostly) accounted for nearly 10 percent.

Since the white-footed mouse lives mostly in the woods, it is adapted to woodland or semiwoodland types of foods, such as nuts, seeds, and insects. Cultivated foods and grass seeds, often eaten by other common small mammals such as the house mouse and deer mouse, are of relatively little importance to *P. leucopus*, corn forming only 16.8 percent of the food of this species in cornfields. Foods of the white-footed mouse in such open habitats as weedy fields, grassy fields, and corn are shown in Table 119. Unidentified seeds and miscellaneous vegetation were most important in weedy and grassy fields, and in cornfields the most important foods were corn, lepidopterous larvae, Coleoptera, and unidentified seeds.

Food habits were also summarized on a seasonal basis (Table 120). Ash seeds were important in winter, but miscellaneous vegetation and unidentified seeds constituted a major portion of the food in winter, spring, and fall. Lepidopterous larvae were important from spring throughout the remainder of the year. Black cherry pits (abundant on the ground from the previous fall) were important in spring and summer. Coleoptera, mostly Carabidae and Scarabaeidae, became a significant food in summer.

The foods of juveniles (Table 121) and adults were compared and found to be similar. The four most abundant items eaten by juveniles were among the first five most important items eaten by adults.

White-footed mice store considerable food for winter use, and large amounts of nuts, seeds, acorns, and other seeds may be found in hollow trees, stumps, branches, beneath rubbish, in buildings, or in other suitable locations. The pits of the black cherry appear to be favorite storage items; the mice eat the seeds from inside the pits.

Among baits effective in catching white-

Table 117

Foods eaten by *Peromyscus leucopus* (n = 489)
from Pike County, Indiana
(from Jones, 1970)

Food Item	Percent Volume	Percent Frequency
Starchy material	30.1	77.3
Insects	14.5	78.6
Lepidopterous or Hymenopterous larvae	9.2	42.2
Seeds (unidentified)	7.5	41.0
Prunus (black cherry) seeds	5.3	21.4
Rubus sp. (blackberry) seeds	3.7	10.0
Oxalis (wood sorrel) seeds	3.6	9.4
Plant (unidentified)	3.3	23.3
Hair	2.2	41.2
Chilopoda (centipede)	1.9	13.7
Green vegetation	1.8	12.7
Apocynum (Indian hemp) seeds	1.6	7.9
Geranium (cranesbill) seeds	1.5	5.0
Mollusca	1.2	8.9
Acer (maple) seeds	1.2	8.3
Unknown	0.9	8.3
Arachnida	0.8	9.8
Flesh	0.8	4.8
Pinus (pine) seeds	0.8	4.8
Endogone	0.7	6.0
Fraxinus (ash) seeds	0.7	4.4
Rhus (sumac) seeds	0.6	2.3
Ulmus (elm) seeds	0.5	3.3
Lespedeza (bush clover) seeds	0.5	3.1
Rosa (rose) seeds	0.5	2.9
Rumex sp. (dock) seeds	0.4	3.7
Celastrus (bittersweet) seeds	0.4	2.9
Populus (cottonwood) seeds	0.4	2.5
Rhus (poison ivy) seeds	0.4	2.5
Sassafras (sassafras) seeds	0.4	1.5
Pebbles	0.3	7.3
Lonicera (honeysuckle) seeds	0.3	1.5
Grass seeds	0.2	3.3
Panicum (panic grass) seeds	0.2	2.7
Cornus (dogwood) seeds	0.2	2.1
Animal	0.2	1.5
Lathyrus (everlasting pea) seeds	0.2	0.6
Fungus	0.1	3.5
Vitis (grape) seeds	0.1	1.5
Smilax (greenbrier) seeds	0.1	1.2
Carex (sedge) seeds	0.1	1.2
Feathers	0.1	1.0
Lepidium (peppergrass) seeds	0.1	1.0
Setaria (foxtail grass) seeds	0.1	0.6
Robinia (black locust) seeds	0.1	0.6
Melilotus (sweet clover) seeds	0.1	0.6
Pyrus (apple) seeds	0.1	0.2
	100.0	

Table 118

Foods eaten by *Peromyscus leucopus* (n = 272)
from Vigo County, Indiana
(from Whitaker, 1966)

Food Item	Percent Volume	Percent Frequency
Seeds	13.1	38.6
Vegetation	12.0	28.8
Lepidopterous larvae (caterpillars)	11.4	27.9
Mast	8.1	9.5
Prunus serotina (black cherry) seeds	6.9	10.2
Fraxinus (ash) seeds	5.1	6.1
Elymus seeds	4.1	6.1
Coleoptera	3.9	13.6
Setaria (foxtail grass) seeds	3.3	5.1
Green vegetation	3.3	7.7
Animal	3.0	12.5
Chilopoda (centipede)	2.6	9.0
Araneae (spider)	2.1	5.5
Hemiptera	1.9	5.5
Corn	1.6	2.9
Wheat seeds	1.4	1.8
Impatiens (touch-me-not) seeds	1.3	2.2
Ambrosia trifida (giant ragweed) seeds	1.3	1.8
Acrididae (grasshopper), Gryllidae (cricket)	1.3	1.8
Coleopterous larvae	1.2	3.3
Flesh (mouse, bird)	1.2	3.3
Fagus (beech) nuts	1.0	1.1
Gastropoda (slugs and snails)	1.0	3.6
Polygonum (knotweed) seeds	0.9	1.1
Dipterous larvae	0.8	4.7
Rubus (blackberry)	0.8	1.8
Endogone	0.7	1.1
Asclepias (milkweed) seeds	0.5	0.7
Annelida (earthworms)	0.5	1.8
Soybeans	0.4	0.7
Hymenoptera	0.4	0.3
Abutilon (velvetleaf) seeds	0.4	0.3
Diptera	0.4	1.4
Lepidopterous pupae	0.3	0.3
Bromus (brome grass) seeds	0.3	0.3
Carabidae (ground beetle)	0.3	0.3
Chenopodium (pigweed) seeds	0.3	1.4
Erigeron (fleabane) seeds	0.3	0.3
Enchytraeidae (enchytraeid worms)	0.2	1.1
Oxalis (wood sorrel) seeds	0.2	0.3
Formicidae (ant)	0.2	0.7
Nematocera (ribbon worm)	0.1	0.3
Curculionidae (snout beetle)	0.1	0.3
Juncus (rush) seeds	trace	0.7
Calliphorid eggs	trace	0.3
Trifolium (clover) flowers	trace	0.3
Rumex (dock) seeds	trace	0.3
	100.0	

Table 119

Major foods eaten by *Peromyscus leucopus* in three habitats
(expressed in percent volume)
(sample sizes ranged from 25 to 33 animals)

	Weedy field	Grassy field	Corn
Unidentified seeds	20.1	19.3	8.6
Miscellaneous vegetation	17.1	12.6	3.8
Ambrosia seeds	9.5	—	—
Hemiptera	4.8	—	—
Lepidopterous larvae	4.8	8.1	14.4
Coleopterous larvae	4.4	—	—
Unidentified animals	3.8	5.9	1.2
Coleoptera	3.3	3.1	9.7
Green vegetation	2.3	0.9	—
Chilopoda	1.8	3.9	1.2
Flesh	1.5	3.7	—
Setaria seeds	0.6	8.1	2.4
Corn	—	—	16.8
Spider	—	0.7	4.4

Table 120

Seasonal variation in foods eaten by *Peromyscus leucopus*
from Vigo County, Indiana
(expressed in percent volume)

	Winter	Spring	Summer	Fall
n	83	65	47	77
Miscellaneous vegetation	14.2	13.9	6.4	11.6
Unidentified seeds	9.8	17.9	8.2	15.6
Elymus seeds	8.1	5.2	0.0	1.4
Setaria seeds	7.0	0.0	1.3	3.2
Lepidopterous larvae	4.4	17.7	16.9	10.3
Wheat seeds	4.3	0.3	0.0	0.0
Green vegetation	3.4	4.5	1.8	1.1
Coleopterous larvae	3.3	0.5	0.2	0.2
Coleoptera	3.1	1.0	10.5	3.2
Spider	2.4	0.3	4.3	1.8
Chilopoda	2.1	4.3	3.2	1.5
Prunus	1.8	11.8	11.3	5.6
Hemiptera	1.3	2.2	2.4	2.1
Earthworms	0.2	1.1	0.9	0.0
Corn	0.1	0.0	3.9	3.1
Soybeans	0.0	1.2	0.0	0.5
Endogone	0.0	0.0	3.9	0.0
Ambrosia seeds	0.0	0.0	0.0	4.5

Table 121
Foods eaten by 15 juvenile white-footed mice from Indiana

Food item	Percent Volume	Percent Frequency
Lepidopterous larvae	17.7	40.0
Vegetation	13.0	33.3
Prunus serotina (black cherry) seeds	10.0	13.3
Mast	6.6	6.7
Fagus grandifolia (beech) nuts	6.6	6.7
Polygonum (knotweed) seeds	6.6	6.7
Setaria (foxtail grass) seeds	6.6	6.7
Seeds	6.0	20.0
Grass seeds	5.7	6.7
Coleopterous larvae	4.7	6.7
Dipterous larvae	3.7	6.7
Coleoptera	3.0	13.7
Formicidae (ants)	2.7	6.7
Green vegetation	2.7	6.7
Rubus (blackberry) seeds	2.0	6.7
Enchytraeid worm	1.3	6.7
Gastropoda (slugs)	1.0	6.7
	99.9	

footed mice are peanut butter, suet, apple, dry or moist rolled oats, and bacon.

Feeding platforms are frequently established on top of old birds' nests, particularly those of the size made by American robins, mockingbirds, gray catbirds, and brown thrashers. Such feeding platforms are usually evident in multiflora rose fencerows and a cupful of debris left from the feeding of the mice on rose hips may be present in or on a single nest.

REPRODUCTION. The gestation period of *P. leucopus* is about 21 to 23 days, but may be extended in nursing females. In Indiana, the species evidently breeds throughout the year (Table 122). We have examined gravid females collected in each month of the year, but relatively few were taken from November to February. Most young are probably born from May to August. Females produce multiple litters, but we have no details on this aspect of breeding biology. We have embryo counts from 46 gravid females, each of which contained from 2 to 7 embryos, as follows: 2 embryos (2); 3 (8); 4 (14); 5 (17); 6 (4); 7 (1). The average number of embryos per female was 4.3.

The numbers of placental scars were tabulated for 36 female white-footed mice. One each had 2, 3, 9, and 12 scars; 10 had 4; 7 had 5; 7 had 6; 2 had 7; and 6 had 8. A gravid female trapped 25 April had 3 embryos and 4 placental scars. Another taken 28 November had 3 embryos and 8 placental scars. The female with 12 placental scars was captured on 13 December. Nixon A. Wilson took a female and 3 young (one measured 125 mm in total length) from a nest on 4 October. The female contained 4 embryos 27 mm in length.

Engels (1933) mentioned a nest containing a female and 3 young that was about 20 feet above the ground in a willow tree. The nest cavity was about 2 feet deep and contained an accumulation of 6 inches of droppings and debris at the bottom. The nest was composed of grasses and hair. Lyon (1923) found a nest constructed of torn bits of paper in a discarded pasteboard box on the ground. The nest contained a female with several young covered with hair but unable to walk. A few hours later, the young had been moved (presumably by the parent) from the site. Evermann and Butler (1894b) reported that nursing young cling tightly to the female. Evermann stated that he had "often caught an old female with young hanging to her teats and carried her by the tail for many rods before the young would drop off." Soon after Hahn (1908b) placed a female with three young in a cage, the adult ate her offspring.

Table 122

Reproductive data from adult female white-footed mice from Vigo County
random trapping program

Months	Number adult females examined	Number pregnant	Average number embryos per pregnant female	Number with placental scars	Average number placental scars
Jan.-Feb.	26	2	3.00	18	5.75
March-April	27	9	3.88	13	4.75
May-June	2	1	5.00	1	5.00
July-August	14	6	4.83	6	5.20
Sept.-Oct.	5	1	6.00	4	6.33
Nov.-Dec.	34	2	4.00	19	6.75

PARASITES. Lyon (1923) mentioned that from 5 to 10 percent of the white-footed mice he trapped in Porter County in the fall of 1922 were infested with *Cuterebra* larvae. We do not know how many mice he trapped, but 49 specimens (National Museum of Natural History) collected by him between 26 September and 13 October 1922 are probably part (or all?) of the catch. Only one male was infested with a *Cuterebra;* most of the parasites were in "nursing females." Each infested mouse was host to a single larva.

Test and Test (1943) reported *Cuterebra angustifrons* from *P. leucopus* collected from 26 to 30 August 1941 in Turkey Run State Park (Parke County). Of 108 mice of all ages examined, 31 (28.7 percent) were infested with 1 to 3 cuterebrid larvae or had holes in the skin where larvae had recently emerged. Most of the larvae occurred in the inguinal region (the scrotal sac of males being a common site), but some were in the axilla or belly region. The incidence of infestation in males was 29.7 percent, females, 27.3 percent. Most mice were parasitized by a single larva. We have noted numerous white-footed mice with cuterebrid larvae; these animals were captured from June to September plus one on 17 November, which seems quite late in the season.

Whitaker and Corthum (1967) published data on fleas and Whitaker and Wilson (1968) reported on mites from Indiana white-footed mice. Information from these papers plus additional data are included in Table 123. Two fleas *(Orchopeas leucopus, Epitedia wenmanni)*, the mite *Androlaelaps fahrenholzi*, one chigger *(Euschoengastia pero-*

mysci), and the tick *Dermacentor variabilis* are the major ectoparasites of the white-footed mouse in Indiana, although a number of additional species have been found. *Hirstionyssus talpae*, reported by Whitaker and Wilson (1968), has now been reidentified a *H. utahensis.*

One species of louse *(Hoplopleura hesperomydis)* has been taken on white-footed mice in Indiana. It is the common louse on *Peromyscus* and has been found in Indiana only on *P. leucopus* (the type host) and *P. maniculatus.* Wilson (1961) previously reported this louse from Indiana *P. leucopus.* He also listed the tick *Dermacentor variabilis*, the five fleas included in Table 123, and the fleas *Peromyscopsylla hesperomys* (6 specimens) and *Corrodopsylla curvata* (1 specimen).

Internal parasites recovered from 295 white-footed mice included 47 nematodes, 41 cestodes, and 1 trematode, all yet unidentified.

DECIMATING FACTORS. The white-footed mouse is undoubtedly a common prey item of many nocturnal avian and mammalian predators. We have records of predation on this mouse by domestic cats and dogs, by the gray fox, the red fox, the long-tailed weasel, and the mink. The remains of *Peromyscus* sp. (some no doubt *P. leucopus*) have been identified in the pellets of the following Indiana owls: barn owl, short-eared owl, long-eared owl, screech owl, great horned owl, saw-whet owl.

TAXONOMY. The subspecies in Indiana is *Peromyscus leucopus noveboracensis* (Fisch-

Table 123

Ectoparasites and other associates of *Peromyscus leucopus* (n = 272) from Indiana

Parasites	Parasites		Hosts Parasitized	
	Total	Average	Total	Percent
Fleas (Siphonaptera)				
Orchopeas leucopus	140	0.51	58	21.3
Epitedia wenmanni	43	0.16	38	14.0
Peromyscopsylla scotti	7	0.03	5	1.8
Ctenopthalmus pseudagyrtes	5	0.02	5	1.8
Stenoponia americana	4	0.01	4	1.5
Sucking Lice (Anoplura)				
Hoplopleura hesperomydis	27	0.10	14	5.1
Flies (Diptera)				
Cuterebra sp.	5	0.02	5	1.8
Mites (Acarina) other than chiggers				
Androlaelaps fahrenholzi	156	0.57	60	22.1
Hirstionyssus utahensis	20	0.07	3	1.1
Radfordia subuliger	16	0.06	9	3.3
Dermacarus hypudaei	1	0.004	1	0.4
Ornithonyssus bacoti	2	0.01	1	0.4
Radfordia hylandi	1	0.004	1	0.4
Laelaps kochi	1	0.004	1	0.4
Myocoptes musculinus	2	0.01	1	0.4
Chigger Mites (Trombiculidae)				
Euschoengastia peromysci	63	0.23	11	4.0
Euschoengastia setosa	1	0.004	1	0.4
Miyatrombicula jonesae	1	0.004	1	0.4
Ticks (Ixodides)				
Dermacentor variabilis	88	0.32	27	9.9

er). A series of 29 specimens from Posey County has a shorter average tail length than 52 specimens from Porter County and 18 specimens from Ripley and Jefferson counties. The Posey County animals may exhibit a trend toward *Peromyscus leucopus leucopus* (Rafinesque).

SELECTED REFERENCES. Hamilton, 1941b; King, 1968; Klein, 1960; McCarley, 1954; Nicholson, 1941; Osgood, 1909; Synder, 1956; Whitaker, 1963b, 1966.

Eastern Woodrat
Neotoma floridana (Ord)

Wood Rat, Allegheny Wood Rat, Allegheny Cave Rat

Neotoma pennsylvanica: Hahn, 1909
Neotoma magister: Kirkpatrick and Conaway, 1948
Neotoma floridana: Evermann and Butler, 1894b

DESCRIPTION. The woodrat is about the size of the familiar Norway rat, but the woodrat has longer, softer fur, larger ears, and a more heavily haired tail. The woodrat is grayish or buffy gray above, with some blackish color along the back, so that the sides are usually paler than the dorsum. The feet and underparts are white. Some animals show varying amounts of buffy color on the undersides. The tail is distinctly bicolored, dark above and whitish below. In many respects, the woodrat looks much like a very large white-footed mouse or deer mouse. Woodrats and Norway rats are frequently confused with each other. One reason appears to be that most people do not expect to find Norway rats in habitats away from buildings, thus any rat observed away from human habitations is thought to be a woodrat.

Weights and measurements are shown in Table 124. The dental formula is

$$I \frac{1}{1} C \frac{0}{0} P \frac{0}{0} M \frac{3}{3} = 16.$$

STATUS AND DISTRIBUTION. Evidently Cope (1872) first mentioned the woodrat from Indiana in his discussion of the fauna of Wyandotte Cave (Crawford County). He wrote, "The rats also have brought into fissures and cavities communicating with the cave, seeds, nuts, and other vegetable matter, from time immemorial, which furnished food for insects." Packard (1888) also made reference to rats in Wyandotte Cave: "A 'cave rat' was described to me by Mr. Rothrock as having been seen in the main Wyandotte Cave. It was said to be of the same color as the domestic rat, but with a body longer, somewhat like a weasel's; the whiskers are larger than those of a rat and the 'ears are nearly twice as large'; it is probably a Neotoma." In 1897, Blatchley mentioned the rats in Wyan-

Table 124

Weights and measurements of
Neotoma floridana from Indiana

	Males	Females
Total length (mm)		
n	13	17
x̄	389.6	389.6
range	365-419	348-431
SD	18.5	18.8
SE	5.1	4.6
Tail length (mm)		
n	13	17
x̄	170.8	174.0
range	141-191	155-186
SD	13.4	9.7
SE	3.7	2.4
Hind foot (mm)		
n	13	18
x̄	41.9	41.8
range	37-44	39.0-45.5
SD	1.9	1.8
SE	0.5	0.4
Weight (grams)		
n	13	17
x̄	324.5	293.2
range	240.0-383.5	193.6-361.9
SD	40.0	46.1
SE	11.1	11.2

dotte Cave: "The cats have exterminated the 'rats' *(Neotoma)* mentioned by Cope and Packard as being inhabitants of the cave."

In the summer of 1930, Paul F. Hickie and Thomas Harrison (then students at the University of Michigan) conducted a survey of mammals around the perimeter of Indiana for the Indiana Department of Conservation and the University of Michigan Museum of Zoology. They searched for woodrats in southern Indiana and were successful in collecting the first specimens from the state. We feel it is of interest to quote their account.

The vicinity of Wyandotte Cave was selected as the most likely territory, especially as one of the guides at the cave, in answer to a questionnaire, had written rats occurred in the cave. Inquiry there solicited the information that they occurred in Wyandotte Cave, but traps set in the cave in places where they were said to have been seen yielded only a white-footed mouse, a new specimen for the cave, but no woodrats. The traps were placed nearly half a mile in from the entrance. The guide was unable to find even traces of rats.

Eastern woodrat. Photo by Mumford

The first real inkling of their presence came from a man who had prospected in the West for gold and knew them there, where they are common. He had seen their piles of sticks in the mouths of caves along the cliff above his home in Crawford County and had even caught two while trapping mink and weasels in the winter. His aid was solicited, but all to no avail. He was unable to locate the piles of sticks, and traps placed in that locality yielded nothing.

From there the search shifted on to the east a few miles, near Road 62 and just within Harrison County, where it was reported there was a small cave in which they had once abounded in great numbers. A guide offered his services and our party scoured the steep hillside in search of the cave. Failing to find the cave, another guide was procured, but again the cave eluded us. Finally we left with the understanding that we were to be called when the cave was located.

One other locality seemed to offer possibilities. Mr. C. C. Deam, Research Forester of the Indiana Conservation Department, reported high cliffs and a buzzard's roost at Tobacco Landing. Going southward from Laconia, a narrow rocky road leads down to the Landing, a lonely place graced by a single dwelling and a light for guiding Ohio River steamers. The house stands at the base of a high cliff and overlooks the Ohio River from a safe distance above its spring floods. A series of interrupted ledges traverse the side of the cliff and along these are found a number of small caves. The first cave we investigated showed unmistakable signs of the presence of rats. Piled on top of a large boulder was a collection of debris—small sticks, fresh twigs and leaves, corn cobs, bones of mammals, pokeberries, nuts, etc. Near by was another rock on which a pile of small stones had been collected. We continued our search and soon located a nest in an obscure niche. It was composed of the bast fibers of trees loosely formed into a deep, thick-walled cup. There could be no doubt now of the presence of *Neotoma*. The penetrating gleam of the flashlight moved on, then stopped suddenly. There sat a woodrat in its full glare, blinking serenely out, apparently unalarmed and entirely at ease.

To avoid disturbing it, the flash was immediately snapped off. We were too close for a shotgun and the .22 with shot loads was in the car at the Landing. We went for it and fifteen minutes later when we returned the rat was still resting in the same place. By a bit of cooperation, one holding the flash and the other shooting, it soon entered our collection.

On our return trip from Tobacco Landing, we were informed that the cave we had searched for so long had been found and a rat had even been seen. We went to it immediately, and though it was five

hours since the rat had been seen, it was still in about the same place. At first only its nose could be seen, but it became curious and edged out a trifle too far. At the report of the gun it toppled over and we had another specimen.

Subsequent trapping at Tobacco Landing yielded two more specimens. It is probable that *Neotoma* occurs in suitable habitats throughout this region. The four specimens were all from Harrison County, but since the limestone cliffs and caves extend into the adjoining Counties of Spencer, Perry, Crawford, Floyd and Clark, there is great likelihood that *Neotoma* will eventually be found in them, or even at some distance north of the Ohio River. Judging from their habits, it is unlikely that they would be able to survive long the attacks of their enemies, the carnivorous and predacious birds and mammals in the absence of safe hiding places in caves and under ledges along inaccessible limestone cliffs. [Hickie and Harrison, 1930]

C. M. Kirkpatrick and C. H. Conaway were evidently the next researchers to obtain woodrat specimens at Tobacco Landing. They wrote (1948):

By following the directions given by Hickie and Harrison (1930), we arrived at perhaps the same spot where they first captured woodrats in Indiana which is Tobacco Landing in Harrison County. On the warm night of December 27, 1946, a total of 8 of these unsuspicious creatures came into our traps, of which 6 were taken alive. They exhibited no fear of new, wooden live traps, but entered them readily for ear corn bait. All of the *Neotoma* taken were adults of which 3 were males and 5 were females.

The same authors obtained additional information regarding the woodrat in Indiana:

In addition to the local occurrence of *Neotoma* at Tobacco Landing, we have proof of their presence on the Harrison State Forest where the limestone escarpment borders the Ohio River. On two occasions unmistakable signs of their activity were found there and such identifiable parts as feet, toes, and vibrissae were left in our steel traps. No signs of these rats were noted along similar cliffs along the Ohio River in Crawford County, but definite evidence of their occurrence was found in Orange County. In a small cave on a hill just west of Valeene many piles of debris consisting of wood, bones, rocks, and scattered nuts were found, as well as holes in the cave floor and walls.

Once the presence of woodrats at Tobacco Landing was known to mammalogists, numerous persons visited the site. We have examined specimens taken there on 6 May 1951, 6 February 1954, 22 December 1957, 9 March and 7 December 1958, and 8 March 1959. Mumford and M. P. Kahl, Jr., live-trapped a *Neotoma* there on 6 February 1954, noted abundant signs of the animals, and secured some photographs of woodrats inside the cave. There are few recorded visits to the cave since 1959. When we last were there (19 March 1973), about 4 to 6 feet of the floor of the cave had been removed, along with the large boulders and other rubble that gave much shelter to the rats earlier. We heard rumors that people had excavated the cave in search of Indian artifacts. We found two *Neotoma* nests in crevices inside the cave, but saw no woodrats.

Jay H. Schnell trapped a woodrat on the Harrison–Crawford State Forest (Harrison County) on 21 March 1954. The site is possibly the same one where Kirkpatrick and Conaway found woodrats in 1946. Subsequently, others have taken specimens at this locality, which we last visited on 20 March 1973. Woodrat signs were still obvious on that date. We have also located woodrats at two other sites on the Harrison–Crawford State Forest (both localities are in Harrison County) and suspect that in the general vicinity there are other populations.

There have been persistent reports of woodrats in Crawford County, aside from those mentioned in Big Wyandotte Cave. Lewis Lamon, a spelunker who has explored some 200 Indiana caves, is confident he observed woodrats in the county some years ago. Donald W. Ash reported woodrats in Wildcat Cave, near Wyandotte. In late December 1969, we explored (with James L. Mumford) some escarpments parallel to the Ohio River north of Fredonia. We found debris in crevices in the outcrops and what appeared to be droppings of *Neotoma*. None of the signs was fresh. On 2 April 1973, we again visited the site and set 60 rattraps. This time, we found numerous (but old) signs of woodrats, including pieces of bone, metal, sticks, leaves on top of rock ledges. We found a nest in a deep crevice. But we observed no woodrats and captured none.

We went to Big Wyandotte Cave on 3 April 1973, and one of the guides took us into the cave to show us the spot where woodrats had been seen and one had been live-trapped and released. Also, a woodrat, found dead in the cave, had electrocuted itself by gnawing through the insulation on some wires forming the lighting system in the cave. This animal had been buried nearby. Although we searched the burial site carefully and detected the smell of a dead animal, we were unable to locate the specimen. About 1,700 feet inside the cave (and more than 300 feet below the surface) were *Neotoma* tracks in the dust covering the cave passage. At the site where the live animal had been held in a cage for a time, then released, there was an area approximately 30 feet square of which every square inch was covered with tracks. The guide told us that when the confined animal was there, other woodrats visited the cage from time to time; this observation was based on the occurrence of fresh tracks after all tracks had been erased. There is no doubt in our minds that the guides had observed *Neotoma;* their descriptions were quite accurate. We carefully searched for nests and the presence of green twigs along the cave passages, but found neither.

The eastern woodrat may eventually be found in several new localities, for no one has conducted intensive research on the distribution of this species in Indiana. Richard L. Powell told us he has noticed signs of woodrats in a cave near Hardinsburg (Washington County). Ted Chandik observed a rat-like animal in Donaldson's Cave (Lawrence County) in 1958. On 20 February 1954, Mumford observed droppings and debris on ledges in May's Cave, southwest of Bloomington (Monroe County); the signs were not fresh. Spelunkers have reported rats in Sullivan's Cave (Lawrence County), but we have no precise date for the observation, which was probably in the mid-1950s. Old signs of *Neotoma* (mostly droppings) were observed in Sullivan's Cave by Mumford, R. D. Kirkpatrick, and L. Kimball on 1 March 1955. Bader and Hall (1960) discovered woodrat bones and an old nest of this species in Sullivan's Cave.

There is no doubt that the eastern woodrat once enjoyed a wider distribution in south-central Indiana. Richards (1972) summarized the "Recent fossil" remains of *Neotoma* found in 11 caves in Harrison, Jennings, Lawrence, Monroe, Orange, and Owen counties. He concluded that "*Neotoma* dis-

Map 41.   The Eastern Woodrat, *Neotoma floridana*, in Indiana

tribution in the past was most likely concurrent with the limits of both of Indiana's karst areas, according with its cave and bluff crevice habitat." The woodrat bones were associated with bones of now extirpated Indiana mammals, such as the black bear, porcupine, spotted skunk, and elk. These remains prove that at some earlier time the eastern woodrat occurred at least 70 miles farther north than Wyandotte Cave, its known, northernmost locality today. The cause of the depopulation of much of the Indiana range is unknown.

All of the intact specimens of woodrats we have examined were taken at four sites in Harrison County, between 1930 and 1973. The recent observation in Big Wyandotte Cave adds that area to the currently known distribution of the species, which does not appear to be common at any of the sites. It would seem that careful monitoring of the remaining population would be an excellent study, for we do not know whether the species is declining or increasing (either in range or in numbers).

HABITAT.   In Indiana, the eastern woodrat is apparently restricted to caves and limestone escarpments in the heavily forested hills of south-central Indiana. Red cedar appears to be an important tree to the species, which makes its nest of the shredded bark and makes heavy use of the twigs. We are not certain of the food value of red cedar twigs, but where *Neotoma* occurs green juniper sprigs are scattered all along runs used by the rats and are strewn throughout caves inhabited by them. Perhaps the cedar is a food supply, but we do not know why such a quantity of twigs is found on the ground. Caves used by woodrats are dry and have numerous fissures, crevices, and ledges along their length. We have found one woodrat family living in an abandoned building.

HABITS.   Woodrats are essentially nocturnal when foraging for food outside their cave and cliff retreats. But they can often be observed inside the caves (and sometimes in deep fissures in escarpments) during the daytime. We do not know the extent of daytime activity inside caves, but casual observations indicate that woodrats may be moving about throughout the day. At times, we have found individuals resting in nests, but at other times they have been observed moving along ledges or in and out of fissures. Some of these movements, of course, could be a result

Bluffs along Ohio River in Harrison County, home of eastern woodrat. Photo by Whitaker

of our disturbance. The rats evidently forage widely outside the cave at night. At Tobacco Landing they had gathered many fish and turtle bones and deposited them in the cave. The nearest source of such items was 100 yards away, along the Ohio River.

Woodrats move about over the escarpments, leaving tracks in the dust that collects in narrow, protected ledges. Woodrats are no doubt excellent climbers, and the rough surfaces of rock ledges and cave walls do not hamper movements. From the abundance of red cedar twigs noted in the caves, along runways on the escarpments, and scattered throughout the forest along paths followed by the rats, woodrats must be good tree climbers. They cannot gather the twigs in any other way. They no doubt also climb to obtain other food items, such as wild grape, pokeberries, and the like, that they store in the caves in the fall.

Rats of the genus *Neotoma* are noted for their habit of gathering all sorts of items, which they transport to a particular site and pile into "middens." We observed several such middens at Tobacco Landing, where the rats usually heaped the material on top of a large boulder lying on the cave floor. On 19 March 1954, Mumford examined the materials in such a midden there, and found the following: the seeds and fruit of black walnut, hickory, coffee tree, wild grape, tulip poplar, buckeye, redbud, ailanthus, oak, pokeweed, corn, persimmon, and sugar maple; other plant materials, including unidentified dead leaves, leaves of pokeberry, willow, redbud, white oak, sugar maple, chestnut oak, and elm, red cedar sprigs and unidentified twigs, sycamore bark, tendrils from wild grape, and bits of charcoal; and miscellaneous items, including fish bones, turtle bones and shell, bits of glass, lead foil, small paint can, small cardboard box, cellophane, cigarette butt, rubber band, .22 cartridge case, shotgun shell, bottle cap, large mammal dropping, plastic buckle, metal buckle, cigarette package, crow feather, metal teaspoon, bits of cloth, grasshopper head, and a snail shell. In the center of this pile of debris was a globular nest (evidently in use) composed of grasses and shredded bark.

Two or more woodrats were observed for nearly an hour as they climbed about the cave walls and appeared or disappeared along horizontal cracks there. The animals were unafraid and appeared curious. Other observers have noted this curiosity. One rat permitted its nose to be touched with a lighted flashlight without showing alarm. On a later visit to another cave, Whitaker captured an adult woodrat by hand. Burrows, evidently dug by the rats, beneath boulders scattered about the cave floor showed signs of heavy, recent use.

Kirkpatrick and Conaway maintained four of their captive woodrats in the laboratory for approximately three months. They made the following observations:

From the first our live specimens were docile and curious. They permitted stroking and took food from our fingers within a few hours after their capture, but would never permit themselves to be picked up. When agitated they would stamp the hind feet to make a thumping sound. As long as we held them captive, no woodrat would ever tolerate another of either sex in the same cage. When placed together, their peaceful and drowsy attitude instantly changed to one of combat. Standing on their hind legs and propped up by the tail, they sparred and jousted with the forefeet, constantly grinding their teeth with a soft rasping noise and vibrating the vibrissae at a tremendous rate. Apparently it was the purpose of each individual to catch the other off balance and then use the advantage to inflict an injury, although we could never detect a wound as a result of these encounters. To our knowledge no sounds were ever uttered by our captive woodrats.

We have observed numerous woodrat nests inside the caves. In some cases, nests were on top of exposed ledges about 5 feet from the cave floor. Other nests were in shallow or deep crevices in the cave walls (and along rocky escarpments). One nest was in the midst of a debris pile atop a boulder. The only nest we observed in a building was within a huge pile of debris (paper, cardboard, sticks, leaves, glass, wire, metal) stacked on top of an old closet in the corner; this nest was about 7 feet from the floor. All nests examined closely were constructed mainly of the shredded bark of red cedar. Nests in exposed situations were globular, about 8 to 9 inches in diameter with a rather large hole on one side, so that that side of the nest was mostly open. A nest was constructed on the same spot where an earlier nest had been burned by vandals.

FOOD. The woodrat evidently feeds on a wide variety of vegetable foods. Food is transported back to the caves and stored in fissures in the cave walls. Such caches that we observed were composed mainly of the entire fruit heads of pokeberry and wild grape. Kirkpatrick and Conaway noted that their captives "accepted a variety of vegetables, grains, and nuts" and "One individual ate peanut butter avidly while the others showed little interest in it." A captive kept by Mumford ate lettuce, carrot, celery, corn, apple, and peanut butter. Of these, the apple seemed to be most preferred. Bits of *Peromyscus* flesh were eaten avidly. The animal would hold food in its forefeet and sit on its haunches and eat, much like a squirrel. Food was manipulated expertly with the front feet. It even picked up a single apple seed in one front foot, held it with both forepaws, peeled off the outer coat and ate the inside portion. Twice, after holding gobs of peanut butter in the front feet and eating that food, the rat carefully licked and cleaned the front feet.

We examined the stomach contents of only five Indiana woodrats. Miscellaneous vegetation (roots, twigs, dead leaf parts, etc.) formed about 7 percent of the total volume. Unidentified seeds or nuts composed 35 percent, and 58 percent consisted of cuttings of stems and leaves of green plants, including violets and clover. We have no direct proof

that the woodrats are eating red cedar. On 1 May 1974, we observed the usual abundance of red cedar twigs in a small cave in Harrison County; in addition, numerous green, fresh leaves of twinleaf were lying about on the ledge. This was the only time during several visits that we had observed twinleaf being cut and transported into the cave by the rats.

REPRODUCTION. The gestation period for woodrats is about 33 to 42 days. A female taken on 9 March 1958 contained two embryos measuring 45 mm in crown-rump length. A female trapped on 21 March 1954 had four very small embryos and another female taken 21 March 1973 showed four small uterine enlargements. We observed a female with a litter of three young (their eyes not yet open) on 3 April. On 1 May we found an adult and two half-grown young in a nest in a cave. These young were gray above and white below, lacking the buffy tones of the adults. Males collected on 8 and 20 March had testes 13 by 23 and 12 by 24 mm respectively. We can find nothing else recorded regarding reproduction in Indiana *Neotoma*.

The female we found with three young in a large debris pile on 3 April was not visible to us until we took a stick and began probing into the material. The adult woodrat ran out, three young clinging to her teats, and went along the horizontal boards forming the

Litter of woodrats from old building in Harrison State Forest, Crawford County. Photo by Mumford

framework of the building. The young all soon became detached and we captured them. The female came to the wooden floor of the building and escaped into a burrow beneath it. We placed two of the young back at the edge of the debris pile containing the nest and left for two and a half hours. When we returned, the young were gone, evidently having been moved by the female, and the nest was empty. One of this litter, kept captive for five days, measured 152-59-28 mm in standard measurements and weighed 32.8 grams.

The 1 May observation of an adult and two young in a nest inside a cave was also rather brief. Soon after we shined the beam of our flashlights on the family they left the nest and moved about along the cave walls and ledges. One young was noticed sitting on its haunches, holding the green leaves of a twin-leaf plant in its forepaws, feeding on the leaf. Later, this same young came up behind the female along the cave wall, got a nipple in its mouth and began nursing. We were attempting to obtain photographs during this time. The female moved along the wall, got into a nest momentarily, then left it; the young, still hanging on, followed her.

PARASITES. Wilson (1961) reported two species of ticks, *Dermacentor variabilis* and *Ixodes woodei*, from Indiana woodrats. He took 2 specimens of the former and 22 of the latter from woodrats and woodrat nests (Harrison County). Although *Ixodes woodei* had been found on other species of *Neotoma*, these were the first recorded from *N. floridana*. Wilson also found 13 specimens of the flea *Epitedia cavernicola* on the woodrat and collected 92 specimens of this flea from rat nests. He took 8 specimens of another flea, *Orchopeas* sp., from one rat and 21 more from nests. This species appears to be *O. sexdentatus*. *Neotoma floridana* is evidently the normal host for both fleas. One specimen of the flea *Epitedia wenmanni* was taken from a woodrat, and a single specimen of another flea, *Ctenophthalmus pseudagyrtes*, was recovered from a nest.

We have examined ten adult Indiana woodrats for ectoparasites (Table 125). The two fleas *Orchopeas sexdentatus* and *Epitedia cavernicola* and chiggers appear from this small sample to be the main ectoparasites of Indiana woodrats.

DECIMATING FACTORS. The only direct evidence we have regarding potential danger

Table 125

Ectoparasites and other associates of *Neotoma floridana* (n = 10) from Indiana

Parasites	Parasites		Hosts Parasitized	
	Total	Average	Total	Percent
Fleas (Siphonaptera)				
Orchopeas sexdentatus	86	8.60	10	100.0
Epitedia cavernicola	43	4.30	10	100.0
Peromyscopsylla hesperomys	1	0.10	1	10.0
Mites (Acarina) other than chiggers				
Androlaelaps fahrenholzi	5	0.50	2	20.0
Ornithonyssus bacoti	5	0.50	1	10.0
Eulaelaps stabularis	1	0.10	1	10.0
Cyrtolaelaps sp.	1	0.10	1	10.0
Proctolaelaps sp.	1	0.10	1	10.0
Hypoaspis leviculus	1	0.10	1	10.0
Chigger mites (Trombiculidae)				
Euschoengastia setosa	55	5.50	6	60.0
Neotrombicula lipovskyi	44	4.40	3	30.0
Euschoengastia peromysci	2	0.20	1	10.0
Cheladonta ouachitensis	1	0.10	1	10.0
Ticks (Ixodides)				
Dermacentor variabilis	2	0.20	1	10.0
Ixodes woodei	1	0.10	1	10.0

to Indiana woodrats involves man's activities. The one act of vandalism was mentioned above: a nest, which we found when we did not have a camera, was revisited later for photographing and was found to have been burned in the meantime; evidently someone had simply held a match to the dry tinder material of the nest. Also, at least one woodrat electrocuted itself in Big Wyandotte Cave by gnawing wires. No dead woodrats were observed. Man and his activities (especially excessive spelunking) may pose some threat to this uncommon mammal. Undoubtedly, predatory birds and mammals and snakes occur in the woodrat's habitat and may take their toll.

TAXONOMY. The subspecies in Indiana is *Neotoma floridana magister* Baird.

SELECTED REFERENCES. Chamberlain, 1928; Hamilton, 1953; Hickie and Harrison, 1930; Lay and Baker, 1938; Murphy, 1952; Pearson, 1952; Poole, 1940; Rainey, 1956; Richards, 1972; Svihla and Svihla, 1933.

Meadow Vole
Microtus pennsylvanicus (Ord)

Eastern Meadow Vole, Pennsylvania Meadow Mouse, Field Mouse, Marsh Mouse, Meadow Mouse, Vole, Common Vole, Buffalo Mouse, Pennsylvania Vole

Arvicola riparius: Plummer, 1844
Arvicola pennsylvanicus: Cox, 1893
Microtus pennsylvanicus: Bailey, 1900

DESCRIPTION. The four species of voles in Indiana are all large-headed, heavy-bodied, short-tailed mice with short legs, and have short ears that are mostly hidden by the fur of the head. The meadow vole, *Microtus pennsylvanicus*, is the largest of these species and usually has a dull, dark chestnut-colored dorsum and a silvery (sometimes buffy) underside. The back color varies considerably, both seasonally and geographically, so that some individuals (especially immatures) are difficult to distinguish externally from the prairie vole, *Microtus ochrogaster*. The meadow vole usually has a tail that is longer (from 36 to 45 mm) than the prairie vole's tail (from 28 to 37 mm). The woodland vole *(Microtus pinetorum)* and the southern bog lemming *(Synaptomys cooperi)*, the other Indiana voles, both have much shorter tails (about the same length as the hind foot).

The best character for separating the meadow vole from the prairie vole is the number of enamel loops on the grinding surface of the upper molar teeth (see Figs. 29 and 30). The meadow vole has five closed enamel loops on the middle molar; the

Meadow vole. Photo by Anthony Brentlinger, ISU AV Center

prairie vole has only four. The meadow vole has three, four, or five triangles between the anterior and posterior loops, the prairie vole has two.

Among Indiana specimens, we have seen one blond specimen (Natural Museum of Natural History 267705) of the meadow vole and another that appeared to be partially melanistic. A third specimen has a white mark on the forehead. Evermann and Butler (1894b) mentioned a "partial albino." Meadow voles from northwestern and western Indiana usually average darker in color than those from elsewhere in the state, but dark individuals may occur almost anyplace. In southeastern Indiana, we have noticed that meadow voles tend to be paler in color and some approach the back color of the prairie vole, with which they occur in old fields. The palest meadow vole we have examined was taken in southwestern Indiana (Gibson County), where the species appears to be rare or absent in most sections.

Measurements and weights of Indiana meadow voles are summarized in Table 126. Data in the table include only specimens measuring 135 mm or more in total length or having a minimum weight of 25 grams. We considered such animals to be "adults" based on reproductive data. The dental formula is

$$ I\ \frac{1}{1}\ C\ \frac{0}{0}\ P\ \frac{0}{0}\ M\ \frac{3}{3}\ =\ 16. $$

STATUS AND DISTRIBUTION. John Plummer (1844) mentioned the meadow vole (under the vernacular name marsh mouse) in Wayne County, but wrote nothing about its status. Haymond (1870) simply stated that the species was "common in the fields and meadows" of Franklin County. Quick and Butler (1885) called the meadow vole "the most common" mammal in southeastern Indiana. They noted that it varies in numbers with the seasons, and in some years fencerows of wheat and barley fields were traversed by networks of runways. They found it "very common" in 1878 and 1879, but in 1880 "most of them disappeared, and for a long time they were very scarce. They have slowly increased in numbers and are now as numerous, perhaps, as ever." In Randolph County it was considered "common everywhere" by Cox (1893). Evermann and Butler (1894b) stated that this vole was "apparently common wherever reported," and they considered it "the most common meadow mouse" (in comparison with the prairie vole). They had records of the meadow vole from Carroll, Clinton, Franklin, Randolph, and Vigo counties. Although Hahn (1907a) did not indicate the status of this vole along the Kankakee River where he trapped in August 1905, he collected several specimens at Roselawn and Mt. Ayr (Newton County) and at Hebron (Porter County), and the species was probably fairly common at those sites. McAtee (1907) recorded the meadow vole as "common" in the Bloomington (Monroe County) area. Its status and distribution in Indiana were scarcely mentioned by Hahn (1909), who wrote only

Table 126

Weights and measurements of *Microtus pennsylvanicus* from Indiana

	Males	Females
Total length (mm)		
n	148	73
x̄	155.8	154.4
range	126-190	132-183
SD	12.46	10.88
SE	1.02	1.27
Tail length (mm)		
n	146	73
x̄	41.36	40.44
range	30-56	30-54
SD	5.25	4.91
SE	0.43	0.57
Hind foot (mm)		
n	149	71
x̄	20.4	19.9
range	17-24	17-23
SD	1.13	1.23
SE	0.09	0.14
Weight (grams)		
n	104	60
x̄	38.2	38.8
range	25.1-62.7	24.4-63.2
SD	8.59	8.34
SE	0.84	1.08

that its range included all of Indiana, "but it can not be found in every locality." In discussing the status of this vole at Lake Maxinkuckee (Marshall County), Evermann and Clark (1911) stated, "The Meadow Mouse is abundant in all suitable situations about the lake." Engels (1933) reported *M. pennsylvanicus* as "fairly common" in St. Joseph County.

Lyon (1936) noted that the species was "found throughout the northern three-fourths of Indiana." He listed records for 16 counties, but knew of specimens from only 8 of these. Mumford was able to trap only 4 specimens in Jackson County between 1952 and 1955, but 19 additional individuals were represented in mammal remains identified from owl pellets collected in that county (Mumford and Handley, 1956). The meadow vole has been common in Tippecanoe County since at least the mid-1940s, when data collecting, for the most part, was initiated (Kirkpatrick and Conaway, 1947). In 1948,

Kirkpatrick and Conaway recorded additional specimens from other counties. Lindsay (1960) collected only a few meadow voles in Ripley and Jefferson counties, but took 46 prairie voles during the same period.

The meadow vole is common to abundant in northern Indiana, but less common to the south and west. We have seen only 5 specimens (Gibson and Vanderburgh counties) from the counties southwest of a line connecting Vigo and Clark counties (Map 42). The meadow vole has been collected in large numbers in Vigo County, where several hundred have been taken in the Clear Creek valley, west of Terre Haute. Hoffmeister and Mohr (1957) knew of no specimens of *M. pennsylvanicus* from Illinois south of a line connecting Havana and Kankakee. Whitaker, however, trapped several specimens of the meadow vole along Clear Creek, just west of the Illinois-Indiana state line and about 80 miles south of the known Illinois range as shown by Hoffmeister and Mohr. Clearly, more fieldwork is required to determine the status of this vole along the Illinois-Indiana state line south of Vigo County. It would seem quite likely that the meadow vole occurs in several additional southwestern Indiana localities. We have examined specimens from 74 counties.

Sometimes the meadow vole occurs in large numbers, but we have no specific population estimates for Indiana. During the winter of 1972–73, there was a high population of the meadow vole in Tippecanoe County. From November to April the species was observed in numbers in old fields. Mumford and others saw at least 50 animals in two hours in a fallow field of tall grasses. (Some numbers taken per 100 trap-nights in selected habitats are given in Tables 127, 128). The species exhibits well-developed 3- to 4-year cyclic peaks in populations (Hamilton, 1937c; Keller and Krebs, 1970). Krebs, Keller, and Tamarin (1969) studied population changes in a large grassy field near Bloomington. They used three fenced and one unfenced grid and mark-release live trapping to collect demographic information. In one case, a fenced population increased to three times the size of its unfenced control. The fence caused the increase by preventing dispersal, and led the authors to the conclusion that dispersal is probably necessary for

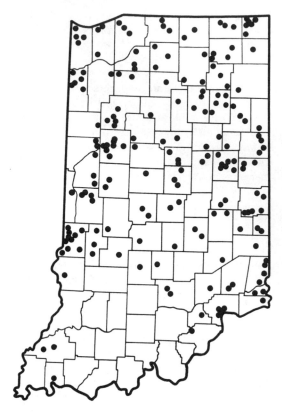

Map 42. The Meadow Vole, *Microtus pennsylvanicus*, in Indiana

normal population control in these voles. They captured from 0 to 8.19 animals per 100 trap-nights (see Table 135 under *Microtus ochrogaster*).

Hamilton (1937c) suggested that increased population size was related to a longer reproductive season, an acceleration of the breeding rate and an increased number of young per litter. Keller and Krebs (1970) found that an expanded breeding season was associated with cyclic increases of both the meadow vole and the prairie vole.

HABITAT. Hahn (1907a) commented on the habitat of the meadow vole along the Kankakee River, noting that "this species is found in places which are submerged during the winter and spring months." He wondered how the animals there kept from drowning, but surmised that they retreated to higher ground during flood times. He trapped "at one place where a low hill covered with bluegrass was bordered by a marsh overgrown with coarse, high marsh grass." He wrote, "On the hill I did not get a single meadow mouse, while in the marsh I got five and saw many runways." Later (Hahn, 1909) he elaborated on the description of the marsh mentioned above: "The grasses there grow up rank and fall down, become coated with a film of mud, and form a dense mat year after year. Under this mat of dead and decaying grass I found runways and caught the Pennsylvania vole in abundance." He also discussed the habitat of this vole elsewhere in Indiana. "In the southern part of the State, where there are fewer marshes, they often live along the grassy banks that line the smaller streams. They are sometimes found under corn and wheat shocks also, being therefore independent of the swamps."

Evermann and Clark (1920) remarked on the meadow vole about Lake Maxinkuckee:

The Meadow Mouse is abundant in all suitable situations about the lake. The extensive areas of semi-marshy grassy land supply an ideal habitat for this noxious but interesting little animal. Wherever there are meadows or marsh ground covered with grasses these mice will be found, their labyrinthine runways forming an intricate network under the dead grass where their nests are common and usually quite conspicuous. These runways are very common in the low marshy meadows such as are usually submerged during the winter and spring, during which time the mice must retreat to higher ground.

Engels (1933) noted that in St. Joseph County all of the specimens of meadow vole collected "were taken in marshes, low meadows, or in rank grass at the foot of hills." The only specimens taken by Mumford in Jackson County were four trapped in "small marshy areas around ponds" in cattails and sedges (Mumford and Handley, 1956). In Jefferson and Ripley counties, Lindsay (1960) captured meadow voles mostly in "weed fields not cultivated for several years," and a few were taken in fencerows.

As pointed out by Pearson (1959) and Getz (1961a), *Microtus pennsylvanicus* is closely associated with moist areas supporting grasses and sedges. It also occurs in relatively dry, upland fields in southern Indiana and is frequently locally common in cultivated fields. We have trapped it in marshes, low meadows, fencerows, damp fallow fields, and along ditches, lake shores, and streams. Specimens have been taken in clover fields, wheat

stubble, abandoned gardens, or lawns overgrown with dense grasses. Meadow voles are often captured in summer and fall in low sites that remain completely inundated for long periods in spring. We have seldom taken this species in woodlands in Indiana except along heavily vegetated stream edges or moist areas, but it does occur along woodlot borders and in grassy areas surrounded by woods. In the pothole country of Steuben County, we have observed this vole on floating mats of vegetation (mostly cattails) in the center of ponds. The voles could not have reached such sites without swimming to them from shore.

In mid-October 1974, we trapped in Porter County, in the sand dunes and associated habitats along Lake Michigan. We captured a few meadow voles in the sparse, pure stands of beachgrass growing on pure sand of the foredunes. Along the base of the first line of higher dunes in mixed vegetation dominated by beachgrass and purpletop grass, we trapped a few additional animals. But the largest number of meadow voles was captured in a flat, moist depression behind the foredunes in a pure stand of beachgrass. It is interesting that Lyon did not trap any meadow voles in the dunes of Porter County where he worked in the fall of 1922. He did take several prairie voles, a species we did not capture.

During a random trapping study in Vigo County, 26 meadow voles were taken. The species was consistently found in only one habitat (grassy field), where 0.65 per 100 trap-nights were captured. It was represented in low numbers in five other habitats: weedy field, corn stubble, wheat stubble, river-bottom woods, and brushy field (Table 127). In the grassy field habitats, all 16 voles trapped were in the 12 plots with good cover, although there were 15 plots with fair cover, and 6 plots with poor cover. Significantly more (14, or 2.33 per 100 trap-nights) were taken in 8 plots with moist soil than in 13 plots with dry soil (2, or 0.21 per 100 trap-nights) ($X^2 = 31.80$, 2 df). Getz (1961a) concluded that moisture was not the dominant limiting factor for meadow voles on his study area, but Lyon (1936), Hamilton (1943), and DeCoursey (1957) thought that *M. pennsylvanicus* tended to inhabit more moist areas than did *M. ochrogaster*.

Table 127

Numbers of *Microtus pennsylvanicus* taken in random plots
in various habitats in Vigo County, Indiana
(from Whitaker, 1967a)

	Number of plots	Trap-nights	Number of meadow voles taken	Number per 100 trap-nights
Grassy field	33	2,475	16	0.65
Weedy field	29	2,175	4	0.18
River bottom woods	15	1,125	1	0.09
Wheat stubble	37	2,775	2	0.07
Corn stubble	50	3,750	2	0.05
Brushy field	23	1,725	1	0.06

Vigo County is on or near the edge of the known geographic range of *M. pennsylvanicus*; this might influence its habitat preference there. If soil moisture is a major limiting factor in the occurrence of meadow voles, one might expect to find the species only in more moist habitats. This may be what is occurring in Vigo County, where there are three major soil types — upland silt loam, bottomland silt loam, and sandy loam. The prairie vole occurred in good and fair cover in weedy and grassy fields in all three soil types, while the meadow vole was taken only in good cover and only on the bottomland silt loam (Whitaker, 1968). This special combination of factors appears to explain, at least in part, why the meadow vole does not occur far westward. Bottomland silt loam does not occur far westward, particularly in abundance. It would be interesting to see how far south *M. pennsylvanicus* extends in the area of the bottomland silt loam. In Monroe County, in a more internal part of the range of both species, the two species occurred together, seemingly in identical habitats (Krebs, Keller, and Myers, 1971).

Zimmerman (1965) likewise studied the occurrence of meadow voles in Vigo County (Table 128). He found a definite correlation between *M. pennsylvanicus* and grassy fields ($X^2 = 28.23$, 2 df). The species was taken only where grasses made up at least 50 percent or more of the vegetation. Meadow voles also showed a positive correlation with specific grasses, particularly the bluegrass *Poa compressa*. Where these grasses occurred, they were usually one of the dominants; these are grasses of established meadows. Meadow voles did not have a positive correlation with

foxtail *(Setaria faberi)*, an early seral plant. Also, the meadow vole showed no correlation with tumble-grass *(Panicum capillare)*, English plantain *(Plantago lanceolata)*, yarrow *(Achillea millefolium)*, meadow fescue *(Festica elatior)*, and Japanese chess *(Bromus japonicus)*. Zimmerman likewise found a significant correlation between *M. pennsylvanicus* and better cover ($X^2 = 28.70$, 2 df). Zimmerman concluded that optimum habitat of the meadow vole at Terre Haute was in areas where grasses formed 50 percent or more of the vegetation and cover was fair to good. The prairie vole required less herbaceous ground cover and was found in fields with more variety among the plant species.

Keller and Krebs (1970) studied the prairie vole and the meadow vole near Bloomington and found the two occurring together in some grassy field plots but not in others (see further discussion under *Microtus ochrogaster*). Study of their data reveals that the meadow vole was more apt to be found in floodplain, poorly drained soils with much grass, whereas the prairie vole was more abundant in better-drained upland soils with greater mixtures of plants.

ASSOCIATED SPECIES. The meadow vole in Vigo and Newton counties often occurs with the prairie vole in drier parts of its habitat, and often with the masked shrew in its more typical habitats. The meadow vole sometimes invades wheat stubble and clover fields, and is often common in hayfields. In southern Indiana, the southeastern shrew may also occur with the meadow vole. The house mouse often occurs with *M. pennsylvanicus*, especially in the earlier seral stages

Table 128

Comparison of abundance of grasses, plants and type of cover in plots
where *Microtus ochrogaster* and *Microtus pennsylvanicus* were trapped
near Terre Haute, Indiana, 1964-1965 (from Zimmerman, 1965)

| | | *M. ochrogaster* | | *M. pennsylvanicus* | |
	Plots	No.	No./100 trap-nights	No.	No./100 trap-nights
Abundance of grasses					
75% or more	22	16	0.48	32	0.97
50-74%	27	10	0.25	11	0.27
25-49%	13	21	1.08	0	0
	62	47	0.51	43	0.46
Plants					
Poa	39	18	0.31	40	0.68
Panicum	17	7	0.27	22	0.86
Setaria	13	21	1.08	0	0
Plantago	38	23	0.40	31	0.82
Trifolium	9	15	1.11	0	0
Achillea	18	11	0.41	20	0.74
Cover					
Good	29	20	0.46	38	0.87
Fair	27	20	0.49	5	0.12
Poor	6	7	0.78	0	0
	62	47	0.51	43	0.46

and in clover and wheat stubble. The meadow jumping mouse is another form often taken in the same traplines with meadow voles.

HABITS. Meadow voles are active both day and night, but are especially active near dawn and dusk. They do not hibernate. They forage for food along well-established and maintained runways on top of the ground. Such runways are constructed by the voles, are devoid of any vegetation, and are about 1.5 inches wide. Runways are mostly hidden beneath the grasses and other vegetation, but often emerge from such cover (depending upon the density of the ground vegetation) and cross open areas. The voles can move quite swiftly along these runs and no doubt they become familiar with them from constant use. When a meadow vole is disturbed while foraging, it runs rapidly along the runways to an underground burrow or other safe retreat. Sections of grass stems and fecal pellets are scattered along the runways, and at certain sites there are accumulations of droppings. Underground burrows are also constructed and used at all seasons. At certain times of the year in good meadow vole

habitat one can find much evidence of digging and piles of loose soil lying about the burrow entrances. There appears to be a considerable amount of such activity beneath deep snow, as evidenced by the signs remaining after the snow melts away.

Nests of shredded grasses are constructed on the surface of the ground, in underground burrows, or beneath the protection of some object lying on the ground. Nests are somewhat globular and about 6 inches in diameter; often they can be seen in a clump of grass, but in good cover such nests may be inconspicuous. The opening to the nest is usually from below and is connected with the runways radiating out from the nest. Quick and Butler (1885) observed nests "in thickets, brier patches, swampy places on tussocks of grass, in a log or fence corner, under piles of rubbish. . . ." In "clover meadows" they noted that many nests were "on the open ground." Nests they observed were constructed of bluegrass and other grasses.

Meadow voles are good swimmers, at least for short distances, an advantage where they occupy wet places or areas that are flooded temporarily. Hahn (1909) wondered whether meadow voles might use underground burrows filled with water, for he wrote:

I have found their runways elsewhere in boggy places, running along under the dry grass for some distance, then going through underground tunnels filled with water, and perhaps leading to a nest under some upraised hummock. I have never found the mice at home in such a place, but there is strong evidence that they do at times occupy nests that can be reached only by swimming through tunnels that are filled with water.

We noted that a captive animal was capable of standing upright on its hind feet and was able to hold that position at least for several seconds. It also used an exercise wheel provided in its cage. A captive kept by Plummer gnawed the wood of its cage. From our observations and those of others, it appears that meadow voles are very active animals. During the fall and winter, one can often see many individuals moving about in the runways during the day. We get the impression that the species may be more diurnal in cold weather than in warm weather, for on cold winter days we have noted many voles running about while we were hunting in old fields.

Meadow voles produce several types of vocalizations, including squeaks, squeals, and a growling sound. They also chatter their teeth quite audibly. No doubt these sounds are important in communication between voles, but we have no details regarding their function.

FOOD. Most earlier authors that mentioned anything about food habits of this vole

Meadow vole. Photo by Whitaker

remarked on its preference for grasses. Hahn (1909) thought it possible that seeds and grain (wheat and corn) were also taken, especially in winter. Evermann and Clark (1920) discussed the utilization of corn, as follows: "When the corn is cut and left in shocks in the field these mice establish themselves in nearly every shock, building a nest near the center and feeding destructively upon the corn. The amount of damage done in this way to the average field of corn is very considerable. . . ." Two captives kept for three weeks by Mumford ate the following foods: carrot, bluegrass, cabbage, rolled oats, celery, shelled corn, bread, apple cores (apparently a favorite food), potato peelings, banana, lettuce, peanut butter, red clover, dandelion. Both refused to eat pieces of *Microtus* flesh left in their cage overnight. A captive kept by Plummer (1844) "refused meat and worms."

During the winter of 1958–59, Robert Kern, a Christmas tree grower at Rochester (Fulton County) showed Mumford many pine trees that had been girdled extensively and killed by meadow voles. Kern estimated that during that winter (which was characterized by considerable snow cover) he lost a thousand trees. Trees as large as 2 inches in diameter had been girdled and gnawed until they had diameters of only 1 inch. Voles of various species, under the collective name of "orchard mice," have done considerable damage by girdling young fruit trees in various sections of Indiana, and control programs by trapping or poisoning have been in operation for many years.

The formation of runways used by meadow voles results partially from their feeding habits, as described by Hahn (1909):

The grass is eaten away in a path just large enough for the animal to pass through comfortably and care is taken that it shall be where the long stems have fallen over so that they form a roof for the runway. These paths are extended nightly and often ramify and reunite in a bewildering maze of endless passages. However, the animals do not depend altogether on elongations of these pathways for their food. Often they find a bunch of particularly juicy grass and there they sit and eat their fill. Usually they are not "clean eaters," but leave sections of the grass blades, either because they are too tough or because it does not seem to the creatures profitable to pick up dropped food when there is so much at hand.

As mentioned earlier, these cuttings left by the voles are telltale signs of their presence in an area. Cuttings may be of various lengths, ranging from 1 to 4 inches, and may be strewn along the runways or dropped in piles. Whitaker noticed in Vigo County that short lengths of grass cuttings had been slit lengthwise, suggesting that perhaps the voles were cutting the grass open to feed on the soft interior. Quick and Butler (1885) commented on the meadow vole's habit of cutting down standing stalks of grass to get to the fruiting heads and leaving piles of 4-inch sections of cut stems.

Zimmerman (1965) studied the stomach contents of 43 meadow voles from randomly selected plots at Terre Haute (Table 129). The most common food (32.1 percent of the total volume) and the most common plant in the plots from this sample was Canada bluegrass. Other plants with high abundance indices eaten in large amounts by meadow voles were muhly, tumble-grass, and plantain, constituting 14.6 percent, 24.7 percent, and 5.8 percent by volume respectively. Information on relative availability of some of these foods is given in Table 130. Canada bluegrass, muhly, and tumble-grass were eaten in greater amounts than their availability would indicate, while other foods were eaten at lower rates. Yarrow was eaten

Cuttings of meadow vole. Photo by Whitaker.

in small amounts, while aster, goldenrod, Japanese chess, and common ragweed were not eaten. Some of these may have been avoided because they were dry or dead at the time of the study. Plants eaten were green and succulent. The presence of insect material (3.6 percent) in the stomachs indicates that meadow voles at Terre Haute are not entirely herbivorous.

Table 129

Foods eaten by *Microtus pennsylvanicus* (n = 43)
from Terre Haute, Vigo County, Indiana
(from Zimmerman, 1965)

Food item	Percent Volume	Percent Frequency
Poa compressa (Canada bluegrass)	32.1	60.5
Panicum capillare (tumble-grass)	24.7	34.9
Muhlenbergia sobolifera (muhly)	14.6	35.9
Miscellaneous vegetation	7.4	34.9
Plantago lanceolata (narrow-leaved plantain)	5.8	23.0
Achillea millefolium (yarrow)	4.7	9.3
Microtus flesh	2.1	6.9
Endogone	2.1	4.6
Taraxacum officinale (dandelion)	2.1	4.6
Lepidopterous larvae	1.7	9.3
Oxalis sp. (yellow wood sorrel)	1.6	6.9
Miscellaneous Coleoptera	1.5	8.4
Phleum pratense (timothy)	1.4	2.3
Roots	0.4	2.3
Insects	0.4	4.6

Table 130
Availability of plant foods eaten by
Microtus pennsylvanicus
from Terre Haute, Indiana, 1964-1965
(from Zimmerman, 1965)

Plants	Abundance index	Percent volume
Poa	6.70	32.1
Muhlenbergia	6.30	14.6
Panicum	2.90	24.7
Achillea	2.90	4.7
Plantago	2.25	5.8
Daucus	0.70	—
Aster	0.55	—
Solidago	0.55	—
Bromus	0.50	—
Ambrosia	0.40	—
Rumex	0.35	—
Taraxacum	0.30	2.1
Phleum	0.20	1.4
Asclepias	0.20	—
Oxalis	0.20	1.6

REPRODUCTION. The gestation period in *Microtus pennsylvanicus* is about 21 days. Although we have no specific information on the subject from Indiana, females probably produce numerous litters per year, as they do in other parts of their range. It appears that the meadow vole breeds throughout most of the year in Indiana, although we have examined no gravid females from 31 December to 11 February. A female taken on 19 January (Vanderburgh County) had recently suckled young, as evidenced by the absence of hair surrounding the nipples. Keller and Krebs (1970), working in Monroe County, found that breeding occurred mainly from March through October, but increased winter breeding occurred during the increasing phase of the population cycle. The individuals breeding in winter were mainly the larger members of the population. Our data also indicate that most gravid females were taken from March through November (Table 131). There may be a cessation of breeding in midwinter, but we think it probable that gravid meadow voles may be taken in each month of the year somewhere in Indiana. The phase of the population cycle, prevailing weather conditions, and available food may have an effect on reproduction.

Corthum (1967) examined 153 gravid

meadow voles trapped in Vigo County; the number of embryos per female ranged from 1 to 9, and the mean was 4.46. Keller and Krebs (1970) found a mean of 4.54 embryos per female in 152 gravid females. We have examined 48 pregnant meadow voles, in which the mean number of embryos per female was 4.81; the number of embryos ranged from 2 to 8 (SD = 1.39; SE = 0.20). Three gravid females each had 2 embryos; 5 had 3; 9 had 4; 19 had 5; 7 had 6; 3 had 7; and 2 had 8. The average litter size (judging from embryo counts) is larger in the meadow vole than in the prairie vole (see under that species). Corthum (1967) found that placental scars persisted for 44 to 49 days in the meadow vole and 42 to 45 days in the prairie vole.

The testis size in meadow voles averages large throughout the year, but decreases from November to January. If testis size is any indication of breeding season, a midwinter decrease in reproductive activity is suggested and correlates with the decreased number of gravid females observed at that season. Quick and Butler (1885) reported that meadow voles bred from February to December around Brookville (Franklin County).

PARASITES. Information on ectoparasites of Indiana meadow voles is shown in Table 132. Included are data from Whitaker and Wilson (1968) for Vigo County, but data reported by Whitaker and Corthum (1967) are excluded from the table since only fleas were tabulated in the latter study. The most abundant ectoparasite on the meadow vole in Indiana is the tiny listrophorid mite *Listrophorus mexicanus* (= *L. leuckarti* of Whitaker and Wilson). It is a minute, cigar-shaped mite that clings to individual hairs; often several hundred are present on one vole. The laelapid mite *Laelaps kochi* is the second most abundant form, followed by *Androlaelaps fahrenholzi*; both are larger mites which can be seen moving about in the fur. The hypopus *Dermacarus hypudaei*, the myocoptid mite *Myocoptes japonensis*, the macronyssid mite *Ornithonyssus bacoti*, and the myobiid mite *Radfordia lemnina* were less abundant, but yet were important mites of this vole.

Only seven ticks, all *Dermacentor variabilis*, were taken from *M. pennsylvanicus* during the present studies. Ticks collected by Wilson (1961) from this species were a single

Table 131

Reproductive information from *Microtus pennsylvanicus* from Indiana

Month	Adult Females			Adult Males		
	Number examined	Pregnant		Number examined	Testis size (mm) Average	
		No.	Percent		Length	Width
Jan.	5	—	—	6	6.9	4.4
Feb.	10	1	10.0	13	10.4	7.0
March	3	3	100.0	8	13.2	7.5
April	12	8	66.7	4	14.3	8.8
May	8	5	62.5	1	4.5	3.0
June	3	3	100.0	6	10.5	6.3
July	4	4	100.0	9	15.0	9.5
August	1	1	100.0	8	14.3	9.0
Sept.	17	9	52.9	26	11.8	7.0
Oct.	11	7	63.6	12	11.5	7.0
Nov.	9	6	66.7	17	8.8	5.4
Dec.	1	1	100.0	5	8.6	4.0

Table 132

Ectoparasites and other associates of *Microtus pennsylvanicus* (n = 91) from Indiana

Parasites	Parasites		Hosts parasitized	
	Total	Average	Total	Percent
Fleas (Siphonaptera)				
Peromyscopsylla hamifer	12	0.13	4	4.4
Epitedia wenmanni	2	0.02	2	2.2
Megabothris asio	1	0.01	1	1.1
Sucking Lice (Anoplura)				
Hoplopleura acanthopus	230	2.53	26	28.6
Mites (Acarina) other than chiggers				
Listrophorus mexicanus	17,172	188.70	43	47.3
Laelaps kochi	268	2.95	45	49.5
Androlaelaps fahrenholzi	93	1.02	24	26.4
Dermacarus hypudaei	79	0.87	9	9.9
Myocoptes japonensis	57	0.63	12	13.2
Ornithonyssus bacoti	32	0.35	9	9.9
Radfordia hylandi	23	0.25	10	11.0
Laelaps alaskensis	8	0.09	5	5.5
Haemogamasus liponyssoides	4	0.04	3	3.3
Chigger Mites (Trombiculidae)				
Euschoengastia peromysci	39	0.43	5	5.5
Eutrombicula alfreddugesi	1	0.01	1	1.1
Neotrombicula whartoni	1	0.01	1	1.1
Neotrombicula lipovskyi	1	0.01	1	1.1
Ticks (Ixodides)				
Dermacentor variabilis	7	0.08	3	3.3

D. variabilis (Brown County), and three specimens of *Ixodes muris* (Lagrange County).

Wilson found the louse *Hoplopleura acanthopus* to be common on meadow voles and prairie voles throughout Indiana, and recorded 461 individuals from the former. This louse was commonly found during the present studies, also (Table 132). Wilson took a second species of sucking louse *(Polyplax alaskensis)* from *M. pennsylvanicus*. This louse, represented by only 12 specimens, was taken only on meadow voles and only in northern Indiana (Lagrange, Porter, and Steuben counties).

Wilson found *Ctenophthalmus pseudagyrtes* (26 specimens) to be the most common flea on meadow voles, followed by *Megabothris asio* (14 specimens). He found only two specimens of *Epitedia wenmanni* (Noble and Porter counties), one of *Atyphloceras bishopi* (Union County), and one of *Peromyscopsylla hamifer* (Newton County). Only 15 individuals, including three species of fleas, were taken during the present studies, but Whitaker and Corthum (1967) also found *C. pseudagyrtes* to be the most common flea on the meadow vole from Vigo County, where 13 of 282 (4.6 percent) each had one flea. *Epitedia wenmanni* (6 specimens) was the second most abundant flea in the *M. pennsylvanicus* sample from Vigo County, and 5 *Orchopeas leucopus* were taken along with a single individual of *Peromyscopsylla hamifer*.

A total of 122 meadow voles (54 from Vigo County) was examined for cestodes and trematodes by Whitaker and Adalis (1971). Six trematodes were found in one of the voles but were lost. One unidentified cestode larva (bladderworm) was found in one, and 30 adult cestodes were found in 18 of the voles. Twelve cestodes from seven voles were identified as *Andrya macrocephala*, 4 as *Paranoplocephala troeschi*, 3 as *P. infrequens*, and 1 as *Cladotaenia* sp. A total of 141 unidentified nematodes was found in this species. These were in 7 voles (5.7 percent of those examined, an overall average of 1.16 per vole).

Fish (1971) took 152 acanthocephalans *(Moniliformis clarki)* from 19 of 124 meadow voles (15.3 percent) from Vigo County. All the infected voles came from one field, however, and none has been taken elsewhere in Indiana to our knowledge.

DECIMATING FACTORS. Meadow voles are preyed upon by numerous avian and mammalian predators. Price (1942) recorded remains of this vole in pellets of the barred owl. Kirkpatrick and Conaway (1947) found meadow vole skulls in the pellets of the barn owl, long-eared owl, short-eared owl, and great horned owl. Long-eared owl pellets analyzed by George (1955) also contained meadow vole skulls. No doubt other owls feed on this vole, but the published information on Indiana species that we have noted does not separate the various species of *Microtus* in the analyses. Mumford and Danner (1974) recorded the meadow vole as prey of the marsh hawk.

Various persons have studied the food habits of red and gray foxes in Indiana, but in many cases did not separate the species of *Microtus* in their tabulations. From our studies, we have found meadow voles in the stomachs of red fox (1 of 14), mink (1 of 5), least weasel (1 of 1), gray fox (3 of 34), and opossum (2 of 84). Domestic cats often kill meadow voles. No doubt other mammals also take this common vole. Lyon (1930) once found a pile of 7 dead meadow voles and a deer mouse. From the evidence, he thought the cache may have been that of a weasel.

TAXONOMY. The subspecies in Indiana is *Microtus pennsylvanicus pennsylvanicus* (Ord). Except for the color variations already mentioned above, meadow voles from throughout Indiana are fairly uniform in color and size.

SELECTED REFERENCES. Bailey, 1924; Corthum, 1967; Hamilton, 1937a, 1937c, 1941a; Keller and Krebs, 1970; Krebs, Keller, and Myers, 1971; Krebs, Keller, and Tamarin, 1969; Whitaker and Adalis, 1971; Zimmerman, 1965.

Prairie Vole
Microtus ochrogaster (Wagner)

Meadow Mouse, Prairie Meadow
Mouse, Yellow-bellied Vole, Buff-bellied
Meadow Mouse, Middle Western
Prairie Vole

Arvicola xanthognata: Plummer, 1844, (probably)
Arvicola austerus: Quick and Langdon, 1882
Microtus austerus: Bailey, 1900
Pedomys ochrogaster: Lindsay, 1958
Microtus ochrogaster: Hahn, 1908b

DESCRIPTION. The prairie vole is usually grayish brown above, and the mixture of black and brownish-yellow tips of the longer hairs gives the dorsum a salt and pepper (grizzled) appearance. The sides are paler than is the back, and the underside is usually buffy (ranging from pale buff to ochraceous or fulvous); some specimens have silvery undersides. The pelage of the prairie vole appears coarser and less shiny than that of the meadow vole. As mentioned under *Microtus pennsylvanicus*, the best method of separating these two species is by dental characteristics.

There are several records of abnormally colored prairie voles from Indiana. A specimen (National Museum of Natural History 156887) taken at Montmorenci (Tippecanoe

County) in 1891 is blond. An albino from Wayne County was reported by DeBlase and Humphrey (1965). Mumford (1964) collected a melanistic prairie vole in Washington County; Larry L. Roop obtained two additional melanistic animals at the same site in 1964. A specimen from Dearborn County (Indiana State University 1374) has mixed silvery and buff hairs on the venter, some small patches of silvery color on the back and sides, and a rather prominent silvery "collar" extending across the dorsum behind the ears. Although the typical belly color of the prairie vole is buffy, we have examined numerous specimens with silvery venters; these specimens were taken in the following counties: Clay, Delaware, Grant, Hamilton, Harrison, Jennings, Johnson, LaPorte, Lawrence, Madison, Porter, Ripley, Washington, and Wayne. We have also examined a very dark specimen from Porter County and pale specimens from LaPorte, Pike, and Sullivan counties. The variation in pelage color both in prairie voles and in meadow voles sometimes renders it difficult to identify a particular specimen to species without examining the molar teeth.

Weights and measurements are summarized for prairie voles from various sections of Indiana in Table 133. Males and

Prairie vole. Photo by Tom French

females were similar in size, and no meaningful differences were evident between the regional samples. The dental formula is

$$I \frac{1}{1} C \frac{0}{0} P \frac{0}{0} M \frac{3}{3} = 16.$$

STATUS AND DISTRIBUTION. Plummer (1844) appears to be the first to record the prairie vole from Indiana (Wayne County), although he preserved no specimen. Haymond (1870) did not list it from Franklin County, nor did Cox (1893) record it from Randolph County. Evermann and Butler (1894b) knew of specimens from Franklin and Vigo counties, noting that in Franklin County "A few specimens have been taken, but it does not

appear to be abundant." Hahn did not trap this species along the Kankakee River in 1905, but noted that specimens had been taken at LaPorte (LaPorte County). In the Bloomington (Monroe County) area, it was considered "Probably common" by McAtee (1907). Between September 1906 and September 1907, Hahn found the prairie vole to be more abundant than the woodland vole or the southern bog lemming on the Indiana University Farm (near Mitchell, Lawrence County). Hahn (1909) remarked that the geographic range of the prairie vole included all of Indiana, but that the vole "does not seem to occur everywhere in the northern part of the State." He knew of records for 8 counties.

Evermann and Clark (1920) did not record

Table 133

Weights and measurements of *Microtus ochrogaster* from Indiana
(geographical variations indicated)

	Males				Females			
	Total length	Tail length	Hind foot	Weight	Total length	Tail length	Hind foot	Weight
Northwestern Indiana (Porter, Newton, and Pulaski counties)								
n	32	32	30	18	17	17	17	12
x̄	139.4	33.1	18.7	34.5	144.5	33.2	19.0	35.1
range	119-163	25-48	17-21	26.9-44.6	130-163	27-48	17-21	27.2-48.8
SD	11.18	4.23	2.39	6.89	8.73	5.91	1.44	7.85
SE	1.97	0.74	0.66	1.64	2.11	1.43	0.4	2.27
West-central Indiana (Warren, Tippecanoe, and Montgomery counties)								
n	31	30	31	25	21	21	21	19
x̄	141.0	30.7	18.9	35.9	137.6	30.9	18.7	36.5
range	130-165	20-41	16-22	23.0-47.2	124-155	22-36	17-22	24.5-50.0
SD	9.87	3.99	1.19	6.02	14.44	3.63	1.44	5.83
SE	1.77	0.73	0.21	1.20	3.15	0.79	0.31	1.38
West-central Indiana (Vigo, Sullivan, and Clay counties)								
n	42	43	43	31	47	47	47	35
x̄	141.5	31.4	18.9	33.1	141.2	31.3	18.8	34.4
range	126-160	20-38	16-20	24.0-45.2	112-161	20-38	17-21	25.7-53.6
SD	10.46	4.70	1.01	5.82	10.63	3.64	1.12	8.91
SE	1.61	0.71	0.15	1.05	1.54	0.53	0.16	1.50
Southwestern Indiana (Pike, Gibson, Posey, Vanderburgh, and Warrick counties)								
n	29	29	29	3	37	37	45	13
x̄	140.9	31.4	18.9	42.9	139.7	31.2	18.4	35.1
range	126-161	27-40	16-20	36.9-46.1	126-154	26-35	16-20	27.6-45.5
SD	8.98	3.60	1.14	5.20	1.39	2.79	7.86	5.3
SE	1.66	0.67	0.2	3.00	1.15	0.46	1.17	1.4
Southeastern Indiana (Jennings, Ripley, Dearborn, Ohio, Clark, and Jefferson counties)								
n	47	47	47	26	36	35	34	14
x̄	143.65	33.4	19.02	32.5	143.7	33.4	19.4	34.3
range	129-161	23-42	16-22	25.5-43.8	131-166	29-42	18-22	26.7-42.2
SD	9.05	4.80	1.42	8.64	8.43	4.08	1.21	4.99
SE	1.32	0.70	0.20	1.69	1.40	0.68	0.20	1.33

the prairie vole about Lake Maxinkuckee (Marshall County) between 1899 and 1913, nor have we examined a specimen from that county. Marcus W. Lyon, Jr., trapped 7 prairie voles in the dunes of Porter County in the fall of 1922 (Lyon, 1923), but there are 13 additional specimens taken there by Lyon in 1923 and 1924 in the National Museum of Natural History. Engels (1933) thought that *M. ochrogaster* was probably "not uncommon" in St. Joseph County. Lyon (1936) summarized the distribution of this vole in Indiana by stating, "It is found throughout practically all of Indiana, though there are no records from the northeastern corner of the state." He also wrote, "The Prairie Meadow Mouse was probably originally confined to the natural prairie region of northwestern Indiana, but with the artificial making of fields everywhere in the state it is the common meadow mouse in upland fields, preferring drier locations than does the Pennsylvania Meadow Mouse." He listed records from 16 counties. During the winter of 1946–47, the prairie vole reached a high population level in Tippecanoe County, as evidenced by the large numbers of this vole eaten by four species of owls (Kirkpatrick and Conaway, 1947, 1948; details of their data will be discussed later). In the early 1950s, Mumford found the prairie vole to be common in Jackson County (Mumford and Handley, 1956). Lindsay (1960) also found the species to be common in Jefferson and Ripley counties during the same period. We have examined specimens from 68 counties, and no doubt the species occurs in many more counties. It is definitely more abundant in the southern half of Indiana than in the northern half, but local populations may be periodically high in the latter. We still consider the prairie vole to be rare in the northeastern corner of the state, and suspect that in this region populations may be more scattered; there is also the possibility that the vole simply does not occur in some extreme northeastern counties (Map 43).

The prairie vole is an abundant species in Indiana and probably ranks close behind the house mouse, the white-footed mouse, and the deer mouse in total numbers. The meadow vole may be nearly as abundant as the prairie vole. We have summarized some of our data on numbers of prairie voles taken

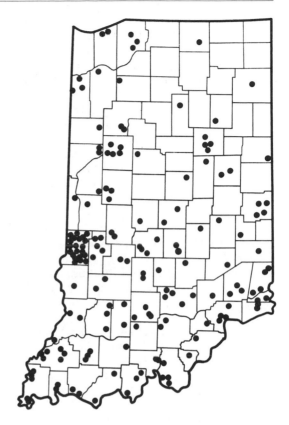

Map 43.   The Prairie Vole, *Microtus ochrogaster*, in Indiana

per 100 trap-nights in some Vigo County habitats (Table 134). Keller and Krebs (1970) also recorded the numbers of this vole taken per 100 trap-nights in six grassland plots near Bloomington (Table 135). Numbers varied greatly, from 0 to 18.06 over eight collecting periods. *Microtus ochrogaster* (and *M. pennsylvanicus*) are cyclic and reach population peaks at intervals of three to four years. Krebs found that both species appeared to follow synchronous cycles on his study area, although density estimates for the two species differed. The abundance of the prairie vole near Lafayette (Tippecanoe County) during the winter of 1946–47 is emphasized by the fact that 28 were taken in 92 trap-nights and 557 prairie voles were identified among 1,098 prey items in the pellets of four species of owls (Kirkpatrick and Conaway, 1947, 1948). Lindsay (1958) noted that the prairie vole was more abundant in Ripley County during the winter of 1952–53 than in the following year. And we have witnessed the dramatic fluctuations of number of this vole at Lafayette over the past twenty years.

HABITAT. The prairie vole seems to prefer relatively dry fields, either cultivated (hay, clover, etc.) or noncultivated, that support a cover of grasses or weeds. Overgrown fields with scattered sprouts or a few larger trees are also inhabited by this vole, but it generally shuns the woods. Prairie voles have been trapped in heavily grazed pastures and, very rarely, even in harvested soybean fields, where ground cover was quite sparse or almost entirely lacking. The best catches of prairie voles are usually made in fallow fields or hay fields. Lyon (1923) trapped three specimens "in a wooded dune, though near a meadow" in traps placed in underground runs. Lindsay (1958) trapped five specimens "from a small open area in one corner of a wooded region."

Hahn (1908b) noted that *M. ochrogaster* was "found in the fields wherever there is a growth of grass dense enough to afford cover" in Lawrence County. Later he wrote, "I have seldom seen it far from fencerows, old pastures or meadows where the grass grows thick and tall and forms the roof and walls of the runways made by these mice" (Hahn, 1909). Lyon trapped specimens in an interdunal meadow in Porter County "in traps placed at random on the ground as no runways were discernible." He took the species in only one of four such meadows sampled, however, and wondered if colonies might not be local in distribution. Hahn and Lyon both noted that the prairie vole was the common vole in upland fields in the state. In Jackson County, it "was plentiful in all habitats trapped except woods and marshes" and "seemed equally abundant in abandoned fields of broom grass and in cultivated fields" (Mumford and Handley, 1956).

Lindsay (1958) trapped the majority of his prairie vole specimens in southeastern Indiana "in cultivated fields where considerable cover remained or in weed fields" which had not been cultivated for two or three years. He described the vegetation of one such weed field.

The plant species 12 inches or more high included aster *(Aster latifolius)*, patience-dock *(Rumex patientia)*, evening-primrose *(Oenothera biennis)*, white top *(Erigeron annus)*, common groundsel *(Senecio vulgaris)* and crowfoot *(Ranunculus abortivus)*. Vegetation 4 to 12 inches in height included wild onion *(Allium vineale)*, early wintercress *(Barbarea verna)*, henbit *(Lamium amplexicaule)*, cranesbill *(Geranium carolinianum)*, cheat *(Bromus secalinus)*, pepper grass *(Lepidium virginicum)* and wood-sorrel *(Oxalis corniculata)*. Plants 3 inches or less in height, through which runways were made, included whitlow-grass *(Draba verna)*, chickweed *(Cerastium arvense)*, rock-cress *(Arabis sp.)*, Venus's looking-glass *(Specularia perfoliata)*, annual bluegrass *(Poa annua)*, corn-speedwell *(Veronica arvensis)*, hoary plantain *(Plantago virginica)*, knotweed *(Polygonum aviculare)* and wormseed-mustard *(Erysimum cheiranthoides)*.

Zimmerman (1965) studied voles in Vigo County, where he found a definite correlation between the presence of the meadow voles and high amounts of grass in fields (Table 128), but the prairie vole was not so restricted. Areas with only 25 to 75 percent grasses yielded more prairie voles than areas with 76 to 100 percent grasses ($X^2 = 15.76$, 1 df). The prairie vole did show a positive correlation with grasses, particularly Canada bluegrass and giant foxtail. Foxtail was associated with weedy plants and was often the dominant grass in plots with only 25 to 49 percent grasses. Clover, often found with foxtail, also showed a positive correlation with the prairie vole. In general, Zimmerman found the prairie vole in areas with less cover and fewer grasses (that is, more forbs) than the meadow vole. During the random trapping program in Vigo County by Whitaker (1967a), the prairie vole was relatively abundant in grassy, weedy, and cultivated fields (Table 134). None were taken in upland or river-bottom woods (54 and 15 plots respectively), brush (16 plots), plowed field (48 plots), soybean fields (16 plots), or soybean stubble (22 plots). Of prairie voles trapped in cultivated fields, five were in lespedeza and five in clover. In 20 plots with good cover in grassy, weedy, or cultivated fields, 1.38 prairie voles per 100 trap-nights were captured; none were caught in 14 plots with poor cover. This difference was significant; better cover yielded more prairie voles ($X^2 = 15.72$, 2 df), although Zimmerman found no such correlation. Whitaker also summarized data regarding soil moisture and catches of prairie voles. Two voles were trapped in 2 plots with wet soil (1.33 per 100 trap-nights). In the 62 plots with dry soil, 37, or 0.80 voles per 100 trap-nights were taken, and in 20 plots with moist soil 16 voles, or 1.07 per 100 trap-nights were taken. We cannot conclude that the prairie vole was affected appreciably by soil moisture in this study.

In a remnant, sand prairie (Little Bluestem Prairie) 5 miles north of Terre Haute (Vigo County), prairie voles and deer mice were practically the only small mammals trapped. The area contains mainly clumps of little bluestem and a few other plants, with bare sand between the clumps, and is probably characteristic of a major presettlement habitat and mammalian community in this section of Indiana.

Keller and Krebs (1970), who studied *Microtus* near Bloomington, trapped in 15 grassland study areas varying in size from 0.4 to 14.6 acres. Although they captured prairie voles and meadow voles at different rates on various areas (Table 135), their data reveal that the prairie vole was much more abundant on better-drained sites, generally with mixed vegetation (rather than more uniform grass stands), which do not flood. These results correlate well with those of Zimmerman, who found that the prairie vole eats a greater variety of plant foods than does the meadow vole and inhabits sites where vegetation is more varied.

In Kansas, Martin (1956) thought that the yield of grasses and the amount of debris and ground cover might be critical factors in the distribution of the prairie vole. He took most of his specimens in ungrazed or unmown grasslands, and seldom found the species in mown grasslands, alfalfa, or other croplands or stubble, in fields in early successional states, or in areas containing woody vegetation. Jameson (1947), who also studied this vole in Kansas, found it in areas where the dominant plants in summer were grasses or clover.

The prairie vole has been trapped in a variety of sites in Indiana, as noted by the following label notations: gravel pit, under corn shock, field of tall grass, railroad embankment, roadside ditch, old field, weedy stubble field, ditch or stream bank, wheat-clover-stubble, corn stubble, soybean stubble, fencerows (bordering woods, cornfield, clover fields), upland pasture, brushpile, abandoned garden, alfalfa field, clover field, field of 3-year-old fescue, wet and grassy field, marsh, marsh border, bog, closely mown old field, in building, field of prairie grasses, grassy spot in woods, old house site. In many counties, railroad grades are among the best places to trap this vole. Hahn (1908b) wrote, "Its fossorial habits lead it, doubtless accidentally, into caves. I found the skulls of two individuals in the Shawnee [=Donaldson's] Cave and later trapped another there."

ASSOCIATED SPECIES. The meadow vole is often found with the prairie vole in the wetter parts of the latter's habitat, especially when dense grassy ground cover is present.

Table 134

Numbers of *Microtus ochrogaster* taken in random plots
in various habitats in Vigo County, Indiana
(from Whitaker, 1967a)

	Number of plots	Trap-nights	Number of prairie voles taken	Number per 100 trap-nights
Grassy Field	33	2,475	25	1.01
Weedy Field	29	2,175	20	0.92
Cultivated Field	22	1,650	10	0.61
Winter Wheat	9	675	2	0.30
Wheat Stubble	37	2,775	6	0.22
Brushy Field	23	1,725	2	0.12
Corn	38	2,850	3	0.11
Pasture	17	1,275	1	0.08
Corn Stubble	50	3,750	2	0.05

Table 135

Numbers per 100 trap-nights of *Microtus pennsylvanicus*
and *Microtus ochrogaster* caught in different habitat situations
(from Keller and Krebs, 1970)

	1965		1966			1967		
	Apr 13- Aug 9	Aug 14- Dec 14	Jan 3- Apr 20	Apr 23- Aug 23	Aug 27- Dec 25	Jan 7- May 1	May 6- Sept 4	Sept 9- Jan 11
Microtus pennsylvanicus								
Terrace, grassland	0.93	0.14	0.97	1.25	0.14	—	0.37	2.78
Floodplain, fescue	1.20	2.54	4.44	2.75	2.24	1.87	0.56	3.15
Bottomland, fescue	0.56	—	4.74	8.19	5.69	1.13	1.11	3.33
Floodplain, fescue	0.90	3.85	2.39	3.06	7.69	0.09	0.09	0.28
Floodplain, fescue	2.12	5.76	4.38	3.68	2.92	0.56	0.97	2.78
Floodplain, grass	0.89	3.81	4.29	1.90	2.15	1.60	0.97	2.19
Floodplain, fescue	2.53	4.44	4.44	7.14	5.56	1.67	6.11	1.67
Floodplain, mixed vegetation	0.28	—	1.67	1.11	0.74	0.93	0.37	1.67
Microtus ochrogaster								
Grassland	3.41	0.97	7.50	18.06	2.92	0.83	1.02	0.28
Floodplain, fescue	0.65	1.06	1.48	2.09	2.24	0.37	0.09	0.29
Bottomland, fescue	0.56	—	0.28	0.28	1.81	—	—	0.56
Floodplain, fescue	—	2.72	0.25	1.57	2.96	—	0.28	0.93
Floodplain, grass	0.36	0.32	0.24	2.62	1.94	0.06	0.29	0.35
Floodplain, mixed vegetation	1.11	0.56	2.22	4.44	0.74	—	0.37	—

The house mouse is often found with the prairie vole in cultivated areas, and in dry old fields the least shrew is likely to be found with this vole. However, the most common associate in Indiana is the deer mouse, found with the prairie vole in more open habitats. In some sites, the short-tailed shrew, the meadow jumping mouse, and other small mammals may occur with the prairie vole. On one occasion, Mumford trapped the prairie vole, meadow vole, woodland vole, and southern bog lemming in the same abandoned garden in a single night.

HABITS. The habits of the prairie vole are quite similar to those of the meadow vole. Both construct and maintain conspicuous runways, both leave plant cuttings and droppings along their runways, and they construct similar appearing nests. To our knowledge, these voles are similar in their diurnal and nocturnal activity patterns.

Plummer (1844) remarked that "One of these little animals was found in its large nest lined with rabbit's fur, on the outside of the wall of a well thirty feet below the surface of the earth." The nest is usually made of dry grasses. Hahn (1908b) wrote, "The nest is generally placed underground, but sometimes an old log or board is the only covering. . . . Two or more tunnels usually lead to it, for this species, like *M. pennsylvanicus*, uses underground runways." A nest found by Hahn (1909) was described by him as follows:

One that I found was in a little depression under a discarded railroad tie lying on the side of an embankment. At the time of discovery, about 4 p.m. on April 11, the mother was not at home, and I carefully replaced the tie over the nest containing three hairless and blind young. Early the next morning the old mouse was again absent but about ten o'clock I found her nursing her offspring. She began to run with the young still clinging to her teats, but the whole family was captured. They were confined in a roomy wire cage with plenty of dry grass and cotton for a nest and fresh grass, bread and water for food. Nevertheless, the next morning the cage contained only the mother; she had eaten her children. The old mouse lived only two days longer. She showed a surprising ability to climb, not only going up the sides of the cage, but creeping, fly-like, across the wire top with her claws hooked in the meshes of the wire and her body hanging downwards."

FOOD. Hahn (1909) made a few observations on the food habits of this vole in Indiana.

"It is very fond of wheat when it is just ripening and has an ingenious method of getting at the heads. The stalks are not stiff enough for the mice to climb and interference with other heads prevents the wheat from falling over when the stalk is cut at its base. Therefore, the mice raise themselves on their haunches and cut the stalks as high as they can reach and when the cut end falls to the ground they cut off another section three or four inches long and repeat the process until the head is in reach. This work has been attributed to *M. pennsylvanicus*, and that species may be guilty also, but I have caught the prairie vole near freshly cut stems when none of the other species were to be found in the locality. Wild seeds and berries are eaten also, but the principal food of this species is grass.

Hahn trapped prairie voles by using dry oatmeal, nuts, cheese, bread, or grain as bait.

One he trapped in a cave "had been eating a pasteboard box." And he mentioned that the voles occasionally damaged orchard trees by stripping the bark from the young trees in the winter.

Zimmerman (1965) made a comparative study of the food habits of the prairie vole and meadow vole in Indiana (Vigo County). He found that the former ate a greater variety of food, including many kinds of herbaceous plants, than did the latter (Table 136). The most common food of the prairie vole was Canada bluegrass. Other important foods were red clover, lespedeza, tumble-grass, and roots. Common foods of the prairie vole not eaten by the meadow vole were red clover, lespedeza, fleabane, meadow fescue, and alfalfa. Martin (1956) suggested that the food of the prairie vole consisted chiefly of those plants most common in the habitat, and this was partially true. Zimmerman calculated an

Table 136

Foods eaten by prairie voles from Terre Haute, Indiana
(from Zimmerman, 1965)

Food Item	Percent Volume	Percent Frequency
Poa compressa (Canada bluegrass)	15.8	36.2
Miscellaneous vegetation	13.1	38.3
Unidentified roots	10.0	14.8
Trifolium pratense (red clover)	9.7	12.7
Lespedeza sp.	6.7	10.6
Panicum capillare (tumble-grass)	6.4	8.5
Trifolium pratense (red clover) roots	5.2	6.3
Erigeron sp. (whitetop or fleabane)	5.0	8.5
Plantago lanceolata (English plantain)	4.6	12.8
Festuca elatior (meadow fescue)	4.0	8.0
Medicago sativa (alfalfa)	3.6	8.5
Unidentified seeds	2.2	4.2
Lepidopterous larvae	1.9	4.2
Chenopodium sp. (pigweed)	1.8	4.2
Oxalis sp. (wood-sorrel)	1.5	2.1
Unidentified insects	1.4	10.6
Miscellaneous Coleoptera	1.4	8.4
Setaria faberii (giant foxtail) seeds	1.2	4.2
Rumex crispis (curly dock)	1.1	2.1
Microtus flesh	1.0	2.1
Polygonum sp. (smartweed)	0.8	4.2
Muhlenbergia sobolifera (muhly)	0.8	4.2
Endogone	0.6	2.1
Phleum pratense (timothy)	0.4	2.1
Taraxacum officinale (dandelion)	trace	2.1
Achillea millefolium (yarrow)	trace	2.1
	100.2	

abundance index as an indication of availability for major plants in the *Microtus* habitats he trapped. Bluegrass had the highest abundance index and constituted 15.8 percent of the total volume of food (Table 137). Other abundant foods eaten were English plantain, red clover, tumble-grass, and lespedeza.

A few plants (yarrow, muhly, giant foxtail) had high abundance indices but were not eaten in large amounts by the prairie vole. Yarrow was also eaten in comparably small amounts by the meadow vole. Other plants such as aster, goldenrod, Japanese chess, and common ragweed were not eaten by either species of *Microtus*. In contrast, plants such as curly dock, alfalfa, fleabane, pigweed, and wood-sorrel had low abundance indices but were eaten in larger amounts than would be expected. It appeared that these plants were favored by the prairie vole. These results indicate some selectivity by *M. ochrogaster* among the various food plants available to it.

Table 137
Availability of plant foods eaten by prairie voles from Terre Haute
(from Zimmerman, 1965)

Plants	Abundance index	Percent volume
Poa	3.10	15.8
Setaria	2.86	1.2
Plantago	2.79	4.6
Muhlenbergia	2.48	0.8
Achillea	1.55	—
Trifolium	1.52	14.9
Panicum	1.38	6.4
Festuca	1.10	4.0
Lespedeza	1.07	6.7
Bromus	0.83	—
Taraxacum	0.83	—
Digitaria	0.83	—
Solidago	0.72	—
Andropogon	0.69	—
Polygonum	0.69	0.8
Aster	0.69	—
Ambrosia	0.66	—
Asclepias	0.62	—
Rumex	0.55	1.1
Medicago	0.48	3.6
Chenopodium	0.45	1.8
Erigeron	0.41	5.0
Oxalis	0.34	1.5
Phleum	0.28	0.4
Melilotus	0.24	—

The prairie vole ate a relatively large amount of insect material (4.7 percent of the volume), including beetle larvae and caterpillars, indicating that it is not entirely herbivorous. It is believed that the *Microtus* flesh found in stomachs was from eating voles in traps, for several of the trapped voles had been partially devoured.

REPRODUCTION. The gestation period in *M. ochrogaster* is about 21 days. We have examined gravid prairie voles in each month of the year, although it appeared that fewer pregnancies occurred in the December–January, April, and June–July periods (Table 138). Most females gravid in winter were from southern Indiana. We obtained the highest pregnancy rates from September to November. In our sample of 85 gravid prairie voles, the number of embryos per female ranged from 1 to 7, with a mean of 3.48. Three females each had 1 embryo, 12 had 2, 31 had 3, 25 had 4, 9 had 5, 4 had 6, and 1 had 7. The average number of embryos per female was low in winter, increased through May, decreased to a low in July, then increased to a high in October. Thus, although the species bred throughout the year, the greatest number of pregnancies and the highest numbers of young occurred in spring and fall. We observed a copulation plug in a female taken on 12 August.

The smallest female with embryos weighed 23.4 grams; the shortest gravid female was 128 mm in total length. Females were divided into four size and weight classes to analyze differences in these categories. Weight classes were 20 to 29, 30 to 39, 40 to 49, and 50 and more grams. Females for which we had no weights were placed in size classes by total length, as follows: 128 to 139, 140 to 149, 150 to 159, and 160 and more mm. Larger females generally had larger numbers of embryos; the smallest size class (10 specimens) averaged 3.00, the next larger class (35 specimens) averaged 3.45, the next larger class (28 specimens) averaged 3.54, and the largest class (9 specimens) averaged 4.00 embryos per gravid female.

Keller and Krebs (1970) found that in the Bloomington area most breeding took place from March through October, and that larger females were more apt to breed in winter

Table 138

Reproductive information from adult female
prairie voles from Indiana

Month	Number examined	Number pregnant	Percent pregnant	Average number embryos per pregnant female
January	20	5	25.0	2.40
February	15	7	46.7	3.00
March	21	10	47.6	3.50
April	13	3	23.1	4.00
May	6	3	50.0	4.33
June	8	2	25.0	3.00
July	18	4	22.2	2.00
August	17	7	41.2	3.43
September	12	11	91.7	3.82
October	25	15	60.0	4.53
Novermber	28	14	50.0	3.29
December	23	4	17.4	2.25
	206	85	41.3	3.48

than smaller females. Of 160 gravid prairie voles they examined, the mean number of embryos per female was 3.27. Embryo counts per female averaged larger in summer than at other seasons, and larger females averaged a larger number of embryos than smaller females.

Corthum (1967) recorded a mean of 3.89 embryos per female in 134 gravid prairie voles from Vigo County and noted that visible placental scars disappeared about 42 to 45 days after parturition.

We also collected data on testis size in male prairie voles. Testis size remained relatively large throughout the year, as expected for a species that breeds in every month. There was a midwinter decrease, however, that coincided with the period of lowest pregnancy rate. Testis size then increased in February and March, decreased through early summer, but again increased in late summer and fall (Table 139).

PARASITES. On 63 Indiana (Vigo County) prairie voles examined for mites by Whitaker and Wilson (1968), *Laelaps alaskensis* was the most abundant species. This was followed by *Laelaps kochi*, *Androlaelaps fahrenholzi*, and *Dermacarus hypudaei*, plus a few other species. These and additional data are included in Table 140. Wilson (1957) had previously reported the mites *Haemogamasus longitarsus* (=*H. barberi*) and

Laelaps kochi on specimens of this vole from Harrison County.

Wilson (1961) reported 41 ticks (*Dermacentor variabilis*) and 313 lice (*Hoplopleura acanthopus*) from 60 Indiana prairie voles. In 1957 he recorded the flea *Stenoponia americana* (Harrison County), and in 1961 added four additional species of fleas: 13 individuals of *Ctenophthalmus pseudagyrtes* (the most important species), 3 of *Atyphloceras bishopi* (Clay County), 1 of *Epitedia wenmanni* (Fountain County), 1 of *Orchopeas leucopus* (Jackson County).

Table 139

Testis measurements of prairie voles
from Indiana

Month	Number examined	Testis size (mm) Average	
		Length	Width
January	14	10.35	6.35
February	13	11.61	6.92
March	14	11.60	7.57
April	10	11.00	7.20
May	0	—	—
June	2	10.50	6.50
July	3	13.60	8.33
August	10	11.90	7.20
September	19	11.20	6.73
October	16	10.88	6.80
November	27	9.10	5.90
December	9	8.44	5.30

Table 140

Ectoparasites and other associates of *Microtus ochrogaster* (n = 70) from Indiana

Parasites	Parasites		Hosts Parasitized	
	Total	Average	Total	Percent
Fleas (Siphonaptera)				
Ctenophthalmus pseudagyrtes	2	0.03	2	2.9
Sucking Lice (Anoplura)				
Hoplopleura acanthopus	28	0.40	10	14.3
Mites (Acarina) other than chiggers				
Dermacarus hypudaei	355	5.07	14	20.0
Androlaelaps fahrenholzi	184	2.63	16	22.9
Laelaps kochi	55	0.79	17	24.3
Myocoptes japonensis	42	0.60	6	8.6
Listrophorus mexicanus	20	0.29	3	4.3
Laelaps alaskensis	19	0.27	3	4.3
Radfordia hylandi	19	0.27	3	4.3
Myocoptes musculinus	5	0.07	2	2.9
Trichoecius tenax	3	0.04	2	2.9
Eulaelaps stabularis	2	0.03	2	2.9
Orycteroxenus soricis	2	0.03	2	2.9
Pygmephorus rackae	2	0.03	1	1.4
Haemogamasus longitarsus	1	0.01	1	1.4
Ornithonyssus bacoti	1	0.01	1	1.4
Haemogamasus liponyssoides	1	0.01	1	1.4
Bakerdania sp.	1	0.01	1	1.4
Chigger Mites (Trombiculidae)				
Euschoengastia setosa	11	0.16	3	4.3
Eutrombicula alfreddugesi	5	0.07	3	4.3
Neotrombicula whartoni	1	0.01	1	1.4
Ticks (Ixodides)				
Dermacentor variabilis	13	0.19	8	11.4

Whitaker and Corthum (1967) examined 142 Indiana (Vigo County) prairie voles for fleas. Of 27 found, 25 were *Ctenophthalmus pseudagyrtes*, the only important flea on Indiana prairie voles. Single specimens of *Stenoponia americana* and *Epitedia wenmanni* were also recorded from this sample.

Whitaker and Adalis (1971) examined 157 prairie voles for internal parasites and recorded 227 cestodes in 42 specimens. Cestodes identified were *Andrya macrocephala* (22), *Paranoplocephala troeschi* (25), *P. infrequens* (5), and *Taenia taeniaeformis* (1). The *Taenia* occurred as cysts in the liver and the other cestodes were from the intestines. Fish (1971) reported 442 acanthocephalans *(Moniliformis clarki)* from 36 of 156 prairie voles. All of the infected voles were from one population on the south edge of Terre Haute.

DECIMATING FACTORS. Prairie vole remains have been identified in the pellets of the barn owl, screech owl, long-eared owl, short-eared owl, great horned owl, and marsh hawk (Kirkpatrick and Conaway, 1947; George, 1955; Mumford and Danner, 1974). A barred owl found dead along the highway in Warrick County on 28 February contained 3 complete prairie voles in its gullet. Undoubtedly other birds of prey feed on this common mammal. We have found *M. ochrogaster* remains in 6 of 14 red fox stomachs, in which this vole accounted for 21.3 percent of the volume of food present. We also identified prairie voles in 4 of 8 coyote stomachs, 5 of 34 gray fox stomachs, 1 of 7 striped skunk stomachs, and 3 of 83 opossum stomachs. We have seen numerous specimens in various museum collections that were captured by domestic cats and dogs, according to label notations. Attempts are made to control *M. ochrogaster* and other voles in orchards by poisoning and trapping in order to decrease damage to young trees.

TAXONOMY. Bole and Moulthrop (1942) fixed the type locality of *Microtus ochrogaster ochrogaster* (Wagner) at New Harmony, Posey County, Indiana. Thus, the prairie vole shares with the Indiana bat the distinction of having its type locality in Indiana. Bole and Moulthrop thought that *M. o. ochrogaster* occupied most of the state, but that *M. o. ohionensis* Bole and Moulthrop occurred in the east-central portion. The latter subspecies supposedly is characterized partly by its silvery venter (in contrast to the buffy venter of *M. o. ochrogaster*). However, we have examined silver-bellied prairie voles from 17 counties scattered throughout the range of the species in Indiana and do not consider this characteristic valid for separating *ohionensis* from *ochrogaster*. In fact, Mumford examined silvery bellied prairie vole specimens in the National Museum of Natural History from Colorado, Iowa, Kentucky, Missouri, Montana, Nebraska, South Dakota, Wisconsin, and Wyoming.

SELECTED REFERENCES. Corthum, 1967; Jameson, 1947; Keller and Krebs, 1970; Krebs, Keller, and Myers, 1971; Krebs, Keller, and Tamarin, 1969; Martin, 1956; Whitaker and Adalis, 1971; Zimmerman, 1965.

Woodland Vole
Microtus pinetorum (Le Conte)

Pine Mouse, Mole Mouse, Blue-grass Vole, Southern Pine Mouse, Pine Vole

Arvicola scalopsoides: Kennicott, 1857 (possibly)
Arvicola Pinetorum: Quick and Langdon, 1882 (not 1832, as in Lyon, 1936)
Pitymys pinetorum: Evermann and Clark, 1920
Microtus pinetorum: Bailey, 1900

DESCRIPTION. The woodland vole has glossier, shorter, finer (more molelike or shrewlike) fur than do the other species of microtines found in Indiana. It lacks the coarse, long, scattered guard hairs of other Indiana voles. This type of pelage is in keeping with the more subterranean habits of the woodland vole. Its color above is brownish, usually tinged with reddish or cinnamon; the venter is paler, usually buffy or silvery in color. Pelage color varies from one part of Indiana to another. Immatures and winter-pelaged adults may be darker and duller. The eyes and ears are small, and the tail is about equal to or less than the length of the hind foot. Among other Indiana microtines, only the southern bog lemming (*Synaptomys cooperi*) has such a short tail, but it can be separated from the woodland vole by its grooved upper incisors. Although Fish and Whitaker (1971) reported a specimen of *Microtus pinetorum* with grooved upper incisors, this is very unusual.

Weights and measurements are shown in Table 141. The dental formula is

$$I \frac{1}{1} \ C \frac{0}{0} \ P \frac{0}{0} \ M \frac{3}{3} = 16.$$

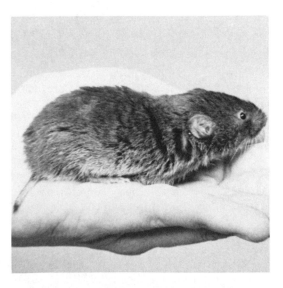

Woodland vole. Photo by Anthony Brentlinger, ISU AV Center

Table 141

Weights and measurements of
Microtus pinetorum from Indiana

	Males	Females
Total length (mm)		
n	11	8
x̄	117.2	121.7
range	109-138	111-143
SD	9.9	11.7
SE	3	4
Tail length (mm)		
n	11	8
x̄	17.8	16.5
range	15-20	14-19
SD	2	1.9
SE	0.6	0.6
Hind foot (mm)		
n	11	8
x̄	16	15.8
range	15-18	13-17
SD	1.0	1.4
SE	0.3	0.5
Weight (grams)		
n	11	9
x̄	25.5	27.2
range	23.3-29.5	22.7-33.8
SD	2.2	3.7
SE	0.7	1.2

STATUS AND DISTRIBUTION. E. R. Quick evidently collected and preserved the first woodland vole specimens from Indiana (Evermann and Butler, 1894b). There are two specimens in the National Museum of Natural History taken by Quick at Brookville (Franklin County) in March and April 1879. "In certain localities they are some years plentiful enough," according to Evermann and Butler in discussing the status of this vole in Franklin County. These authors knew of records from only 4 counties. *Microtus pinetorum* was considered "an abundant vole" by Hahn on his study area near Mitchell (Lawrence County), and in 1909 he listed records from 7 Indiana counties (Hahn, 1908b, 1909). Evermann and Clark (1920) knew of only one specimen taken at Lake Maxinkuckee and thought the species was probably not common there. M. W. Lyon, Jr., trapped 2 woodland voles in the dunes of Porter County in October 1922 (Lyon, 1923), but trapped 10 more in October and November 1923 and another in November

1924 there, perhaps indicating some local abundance. In St. Joseph County, the species was thought to be "not numerous" by Engels (1933). Lyon (1936) stated that M. *pinetorum* was found throughout Indiana, but he had specimen records from only 6 counties and other records from 9 additional counties. Kirkpatrick and Conaway (1948) recorded 7 specimens from a large orchard near Aurora (Dearborn County). Lindsay (1958) found the woodland vole relatively common in southeastern Indiana in the early 1950s and trapped 18 in Ripley County, 2 in Jefferson County, and 1 in Scott County. We have not found this vole to be overly common anywhere we have trapped in the state, although we have usually been able to get specimens without much difficulty when traps were properly set in underground woodland burrows. There are specimens from 34 counties (Map 44).

Woodland voles sometimes occur in considerable numbers in deciduous forests, as

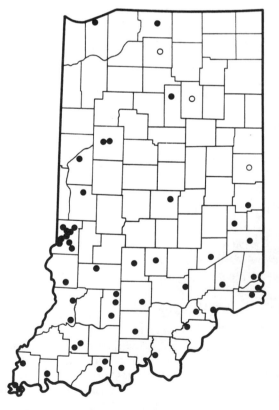

Map 44. The Woodland Vole, *Microtus pinetorum*, in Indiana

Hahn evidently found the species in Law-rence County in the early 1900s. On 11 February 1884, Quick and Butler (1885) captured 11 woodland voles by hand in two hours in Franklin County. It appears that the woodland vole may be much more common in southern Indiana than in northern Indiana, but its true status needs to be more adequately determined by using specialized trapping techniques to capture this species.

HABITAT. Woodland voles will live in a variety of habitats. In Indiana they have been taken in orchards, old corn stubble, pasture, railroad embankment, fencerows, pine plantations, brushy, grassy, and cultivated fields, upland and lowland deciduous forests (including floodplains), upland mixed coniferous and deciduous forests, on lawns, and about the borders of cypress swamps and ponds. However, as Hahn (1909) and Lyon (1936) stated, the woodland vole's major habitat is deciduous forest with soft soil and leaf mold that enables the animals to burrow more easily. In what is now Spring Mill State Park (Lawrence County), Hahn (1908b) noted that "It lives on the rocky hills, about the caves, in the heavy woods where the carpet of dead leaves is several inches deep, and in the fields." Pine or other pure evergreen forests are very seldom inhabited by this vole. Whitaker has taken a number in Indiana along woodlot borders where grassy vegetation was encroaching on the forest floor. Lindsay (1958) took 12 specimens "in somewhat open areas within a hydro-mesophytic forest" (Ripley County) where the ground cover was chiefly panic-grass and other grasses (unidentified); other herbaceous plants there were sedge, poison ivy, summer grape, and bograss. Lyon (1923) trapped a woodland vole in an area of damp sphagnum and cranberry at the edge of an interdunal pond in the dunes region (Porter County). Quick and Butler (1885) found the species on the "higher part of a steep, partially wooded hill" (Franklin County). Here the animals were found beneath logs, stumps, leaves, and stones. This habitat was further described by Quick and Butler as "woods pastures" where bluegrass grew on the sparsely wooded, dry hillsides and there was little or no undergrowth.

Of 12 woodland voles taken in Vigo County during a random trapping program, 8 were in upland woods, 3 in grassy fields, and 1 in a river-bottom woods. Several of those taken in upland woods were from areas where the woody vegetation was dense. All 8 were from plots having fair to poor herbaceous cover (no upland woods plots had good cover). All were taken from the 39 plots containing leaf mold; none was taken in 19 plots without leaf mold. The 3 woodland voles from the grassy field were all from a single, shaded plot at the edge of a deep woods; the plot contained some woody vegetation. The soil was moist where 9 of the 12 were taken; 1 was taken where the soil was very dry, and 2 where the soil was dry. In August 1977, we trapped several woodland voles on the surface of the ground along the floodplain of a creek (Fountain County). Vegetation here consisted of nettles, touch-me-not, giant ragweed, knotweed, pokeberry, sneezeweed, ironweed, and other plants and sprouts. Trees growing along the area were black walnut, hackberry, silver maple, butternut, and mulberry.

In some strip-mined land (Pike County) and old fields (Spencer County) woodland voles appeared to be associated with dense honeysuckle or honeysuckle / black locust vegetation. And on top of the highest elevations in the Clark County State Forest, in March 1955, woodland vole burrows were numerous beneath the stands of chestnut oak and Virginia pine.

ASSOCIATED SPECIES. The major species of small mammals found with the woodland vole in forested habitats are the short-tailed shrew and the white-footed mouse. The short-tailed shrew and the woodland vole occupy similar niches in woodlands, and both may have their burrows in the same area. Vole burrows are rounded (in cross-section) and are larger than shrew burrows, which are somewhat flattened dorsoventrally. The short-tailed shrew and the white-footed mouse have been trapped in woodland vole burrows by Lyon (1936) and by Whitaker. Whitaker also caught a meadow jumping mouse and several salamanders (*Ambystoma texanum* and *Plethodon glutinosus*) in vole burrows (Vigo County). In various other vegetation types, the prairie vole and meadow vole, the meadow jumping mouse, the southern bog lemming, the house mouse and deer mouse, and the masked shrew have been taken in the same traplines with woodland voles.

A small number of traps set for one night along prominent surface runs in an abandoned garden grown up to tall, dense bluegrass and scattered weeds (Decatur County) captured woodland voles, prairie voles, meadow voles, and southern bog lemmings. Lindsay trapped woodland voles, prairie voles, meadow voles, and white-footed mice in the same habitat in Ripley County.

HABITS. The woodland vole is a somewhat colonial, burrowing species. Relatively little is known of its habits or behavior, but it is evidently active both day and night. Hahn (1908b) thought it was "largely diurnal" and mentioned observing the animals during the daytime. Later he wrote:

Sometimes in walking quietly through the woods you may hear a dead leaf rustle as though moved by the wind. If you look quickly and keenly toward it you may distinguish a brown head, set with two tiny, bead-like eyes, disappearing into a hole under the leaves. If you examine the place closely you will probably find the entrance to the labyrinthian tunnels of these mice and very likely you can also find where the animal has been cutting the stem of a green violet or some other tender plant. [Hahn, 1909]

Lindsay (1958) also recorded observations of woodland voles aboveground during the day. Many authors consider the species to spend most of its time in burrows below the ground, but there is enough circumstantial evidence from observations, trapping, and the appearance of woodland vole remains in the stomachs of several avian predators to indicate that considerable time must be spent aboveground. We have trapped several in surface runs during the daylight hours.

Presumably woodland voles feed in part by foraging beneath and among the leaves on the forest floor, especially beneath logs and about the leaf mold. This is the only method by which it could obtain some of the food found in stomachs examined by us. Certainly much time is spent inside the burrow system, which may be extensive. If one looks along the shallow burrows of the woodland vole, he will see neat, round openings to the surface; there is no soil about these openings. Hahn saw foraging woodland voles scurry back into these openings when he disturbed them during the day. These burrows are usually confined to the softer, loose soils, for woodland voles do not have the powerful digging front feet possessed by moles. The voles are said to push the soil from the burrow with their forefeet; evidently the excavated soil is scattered about, rather than being left in mounds at entrances to the burrow system. Many burrows are just below the ground surface, and the top of the burrow is often pushed up to form a small, low ridge along the ground, although under the forest floor litter of leaves, twigs, and other ground cover, the ridges may not be visible until the covering material is scraped aside. Deeper burrows are also constructed, some to a depth of at least 18 inches. Burrows made by the eastern mole may also be used by the woodland vole. Lindsay found burrows of woodland voles to be 2 to 4 inches beneath the ground surface, but this was in a wet woods where the water table was high much of the year.

Hahn (1909) stated that the nest "is always placed under ground or under an old stump or log and is made of fine, dry grass, root fibers or leaves." Quick and Butler (1885) found this vole during the winter in nests "beneath a pile of leaves or an old stump." They found that a single animal usually occupied such nests, which were globular, 4 to 6 inches in diameter, and constructed of bluegrass. Underground nests are placed in an enlarged portion of the burrow and are sometimes composed of shredded vegetation.

In some habitats woodland voles may construct extensive burrow systems in limited areas but may avoid adjacent, similar looking habitat. The home range is evidently small. Burt (1940) calculated it at a quarter of an acre. Benton (1955) found the average home range diameter of 13 individuals studied in New York to be only 21 yards. It has been noted that occupied areas may be abandoned after a time for no apparent reason.

Microtus pinetorum has been captured by hand during the day by turning over stones, logs, stumps, and leaves. When suddenly uncovered in this way, the animals appear dazed and may pause for a brief time, during which they can usually be grabbed. Nixon A. Wilson captured woodland voles by hand about the border of Hovey Lake (Posey County) on 14 and 15 May; the lake was flooded at the time, and small mammals may have been forced out of their regular haunts and were sheltering beneath available structures. By turning over logs, Wilson observed 8 woodland voles, 2 masked shrews, 1 short-tailed shrew, and 2 white-footed mice.

Since woodland voles spend so much of their time underground, they are usually difficult to trap in numbers by conventional methods. One way to increase the catch is to locate the burrows, by observing the upraised ridges marking their location or by probing with the fingers into the soft, moist forest earth. A rectangular hole is then dug into the burrow from above so that a regular snap-back mousetrap can be lowered into the burrow with the trap treadle at a level with the surface of the runway and directly in it, so that the vole must run over the treadle when running through the tunnel. It is best to cover the set with a piece of bark or other object, but we have taken woodland voles in such sets without any covering.

FOOD. The woodland vole is said to feed mainly on roots, bulbs, tubers, bark, seeds, nuts, acorns, and insects; it stores food for winter. Hahn (1908b) found seeds, roots, and insects in the few stomachs of specimens he examined from Lawrence County. Quick and Butler reported that winter foods of *Microtus pinetorum* in southeastern Indiana included the roots of young hickories, young sprouts of white clover, fruit of hawthorn, and the tuberous roots of wild violet. They reported deposits that contained a gallon of stored vio-

let tubers; some were stored 18 inches below the surface of the ground. Hahn reported that woodland voles ate sweet potatoes and "white" potatoes from gardens and also fed on sprouting corn. He further commented on the damage done by these voles during the winter to young orchard trees. In one instance manure and coarse stalks had been piled about the bases of the orchard trees for protection; but during the winter, voles partially or completely girdled about half of the trees.

From other states, there are additional reports of plant foods, mostly stored in burrow chambers. Saunders (1932) found tubers of squirrel corn and Schmidt (1931) mentioned tubers of Dutchman's breeches. Foods reported by Hamilton (1938) included tubers of quackgrass, broad-leaved dock, stems of barnyard grass, witch grass, sandbur, and smartweed, and leaves of buttercup.

We have examined the stomach contents of 25 woodland voles taken in Indiana (Table 142). Of these, 3 were collected in winter, 4 in spring, 5 in summer, and 13 in fall. Our analyses mostly substantiate general statements in the literature. Various plant parts (stems, leaves, roots, nuts) constituted 92 percent of the food in our sample. The fungus *Endogone* represented 3 percent and insect material nearly 5 percent of the identified foods. It seemed of interest that hickory nuts, beechnuts, and black cherry seeds were present. In a burrow in a forest area from which *M. pinetorum* was taken in October,

Table 142

Foods eaten by *Microtus pinetorum* (n = 25) from Indiana

Food Item	Percent Volume	Percent Frequency
Roots, tubers	30.6	44.0
Green vegetation	20.0	32.0
Mast	12.4	20.0
Unidentified seeds	8.4	12.0
Grass	4.8	8.0
Prunus serotina (black cherry) pits	4.0	4.0
Carya (hickory) nuts	4.0	4.0
Galium (bedstraw) leaves and stems	4.0	4.0
Fagus (beech) nuts	4.0	4.0
Insects	3.2	8.0
Endogone	3.0	4.0
Coleoptera	1.6	4.0
	100.0	

fresh, green cuttings (apparently made by woodland voles) of sedge, black maple, and spleenwort were noted.

M. W. Lyon, Jr., and W. D. Fitzwater both found that pieces of apple made an excellent bait for trapping woodland voles.

REPRODUCTION. Woodland voles evidently produce young mostly from late February or early March through September or October. We have relatively little data for Indiana specimens. Hahn (1909) reported from 2 to 4 embryos in gravid females he saw. A female captured in Ripley County on 15 November contained 2 embryos measuring 20 mm in crown-rump length. According to Hamilton (1938), the gestation period is about 20 to 21 days and weaning takes place about 17 days after birth. Litter size usually ranges from 2 to 4; the 3 gravid females from Indiana that we examined each contained 2 embryos. Roberts and Early (1952) reported one litter of 8 young. Of 14 litters born in captivity, 4 contained 2 young, 9 contained 3 young, and 1 contained 4 young (Hamilton, 1938), an average of 2.8 per litter. Females probably have 3 to 4 litters per year. The number of young per litter is somewhat lower than that for other species of *Microtus* in Indiana, probably because the subterranean environment affords the young a greater chance of survival. Raynor (1960) reported an instance where 3 females with their litters were found in a single nest. If this is a common occurrence, perhaps accounts of large litters could be the result of multiple litters found together.

Males with enlarged testes (4 x 6 to 5 x 8 mm.) have been trapped in January, April, July, September, and October, probably indicating a long breeding season, as mentioned above.

PARASITES. Of 26 woodland voles examined for internal parasites, unidentified cestodes and nematodes were found in 3 each. Fish (1971) took 15 acanthocephalans (*Moniliformis clarki*) from a woodland vole taken in Vigo County.

External parasites were found on 23 of 26 woodland voles examined (Table 143). Some of these have previously been recorded in the literature (Whitaker and Wilson, 1968; Whitaker and Corthum, 1967). Although our sample size is small, the variety of species of

parasites taken is relatively large. Perhaps this wide variety of parasites is correlated with the subterranean habitat of this vole. The most common ectoparasites, however, are a chigger (*Euschoengastia ohioensis*) and the ubiquitous mite *Androlaelaps fahrenholzi*. A number of hypopi of *Dermacarus* were found, but most were on a single specimen. The only flea recorded was the species commonly found on *Blarina brevicauda* (which often uses burrows of the woodland vole). Four species of the phoretic genus *Pygmephorus* were taken on woodland voles. Wilson (1957, 1961) has reported the mite *Haemogamosus longitarsus*, two fleas *Ctenophthalmus pseudagyrtes* and *Stenoponia americana*) and a tick (*Dermacentor variabilis*) on four specimens collected in Harrison and Posey Counties.

DECIMATING FACTORS. Presumably the woodland vole has few natural predators. However, the fact that hawks and owls prey on woodland voles indicates that there is considerable aboveground activity by *M. pinetorum*. Pearson and Pearson (1947) and Latham (1950) recorded six species of owls, four species of hawks, the red fox, the gray fox, and the opossum as predators on woodland voles. Parmalee (1954) added the barn owl, Llewelyn and Uhler (1952) the mink and raccoon, and Barbour (1951) the rat snake as predators. We have records of at least three woodland voles being captured by domestic cats, and Quick and Butler (1885) mentioned this predator. Perhaps the presence of woodland vole skulls in hawk and owl pellets examined by various authors in Indiana has been overlooked, because of their close resemblance to the skulls of the prairie vole. We examined one woodland vole that was found in a pitfall trap set for insects. Several other individuals have been found dead.

TAXONOMY. Other authors have mapped *Microtus pinetorum auricularis* Bailey as occupying the northern quarter of Indiana and *M. p. scalopsoides* (Audubon and Bachman) as occupying the remainder of the state (Hall and Kelson, 1959). Most of the specimens from the Ohio River valley appear to be typical *auricularis*, but specimens from extreme northern Indiana are consistently duller in color. The few specimens examined from the remainder of Indiana appear to be intergrades (Mumford, 1969c). On the basis of the subspecies concept expressed by Whitaker (1970a), we see no evidence of a major break in gene flow between groups of Indiana populations. There does appear to be a clinal gradation of characters. The taxonomy of *M. pinetorum* requires more study.

SELECTED REFERENCES. Benton, 1955; Hamilton, 1938; Miller and Getz, 1969; Paul, 1970; Pascal, 1974; Valentine and Kirkpatrick, 1970.

Table 143

Ectoparasites and other associates of *Microtus pinetorum* (n = 26) from Indiana
(27 examined for chiggers)

Parasites	Parasites		Hosts Parasitized	
	Total	Average	Total	Percent
Fleas (Siphonaptera)				
Ctenophthalmus pseudagyrtes	8	0.31	5	19.2
Sucking Lice (Anoplura)				
Hoplopleura acanthopus	7	0.27	2	7.7
Mites (Acarina) other than chiggers				
Androlaelaps fahrenholzi	117	4.50	14	53.8
Dermacarus hypudaei	70	2.69	5	19.2
Ornithonyssus bacoti	13	0.50	1	3.8
Bakerdania sp.	11	0.42	1	3.8
Laelaps alaskensis	10	0.38	5	19.2
Haemogamasus longitarsus	9	0.35	6	23.1
Laelaps kochi	9	0.35	3	11.5
Radfordia hylandi	7	0.27	1	3.8
Eulaelaps stabularis	3	0.12	3	11.5
Myocoptes musculinus	2	0.08	2	7.7
Anoetidae	2	0.08	1	3.8
Myocoptes japonensis canadensis	1	0.04	1	3.8
Cyrtolaelaps sp.	1	0.04	1	3.8
Pygmephorus equitrichosus	32	1.23	—	—
Pygmephorus hastatus	2	0.08	—	—
Pygmephorus scalopi	2	0.08	—	—
Pygmephorus whitakeri	2	0.08	—	—
Chigger Mites (Trombiculidae)				
Euschoengastia ohioensis	69	2.56	5	18.5
E. peromysci	13	0.48	1	3.7
Neotrombicula lipovskyi	3	0.11	1	3.7
Ticks (Ixodides)				
Dermacentor variabilis	2	0.08	2	7.7

Muskrat
Ondatra zibethicus (Linnaeus)

Common Muskrat

Fiber zibethicus: Wied, 1839
Ondatra zibethica: Evermann and Clark, 1920
Ondatra zibethicus: Mumford and Handley, 1956

DESCRIPTION. The muskrat is the largest of the cricetid rodents in Indiana. It is a chunky, dark reddish brown animal, with a long, essentially naked, scaly, laterally compressed tail. The pelage is dense and shiny, especially in winter, and consists of a thick coat of underfur over which lies a covering of long, glossy guard hairs. The sides are yellow-tinged and the belly is a dingy whitish yellow. The ears and eyes are relatively small for an animal of this size. The feet and tail are dark. The hind feet bear webbed toes and are much larger than the front feet. The anterior face of the upper incisors are yellowish orange. We have records of several albinos from Indiana and of other individuals that were uniformly pale tan. Partially albino specimens have also been examined; in these animals the pelage is blotched with large patches of brown and white. Extremely dark individuals are sometimes encountered and Evermann and Clark (1920) wrote (concerning Lake Maxinkuckee, Marshall County) that "Black pelts, which constitute a small proportion of the catch, bring much higher prices."

Brooks (1959) weighed 5,544 Indiana musk-

Color variations in muskrats. Photo by David W. Berrey

rats and found the adult males to average 1,215 grams and adult females to average 1,247 grams. Additional information is given in Table 144. The dental formula is

$$I \frac{1}{1} C \frac{0}{0} P \frac{0}{0} M \frac{3}{3} = 16.$$

STATUS AND DISTRIBUTION. The muskrat is common throughout the state where suitable habitat is present (Map 45); thus it is most abundant in northern Indiana, where lakes and marshes are most numerous. The largest populations are usually found in the larger marshes. Lyon (1936) noted that 586,000 muskrats were taken in Indiana during the 1931–32 fur season. Brooks (1959) reported that the average annual reported catch of muskrats for the seven years of 1952 to 1958 was 199,000. Of these, 75 percent were taken in northern Indiana. Specimens are in collections from 65 counties.

Before so many of the marshes and other water areas in Indiana were drained, musk-

Muskrat. Photo by Roger W. Barbour

Table 144
Weights and measurements of
Ondatra zibethicus from Indiana

	Males	Females
Total length (mm)		
n	35	23
x̄	537.2	515.9
range	463-631	447-598
SD	42.8	37.1
SE	7.2	7.7
Tail length (mm)		
n	35	23
x̄	230.5	221.9
range	192-273	186-260
SD	21.8	20.3
SE	3.7	4.2
Hind foot (mm)		
n	34	22
x̄	78.4	77.5
range	65-95	66-88
SD	5.2	4.8
SE	0.88	1.0
Weight (grams)		
n	23	40
x̄	988.6	1107.0
range	724-1498	618-1525
SD	223.5	243.7
SE	46.6	38.5

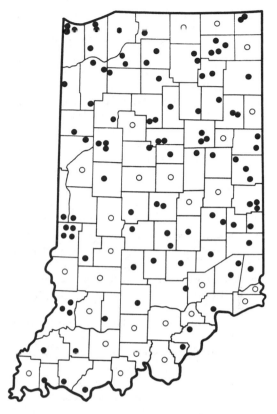

Map 45.   The Muskrat, *Ondatra zibethicus*,
in Indiana

rats probably occurred in tremendous numbers in northwestern Indiana. The Grand Marsh of the Kankakee River originally covered about 500,000 acres, and much of it was prime muskrat habitat. It was said that good trappers could take 35 muskrats per day in Lake County in 1811; one man is credited with capturing 10,000 in one year (Dinwiddie, 1884). Josiah Granger lived on Jerry Island, along the Kankakee River, in 1852 and kept a diary in which he recorded hunting, fishing, and trapping exploits, bird and mammal observations, and weather data (Reed, 1920). On 20 February, he caught 36 muskrats in 42 traps. On 15 and 24 March, he trapped 34 and 40 respectively, but on 26 March his diary read: " . . . got a boat full of rats . . . yesterday." Hahn (1909) stated that L. N. Lamb sometimes caught more than 80 muskrats per night in his line of 100 traps in 1871, after "the Kankakee valley burned off." Another trapper told Hahn that when he came to the Kankakee country in 1865, musk-

rat houses were so closely spaced that it was possible to open three or four of them at a time from an anchored boat. And as recently as 1904 an acquaintance of Hahn said he trapped 300 muskrats in 30 days "in the Kankakee in Newton and Lake counties." This same season, another trapper took 700 during the fall and winter in Jasper and Porter counties.

Mumford talked to Roy Granger, at Roselawn, in 1952. Granger said that he and his father took more than 5,000 muskrats one year and more than 300 in one night. He said that he once speared 72 through the ice in one day. This was probably in the early 1900s; even allowing for inflated figures of the kills, muskrats must have still been extremely abundant.

During the period 1834 to 1884, the annual catch of muskrats in Lake County was said to have been from 20,000 to 40,000 (Ball, 1884). For the years 1952 to 1958, the average annual catch reported from 12 counties (including Lake) in northwestern Indiana was 19,000 (Brooks, 1959).

Meager records kept by fur traders between 1800 and 1811 in St. Joseph County and at Fort Wayne (Allen County) do not bear out this abundance. Possibly muskrats taken in northwestern Indiana went to other markets, such as the Chicago area. William Burnett bought only 2,014 muskrat skins in 1800 and 1801 at his trading post on the St. Joseph River (Engels, 1933). At Fort Wayne, John Johnston received 5,379 muskrat skins from 1804 to 1811. Records show that he shipped only 11 skins in 1804, but 2,715 in 1811. There is the possibility that muskrats were not sought after as much as beaver and other species during the early 1800s. Beavers were undoubtedly quite scarce in this portion of Indiana at that time and trappers may have turned to muskrats for their revenue later. It may also be possible that the muskrats increased in numbers markedly between 1800 and 1900.

In other portions of the state, local areas supported good numbers of muskrats. B. W. Evermann counted 140 muskrat houses on Five-mile Pond, near Terre Haute (Vigo County) in 1893. Concerning the status of the muskrat in southeastern Indiana in 1885, Butler (1885) wrote "From all that I can learn, I do not think it is less common than at the time of the early settlement of this region." This section of Indiana was not as susceptible to large-scale drainage, nor did it contain large marshes such as were found in northern Indiana. At Lake Maxinkuckee a trapper caught between 60 and 70 muskrats during the winter of 1896–97. Two men who trapped different parts of the lakeshore in the fall of 1900 had taken 30 and 50 by 9 November. Two men took 103 from one portion of the lake by 1 November 1903; they caught 28 in one night (Evermann and Clark, 1911). In St. Joseph County, a boy captured 300 muskrats at Sousley's Lake during the winter of 1931–32 (Engels, 1933). And Brennan (1923) mentioned that muskrats were "living by the thousands in the great marshes . . . of the Indiana Dunes" in earlier years.

Despite the inferential data (based on numbers of houses) and historical accounts, there is little information on muskrat populations in Indiana. Again, Brooks (1955) gathered the most significant information.

On the Willow Slough area, 400 acres were trapped in the fall of 1954. A total of 1,984 muskrats was taken (4.96 per acre). There were 10.5 muskrats per acre taken in 28 acres of cattail / burreed. Two areas (22 and 64 acres) of cattails only, but with sufficient water, each produced 10.3 per acre. The next highest catches per acre (9.4 and 7.9) were both from pure cattail stands, of 16 and 14 acres (Table 145).

HABITAT. Marshes and other water areas with an abundance of emergent vegetation are the preferred habitats of muskrats, but the species also occurs along streams and ditches and about lakes and ponds. Muskrats will even take up residence in small ponds that may later dry up, as George Dellinger reported.

In a close cropped pasture . . . lies a small depression that is dry most of the year. In February 1951, just three days after some heavy rains, I passed by and noticed a strip of muddy water extending out from one bank while the rest of the water was quite clear. As I could not see any livestock in the pasture which may have muddied the water, I stopped to investigate. The pond was approximately fifty feet wide and not over ten inches deep. No typical pond vegetation was present; water does not stand in the depression often or long enough to drown out the blue grass on the bottom. Just below water level were two dens in the process of construction. I cut a small branch . . . and prodded into each hole to determine the extent of their depth. Neither were over three feet deep. The first was found to harbor a muskrat which swam out and entered the second hole. Upon prodding this hole, two rats came out and swam over into the clear water. The only means of reaching this pond was overland through open fields from Walnut Fork Creek about one-half mile to the east.

Brooks (1955) provided the best data on habitats in northwestern Indiana. On the Willow Slough Fish and Wildlife Area (Newton County) he found that cattail / burreed was the most productive habitat, followed in importance by cattail predominantly, cattail with some bulrush, and duck potato / sedge / water lily (with no cattail). Population figures, based on trapping in these communities, have been given above. Evidently a good stand of cattails and water of sufficient depth are the most important characteristics of good muskrat habitat. In nonmarsh habitat

Table 145

Muskrats trapped in various habitats,
Willow Slough Fish and Wildlife Area,
Newton County, Indiana, 1954

Vegetation Type	Number of Acres	Number of Muskrats Caught per Acre	Number of Areas
Cattail / burreed	28	10.5	1 area
Cattail, with sufficient water	86	10.3, 10.3	2 areas
Cattail, with sufficient water, but much vegetation removed by muskrats	30	7.9, 9.4	2 areas
Cattail, with some bulrush	27	3.9	1 area
Cattail mostly, sufficient water, adverse weather when trapping	45	3.0, 2.2	2 areas*
Cattail, with shallow water	106	2.8, 1.7, 1.6	3 areas
No cattail; duck potato / sedges / water lilies	78	0.9	1 area

*Considered to be overpopulated with muskrats

in southeastern Indiana, Butler (1885) found muskrats to be "abundant about the estuaries of creeks whose banks are covered with a luxuriant growth of vegetation."

ASSOCIATED SPECIES. In the study by Brooks, the other fur-bearing mammals trapped were the mink, the raccoon, the opossum, and the beaver. In 1953, 21 minks and 17 raccoons were trapped; in 1954 there were 15 minks and 39 raccoons taken. Only 3 opossums were captured in 1953 and 12 in 1954. Beavers (12) were taken only in 1954. Smaller mammals inhabiting the best muskrat habitats include primarily the meadow vole and the star-nosed mole; in drier sites about the marshes, short-tailed shrews, masked shrews, meadow jumping mice, and other small species occur. A nest of the masked shrew has been found in a muskrat house.

HABITS. The muskrat is mostly nocturnal, but also is active by day, especially in spring and fall. It spends most of the daylight hours in burrows or houses that it constructs in or near water. The houses are the most conspicuous indicators of the muskrat's presence on a marsh. Houses are built in shallow water and are constructed of emergent and submerged vegetation, cattail being a favorite when it is available. Houses are roughly circular, average from 4 to 5 feet in diameter at

Ditch in Newton County, home of muskrats.
Photo by David W. Berrey

the water level, and extend 2 to 3 feet above the water surface. They have walls about 1 to 1.5 feet thick. Sometimes structures twice the average size are built. Inside the house is an irregularly shaped chamber above the water level. An underwater entrance leads to one side of this chamber; the entrance also serves as a plunge hole into which the muskrat dives when danger threatens. Normally the chambers are dark. Brooks (1959) examined several houses and found that the chambers were usually a foot in diameter and about 6 to 8 inches high. Larger houses sometimes had two chambers. Nests of dry, shredded cattail leaves and other rather soft vegetation were in them. A house examined by Butler had a chamber 22 inches in greatest length and 16 inches in least length; it averaged 12 inches wide; its greatest height was 12 inches.

On the Jasper-Pulaski Fish and Wildlife Area (Jasper County) the majority of houses were in water varying from 1 to 2 feet deep (Brooks, 1959). The animals usually clear the emergent vegetation (including roots) away from the immediate vicinity of the house and much of this material goes into house construction. Brooks stated that from an airplane these houses look like doughnuts on a tray, with the houses as the centers, surrounded by circular, cleared areas. Cattails, burreed, bulrushes, rice cutgrass, watershield, wool grass, smartweed, hornwort, and other plants are used in building. Butler also examined houses in which "swamp grass, sedge, coarse weeds and mud" had been added to the usual materials. In addition, he found freshwater algae, small pieces of driftwood, a few pieces of shingles, and two wooden barrel staves incorporated into houses. Most of the mud was in the lower part of the houses and was thought to have been partly transported on the roots of plants. It is interesting that Butler made the comment that muskrats did not construct houses in that part of the state (Franklin County) until after they took up residence in a 15-mile segment of the destroyed and abandoned Whitewater Valley Canal (completed in 1846), after 1866. Before this, they lived in burrows in river banks. At Lake Maxinkuckee, Evermann and Clark (1920) noted a preference for muskgrass and bulrush in house construction, some houses being constructed almost entirely of the former. They also observed that both yellow and white water lilies, pondweed, water milfoil, hornwort, cattail, iris, and other plants were used, and commented on the use of "considerable mud" in certain houses.

Muskrat house, Vigo County. Photo by Whitaker

House sites are often on a stump, in or on some brush, about a tree in the water, along a fence, or on or about some other object in the water. Butler noted a house built on a barrel standing on end in shallow water. Where no such foundation is present, the muskrats cut vegetation and make a raft, which sinks to the bottom and serves as an anchor for the rest of the house. Evermann and Clark found two muskrat houses built above the water about a foot, on the cross-timbers supporting piers. Both were built mainly of muskgrass. When disturbed, the muskrats in these houses would drop quietly into the water and swim away.

There are two major peaks of house construction—in spring and in late summer or early fall. Houses do not persist for more than a season unless they are well anchored to some durable object and constantly repaired. Rain, wind, and waves quickly destroy them, and the material from which they are made rots rapidly. In the spring, some new houses are built and others are repaired for rearing of the young. Depending upon the season, from one to ten animals may occupy a house, but four to five usually do so. This number can construct a house in one or two nights. In the spring breeding season, only one pair is found per house. Butler destroyed one house while making his examination of it; within a week a new house twice the size of the original was built on the same site.

Bank burrows are commonly used and muskrats seem to prefer to construct these burrows in vertical banks. Butler noted that most bank burrows were excavated in loamy or light clay banks and it was exceptional to find one in sandy or gravelly soil. Along the Whitewater Canal, he found that each bank burrow had two openings, usually 18 to 24 inches apart. He thought one was at the high-water mark and the second at the low-water mark. From the entrance, the tunnels led backward and sloped upward to enlarged galleries, where the nest was constructed. A small passage then led from this chamber to the surface of the ground above. Burrows usually extended 15 to 20 feet in a straight line. Both Brooks and Butler remarked on the preference of muskrats for bank burrows. Brooks reported that such burrow systems tended to be more complex with continued use, with additional nest chambers and tunnels being constructed. Brooks found that most simple systems had a burrow entrance that opened under the water. Herbst (1966) excavated completely two burrow systems, which contained 18 and 27 feet of tunnel. Each had two underground entrances, with long, sloping galleries that extended above the water level. Along these galleries, small side excavations "the size of one muskrat" were spaced. Side tunnels about 2 feet long and ending in small chambers containing bits of plants were frequently found. The main living quarters was an elliptical chamber with a bed of shredded vegetation. Permanent dens have been found along small ditches not more than a foot wide and with water only 6 inches deep.

Where muskrats live for some time, they tend to enter and leave the water repeatedly at certain places. This forms obvious worn areas in the soil along the water known as "slides," and trapping of these animals can be facilitated by placing the traps in the water at the base of such runways. In muddy areas, the footprints, and the drag mark made by the tail between the foot tracks, can be seen.

Tagging studies by Brooks revealed that many muskrats spend their entire lives within a radius of 200 yards of their birthplace. In late summer and fall, however, individuals wander and some have been observed more than a mile from water. This fall dispersion no doubt prevents overcrowding on the home marsh and is a mechanism for invading and becoming established in new areas. A similar movement may occur in early spring, as animals become quite intolerant of each other and explore for more suitable areas to bear and rear their young. During these overland travels into unfamiliar territory, muskrats are more vulnerable to predation and accidents; many are killed by automobiles. Spring and fall reports of muskrats in cities, residential areas, and other nonaquatic sites are probably mostly of wandering animals.

Muskrats remain active under the ice in winter, taking advantage of air trapped between the ice and the water. They enter and leave the water where the current prevents freezing, where the ice is broken, or where spaces occur in ice enclosing a tree or other object. Hunters take advantage of muskrats in winter; when the water is covered with clear ice of the correct thickness, the hunters walk out to the houses, give them a few kicks (causing the muskrats to leave them), then spear the animals as they surface after leaving their houses. Some muskrats are simply speared as they move along their regular runways.

On warm, quiet afternoons muskrats may sun themselves while resting on logs, feeding platforms, and other structures or on the bank at the edge of the water. Disturbed animals plunge into the water and swim toward a burrow. If they cannot reach a burrow quickly, they may remain submerged, coming to the water's surface at brief intervals and showing only their eyes and nose as they breathe. The observer can often follow a swimming muskrat's path by the line of air bubbles that rise to the surface in its wake.

A cornered muskrat may put up a good fight, whether confronted by a dog or by man. We have noticed that individuals encountered on land far from their homes were quite aggressive and would readily approach us when we attempted to capture them. Their sharp incisors are good weapons for fighting and one sometimes sees badly scarred individuals that have been involved in fights. Much fighting among muskrats takes place in the spring and is correlated with the onset of reproductive activities.

Some animals tagged in Indiana were known to be alive in their fourth year, but these individuals had extremely long lifespans. Approximately two-thirds of the young produced in the spring live until the fall trapping season. Only 10 to 15 percent reach an age of one year. During the trapping season, about 80 percent of the catch is composed of animals born during the previous spring and summer.

FOOD. Muskrats are primarily vegetarians, but will eat animal matter, even carrion, under certain conditions. Probably most emergent plants in a muskrat marsh are eaten by the animals, but cattails, burreed, bulrush, water lilies, pondweeds, smartweeds, duck potato, water plantain, rice cutgrass, hornwort, sedges, grasses, swamp loosestrife, buttonbush, and woolgrass have been specifically mentioned by various workers in Indiana. Other plant foods include red clover, wheat, corn, apples, parsnips, beets, carrots, turnips, and willow. The bark or roots are consumed from several of the plants listed above. The animals eat the seeds, stems, and roots of both yellow and white water lily (Evermann and Clark, 1920). Muskrats seem especially fond of corn when the ears are in the milk stage; Butler noted that sometimes the animals even cut the corn stalks and carried them back to their houses. And corncobs have been noted about burrow entrances, suggesting that ear corn is also transported by some individuals. In late December, well-used trails in the snow revealed that muskrats were foraging up to 50 yards into a picked cornfield along a creek. It was also noted in early October that a much-used trail led from the edge of a pond to a supply of fallen apples beneath a tree 135 feet from the pond. We have one report of muskrats eating acorns.

Animal foods include winter-killed fishes, frogs, crayfishes, mussels, and other dead animals. Butler noted that dead ducks, geese, coots, chickens, and turtles were eaten, and one muskrat ate part of another muskrat that had been caught in a trap. Butler listed various species of mussels among the foods of muskrats in southeastern Indiana. Among them were *Anodonta plana, A. decora, A. imbecillus, Unio luteolus, U. parvus, Margaritana rugosa, M. complanata, Unio occidens, U. lachrymosus, U. plicatus,* and *U. multiplicatus.* He estimated that about one-half of the mussels taken by muskrats were composed of the three species of *Anodonta.* Evermann and Clark (1920) observed the habits of muskrats feeding on freshwater mussels in Lake Maxinkuckee. They mentioned that in fall and early winter, piles of mussel shells could be found on objects projecting out into the water, such as a log, a pier, or a fallen treetop. Some of these piles contained a bushel or more of shells. On 24 September they examined one of these piles of discarded shells in some detail; it was offshore several feet and in water about 18 inches deep. About one-half of the shells were counted and examined. These 532 shells represented four species, as follows: *Lampsilis luteola,* 358; *Unio gibbosus,* 167; *L. iris,* 6; *L. multiradiata,* 1. In winter, they observed muskrats far out, diving through cracks in the ice to obtain mussels. The animals would emerge with a mussel, then sit on the edge of the ice and eat it. One was seen feeding in this fashion a thousand feet from the shore. Sometimes it would dive five to six times without securing a mussel. While feeding, the muskrats sat on their haunches, manipulated the shell with their forefeet, and with much chewing and clawing usually managed to open the shell. They were sometimes unsuccessful in opening mussels. From examination of the mainly unbroken shells, it appeared that the muskrats inserted their claws or teeth between the valves in such a way as to cut or tear loose the adductor muscle. H. P. Weeks, Jr., saw muskrats eating snails in the White River. Animal material is usually taken in greatest abundance in late fall, winter, and early spring, when succulent plants are not readily available.

In winter, muskrats may form feeding structures, called push-ups, on top of the ice. Brooks (1959) described the process as follows. The animal must first gnaw a hole through the ice from the underside; sometimes the site of an air bubble is chosen. The hole is enlarged so that the muskrat can crawl through it. Then the animal collects masses of submerged vegetation and constructs a small house over the hole, leaving space enough for the muskrat to sit on the edge of the ice inside the shelter to feed. The wet vegetation soon freezes and forms a protective feeding shelter until warmer weather quickly destroys it. At other times of the year, the animals commonly use feeding platforms, small semifloating rafts of cut vegetation resting on bent-over, uncut emergent plants. Such structures are usually roughly 12 to 15 inches in diameter. One can find refuse on them, and Mumford once found a litter of newborn young on a feeding platform.

REPRODUCTION. Pair formation is apparently initiated mostly by the female, which will swim back and forth before the male and utter squeaking notes. Courtship begins in February and copulation has been observed as early as 10 March. During this period, the males are said to give grunting sounds. Butler (1885) mentioned that on warm nights in early spring one could hear the "squealing of the females" and the "grunts of the males." The gestation period is usually about 28 to 30 days. In his studies on the Willow Slough Fish and Wildlife Area, Brooks found no litters that he considered to have been born before late April. Herbst found four newborn

litters on 12 April in Tippecanoe County. Most young are probably born in May and June, but there are records of gravid females in late fall and even in early winter. A gravid female was trapped in November in Noble County; another with 7 embryos was taken in late December (Pulaski County). Butler found a litter not over one-third grown in September in southeastern Indiana. One young about two weeks old was found at Lafayette on 8 November. Brooks thought the normal "breeding season" (undefined) in Indiana was from about mid-April to mid-August.

Relatively few gravid females have been examined from Indiana. Brooks gathered data on litter size by examining nests inside houses in spring and early summer. He examined 44 litters in 1954 at Willow Slough; litter size ranged from 3 to 10. He considered only 23 of these litters complete, and the average number per litter was 6.9. In 1955, he observed 8 litters that ranged from 3 to 8 young. The 6 litters that he thought were complete averaged 6.0 young per litter. Evidently one of the problems in determining whether a litter is complete is that all young of a litter are not always born on the same day; it may require two or even three days to complete the births of a single litter. Brooks located two nests in one muskrat house; each nest contained 5 young and the nests were connected by a tunnel. He thought all young were part of one litter. Five young in one nest ranged from 30 to 32 grams each, while 5 young in the second nest varied from 42 to 46 grams each. For all of his studies, litter size ranged from 1 to 12 and averaged 6.2 young.

Young muskrats at birth are blind, nearly naked, and helpless. They are reared in dry, warm nests of soft vegetation in the chambers of muskrat houses or burrows. Brooks examined more than 400 young in nests and found that at birth they averaged 22 grams. After two weeks in the nest, their eyes open. They swim about when three weeks old, but have difficulty diving. At about four weeks, young are weaned and on their own; at this time they average about 200 grams. If the female produces a second litter, the young are driven from the house or burrow and must find new living quarters. Indiana muskrats usually have two or three litters per season. The young from the last litter may stay with the parents until the next breeding season. Females evidently come into heat about every 30 days during the breeding season (April to August), so are capable of producing four to five litters per year.

The young grow rapidly and in good habitat equal the size of the adults when four to five months old. None of the 148 young muskrats tagged in their nests showed evidence of giving birth before the fall trapping season. Weights of approximately 3 pounds were attained in a sample of 88 tagged young of both sexes in 250 days. In a four-year study during which 5,544 fall-trapped muskrats (of all sex and age classes) were weighed, it was found that subadult males averaged 3 pounds 1 ounce and subadult females 2 pounds. The exact ages of these young were unknown.

At two weeks of age, young are covered with dark, lead gray fur; this pelage is replaced by adult-colored hair at about three months of age. At birth, young have round tails, which first become laterally flattened at about the time of weaning and reach their full shapes at about three months of age.

Adult females exhibit varied behavior patterns concerning defense of their young. Some females attempt to defend them vigorously against any predator. Young have, on the other hand, been found in cold, wet places where they appeared uncared for by the females. Young are evidently quite hardy.

Reproductive success in muskrats depends upon habitat conditions and populations of the animals. Overpopulation tends to produce smaller litters and fewer litters per female. Stress and strife brought on by too dense a population of animals cause these decreases. The animals fight to defend territories, and more frequent encounters between individuals cause innumerable squabbles, which decreases breeding efficiency. Males, especially, become quite territorial during the breeding season and probably center their territorial defense about the burrow or house, whichever they are using for nesting.

We have little data on the testis sizes of adult males at various seasons. Single males taken 14 and 27 March each had testes 12 by 18 mm. Another male taken 21 April had testes measuring 12 by 30 mm. And two collected on 11 July had testes 17 by 23 and 15 by 25 mm.

PARASITES. Wilson (1961) examined 7 Indiana muskrats for fleas, lice, and ticks, but none were found. Whitaker and Wilson (1968) found one specimen of the mite *Ondatralaelaps multispinosus* on a Vigo County muskrat, and also reported a species of the hypopial form of a mite of the genus *Dermacarus* from a muskrat taken in Vermillion County. This mite was described as a new species (*ondatrae*) by Rupes and Whitaker (1968). The type locality is 5 miles southwest of Clinton. Whitaker has seen large numbers of specimens from muskrats taken in Erie County, Ohio, and Conrad Yunker has recently been successful in rearing adults of this species in the laboratory. In the paper by Whitaker and Wilson (1968), this mite was listed as species "O" (= *Zibethacarus*).

Bauer and Whitaker (1981) examined 40 muskrats from Indiana for ectoparasites. The major species found (Table 146) were *Listrophorus americanus*, *L. dozieri*, *L. faini*, *L. ondatrae*, *L. validus* (Listrophoridae), *Zibethacarus ondatrae* (Glycyphagidae), and *Laelaps multispinosa* (Laelapidae). *Zibethacarus ondatrae* exists on the muskrat in the hypopial (transport) stage. No adults of this species were found.

One individual chigger, one flea, and one each of four different mite species were the only other parasites taken, and none of these can be considered as regularly occurring on Indiana muskrats, even though two of the mites, *Radfordia zibethicalis* and *Myocoptes ondatrae*, are muskrat parasites. The other four species can be considered as stragglers or accidentals, presumably having wandered onto the muskrats. *Radfordia zibethicalis* was previously reported from North America only from *Ondatra* from Texas, whereas this is the first report of *Myocoptes ondatrae* from North America. *Myocoptes ondatrae* was described from *Ondatra zibethicus* from the Old World (Lukoschus and Rouwet, 1968). In addition, these are the first records from Indiana for the five species of *Listrophorus* listed above.

Five of the six known species of *Listrophorus* parasitizing North American muskrats were identified from the muskrats collected in Indiana. *Listrophorus americanus*, *L. dozieri*, *L. faini*, and *L. validus* parasitized all 40 muskrats examined, whereas *L. ondatrae* was found on only 2 of the 40. This situation would appear to violate Gause's Prin-

Table 146
Ectoparasites and other associates of *Ondatra zibethicus* (n = 40) from Indiana
(from Bauer and Whitaker, 1981)

Parasites	Parasites		Hosts Parasitized	
	Total	Average	Total	Percent
Fleas (Siphonaptera)				
Orchopeas howardii	1	.03	1	2.5
Mites (Acarina) other than chiggers				
Listrophorus americanus	10,828	270.70	40	100.0
Listrophorus dozieri	7,256	181.40	40	100.0
Listrophorus faini	7,218	180.45	40	100.0
Listrophorus ondatrae	126	3.15	2	5.0
Listrophorus validus	1,866	46.65	40	100.0
Zibethacarus ondatrae	4,689	117.23	25	62.5
Laelaps multispinosa	995	24.88	29	72.5
Radfordia zibethicalis	1	.03	1	2.5
Marsupialichus brasiliensis	1	.03	1	2.5
Androlaelaps fahrenholzi	1	.03	1	2.5
Myocoptes ondatrae	1	.03	1	2.5
Chigger Mites (Trombiculidae)				
Euschoengastia peromysci	1	.03	1	2.5

ciple, which states that closely related species cannot exist for extended periods in the same ecological niche. However, the various species of *Listrophorus* were adapted for and had their centers of abundance on different parts of the muskrat.

DECIMATING FACTORS. Minks can be important predators on muskrats. They sometimes enter muskrat houses by making a hole through the side into the central cavity. Minks frequently eat muskrats caught in steel traps. Raccoons, dogs, and red foxes prey on *Ondatra*, and dogs are especially destructive in late summer when water levels recede so that the houses are more accessible. Heavy rains, winds, and waves may destroy houses and drown the young. Highway kills are numerous, especially where heavily traveled roads border good muskrat habitat. Drainage, however, remains the only real threat to the species.

Raccoons obtain mostly young muskrats, which they take from their nests after tearing holes in the sides of muskrat houses. Kase (1946a) examined the stomachs of 211 red foxes taken in northern Indiana and found muskrat remains in only 5. Muskrat carcasses are sometimes found about the entrance to a fox den containing young, so adult foxes are able to prey on muskrats to some extent. F. H. Montague, Jr., and his wife saw a red-tailed hawk capture a muskrat. Tom Stankus saw a great horned owl with a dead muskrat.

The role of disease among Indiana muskrats is largely unknown, but muskrats are susceptible to several diseases, such as tularemia, pneumonia, and a virus known as Errington's disease. Some die of "shock disease" when being trapped and handled.

Weather can be an important factor in the welfare of muskrats. Sufficient water must be present in the habitat and droughts can present serious problems. Severe drought may dry up certain habitats, causing the animals to become more and more crowded as water recedes; finally, after much friction between individuals because of lack of space, the animals may be forced to abandon an area completely. A few animals may remain in burrows beneath the mud after all surface water is gone, but they may not be able to persist long unless rainfall again fills the ponds. The flooding of houses and burrows also takes a toll of small young.

Brooks (1959) related how a trapper in Lagrange County took advantage of drought conditions during the hunting season. The trapper owned a dog that was skilled in digging out and killing muskrats. On one marsh nearly devoid of water in the fall, the trapper and his dog took more than 50 animals per day for several days.

Shallow water areas that freeze to the bottom in winter cause many problems, since muskrats generally do not store food for the winter. They may find it difficult or impossible to dig for roots and other foods when ice interferes, and may starve if ice persists for long periods.

TAXONOMY. *Ondatra zibethicus zibethicus* (Linnaeus) is the subspecies found in Indiana.

SELECTED REFERENCES. Bauer and Whitaker, 1981; Brooks, 1959; Butler, 1885.

Southern Bog Lemming
Synaptomys cooperi Baird

Lemming Mouse, Stone Lemming Mouse, Illinois Lemming Mouse, Cooper's Mouse

Synaptomys cooperi: Coues, 1874

DESCRIPTION. The southern bog lemming is a small microtine rodent with a very short, sparsely furred tail (about the length of the hind foot) and with shallow grooves on the upper incisors. The ears are short and the eyes are small. The upperparts are yellowish brown to cinnamon brown, grizzled with blackish. The underparts are silvery. This species can be separated from all other Indiana rodents except *Microtus pinetorum* by its short tail and from *M. pinetorum* by its grooved upper incisors (see Fig. 32).

Synaptomys cooperi specimens from Indiana vary in color, as noted by Quick and Butler (1885) and by Hahn (1909). Quick and Butler reported that animals just reaching maturity were darkest and that one old female with a reddish brown back was dark ash color below. They mentioned that young animals had finer, shorter, glossier fur than did adults. Hahn noted that summer-collected specimens tended to be decidedly rusty colored on the dorsum and had the short fur of the back tipped with a ferruginous color. Winter-taken specimens were paler, usually with the short hairs on the dorsum tipped with cinnamon or fulvous. The sides are paler than the back. We have examined specimens that were quite pale above, but do not know the age of such animals. The

Southern bog lemming. Photo by Roger W. Barbour

palest specimen (male, 23 January; Fountain County) is mostly grayish-white above and gray below. Two other specimens from the same area are rufous reddish or grayish brown above. An immature (Parke County) is almost slate gray, with reddish tipped hairs on the dorsum and a silvery belly.

The southern bog lemming has six plantar pads on each hind foot. Mammary glands usually number six, occasionally four. Old males have glands on their sides immediately anterior to the hind limbs. Whitish hairs grow from these glands. In some individuals these hairs are white to the tips; but in others they are white only at the base, and may be seen by parting the hair. Internally, the glands appear oval and are 3 to 8 mm long.

Weights and measurements are given in Table 147. The dental formula is

$$I \; \frac{1}{1} \; C \; \frac{0}{0} \; P \; \frac{0}{0} \; M \; \frac{3}{3} \; = \; 16.$$

STATUS AND DISTRIBUTION. Coues (1874) first mentioned the southern bog lemming

Table 147
Weights and measurements of
Synaptomys cooperi from Indiana

	Males	Females
Total length (mm)		
n	48	30
x̄	117.4	116.8
Range	99-135	99-134
SD	7.35	8.57
SE	1.06	1.57
Tail length (mm)		
n	48	30
x̄	18.5	18.7
Range	14-27	13-24
SD	2.95	2.76
SE	0.42	0.50
Hind foot (mm)		
n	48	30
x̄	18.6	18.5
Range	15-20	16-20
SD	1.09	1.14
SE	0.16	0.21
Weight (grams)		
n	46	31
x̄	29.2	27.5
Range	20.4-45.4	14.3-51.6
SD	5.66	6.97
SE	0.83	1.25

from Indiana in referring to a specimen taken by Rufus Haymond in Franklin County. Quick and Butler (1885) noted that this specimen was taken in 1866. We have been unable to determine the whereabouts of this specimen, but it may be an undated one in the National Museum of Natural History. Evidently Haymond was unaware of the true identity of his specimen, for he did not list the species from Franklin County (Haymond, 1870). A second specimen was taken in the county in either 1878 or 1879 (Haymond, 1882; Quick and Butler, 1885) and at least six specimens collected in 1879 are in the National Museum of Natural History. In discussing the importance of Edgar R. Quick's collecting of a series of *Synaptomys*, Quick and Langdon (1882) wrote:

The interest that attaches to Mr. Quick's discovery may be inferred from the fact that Dr. Coues was able to obtain but eighteen specimens for study, from the Smithsonian collections, while preparing his elaborate monograph on the family. In European collections, the species was almost, or quite, unknown. Through Mr. Quick's liberality, specimens have been placed in the museums of the Zoological Society of London, the Royal Society of London, the Royal Society of Berlin, and in the Cincinnati Society of Natural History.

Evermann and Butler (1894b), knew of specimens from only Brown and Franklin counties. By 1909, Hahn was able to list specimens from 6 Indiana counties. A. B. Howell (1927) added specimens from 2 more counties and Engels (1933) from another. Based on extant specimens known to Lyon (1936), the distribution of the southern bog lemming in Indiana included Franklin, Jay, Lawrence, Monroe, Newton, Ohio, Porter, and St. Joseph counties. Lyon never trapped one in the state. More extensive mammal collecting over the past 40 years has resulted in specimens now being known from 48 counties (Map 46), and the bog lemming occurs throughout the state.

This vole appears to be colonial and to occur in abundance only in small, local areas. Judging from the relatively few we have taken (76) in snap traps, the species must occur in fairly low numbers, although one must take into account that it is a difficult animal to trap by the methods we have employed. It seldom is attracted to bait. Be-

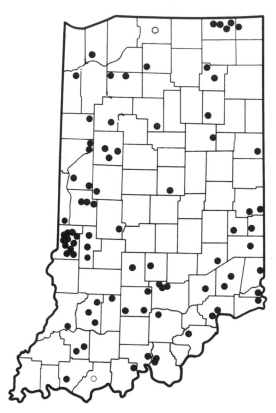

Map 46.   The Southern Bog Lemming, *Synaptomys cooperi*, in Indiana

tween 1878 and 1885, Quick collected more than 25 specimens from a small area southeast of Brookville (Franklin County). Haymond (1882) wrote that Quick "found a large colony inhabiting an aboriginal stone mound, on 'Brown's Hill,'" in reference to these animals. Quick and Butler (1885) further commented on the bog lemmings there: "In 1879 they were very common on Brown's Hill, many of them frequenting the remains of an old stone mound." Evermann and Butler (1894b) reported that Quick found this species "in numbers" in 1878; this comment no doubt refers to the above reference, but there is a discrepancy in dates.

Some idea of relative abundance of bog lemmings to other voles can be inferred from the analyses of owl pellets from three species of owls in Tippecanoe County. The remains of 13 bog lemmings were found in 145 pellets of the barn owl, 3 in 83 pellets of the long-eared owl, and 1 in 102 pellets of the great horned owl. Comparable figures for prairie voles and meadow voles from the same sam-

ples respectively were 121, 71; 95, 22; and 63, 1. Seven bog lemmings were represented among 270 small mammals identified in owl pellets from Jackson County (Mumford and Handley, 1956). The best trapping success we have enjoyed was from 21 to 23 September 1962, when Mumford captured 10 bog lemmings in 150 trap-nights (Washington County) in a 3-year-old fescue field. The species may be fairly easy to obtain in a locality one year and be impossible to catch there the following year. We do not know if this represents a cyclic population phenomenon or whether the animals move about in search of optimum habitat. We suspect that population cycles are involved, for some habitats where we have taken the species have not changed that much from year to year.

HABITAT.   Quick and Butler (1885) wrote, "The mouse is found on hillsides in high, dry, blue grass pastures, where flat stones are irregularly scattered over the surface; it especially prefers what are known as 'woods pastures', containing little or no undergrowth." They mention that Haymond took his specimen in a "hillside pasture field, with no trees" and that many of their specimens came from a "steep rocky hill sparsely covered with timber." The two specimens that W. L. Hahn collected in the Kankakee River valley were "taken in dense bluegrass by the side of the road." In writing about the University Farm (now within Spring Mill State Park), Hahn (1908b) stated, "This animal is restricted to fields in which a dense growth of grass is allowed to grow up and remain uncut." Later (Hahn, 1909) he wrote, "In Indiana I have but a single specimen recorded from a swamp. That one was taken in a tamarack swamp near the LaGrange-Noble County line west of Wolcottville. At other places they seem to be confined to areas covered with dense blue grass." Engels (1933) reported that one of his students trapped five specimens "in rank grass several feet from the bank of a small creek" in St. Joseph County. Some specimens have been trapped in orchards (Kirkpatrick and Conaway, 1948). In Jackson County, Mumford found that well-drained upland home sites (then abandoned) were excellent bog lemming habitats. Such sites were reverting back to briers and brush, but had a lush stand of bluegrass forming the dominant ground cover. Lindsay (1960) captured this vole in weed fields with bluegrass and in fencerows.

Despite the vernacular name, *Synaptomys cooperi* has rarely been trapped in bogs or other wet areas in Indiana. Most of the individuals we have taken have been in grassy fields, especially fields containing bluegrass or little bluestem. Kirkpatrick and Conaway (1948) reported the taking of a specimen in an old cranberry bog (Warren County), and we have mentioned above Hahn's record from a tamarack area. Mumford captured one along the outlet from a pond, where the soil was saturated and water stood in some of the runways; the dead, weedy vegetation had fallen and was mildewed. We trapped a specimen along the river bank at the edge of a tamarack swamp (Lagrange County). Others were taken in old fields where bluestem was a dominant plant. In other parts of its range, the bog lemming occurs in woodlands, and we have trapped a number in sunken cans in Indiana woodlands, but none by means of mousetraps sunken in burrows. Mumford found one dead, on top of the snow, in a woods (Union County), but the animal had been injured and could have been dropped there by a predator.

Other trapping sites, from specimen labels, are as follows: clearing in woods; grassy woods; border of ditch and weedy stubble field; bluegrass lawn; old field; overgrown garden; dry, open field along dry stream; fencerow at edge of unkept cemetery; old field at edge of pine plantation; brushy roadside along creek; upland field of *Andropogon* (bluestem); marsh; fencerow bordering hayfield; old field border; fencerow of shrubs and grasses near edge of marsh; small wooded floodplain along creek.

ASSOCIATED SPECIES. The small mammals most often trapped with the bog lemming in Indiana are the prairie vole, the meadow vole, the house mouse, the masked shrew, and the least shrew. At other times, the white-footed mouse, the deer mouse, the meadow jumping mouse, and the short-tailed shrew have been taken in the same traplines. Where Quick obtained his large series of specimens in Franklin County, he and Butler noted that "No other species were commonly met with in this locality at the same time." Later, in the same paper, they wrote that the bog lemming and the woodland vole occurred together.

HABITS. Specimens have been trapped during the day and at night, but we know relatively little about the activity patterns of this species. It uses the runways constructed by *Microtus* and in some sites makes its own runways in bluegrass. In Jackson County, such runs alternately were beneath the fallen grass and on top of it. The runways were not bare, as is usually the case in *Microtus*, but were lined with living bluegrass. *Microtus* was absent at this site.

During the daytime, bog lemmings hide beneath objects lying on the ground. Quick and Butler reported that *Synaptomys* was "Most frequently found by turning over stones and logs, beneath which it remains concealed, especially in winter." These rodents were difficult to catch by hand in such situations, for when uncovered, "they were off like a flash for their subterranean paths." Burrows examined by Quick and Butler were usually relatively short but "sinuous and intricate." Bog lemmings are commonly trapped in subterranean burrows in New York state woodlands.

Nests, according to Quick and Butler, were always under cover, "generally in hollow logs or stumps, and composed of fine grasses." They thought the nests were not so securely built as the nests of some other voles. Hahn (1909) found a nest on top of the ground "with no cover except a very thin veil of dry grass blades." The nest was conical, about 10 inches in diameter and 5 inches tall. It was inconspicuous, because it was constructed of moss and grass and was situated in a hummocky place among some sumac bushes. It was lined, with fine, dry grasses. Mumford observed a bog lemming that spent several weeks during the fall in a nest under a large sheet of corrugated metal roofing lying on the ground. The nest was nearly globular and composed of dry grasses. Runways radiated out under the roofing from the nest to the surrounding grassy areas.

Hahn attempted to rear three young bog lemmings (total lengths 62 to 64 mm) but all died within three days.

FOOD. Green plants, especially bluegrass and other grasses, appear to be favored summer foods of this species. Roots of these plants and of others are eaten more abundantly in the winter. Quick and Butler noted that in winter bog lemmings fed chiefly on bluegrass and the more tender portions of white clover. They also found large quantities of the tuberous roots of wild artichoke stored by the voles for winter. Hahn (1909) thought that bog lemmings ate grass "more exclusively than any other species that I know."

We have examined the stomachs of 16 Indiana specimens, 14 of which contained 100 percent green vegetation we did not attempt to identify. One of the additional animals contained, by volume estimate, 2 percent mite, 8 percent vegetation, and 90 percent the fungus *Hymenogaster*; the other contained 100 percent grass seeds.

When feeding, *Synaptomys* cuts plant stems into pieces about 3 inches long. Other voles also produce similar, but shorter, cuttings. The animals stand on their hind legs to reach up and cut the grasses and other plants; the plant then drops down and the voles cut off successive sections. Bog lemming runways often contain bright green fecal pellets.

REPRODUCTION. Connor (1959) reported the gestation period of *Synaptomys cooperi* to be about 23 days. Females entered estrus shortly after parturition, so successive pregnancies could occur over a short time. Quick

Table 148

Ectoparasites and other associates of *Synaptomys cooperi* (n = 65) from Indiana
(from Wassel, Tieben, and Whitaker, 1978)

Parasites	Parasites		Hosts Parasitized	
	Total	Average	Total	Percent
Fleas (Siphonaptera)				
Ctenophthalmus pseudagyrtes	16	0.25	9	13.8
Megabothris asio	1	0.02	1	1.5
Sucking Lice (Anoplura)				
Hoplopleura acanthopus	183	2.82	11	16.9
Mites (Acarina) other than chiggers				
Listrophorus synaptomys	1,657	25.49	20	30.8
Dermacarus hypudaei	623	9.58	24	36.9
Laelaps alaskensis	533	8.20	55	84.6
Androlaelaps fahrenholzi	13	0.20	9	13.8
Laelaps kochi	13	0.20	2	3.1
Ornithonyssus bacoti	12	0.18	2	3.1
Bakerdania sp.	10	0.15	6	9.2
Euryparasitus sp.	10	0.15	5	7.7
Anoetidae	3	0.05	2	3.1
Haemogamasus liponyssoides	3	0.05	1	1.5
Myocoptes japonensis	3	0.05	1	1.5
Radfordia hylandi	3	0.05	3	4.6
Proctolaelaps sp.	1	0.02	1	1.5
Pygmephorus mustelae	1	0.02	1	1.5
Pygmephorus scalopi	1	0.02	1	1.5
Pygmephorus sp.	1	0.02	1	1.5
Xenoryctes latiporus	1	0.02	1	1.5
Chigger Mites (Trombiculidae)				
Euschoengastia peromysci	299	4.60	24	36.9
Euschoengastia ohioensis	26	0.40	8	12.3
Eutrombicula alfreddugesi	8	0.12	1	1.5
Euschoengastia setosa	5	0.08	1	1.5
Ticks (Ixodides)				
Dermacentor variabilis	381	5.86	28	43.1
Ixodes muris	9	0.14	2	3.1
Ixodes dentatus	5	0.08	4	6.2

and Butler reported that breeding took place among bog lemmings from February to December, but these authors supplied no details. We have summarized embryo counts for 16 gravid females collected from March to December. Each contained from 2 to 6 embryos and averaged 3.25. Quick and Butler wrote that not more than 4 young per litter were produced by the bog lemmings they examined. Hahn found a nest with 4 young. We have examined a lactating female taken on 22 January (Benton County), thus it appears that the species can breed throughout all (or most) of the year in Indiana.

PARASITES. The most abundant ectoparasites on *Synaptomys cooperi* in Indiana are the mites *Listrophorus synaptomys*, *Dermacarus hypudaei*, and *Laelaps alaskensis*, the chigger *Euschoengastia peromysci*, the tick *Dermacentor variabilis*, and the louse *Hoplopleura acanthopus* (Table 148). *Laelaps alaskensis* was previously reported by Whitaker and Wilson (1968) and by Wilson (1957), who also reported the louse. *Listrophorus synaptomys* was recently described as new by Fain *et al.* (1974). Numerous other species of ectoparasites taken in smaller numbers are listed in Table 148. In addition, another new listrophorid, *Quasilistrophorus microticolus*, was described by Fain, Whitaker, and Lukoschus (1978). It is primarily from *Arborimus* from Oregon, but Lukoschus found 3 individuals on *S. cooperi* from Bicknell (Knox County), Indiana.

Whitaker and Adalis (1971) found 31 trematodes (*Quinqueserialis hassalli*) in 1 of 13 bog lemmings examined from Indiana.

DECIMATING FACTORS. The skull of a bog lemming was found in the stomach of an unidentified hawk (Evermann and Butler, 1894b). *Synaptomys* remains have also been identified in the pellets of the barn owl, the long-eared owl, and the great horned owl. No doubt other species of owls also capture and eat bog lemmings. T. W. Hoekstra found the skull of *Synaptomys* in the scat of an unidentified fox. Several specimens have been found dead along roads, where they may have been left by predators or struck by vehicles. A specimen was found in a window well on the Earlham College campus. Rufus Haymond confined a bog lemming with a short-tailed shrew, which killed and partially ate the vole.

TAXONOMY. *Synaptomys cooperi cooperi* Baird is found throughout most of Indiana, but specimens from along the Ohio River upstream to Clark County, from southwestern Indiana (Daviess and Pike counties), and from northwestern Indiana (Newton and Porter counties) approach *S. c. gossi* (Coues). The few specimens from west-central Indiana, however, seem nearer to *S. c. cooperi* in all characteristics except their wide incisors. Wetzel (1955) mapped western Indiana and the Ohio River valley as gradational areas, but he saw little Indiana material. Specimens from extreme southeastern Indiana (Jefferson County) are similar to *S. c. cooperi* rather than to *S. c. kentucki* Barbour.

SELECTED REFERENCES. Buckner, 1957; Burt, 1928; Connor, 1959; Fain, Whitaker, and Lukoschus, 1978; Howell, 1927; Linsdale, 1927; Stegeman, 1930; Wassel, Tieben, and Whitaker, 1978.

Family Muridae

Norway Rat
Rattus norvegicus (Berkenhout)

Brown Rat, Common Rat, House Rat,
Common House Rat

Mus decumanus: Plummer, 1844
Mus norvegicus: Elliott,1907
Epimys norvegicus: Evermann and Clark, 1920
Rattus norvegicus: Lyon, 1923

DESCRIPTION. The Norway rat is a relatively large, well-known rodent, but there appears to be considerable confusion in Indiana regarding its color variations and the separation of it from the woodrat (*Neotoma floridana*). The Norway rat usually has grayish upperparts, more or less grizzled with blackish. However, some individuals tend to be reddish or more brownish, and the amount of black varies. Certain specimens are completely blackish. The underparts are usually gray (sometimes buffy or whitish), and tend to be darkest in those animals with blackish upperparts. Plummer (1844) examined albinos from the Richmond (Wayne County)

Norway rat. Photo by Roger W. Barbour

area. The scaly tail is nearly naked and is almost as long as the head and body lengths combined. The ears and eyes are relatively small. The woodrat has large ears and eyes, a furred tail (gray above, white below), less coarse pelage, and its color is usually buffy gray or brownish above and white below. The skull of the Norway rat has three rows of cusps on the grinding surfaces of the cheek teeth, the woodrat has two rows.

Weights and measurements are shown in Table 149. The largest specimen we have seen was a captive male, originally trapped in the wild, that weighed 651 grams and measured 489 mm in total length when killed. (This individual is not included in the table, since it was kept in captivity.) The dental formula is

$$I \frac{1}{1} C \frac{0}{0} P \frac{0}{0} M \frac{3}{3} = 16.$$

STATUS AND DISTRIBUTION. It is interesting that little appears in the literature regarding the Norway rat in Indiana. Evidently it is not an animal that people are interested in, except for its destructive habits. Wied (1862) did not record the Norway rat at New Harmony (Posey County) during the winter of 1832–33. With reference to Wayne County, Plummer (1844) wrote the following: "This universally despised creature made its appearance here in 1835. White varieties of this rat have several times been brought to me as a new species; they have always proved to be albinos." Haymond (1870) wrote about the Norway rat in Franklin County: "The brown or Norway rat is here, as elsewhere, extremely numerous. It is one of the hardiest and most energetic animals, constantly increasing in numbers notwithstanding the utmost exertion of all its enemies, man inclusive. They first appeared in Brookville in the summer of 1827." According to E. J. Chansler, the Norway rat was said to have been first seen in Knox County in 1840 (Butler, 1895). Evermann and Butler (1894b) considered

Table 149

Weights and measurements of
Rattus norvegicus from Indiana

	Males	Females
Total length (mm)		
n	30	47
x̄	379.0	373.5
range	315-439	341-416
SD	30.5	20.2
SE	5.6	2.9
Tail length (mm)		
n	29	47
x̄	169.2	166.1
range	137-202	141-195
SD	16.0	14.3
SE	3.0	2.1
Hind foot (mm)		
n	29	47
x̄	39.4	39.1
range	32-48	33-45
SD	3.5	2.6
SE	0.7	0.4
Weight (grams)		
n	29	47
x̄	292.0	249.7
range	178.9-409.0	179.9-396.5
SD	59.8	71.4
SE	11.1	10.3

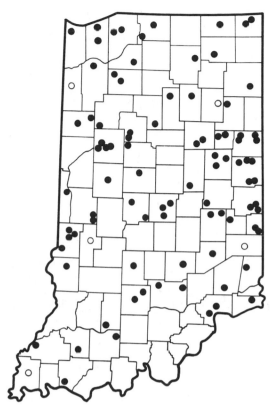

Map 47. The Norway Rat, *Rattus
norvegicus*, in Indiana

R. norvegicus "our common rat," but did not elaborate on its status or distribution. Hahn (1907a) found it "abundant about houses and farm buildings" in portions of the Kankakee River valley in 1905. In Monroe County, it was classed as "abundant" by McAtee in 1907. Evermann and Clark (1920) called it "all too common" at Lake Maxinkuckee (Marshall County). In the dunes of Porter County, Lyon (1923) neither saw nor captured any specimens during the fall of 1922. He wrote, "Residents say rats are sometimes found about the outbuildings of the store at Waverly Beach. As the region becomes more populated rats will probably form a constant part of the fauna." It had become a pest throughout St. Joseph County by 1933. Hahn (1909) and Lyon (1936) had little to say about it in Indiana and Lyon listed records for only 9 counties. The Norway rat is abundant throughout Indiana, but numerical data regarding populations are lacking. Specimens from 54 counties are in museums (Map 47).

We have found no information regarding the population of Norway rats in Indiana, but it is well known that rat control measures have been undertaken in various cities, about garbage dumps, at granaries and grain storage elevators, and at other sites. In earlier years, before sanitary land-fill methods were used to dispose of garbage, Norway rat populations at dumps increased rapidly and were periodically kept under control by poisoning. Local residents often visited the dumps to shoot rats, frequently killing dozens in a day. We have trapped 15 rats from a dump in several days and 21 from a grain elevator over a longer period. In both cases, many more rats were present but could not be trapped. We suspect that there are at least 2,000,000 rats in rural areas of Indiana. We have no data for nonrural areas. In several states, authors have estimated that one rat per person may be present.

HABITAT. *Rattus norvegicus* is usually associated with man and his activities. Thus, large populations of Norway rats are found in cities (in sewers, about garbage, and in trash dumps), about grain and other food storage facilities, and in and about farm buildings. Other colonies are formed in and about the borders of cultivated fields, along ditch banks, and in other areas some distance from human habitations. Probably such "feral" populations tend to be smaller than those associated with more abundant food, cover, and protection.

One colony in Cass County was situated along a shallow ditch bordering a cornfield; after the corn was picked, the rats evidently moved out to the ditch and excavated many burrows in the bluegrass sod along the fence. A summer colony was observed in Vigo County along a dike at the edge of a ditch. Extensive rural roadside garbage and rubbish dumps have been noted that were infested with Norway rats. Engels (1933) reported a colony established on an island in a lake at Notre Dame. Kirkpatrick and Conaway (1948) observed "field-living populations" of this rat "along fence rows and ditches" in various parts of Tippecanoe County during the fall and winter of 1946. Lindsay (1960) reported its living in corn shocks in southeastern Indiana.

HABITS. This rat is likely to be found living beneath buildings, especially grain storage bins (and corncribs), where it excavates extensive burrow systems and creates a maze of well-used runways. Runways are often along the base of the building walls, and when used enough are barren paths. Burrows usually have mounds of excavated earth at their entrances. Burrows are numerous when a thriving colony is extant. Corncribs are sometimes literally undermined with a network of burrows and tunnels. Burrows may be dug to a depth of 18 inches; they are usually 3 to 4 feet long, but may reach 6 feet in length.

The Norway rat is essentially nocturnal, but considerable activity also takes place during the day, particularly at dusk and dawn. We have trapped immatures in surface runways during the day; on that occasion (at the Jasper-Pulaski Fish and Wildlife Area), we were told by area personnel that each afternoon about four o'clock the rats could be seen running along the ground at the side of a building. Our animals were caught in snap traps set across the well used runs shortly before 4 P.M.

The tracks of this species can be found in the mud along streams and ditches. Evidently such movements are quite extensive; perhaps the waterways are used as travel lanes (and a source of food?). Dellinger (1951) captured Norway rats in muskrat traps set 2 inches below the surface of the water. He found *Rattus* using drainage tiles a mile from any buildings.

In addition to the burrows and runways, other obvious signs are left by populations of this rat. The animals do much gnawing, making holes in walls, at the corner of doors, in foundations, and in other wooden structures. They may enter buildings by enlarging holes through which pipes have been run. Where the animals are numerous, dark stains will be found about holes gnawed through the wood. Rats tend to strew garbage, food refuse, and other materials about, and the plentiful droppings are deposited anywhere except in the nest area.

Norway rats generally forage on the ground, but have been known to reach the upper floors (and attics) of buildings. They are good swimmers, which probably enables them to live and travel in sewers, sometimes even getting into the water lines. We have reports of rats surfacing inside toilet bowls in occupied houses. Adults are wary, and are often difficult to trap. The Norway rat is a hardy, adaptable, and aggressive species.

Nests are constructed in a variety of hidden sites, such as at the end of a ground burrow, in the hollow wall of a building, beneath a building or other large object, and in piles of rubbish, boxes, or other items offering suitable protection. Nests are not particularly well constructed and may consist of any soft materials, such as shredded vegetation, paper, cloth, or insulation materials.

This is a highly colonial species, with members of the colony at times exhibiting some type of cooperation, such as feeding together in numbers or driving strange rats away. The home range of an individual may be relatively small; David E. Davis found that in the city of Baltimore, Maryland, home ranges were about 150 feet in diameter. At times, Norway rats emigrate some distances.

In general, most of the habits (and feeding behavior) of this species are detrimental to man. About the only value derived from this common and widely despised pest is in the use of countless specimens of the laboratory white rat (a mutant) that has contributed so much to biological research throughout the world.

ASSOCIATED SPECIES. In many of the places where the Norway rat lives, its closest associate is probably the house mouse. Both have somewhat similar life styles. Old buildings occupied by rats may also house various bats (mainly the big brown bat and the little brown myotis). Populations of rats living in fields, along ditches, and in other areas more or less uninhabited by man are found with many other species of native mammals. Muskrats, minks, raccoons, and opossums are attracted to ditches and streamsides. In cultivated fields, the house mouse, deer mouse, voles, jumping mouse, ground squirrels, and eastern mole also live. In northeastern Indiana, the star-nosed mole also forages along streams and about the borders of lakes and marshes where Norway rats sometimes occur. Evidently the Norway rat is more aggressive than the black rat *(Rattus rattus)*. Plummer (1844) noted in Wayne County that "In a few years after the incursion of the brown or

Norway rat, the black rat became totally unknown." In Franklin County, Haymond (1870) noted that when the Norway rat appeared in 1827, the black rat "was numerous." He wrote, "it was, however, but a year or two after the Norway rat appeared, until they were all gone—all eaten up by this predatory stranger."

FOOD. There have been few studies of the stomach contents of Norway rats. The foods found in the stomachs of 115 rats from Indiana were summarized by Whitaker (1977). Most of these animals were collected on and around farms and grain storage areas, and this is reflected in the food habits data (Table 150). The major food was grain (mostly wheat), which made up about 40 percent of the volume, followed by corn (20 percent volume). When the amounts of sorghum and soybean were added to the wheat and corn, cultivated crops constituted 62 percent of the volume of identified foods. It should be mentioned that this was processed grain, not that left in the field after harvesting. Most other food items were of plant origin. The

Table 150

Foods eaten by *Rattus norvegicus* (n = 115) from Indiana
(from Whitaker, 1977)

Food Item	Percent Volume	Percent Frequency
Grain seeds (mostly wheat)	39.7	46.1
Corn	20.2	27.8
Flesh	6.3	10.4
Green Vegetation	5.3	12.2
Mast	5.0	6.1
Unidentified material	5.0	2.6
Miscellaneous vegetation	4.8	12.2
Trifolium (clover) flowers	3.9	8.7
Garbage	3.2	5.2
Grass seeds	2.1	3.5
Unidentified seeds	1.2	1.7
Sorghum seeds	1.1	1.7
Soybean seeds	1.1	1.7
Muscoidea	0.6	1.7
Dipterous larvae	0.2	3.5
Coleoptera	0.1	2.6
Formicidae (ant)	0.1	2.6
Annelida (earthworm)	0.1	0.9
Insect	0.1	3.5
Coleopterous larvae	0.1	2.6
Adult Lepidoptera	0.1	0.9
	100.3	

volume of animal material (mostly flesh) was 7.7 percent. Garbage made up 3.2 percent of the total volume, but some other materials (particularly flesh and unidentified items) may also have been garbage.

In addition to the foods listed in the table, one stomach each contained the following: unidentified insect larvae, moth pupae, Hemiptera, pigweed seeds, feathers, leaf-hoppers, harvestmen, Cryptophagidae (Coleoptera), Diptera.

We have made some calculations with regard to the amount of food that Norway rats might consume throughout rural Indiana in a year. There are about 75,000 major farms and approximately 770 granaries in the state. We estimate that perhaps 25 rats occur per farm and about 80 per granary (these figures may be low). If each rat eats about 15 grams of food (60 percent of which is grain) per day, in a year about 7,000 tons of grain would be consumed by this species in Indiana.

In addition to direct food consumption, Norway rats despoil and contaminate food-stuffs and grain and cause other types of damage. For example, they chew or destroy stored clothing, furs, carpeting, leather goods, meats, foodstuffs, and other items. Gnawing on wires increases the fire hazard, and the gnawing of lead water pipes may affect water systems. The rats also destroy insulation. In dwellings, the woodwork, doors, floors, and other wooden parts may be damaged by gnawing activities.

REPRODUCTION. Although *R. norvegicus* has long been a numerous species, there is very little published information concerning its reproduction in Indiana. Lindsay (1958) examined a female with 11 embryos. Reproductive data for 143 Indiana-taken Norway rats (many from Lawrence and Vigo counties) are presented in Table 151. Of these, 48 were adult females and 29 were adult males. Most of the females were taken in April, June, and August; nearly half of the males were taken in April. The reputedly high reproductive rate of the species is borne out by our sample: 12 of the females were gravid and 30 had placental scars; 2 individuals had both placental scars and embryos. One female contained 17 embryos, 8 of which were being resorbed. Another specimen was so badly damaged that a complete embryo count could not be made. The 10 remaining gravid females averaged 8.3 embryos each, as follows: 1 had 5 embryos; 2 had 7; 3 had 8; 1 had 9; 2 had 10; 1 had 11.

From 4 to 12 (average 7.4) placental scars were counted in 19 female Norway rats. However, 10 individuals exhibited a larger number of scars: 2 had 14, 2 had 27, 1 each had 23, 24, 26, 29, and 39. We do not know how long placental scars persist in Norway rats, but in *Microtus* scars are not visible after 40 to 44 days (Corthum, 1967). Evidently placental scars in this rat are retained for a much longer time. To determine how long placental scars persist in this species, albino Norway rats were kept in captivity after giving birth and were sacrificed after 30, 40, 50, 60, 80, and 100 days. Placental scars had become smaller after 80 days, but were still clearly

Table 151

Reproductive data from *Rattus norvegicus* from Indiana

Month	Adult Females			Adult Males		
	Number examined	Number pregnant	No. with placental scars	Number examined	Testis size (mm) Average Length	Width
Feb.	4	0	2	1	20.0	10.0
March	1	0	0	1	19.0	11.0
April	10	2	9	13	19.4	10.0
May	1	1	0	2	18.0	14.5
June	16	3	10	4	19.7	12.3
July	5	3	2	2	20.0	12.0
August	8	2	4	6	19.2	11.6
Sept.	2	1	1	0	—	—
Oct.	1	0	1	0	—	—

evident and black even after 100 days. Davis and Emlen (1948) found that the scars persisted at least a year in this species. We thus assume that the larger numbers of scars in the wild rat sample above may represent from two to four litters, possibly produced in rapid succession.

Gravid females were examined from April through September, but few specimens were available for some of these months and none were taken in November, December, or January. Aside from the above study we can find practically nothing from Indiana regarding breeding in *Rattus norvegicus*. A female taken in Boone County on 28 February contained 5 embryos measuring 35 mm in crown-rump length.

In our sample, 66 of the 143 specimens were juveniles. Although few specimens were taken in some months, juveniles were present much of the year. There may be a brief midwinter cessation in breeding, for the 5 specimens taken in February were all adults. Two females taken in February still had placental scars, but we do not know whether these represent midwinter litters or simply prolonged retention of scars. The fact that one female contained 39 placental scars indicates that four separate litters were probably represented. Since the gestation period of *R. norvegicus* is about 21 days, 63 days would be required from the birth of the first litter to enable a female to accumulate three additional sets of scars (from three more litters). The two females with placental scars taken on 11 February, then, could indicate that young were produced about 8 December.

One female, evidently near term, contained 6 embryos, measuring 60, 61, 62, 63, 66, and 66 mm in total length. An additional embryo was being resorbed. These same young had tail lengths from 13 to 16 mm and hind foot lengths of 7 to 8 mm. Probably newborn young are near the size of members of this litter.

The 29 adult males taken from February through August had testes averaging about 20 mm in length throughout this period. We have examined a male taken on 22 December that had testes 22 mm long. More data are required on testis development of males in other months of the year.

Our data do indicate, however, that the re-

productive rate of the Norway rat in Indiana is high, with breeding probably occurring throughout most of the year. Given suitable conditions, this rat can quickly reach a high population level.

PARASITES. Whitaker (1977) reported on the ectoparasites of 146 Norway rats taken in Indiana (Table 152). The most abundant parasite was a sucking louse (*Polyplax spinulosa*), found on 48 percent of the specimens. The two next most common species (both probably parasitic) were a laelapid mite (*Androlaelaps fahrenholzi*) and a myobiid mite (*Radfordia ensifera*), in that order. Another numerous species, probably nonparasitic, was a mite of the genus *Trichouropoda*; it evidently represents a species similar to *T. orbicularis*. Fleas were not found on the rats examined. A single chigger (*Eutrombicula alfreddugesi*) and only two ticks (*Dermacentor variabilis*) were recorded. A surprising facet of this study is that the rats examined harbored relatively few ectoparasites, except for sucking lice. Only 86 of the 146 specimens harbored ectoparasites or other associates of any kind.

A fairly large number of parasites and other associates was taken, although not all have been identified to species, and many were not parasites. Parasitic species consisted of 1 louse, 11 mites, and a tick. Many of the taxa taken in low numbers must be considered as stragglers or accidentals, presumably having wandered onto the rats either before or after death. A few types such as *Trichouropoda* sp. and the species of *Macrocheles* and *Pygmephorus* appear to be regular, though not abundant, associates. The latter two of these apparently have phoretic relationships with the rats.

The two most common species of mites on rats from Indiana were *Androlaelaps fahrenholzi* and *Radfordia ensifera*. *Androlaelaps fahrenholzi* is a common mite on many species of mammals. It seems peculiar that it was not reported on rats from Louisville, Kentucky (Goode and Kotcher, 1949), since it is large and easily seen. *Radfordia ensifera*, a myobiid mite, is small and easily overlooked. One needs to use a dissecting microscope to examine the hair and skin of the hosts while brushing the hair back with dissecting needles to find mites of this species. We suspect

Table 152

Ectoparasites and other associates of *Rattus norvegicus* (n = 146) from Indiana

Parasites	Parasites		Hosts Parasitized	
	Total	Average	Total	Percent
Sucking Lice (Anoplura)				
Polyplax spinulosa	2,056	14.08	70	47.9
Mites (Acarina) other than chiggers				
Androlaelaps fahrenholzi	212	1.45	44	30.1
Radfordia ensifera	69	0.47	17	11.6
Trichouropoda sp.				
near *orbicularis*	40	0.27	16	11.0
Pygmephorus whitakeri	24	0.16	1	0.7
Proctolaelaps hypudaei	23	0.16	6	4.1
Hypoaspis sp.	21	0.14	6	4.1
Anoetidae	18	0.12	9	6.2
Androlaelaps casalis	18	0.12	15	10.3
Tyroglyphidae	13	0.09	5	3.4
Chortoglyphidae	11	0.08	8	5.5
Ornithonyssus bacoti	8	0.05	4	2.7
Macrocheles merdarius	6	0.04	3	2.1
Pygmephorus designatus	5	0.03	1	0.7
Ornithonyssus sylviarum	4	0.03	4	2.7
Zibethacarus ondatrae	4	0.03	1	0.7
Euryparasitus sp.	4	0.03	3	2.1
Macrocheles mammifer	3	0.02	3	2.1
Phytoseiidae	3	0.02	3	2.1
Hypoaspis lubrica	3	0.02	2	1.4
Androlaelaps morlani	1	0.01	1	0.7
Hirstionyssus butantanensis	1	0.01	1	0.7
Androlaelaps sp.	1	0.01	1	0.7
Glycyphagidae (adult)	1	0.01	1	0.7
Pygmephorus scalopi	1	0.01	1	0.7
Pygmephorus mahunkai	1	0.01	1	0.7
Cheyletus eruditus	1	0.01	1	0.7
Macrocheles sp.	1	0.01	1	0.7
Chigger Mites (Trombiculidae)				
Eutrombicula alfreddugesi	1	0.01	1	0.7
Ticks (Ixodides)				
Dermacentor variabilis	2	0.01	1	0.7

that it was simply overlooked in the Louisville studies, especially since few other small mites were taken in numbers in that study.

Data from Indiana rats (mostly from central Indiana) can be compared to Goode and Kotcher's data from Louisville, just across the Ohio River from southern Indiana. The louse *Polyplax spinulosa* was the most common parasite taken during both studies. The percentage of hosts parasitized was lower in Indiana, but the overall average number per host was higher. However, there the similarity ended; of the four most abundant mites and fleas of rats from Louisville (the fleas

Nosopsyllus fasciatus and *Xenopsylla cheopis* and the mites *Ornithonyssus bacoti* and *Laelaps echidnina*), three were not found at all on Indiana rats, whereas *Ornithonyssus bacoti*, was found in low numbers (0.05 per rat, and on 2.7 percent of the Indiana rats). This is a common mite on the house mouse in Indiana (Clark, 1971; Whitaker, 1970b), but is much less common on *Rattus* in Indiana or in Louisville (0.43 per rat, and on 10.5 percent of the Kentucky rats). It is not clear why rat fleas were not found on Indiana rats; perhaps these fleas are more common in the south. It would be instructive to search for this flea on rats from extreme southern Indiana. Perhaps rat fleas tend to move off the dead host faster than other fleas, but this seems unlikely; some fleas would surely have been taken if they were common on central Indiana rats.

Other authors have reported ectoparasites of Indiana *R. norvegicus*. Wilson (1961) examined 69 specimens for fleas, ticks, and sucking lice. He reported 292 lice *(Polyplax spinulosa)* on this species from Lagrange, Marion, and Tippecanoe counties, 2 ticks *(Dermacentor variabilis)*, and 4 fleas *(Ctenopthalmus pseudagyrtes, 1; Orchopeas howardii, 1; O. leucopus, 2)*. However, 44 of the lice were from laboratory rats (Marion County) rather than from wild individuals. Cable (1943) and Wallace (1925) reported the fleas *Ctenocephalides felis, Xenopsylla cheopis,* and *Nosopsyllus fasciatus* from Marion County.

The two latter species are typically found on Norway rats. Some of the ectoparasites and associates found on *R. norvegicus* in other parts of the country were not taken (or occurred in low numbers) in the study by Whitaker (1977). Such forms among the mites were *Alliea laruei, Liponyssoides sanguineus, Eulaelaps stabularis, Laelaps echidnina,* and *Laelaps nuttalli*. The latter two species are very common parasites of *Rattus norvegicus* in many localities, yet none were found in Indiana. *Laelaps echidnina* was recorded in 25 separate papers from North American localities (Whitaker and Wilson, 1974); most of these records were from southern states and a few were from northeast seacoast states. However, *L. echidnina* is found on Norway rats in Ohio (Masters, 1960) and in Quebec (Firlotte, 1948). Rats from Providence, Rhode Island, were examined and 21 percent were found to be infested with *L. echidnina*. Large numbers of this species were found on *R. norvegicus* from New Jersey (Thomas, 1956). No difference was discerned in abundance on old versus young rats, but average numbers per rat were much higher in warmer months than in colder months. Sixty-nine mites of this species were included among 3,473 ectoparasites from 392 live-trapped Norway rats from Louisville, Kentucky (Goode and Kotcher, 1949). All of the 12 reports of *L. nuttalli* are for southern states.

Internal parasites have been collected from a sample of 145 Norway rats collected in Indiana. Of this sample, 74 rats were infected with nematodes and 29 with cestodes. None of the 2,045 nematodes (27.6 per infected host) or 269 cestodes (9.3 per infected host) have been identified to species.

DECIMATING FACTORS. Norway rat remains have been identified in the pellets of the barn owl and the great horned owl (Kirkpatrick and Conaway, 1947). No doubt other avian predators prey on this species. Dogs and domestic cats are known predators and perhaps are the most important in Indiana, because most rat populations are in proximity to man and his pets. A badger taken in Wayne County had the remains of a *Rattus norvegicus* in its digestive tract. We have found this rat in one stomach of the gray fox. Minton (1944) observed a black rat snake capture a Norway rat in a building. Man is certainly the worst enemy of this rat, and constant poisoning campaigns have been waged in attempts to keep it under control. Immediately after the harvesting of grain crops in the fall, an increase in the numbers of rats killed on roads by motor vehicles is noticed; evidently the animals are forced to find new living quarters and their movements take them across various types of roadways.

George Dellinger wrote the following account of rat eradication on the farm.

The most satisfactory method of reducing rat populations on farms is by the trap, water and club. These were always my Dad's favorites. Once each year, following the rainy season when hundreds of rats would be driven into the buildings from brush piles and other outlying natural shelters, my father would declare an anti-rat week. In this, he and we four boys, moved all the sacked feed and bales, gassed the corn crib with $C + C_o$, and drowned out all the subterranean runways killing every rat as it was exposed. Few ever escaped and those which did must have moved out as several months would pass before we would see any renewed rat activity.

TAXONOMY. *Rattus norvegicus norvegicus* (Berkenhout) is probably the subspecies found in Indiana.

SELECTED REFERENCES. Clark, 1971; Davis, 1953; Davis and Emlen, 1948; Davis, Emlen, and Stokes, 1948; Hamilton, 1947; Perry, 1944; Pisano and Storer, 1948; Silver, 1927; Whitaker, 1977.

House Mouse
Mus musculus Linnaeus

Common Mouse, Domestic Mouse

Hesperomys indianus: Wied, 1862
Mus musculus: Plummer, 1844

DESCRIPTION. The house mouse is a grayish, medium-sized, long-tailed, long-eared mouse with a nearly naked tail. This mouse tends to be much the same color above and below, but there are many variations and numerous individuals are paler on the underside than above. In Indiana, the house mouse is most likely to be confused with the white-footed mouse, the deer mouse, or the western harvest mouse. Normally all three latter species have a white or whitish belly, rather than grayish, and all have more hair on the tail than the house mouse has. The house mouse can also be separated from those listed above by its three rows of cusps on the grinding surfaces of the molariform teeth, rather than two rows (see Fig. 27). The harvest mouse has deeply grooved upper incisors. *Mus* has anal scent glands which secrete a characteristic musky odor easily detected by the human nose.

We have noted some variations in color among house mice from Indiana. A few taken in Jackson County had whitish to pale buff bellies. A specimen from Vermillion County is a tan or blond individual. Many house mice tend to be grayish brown, rather than grayish, and we have noted a few with nearly black upperparts. The familiar laboratory white mouse is an albinistic strain of the house mouse, but we have had no records of complete wild albinos in the state. McAtee (1907) collected a house mouse that "had a well marked gray spot on the forehead," and we have examined a specimen with a white forehead spot. We have seen one specimen with the terminal 5 mm of its tail white. Brechner and Kirkpatrick (1970) reported on molt in Indiana *Mus*.

Weights and measurements are shown in Table 153. The dental formula is

$$I \frac{1}{1} C \frac{0}{0} P \frac{0}{0} M \frac{3}{3} = 16.$$

STATUS AND DISTRIBUTION. Although Wied (1862) did not mention the house

House mouse. Photo by Whitaker

Table 153
Weights and measurements of *Mus musculus* from Indiana

	Males	Females
Total length (mm)		
n	171	147
x̄	158.4	161
range	133-188	143-192
SD	10.6	11.6
SE	0.8	0.9
Tail length (mm)		
n	171	147
x̄	75.2	74.8
range	63-89	58-92
SD	5.5	8.2
SE	0.4	0.6
Hind foot (mm)		
n	171	174
x̄	16.9	16.8
range	15.0-19.5	15-20
SD	0.8	0.8
SE	0.06	0.06
Weight (grams)		
n	170	144
x̄	16.8	18
range	13-25	13.0-27.6
SD	2.9	3.5
SE	0.2	0.3

mouse from New Harmony (Posey County), where he visited during the winter of 1832–33, he later described a new species, *Hesperomys indianus* (= *Mus musculus*), from specimens evidently obtained there at that time (Hatt, 1930). The specimen, later identified as that of a house mouse, is evidently the one now in the American Museum of Natural History (No. 575). There is no record of when this mouse was introduced into Indiana, but it may have arrived about the time of the first white settlers. Plummer (1844) knew of it in Wayne County and wrote, "This little animal still maintains its possession of our dwellings, but its numbers have evidently been diminished since the introduction of the brown rat" (*Rattus norvegicus*). Haymond (1870) described the status of *Mus* in Franklin County by stating that it was "common everywhere." It had not yet been identified from Randolph County by Cox (1893). Evermann and Butler (1894b) simply wrote, "Our common species. Introduced—cannot learn the date of its introduction." McAtee (1907) classified it as abundant in the Bloomington (Monroe County) area.

Hahn (1909) was of the opinion that the house mouse was found "in almost every house and barn in the State" and in fields. *Mus musculus* was "all too common" at Lake Maxinkuckee (Marshall County), according to Evermann and Clark (1920). In 1922, Lyon (1923) did not find many house mice in the dunes region of Porter County. He wrote, "In spite of the large number of week-end visitors to the dunes who leave much food scattered about, and the numerous cottages toward Waverly Beach the house mouse does not appear to be common in the region. . . . W. D. Richardson states that the only mice he has observed in his cottage are deer mice." Engels (1933) found house mice "very common in buildings" in St. Joseph County, and he noted, "In the fields west of the Notre Dame Stadium they are much more common than the native mice." Lyon (1936) makes no mention of the status of *Mus* in Indiana; he mapped records from only 8 counties. Lindsay (1960) considered the house mouse a "common nuisance" in the section of southeastern Indiana where he worked.

Population data on Indiana *Mus musculus* were gathered by Barrett and Darnell (1967), who sampled a 22.5-acre red clover field near Princeton (Gibson County) in July and August 1962. On three grids totaling 7.92 acres in this field, 83 house mice were trapped and released during the week of 24 to 30 July. In addition, 16 prairie voles and 24 deer mice were captured at the same time, but *Mus* constituted approximately 68 percent of the total combined population of these three species. Data on numbers of house mice taken per 100 trap-nights for various habitats in Vigo County are shown in Table 154. Today, *Mus musculus* is probably the most common species of mammal in Indiana and is found throughout the state. We have examined specimens from 84 counties (Map 48).

In Vigo County, *Mus* populations were highest in late summer and fall and lowest in early spring. This conclusion is based on data from all habitats combined, including those (weedy and grassy fields) that remain throughout the year. Lack of breeding in winter and small litter size in early spring af-

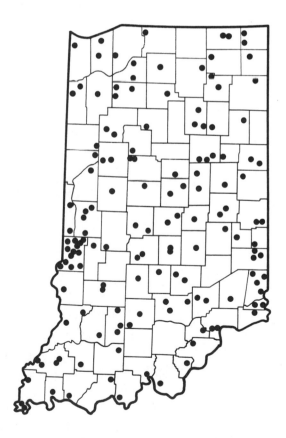

Map 48.   The House Mouse, *Mus musculus*, in Indiana

fected populations. The numbers of *Mus* taken in its eight major habitats (as shown in Table 154) for two-month periods throughout the year are shown in Table 155 (weedy and grassy fields have been combined). The ephemeral nature of some of the habitats is apparent. Some plots were trapped only from March through June; most of the cultivated fields were trapped in late summer and fall.

HABITAT. Most authors writing about the house mouse in Indiana have mentioned its occurrence in buildings, but as early as 1907 Hahn noted that *Mus* was found "in the fields as well as in buildings" along the Kankakee River, and McAtee (1907) observed that this mouse inhabited fields near Bloomington. It is certainly a common species about rural, suburban, or city buildings and about garbage dumps and other debris-laden habitats. But the house mouse is also a common animal in fields and other open areas a mile or more from buildings. That it inhabits such diverse habitats reflects the adaptability of this non-native mammal.

Away from buildings, the house mouse is primarily a species of cultivated fields where adequate cover exists. In Indiana, it is abundant in cornfields with much grassy and

weedy vegetation in and between the rows. It perhaps reaches its greatest abundance in winter wheat fields or in wheat fields in the spring and early summer after the wheat has formed dense cover. The house mouse also may be abundant after the wheat has been harvested and the succeeding crop (usually clover or alfalfa) has again formed dense vegetation. The species is also sometimes abundant in fields allowed to lie fallow for one to two years, especially if dense stands of foxtail, pigweed, and other weeds are present. *Mus* takes advantage of the early successional stages of vegetation associated with farming operations where there is good ground cover. It is essentially an opportunistic migrant, moving into an area when short-term, dense vegetation occurs, but disappearing when the vegetation is removed. It finds agricultural lands where crops are grown in a relatively short time then harvested an ideal habitat.

Data on this species in various habitats in Vigo County, based on a random trapping program (25 × 25-meter plots, 25 traps per plot), are shown in Table 154. It is apparent that the house mouse abounds in cultivated fields. Habitats with woody vegetation were

Table 154

House mice taken in random plots in various habitats in Vigo County, Indiana (from Whitaker, 1967a)

	Number of plots	Trap-nights	Number of *Mus* taken	Number per 100 trap-nights
Winter wheat	9	675	42	6.22
Corn	38	2,850	˙139	4.88
Grassy field	33	2,475	74	2.99
Wheat stubble	37	2,775	82	2.95
Weedy field	29	2,175	63	2.90
Corn stubble	50	3,750	78	2.08
Soybeans	16	1,200	25	2.08
Misc. cultivated fields	22	1,650	33	2.00
River-bottom woods	15	1,125	2	0.18
Brushy field	23	1,725	2	0.12
Plowed field	48	3,600	1	0.03
Upland woods	54	4,050	0	0
Brush	16	1,200	0	0
Pasture	17	1,275	0	0
Soybean stubble	22	1,650		
	429	32,175	541	

avoided, only four animals being taken in 108 such plots, two each in river-bottom woods and two in brushy field. Six of the eight habitats in which this species thrived were cultivated annually. One of the remaining two habitats (weedy field) was most often in an early seral stage, just after the field had been cultivated. Only grassy field, the poorest of the habitats for the species in terms of abundance, represented a later seral stage.

Among the eight habitats in which *Mus* was important, there were 54 plots with good, 126 with fair, and 54 plots with poor cover. These plots yielded 223, 279, and 34 house mice (5.51, 2.95, and 0.84 per 100 trap-nights) respectively. Thus, significantly fewer mice were taken in areas with less ground cover ($X^2 = 86.31$, 2 df). This relationship explains the lack of house mice in one cultivated habitat (soybean stubble). In most cases, when soybeans were harvested, practically no stubble was left. In corn and wheat stubble, much herbaceous vegetation was left in some fields and very little in others. Stubble fields with much ground vegetation supported the house mouse.

In the only two noncultivated habitats which the species regularly occupied (weedy field and grassy field) populations were highest from November through February and lowest from March through August (Table 155). All other habitats in which *Mus* was found were cultivated and therefore temporary. Winter wheat was present only from March to June, but harbored high *Mus* populations during that time. This high population continued through the September-October period in wheat stubble, where *Mus* fed on the abundant wheat seeds on the ground. Corn was important as a habitat from July to December. *Mus* remained at a relatively constant population level in corn stubble from November through April, or during the period when this habitat was present. *Mus* was abundant in sorghum fields, which matured in July and August. Since all cultivated habitats were temporary, and since no house mice were taken in plowed fields, it follows that the species moved away from these areas when they were plowed. It is thought by some workers that many house mice enter houses and other buildings in the fall (Schwarz and Schwarz, 1943). This is cer-

tainly true, as evidenced by the invasions of house mice into rural houses in Vigo County. However, not all house mice enter buildings, and populations occur where there are no buildings for some distance. The great fall increase in *Mus* populations in weedy fields and grassy fields is undoubtedly a result of movement. Many animals remain in cornfields after the harvest, but only if ample litter or herbaceous vegetation covers the ground. Probably the majority of the house mice present at harvest time remain in the same area if adequate ground cover exists; if not, the animals move to areas with such cover.

There were 212 plots with dry soil in which 473 mice (2.97 per 100 trap-nights) were taken, and 20 plots with moist soil in which 63 mice (4.20 per 100 trap-nights) were taken. All the plots with moist soil were in weedy and grassy fields. It is not known whether the high mouse populations there were directly due to the soil moisture or to the increased cover, which was probably influenced by moisture.

Specific trap sites where house mice have been captured around the state, as noted on specimen labels, are buildings (including a greenhouse), brush about farm buildings, corn crib, fencerows, apple orchard, brush pile in field, along railroad right-of-ways (often a good trapping site), clover field, alfalfa field, grassy border of cornfield, edge of stubble field, ditch along border of hayfield, fallow field, dense weeds at pond border, low grassy area near river, marsh border, grassy field, pine plantation, gravel pit.

ASSOCIATED SPECIES. The house mouse most often occurs with the deer mouse, the prairie vole, the meadow vole (sometimes), and the harvest mouse (in northwestern Indiana). In cultivated fields which are plowed annually for crops, such as corn and wheat, the house mouse is found where ground cover is adequate, and the deer mouse is its counterpart where there is less ground cover. However, the two species overlap broadly. The house mouse is able to take advantage of early plant succession and quickly forms large populations in such habitats. If the ground cover in these areas remains adequate over longer periods of time, the prairie vole and / or the meadow vole tend to replace the

Table 155

Numbers of House Mice taken during Vigo County random trapping program, by season and habitat in eight habitats (weedy and grassy fields here combined) in which *Mus* was abundant (TN = trap-nights) (from Whitaker, 1967a)

	Jan. Feb.	March April	May June	July Aug.	Sept. Oct.	Nov. Dec.
Winter wheat						
Trap-nights	0	375	300	0	0	0
Mus		25	17			
No./ 100 TN		6.67	5.67			
Corn						
Trap-nights	225	150	0	975	1,050	450
Mus	6	0		32	72	29
No. / 100 TN	2.67			3.28	6.86	6.44
Wheat Stubble						
Trap-nights	450	525	75	525	675	525
Mus	13	3	4	36	25	1
No. / 100 TN	2.89	0.57	5.33	6.86	3.70	0.19
Weedy Fields & Grassy Fields						
Trap-nights	900	900	825	450	600	975
Mus	28	0	8	3	21	77
No. / 100 TN	3.11		0.97	0.67	3.50	7.90
Corn Stubble						
Trap-nights	1,275	1,725	75	0	150	525
Mus	29	33	0		3	13
No. / 100 TN	2.27	1.91			2.00	2.48
Soybeans						
Trap-nights	150	225	0	375	300	150
Mus	8	0		8	6	3
No. / 100 TN	5.33			2.13	2.00	2.00
Misc. cultivated fields						
Trap-nights	75	300	225	150	525	375
Mus	0	3	5	10	14	1
No. / 100 TN		1.00	2.22	6.67	2.67	0.27
Totals						
Trap-nights	3,075	4,200	1,500	2,475	3,300	3,000
Mus	84	64	34	89	141	124
No. / 100 TN	2.73	1.52	2.27	3.60	4.27	4.13

house mouse as the dominant species. Again, from early to late plant successional stages, there is considerable overlap among these species.

Whitaker (1967a) examined the interrelationships between *Mus* and other small mammalian associates. It appeared that the white-footed mouse inhibited populations of *Mus* when the two occurred together. It is possible that this factor helps limit *Mus* to cultivated areas, where *Peromyscus leucopus* does not flourish.

The major associate of *Mus* in Indiana is the deer mouse, *Peromyscus maniculatus*.

The house mouse moves about in search of habitats containing adequate amounts of herbaceous ground cover, while the deer mouse is relatively sedentary, uses the soil as its principal cover, and remains in cultivated fields throughout the agricultural cycle. *Mus* and *P. maniculatus* react to one another in different ways in different habitats. In grassy and weedy fields the two occurred together about as often as would be expected by chance, and both species were more abundant when together than when alone. This was apparently related to the excellent, but short-term, conditions of those habitats. Both species were able to reach large population size quickly, the deer mouse by being there in the beginning and the house mouse by immigration and a rapid reproductive rate. However, in longer lasting cultivated habitats, such as corn, corn stubble, and soybeans, the two occurred together less often than would be expected by chance, and both were less abundant when together than when alone. It appeared that in this latter situation, both ecological separation and competitive exclusion were acting. In wheat stubble, the deer mouse occurred at higher rates and the house mouse at lower rates when the two were together than when alone. This is probably because *Mus* had to invade and compete with the already established *P. maniculatus* in a habitat often marginal for *Mus* because of the lack of ground cover.

The house mouse and the prairie vole occurred together in weedy and grassy fields about as often as expected, and *Mus* was unaffected or occurred in greater numbers with *Microtus ochrogaster* than when alone, indicating no detrimental effects. The two probably occupied essentially separate niches in these habitats.

HABITS. The house mouse is mostly nocturnal, although we have trapped specimens in fields during the daytime. One was trapped between 1:30 and 5:20 P.M. on 19 September, and two were trapped on 27 December between 12:30 and 2 P.M. on a clear, sunny, calm, relatively warm day. The house mouse moves about on the ground under the herbaceous cover of cultivated fields, feeding on grain, weed seeds, and insects. It usually does not make conspicuous runways, but does make extensive use of the runs of voles and other small mammals. It is a good climber, jumper, and swimmer. In buildings, house mice easily reach upper floors. Young may forage together, for we once captured two in a snap-trap at the same time in an old garden.

Seasonal movements of *Mus* have been mentioned in our discussion of habitat, although we have no data on distances involved. House mice invade all types of buildings in the fall and early winter, often entering occupied human dwellings. Since many house mice also remain during the winter, it appears that some of the movement into

buildings is in response to lack of cover in surrounding areas. Once inside buildings, the mice are likely to do extensive gnawing of paper, cardboard, clothing, or other materials, consume and despoil various stored foods, leave much litter about, and deposit feces and urine in abundance. Also, the characteristic odor of this mouse frequently pervades the atmosphere of buildings where large populations assemble. *Mus* is difficult to exclude from buildings, for it can enter very small openings, and it can sometimes be difficult to control.

There is practically nothing in the literature on Indiana mammals concerning the habits of the house mouse. Nests are found in underground burrows, in rubbish, or in buildings, and are usually loose, rather globular masses of grasses, to which have been added feathers, mammal hair, shredded paper, cloth, or other soft materials.

The usual sound made by the house mouse is a short, high-pitched squeak. On the night of 8 July 1958, Mumford and Nixon A. Wilson were setting mousetraps in an abandoned barn. They became aware of a faint, whimpering sound, which was finally traced to a house mouse running about along the walls of the building. Perhaps this vocalization is the basis for published reports of "singing" house mice. Young house mice raised by McAtee became perfectly tame and fearless.

FOOD. Whitaker (1966) examined the stomachs of 478 house mice from Indiana (Table 156) and found seeds of foxtail grass *(Setaria)* to be the most important food (20.2 percent of the food by volume and appearing in 25.3 percent of the stomachs). Various seeds, especially those of grasses (excluding cultivated species), collectively made up 42 percent of the diet. Seeds of cultivated plants—corn, wheat, sorghum, and soybeans—constituted 22.9 percent. Of the animal foods, lepidopterous larvae were a major item, accounting for 15 percent of all food in the stomachs. These larvae, the second most important food, occurred in nearly 45 percent of the stomachs. Animal foods constituted 24.1 percent of all foods. Miscellaneous vegetation, consisting of roots, stems, leaves, and other plant parts, accounted for about 10 percent of the material. The fungus *Endogone* was a relatively minor food.

Table 156

Foods eaten by *Mus musculus* (n = 478)
from Vigo County
(from Whitaker, 1966)

Food Item	Percent Volume	Percent Frequency
Setaria (foxtail grass) seeds	20.2	25.3
Lepidopterous larvae, pupae	14.6	43.7
Corn	13.0	16.3
Miscellaneous vegetation	8.4	20.3
Wheat seeds	7.4	10.5
Panicum (witch grass) seeds	3.7	4.2
Digitaria (crabgrass) seeds	3.5	4.6
Ambrosia trifida (giant ragweed) seeds	2.8	3.6
Coleopterous larvae	2.1	3.8
Seeds	2.1	4.6
Endogone	2.0	6.3
Green vegetation	2.0	4.8
Echinochloa (barnyard grass) seeds	1.8	3.6
Sorghum halepense (Johnson grass) seeds	1.7	4.2
Coleoptera	1.6	3.8
Cultivated Sorghum seeds	1.6	1.7
Polygonum (knotweed) seeds	1.4	1.9
Bromus (brome grass) seeds	1.3	1.5
Erigeron (fleabane) seeds	1.1	1.5
Animal material	1.0	5.2
Soybeans	0.9	1.7
Hemiptera	0.9	1.9
Chilopoda (centipedes)	0.7	1.9
Formicidae (ant)	0.6	1.3
Annelida (earthworm)	0.5	1.3
Limacidae (slugs)	0.5	1.0
Elymus seeds	0.5	0.6
Enchytraeidae (enchytraeid worms)	0.4	0.4
Flesh (mouse, bird)	0.3	0.8
Corn stamens	0.2	0.4
Scarabaeidae (scarab beetle)	0.2	0.4
Araneae (spider)	0.2	0.8
Hymenoptera	0.2	0.2
Amaranthus (amaranth pigweed) seeds	0.2	0.2
Carabidae (ground beetle)	0.1	0.4
Dipterous larvae	0.1	1.9
Potentilla (cinquefoil) seeds	0.1	0.2
Diptera	0.1	0.4
Rumex (dock) seeds	trace	0.2
Moss	trace	0.2
Acrididae (grasshoppers)	trace	0.2
Nematoda (nematodes)	trace	0.2
Chenopodium (pigweed) seeds	trace	0.2
Collembola (springtails)	trace	0.2
Fungus	trace	0.2

Foods of *Mus* in major habitats are summarized in Table 157. Important foods in soybean fields were foxtail seeds, lepidopterous larvae, and Johnson grass seeds. Soybeans made up only 3.5 percent of the volume for the house mouse, while soybeans were the major food for the deer mouse in this habitat. In wheat fields, lepidopterous larvae and wheat seeds were the major foods of *Mus*, and in sorghum fields, the major food was sorghum seeds. In corn or wheat stubble, food habits of the house mouse and the deer mouse were rather similar, with the cultivated grain being most important, followed by lepidopterous larvae.

In weedy fields, the most important foods of *Mus* were seeds of giant foxtail and giant ragweed, both characteristic of this habitat. In grassy fields, tumble-grass *(Panicum)* seeds were of greatest importance, followed closely by foxtail seeds.

Food habits of the house mouse also changed with the season, but these changes were much influenced by seasonal farming practices. One strictly winter food of *Mus* was *Panicum* (13 percent). Cultivated sorghum seeds (9.2 percent) were eaten only in fall, and Johnson grass occurred in stomachs only in summer and fall.

Corn is available in Indiana fields throughout the year, at least to a degree, but is particularly important in winter, after it has matured and been harvested. At that time there is much loose corn and even whole ears on the ground. There are relatively few other foods available in these cornfields, except foxtail seeds, which also were important in winter. Numerous seeds were available in the soil in winter, but these were apparently not too heavily consumed (Houtcooper, 1972).

The most important winter foods of *Mus* were corn and foxtail seeds. Lepidopterous larvae became important as the season progressed, and there was a decline in corn consumption as the previous year's cornfields were plowed. Corn formed only a minor portion of spring food. Wheat seeds were avail-

Table 157

Percent volumes of important foods of *Mus musculus* from major habitats of Vigo County, Indiana (Sample sizes ranged from 23 to 127 animals) (from Whitaker, 1966)

	Soybeans	Wheat	Wheat Stubble	Corn Stubble	Weedy Field	Grassy Field	Corn
Setaria seeds	48.9	4.0	5.5	7.1	19.3	26.6	34.4
Lepidopterous larvae	19.3	27.1	26.6	11.6	7.7	8.1	10.4
Sorghum halepense seeds	12.6	—	—	—	—	—	—
Soybeans	3.5	0.6	—	2.8	—	—	—
Miscellaneous Vegetation	1.5	3.3	12.0	8.4	12.4	8.3	7.6
Endogone	0.7	0.4	8.4	—	—	0.2	1.3
Coleoptera	0.7	0.6	0.7	0.7	5.6	2.1	1.7
Green Vegetation	0.4	11.5	0.2	1.5	1.1	0.6	1.5
Wheat seeds	—	24.9	34.3	—	—	—	—
Coleopterous larvae	—	6.7	0.4	1.6	9.2	0.2	0.1
Earthworms	—	3.6	—	1.0	—	—	—
Corn	—	2.4	—	58.8	1.8	—	16.5
Seeds	—	1.9	2.0	2.3	3.6	0.2	2.7
Digitaria seeds	—	—	1.4	—	—	3.2	6.1
Flesh	—	—	—	0.3	0.1	—	2.2
Ambrosia seeds	—	—	—	—	21.8	—	—
Hemiptera	—	—	—	—	1.1	1.0	0.9
Animal	—	—	—	—	0.6	1.0	1.5
Echinochloa seeds	—	—	—	—	0.2	4.4	4.0
Chilopoda	—	—	—	—	0.2	—	trace
Panicum seeds	—	—	—	—	—	28.9	—

able in the fields after harvest and formed a small portion of the diet all year. Since cover was necessary for *Mus* to become abundant, harvested wheat fields became important in summer when clover, lespedeza, and grasses began to form cover in the fields. Lepidopterous larvae were still important in summer and into the fall, but declined as fall progressed. Foxtail seeds again became the most important food by fall.

Food habits of obvious juveniles (individuals less than 12 grams) were summarized separately for comparison with adults (Table 158). The major food of both juveniles and adults was foxtail seeds. Although the order was different, the six most abundant foods

were the same for both age groups. A direct comparison was also made on small samples (6 juveniles, 7 adults), taken 11-13 December in the same field; 5 of the 6 juveniles, and 6 of the 7 adults had fed only upon *Panicum* seeds. The remaining adult had eaten 50 percent *Panicum* and 50 percent miscellaneous vegetation, while the remaining juvenile had eaten 60 percent *Panicum* and 40 percent miscellaneous vegetation. Thus, these data also support the conclusion that there was no difference between adult and juvenile feeding habits.

REPRODUCTION. Relatively little information exists on reproductive habits of feral *Mus*

Table 158

Foods eaten by 150 juvenile house mice from Indiana
(from Whitaker, 1966)

Food Item	Percent Volume	Percent Frequency
Setaria (foxtail grass) seeds	24.8	31.3
Panicum (witch grass) seeds	11.3	12.7
Miscellaneous vegetation	10.6	18.6
Lepidopterous larvae	9.1	14.6
Corn	7.9	10.0
Wheat seeds	7.1	10.7
Seeds	3.6	4.0
Polygonum (knotweed) seeds	3.1	3.3
Endogone	2.8	7.3
Digitaria (crabgrass) seeds	2.7	3.3
Ambrosia trifida (giant ragweed) seeds	2.5	4.0
Grass seeds	2.1	2.7
Coleoptera	1.8	4.0
Green vegetation	1.6	3.3
Unidentified material	1.5	3.3
Sorghum seeds	1.3	1.3
Echinochloa (barnyard grass) seeds	1.1	1.3
Hemiptera	0.8	2.0
Bird flesh	0.7	0.7
Enchytraeidae (enchytraeid worms)	0.7	0.7
Sorghum halepense (Johnson grass) seeds	0.6	0.7
Formicidae (ant)	0.4	0.7
Lepidoptera cocoon	0.4	0.7
Scarabaeidae (scarab beetle)	0.3	0.7
Coleopterous larvae	0.3	2.0
Bromus (brome grass) seeds	0.3	0.7
Insect larvae	0.2	0.7
Araneae (spider)	0.1	0.7
Dipterous adults	0.1	0.7
Chilopoda (centipedes)	0.1	0.7
Dipterous larvae	0.1	2.0
Gastropoda (slug)	trace	0.7
	100.0	

populations. In other states, Pearson (1963) reported breeding throughout the winter one year just before a population peak, and in other years a cessation of reproductive activity between December and April in the same area. Breaky (1963) reported a breeding season extending from 15 April to 15 December and gave information on percentages of pregnancies and placental scars in adult females. Lidicker (1966) presented breeding information on a California island population as it declined to extinction.

Whitaker took 48 pregnant house mice during random trapping studies in Vigo County (Table 159). The average number of embryos per female was 6.02, with a range of 3 to 10. None of 17 adult females taken in December and January were gravid, nor were 8 adult females taken in May or June. More data are needed, but it would appear that smaller litters were produced during the early spring than during the summer and fall. The average number of embryos in 10 pregnant females taken in February, March, and April was 4.7, while the average was 6.37 in 38 pregnant females taken from July through November. Not enough females were taken in the various habitats to draw reliable conclusions, but females trapped in cornfields had the highest average number (6.81) of embryos. The average number of placental scars per female was 6.33, similar to the average number of embryos per pregnant female. The percentage of juveniles in the population was lowest during late spring.

Males appear to have rather large testes throughout the year, and perhaps additional collecting will reveal that breeding does occur at all seasons.

There are scant data on reproduction of *Mus* in Indiana from other sources. The number of embryos in 11 gravid females from various parts of Indiana averaged 6.1 and ranged from 3 to 10. Dates of collection of this sample ranged from 18 February to 27 November. McAtee (1907) mentioned finding 13 "practically hairless" young in a nest in a field. We once found a female with 4 young in a nest. Other data on litter size are lacking, and it appears that mammalogists simply do not spend much time working with *Mus musculus*.

PARASITES. Whitaker (1970b) examined 467 house mice from Vigo County for external parasites. Except for 11 species of mites, few ectoparasites were found. One specimen yielded about 15 larval ticks, two each hosted a flea, one had 2 lice, and many were infested with mites (Table 160). Of the mites, *Androlaelaps morlani*(?), *Dermacarus hypudaei*, *Eulaelaps stabularis*, *Haemogamasus longitarsus*, and *Listrophorus mexicanus* (reported as *L. leuckarti* by Whitaker, 1970b) were represented by only 1 or 2 specimens each, and *Hirstionyssus butantanensis* (reported as *H. talpae* by Whitaker, 1970b) by only 4, so these species were not considered important parasites. Some of the more important mites were the myobiids *Myobia musculi* and *Radfordia affinis*, the macronyssid *Ornithonyssus bacoti*, and the laelapid *Androlaelaps fahrenholzi*. From 3 mice were recovered 58 specimens of the hypopial form of the mite *Xenoryctes latiporus* (= *Dermacarus heptneri*, Rupes and Whitaker, 1968), first described from *Mus* taken during these studies (Fain and Whitaker, 1973). This

Table 159

Reproductive data from adult female house mice
from Vigo County random trapping program

Months	Number examined	Number pregnant	Average number embryos	Number with placental scars	Average number placental scars
Jan.-Feb.	12	2	4.00	4	5.00
March-April	18	8	4.88	9	5.00
May-June	8	0	0.00	7	6.14
July-Aug.	26	16	6.69	17	6.09
Sept.-Oct.	27	14	6.07	13	6.67
Nov.-Dec.	31	8	6.25	17	7.29

Table 160

Ecto- and endoparasites of *Mus musculus* from Vigo County, Indiana
(from Whitaker, 1970)

	Parasites		Hosts Parasitized	
	Total	Average	Total	Percent
External parasites (467 individuals examined)				
Fleas (Siphonaptera)				
Orchopeas leucopus	1	.002	1	0.2
Ctenophthalmus pseudagyrtes	1	.002	1	0.2
Sucking Lice (Anoplura)				
Hoplopleura captiosa	2	.004	1	0.2
Mites (Acarina) other than chiggers				
Myobia musculi	161	0.34	36	7.7
Radfordia affinis	73	0.16	35	7.5
Ornithonyssus bacoti	38	0.08	18	3.9
Myocoptes musculinus	37	0.08	16	3.4
Androlaelaps fahrenholzi	28	0.06	14	3.0
Xenoryctes latiporus	58	0.12	3	0.6
Dermacarus hypudaei	2	0.004	2	0.4
Hirstionyssus butantanensis	4	0.01	2	0.4
Eulaelaps stabularis	1	0.002	1	0.2
Listrophorus mexicanus	1	0.002	1	0.2
Androlaelaps morlani (?)	1	0.002	1	0.2
Ticks (Ixodides)				
Larval ticks	15	.03	1	0.2
Internal parasites (489 individuals examined)				
Heligmosomoides polygyrus	653	1.34	56	11.5
Cestodes	187	0.38	43	8.8
Syphacia sp.	76	0.16	8	1.6
Protospirura sp.	15	0.03	11	2.2
Cuterebra larvae	1	0.002	1	0.2
Ascarid larvae	1	0.002	1	0.2
Heterakis sp.	1	0.002	1	0.2

mite is tiny and can be easily overlooked, hence it may be more abundant than indicated. Mites of this type cling tenaciously to individual hairs; one must separate the hairs with dissecting pins and examine them individually to find the hypopi.

Liponyssoides sanguineus was reported from Indianapolis by Pratt and Good (1954). They list no definite host, but imply that it was taken on the house mouse. We have not taken this species.

Indiana house mice appear to be relatively free of fleas; one each of *Orchopeas leucopus* and *Ctenophthalmus pseudagyrtes* were found on 470 specimens. One specimen of a third flea *(Epitedia wenmanni)* was reported by Whitaker and Corthum (1967), and Wilson

(1961) recorded a specimen each of *E. wenmanni* and *O. leucopus* from Indiana house mice.

Wilson (1961) recorded four specimens of the louse *Hoplopleura captiosa*, and Whitaker found two additional specimens on one mouse. This louse is now known from Carroll, Tippecanoe, and Vigo counties.

The house mouse is the principal host for *Myobia musculi* and *Myocoptes musculinus*.

External parasites, as a group, were most abundant in fall and summer, and least abundant in winter ($X^2 = 29.47$, 3df). *Myobia musculi*, *Radfordia affinis*, and *Myocoptes musculinus* were fall and winter mites, *Myocoptes* occurred only during those seasons. *Ornithonyssus bacoti* was taken at its greatest rate in the fall. With the exception of *A. fahrenholzi,* all species were at their lowest abundance in winter.

Clark (1971) studied ectoparasites of 66 and endoparasites of 64 house mice from an inhabited building at Terre Haute. His data were compared to those from feral house mice collected by Whitaker (1970b). The mice from the building had a lower diversity, a lower total number per individual, and a lower incidence of parasites.

Internal parasites in the 489 house mice examined by Whitaker were all nematodes and cestodes, of which nematodes were most abundant. The most common nematode was *Heligmosomoides polygyrus,* which was generally red and tightly coiled when observed among materials from the intestinal tract. The 56 mice infected with this nematode were host to a total of 653 (from 1 to more than 100 per mouse). Eight of the mice contained more than 25 worms each. Although *H. polygyrus* was found mostly in house mice, a few were present in deer mice. Most of the nematodes of the genus *Protospirura* were in the stomach rather than the intestine. One mouse was host to a nematode of the genus *Heterakis* and another to a larval ascarid nematode. Although cestodes were important parasites of house mice, none has been identified and they are treated here as a group. One mouse had five objects beneath the skin of the head that appeared to be larval cestodes. A single specimen was host to a botfly larva (*Cuterebra* sp.). Adalis and Scherich (1971) reported on the cecal helminths *Syphacia obvelata* and *Aspiculurus tetraptera* in *Mus* from Indiana.

DECIMATING FACTORS. Domestic cats and dogs commonly prey on the house mouse. Mangus (1950) recorded the remains of *Mus* in stomachs of the red fox. Kirkpatrick and Conaway (1947) reported house mouse skulls in pellets of the barn owl, but found none in pellets of the short-eared, long-eared, or great horned owl. We have found *Mus* in the digestive tracts of screech owls and great horned owls and in the pellets of long-eared owls.

TAXONOMY. *Mus musculus domesticus* Rutty probably occurs throughout Indiana, but Bole and Moulthrop (1942) considered southern Ohio to be occupied by *M. musculus brevirostris* Waterhouse.

SELECTED REFERENCES. Caldwell and Gentry, 1965; Clark, 1971; Evans, 1949; King, 1957; Schwarz and Schwarz, 1943; Whitaker, 1966, 1967a, 1970b.

Family Zapodidae

Meadow Jumping Mouse
(*Zapus hudsonius*)

Jumping Mouse, Hudson Bay Jumping Mouse, Short-footed Jumping Mouse

Gerbillus canadensis: Wied, 1839
Jaculus labradorius: Wied, 1862
Jaculus Hudsonicus: Tenney, 1872
Zapus hudsonicus: Butler, 1892a
Zapus hudsonius: Butler, 1895

DESCRIPTION. The meadow jumping mouse is a medium-sized, yellowish mouse with a very long, thin tail much longer than the body length. The middorsal region is yellowish brown or olive brown, the sides are yellowish with scattered dark hairs, and the underparts are white. The ears are small and rounded. The hind feet are much elongated and larger than the front feet. The three large molariform teeth on either side of the upper jaw have a rather complicated cusp pattern. Anterior to these teeth is a very small ("peg") tooth. The upper incisors are deeply grooved (see Fig. 33) and covered with an orangish enamel. The infraorbital foramina are large and oval.

Meadow jumping mouse. Photo by Dennis E. Clark

Weights and measurements are shown in Table 161. The dental formula is

$$\text{I } \frac{1}{1} \text{ C } \frac{0}{0} \text{ P } \frac{1}{0} \text{ M } \frac{3}{3} = 18.$$

STATUS AND DISTRIBUTION. Wied (1862) reported this mouse from New Harmony (Posey County). John Plummer (1844) observed one in Wayne County in 1843 and wrote, "It must be comparatively rare, as I have not yet met with any of our farmers who are acquainted with it." Evermann and Butler (1894b) had reports or records from Carroll, Howard, Knox, Lagrange, Starke, Vigo, and Wabash counties. It was reported to be "rather common" in Starke County, "not uncommon" in Knox County, and "rare" in Howard County. By 1909, Walter Hahn was able to list records of *Zapus hudsonius* from a few additional counties and he stated that it was found in every section of the state but was "nowhere abundant." He also wrote:

The writer spent the first twenty years of his life on a farm in southeastern Indiana, where he was familiar with most of the animals, yet he never saw a jumping mouse. Later, in collecting more than 300 small mammals in the State, but one jumping mouse has been obtained through his personal efforts. This is in accord with the experience of most other naturalists, although a number of specimens may sometimes be obtained in one season where

they had not previously been seen. They are said to be most easily captured in some localities by following the mower as the grass of a low meadow is being cut.

Hahn also quoted from W. B. Van Gorder regarding the occurrence of the meadow jumping mouse in Noble County, as follows: "In Albion Township in 1895 I took the first jumping mouse I ever saw. In 1907 I saw another, and in 1908, . . . four of them came to my notice."

In writing about the Lake Maxinkuckee (Marshall County) region of Indiana, Evermann and Clark (1911) stated, "It is frequently reported from this part of the state, particularly from the vicinity of Yellow River. It is also said to be seen occasionally about Rochester a few miles southeast of the lake. Our only definite records for the lake are a weather-worn skull found on Long Point in 1906, and one found dead near the ice houses on the west side of the lake August 26, 1906." Engels (1933) reported the species as "never very numerous" in St. Joseph County.

In 1936, Marcus W. Lyon, Jr., wrote that the jumping mouse was "apparently found throughout Indiana, though none have as yet been reported from or taken in the southeastern counties. The animal is nowhere common in the state. . . . In the dunes region of Porter County, I took one *Zapus* in a total of some

Table 161

Weights and measurements of
Zapus hudsonius from Indiana

	Males	Females
Total length (mm)		
n	41	29
x̄	198.9	206.2
range	180-220	185-234
SD	10.2	10.4
SE	1.6	1.9
Tail length (mm)		
n	41	29
x̄	116.6	120.7
range	105-129	101-137
SD	7.1	7.4
SE	1.1	1.4
Hind foot (mm)		
n	38	29
x̄	28.2	28.5
range	26-30	25-31
SD	1.1	1.5
SE	0.2	0.3
Weight (grams)		
n	38	29
x̄	17.5	18.8
range	15-25	15.2-30.1
SD	2.4	3.5
SE	0.4	0.6

200 mammals . . . and Paul Hickie took two out of a total of seven mammals trapped near Mongo, LaGrange County." Lyon listed records or reports from 20 counties.

We have examined specimens of the meadow jumping mouse from 55 Indiana counties fairly well distributed throughout the state, although there are specimens from only Jefferson County along the Ohio River between Spencer County and the Ohio-Indiana state line (Map 49).

Jumping mice may be locally abundant at times. On 9 May 1961, Mumford and one of his classes saw 19 jumping mice and captured 7 by hand in an area 30 by 200 yards along a narrow, wooded floodplain of a creek (Tippecanoe County). Jumping mice have inhabited this area since at least 1947. In a small brushy old field tract near Terre Haute (Vigo County), it is one of the most abundant small mammals. During three trapping sessions, 57 individuals (1.19 per 100 trap-nights) were taken. We have also trapped

some numbers of this mouse in stands of *Impatiens* and other heavy herbaceous vegetation in the wooded portions of Turkey Run State Park (Parke County), where 45 (1.42 per 100 trap-nights) were taken.

HABITAT. The meadow jumping mouse is most often found in old fields, damp old fields, or (sometimes) in woodland, but appears to be most influenced by the amount of herbaceous ground vegetation. It is often found in moist situations, but this appears to be related to the lack of disturbance by man and the presence of ground cover, rather than directly to moisture. It often becomes abundant in areas of the proper kind of dense permanent ground cover regardless of the amount of ground moisture. *Zapus hudsonius* is sometimes common in open, woodland glades such as those at Turkey Run State Park, where it is abundant in the dense stands of *Impatiens* along streams. Occasional specimens are taken in areas support-

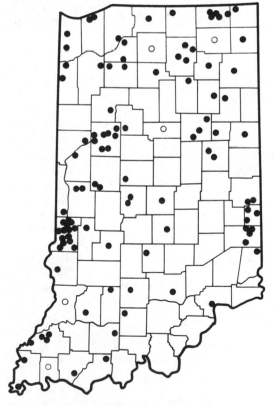

Map 49. The Meadow Jumping Mouse,
Zapus hudsonius, in Indiana

Floodplain habitat of meadow jumping mouse in Warren County. Photo by Mumford

ing less vegetation, but this is not normally the case.

Label notations indicating where specimens were trapped reflect the varied habitats of this species: grassy woods border, mature deciduous forest, in pine plantation, grassy opening in woods, wooded floodplain along creek, high brush, brushy second growth, brushy fencerow in upland area, fallow field, grassy area in cornfield, grassy marsh border, cattail marsh, grassy fencerow, fencerow of weeds and multiflora rose along cornfield, rank weeds along small creek, along ditch bank, along railroad grades with weeds and some brush, soybean field, alfalfa field, low spot in hayfield, in garden, in building, grassy meadow.

ASSOCIATED SPECIES. The meadow jumping mouse in Indiana most often occurs in open fields with the meadow vole, the masked shrew, and the house mouse. Since the jumping mouse has been taken in such diverse habitats, most other small mammals have at some time been taken in the same traplines with it. In woodlands, the usual associates are the short-tailed shrew and the white-footed mouse. At some locations, the woodland vole also shares the habitat and two jumping mice have been trapped in the underground burrows of these voles. At a site near Lafayette, the bog lemming, the meadow vole, and the jumping mouse were all taken by hand in a floodplain area.

HABITS. The meadow jumping mouse is most active at night, but can also be found during the day. In our experience, there is much diurnal activity in late April and May, the times when we have observed many individuals during daylight hours. Under certain weather conditions at this time of year, the mice appear to be active throughout the day. Possibly the apparent increase in daytime activity during this period is correlated with their recent emergence from hibernation.

Jumping mice spend considerable time each year in hibernation. The latest fall date we have for one aboveground is 20 November, and the earliest spring date is 4 April. Individuals were collected on 8 and 12 November and 31 were taken during October, 21 being trapped between 1 and 15 October. Most animals have entered hibernation by the last half of October. Whitaker (1963a) found by continuous trapping in New York that the last jumping mouse was taken on 18 October, 1 November, and 20 October, for three successive years. A specimen from Wayne County, Indiana, taken on 8 November, was "found in hibernation," according to label notations. Although we have 7 records of jumping mice seen or trapped from 4 to 29 April, there are 25 such records for May. Our data suggest that jumping mice emerge from hibernation in late April and early May. Only two April records are earlier than the 23rd. In Whitaker's New York study, the first meadow jumping mice were trapped on 30 April, 2 May, 25 April, and 25 April in four successive years. Males emerge from hibernation earlier than females do, and Whitaker took first females an average of 15.5 days after first males in the above years. From available data, it appears that Indiana *Zapus hudsonius* emerge from hibernation slightly earlier and enter hibernation slightly later than those in New York. The deposition of sufficient body fat to allow successful hibernation has not been investigated in detail in Indiana jumping mice. Only 8 of 68 taken the last half of September and 2 of 14 trapped in October and November had accumulated significant amounts of fat. About the same results were obtained by Whitaker during his New York studies. Since it takes about two weeks for jumping mice to put on adequate fat and since so few animals taken in fall are obviously fat, Whitaker postulated that jumping mice put on a layer of fat quickly then immediately enter hibernation, and that this process may occur any time during September or October. (For further discussion on this matter, his paper should be consulted.)

When an observer flushes a jumping mouse in its daytime habitat, the mouse will usually make a few jumps of 1 to 2 feet then crouch on the ground. One can often capture the mouse by quietly approaching the hiding spot and cupping his hands over it. Under these conditions, jumping mice appear to depend upon camouflage and remain quiet for protection. When chased persistently, however, the mice may be quite active, darting about and jumping this way and that until they locate and enter a burrow or other safe retreat. One was observed entering a burrow near the edge of the water along a creek.

Over a hundred years ago, Tenney (1872) published a lengthy account of a hibernating jumping mouse he found near Vincennes (Knox County). The animal was dug out of the ground on 18 January and was "apparently dead." A portion of Tenney's account follows:

It was coiled up as tightly as it could be, the nose being placed upon the belly, and the long tail coiled around the ball-like form which the animal had assumed. I took the little mouse into my hand. It exhibited no motion or sign of life. Its eyes and mouth were shut tight, and its little fore feet or hands were shut and placed close together. Everything indicated that the mouse was perfectly dead, excepting the fact that it was not rigid as perhaps a dead mouse would be in the winter. I tied the mouse and nest in my hankerchief and carried them to Vincennes. Arriving at Dr. Patton's office I untied my treasures, and took out the mouse and held it for some time in my hand; it still exhibited no sign of life; but at length I thought I saw a very slight movement in one of the hind legs. Presently there was a very slight movement of the head, yet so feeble that one could hardly be sure it was real. Then there came to be some evidence of breathing, and a slight pressure of my fingers upon the tail near the body was followed by an immediate but feeble movement of one of the hind legs. At length there was unmistakable evidence that the animal was breathing, but the breathing was a labored action, and seemingly performed with great difficulty. As the mouse became warmer the signs of life became more and more marked; and in the course of the same afternoon on which I brought it into the warm room it became perfectly active, and was as ready to jump about as any other member of its species.

He kept the mouse in captivity at least until April and it went in and out of hibernation several times. Tenney found that this mouse was "capable of passing into the deepest lethargic state in a single night, and of returning, when warmed, to activity again on the succeeding day." Tenney was much impressed by the state of "profound lethargy" the mouse was in at the time it was discovered.

Hahn (1909) reported that "Mr. Chansler found one in midwinter near Bicknell, hibernating in an underground nest on a side hill near some damp woods. It seemed very stupid and inactive, but ran about some when dug out." We do not know the date on which this animal was observed.

Evidently jumping mice construct globular nests of grasses on top of the ground and in underground burrows. Tenney reported that the nest used for hibernation was "about two feet below the surface of the ground, carefully made of bits of grass." His captive gnawed paper into bits and constructed a nest "perhaps five or six inches in diameter." The center of the nest, where the mouse slept, was hollow. Nest construction took place at night.

Jones and Whitaker (1976) reported a nest containing a hibernating jumping mouse in a woodchuck burrow in Vigo County. The burrow was found on 22 January 1974 in a dike along the Wabash River. The nest was about 14 cm in diameter and was entirely of the leaves of the grass *Festuca*, the principal plant on the dike. The only ectoparasites found on the mouse were eight mites, *Androlaelaps fahrenholzi*. The digestive tract of the mouse was empty except for nine fecal pellets in the large intestine which had been there for some time. A number of invertebrates were found in the nest, but only two species were regular parasites of *Zapus hudsonius*. They were *Androlaelaps fahrenholzi*, and adults of *Dermacarus*, probably *newyorkensis*. Whitaker found another jumping mouse in hibernation in Indiana, in December in a nest of oak leaves about two feet below the surface in a cinder pile in Clay County.

Zapus makes no runways and seems to leave little sign of its presence, other than little piles of match-length grass stems and seed heads when feeding on timothy and a few other grasses. When startled, the jumping mouse will sometimes jump aimlessly here and there, reminding one of the actions of a frog trying to escape capture. Usually, however, the mouse will hop off quickly in a series of leaps about 2 feet each, then hide in a clump of vegetation. Some authors credit the jumping mouse with leaps of 6 or 8 feet, but in the habitats where we have observed it, such jumps would be difficult to make because of the dense vegetation. This species probably seldom makes leaps much over 3 to 4 feet. Longer leaps mentioned in the literature probably refer to the woodland jumping mouse, *Napaeozapus insignis* (not found in Indiana), rather than to this species. A meadow jumping mouse captured on 20 November was actively jumping about at 8:00 A.M. One found along a small creek was chased about over an area 6 by 10 feet before it entered the water and began to swim the 6 feet across the creek. It swam about 2 feet and returned to the bank near where it started. When closely pursued again, it again entered the creek; when it was halfway across, the observers closed in on it. This caused it to dive completely beneath the water and swim nearly a foot before surfacing, when it was captured.

Jumping mice live well in captivity, and we have maintained them for various periods in the laboratory. Tenney described how his captive cleaned itself: "Soon after it was fairly established in its new and more commodious quarters, it began to clean every part of its body in the most thorough manner, washing itself very much in the same manner as a cat washes. On coming to the tail it passed that long member, for its whole length, through the mouth from side to side, beginning near the body and ending at the tip." When this animal was disturbed in its nest it "vigorously" repelled the intrusion "by striking with its fore feet with the greatest rapidity," but apparently did not attempt to bite.

The meadow jumping mouse may be rather social, for several have at times been observed in a small area. W. B. Van Gorder made the following remarks on an observation he made in Noble County in 1908: ". . . while watching for birds in a willow swamp four of them (jumping mice) came to my notice only a few feet away. They were playing and running about and were very sportive and interesting, when all at once they bounded away like so many little kangaroos." We do not have a precise date for this sighting. The 19 animals reported by Mumford and his class in a relatively small area were seen on 9 May.

FOOD. Earlier authors writing about the meadow jumping mouse in Indiana gave very little precise data on food habits. Tenney noted that his captive ate corn. A specimen taken in late November had a distended stomach filled with a whitish, cheesy mass, which could not be identified. Whitaker and Mumford (1971b) reported on the foods found in the stomachs of 131 meadow jumping mice collected in Indiana (Table 162). Seeds of touch-me-not *(Impatiens)* were the single most important food, followed by the fungus *Endogone*, seeds of foxtail grass, unidentified grass seeds, and seeds of purple-top grass. Seeds of *Impatiens* are available in the late summer and fall and can often be easily identified because of the blue endosperm of the seed (even in unopened stomachs it is visible through the stomach wall). *Endogone* is eaten by several kinds of small mammals, but is a particularly common food of both the meadow jumping mouse and the woodland jumping mouse, forming about 12 percent of the diet of the former and about 35 percent of the diet of the latter (Whitaker, 1963a). This is particularly interesting since little is known about the biology or occurrence of the fungus, and it is of questionable food value. It is not known how the mice find *Endogone*, since we have been unable to locate it in any abundance. The question is sometimes raised whether *Endogone* might be ingested along with other food. This does not appear to be the case. *Endogone* is not found consistently with any other food, and, more important, *Endogone* spores often make up a very large portion of the stomach contents. Percent volume estimates of *Endogone* in 17 of the 131 *Zapus* stomachs examined were 100, 85, 80 (3 stomachs), 70, 60 (3), 55 (2), and 50 (6). Also, 50.4 percent of the mice had some *Endogone* in their stomachs; this is a higher rate of occurrence than for any other food. These data indicate that the fungus is sought out and eaten by the mice. Undoubtedly they locate it by olfaction.

To get an indication of the potential energy value of *Endogone*, this fungus was collected from the stomachs and intestines of four jumping mice and burned in a Parr Oxygen Bomb Calorimeter. The samples from the stomachs and those from the intestines were each divided into two equal masses, weighed, and burned. The two masses from the stomachs averaged 2,735.50 calories per gram (2,610.31 and 2,860.69), while the two masses from the intestines averaged 2,266.44 calories per gram (2,169.42 and 2,363.46), or

significantly less than the material in the stomachs (t = 9.23, 2 df). For comparison, some calorific measurements of seeds obtained by Kendeigh and West (1965) are: barnyard grass, 4,819 (hulled); Virginia wild rye, 4,695; giant foxtail, 4,585 (hulled); corn, 4,317; Pennsylvania smartweed, 4,515; black ash, 5,625. It would appear that *Zapus hudsonius* is getting energy from *Endogone*, but that the potential amount of energy in this fungus is much less than that in many kinds of seeds.

Another fungal food, *Hymenogaster*, was occasionally eaten. This fungus forms pea-sized oval bodies attached to the bases of plants.

Seeds are the mainstay of the diet of the meadow jumping mouse in Indiana and in New York, with specific kinds of seeds being eaten progressively as they ripen. Seeds made up a total percentage volume of 66.7 in 131 Indiana jumping mice (Table 162). This mouse exhibits an interesting behavior adaptation for obtaining seeds from certain grasses (notably timothy); the mouse reaches up as far as it can, cuts off the grass stem, which it then grasps and pulls down; it repeats the process until the seed head is reached, then it strips the seeds, leaving the rachis and glumes. Apparently the jumping mouse also sometimes climbs the grass stem, cuts off the top and brings this to the ground to eat. Contrary to early reports, this mouse apparently does not store food.

REPRODUCTION. The gestation period for *Zapus hudsonius* is about 18 days. Few data on reproduction have been gathered in Indiana. Six gravid jumping mice were collected, one each on 20 May, 2 June, 21 June, 5 July, 21 July, and 16 August. The number of embryos per female averaged 5 and ranged from 4 to 6. Another female with 6 embryos was examined, but we do not have the precise collection date. A female taken on 9 May carried a copulation plug. None of 17 females captured in September were pregnant, but 3 had placental scars.

Testis sizes in male meadow jumping mice were recorded for numerous specimens, by month collected, but our sample was not large for each month (Table 163). Male jumping mice have large testes (averaging at least 3 × 6 mm) from at least April through August,

Table 162
Foods eaten by *Zapus hudsonius* (n = 131) from Indiana
(from Whitaker and Mumford, 1971b)

Food Item	Percent volume	Percent frequency
Impatiens (touch-me-not) seeds	21.4	27.5
Endogone	15.6	50.4
Setaria (foxtail grass) seeds	10.0	10.7
Grass seeds	9.6	18.3
Triodea flava (tall redtop) seeds	9.0	13.7
Lepidopterous larvae	5.7	13.7
Miscellaneous vegetation	4.6	15.3
Phleum pratense (timothy) seeds	3.7	3.8
Green grass seeds	3.4	6.1
Hymenogaster	1.8	4.6
Seeds (unidentified)	1.7	4.6
Dactylus glomerata (orchard grass) seeds	1.5	1.6
Gastropoda (slugs)	1.3	1.6
Curculionidae (snout beetle)	1.1	2.3
Green vegetation	1.0	1.6
Cerastium (chickweed) seeds	0.9	4.6
Rumex acetosella (sheep sorrel) seeds	0.8	2.3
Bromus (brome grass) seeds	0.8	0.8
Panicum (witch grass) seeds	0.8	0.8
Elymus (wild rye) seeds	0.8	0.8
Echinochloa (barnyard grass) seeds	0.6	0.8
Rubus (blackberry) fruit	0.6	1.6
Animal	0.5	2.3
Oxalis (wood sorrel) seeds	0.5	0.8
Coleopterous larvae	0.4	2.3
Poa (bluegrass) seeds	0.4	1.5
Mast	0.3	0.8
Chenopodium (pigweed) seeds	0.3	0.8
Carabidae (ground beetle)	0.2	0.8
Prunus serotina (black cherry) seeds	0.2	0.8
Chrysomelidae (leaf beetles)	0.2	1.5
Coleoptera	0.2	1.5
Festuca (fescue) seeds	0.2	0.8
Leerzia (rice cutgrass) seeds	0.1	0.8
Reduviidae (assassin bug)	trace	0.8
Dipterous larvae	trace	1.5
Polygonum (knotweed) seeds	trace	0.8
	100.2	

and no doubt most of the insemination of females takes place during this period. Testis size was smaller in September and October. This, coupled with the fact that none of 17 females taken in September were gravid, indicates that little copulation takes place in August.

We have examined relatively few very young meadow jumping mice. (The adult state is reached at about 14–15 grams.) A jumping mouse trapped on 18 June weighed 6.7 grams and was 159 mm in total length. Another measured 170 mm in total length and weighed 8.1 grams on 25 June. On 12 October one was taken that was 168 mm in total length, and other animals 170 mm in total length were collected on 12 July and 3 October. Eight additional specimens measuring from 171 to 180 mm in total length were taken between 1 August and 6 October. It appears that young jumping mice do not wander away from the nest (at least they have not been trapped) until they are fairly well grown.

PARASITES. Test and Test (1943) reported finding a *Cuterebra* sp. (possibly *angustifrons?*) larva in the inguinal region of a jumping mouse trapped in Parke County between 26 and 30 August 1941. The only other record we have for this parasite is for a specimen captured on 16 August 1977 (Fountain County) by us; it was infected with a single *Cuterebra* larva.

Whitaker and Corthum (1967) found no fleas on 21 meadow jumping mice they examined, and Whitaker and Mumford (1971b) recorded a single flea *(Orchopeas leucopus)* from an additional 100 animals. We found only 3 ticks *(Dermacentor variabilis)* on these same 100 specimens (Table 164). Several species of mites occur on Indiana *Zapus*. Whitaker and Wilson (1968) reported an estimated 452 hypopial mites *(Dermacarus hypudaei = D. newyorkensis)* on 29 specimens from Vigo County. This mite is very common on *Zapus* throughout much of North America. Whitaker and Wilson also recorded 2 specimens of the mite *Androlaelaps fahrenholzi* on Vigo County jumping mice.

We found 60 of the 100 Indiana jumping mice we examined to harbor, by conservative estimate, 4,275 *Dermacarus newyorkensis*, an average of 42.7 per mouse. The next most common mite was *Androlaelaps fahrenholzi* (2.1 per mouse for 22 infested animals). Additional mites were 8 individuals of *Or-*

Endogone, an important fungal food of the meadow jumping mouse. Photo by Mark Oster

Table 163
Testis size of *Zapus hudsonius* from Indiana

| Month | Number examined | Testis size (mm) | |
		Average Length	Width
April	1	3	6
May	8	3.2	6.3
June	1	3	7
July	20	3.4	6
August	6	3.3	6.6
September	11	2.0	4.4
October	5	2	4.6

nithonyssus bacoti and 1 each of the myobiid *Radfordia* sp. (immature but probably *ewingi*) and of *Macrocheles* sp.

Six of 115 meadow jumping mice examined for chiggers (Whitaker and Loomis, 1979) were infested as follows: *Euschoengastia peromysci* (12); *Neotrombicula whartoni* (5); *Eutrombicula alfreddugesi* (3); *Leptotrombidium peromysci* (1).

Of 127 Indiana meadow jumping mice examined for endoparasites, 2 contained 158 unidentified trematodes and 7 contained 79 unidentified cestodes.

DECIMATING FACTORS. Domestic cats are known predators on *Zapus* and at least 2 Indiana specimens were brought in by cats. Hahn (1907a) took a specimen "from the stomach of a bull snake, *Pituophis sayi*," in the Kankakee River valley. Edna Banta, former naturalist at McCormick's Creek State Park, told Mumford that she once raised a family of jumping mice whose nest had been plowed out of the ground. We have a few records of jumping mice found dead on roads, where they were probably struck by vehicles, for we have noted several *Zapus* along roads at night. Undoubtedly owls take jumping mice, but most of our owl pellet analyses involve winter food habits and hibernating mice are not then vulnerable to owl predation.

TAXONOMY. Hall and Kelson (1959) indicated that both *Zapus hudsonius americanus* (Barton) and *Z. h. intermedius* Krutsch occur in Indiana. Indiana specimens are rather uniform and not readily separable from specimens from Maryland, Virginia, and other eastern states. We prefer to consider the Indiana population *Z. h. americanus*, although

there may be a trend toward Z. h. intermedius along the western border of the state.
Gwilym S. Jones is currently studying the
classification of the genus Zapus.

SELECTED REFERENCES. Hamilton, 1935;
Jones and Whitaker, 1976; Morrison and
Ryser, 1962; Quimby, 1951; Whitaker, 1963a;
Whitaker and Loomis, 1979; Whitaker and
Mumford, 1971b.

Table 164

Ectoparasites and other associates of Zapus hudsonius (n = 100) from Indiana
(115 examined for chiggers)

Parasites	Parasites		Hosts Parasitized	
	Total	Average	Total	Percent
Fleas (Siphonaptera)				
Orchopeas leucopus	1	0.01	1	1.0
Mites (Acarina) other than chiggers				
Dermacarus newyorkensis	4,275	42.75	60	60.0
Androlaelaps fahrenholzi	209	2.09	22	22.0
Ornithonyssus bacoti	8	0.08	3	3.0
Radfordia sp.	1	0.01	1	1.0
Macrocheles sp.	1	0.01	1	1.0
Chigger mites (Trombiculidae)				
Euschoengastia peromysci	12	0.10	2	1.7
Neotrombicula whartoni	5	0.04	1	0.9
Eutrombicula alfreddugesi	3	0.03	2	1.7
Leptotrombidium peromysci	1	0.01	1	0.9
Ticks (Ixodides)				
Dermacentor variabilis	3	0.03	2	2.0

Order CARNIVORA

Family Canidae

Coyote
Canis latrans Say

Prairie Wolf, Brush Wolf, Wolf

Canis latrans: Butler, 1895

DESCRIPTION. Coyotes are doglike animals with pointed noses and ears and tan to whitish legs and feet. The outsides of the ears are reddish or rusty colored. The body may be mostly gray, yellowish gray, or reddish gray, mixed with varying amounts of black above; the throat and undersides are whitish or grayish. The tail is quite bushy and relatively short; above, it usually is similar in color to the back, but may be more grayish with a blackish spot on the dorsal surface near the base and it may have a black tip. The underside of the tail is paler than the dorsal surface. The pelage is coarse and long. An albino specimen has been reported from Union County.

The coyote, red fox, gray fox, and raccoon all have six upper molariform teeth on each side (see Fig. 5). The raccoon skull is much smaller (short rostrum and rounded braincase) than coyote or fox skulls. The coyote skull is considerably larger than that of either fox. Fox skulls have dorsal crests divided anteriorly; the coyote skull has a single dorsal crest. Coyote skulls are most likely to be confused with skulls of the domestic dog, or with coyote-dog (coydog) hybrids. The distance between the first two molariform teeth di-vided into the length of the molariform tooth row is usually about 3.7 in the coyote, less than 3.0 in dogs, and from 3.1 to 3.6 in hybrids.

Weights and measurements are shown in Table 165. The dental formula is

$$I\ \frac{3}{3}\ C\ \frac{1}{1}\ P\ \frac{4}{4}\ M\ \frac{2}{3}\ =\ 42.$$

STATUS AND DISTRIBUTION. The coyote originally occurred in both northwestern and parts of western Indiana in fairly good numbers. Packs of twenty were reported in Lake County, and David Thomas recounted that thirteen were killed on Christmas Day, 1816, at Fort Harrison (Vigo County). In 1883, LaPorte County paid bounties on 51 "coyotes" (Haller, 1950). Some of these animals, however, could have been gray wolves (*Canis lupus*). In writing about Lake County, Dinwiddie (1884) stated, "In the early settlement of the county Prairie Wolves were very numerous and bold. They were mostly the common brownish wolf, but there were a few nearly black." It is obvious that the coyote was never extirpated from Indiana; they persisted despite persecution by settlers and began to exhibit an increase by 1909 (Hahn, 1909). With the elimination of most of Indiana's forests, the coyote was able to move away from the prairie regions and invade

Coyote. Photo by Jon Farrar

other sections of the state. This trend is evident from the fact that Lyon (1936) had reports of coyotes from 32 counties. Since 1936, the coyote has continued to increase, judging from reports, animals killed, and bounty records. From 1849 to 1948, there were 1,325 "coyotes" bountied in 17 counties (Haller, 1950). In 1946, bounties were paid on 102 coyotes in 9 Indiana counties.

Populations of coyotes sometimes are present in a locality for several years; one such site near Romney (Tippecanoe County) has been the source of animals shot from at least 1965 to 1978. An earlier concentration occurred near West Point (Tippecanoe County). In the Parr–Fair Oaks–Demotte area of northwestern Jasper County, 10 to 12 coyotes were reportedly killed annually for several years before 1969 (*fide* Larry E. Lehmann). This region for years seemed to be one of the optimum areas for the coyote in Indiana. From November 1966 to January 1968, 7 were bountied from Jasper County (letter from Lehmann to Mumford).

Coyotes now occur throughout Indiana, having successfully invaded the hilly, wooded south-central portion in recent times. They can now be expected to appear in any county (Map 50).

Many early references to coyotes in Indiana (they were usually listed as "wolves") cannot be properly evaluated because they may refer to the coyote, gray wolf, or red wolf—all once found in the state. However, since the settlement of Indiana by the white man, most such accounts probably refer to coyotes. In more recent years, there has been an increasing number of records of coyote-dog hybrids. Some of these hybrids are quite large (50 pounds) and many residents mistakenly believe that these animals are gray wolves. Since all degrees of dog or coyote characteristics may be visible in any particular hybrid animal, some interesting and puzzling specimens are sometimes produced.

Population data are few, and no intensive study has been conducted on the coyote in Indiana. Leonard "Dutch" Schwartz trapped 16 coyotes on the Willow Slough Fish and Wildlife Area (Newton County) in one winter. During the winter of 1976–77, about 100 coyotes were trapped or shot in a relatively small area of northern Montgomery County and southern Tippecanoe County. The following winter, about 50 coyotes were known to have been taken in the same general area.

HABITAT. Although numerous accounts of coyotes killed in Indiana have been pub-

Table 165

Weights and measurements of
Canis latrans from Indiana

	Males	Females
Total length (mm)		
n	24	15
x̄	1190.0	1185.6
range	1025-1320	1030-1450
SD	65.4	104.7
SE	13.3	27.0
Tail length (mm)		
n	24	15
x̄	342.7	340.2
range	290-395	295-387
SD	29.3	28.2
SE	6.0	7.2
Hind foot (mm)		
n	22	15
x̄	199.9	187.5
range	180-210	169-203
SD	8.5	12.6
SE	1.8	3.2
Weight* (pounds)		
n	29	22
x̄	30.9	25.6
range	17.75-38.5	19-32
SD	4.3	3.2
SE	0.8	0.7

*A series of 42 male coyotes from Montgomery County taken during 1976 averaged 29.5 lbs (range 16-46; SD=6.9, SE=1.1), whereas 17 females averaged 27.2 lbs (range 18-33; SD=4.0, SE=1.0).

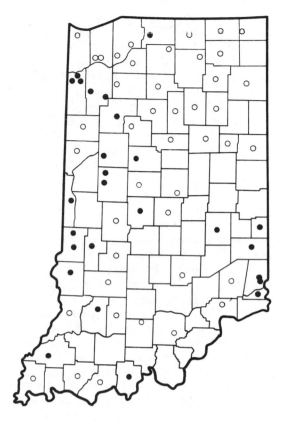

Map 50.   The Coyote, *Canis latrans*, in Indiana

lished in newspapers and magazines, few data are available on the habitats in which the animals were encountered. Most coyote hunters evidently located the animals in the brushy portions of cultivated or overgrown areas, and mentioned finding them in the brush or note that their tracks led into brushy sites. Near Lafayette, a family of coyotes lived in a rather extensive, brushy series of old gravel pits in the late summer of 1972. They probably had a den there. Coyotes are also reported from the forested regions of southern Indiana, but brushy openings, creek bottoms, and other favorable sites occur in that section of the state. Vague references in early historic accounts mention coyotes "on the prairie," and no doubt in presettlement times most Indiana coyotes were found on the prairies or prairie fringes. Even today, reports of coyotes are received more commonly from the northwestern section of the

state, which was once prairie, than from other sections.

Waste areas, some with dense, low vegetation, appear to supply good conditions for coyotes in Indiana. Coyotes have recently invaded a waste area in Clark County, Illinois, just west of Terre Haute, Indiana. Here coyotes have been seen or heard several times. There are reports of coyotes in abandoned strip-mined lands in southwestern Indiana.

Standing corn is evidently an important vegetation type for coyotes in parts of the state. An animal trapped and fitted with a radio transmitter by S. D. Ford spent much of its time during the day in the fall in a cornfield until the corn was picked. Two coyotes were trapped in a popcorn field in Gibson County.

HABITS.   Little information has been obtained on the habits of Indiana coyotes. They are mostly nocturnal, spending the day bedded down in the cover of a brushy area, fencerow, stubble field, weed field, or cornfield. Judging from the number of observations made during the daytime, coyotes move about, and possibly hunt, to some extent also during daylight hours. A female coyote killed in February was flushed by hunters from a daytime retreat (a weed patch) it shared with a red fox. In early morning and late evening, coyotes are sometimes seen in open areas, such as airports. One of a group of five was struck by an airplane on the Purdue University Airport in 1977. Airport personnel complained that the animals had been repeatedly observed on the runways. Perhaps the coyotes were attracted there by the open space and by the numerous ground squirrels and mice available for food.

Until fairly recent years, there were few reports of coyotes heard howling in Indiana. Earlier, when the state coyote population was low, the animals appear to have been much more secretive and quiet. C. M. Kirkpatrick and S. R. Esten both reported howling having been heard on the Jasper-Pulaski Fish and Wildlife Area in the early 1930s. From time to time up to the 1960s howling was reported. Then in the 1960s and into the 1970s, more and more coyotes were heard. No doubt some of the increase in reports resulted from the greatly increased coyote population that occurred in the 1960s. And some of the increased frequency of howling may have been a function of social activity. The coyotes living near the Purdue University campus frequently howled in response to the sound of a train whistle nearby. Other loud sounds will also entice coyotes to howl.

There are several published accounts in popular magazines and newspapers of coyote chases by dogs. One coyote was reportedly chased "2 days" before it was killed (*Outdoor Indiana*, January 1936). Another was pursued by dogs for 6 miles (*Plymouth Pilot*, 2 March 1959). Fox hounds chased another coyote 25 miles over a four-hour period before the coyote was killed (*Indianapolis Star*, October 1966). An account of a fight between a coyote and a female German shepherd was described in *Outdoor Indiana* (July 1934). The coyote was captured alive and kept captive for some time at the Jasper-Pulaski Fish and Wildlife Area. Numerous hunters and trappers in Indiana feel that the coyote displaces foxes in an area. There is considerable concern that in counties where coyotes are still invading, the fox population will decrease drastically. We know of no quantitative data to support this belief.

Although most of the observations of coyotes in Indiana in recent years have been of single animals or small groups, there have been some reports of larger assemblages. Six animals seen together in July (Gibson County) by Terry Tichenor probably represented a family. There are earlier reports of "packs" containing as many as twenty animals.

One difficulty in assessing the observations of coyotes in Indiana has been the determination of whether the observer saw a coyote, a dog, or a dog-coyote hybrid. Coyotes usually carry the tail down when running. Eric Edberg noticed that when a coyote is sneaking it tucks the tail, lowers its ears, and keeps its nose near the ground. Some of the animals reported to us (and some of the specimens and photographs we have examined) were simply too large and abnormally colored to be coyotes.

C. W. Bussel reported that packs of coyotes were found in February (thought to be the mating season) in northwestern Indiana. David Thomas implied that several coyotes might be found together, and historical accounts mention "packs." No recent observations of packs of animals have come to our attention, although in the late 1800s as many as "20 in a drove" were reported (Anderson, 1922). A pack of prairie wolves was recorded in LaPorte County in the winter of 1832.

Dens are usually burrows in the ground. Coyotes may dig their own or modify a burrow system excavated by another mammal, such as a woodchuck. The den may be in a concealed site, such as under a stump, and have two or three entrances. Mounds of excavated soil are frequently found at the burrow entrances. Once a den is established, it may be used for several years. W. E. Madden told us of a coyote den occupied for four consecutive years in a sandy ("blowout") area that had been planted with pine trees years ago (Newton County). We have reports of other dens being used for at least two years each. At least one of these was located in a thicket.

Some coyotes reportedly have constructed their dens in old, overgrown gravel pits and in strip-mined areas. Dens are also located in wooded areas and in sites where there are dense plantings of multiflora rose.

A trapper in Gibson County captured single coyotes in the same trap on 17 and 20 December. We have reports of two animals seen traveling together on 14 December, 13 January, and 20 January. These were possibly mated pairs. Two of three coyotes running together in late March were shot; one was a male, the other a female. A trapper reported that when he found a coyote in one of his traps there were two or three other coyotes lingering nearby.

FOOD. Most general accounts of coyotes in Indiana in earlier times refer to the destruction of poultry, pigs, lambs, and game animals by the "wolves," and one person mentioned that coyotes were especially adept at killing turkeys (Hahn, 1909). Coyotes are opportunistic feeders and can subsist on a wide variety of animals (mostly mammals). A considerable amount of mammalian food is taken as carrion. Some plant materials are also eaten. There has been no systematic work conducted on the food habits of the coyote in Indiana. Such a study is currently under way by S. D. Ford.

The coyote captures small prey by pouncing upon it with its feet, but usually kills larger prey by rushing it from the front and slashing the throat, killing with the canine teeth. Coyotes often hunt in groups of three or four, and they may partially cover a larger kill after feeding on it, and feed on it again later.

Conservation Officer Donald Smith told us that he had examined the stomach contents of a few Indiana coyotes and found that they contained mostly voles and other small rodents. A coyote killed near West Point had nothing but 14 prairie voles and 2 mice (*Peromyscus* sp.) in its stomach. James Eloff, while tracking a coyote, found remains of a mourning dove killed by the coyote. We examined the stomachs of 11 other Indiana coyotes. In 4 of them, nothing but prairie voles (total of 16 specimens) was present. Cottontail remains were found in 4, opossum remains in 2, and domestic cow in 1; in each

case, these foods were apparently taken as carrion. One stomach each contained persimmon, voles (*Microtus* sp.), deer mice, and grasshoppers.

We still receive numerous complaints of coyotes killing livestock, and more attention needs to be paid to these reports. We have good evidence that at least some of the alleged killings by coyotes were due to dogs. It is extremely difficult to determine after the fact whether a coyote, a dog, or a coyote-dog hybrid is responsible for damage to livestock. All may kill in a similar fashion, and distinguishing between the tracks of dogs and coyotes is practically impossible. Dog owners and farmers may be quick to blame coyotes for killings actually done by domestic dogs. On the other hand, there is no doubt that the coyote is capable of killing poultry and small livestock. Clearly, more information is needed before the role of the coyote can be better assessed.

Another problem that confronts us in determining food habits from stomach analyses is whether a certain food item was taken as carrion or represents an animal killed by the coyote.

REPRODUCTION. Pairs of coyotes are seen in late winter, and copulation probably occurs in January and February. There is considerable evidence from other states that a mated pair remains together for prolonged periods—perhaps even life (Young and Jackson, 1951). The gestation period is about 60 to 63 days. One litter, averaging from 5 to 7 young, is produced each year.

The young are usually born in underground burrows, sections of which are enlarged to form a chamber about 3 feet in diameter to accommodate the family. C. W. Bussel noted that dens were frequently constructed on knolls or other elevated places on the prairie. Evidently this allows the adults to more easily detect potential danger (Hahn, 1909). There are also reports of young being born in hollow logs. Bussel told Hahn that coyotes defended the den site against dogs venturing near it. He also thought the young were "moved about a great deal" after they were a month old, especially after man or dogs came near the den.

David M. Brooks examined a gravid female

Table 166

Ectoparasites and other associates of *Canis latrans* (n = 15) from Indiana

Parasites	Parasites		Hosts Parasitized	
	Total	Average	Total	Percent
Fleas (Siphonaptera)				
Cediopsylla simplex	18	1.2	2	13.3
Chigger Mites (Trombiculidae)				
Eutrombicula alfreddugesi	9	0.60	1	6.7
Ticks (Ixodides)				
Ixodes cookei	4	0.27	1	6.7
Dermacentor variabilis	2	0.13	1	6.7

(Newton County) on 7 February, but did not record the number of young. A female killed on 5 March (Sullivan County) contained 5 embryos.

PARASITES.   Four kinds of external parasites were found on fifteen Indiana coyotes examined to date — a flea, a chigger, and two ticks (Table 166).

The intestinal tracts of eleven coyotes have been examined for internal parasites. Nine of them harbored a total of 123 cestodes (11.2 per host). Seven yielded 59 nematodes (5.4 per host).

DECIMATING FACTORS. Man and the automobile are the major enemies of the coyote in Indiana.

TAXONOMY.   *Canis latrans thamnos* Jackson may be the subspecies inhabiting most of Indiana, although *C. l. frustror* Woodhouse could also be present (Hall and Kelson, 1959).

SELECTED REFERENCES.   Sperry, 1941; Whiteman, 1940; Young and Jackson, 1951.

Red Fox
Vulpes vulpes Linnaeus

Vulpes fulvus: Haymond, 1870
Vulpes fulva: Evermann and Clark, 1920
Vulpes vulpes: Cox, 1893

DESCRIPTION. The red fox is a bushy tailed, doglike animal with a pointed muzzle and large, pointed ears. It is usually reddish, reddish orange, or yellowish red above. The muzzle, neck, and shoulders are usually orange red, and the flanks, rump, and tail are golden brown. The legs and the outsides of the ears are black. The cheeks, throat, underparts, insides of the ears, and tail tip are white. Color variations occur from time to time. Melanistic animals are basically black. The "silver fox" is a pelage variation in which the guard hairs are black, with frosted or white tips. The "cross fox" pelage shows a darkish band across the shoulders at right angles to the dark middorsal coloration, thus forming a cross. A photograph of a cross fox,

killed near Greenwood, appears in *Outdoor Indiana* (February 1951). Another unusual form of pelage is the so-called Sampson fox, in which the guard hairs are absent and the animal appears to have been singed. Newborn red foxes have short, soft, dark gray pelage.

In Indiana, the skulls of foxes, coyotes, and domestic dogs have 6 upper and 7 lower molariform teeth. The coyote skull is much larger than those of either species of Indiana fox. The temporal ridges on the red fox skull meet posteriorly to form a V-shaped pattern (see Fig. 12); these same ridges on the gray fox skull meet posteriorly to form a U-shaped pattern (see Fig. 11).

Weights and measurements are shown in Table 167. The dental formula is

$$\text{I } \frac{3}{3} \text{ C } \frac{1}{1} \text{ P } \frac{4}{4} \text{ M } \frac{2}{3} = 42.$$

Young red fox. Photo by Fredrick H. Montague, Jr.

STATUS AND DISTRIBUTION. We have been unable to determine just when the red fox first appeared in Indiana. According to Hahn (1909), Lyon (1936), and Hall and Kelson (1959), the red fox may have been introduced into the eastern United States by early settlers for hunting purposes. Wied (1862) saw only the gray fox at New Harmony in the winter of 1832–33. The red fox was not listed from Wayne County by Plummer (1844). In writing of Franklin County, Haymond (1870) stated, "It is only within the last ten or fifteen years that the red fox has been observed in this county. Previously to that time we had none but the common gray variety." But fifteen years later the red fox was the common fox in this country (Butler, 1885). Cox (1893) noted that "A few are taken each year" in Randolph County. E. J. Chansler knew of no record for Knox County before 1870 (Hahn, 1909), though the species was common there from 1880 to 1895 (Butler, 1895). In 1894, Evermann and Butler were able to publish relatively few records for the red fox in Indiana. It was considered "rather common" in

Carroll, Monroe, and Vigo counties. In Vigo County, several fox drives were conducted each winter "and from none to three or four foxes caught each time." Evermann and Butler also listed records for Lagrange, Randolph, and Wabash counties, and noted that the red fox was now "numerous" in Franklin County. Butler (1895) quoted W. W. Pfrimmer as informing him that in Newton County the red fox was "plentiful" along the Iroquois River but elsewhere in the county was "rare."

Hahn (1907a) wrote the following about the status of the red fox in the portion of the Kankakee River valley he studied in the summer of 1905: "The red fox is not common in the marshes, though occasionally taken there. At Mountayr they were very abundant and troublesome." In the Bloomington area (Monroe County), this fox was "not rare," and "traces of these animals are not hard to find in many parts of the county" (McAtee, 1907). Where Hahn worked near Mitchell in 1906–07, he did not see or capture a red fox, but stated that "it is said to be quite as numerous as the other species." Hahn (1909) presented

Table 167
Weights and measurements of *Vulpes vulpes* from Indiana

	Males	Females
Total length (mm)		
n	195	126
x̄	1052.4	951.4
range	895-1110	890-1000
SD	649.4	34.2
SE	46.5	3.04
Tail length (mm)		
n	196	125
x̄	376.6	356
range	320-410	320-382
SD	32.44	16.6
SE	2.31	1.49
Hind foot (mm)		
n	185	127
x̄	160	150
range	100-180	135-160
SD	7.15	5.96
SE	0.52	0.52
Weight (grams)		
n	194	125
x̄	4887.3	3973.5
range	3402-6350	3402.0-5443.2
SD	506.1	347.6
SE	36.3	31.09

a discussion of the status of the red fox in Indiana and other eastern states. He wrote, "I think there can be no doubt that this species has been introduced into Indiana since the coming of the white man." He then mentioned the early records from the state (mentioned above) and went on to state:

At the present time these foxes do not seem to be diminishing in numbers. Most of the evidence I have on this point was collected during the summer of 1905. At that time they had become very bold and numerous in the fertile, thickly settled valley of the Ohio River between Rising Sun and Aurora. In a distant part of the State, at Mountayr, Newton County, they were also a pest. . . . In 1908 they were very abundant and bold near Bascom, Ohio County.

In the Lake Maxinkuckee region (Marshall County) Evermann and Clark (1911) found the red fox rare. They wrote, "The only foxes actually seen by us about the lake were a family of three young and their mother found April 18, 1901. . . ."

In reference to a portion of Porter County, Lyon (1923) wrote, "This animal is apparently not rare in the dunes though not very frequently seen. Residents state that a small number are obtained each season for their fur. One was seen by my wife October 1, 1922." Engels (1933) knew of no records of the red fox in St. Joseph County but thought it had undoubtedly occurred there. He made reference to the fact that fur trader William Burnett had included among a list of furs he obtained along the St. Joseph River in 1800–1801 a fur known as "Redskin." Engels wondered whether this was the name applied to red fox skins. A check of Burnett's records reveals that he listed "Fox, 107; Redskin, 518." We note that deerskins were not mentioned at all and wonder if these were the skins in question. From current evidence, it seems unlikely that the red fox was present in St. Joseph County by 1800. Lyon (1936) had little to say about the status of the red fox in the state but commented that it "probably occurs or has occurred in every county in Indiana." And he later noted, "There is some question as to whether the Red Fox is an original native of Indiana. . . . Most observers in Indiana are inclined to the belief that the Red Fox is a late invader in the state and only appeared when the country became half settled, conditions well suited to its life." Leopold (1929) discussed the possible northward migration of the red fox in Indiana about 1913.

During the 1931–32 season, 2,964 "foxes" were reportedly taken in Indiana, but there was no breakdown into species. Red fox skins at that time sold for $1.75 to $4.00 each (Lyon, 1936).

It is very difficult to determine population fluctuations in numbers of red foxes in Indiana over the past 100 years. Bounties paid on foxes from 1875 to 1948 were summarized by Haller (1950). During this period, bounties were paid in at least 40 different years and on 89,618 foxes. It was impossible to separate red fox from gray fox bounty payments, so any discussion of populations must simply be confined to "foxes." Haller noted that bounty payments indicated population peaks of foxes in northern Indiana in 1926, 1934, and 1946. Population peaks in southern Indiana occurred about 2 years later in each case. Fur buyers purchased 1,820 red fox

Map 51. The Red Fox, *Vulpes vulpes,* in Indiana

pelts from 1952 to 1957. Of these, 57 percent were bought in southern Indiana. But it should be remembered that during this period bounties were being paid by various counties throughout the state. The price paid per pelt during this period averaged 32 cents and ranged from 27 to 40 cents annually. The largest proportion of pelts was purchased in south-central Indiana, followed by the north-central, southwest, northeast, southeast, and northwest districts, in that order. Haller determined that about 48 percent of the foxes taken in fur season were bountied. Because of the lack of systematic and complete fur buyer records and the difficulties of using bounty payment data, there appears to be no information available that enables us to estimate fox populations in Indiana. The red fox may be locally common or rare. Warren S. Rowe told us that during the 1953–54 trapping season, 17 red foxes were taken on 1,280 acres of the Willow Slough Fish and Wildlife Area (Newton County).

HABITAT. The usual habitat of *Vulpes vulpes* is open, dry land, such as old fields, pastures, brushy tracts, farmland, and other unforested areas. Even where rather intensive cultivation is carried out, red foxes are numerous; they evidently find sufficient refuge in waste areas or fencerows and along railroads or ditch banks. They may frequently be seen (even in daytime) some distance from cover, in soybean stubble, in winter wheat, or on plowed ground. They make extensive use of forest edges and small woodlands and are able to penetrate into all of the forested areas of Indiana along streams, roads, power lines, trails, cultivated sections, and other more open areas.

Hahn (1907a) noted that the red fox "is not common in the marshes, though occasionally taken there" along the Kankakee River. Relatively little can be found in the Indiana literature on habitat of the red fox in the state. Haller (1951c) gathered considerable information on winter habitat use by this fox in Greene County during 1950–51. He walked 68,330 yards following red fox trails in the snow (Table 168). The part of western Greene County worked by Haller was "in or near strip mine areas in the glaciated region."

HABITS. The red fox is mostly nocturnal and spends much of the day bedded down in various places that are relatively open. But it is not unusual to see it hunting or traveling during the daytime. Daytime beds are located in stubble fields, fallow fields, pastures, dry marsh borders, fencerows, thickets, and other sites providing some cover. On sunny days, the foxes often lie in the sun. On windy and colder days, they usually bed down on the lee side of a knoll, ditch bank, or gulley. Hunters frequently report red foxes in the rugged old fields of southern Indiana, where broom grass forms much of the cover. Here, they often lie on the sunny slopes in winter and early spring. Kase (1944) reported a female red fox and a female coyote flushed from the same weed patch in February (Montgomery County).

Activity does not cease in winter, and the tracks of red foxes in the snow are among the most common mammal signs noted at that season. Individual foxes may travel a considerable distance in a single night. Lyon noted where one had walked for half a mile along

Table 168

Cover types used by Indiana red foxes in winter
(from Haller, 1951c)

Cover Type	Number of Trails	Total Length (yards)	Average Trail Length in Cover Type
Strip-mine spoils	22	28,800	1,309
Hay fields	2	700	350
Woods	10	3,370	337
Cornfields	11	3,260	296
Soybean stubble	7	1,340	191
Wheat stubble	5	1,500	300
Pasture	11	6,000	545
Fallow fields	4	2,650	662
Plantation	1	100	100
Pond edge	7	2,260	323
Stream edge	9	5,200	578
Fencerow	9	11,300	1,255
Railroad grade	3	1,850	617

the fore dunes of Lake Michigan. F. H. Montague, Jr. (1975), obtained some travel data from red foxes equipped with radio transmitters: two juveniles moved 2.6 miles per night in early fall; an adult male moved 5.6 miles per night during January. Montague found that on his study area (White County) red foxes traveled extensively in the open croplands. These same juveniles occupied a common range of 0.64 square miles during the period they were radio-tagged, while the adult male occupied an area of approximately 1 square mile. Foxes often travel along old roads, ditch banks, fencerows, woods trails, railroads, and woodland borders. Their tracks also reveal that they move long distances over open fields with no cover, even in winter.

Red foxes spend some time (especially during the breeding season) in ground burrows. Although foxes can excavate their own dens, they often take over a burrow system constructed by a woodchuck or other mammal and modify it for their own use. Kirkpatrick *et al.* (1969) excavated a burrow that contained a juvenile red fox and an adult woodchuck. The woodchuck was found about 5 feet from the entrance and the fox about 9 feet. Dens have been observed in old fields, along fencerows, on grassy or wooded hillsides, along ditch banks, in pastured woodlots, in caves, on sandy knolls, in grassy fields, in brushy thickets, in broken drainage tiles,

under buildings, in oat fields, and in pastures. Six dens found by Haller (in Greene County) were situated an average distance of 473 yards from the nearest farm building and 27 yards from the edge of the cover type in which located. Den sites are normally well drained and no nesting material is carried into the den, which usually has at least two entrances. Burrow systems may be 20 to 25 feet long. Occupied red fox dens are characterized by their strong odor of fox urine and by the remnants of food items strewn about the entrance. We have noticed that in northwestern Indiana red foxes often construct their dens on sandy knolls or ridges where digging is easy and vision from the den is good. Dellinger noted that the red fox in Montgomery County tended to locate its den "in open fields, fence rows, and open hillsides as well as open woodland." And he also observed that red foxes seemed "only to use a den to rear their young and occasionally thereafter on extremely bad days."

The red fox has always been considered a cunning animal, and there are countless stories (folklore to fairy tales) about the stealth and slyness of this species. Certainly, it has been able to survive, to increase its numbers, and to adapt to man and his activities in Indiana. Despite years and years of campaigns waged to eradicate or decrease them in the state, red foxes are still an important part of the mammalian fauna. They depend upon their running ability (rather than fighting) to escape dogs, for we have several records of dogs catching and killing foxes. There are many tales of methods used by foxes to throw dogs off their scent. These include doubling back along their trail, walking along the top of a rail fence and then jumping far to one side, and taking advantage of the terrain and various obstacles, natural or manmade, that may impede the progress of the pursuing dogs. The red fox has tremendous stamina and will lead dogs on chases that last for hours.

The red fox seems to be inquisitive and will sometimes allow man to approach quite closely. Whitaker once had a fox approach him in a field until they were perhaps 250 feet apart. The fox became aware of him and started to withdraw, but Whitaker dropped to the ground. The fox made a large semicircle and approached Whitaker from the opposite side until only 50 feet away, then simply stood and watched for a minute. Foxes can be lured to within gunshot range by hunters using predator calls, which sound like a rabbit in distress. Night hunting (and some day hunting) with predator calls is considered quite a sport in Indiana. The usual call of the red fox is a "barking" sound, somewhat reminiscent of the call of a crow, but the fox also emits other sounds. John F. Senft observed a red fox chasing a gray fox and heard a growling noise, but he was unable to determine which species made this sound.

Foxes have locations within their territories where they repeatedly urinate on some stick, post, stump, clump of grass, or other object to form scent markings. Such markings signify to other foxes that the particular locality is occupied by a resident fox. We have practically no data on territoriality of red foxes in Indiana.

FOOD. The red fox hunts mainly by stealthily stalking its prey. Mice, rabbits, and other animals are often captured, either while resting or while moving about, by foxes pouncing on them. Prey is usually caught with the front feet and is quickly dispatched by biting behind the head. Haller made observations of successful kills by red foxes while following their trails in the snow. During the winter of 1950–51, he summarized the feeding habits along 26 red fox trails in a strip-mined area of western Greene County. He calculated that along the average trail of 2,628 yards the fox captured 5.7 mice, 0.1 rabbits, and 0.07 songbirds. Chickens, garbage, corn, and turtle were also eaten, but in very small amounts. It was noted that "red foxes largely confined their efforts to the more open types of cover as compared to the gray fox." Songbirds were obtained while they were roosting. On three occasions, foxes passed within 10 feet of roosting bobwhites without disturbing the quails. A red fox stalked some feeding bobwhites once, but did not make a kill. Rabbits were captured in their forms by the foxes jumping on them. Several times foxes passed within 6 feet of rabbits in their forms and were apparently unaware of the rabbits. Corn, berries, and other miscellaneous food items were eaten from plants or dug out of the snow.

Foxes have often been persecuted for their habit of feeding on domestic poultry. A man at Mount Ayr complained that red foxes killed 150 of his chickens in the spring and summer of 1905. "He dug up some of the chickens they had buried and poisoned them and afterwards found the carcasses of four foxes which had been poisoned and he believed others were killed which he did not find" (Hahn, 1907a). Regarding the general feeding habits of the red fox and possibly summing up the prevailing feelings about it in Indiana, Hahn (1909) wrote,

It can not be questioned that foxes are among our most destructive animals. At the same time, there is a dash and wit about their thievery that makes one feel somewhat lenient toward them. A fox would about as soon take a chicken from a farmyard when there are two or three men in sight as at any other time, and he seldom fails to make a successful getaway with his booty. The chicken yard suffers most from their depredations, but other poultry are also relished and rarely a young pig or lamb is the victim. The stealing is usually done in daylight, although geese and ducks or other poultry roosting on the ground are not safe at night.

Dellinger observed that most cases of fox predation on poultry that he knew about occurred in spring and early summer when the foxes were rearing young.

Kase (1946a) reported on the stomach contents of 211 red foxes from 22 Indiana counties, mostly in the northern half of the state.

When possible, prey items were identified to species (Table 169). Most of the insects were grasshoppers, but some lepidopteran and dipteran larvae and a flea were included. Non-food items were as follows: weed seeds, bits of grasses, small grains, straw, tree leaves, rotten wood, bark, charcoal, wax paper, string, red fox hair (in 31 stomachs), red fox toes, fragments of red fox skin. Haller (1951a, 1951b, 1952a) published his analyses of 215 stomachs of red foxes collected in Indiana (Table 170).

Mangus (1950) identified the contents of the stomachs of 80 red foxes from Tippecanoe County, taken in December, January, and February (Table 171). Among the mice identified were the woodland vole and the southern bog lemming. Microtines occurred about twice as often as mice of the genus *Peromys-*

cus. Mangus found the remains of 11 shrews in 6 stomachs and listed by species only *Cryptotis parva,* which he called the "short-tailed shrew." We do not know whether he confused the least shrew and short-tailed shrew. Two stomachs contained a total of 14 grasshoppers (*Melanoplus* sp.), and a beetle (*Hapalus caliginosus*) was found in another stomach. Species of plants identified were corn, pokeberry, bedstraw (*Galium* sp.), horse gentian (*Lonicera* sp.), and maple-leaved goose-foot (*Chenopodium* sp.). One stomach was completely filled with bark.

We examined the stomach contents of 14 Indiana red foxes and found that the prairie vole occurred most frequently, followed by beetles (Scarabaeidae; Coleoptera), unidentified animal material, cottontail, and short-tailed shrew in that order (Table 172).

Table 169

Occurrence of prey items in 211 red fox stomachs from 22 Indiana counties
(from Kase, 1946a)

Prey Items	Number of Times Occurring	Prey Items	Number of Times Occurring
Mammals:		Eastern Bluebird	1
Cottontail	187	Starling	2
Mice (*Peromyscus* sp.)	59	House sparrow	1
Voles / bog lemmings	70	Meadowlark	3
House mouse	3	Dark-eyed Junco	1
Mice, unidentified	11	Tree Sparrow	10
Opossum	3	Swamp Sparrow	1
Fox squirrel	5	Song Sparrow	10
Muskrat	5	Lapland longspur	1
Hog carrion	22	Black duck	1
Cow carrion	1	Bobwhite	14
Sheep carrion	4	Ring-necked pheasant	5
Pig	2	Bird, unidentified	32
Least shrew	1	Fishes:	
Short-tailed shrew	2	Bullhead	1
Shrew, unidentified	4	Amphibians:	
Woodchuck	1	Salamander	1
Striped skunk	4	Insects:	7
Mammal, unidentified	23	Plants:	
Birds:		Grass (green blades)	1
Domestic chicken	41	Wheat / Rye (green	
Guinea	1	(blades)	8
Domestic pigeon	1	Corn	16
Mourning dove	4	Pokeberry	1
Dove or Pigeon	3	Apple	2
Screech Owl	1	Wild rose	1
Red-bellied woodpecker	1	Wild grape	1
Tufted titmouse	1	Persimmon	6
Wren	1	Unknown	12

Table 170

Occurrence of prey items in 215 red fox stomachs from Indiana
(from Haller, 1951a, 1951b, 1952a)

Prey Items	Number of Times Occurring	Prey Items	Number of Times Occurring
Mammals:		Meadowlark	1
Cottontail	140	Ring-necked pheasant	1
Voles / bog lemmings	40	Bird, unidentified	11
Mice (*Peromyscus* sp.)	21	Insects:	
House mouse	1	Grasshopper	7
Mice, unidentified	49	Beetles	1
Fox squirrel	7	Plants:	
Gray squirrel	1	Grass	72
White-tailed Deer	1	Clover	3
Striped skunk	2	Wheat (green leaves)	9
Pig carrion	9	Straw	3
Hog	2	Smartweed	1
Sheep	2	Apple	3
Mammal, unidentified	1	Black cherry	6
Milk	10*	Wild grape	8
Birds:		Black raspberry	3
Domestic chicken	40	Blackberry	3
Eggshell	1	Persimmon	2
Mourning Dove	2	Beechnut	1
Bobwhite	2	Corn	2
Cardinal	1	Bluegrass leaves	1
Rufous-sided Towhee	1	Unknown	1

*There were 41 juveniles in the sample.

Table 171

Occurrence of prey items in 80 red fox stomachs
from Tippecanoe County, Indiana
(from Mangus, 1950)

Prey Items	Number of Times Occurring	Prey Items	Number of Times Occurring
Mammals:		Birds:	
Cottontail	62	Chickens	9
Mice (*Peromyscus* sp.)	17	Songbirds	6
Voles / bog lemmings	35	Birds, unidentified	12
House mouse	2	Insects:	
Mice, unidentified	6	Grasshoppers	2
Opossum	1	Beetles	1
Raccoon	1	Plants:	
Striped skunk	2	Wheat (green leaves)	5
Woodchuck	2	Leaves	4
Shrew, unidentified	7	Seeds	8
Swine carrion	9	Miscellaneous:	
Red fox carrion	1	Soil and bark	7
Raccoon carrion	1	Straw and grass	26
		Red fox hair	11

Table 172

Foods eaten by *Vulpes vulpes* (n = 14) from Indiana

Food Items	Percent Volume	Percent Frequency
Prairie vole	26.3	35.3
Eastern cottontail	14.3	11.7
Scarabaeidae (adult beetle)	10.7	11.7
Virginia opossum	7.1	5.8
Bird, unidentified	6.8	14.3
Short-tailed shrew	5.4	11.7
Grasshopper (Acrididae)	4.3	5.8
Fox squirrel	3.9	5.8
White-tailed deer	3.9	5.8
Mouse (*Peromyscus* sp.)	2.9	5.8
Cricket (Gryllidae)	2.5	5.8
Deer mouse	2.1	5.8
Carabidae (ground beetle)	1.8	5.8
Animal, unidentified	1.8	17.6
Vole (*Microtus* sp.)	1.8	5.8
Meadow vole	1.1	5.8
Lepidopterous larvae	1.1	5.8
House mouse	0.7	5.8
Coleoptera	0.7	11.7
Diptera	0.4	5.8
Vegetation	0.4	5.8
Corn	0.1	5.8
	100.1	

Foraging red foxes investigate much of their environment, as evidenced by their tracks in mud, dust, or snow. They appear to spend considerable time hunting about the water's edge. In fall and winter they dig about the edges of bales of hay left in the fields, searching for mice and voles beneath the bales. Trappers take advantage of this habit by burying steel traps around such bales. Red fox tracks are frequently noted in the soft, loose soil on the tops of large ant-hills. We do not know why they investigate such sites, but they may be scent-marking stations. Evermann and Clark (1920) reported a red fox standing on a maple tree that leaned nearly horizontally out over a river. On an early September evening (5:45) a red fox was seen sitting quietly in a close-cropped low pasture among the beef cattle, within 20 yards of a busy highway. It paid no attention to two observers that stopped their car to watch it for several minutes. Foxes also indulge in play, and Dellinger related the following account of a red fox observed by his brother.

In the early morning, a fox was seen trotting across a pasture in which were several sows and their litters. At the fox's approach, the pigs scampered away and the fox bounded after them. It circled ahead of them and turned them back then romped around them again and headed them off. The fox repeated this several times and did not at any time make a pass at any of them even though they were only a week old and still quite small. Its run was not the sweeping gallop of a running fox but a bounding, very like a romping puppy. After a few circles, the fox gave up and loped off in its original direction.

Red foxes often cache prey they capture. Hahn made reference to their caching chickens they had killed. When following fox trails in the snow, Haller observed that "the caching or storage of food by foxes was only apparent when the cottontail rabbit was obtained. When such occurred, the fox merely shoved the remains into the snow and pawed a few pieces of vegetation over the item and added a covering of snow. In the few cases observed, the fox never came back to utilize the food cached." Thomas W. Hoekstra found the cache of a red fox (Martin County) on 25 June that contained an eastern chipmunk, two eastern moles, and a vole (*Microtus* sp.). Ralph D. Kirkpatrick *et al.* (1969) found two banded, freshly killed coturnix quail beneath a decaying log four feet from the entrance of an active red fox den. The quail had been released nearby the previous day.

Haller also made observations on the food refuse found about active dens in the spring. At five dens in Greene County and four dens in Dubois County he listed the following: domestic chicken, cardinal, blue jay, rufous-sided towhee, mourning dove, cottontail, fox squirrel, woodchuck, opossum, striped skunk, eastern mole, short-tailed shrew, *Peromyscus* sp., *Microtus* sp., house mouse, box turtle. We have one report of the killing of a chukar by a red fox.

REPRODUCTION. Male and female red foxes may be seen traveling together in December, and copulation evidently begins during that month. Hoffman and Kirkpatrick (1954) studied reproduction in 52 female and 52 male red foxes bountied in Tippecanoe County during the winter of 1947–48 and in early 1949. They reported:

Of 52 vixens examined from December 17 to February 24 during two winters, 31 were pregnant and

four were either in or near estrus. . . . In Indiana some red fox matings take place in December. . . . The latest date for an estrus or near estrus female . . . was February 14. . . . Seven of 17 males studied were producing fully formed sperm and 14 were producing either sperm or spermatids. This clearly indicates that active spermatogenesis does occur between December 20 and February 10.

Gravid red foxes have been collected from 2 January to 26 February, but undoubtedly pregnancy extends into March, or even April. The 31 gravid vixens examined by Hoffman and Kirkpatrick contained from 4 to 12 (average 6.8) uterine enlargements or embryos each. A female taken 16 February had 13 embryos measuring 55 mm in crown-rump length. R. D. Kirkpatrick found 9 embryos in a female killed 16 February (Grant County) and another vixen taken on 26 February (Randolph County) contained 8 embryos.

We have relatively little data concerning litter size. It is sometimes difficult to make accurate counts of young at dens. Evermann and Clark (1920) reported the killing of a vixen occupying a den with her three young. A female and four young estimated to be from 4 to 5 weeks old were removed from a den on 18 April. An immature male from this group weighed 1,765 grams and was 617 mm in total length (Kirkpatrick and Conaway, 1948).

Table 173

Ectoparasites and other associates of *Vulpes vulpes* (n = 14) from Indiana

Parasites	Parasites		Hosts Parasitized	
	Total	Average	Total	Percent
Fleas (Siphonaptera)				
Cediopsylla simplex	14	1.00	4	28.6
Ctenocephalides canis	1	0.07	1	7.1
Epitedia wenmanni	1	0.07	1	7.1
Sucking Lice (Anoplura)				
Neohaematopinus sciuri	1	0.07	1	7.1
Mites (Acarina) other than chiggers				
Hirstionyssus utahensis	1	0.07	1	7.1
Scalopacarus obesus	1	0.07	1	7.1
Chigger Mites (Trombiculidae)				
Neotrombicula whartoni	40	2.86	1	7.1
Myatrombicula jonesae	6	0.43	1	7.1
Ticks (Ixodides)				
Ixodes cookei	20	1.43	9	64.3
Dermacentor variabilis	5	0.36	2	14.3

We observed a young about one-third grown on 5 May. Frank D. Haller reported a minimum of twenty young at six dens he observed. At four other dens he found from three to six young each.

PARASITES AND DISEASES. Wilson (1961) reported the ticks *Dermacentor variabilis* and *Ixodes cookei* and the flea *Cediopsylla simplex* from Indiana red foxes. We examined 14 red foxes for external parasites, of which the only regularly occurring forms were the tick *Ixodes cookei* and the flea *C. simplex* (Table 173). One fox was host to 40 chiggers (*Neotrombicula whartoni*).

Kase (1946a) found at least three species of ascarids in 40 of 211 red fox stomachs he examined. Of these, 24 were *Physaloptera* sp., 10 were *Toxocara canis,* 3 were *Toxascaris leonina,* and 3 were unidentified.

The Indiana State Board of Health examined 60 rabid "foxes" from 1947 to 1956 (Brooks, 1959a); some of these may have been gray foxes. Mange seems to be common in Indiana foxes.

DECIMATING FACTORS. Natural enemies of the red fox in Indiana are few, but hunting, trapping, dogs, and automobiles take their toll. Fox hunting is still a popular sport. Animals are hunted by day or night with dogs, called within shooting range (mostly at night) with predator calls, hunted from airplanes, or killed in drives composed of many people who encircle likely habitat and hunt it out on foot.

TAXONOMY. There has long been some controversy over the classification of the red fox. Recently, the name *Vulpes vulpes* Linnaeus has been assigned to North American specimens formerly named *V. fulva* (Desmarest), because European and North American animals are currently thought to be conspecific.

SELECTED REFERENCES. Brooks, 1959; Hoffman and Kirkpatrick, 1954; Kase, 1946a; Richards and Hine, 1953; Sheldon, 1949, 1950.

Gray Fox
Urocyon cinereoargenteus (Schreber)

Canis cinereo-argenteus: Wied, 1839
Canis virginianus: Wied, 1839
Canis cinereo-argentatus: Plummer, 1844
Vulpes Virginianus: Haymond, 1870
Urocyon cinereo-argentatus: Evermann and Butler, 1894b
Urocyon cinereoargentatus: Hahn, 1909
Urocyon cinereoargenteus: Hahn, 1908b (*Urocyan cinereoargenteus,* Adams, 1950, a misprint for *Urocyon*)

DESCRIPTION. This smaller relative of the red fox is basically grizzled grayish above and on the sides with a whitish belly and throat. On either side of the throat is a rather extensive rufous patch. Some buffy color may show through the gray of the back, for the basal portion of the dorsal hairs is buffy. This same color is present between the gray sides and the white belly and along the lower tail surface. The bushy tail has a black stripe along its upper surface, and a black tip. The feet and legs are rusty yellowish, similar to the color of the sides of the neck and the

backs of the ears. The chin and the sides of the muzzle are black. We have seen at least five melanistic individuals.

The skull of the gray fox is most likely to be confused with that of the red fox; both

Gray fox. Photo by Roger W. Barbour

have the same number of teeth. The well-developed temporal ridges on the gray fox skull meet posteriorly to form a U shape (see Fig. 11); the same ridges on the red fox skull meet posteriorly to form a V shape (see Fig. 12).

Weights and measurements are shown in Table 174. The dental formula is

$$I \frac{3}{3} \ C \ \frac{1}{1} \ P \ \frac{4}{4} \ M \ \frac{2}{3} \ = \ 42.$$

STATUS AND DISTRIBUTION. Wied (1862) reported the gray fox from New Harmony (Posey County). Plummer (1844) wrote about the species in Wayne County: "The gray fox is still found in the more wooded parts of the county. During earthquakes felt here in 1811 and 1812, it is said great numbers of foxes were started out of their retreats." In Franklin County, Haymond (1870) reported that "These foxes are numerous; probably as

Table 174

Weights and measurements of *Urocyon cinereoargenteus* from Indiana

	Males	Females
Total length (mm)		
n	56	56
x̄	943.7	922.37
range	805-1065	819-1004
SD	46.46	41.05
SE	6.2	5.48
Tail length (mm)		
n	56	56
x̄	338.9	330.30
range	220-440	262-425
SD	34.8	28.09
SE	4.65	3.75
Hind foot (mm)		
n	56	54
x̄	136.9	133.85
range	125-150	117-143
SD	5.65	5.98
SE	0.75	0.81
Weight (grams)		
n	51	52
x̄	4399.4	4009.2
range	3402-5896.8	3275-4762.8
SD	542.2	383.1
SE	75.9	53.13

much so as they ever were." The gray fox was not recorded from Randolph County by Cox (1893). Evermann and Butler (1894b) recorded this fox only from Franklin County, repeated Haymond's statement of 1870, and added: "They are still found but are rare. Their shy habits perhaps make them appear less numerous than they are." Butler (1895) reported the species from Knox County and quoted E. J. Chansler, who reported it was "common to fifteen years ago" but was "now rare." Hahn (1907a) did not report the gray fox from the Kankakee River valley, and McAtee (1907) did not list it from the Bloomington area. In writing about the Mitchell (Lawrence County) region, Hahn (1908b) noted, "The gray fox is still common in this locality, although almost exterminated throughout the State."

Hahn (1909) wrote the following regarding the status of the gray fox in Indiana: "The gray fox was formerly common in nearly all parts of the State, but it is fast disappearing. Wied states that it was abundant at New Harmony in 1832." Hahn then mentioned the records of Plummer, Haymond, and Butler that we mentioned above and goes on to say,

Prof. Van Gorder states that it formerly occurred in Noble County, but is now rare or extinct. Mr. I. W. Burton, of Roselawn, and others familiar with the Kankakee region, have told me that the gray fox never inhabited the swamps, but that it has been known to occur in the higher woods in that part of the state. At present I know of but two localities in which these foxes still live, although there are doubtless others. These places are the rough, partially wooded hills along Willow Creek in Ohio County and the rough land along the East Fork of White River near Mitchell.

Evermann and Clark (1920) did not mention the gray fox from the Lake Maxinkuckee region, nor did Lyon (1924) list it from the dunes region of Porter County. In St. Joseph County, it was considered "once common . . . but not known here for many years" by Engels (1933). He evidently based this statement on an anonymous list of mammals of the county, published in 1880, that mentioned that the gray fox was "less common than formerly," and this list may have been inaccurate. In light of the foregoing reports, it is interesting that Lyon (1936) made the following statement: "The Gray Fox was the original fox of Indiana and probably is the species referred to by early writers in speaking of 'foxes.' Even at the present time it is probably found in every county of the state in spite of encroaching civilization and intensive persecution." Lyon's information was based mostly on a questionnaire he had sent to "State Game Wardens and County Agricultural Agents." The distribution map Lyon published does not show any records for many counties in the northern half of the state.

Barnes (1946a) considered the gray fox rare in northern Indiana in 1942 and noted that the highest 1945 kill was made in the south-central portion of the state. This region includes most of the forested hills in the unglaciated part of Indiana. In 1948, bounties were paid in Harrison County on 208 gray foxes and 161 red foxes. The same year, in Shelby County, only 66 gray foxes were included among 365 foxes bountied. Gilbert Heishman told Mumford that gray foxes outnumbered red foxes 2 to 1 in Harrison County in 1953. Dellinger (1951) noted that in Montgomery County the numbers of gray foxes and red foxes had changed within the past decade. He wrote,

Eight to ten years ago the red fox outnumbered the grays several times. Since that time the ratio has reversed. In my first year of trapping fox, 1943, I took fourteen foxes of which twelve were red. This same general ratio held true for the next two years. In 1947 of eleven foxes trapped six were red. Each year since the ratio has fallen a little lower. In 1949 of twenty-one foxes taken three were reds. In 1950, of fifteen foxes only two were reds. Also a study of tracks in the snow will show a ratio of two grays for each red.

In Jackson County, bounties were paid on 472 foxes in 1953; of these, it was estimated that 10 percent were gray foxes, according to the county auditor. Observations made by Mumford in the wooded hills region of the county suggested that both species were present in about equal numbers (Mumford and Handley, 1956). In the early 1950s, Lindsay (1960) noted that gray foxes were less common than red foxes in Jefferson and Ripley counties.

Of 18 foxes trapped on 1,280 acres of the Willow Slough Fish and Wildlife Area (Newton County) in the winter of 1953–54, only 2 were gray foxes (fide Warren S. Rowe). On Willow Slough during the winter of 1959–60, only 2 of 39 foxes killed were gray foxes (fide D. M. Brooks). Neither Lyon (1936) nor Rand and Rand (1951) knew of the presence of gray foxes in Porter County, but Raymond Grow observed a den with young near Baileytown in 1958. It appears that the gray fox has been increasing in numbers over much of the northern half of Indiana during the past 40 years.

Data from annual reports of Indiana fur buyers have been summarized for the years 1954 through 1963. Although annual prices paid for pelts and bounties had much to do with the numbers sold to buyers, these figures are of interest, for they probably reflect the gray fox populations in the six sections into which the state was divided for analysis of these data. Of 2,615 gray foxes purchased during this period, 38.2 percent were from south-central, 19.5 percent from central, 15.9 percent from southwest, 14.0 percent from southeast, 6.8 percent from northeast, and 5.6 percent from northwest Indiana. We suspect that the relative abundance of gray foxes in Indiana today is similar to that reflected in the above data. The species is found throughout the state where habitat conditions are suitable, but is still most common in the southern half. Gray foxes are far more abundant than red foxes in Vigo County. We have examined specimens from 44 counties (Map 52).

HABITAT. The gray fox prefers brushy and wooded habitats to the open areas that attract red foxes. Plummer (1844) noted that gray foxes inhabited the "more wooded parts" of Wayne County, and Butler (1895) mentioned their occurrence in dense thickets and woodlands. Their relative abundance in southern Indiana is no doubt favored by the hilly, wooded terrain and the recent development of large areas of brushland on stipped coal lands and abandoned fields.

Frank D. Haller (1951b) gathered information on the winter habitat of gray foxes by following their trails in the snow (Greene County), from 21 November to 13 March. In the western part of the county, "in or near strip mine areas in the glaciated region," he was able to track foxes on six trails for a total of 8,655 yards. The total length of trails in

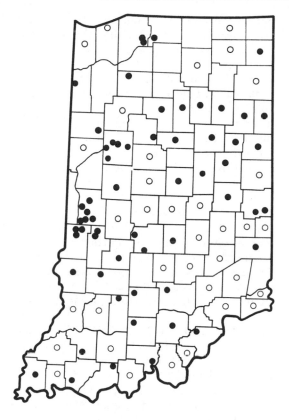

Map 52. The Gray Fox, *Urocyon cinereoargenteus*, in Indiana

each cover type was as follows: strip-mine spoils, 4,700 yards; plantation, 2,150; pond edge, 800; woods, 725; pasture, 200; cornfields, 50; railroad grade, 30. Two trails followed for 4,700 yards in eastern Greene County, "in unglaciated hill country, characterized by large woods and submarginal farming practices," revealed the foxes had traveled the following distances (in yards per habitat): woods, 2,700; pasture, 900; wheat stubble, 500; cornfields, 300; road, 300.

HABITS. Daytime observations of the gray fox are by no means rare, but this species is mostly nocturnal. It evidently spends a considerable part of the day in dens or other hidden retreats; relatively few gray foxes are seen by man. One gray fox shot by hunters was resting by day in a brush pile. Where hunters engage in fox drives, the numbers of gray foxes shot are generally low and there seems to be considerable evidence that the foxes simply retreat to dens rather than allow

themselves to be driven. This behavior is in keeping with the basic shyness of the gray fox. Dellinger noted that in Montgomery County, where he had seen 40 foxes killed on fox drives over a three-year period, only 1 gray fox was included. We have talked to hunters who use dogs to chase foxes, and who complained that gray foxes do not run well ahead of dogs but tend to enter their burrows rather quickly once a chase is begun.

F. H. Montague, Jr. (1975), using radio telemetry, calculated the home range of an adult male (24 November-15 January) to be 227 acres and that of an adult female (24 May-7 August) to be 358 acres.

Hahn (1909) described an encounter with a gray fox, as follows:

I chanced to glance out the window one quiet Sunday morning when the hounds were baying in the distance, just in time to see a gray fox trotting up a woodland path. It stopped about 30 yards away and listened, then made a detour to avoid the house, stopping several more times nearby, apparently oblivious of my presence, although in the meantime I had quietly left the house and was in full view of the animal. It seemed to have used that path before, for it made for a place where there was a break in the close barbed wire fence, then crossed the road, sprang upon the rail fence, ran along its top for a rod, stopping to listen again, and then, as the hounds were coming nearer, it went off across a meadow at an easy trot.

Gray foxes live in burrows that they may excavate themselves and in rocky ledges, in caves, and beneath buildings, piles of rocks, or similar structures. Five dens found in one season (Greene County) by F. D. Haller were all "situated in rock ledges or rock piles," and two other dens he located were "in rock outcrops in woods." The latter were located an average of 100 yards from farm buildings and 40 yards from the edge of some cover. Mumford located a den beneath a pile of discarded slabs left in the woods by a portable sawmill operation. There are a few records of dens in the bases of hollow trees. In speaking of gray fox dens in Indiana, Hahn (1909) wrote,

. . . the dens do not differ from those of the red fox, but they are never placed out in the open fields as are those of the latter species. At Mitchell I found a den not more than 150 yards from an inhabited house, but it was in dense woods on top of a little knoll where there was little likelihood of its being discovered. Another den, likewise near a house, was in the bottom of a sinkhole which seemed to have connection with quite an extensive cavern. Some hunters ran a fox into this latter refuge one night and attempted to dig it out, but gave up the task when they discovered after more than an hour's work, that the den was in a rock lined cavern, too small for a man to enter, but probably of considerable length.

Dellinger observed dens of both red foxes and gray foxes in Montgomery County and had this to say regarding them.

"However, the gray tends more commonly to den in open woods or thickets and use a den throughout the year. . . . I believe the most characteristic feature of the den of the gray fox is the ever present pile of freshly extruded soil. They seem to daily enlarge or clean out their den. This characteristic may lead one to confuse the woodchuck den with the gray fox den. However, if tracks cannot be found in the fresh soil, then a couple return visits the next week prove conclusive. The gray fox will still have a fresh soil pile while the woodchuck's den will have little or no new soil. The fox practices this habit throughout the year. In the dead of winter their dens will be found by these fresh diggings. Even old unused dens may be found, cleaned out. This occurs in all types of weather—deep snow, zero, moderating—and for no apparent reason. On close study of one of these dens, it is obvious that they did not enter further than a few feet in any of the dens yet each opening of a series of dens may be freshly cleaned out.

The gray fox has frequently been observed in the low branches of trees, especially trees that lean. An adult gray fox, found in the base of a hollow snag, jumped from the top of the snag when the hollow was probed with a pole. We have already mentioned the individual Hahn saw walking along the top of a rail fence. Hahn also described how he trapped a gray fox that had crossed a flooded creek on a fallen log. Although the gray fox appears to spend little time near water, it may wade to cross small creeks. We recorded crayfish among the food items found in gray fox stomachs in Indiana, so perhaps this fox hunts along water areas to some extent. It is possible, of course, that crayfish may be captured some distance from water. When following gray fox trails in the snow, Haller observed that some time was spent along the edges of ponds. Mumford and several others once (30 December 1957) observed a gray fox out on the pack ice of Lake Michigan a half mile from shore. It was evidently searching for dead and sick ducks and gulls, which were observed.

According to Hahn, the bark of the gray fox is similar to that of the red fox, but has less volume. Another vocal sound, which was recorded on tape and sent to us for identification, is a loud, rather high-pitched yowling call of about 2 seconds duration, repeated frequently. The call is difficult to describe, but reminds one of an animal howling with pain or the calls given by some monkeys. In the case we know about, it was given at night, in the spring. Gray foxes can be called within close range by squeaking noises. Mumford became aware of this one day while he was sitting in a wooded area making squeaking sounds on the back of his hand in attempts to call up a worm-eating warbler. After a minute, he was aware of a movement to one side and saw an adult gray fox standing within 20 yards, watching him. Hunters make use of the foxes' curiosity by using commercial predator calls to attract the animals to within gunshot range. Some hunters have told us that at night a gray fox will come directly to this sound and will approach to within a few yards from the hiding hunter, even while in the beam of a powerful flashlight.

Evidently several persons have kept captive gray foxes as pets. One female we observed, which had been captured when she weighed only one pound, had the run of a house. She was housebroken, was quite tame, and played with cats and dogs. Hahn (1909) mentioned young that were kept as pets "for some time."

John F. Senft told us that one day he was in a wooded area in Tippecanoe County when he heard some growling sounds. Soon, he saw a red fox chasing a gray fox. The foxes became aware of Senft's presence and stopped. When the red fox ran, the gray fox (which had by now turned) chased it. We have noticed that when pressed the gray fox can run swiftly, at least for short distances. Mumford, driving along a country road at night, saw a gray fox in the road. The fox appeared to be jumping or "bouncing" along. As the car came closer, the fox lowered its body and ran very fast, turning off into the roadside ditch as the car came near.

FOOD. There are general references in the literature regarding food of gray foxes. In general, the public has considered both species of foxes as pests and a threat to their poultry and livestock. This feeling is reflected in the fact that as early as 1875 Indiana initiated a bounty on foxes. Over the years, relatively few data have been accumulated on the food habits of the gray fox in our state.

Hahn (1908b) made the following observation in what is now Spring Mill State Park. "When snow was on the ground the track of one of these foxes entered the Twin Cave nearly every night, for what purpose I cannot say, as the cave contained no food, unless the fox was able to catch bats." John C. Kase (1946c) and Frank D. Haller (1951a, d, 1952a) analyzed the foods in the stomachs of 66 gray foxes collected in Indiana (Table 175). Haller also gathered information on winter food habits by following fox trails in the snow. Along six trails in Greene County, he found

evidence of foxes feeding on mice 21 times, songbirds 6, corn 5, pokeberry 1, and cottontail 1. At five gray fox dens with young, Haller found remains of 3 rabbits, 3 chickens, and a woodchuck. He noted that relatively little food was observed about the entrances, even when litters of young occupied the dens. Dellinger (1951) mentioned the same fact. This is in contrast to the habits of the red fox.

Dellinger thought that raids on poultry were usually made in spring and early summer, when the fox litters were in the dens. Cletus Rush, a farmer in Tippecanoe County, told us that gray foxes captured several of his chickens in broad daylight, while he watched them. The foxes had a den near his barn. A den containing young was found beneath a chicken house near Kokomo. Haller found tracks in the snow where a gray fox had flushed a cottontail, followed it into a burrow, and captured it. Whitaker was squirrel hunting one afternoon in late August about a half

Table 175

Occurrence of foods in 66 Indiana gray fox stomachs
(from Kase, 1946c; Haller, 1951a,d, 1952a)

Food Item	Number of stomachs in which present	Food Item	Number of stomachs in which present
Mammals:		persimmon	12
eastern cottontail	51	pokeberry	1
vole (*Microtus* spp.)	10	ground cherry	1
mouse (*Peromyscus* spp.)	20	unidentified	9
house mouse	1	Birds:	
mice spp.	15	bobwhite	1
short-tailed shrew	1	cardinal	4
shrew spp.	1	marsh hawk	1
fox squirrel	9	rufous-sided towhee	2
gray squirrel	1	robin	2
domestic hog	3	song sparrow	2
Reptiles:		mourning dove	2
snake (genus *Elaphe*)	1	domestic pigeon	1
Plants:		dove or pigeon	2
corn	14	domestic chicken	11
hickory nuts	3	birds spp.	17
beechnuts	1	Insects:	
grasses	18	grasshoppers	7
apple	7	beetles	2
pear	1	Miscellaneous:	
raspberry	1	gray fox fur and toes	1
wild rose (*Rosa* spp.)	1	striped skunk toes, hairs	1
black cherry	1	black walnut shavings	1
wild grape	6		

Table 176

Foods eaten by *Urocyon cinereoargenteus* (n = 34) from Indiana

Food Item	Percent Volume	Percent Frequency
Corn	24.0	41.0
Eastern cottontail	16.0	17.6
Prairie vole	10.7	14.7
Meadow vole	7.5	8.8
Bird	7.1	11.7
Fox squirrel	5.9	8.8
Acrididae (grasshopper)	5.9	17.6
Pawpaw fruit	3.4	5.8
Crayfish	2.9	2.9
White-tailed deer	2.8	2.9
Flesh, probably carrion	2.1	2.9
Carabidae (ground beetles)	1.5	2.9
Phytolacca (pokeweed) seeds	1.5	2.9
Vegetation	1.2	11.7
Wheat	1.1	2.9
Pentatomidae (stink bugs)	1.0	2.9
Coreidae (squash bugs)	0.9	5.8
Chrysemys picta (painted turtle)	0.8	2.9
Norway rat	0.8	2.9
Persimmon	0.6	8.8
Mast	0.6	2.9
Vertebrate, internal organs	0.6	2.9
Grass	0.3	2.9
Seeds, unidentified	0.3	2.9
Lepidopterous larvae (caterpillars)	0.2	2.9
Coleoptera (beetles)	0.2	2.9
Dried leaves	0.2	5.8
Acorns	0.2	2.9
Scarabaeidae (June beetles)	0.2	2.9
Eastern mole	0.1	2.9
Root	trace	2.9
Gryllidae (crickets)	trace	2.9
Cicadellidae (leafhoppers)	trace	2.9
	100.6	

hour before sunset. As he started to stalk a squirrel that was dropping fragments of beechnuts while feeding in a beech tree, a gray fox appeared. The fox moved beneath the tree containing the squirrel and, peering into the tree, walked in circles several times where the cuttings dropped by the squirrel were falling. After 3 to 4 minutes, the fox left the area. An adult gray fox shot on 31 August had vole, corn, and a dozen large grasshoppers in its stomach (Mumford and Handley, 1956). Helen Hendricks (1970) watched a gray fox that came into her yard at dusk and ate cookies, doughnuts, and other snacks put out for it at a bird feeding station. Later, two adults and two young visited the site.

We have examined the foods in the stomachs of 34 Indiana gray foxes (Table 176). The five most important foods, by percent volume, were corn, cottontail, prairie vole, meadow vole, and birds.

REPRODUCTION. Copulation in gray foxes probably takes place mainly in January and February. The gestation period is 51 days. We have examined no gravid females from Indiana. We have records of 3, 3, 3, 3, 4, and 5 young in 6 litters in dens. Hahn mentioned a litter obtained by digging them out of a den (Lawrence County) in mid-March. Three young taken from a den (Jackson County) on 8 May each weighed 424 grams. All had their eyes open and were dark gray in color; one was paler than the others. All showed a trace of reddish color at the bases of the ears. By 11 June, they had adult markings. On 29 May a litter was taken from another den (Howard County). A male taken at Brookville (Franklin County) on 4 February had testes 30 by 35 mm.

PARASITES. There appears to be little in the earlier literature concerning parasites of the gray fox in Indiana. When Kase and Haller did their food habits study of foxes, they reported that 17 of 66 stomachs contained roundworms *(Physaloptera)*. Wilson (1961) reported 1 specimen of the tick *Dermacentor variabilis*, 6 of the tick *Ixodes cookei*, and the fleas *Cediopsylla simplex* (13) and *Ctenocephalides canis* (1).

Of 42 gray foxes we examined for external parasites, 39 were parasitized by 4 species of mites, 2 chiggers, a louse, 11 fleas, and 2 ticks (Table 177). The most abundant parasites were the mite *Androlaelaps fahrenholzi*, the louse *Suricatoecus quadraticeps*, the flea *Cediopsylla simplex*, and the tick *Ixodes cookei*.

DECIMATING FACTORS. Man is the major enemy of the gray fox, and through hunting, trapping, and poisoning has long waged campaigns aimed at decreasing fox populations. Until recent years, the pelts were of little value; gray fox pelts have never commanded the price paid for red fox pelts, which are softer and more in demand. We have examined numerous gray foxes killed by motor vehicles. The role of disease in Indiana populations is unknown, but certainly rabies and probably other forms are important at certain times at certain places.

TAXONOMY. The subspecies in Indiana is probably *Urocyon cinereoargenteus cinereoargenteus* (Schreber).

SELECTED REFERENCES. Layne, 1958; Sheldon, 1949; Sullivan, 1956; Wood, 1958.

Table 177

Ectoparasites and other associates of *Urocyon cinereoargenteus* (n = 42) from Indiana

Parasites	Parasites		Hosts Parasitized	
	Total	Average	Total	Percent
Fleas (Siphonaptera)				
Cediopsylla simplex	48	1.14	17	40.5
Chaetopsylla lotoris	17	0.40	7	16.7
Ctenocephalides felis	6	0.14	3	7.1
Odontopsyllus multispinosus	3	0.07	2	4.8
Orchopeus howardii	3	0.07	2	4.8
Ctenophthalmus pseudagyrtes	2	0.05	2	4.8
Epitedia wenmanni	2	0.05	2	4.8
Orchopeas leucopus	2	0.05	1	2.4
Ctenocephalides canis	1	0.02	1	2.4
Oropsylla arctomys	1	0.02	1	2.4
Tamiophila grandis	1	0.02	1	2.4
Biting Lice (Mallophaga)				
Suricatoecus quadraticeps	167	3.98	10	23.8
Mites (Acarina) other than chiggers				
Androlaelaps fahrenholzi	24	0.57	6	14.3
Dermacarus hypudaei	7	0.17	2	4.8
Ornithonyssus bacoti	4	0.10	1	2.4
Cyrtolaelaps sp.	1	0.02	1	2.4
Chigger Mites (Trombiculidae)				
Neotrombicula lipovskyi	150	3.57	1	2.4
Neotrombicula whartoni	1	0.02	1	2.4
Ticks (Ixodides)				
Ixodes cookei	154	3.67	20	47.6
Dermacentor variabilis	1	0.02	1	2.4

Family Procyonidae

Raccoon
Procyon lotor

Coon

Procyon Lotor: Wied, 1839

DESCRIPTION. The raccoon is a rather chunky, grayish mammal with a black mask and a relatively long, bushy tail marked with alternate rings of black and pale (often yellowish) fur. The ears are rounded. The hind legs are noticeably longer than the front legs, so that raccoons walk in a rather peculiar position with the rump elevated above the front quarters. Pelage color varies considerably and we have examined several albinos. Photographs of "albino" raccoons taken in Indiana have been published in *Outdoor Indiana* (April 1938, p. 27; April 1940, p. 19; January 1952, p. 22). One of these animals appears, from the photograph, to be blond colored overall, with rings visible on the tail. Other blond specimens are in collections at Earlham College and Purdue University. Small numbers of Indiana raccoons exhibit a very dark, nearly black, pelage. In those animals, the black mask is more obscure. Butler (1895) quoted E. J. Chansler as saying "The fur traders say they generally get two or three black 'coons each winter" in Knox County. In the Joseph Moore Museum (Earlham College) is a melanistic specimen

from Franklin County. Other variations include individuals with mostly the normal, grayish pelage but with a broad, black stripe down the entire length of the back. Still other variations are reddish animals. Hunters and other Indiana residents frequently remark on these color variations and sometimes also talk about raccoons with extra long legs. Sometimes laymen separate "swamp 'coons" from raccoons found in upland areas.

The raccoon skull has 6 upper and 6 lower molariform teeth (see Fig. 5); this is the only Indiana carnivore with 6 lower molariform teeth, but foxes and coyotes have 6 upper teeth of this type. Raccoon skulls are shorter (especially the rostrum) than canid skulls and have relatively wider braincases. In raccoons, the posterior portion of the braincase is usually rounded but low sagittal crests and supraoccipital ridges may be present (especially on older animals). Canid skulls usually have well developed sagittal ridges and supraoccipital crests; these are most obvious in the coyote.

Weights and measurements data are shown in Table 178. The dental formula is

$$I \frac{3}{3} C \frac{1}{1} P \frac{4}{4} M \frac{2}{2} = 40.$$

STATUS AND DISTRIBUTION. The raccoon must have been an important part of the mammalian fauna of presettlement Indiana. Barce (1922) stated that La Fountaine obtained 500 skins in less than 30 days at Ft. Wayne (Allen County) in the winter of 1789–90. While touring in what is now Indiana in 1816, David Thomas noted that "Raccoons are in great plenty, and very destructive to corn" (Lindley, 1916). Wied (1862) recorded the raccoon as plentiful (*"gemein"*) at New Harmony (Posey County) during the winter of 1832–33. In Wayne County, Plummer (1844) found raccoons common and stated that they were "often hunted for amusement." A. B. Cole, a fur buyer in Noblesville (Hamilton County),

Raccoon. Photo by Mumford

Table 178
Weights and measurements of *Procyon lotor* from Indiana

	Males	Females
Total length (mm)		
n	78	52
x̄	771	736.09
range	664-853	550-844
SD	39.38	49.73
SE	4.45	6.9
Tail length (mm)		
n	78	52
x̄	210.7	206.48
range	159-254	146-249
SD	22	25.8
SE	2.49	3.59
Hind foot (mm)		
n	78	52
x̄	110.88	107.28
range	85-124	92.8-118.0
SD	7.48	4.98
SE	0.84	0.69
Weight (grams)		
n	72	47
x̄	6,261.9	5,618.77
range	4082.4-6810.0	4377.2-8250.0
SD	1,499.27	934.1
SE	176.7	136.26

bought 3,238 raccoon pelts for $2,006.62 in 1859 (Anonymous, 1906). About Franklin County, Haymond (1870) wrote, "It is the general opinion of our people that the raccoons are as numerous as they ever were; probably more so; but as their skins are of little value, they are not hunted as much as formerly, which may account for their abundance." Stewart (1872) noted that in Carroll County raccoons were "very plenty [sic]; and one year they actually destroyed the corn crop of Joseph McCain!" Raccoons were common and trapped for their fur in Randolph County (Cox, 1893). By 1894, they were said to have declined in Carroll, Franklin, Monroe, and Vigo counties and were listed for only 7 counties (Evermann and Butler, 1894b).

McAtee (1907) considered the raccoon common in the Bloomington area, and wrote, "Every one of the numerous caves in this region has at least one 'coon living in it and evidences of these animals are plentiful along every stream. Mayfield's, Strong's and Truitt's caves are favorite haunts." Along the Kankakee River where he worked in 1905, Hahn (1907a) found the raccoon "abundant" and noted that "many are trapped for fur each year." For some reason, Hahn (1908b) did not include the raccoon in his list of mammals on his forested study area near Mitchell (Lawrence County), where it should have been common. However, in 1909 he mentioned a raccoon specimen from this area; evidently he simply failed to add the raccoon to his 1908 list. In 1909 he wrote about the status of Indiana raccoons as follows: "They were very numerous in the great woods of southern Indiana in the early days and were also found in the timbered swamps to the north, but were not abundant on the prairies. At the present time I do not think they have been completely exterminated in any county of the State, but they are not abundant in thickly settled counties like Marion or in the prairie regions like Benton County."

In the Lake Maxinkuckee area (Marshall County) Evermann and Clark (1911) noted that "The Raccoon appears to be somewhat common, especially in the large stretch of heavy woodland east of the lake." They also stated that raccoons are said to be common along the Kankakee. Regarding prices paid for raccoon pelts, they wrote: "In 1912 their pelts brought $1.50 to $2.00 each. One trapper at Maxinkuckee secured two raccoons in the winter of 1911, two in 1912, and one in 1913. The pelts sold for $1.00 to $2.50 each. Another secured about 12 in 1911–12, worth $1.50 to $2.75 each, 16 in 1912–13, worth $1.50 to $3.00 each, and eight in 1913–14, which he sold at $1.50 to $2.50 each."

The raccoon may have been relatively rare in the dunes area of Porter County in the early 1920s. Lyon (1923) wrote, "Residents state that a few 'coons' are taken each season for their fur. I have no personal knowledge of the animal and I have never been fortunate enough to find foot prints that might have been made by it." Engels (1933) stated that raccoons "were undoubtedly common in St. Joseph County up to quite recent times," but he appears to have been influenced by Hahn's remarks regarding the abundance of raccoons along the Kankakee River. No specific record is given for the county. Lyon (1936) did not comment on the status of the raccoon in Indiana. His range map depicted observations or records from nearly all counties, but he knew of specimens from only 6. He mentioned that "The price of raw Indiana Raccoon skins ranges from $1.50 to $3.00" and 27,391 skins were taken in Indiana during the 1931–32 season.

In Jackson County, the raccoon was very abundant in the early 1950s. A trapper told Mumford that he took 81 from 15 November to 4 December 1953. This trapper complained that the raccoons ruined his mink sets. Another trapper caught 21 raccoons within three-fourths of a mile along the White River (Mumford and Handley, 1956). Lindsay (1960) thought the raccoon was common in the counties of southeastern Indiana where he worked in the early 1950s.

Brooks (1959) collected considerable data on Indiana raccoons and summarized information on their status and distribution in the state. He was of the opinion that raccoons were then more abundant than they were in earlier years when habitat conditions would seem to have been better for them. He wrote:

Indiana is one of the foremost states in the production of raccoons, being surpassed in an annual harvest probably only by Missouri. While common throughout the entire state and present in every county, raccoons are not equally numerous in all sections. Harvest data, which has been collected by the Sportsman's Questionnaire for many years, was used to determine the relative abundance and harvest in different parts of the state.

Analyses of this information revealed that "generally the northern third of the state has a fair raccoon kill, the southern third poor, and the best is found to be in the central portion." Exceptions to this pattern occurred where local habitat conditions were variable. The raccoon has benefited from cultivated crops, especially corn, and this helps explain the relative abundance of the species in central Indiana, where streams, ditches, woodlots, and cultivated fields are interspersed. Raccoon hunters know that in the fall if they release their dogs after dark in an area where a cornfield adjoins a wooded area, their chances of finding a raccoon are increased considerably compared to some other habitats.

Brooks noted that large urban areas usually supported low raccoon populations, as did the sandy soils of low fertility (northwestern Indiana), the extensive woodlands of southern Indiana, and large open fields and prairie areas. Brooks discussed the status of the raccoon in Indiana, noting that it was one of the few game animals that had increased, rather than decreased, in numbers over the years. In the 1930s the raccoon population in the state declined drastically and there was much concern regarding this animal's future. Many organizations raised and liberated raccoons and other raccoons were imported and released in the state. In the early 1940s, the raccoon population began a marked increase and may have reached numbers above any previously recorded for the state. It is doubtful that restocking had much to do with this increase, for raccoons increased in both stocked and unstocked areas, as well as in neighboring states. Raccoons also became numerous in northern areas where they were formerly rather rare. Apparently the population enjoyed an increase into the late 1950s. Annual catches of 101,655 (1953), 98,981 (1954), 108,052 (1955), 102,576 (1956), and 90,153 (1957) were reported. Raccoons accounted for 29 percent of the value of furs taken in Indiana during this period (Brooks, 1959).

Larry E. Lehman conducted research on Indiana raccoons for over a decade. Between 1967 and 1972, he worked on the Jasper-Pulaski Fish and Wildlife Area, northwest of Medaryville. His study area of 2,000 acres of shallow marshes interspersed with wooded ridges and uplands was known to harbor large numbers of raccoons. Annual July population estimates varied with 1 raccoon to every 1 to 7 acres on sample plots ranging from 188 to 310 acres (Lehman, 1977). A second study area chosen by Lehman was near Maumee (Jackson County), approximately 25 miles southeast of Bloomington. The study area was in the Salt Creek drainage, where permanent water was available and there was a good interspersion of croplands, floodplain, and timbered areas. On this site there was 1 raccoon to 15 to 45 acres (Lehman, 1976).

Data were collected on the numbers of raccoons observed dead on Indiana roads each year for a ten-year period. The lowest number (12 per 1,000 miles) was noted in 1975 and the highest (19 per 1,000 miles) in 1974.

Raccoon pelts brought high prices in the mid-1970s, and there was increased hunting of the animals. But despite the increased hunting pressure, the population appeared to maintain itself fairly well. Perhaps where the raccoon has adequate escape cover (den trees, burrows, etc.) it is difficult to deplete drastically the species by legal hunting. Illegal and unsportsmanlike practices of cutting down den trees, digging out ground burrows, taking in excess of the legal limit, and taking raccoons out of season do occur. However, the apprehension of illegal raccoon hunters is difficult, especially when the hunters are familiar with the terrain. Many hunting clubs feel that Indiana should have more raccoons and that the raccoon population of the state has declined. We feel that this may be true in local areas, but by and large the raccoon is still common. We have examined specimens from 60 counties (Map 53).

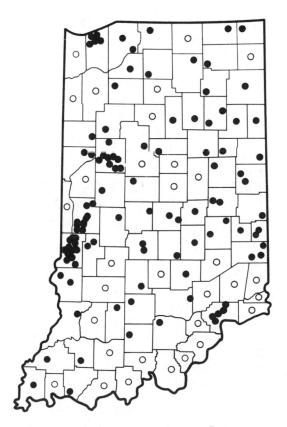

Map 53. The Raccoon, *Procyon lotor,* in Indiana

HABITAT. Raccoons are usually encountered in wooded areas near water and travel along small ditches and tiny creeks as well as the largest rivers. Tracks of this species seem always present in such places. The species also occupies other habitats, such as grassland and farmland, where it finds shelter in drainage tiles, woodchuck burrows, or buildings. Early accounts indicate the raccoon was originally confined mainly to the forested portions (including swamps) of Indiana. As the forest areas diminished, and as the marshes and swamps were drained throughout the state, many thought the number of raccoons would be greatly decreased. But this has not been the case. The raccoon is an adaptable animal, and has prospered despite continued drainage of land and destruction of timber. The raccoon simply learned to live with man and with man's activities, even in urban areas. Indeed, it is not unusual to find raccoons living in cities.

HABITS. The raccoon is terrestrial, arboreal, and semiaquatic, depending upon the occasion. Much time is spent in traveling on the ground along waterways, fencerows, or roadways, and it commonly searches for food around water areas. We have seen raccoons on several occasions wading along the edge of a pond or lake. The caves of southern Indiana are extensively explored by the raccoon; tracks are often seen inside the caves more than a quarter of a mile from entrances. An underground concrete culvert 401 feet long (with side passages of 72 and 217 feet) was repeatedly explored by raccoons. A propensity for swimming permits the raccoon to inhabit swamps and other areas subject to inundation. Though it probably obtains little of its food by climbing, it uses trees for escape, denning, and sunning. Raccoons often travel in groups, probably composed of females with their young. Hunters' dogs may tree two to five at a time in the same tree during the fall.

Dens are usually in large hollow trees, where available, and in late summer one can sometimes observe families of raccoons moving about the limbs of a den tree just before and at dusk. The young often seem to be playing, which perhaps improves their arboreal abilities. The den itself may be in the main trunk of the tree, or, more often, in a large limb. The den cavity is often a foot or more in diameter, and no nesting material is added; the raccoon simply uses the rotten wood and other accumulated debris already there for nesting. Dellinger (1951) observed a den situated at least a mile from open water, but this may be an exception. When good den trees are not available, raccoons may nest in a hollow log, in a rock crevice, under a stump, or in some other protected place. Rabbit hunters flushed one from its daytime bed in a brush pile. In cities, raccoons may live under buildings, in house attics, fireplace chimneys, garages, or den trees and burrows in less disturbed areas. One family lived in the brick chimney of an occupied house.

Lehman studied the home ranges of raccoons by telemetry on his two Indiana study areas (mentioned above). At Jasper-Pulaski the average home range was about 50 acres, and at the Maumee study area home ranges averaged approximately 200 acres. Lehman found the following average minimum home range (in acres) for sex and age classes at Jasper-Pulaski: 21 adult females (27.3); 4 adult males (142.3); 3 yearling females (15.3); 5 yearling males (15.0); 11 juvenile females (11.5); 17 juvenile males (14.0). Home range size is undoubtedly correlated with available food, den sites, and other characteristics of the habitat, and with the density of the raccoon population in the habitat.

Lehman obtained nightly travel information for five raccoons equipped with radio transmitters. A juvenile female tracked by telemetry for two weeks in August and September, traveled an average of 5,100 feet per night. An adult male tracked for two weeks in April and May averaged 5,100 feet per night. A yearling female moved an average of 3,000 feet per night during two weeks in May. Two adult females, tracked for two and three weeks in May and June, moved average distances of 9,500 and 7,500 feet per night. Some information on movements of imported raccoons released in Indiana was obtained in 1976, when 456 raccoons were obtained from Texas and released in five southwestern Indiana counties. Five animals fitted with radio collars and released in Gibson County were all found dead within 37 days after release. All were within one-half mile of the release site. Five other animals with radios were released in Pike County. All were dead within

9 months—four within 4 miles of where released and one 38 miles away. Few of the other 446 raccoons (all with ear tags) were recovered. Of those that were recovered, most had not moved far from where released, a few had moved several miles, and one was shot 58 miles away (Anonymous, 1977).

Raccoons appear to enjoy sunning, especially in early spring when warm days occur. Dellinger made several observations regarding this behavior and we have frequently noted it. Dellinger (1951) wrote:

A sunning raccoon is very versatile in the positions it can assume. It may lie sprawled out lengthwise or crosswise over a limb with four legs dangling over the sides, draped through an upright fork, sprawled flat on its back on a broad limb with four feet sticking up at all angles, or sitting in a reclining position on the limb base and leaning back against the trunk like a pompous old man sitting on the porch with his chair tipped back against the house front.

Not only do raccoons sun themselves in exposed sites on warm days, but they also appear to choose such sites simply to sleep in the daytime. Brooks mentioned that during mild weather raccoons often bedded down on top of leaf nests built by squirrels, in open weed fields, along brushy fencerows, or in dry cattail marshes. Butler (1895) quoted W. W. Pfrimmer, who reported that raccoons "bed up like hogs, two in a bed, on the edge of the marshes."

Some of our observations of sleeping raccoons found in the daytime are as follows: On 31 March (a clear, windy day, temperature 55°F) one curled up 30 feet from the ground in a pine tree in a pine planting at four o'clock in the afternoon. The top of the tree was missing and the animal was lying supported by a whorl of branches at the point where the top was broken off. The raccoon was shaken from the tree and it ran into a burrow in the ground 75 feet away. At 6:30 A.M. on 26 April, a raccoon was seen curled up at the base of a large limb at the trunk of a tree, about 35 feet from the ground. The morning was sunny and cool. Another animal was found asleep on top of a fox squirrel's nest, at the trunk of a tree, 25 feet from the ground, on 2 May. A photographer climbed the tree adjacent to the nest tree and took pictures of the animal, which was not disturbed.

On 6 May, a raccoon was curled up, asleep, 25 feet from the ground, on top of a relatively small, slightly ascending branch, 5 or 6 feet from the tree trunk. Another was seen asleep on top of a squirrel's nest on 17 June. On several other occasions (date not recorded) we have seen raccoons in spring lying on large limbs of cottonwoods and willows about the edge of the marshes on the Willow Slough Fish and Wildlife Area. We have no reports of raccoons sunning or sleeping in exposed sites during the fall.

George Dellinger made some observations on a family of raccoons that lived near his home. Starting about the middle of March, he watched an adult raccoon climb down the tree daily around sunset and walk away. The animal (presumably a female) would return to the den within a few minutes to an hour. She evidently was going each trip to a log, upon which she defecated day after day. During late May, the young were often seen lying out on limbs of the tree on warm, sunny days. Larry Lehman also noted that raccoons repeatedly visited certain sites (often a fallen log) to defecate.

The raccoon is capable of making several types of calls, including loud screams which are often attributed to "bobcats" or other mammals. The young utter a whimpering, chattering call. Sometimes the location of a litter in a den can be determined by such calls. Evermann and Clark (1920) often heard raccoons giving "a shivering call not unlike that of a screech owl" on spring nights. During the mating season, raccoons are frequently heard giving squalls and shrieks and other loud sounds. Hunters also are familiar with the loud screams uttered by raccoons when fighting their dogs.

The raccoon is an inquisitive animal and tends to explore and examine many things within its home range. For example, a bright piece of metal foil is often wrapped about the pan of a steel trap placed in shallow water; the raccoon reaches a foot out to examine the foil and is captured. Raccoons walk along the tops of fallen logs and across bridges. Hollow logs, trees, and other retreats are visited by raccoons, perhaps in search of food or potential dens. Trees that have been climbed repeatedly by raccoons usually show long scratches on the bark (or dead wood if the bark is gone) and can be recognized easily.

Another obvious sign left by raccoons is an abundance of tracks, usually in the mud, and of droppings. The animals appear to investigate even small water holes and temporary pools, possibly in search of crayfish and frogs.

The seasonal movements of raccoons have not been studied in detail in Indiana. However, there are general observations (mostly concerning animals killed on roads) that reveal certain activity periods. During the breeding season, males travel long distances in search of females. This period, usually February in Indiana, is marked by an increased number of dead raccons noted along roadways. There is a pronounced movement of raccoons also in early fall, when the number of animals killed on roads reaches its highest peak. It is thought that many of the animals killed at this time are young leaving their range to find new quarters.

The raccoon is essentially nocturnal, but becomes quite active at dawn and dusk. Each of the animals radio-tagged by Lehman (1977) "began nocturnal activity prior to sunset and remained active until dawn." Most daytime observations are of animals sleeping or resting, although occasionally one finds a raccoon wandering about. Raccoons are not true hibernators, but may remain in dens for short periods during inclement weather. In the fall the animals get quite fat, and they are able to sustain themselves for varying lengths of time without food in winter. In other states several to many raccoons have been found using the same winter den, but we have no data on this behavior in Indiana animals.

Raccoons are not swift runners. Many raccoon "chases" by dogs at night are probably the result of the dogs following the scent of the hunted animals; the raccoon may already be in a tree before the "chase" begins. In fact, some hunters simply drive about at night shining spotlights on roadside trees, in which they often find raccoons and shoot them. Since a raccoon can easily be captured by dogs, when pursued it usually climbs a tree for protection when the dogs get close. If the raccoon is captured on the ground, a fight may ensue. Raccoons are good fighters when they have their backs protected, and many raccoon hunting dogs exhibit split ears sustained in such fights. Some dogs, however, can easily kill a raccoon on the ground. In the water, the raccoon seems to have an advantage and frequently tires the dogs sufficiently so that it can escape. Hahn (1909) relates an observation he made: "I once saw an old female, standing in a shallow pool of water with her back to an overhanging bank, keep four husky dogs at bay for ten or fifteen minutes." Although the raccoon is normally not aggressive toward man, Audubon and Bachman (1851) wrote the following account:

We once met one of these animals whilst we were travelling on horseback from Henderson to Vincennes, on the edge of a large prairie in a copse, and on approaching it ran up a small sapling from which we shook it off with ease; but as soon as it reached the ground it opened its mouth and made directly towards us, and looked so fierce, that drawing a pistol from our holsters, we shot it dead when it was only a few feet from us.

Hahn (1909) kept several raccoons captive and recorded some observations on them. Five young weighing "perhaps eight or ten ounces each" were kept for some weeks. "They showed very great differences of disposition and only one became really tame. He remained a pet until late summer, when he escaped. Two or three days later he came back and began paddling in his dish, which was his way of asking for food. He was chained up and remained until October, when he again escaped and was not seen afterward." Hahn (1909) also wrote, "One that I once had as a pet liked nothing better than a dish of water in which he dabbled with his feet, sometimes washing his nose and lips also, but generally watching something else and paying little attention to the water as long as he could keep his feet in it." Several persons we know have kept young raccoons for a time, but usually they found the pets too difficult to manage when they approached adult size. Pet raccoons given the run of a house will soon make tatters of the curtains and may damage other furnishings on occasion. The animals are quite strong and are able to get into food containers or remove the lids from garbage cans. They can stand upright on their hind feet to reach higher objects. Their fingers are quite dexterous and this enables raccoons to remove the tops from wood duck nesting boxes and to capture and hold food.

FOOD. The omnivorous diet of the raccoon is widely known. The species eats a great variety of plant and animal foods, including carrion and garbage. It raids the garden on the one hand and kills poultry on the other. Hahn (1909) made observations on one of his captive raccoons.

He would eat anything the cats would eat and was fond of milk, but he resented any interference when eating and was always less tractable with strangers than with those he knew. Besides his ordinary food, he once caught a salamander and ate it, and another time a garter snake. However, the delicacy he most esteemed was crayfish, and it was always difficult to persuade him to leave when he was taken to the creek to catch them. This he did with his hands without being pinched by their chelae, but I am unable now to say just how the feat was accomplished. He showed a disposition to attack poultry, but was never given an opportunity to do so.

Evermann and Clark (1920) mentioned the depredations of raccoons on cornfields "at roasting-ear time" and their feeding on fresh-water mussels. Other authors have mentioned that raccoons eat cultivated fruits and berries, persimmons, acorns, nuts, fish, snails, eggs, small birds and mammals, and honey. And their taste for sweet corn from the stalk is well known. C. M. Kirkpatrick once saw a young raccoon feeding on acorns 20 feet up in a chestnut oak. At 6:45 P.M. (15 minutes after sundown) on the evening of 29 September, we watched three small raccoons feeding on acorns about 20 feet from the ground among the branches of a black oak. Whitaker has seen similar behavior on several occasions. When Mumford was trapping and banding ducks at the Hovey Lake Fish and Wildlife Area in the late 1940s, raccoons often entered the traps and killed many ducks. After ten raccoons were captured at one ducktrap in a two-week period, the banding operation was suspended there. A raccoon would kill as many as ten ducks at one time, but feed on only one or two of them. Usually, every duck in the trap would be killed. On all of the areas where wood duck nesting boxes have been erected on tree trunks, raccoons have been a problem. The wooden boxes are damaged by raccoons, which are sometimes able to remove the lids. Duck eggs, young ducklings, and even adults have been eaten from these boxes. On the Jasper-Pulaski Fish and Wildlife Area, raccoons interfere with the nesting of Canada geese. The raccoons prey on nests with eggs or young, often rolling the eggs out of the nest even though they may not be broken or eaten.

We have examined the stomach contents of 41 Indiana raccoons, in which were found 43 categories of food (Table 179). The most important foods, by volume, were corn, earthworms, and mast. Vegetable material accounted for 66 percent of the total volume, insects 9.2 percent, other invertebrates 15.1 percent, and vertebrates 9.4 percent. Among the vertebrates, mammals made up 7.2, amphibians 1.7, and birds 0.5 percent.

Lehman (1977) examined 66 raccoon scats collected during summer and fall on the

Table 179

Foods eaten by *Procyon lotor* (n = 41) from Indiana

Food Item	Percent Volume	Percent Frequency
Corn	28.1	34.1
Annelida (earthworm)	11.6	21.9
Mast	9.9	9.7
Grain seeds (mostly wheat)	4.8	7.3
Grape	4.6	4.8
Vegetation	3.6	21.9
Gryllidae (cricket)	2.7	9.7
Muskrat	2.4	2.4
Eastern Cottontail	2.4	2.4
Trifolium (clover) seeds & flowers	2.4	2.4
Opossum	2.4	2.4
Ambrosia trifida (giant ragweed) seeds	2.4	2.4
Prunus serotina (black cherry) pits	2.4	2.4
Cornus racemosa (gray dogwood) berries	2.4	2.4
Asimina triloba (pawpaw)	2.3	2.4
Isopoda (sowbug)	2.0	2.4
Acrididae (grasshopper)	2.0	4.8
Rana clamitans (Green Frog)	1.5	2.4
Rubus (blackberry) fruit	1.5	2.4
Coleoptera	0.9	7.3
Lepidopterous pupae	0.9	4.8
Carabidae (ground beetle)	0.8	9.7
Sorghum	0.7	4.8
Tipulid larvae (crane fly)	0.6	2.4
Gastropoda (snail)	0.6	4.8
Bird	0.5	2.4
Scarabaeidae (scarab beetle)	0.5	2.4
Grass	0.5	2.4
Decapoda (crayfish)	0.4	4.8
Seeds	0.4	2.4
Araneae (spider)	0.4	2.4
Lepidoptera	0.2	2.4
Insect	0.2	2.4
Bufo woodhousei (Fowler's Toad)	0.2	2.4
Nemobius fasciatus (Gryllidae)	0.1	2.4
Formicidae (ant)	0.1	9.7
Phalangidae (harvestman)	0.1	2.9
Pentatomidae (stinkbug)	0.1	2.4
Reduviidae (assassin bug)	0.1	2.4
Photurus (Lampyridae) larvae	trace	2.4
Hymenoptera	trace	2.4
Tetramorium caespitosum (ant)	trace	2.4
	99.7	

Jasper-Pulaski Fish and Wildlife Area. The following foods occurred in the percent frequency shown: crayfish, 54; vegetable matter, 41; insects, 26; snails, 18; corn, 6; hair, 18; feathers, 4. Since the study area where Lehman worked is mostly marsh, swamp, and woodlands, raccoons depended mainly on noncultivated foods. Hence, the low incidence of corn, although corn otherwise appears to be an important food for raccoons throughout Indiana. On the Jasper-Pulaski study tract, little corn was available to the animals.

The belief persists that raccoons wash their food, and part of the scientific name (*lotor*) means "washer." But even though raccoons do dabble and play with their food in the water, the food is probably not being washed. When a raccoon is feeding along a stream or other body of water, it walks along in the water's edge and with its front feet reaches into crannies among rocks, vegetation, and drift material in search of crayfish or other food. The toes of the forefeet of raccoons are long and can be manipulated like fingers to pick up small items. When a raccoon captures a crayfish, the prey is often held between the front feet and rubbed or rolled about under water. This gives the appearance of washing it, but it may be that the manipulation serves to kill or disable the crayfish or to break it up for more easy consumption. Possibly the large pinching claws of the prey are broken off in this fashion, for they are usually discarded when the crayfish is eaten. Captive raccoons handle crayfish and other foods in a similar fashion, frequently taking food to the water dish and dabbling with it.

Raccoons sometimes become a nuisance in campgrounds, city parks, cemeteries, residential areas, and other places where they are protected. They raid garbage and trash cans, dumping the cans and littering the contents about. The animals may become bold in public camping areas and may even enter tents or trailers for handouts or in search of food. Where man is in such close contact with raccoons, there is some danger of diseases being spread from raccoons to man or to man's pets. And sick raccoons, when handled, frequently bite people, causing much concern about rabies or other infectious diseases.

REPRODUCTION. Brooks (1959) stated that most female Indiana raccoons are bred in late January and early February, with some copulations occurring as late as May. He thought that yearling females especially, and females not bred earlier, were bred in May. The gestation period is about 63 days, so many Indiana litters are born in April and May. Lehman (1968) recorded young he estimated to be born the first half of September. Females have a single litter per year. A certain percentage of yearling females breed, but males do not breed until their second year. Brooks reported that litter size varied from 1 to 9 and averaged 4 or 5. We have records of 12 gravid females, which contained from 1 to 5 and averaged 3.3 embryos each. Brooks summarized the number of placental scars in the reproductive tracts of 33 females collected during the 1952–53 season. Scar counts per female ranged from 2 to 9 and averaged 5.1. A sample of 15 females taken during the 1960–61 season averaged 3.5 scars each. During the 1962–63 season, Brooks obtained the reproductive tracts of 1,188 female raccoons sold to fur buyers. Of these, 25 percent (296) had produced young. The average number of placental scars per female in this group was 3.8. Brooks found that placental scars persisted until at least 17 March.

We have relatively little information on numbers of young in litters observed with females. Seven litters reported averaged 4.3 young. The number of young born per litter would be expected to be smaller than the average number of embryos or placental scars per female. No doubt our sample size of observed litters is too small to reveal this difference.

Lactating females have been collected as early as 31 March, but some females no doubt are lactating earlier in the season. Two females taken on 10 March each contained embryos 30 mm in crown-rump length. The earliest date for parturition we have on record is that of two young raccoons, estimated to be about 7 weeks old, found in a wood duck nesting box on 29 March.

Brooks noted that a raccoon at birth weighed about 2 ounces (57 grams). At birth, the young are not densely furred. The rings on the tail may be apparent, but the ring colors at this stage are composed of pigmented skin rather than hairs. The eyes of the young open at about 3 weeks of age; at this time the face mask and the furred rings of the tail are appearing. We examined one young raccoon on 24 April that weighed 120.5 grams and measured 185 mm in total length. No tail rings were visible, but there was a faint suggestion of a face mask. The body was sparsely haired and the dorsum was a silvery gray color. Young remain in the den until about 10 weeks of age and are weaned at about 14 weeks. Family groups composed of the adult female and her litter remain together into the fall, but the male takes no part in rearing the family. Lehman (1977) concluded that young 10 to 12 weeks of age "were highly dependent upon their female parent for survival." Raccoon hunters have told us that their dogs tree numerous litters in September.

PARASITES AND DISEASES. Wilson (1957) recorded two species of ticks (*Ixodes cookei* and *I. texanus*) and a flea *(Chaetopsylla lotoris)* from Indiana raccoons. Wilson and Mumford once removed more than a hundred ticks from the carcass of a raccoon found dead on the road (Putnam County, on 24 February). Brooks (1959) did not include any data on ectoparasites, but he mentioned one raccoon suspected of having "tick paralysis."

On 54 Indiana raccoons examined we recorded 14 species of ectoparasites (Table 180). The 4 species that each occurred on more than 10 percent of the hosts were the biting louse *Trichodectes octomaculatus* and 3 ticks (*Ixodes cookei, I. texanus, Dermacentor variabilis*). One raccoon was host to an estimated 14,000 laelapid mites of the genus *Hirstionyssus*. These mites were preserved poorly and cannot be definitely identified to species. *H. staffordi*, usually found on skunks and common on the striped skunk in Indiana, may have been the species represented.

We have endoparasites from 30 Indiana raccoons. Included are 195 cestodes from 14 animals, 256 trematodes from 6, and 646 nematodes from 26 animals in this sample. None of these parasites have been identified.

Late in 1955, the number of sick and dead raccoons found on the Willow Slough Fish and Wildlife Area (Newton County) indicated a disease problem. The clinical behavior of several sick animals suggested rabies. In addition, other sick animals not exhibiting rabies symptoms also died. Only 2 of 37 raccoons submitted to the U.S. Public Health Laboratory, Indianapolis, during 1956 tested positive for rabies. An attempt was made to obtain sick raccoons from throughout the

Table 180

Ectoparasites and other associates of *Procyon lotor* (n = 54) from Indiana

Parasites	Parasites		Hosts Parasitized	
	Total	Average	Total	Percent
Fleas (Siphonaptera)				
Ctenocephalides felis	24	0.44	5	9.3
Orchopeas howardii	6	0.11	5	9.3
Chaetopsylla lotoris	5	0.09	5	9.3
Biting Lice (Mallophaga)				
Trichodectes octomaculatus	1,609	29.80	29	53.7
Mites (Acarina) other than chiggers				
Hirstionyssus staffordi (?)	14,000	259.26	1	1.9
Androlaelaps fahrenholzi	10	0.19	4	7.4
Androlaelaps casalis	1	0.02	1	1.9
Ornithonyssus wernecki	1	0.02	1	1.9
Hypoaspis leviculus	1	0.02	1	1.9
Chigger Mites (Trombiculidae)				
Neotrombicula whartoni	5	0.09	1	1.9
Neotrombicula microti	4	0.07	1	1.9
Ticks (Ixodides)				
Ixodes texanus	159	2.94	24	44.4
Ixodes cookei	24	0.44	9	16.7
Dermacentor variabilis	23	0.43	6	11.1

state in 1956 in order to obtain more information on diseases in this species. Canine distemper was found in one or more animals from 18 counties scattered throughout the state, and in 24 of 32 animals examined (Robinson, *et al.*, 1957).

Among the 24 animals with distemper, 16 had a viral type of pneumonia and 6 had a viral type of encephalitis commonly associated with distemper. In addition, 2 specimens had primary toxoplasmosis and 1 had meningitis.

Cultures from the visceral organs of 25 raccoons from this sample yielded *Streptococcus* in 3 and *Pasteurella, Proteus,* and *Pseudomonas* in 2 each. Gross examinations for endoparasites of 25 animals revealed *Ancylostoma* in 4, *Toxocara* in 7, *Taenia* in 7, *Physaloptera* in 15, and *Capillaria* in 3.

In April 1973, several raccoons captured and examined in West Lafayette (Tippecanoe County) were found to have distemper (*Lafayette Journal and Courier*, 10 April 1973). Rabies was not diagnosed in any of these animals. There have been other cases of sick, sluggish, or otherwise abnormal behavior of raccoons in the same area, a heavily wooded city park.

Of 942 Indiana raccoons submitted to the Indiana Department of Health from 1970 to 1976, none tested positive for rabies.

DECIMATING FACTORS. Other than the diseases, to which an unknown percentage of raccoons succumb, man appears to be their worst enemy. Man has long trapped and hunted the raccoon for its fur and, to a lesser extent, for its flesh. Before Indiana was settled, the Indians ate raccoons, as recorded by early travelers through the state. Having eaten numerous raccoons, we can vouch for the fact that the meat is tasty, if prepared properly. As much fat as possible should be removed from the carcass before it is cooked. Years ago, a man in Mt. Vernon (Posey County) had a reputation for his skill in preparing barbecued raccoon, and Mumford enjoyed this culinary delight on one occasion. Large numbers of raccoons are killed on roads by automobiles and other vehicles. We have been unable to obtain information on predation by native animals, although domestic dogs are a threat.

The winter of 1977–78 was markedly unusual for Indiana, with long periods of cold temperatures and 40 to 50 days with continuous snow cover. In late winter, numerous persons reported weak and dead raccoons. Several of those found dead were at the bases of trees; the animals were evidently too weak to climb. Other weakened animals were observed along a road that had been plowed free of snow, which was piled on either side; the animals were unable to climb the snowbanks to escape from the road.

TAXONOMY. Goldman, in Goldman and Jackson (1950), considered Indiana to be inhabited by only *Procyon lotor lotor* (Linnaeus). Hall and Kelson (1959) indicate that *P. l. hirtus* Nelson and Goldman is the form occurring in northwestern Indiana. The status of these subspecies cannot be worked out until more specimens are available for determination. We do not know the extent of the importation of raccoons into Indiana over the years, but it may have been quite large. When raccoons declined so drastically in the 1930s, there appears to have been a widespread effort by various clubs, agencies, and individuals to buy animals from other states for release in Indiana. As early as 1940 (*Outdoor Indiana*, Vol. 7, p. 20) it was noted that tagged animals were being recovered some distance from the release sites. In 1963, a local group purchased 86 Texas raccoons and released them near New Harmony. More than $1,000 was spent in 1967 to purchase 150 Texas raccoons for release at Corydon (Harrison County); the number actually released is not available, but only 1 tagged animal was recovered (30 miles from the release site) according to Lehman. Lehman told us that raccoons had also been purchased from Florida and Wisconsin for Indiana releases. Between April and June 1976, the Indiana Division of Fish and Wildlife released 456 Texas raccoons in Gibson, Pike, Posey, Spencer, and Warrick counties. We know from conversations with raccoon hunters and members of various clubs that many more animals have been imported. It is possible that some of these introduced raccoons have been collected and donated to museums. Thus some of the animals from distant states could represent other subspecies.

SELECTED REFERENCES. Baker, Newman, and Wilke, 1945; Giles, 1939, 1940, 1942, 1943; Goldman and Jackson, 1950; Hamilton, 1936a; Stains, 1956; Stuewer, 1943a, b; Twichell and Dill, 1949.

Family Mustelidae

Least Weasel
Mustela nivalis Linnaeus

Weasel, Allegheny Weasel, Allegheny
Least Weasel

Mustela pusilla: Plummer, 1844 (probably)
Putorius pusillus: Kennicott, 1859 (probably)
Putorius allegheniensis: Hahn, 1909
Mustela rixosa: Dice, 1928
Mustela nivalis: Whitaker and Zimmerman,
1965

DESCRIPTION. Weasels are slender, long-bodied animals with long necks, small heads (not much larger than the neck), and short legs. The least weasel (*Mustela nivalis*), the smaller of the two weasels found in Indiana, is the smallest carnivore in the world. It is about 6 to 8 inches in total length but has a tail only about an inch long. In summer, the pelage is brown above and white below. In winter, some animals turn white except for scattered blackish hairs in the tail tip. In the larger long-tailed weasel (*Mustela frenata*), the tail tip is solid blackish in both summer and winter.

The skull of the least weasel is difficult to

Least weasel. Photo by Durward L. Allen

distinguish from other *Mustela* skulls except for size. Its small size (less than 33 mm total length) serves to separate *M. nivalis* from the other two Indiana species of the genus. The skulls of *M. frenata* and *M. vison* are 39 mm or greater in length.

Weights and measurements are shown in Table 181. The dental formula is

$$I \frac{3}{3} C \frac{1}{1} P \frac{3}{3} M \frac{1}{2} = 34.$$

STATUS AND DISTRIBUTION. The weasel that Plummer (1844) mentioned from Wayne County under the name *Mustela pusilla* may or may not have been *M. nivalis*. Lyon (1936)

Table 181

Weights and measurements of
Mustela nivalis from Indiana

	Males	Females
Total length (mm)		
n	34	17
x̄	184.5	173.1
range	144-209	149-188
SD	13.8	11.46
SE	2.36	2.78
Tail length (mm)		
n	35	16
x̄	30.62	27.8
range	21-40	18-33
SD	4.08	3.88
SE	0.69	0.97
Hind foot (mm)		
n	31	15
x̄	21.35	18.93
range	18-26	18-22
SD	1.83	1.38
SE	0.33	0.35
Weight (grams)		
n	26	10
x̄	44.6	31.96
range	25.7-67.9	21.5-51.9
SD	12.91	9.05
SE	2.5	2.86

thought that Plummer probably intended the species to be *M. frenata.* Plummer wrote, "This small weasel is frequently brought into town to be sold, being generally taken while young." The implication was that most of the specimens Plummer saw were small ("young"). Since there are a dozen specimens of *M. nivalis* from Wayne County in the collections of the Joseph Moore Museum, it seems quite likely to us that at least some of Plummer's specimens were indeed *M. nivalis.* The first preserved specimen, however, was not collected until 7 February 1927, in Wells County (Dice, 1928). Lyon (1933, 1939) recorded single specimens from Pulaski, St. Joseph, and Wells counties and later (Lyon, 1940) added two additional specimens from Pulaski County. Kirkpatrick and Conaway (1948) reported specimens from Steuben and Tippecanoe counties.

Through the years, more specimens have been collected and we now have a much better picture of the status and distribution of this small animal. It probably is less rare than previously thought. At Lafayette, Richmond, and Terre Haute, where there has been considerable mammal collecting, 9, 12, and 4 specimens have been obtained respectively. At Lafayette, several other least weasels were captured alive and released. We know of specimens in museums from 35 counties (Map 54). the southernmost specimen record is from the Muscatatuck National Wildlife Refuge (Jennings County). Leland Chandler reported to us a sight observation of a specimen from Ripley County. We suspect that intensive trapping and collecting aimed at capturing this weasel are needed to provide data concerning its true status.

HABITAT. The first least weasel specimen collected in the state was captured by a dog as the weasel ran from under a corn shock. A least weasel was killed in a burrow beneath a quail coop on the Jasper-Pulaski Fish and Wildlife Area. Another was taken in a gravel pit, and two were plowed out of the ground. Several were trapped at Lafayette in weedy bluegrass pastures, where ground squirrel colonies were present. One entered a mousetrap set across what appeared to be a vole *(Microtus)* runway in a shallow, weedy ditch bordering a grassy meadow. Several least weasels have been taken from build-

ings, even in suburban areas. One was seen entering a mole *(Scalopus)* tunnel (Kirkpatrick and Conaway, 1948). In an abandoned weedy, brushy field at Lafayette, one lived in burrows beneath some large slabs of concrete. Those from Vigo County were taken in mixed grassy / shrubby fields. One had fallen into a freshly dug grave in a cemetery.

ASSOCIATED SPECIES. *Mustela nivalis* probably is associated with numerous small mammals that it preys on, particularly *Microtus* and *Peromyscus.* The frequency with which this weasel has been found in and about buildings suggests that house mice, and perhaps Norway rats, were being sought. This weasel also inhabits areas where thirteen-lined ground squirrel colonies are established.

HABITS. Little is known of the least weasel. C. M. Kirkpatrick caught four in live traps set for thirteen-lined ground squirrels in July 1958. The weasels entered traps in

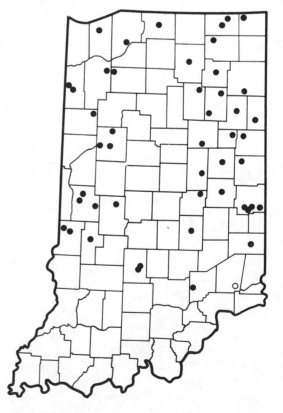

Map 54.   The Least Weasel, *Mustela nivalis,*
in Indiana

which mice were sometimes captured, but no evidence of other animals was found in traps containing weasels. Ground squirrel or mouse scent left on the traps may have attracted the weasels, two of which died in the traps. Evidently least weasels explore various sites for possible food or for shelter. For example, individuals have been found under a corn shock, dead in a bird feeder, in a can in a garage, beside a woodpile in a suburban yard, in a drain tile beneath a farm road, in a granary, in occupied houses, and beneath a coop housing quails. The presence of least weasels in these places may indicate that they were searching for food.

Nests are evidently in burrows underground and may be composed of grasses or other vegetation plus fur and feathers of the weasel's prey. Lyon (1933) mentioned a nursing female least weasel plowed out of a shallow hole in the ground "in the autumn."

Least weasels are active throughout the year and appear to be more nocturnal than diurnal, although we have several records of weasels being observed during the day. We know little about their movements. One was trapped in a *Microtus* runway through rather dense grasses. The tracks of another that lived in an old field were followed one February morning after a light snow the afternoon before. The weasel had foraged 195 feet from the den in one direction and had crossed a small, frozen cattail marsh. In the other direction from the den, its tracks led 360 feet. The path it took meandered about among the cattails, weeds, and clumps of grasses and nowhere followed a straight line. The night these tracks were made the temperature had reached a low of −4°F. James L. Mumford had originally found this animal, when he saw it looking out of its burrow in the daytime.

This weasel was live-trapped and kept for six days. When startled it gave a short, explosive squeak. It slept rolled into a circle, with its head resting on its flank. Most of the daylight hours were spent in a darkened box provided for the animal. Food was usually taken into the box to eat. Kirkpatrick and Conaway (1948) described the behavior of a least weasel kept in captivity for ten months. They noted that it "never forsook its viciousness." A third least weasel, kept captive for about four hours, was observed much of that

period. It gave a loud squeak and a hissing sound, which can be imitated by forcefully taking air into one's mouth through rounded lips. On one occasion, the animal appeared to stamp its feet when disturbed. If one placed a finger near the side of the cage, the weasel always lunged at it, noisily striking the wire of the cage and uttering vocal sounds. Others have noted that disturbed least weasels discharge a fetid, musky odor from their anal scent glands.

FOOD. The major food of this species is probably small mammals, primarily mice. A captive weasel kept by Mumford would pick up dead deer mice by the back of the head and carry them into a nest box. Kirkpatrick and Conaway also noted that food "was usually carried into a small box and eaten or stored there." A captive least weasel they studied killed and ate mice and half-grown albino rats, but "showed fear of a bat and of a small snake which were placed in its cage." It refused to eat butterflies and shrews (*Blarina*). The captive we observed readily ate dead deer mice and squirrel liver.

The killing of live prey by captives was observed by Kirkpatrick and Conaway and by Mumford. The former authors wrote,

Live mice and half-grown albino rats offered to the weasel were dispatched by biting behind the right ear. In killing the rats, which weighed more than the weasel, a violent struggle usually took place with the weasel astride the victim's back, gripping with all feet as they rolled and tossed about. The rats were frequently tugged about by the nose before a satisfactory head hold was obtained.

Mumford watched a captive female least weasel after a live prairie vole had been placed in her cage. The weasel periodically attacked the vole, with no visible damage to the latter. The vole would resist attack by backing into a corner of the cage, standing up on its back feet and fending off the weasel. The weasel did not seem to be able to see the vole the length of the cage (about 10 inches), but appeared to hunt for it by scent. Four hours after the vole was placed in the cage, it was dead.

We have examined the stomachs of two Indiana least weasels killed in March. One contained nothing but vole (*Microtus*) remains. The other stomach held only vegeta-

Table 182

Ectoparasites and other associates of *Mustela nivalis* (n = 8) from Indiana

Parasites	Parasites		Hosts Parasitized	
	Total	Average	Total	Percent
Biting Lice (Mallophaga)				
Stachiella kingi	466	58.25	4	50.0
Mites (Acarina) other than chiggers				
Myocoptes japonensis	25	3.13	1	12.5
Androlaelaps fahrenholzi	6	0.75	2	25.0
Listrophorus mexicanus	6	0.75	1	12.5
Zibethacarus ondatrae	3	0.38	1	12.5
Laelaps alaskensis	1	0.13	1	12.5
Chigger Mites (Trombiculidae)				
Euschoengastia peromysci	1	0.13	1	12.5
Ticks (Ixodides)				
Dermacentor variabilis	5	0.63	1	12.5
Ixodes cookei	1	0.13	1	12.5

tion, about one-fourth of which was grass stems and seeds and the remainder was mast.

REPRODUCTION. Unlike the other two species of the genus *Mustela* in Indiana, *M. nivalis* does not exhibit delayed implantation. Heidt (1970) determined that the gestation period for nine least weasel litters ranged from 34 to 36 days. The number of young per litter varied from 1 to 6 (average 4.7). We examined a female taken on 4 July (Tippecanoe County) that contained 6 embryos measuring 10 mm in crown-rump length. We have no other data on embryos or litters from Indiana. In other states, litters have been reported in many months. Males we examined had fairly large testes in February, March, May, July, November, and December; a September specimen had smaller testes. Perhaps males are capable of inseminating females at various or for extended periods of the year. Reproduction in this species deserves further attention.

PARASITES. We examined eight least weasels for external parasites and found five species of mites, one louse, one chigger, and two ticks (Table 182). Only the biting louse *Stachiella kingi* was common. Only one unidentified cestode was collected from twelve weasels examined.

DECIMATING FACTORS. We have records of least weasels captured by domestic dogs and three by domestic cats. The incidence of such captures probably reflects the amount of time this weasel spends about buildings, where cats and dogs presumably find it more easily. Larry L. Calvert, while tracking a red fox in the snow, found where the fox killed a least weasel then discarded it along the trail. Merlin Shoesmith found a dead least weasel at the mouth of an active red fox den. Several specimens we examined were found dead. One was found dead in a bird feeder; when it was skinned, one or two small punctures through the skin were found in the neck region. Two specimens were killed during plowing operations. Another had fallen into a freshly dug grave. We have examined the skull of a least weasel from the pellet of an unidentified (possibly great horned) owl.

TAXONOMY. For a long time, the small weasel in North America had the name *Mustela rixosa*. Recently it has been assigned the Old World species name *M. nivalis*. The subspecies in Indiana is probably *M. n. allegheniensis*.

SELECTED REFERENCES. Hatt, 1940; Heidt, 1970; Heidt, Petersen, and Kirkland, 1968; Polderboer, 1942.

Long-tailed Weasel
Mustela frenata Lichtenstein

Weasel, Common Weasel, New York Weasel

Putorius noveboracensis: Haymond, 1870
Putorius longicauda: Cox, 1893
Putorius erminea: Evermann and Butler, 1894b
Mustela noveboracensis: Evermann and Clark, 1911
Mustela frenata: Kirkpatrick and Conaway, 1948

DESCRIPTION. The long-tailed weasel is brown above and white below in summer. Individuals vary in the amount of white in the underparts, and some have the white slightly to almost completely replaced with a yellowish color. The tail is relatively longer than that of *Mustela nivalis* and has a black tip. In winter, a few long-tailed weasels turn white except for the black tail tip. Hall (1951) reported that only some animals in the northern third of Indiana became white. Lyon (1936) was told by A. F. Didelot, a trapper in Porter County, that only 2 of 200 weasels he had captured there were white. Brooks (1959) stated that less than 5 percent of the weasels bought in northern Indiana were in the white pelage. Hahn (1909) had reports of white animals (Knox and Monroe counties), and Mumford and Handley (1956) mentioned them from Jackson County. In addition, we have seen white pelaged Indiana specimens from Delaware, Elkhart, LaPorte, and Tippecanoe counties.

The skulls of members of the genus *Mustela* are quite similar, but are separable on the basis of size. In *M. frenata* the total length of the skull is about 44 to 51 mm in males and about 39 to 44 mm in females. Males are considerably larger than females.

Weights and measurements are given in Table 183. The dental formula is

$$I \frac{3}{3} \ C \frac{1}{1} \ P \frac{3}{3} \ M \frac{1}{2} = 34.$$

Table 183
Weights and measurements of *Mustela frenata* from Indiana

	Males	Females
Total length (mm)		
n	25	11
x̄	360	292.7
range	252-400	191-343
SD	32.6	38.5
SE	6.5	11.61
Tail length (mm)		
n	23	11
x̄	121.39	93.1
range	99-144	91-104
SD	11.13	6.4
SE	2.32	1.93
Hind foot (mm)		
n	25	11
x̄	42.4	34.2
range	32-49	28-38
SD	4.3	3.06
SE	0.87	0.92
Weight (grams)		
n	19	6
x̄	200	94.4
range	102.3-283.5	83.2-109.2
SD	53.26	10.31
SE	12.2	4.2

Long-tailed weasel, winter pelage. Photo by B. Burkett, U.S. Fish and Wildlife Service

STATUS AND DISTRIBUTION. Wied (1862) recorded the long-tailed weasel from Posey County. Haymond (1870) discussed this weasel in Franklin County, as follows: "The common weasel, probably the most rapacious, blood-thirsty and cruel of all carnivorous animals, is still found here, though in small numbers." In Randolph County, it was considered "formerly abundant, now rather rare" by Cox (1893). B. W. Evermann reported it from Carroll, Monroe, and Vigo counties, "but never found it common" in any of them, but it was considered not uncommon in Franklin County (Evermann and Butler, 1894b). Hahn (1907a) wrote that weasels "are abundant at most points in the Kankakee River Valley and are trapped for fur, although their skins are not very valuable." In the Bloomington (Monroe County) area, McAtee (1907) thought the long-tailed weasel was rare. And on Hahn's study area near Mitchell (Lawrence County) in the early 1900s weasel tracks "were very numerous." Hahn thought this weasel was found in every county of the state in 1909.

Evermann and Clark (1911) listed the long-tailed weasel as "not rare" about Lake Maxinkuckee, but remarked that "it is not often seen." They also wrote, "It is said to occur in limited numbers on the higher ground back from the Kankakee River." This weasel was evidently numerous in the dunes region of Porter County in the early 1920s. Lyon (1923) reported it as "fairly common" in that area and wrote that "Mr. A. F. Didelot . . . trapped about 200 . . . in the past three winters in the region of the dunes and near Chesterton." Engels (1933) thought the species was probably common throughout St. Joseph County. In 1936, Lyon stated that "It is found in every county in Indiana" but he listed specimens from only 5 counties. Old trappers and hunters talked to in Jackson County between 1952 and 1954 told Mumford that they had seen few weasels during the past 15 years. Franklin Brothers, fur buyers in Seymour, purchased 12 to 15 weasels during the fur season of 1953-54 and thought that weasels were decreasing. Lindsay (1958) noted that reports of weasels in the portion of southeastern Indiana where he worked (mostly Ripley County) were uncommon and attributed this to the low price offered for weasel pelts by fur dealers.

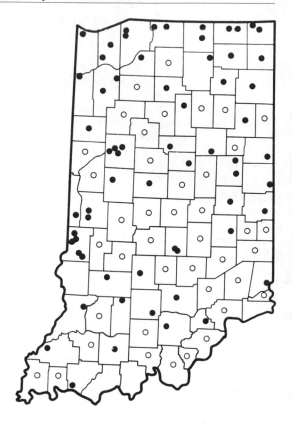

Map 55.   The Long-tailed Weasel, *Mustela frenata*, in Indiana

Long-tailed weasels are still probably found throughout the state, but more are reported from the northern half. Specimens are preserved from 47 counties (Map 55).

Population data on Indiana weasels are largely lacking. The numbers of skins sold to fur dealers for certain years are available, but probably reflect fur prices (which vary from time to time) rather than populations. The reference by Lyon to a trapper catching 200 long-tailed weasels in three winters (Porter County) certainly indicates local abundance. Lyon also stated that in 1932 Indiana fur buyers paid from 10 to 40 cents each for weasel pelts. Brooks (1959) mentioned that the highest prices paid by Indiana fur buyers for weasel pelts was $2.50 to $3.00 each, in the 1919-20 season, and "during the past five years" (1953–57) pelts had averaged 70 cents each. And over this same 5-year period, an average of 684 weasels per year were reported bought by Indiana fur buyers. The numbers of weasels bought annually from

1952 to 1957 were 900, 1,022, 625, 686, 719, and 366 respectively. Prices paid per animal ranged from 65 to 80 cents.

From 1952 to 1963, there were 6,631 weasels sold to Indiana fur buyers. Of this number, 32.1 percent were purchased in 17 counties in the northeastern corner, 18.6 percent in 17 counties in north-central, and 13.1 percent in 12 counties in the northwestern portion of Indiana. These data indicate that weasels were more abundant in the northern half of Indiana than in the southern half.

HABITAT. Weasels are found in practically all habitats. Although they are frequently seen near water, they are much less aquatic than the mink; some authors have suggested that the long-tailed weasel avoids water. *Mustela frenata* is a fairly good climber, but we have little data regarding the amount of time it spends in arboreal sites. Hahn (1909) mentioned that this weasel also used caverns. In the wooded hills of Harrison County, Gilbert Heishman trapped weasels about limestone escarpments, and three young were plowed out of a field in that county. Russel Bruner, a trapper in Crawfordsville, took them in traps set in water for minks and muskrats, at dens in fields and woods, and in hollow trees and tile drains (Dellinger, 1951). They frequent barns and other farm buildings, where they are probably attracted by rats, mice, and poultry, or even bats (Mumford, 1969a). Two were trapped in a 40-acre deciduous woods at Lafayette.

ASSOCIATED SPECIES. Since this weasel makes use of most mammal habitats in Indiana, its associates include many other mammal species. We have trapped the limestone escarpments in Harrison County where Gilbert Heishman told us long-tailed weasels were found. Our traps took white-footed mice in large numbers and a few eastern woodrats, both of which are probably prey of the weasel.

HABITS. Most weasel activity is at night, but it is not unusual to see long-tailed weasels during the daytime. Hahn (1909) wrote, "I have known in a number of instances, of persons seeing them about a barn or garden during daylight." Whitaker observed one running along a log in the woods about midmorning in October. Henry A. Link watched one pursuing eastern chipmunks in

and out of burrows at midday. Malcolm F. Bundy found a weasel in his barn killing bats during the day. Evermann and Clark (1920) reported an account of a weasel chasing an eastern cottontail. During the morning of 29 June 1965, Mumford was making a bird census along the edge of an extensive marsh in the Indiana Dunes State Park (Porter County). He became aware of much scolding by songbirds nearby and quietly watched for signs of the disturbance. Soon, a weasel was noted moving along the ground at the edge of the marsh; a rufous-sided towhee and several other small birds were moving along behind it, calling and scolding. The weasel seemed unhurried and walked along the top of a fallen sapling about four inches in diameter, then disappeared into a thicket. It did not seem to be carrying anything. C. M. Kirkpatrick observed a weasel during the day inside a large, outdoor pen housing ring-necked pheasants.

We have obtained relatively few records of long-tailed weasels being observed at night. George Dellinger shot one from a small tree at night while he was hunting raccoons. The weasel was detected by its eyeshine in the beam of a head lantern. George R. Parker's dog treed a weasel in a cavity at the base of a tree while hunting raccoons on a warm January night. And we have had persons tell us of having seen long-tailed weasels in trees, usually at night. This weasel evidently can climb quite well, for the one that Bundy watched killing bats in a barn was running about in the barn rafters, where the bats were hanging. We have seen a weasel specimen that Marion T. Jackson found 8 feet above the ground in a hole in a dead tree snag. Gwilym S. Jones reported that a weasel climbed a tree to escape him.

Foraging weasels evidently enter many types of openings and crannies in search of prey. Hahn (1909) reported on the habits of hunting weasels which he tracked in the snow. He wrote,

They wind in and out among the trees, entering the base of a hollow tree, a hollow log there, next a deserted woodchuck hole and then a natural cavern. But they almost always emerge at the same or another entrance and go on. Indeed they probably have no permanent homes except in the breeding season, but hunt till tired and satiated, then enter some convenient shelter for sleep, only to emerge and go on to another den miles away.

The slender body, short legs, and small head of the weasel enable it to enter small openings in search of food. Thus, it can move about in underground burrows, hollow trees, cavities in rocky escarpments or among the exposed roots of trees along ditches or streams, about woodpiles or debris piled on the ground, and many other places.

Dens or shelters are in a variety of sites. Engels (1933) mentioned trapping a weasel in a runway "to its den in a pile of rocks at one end of a culvert." Ray Bennett told us of finding seven weasels under an old stump. Evermann and Clark mentioned one that took up temporary residence beneath the floor of a tent. W. L. Hahn trapped one in a hole at the base of a tree. Others have been caught entering or leaving drainage tiles. Weasels are frequently found in buildings and may sometimes make their dens in or beneath them. Most dens are probably in underground burrows. Quite often the den of a long-tailed weasel will contain debris (fur, feathers, etc.) from its prey.

Much has been written about the hunting and killing done by weasels. Haymond (1870), who termed weasels "blood-thirsty and cruel," also stated that "When they make an attack upon the poultry or rats of a barn they continue to stay as long as anything is left with life, unless prevented by fatigue or the approach of daylight." Perhaps his comments are somewhat exaggerated, but weasels are known to be persistent when pursuing prey. Hahn (1909) wrote, "Weasels are the most blood-thirsty of all our mammals. Like the mink, they will invade a chicken-house and kill a large number in a single night." When long-tailed weasels are intent on chasing their prey, they pay little attention to observers, even near them. The weasels appear to reach a frenzied state and will persist in the chase even though one tries to drive them away. Malcolm F. Bundy had to shoot one in his barn because it continued to catch and kill bats (*Eptesicus fuscus*) while he watched close by and tried to discourage it. C. M. Kirkpatrick chased one that had killed many young pheasants in a large outdoor pen. While being shot at and closely pursued, the weasel killed several young pheasants that crossed its path. A weasel observed pursuing an eastern cottontail evidently followed the scent of the rabbit during the chase (Evermann and Clark, 1920). Hahn "often" noted tracks in the snow left by a long-tailed weasel following a rabbit.

Grosjean (1942) described the intensity and persistence of a weasel in pursuit of a rabbit:

On August 12, 1941, I heard a commotion in my yard at Lake James, Indiana. I investigated and found that a New York Weasel was after a young rabbit. They passed by me several times in their mad rush back and forth. I tried to frighten the weasel, but it paid no attention to me. Judging by the squeals of the rabbit, the weasel had wounded it several times, apparently in the throat. At last the rabbit gave in. As I came close, the weasel let go of the rabbit, but would not go far away. It kept returning, again and again, and tried several times to drag the rabbit away from in front of me. It ran over my shoe two or three times; I even put my finger on the animal. It was not afraid and apparently had no intention of losing its prey. The weasel had made five large holes in the rabbit's throat, but there was no obvious bleeding. After the rabbit was killed, the weasel still remained and was so engrossed that we placed half a minnow trap over him and the dead rabbit. We then shoved a pane of glass under the trap, turned all over, and fitted the other half of the trap into place. The weasel and the dead rabbit were immersed in the lake until the weasel drowned. Its skin is now in the Field Museum of Natural History.

Aside from tracks (mostly noticed in the snow), the long-tailed weasel appears to leave little visible sign of its presence. This probably accounts for our lack of data regarding its habits. George R. Parker was raccoon hunting on a January night when his dogs treed a weasel in a cavity in the base of a tree. Parker watched the weasel inside the hole for some time and reported that it was making a high-pitched, chirping sound.

FOOD. Small mammals and birds probably make up much of the weasel's diet. We have examined the stomach contents of five Indiana long-tailed weasels. Each contained a single food item, as follows: meadow jumping mouse, unidentified mouse flesh, *Microtus* flesh, white-footed mouse, unidentified bird. George Dellinger trapped a weasel that had evidently killed a trapped cottontail; we have mentioned earlier that this weasel chases rabbits. Raymond Moffatt saw a long-tailed weasel chasing an adult gray squirrel. The chase took place "up and down trees and on the ground with both the squirrel and weasel squealing at every bound" (Allen, 1952a). There are numerous reports of weasels entering pens or buildings and killing numerous chickens. A weasel captured in a trap set for birds probably was attracted by the birds therein (Engels, 1933). We have reports of a weasel killing a flying squirrel in a live-trap and of a chukar partridge being killed by a weasel.

Food is cached by weasels and there appears to be some uncertainty as to whether or not this stored food is eaten later.

REPRODUCTION. Fertilization is delayed after copulation in this species. Brooks (1959) observed copulation on 15 April. Males col-

lected 21 May, 22 June, 26 June, and 25 July had testes 7, 14, 14, and 15 mm long respectively. Another taken on 22 May had scrotal testes (no measurements). A lactating, nongravid female was captured on 4 May. Young were observed at a den on 14 June and Charles Black obtained a female with three young nearly full-grown in June.

PARASITES. We found 18 species of ectoparasites and other associates on our relatively small sample (16) of Indiana long-tailed weasels (Table 184). The most abundant forms were *Neotrichodectes minutus* (a biting louse), and two listrophorid mites, *Lynxacarus mustelae* and *L. nearcticus*. Wilson (1961) reported a tick *(Ixodes sculptes)* from a weasel taken in Tippecanoe County.

DECIMATING FACTORS. We have records of domestic dogs capturing long-tailed weasels. Most weasels are probably taken by man in

Table 184

Ectoparasites and other associates of *Mustela frenata* (n = 16) from Indiana

Parasites	Parasites		Host Parasitized	
	Total	Average	Total	Percent
Fleas (Siphonaptera)				
Ctenophthalmus pseudagyrtes	6	0.38	4	25.0
Sucking Lice (Anoplura)				
Hoplopleura erratica	7	0.44	1	6.3
Biting Lice (Mallophaga)				
Neotrichodectes minutus	43	2.69	6	37.5
Mites (Acarina) other than chiggers				
Lynxacarus mustelae	1,971	123.19	4	25.0
Lynxacarus nearcticus	17	1.06	1	6.3
Androlaelaps fahrenholzi	4	0.25	3	18.8
Xenoryctes latiporus	4	0.25	1	6.3
Haemogamasus reidi	3	0.19	1	6.3
Dermacarus hypudaei	2	0.13	2	12.5
Zibethacarus ondatrae	2	0.13	1	6.3
Laelaps multispinosa	1	0.06	1	6.3
Dermacarus hylandi	1	0.06	1	6.3
Aplodontopus sciuricola	1	0.06	1	6.3
Pygmephorus designatus	1	0.06	1	6.3
Haemogamasus liponyssoides	1	0.06	1	6.3
Chigger Mites (Trombiculidae)				
Eutrombicula alfreddugesi	7	0.44	2	12.5
Euschoengastia peromysci	1	0.06	1	6.3
Ticks (Ixodides)				
Dermacentor variabilis	12	0.75	1	6.3

his trapping and hunting activities, and some are killed on roads by vehicles.

TAXONOMY. The subspecies in Indiana is *Mustela frenata noveboracensis* (Emmons).

SELECTED REFERENCES. Hall, 1951; Hamilton, 1933b; Polderboer, Kuhn, and Hendrickson, 1941; Quick, 1944; Sanderson, 1949; Wright, 1942, 1947, 1948.

Mink
Mustela vison Schreber

Common Mink, Little Black Mink, Large Brown Mink, Southeastern Mink

Putorius vison: Plummer, 1844
Putorius nigrescens: Haymond, 1870
Lutreola vison: McAtee, 1907
Mustela Vison: Wied, 1839

DESCRIPTION. Minks are usually a uniform, dark brown color above and below. The color on the lower part of the back tends to be darker than that on the forequarters, and part of the tail is sometimes blackish, especially the tip. Pelage color varies from tan, pale brown, and rich brown to blackish. We have noted at least one specimen with scattered whitish hairs over the dorsum. There is often a white chin spot present, and some specimens also have small patches of white on the throat, chest, belly, or just anterior to the anus. Although the body proportions of the mink are similar to those of the weasels, the mink has a much bushier tail and is larger. Trappers and fur buyers frequently comment about "cotton minks," which are animals with abnormal pelage. Such specimens may have normal colored guard hairs but the underfur may be pale, of poor quality, and resemble cotton because the basal portion of the underfur is whitish. This condition may extend over much of the pelt, but it is most likely to be noticed just above the base of the tail. If one blows on the fur in this region, parting the overlying guard hairs, the condition of the underfur can be readily seen. Cotton minks have no value on the fur market. Minks, unlike weasels, do not turn white in winter.

Weights and measurements are shown in Table 185. The dental formula is

$$\text{I } \frac{3}{3} \text{ C } \frac{1}{1} \text{ P } \frac{3}{3} \text{ M } \frac{1}{2} = 34.$$

Table 185

Weights and measurements of *Mustela vison* from Indiana

	Males	Females
Total length (mm)		
n	18	8
x̄	577.4	503.8
range	475-629	480-530
SD	39.33	16.58
SE	9.27	5.86
Tail length (mm)		
n	18	8
x̄	188.83	165
range	148-224	149-181
SD	18.34	12.16
SE	4.32	4.3
Hind foot (mm)		
n	18	8
x̄	64.5	54.75
range	48-94	54-60
SD	10.26	3.01
SE	2.42	1.06
Weight (grams)		
n	11	6
x̄	1,111.8	551.5
range	997.2-1362.0	453.6-680.4
SD	136.84	93.6
SE	41.26	38.2

STATUS AND DISTRIBUTION. Wied (1839) recorded the mink from New Harmony (Posey County). Plummer (1844) noted that "Minks are quite an annoyance to our husbandmen" in Wayne County. We assume he was referring to the mink's depredations on poultry, for Haymond (1870) wrote: "These animals are very destructive to poultry, and therefore very unpopular with our good housewives." Haymond, however, thought there were two species of minks in Franklin County—the common mink and the little black mink. He stated, "These minks are both common—the former the most numerous." The mink was considered "common in some localities" in Randolph County (Cox, 1893). Evermann and Butler (1894b) listed the mink from 8 counties, Evermann noting that he had "seen it occasionally" in Carroll, Monroe, and Vigo counties. They further noted that in Franklin County it was "not uncommon in certain localities." Blatchley (1898) considered the mink rather common in Lake and Porter counties.

In the summer of 1905, Hahn (1907a) found the mink "abundant in the wooded swamps" along the Kankakee River. In the Bloomington area, it was thought to be "rather rare" by McAtee (1907). And Hahn (1908b) frequently saw tracks on his study tract in Lawrence County. When Hahn wrote *Mammals of Indiana* (1909), he commented, "Minks were once numerous throughout most of Indiana. They have been trapped and hunted for their fur to such an extent that they are now considerably reduced in numbers, but even yet are by no means rare where swamps and woods remain." Evermann and Clark (1911) noted, "The Mink is not common in the immediate vicinity of Lake Maxinkuckee, but it is said to be more plentiful a few miles to the westward and along Yellow and Tippecanoe rivers." Lyon (1923) remarked that trappers caught a number of minks in the dunes region of Porter County each year. In St. Joseph County, *Mustela vison* was "rather common in the marshes and along the lakes and streams: and was very numerous about Sousley Lake in 1931–32" (Engels, 1933). Lyon (1936) wrote that the mink was probably in every county of Indiana "where living conditions for it are suitable," but he knew of specimens from only 6 counties. During the 1931–32 season, Indiana trappers captured 18,108 minks in the state. Trappers reported "fair success" in taking minks in Jackson County during the seasons of 1952–53 and 1953–54 (Mumford and Handley, 1956).

In 1859, a Noblesville fur buyer bought 1,126 mink pelts for $687.50 (Anonymous, 1906). Brooks (1959) reported that the mink population declined between the 1940s and 1950s. Indiana fur buyers purchased an average of 6,997 minks per year from 1954 to 1957. For the years 1942 to 1953, this average

was 16,923, and from 1958 to 1963 it was 8,592. In 1965, one trapper in southern Vigo County took 74 minks along the Wabash River. The mink is still probably common to uncommon throughout the state where suitable habitat occurs. Low fur prices the past several years may have taken some trapping pressure off the mink in Indiana. We have examined specimens from 38 counties (Map 56).

HABITAT. Water is the one essential of any habitat suited to minks, although the animals forage into dry land areas when feeding or seeking mates. The borders of lakes, marshes, and ponds, or the banks of rivers, ditches, and smaller streams and creeks, are favorable haunts. Wooded and unforested areas are both inhabited by minks. Banta (1907) noted mink tracks in Mayfield's Cave, and W. S. Blatchley reported mink sign in caves (McAtee, 1907). Minks sometimes make their dens in muskrat houses and Kirkpatrick and

Map 56. The Mink, *Mustela vison*, in Indiana

Conaway (1948) reported trapping a mink at a small hollow in the base of a tree. Minks enter buildings, but presumably only in search of food.

ASSOCIATED SPECIES. In Indiana, the mink is closely associated with the muskrat. Minks may use muskrat burrows and houses, and feed on muskrats. This association is amply demonstrated by the fact that *Zibethacarus ondatrae*, the usually host-specific mite of the muskrat, was found on five of twelve Indiana minks examined by us. Other mammals commonly present in at least some mink habitats are the beaver, the raccoon, and various mice, voles, and shrews.

HABITS. Minks are excellent swimmers and divers, capable of diving to depths of 15 feet or more and swimming under water for 100 yards. When foraging along streams, they explore holes, hollow logs and trees, root tangles, piles of brush, and other dark recesses where prey may be found. Hahn (1909) wrote, "In the water they swim and dive with the agility and speed of an otter. On land, they hunt with the stealth of a cat and run with the speed of a coyote." Perhaps

Hahn colored this account a bit, but he makes the point that the mink is a good hunter. He also stated that minks may travel long distances in search of food and relates that one hunter wrote him that he (the hunter) once tracked a mink nearly all day in the snow for about 20 miles.

The mink is mostly nocturnal, but there are numerous daytime observations, both of family groups and of lone individuals. Evermann and Butler (1894b) observed three minks in the daytime "about a drift pile" within the city limits of Brookville. J. T. Scovell was going down the Tippecanoe River by boat in July when he saw a "family of young minks" on a mass of drift along the stream. "They were moving about on the drift from one part to another. As the boat approached, the two old minks swam out toward it, and as the boat floated by they made a wheezy noise which they continued until the boat was some distance below them when they returned to the drift, into which the young had disappeared" (Evermann and Clark, 1920). On several occasions, Mumford, while duck hunting by floating in a boat, has observed single minks

Mink. Photo by Jon Farrar

hunting along streams in the early morning. The animals entered all dark crannies among overhanging roots, cutbanks, and loose piles of drift materials along the bank. Evidently some of the daylight activity of minks is play, for Dellinger mentions that he talked to numerous avid fishermen and trappers who had watched minks during the day. They reported that often the mink observed "seemed only to be romping about like a playful puppy." Dellinger (1951) also wrote the following:

One lady told the following account of her family's experience with a family of mink. She and her husband were fishing along Walnut Fork Creek just south of highway 32 and their two very young daughters were playing along the bank several yards upstream. Suddenly one of the girls screamed and when they turned and looked they saw a medium sized mink approaching the child and but a few feet away. It stopped about six feet away and surveyed the frozen girl until the father rushed towards them shouting. He had thought the mink might be rabid and was attacking the child. At his shout the mink fled back into the thick brush of a fallen tree. . . . Within an hour after the experience the mink was seen to reappear from the fallen tree, survey the group, then meander down to the water and return to the fallen tree. It promptly reappeared but this time was followed by four rat-sized babies. For the next two hours, the five played in and out of the water and all along the bank and paid no heed to the quiet fishermen but fifty feet down the bank. After two hours play they re-entered the brush of the fallen tree and did not reappear.

C. M. Kirkpatrick and C. H. Conaway came upon a female and litter of young during the day and caught two of the young. When the young called, the female rushed the observers and was shot. Such observations suggest that adult minks possess a strong attachment for their young and will probably fight to defend them if necessary.

Minks often move along with a loping gait or by means of a series of bounds 16 to 18 inches long, and, even when disturbed, may not move swiftly. Males evidently travel more than females, both in search of food and during the mating season. Brooks stated that often a male will have a hunting circuit of several miles which may take him a week to complete, and thus each day is spent in a different den. Dellinger, who did considerable mink trapping, stated, "The mink, especially the males, are ramblers who seem to be traveling all the time. It seems each mink has a route which leads back to the starting point and which it follows time after time—making a circuit every four to seven days." The mink is a good traveler on land as well as along waterways.

Although the mink is not noted for being a good climber, there are several records of minks being treed by raccoon hunting dogs at night. Dellinger was told by hunters that such animals seldom remained in the tree very long, but would jump out, perhaps take to a second or third tree, and finally escape into a safe retreat.

Mink dens are usually ground burrows near the water's edge and may be constructed by the animal itself or by other mammals (often muskrats). Burrows made by minks are commonly 3 to 4 inches in diameter and from 10 to 12 feet long. Other den sites are hollow trees and logs, tile drains, muskrat houses, and holes under bridge abutments, rocks, and brush piles. Rabbit hunters occasionally flush a mink from daytime retreats in brush piles. Brooks (1959) noted that when muskrat houses were appropriated by minks the muskrats were usually driven away or killed by the invaders. He cited one instance, however, where a single muskrat house sheltered a mink and a litter of muskrats simultaneously. The nesting chambers of the two species were about 2 feet apart, but not connected. Nests are built inside the dens. Brooks described a mink nest as being "about one foot in diameter, made of dried grass or leaves, and often lined with fur and feathers of his victims."

Minks are inherently timid and elusive and, as most fur trappers know, may be difficult to trap. They evidently shun trap sites where human scent is left about, and once they have escaped from a trap they may avoid that spot for long periods of time. In some habitats, minks leave little visible sign of their presence. Tracks in the mud or snow are the most obvious and common signs.

The mink may discharge the contents of its anal scent glands when disturbed or excited. The secretion from these glands is thought by many to be more disagreeable to humans than the similar discharge of the striped skunk. The mink's secretion, to us, seems sweeter than that of the skunk, but has a strong, fetid, musky character. Mark Fitzsimmons noted that live-trapped minks may emit loud squeals when handled by humans.

FOOD. Animal foods constitute the diet of the mink. Although most food is obtained in natural habitats, the mink also is not above taking poultry. Hahn (1909) wrote about the food habits of minks as follows:

They destroy great numbers of mice and also many of the smaller game animals, such as muskrats, rabbits and squirrels. Song and game birds are also killed. However, the greatest harm done by these animals is in the poultry yards. Prof. Cox has recorded the killing of 24 half-grown chickens by a mink in a single night. I have heard of one of the animals killing twelve chickens one night and seven in the same poultry house the next night. In both instances the animal was frightened away or might have killed more. Where they come upon such a supply of food as this, they never eat much of the flesh, but suck the warm blood.

Evermann and Clark (1911) followed the tracks of a mink in the snow at Lake Maxinkuckee on a winter day. The animal had moved along the shore, then out onto the ice of the lake for "several rods to an open place where it evidently fed for a time, after which it returned on the ice to the shore and then followed the lake shore" to a point where "it was found under the edge of the ice and killed." They observed a mink feeding on 7 September 1907 and wrote,

It was watched for some time and was evidently feeding. It would dive and remain under a few seconds, then come up not far from where it went under. After remaining on the surface a minute to two, swimming and turning about in a narrow area, apparently eating what it had brought up, it would dive again. Often the entire length from nose to tip of tail could be seen just above the water surface. When it dived it humped its back, going under head first, the entire length of the tail (except the tip) which seemed to be quite long, often coming entirely out of the water. After feeding for more than 20 minutes it swam to its burrow on shore near the steamer slip. What it was feeding on was not determined.

The same authors also noted that on 17 December 1901 "a mink dragged three ducks from the ice on the lake to a hole under a stone wall." Like the weasels found in Indiana, the mink also stores food.

Dellinger found seven muskrats in his traps during one season that were so badly damaged by some predator (he thought mink) that the pelts were worthless for fur. Three of the muskrats had the top of the head eaten away. Fresh mink sign was evident in six of the seven instances and furnished good circumstantial evidence that minks were indeed the culprits. Dellinger also from time to time found the remains of birds along the ditches where he trapped, and believed that minks were also responsible for these kills. In most cases, prey remains consisted of "a small pile of intestines and such few feathers as were held down by the intestines." Such prey had been taken to a secluded site (under a bush or overhanging bank) before being eaten. C. M. Kirkpatrick reported to us two occasions when "dozens" of penned ring-necked pheasants were killed by minks.

David M. Brooks (1959) studied minks on the Jasper-Pulaski Fish and Wildlife Area. He noted that "in summer, mink fed almost exclusively on bullheads and crayfish. With the coming of winter, frogs and crayfish hibernate in the mud, fish tend to go to deeper water, and much of the mink's summer food becomes inaccessible. Birds and small mammals are then more frequently used for food." Brooks also commented on predation on muskrats by minks, noting that many muskrats may be damaged in traps by attacks of minks. He thought that muskrats unhampered by a trap were sometimes able to defend themselves successfully from a mink. In such cases, the muskrat usually had the advantage of having its hindquarters protected by a root tangle or a burrow. Brooks noted that muskrat carcasses that had been fed upon by minks could be easily recognized. He wrote, "The muskrat's chest is first torn open and then the mink eats out the heart, liver and lungs. The stomach and intestines usually are not consumed." The mink then feeds on the forequarters and hindquarters, "eating the bones and meat, but leaving most of the hide. The head, feet and tail are left intact with half or more of the torn and mangled hide. Mink seem to prefer the bloodiest part of their victims and often, if abundant food is easily obtained, only the heart, liver and lungs are eaten." In early fall, Brooks found that mink sign decreased along the waterways. He thought at this season minks hunted the uplands, feeding on mice. As the weather became cooler, the minks returned to the edge of the water. Minks also fed on fresh carrion and took crippled ducks. Evidently uninjured coot are killed and eaten. Minks will frequently take a coot they have killed to the top of a muskrat house, where they will eat it. However, the gizzard of the coot is seldom eaten and one may find several of these organs on muskrat houses where minks repeatedly feed. Snapping turtle eggs are also eaten by minks.

We examined the stomach contents of only five Indiana minks, which contained the following percentage volumes of various foods: muskrat (20 percent), eastern cottontail (20 percent), meadow vole (20 percent), least shrew (16 percent), eastern mole (10 percent), unidentified bird (6 percent), chorus frog *(Pseudacris triseriata)* (4 percent), snail (2 percent), vegetation (2 percent).

REPRODUCTION. The gestation period in the mink is difficult to determine, for delayed implantation occurs in this species. Gestation is thought to be about 40 to 75 days. Brooks (1959) stated that the breeding season in Indiana was during March, when males may travel long distances to locate receptive females, and young are born in late April or early May. One litter per year is probably produced and litter size usually varies from three to six (rarely more). Kirkpatrick and Conaway found a female nursing three young one-third grown on 11 June. Dellinger related an observation of an adult with four rat-sized young (no date). And Evermann and Clark (1920) reported a family of minks seen in July (no date; no number of young). Evidently family groups remain together during the summer.

Males taken 27 November, 13 January, and 23 March had testes 13, 21, and 25 mm in total length respectively. Another taken in January (no date) had testes 28 mm long.

PARASITES AND DISEASES. By far the most abundant ectoparasite on the twelve minks examined by us (Table 186) was the tiny listrophorid mite *Lynxacarus nearcticus.* Other external parasites present in numbers were a tick *(Ixodes cookei)*, a glycyphagid mite *(Zibethacarus ondatrae)*, a laelapid mite *(Androlaelaps fahrenholzi)*, and a louse *(Stachiella larseni)*. It is particularly interesting that five of the specimens were infested with *Zibethacarus ondatrae*, normally found on the muskrat. Presumably the minks acquired this parasite from using muskrat burrows or by feeding on muskrats.

Table 186

Ectoparasites and other associates of *Mustela vison* (n = 12) from Indiana

Parasites	Parasites		Hosts Parasitized	
	Total	Average	Total	Percent
Fleas (Siphonaptera)				
Ctenocephalides felis	1	0.08	1	8.3
Ctenophthalmus pseudagyrtes	1	0.08	1	8.3
Biting Lice (Mallophaga)				
Stachiella larseni	550	45.83	6	50.0
Mites (Acarina) other than chiggers				
Lynxacarus nearcticus	3,285	273.75	6	50.0
Zibethacarus ondatrae	121	10.08	5	41.7
Androlaelaps fahrenholzi	50	4.17	4	33.3
Laelaps kochi	2	0.17	2	16.7
Marsupialichus brasiliensis	1	0.08	1	8.3
Laelaps multispinosa	1	0.08	1	8.3
Chigger Mites (Trombiculidae)				
Neotrombicula whartoni	2	0.17	2	16.7
Ticks (Ixodides)				
Ixodes cookei	191	15.92	5	41.7

Internal parasites collected from ten mink specimens included 54 trematodes (in two animals), 1 nematode, and 2 cestodes.

Although canine distemper was suspected as the cause of deaths of Indiana minks in the winter of 1956–57, it was not definitely established. Brooks (1959) wrote,

Canine distemper, recently found to be present in the raccoon population in many sections of the state, is a serious disease of mink. The habitat of mink and raccoon overlap and undoubtedly many mink have contracted and died from this disease. There has been a marked decrease in the number of mink trapped during the past four years in areas where canine distemper was found to be present in raccoon.

All of 22 minks tested for rabies by the Indiana State Board of Health from 1970 to 1976 were negative for this disease.

DECIMATING FACTORS. Minks are frequently found dead, but to our knowledge none of these animals has been diagnosed as to cause of death. During the 1955–56 trapping season, eight dead minks were found on the ice at the Willow Slough Fish and Wildlife Area. D. M. Brooks thought that some of them had possibly been killed by dogs. We have recorded several dead minks killed by vehicles. Habitat destruction, especially drainage of wetlands, is the worst enemy of the mink in Indiana.

TAXONOMY. According to Hall and Kelson (1959) *Mustela vison mink* Peale and Beauvois and *M. v. letifera* Hollister occur in the state; the latter is confined to the northwestern corner, but we see no reason to recognize more than one subspecies in the state.

SELECTED REFERENCES. Enders, 1952; Errington, 1943; Gorham and Griffiths, 1952; Hamilton, 1936b, 1940; Hansson, 1947; Hollister, 1913; Korschgen, 1958; Marshall, 1936; Sealander, 1943; A. Svihla, 1931.

Badger
Taxidea taxus (Schreber)

American Badger

Taxidea americana: Evermann and Butler, 1894b
Taxidea taxus: Hahn, 1907a

DESCRIPTION. The badger has short legs and tail, a heavy, rather flattened body, and is grayish to grayish buff in color. The feet are black; the broad front feet have long, strong claws for digging. A narrow white stripe runs from the nose to the shoulders. The face is black and white and there is a black patch in front of each ear. The underside is whitish to yellowish. A black individual was taken in Noble County in 1880 (Evermann and Butler, 1894b).

The skull is massive, about 120 mm in total length, 80 mm in zygomatic width, and has a triangular braincase (see Fig. 15). The hard palate extends far behind the posterior edge of the last molariform teeth. This is the only Indiana carnivore skull more than 100 mm long with 4 upper molariform teeth.

Weights and measurements are shown in

Table 187. The dental formula is

$$I \frac{3}{3} C \frac{1}{1} P \frac{3}{3} M \frac{1}{2} = 34.$$

STATUS AND DISTRIBUTION. The earliest report of a badger in Indiana that we have knowledge of is that of Ebenezer M. Chamberlain for Elkhart County, in 1833 (Anonymous, 1919). The badger was considered "almost extinct" in Lake County in 1884 (Ball, 1884). Evermann and Butler (1894b) were the first biologists to publish a summary of records known to them up to that time. They mentioned one killed in Vermillion County in 1880. S. D. Steininger told them of the occurrence of badgers in DeKalb, Elkhart, Kosciusko, Lagrange, Noble, and Steuben counties. Four were said to have been captured in Lagrange County "within the last ten years, the last one in 1887." In 1888, "three were caught in the northeast part of Elkhart County." Another was taken in that county in 1889. One was killed in Noble County in 1880. They mentioned an unver-

Badger. Note the "flattened" body. Photo by Luther C. Goldman, U.S. Fish and Wildlife Service

ified record from Grant County. On 28 July 1889, a badger was killed near Metamora (Franklin County), and two others were reportedly taken there the preceding year.

Butler (1895) noted that the badger was "occasionally found" in Newton County and that one was killed in Benton County about 1874. When W. L. Hahn wrote *Mammals of Indiana* (1909), he cited the records of Evermann and Butler and stated, "The badger has never been very abundant in Indiana." Hahn had been informed of other reports and records of Indiana badgers and added the following:

Prof. Van Gorder says the badger was supposed for a long time to be extinct in Noble County, but that he saw one taken in Green township in the spring of 1895, and one or two have been reported in the county since that time. Mr. I. N. Lamb saw one near English Lake in 1871. Mrs. Anderson mentions their occurrence in Benton County and Mr. Upson saw one in LaGrange County in the spring of 1908.

Brennan (1923) observed a badger in the dunes of Porter County in 1918. Evermann and Clark (1911), writing about the Lake Maxinkuckee region of Marshall County, stated, "Never more than very rare in Indiana and now probably extinct in this part of the state." They noted that "old residents say that it was formerly found in Marshall County."

Lyon (1932) summarized all badger records from Indiana then known to him. Counties from which he listed records for the period 1926 to 1931 included Cass, Elkhart, Jasper, Kosciusko, Lake, Porter, St. Joseph, and Whitley. In 1936, when Lyon published his *Mammals of Indiana*, he was able to add little to his 1932 data, although he included reports (unsupported by specimens) from additional counties in the northern one-third of the state. Except for the old records from Vermillion County (1880) and Franklin County (1889), the southern known border of the occupied range of the badger was marked by Benton, Howard, and Grant counties. Up to 1936, there appeared to be no indication of range extension. No doubt, the badger was rare in Indiana from 1900 to 1936.

In 1942, Barnes wrote that the badger is "a scarce animal in Indiana" and that catches "generally occur in the northern part of the state." He noted that 61 were reportedly

Table 187

Weights and measurements of
Taxidea taxus from Indiana

	Males	Females
Total length (mm)		
n	11	8
x̄	753.7	689.12
range	605-843	614-787
SD	69.9	59.32
SE	21.07	20.9
Tail length (mm)		
n	11	8
x̄	148.18	124.12
range	115-250	115-139
SD	38.58	15.31
SE	11.6	5.41
Hind foot (mm)		
n	11	7
x̄	108.1	101.85
range	93.0-120.5	85-115
SD	9.08	10.04
SE	2.73	3.79
Weight (grams)		
n	11	7
x̄	7,376.8	6,996.3
range	3,628.8-12,100.0	3,175.2-9,072.0
SD	3,455.7	1,967.9
SE	1,041.9	743.8

taken in Indiana in 1942 and 172 in 1943. Brooks (1956) conducted a survey of badger distribution in Indiana by sending questionnaires to conservation officers in each county. As of 1955, badgers were reported from 33 counties, including Dubois and Crawford in southern Indiana. Brooks thought that the badger was probably most numerous in the northeastern section of the state and most rare in the southern half. He estimated the largest county population to be 50 (Lagrange County). Estimates for other counties were as follows: Kosciusko, 10 to 35; Noble, 25; Warren, 12; Owen, 10; Marshall, 10. The statewide population was estimated at 350.

By plotting records we have accumulated from various sources, it appears that badgers did not extend their range much during the 1940s, but an increased number of reports was obtained in the 1950s, including records from 9 counties in the southern half of Indiana. The most marked increase in reports and range extension occurred in the 1960s.

Badgers were also reported from new areas during the 1970s, but the rate of range extension appears to have slowed by then. From 1952 through 1963, there were 71 badgers reported sold to fur buyers. The numbers purchased per year for this period were 9, 4, 0, 8, 4, 3, 0, 7, 6, 7, 18, and 5. Of the 71 badgers sold over this period, 30 were from northeastern, 13 from northwestern, and 11 from southwestern Indiana. We know that not all badgers killed are sold to fur buyers.

We have no records of badgers for Vermillion County from 1880 to 1959, but since 1950, the species has been recorded from Vermillion County southward in 10 counties along the southwestern side of Indiana. Likewise, we have no records from Franklin County from 1889 to 1949 (Brooks, 1956). The first records for counties near Franklin (Dearborn, Henry, Rush, Union, Wayne) were obtained in the 1950s and 1960s. Of course, over the years badgers may have occupied various counties for which we have no reports. And since 1936, the badger has spread southward through the center of the state from Howard County to Bartholomew County (with one report for Crawford County). The spread of the badger has been similar to that of another prairie mammal, the thirteen-lined ground squirrel. We have examined badger specimens from 26 counties, but there are reports of the species from many other counties (Map 57). The badger is on the list of protected mammals in Indiana.

HABITAT. Lyon reported a badger trapped at the mouth of a woodchuck burrow. Dellinger mentioned one trapped at its burrow "in a thicket," and another, also taken at a burrow entrance, "was using several dens . . . in the banks of an old gravel pit" where grass had revegetated. Bee Wright trapped three in old fields near Bloomingdale (Parke County). In the fall of 1959, a badger excavated a dozen holes in a fallow field sparsely overgrown with aster, goldenrod, sweet clover, and other plants in Lagrange County. The area was a dry, east slope of one of the many gravelly moraines so common in northeastern Indiana. This type of terrain no doubt affords the most favorable habitat for badgers in Indiana and is probably one of the reasons that most of the animals are in this section. Such areas are not conducive to intensive cultiva-

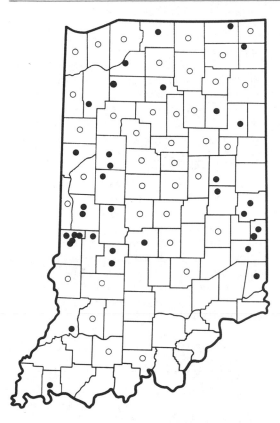

Map 57.　The Badger, *Taxidea taxus*, in
Indiana

sects, and other animals. No doubt raccoons, striped skunks, opossums, and other mammals also use burrows made by badgers.

HABITS. The badger is an accomplished burrower, as evidenced by its body form and its powerful digging front feet. Burrows are quite large and are usually broader than high to accommodate the shape of the badger itself. Large amounts of soil are usually piled about the burrow entrances, for much excavation is done in constructing a suitable den. A den where a badger was trapped in Union County was examined by Mumford. It was in a pasture along a small stream at the edge of a small clump of trees, halfway up the slope. The soil was sandy and gravelly at the site. The den had three (possibly four) entrances. Dale N. Martin and Mumford visited another den in Lagrange County. Many burrows of various depth were found dug into the slope of a low sandy / gravelly ridge in a field that had been fallow for three years. The shallow holes were rather small and may have been excavated by the animals while feeding. Several larger burrows were deep and extended out of our vision beneath the ground. At the entrance to each of these deeper burrows was a sizable mound of soil and small stones which had been removed from the tunnels. The deep burrows were, in cross section, flat on the bottom, wider than high, and rounded on top. A characteristic musky odor (mentioned by Dellinger, 1951) was evident at both of these dens. Mrs. Joanna Baker described to us (in a letter) several shallow depressions she had noticed made by a badger at entrances to thirteen-lined ground squirrel burrows. She saw no such digging at entrances to eastern chipmunk burrows nearby. The digging of badgers is sometimes quite extensive and often indicates (along with tracks) the presence of these animals in an area.

The badger is mostly nocturnal, but not strictly so, and we have several reports of animals observed during the day. It appears to be quite wary during the day and usually retreats quickly underground when disturbed. But Jon F. Heisterberg and Steven D. Ford approached to within 20 yards of a badger near its den; the badger stood upright on its haunches and looked about before entering its burrow. Dale N. Martin also observed that a badger he saw several times did

tion, and abundant cover plus soils suited to easy digging are at hand. Also, chipmunks and thirteen-lined ground squirrels are plentiful and available as food. The area from which three badgers were taken in Owen County was in the edge of the hills not far from the unglaciated portion of the state. Here, dispersion could have occurred along the relatively flat, narrow stream valleys. James A. Hughes reported the trapping of three badgers "along streams" in Hendricks County. Other habitats from which badgers have been reported include an abandoned gravel pit, a hayfield, a railroad right-of-way, and in cities (Indianapolis, Terre Haute, West Lafayette).

ASSOCIATED SPECIES. In the badger's habitat, it is probably most closely associated with the woodchuck, the thirteen-lined ground squirrel, the red fox, the eastern cottontail, and various smaller species. Badgers feed on other mammals, especially ground squirrels and chipmunks, and on birds, in-not remain out of its burrow long after it detected his presence.

We have heard of several badgers being cornered on the ground by dogs. The fact that the badger is not a fast runner probably renders it vulnerable to this type of harassment. Badgers usually walk slowly, with a waddling gait, but sometimes run with an awkward galloping motion. When threatened they may stand their ground and fight, emitting hisses, snarls, and squeals and sucking in air noisily. A man related how his dog, which was adept at killing raccoons and woodchucks, was unable to kill a badger. When fighting, badgers may gnash their teeth and raise the long hairs along the back. They also can emit a foul-smelling musk from their anal scent glands, but the musk is not forcibly ejected for some distance as it is by the striped skunk. The badger probably does little climbing, although Greg Lancaster told us that his dogs once treed a badger 12 feet up in a tree with many limbs. The dogs of raccoon hunters sometimes catch badgers on the ground at night. Three badgers (a family group?) found on the ground during the day stood their ground when the farmer who found them got off his tractor and approached them.

The badger does not hibernate, but may remain in its burrow (sometimes plugged) during inclement weather. Tracks have been observed in the snow. We have been unable to obtain much information regarding the winter activity of badgers. The animal is evidently so difficult to observe or so nocturnal in habits that few persons ever see one, unless it is in a trap or dead along the road. Some feel that badgers are somewhat nomadic, using a den for a time, then moving on. This may be especially true of males, for we have noticed that most badgers killed on roads have been males. Their travels evidently take them into contact with man. Clifford Barnes shot a badger that appeared on his lawn one night in a rural area. We know of at least three animals that were found in cities.

One would not expect the badger to make a good pet, but in the January 1937 *Outdoor Indiana* is a photograph of an eleven-year-old boy with his pet badger. The strength of a badger is tremendous. Badgers are equipped with a strong skull, large teeth, and long front claws—all formidable weapons of defense.

Perhaps pets are best obtained when very young, so that they will be more likely to be tame when handled.

Several persons have related to us their observations of badgers captured in steel traps. Freeman Retherford caught one that dug a semi-circular excavation 8 inches deep and almost 10 inches wide. Others have told us that badgers attempted to cover themselves by digging when caught in a trap. That this is probably true is supported by the account given to us by Dale N. Martin. Martin had set a trap for a fox and one morning found the trap missing but found a deep hole at the site. He dug about with his hands in the sandy soil in the hole but could not locate the trap, which he assumed was gone. Nineteen days later, when he again visited the site, he noticed a hole about 3 inches in diameter at the bottom of the larger depression. A live badger, with a badly damaged foot, was still in the trap and was released. The hole it had dug was about 2.5 feet deep (the length of the trap chain).

The badger is probably a fairly good swimmer; we have a record of one found floating on some driftwood during a flood. The animal was lassoed and captured.

FOOD. We have been unable to obtain many Indiana badger specimens for food habits analysis. Elsewhere, badgers obtain much of their food by digging out small rodents, and they feed on other animals as well. Mrs. Baker's observations of badgers excavating the entrance burrows to thirteen-lined ground squirrel dens have been mentioned above. Of three Indiana specimens we examined, one contained the remains of a Norway rat, and another contained portions of a woodchuck; the third had eaten eastern cottontail (50 percent of volume of food), eastern chipmunk (40 percent), and meadow vole (10 percent). Ralph D. Kirkpatrick reported to us that a badger he examined contained three young cottontails in its stomach.

REPRODUCTION. There is meager information concerning reproduction from Indiana records and specimens. Badgers have delayed implantation, thus the gestation period is difficult to determine. Mating probably occurs in the fall. Jackson (1961) reported that the nest of a badger is about 2 to 2.5 feet in diameter and is placed in a chamber of the underground burrow system; nests may be located 2 to 6 feet below the ground surface. Evidently one litter per year is produced and litter size varies from one to five, usually two to three. Young are probably born about April or May.

Nixon A. Wilson reported that an adult female and five young were dug from a den near Waveland (Montgomery County) about 1954. Dennis Lehr flushed an adult and three half-grown young from a hayfield (Owen County) in July. One female we examined that had been taken on 17 May had four placental scars. A 16-pound male killed on 3 November had abdominal testes 12 by 20 mm. Another male, taken 1 July, had testes measuring 17 by 51 mm.

PARASITES. Wilson (1961) reported the tick *Ixodes cookei* from the badger in Indiana. All eleven Indiana badgers we examined were parasitized. Ticks *(Ixodes cookei, Dermacentor variabilis)* were found on all specimens. Except for numerous individuals of the mite *Hirstionyssus staffordi* (found mostly on one badger), the biting louse *Neotrichodectes interruptofasciatus* and the mite *Androlaelaps fahrenholzi* were the most abundant parasites found (Table 188).

Three of four specimens examined for endoparasites contained 4, 6, and 8 nematodes in their intestines.

DECIMATING FACTORS. Man is the only known enemy of the badger in Indiana. Numerous animals are killed by motor vehicles, trapped, or shot. Even though the badger has been placed on the protected list in Indiana, illegal killing persists. In some cases the persons responsible do not know the game laws, and in other cases the animals are killed because of the difficulty of releasing them unharmed from steel traps (usually set for foxes) in which they are captured accidentally. In recent times, badger pelts have been worth little on the fur market, so trappers have not trapped specifically for them. In earlier times, the hair was said to have been used for making shaving brushes.

TAXONOMY. According to Long (1972), most Indiana badgers can be assigned to the subspecies *Taxidea taxus taxus* (Schreber), but one specimen from Mongo, (Lagrange County) was assigned to *T. t. jacksoni* Schantz.

SELECTED REFERENCES. Davis, 1946; Errington, 1937; Hamlett, 1932; Snead and Hendrickson, 1942.

Table 188

Ectoparasites and other associates of *Taxidea taxus* (n =11) from Indiana

Parasites	Parasites		Hosts Parasitized	
	Total	Average	Total	Percent
Fleas (Siphonaptera)				
Oropsylla arctomys	7	0.64	1	9.1
Biting Lice (Mallophaga)				
Neotrichodectes interruptofasciatus	454	41.27	4	36.4
Mites (Acarina) other than chiggers				
Hirstionyssus staffordi	1,202	109.27	3	27.3
Androlaelaps fahrenholzi	86	7.82	4	36.4
Haemogamasus liponyssoides	1	0.09	1	9.1
H. reidi	1	0.09	1	9.1
Ticks (Ixodides)				
Dermacentor variabilis	48	4.36	4	36.4
Ixodes cookei	43	3.91	9	81.8

Striped Skunk
Mephitis mephitis (Schreber)

Eastern Skunk, Illinois Skunk, Skunk,
Polecat, Common Skunk, Striated
Weasel

Mephitis mesomelas: Wied, 1839
Mephitis Americana: Plummer, 1844
Mephitis Chinga: Audubon and Bachman,
1846
Mephitis mephitica: Haymond, 1870 (note
errata page)
Mephites mephitica: Quick and Langdon,
1882
Mephitis avia: Bangs, 1898
Chinca putida: Howell, 1901
Chincha mesomelas: Howell, 1901
Mephitis putida: Hahn, 1908b
Mephitis nigra: Lyon, 1923
Mephitis mephitis: McAtee, 1907

DESCRIPTION. The body and legs of the
striped skunk are black. The head is mostly
black, usually with a narrow white stripe on
the forehead. The back is partly black with a
V-shaped white stripe of varying width and
length from the nape to the tail and extending down onto the sides. This dorsal white
stripe is sometimes absent or represented by
small white areas. The long, bushy tail is
black and white and may have a white tip. A
white skunk was taken at Geneva, Indiana
(photo in *Outdoor Indiana* 19:24, 1952), and

Striped skunk. Photo by Karleton Crain

all-black individuals have been reported
(Evermann and Butler, 1894b). Skunks are
quite variable with regard to the amount of
white in the pelage. Fur buyers pay a higher
price for pelts with the least amount of white,
for the black portions of the hides are most
valuable. Buyers divide skunk pelts into
several classes: Blacks, Stars, Shortstripes,
Longstripes, Broadstripes. Blacks have no
white, and Stars have white only on the head
or perhaps no farther back than the forelegs.
Shortstripes may have white stripes reaching
posteriorly to the middle of the pelt, and
Longstripes have white stripes reaching the
tail. The entire back is white in Broadstripes
(Brooks, 1959). Skunks have short legs,
pointed muzzles, and small ears. Fourteen is
the full complement of teats, but some individuals have less.

This is one of three genera of wild Carnivora in Indiana with four upper molariform
teeth per side. The others are *Taxidea* and
Mustela (the domestic cat also has four). The
skunk's skull can immediately be distinguished from the others by its shape. The
back of the skull is flat, but its profile over the
orbits abruptly angles downward. Also, in the
skunk the bony palate ends at the posterior
border of the molariform teeth; it extends beyond them in *Mustela* and *Taxidea* (see Figs.
13, 14).

Weights and measurements are given in
Table 189. The dental formula is

$$I \frac{3}{3} C \frac{1}{1} P \frac{3}{3} M \frac{1}{2} = 34.$$

STATUS AND DISTRIBUTION. David Thomas
(1819) may have been the first to report
striped skunks from Indiana, unless the
"Cat" skins purchased by William Burnett in
1800–1801 were possibly *Mephitis* pelts
(Engels, 1933). Plummer (1844) wrote about
the striped skunk in Wayne County: "This
disgusting animal, though recently killed
here, is not common." Haymond (1870) stated
that skunks "are much more common in this
region than formerly, and seem to be increasing yearly" (Franklin County). Cox wrote that
skunks were only occasionally found in Randolph County in 1893, but that they were

Table 189
Weights and measurements of
Mephitis mephitis from Indiana

	Males	Females
Total length (mm)		
n	15	11
x̄	596.6	571.9
range	489-635	447-630
SD	61.25	46.6
SE	15.81	14.07
Tail length (mm)		
n	15	11
x̄	226.8	214.1
range	159-290	174-258
SD	37.33	27.1
SE	9.63	8.19
Hind foot (mm)		
n	15	11
x̄	64.6	61
range	48-71	54-68
SD	7.17	4.6
SE	1.85	1.4
Weight (grams)		
n	11	6
x̄	1,846.7	1732.6
range	1022-2810	907.2-2086.5
SD	734.6	457.5
SE	221.5	186.8

formerly abundant there. Striped skunks were reported to be "not uncommon" in Carroll, Monroe, and Vigo counties, "though less so than formerly," and "still abundant" in Franklin County (Evermann and Butler, 1894b). Blatchley (1898) noted that striped skunks were "rather common" in Lake and Porter counties, "and yield a considerable annual revenue to the professional trapper."

In the summer of 1905, Hahn found the species common in the Kankakee River region where he worked. According to McAtee (1907), the striped skunk was common in the Bloomington (Monroe County) area. In the Mitchell (Lawrence County) region "skunks seemed to be common" (Hahn, 1908b). In 1909, Hahn wrote, "The opinion of most of my correspondents seems to be that skunks are growing scarce. However, I feel quite sure that these animals are as abundant or more abundant about my boyhood home in Ohio County than they were twenty years ago. . . . I do not think that they have been

completely exterminated in any county of the State." In the Lake Maxinkuckee region (Marshall County), Evermann and Clark (1911) listed the skunk as "not common . . . but it is apparently becoming more frequent." In the dunes region of Porter County, where M. W. Lyon, Jr., conducted fieldwork in the fall of 1922, skunks were reportedly "fairly common . . . and a number are taken each season for fur. By November 30, 1922, R. W. Sabinske had taken seven" (Lyon, 1923). Engels (1933) considered the skunk "a common and well-known resident" of St. Joseph County. Skunks were present in every county of Indiana according to Lyon (1936), but Lyon gave no other data regarding status, other than reporting that 183,234 skunks were taken by Indiana trappers during the winter of 1931–32. He listed preserved specimens from only six counties, but this relative scarcity of specimens no doubt reflects the reluctance of most persons to handle skunks—either dead or alive.

During the late 1930s and early 1940s, a disease thought to be encephalitis drastically reduced the population of striped skunks in Indiana, and though they have evidently enjoyed a rather steady increase over the past 30 years, they may not yet be back to former numbers. Lack of good data hampers this evaluation.

In the early 1950s skunks were fairly common in Jackson County, as evidenced by observations and by animals killed on roads. Brooks (1959) compiled figures on the numbers of skunks bought by Indiana fur dealers from 1953 to 1957. The totals for these years were 2,457, 1,283, 1,073, 777, and 551 respectively. The annual value of pelts no doubt influenced the numbers of skunks killed and sold. Prices were relatively high in the early 1930s, but have declined drastically since that period. Lindsay (1960) had the following to say regarding the status of the striped skunk in Jefferson and Ripley counties in the early 1950s: "In the area investigated this species was much less common the last few years than approximately 30 years ago, when the author frequently accompanied skunk hunters at night. At that time it was not unusual for six to eight skunks to be taken in a single evening with the aid of a good dog." Ed Wagner thinks skunks increased from 1972 to 1973 on the Muscatatuck National Wildlife Refuge (Jackson and Jennings counties).

Today, the striped skunk probably occurs throughout the state, but may be rare locally. In one study of 691 mammals observed dead on roads, 73 were skunks. More than 400 skunks were submitted to the Indiana State Board of Health between 1970 and 1976 to be examined for rabies. However, since the skunk is known to be a high-risk species as a carrier of rabies, perhaps a disproportionate number was examined. Specimens are in collections from 32 counties (Map 58).

HABITAT. There is practically nothing in the literature concerning the habitat of Indiana skunks. McAtee (1907) and Hahn (1909) both mentioned that the animals lived in sinkholes, and Hahn also referred to the skunk's feeding in old pastures. Brooks (1959) stated, "They prefer gently rolling land interspersed with open grassy fields, brush land, woods and water." We have noted that striped skunks occur in a variety of habitats, including fields or woods and along fencerows, streams, and dry ravine banks. Weedy and brushy fields and brushy pastures seem attractive to them. They evidently enter caves on occasion, for their odor has been detected in several caverns. Most of our daytime observations were made in weed fields or along roads through brushy woods borders. Dellinger (1951) mentioned that skunks were found in fields and open woodland pastures. Judging from the many complaints we receive, skunks are not uncommon about farm buildings, churches, and even suburban and city residences, where the animals frequently establish their dens under buildings.

HABITS. The skunk is almost entirely terrestrial, although it is said by some to climb, though infrequently, and to enter water when pursued. It is often observed by day, especially during the late afternoon, but is mostly nocturnal. Females with their litters have been seen traveling by daylight. Young follow the females single file. The usual gait of skunks is a waddling, plodding one; at times they may move at a slow trot. When foraging in open areas, they usually keep their noses near the ground as they amble along a trail or fencerow. Their eyesight appears to be poor and we have had a foraging animal walk up to our feet and pass, unhurriedly, as though unaware of our presence. Presumably, the striking black and white coloration of the skunk serves quite well as a warning to potential predators to stay their distance, and thus skunks need not worry much about running to escape enemies.

The ability of the skunk to defend itself by means of a discharge from its anal scent glands is well known. The skunk can eject the musk for distances up to six feet or more. Even baby skunks have this ability, although there is much less musk and the odor is less disagreeable. When approached, a skunk may waddle away or, if sufficiently disturbed, may lower the head, arch the back, and raise the tail in preparation for spraying the scent. Usually the hair on the back and tail is raised at this time, also. The animal may then stamp or scratch on the ground with its front feet. Continued disturbance may cause the animal to spray the contents of its anal scent glands at the intruder. The material ejected contains a sulphur-alcohol compound (butylmercaptan), which is responsible for the strong odor (Jackson, 1961). The spray may cause cough-

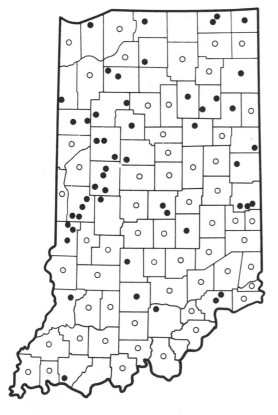

Map 58.   The Striped Skunk, *Mephitis mephitis,* in Indiana

ing, choking, nausea, and even temporary blindness (if it enters the eyes) in humans. Evidently the skunk is quite accurate in directing the spray, as more than one of our friends can attest. The odor is quite persistent and may be detected for about a mile, depending upon atmospheric conditions. There seems to be some question regarding how much time is required for an animal that has emptied its scent glands to refill them; some think at least a week is needed to replenish them.

For the most part, skunks live in underground burrows, which they may construct themselves. Most often they appear to use burrows dug by woodchucks or other larger mammals. Burrows may have more than a single opening. Grasses are gathered and transported into the den for the construction of a nest. Dellinger (1951) was of the opinion that occupied dens usually had leaves or grass stuffed loosely into the entrance, and thus appeared to be unused. Active dens can also be detected by the characteristic odor or by the presence of skunk hairs about the entrance. Dens are often under buildings, both occupied and unoccupied by humans. One nest was found in a burrow under a stump. During the coldest periods of winter, skunks may remain inactive in their dens but they do not hibernate. The Indiana specimens we have examined were collected from 7 February to 31 December. The animals accumulate much body fat in the fall and are thus able to fast for considerable periods if necessary. A male collected on 19 August was very fat. It is not unusual to find more than one animal per den in winter; Hahn (1909) reported seven in a single den in February. Perhaps some of these groups represent families. Skunks also take shelter in small culverts and drainage tiles.

Skunks may be handled without causing them to spray, but there is considerable disagreement on this subject. Some say the tail can be held down or the animal can be lifted off the ground to prevent its ejecting the scent. Animals captured in live traps can be safely transported after the trap has been covered with a burlap bag or other material that darkens the interior of the trap and quiets the animal. There appears to be much variation in the behavior of individual skunks with regard to their scenting when handled; a "foolproof" method may not always work.

Skunks often make good pets, but some become difficult to control or handle as they grow older. Young, de-scented individuals offer the best prospects for a suitable pet. Haymond (1870) wrote, "The young kittens are very pretty little animals, and make pleasant pets, provided they are not *kept too long*" (italics his). We were once called to remove an adult pet skunk from the basement of a house, where it had become impossible to control and had finally done extensive damage to the walls by chewing and scratching. This animal was said to have been quite satisfactory as a pet when it was younger.

FOOD. Insects (adult and larvae) make up much of the food of the striped skunk. Hahn (1909) described some of the feeding signs left by skunks and reported his observations of an animal, as follows:

Last summer while setting traps for field mice in an old pasture, I noticed a great many small conical holes going down through the grass and into the hard ground for an inch or two. It was evident that some animal had been searching for grubs and insects there. I was uncertain at first as to what sort of animal had been doing the work, but one evening about sun-down I saw a large skunk come out of a sinkhole and begin nosing around in the grass. I watched it for some time, going up to within eight or ten yards of it (I feared to go nearer). It went about, watching me over its shoulder and appearing uneasy because of my presence, but not running away. It would thrust its nose down through the close mat of short blue grass, apparently being able to make a hole into the hard earth with its snout alone, although it used both claws and teeth to work deeper when necessary. I could not see what it was eating, but grubs and other insect larvae were probably abundant there.

Hahn also mentioned that in the tobacco growing regions of Indiana, skunks were "indefatigable in their search for tobacco worms," although they break many leaves from the tobacco plants while feeding. George Dellinger also mentioned "little funnel shaped diggings, overturned or broken up cattle chips (dung)" as indications of the presence of striped skunks. Fredrick H. Montague, Jr., told Mumford that he once watched a skunk feeding in an old pasture for more than an hour. The animal went from one pile of dried cow dung to another, turning over each chip in search of food beneath.

Skunks also feed on animal materials of various kinds, including eggs and poultry, and one of the specimens we examined was killed in a chicken house. An immature collected on 4 November had the stomach full of grasshoppers and plant material. Mumford observed a skunk along the highway one afternoon feeding on a bag of potato chips, no doubt discarded by a passing motorist. McAtee (1907) quoted B. W. Evermann, who noted that the striped skunk "has the habit of visiting smoke houses." Perhaps in earlier years, when farmers smoked their own winter meat, the process attracted skunks.

We examined the foods in seven skunk stomachs and found that the mammal remains (57.2 percent) were about equally divided among prairie voles, muskrats, short-tailed shrews, and eastern cottontails. Insect remains (42.5 percent) consisted of Acrididae (27.1 percent), Scarabaeidae (10.7 percent), scarabaeid larvae (2.9 percent), Carabidae (0.7 percent), lepidopterous larvae (0.7 percent), and Gryllidae (0.4 percent). Lespedeza leaves made up 0.1 percent, and unidentified vegetation a like amount.

REPRODUCTION. The gestation period of the striped skunk is about 63 days. A single litter is born each year. Copulation probably occurs in late February and early March, but we have examined no gravid skunks from Indiana and have obtained relatively little information regarding reproduction. McAtee (1907) reported the capture of four young, each about 8 inches long, on 14 June (Monroe County). A nest containing six young was dug out from under a stump on 5 May. And a female and her five young were trapped beneath a chicken house on 2 June. Four of this litter ranged from 220 to 258 grams each and from 290 to 295 mm in total length. A specimen taken in Wayne County on 15 May measured 160 mm in total length; its eyes were not yet open. An adult male taken on 14 February had testes 21 mm long; another male captured on 16 March had 19-mm testes.

PARASITES AND DISEASES. Wilson (1957, 1961) reported two ticks (Ixodes cookei, Dermacentor variabilis) and a louse (Neotrichodectes mephitidis) from Indiana striped skunks. The important ectoparasites on the ten skunks we examined (Table 190) were the biting louse (Neotrichodectes mephitidis), two mites (Hirstionyssus staffordi, Androlaelaps fahrenholzi) and the tick (Ixodes cookei).

Of nine skunks examined for endoparasites, three yielded 46 cestodes, two were infected with 56 trematodes, and all contained nematodes (totaling 297). None of these parasites have been identified.

Skunks are susceptible to canine distemper, rabies, and encephalitis. Between 1947 and 1956, the Indiana State Board of Health diagnosed 24 animals as rabid. And 164 of 406 skunks submitted to the State Board of Health for examination from1970 to 1976 tested positive for rabies. The striped skunk now leads all other Indiana (and U.S.) mammals (including domestic) in the number of rabies cases per year. This distinction

Table 190

Ectoparasites and other associates of *Mephitis mephitis* (n=10) from Indiana

Parasites	Parasites		Hosts Parasitized	
	Total	Average	Total	Percent
Fleas (Siphonaptera)				
Ctenocephalides felis	2	0.20	1	10.0
Biting Lice (Mallophaga)				
Neotrichodectes mephitidis	3,420	342.00	7	70.0
Mites (Acarina) other than chiggers				
Hirstionyssus staffordi	613	61.30	8	80.0
Androlaelaps fahrenholzi	68	6.80	3	30.0
Chigger Mites (Trombiculidae)				
Neotrombicula whartoni	1	0.10	1	10.0
Ticks (Ixodides)				
Ixodes cookei	43	4.30	7	70.0

formerly was held by the domestic dog until widespread rabies inoculation programs decreased the incidence of the disease in this pet.

DECIMATING FACTORS. Most of the skunks observed in Indiana are those lying dead along roads where they have been killed by vehicles. Man is probably the most important predator and frequently eliminates skunks from certain sites. Some dogs are known to kill skunks. Mangus (1950) found the remains of 2 skunks in 80 red fox stomachs he examined. It appears that the great horned owl is one of the most important natural predators of skunks in Indiana. We have examined at least 5 of these owls that reeked of skunk scent, and an additional record has been supplied by H. P. Weeks, Jr. A great horned owl, carrying a striped skunk, collided with some power lines; the remains of the electrocuted owl and its prey were found on the ground.

Although skunk fur is quite thick and lustrous, the demand for it declined some years ago. As a result, skunks were for many years not harvested in large numbers by hunters and trappers. This probably was a factor contributing to the increase in Indiana skunks. Skunks are not sought as food, although some authors have written that the flesh is "tender and white like that of a young chicken, and very palatable." The strong aversion the average person has against skunks would probably preclude any desire to eat its flesh.

TAXONOMY. *Mephitis mephitis nigra* (Peale and Beauvois) occupies all except the northwestern corner of Indiana, where *M. m. avia* Bangs is said to occur. Bangs (1898) described *Mephitis avia*, and recorded a specimen from Fowler (Benton County). Hall (1936) reduced *avia* to subspecific rank under *Mephitis mephitis*. More specimens are needed from the northwestern quarter of the state in order to delineate the ranges of these races.

SELECTED REFERENCES. Allen, 1939; Allen and Shapton, 1942; Cuyler, 1924; Hamilton, 1936c, 1937b; Kelker, 1937; Selko, 1937, 1938a, b; Shaw, 1928; Stegeman, 1937.

Family **Felidae**

Bobcat
Felis rufus (Schreber)

American Wild Cat, Wild Cat, Catamount, Bay Lynx

Felis rufa: Wied, 1839
Lyncus rufus: Plummer, 1844
Lynx Rufus: Audubon and Bachman, 1846
Lynx ruffus: Hahn, 1909
Lynx rufa: Evermann and Clark, 1920
Felis rufus: Mumford and Whitaker, this publication.

DESCRIPTION. The bobcat is a rather long-legged, stubby-tailed, moderate-sized wildcat with large cheek tufts. Pelage color varies, but is normally reddish-brown above and whitish below, spotted blackish throughout. The pointed ears have inconspicuous hair tufts and the dorsal tip of the tail is black. Many Indiana residents mistake feral domestic cats for bobcats, but domestic cats are considerably smaller and normally have long tails.

The bobcat skull is short, wide, has a very short rostrum, and is the only Indiana carnivore skull with 3 upper molariform teeth. In Indiana only the domestic cat skull is likely to be confused with that of a bobcat, but the former is much smaller and has 4 upper molariform teeth.

WEIGHTS AND MEASUREMENTS. Wied (1862) recorded meager data on Indiana bobcats. He reported one male "three feet" in total length and a female that was only 525 mm long (including the hairs on the tail tip). He also gave the weight of a female as 15 pounds. In *Outdoor Indiana* (Vol. 5, March

1938, p. 30) is a photograph of the skin of a bobcat killed in Morgan County; the bobcat reportedly weighed 16 pounds. The 27 November 1975 *Tell City News* contains a photograph of an unsexed bobcat killed in Perry County that reputedly weighed 16.5 pounds. The skull of an unsexed bobcat killed in the fall of 1970 (Monroe County) measured 140 mm in total length and 107 mm in zygomatic breadth. Jackson (1961) gave the following measurements for adult bobcat specimens: total length, 875 to 1,000 mm; tail length, 100 to 120 mm; hind foot, 215 to 250 mm. He also gave 16 to 25 pounds as the range of weights. The dental formula is

$$I \frac{3}{3} C \frac{1}{1} P \frac{2}{2} M \frac{1}{1} = 28.$$

STATUS AND DISTRIBUTION. The bobcat formerly occurred throughout Indiana. Its current status is hopelessly confused by reports of "wild cats" (many of them domestic cats) and by a lack of specimens, photographs, or other undisputed evidence. The bobcat is probably quite rare in Indiana and most likely to be encountered in the southern half of the state.

Adams (1950) listed bobcat bones from the Angel Mounds archaeological site (Vanderburgh County). Wied reported that the bobcat was not rare at New Harmony (Posey County) in 1833, but his account is confused with the lynx (Hahn, 1909). Dinwiddie (1884) wrote the following concerning Lake County: "In 1837 or 1838 a Wild-cat was killed at the head of Cedar Lake. From 1855 to 1867 two were often seen and heard in Pleasant Grove and vicinity, and in the latter year one was killed at Bostwick Prairie." Plummer (1844) wrote about the species in Wayne County: "This wild cat, once common, has seldom been seen since 1823." A fur buyer purchased 48 bobcat skins at Noblesville (Hamilton County) in 1859. Rufus Haymond (1870) reported that "Occasionally there is a wild cat seen in that county, but they are rare" in Franklin County. In discussing bobcats in the same county, Evermann and Butler (1894b) noted that 1869 "was about the end of their existence in this county. Wild cat reports are seen in the papers almost every winter. Definite records are needed." Butler (1895) reported a bobcat killed at Bicknell (Knox

County) in 1832 and another reported in the same county in the spring of 1894. He also included a report of a 56-pound bobcat killed near Bluffton (Wells County) in November 1894, but the source of this report (Fletcher M. Noe) is known to be unreliable.

Hahn (1909) mentioned several Indiana records of bobcats and also reports of the "catamount" and "lynx." There is no way to determine what species were being discussed, but probably most accounts were of bobcats. Among his records are the following: one at Wheatland (Knox County) 10 January 1900 and an adult and two young killed in the same county in 1894. He quoted Mrs. Annie Anderson, of Oxford concerning "lynxes" in Benton County:

In August, 1870, when I was about ten years old, my brother and I were gathering berries on the banks of Pine Creek, about four miles south of Oxford, when I spied in some hazel brush what I thought to be a maltese cat. I called to the kitty and started to catch it, when my brother stopped me, saying that he did not like the looks of its eyes. It was standing still, staring at us, evidently as much surprised as we were. In the following autumn some hunters killed a lynx in the same place, and it proved to [sic] my maltese kitty or one like it. I have not heard of any since until about three years ago (1905) some boys killed a bobcat about a mile from the same place.

Hahn also reported that T. F. Upson killed a "bobcat" near Lima (Lagrange County) in the fall of 1857 and knew of none in that vicinity since. R. S. White, Jr., killed a "catamount" in the winter of 1906 on Pigeon Creek (Warrick County). This was the latest record Hahn knew about, except for newspaper reports of animals killed and not positively identified to species. Hahn concluded, "Nevertheless it is very probable that a few wildcats remain at the present time in the less accessible swamps and woods in various parts of the State."

Bee Wright trapped a male bobcat near Bloomingdale (Parke County) about 1913. Nixon A. Wilson and Mumford examined the skin in Wright's possession on 5 November 1959 (the skin was later sold to a tourist). In writing about the Lake Maxinkuckee (Marshall County) region, Evermann and Clark (1911) stated, "The Wild Cat or Lynx was probably not uncommon in this country [sic] up to about 1850. They are now rarely seen. We have authenticated accounts of their occurrence west of Lake Maxinkuckee as late as 1870, or later." Lyon (1936) reported that bobcats had been seen in Brown County during the period 1914 to 1918. One was killed during the 1937–38 hunting season near Martinsville (Morgan County) and a photograph of the skin was published (*Outdoor Indiana*, March 1938, p. 30). William B. Barnes reported a specimen (mounted and in private ownership) killed near Martinsville "a few years" before 1959. And from 1952 to 1957, bobcats were reportedly killed in Jennings, Lagrange, Morgan, and Warren counties (Brooks, 1959). In the fall of 1970, a deer hunter shot a bobcat in Monroe County; a picture of the skull of this specimen (PUWL 2774) is shown here. In late November 1975, Allen Goffinet shot a bobcat 5 miles southeast of Bristow (Perry County). The *Tell City News*, 27 November 1975, had a photograph of this animal.

We have received other reports of bobcats being observed or killed. Most reports have come from southern Indiana, but some are from the northern half. It appears that this secretive species may persist in local areas. There is also the possibility that bobcats move about, appearing in a locality for a time, then leaving it. Perhaps in the future more photographs or specimens can be obtained for verification of records. For the present, we have no way of determining the numerical status of this species in Indiana. It has been placed on the protected list of Indiana mammals.

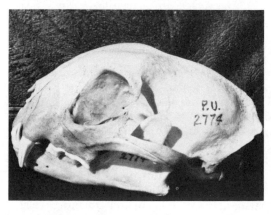

Skull of bobcat shot in Monroe County in 1970. Photo by David W. Berrey

HABITAT. The area in Monroe County where the specimen was shot is hilly and well forested, with considerable rather remote sections. Much of the country around Bristow (Perry County) is also hilly terrain. Persistent reports of bobcats in Brown and Morgan counties have come from similar areas. The animal caught in the winter of 1937–38 near Martinsville was evidently inhabiting an old stone quarry. In the south-central hill region of Indiana are numerous sites where rock outcrops, rocky ledges, and caves abound. This type of habitat, much of which is also heavily forested, would appear ideal for bobcats. The species occupies similar habitat in southern Ohio and Illinois. According to Hoffmeister and Mohr (1957), bobcats in Illinois inhabit wooded bottomlands and timbered slopes and bluffs. In other parts of its range, the bobcat prefers woodlands and brushy country, especially where the land is broken, rocky, or swampy.

ASSOCIATED SPECIES. The bobcat probably has no well defined association with other mammals other than occurring generally with other woodland species and as a predator on smaller mammals.

HABITS. There are few published observations on Indiana bobcats. Elsewhere, the species is shy and retiring, and often lives in areas over long periods without being observed by people living in the areas. The bobcat is mostly nocturnal. It has a catlike walk, but it can trot or run in bounding leaps of 6 to 8 feet. Bobcats climb well, either to take refuge from dogs or to gain a vantage point for hunting or observations. Allen Goffinet reported that the bobcat he shot leaped out of an overhanging tree and began to attack his beagle hounds. Audubon and Bachman (1849) described how the bobcat sometimes eluded dogs on its trail by walking up and down a fallen log, then leaping from the log into a tree. They included an observation made by Audubon in southern Indiana.

One fine morning in autumn, when we had crossed the Ohio River at Henderson, in Kentucky, with the view of shooting some wild turkey, geese, and perhaps a deer, we chanced to seat ourselves about fifty yards from a prostrate tree, and presently saw a Wild Cat leap on to it and go through the manoeuvres we have described in a preceding page.

Bobcat. Photo by Roger W. Barbour

He did not see us, and had scarcely reached one of the higher branches of a tall white-oak, after springing into it from the fallen tree, when we heard the dogs, which soon came up, with the hunters following not far behind. They asked, when they perceived us, whether we had seen the "Cat" that had given them the slip. Always willing to assist the hunter who had lost his game, and having no particular liking towards this species, we answered in the affirmative, and showed them the animal, closely squatted on a large branch some distance from the ground. One of the party immediately put his rifle to his shoulder and pulled the trigger: the Cat leaped from the branch into the air, and fell to earth quite dead.

This event undoubtedly happened shortly after 1800, when Audubon was living in Henderson.

Bobcats are quite vocal at times, uttering screams and growling sounds, some of them similar to those of the domestic cat, and are said to be especially noisy when fighting. We suspect some of the nocturnal sounds attributed to bobcats in Indiana have been those of raccoons, foxes, and other mammals.

Dens are located in rock crevices, hollow trees, and other protected places, and nesting materials (usually vegetation) are carried into the den.

FOOD. We have no data from Indiana. In other states, the bobcat feeds heavily on rabbits and hares, other mammals, and birds.

REPRODUCTION. There are no data from Indiana. The gestation period is about 62 days and copulation normally occurs in early spring. Litter size ranges from one to four, but usually two young are produced.

PARASITES. We have no information from Indiana specimens. Ectoparasites reported from bobcats taken elsewhere include the tick *Dermacentor variabilis*, the fleas *Cediopsylla simplex* and *Odontopsyllus multispinosus* (both found on rabbits), and the mite *Lynxacarus morlani*.

DECIMATING FACTORS. Man is the only important enemy of the bobcat in Indiana. Full protection was given the bobcat in Indiana some years ago, but animals are still occasionally shot or trapped.

TAXONOMY. The subspecies in Indiana is probably *Felis rufus rufus* (Schreber).

SELECTED REFERENCES. Foote, 1945; Marston, 1942; Peterson and Downing, 1952; Pollack, 1950, 1951a, b; Rollings, 1945; Young, 1958.

Order **ARTIODACTYLA**

Family **Cervidae**

White-tailed Deer
Odocoileus virginianus (Zimmermann)

Virginia Deer, Red Deer, Deer

Cervus virginianus: Wied, 1839
Cariacus virginianus: Evermann and Butler, 1894b
Dama virginiana: Hall and Kelson, 1959
Odocoileus virginianus: Hahn, 1907a

DESCRIPTION. The white-tailed deer requires no extensive description for it is such a well-known animal. It is the largest wild mammal presently extant in Indiana (assuming the introductions of elk have been unsuccessful). From April to January (sometimes into February), males carry antlers; those of young bucks are simple spikes on either side. Antlers on does are extremely rare. The ears are large. The summer pelage is reddish brown above and whitish below. The winter pelage is grayer and more dense than the summer coat. Winter pelage is shed from late April to late May. Deer older than one year retain the summer pelage until the last week of August, when the fall molt begins. The winter coat is acquired by the third week of September. Fawns molt from the second week of September through the first week of October. Newborn fawns are brownish red above and white below with white spots over the body; these spots disappear when the first winter pelage is acquired in the fall.

Atypical color in deer almost always in-

volves abnormal patches of white in the pelage. This is frequently in the form of spotting or blotches; some animals appear all white.

MEASUREMENTS AND WEIGHTS. There are few data concerning complete measurements of Indiana deer. Since all refer to recent specimens (which were introduced from several states), we do not know what measurements were typical in the original population that inhabited Indiana. Allen (1952b) compiled total length data on 599 deer of both sexes shot by hunters in 1951. The data

White-tailed deer. Photo by Larry E. Lehman

479

were divided into five major herd areas and were presented by Allen as averages only. For animals more than 1.5 years old, average total length ranged from 1,572 to 2,134 mm for males and 1,499 to 1,791 mm for females. Hamilton (1957) presented partial measurements for 34 males 1.5 years old and older. Total lengths ranged from 1,625 to 1,900 mm and hind foot lengths ranged from 475 to 525 mm. Tail lengths for a few animals ranged from 237 to 310 mm. We have been unable to find any information on ear measurements.

Allen (1955) reported that the average whole weights for males and females, of a sample of 1,000 deer of all ages and both sexes killed during the hunting season, were 157 and 110 pounds respectively. The largest male weighed 329 pounds.

Weight is variable with season. Hoekstra (1971) summarized weight data for 115 adults (2.5 years and older) at the Crane Naval Weapons Support Center (Martin County). These were whole weights obtained from freshly killed or live, immobilized animals. Average weights in pounds for 3-month periods were as follows: March-April-May, males 143, females 139; June-July-August, males 151, females 136; September-October-November, males 203, females 141; December-January-February, males 180, females 135. Kirkpatrick *et al.* (1976) provided additional information on the live weights of Crane deer. Both sexes are heaviest in the fall; males are lightest in the spring. Females are lighter in the summer than in spring (when they are carrying young). Seasonal weight trends are the same for all age classes. In fawns, seasonal weight changes are the same for both sexes, the males being slightly heavier. Adult females lose about 4 percent of their fall body weight by spring. During the period 1967 to 1970, the fall weight loss in Crane buck deer over the winter approached 30 percent.

There is a considerable amount of information on weights of hog-dressed deer killed during annual hunts at Crane. Hog-dressed deer (carcasses with the viscera removed) are approximately 25 percent lighter than whole deer. These fall data have been summarized for seven years (1962–69), by age classes for 5,378 deer (Kirkpatrick *et al.*, 1976). Males were heavier than females in all age classes.

Females reached weights near their maximum in their second year, but males increased their average weights through the fourth year. Six-month old fawns averaged 68 and 64 pounds for males and females respectively. Males 1.5 years old averaged 112 pounds, females 99 pounds. Males 2.5 years and older averaged from 140 to 169 pounds per year; females in the same category ranged from 105 to 112 pounds.

The dental formula is

$$I \ \frac{0}{3} \ C \ \frac{0}{1} \ P \ \frac{3}{3} \ M \ \frac{3}{3} \ = \ 32.$$

STATUS AND DISTRIBUTION. The white-tailed deer is now found throughout Indiana and is locally common (Map 59). The heaviest concentrations are probably in the northern one-fourth and southern one-third of the state. Good populations have built up through the years on some military installations and on various fish and wildlife areas. Indiana initiated a deer hunting season in 1951, after a closed period of 58 years. Specimens are in collections from 22 counties.

Before Indiana became a state, the white-tailed deer was probably found in some numbers in the region, although there is little evidence on record other than brief comments of early travelers and of authors of county histories. People taking the usual trail from Vincennes, Indiana, to Louisville, Kentucky, in the 1790s frequently saw deer enroute. Much of this trail was through mature forest. John Tipton left Corydon (Harrison County) on 12 September 1811 and trekked northwestward, reaching Pine Creek on 5 November. Numerous deer were encountered and 9 were shot during that period. In November 1819, some Indians at Vincennes sold a 140-pound buck white-tailed deer for two dollars and venison was being sold at the rate of 25 cents for 30 pounds (Faux, 1823). An estimated 20,000 deer were present in Morgan County in 1820 (Sandburg, 1939), but we have no way of knowing how this figure was obtained by the reporter, Noah Major. At Hindostan (Martin County) deer meat sold for 20 cents "a haunch" in 1822–23, and two hunters using dogs killed 16 deer there (Blaney, 1824). Deer were abundant in LaPorte County in

Map 59.   The White-tailed Deer, *Odocoileus virginianus*, in Indiana

1836, and at one time venison "could hardly be sold."

During the winter of 1840–41, more than 50 deer took refuge in a grove west of Oxford (Benton County), where 9 were killed in half a day. But when the last deer seen in the vicinity was shot at Parish Grove in 1874, it sold for fifteen dollars (Birch, 1942). Few deer were killed in Lake County from 1874 to 1884 (Demmon *et al.*, 1934). Dinwiddie (1884) wrote that deer, "once numerous are still occasionally seen and more rarely shot on the islands of the Kankakee marshes" (Lake County). In the Indiana dunes in the early 1860s, as many as 20 deer could be seen at one time, but the last was reportedly shot there in the early 1870s (Brennan, 1923). One was killed near Michigan City in 1880. A buyer purchased 1,130 deer skins for $757.25 at Noblesville (Hamilton County) in 1859. Before 1850, one could see herds of 10 to 20 deer in Jackson County.

Hunters used to hold deer drives by form-

ing large circles of men around good habitat, then walking toward the center of the circle to make it smaller (fox drives are still conducted this way) and shooting the deer as they attempted to escape. Such a hunt in Warren County in the early 1840s resulted in about 300 deer being circled; many escaped, but about 160 were reportedly killed (Goodspeed, 1883). Ball (1900) mentioned the hunting of deer in the same fashion in Lake County. He also reported that in Jasper and Newton counties as many as 70 deer could be seen at one time in 1843 and 1844. And in Pulaski County, what was considered the last deer was shot in the winter of 1880–81.

Many other historical accounts can be found in the *Indiana Magazine of History*, in county histories, and in other published works. The evaluation of these stories is, of course, impossible, but certainly they attest to the abundance of white-tailed deer that once must have occurred in Indiana.

It appears that the white-tailed deer was extinct in Indiana by 1900. A restocking program was initiated in 1934, when 35 deer were released in 7 Indiana counties. A few deer were said to have been present in Harrison County in 1934. Evidently these were animals that entered Indiana on their own, perhaps across the Ohio River. Between 1934 and 1942, there were 296 animals released and through 1955 more than 400 had been reintroduced into a total of 22 counties (Allen, 1955).

In 1943, an estimated 900 deer were present in the state. This number had reached an estimated 1,200 a year later, when deer were reported from 35 counties. The 1946 population was calculated to be more than 2,900, but may have actually been nearly twice this number (considering the uncounted animals on military reservations, state parks, state and federal forest lands). By this time, deer damage to crops was becoming frequent. The 1949 population estimate was over 2,500, but by 1951 it was nearly 5,000. In November 1951, the first deer season of the 1900s was opened in Indiana.

Once established, the deer began to extend its range; it was helped by the trapping and transplanting of deer into many new areas by state biologists. By 1966, deer were probably present in each of Indiana's 92 counties, and today they enjoy this same type of distribution.

Population figures on a statewide basis are not available for the past several years. The best population data for deer in Indiana are those from studies conducted on the Crane Naval Weapons Support Center (formerly the Crane Naval Ammunition Depot), Martin County. This research was reported on by White (1968), Hoekstra (1971), Stormer (1972), and Kirkpatrick *et al.* (1976). The Crane military reservation was not opened to deer hunting until 1960, but aerial population surveys were initiated there in 1956 by the Indiana Division of Fish and Wildlife (Hamilton, 1956). In 1963, various Purdue University graduate students began deer research at Crane. Subsequently, Stormer *et al.* (1974) summarized data on the fall deer population from 1960 to 1971. Their paper presents the various problems encountered in censusing by different methods (pellet-group counts, recovery of tagged deer, roadside counts, kill-hunting effort). From 1960 to 1962, there were an estimated 52 deer per square mile on Crane. Slightly more deer were probably present in 1961 (the highest population recorded). From 1964 to 1968, there were about 41 deer per square mile. Hunting in 1968 and 1969 resulted in a decline to 26 per square mile in the fall of 1969 and 21 per square mile in 1970.

Aerial surveys taken on the Tippecanoe River State Park in December 1955, January 1957, and December 1958 resulted in estimates of the deer population there at 6.7, 8.3, and 4 per square mile, respectively. Problems of accuracy were encountered in the aerial censusing. Through the use of pellet-group counts, the following deer per square mile were calculated for various areas in 1964: Brownstown Ranger District, 3.4; Pigeon River Fish and Wildlife Area, 5.0; Harrison State Forest, 5.5; Winamac Fish and Wildlife Area, 8.0; Glendale Fish and Wildlife Area, 13.5; Tell City Ranger District, 30.0; Crane Naval Ammunitions Depot, 69.4. It should be mentioned that Stormer *et al.* (1974) estimated only 41 deer per square mile on Crane in 1964; thus different census methods are likely to give different results.

HABITAT. In Indiana, the white-tailed deer occupies woodlands, woodland borders, brushy areas, swamps, and agricultural land where there is adequate cover. Probably the best habitat includes a water source, mixed forest, brushy areas, some open land (croplands appear important in many sections of the state), and pine plantations. That deer are present even in counties that are intensively cultivated is an indication of the adaptability of the species, which originally was primarily a forest-inhabiting animal. In parts of the former prairie region, deer frequent vegetation (weeds to trees) along drainage ditches.

ASSOCIATED SPECIES. Because of its wide range of habitats, the white-tailed deer probably occurs, at some places, at some times, with almost every other species of Indiana mammal.

HABITS. The white-tailed deer is largely nocturnal or crepuscular, and spends much of the daytime lying in beds situated in brush, in tall grass and weeds, or in wooded areas. Several animals may bed within a small area. On a hot (95°F) July afternoon, a doe and fawn were flushed from their beds among the weeds in a fallow field. The beds, well shaded and in weeds about 3 feet tall, were 50 yards from the edge of the field. In warm weather, deer may bed down in relatively open sites. At dusk, activity is great, as animals move away from their protective covers and into open fields, along roadsides, and to other areas of sparse vegetation to feed and drink. Evidently activity does not continue throughout the night. Fred A. Stormer observed that deer bedded down and rested before midnight, then actively fed again, followed by another bedding period, then a last active period at dawn. It is not unusual to see some individuals active during the day. Deer seem to move about more on dark or stormy days. A doe was observed feeding on spatterdock while wading belly-deep in a marsh at midday, on a clear, hot day (14 July).

On Crane, Stormer (1972) found that most often two to four deer were seen together. Occasional larger groups were generally thought to be feeding congregations. The highest proportion of deer observed in groups was from March to mid-May, when 71 groups were noted per 100 observations.

Indiana deer generally do not come together in winter groups at "yards" as deer do in some other states. Yarding is not usually necessary in Indiana because some food is available throughout the year and heavy snows that lie on the ground for long periods do not normally occur in this state. During the winter of 1977–78, however, yarding was evident. H. P. Weeks, Jr., reported as many as 50 to 60 deer in yards. And in the winter of 1978–79, we obtained reports of the yarding of smaller numbers. Even when yarding does not occur, herds containing as many as 20 animals have been observed. Although yarding is not a characteristic behavior of Indiana white-tailed deer, on the Crane area the animals do tend to make more use of pine plantations during the winter than at other seasons. This winter preference for pine plantings is noticeable whether snow is on the ground or not, and is possibly an attempt to escape wind. Also, pines offer more protection from observation after the deciduous trees drop their leaves. On winter days, deer tend to bed down on south-facing slopes, where they can take advantage of sunshine and still escape the generally north winds. Deer beds are rather circular and about 3 feet in diameter. Their presence in snow is quite obvious because the snow is packed and partially melted by the heat of the body. In weedy areas, the vegetation is flattened and smoothed down by the weight of the resting animal.

During the rutting season, male deer paw the ground and create barren, somewhat circular patches 3 to 5 feet in diameter, called scrapes. Scrapes become noticeable in October and their use increases markedly from mid-October to the first week of November. On Crane, it was noted that scrapes still being visited in late November were not used the first week of December.

Deer are strong swimmers and encounter no difficulty in crossing the Ohio River. In marshy areas they readily jump into the water to escape danger and will cross wide expanses of wet marsh. One can follow their trails and will note that they frequently enter the water. Established travel lanes are a conspicuous part of good deer habitat. Well-used trails become devoid of vegetation after a time and are often cut deeply into the soil. Such trails are usually 10 to 12 inches wide. One can find trails that lead up to a fence, then continue on the opposite side of the fence. This reveals the deer's ability to jump such obstacles—sometimes clearing fences that are 8 to 9 feet tall.

White-tailed deer have several vocal sounds. Young deer give sort of bleating calls. Adults most frequently "snort" and when disturbed may give this call several times.

During the fall, when their antlers are losing their "velvet" coat, deer do much rubbing of the antlers against trees or shrubs. A particular tree or sprout may be used as a rubbing post time after time, until it loses much of its bark and some of its small branches. The rubbing was long thought to facilitate the removal of velvet from the antlers, but also appears to be a means of territorial marking.

Some data on the home range of deer have been gathered by Hoekstra (1971). He found that the average distance an individual was observed from its center of activity was 0.4 mile for does and 0.8 mile for fawns. Adult males ranged from 0.6 to 1.2 miles. Thus, in good habitat, where the essentials for an animal are found in close proximity, the individual does not have to travel far from day to day.

LONGEVITY. From studies on the Crane herd it has been possible to make some estimates on life expectancy of deer. Hoekstra (1971) calculated the life expectancy of male fawns to be 1.6 years; that of female fawns was 2.4 years for the years 1967 and 1968. Most males were gone from the population after 10.5 years, but some females reached the age of 14.5 years. The proportions of fawns, yearlings, and adults in the annual kill at Crane for the years 1961 through 1964 and 1966 through 1969 were presented by Kirkpatrick *et al.* (1976). These average percentages, of a sample of more than 7,100 deer, were as follows: fawns, 43.4 percent; yearlings, 24.5 percent; adults, 32.0 percent.

ACTIVITY. Hoekstra (1971) studied the roadside activity of deer at Crane, where the road shoulders are kept in grass and forbs and free of encroachment of brush, and thus are attractive to grazing animals. As expected, the presence of deer along the roads varied from season to season. Females showed a high usage during March and April, when new grass was probably a major attraction. Roadside activity then reached a low level in May and remained low through July. From July to

October the usage of roadsides increased. Males showed a high use in April, a low in May, an increase in June, followed by a slight, progressive decrease to September; usage increased in October.

Roadside counts of deer taken from an hour before sunset to an hour after sunset provided information on evening activity. For males, the April peak occurred in the hour before sunset. The activity peak in June was at sunset, and the August and October peaks were one-half hour after sunset. For females, the April peak was at sunset, while June, August, and October peaks were one-half hour after sunset. Hoekstra concluded that evening activity was probably stimulated by the temperature changes from the daily maximum, rather than by the actual temperatures at the time of observation.

Other activity data were gathered by recording the time of death for each of 48 deer killed by vehicles on roads in Steuben County. Kills occurred most frequently between 6 and 7 A.M. and 6 to 8 P.M., probably indicating times of greatest movement. An analysis of the seasonal occurrence of 123 vehicle-killed deer on roads in Owen and Putnam counties revealed that the greatest number of kills occurred in November.

MOVEMENTS. The movements of 29 yearling males and 54 adult females were studied by tagging each animal and recording the distance between the site where marked and the site where it was next captured (or killed). It is interesting that 62 percent of the yearling males were recovered more than 2,000 yards (1.1 miles) from where first captured. Only 30 percent of the adult females moved the same distance, indicating that the males probably had a greater tendency to disperse.

Other data gathered on marked deer showed that some animals moved considerable distances. Individual animals varied in this respect. One male had an average movement radius of 461 yards (0.3 mile) between its seventh and sixteenth month of life. But during its seventeenth month it was observed twice more than 5,800 yards (3.3 miles) from its previous center of activity. A yearling male marked in July was killed that fall 3,750 yards (2.1 miles) from its capture site. A week-old male tagged in June 1968 was recaptured in September 1970 more than

8,300 yards (4.7 miles) from where it was marked. Another yearling male moved 4,350 yards (2.5 miles) within a month after being marked. Twenty days later, it was seen 1,833 yards (1.04 miles) from the above spot, and in August 1971 the same animal was observed 3.3 miles from the original capture site. Yet another yearling male moved 7.3 miles within a month of being tagged. A week later it was back at the capture site, but the following night was seen 1,250 yards (0.7 mile) away. Other yearling males did not move such distances. Not all long-distance movements were of males. Two does moved more than 4,500 yards (2.6 miles) from where they were marked. Other females moved 2.4 miles, 2.7 miles, 4 miles, and 8 miles. The latter had been tagged three years before it was found dead. Such long-distance movements are certainly thought to be beyond the home ranges of the animals involved and therefore must indicate dispersal.

FOOD. White-tailed deer eat a wide variety of vegetable matter, so undoubtedly seasonal availability influences food habits at specific localities. Sotala and Kirkpatrick (1973) did the most comprehensive study of the food habits of Indiana deer. They examined the rumina from 132 animals taken in Martin County (Table 191). Of the 116 taxa identified (all but 9 at least to genus), 5 vines accounted for about one-fourth of the annual volume of food. These vines were Japanese honeysuckle, poison ivy, Virginia creeper, greenbrier, and grape. Japanese honeysuckle was the most heavily used throughout the year. The 19 plant foods that each contributed more than 1.0 percent to the annual volume of food made up 82.2 percent of this annual volume. Allen (1953) tabulated food items in 191 deer rumina from southern Indiana (Table 192).

Deer also eat rye, wheat, green beans, canteloupe, tomatoes, watermelons, tobacco (*Nicotiana*), and probably other cultivated plants. Crop damage by deer in Indiana has been reported on corn, soybeans, orchards, gladiolus, melons, and Christmas tree plantations. Probably much of the damage to the latter are through rubbing and polishing of antlers on small pines. Mumford saw a deer in water up to its belly feeding on spatterdock on the Jasper-Pulaski Fish and Wildlife Area. One observer reported to us that he saw

Table 191
Foods from 132 White-tailed Deer rumina, Martin Co., Indiana
(by percent volume and percent frequency)
(from Sotala and Kirkpatrick, 1973)

Food	Spring		Summer		Fall		Winter	
	Vol.	Freq.	Vol.	Freq.	Vol.	Freq.	Vol.	Freq.
Grass/Grasslike leaves	18	62	—	—	2	70	28	88
Poison ivy *(Rhus radicans)*	13	67	8	81	—	—	—	—
Unidentified leaves	8	86	9	100	2	72	2	67
Goldenrod *(Solidago* spp.)	8	76	3	45	—	—		
Virginia creeper *(Parthenocissus quinquefolia)*	7	57	12	77	2	15		
Cinquefoil *(Potentilla* spp.)	6	90	2	58	—	—		
Greenbrier *(Smilax* spp.)	5	52	4	71	4	81	4	42
Japanese honeysuckle *(Lonicera japonica)*	4	52	6	55	11	77	10	58
English plantain *(Plantago lanceolata)*	3	38	—	—	4	55	19	64
Moth wings *(Polyporus versicolor)*	3	14	—	—				
Grape *(Vitis* spp.)	2	33	9	68	2	36	—	—
Sumac *(Rhus copallinum/glabra)*	2	24	1	39	—	—	2	24
Ash *(Fraxinus* spp.)	2	14	—	—				
Black cherry *(Prunus serotina)*	2	38	3	52				
Bramble *(Rubus* spp.)	1	29	2	32				
Elm *(Ulmus* spp.)	1	19						
Hickory *(Carya* spp.)	1	43						
Sugar maple *(Acer saccharum)*	1	24						
Christmas fern *(Polystichum acrostichoides)*	1	19	—	—	—	—	3	64
Periwinkle *(Vinca minor)*	1	19	—	—	1	6	6	30
Red maple *(Acer rubrum)*	1	14	2	29	—	—		
Sweet clover *(Melilotus* spp.)			6	71	2	47		
Unidentified fungi			5	42	2	28		
Jewelweed *(Impatiens* spp.)			3	29	—	—		
Sassafras *(Sassafras albidum)*			3	58	1	38		
American plum *(Prunus americana)*			3	3	—	—		
Deerberry *(Vaccinium stamineum)*			2	3	—	—		
Korean lespedeza *(Lespedeza stipulacea)*			2	52	—	—		
Wild crab and apple *(Pyrus* spp.)			2	10	14	45		
Evening primrose *(Oenothera* spp.)			1	6	—	—		
Smooth Solomon's seal *(Polygonatum biflorum)*			1	6	—	—		
Persimmon *(Diospyros virginiana)*					19	77	3	27
Red oak *(Quercus borealis)*					17	36	—	—
Black Oak *(Quercus velutina)*					5	15	—	—
Coralberry *(Symphoricarpos orbiculatus)*					3	30	—	—
White oak *(Quercus alba)*					2	6	2	6
Oak *(Quercus* spp.)					7	12	7	12
Wild onion *(Allium* spp.)					3	18	3	18
Oxeye daisy *(Chrysanthemum leucanthemum)*					2	45	2	45
Wild carrot *(Daucus carota)*							1	21
Red cedar *(Juniperus virginiana)*							1	12

Table 192
Foods eaten by 191 White-tailed Deer, Indiana, by frequency of occurrence
(from Allen, 1953)

Species	1-3 Nov. 1951 (111 rumina)		6-8 Nov. 1952 (80 rumina)	
	Number	Percent	Number	Percent
Acorns	101	90.9	26	32.5
White oak *(Quercus alba)*	40	36.9	5	6.2
Red oak *(Quercus borealis)*	26	23.4	6	7.5
Pin oak *(Quercus palustris)*	21	18.9	18	10
Chestnut oak *(Quercus montana)*	14	12.6	2	2.5
Black oak *(Quercus velutina)*	3	2.7	—	—
Swamp white oak *(Quercus bicolor)*	1	0.9	—	—
Quercus spp. fragments	34	30.6	8	10
Sumac *(Rhus* spp.)	50	46.8	29	36.3
Japanese honeysuckle *(Lonicera japonica)*	37	33.3	10	12.5
Korean lespedeza *(Lespedeza stipulacea)*	31	27.9	—	—
Persimmon *(Diospyros virginiana)*	29	26.1	15	18.7
Apple spp.	19	17.1	—	—
Corn *(Zea mays)*	19	17.1	45	56.2
Coralberry *(Symphoricarpos orbiculatus)*	17	15.3	18	22.5
Wild crabapple spp.	15	13.5	30	37.5
Pokeberry *(Phytolacca)*	13	11.7	12	15
Grape *(Vitis* spp.)	13	11.7	14	17.5
Beggarticks *(Bidens frondosa)*	9	8.1	8	10
Soybean *(Glycine max)*	11	9.9	11	13.7
Hogpeanut *(Amphicarpa* spp.)	8	7.2	17	21.2
Trumpet creeper *(Campsis radicans)*	7	6.3	—	—
Smartweed *(Polygonum persicaria)*	7	6.3	11	13.7
Ground cherry *(Physalis pubescens)*	4	3.6	5	6.2
Tickclover *(Desmodium* spp.)	4	3.6	2	2.5
Lespedeza spp.	4	3.6	24	30
Sweet clover *(Melilotus* spp.)	4	3.6	—	—
Bittersweet *(Celastrus scandens)*	3	2.7	—	—
Poison ivy *(Rhus toxicodendron)*	3	2.7	7	8.7
Red cedar *(Juniperus virginiana)*	3	2.7	—	—
Aster spp.	2	1.8	3	3.7
Beechnuts *(Fagus grandiflora)*	2	1.8	3	3.7
Hay	2	1.8	—	—
Honey locust *(Gleditsia triacanthos)*	2	1.8	2	2.5
Dewberry leaves *(Rhubus* spp)	1	0.9	—	—
Unidentified	1	0.9	1	1.2
Hawthorn *(Crataegus* spp.)	1	0.9	1	1.2
Crabgrass *(Digitaria* spp.)	1	0.9	1	1.2
Ironwood buds *(Ostrya virginiana)*	1	0.9	—	—
White ash buds *(Fraxinus americana)*	1	0.9	—	—
Spanish needles *(Bidens bipinnata)*	1	0.9	—	—
Wild bean *(Phaseolus* spp.)	1	0.9	—	—
Pigweed *(Amaranthus* spp.)	1	0.9	3	3.7
False buckwheat *(Polygonum scandens)*	1	0.9	1	1.2
White pine, needles *(Pinus strobus)*	1	0.9	—	—
Hazelnut catkin *Corylus americana)*	1	0.9	1	1.2
Maple leaves *(Acer* spp.)	1	0.9	—	—
Common milkweed *(Asclepias syriaca)*	1	0.9	3	3.7
Black locust *(Robinia pseudoacacia)*	1	0.9	2	2.5
Oats *(Avena* spp.)	1	0.9	—	—
Alfalfa *(Medicago sativa)*	1	0.9	—	—

Table 192 continued

Species	1-3 Nov. 1951 (111 rumina)		6-8 Nov. 1952 (80 rumina)	
	Number	Percent	Number	Percent
Sycamore, seeds *(Platanus occidentalis)*	1	0.9	—	—
Alfalfa, red clover, sweet clover			20	25
Greenbrier *(Smilax* spp.)			22	27.5
Pumpkin *(Cucurbita* spp.)			6	7.5
Sassafras *(Sassafras albidum)*			3	3.7
Flowering dogwood *(Cornus florida)*			2	2.5
Buttonweed *(Diodia teres)*			2	2.5
Paspalum spp.			2	2.5
Black cherry *(Prunus serotina)*			2	2.5
Black gum *(Nyssa sylvatica)*			1	1.2
Knotweed *(Polygonum virginianum)*			1	1.2
Panic grass *(Panicum* spp.)			1	1.2
Velvet-leaf *(Abutilon theophrasti)*			1	1.2
Curled dock *(Rumex crispus)*			1	1.2
New Jersey tea *(Ceanothus americana)*			1	1.2
Yellow foxtail-grass *(Chaetochloa glauca)*			1	1.2
Puffball			1	1.2

a deer standing in shallow water in a stream picking up and eating acorns from the stream bottom. H. P. Weeks, Jr., has noticed that deer may eat persimmon seeds and not the pulp of this fruit.

Deer tend to feed rather hurriedly, then retire to a safer site to rest quietly. At this time, some food is regurgitated and chewed again (chewing the cud).

Salt is attractive to deer in many locations. The animals will travel some distance for salt and will frequent natural salt licks. Trails radiating from these licks become well used and worn bare by the hooves of the animals. Around salt blocks placed for deer the salt-impregnated earth may at times be eaten to a depth of more than a foot and a diameter of 6 to 8 feet. Salt was most effective in attracting deer for trapping in spring and fall.

Hamilton (1964) conducted a study of woody browse availability and use by deer on seven areas in Indiana during the spring of 1964. The five southern Indiana areas studied were the Brownstown Ranger District, the Crane Naval Ammunition Depot, the Harrison State Forest, the Glendale Fish and Game Area, and the Tell City Ranger District. Northern localities sampled were the Pigeon River and Winamac fish and game areas. A compilation of the browse usage on five of these areas is presented in Table 193.

On the five southern Indiana study sites, the key browse species appeared to be smooth sumac, dwarf sumac, sassafras, flowering dogwood, and red cedar. These plants constituted from 35.8 to 75 percent of all foods eaten. On the northern areas, key browse species appeared to be aspen, staghorn sumac, smooth sumac, red osier dogwood, and soft maples. Additional details of this study can be obtained from Hamilton's report.

White (1968) reported that the most important species of woody plant browse at Crane were flowering dogwood, sassafras, smooth sumac, sugar maple, hophornbeam, greenbrier and willow.

REPRODUCTION. The mating season (rut) of deer evidently occurs mostly in October and November, but there are variations. For five years on the Crane area conception dates ranged from about 30 October to 12 January, but showed a peak the third week of November. About 88 percent of the does were bred in November. The gestation period averages 201 days, but is somewhat variable. Fawn and yearling does breed somewhat later in the year than do adult does. Some fawns are bred when they are 6 to 7 months old (Hamilton, 1957). From 6 to 8 November 1952, it was found that 68 of 99

Table 193

Utilization (percent volume) of woody browse by White-tailed Deer
on selected areas in Indiana, spring 1964 (from Hamilton, 1964)

Browse Species	Brownstown	District and Percentage of food eaten			
		Pigeon River	Harrison	Winamac	Glendal
Silver Maple (Acer saccharinum)	37.7	—	—	—	—
Dwarf Sumac (Rhus)	18.9	—	2.3	4.7	—
Black Gum (Nyssa sylvatica)	11.3	—	—	—	—
Red Cedar (Juniperus virginiana)	7.5	—	15.9	—	—
Quercus spp.	7.5	—	—	—	10.1
Vaccinium spp.	7.5	1.6	—	—	—
Flowering Dogwood (Cornus florida)	7.5	—	4.5	—	15.7
Sassafras (Sassafras albidum)	1.9	—	52.3	7.0	33.3
Staghorn Sumac (Rhus typhina)		88.4	—	—	—
Aspen (Populus spp.)		4.8	—	16.3	—
Black Locust (Robinia pseudoacacia)		0.8	—	—	—
Red Osier Dogwood (Cornus stolonifera)		1.6	—	—	—
Soft Maple (Acer spp.)		1.6	—	—	5.4
Viburnum spp.		0.4	—	4.7	—
Smooth Sumac (Rhus glabra)		0.4	—	—	—
Hawthorn (Crataegus spp.)		0.4	—	—	—
Raspberry (Rubus spp.)			22.7	—	1.0
Coralberry (Symphoricampos orbiculatus)			2.3	—	—
Red Maple (Acer rubrum)				18.6	—
New Jersey Tea (Ceanothus americanus)				4.7	—
Prunus spp.				41.9	—
Salix spp.				2.3	—
Crabapple (Malus spp.)					10.1
Wahoo (Euonymus atropurpureus)					14.8
Black Walnut (Juglans nigra)					9.5

adult females examined were lactating or suckling young. At Crane, on 25 and 26 November 1961, 86 females were killed by hunters. Of these, 34 were 6-month old fawns. Fifteen of the does were lactating.

Probably most fawns are born from mid-May to early July, with about 87 percent of the births between mid-May and mid-June. These data were derived from the examination of 101 gravid does killed on the Crane area. There were evidently few if any births before the middle of May. Approximately 20 percent occurred the last half of May, 67 percent the first half of June, 9 percent the last half of June and 5 percent after 1 July. Females bred for the first time usually produce one fawn per litter; thereafter two per litter are the rule, but triplets are by no means rare. The embryos found in 350 dead does between 1959 and 1966 showed that 116 had one embryo, 209 had two embryos, and 25 had three embryos. In another instance, a female examined held four embryos.

Observations of females with young yield different results. Over a ten-year period (1957-1966), more than 1,000 does with fawns were tabulated by observers. Of these, 53 percent were accompanied by a single fawn, 43 percent had twins, and 4 percent were with three fawns. It is evident that observations of does with their young would be expected to yield different results than counts of embryos in gravid females. Infant mortality is a factor that would decrease litter size. Also, observers might not always see the entire number of fawns accompanying a doe. It might be interesting to gather data on the average litter size in deer from good, average, and poor habitats in Indiana to determine whether a significant difference in number of young produced may exist. Fawns begin accompanying their mothers when about two months old. At Crane, this is usually during the last two weeks of July.

We have been unable to find any weights for newborn fawns from Indiana, but White

(1968) compiled weight and growth for some animals. He found that embryo weights in mid-April were about 3 pounds, while those examined a month later weighed 5 to 6 pounds each. Other authors give birth weights ranging from 6 to 8 pounds, and report that single fawns may average heavier than members of twin fawns. White examined does killed on 13 and 15 May that contained, respectively, a single embryo weighing 5 pounds 14 ounces, and twin embryos weighing 5 pounds each. Additional data on fawn weights were gathered as follows: 18 June, two fawns, 13 and 15 pounds; 22 June, one fawn, 28.5 pounds; 29 July, one fawn, 40 pounds; 20 August, one fawn, 55 pounds; 7 October, one fawn, 80 pounds; 31 October, one fawn, 70 pounds. Evidently the birth weight is tripled during the first month, then increased by about twelve times during the first six months of life.

SEX RATIOS. There is evidently an unequal number of males and females in white-tailed deer, at least on the Crane area, in Indiana. Data compiled in 1964, 1965, 1970, and 1971 revealed that of 148 fetuses examined 81 were male and 67 female. The preponderance of males is similar to that reported by other authors (Severinghaus and Cheatum, 1956; Haugen, 1975) for other states. There appeared to be a differential loss of male and female fawns on Crane. For eight annual hunts, the sex ratio for fawns averaged 108 males to 100 females. Since there is probably no bias due to hunter selection of males over females for fawns, males seem to have a slightly higher mortality rate than females. Yearling deer at Crane over eight annual harvests averaged 101 males killed per 100 females. Among adult deer on the same area, adult females outnumbered adult males nearly 2 to 1 (100 to 52) for the same period.

Several factors probably contribute to the higher loss rate of males from the population. On Crane, 37 of 64 fawns killed over a three-year period by automobiles were males. Perhaps male fawns are more active and move about more, and thus are more susceptible to accidents. Mature bucks may have a higher mortality because of weight losses, physiological stress, and injury during the breeding season. Hunter selection can affect

sex ratios obtained from the examination of deer harvested, but on Crane both sexes have always been legal. Obviously, no one can determine whether hunter bias has operated there. Yearling males show a tendency to disperse more widely than do females; thus some males may have strayed outside of the Crane installation where a "bucks only" hunting season has usually been in effect.

ANTLER GROWTH. Most adult male deer have shed their antlers by early January. Some second-year bucks lose their antlers later, and some males were seen with antlers until early February. Antler growth begins in April, but is most rapid from May to July, during which time the antlers reach nearly full development. Adult males begin antler development two weeks earlier than males in their first year of life. New antlers are in the velvet stage, and sloughing of the velvet takes place generally during the last week of August and the first half of September. Occasionally an individual may retain the velvet longer. An adult doe with a 6-inch spike antler on one side of the head was examined during one hunt on Crane.

There is considerable literature on the correlation of antler growth and development and the age of individual deer. On Crane, yearling males commonly had antlers with 4 points; some had 8 points, but the average number of points varied annually. Most 8-point bucks were in their fourth or fifth year of life. Most males three, four, and five years old had 8 points in all of the years studied. Males with 10 points were in at least their fifth year, and 12-point bucks were generally in their sixth year of life. Antler size often reflects the nutritional value of the habitat where deer live, and thus antler growth and type may vary considerably from one location to another. During the 1951 hunting season in Indiana, several bucks with 16 to 20 antler points were examined (Allen, 1952b).

PARASITES AND DISEASES. White (1967) reported the lone star tick (*Amblyomma americanum*) from white-tailed deer in Indiana. Hoekstra (1971) noted that large numbers of the larvae and nymphs of this tick were found in the ears of deer beginning the first of April; these parasites remained on the deer throughout the summer but decreased in September and October, after which none were found. Immatures were confined mainly to the ears; larval and adult forms were commonly observed on the ears and head and around the anus. Adults and larval ticks were also occasionally found on antlers in the velvet, on the scrotum, and on the udder, between May and July. The largest numbers of larval and adult ticks were noted during May and June; moderate numbers were seen during July and August. *Amblyomma americanum* was the only tick found on deer at Crane in 120 collections of parasites made in 1967 and 1968. *Dermacentor variabilis* occurred commonly on foxes and raccoons at Crane, but was not found on deer.

A large number of the mallophagan louse *Tricholipeurus parallelus* was found on a single female deer in 1971.

The most common internal parasite of deer at Crane was the lungworm *Muellerius minutissimus*, found in 33 of 44 animals examined. The stomach worm *Ostertagia trifurcata* was found in 7 of 9 deer examined by White (1968).

White (1968) reported the mallophagan louse *Damalinia* sp. (=*Tricholipeurus*) from 1 deer, a nematode (*Setaria* sp.) from 5 deer, the bladderworm *Taenia hydatigena* (=*Cysticercus tenuicollis*) from 1 deer, and *Anaplasma* sp. from 6 to 28 deer.

During our studies, only 4 deer from Indiana were examined for ectoparasites; these yielded two species of biting lice, *Tricholipeurus lipeuroides* (9 individuals on 3 of the deer) and *T. parallelus* (58 on 4 deer).

Diseases found in deer were lipomatosis (in a 3-year-old male; photo in White's dissertation), fibrosarcoma, and hemorrhagic septicemia. A hemorrhagic disease was diagnosed in deer on the Kingsbury Fish and Wildlife Area. An unidentified epizootic has been reported from deer in Howard County.

DECIMATING FACTORS. Although disease does not appear to play an important role in the health of Indiana deer, other agents take their toll. Among these are dogs, drowning, cars and other vehicles, trains, locked antlers, falls, and fences. One deer was found, dead, wedged tightly in the low crotch of a tree. Poaching has always been a serious problem in the management of Indiana white-tailed deer, and is likely to continue to take a certain percentage of the population annually.

TAXONOMY. *Odocoileus virginianus borealis* (Miller) possibly occupies practically all of the state. Liberated animals were obtained from Michigan, North Carolina, Pennsylvania, and Wisconsin, and no complete specimens of native deer are known to be preserved in museum collections. Hall and Kelson (1959) consider North Carolina to be occupied by *Odocoileus virginianus virginianus* Zimmerman and place the boundary between *virginianum* and *borealis* at the Ohio River. Deer cross the Ohio River freely, and intergrades probably occur in the Ohio River valley.

SELECTED REFERENCES. Allen, 1955; Hamilton, 1964; Hoekstra, 1971; Kirkpatrick, White, Hoekstra, Stormer, and Weeks, 1976; Stormer, 1972; Stormer, Hoekstra, White, and Kirkpatrick, 1974; White, 1968.

Appendixes
A

Species of Ectoparasites Known from Wild Mammals of Indiana

INSECTA
  Fleas (Siphonaptera)
    Amphipsyllidae
      Odontopsyllus multispinosus (Baker, 1898)
    Ceratophyllidae
      Dactylopsylla ignota (Baker, 1895)
      Megabothris asio (Baker, 1904)
      Nosopsyllus fasciatus (Bosc d'Antic, 1801)
      Opisocrostis bruneri (Baker, 1895)
      Orchopeas howardii (Baker, 1895)
      O. leucopus (Baker, 1904)
      O. sexdentatus (Baker, 1904)
      Oropsylla arctomys (Baker, 1904)
    Pulicidae
      Cediopsylla simplex (Baker, 1895)
      Ctenocephalides canis (Curtis, 1826)
      C. felis (Bouche, 1835)
      Xenopsylla cheopis (Rothschild, 1903)
    Vermipsyllidae
      Chaetopsylla lotoris (Stewart, 1926)
    Hystrichopsyllidae
      Atyphloceras bishopi Jordan, 1933
      Conorhinopsylla stanfordi Stewart, 1930
      Corrodopsylla curvata (Rothschild, 1915)
      C. hamiltoni (Traub, 1944)
      Ctenophthalmus pseudagyrtes Baker, 1904
      Doratopsylla blarinae C. Fox, 1914
      Epitedia cavernicola Traub, 1957
      E. wenmanni (Rothschild, 1904)
      Nearctopsylla genalis (Baker, 1904)
      Rhadinopsylla orama Smit, 1957
      Stenoponia americana (Baker, 1899)
      Tamiophila grandis (Rothschild, 1902)
    Ischnopsyllidae
      Myodopsylla insignis (Rothschild, 1903)

      Nycteridopsylla chapini Jordan, 1929
    Leptopsyllidae
      Peromyscopsylla hamifer (Rothschild, 1906)
      P. hesperomys (Baker, 1904)
      P. scotti I. Fox, 1939

  Sucking Lice (Anoplura)
      Enderleinellus longiceps Kellogg and Ferris, 1915
      E. marmotae Ferris, 1919
      E. suturalis (Osborn, 1891)
      E. tamiasciuri Kim, 1966
      Haematopinoides squamosus Osborn, 1891
      Hoplopleura acanthopus (Burmeister, 1893)
      H. captiosa Johnson, 1960
      H. erratica (Osborn, 1896)
      H. hesperomydis (Osborn, 1891)
      H. sciuricola Ferris, 1921
      H. trispinosa Kellogg and Ferris, 1915
      Neohaematopinus sciuri Jancke, 1931
      N. sciurinus Mjöberg, 1891
      N. sciuropteri Osborn, 1891
      N. semifasciatus Ferris, 1916
      Polyplax alaskensis Ferris, 1933
      P. spinulosa Ferris, 1923

  Biting Lice (Mallophaga)
      Geomydoecus illinoensis Price and Emerson, 1971
      Neotrichodectes interruptofasciatus (Kellogg and Ferris, 1915)
      N. mephitidis (Packard, 1872)
      N. minutus (Paine, 1912)
      Stachiella kingi (McGregor, 1917)
      S. larseni Emerson, 1962
      Suricatoecus quadraticeps (Chapman, 1897)

491

Trichodectes octomaculatus Paine,
1912
Tricholipeurus lipeuroides (Megnin,
1884)
T. parallelus (Osborn, 1896)

Beetles (Coleoptera)
Leptinidae
Leptinus americanus LeConte, 1866
Platypsyllidae
Platypsylla castoris Ritsema, 1869

True Bugs (Hemiptera)
Cimicidae
Cimex adjunctus Barber, 1939

Flies (Diptera)
Cuterebridae
Cuterebra sp.
Cuterebra angustifrons Dalmat

ACARINA
Mites (other than chiggers)
Atopomelidae
Didelphilichus serrifer Fain, 1970
Cheyletidae
Cheletonella vespertilionis Womersley,
1941
Cheyletiella parasitivorax (Megnin,
1878)
Cheyletus eruditus (Schrank, 1781)
Eucheyletia bishoppi Baker, 1949
Chirodiscidae
Histiophorus mingaudi (Trouessart,
1896)
Olabidocarpus whitakeri McDaniel
and Coffman, 1970
Chortoglyphidae
Aplodontopus micronyx Fain and
Spicka, 1977
A. sciuricola Hyland and Fain, 1968
Glycyphagidae
Dermacarus hylandi Fain, 1969
D. hypudaei (Koch, 1841)
D. newyorkensis Fain, 1969
D. reticulosis Spicka and Gerrits, 1977
D. tamiasciuri Rupes, Yunker, and
Wilson, 1971
Echimyopus orphanus Fain and Phil-
lips, 1977
Marsupialichus brasiliensis Fain, 1969
Orycteroxenus canadensis Fain, Kok,
Lukoschus and Clulow, 1971
O. soricis (Oudemans, 1915)

Scalopacarus obesus Fain and
Whitaker, 1973
Xenoryctes latiporus Fain and
Whitaker, 1973
Zibethacarus ondatrae (Rupes and
Whitaker, 1968)
Laelapidae
Androlaelaps casalis (Berlese, 1887)
A. fahrenholzi (Berlese, 1911)
A. geomys (Strandtmann, 1949)
A. morlani (Strandtmann, 1949)
Eulaelaps stabularis (Koch, 1836)
Haemogamasus ambulans (Thorell,
1872)
H. harperi Keegan, 1951
H. liponyssoides Ewing, 1925
H. longitarsus (Banks, 1910)
H. reidi Ewing, 1925
Hirstionyssus blarinae Herrin, 1970
H. butantanensis (Fonseca, 1932)
H. geomydis (Keegan, 1946)
H. longichelae Allred and Beck, 1966
H. staffordi Strandtmann and Hunt,
1951
H. talpae Zemskaya, 1955
H. utahensis Allred and Beck, 1966
Hypoaspis leviculus (Eads, 1951)
H. lubrica Voigts and Oudemans, 1904
Laelaps alaskensis Grant, 1947
L. kochi Oudemans, 1936
L. multispinosa (Banks, 1910)
Myonyssus jamesoni Ewing and Baker,
1947
Listrophoridae
Asiochirus blarinae Fain and Hyland,
1972
Geomylichus floridanus (Radford,
1949)
Listrophorus americanus Radford,
1944
L. dozieri Radford, 1944
L. faini Dubinina, 1972
L. mexicanus Fain, 1970
L. ondatrae Fain, Kok, and Lukoschus,
1970
L. synaptomys Fain, Whitaker,
McDaniel, and Lukoschus, 1974
L. validus Banks, 1910
Lynxacarus mustelae (Megnin, 1885)
L. nearcticus Fain and Hyland, 1973
Quasilistrophorus microticolus Fain,
Whitaker, and Lukoschus, 1978
Macrochelidae
Macrocheles mammifer Berlese

M. merdarius (Berlese)
Macrocheles n.sp.
Macronyssidae
  Macronyssus crosbyi (Ewing and
    Stover, 1915)
  M. jonesi (White, 1966)
  M. macrodactylus Radovsky and Beck,
    1971
  Ornithonyssus bacoti (Hirst, 1913)
  O. sylviarum (Canestrini and Fanzago,
    1877)
  O. wernecki (Fonseca, 1935)
  Steatonyssus ceratognathus (Ewing,
    1923)
  S. furmani Tipton and Boese, 1958
  S. occidentalis (Ewing, 1933)
Myobiidae
  Acanthopthirius caudatus eptesicus
    Fain and Whitaker, 1976
  A. gracilis Fain and Whitaker, 1976
  A. lasiurus Fain and Whitaker, 1976
  A. lucifugus Fain and Whitaker, 1976
  Amorphacarus hengererorum Jame-
    son, 1948
  Archemyobia inexpectatus Jameson,
    1955
  Blarinobia cryptotis McDaniel, 1967
  B. simplex (Ewing 1938)
  Eadiea condylurae Jameson, 1949
  Myobia musculi (Schrank, 1781)
  Protomyobia americana McDaniel,
    1967
  P. claparedei (Poppe, 1896)
  Pteracarus completus completus Dus-
    babek and Wilson, 1973
  Radfordia affinis (Poppe, 1896)
  R. ensifera (Poppe, 1896)
  R. hylandi Fain and Lukoschus, 1977
  R. subuliger Ewing, 1938
  R. zibethicalis (Radford, 1936)
Myocoptidae
  Mycoptes japonensis japonensis Rad-
    ford, 1955
  M. j. canadensis Radford, 1955
  Myocoptes musculinus (Koch, 1844)
  M. ondatrae Lukoschus and Rouwet,
    1968
  Trichoecius tenax (Michael, 1889)
Pygmephoridae
  Bakerdania equisetosa Cross, 1970
  B. plurisetosa Mahunka, 1975
  Pygmephorus brevicauda Smiley and
    Whitaker, 1979
  P. designatus Mahunka, 1973

P. equitrichosus Mahunka, 1975
P. faini Smiley and Whitaker, 1979
P. hamiltoni Smiley and Whitaker,
  1979
P. hastatus Mahunka, 197*
P. horridus Mahunka, 1973
P. johnstoni Smiley and Whitaker,
  1979
P. mahunkai Smiley and Whitaker,
  1979
P. moreohorridus Mahunka, 1975
P. mustelae Rack, 1975
P. rackae Smiley and Whitaker, 1979
P. scalopi Mahunka, 1973
P. spinosus Kramer, 1877
P. tamiasi Mahunka, 1975
P. whartoni Smiley and Whitaker, 1979
P. whitakeri Mahunka, 1973
Spinturnicidae
  Spinturnix americanus (Banks, 1902)
  S. bakeri Rudnick, 1960
  S. globosus (Rudnick, 1960)

Chiggers (Trombiculidae)
  Cheladonta ouachitensis Lipovsky,
    Crossley, and Loomis, 1955
  Eutrombicula alfreddugesi (Oude-
    mans, 1910)
  Euschoengastia hamiltoni Brennan,
    1947
  E. marmotae Farrell, 1956
  E. ohioensis Farrell, 1956
  E. peromysci (Ewing, 1929)
  E. pipistrelli Brennan, 1947
  E. setosa (Ewing, 1937)
  E. trigenuala Farrell, 1956
  Leptotrombidium myotis (Ewing,
    1929)
  L. peromysci Vercammen-Grandjean
    and Langston, 1976
  Microtrombicula trisetica (Loomis and
    Crossley, 1963)
  Miyatrombicula cynos (Ewing, 1937)
  M. jonesae (Brennan, 1952)
  Neotrombicula fitchi (Loomis, 1954)
  N. lipovskyi (Brennan and Wharton,
    1950)
  N. microti (Ewing, 1928)
  N. sylvilagi (Brennan and Wharton,
    1950)
  N. whartoni (Ewing, 1929)
  Walchia americana (Ewing, 1942)

Ticks (Ixodoidea)
  Argasidae—Soft Ticks
    Ornithodorus kelleyi Cooley and
      Kohls, 1941
  Ixodidae—Hard Ticks
    Amblyomma americanum Linnaeus,
      1758
    Dermacentor variabilis (Say, 1821)
    Haemaphysalis leporis-palustris (Pac-
      kard, 1869)

Ixodes cookei Packard, 1869
I. dentatus Neumann, 1899
I. marxi Banks, 1908
I. muris Bishopp and Smith, 1937
I. sculptus Neumann, 1904
I. texanus Banks, 1909
I. woodi Bishopp, 1911

B

New Species of Ectoparasites Collected during Our Studies
of Indiana Mammals
(all Acarina: Mites, other than chiggers)

Chirodiscidae
  Olabidocarpus whitakeri McDaniel and
    Coffman, 1970
    from *Myotis austroriparius*, Greene
    County
Chortoglyphidae
  Aplodontopus micronyx Fain and Spicka,
    1977
    from pits in tail skin of *Spermophilus
    tridecemlineatus*, Vigo County
Glycyphagidae
  Dermacarus reticulosus Spicka and Ger-
    rits, 1977
    from *Spermophilus tridecemlineatus*, the
    La Salle Fish & Game Area, Newton-
    Lake County border
  Scalopacarus obesus Fain and Whitaker,
    1973
    New genus and new species
    from *Scalopus aquaticus*, Parke and Vigo
    counties
  Xenoryctes latiporus Fain and Whitaker,
    1973
    from *Scalopus aquaticus* and *Sper-
    mophilus tridecemlineatus*, Newton
    and Vigo counties
  Zibethacarus ondatrae Rupes and
    Whitaker, 1968
    from *Ondatra zibethicus*, Vermillion
    County
Listrophoridae
  Listrophorus synaptomys Fain, Whitaker,
    McDaniel, and Lukoschus, 1974
    from *Synaptomys cooperi*, Vigo, Harri-
    son, and Dearborn counties

Quasilistrophorus microticolus Fain,
    Whitaker, and Lukoschus, 1978
    from *Synaptomys cooperi*, Knox County
    (and from *Arborimus albipes* and *A.
    longicaudus*, Lincoln and Curry coun-
    ties, Oregon)
Macrochelidae
  Macrocheles n. sp. (to be described by G.
    W. Krantz)
    from *Spermophilus tridecemlineatus* and
    Marmota monax, Vigo County
Myobiidae
  Acanthopthirius caudatus eptesicus Fain
    and Whitaker, 1976
    New subspecies
    from *Eptesicus fuscus*, Lawrence and
    Jefferson counties
  Acanthopthirius gracilis Fain and
    Whitaker, 1976
    from *Myotis keenii*, Greene and Vigo
    counties
  Acanthopthirius lasiurus Fain and
    Whitaker, 1976
    from *Lasiurus borealis* and *L. cinereus*,
    Lawrence and Vanderburgh counties
  Acanthopthirius lucifugus Fain and
    Whitaker, 1976
    from *Myotis lucifugus*, Lawrence County
Pygmephoridae
  Bakerdania plurisetosa Mahunka, 1975
    from *Scalopus aquaticus*, Parke County
  Pygmephorus brevicauda Smiley and
    Whitaker, 1979
    from *Blarina brevicauda*, Vigo County

Pygmephorus designatus Mahunka, 1973
 from Sylvilagus floridanus and Cryptotis
 parva, Vermillion County
Pygmephorus equitrichosus Mahunka,
 1975
 from Sorex cinereus, Posey County
Pygmephorus faini Smiley and Whitaker,
 1979
 from Blarina brevicauda, Vigo County
 (and from B. brevicauda from Minnesota, and B. telmalestes from Virginia)
Pygmephorus hamiltoni Smiley and
 Whitaker, 1979
 from Blarina brevicauda, Vigo County
 (and from B. brevicauda from North
 Carolina)
Pygmephorus hastatus Mahunka, 1973
 from Scalopus aquaticus and Blarina
 brevicauda, Parke and Vigo counties
Pygmephorus horridus Mahunka, 1973
 from Scalopus aquaticus and Blarina
 brevicauda, Parke and Vigo counties
Pygmephorus johnstoni Smiley and
 Whitaker, 1979
 from Blarina brevicauda, Vigo County
 (and from soil from Ohio; and from
 Neurotrichus gibbsi from Oregon)

Pygmephorus mahunkai Smiley and
 Whitaker, 1979
 from Rattus norvegicus and Scalopus
 aquaticus, Vigo County
Pygmephorus moreohorridus Mahunka,
 1975
 from Condylura cristata, Lagrange
 County
Pygmephorus rackae Smiley and Whitaker,
 1979
 from Blarina brevicauda, Vigo County
 (and from B. brevicauda from Minnesota, and Geomys bursarius from
 Missouri)
Pygmephorus scalopi Mahunka, 1973
 from Scalopus aquaticus and Blarina
 brevicauda, Parke and Vigo counties
Pygmephorus tamiasi Mahunka, 1975
 from Tamias striatus, Pulaski County
Pygmephorus whartoni Smiley and
 Whitaker, 1979
 from Scalopus aquaticus, Vigo County
Pygmephorus whitakeri Mahunka, 1973
 from Scalopus aquaticus, Parke County
 (and from Parascalops breweri, Mil-
 ford Gorge, Otsego County, New York)

C

Pygmephorid Mites of Wild Mammals of Indiana

	Hosts examined	Pygmephorus identified*
Bakerdania equisetosa Cross, 1970		
Reithrodontomys megalotis	180	1
B. plurisetosa Mahunka, 1975		
Scalopus aquaticus	104	5
Pygmephorus brevicaudae Smiley and Whitaker, 1979		
Blarina brevicauda	92	1
P. designatus Mahunka, 1973		
Blarina brevicauda	92	3
Cryptotis parva	108	6
Rattus norvegicus	146	5
Scalopus aquaticus	104	1
Sylvilagus floridanus	131	1
P. equitrichosus Mahunka, 1975		
Blarina brevicauda	92	2
Microtus pinetorum	26	32
Sorex cinereus	40	1
P. faini Smiley and Whitaker, 1979		
Blarina brevicauda	92	2
P. hamiltoni Smiley and Whitaker, 1979		
Blarina brevicauda	92	27

P. hastatus Mahunka, 1973		
Blarina brevicauda	92	1
Microtus pinetorum	26	2
Scalopus aquaticus	104	2
Tamias striatus	81	1
P. horridus Mahunka, 1973		
Blarina brevicauda	92	6
Scalopus aquaticus	104	1
P. johnstoni Smiley and Whitaker, 1979		
Blarina brevicauda	92	3
P. mahunkai Smiley and Whitaker, 1979		
Rattus norvegicus	146	1
Scalopus aquaticus	104	1
P. moreohorridus Mahunka, 1975		
Condylura cristata	21	1
P. mustelae Rack, 1975		
Synaptomys cooperi	65	1
P. rackae Smiley and Whitaker, 1979		
Blarina brevicauda	92	16
Microtus ochrogaster	70	1
P. scalopi Mahunka, 1973		
Blarina brevicauda	92	5
Microtus pinetorum	26	2
Rattus norvegicus	146	1
Scalopus aquaticus	104	64
Synaptomys cooperi	65	1
P. spinosus Kramer, 1877		
Blarina brevicauda	92	1
P. tamias Mahunka, 1975		
Tamias striatus	81	1
P. whartoni Smiley and Whitaker, 1979		
Scalopus aquaticus	104	1
P. whitakeri Mahunka, 1973		
Blarina brevicauda	92	4
Geomys bursarius	85	1
Microtus pinetorum	26	2
Rattus norvegicus	146	24
Scalopus aquaticus	104	15
Sorex sp.	1	1

*These are only the numbers actually identified for each. Number may be greater as unidentified pygmephorids, if any, may include more of this species. April 1980

D

Trees, Shrubs, and Other Plants Associated with Indiana Mammals

TREES AND SHRUBS

ailanthus (tree of heaven)	*Ailanthus altissima*
alder (speckled)	*Alnus rugosa*
apple	*Malus*
ash	*Fraxinus*
black ash	*Fraxinus nigra*
green ash	*Fraxinus pennsylvanica*
pumpkin ash	*Fraxinus profunda (tomentosa)*
white ash	*Fraxinus americana*

aspen	*Populus*
quaking aspen	*Populus tremuloides*
basswood	*Tilia*
American basswood	*Tilia americana*
white basswood	*Tilia heterophylla*
beech, American	*Fagus grandifolia*
beech, blue	*Carpinus caroliniana*
birch	*Betula*
river birch	*Betula nigra*
yellow birch	*Betula lutea (alleghaniensis)*
bittersweet	*Celastrus scandens*
blackberry	*Rubus*
blueberry	*Vaccinium*
buckeye	*Aesculus*
yellow buckeye	*Aesculus octandra*
butternut	*Juglans cinerea*
buttonbush, common	*Cephalanthus occidentalis*
catalpa, northern	*Catalpa speciosa*
cedar, eastern red	*Juniperus virginiana*
cherry, black	*Prunus serotina*
chestnut, American	*Castanea dentata*
coffeetree (Kentucky)	*Gymnocladus dioica*
coralberry	*Symphoricarpos orbiculatus*
cottonwood	*Populus*
(eastern) cottonwood	*Populus deltoides*
swamp cottonwood	*Populus heterophylla*
crab (crab apple)	*Malus*
cranberry	*Vaccinium*
cranberry, high bush	*Viburnum trilobum*
creeper, trumpet	*Campsis radicans*
creeper, Virginia (woodbine)	*Parthenocissus quinquefolia*
crossvine	*Bignonia capreolata*
cypress, bald	*Taxodium distichum*
deerberry	*Vaccinium stramineum*
dewberry	*Rubus*
dogwood	*Cornus*
flowering dogwood	*Cornus florida*
gray dogwood	*Cornus racemosa*
red-osier dogwood	*Cornus stolonifera*
elder (elderberry)	*Sambucus*
elder, box	*Acer negundo*
elderberry (elder)	*Sambucus*
elm	*Ulmus*
American elm	*Ulmus americana*
Chinese elm	*Ulmus parvifolia*
red elm	*Ulmus rubra*
rock (cork) elm	*Ulmus thomasii*
gooseberry, wild	*Ribes*
grape	*Vitis*
pigeon grape	*Vitis cinerea*

summer grape	*Vitis aestivalis*
sweet winter grape	*Vitis*
greenbrier	*Smilax*
gum, black	*Nyssa sylvatica*
gum, sweet	*Liquidambar styraciflua*
hackberry	*Celtis occidentalis*
haw, possum	*Ilex decidua*
hawthorn	*Crataegus*
hazel, witch	*Hamamelis virginiana*
hazelnut (American)	*Corylus americana*
hemlock (eastern)	*Tsuga canadensis*
hickory	*Carya*
bitternut hickory	*Carya cordiformes*
mockernut hickory	*Carya tomentosa*
pignut hickory	*Carya glabra*
shagbark hickory	*Carya ovata*
shellbark hickory	*Carya laciniosa*
holly, Indiana (Michigan)	*Ilex verticillata*
holly, mountain	*Nemopanthus mucronata*
honeysuckle	*Lonicera*
Japanese honeysuckle	*Lonicera japonica*
hornbeam, hop-(ironwood)	*Ostrya virginiana*
huckleberry	*Gaylussacia*
hydrangea	*Hydrangea arborescens*
ironwood (hop-hornbeam)	*Ostrya virginiana*
ivy, poison	*Rhus radicans (toxicodendron),* *Toxicodendron radicans*
leatherleaf	*Chamaedaphne calyculata*
leatherwood	*Dirca palustris*
locust	*Robinia, Gleditsia*
black locust	*Robinia pseudoacacia*
honey locust	*Gleditsia triacanthos*
thornless honey locust	*Gleditsia*
water locust	*Gleditsia aquatica*
maple	*Acer*
black maple	*Acer nigrum*
red maple	*Acer rubrum*
silver maple	*Acer saccharinum*
sugar maple	*Acer saccharum*
mulberry	*Morus*
nannyberry	*Viburnum lentago*
New Jersey tea	*Ceanothus americanus*
ninebark	*Physocarpus opulifolius*
oak	*Quercus*
black oak	*Quercus velutina*
bur oak	*Quercus macrocarpa*
chestnut oak	*Quercus prinus*
chinquapin oak	*Quercus muhlenbergii*

jack (blackjack) oak	*Quercus marilandica*
overcup oak	*Quercus lyrata*
pin oak	*Quercus palustris*
post oak	*Quercus stellata*
red (northern) oak	*Quercus rubra*
red (southern) oak	*Quercus falcata*
scarlet oak	*Quercus coccinea*
Shumard oak	*Quercus shumardii*
swamp chestnut oak	*Quercus michauxii*
swamp white oak	*Quercus bicolor*
white oak	*Quercus alba*
orange	*Citrus*
Osage orange	*Maclura pomifera*
pawpaw	*Asimina triloba*
pear	*Pyrus*
pecan	*Carya illinoensis*
persimmon	*Diospyros virginiana*
pine	*Pinus*
jack pine	*Pinus banksiana*
Scotch pine	*Pinus sylvestris*
Virginia pine	*Pinus virginiana*
white pine	*Pinus strobus*
plum, wild (American)	*Prunus americana*
poison ivy	*Rhus radicans (toxicodendron)*
pondbrush (swamp privet)	*Forestiera acuminata*
poplar	*Populus*
poplar, tulip (tulip tree)	*Liriodendron tulipifera*
possum-haw	*Ilex decidua*
privet, swamp (pondbrush)	*Forestiera acuminata*
prune	*Prunus*
raspberry	*Rubus*
redbud	*Cercis canadensis*
rose	*Rosa*
multiflora rose	*Rosa multiflora*
rosemary, bog	*Andromeda glaucophylla*
sassafras	*Sassafras albidum*
serviceberry	*Amelanchier*
spicebush	*Lindera benzoin*
spirea	*Spirea*
St. Johns wort	*Hypericum*
sugarberry	*Celtis laevigata*
sumac	*Rhus*
dwarf (shining) sumac	*Rhus copallina*
poison sumac	*Rhus vernix*
smooth sumac	*Rhus glabra*
staghorn sumac	*Rhus typhina*
sycamore	*Platanus occidentalis*
tamarack	*Larix laricina*
tea, New Jersey	*Ceanothus americanus*

tree of heaven (ailanthus)	*Ailanthus altissima*
tulip poplar (tulip tree)	*Liriodendron tulipifera*
viburnum, maple-leaved	*Viburnum acerifolium*
wahoo	*Euonymus atropurpureus*
walnut, black	*Juglans nigra*
willow, black	*Salix nigra*
witch-hazel	*Hamamelis virginiana*
woodbine (Virginia creeper)	*Parthenocissus quinquefolia*
wort, St. Johns	*Hypericum*
yew, American	*Taxus canadensis*

OTHER PLANTS

alfalfa	*Medicago sativa*
anemone, rue	*Anemonella thalictroides*
arrowhead (duck-potato)	*Sagittaria*
artichoke, wild (Jerusalem)	*Helianthus tomentosus*
aster	*Aster laterifolius, Aster pilosus*
heath aster	*Aster ericoides*
woodland aster	*Aster*
avens	*Geum*
banana	*Musa*
barley	*Hortium*
beachgrass	*Ammophila breviligulata*
bean	*Vicia*
bean, wild	*Strophostylus*
beauty, spring	*Claytonia virginica*
bedstraw	*Galium*
pretty bedstraw	*Galium concinnum*
beet	*Beta vulgaris*
beggarticks	*Bidens frondosa*
bellwort	*Uvularia*
bent-grass, reed	*Calamagrostis canadensis*
black-eyed Susan	*Rudbeckia hirta*
blazing-star	*Liatris*
dense blazing-star	*Liatris aspera*
bloodroot	*Sanguinaria canadensis*
bluegrass	*Poa*
annual bluegrass	*Poa annua*
Canada bluegrass	*Poa compressa*
bluestem	*Andropogon furcatus*
big bluestem	*Andropogon gerardi*
little bluestem	*Andropogon scoparius*
bluet	*Houstonia caerulea*
boneset	*Eupatorium perfoliatum*
bracken	*Pteridium aqualinum*
bramble	*Rubus*
breeches, Dutchman's	*Dicentra cucullaria*
broomgrass (broom-sedge)	*Andropogon virginicus*
buckwheat, false	*Polygonum scandens*
bulrush	*Scirpus*

burdock	*Arctium lappa*
bur-reed	*Sparganium*
buttercup	*Ranunculus*
buttonweed	*Diodia teres*
cabbage	*Brassica*
cabbage, skunk	*Symplocarpus foetidus*
cane	*Arundinaria gigantea*
canteloupe	*Cucumis melo*
carrot (wild and domestic)	*Daucus carota*
cattail	*Typha*
common cattail	*Typha latifolia*
narrow-leaved cattail	*Typha angustifolia*
celery	*Spermolepis*
chara (stonewort alga)	*Chara contraria*
cheat	*Bromus secalinus*
cherry, ground	*Physalis*
chess	*Bromus*
Japanese chess	*Bromus japonicus*
chickweed	*Cerastium arvense*
cinquefoil	*Potentilla simplex*
clover	*Trifolium*
red clover	*Trifolium pratense*
white clover	*Trifolium repens*
clover, round-headed bush	*Lespedeza capitata*
clover, white sweet	*Melilotus alba*
cocklebur	*Xanthium canadense*
compass-plant	*Silphium laciniatum*
coreopsis, tall	*Coreopsis tripteris*
corn	*Zea mays*
corn, squirrel	*Dicentra canadensis*
cottongrass (cotton-sedge)	*Eriophorum*
cowslip (marsh marigold)	*Caltha palustris*
crabgrass (finger grass)	*Digitaria*
cranesbill	*Geranium carolinianum*
cress, rock	*Arabis*
crocus	*Crocus*
crowfoot	*Ranunculus arbortivus*
cutgrass, rice	*Leersia oryzoides*
daisy, oxeye	*Chrysanthemum leucanthemum*
dandelion	*Taraxacum officinale*
dock	*Rumex*
broad-leaved dock	*Rumex obtusifolius*
curled (curly) dock	*Rumex crispus*
patience dock	*Rumex patientia*
swamp dock	*Rumex verticillatus*
water dock	*Rumex verticillatus*
dock, prairie	*Silphium terebinthinaceum*
dropseed, prairie	*Sporobolus*
duck-potato (arrowhead)	*Sagittaria latifolia*
ferns	
chain fern	*Woodwardia*

Christmas fern	*Polystichum acrostichoides*
cinnamon fern	*Osmunda cinnamomea*
marginal shield fern	*Dropteris marginalis*
marsh shield fern	*Dropteris thelypteris*
royal fern	*Osmunda regalis*
sensitive fern	*Onoclea sensibilis*
fescue	*Festuca*
meadow fescue	*Festuca elatior*
sheep fescue	*Festuca ovina*
flag (iris)	*Iris*
fleabane, daisy (whitetop)	*Erigeron annuus*
foxtail (foxtail grass)	*Setaria*
giant foxtail	*Setaria faberii*
foxtail grass, yellow	*Chaetochloa glauca*
gentian	*Gentiana*
gentian, horse	*Triosteum*
geranium, wild	*Geranium maculatum*
ginger, wild	*Asarum canadense*
gladiolus	*Gladiolus*
goat's-beard (salsify)	*Tragopogon major*
goldenrod	*Solidago*
hard-leaved goldenrod	*Solidago rigida*
goose-foot	*Chenopodium*
maple-leaved goose-foot	*Chenopodium hybridum*
narrow-leaved goose-foot	*Chenopodium leptophyllum*
grass	
barnyard grass	*Echinochloa crusgalli*
beachgrass	*Ammophila breviligulata*
bluegrass	*Poa*
bottlebrush grass	*Hystrix patula*
brome grass	*Bromus*
broomgrass (broom-sedge)	*Andropogon virginicus*
cord grass (slough grass)	*Spartina michauxiana*
cottongrass (cotton-sedge)	*Eriophorum*
crabgrass (finger grass)	*Digitaria*
foxtail grass	*Setaria*
foxtail-grass, yellow	*Chaetochloa glauca*
Indian grass	*Sorghastrum nutans*
Johnson grass	*Sorghum halepense*
knotgrass	*Paspalum*
muskgrass (chara)	*Chara*
old-witch (tumble) grass	*Panicum capillare*
orchard grass	*Dactylis glomerata*
panic grass	*Panicum microcarpon,*
	Panicum villosissimum
pepper grass	*Lepidium virginicum*
poverty grass	*Danthonia spicata*
quack grass	*Agropyron repens*
reed bent-grass	*Calamagrostis canadensis*
rice cutgrass	*Leersia oryzoides*
slough grass (cord grass)	*Spartina michauxiana*
tumble (old-witch) grass	*Panicum capillare*
whitlow grass	*Draba verna*

witch grass	*Panicum*
wool grass	*Scirpus cyperinus*
ground-cherry	*Physalis virginiana*
groundsel, common	*Senecio vulgaris*
heal-all (self-heal)	*Prunella vulgaris*
hemp, Indian	*Apocynum*
henbit	*Lamium amplexicaule*
hepatica	*Hepatica*
hog-peanut	*Amphicarpa bracteata*
hornwort	*Ceratophyllum*
horsemint	*Monardia punctata*
horseweed	*Erigeron canadensis*
Indian-plantain, tuberous	*Cacalia tuberosa*
iris (flag)	*Iris*
ironweed	*Vernonia*
ivy, English	*Hedera helix*
jack-in-the-pulpit	*Arisaema triphyllum*
Joe-Pye weed	*Eupatorium*
knotgrass	*Paspalum*
knotweed (smartweed)	*Polygonum aviculare*
knotweed, Virginia	*Polygonum virginianum*
lambs-quarters (pigweed)	*Chenopodium album*
larkspur, rock	*Delphinium*
lespedeza	*Lespedeza*
Korean lespedeza	*Lespedeza stipulacea*
lettuce	*Lactuca*
prickly lettuce	*Lactuca scariola*
wild lettuce	*Lactuca canadensis*
licorice, wild	*Galium circaezans*
lily, water (white, yellow)	*Nymphaea, Nuphar*
lizard's-tail	*Saururus cernuus*
looking-glass, Venus'	*Specularia perfoliata*
loosestrife, swamp	*Decodon verticillatus*
marigold	*Tagetes*
marigold, marsh (cowslip)	*Caltha palustris*
mayapple	*Podophyllum peltatum*
mayflower, Canada	*Maianthemum canadense*
milfoil, water	*Myriophyllum*
milkweed	*Asclepias*
blunt-leaved milkweed	*Asclepias amplexicaulis*
common milkweed	*Asclepias syriaca*
swamp milkweed	*Asclepias incarnata*
whorled milkweed	*Asclepias verticillatus*
mint	*Mentha*
moonseed, Canada	*Menispermum canadense*
moonseed, red-berried (Carolina)	*Cocculus carolinus*
muhly	*Muhlenbergia sobolifera*
mullein	*Verbascum thapsus*

muskgrass (chara)   *Chara*
mustard, wormseed   *Erysimum cheirunthoides*

needles, Spanish   *Bidens bipinnata*
nettles
  false nettle   *Boehmeria cylindrica*
  stinging nettle   *Urtica dioica*
  wood nettle   *Laportea canadensis*

oats   *Avena sativa*
onion, wild   *Allium*

parsnip (domestic and wild)   *Pastinaca sativa*
partridge berry   *Mitchella repens*
partridge pea   *Cassia fasciculata*
passion-flower, yellow   *Passiflora lutea*
peas
  everlasting pea   *Lathyrus latifolius*
  garden pea   *Pisum*
  partridge pea   *Cassia fasciculata*
peanut   *Arachis hypogaea*
peppergrass   *Lepidium virginicum*
periwinkle   *Vinca minor*
petunia   *Petunia*
phlox, blue   *Phlox divaricata*
pigweed (lambs-quarters)   *Chenopodium album*
pigweed, amaranth   *Amaranthus*
pitcher plant   *Sarracenia purpurea*
plantains
  English (narrow-leaved) plantain   *Plantago lanceolata*
  hoary plantain   *Plantago virginica*
  tuberous Indian-plantain   *Cacalia tuberosa*
  water plantain   *Alisma triviale*
pokeweed   *Phytolacca americana*
pondweed   *Potamogeton*
popcorn   *Zea mays*
potato   *Solanum tuberosa*
potato, duck (arrowhead)   *Sagittaria*
potato, sweet   *Ipomoea batatas*
prickly-pear (cactus)   *Opuntia humifusa*
primrose, evening   *Oenothera biennis*
pumpkin   *Cucurbita*
purpletop (tall redtop)   *Triodea flava*
purslane, common   *Portulaca oleaceae*
pussytoes   *Antennaria*

quackgrass   *Agropyron repens*

ragweed   *Ambrosia coronopifolia*
  common (lesser) ragweed   *Ambrosia artemisiifolia*
  great ragweed   *Ambrosia trifida*
rattlesnake-master (eryngo)   *Eryngium aquaticum*
redtop   *Agrostis stolonifera*
redtop, tall (purpletop)   *Triodea flava*

rockcress	*Arabis*
rush	*Juncus*
bog rush	*Juncus effusus*
Russian thistle	*Salsola pestilex*
rye	*Secale cereale*
rye, Virginia wild	*Elymus virginicus*
rye, wild	*Elymus*
salsify (goat's beard)	*Tragopogon major*
sandbur	*Cenchrus pauciflorus*
sedge	*Carex, Carex grayii*
self-heal (heal-all)	*Prunella vulgaris*
senna, wild	*Cassia marilandica*
skunk-cabbage	*Symplocarpus foetidus*
slough-grass (cord-grass)	*Spartina michauxiana*
smartweed (knotweed)	*Polygonum (Persicaria)*
Pennsylvania smartweed	*Polygonum pennsylvanicum*
sneezeweed	*Helenium*
snowberry	*Gaultheria hispidula*
Solomon's seal, false	*Smilacina*
Solomon's seal, smooth	*Polygonatum biflorum*
sorghum	*Sorghum*
sorrel, sheep	*Rumex acetosella*
sorrel, wood	*Oxalis corniculata*
soybean	*Glycine max*
spatterdock (yellow water lily)	*Nuphar advena*
speedwell, corn	*Veronica arvensis*
sphagnum	*Sphagnum*
spleenwort	*Asplenium*
ebony spleenwort	*Asplenium platyneuron*
spring beauty	*Claytonia virginica*
spurge, flowering	*Euphorbia corollata*
squash	*Cucurbita*
strawberry	*Fragaria virginiana*
sundew	*Drosera rotundifolia*
sunflower	*Helianthus*
tall sunflower	*Helianthus giganteus*
Susan, black-eyed	*Rudbeckia hirta*
sweet potato	*Ipomoea batatas*
thistle	*Cirsium*
Canada thistle	*Cirsium arvense*
Russian thistle	*Salsola pestifex*
tick-clover (tick-trefoil)	*Desmodium*
timothy	*Phleum pratense*
tobacco	*Nicotiana tabacum*
tomato	*Lycopersicon*
toothwort	*Dentaria*
cutleaf toothwort	*Dentaria laciniata*
slender toothwort	*Dentaria heterophylla*
touch-me-not (jewelweed)	*Impatiens*
pale touch-me-not	*Impatiens pallida*
spotted touch-me-not	*Impatiens capensis*
trefoil, tick (tick-clover)	*Desmodium*

trillium (wake-robin)	*Trillium erectum*
tulip	*Tulipa*
turnip	*Brassica rapa*
twinleaf	*Jeffersonia diphylla*
velvetleaf	*Abutilon theophrasti*
vervain	*Verbena*
violet	*Viola*
Missouri violet	*Viola missouriensis*
primrose-leaved violet	*Viola primulifolia*
wild violet	*Viola cucullata*
wake-robin (trillium)	*Trillium erectum*
waterleaf	*Hydrophyllum*
waterlily (white and yellow)	*Nymphaea, Nuphar*
watermelon	*Citrullus*
water-milfoil	*Myriophyllum*
watershield	*Brassenia schreberi*
wheat	*Triticum aestivum*
wheat, wild	*Elymus canadensis*
whitetop (daisy fleabane)	*Erigeron annuus*
whitlow-grass	*Draba verna*
windflower	*Anemone quinquefolia*
winter-cress, early	*Barbarea verna*
witch-grass	*Panicum*
woolgrass	*Scirpus cyperinus*
wood-sorrel	*Oxalis corniculata*
yam	*Dioscorea villosa*
yarrow	*Achillea millefolium*

E

Other Animals Mentioned in the Text

AMPHIBIANS, FISHES, AND REPTILES

bullhead (catfish)	*Ictalurus*
cave blindfish	*Amblyopsis spelea*
chub, creek	*Semotilus atromaculatus*
frog, chorus	*Pseudacris triseriata*
gar (gar pike)	*Lepisosteus*
racerunner, six-lined	*Cnemidophorus sexlineatus*
salamanders	
cave salamander	*Eurycea lucifuga*
red-backed salamander	*Plethodon cinereus*
slimy salamander	*Plethodon glutinosus*
small-mouthed salamander	*Ambystoma texanum*
tiger salamander	*Ambystoma tigrinum*
snakes	
black rat snake (rat snake)	*Elaphe obsoleta*
bull snake	*Pituophis melanoleucus (sayi)*
garter snake	*Thamnophis sirtalis*
prairie king snake	*Lampropeltis calligaster*

rat snake (black rat snake)	*Elaphe obsoleta*
toad, Fowler's	*Bufo woodhousei*
turtles	
Blanding's turtle	*Emydoidea blandingi*
eastern box turtle	*Terrapene carolina*
snapping turtle	*Chelydra serpentina*
spotted turtle	*Clemmys guttata*

BIRDS

bluebird, eastern	*Sialis sialis*
bobwhite	*Colinus virginianus*
cardinal	*Cardinalis cardinalis*
catbird, gray	*Dumetella carolinensis*
chicken, domestic	*Gallus*
chicken, greater prairie	*Tympanuchus cupido*
chukar	*Alectoris graeca*
coot, American	*Fulica americana*
crow, common	*Corvus brachyrhynchus*
cuckoo, yellow-billed	*Coccyzus americanus*
dove, mourning	*Zenaidura macroura*
duck, wood	*Aix sponsa*
flicker, common	*Colaptes auratus*
goldfinch, American	*Spinus tristis*
goose, Canada	*Branta canadensis*
goshawk	*Accipiter gentilis*
guinea, domestic	*Numida*
hawks	
Cooper's hawk	*Accipiter cooperii*
marsh hawk	*Circus cyaneus*
red-tailed hawk	*Buteo jamaicensis*
rough-legged hawk	*Buteo lagopus*
heron, yellow-crowned night	*Nyctanassa violacea*
jay, blue	*Cyanocitta cristata*
kestrel, American (sparrow hawk)	*Falco sparverius*
killdeer	*Charadrius vociferus*
martin, purple	*Progne subis*
mockingbird	*Mimus polyglottos*
owls	
barn owl	*Tyto alba*
barred owl	*Strix varia*
great horned owl	*Bubo virginianus*
long-eared owl	*Asio otus*
saw-whet owl	*Aegolius acadicus*
screech owl	*Otus asio*
short-eared owl	*Asio flammeus*
pheasant, ring-necked	*Phasianus colchicus*
phoebe, eastern	*Sayornis phoebe*
pigeon, domestic	*Columba livia*
plover, American golden	*Pulvialis dominica*
quail, migratory (coturnix)	*Coturnix coturnix*
robin, American	*Turdus migratorius*
sapsucker, yellow-bellied (red naped)	*Sphyrapicus varius*

sparrows
  house (English) sparrow
  song sparrow
swift, chimney
thrasher, brown
thrush, wood
titmouse, tufted
towhee, rufous-sided
turkey
warblers
  prairie warbler
  prothonotary warbler
  yellow warbler
woodcock, American
woodpeckers
  pileated woodpecker
  red-bellied woodpecker
wren, Carolina

Passer domesticus
Melospiza melodia
Chaetura pelagica
Toxostoma rufum
Hylocichla mustelina
Parus bicolor
Pipilo erythrophthalmus
Meleagris gallopavo

Dendroica discolor
Protonataria citrea
Dendroica petechia
Philohela minor

Dryocopus pileatus
Centurus carolinus
Thyrothorus ludovicianus

MAMMALS

anteater, spiny (echidna)
bandicoot
bat, horseshoe
bat, Townsend's big-eared
bear, black
beaver, giant
bison
cat, domestic
cow
dog, domestic
echidna (spiny anteater)
elk (wapiti)
fisher
jackrabbit, white-tailed
lamb (domestic sheep)
lion, mountain
lynx
mammoth
mastodon
mole, hairy-tailed
mole, shrew
mouse, eastern harvest
mouse, woodland jumping
muskox
myotis, small-footed
nutria
opossum
otter, river
Phenacomys (vole)
pig, domestic
platypus, duck-billed
porcupine
rat, black

Tachyglossus, Zaglossus
family Peramelidae
Rhinolophus sp.
Plecotus townsendii
Ursus americanus
Castoroides
Bison bison
Felis catus
Bos taurus
Canis familiaris
Tachyglossus, Zaglossus
Cervus elaphus
Martes pennanti
Lepus townsendii
Ovis aries
Felis concolor
Felis lynx
Mammuthus
Mammut
Parascalops breweri
Neurotrichus gibbsii
Reithrodontomys humulis
Napaeozapus insignis
Ovibos, Symbos
Myotis leibii
Myocastor coypus
Didelphis azarae
Lutra canadensis
Arborimus
Sus scrofa
Ornithorhynchus anatinus
Erethizon dorsatum
Rattus rattus

rat, vesper	*Nyctomys sumichrasti*
rabbit, San Juan	*Oryctolagus cuniculus*
sheep, domestic	*Ovis aries*
shrew, short-tailed (swamp)	*Blarina telmalestes*
skunk, eastern spotted	*Spilogale putorius*
sloth, ground	*Megalonyx*
wapiti (elk)	*Cervus elaphus*
wolf, gray (timber)	*Canis lupus*
wolf, red	*Canis rufus*
wolverine	*Gulo gulo*
wombat	*Lasiorhinus, Phascolomis*

References

Adalis, D., and L. Scherich. 1971. A study of cecal helminths of the house mouse, *Mus musculus* L., in Delaware County, Indiana. Proc. Ind. Acad. Sci., 80:485. (Abstract.)

Adams, W. R. 1950. Food animals used by the Indians at the Angel Site. Proc. Ind. Acad. Sci., 59:19-24.

Allan, P. F. 1947. Blue jay attacks red bat. J. Mammal., 28:180.

Allen, D. L. 1939. Winter habits of Michigan skunks. J. Wildl. Mgmt., 3:212-218.

———. 1943. Michigan Fox squirrel management. Mich. Dept. Conserv. Game Div. Publ. No. 100. 404pp.

Allen, D. L., and W. W. Shapton. 1942. An ecological study of winter dens, with special reference to the eastern skunk. Ecology, 23:59-68.

Allen, E. G. 1938. The habits and life history of the eastern chipmunk, *Tamias striatus lysteri*. N.Y. State Mus. Bull. No. 314:7-119.

Allen, G. M. 1916. Bats of the genus *Corynorhinus*. Bulletin Museum of Comparative Zoology, 60:333-356.

Allen, H. 1864. Monograph of the bats of North America. Smithsonian Miscellaneous Collections, 7:53.

———. 1894. A monograph of the bats of North America. U.S. National Museum Collections, 43:86.

Allen, J. A. 1898. Revision of the chickarees, or North American red squirrels (subgenus *Tamiasciurus*). Bulletin American Museum Natural History, 10:258.

Allen, J. M. 1952a. Gray and fox squirrel management in Indiana. Ind. Pittman-Robertson Bull. No. 1:1-112. Ind. Dept. Conservation.

———. 1952b. Hunter interview and kill examination. Ind. Pittman-Robertson Wildl. Res. Rept., 12:226-237. (Mimeo.)

———. 1953. White-tailed deer investigation. Ind. Pittman-Robertson Wildl. Res. Rept., 14:99, 101. (Mimeo.)

——— (editor). 1955. White-tailed deer. *In* Indiana Pittman-Robertson Wildlife Restoration 1939-1955. Indiana Department of Conservation, Division of Fish and Game. Bull. No. 3:36-54.

———. 1959. 1958 Sportsman's Questionnaire. Ind. Pittman-Robertson Wildl. Res. Rept., 20:52-60. (Mimeo.)

Anderson, A. 1922. Indiana Magazine of History, 18:349-353.

Anonymous. 1880a. Fauna of Laporte County. *In* History of Laporte County, Indiana. C. C. Chapman and Co., Chicago. p.303.

———. 1880b. History of St. Joseph County, Indiana. C. C. Chapman and Co., Chicago. p.340.

———. 1881. History of Elkhart County, Indiana. C. C. Chapman and Co., Chicago. p.338.

———. 1905. The journal of John Tipton. Ind. Quarterly Magazine of History, 1:9-15 and 2:74-79.

———. 1906. Wild animals of Indiana. Ind. Mag. Hist., 2:13-16.

———. 1919. Journal of Ebenezer Mattoon Chamberlain. Ind. Mag. Hist., 15:233-259.

———. 1938. Outdoor Indiana, 5:27, 30.

———. 1939. Outdoor Indiana, 6:12, 25.

———. 1940. Outdoor Indiana, 7:19.

———. 1952. Outdoor Indiana, 19:22.

———. 1977. Hoosier Conservation, 17:8.

Anthony, E. L. P., and T. H. Kunz. 1977. Feeding strategies of the little brown bat, *Myotis lucifugus*, in southern New Hampshire. Ecology, 58:775-786.

Arlton, A. V. 1936. An ecological study of the common mole. J. Mammal., 17:349-371.

Audubon, J. J., and J. Bachman. 1846–1854. The viviparous quadrupeds of North America, Vols. I–III.

———. 1849. The quadrupeds of North America. V. G. Audubon, New York. Vol. 1:272.

———. 1851. The quadrupeds of North America, Vol. 2:77.

Bader, R. S., and J. S. Hall. 1960. Mammalian remains from an Indiana cave. J. Mammal., 41:111-112.

Bailey, V. 1893. The prairie ground squirrels or Spermophiles of the Mississippi Valley. U.S.D.A. Div. Ornithology and Mammalogy, Bull. No. 4, 69pp.

———. 1900. Revision of American voles of the

genus *Microtus*. North American Fauna, 17, 88pp.

———. 1924. Breeding, feeding, and other life habits of meadow mice *(Microtus)*. J. Agr. Res., 27:523-535.

Baird, S. F. 1857. Mammals. Explorations and surveys for a railroad from the Mississippi River to the Pacific Ocean. War Dept., Vol. 9.

Baker, R. H., C. C. Newman, and F. Wilke. 1945. Food habits of the raccoon in eastern Texas. J. Wildl. Mgmt., 9:45-48.

Ball, T. H. (editor and publisher). 1884. Lake County, Indiana 1884; an account of the semicentennial celebration of Lake County, Sept. 3 and 4, with historical papers . . . Lake County Star, Crown Point. 488pp.

———. 1895. Extinct fauna of Lake County. Proc. Ind. Acad. Sci. 4:54-57.

———. 1900. Northwestern Indiana from 1800 to 1900. Donohue and Henneberry, Chicago. 570pp.

Bangs, O. 1894. *Synaptomys cooperi* Baird in eastern Massachusetts with notes on *Synaptomys stonei* Rhoads as to the validity of this species. Proc. Biol. Soc. Washington, 9:101.

———. 1896a. A review of the weasels of eastern North America. Proc. Biol. Soc. Washington, 10:13.

———. 1896b. A review of the squirrels of eastern North America. Proc. Biol. Soc. Washington, 10:149-166.

———. 1898. Description of two new skunks of the genus *Mephitis*. Proc. Biol. Soc. Washington, 12:31-33.

———. 1899. A new race of chickaree. Proc. New England Zool. Club, 1:28.

Banta, A. M. 1907. The fauna of Mayfield's Cave. Carnegie Inst. Wash. Publ. No. 67:12-21.

Barbour, R. W. 1951. The mammals of Big Black Mountain, Harlan County, Kentucky. J. Mammal., 32:100-110.

Barbour, R. W., and W. H. Davis. 1969. Bats of America. The Univ. Press Kentucky. 286pp.

Barce, E. 1922. The land of the Miamis. The Benton Review Shop, Fowler, Indiana. pp.12-41.

———. 1925. Annals of Benton County. Privately published, Fowler, Indiana.

Barnes, W. B. 1946a. 1945 Sportsman's Questionnaire. Ind. Pittman-Robertson Wild. Res. Rept., 7:21-54. (Mimeo.)

———. 1946b. The Sportsman's Questionnaire method of estimating the game kill in Indiana. Transact. N. Amer. Wildl. Conf., 11:339-348.

———. 1952. Zoogeographic regions of Indiana. Amer. Midl. Nat., 48:694-699.

———. 1955. Land acquisition, development and maintenance projects. *In* Indiana Pittman-Robertson Wildlife Restoration 1939-1955. pp.198-216.

Barnett, E. M. 1955. A study of sexual development in the male gray squirrel with reference to some skeletal measurements. MS thesis, Purdue Univ., August 1955. 62pp.

Barrett, G. W., and R. M. Darnell. 1967. Effects of dimethoate on small mammal populations. Amer. Midl. Nat., 77:164-175.

Bartlett, C. H., and R. H. Lyon. 1899. LaSalle in the Valley of the St. Joseph. An historical fragment. Tribune Publ. Co., South Bend. 119pp.

Bauer, C. A., and J. O. Whitaker, Jr. 1981. Ectoparasites of muskrats from Indiana with special emphasis on the spatial distribution of coexisting mites of the genus *Listrophorus*. Amer. Midl. Nat., 105:112-123.

Baumgartner, L. L. 1939. Fox squirrel dens. J. Mammal., 20:456-465.

———. 1943. Fox squirrels in Ohio. J. Wildl. Mgmt., 7:193-202.

Beer, J. R. 1955. Survival and movements of banded big brown bats. J. Mammal., 36:242-248.

Beer, J. R., and A. G. Richards. 1956. Hibernation of the big brown bat. J. Mammal., 37:31-41.

Bekoff, M. 1977. *Canis latrans*, Mammalian Species No. 79:1-9.

Belwood, J. J., and M. B. Fenton. 1976. Variation in the diet of *Myotis lucifugus* (Chiroptera: Vespertilionidae). Canadian J. Zoology, 54:1674-1678.

Bendell, J. F. 1961. Food as a control of a population of white-footed mice, *Peromyscus leucopus noveboracensis* (Fischer). Canadian J. Zoology, 37:173-209.

Benton, A. H. 1955. Observations on the life history of the northern pine mouse. J. Mammal., 36:52-62.

Benton, A. H., and J. Scharoun. 1958. Notes on a breeding colony of *Myotis*. J. Mammal., 39:293-295.

Birch, J. S. 1942. History of Benton County and historic Oxford. Crow and Crow, Inc. Oxford. 386pp.

Birkenholz, D. E. 1967. The harvest mouse *(Reithrodontomys megalotis)* in central Illinois. Trans. Ill. Acad. Sci., 60:49-53.

Bishop, S. C. 1947. Curious behavior of a hoary bat. J. Mammal., 28:293-294, 409.

Blair, W. F. 1940a. Notes on home ranges and populations of the short-tailed shrew. Ecology, 21:284-288.

———. 1940b. A study of prairie deer mouse populations in southern Michigan. Am. Midl. Nat., 24:273-305.

Blaney, W. N. 1824. An excursion through the United States and Canada, 1822-23, by an English gentleman, (Capt. Blaney). *In* Lindley, 1916, pp. 276-290.

Blatchley, W. S. 1897. Indiana caves and their

fauna. 21st. Annual Report Ind. Dept. Geology and Natural Resources. pp.121-212.

———. 1898. Notes on the fauna of Lake and Porter counties. 22nd Annual Report Ind. Dept. Geology and Natural Resources. pp.89-91.

———. 1910. An illustrated descriptive catalogue of the Coleoptera or beetles (exclusive of the Rhynchophora) known to occur in Indiana. With bibliography and description of new species. Nature Publ. Co., Indianapolis. 1386pp.

Bliss, L. C., and S. W. Cox. 1964. Plant community and soil variation within a northern Indiana prairie. Amer. Midl. Nat., 72:115-128.

Blossom, P. M. 1932. A pair of long-tailed shrews (Sorex cinereus cinereus) in captivity. J. Mammal., 13:136-143.

Bole, B. P., Jr., and P. N. Moulthrop. 1942. The Ohio recent mammal collection in the Cleveland Museum of Natural History. Scientific Publ., Cleveland Mus. Nat. Hist., 5:83-181.

Bowles, V. 1962. Examination of owl pellets. Ind. Audubon Quarterly, 40:34-37.

Bradt, G. W. 1938. A study of beaver colonies in Michigan. J. Mammal., 19:139-162.

———. 1939. Breeding habits of beaver. J. Mammal., 20:486-489.

Breaky, D. R. 1963. The breeding season and age structure of feral house mouse populations near San Francisco Bay, California. J. Mammal., 44:153-168.

Brechner, R. E., and R. D. Kirkpatrick. 1970. Molt in two populations of the house mouse, Mus musculus. Proc. Ind. Acad. Sci., 79:449-454.

Brennan, G. A. 1923. The wonders of the dunes. The Bobbs-Merrill Co., Indianapolis. 326pp.

Brisbin, I. L. 1966. Energy-utilization in a captive hoary bat. J. Mammal., 47:719-720.

Brooks, D. M. 1955. Furbearer investigation. Ind. Pittman-Robertson Wildl. Res. Rept., 16:15-26. (Mimeo.)

———. 1956. Conservation officers' mammal questionnaire. Ind. Pittman-Robertson Wildl. Res. Rept., 16:202-212. (Mimeo.)

———. 1959. Fur animals of Indiana. Ind. Pittman-Robertson Bull. No. 4, Ind. Dept. of Conservation. 195pp.

Brown, L. G., and L. E. Yeager. 1945. Fox squirrels and gray squirrels in Illinois. Bull. Ill. Nat. Hist. Survey, 23:449-536.

Buckner, C. H. 1957. Home range of Synaptomys cooperi. J. Mammal., 38:132.

Burt, W. H. 1928. Additional notes on the life history of the Goss lemming mouse. J. Mammal., 9:212-216.

———. 1940. Territorial behavior and population of some small mammals in southern Michigan. Misc. Publ. Mus. Zool. Univ. Mich. No. 45. 58pp.

Bushong, C. 1959. More rabbits—the easy way. Ind. Dept. Conservation Research & Mgmt. Report, 13pp.

Buskirk, W. H. 1963. Bat skulls found in owl pellet. Ind. Audubon Quarterly, 41:38.

Butler, A. W. 1885a. The muskrat. American Field, 24:513-537.

———. 1885b. Observations on the muskrat. American Naturalist, 19:1044-1055.

———. 1885c. Observations on faunal changes. Bull. Brookville Soc. Nat. Hist., No. 1:5-10.

———. 1887. Zoological Miscellany. J. Soc. Nat. Hist., Cincinnati, 9:261.

———. 1888. Zoological Miscellany. J. Soc. Nat. Hist., Cincinnati, 10:214.

———. 1892a. Our smaller mammals and their relation to horticulture. Transactions Ind. Horticultural Soc. for 1891. pp.117-123.

———. 1892b. On Indiana shrews. Proc. Ind. Acad. Sci., 1:161-163.

———. 1895. The mammals of Indiana. Proc. Ind. Acad. Sci., 4:81-86.

———. 1898. The birds of Indiana. In 22nd Annual Report Ind. Dept. Geology and Natural Resources. pp. 515-1187.

Cable, R. M. 1943. The Indiana rat flea, Xenopsylla cheopis. Proc. Ind. Acad. Sci., 52:201-202.

Cagle, F. R., and L. Cockrum. 1943. Notes on a summer colony of Myotis lucifugus lucifugus. J. Mammal., 24:474-492.

Caldwell, L. D., and J. B. Gentry. 1965. Interactions of Peromyscus and Mus in a one-acre field enclosure. Ecology, 46:189-192.

Caldwell, R. S., and G. S. Jones. 1973. Winter congregation of Plethodon cinereus in ant mounds, with notes on their food habits. Amer. Midl. Nat., 90:482-485.

Catlett, R. H., and H. S. Shellhammer. 1962. A comparison of behavioral and biological characteristics of house mice and harvest mice. J. Mammal., 43:133-144.

Chamberlain, E. B. 1928. The Florida wood rat in South Carolina. J. Mammal., 9:152-153.

Choate, J. R. 1970. Systematics and zoogeography of middle American shrews of the genus Cryptotis. Univ. Kans. Publ. Mus. Nat. Hist., 19:195-317.

Christian, J. J. 1950. Behavior of the mole (Scalopus) and the shrew (Blarina). J. Mammal., 31:281-287.

———. 1956. The natural history of a summer aggregation of the big brown bat, Eptesicus fuscus. Amer. Midl. Nat., 55:66-95.

Clark, D. E. 1971. Parasites of Mus musculus taken from an inhabited building in Terre Haute, Vigo County, Indiana. Proc. Ind. Acad. Sci., 80:495-500.

Cockrum, E. L. 1949. Range-extension of the

swamp rabbit in Illinois. J. Mammal., 30:427-429.

Cockrum, W. M. 1907. Pioneer history of Indiana. Oakland City Journal Press. 638pp.

Collett, J. 1890. Bats in the Wyandotte Cave, Indiana. American Naturalist, 24:189-190.

Conaway, C. H. 1947. The life history and ecology of the pocket gopher in Indiana. BS thesis, Purdue Univ., June 1947. 35pp.

———. 1958. Maintenance, reproduction and growth of the least shrew in captivity. J. Mammal., 39:507-512.

———. 1959. The reproductive cycle of the eastern mole. J. Mammal., 40:180-194.

Condrin, J. M. 1936. Observations on the seasonal and reproductive activities of the eastern chipmunk. J. Mammal., 17:231-234.

Connor, P. F. 1959. The bog lemming Synaptomys cooperi in southern New Jersey. Mich. State Univ. Publ. Mus. Biol. Ser. 1. pp.161-248.

Constantine, D. G. 1966. Ecological observations on lasiurine bats in Iowa. J. Mammal., 47:34-41.

Cope, E. D. 1872. Observations on Wyandotte Cave and its fauna. American Naturalist, 6:406-422.

Cope, J. B. 1949. Rough-legged hawk feeds on shrews. J. Mammal., 30:432.

Cope, J. B., W. W. Baker, and J. Confer. 1961. Breeding colonies of four species of bats of Indiana. Proc. Ind. Acad. Sci., 70:262-266.

Cope, J. B., E. Churchwell, and K. Koontz. 1961. A method of tagging bats with radioactive Gold-198 in homing experiments. Proc. Ind. Acad. Sci., 70:267-269.

Cope, J. B., and D. R. Hendricks. 1970. Status of Myotis lucifugus in Indiana. Proc. Ind. Acad. Sci., 79:470-471.

Cope, J. B., and S. R. Humphrey. 1967. Homing experiments with the evening bat, Nycticeius humeralis. J. Mammal., 48:136.

———. 1977. Spring and autumn swarming behavior in the Indiana bat, Myotis sodalis. J. Mammal., 58:93-95.

Cope, J. B., K. Koontz, and E. Churchwell. 1961. Notes on homing of two species of bats, Myotis lucifugus and Eptesicus fuscus. Proc. Ind. Acad. Sci., 70:270-274.

Cope, J. B., and R. Mills. 1970. Big brown bat Eptesicus fuscus movement in Tunnel Cave, Clifty Falls State Park, Indiana. Proc. Ind. Acad. Sci., 79:439-440. (Abstract.)

Cope, J. B., and R. E. Mumford. 1955. A preliminary report on bat banding in Indiana. Proc. Ind. Acad. Sci., 64:284-286.

Cope, J. B., R. E. Mumford, and N. A. Wilson. 1958. Some observations on a summer colony of Myotis lucifugus. Proc. Ind. Acad. Sci., 67:316-321.

Cope, J. B., A. R. Richter, and R. S. Mills. 1974. A summer concentration of the Indiana bat, Myotis sodalis, in Wayne County, Indiana. Proc. Ind. Acad. Sci., 83:482-484.

Cope, J. B., and W. B. Telfair. 1970. Radiotelemetry with the big brown bat (Eptesicus fuscus). Proc. Ind. Acad. Sci., 79:466-469.

Corthum, K. W., Jr. 1967. Reproduction and duration of placental scars in the prairie vole and the eastern vole. J. Mammal., 48:287-292.

Coues, E. 1874. Synopsis of Muridae of North America. Proc. Acad. Nat. Sci., Philadelphia, 26:173-196.

Cox, S. 1860. Recollections of the early settlement of the Wabash Valley. Lafayette, Ind. 160pp.

Cox, U. O. 1893. A list of the birds of Randolph County, Indiana, with some notes on the mammals of the same county. Ornithologist and Oologist, 18:2-3.

Criddle, S. 1939. The thirteen-striped ground squirrel in Manitoba. Canadian Field-Nat., 53:1-6.

Cuyler, W. K. 1924. Observations on the habits of the striped skunks (Mephitis mesomelas varians). J. Mammal., 5:180-189.

Davis, D. E. 1953. The characteristics of rat populations. Quart. Rev. Biol., 28:373-401.

Davis, D. E., and J. T. Emlen, Jr. 1948. The placental scar as a measure of fertility in rats. J. Wildl. Mgmt., 12:162-166.

Davis, D. E., J. T. Emlen, Jr., and A. W. Stokes. 1948. Studies on home range in the brown rat. J. Mammal., 29:207-225.

Davis, W. B. 1941. The short-tailed shrews (Cryptotis) of Texas. J. Mammal., 22:411-418.

———. 1946. Further notes on badgers. J. Mammal., 27:175.

Davis, W. B., and L. Joeris. 1945. Notes on the life history of the little short-tailed shrew. J. Mammal., 26:136-138.

Davis, W. H., and H. B. Hitchcock. 1965. Biology and migration of the bat, Myotis lucifugus, in New England. J. Mammal., 46:296-313.

Davis, W. H., and W. Z. Lidicker, Jr. 1956. Winter range of the red bat, Lasiurus borealis. J. Mammal., 37:280-281.

Davis, W. H., and R. E. Mumford. 1962. Ecological notes on the bat Pipistrellus subflavus Amer. Midl. Nat., 68:394-398.

Deam, C. C. 1940. The Flora of Indiana. Ind. Dept. Conserv., Div. of Forestry. 1236pp.

DeBlase, A. F., and J. B. Cope. 1967. An Indiana bat impaled on barbed wire. Amer. Midl. Nat., 77:238.

DeBlase, A. F., and S. R. Humphrey. 1965. Additional record of an albino prairie vole. J. Mammal., 46:501.

DeCoursey, G. E., Jr. 1957. Identification, ecology

and reproduction of *Microtus* in Ohio. J. Mammal., 38:44-52.

Dellinger, G. P. 1951. Mammals of Montgomery County. BS thesis, Purdue Univ. 78 pp.

Demaree, H. A., Jr. 1978. Population ecology and harvest of the cottontail rabbit on the Pigeon River Fish and Wildlife Area 1962-1970. Ind. Pittman-Robertson Bull. No. 10., Ind. Dept. Nat. Res., Div. Fish and Game. 109pp.

Demmon, A. M., J. Little, P. M. McNay, and A. G. Taylor. 1934. History of Lake County. Vol. XI. Public. Old Settler and Historical Assoc. Lake County, The Lake County Hist. Soc. Lake Co. Star Press. 342pp.

Denney, R. N. 1952. A summary of North American beaver management 1946-1948. Colorado Game and Fish Dept., Denver. 58pp.

de Vos, A. 1964. Range changes of mammals in the Great Lakes region. Amer. Midl. Nat., 71:210-231.

Dice, L. R. 1928. The least weasel in Indiana. J. Mammal., 9:63.

Dinwiddie, E. W. 1884. The fauna of Lake County. *In* Lake County, Indiana 1884. T. H. Ball (Editor and Publisher). pp.151-152.

Dubinina, E. V. 1964. Mites of the genus *Histiophorus* (Listrophoridae)—parasites of beavers. Parasit. Sbornik 22. Zool. Inst. Acad, Nauk. SSSR, 111-152. (In Russian, with English summary.)

———. 1967. Mites of the genus *Listrophorus* (Listrophoridae)—parasites of the muskrat. Acad. Sci. U.R.S.S. Zool. Inst. Parasitol. Sbornik., 23:167-176. (In Russian.)

Dury, C. 1890. North American Sciuridae or squirrels. J. Cincinnati Soc. Nat. Hist., 12:67.

Duvernoy, M. 1842. Notices pour servir à la monagraphie du genre Musaraigne. *Sorex.* Cuvier Magazine de Zool, series 2, vol. 4:1-48.

Easterla, D. A., and L. C. Watkins. 1969. Pregnant *Myotis sodalis* in northwestern Missouri. J. Mammal., 50:372-373.

———. 1970. Nursery colonies of evening bats (*Nycticeius humeralis*) in northwestern Missouri and southwestern Iowa. Trans. Missouri Acad. Sci., 4:110-117.

Ecke, D. H. 1955. The reproductive cycle of the Mearns cottontail in Illinois. Amer. Midl. Nat., 53:294-311.

Edgren, R. A., Jr. 1948. Notes on a northern short-tailed shrew. Natural History Miscellanea, Chicago Acad. Sci. No. 25. 2pp.

Elder, W. H., and W. J. Gunier. 1978. Sex ratios and seasonal movements of gray bats (*Myotis grisescens*) in southwestern Missouri and adjacent states. Amer. Midl. Nat., 99:463-472.

Elliott, D. G. 1901. Synopsis of the North American

mammals. Field Columbian Mus. Publ. II, Zool. Series.

———. 1907. A catalogue of the mammals in the Field Columbian Museum. Field Columbian Mus. Publ. 115, Zool. Series, No. 8:504.

Elwell, A. S. 1962. Blue jay preys on young bats. J. Mammal., 43:434.

Enders, R. K. 1952. Reproduction in the mink (*Mustela vison*). Proc. Amer. Phil. Soc., 96:691-755.

Engels, W. L. 1931. Long-tailed shrews in northern Indiana. J. Mammal., 12:312.

———. 1933. Notes on the mammals of St. Joseph County, Indiana. Amer. Midl. Nat., 14:1-16.

English, P. F. 1932. Some habits of the pocket gopher, *Geomys breviceps breviceps*. J. Mammal., 13:126-132.

Errington, P. L. 1937. Summer food habits of the badger in northwestern Iowa. J. Mammal., 18:213-216.

———. 1943. An analysis of mink predation upon muskrats in north-central United States. Iowa Agr. Exp. Stat. Res. Bull. 320:797-924.

Esten, S. R. 1933. Report of wildlife census of the Jasper-Pulaski Game Preserve, March, 1933. Yearbook Ind. Audubon Soc. for 1933. pp.32-39.

Evans, F. C. 1949. A population study of house mice (*Mus musculus*) following a period of local abundance. J. Mammal., 30:351-363.

———. 1951. Notes on a population of the striped ground squirrel (*Citellus tridecemlineatus*) in an abandoned field in southeastern Michigan. J. Mammal., 32:437-449.

Evermann, B. W. 1888. The occurrence in Indiana of the star-nosed mole (*Condylura cristata* L.). American Naturalist, 22:359.

Evermann, B. W., and A. W. Butler. 1894a. Bibliography of Indiana mammals. Proc. Ind. Acad. Sci., 3:120-124.

———. 1894b. Preliminary list of Indiana mammals. Proc. Ind. Acad. Sci., 3:124-139.

Evermann, B. W., and H. W. Clark. 1911. Notes on the mammals of the Lake Maxinkuckee region. Proc. Washington Acad. Sci., 13:1-34.

———. 1920. Lake Maxinkuckee. A physical and biological survey. Ind. Dept. Conserv., Publ. No. 7, Vol. 1:452-480.

Fain, A. 1967. Diagnoses d'Acariens nouveaux, parasites de Rongeurs ou de Singes (Sarcoptiformes). Rev. Zool. Bot. Afr., 76:280-284.

———. 1970. Diagnoses de nouveaux lobalgides et listrophoroides (Acarina: Sarcoptiformes). Rev. Zool. Bot. Afr., 81:271-300.

Fain, A., W. A. M. de Cock, and F. S. Lukoschus. 1972. Parasitic mites of Surinam XVII. Description and life cycle of *Marsupialichus marsupialis* sp. n. from *Didelphis marsupialis*

(Glycyphagidae: Sarcoptiformes). Acarologia, 14:81-93.

Fain, A., and K. Hyland. 1972. Description of new parasitic mites from North American mammals. Rev. Zool. Bot. Afr., 85:174-176.

Fain, A., and J. R. Phillips. 1977. Astigmatic mites from nests of birds of prey in U.S.A. 1. Description of four new species of Glycyphagidae. Intl. J. Acarology, 3:105-114.

Fain, A., and E. J. Spicka. 1977. A reclassification of the genus *Aplodontopus* (Acari: Sarcoptiformes) with a description of *Aplodontopus micronyx* sp. n. from the thirteen-lined ground squirrel, *Spermophilus tridecemlineatus*, in Indiana, U.S.A. J. Parasitology, 63:137-140.

Fain, A., and J. O. Whitaker, Jr. 1973. Phoretic hypopi of North American mammals (Acarina: Sarcoptiformes, Glycyphagidae). Acarologia, 15:144-170.

———. 1976. Notes on the genus *Acanthophthirius* Perkins in North America (Acarina: Myobiidae). Bull. Ann. Soc. r Belge. Entomol., 112:127-143.

Fain, A., J. O. Whitaker, Jr., and F. S. Lukoschus. 1978. *Quasilistrophorus microticolus* g. n. et sp. n. (Acari: Listrophoridae) from North American microtine rodents. J. Parasitology, 64:1097-1099.

Fain, A., J. O. Whitaker, Jr., B. McDaniel, and F. Lukoschus. 1974. *Listrophorus synaptomys*, a new species from *Synaptomys* and *Lemmus* (Acarina: Listrophoridae). Acarologia, 16:319-324.

Faux, W. 1823. Memorable days in America, being a journal of a tour to the United States. *In* Lindley, 1916. pp.291-326.

Fenton, M. B. 1970. Population studies of *Myotis lucifugus* (Chiroptera: Vespertilionidae) in Ontario. Life Sci. Contributions, Royal Ontario Museum, No. 77:34.

———. 1977. Variation in the social calls of little brown bats *(Myotis lucifugus)*. Canadian J. Zoology, 55:1151-1157.

Ferris, G. F. 1921. Contributions toward a monograph of the sucking lice. Part II. Stanford Univ. Publ., Univ. Ser. Biol. Sci., 2:53-134.

Findley, J. S., and C. Jones. 1964. Seasonal distribution of the hoary bat. J. Mammal., 45:461-470.

Firlotte, W. R. 1948. A survey of the parasites of the brown Norway rat. Canadian J. Comp. Med. Vet. Sci., 12:187-191.

Fish, P. G. 1971. Notes on *Moniliformis clarki* (Ward) (Acanthocephala: Moniliformidae) in west central Indiana. J. Parasitology, 58:147.

———. 1974. Notes on the feeding habits of *Microtus ochrogaster* and *M. pennsylvanicus*. Amer. Midl. Nat., 92:460-461.

Fish, P. G., and J. O. Whitaker, Jr. 1971. *Microtus*

pinetorum with grooved incisors. J. Mammal., 52:827.

Fitch, H. S., and L. L. Sandidge. 1953. Ecology of the opossum on a natural area in northeastern Kansas. Univ. Kans. Mus. Nat. Hist. Publ., 7:305-338.

Fitzpatrick, F. L. 1925. The ecology and economic status of *Citellus tridecemlineatus*. Univ. Iowa Studies Nat. Hist. 11(1):1-40.

———. 1927. Report on the food habits of *Citellus tridecemlineatus* (Mitchell). Iowa Acad. Sci., 33:291-293.

Fitzwater, W. D., Jr., and W. J. Frank. 1944. Leaf nests of gray squirrel in Connecticut. J. Mammal., 25:160-170.

Flyger, V. F. 1955. Implications of social behavior in gray squirrel management. Trans. Twentieth North Amer. Wildl. Conf., pp.381-389.

Foote, L. E. 1945. Sex ratio and weights of Vermont bobcats in autumn and winter. J. Wildl. Mgmt., 9:326-327.

Ford, S. D. 1975. Range, distribution, and habitat of the western harvest mouse, *Reithrodontomys megalotis*, in Indiana. MS thesis, Ind. State Univ. 36pp.

———. 1977. Range, distribution, and habitat of the western harvest mouse, *Reithrodontomys megalotis*, in Indiana. Amer. Midl. Nat., 98:422-432.

Foster, G. W., S. R. Humphrey, and P. P. Humphrey. 1978. Survival rate of young southeastern brown bats, *Myotis austroriparius*, in Florida. J. Mammal., 59:299-304.

Francq, E. N. 1969. Behavioral aspects of feigned death in the opossum *Didelphis marsupialis*. Amer. Midl. Nat., 81:556-568.

French, T. W. 1980. Ecological relationships between the southeastern shrew (*Sorex longirostris* Bachman) and the masked shrew (*S. cinereus* Kerr) in Vigo County, Indiana. Ph.D. diss., Indiana State University. 54pp.

Gaige, F. M. 1932. Report of the Director of the Museum of Zoology to the board of regents July 1, 1930 to June 30, 1931. Univ. of Michigan Official Publ. 33. 52pp.

George, E. F. 1955. A report on the analysis of one hundred thirty-two pellets of the long-eared owl. Proc. Ind. Acad. Sci., 64:257-258. (Abstract.)

Getz, L. L. 1961a. Factors influencing the local distribution of *Microtus* and *Synaptomys* in southern Michigan. Ecology, 42:110-119.

———. 1961b. Notes on the local distribution of *Peromyscus leucopus* and *Zapus hudsonius*. Amer. Midl. Nat., 65:486-500.

Gifford, C. 1955. Some observations on the behavior and food habits of two species of

Myotis. Proc. Ind. Acad. Sci., 64:256. (Abstract.)

Giles, L. W. 1939. Fall food habits of the raccoon in central Iowa. J. Mammal., 20:68-70.

——. 1940. Food habits of the raccoon in eastern Iowa. J. Wildl. Mgmt., 4:375-382.

——. 1942. Utilization of rock exposures for den and escape cover by raccoons. Amer. Midl. Nat., 27:171-176.

——. 1943. Evidences of raccoon mobility obtained by tagging. J. Wildl. Mgmt., 7:235.

Ginn, W. E. 1959. Fur buyer report. Ind. Pittman-Robertson Wildl. Res. Rept., 20:27-35. (Mimeo.)

Goldman, E. A., and H. H. T. Jackson. 1950. Raccoons of North and Middle America. U.S. Dept. Interior, Fish and Wildl. Serv., North American Fauna No. 60. 153pp.

Goode, N. E., and E. Kotcher. 1949. Murine typhus fever in Louisville, Kentucky. Public Health Rept., 64:229-237.

Goodspeed, W. A. 1883. History of Warren County. *In* Counties of Warren, Benton, Jasper and Newton, Indiana. F. A. Battey and Co., Chicago. pp.31-211.

Gordon, R. B. 1936. A preliminary vegetation map of Indiana. Amer. Midl. Nat., 17:866-877.

Gorham, J. R., and H. J. Griffiths. 1952. Diseases and parasites of minks. U.S.D.A. Farmers Bull. No. 2050. 41pp.

Gould, E. 1955. The feeding efficiency of insectivorous bats. J. Mammal., 36:399-407.

Grasse, J. E., and E. F. Putnam. 1950. Beaver management and ecology in Wyoming. Wyo. Game and Fish Comm. Bull. No. 6. 52pp.

Griswold, B. J. (editor). 1927. Fort Wayne, Gateway to the West 1802-1813. Ind. Historical Collections, Hist. Soc. Ind. Library and Hist. Dept., Indianapolis. 690pp.

Grizzell, R. A., Jr. 1955. A study of the southern woodchuck *(Marmota monax monax)*. Amer. Midl. Nat., 53:257-293.

Grosjean, M. S. 1942. A persistent weasel. J. Mammal., 23:443.

Gunier, W. J., and W. H. Elder. 1971. Experimental homing of gray bats to a maternity colony in a Missouri barn. Amer. Midl. Nat., 86:502-506.

Guthrie, M. J. 1933. The reproductive cycles of some cave bats. J. Mammal., 14:199-216.

Haberman, C. G., and E. D. Fleharty. 1972. Natural history notes on Franklin's ground squirrel in Boone County, Nebraska. Trans. Kansas Acad. Sci., 74:76-80.

Hahn, W. L. 1907a. Notes on the mammals of the Kankakee Valley. Proc. U.S. Nat. Mus., 32:455-464.

——. 1907b. The mammalian remains of the Donaldson Cave. Proc. Ind. Acad. Sci., 15:142-144.

——. 1908a. Some habits and sensory adaptations of cave-inhabiting bats. Biological Bulletin, 15:135-193.

——. 1908b. Notes on the mammals and cold-blooded vertebrates of the Indiana University Farm, Mitchell, Indiana. Proc. U.S. Nat. Mus., 35:545-581.

——. 1909. The mammals of Indiana. 33rd Annual Report Ind. Dept. Geology and Natural Resources. pp.417-654, 659-663.

Hall, E. R. 1936. Mustelid mammals from the Pleistocene of North America with systematic notes on some recent members of the genera *Mustela, Taxidea* and *Mephitis*. Carnegie Inst. Wash. Publ. No. 473:41-119.

——. 1951. American weasels. Univ. Kans. Publ. Mus. Nat. Hist., 4:1-466.

Hall, E. R., and K. R. Kelson. 1959. The mammals of North America. The Ronald Press Co., New York. 2 vols. 1083pp.

Hall, J. S. 1962. A life history and taxonomic study of the Indiana bat, *Myotis sodalis*. Reading Public Mus. and Art Gallery, Scientific Publ. No. 12. 68pp.

——. 1963. Notes on *Plecotus rafinesquii* in central Kentucky. J. Mammal., 44:119-120.

Hall, J. S., and N. Wilson. 1966. Seasonal populations and movements of the gray bat in the Kentucky area. Amer. Midl. Nat., 75:317-324.

Haller, F. D. 1947. Correlation of farming practices with wildlife production and utilization on Indiana farms. Ind. Pittman-Robertson Wildl. Res. Rept., 8:85-103. (Mimeo.)

——. 1948. Correlation of farming practices with wildlife production and utilization on Indiana farms. Ind. Pittman-Robertson Wildl. Res. Rept., 9:68-76. (Mimeo.)

——. 1949. Correlation of farming practices with wildlife production and utilization on Indiana farms. Ind. Pittman-Robertson Wildl. Res. Rept., 10:58-97. (Mimeo.)

——. 1950. The bounty system in Indiana. Ind. Pittman-Robertson Wildl. Res. Rept., 11:93-125. (Mimeo.)

——. 1951a. Winter food habits of the red and gray fox in southern Indiana. Ind. Pittman-Robertson Wildl. Res. Rept., 12:41-51. (Mimeo.)

——. 1951b. Food habits of the red fox in spring and early summer. Ind. Pittman-Robertson Wildl. Res. Rept., 12:85-91. (Mimeo.)

——. 1951c. Field studies of the winter feeding habits of red and gray foxes. Ind. Pittman-Robertson Wildl. Res. Rept., 12:95-100. (Mimeo.)

——. 1951d. Winter food habits of the gray fox in Tippecanoe County, Indiana. Ind. Pittman-

Robertson Wildl. Res. Rept., 12:91-93. (Mimeo.)

———. 1952a. Food habits of the red and gray fox in summer and early fall. Ind. Pittman-Robertson Wildl. Res. Rept., 12:253-260. (Mimeo.)

———. 1952b. Fox den studies. Ind. Pittman-Robertson Wildl. Res. Rept., 13:30-35. (Mimeo.)

Hamilton, L. H., and W. Darroch. 1916. Jasper and Newton Counties, Indiana. Lewis Publ. Co., Chicago and New York.

Hamilton, R. 1956. White-tailed deer investigation. Ind. Pittman-Robertson Wildl. Res. Rept., 17:14-18. (Mimeo.)

———. 1957. White-tailed deer investigation. Ind. Pittman-Robertson Wildl. Res. Rept., 18:86-94. (Mimeo.)

———. 1960. Survey of occupied deer range in Indiana, 1959. Ind. Pittman-Robertson Wildl. Res. Rept., 20:85-86. (Mimeo.)

———. 1964. White-tailed deer investigation. Indiana Department of Natural Resources Wildlife Research Report, 25:29-61. (Mimeo.)

Hamilton, W. J., Jr. 1929. Breeding habits of the short-tailed shrew, *Blarina brevicauda*. J. Mammal., 10:125-134.

———. 1930. The food of the Soricidae, J. Mammal., 11:26-39.

———. 1931a. Habits of the short-tailed shrew. *Blarina brevicauda* (Say). Ohio J. Sci., 31:97-106.

———. 1931b. Habits of the star-nosed mole, *Condylura cristata*. J. Mammal., 12:345-355.

———. 1933a. The insect food of the big brown bat. J. Mammal., 14:155-156.

———. 1933b. The weasels of New York: Their natural history and economic status. Amer. Midland Nat. 14:289-344.

———. 1934. The life history of the rufescent woodchuck, *Marmota monax rufescens* Howell. Ann. Carnegie Mus., 23:85-178.

———. 1935. Habits of jumping mice. Amer. Midl. Nat., 16:187-200.

———. 1936a. The food and breeding habits of the raccoon. Ohio J. Sci., 36:131-140.

———. 1936b. Food habits of the mink in New York. J. Mammal., 17:169.

———. 1936c. Seasonal foods of skunks in New York. J. Mammal., 17:240-246.

———. 1937a. Activity and home range of the field mouse, *Microtus pennsylvanicus pennsylvanicus* (Ord). Ecology, 18:255-263.

———. 1937b. Winter activity of the skunk. Ecology, 18:326-327.

———. 1937c. The biology of microtine cycles. J. Agr. Res., 54:779-790.

———. 1938. Life history notes on the northern pine mouse. J. Mammal., 19:163-170.

———. 1940. The summer food of minks and raccoons on the Montezuma marsh, New York. J. Wildl. Mgmt., 4:80-84.

———. 1941a. Reproduction of the field mouse *Microtus pennsylvanicus* (Ord). Cornell Univ. Agr. Exp. Stat. Mem. 237. 23pp.

———. 1941b. The food of small forest mammals in eastern United States. J. Mammal., 22:250-263.

———. 1943. The mammals of eastern United States. Comstock Publ. Co., Ithaca, New York. 432pp.

———. 1944. The biology of the little short-tailed shrew, *Cryptotis parva*. J. Mammal., 25:1-7.

———. 1947. Rats and their control. Cornell Univ. Ext. Bull. 353. 34pp.

———. 1953. Reproduction and young of the Florida woodrat, *Neotoma f. floridana* (Ord). J. Mammal., 34:180-189.

———. 1958a. Life history and economic relations of the opossum *(Didelphis marsupialis virginiana)* in New York State. Cornell Univ. Agr. Exp. Stat. Mem. 354. 48pp.

———. 1958b. The food of the opossum in New York State. J. Wildl. Mgmt., 15:258-264.

Hamlett, G. W. D. 1932. Observations on the embryology of the badger. Anat. Rec., 53:283-303.

Handley, C. O., Jr. 1959. A revision of American Bats of the genera *Euderma* and *Plecotus*. Proc. U.S. Nat. Mus., 110:95-246.

Hansson, A. 1947. The physiology of reproduction in mink *(Mustela vison* Schreb.) with special reference to delayed implantation. Acta Zoologica, 28:1-136.

Harrison, T., and P. F. Hickie. 1931. Indiana's swamp rabbit. J. Mammal., 12:319-320.

Hartman, Carl G. 1920. Studies in the development of the opossum, *Didelphis virginiana*. V. The phenomena of parturition. Anat. Rec., 19:1-11.

———. 1923. Breeding habits, development and birth of the opossum. Smithsonian Rept. for 1921. Pub. 2698. pp.347-363.

———. 1928. The breeding season of the opossum *(Didelphis virginiana)* and the rate of intrauterine and postnatal development. J. Morphol. and Physiol., 46:143-215.

Hatt, R. T. 1929. The red squirrel: Its life history and habits, with special reference to the Adirondacks of New York and the Harvard Forest. Bull. New York State College Forestry. Roosevelt Wild Life Annals, 2:1-146.

———. 1930. Identity of *Hesperomys indianus* Wied. J. Mammal., 11:317–318.

———. 1931. Habits of a young flying squirrel *(Glaucomys volans)*. J. Mammal., 12:233-238.

———. 1940. The least weasel in Michigan. J. Mammal., 21:412-416.

Haugen, A. O. 1942. Life history studies of the cottontail rabbit in southwestern Michigan. Amer. Midl. Nat., 28:204-244.

————. 1943. Management studies of the cottontail rabbit in southwestern Michigan. J. Wildl. Mgmt., 7:102-119.

————. 1975. Reproductive performance of white-tailed deer in Iowa. J. Mammal., 56:151-159.

Haymond, R. 1870. Mammals found at the present time in Franklin County, Indiana. 1st Annual Rept. Ind. Geol. Survey. pp.203-208.

————. 1882. Mammals found in Franklin County. In Atlas of Franklin Co., Indiana. J. H. Beers and Co., Chicago. 112pp.

Hays, H. A., and D. C. Bingman. 1964. A colony of gray bats in southeastern Kansas. J. Mammal., 45:150.

Heidt, G. A. 1970. The least weasel Mustela nivalis Linnaeus. Developmental biology in comparison with other North American Mustela. Publ. Mich. State Univ. Biol. Ser., 4:227-282.

Heidt, G. A., M. K. Petersen, and G. L. Kirkland, Jr. 1968. Mating behavior and development of least weasels (Mustela nivalis) in captivity. J. Mammal., 49:413-419.

Henderson, G. 1932. The chipmunk as an enemy of birds. Wilson Bulletin, 44:184-185.

Hendricks, D. E. 1967. The ectoparasites and other arthropod associates of the 13-lined ground squirrel. Purdue Univ. Agr. Exp. Stat., Research Bull. No. 817. 15pp.

Hendricks, H. 1970. Woodchucks in a gray fox burrow. Ind. Audubon Quarterly, 48:118.

Hennepin, L. 1683. A description of Louisiana. Reprint: Scholarly, 1938.

Henning, W. L. 1952. Studies in control of the prairie mole Scalopus aquaticus machrinus (Rafinesque). J. Wildl. Mgmt., 16:419-424.

Herbst, D. L. 1966. Ecological studies of the vertebrate populations of a northern Indiana marsh. MS thesis, Purdue Univ., Jan. 1966. 90pp.

Hess, W. N. 1926. Abnormal growth of the incisor teeth of the woodchuck. Proc. Ind. Acad. Sci., 35:275-276.

Hickie, P. F., and T. Harrison. 1930. The Alleghany wood rat in Indiana. Amer. Midl. Nat., 12:169-174.

Hicks, E. A. 1949. Ecological factors affecting the activity of the western fox squirrel, Sciurus niger rufiventer (Geoffroy). Ecol. Monogr., 19:287-302.

Hilton, D. F. J. 1970. A technique for collecting ectoparasites from small birds and mammals. Canadian J. Zoology, 48:1445-1446.

Hisaw, F. L. 1923a. Feeding habits of moles. J. Mammal., 4:9-20.

————. 1923b. Observations on the burrowing habits of moles (Scalopus aquaticus macrinoides). J. Mammal., 4:79-88.

Hitchcock, H. B. 1965. Twenty-three years of bat banding in Ontario and Quebec. Canadian Field-Nat., 79:4-14.

Hoekstra, T. W. 1971. Ecology and population dynamics of white-tailed deer on Crane Naval Ammunition Depot, Indiana. Ph.D. dissertation, Purdue Univ. 407pp.

Hoffman, R. A. 1952. A histological study of the accessory sex glands of the male fox and gray squirrels as criteria of age and sexual activity. MS thesis, Purdue Univ., Jan. 1952. 73pp.

Hoffman, R. A., and C. M. Kirkpatrick. 1954. Red fox weights and reproduction in Tippecanoe County, Indiana. J. Mammal., 35:504-509.

————. 1956. An analysis of techniques for determining male squirrel reproductive development. Trans. 21st North Amer. Wildl. Conf., 21:348-355.

————. 1959. Current knowledge of tree squirrel reproduction cycles and development. In Symposium on the gray squirrel. Editor: V. Flyger. Proc. 13th Ann. Conf. Southeastern Assoc. Game and Fish Commissioners. pp.363-367.

Hoffmeister, D. F. 1954. Distribution of some Illinois mammals. Nat. Hist. Miscellanea, Chicago Acad. Sci. No. 128. 4pp.

————. 1956. Southern limits of the least weasel (Mustela rixosa) in central United States. Trans. Ill. Acad. Sci., 48:195-196.

Hoffmeister, D. F., and W. L. Downes. 1964. Blue jays as predators of red bats. Southwestern Naturalist, 9:102-109.

Hoffmeister, D. F., and W. W. Goodpaster. 1963. Observations on a colony of big-eared bats, Plecotus rafinesquii. Trans. Ill. Acad. Sci., 55:87-89.

Hoffmeister, D. F., and M. M. Hensley. 1949. Retention of the "color" pattern in an albino thirteen-lined ground squirrel (Citellus tridecemlineatus). Amer. Midl. Nat., 42:403-405.

Hoffmeister, D. F., and C. O. Mohr. 1957. Fieldbook of Illinois mammals. Natural Hist. Surv. Div. Manual 4. 223pp.

Hollister, N. 1911a. A systematic synopsis of the muskrats. North American Fauna 32, 47pp.

————. 1911b. Remarks on the long-tailed shrews of the eastern United States with description of a new species. Proc. U.S. Nat. Mus., 40:377-381.

————. 1913. A synopsis of the American minks. Proc. U.S. Nat. Mus., 44:471-480.

Hooper, E. T. 1942. Geographic variation in the eastern chipmunk, Tamias striatus, in Michigan. Occas. Papers Mus. Zool. Univ. Mich. No. 461. 5pp.

————. 1952. A systematic review of the harvest mice (genus Reithrodontomys) of Latin

America. Misc. Publ. Univ. Mich. Mus. of Zool., 77:1-225.

Houtcooper, W. C. 1972. Rodent seed supply and burrows of *Peromyscus* in cultivated fields. Proc. Ind. Acad. Sci., 81:384-389.

Howard, T. E. 1907. A history of St. Joseph County, Indiana. Lewis Publ. Co., Chicago and New York. Vol. 1:44. 601pp.

Howard, W. E. 1949. Dispersal, amount of inbreeding, and longevity in a local population of prairie deermice on the George Reserve, southern Michigan. Univ. Mich. Contrib. Lab. Vert. Biol. No. 43. 50pp.

Howell, A. B. 1927. Revision of the American lemming mice (genus *Synaptomys*). North American Fauna 50. 38pp.

Howell, A. H. 1901. Revision of the skunks of the genus *Chincha*. North American Fauna 20. 62pp.

————. 1909a. Description of a new bat from Nickajack Cave, Tennessee. Proc. Biol. Soc. Wash., 22:46.

————. 1909b. Notes on the distribution of certain mammals in the southeastern United States. Proc. Biol. Soc. Washington, 22:66.

————. 1910. Notes on the mammals of the middle Mississippi Valley, with description of a new woodrat. Proc. Biol. Soc. Washington, 22:23-24.

————. 1914. Notes on the skunks of Indiana, with a correction. Proc. Biol. Soc. Washington, 27:100.

————. 1915. Revision of the American marmots. North American Fauna 37. 80pp.

————. 1918. Revision of the American flying squirrels. North American Fauna 44. 64pp.

————. 1929. Revision of the American chipmunks. North American Fauna 52. 157pp.

————. 1932. Notes on range of the eastern chipmunk in Ohio, Indiana and Quebec. J. Mammal., 13:166-167.

————. 1938. Revision of the North American ground squirrels, with a classification of the North American Sciuridae. North American Fauna 56. 256pp.

Hubbard, C. A. 1947. (Facsimile edition reprinted, 1968). Fleas of western North America, their relation to the public health. Hafner Publ. Co., New York and London. 533pp.

Humphrey, S. R. 1964. Extermination at Indiana *Myotis lucifugus* nurseries. Bat Research News, 5:34.

————. 1966. Flight behavior of *Myotis lucifugus* at nursery colonies. J. Mammal., 47:323.

Humphrey, S. R., and J. B. Cope. 1964. Movement of *Myotis lucifugus lucifugus* from a colony in Boone County, Indiana. Proc. Ind. Acad. Sci., 73:268-271.

————. 1968. Records of migration of the evening bat, *Nycticeius humeralis*. J. Mammal., 49:329.

————. 1970. Population samples of the evening bat, *Nycticeius humeralis*. J. Mammal., 51:399-401.

————. 1976. Population ecology of the little brown bat, *Myotis lucifugus*, in Indiana and north-central Kentucky. Special Publ. No. 4, Amer. Soc. Mammalogists. 81pp.

————. 1977. Survival rates of the endangered Indiana bat, *Myotis sodalis*. J. Mammal., 58:32-36.

————. 1978. Status, winter habitat, and management of the endangered Indiana bat, *Myotis sodalis*. Florida Scientist, 41:65-76.

Humphrey, S. R., A. R. Richter, and J. B. Cope. 1977. Summer habitat and ecology of the endangered Indiana bat, *Myotis sodalis*. J. Mammal., 58:334-346.

Hunt, T. P. 1959. Breeding habits of the swamp rabbit with notes on its life history. J. Mammal., 40:82-91

Jackson, H. H. T. 1915. A review of the American moles. North American Fauna 38. 100pp.

————. 1928. A taxonomic review of the American long-tailed shrews. North American Fauna 51. 238pp.

————. 1949. Two new coyotes from the United States. Proc. Biol. Soc. Washington, 62:31-32.

————. 1961. Mammals of Wisconsin. Univ. Wisc. Press. 504pp.

Jameson, E. W., Jr. 1947. Natural history of the prairie vole (Mammalian Genus *Microtus*). Univ. Kans. Publ. Mus. Nat. Hist., 1:125-151.

Johnson, A. S. 1970. Biology of the raccoon (*Procyon lotor varius* Nelson and Goldman) in Alabama. Contribution Alabama Cooperative Wildlife Research Unit. Bull. 402. Auburn Univ. Agr. Exp. Stat. 148pp.

Johnson, G. E. 1928. Hibernation of the thirteen-lined ground squirrel, *Citellus tridecemlineatus* (Mitchill). I. A comparison of the normal and hibernating states. J. Exper. Zool., 50:15-30.

————. 1931. Early life of the thirteen-lined ground squirrel. Trans. Kansas Acad. Sci., 34:282-290.

Jones, C. 1967. Growth, development, and wing loading in the evening bat, *Nycticeius humeralis* (Rafinesque). J. Mammal., 48:1-19.

Jones, C., and R. D. Suttkus. 1973. Colony structure and organization of *Pipistrellus subflavus* in southern Louisiana. J. Mammal., 54:962-968.

————. 1975. Notes on the natural history of *Plecotus rafinesquii*. Occas. Papers Mus. Zool. Louisiana State Univ., No. 47. 14pp.

Jones, G. S. 1970. Foods of the white-footed mouse, *Peromyscus leucopus noveboracensis*, from Pike County, Indiana. Proc. Ind. Acad. Sci., 79:172-176.

Jones, G. S., and J. O. Whitaker, Jr. 1976. The fauna of a hibernation nest of a meadow jumping mouse, *Zapus hudsonius*. Canadian Field-Nat., 90:169-170.

Jones, J. K., Jr., D. C. Carter, and H. H. Genoways. 1979. Revised checklist of North American mammals north of Mexico. Occas. Papers Mus. Texas Tech. Univ., No. 62:1-17.

Jones, J. K., Jr., and B. Mursaloglu. 1961. Geographic variation in the harvest mouse, *Reithrodontomys megalotis*, on the central Great Plains and in adjacent regions. Univ. Kans. Publ. Mus. Nat. Hist., 14:9-27.

Jordan, J.S. 1948. A midsummer study of the southern flying squirrel. J. Mammal., 29:44-48.

Joseph, T. 1972. Coccidial immunity studies in the gray squirrel. Proc. Ind. Acad. Sci., 81:341. (Abstract.)

———. 1974a. Coccidia from the opossum, *Didelphis virginiana* (Kerr). Proc. Ind. Acad. Sci., 83:467. (Abstract.)

———. 1974b. *Eimeria indianensis* sp. n. and an *Isospora* sp. from the opossum, *Didelphis virginiana* (Kerr). J. Protozool., 21:12-15.

———. 1975. Evidence of possible superfetation or delayed implantation in the opossum, *Didelphis virginiana*. Proc. Ind. Acad. Sci., 84:478. (Abstract.)

Kase, J. C. 1944. Fox drives in Indiana. Ind. Pittman-Robertson Wildl. Res. Rept., 5:20-29. (Mimeo.)

———. 1946a. Winter food habits of red foxes in Indiana. Ind. Pittman-Robertson Wildl. Res. Rept., 6:10-27. (Mimeo.)

———. 1946b. Foxes must eat, too. Outdoor Indiana, June 1946. 2pp.

———. 1946c. Winter food habits of gray foxes in southern Indiana. Ind. Pittman-Robertson Wildl. Res. Rept., 7:14-20. (Mimeo.)

Kelker, G. H. 1937. Insect food of skunks. J. Mammal., 18:164-170.

Keller, B. L., and C. J. Krebs. 1970. *Microtus* population biology, III. Reproductive changes in fluctuating populations of *M. ochrogaster* and *M. pennsylvanicus* in southern Indiana, 1965-67. Ecol. Monogr., 40:263-294.

Kendeigh, S. C., and G. C. West. 1965. Caloric values of plant seeds eaten by birds. Ecology, 46:553-555.

Kennicott, R. 1857. The quadrupeds of Illinois injurious and beneficial to the farmer. Patent Office Report, 1856:52-110.

———. 1858. The quadrupeds of Illinois injurious and beneficial to the farmer. U.S. Patent Office Rept. Agric., 1857:72-107.

———. 1859. The quadrupeds of Illinois injurious and beneficial to the farmer. U.S. Patent Office Rept. of Agric., 1858:241-256.

King, J. A. 1957. Intra- and interspecific conflict of *Mus* and *Peromyscus*. Ecology, 38:355-357.

———. (editor). 1968. Biology of *Peromyscus* (Rodentia). Spec. Publ. No. 2, Amer. Soc. Mammalogists. 593pp.

Kirkpatrick, C. M. 1943. Rafinesque's bat in Indiana. Amer. Midl. Nat., 29:797.

———. 1950. Crow predation on nestling cottontails. J. Mammal., 31:322-327.

———. 1955. The testis of the fox squirrel in relation to age and seasons. Amer. J. Anatomy, 97:229-256.

———. 1956. Coprophagy in the cottontail. J. Mammal., 37:300.

———. 1960. Unusual cottontail litter. J. Mammal., 41:119-120.

Kirkpatrick, C. M., and E. M. Barnett. 1957. Age criteria in male gray squirrels. J. Wildl. Mgmt., 21:341-347.

Kirkpatrick, C. M., and C. H. Conaway. 1947. The winter foods of some Indiana owls. Amer. Midl. Nat., 38:755-766.

———. 1948. Some notes on Indiana mammals. Amer. Midl. Nat., 39:128-136.

Kirkpatrick, C. M., and R. A. Hoffman. 1960. Ages and reproductive cycles in a male gray squirrel population. J. Wildl. Mgmt., 24:218-221.

Kirkpatrick, C. M., C. M. White, T. W. Hoekstra, F. A. Stormer, and H. P. Weeks, Jr. 1976. White-tailed deer of U.S. Naval Ammunition Depot Crane. Res. Bull. 932, Purdue Univ. Agr. Exp. Stat. 42pp.

Kirkpatrick, R. D. 1961. New observations of Indiana swamp rabbits. J. Mammal., 42:99-100.

———. 1970. Fox bounty in Indiana during the years 1961 through 1968. Proc. Ind. Acad. Sci., 79:187-192.

Kirkpatrick, R. D., and T. W. Landrum. 1975. Preliminary evaluation of a tooth wear aging technique for the big brown bat, *Eptesicus fuscus*. Proc. Ind. Acad. Sci., 84:476-477. (Abstract.)

Kirkpatrick, R. D., D. Martin, and J. D. McCall. 1969. Red fox and woodchuck in same burrow. Ind. Audubon Quarterly, 47:124-125.

Klein, H. G. 1960. Ecological relationships of *Peromyscus leucopus noveborancensis* and *P. maniculatus gracilis* in central New York. Ecol. Monogr., 30:387-407.

Klingener, D. 1964. Notes on the range of *Napaeozapus* in Michigan and Indiana. J. Mammal., 45:644-645.

Klugh, A. B. 1923. Notes on the habits of the chipmunk, *Tamias striatus lysteri*. J. Mammal., 4:29-32.

———. 1927. Ecology of the red squirrel. J. Mammal., 8:1-32.

Komarek, E. V., and D. A. Spencer. 1931. A new

pocket gopher from Illinois and Indiana. J. Mammal., 12:404-408.

Korschgen, L. J. 1958. December food habits of mink in Missouri. J. Mammal., 39:521-527.

Krebs, C. J., B. L. Keller, and J. H. Myers. 1971. *Microtus* population densities and soil nutrients in southern Indiana grasslands. Ecology, 52:660-663.

Krebs, C. J., B. L. Keller, and R. H. Tamarin. 1969. *Microtus* population biology: Demographic changes in fluctuating populations of *M. ochrogaster* and *M. pennsylvanicus* in southern Indiana. Ecology, 50:587-607.

Krutzsch, P. H. 1954. North American jumping mice (Genus *Zapus*). Univ. Kans. Publ. Mus. Nat. Hist., 7:349-472.

Kunz, T. H. 1968. Helminths from the Red Bat, *Lasiurus borealis,* in Iowa. Amer. Midl. Nat., 80:542-543.

Kunz, T. H., E. L. P. Anthony, and W. T. Rumage. 1977. Mortality of little brown bats following multiple pesticide applications. J. Wildl. Mgmt., 41:476-483.

Lafayette Journal-Courier, 10 April 1973, p. A-3.

Landrum, T. W. 1971. Selected aspects of the ecology of the big brown bat *(Eptesicus fuscus)* in Grant County, Indiana. MS thesis, Ball State Univ., August 1971. 63pp.

Langdon, F. W. 1881a. The mammalia of the vicinity of Cincinnati. J. Cincinnati Soc. Nat. Hist., 4:297-313.

———. 1881b. Zoological Miscellany. J. Cincinnati Soc. Nat. Hist., 4:336-337.

———. 1882. A synopsis of the Cincinnati fauna. Zool. Misc. J. Cincinnati Soc. Nat. Hist., 5:185-194.

Latham, R. M. 1950. The food of predaceous animals in northeastern United States. Penn. Game Comm., Harrisburg. 69pp.

LaVal, R. K. 1970. Intraspecific relationships of bats of the species *Myotis austroriparius*. J. Mammal., 51:542-552.

Lay, D. W. 1942. Ecology of the opossum in eastern Texas. J. Mammal., 23:147-159.

Lay, D. W., and R. H. Baker. 1938. Notes on the home range and ecology of the Attwater wood rat. J. Mammal., 19:418-423.

Layne, J. N. 1954. The biology of the red squirrel, *Tamiasciurus hudsonicus loquax* (Bangs), in central New York. Ecol. Monogr., 24:227-267.

———. 1958. Reproductive characteristics of the gray fox in southern Illinois. J. Wildl. Mgmt., 22:157-163.

Layne, J. N., and W. H. McKeon. 1956a. Some aspects of red fox and gray fox reproduction in New York. New York Fish and Game Journal, 3:44-74.

———. 1956b. Notes on red fox and gray fox den

sites in New York. New York Fish and Game Journal, 3:248-249.

Leedy, D. L. 1947. Spermophiles and badgers move eastward in Ohio. J. Mammal., 28:290-292.

Lehman, L. E. 1968. September birth of raccoons in Indiana. J. Mammal., 49:126-127.

———. 1976. Raccoon live trapping and telemetry studies in Indiana. *In* Fish and wildlife in Indiana, 1776–1976 and reports of fish and wildlife studies. Editor: H. E. McReynolds. Proc. of joint meeting Amer. Fisheries Soc. and The Wildlife Soc. pp.33-34.

———. 1977. Population ecology of the raccoon on the Jasper-Pulaski Wildlife Study Area. Bull. No. 9, Ind. Dept. of Nat. Res., Div. Fish and Wildl. 97pp.

Leopold, A. 1929. Report of a game survey of Indiana. 54pp. (Mimeo.)

Lewis, J. B. 1940. Mammals of Amelia County, Virginia. J. Mammal., 21:424.

Lidicker, W. Z., Jr. 1966. Ecological observations on a feral house mouse population declining to extinction. Ecol. Monogr., 36:27-50.

Lindley, H. 1916. Indiana as seen by early travelers; A collection of reprints from books of travel, letters and diaries prior to 1830. Ind. Hist. Comm., Indianapolis. 539pp.

Lindsay, D. M. 1956a. Additional records of *Nycticeius* in Indiana. J. Mammal., 37:282.

———. 1956b. Some bat records from southeastern Indiana. J. Mammal., 37:543-545.

———. 1958. Mammals of Ripley and Jefferson counties, Indiana. Ph.D. dissertation, Univ. of Cincinnati. 104pp.

———. 1959. Mammals of Ripley and Jefferson counties. Proc. Ind. Acad. Sci., 68:360-361. (Abstract.)

———. 1960. Mammals of Ripley and Jefferson counties, Indiana. J. Mammal., 41:253-262.

Lindsey, A. A. 1961. Vegetation of the drainage-aeration classes of northern Indiana soils in 1830. Ecology, 42:432-436.

———. (Editor.) 1966. Natural features of Indiana. Ind. Acad. Sci. 600pp.

Lindsey, A. A., W. B. Crankshaw, and S. A. Qadir. 1965. Soil relations and distribution map of the vegetation of presettlement Indiana. Botanical Gazette, 126:155-163.

Lindsey, A. A., D. V. Schmeltz, and S. A. Nichols. 1969. Natural areas in Indiana and their preservation. Ind. Nat. Areas Surv., Purdue Univ. 594pp.

Linsdale, J. 1927. Notes on the life of *Synaptomys*. J. Mammal., 8:51-54.

Llewellyn, L. M., and F. M. Uhler. 1952. The foods of fur animals of the Patuxent Research Refuge, Maryland. Amer. Midl. Nat., 48:193-203.

Long, C. A. 1972. Taxonomic revision of the North

American badger, *Taxidea taxus*. J. Mammal., 53:725-759.

——. 1973. *Taxidea taxus*. Mammalian Species No. 26:1-4.

Lopp, O. V. 1942. Cottontail rabbit investigation. Ind. Pittman-Robertson Wildl. Res. Rept., 3:16-20. (Mimeo.)

——. 1943. Cottontail rabbit investigation. Ind. Pittman-Robertson Wildl. Res. Rept., 4:14-17. (Mimeo.)

Lowe, C. E. 1958. Ecology of the swamp rabbit in Georgia. J. Mammal., 39:116-127.

Lowery, G. H., Jr. 1974. The mammals of Louisiana and its adjacent waters. La. State Univ. Press. 565pp.

Lukoschus, F. S., and J. G. H. J. Rouwet. 1968. *Myocoptes ondatrae* spec. nov., ein neuer parasit von *Ondatra zibethica* L. (Listrophoridae: Sarcoptiformes). Acarologia, 10:483-492.

Lyon, M. W., Jr. 1923. Notes on the mammals of the dune region of Porter County, Indiana. Proc. Ind. Acad. Sci., 31:209-221.

——. 1924. New records of Indiana mammals. Proc. Ind. Acad. Sci., 33:284-285.

——. 1925. New record of the small short-tailed shrew in Indiana. Proc. Ind. Acad. Sci., 34:391.

——. 1926. Bats. The Audubon Bulletin, Ind. Audubon Soc., pp.13-14.

——. 1930. A pile of *Microtus*. J. Mammal., 11:320.

——. 1931. Bat oil for rheumatism. J. Mammal., 12:313.

——. 1932a. Franklin's ground squirrel and its distribution in Indiana. Amer. Midl. Nat., 13:16-20.

——. 1932b. Remarks on *Geomys bursarius illinoensis* Komarek and Spencer. J. Mammal., 13:77-78.

——. 1932c. The badger, *Taxidea taxus* (Schreber), in Indiana. Amer. Midl. Nat., 13:124-129.

——. 1933. Two new records of the least weasel in Indiana. Amer. Midl. Nat., 14:345-349.

——. 1934a. Distribution of the red squirrel in Indiana. Amer. Midl. Nat., 15:375-376.

——. 1934b. Origins of Indiana's mammals. Proc. Ind. Acad. Sci., 43:27-43.

——. 1936. Mammals of Indiana. Amer. Midl. Nat., 17:1-384.

——. 1939. The least weasel in St. Joseph County. Amer. Midl. Nat., 22:216.

——. 1940. More least weasels in Indiana. Amer. Midl. Nat., 23:253.

——. 1942. Additions to the mammals of Indiana. Amer. Midl. Nat., 27:790-791.

Mahunka, S. 1973. *Pygmephorus* species (Acari: Tarsonemida) from North American small mammals. Parasitol. Hung., 6:247-259.

——. 1975. Further data to the knowledge of Tarsonemida (Acari) living on small mammals in North America. Parasitol. Hung., 8:85-94.

Malecki, II. R. 1949. The parasites of the pocket gopher (*Geomys bursarius illinoensis*) at the eastern limit of its range. MS thesis, Purdue Univ. 41pp.

Malott, C. A. 1922. The physiography of Indiana. *In* Handbook of Indiana geology. Ind. Dept. Conserv. Publ., 21:59-256.

Mangus, L. H. 1950. Winter foods of foxes in Tippecanoe County, Indiana. BS thesis, Purdue Univ., June 1950. 31pp.

Marshall, W. H. 1936. A study of the winter activities of the mink. J. Mammal., 17:382-392.

Marston, M. A. 1942. Winter relations of bobcats to white-tailed deer in Maine. J. Wildl. Mgmt., 6:328-337.

Martin, E. P. 1956. A population study of the prairie vole (*Microtus ochrogaster*) in northeastern Kansas. Univ. Kans. Publ. Mus. Nat. Hist., 8:361-416.

Martin, R. L. 1961. Vole predation on bats in an Indiana cave. J. Mammal., 42:540-541.

Martinson, R. K., J. W. Holten, and G. K. Brakhage. 1961. Age criteria and population dynamics of the swamp rabbit in Missouri. J. Wildl. Mgmt., 25:271-281.

Masters, C. O. 1960. Arthropods of medical importance in Ohio. Ohio J. Sci., 60:332-334.

McAtee, W. L. 1907. A list of mammals, reptiles and batrachians of Monroe County, Indiana. Proc. Biol. Soc. Washington, 20:1-16.

McCarley, W. H. 1954. The ecological distribution of the *Peromyscus leucopus* species group of mice in eastern Texas. Ecology, 35:375-379.

——. 1959. An unusually large nest of *Cryptotis parva*. J. Mammal., 40:243.

McCarley, H. 1966. Annual cycle, population dynamics and adaptive behavior of *Citellus tridecemlineatus*. J. Mammal., 47:294-316.

McClure, H. E. 1942. Summer activities of bats (genus *Lasiurus*) in Iowa. J. Mammal., 23:430-434.

McDaniel, B., and C. C. Coffman. 1970. The labidocarpid bat mites of the United States (Acarina: Listrophoridae). Proc. Helminth. Soc. Wash., 37:223-229.

McDaniel, B., and J. O. Whitaker, Jr. 1972. A new genus and two new species of listrophorid fur mites from North American shrews (Acarina: Listrophoridae). Proc. Entomol. Soc. Wash., 74:426-432.

McManus, John J. 1974. *Didelphis virginiana*. Mammalian Species No. 40. pp.1-6.

Meek, D. (editor). 1960. Bird Notes. Audubon Leaves, 14:9. South Bend Audubon Soc. (Mimeo.)

Merriam, C. H. 1892. The occurrence of Cooper's

lemming mouse (Synaptomys cooperi) in the Atlantic States. Proc. Biol. Soc. Washington, 7:175-177.

———. 1895a. Synopsis of the American shrews of the genus Sorex. North American Fauna 10:57-118.

———. 1895b. Revision of the shrews of the American genera Blarina and Notiosorex. North American Fauna No. 10. 34pp.

———. 1896. Revision of the lemmings of the genus Synaptomys, with descriptions of new species. Proc. Biol. Soc. Washington, 10:55-64.

Miller, D. H., and L. L. Getz. 1969. Life history notes on Microtus pinetorum in central Connecticut. J. Mammal., 50:777-784.

Miller, G. S., Jr. 1895. The long-tailed shrews of the eastern United States. North American Fauna No. 10:35-56.

———. 1896. Genera and subgenera of voles and lemmings. North American Fauna No. 12. 84pp.

———. 1897. Revision of the North American bats of the family Vespertilionidae. North American Fauna No. 13. 141pp.

———. 1907. The families and genera of bats. U.S. Nat. Mus., Bull. No. 57. 282pp.

———. 1924. List of North American recent mammals, 1923. U.S. Nat. Mus., Bull. No. 128. 673pp.

Miller, G. S., Jr., and G. M. Allen. 1928. The American bats of the genera Myotis and Pizonyx. U.S. Nat. Mus., Bull. No. 144. 218pp.

Miller, W. C. 1969. Ecological and ethological isolating mechanisms between Microtus pennsylvanicus and Microtus ochrogaster at Terre Haute, Indiana. Amer. Midl. Nat., 82:140-148.

Mills, R. S., G. W. Barrett, and J. B. Cope. 1976. Bat species diversity patterns in east central Indiana. Proc. Ind. Acad. Sci., 85:409. (Abstract.)

Minton, S., Jr. 1944. Introduction to the study of the reptiles of Indiana. Amer. Midl. Nat., 32:438-477.

Mohr, C. E. 1933. Observations on the young of cave-dwelling bats. J. Mammal., 14:49-53.

Mohr, C. O., and W. P. Mohr. 1936. Abundance and digging rate of pocket gophers, Geomys bursarius. Ecology, 17:325-327.

Montague, F. H., Jr. 1975. The ecology and recreational value of the red fox in Indiana. Ph.D. dissertation, Purdue Univ., August 1975. 268pp.

Moore, J. C. 1943. A contribution to the natural history of the Florida short-tailed shrew. Proc. Florida Acad. Sci. 6:155-166.

———. 1949. Notes on the shrew, Sorex cinereus, in the southern Appalachians. Ecology, 30:234-237.

Morlan, H. B. 1952. Host relationships and seasonal abundance of some southwest Georgia ectoparasites. Amer. Midl. Nat., 48:74-93.

Morrison, P., and F. A. Ryser. 1962. Metabolism and body temperature in a small hibernator, the meadow jumping mouse, Zapus hudsonius. J. Cell. and Comp. Physiol., 60:169-180.

Moseley, E. L. 1928. The number of young red bats in one litter. J. Mammal., 9:249.

Mossman, H. W., R. A. Hoffman, and C. M. Kirkpatrick. 1955. The accessory genital glands of male gray and fox squirrels correlated with age and reproductive cycles. Amer. J. Anatomy, 97:257-301.

Mumford, R. E. 1953a. Bat banding in Indiana caves. Outdoor Indiana, 20:7 10.

———. 1953b. Hoary bat skull in an Indiana cave. J. Mammal., 34:121.

———. 1953c. Status of Nycticeius humeralis in Indiana. J. Mammal., 34:121-122.

———. 1958. Population turnover in wintering bats in Indiana. J. Mammal., 39:253-261.

———. 1960. A survey of Indiana mammals. Outdoor Indiana, 31:1-2.

———. 1961. The mammals of Indiana—history and current status. Ph.D. dissertation, Purdue Univ., Jan. 1961. 285pp.

———. 1964. A melanistic prairie vole. J. Mammal., 45:150.

———. 1967. New distribution records for Sorex longirostris and Citellus tridecemlineatus in Indiana. Proc. Ind. Acad. Sci., 76:397. (Abstract.)

———. 1969a. Long-tailed weasel preys on big brown bats. J. Mammal., 50:360.

———. 1969b. The hoary bat in Indiana. Proc. Ind. Acad. Sci., 78:497-501.

———. 1969c. Distribution of the mammals of Indiana. Monograph No. 1, Ind. Acad. Sci. 114pp.

———. 1973. Natural history of the red bat (Lasiurus borealis) in Indiana. Periodicum Biologorum, 75:155-158.

Mumford, R. E., and L. L. Calvert. 1960. Myotis sodalis evidently breeding in Indiana. J. Mammal., 41:512.

Mumford, R. E., and J. B. Cope. 1958. Summer records of Myotis sodalis in Indiana. J. Mammal., 39:586-587.

———. 1964. Distribution and status of the Chiroptera of Indiana. Amer. Midl. Nat., 72:473-489.

Mumford, R. E., and C. R. Danner. 1974. An Indiana marsh hawk roost. Ind. Audubon Quarterly, 52:96-98.

Mumford, R. E., and C. O. Handley, Jr. 1956. Notes on the mammals of Jackson County, Indiana. J. Mammal., 37:407-412.

Mumford, R. E., and R. D. Kirkpatrick. 1961. Distribution of the 13-lined ground squirrel in Indiana. Proc. Ind. Acad. Sci., 70:275-277.

Mumford, R. E., and C. L. Rippy. 1963. The southeastern shrew (Sorex longirostris) in Indiana. Proc. Ind. Acad. Sci., 72:340-341.

Mumford, R. E., and J. O. Whitaker, Jr. 1975. Seasonal activity of bats at an Indiana cave. Proc. Ind. Acad. Sci., 84:500-507.

Murie, A. 1936. Following fox trails. Misc. Publ. Mus. Zool. Univ. Mich. No. 32. 45pp.

Murphy, M. F. 1952. Ecology and helminths of the Osage wood rat, Neotoma floridana osagensis, including the description of Longistriata neotoma n. sp. (Trichostrongylidae). Amer. Midl. Nat., 48:204-218.

Murray, L. T. 1939. An albino Blarina from Indiana. J. Mammal., 20:501.

Nelson, E. W. 1909. The rabbits of North America. North American Fauna No. 29. 314pp.

Newlin, C. E. 1897. Abnormal incisor growth of rodents. Proc. Ind. Acad. Sci., 6:226-227.

Newman, J. E. 1966. Bioclimate. In Natural features of Indiana. Editor: A. A. Lindsey. Ind. Acad. Sci. pp.171-180.

Nicholson, A. J. 1941. The homes and social habits of the wood mouse (Peromyscus leucopus noveborancensis) in southern Michigan. Amer. Midl. Nat., 25:196-223.

Novakowski, N. S. 1956. Additional records of bats in Saskatchewan. Canadian Field-Nat., 70:142.

Orr, R. T. 1950. Unusual behavior and occurrence of a hoary bat. J. Mammal., 31:456-457.

Osgood, W. H. 1909. Revision of the mice of the American genus Peromyscus. North American Fauna No. 28. 285pp.

Packard, A. S. 1888. The cave fauna of North America, with remarks on the anatomy of the brain and origin of the blind species. Mem. Nat. Acad. Sci., 4:16.

Packard, R. L. 1956. The tree squirrels of Kansas: Ecology and economic importance. Univ. Kans. Mus. Nat. Hist. and State Biol. Surv. Kans. Mus. Publ. 11. 67pp.

Parmalee, P. W. 1954. Food of the great horned owl and barn owl in east Texas. Auk, 71:469-470.

Pascal, D. D., Jr. 1974. An ecological study of the pine mouse, Microtus pinetorum (LeConte), in Clark County, Illinois. MS thesis, Indiana State Univ. 51pp.

Paul, J. R. 1970. The pine vole in North Carolina. Ill. State Mus. Repts. Invest. No. 20. 28pp.

Pearson, O. P. 1944. Reproduction in the shrew (Blarina brevicauda Say). Amer. J. Anatomy, 75:39-93.

——. 1963. History of two local outbreaks of feral house mice. Ecology, 44:450-549.

——. 1964. Carnivore-mouse predation; An example of its intensity and bioenergetics. J. Mammal., 45:177-188.

Pearson, O. P., and A. K. Pearson. 1947. Owl predation in Pennsylvania, with notes on the small mammals of Delaware County. J. Mammal., 28:137-147.

Pearson, P. G. 1952. Observations concerning the life history and ecology of the wood rat, Neotoma floridana floridana (Ord.). J. Mammal., 33:459-463.

——. 1959. Small mammals and old field succession on the Piedmont of New Jersey. Ecology, 40:249-255.

Pence, D. B. 1973. Notes on two species of hypopial nymphs of the genus Marsupialichus (Acarina: Glycyphagidae) from mammals in Louisiana. J. Med. Entomol., 10:329-332.

Perry, J. S. 1944. The reproduction of the wild rat (Rattus norvegicus Erxleben). Proc. Zool. Soc. 115 (I and II). pp.19-46.

Peterson, R. L., and S. C. Downing. 1952. Notes on the bobcats (Lynx rufus) of eastern North America with the description of a new race. Contr. Roy. Ont. Mus. Zool. and Paleont. 33. 23pp.

Petty, R. O., and M. T. Jackson. 1966. Plant communities. In Natural features of Indiana. Editor: A. A. Lindsey. Ind. Acad. Sci. pp.264-296.

Phillips, R. E., and C. M. Kirkpatrick. 1960. Indiana hawks and owls. Ind. Dept. of Conserv. 38pp.

Pisano, R. G., and T. I. Storer. 1948. Burrows and feeding of the Norway rat. J. Mammal., 29:374-383.

Plummer, J. T. 1844. Scraps in natural history (quadrupeds). Amer. J. Sci. Arts, 46:236-249.

Polderboer, E. B. 1942. Habits of the least weasel (Mustela rixosa) in northeastern Iowa. J. Mammal., 23:145-147.

Polderboer, E. B., L. W. Kuhn, and G. O. Hendrickson. 1941. Winter and spring habits of weasels in central Iowa. J. Wildl. Mgmt. 5:115-119.

Pollack, E. M. 1950. Breeding habits of the bobcat in northeastern United States. J. Mammal., 31:327-330.

——. 1951a. Food habits of the bobcat in the New England States. J. Wildl. Mgmt., 15:209-213.

——. 1951b. Observations on New England bobcats. J. Mammal., 32:356-358.

Poole, E. L. 1932. Breeding of the hoary bat in Pennsylvania. J. Mammal., 13:365-367.

——. 1940. A life history sketch of the Allegheny woodrat. J. Mammal., 21:249-270.

Pratt, H. D., and N. E. Good. 1954. Distribution of some common domestic rat ectoparasites in the United States. J. Parasitology, 40:113-129.

Preble, E. A. 1899. Revision of the jumping mice of the genus *Zapus*. North American Fauna No. 15:1-42.

Price, H. F. 1942. Contents of owl pellets. Amer. Midl. Nat., 28:524-525.

Provost, E. E., and C. M. Kirkpatrick. 1952. Observations on the hoary bat in Indiana and Illinois. J. Mammal., 33:110-113.

Pruitt, W. O., Jr. 1954. Notes on a litter of young masked shrews. J. Mammal., 35:109-110.

Quick, E. R. 1881. *Hesperomys leucopus* LeConte. J. Cincinnati Soc. Nat. Hist., 4:337.

Quick, E. R., and A. W. Butler. 1885. The habits of some Arvicolinae. American Naturalist, 19:113-118.

Quick, E. R., and F. M. Langdon. 1882. Mammals found in Franklin County, Indiana. *In* Atlas of Franklin County, Indiana. J. H. Beers and Co., Chicago. pp.9-10.

Quick, H. F. 1944. Habits and economics of the New York weasel in Michigan. J. Wildl. Mgmt. 8:71-78.

Quimby, D. C. 1951. The life history and ecology of the jumping mouse, *Zapus hudsonius*. Ecol. Monogr., 21:61-95.

Radovsky, F. J. 1967. The Macronyssidae and Laelapidae (Acarina: Mesostigmata) parasitic on bats. Univ. Calif. Publ. Entomol., 46:1-288.

Rafinesque, S. 1820. Annals of Nature. 2, 3. *In* Allen, H. 1893. A monograph of the bats of North America. Bull. U.S. Nat. Mus. No. 43. 198pp.

Rainey, D. G. 1956. Eastern wood rat, *Neotoma floridana*: Life history and ecology. Univ. Kans. Mus. Nat. Hist. Publ., 8:535-646.

Rand, A. L., and A. S. Rand. 1951. Mammal bones from dunes south of Lake Michigan. Amer. Midl. Nat., 46:649-659.

Raynor, G. S. 1960. Three litters in a pine mouse nest. J. Mammal., 41:275.

Reed, E. H. 1920. Tales of a vanishing river. John Lane Co., New York. 266pp.

Rerick, J. H. 1882. Counties of LaGrange and Noble, Indiana. F. A. Battey and Co., Chicago. 441pp.

Reynolds, H. C. 1945. Some aspects of the life history and ecology of the opossum in central Missouri. J. Mammal., 26:361-379.

———. 1952. Studies on reproduction in the opossum (*Didelphis virginiana virginiana*). Univ. Calif. Publ. Zool., 52:227-284.

Rice, D. W. 1955. A new race of *Myotis austroriparius* from the upper Mississippi Valley. Quart. J. Fla. Acad. Sci., 18:67-68.

———. 1957. Life history and ecology of *Myotis austroriparius* in Florida. J. Mammal., 38:15-32.

Richards, R. L. 1970. Vertebrate remains from an Indiana cave. Proc. Ind. Acad. Sci., 79:472-475.

———. 1972. The woodrat in Indiana: Recent fossils. Proc. Ind. Acad. Sci., 81:370-375.

Richards, S. H., and R. L. Hine. 1953. Wisconsin fox populations. Tech. Wildlife Bull. No. 6., Wisc. Cons. Dept. 78pp.

Richter, A. R., D. A. Seerley, J. B. Cope, and J. H. Keith. 1978. A newly discovered concentration of hibernating Indiana bats, *Myotis sodalis*, in southern Indiana. J. Mammal., 59:191.

Roberts, H. A., and R. C. Early. 1952. Mammal survey of southeastern Pennsylvania. Penn. Game Comm., Harrisburg. 70pp.

Robinson, V. B., J. W. Newberne, and D. M. Brooks. 1957. Distemper in the American raccoon (*Procyon lotor*). J. Amer. Vet. Med. Assoc., 131:276-278.

Rollings, C. T. 1945. Habits, foods, and parasites of the bobcat in Minnesota. J. Wildl. Mgmt., 9:131-145.

Rongstad, O. J. 1965. A life history study of thirteen-lined ground squirrels in southern Wisconsin. J. Mammal., 46:76-87.

Ross, A. 1961. Notes on food habits of bats. J. Mammal., 42:66-71.

———. 1967. Ecological aspects of the food habits of insectivorous bats. Proc. Western Foundation Vertebrate Zool., 1:205-263.

Rudnick, A. 1960. A revision of the mites of the family Spinturnicidae (Acarina). Univ. Calif. Publ. Entomol., 17:157-283.

Rupes, V., and J. O. Whitaker, Jr. 1968. Mites of the subfamily Labidophorinae (Acaridae, Acarina) in North America. Acarologia, 10:493-499.

Rysgaard, G. N. 1942. A study of the cave bats of Minnesota with special reference to the large brown bat, *Eptesicus fuscus fuscus* (Beauvois). Amer. Midl. Nat., 28:245-267.

Sandburg, C. 1939. Abraham Lincoln: The war years. Harcourt, Brace and Co., Vol. 1:81.

Sanderson, G. C. 1949. Growth and behavior of a litter of captive long-tailed weasels. J. Mammal. 30:412-415.

Sandidge, L. L. 1953. Food and dens of the opossum (*Didelphis virginiana*) in northeastern Kansas. Trans. Kansas Acad. Sci., 56:97-106.

Saunders, W. E. 1932. Notes on the mammals of Ontario. Trans. Roy. Canadian Inst. 18:271-309.

Scheffer, T. H. 1931. Habits and economic status of the pocket gophers. U.S.D.A. Tech. Bull. 244. 26pp.

Schmeltz, L. L., and J. O. Whitaker, Jr. 1977. Use

of woodchuck burrows by woodchucks and other mammals. Trans. Kentucky Acad. Sci., 38:79-82.

Schmidt, F. J. W. 1931. Mammals of western Clark County, Wisconsin. J. Mammal. 12:99-117.

Schneider, A. F. 1966. Physiography. *In* Natural features of Indiana. A. A. Lindsey, editor. Ind. Acad. Sci. pp.40-56.

Schooley, J. P. 1934. A summer breeding season in the eastern chipmunk, *Tamias striatus*. J. Mammal., 15:194-196.

Schorger, A. W. 1947. An emigration of squirrels in Wisconsin. J. Mammal., 28:401-403.

Schwartz, A., and E. P. Odum. 1957. The woodrats of the eastern United States. J. Mammal., 38:197-206.

Schwartz, C. W., and E. R. Schwartz. 1959. The wild mammals of Missouri. Univ. Missouri Press and Missouri Conserv. Comm. 341pp.

Schwarz, E., and H. K. Schwarz. 1943. The wild and commensal stocks of the house mouse, *Mus musculus* Linnaeus. J. Mammal., 24:59-72.

Scott, T. G. 1955. An evaluation of the red fox. Ill. Nat. Hist. Surv., Div. Biol. Notes No. 35:16.

Sealander, J. A. 1943. Winter food habits of mink in southern Michigan. J. Wildl. Mgmt., 7:411-417.

Segal, S. 1960. Bird tragedy at the dunes. Ind. Audubon Quarterly, 38:23-25.

Selko, L. F. 1937. Food habits of Iowa skunks in the fall of 1936. J. Wildl. Mgmt., 1:70-76.

———. 1938a. Hibernation of the striped skunk in Iowa. J. Mammal., 19:320-324.

———. 1938b. Notes on the den ecology of the striped skunk in Iowa. Amer. Midl. Nat., 20:455-463.

Severinghaus, C. W., and E. L. Cheatum. 1956. Life and times of the white-tailed deer. The white-tailed, mule and black-tailed deer, Genus *Odocoileus* their history and management. Pages 57-186, *in* The deer of North America. W. P. Taylor, editor. Stackpole, Harrisburg. 668pp.

Shanks, C. E. 1948. The pelt-primeness method of aging muskrats. Amer. Midl. Nat., 39:179-187.

Shantz, H. L., and R. Zon. 1936. Atlas of American agriculture. U.S. Dept. of Agr., Washington, D.C., p. 5.

Shaw, W. T. 1928. The spring and summer activities of the dusky skunk in captivity with a chapter on the insect food of the dusky skunk by K. F. Chamberlain. N.Y. State Mus. Hdbk. No. 4. 103pp.

Sheldon, W. G. 1949. Reproductive behavior of foxes in New York State. J. Mammal., 30:236-246.

———. 1950. Denning habits and home range of red foxes in New York State. J. Wildl. Mgmt., 14:33-42.

Sherman, H. B. 1930. Birth of the young of *Myotis austroriparius*. J. Mammal., 11:495-503.

Shull, A. F. 1907. Habits of the short-tailed shrew, *Blarina brevicauda* (Say). American Naturalist, 41:495-522.

Silver, J. 1927. The introduction and spread of house rats in the United States. J. Mammal., 8:58-59.

Sly, G. R. 1976. Small mammal succession on strip-mined land in Vigo County, Indiana. Amer. Midl. Nat., 95:257-267.

Smiley, R. L., and J. O. Whitaker, Jr. 1979. Mites of the genus *Pygmephorus* (Acar.: Pygmephoridae) on small mammals in North America. Acta. Zool. Acad. Scient. Hungarical 3-4:383-408.

Smith, C. C. 1940. Notes on the food and parasites of the rabbits of a lowland area in Oklahoma. J. Wildl. Mgmt., 4:429-431.

Smith, C. F. 1936. Notes on the habits of the long-tailed harvest mouse. J. Mammal., 17:274-278.

Smith, P. W., and P. W. Parmalee. 1954. Notes on distribution and habits of some bats from Illinois. Trans. Kansas Acad. Sci., 57:200-205.

Snead, E., and G. O. Hendrickson. 1942. Food habits of the badger in Iowa. J. Mammal., 23:380-391.

Snyder, D. P. 1956. Survival rates, longevity and population fluctuations in the white-footed mouse, *Peromyscus leucopus*, in southeastern Michigan. Misc. Publ. Mus. Zool. Univ. Mich., 95:1-33.

Sollberger, D. E. 1940. Notes on the life history of the small eastern flying squirrel. J. Mammal., 21:282-293.

———. 1943. Notes on the breeding habits of the eastern flying squirrel *(Glaucomys volans volans)*. J. Mammal., 24:163-173.

Sotala, D. J., and C. M. Kirkpatrick. 1973. Foods of white-tailed deer, *Odocoileus virginianus*, in Martin County, Indiana. Amer. Midl. Nat., 89:281-286.

Sowls, L. K. 1948. The Franklin ground squirrel, *Citellus franklinii* (Sabine), and its relationship to nesting ducks. J. Mammal., 29:113-137.

Sperry, C. C. 1941. Food habits of the coyote. U.S. Dept. Interior Fish and Wildl. Serv., Wildl. Res. Bull. 4. 70pp.

Spicka, E. J., and P. H. Gerrits. 1977. *Dermacarus reticulosus*, n. sp. (Acari: Labidophorinae: Glycyphagidae) from *Spermophilus tridecemlineatus* from Indiana, U.S.A. J. Med. Entomol., 14:297-299.

Stains, H. J. 1956. The raccoon in Kansas—natural history, management, and economic importance. Univ. Kans. Mus. Nat. Hist. and State Biol. Surv., Misc. Publ. 10. 76pp.

Stannard, L. J., Jr., and L. R. Pietsch. 1958. Ectoparasites of the cottontail rabbit in Lee

County, northern Illinois. Ill. Nat. Hist. Surv., Biol. Notes No. 38:18.

Stark, R. W. 1964. Indiana pioneer merchant. Outdoor Indiana, 8:6-9.

Stegeman, L. C. 1930. Notes on *Synaptomys cooperi cooperi* in Washtenaw County, Michigan. J. Mammal., 11:460-466.

———. 1937. Some parasites and pathological conditions of the skunk *(Mephitis mephitis nigra)* in central New York. J. Mammal., 20:493-496.

Stewart, J. H. 1872. Recollection of the early settlement of Carroll County, Indiana. Hitchcock and Walden, Cincinnati. 370pp.

Stoddard, H. L. 1920a. The flying squirrel as a bird killer. J. Mammal., 1:95-96.

———. 1920b. Nests of the western fox squirrel. J. Mammal., 1:122-123.

Stombauch, T. A. 1953. A taxonomic analysis of the prairie voles of the subgenus *Pedomys* (Genus *Pitymys*). Ph.D. dissertation, Indiana Univ.

Stormer, F. A. 1972. Population ecology and management of white-tailed deer of Crane Naval Ammunition Depot. Ph.D. dissertation, Purdue Univ. 273pp.

Stormer, F. A., T. W. Hoekstra, C. M. White, and C. M. Kirkpatrick. 1974. Assessment of population levels of white-tailed deer on NAD Crane. Purdue Univ. Agr. Exp. Stat., Research Bull. No. 910. 11pp.

Strecker, J. K. 1924. The mammals of McLennan County, Texas. The Baylor Bull., Baylor Univ., 27:3-20.

Stuewer, F. W. 1943a. Reproduction of raccoons in Michigan. J. Wildl. Mgmt., 7:60-73.

———. 1943b. Raccoons, their habits and management in Michigan. Ecol. Monogr., 13:203-257.

Stullken, D. E. 1950. A study of the influence of ambient temperatures on the respiratory metabolism and certain blood constituents in non-hibernating mammals, hibernating mammals, and the bat. Ph.D. dissertation, Purdue Univ. 96pp.

Stunkard, H. W. 1962. A new final host for the cestode, *Cycloskrjabinia taborensis* (Loewen, 1934) Spassky, 1951. J. Parasitology, 48: Suppl. 2, Sec. 2:48.

Sullivan, E. G. 1956. Gray fox reproduction, denning, range, and weights in Alabama. J. Mammal., 37:346-351.

Svihla, A. 1931. Habits of the Louisiana mink *(Mustela vison vulgivagus)*. J. Mammal., 12:366-368.

———. 1932. A comparative life history study of the mice of the genus *Peromyscus*. Misc. Publ. Mus. Zool. Univ. Mich. No. 24. 39pp.

Svihla, A., and R. D. Svihla. 1933. Notes on the life history of the woodrat *Neotoma floridana rubida* Bangs. J. Mammal., 14:73-75.

Svihla, R. D. 1929. Habits of *Sylvilagus aquaticus littoralis*. J. Mammal., 10:315-319.

———. 1931. Notes on desert and dusky harvest mice *(Reithrodontomys megalotis megalotis* and *R. m. nigrescens)*. J. Mammal., 12:363-365.

Taube, C. M. 1947. Food habits of Michigan opossums. J. Wildl. Mgmt., 11:97-103.

Tenney, S. 1872. Hibernation of the jumping mouse. American Naturalist, 6:330-332.

Terrel, T. L. 1969. The swamp rabbit *(Sylvilagus aquaticus)* in Indiana. MS thesis, Purdue Univ. 145pp.

———. 1972. The swamp rabbit *(Sylvilagus aquaticus)* in Indiana. Amer. Midl. Nat., 87:283-295.

Test, F. H. 1932. Winter activities of the eastern chipmunk. J. Mammal., 13:278.

Test, F. H., and A. R. Test. 1943. Incidence of dipteran parasitosis in populations of small mammals. J. Mammal., 24:506-508.

Tevis, L., Jr. 1950. Summer behavior of a family of beavers in New York State. J. Mammal., 31:40-65.

Thomas, D. 1819. Travels through the western country in the summer of 1816. *In* Lindley (1916).

Thomas, H. A. 1956. The abundance and habits of *Laelaps echidninus* on rats in New Jersey. Jour. N.Y. Entomol. Soc., 64:149-156.

Tipton, V. J., and J. L. Boese. 1958. *Steatonyssus furmani*, a new Nearctic bat mite (Acari: Macronyssidae). Proc. Entomol. Soc. Wash., 60:80-84.

True, F. W. 1896. A revision of the American moles. Proc. U.S. Nat. Mus., 19:1-112.

Tuszynski, R. C. 1971. The ecology of the pocket gopher *(Geomys bursarius illinoensis)* in Indiana. MS thesis, Purdue Univ. 63pp.

Tuszynski, R. C., and J. O. Whitaker, Jr. 1972. External parasites of pocket gophers, *Geomys bursarius*, from Indiana. Amer. Midl. Nat., 87:545-548.

Tuttle, M. D. 1975. Population ecology of the gray bat *(Myotis grisescens)*: Factors influencing early growth and development. Occas. Papers Mus. Nat. Hist. Univ. Kans. No. 36:1-24.

———. 1976a. Population ecology of the gray bat *(Myotis grisescens)*: Factors influencing growth and survival of newly volant young. Ecology, 57:587-595.

———. 1976b. Population ecology of the gray bat *(Myotis grisescens)*: Philopatry, timing and patterns of movement, weight loss during migration, and seasonal adaptive strategies. Occas. Papers Mus. Nat. Hist. Univ. Kans. No. 54, 38pp.

———. 1979. Status, causes of decline, and management of endangered gray bats. J. Wildl. Mgmt., 43:1-17.

Tuttle, M. D., and D. E. Stevenson. 1977. An analysis of migration as a mortality factor in the gray bat based on public recoveries of banded bats. Amer. Midl. Nat., 97:235-240.

Twichell, A. R., and H. H. Dill. 1949. One hundred raccoons from one hundred and two acres. J. Mammal., 30:130-133.

Ubelaker, J. E. 1966. Parasites of the gray bat, *Myotis grisescens*, in Kansas. Amer. Midl. Nat., 75:199-204.

Ubelaker, J. E., and T. H. Kunz. 1971. Parasites of the evening bat, *Nycticeius humeralis*, in Iowa. Texas J. of Sci., 22:425-427.

Uhlig, H. G. 1956. The gray squirrel in West Virginia. Cons. Comm. West Va. Div. Game Mgmt. Bull. No. 3. 83pp.

Ulrey, A. B. 1897. The increasing abundance of the opossum *(Didelphis virginiana* Shaw) in northern Indiana. Proc. Inc. Acad. Sci., 6:279.

Valentine, G. L., and R. L. Kirkpatrick. 1970. Seasonal changes in reproductive and related organs in the pine vole, *Microtus pinetorum*, in southwestern Virginia. J. Mammal., 51:553-560.

Van Gorder, W. B. 1916. Geology of Greene County. 40th Annual Report Ind. Dept. Geology and Natural Resources. pp.240-266.

Verts, B. J. 1960. Ecological notes on *Reithrodontomys megalotis* in Illinois. Nat. Hist. Misc., No. 174:1-7.

Visher, S. S. 1944. Climate of Indiana. Ind. Univ. Publ. Sci. Series No. 13:511pp.

Wade, O. 1927. Breeding habits and early life of the thirteen-lined ground squirrel, *Citellus tridecemlineatus* (Mitchill). J. Mammal., 8:269-276.

———. 1930. The behavior of certain spermophiles with special reference to aestivation and hibernation. J. Mammal., 11:160-188.

———. 1950. Soil temperatures, weather conditions, and emergence of ground squirrels from hibernation. J. Mammal., 31:158-161.

Walker, E. P. 1923. The red squirrel extending its range in Indiana. J. Mammal., 4:127-128.

Walker, E. P., F. Warnick, K. I. Lange, H. E. Uible, S. E. Hamlet, M. A. Davis, and P. F. Wright. 1964. Mammals of the World. Vol. 1:176. The Johns Hopkins Univ. Press, Baltimore.

Wallace, F. N. 1925. Report of the Division of Entomology. Ann. Rept. Yearbook Ind. for 1924. pp.206-228.

Walley, H. D. 1970. Movements of *Myotis lucifugus lucifugus* from a colony in LaSalle County, Illinois. Trans. Ill. Acad. Sci., 63:409-414.

Walley, H. D., and W. L. Jarvis. 1971. Longevity record for *Pipistrellus subflavus*. Trans. Ill. Acad. Sci., 64:305.

Wassel, M. E., G. L. Tieben, and J. O. Whitaker, Jr. 1978. The ectoparasites of the southern bog lemming, *Synaptomys cooperi*, in Indiana. Proc. Ind. Acad. Sci., 87:446-449.

Wassel, M. E., J. O. Whitaker, Jr., and E. J. Spicka, 1980. The ectoparasites and other associates of the cottontail rabbit, *Sylvilagus floridanus*, in Indiana. Proc. Ind. Acad. Sci. for 1979. Vol. 89, pp.418-420.

Watkins, L. C. 1970. Observations on the distribution and natural history of the evening bat *(Nycticeius humeralis)* in northwestern Missouri and adjacent Iowa. Trans. Kansas Acad. Sci., 72:330-336.

———. 1972a. *Nycticeius humeralis*. Mammalian Species No. 23. pp.1-4.

———. 1972b. A technique for monitoring the nocturnal activity of bats, with comments on the activity patterns of the evening bat, *Nycticeius humeralis*. Trans. Kansas Acad. Sci., 74:261-268.

Wayne, W. J. 1956. Thickness of drift and bedrock physiography of Indiana north of the Wisconsin glacial boundary. Ind. Dept. Conserv. Geol. Surv. Rept. of Progress No. 7. 70pp.

———. 1960. Range extension of the Allegheny Woodrat *(Neotoma magister)* in Indiana. Proc. Ind. Acad. Sci., 69:311. (Abstract.)

———. 1966. Ice and land. A review of the Tertiary and Pleistocene history of Indiana. *In* Natural features of Indiana. A. A. Lindsey, editor. Ind. Acad. Sci. pp.21-39.

Weeks, H. P., Jr., and C. M. Kirkpatrick. 1976. Adaptations of white-tailed deer to naturally occurring sodium deficiencies. J. Wildl. Mgmt., 40:610-625.

———. 1978. Salt preference and sodium drive phenology in fox squirrels and woodchucks. J. Mammal., 59:531-542.

West, J. A. 1910. A study of the food of moles in Illinois. Bull. Ill. Lab. Nat. Hist., 9:14-22.

Wetzel, R. M. 1955. Speciation and dispersal of the southern bog lemming, *Synaptomys cooperi* (Baird). J. Mammal., 36:1-20.

Whitaker, J. O., Jr. 1962. *Endogone, Hymenogaster* and *Melonagaster* as small mammal foods. Amer. Midl. Nat. 67:152-156.

———. 1963a. A study of the meadow jumping mouse, *Zapus hudsonius* (Zimmermann), in central New York. Ecol. Monogr., 33:215-254.

———. 1963b. Food of 120 *Peromyscus leucopus* from Ithaca, New York. J. Mammal., 44:418-419.

———. 1966. Food of *Mus musculus, Peromyscus maniculatus bairdii* and *Peromyscus leucopus* in Vigo County, Indiana. J. Mammal., 47:473-486.

———. 1967a. Habitat relationships of four species of mice in Vigo County, Indiana. Ecology, 48:867-872.

———. 1967b. Hoary bat apparently hibernating in Indiana. J. Mammal., 48:663.

———. 1967c. Habitat and reproduction of some of the small mammals of Vigo County, Indiana, with a list of mammals known to occur there. Occas. Papers C. C. Adams Center for Ecological Studies, No. 16. 24pp. West. Mich. Univ.

———. 1968. Relationship of *Mus, Peromyscus* and *Microtus* to the major textural classes of soils of Vigo County, Indiana. Proc. Ind. Acad. Sci., 77:206-212.

———. 1970a. The biological subspecies: An adjunct of the biological species. The Biologist, 52:12-15.

———. 1970b. Parasites of feral housemice, *Mus musculus*, in Vigo County, Indiana. Proc. Ind. Acad. Sci., 79:441-448.

———. 1972a. *Zapus hudsonius*. Mammalian Species No. 11. pp.1-7.

———. 1972b. Food habits of bats from Indiana. Canadian J. Zoology, 50:877-883.

———. 1972c. Food and external parasites of *Spermophilus tridecemlineatus* in Vigo County, Indiana. J. Mammal., 53:644-648.

———. 1973. External parasites of bats of Indiana. J. Parasitology, 59:1148-1150.

———. 1974. *Cryptotis parva*. Mammalian Species No. 43. pp.1-8.

———. 1977. Food and external parasites of the Norway rat, *Rattus norvegicus*, in Indiana. Proc. Ind. Acad. Sci., 86:193-198.

Whitaker, J. O., Jr., and D. Adalis. 1971. Trematodes and cestodes from the digestive tracts of *Synaptomys cooperi* and three species of *Microtus* from Indiana. Proc. Ind. Acad. Sci., 80:489-494.

Whitaker, J. O., Jr., and K. W. Corthum, Jr. 1967. Fleas of Vigo County, Indiana. Proc. Ind. Acad. Sci., 76:431-440.

Whitaker, J. O., Jr., G. S. Jones, and R. J. Goff. 1977. Ectoparasites and food habits of the opossum, *Didelphis virginiana*, in Indiana. Proc. Ind. Acad. Sci., 86:501-507.

Whitaker, J. O., Jr., and R. B. Loomis. 1979. Chiggers (Acarina: Trombiculidae) from the mammals of Indiana. Proc. Ind. Acad. Sci., 88:426-433.

Whitaker, J. O., Jr., and W. A. Miller. 1974. Rabies in bats of Indiana: 1968-1972. Proc. Ind. Acad. Sci., 83:469-472.

Whitaker, J. O., Jr., W. A. Miller, and W. L. Boyko.

1969. Rabies in Indiana bats. Proc. Ind. Acad. Sci., 78:447-456.

Whitaker, J. O., Jr., and R. E. Mumford. 1971a. Notes on a collection of bats taken by mistnetting at an Indiana cave. Amer. Midl. Nat., 85:277-279.

———. 1971b. Jumping mice (Zapodidae) in Indiana. Proc. Ind. Acad. Sci., 80:201-209.

———. 1972a. Food and ectoparasites of Indiana shrews. J. Mammal., 53:329-335.

———. 1972b. Ecological studies of *Reithrodontomys megalotis* in Indiana. J. Mammal., 53:850-860.

———. 1972c. Notes on occurrence and reproduction of bats in Indiana. Proc. Ind. Acad. Sci., 81:376-383.

Whitaker, J. O., Jr., D. D. Pascal, Jr., and R. E. Mumford. 1979. Ectoparasites of the red squirrel *(Tamiasciurus hudsonicus)* and the eastern chipmunk *(Tamias striatus)* from Indiana. J. Med. Entomol., 16:350-351.

Whitaker, J. O., Jr., and L. L. Schmeltz. 1973. External parasites of the woodchuck, *Marmota monax*, in Indiana. Entomological News, 84:69-72.

———. 1974. Food and external parasites of the eastern mole, *Scalopus aquaticus*, from Indiana. Proc. Ind. Acad. Sci., 83:478-481.

Whitaker, J. O., Jr., and G. R. Sly. 1970. First record of *Reithrodontomys megalotis* in Indiana. J. Mammal., 51:381.

Whitaker, J. O., Jr., E. J. Spicka, and L. L. Schmeltz. 1976a. Ectoparasites of squirrels of the genus *Sciurus* from Indiana. *In* Fish and wildlife in Indiana, 1776-1976 and reports of fish and wildlife studies. H. E. McReynolds, editor. pp.77-80.

———. 1976b. Ectoparasites of squirrels of the genus *Sciurus* from Indiana. Proc. Ind. Acad. Sci., 85:431-436.

Whitaker, J. O., Jr., and N. A. Wilson. 1968. Mites of small mammals of Vigo County, Indiana. Amer. Midl. Nat., 80:537-542.

———. 1974. Host and distribution lists of mites (Acari), parasitic and phoretic, in the hair of wild mammals of North America, north of Mexico. Amer. Midl. Nat., 91:1-67.

Whitaker, J. O., Jr., and E. G. Zimmerman. 1965. Additional *Mustela nivalis* records for Indiana. J. Mammal., 46:516.

White, C. M. 1968. Productivity and dynamics of the white-tailed deer on the Crane Naval Ammunition Depot in Martin County, Indiana. Ph.D. dissertation, Purdue Univ. 171pp.

Whiteman, E. E. 1940. Habits and pelage changes in captive coyotes. J. Mammal., 21:435-438.

Wied, M. 1839–1841. Reise in das innere Nord-Amerika in den jahren 1832 bis 1834. Vol. 1 and 2. J. Hoelscher, Coblenz.

————. 1862. Verzeichniss der auf seiner reise in Nord-Amerika beobachteten säugethiere. Rodentia. Archiv. für Naturgeschichte, 1:65-190.

Williamson, E. B. 1900. Biological conditions of Round and Shriner Lakes, Whitley County, Indiana. Proc. Ind. Acad. Sci., 9:151-155.

Wilson, N. A. 1957. Some ectoparasites from Indiana mammals. J. Mammal., 38:281-282.

————. 1958. Another instance of bat versus ant. J. Mammal., 39:438.

————. 1960. A northernmost record of *Plecotus rafinesquii* Lesson (Mammalia, Chiroptera). Amer. Midl. Nat., 64:500.

————. 1961. The ectoparasites (Ixodides, Anoplura and Siphonaptera) of Indiana mammals. Ph.D. dissertation, Purdue Univ. 527pp.

————. 1965. Red bats attracted to insect light traps. J. Mammal., 46:704-705.

Wiseman, G. L., and G. O. Hendrickson. 1950. Notes on the life history of the opossum in southeast Iowa. J. Mammal., 31:331-337.

Womersley, H. 1941. Notes on the Cheyletidae (Acarina: Trombidoidea) of Australia and New Zealand, with descriptions of a new species. Rec. So. Australian Mus., 7:51-64.

Wood, J. E. 1958. Age structure and productivity of a gray fox population. J. Mammal., 39:74-86.

Wright, P. L. 1942. Delayed implantation in the long-tailed weasel *(Mustela frenata)*, the short-tailed weasel *(Mustela cicognani)*, and the marten *(Martes americana)*. Anat. Rec. 83:341-353.

————. 1947. The sexual cycle of the male long-tailed weasel *(Mustela frenata)*. J. Mammal. 28:343-352.

————. 1948. Breeding habits of captive long-tailed weasels *(Mustela frenata)*. Am. Midl. Nat. 39:338-344.

Yerger, R. W. 1953. Home range, territoriality, and populations of the chipmunk in central New York. J. Mammal., 34:448-458.

Young, S. P. 1958. The bobcat of North America. Its history, life habits, economic status and control, with list of currently recognized subspecies. Wildl. Mgmt. Inst. and Stackpole Co., Harrisburg. 193pp.

Young, S. P., and E. A. Goldman. 1944. The wolves of North America. Amer. Wildl. Inst., Washington, D.C. 636pp.

Young, S. P., and H. H. T. Jackson. 1951. The clever coyote. Wildl. Mgmt. Inst., Washington, D.C. 411pp.

Zimmerman, E. C. 1965. A comparison of habitat and food of two species of *Microtus*. J. Mammal., 46:605-612.

Index

Each species account contains, in ordered fashion, the various vernacular names for the animal, the synonymy for that species, a description of the animal (including its weights and measurements), the population status and distribution of the species in the state, its habitat preferences, other species most commonly found in association with the animal, its habits and patterns of behavior, its food habits, its reproductive patterns and activities, parasites and diseases associated with the animal, decimating factors affecting the animal, and the taxonomy of the species. Since to index these factors would create a very unwieldy (and not very helpful) listing, we have listed in the general index only the major items and concepts treated in the materials preceding the species accounts. The second part of this index represents the mammals themselves, their common and scientific names, and includes the page references to the species account for each Indiana mammal.